www.wadsworth.com

wadsworth.com is the World Wide Web site for Wadsworth and is your direct source to dozens of online resources.

At *wadsworth.com* you can find out about supplements, demonstration software, and student resources. You can also send email to many of our authors and preview new publications and exciting new technologies.

wadsworth.com
Changing the way the world learns®

THE ENVIRONMENTAL ETHICS AND POLICY BOOK

Philosophy, Ecology, Economics

THIRD EDITION

Donald VanDeVeer □ Christine Pierce
North Carolina State University

THOMSON
™
WADSWORTH

Australia • Canada • Mexico • Singapore • Spain
United Kingdom • United States

THOMSON

TM

WADSWORTH

To Jackie   –D. V.
To Beth   –C. P.

Publisher: *Holly Allen*
Philosophy Editor: *Steve Wainwright*
Assistant Editor: *Lee McCracken*
Editorial Assistant: *Anna Lustig*
Technology Project Manager: *Susan DeVanna*
Marketing Manager: *Worth Hawes*
Advertising Project Manager: *Bryan Vann*
Print/Media Buyer: *Rebecca Cross*

Permissions Editor: *Bob Kauser*
Production Service: *Buuji, Inc.*
Copy Editor: *Heather McElwain, Buuji, Inc.*
Cover Designer: *Cassandra Chu*
Cover Image: *PhotoDisc*
Cover Printer: *Webcom*
Compositor: *Buuji, Inc.*
Printer: *Webcom*

For more information about our products, contact us at:
Thomson Learning Academic Resource Center
1-800-423-0563

For permission to use material from this text, contact us by:
Phone: 1-800-730-2214   **Fax:** 1-800-730-2215
Web: http://www.thomsonrights.com

ISBN 0-534-56188-8

Wadsworth/Thomson Learning
10 Davis Drive
Belmont, CA 94002-3098
USA

Asia
Thomson Learning
5 Shenton Way, #01-01
UIC Building
Singapore 068808

Australia
Nelson Thomson Learning
102 Dodds Street
South Melbourne, Victoria 3205
Australia

Canada
Nelson Thomson Learning
1120 Birchmount Road
Toronto, Ontario M1K 5G4
Canada

Europe/Middle East/Africa
Thomson Learning
High Holborn House
50151 Bedford Row
London WC1R 4LR
United Kingdom

Latin America
Thomson Learning
Seneca, 53
Colonia Polanco
11560 Mexico D.F.
Mexico

Spain
Paraninfo Thomson Learning
Calle/Magallanes, 25
28015 Madrid, Spain

CONTENTS

III THE OTHER ANIMALS   114

IV CONSTRUCTING AN ENVIRONMENTAL ETHIC   174

A. The Broader, Biotic Community   174

B. Deep Ecology and Social Ecology   259

Ⅴ ECONOMICS, ETHICS, AND ECOLOGY   311

PREFACE TO THE THIRD EDITION

This text is designed for students in university-level courses who wish to explore in depth questions about *how on earth we ought to live,* for example, how we can live responsibly with nonhumans and the planet. Although primarily oriented toward questions of ethics (broadly understanding that notion as any serious question about how we ought to live) and approached philosophically, the volume crosses academic disciplines, and attends seriously to economic reasoning and its implications for environmental policy issues. It seeks to unearth and extract for critical attention the relevant moral or normative presuppositions that underlie policy recommendations, whether they are made, for example, by biologists, ecologists, economists, philosophers, bartenders, or public officials.

Such recommendations are heavily influenced by scientific beliefs; hence, this edition contains important essays by Edward O. Wilson, Norman Myers, Rachel Carson, Garrett Hardin, Richard Lewontin, Stephen R. Palumbi, David Barash, Wes Jackson, a selection by a committee from the National Academy of Sciences, and others. The volume includes a variety of views from economists, some critical of mainstream economic theory: A. Myrick Freeman, Partha Dasgupta, Richard Zeckhauser, ¹Robert Repetto, and Robert Solow. It includes historically important papers or excerpts by various philosophers, historians, and environmentalists, for example, Peter Singer, Paul Taylor, Tom Regan, Kristin Shrader-Fréchette, Karen Warren, Lilly-Marlene Russow, Kenneth Goodpaster, Christopher Stone, Aldo Leopold, Arne Naess,

Bryan Norton, Mark Sagoff, Holmes Rolston III, Ernest Partridge, Vandana Shiva, and Lynn White, Jr.

SOME KEY TOPICS ARE:

- Preserving biodiversity
- Ecological sustainability
- Intergenerational justice
- Climate change
- Moral relations with nonhuman creatures
- Ethical grounds for decision making
- Environmental activism
- Religious perspectives on the environment
- Analysis of arguments in environmental ethics
- Relations to the biosphere at large
- The moral standing of ecosystems
- The deep ecology movement
- Ecofeminism
- Developing nations' criticism of industrialized nations' policies
- Market solutions to problems; efficiency
- Cost–benefit analysis
- Corporate responsibility
- Population pressures; reproductive choice
- The place of private property; the "takings" issue
- The value of forests and wilderness
- Global warming

- Modes of environmental activism
- Altering personal consumer habits

NEW TOPICS IN THE THIRD EDITION INCLUDE:

- Marine environmental ethics
- Genetically modified foods
- Transgenic organisms
- The impact of fast food production
- Patenting life
- Judaism and environmental ethics
- Diverse Christian environmental ethics
- Traditional ecological knowledge
- Evolution and the place of humans

In the selection of essays, in the Previews that introduce and set in context the eighteen subsections, in the seven Sidelights designed to touch on related issues, in the extensive Introduction to Ethical Theory, and with the Glossary, Time Chart, and Internet and other Environmental Resources sections, we have sought to create a volume that:

- Contains a thorough range of views
- Is readable, with down-to-earth examples
- Is scientifically literate and informed
- Is intelligible to curious, intelligent readers
- Ranges from philosophical assumptions to policy
- Explains key terminology and avoids jargon
- Presents diverse, competing views
- Contains the vast majority of materials that instructors desire for courses in environmental ethics or policy

We were duly impressed, and sometimes overwhelmed, by all the knowledge that was or could have been helpful in designing the volume that we wished to create. Our reach sometimes exceeded our grasp. However, we sought to construct a coherent whole from the relevant materials, one which reflects the deepest concerns of citizens of the planet and centers on those of professionals in a variety of fields: biology, genetics, forestry, economics, ecology, philosophy, oceanography, geology, and climatology, for example. Indeed we hope that people from diverse fields may talk and listen to each other more. Doing so could initiate a useful form of erosion, the erosion of stereotypes we have about each other, or about other academic disciplines. We believe that this is an urgent matter.

Our work on this volume has heightened our sadness about some of the ways in which we humans are transforming the planet and our fears about what more may happen to it. There is hope for positive change, but change cannot occur without the adoption of radically different attitudes. Such a transformation can come to pass if we think through, reexamine, and critically appraise our ethical and empirical beliefs about what we are doing and our effects on the milieu of life in which we exist. Ideas, especially the "prevailing" ones, have consequences. However, many of the prevailing ideas are only comforting us about what we are doing as we play roulette with species of ancient lineage and with the biosphere.

ABOUT THE THIRD EDITION

A number of considerations guided us in the preparation of the third edition. There are extremely difficult tradeoffs among many relevant considerations, but we have placed *pedagogical* usefulness high on our list. In general, we have tried to locate contributions that, while not necessarily easy, are usually clear and accessible. Many fine, even path-breaking essays, in the field of environmental ethics are just not accessible to many university students who try to work through them. In one of many scenarios, the students with a science background find close philosophical examination difficult to follow. Others with a more typical liberal arts background may find it difficult, to some extent, getting familiar with relevant science. We have tried to avoid as much as possible the sacrifice of serious content and argument, sacrifices that are characteristic of certain journalistic, diatribe-like essays. In striving for some elusive sense of balance, we have minimized the inclusion of such essays so that a certain viewpoint is represented.

Second, we have strengthened the resources in the section "Western Religions and Cultural Perspectives." It now contains nine essays: the famous Lynn White essay criticizing the historical influence of Christianity on environmental attitudes, four essays defending some version of a Christian approach to environmental questions, one explicating a Jewish perspective, one discussing the influence of stories in traditional cultures, and one reviewing the reliance upon ecological "knowledge" found among close-to-the-land "native peoples." One skeptical essay, by David Barash, questions the inference to a divine Designer from facts about order and "perfection" among living things. The place of humans at the pinnacle of living things is also called in question by evolution; hence, basic presuppositions of many of the earlier essays is put in question. New, extensive anthologies on religion and the environment made it inessential to explore in this volume other influential religions: Buddhism, Islam, Hinduism, and so on.

Third, we have included many selections that attend in large part to global issues (the influences of the northern and the southern hemisphere, global warming, and so on). In this edition we have included essays exploring the revolutionary *global* changes brought about by the use of *genetic engineering* to alter plants and animals. For the first time in all history, one species is interfering in a radical way to create, in a short span of time, genetically new organisms; in short, we have begun to alter the course of evolution. As a result, agriculture has entered a new era. The new section is VI.B Food and Agriculture.

Fourth, we continue to give weight to relevant *sciences*. According to one survey, 60 percent of those surveyed in the United States believe that humans and dinosaurs walked the earth at the same time. It is crucial that students of environmental issues attain some view of the world and of time frames in particular that have some connection to reality. It is difficult to imagine how many people can be receptive to reasonable environmental proposals if they approach them with something like a medieval understanding of the world. It is especially dangerous in a democracy. We saw this hazard in the mid-1980s when many Americans were tempted to favor incarceration of those who were HIV positive, given their belief that the virus was transmitted by sneezing. In general, bad science or ignorance of science (not to mention uncritical acceptance of scientific claims) makes for bad ethics and bad policy choices. As of the new millennium, about 20 million humans have died from AIDS, many no doubt because of the mentioned widespread ignorance and denial of the facts about HIV. Some grasp of evolutionary and conservation biology, paleontology, traditional economics, and ecological economics all have their importance. Notably, in 1996, the Pope expressed a qualified endorsement of evolution, some 137 years after the publication of Charles Darwin's *Origin of Species*. A crucial task today for the citizen who is not a scientist in the appropriate field (virtually all of us, including most scientists) is to choose on which authorities to rely—amidst the cacophony of competing voices. Some of these voices are out to protect perhaps legitimate, but often narrow, private interests, and misreport what is often a consensus view among scientists—at least those who have refused to subordinate their minds and voices to the service of governments, corporations, or ecclesiastical interests.

Fifth, we have tried better to indicate, or reflect, recent and *newer* directions in which current discussion in the field has headed, for example, debates over holism and individualism, the immense power of large corporations and corporate responsibility, new directions in ecological economics, the effect of global trade agreements, the concept of sustainability, our myopia about life in the oceans, debates over highly theoretical attempts to settle on moral principles and then simply "apply" them to environmental problems (or leave it to others to do so). We note also a contrasting insistence that ethicists work more "from the bottom up," less "from the top down," and to do so in a more practical, pragmatic, one-issue-at-a-time-in-context manner.

Sixth, we again provide *learning aids to students*. We provide some guidance about how to use the Internet to investigate issues (and perhaps to find help in doing papers). This task is less urgent with the third edition as the use of search engines is no longer radically new. Various useful web sites are listed however. There are many philosophical and scientific terms to understand in this cross-disciplinary field; they are not all in our *Glossary* but many basic ones are listed. To foster a sense of the right *time frame* (or temporal scale) in thinking about evolutionary change, about the extinction of species, and the periods of recovery from extinction, we have provided a *Time Chart*. Getting a sense of temporal perspective can be eye opening and mind-boggling, especially for most of us whose education has focused on the last 3 or 4 thousand years, a rapid wink of the geological eye. Philosophical education, other areas of the humanities, and much in the sciences as well, often proceeds as if the world began with the Pre-Socratics (the 5th century B.C.E.).

In addition to updates and one new Preview, the following are *fifteen* new essays or book excerpts in this third edition:

Robert Gordis, "Judaism and the Environment"

Robin Attfield, "Stewardship vs. Exploitation"

Sallie McFague, "The World as God's Body"

Jay B. McDaniel, "Of God and Pelicans"

R. E. Johannes, "Traditional Ecological Knowledge"

David P. Barash, "Why Bad Things Have Happened to Good Creatures"

Elliot Norse, "Marine Environmental Ethics"

Ernest Partridge, "Future Generations"

Michael Pollan, "A Plant's-Eye View of the World"

Claudia Mills, "Patenting Life"

Stephen R. Palumbi, "Brute-Force Genetic Engineering"

Richard Lewontin, "Genes in the Food!"

Wes Jackson, "Nature as the Measure for a Sustainable Agriculture"

Eric Schlosser, "What's in the Meat?"

The National Academy of Sciences, "Climate Change"

We are grateful to many people for their feedback about the proposed structure of this volume and for their sometimes detailed comments and criticisms of the evolving contents and writing. Some comments were like vaccinations: they stung, but were good for us. Of course, we had to follow our best judgment. However, we very much valued responses of all sorts, and have not the slightest doubt that the book is better than it would have been in the absence of the diverse and sometimes extensive responses that we received. Our editor at Wadsworth, Peter Adams, went to considerable length to ensure that good feedback was made available. Regarding the editing, we profited from the extensive remarks of Talbot Page and Anthony Weston in preparing the first edition. Over the years we have benefited from the suggestions or assistance of Claudia Card, Robin Attfield, Dale Jamieson, J. Baird Callicott, Eric Katz, Bryan Norton, Mark Sagoff, Tom Regan, John Meidell, and Beth Timson. At various times colleagues bailed us out of computer or other difficulties, namely, David Auerbach and Ann Rives. We are most indebted in this third edition to Harold Levin for his good cheer and generous computer assistance. We have been fortunate to have an outstanding research assistant, Barry Chance, who greatly smoothed our path.

We would be remiss if we did not acknowledge the contributions of our reviewers for the second edition: Paul J. Carrick, Harrisburg Area Community College and Pennsylvania State University, Harrisburg; Louisa Moon, Mira Costa College; Bryan Norton, Georgia Institute of Technology; Lilly Russow, Purdue University; Deborah Slicer, University of Montana; and Bruce Waller, Youngstown State University. We are grateful for the insight and attention the following reviewers gave us on this third edition: Daniel Holbrook, Washington State University; Edward Johnson, University of New Orleans; and Joan McGregor, Arizona State University.

We are also indebted to the many instructors who have used our anthology, *People, Penguins, and Plastic Trees: Basic Issues in Environmental Ethics* (the first and second editions), and the predecessors to this volume. We thank them for their usage and comments.

We welcome responses to this collection, especially by email, on ways to make future editions of this volume more useful. Our addresses are

Don_VanDeVeer@ncsu.edu
Chris_Pierce@ncsu.edu

INTRODUCTION

Don't look back. Something might be
gaining on you.

Satchel Paige

Ethical enlightenment is often a matter of
recognizing, sometimes to the surprise
and discomfiture of whole cultures, that
there exist whole realms of moral dilemmas, responsibilities, and obligations that
have been simply missed, even by the
moral giants of earlier generations of the
culture. Looking back, for example, it is
almost incomprehensible to us that our
Declaration of Independence was written
by a slaveholder.

Mark Sagoff

The disaster of the terrorist attack upon the
United States on September 11, 2001 was recognizable instantly, much of it viewed as it
happened, in America especially but also
around the world. However, individually and
collectively we are not very good at recognizing slowly emerging catastrophes. People seldom notice the onset of cancer. The first stages
of the death of a lake tend to fall beneath the
threshold of attention. The dying of a forest
may occur slowly and imperceptibly, until
nothing can be done to save it. If we have been
causing the catastrophic warming of the planet
by our industrial activities in the last two centuries, we may not realize it "for sure" until
tragedy is upon us. And if we have not properly valued the lives of the hundreds of thousands, perhaps millions, of species becoming
extinct during our, and the next, generation,
the products of billions of years of evolution
may be gone because we have chosen, half-
wittingly, to play Russian roulette with the
planet in the name of wealth maximization,

efficiency, "growth," or some other demanding
modern divinity. To have a clue about "what
on earth we are doing," we need a clear, well-
reasoned basis for deciding how to *evaluate*
what we are doing. The price of our not doing
so is already being paid by virtually all species
of living creatures, as well as our own.

For reasons made clear in various parts of
this volume, much under the sun is going
awry, or has already done so. This claim is not
entirely uncontroversial. Why think so? What
exactly are we doing to the planet that we
ought not to be doing or that we ought to be
doing differently? There is much dispute about
how to deal appropriately with our nonhuman
surroundings: the other animals, the forests,
the air, and the oceans, for example.

Indeed, one of the fundamental questions
explored in this volume is whether living
beings other than humans have a value of
their own, not reducible to their instrumental
value (the value of something as a means to an
end) to human beings. As we shall put the
point, do such nonhumans have "moral
standing"? If so, just what value should we
assign to, or recognize in, such beings, and
why? Or can we determine what is the "right
thing to do" to "nature" or nonhuman entities
solely on the basis of considering the short- or
long-term interests of humans of this and/or
future generations? These questions, and
diverse answers to them, underlie competing
views concerning a host of important issues.
The belief that certain nonhumans do have
moral standing has motivated the formulation
of a new "environmental ethic" and a critique
of traditional moral philosophy and economic
theory, both of which historically have

assumed that all and *only* humans "count" (an assumption labeled *anthropocentrism*). Traditional moral philosophy and economic theory have also come in for a good deal of criticism from those who maintain that, when we consider the long-term interests of current and future generations of humans, traditional theories are indefensible; in this view, an intelligent, enlightened anthropocentrism is all we must endorse.

In the last two decades especially, a further criticism has developed among nonanthropocentrists, a criticism of those who, although they recognize certain nonhumans as having a kind of inherent worth of their own, still restrict the bearers of value to *individual* animals or plants. Some environmental thinkers believe that such a view cannot account for the value of ecosystems, habitats, systems of life, indeed, the existence of a biodiverse and ecologically sustainable planet. So, from this critical stance, if we are to formulate the right view to take about our planet or the biosphere, we must surrender both the anthropocentric assumption that all and only humans possess inherent worth or value and the widely held assumption that only *individuals* have such value. The wrong view on these matters is not only intellectually indefensible; acting on this view promises to destroy the biosphere, and perhaps more quickly than people realize who are unaware of the current rate of extinction of nonhumans, the connections between modern industrialization as often practiced, and its destructive effects on our global climate.

The development of a comprehensive, reasoned view about how we ought to be dealing with our nonhuman environment may be labeled an "environmental ethic." We would not quarrel with those who wish to speak of an "ecological ethic" or a moral philosophy of the environment." In the final analysis, this volume is philosophical in the somewhat restricted sense in which professional philosophers use that term, and not in the loose and popular sense in which the editors' university once offered a course in the "philosophy of home decorating." Indeed, the materials presented herein were chosen with the aim of setting out those relevant facts, moral principles, and other considerations that foster the formulation of such an ethic.

Problems about pollution, pesticide use, smog, worries about running out of fossil fuels, and so on are now familiar. However, because of rapid growth in the human population, our commandeering of remaining animal habitats, the great increase in carbon emissions, the spread of the "cattle culture" (consequent demand for land for grazing or growing grain and resulting destruction of the rain forest), we are now bumping up against certain of nature's thresholds for the first time since humans came to exist on this planet some 3 to 5 million years ago (on these thresholds see Essay 89, by Robert Goodland). Our activities are more intense; our population has increased to over 6 billion from about 1 billion in the early 1800s. The most recent time for our population to double has been less than 50 years. We are many! Our impact is greater. Thus our decisions, our modes of determining policy and designing social institutions, are more important than ever. As a cartoon character used to say, "Time's a' wasting."

Successful formulation of a new environmental ethic will require attention to the best science available. For reasons suggested in Part 1, "An Introduction to Ethical Theory," empirical assumptions will play a crucial role in the formulation and defense of normative or moral conclusions about what we ought to be doing with regard to environmental policies. Indeed, we believe that philosophers, scientists, analysts, and formulators of public policy are doomed to important failures if they follow a different path.

Scientists, like others, are often guided by normative assumptions, however, of which they may be only dimly aware and that often lie hidden.[1] In contrast to some volumes concerned with environmental issues, we give a prominent place to the *unearthing and critical examination of moral or evaluative principles,* which are often invoked either explicitly (openly) or tacitly. Further, one cannot be in a position to decide whether a new ethic, a new "environmental ethic," is needed unless one has an understanding of the leading and dominant points of view until recent decades, at which time they began to come under assault. For those reasons, a somewhat extensive and detailed (to newcomers) review of the leading, competing ethical outlooks is provided in the "Introduction to Ethical Theory." A complete first reading may be usefully followed by a rereading of relevant parts as the occasion arises. Some instructors in college or university courses will choose to assign parts of it in a piecemeal fashion, or use it only for reference. In this regard some of the essays can be read easily and easily understood by the typical advanced undergraduate student. Others are more like a steep, curved road and require slow, careful driving, perhaps with a rest stop thrown in, as one gets weary of completing the whole trip without a break. Sometimes a guide is crucial.

A word is in order about how we chose the essays or excerpts and also what led us to order them as we did. First, the range of materials available on the issues discussed herein is extensive. Ideally, a person fully knowledgeable in biology, geology, meteorology, climatology, ethics, political philosophy, forestry, botany, economics, decision theory, and a few other domains would make a good editor. This editorial pair failed to qualify even collectively in this respect. Still, we refused to "stay on our own turf," as might more proper academicians. No doubt we are, therefore, still unaware of some of the best essays deserving consideration. In addition to our own limitations, there is a kind of holistic consideration in choosing essays; we aimed for some degree of balance and diversity, not among all views, but among those that we believe deserve a

hearing. Sheer lack of space also led to some painful omissions, as well as a few painful deletions of first-rate essays in moving to the third edition of this volume. In some cases the historical influence of an essay led to its inclusion, even if we thought that it was not the most sophisticated or the most illuminating one available; in some cases we opted for essays of high quality that have not been so influential, at least not yet.

We comment now about our ordering of the materials and briefly identify the focal points of the different sections in the seven parts of this volume.

After the initial survey, in Part I, of the leading ethical theories, the vocabulary and ingredients of moral argument, some reflection on the relation of moral and empirical claims, and the relevance of science to normative policy conclusions, we turn in Part II, "Western Religious and Cultural Perspectives," to a limited examination of the influence of the Judeo-Christian tradition on our environmental attitudes and policies over the last 2000-plus years. A focal point concerns historian Lynn White's famous essay (4), which traces some of the historic roots of our current environmental crises to the influence of that tradition. Essay 5 by Andrew Linzey, Christian theologian, agrees with White but is hopeful about a Judeo-Christian environmentalism. Nina Rosenstand's essay (10) sketches certain Greco-Roman influences, Romantic attitudes toward nature, as well as those of certain American Indians. The views of Aristotle, Descartes, Bentham, J. S. Mill, Darwin, and others emerge elsewhere in this book.

After the broad sweep of Part II, Part III, "The Other Animals," focuses on our dealings with those living nonhuman entities in "the environment," some of which closely resemble us and some of which are, in fact, loved by humans more than humans love, or care about, many members of their own species. It is tempting to think that if we ought to respect, attribute rights to, or acknowledge duties toward any entities in the not-members-of-our species category, those entities would be the animals, or at least some subset of them—given the way in which some especially enter our culture, and are sometimes members of our communities. So it seems natural to begin one's reflections there. Part III thus begins the exploration of just what our stance toward animals should be, which ones are owed duties, if any, and on what grounds?

Part IV, "Constructing an Environmental Ethic," examines the arguments underlying the assumption that we have stringent duties to nonhuman animals (itself a nontraditional view) and at most to them. Indeed, this view is attacked or questioned on at least two fronts. First, some claim that it is not merely some set of animals (for example, those that are sentient or are subjects of a life) to which we owe duties not to harm (or, for example, respect or aid), but a wider range of entities in the nonhuman environment—for example, all living creatures. Thus, defenders of "biocentric" views may attribute a kind of noninstrumental or intrinsic worth both to plants and animals, if not the inanimate parts of the planet that interact in a crucial, life-supporting way with living creatures. "Biocentric egalitarians" may attribute "equal inherent worth," in some sense, to all living creatures (not necessarily implying that all merit equal *treatment*). Thus these philosophers, and others, view "animal liberationists" (such as Peter Singer or Tom Regan) as stopping short in their recognition of beings that possess moral standing (on this latter concept, see the Preview to Part III). Another deep source of disagreement is that between those who think that intrinsic value is attributable not to nonhuman *individuals* only (such as animals or trees) but rather to certain complexes, for example, to ecosystems or habitats or perhaps to the planet as a whole—and those who take a more "individualist" view of things. The for-

mer may discount, or even deny, that individual animals and other entities possess intrinsic value. The latter are often accused of only extending those bounds of moral concern that were defined more narrowly by traditional theories of rights or the theory of Utilitarianism (see Part I). Holistically oriented critics, especially, claim that a more radical, new ethic is needed that goes beyond extending (compare "extensionist views") moral standing to nonhuman individuals.

If we allow that certain nonhuman entities have moral standing, the nature of conflicts of interest becomes considerably more complicated. Some essays in Part IV struggle with questions about how to resolve such conflicts. Others focus on the views of *Deep Ecologists* who bring their own brand of criticism to traditional anthropocentric orientations as well as dissent from other environmentalist views. In recent years some feminists have both defended certain views described as *ecofeminist* and explored the question of how feminist concerns mesh or do not mesh with those of certain environmentalists—for example, those who think that the metaphor "Mother Earth" is useful in exploring questions of environmental policy, or the question of whether the exploitation of women is connected to human exploitation of nature. Vandana Shiva (Essay 36) focuses on the special conflicts for women in third world nations who may be caught between prodevelopment forces and those who call for something other than "slash-and-burn" approaches to economic growth.

As noted, two important sources of disagreement among those who defend this or that ground as the proper basis of decision making for environmental policy concern (1) whether some nonhumans have moral standing, and (2) whether individuals or certain "wholes" (such as species) do. However, it is important to keep in mind that there are many *within* the anthropocentrist camp (for example, those who rely only on the consideration of what is in the long-term interests of members of our species) who also are highly critical of traditional economics and traditional moral philosophy as well. They are critical of anyone who ignores questions about what practices are ecologically sustainable in the long run, as well as what will promote the well-being of, and justice toward, future generations of human beings. They typically are critical of the way in which traditional ethics and economics has underplayed the dependency of humans on the larger ecosystems in which they live. In this respect anthropocentrists may reach substantial agreement with nonanthropocentrists about the *instrumental* value of nonhuman living and nonliving dimensions of our "environment." To emphasize a point, persistent environmental disagreements and disputes may be but are *not* necessarily over the question of what beings have moral standing. This point becomes more evident in Parts V and VI in this volume.

A common view among economists and many others is that we should let the market decide how to deal with environmental problems, such as scarcity of resources and sinks (places or methods to dispose of our waste). Why should we do that? The answer is that, at least under certain idealized conditions, the market will maximize "consumer satisfaction" or, one might say more neutrally, "human satisfaction." And some would say that that is no different from "utility maximization," thus making clear the utilitarian antecedents of modern economic theory. Such a procedure tends to assign value only on the basis of individual humans' willingness and ability to pay in actual or hypothetical markets. But we may ask whether the value of a rain forest or a species should be equated with its market value during a particular time slice.

Traditional economic theory thus offers a procedure, a theory-laden but widely accepted one, for dealing with environmental questions. It receives initial attention in Section V.A, "Letting the Market Decide."

When we do not leave matters to the market, but rather demand that government agencies (or even corporations) formulate and implement policy with respect to some environmental issue (such as the radical reduction of fish stocks off the northeast coast of the United States and Canada) it is usually assumed that the relative costs and benefits of alternative policies should be weighed and perhaps that what should be done is to maximize benefits minus costs. These matters are the focus of V.B, "Cost–Benefit Analysis." However, serious questions arise about what we should count as costs and as benefits, how this is in fact done, what is done arbitrarily, and what such procedures omit. Indeed, the tendency to focus on what is more readily quantifiable, on what appears to be scientific and rational, is a source of worry. Sometimes a nation can squander its important natural assets without this loss showing up much in its national accounting procedures. Given the heroic effort economists make to measure the actual gains and losses related to various social arrangements and, further, the enormous influence economists have in the formulation of public policy, these questions are of great practical and theoretical importance. Section V.B explores some proposed new measures of how a nation is doing, ones with which users try to measure ecological, as well as economic, gains and losses.

Sections V.C, "From the Commons to Property," and V.D, "Human Population and Pressure on 'Resources,'" turn more directly to specific environmental problems and to questions of specific policy, especially concerns about human population pressures and environmental "resources" (see V.D). Ironically, the Earth Summit at Rio de Janeiro in 1992 managed to avoid addressing what is, arguably, the major source of the rapid destruction of the earth's ecosystems and elimination of extraordinary numbers of the earth's species during this era, namely the vast increase in the *population* of the very adaptive, intelligent, and omnivorous species of which we are members. Questions of environmental policy are, thus, closely connected to questions about the desirability of controlling human population growth and the permissibility (do individual humans have "right to procreate" no matter what the consequences?) or obligation to do so. The regular political denial of this problem is, then, a further practical obstacle. Issues concerning the supply of natural resources and places for our wastes, "sources and sinks," are only made more urgent by population increases. One essayist, however, argues that resources are infinite, so we need not worry.

Both certain proposed solutions to some environmental problems and the explanations of some problems are tied to questions about the appropriate distribution of *property rights* (see V.C). In a famous essay, "The Tragedy of the Commons" (Essay 47), Garrett Hardin urges that many of our problems derive from the fact that certain goods are jointly owned or held in common, such as the oceans, the air, and certain lands. It is predictable, Hardin maintains, that such "commons" are often exploited, because it is in the self-interest of anyone to partake of the benefits in question and to pass on the costs to others. But is the remedy to such problems to privatize such commons or to mutually agree to coercively enforceable restraints—as Hardin suggests? Dissenting views, the concept of property rights, and questions about the justification of the state's "taking" property, and what constitutes a "taking" are explored in this section.

One of the most important and controversial proposals in recent years is that we humans must adopt practices that are *ecologically sustainable*—on one interpretation: practices that can be carried on indefinitely with no net harm to our environment—in large part because we have some duties to future generations. The most plausible formulation of this kind of proposal is controversial; its implications are as well. Some commentators claim that we have, at best, just another meaningless buzzword or, at worst, a demand that we give up the legitimate ideal of continued economic growth. The direction taken on certain fundamental environmental policies in the coming decades, or more, depends in part on the resolution of the nest of disputes surrounding questions about sustainability. A vigorous intellectual crossfire among economists and philosophers is found in V.E, "Future Generations and Sustainability Questions." The dividing lines are not between these two groups.

The content of Section VI.A, "Preserving Biodiversity," is self-evident. "Biodiversity" generally is defined not merely in terms of species diversity, but we merely flag that issue here. The moral questions about whether we have duties to individual plants or animals, to species, or to entire ecosystems seem all the more urgent given certain facts. As we chainsaw and burn our forests, over 70 species become extinct each day, about 27,000 per year. At this moment we are turning the earth into a more sterile, more homogeneous place; 20 percent of the earth's species, species that have come down to this time over a span of about 3.5 billion years, will become extinct in the next 30 years.[2] Facts about the rates and nature of extinction are well delineated in the essay (64) here by E. O. Wilson, and in VI.C by Norman Myers (Essay 77). As these losses happen comparatively slowly by usual standards (not geological time frames—in which the losses are astonishingly rapid) we tend to be blind to what is going on—especially the rapid changes in the biosphere in the last 30 to 50 years or so. Some puzzles about the very concept of species and various grounds for preserving or not preserving species are also explored in Section VI.A.

Aside from unpredictable events such as war and disease, worldwide ongoing practices such as the growing and harvesting of food has an enormous impact on our environment. The devastation of cod populations off the northeast coasts of Canada and the United States resulted from unrestrained harvesting. In this last century, partly due to human population growth, we have seen the virtual extinction of many species. Small farms disappear rapidly. Large factory-like farms tend to grow very few types of plants. Such monocultures are more vulnerable to disease. Large companies that sell, for example, french fries, determine market demand and, thus, which potatoes farmers can profitably grow and sell. Our personal eating habits ["want fries with that?"] collectively alter the world. Corporate decisions then have a powerful influence on the diversity or lack of diversity on existing forms of life. To minimize disease or enhance product life, and to maximize profits, more corporations have begun to develop genetically modified plants. This involves transferring genes from other organisms to host plants to alter their characteristics. Newly created organisms include strawberries modified with flounder genes to produce strawberries with a capacity to withstand colder temperatures. In the works are bacteria modified to be sensitive to TNT for use in detecting explosives. Some of these projects are changing our landscape and the practices of agriculture. Some run the risk of producing unforeseen, out-of-control alterations of the natural world—potentially having radical effects on the course of evolution, arguably for the first time in the history of the world. Some think that this is another instance in which private interests [corporate ones] are passing on costs to others. There is something new under the sun and the essays in VI.B, most by scientists, elaborate and discuss these matters. Another essay by philosopher Claudia Mills discusses the related issue of whether corporations or others should be allowed to patent forms of life.

In Section VI.C, "Wilderness and Forests," a central point is related to the preservation of biodiversity. Old-growth forests, and especially tropical rain forests, constitute the habitats of an astonishingly large number of the world's species. Whether developed nations can expect developing nations to not exploit such areas, when the United States and others have a small percentage of the world's population but consume most of the world's resources, is another important issue. Indeed, our hamburger habit contributes to rain forest destruction. Although the record of the United States in some environmental matters has been, in a number of respects, admirable, there is much criticism of the policy of the U.S. Forest Service and its practice of massive clear-cutting and selling off the trees to logging companies at fees below the actual costs of putting in roads to, and maintaining, the forests. One wonders whether the American people would remain so acquiescent if the Lincoln Memorial, the Vietnam Memorial, or Yellowstone Park were being sold off for the benefit of private corporations—or how Canadians would accept the selling off of Stanley Park in Vancouver, or Londoners the paving of their beautiful city parks. The Forest Service policy is discussed by Perri Knize and Bryan Norton (Essays 78 and 79).

An extremely powerful set of players on the international stage are the world's corporations. Talk of environmental policy, what affects it, and so on, is unrealistic without attention to the influence of these mega-agents. When, for example, large corporations engaged in mining in the United States walk away from their operations leaving large, arsenic-poisoned lakes or ponds—having made land purchases from the U.S. government at $5 an acre—questions arise about the proper role of corporations. The effects of corporate activity are not always environmentally destructive; some argue for laissez-faire, less or no "interference" from "meddling," "do good," "ineffectual," "bureaucratic" government agencies. Some argue that the only duty of corporate boards of directors is to maximize corporate profits—but within what constraints? Such is the familiar battle cry of conservatives. The governments of developing countries come close to giving corporations *carte blanche,* believing that the national per capita income will be increased and that this is, therefore, the path to take. Does this happen? Is it a good thing? Must we choose *between* attributing some blame to corporations and some blame to governments? Why not both? These matters are discussed in VI.D.

Section VI.E, "Sliding to Global Catastrophe," all too briefly touches on some very large issues concerning how we degrade the planet and its ecosystems, sometimes on a global scale. We begin with an excerpt (Essay 88) from Rachel Carson's awareness-raising book, *Silent Spring,* about the accumulation of enormous numbers of new chemicals in our environment, a phenomenon especially since World War II. There is still too little knowledge today of their interaction in the environment; arguably, we are allowing the poisoning of the commons, and indirectly the premature death and avoidable debilitation of millions or billions of living creatures. There are significant benefits, to be sure, to some, but there are questions about whether we know enough even to be capable of adding up the costs and the benefits—or consider the fairness of the distribution of them.

The other issue discussed here is the dispute over global warming. The increase is alleged to be due, in part, to humanly generated carbon emissions and the consequent *intensification* of the "greenhouse effect." This latter problem, in the worst case, could make World War II seem like a minor event in terms of the sheer amount of morbidity and mortality that could result. So far, this issue has been largely ignored by the public and most politicians and denied by various corporate interests—insurance companies being a notable, and perhaps instructive, exception. The evidence suggests, however, the *prospect of events of low to moderate probability occurring, which would involve, as we have noted, horrendous losses of both humans and other living things.* What (1) the evidence suggests, and (2) what we

should be doing about such matters given some crude agreement about (1) are explored in the debate between Patrick Michaels and Christopher Flavin (Essays 90 and 91).

In becoming more aware of the way things are, it seems perfectly natural to become more than a bit discouraged about what has happened, and what cannot be halted. After all, much of what is occurring has momentum, like a battleship, and cannot be stopped or redirected quickly. Still, things can be done to alter policy, and, in fact, some are being done. Part VII, "Varieties of Activism," considers questions about what one might do, assuming that one has done his or her "theoretical homework" and formulated a reasoned view about possible solutions. The options range from making personal changes in one's lifestyle, minor or major (compare giving up rhinohorn aphrodisiacs, ivory piano keys, our battery powered gadgets, or the use of a car!), to lobbying or educating to persuade others to change public policy and alter our political and economic institutions, or engaging in serious civil disobedience as have some of the courageous members of Earth First! or the Sea Shepherds. Regarding the effort to make personal, environment-friendly, lifestyle changes, we do *not* focus on "101 Things One Can Do to Save the Environment." Rather, one essay (98), by Guy Claxton, focuses on the psychological difficulty of altering one's deeply ingrained personal habits—even when one aspires to do so. We trust that this is a familiar problem—given the frequency of attempts to quit smoking, to lose weight, to quit watching so much television, to exercise, and so on.

A final word about the order of the readings. They can be read chronologically, and in many sections we ordered them with that in mind. The reader can move from the simpler to the more complex materials; the order in some sections reflects the difficulty of the content. We gave the heaviest consideration to pedagogical considerations, namely what we determined to be a useful order of investigation, reflection, teaching, and learning (especially the natural rhythms of learning)—not necessarily learning over a 2- or 3-day period, but sequences that help to "put things in place" over a long time period (or span of material). Because the essays can be referred to by number, an instructor's contriving, and specifying, an alternative order of reading should not be difficult.

NOTES

1. The hideous experimentation of Nazi scientists and physicians on Jews and gypsies constitutes one example. The fudging of data on so-called IQ tests by American scientists during the 1920s and 1930s to support racist and ethnic preconceptions is documented by Stephen Jay Gould in *The Mismeasure of Man*. Government officials and physicians cooperated from the 1930s to the 1960s not to treat, and simply to observe, black men in the southern United States who were infected with syphilis (see James Jones, *Bad Blood*). And the lack of research on the causes and treatment of breast cancer in the United States probably reflects a certain sexist bias inside and outside the scientific professions, in view of the fact that breast cancer affects one out of nine women in the United States. One may hold the *belief* that one has a method that ensures the elimination of bias and irrationality, which in part fosters one's unwillingness to look critically and reasonably at certain of one's own inferences or beliefs. The point is, we think, well supported in the history of science, philosophy, and other disciplines.

2. The figures are from E. O. Wilson, *The Diversity of Life* (Cambridge, MA: Harvard University Press, 1992).

PROLOGUE: WORLD SCIENTISTS' WARNING TO HUMANITY

Issued in Washington, DC, by the Union of Concerned Scientists on the 18th of November, 1992, on behalf of over 1,600 scientists, including a majority of the living Nobel Laureates in the sciences.

Human beings and the natural world are on a collision course. Human activities inflict harsh and often irreversible damage on the environment and on critical resources. If not checked, many of our current practices put at serious risk the future that we wish for human society and the plant and animal kingdoms, and may so alter the living world that it will be unable to sustain life in the manner that we know. Fundamental changes are urgent if we are to avoid the collision our present course will bring about.

THE ENVIRONMENT

The environment is suffering critical stress:

The Atmosphere

Stratospheric ozone depletion threatens us with enhanced ultraviolet radiation at the earth's surface, which can be damaging or lethal to many lifeforms. Air pollution near ground level, and acid precipitation, are already causing widespread injury to humans, forests, and crops.

Water Resources

Heedless exploitation of depletable groundwater supplies endangers food production and other essential human systems.

Heavy demands on the world's surface waters have resulted in serious shortages in some 80 countries, containing 40 percent of the world's population. Pollution of rivers, lakes and groundwater further limits the supply.

Oceans

Destructive pressure on the oceans is severe, particularly in the coastal regions that produce most of the world's food fish. The total marine catch is now at or above the estimated maximum sustainable yield. Some fisheries have already shown signs of collapse. Rivers carrying heavy burdens of eroded soil into the seas also carry industrial, municipal, agricultural, and livestock waste—some of it toxic.

Soil

Loss of soil productivity, which is causing extensive land abandonment, is a widespread by-product of current practices in agriculture and animal husbandry. Since 1945, 11 percent of the earth's vegetated surface has been degraded—an area larger than India and China combined—and per capita food production in many parts of the world is decreasing.

Forests

Tropical rain forests, as well as tropical and temperate dry forests, are being destroyed rapidly. At present rates, some critical forest types will be gone in a few years, and most of the tropical rain forest will be gone before the end of the next century. With them will go large numbers of plant and animal species.

Living Species

The irreversible loss of species, which by 2100 may reach one-third of all species now living, is especially serious. We are losing the potential they hold for providing medicinal and other benefits, and the contribution that genetic diversity of lifeforms gives to the robustness of the world's biological systems and to the astonishing beauty of the earth itself.

Much of this damage is irreversible on a scale of centuries, or permanent. Other processes appear to pose additional threats. Increasing levels of gases in the atmosphere from human activities, including carbon dioxide released from fossil fuel burning and from deforestation, may alter climate on a global scale. Predictions of global warming are still uncertain—with projected effects ranging from tolerable to very severe—but the potential risks are very great.

Our massive tampering with the world's interdependent web of life—coupled with the environmental damage inflicted by deforestation, species loss, and climate change—could trigger widespread adverse effects, including unpredictable collapses of critical biological systems whose interactions and dynamics we only imperfectly understand.

Uncertainty over the extent of these effects cannot excuse complacency or delay in facing the threats.

POPULATION

The earth is finite. Its ability to absorb wastes and destructive effluent is finite. Its ability to provide food and energy is finite. Its ability to provide for growing numbers of people is finite. And we are fast approaching many of the earth's limits. Current economic practices which damage the environment, in both developed and underdeveloped nations, cannot be continued without the risk that vital global systems will be damaged beyond repair.

Pressures resulting from unrestrained population growth put demands on the natural world that can overwhelm any efforts to achieve a sustainable future. If we are to halt the destruction of our environment, we must accept limits to that growth. A World Bank estimate indicates that world population will not stabilize at less than 12.4 billion, while the United Nations concludes that the eventual total could reach 14 billion, a near tripling of today's 5.4 billion. But, even at this moment, one person in five lives in absolute poverty without enough to eat, and one in ten suffers serious malnutrition.

No more than one or a few decades remain before the chance to avert the threats we now confront will be lost and the prospects for humanity immeasurably diminished.

WARNING

We the undersigned senior members of the world's scientific community, hereby warn all humanity of what lies ahead. A great change in our stewardship of the earth and the life on it is required, if vast human misery is to be avoided and our global home on this planet is not to be irretrievably mutilated.

WHAT WE MUST DO

Five inextricably linked areas must be addressed simultaneously.

1. We must bring environmentally damaging activities under control to restore and protect the integrity of the earth's systems we depend on. We must, for example, move away from fossil fuels to more benign, inexhaustible energy sources to cut greenhouse gas emissions and the pollution of our air and water. Priority must

be given to the development of energy sources matched to Third World needs—small-scale and relatively easy to implement. We must halt deforestation, injury to and loss of agricultural land, and the loss of terrestrial and marine plant and animal species.

2. We must manage resources crucial to human welfare more effectively. We must give high priority to efficient use of energy, water, and other materials, including expansion of conservation and recycling.

3. We must stabilize population. This will be possible only if all nations recognize that it requires improved social and economic conditions, and the adoption of effective, voluntary family planning.

4. We must reduce and eventually eliminate poverty.

5. We must ensure sexual equality, and guarantee women control over their own reproductive decisions.

The developed nations are the largest polluters in the world today. They must greatly reduce their overconsumption, if we are to reduce pressures on resources and the global environment. The developed nations have the obligation to provide aid and support to developing nations, because only the developed nations have the financial resources and the technical skills for these tasks.

Acting on this recognition is not altruism, but enlightened self-interest: whether industrialized or not, we all have but one lifeboat. No nation can escape from injury when global biological systems are damaged. No nation can escape from conflicts over increasingly scarce resources. In addition, environmental and economic instabilities will cause mass migrations with incalculable consequences for developed and underdeveloped nations alike.

Developing nations must realize that environmental damage is one of the gravest threats they face, and that attempts to blunt it will be overwhelmed if their populations go unchecked. The greatest peril is to become trapped in spirals of environmental decline, poverty, and unrest, leading to social, economic, and environmental collapse.

Success in this global endeavor will require a great reduction in violence and war. Resources now devoted to the preparation and conduct of war—amounting to over $1 trillion annually—will be badly needed in the new tasks and should be diverted to the new challenges.

A new ethic is required—a new attitude towards discharging our responsibility for caring for ourselves and for the earth. We must recognize its fragility. We must no longer allow it to be ravaged. This ethic must motivate a great movement, convincing reluctant leaders and reluctant governments and reluctant peoples themselves to effect the needed changes.

The scientists issuing this warning hope that our message will reach and affect people everywhere. We need the help of many.

We require the help of the world community of scientists—natural, social, economic, political;

We require the help of the world's religious leaders; and

We require the help of the world's peoples.

We call on all to join us in this task.

Among the hundreds of prominent scientists who signed the Warning were 101 Nobel Prize winners—the majority of the living recipients in the sciences:

Philip Anderson	Nicholas Bloembergen
Christian Anfinsen	Baruch Blumberg
Werner Arber	Norman Borlaug
Julius Aschod	Adolph Butenandt
David Baltimore	Georges Charpak
George Bednorz	Stanley Cohen
Baruj Benacerraf	John Comforth
Sune Bergstrom	E. J. Corey
Hans Bethe	Jean Dausset
Michael Bishop	Gerard Debreu
Konrad Bloch	Johann Deisenhofer

Renato Dulbecco	Roald Hoffman	Joseph Murray	Herbert Simon
Manfred Eigen	Robert Holley	Louis Neel	George Snell
Gertrude Elion	Francis Jacob	Erwin Neher	Roger Sperry
Richard Ernst	Jerome Karle	Marshall Nirenberg	Jack Steinberger
Val Fitch	Henry Kendall	George Palade	Donnall Thomas
William Fowler	John Kendrew	Linus Pauling	Jan Tinbergen
Jerome Friedman	Maus von Klitzing	John Polanyi	Samuel C. C. Ting
Kenichi Fukui	Aaron Klug	George Porter	James Tobin
Carlton Gajdusek	Leon Lederman	Ilya Prigogine	Alexander Todd
Murray Gell-Mann	Yuan T. Lee	Edward Purcell	Susumu Tonegawa
P. G. de Gennes	Jean-Marie Lehn	T. Reichstein	John Vane
Donald Glaser	Wassily Leontief	Burton Richter	Harold Varmus
Sheldon Glashow	Rita Levi-Montalcini	F. Robbins	George Wald
Roger Guillemin	William Lipscomb	Carlo Rubbia	E. T. S. Walton
Herbert Hauptman	James Meade	Abdus Salam	James Watson
Dudley Herschbach	Simon van der Meer	Fredrick Sanger	Thomas Weller
Gerard Herzberg	Hartmut Michel	Melvin Schwartz	Torsten Wiesel
Anthony Hewish	Cesar Milstein	Julian Schwinger	Maurice Wilkins
George Hitchings	Franco Modigliani	Glen Seaborg	G. Wilkinson
Dorothy Hodgkin	Nevil Mott	Kai Siegbahn	

I

AN INTRODUCTION TO ETHICAL THEORY

> The creatures with which we are particularly concerned were, not so long ago, gregarious to a fault, noisy, quarrelsome, arboreal, bossy, sexy, clever, tool-using, with prolonged childhoods and tender regard for their young. One thing led to another, and in a twinkling their descendants had multiplied all over the planet, killed off their rivals, devised world-transforming technologies, and posed a mortal danger to themselves and to the many other beings with whom they share their small home.
>
> *Carl Sagan and Ann Druyan[1]*

> I dislike arguments of any kind. They are always vulgar, and often convincing.
>
> *Oscar Wilde*

1. MORAL ARGUMENT AND ETHICAL THEORY

1.1 DISTINGUISHING MORAL AND EMPIRICAL CLAIMS

Determining how we ought to live our "private" lives is hard enough; designing a just and sustainable nation is harder. Designing a just, sustainable, and biodiverse way to live on planet Earth is no mean task; it is not obvious that we members of *Homo sapiens* are up to the challenge—as we bicker during the largest extinction spasm since the last ice age and during massive, human-induced, risky changes in those processes that have hitherto supported life on earth.

Let us think about the importance of the meaning of key terms in assessing claims. To do so we make use of a comment of Charles Darwin. Darwin (1809–1882), author of *On the Origin of Species*, is one of the most influential thinkers the planet has ever seen. Because he was a notorious opponent of slavery and was known to heap "abuse" on those who readily took the whip to their horses, it may come as a surprise to read his words, "I want *practice* at mistreating the female sex."[2] The context of his remark is illuminating and exculpatory. He and a few fellow scientists (male) had managed to inflict a long, perhaps tedious, discussion of biological issues on their spouses (female). The context reveals that Darwin had used 'want' in its now archaic sense of 'lack' (to find someone "wanting in common sense" meant that he or she lacked common sense). Darwin, a generous man, did not mean that he *desired* practice at mistreating females. His remark did not suggest misogyny on his part after all, and our frequent desire to find flaws in great people must wait for another day. What, one might wonder, is the point of this piece of Darwiniana? It is simply that we often talk past each other, or simply do not grasp what someone is asserting unless we pay careful attention to the meaning of the words being used.

To begin our exploration of ethical theory and its relation to environmental issues, we need to reflect on the meaning of key terms such as *moral, ethical,* and *empirical.* Ultimately, we want to have some reasonably clear concept of just what "environmental ethics" is and its role in the larger intellectual scheme of things, assuming that there is a larger scheme of things.

A widespread view is that morality is about certain kinds of behavior, such as truth telling, sexual behavior, or the use of force. But it is difficult to define *morality* or *ethics* in terms of kinds of behavior. Let us consider some paradigm (perfectly clear, noncontroversial) examples of moral or ethical claims:

Rape is wrong.

Child abuse is contrary to one's duty.

We should not let people starve to death.

It is sometimes all right to lie.

Jeffrey Dahmer was an evil man.

Human life is very valuable.

By way of contrast, consider this list of sentences:

Rape is occurring as one reads this sentence.

Child abuse is absent in the Dominican Republic.

Thousands of people have died in Rwanda.

Lying is often motivated by the desire to avoid feeling shame.

Jeffrey Dahmer was an avowed heterosexual.

In 1992 there were over 5.4 billion people on earth.

The claims in the second list are matters of common sense or subject to scientific assessment (probably only the second sentence is false). What they seem to have in common is that they are all claims about the world (or some small aspect of it) and they are claims about the way the world *is, was,* or *will be.* Their truth or falsity is not simply a "matter of definition" or something to be ascertained merely from an examination of the meanings of the words (compare "It's raining or it's not," "Red is a color," "What will be, will be"). We shall label the claims about the world *empirical claims.* Such a use of the term *empirical* is common practice, but other terms are often used to refer to the same types of claims, for example, *descriptive, contingent, scientific, positive,* and *factual.* The important point is not to fight over who gets to choose the label, but rather to be clear about what kind of claim we are assessing. As we have characterized them, empirical claims may be true or false; that is, being true is not a necessary feature for a claim to be an empirical claim. By *factual claim,* some mean what we here mean by *empirical claim;* others use *factual claim* to mean a *true,* empirical claim.

Given the preceding, the following are empirical claims:

If the invertebrates all died, the species *Homo sapiens* would die out within a year.

Stories about a hole in the ozone layer are, like the story about the Holocaust, concocted to scare decent, hardworking citizens.

It takes about 500 years for an inch of topsoil to accumulate.

Stereotypes about "eggheads" and "nerds" suggest that those who use such terms have a certain prejudice against those who think hard or thoroughly about certain matters.

The earth is about 4.5 billion years old.

Obviously, we cannot ascertain the truth or falsity of many empirical claims without scientific inquiry. Although humans have been on this planet for several million years (and "prehuman hominids" even longer), it is only in the last few geological "moments," so to speak, namely the last three centuries, that we have acquired certain substantial empirical knowledge about our planet, such as some knowledge of its age, of the ice ages, of prior mass extinctions, of atomic structure, of the evolution of life, of the transmission of genes, of continental drift. This is a point of enormous import for making decisions about the environment, one to which we shall return.

Now we are in a better position to inquire how moral or ethical claims differ from empirical ones. What makes a moral or ethical claim a moral or ethical claim? The feature that seems to characterize, and in fact be definitive of, a moral claim is that it is about what someone (a person, a church, a corporation) *ought* or *ought not to do*—or a claim about the merit or demerit of someone's character.[3] Look once more at the initial set of claims, which seem to include noncontroversial examples of moral claims. Empirical claims are, then, claims about what is, was, or will be the case and whose truth or falsity depends on what did, does, or will happen. In contrast, moral (or "ethical" or "normative") claims are primarily about what ought or ought not to be done (or to have been done).[4] Thus, moral and empirical claims seem to be of logically different sorts. Shortly we shall consider further the relationship between the two.

Given our functional, but not fastidious, working conception about what is a moral or ethical claim, the following are moral claims:

Children should be eliminated from television advertisements.

White males should be exterminated.

Inefficiency ought to be maximized.

Species' diversity ought to be minimized.

It's all right to torture cats for fun.

Arguably, all the preceding claims are unreasonable; so, in saying that a claim is a moral one, we speak only of the *kind* of claim it is and not of the assessment to be made of that claim (notice that the term *moral* may also be used evaluatively as in "the moral thing to do"—in which *moral* is contrasted with *immoral*). The question of what sort of rational assessment of moral claims may be made is another one to which we shall return.

Our working definition of *moral claim* remains deficient in one respect. It requires us to say that "Keep your elbows off the table when dining" and "It's impermissible to drool when in polite society" are moral claims; our (linguistic) intuitions, however, suggest otherwise. We may wish to preserve some sort of etiquette-versus-morality contrast by recognizing a distinction between comparatively urgent and nonurgent moral claims (classifying claims of etiquette in the latter category). Ultimately, a more thorough account may need to insist that we cannot entirely succeed in explicating the concept of a moral claim without taking into account the kinds of reasons people are prepared to give in defense of their judgments. Given these distinctions, a few points of interest emerge. One is that we cannot identify moral claims by their subject matter. We cannot, for example, rightly say that moral claims are always about sex, the use of force, killing, or truth telling. The following may be, and often are, claims about what someone ought to do:

The United States ought to maximize its self-interest.

Japan ought to maximize its self-interest.

We ought not let any species become extinct.

Brazil ought to cut down its tropical forests to provide jobs for poor people.

The Federal Reserve in the United States ought to raise interest rates.

A hysterectomy is contraindicated.

Corporations ought radically to reduce CO_2 production.

In brief, based on the analysis given, a considerable number of claims of intuitively diverse sorts are to be classified as moral or ethical. Indeed, many leading "policy" issues are moral issues; they are questions about what we ought to do, or cease doing. Questions of what public policy ought to be, or of what laws we should or should not have, are moral questions, and they can be thought of as part of moral philosophy (we do not suggest for a moment that they should be explored only by professional moral philosophers). Some important questions in this volume are, then, moral or ethical in nature:

How ought we to treat animals?

Should we have a national biodiversity policy?

What should we do about the holes in the ozone layer?

What should we do about global warming?

What should we do to slow population growth?

What should we do about mass starvation?

Should we eliminate old-growth forests in order to provide jobs?

The last two lists suggest that an issue may be both "medical" *and* "moral," or "economic" *and* "moral," or "biological" *and* moral," or "political" *and* "moral." There is, then, a kind of remark that ought to be regarded with great suspicion, namely the kind in which an "authority" in one field says in an authoritative tone, "But that is a question of economics" (or "science," or "philosophy," or "law," or "chemistry," or "demography"). Many of these categories are *not mutually exclusive* and insights from different fields may be relevant. Claims implying otherwise often perform only the function that saying "shut up" performs; the latter does not normally foster rational inquiry.

The extent to which we routinely engage in moral and other sorts of evaluation is rarely acknowledged. Indeed, many people seem to hold the belief that they rarely, if ever, make moral or ethical judgments. This is surpassing strange. There seem to be at least two reasons for this. First, there are a small number of terms that seem "explicitly moral," namely *right, wrong, ought, duty, has a right, wicked, evil, irresponsible, permissible,* and so on. It is tempting to think that in the absence of such language, there is no moral claim being made. But we should consider the many (often apparently empirical) terms that are used in an evaluative manner, indeed to make moral judgments about what ought to be done or, perhaps, what is permissible to do. Consider these claims:

This policy is old-fashioned.

Senator Watt is defending his usual Neanderthal stance.

Your proposal is idiotic.

Where did Baker meet that bimbo?

Not to allow clear-cutting would be inefficient.

Your remark to Lakesha was ugly.

Stop being obsessive.

The economy is anemic.

The U.S. policy on global population control is myopic.

Well, yes, if abortion is legally prohibited, then there will be the side effect that some women will die using coat hangers in attempts to self-abort.

This is not a novel to be tossed aside lightly; it should be thrown with great force.[5]

It is rather evident that these claims are either moral (or at least evaluative) claims or clearly imply such. None, of course, uses the explicit moral language we noted earlier. Many terms have both an evaluative and a nonevaluative use; indeed, some began their lives, so to speak, as descriptive or empirical terms but came to be used primarily in an evaluative manner. One example involves the terms *idiot, imbecile,* and *moron.* At one time they were adopted by those who believed in the reliability of IQ tests to refer, respectfully, to those thought to have an IQ of 1 to 25, 26 to 50, or 51 to 75. We all know, however, that any fourth grader is evaluating and not merely describing when he or she says. "You're acting like a moron." We also often use the language of medicine (*sick, myopic*) or aesthetics (*ugly*) or other terms (*beastly, unnatural, primitive, state of the art*) to make evaluations.

A second possible, more indirect, reason for the widespread failure to recognize the extent of moral evaluation is found in the fact, as we might put it, that "morality gets a bad rap." The stereotypical image of "the moralist" or "the moralizer" is that of a person who tends to make unreasonable, harsh, moral judgments and is overly ready to use the coercive power of the law to see to it that everyone obeys the judgment. Most of us are rightly appalled by such people and go to extreme lengths to avoid *appearing* to be like them; for example, we avoid the use of explicit moral language and comfort ourselves with the notion that we do not even make moral claims. We kick them out the front door and sneak them in the back.

Another more obscure reason for refusing to be explicit about our moral judgments we only note in passing. From the 1920s through the 1940s especially, the Logical Positivist movement insisted, most roughly, that *only* empirically testable or verifiable claims were "cognitively meaningful."[6] In brief, it was held that everything else (poetry, moral claims, metaphysics, and religious claims) was either nonsense, the mere expression of emotion, commanding, or prescribing, or at least not anything to which rational discrimination was relevant (the frequently invoked, obscure, undefined "fact-versus-mere-opinion" distinction seems to be a cultural by-product, one known to haunt universities and a fair number of writings in the natural and social sciences). If one believed that one could not rationally choose among competing moral claims or that to make them is to speak nonsense, it would be natural to avoid the appearance of engaging in moral decision making. We note two difficulties with the thesis mentioned. It itself is not empirically verifiable; is the thesis nonsense? Second, it seems to imply that the two claims—(1) we ought to destroy life on earth, and (2) we ought not to destroy life on earth—are equally reasonable, or equally nonsense. On the face of it, such a claim is absurd. In our view, of course we make judgments about what people, ourselves included, and governments ought or ought not to do, and of course not all moral claims are equally reasonable. That fact settles nothing; that is where the interesting arguments *begin,* and no one should apologize for exploring them. As Socrates said about 2400 years ago, "We are discussing no small matter, but how we ought to live."[7]

1.2 JUSTIFICATION, EXPLANATION, PREDICTION, AND DESCRIPTION

We engage in a small number of intellectual activities. They are largely exhausted by listing these four categories: *moral justification, explanation, prediction,* and *description.* To think more clearly about trying to justify claims about what we ought to do regarding environmental issues, we need to consider the nature of explanation, description, and so on and explore briefly how these activities are related to one another. By so doing, we will better identify the role of moral argument and the respective roles of empirical and moral assumptions. Sometimes we simply want to *describe* the world:

In 1992, two out of three Japanese who were surveyed believed that one could become HIV infected by being bitten by mosquitoes.

Some airplanes purchased by the U.S. military cost almost $1 billion apiece.

Philosophers can be overbearing.

There are more than 43,000 students at Texas A&M University.

Fourteen years after evidence strongly suggested that CFCs are severely destructive to the ozone layer, the DuPont Corporation agreed to stop producing them.

Much of science aims simply at creating a correct *description* of the world (the sample claims just given happen to be true); doing so may be revolutionary. Consider, for example, the transforming impact of the establishment of descriptive claims such as these: The earth is not the center of the universe; humans evolved from far more simple forms of life.

Future-tensed true descriptions are the sorts of predictions at which science aims. Correct *prediction* is often possible when another scientific aim is achieved, namely, obtaining satisfactory *explanations* of events and processes. One influential, but by no means uncontroversial, view is that satisfactory scientific explanation must fit the "covering law model"; that is, such an explanation must be stated as an argument in which:

1. The conclusion is a statement that the event to be explained occurred.

2. The premises state that certain initial conditions were satisfied and state a scientific law.

3. The premises are all true.

4. The argument is valid (the conclusion must be true if the premises are).

A crude example explaining why some water turned to steam is this:

Under normal conditions of pressure, water, if heated to 100°C, will undergo a change of state and turn to steam.

This water was heated to 100°C.

This water turned to steam when so heated.

This is one simple example of the kind of causal story that is commonly regarded as necessary for giving a *scientific* explanation of an event; note that it is stated in the form of an *argument*. Arguments can be assessed in two main ways: (1) by assessing them for *validity*, and (2) by assessing the plausibility of their premises.

We suggest that the main activities of the sciences fall into the categories of describing, explaining, and predicting. Explaining and predicting, when fleshed out, take the form of making a claim and defending it, that is, setting out an argument, as noted. These arguments consist of empirical claims of one level of generality or another (or occasional logical truths or tautologies).[8]

There is another activity in which we engage that often *also* takes the form of making a claim and defending it with arguments (reasons). We try to identify justifications for moral judgments in cases of controversy between people and in cases about which we ourselves are morally perplexed.

To *justify* a moral claim is basically to give good reasons for the claim. Often the claim in question will be to the effect that a certain act is right (or wrong, as the case may be) either in the sense of being a duty or in the sense of being permissible. Many actions seem both morally justifiable *and* explainable, such as Ivan's giving his dad a birthday present, Maria's choosing a business or going to college, or Michael Jordan's choosing a career in professional basketball.

But to explain and to justify are not the same thing. There may be an explanation of why U.S. serial killer Jeffrey Dahmer killed a number of innocent people and ate some of their body parts, but surely there is no moral justification for his doing so (so we insist, without here offering any argument). We note that if certain explanations of actions are obtainable, then they also *may* serve to *excuse* the agents from blame. But to find that an agent is excused from blame for an act is not the same as finding that the act was right, that it was morally justified. For example, a killer may be determined to have been insane at the time of committing a murder; in such a case she or he may be judged not responsible for her or his act and, hence, not to blame. It does not follow that murder is acceptable.

1.3 MORAL ARGUMENT: THE INTERPLAY OF MORAL AND EMPIRICAL CLAIMS

Many important "environmental controversies" are moral or ethical in nature, questions about what moral agents ought or ought not to do. A *moral agent* is a being capable of reflecting on reasons, weighing them, and deliberately choosing—normally a member of *Homo sapiens*.[9] Positions on these controversies take the form of normative or moral assertions; for example, we *ought* radically to curtail the practice of eating beef, because the cattle culture plays a huge role in the destruction of the rain forests and of the ecological balance of natural habitats around the planet. To give reasons for one's claim is to make statements that can function as premises in an argument (for example, we ought not to destroy the rain forests, or we ought not to do anything to contribute to global warming). The argument will be a *moral argument*, because all we shall mean by that expression is an argument with a moral *conclusion*.[10] So the following is a moral argument:

Informally stated: That creosote plant should not be destroyed, because it is very valuable.

More formally and fully stated:

We ought to go to great lengths to avoid destroying rare living organisms.

This plant in the Joshua tree forest in California is an 11,700-year-old cre-osote bush and is, hence, the world's oldest living organism.

Thus, we ought not destroy this creosote bush.

So, we have a moral argument; we may also have an argument about public policy, an ecological argument, an argument about flora. Is it a good argument? That question is not so simple to answer. We only note that the argument has at least two virtues; its second premise is true and it is *valid* (in the technical sense of being one in which the conclusion must be true if the premises are). We will further consider how to assess arguments at a later point. Many scientists and ordinary citizens have concluded that we ought to be acting quite differently from the way we have been with regard to preserving biodiversity, halting destruction of the ozone layer, warding off massive global warming, destroying coral reefs, polluting the air, and trashing the oceans. Many others defend policies that are directly to the contrary. Do these normative or moral conclusions just fall from the sky, just spill out of scientific theories and assumptions, or are they not subject to rational assessment? Let us explore this question.

Because, as we noted earlier, moral and empirical claims seem to be of logically different sorts, it is tempting to think that an observation of eighteenth-century Scottish philosopher David Hume is correct. In a famous passage, after examining the writings of other moral philosophers, Hume noted,

> In every system of morality, which I have hitherto met with, I have always remark'd that the author proceeds for some time in the ordinary way of reasoning, and establishes the being of a God, or makes observations concerning human affairs; when of a sudden I am surpriz'd to find, that instead of the usual copulations of the propositions, *is* and *is not*, I meet with no proposition that is not connected with an ought, or an ought not. This change is imperceptible; but is,

however, of the last consequence. For as this *ought* or *ought not*, expresses some new relation or affirmation, 'tis necessary that it should be observed and explained; and at the same time that a reason should be given, for what seems altogether inconceivable, how this new relation can be a deduction from others, which are entirely different from it.[11]

Hume seems to be asserting that we cannot rightly infer any normative claim from any set of purely empirical premises. Indeed, it seems correct that we cannot validly infer that

Rape is wrong (or right).

from

Rape will occur (or did or does).

And we cannot validly infer that

It is wrong to generate and use leaded gasoline.

from

The use of leaded gasoline causes brain damage among children who are heavily exposed to it.

Most informally stated arguments are, however, *enthymematic* ones; that is, either the conclusion or one or more of the premises are not explicitly stated. In our last example, the argument *as stated* is invalid: The conclusion does not necessarily follow from the premises.[12] However, we might reasonably presume that the proponent of the argument is making a moral assumption and that when it is added to the original argument, the *revised* (thus, *different*) argument is valid; the likely assumption may be (something like) that it is wrong to do that which is known to cause nontrivial harm to children. If we were trying to be fastidiously complete, we might also state explicitly another tacit assumption, namely, that to cause brain damage is to cause nontrivial harm.

We are urging two key points about our recent discussion. One is that Hume seems to be correct. No moral conclusion validly follows from a set of purely empirical premises.[13] Many premises are paraded as purely empirical or purely scientific but are, in fact, *value laden* and are not, thus, subject to Hume's strictures. Here are a few claims that seem to be purely empirical but that may not be:

It is inefficient to install scrubbers on those SO_2-emitting smokestacks.

Lethal Dosage 50 tests impose gratuitous pain on the animal subjects.[14]

Abortion is the murder of a fetus.[15]

Those tree-hugging environmentalists want to halt growth.

These are my children.

Resources are unlimited.

The proposal to limit the size of one's family is un-American.

Those are weeds.

That nation exceeded its carrying capacity.

In these examples much depends on the interpretation of the key terms *inefficient, gratuitous, murder, growth, my, resource, un-American,* and so on.

Hume's claim that there is an "is-ought gap" or that there is a gulf between facts and values, as is sometimes said, is controversial. The matter is relevant to other arguments in this volume, such as attempts to derive some moral ideal from facts about the natural world (compare: "What's right is what is natural" and "What is right is whatever is conducive to the survival of the fittest" and "Whatever is unnatural is wrong"). It is also relevant to the assessment of various specific arguments, such as, Japanese representatives at an international conference on whaling arguing that they should be allowed to continue the killings *because* that is a very ancient practice for Japan. The familiar argument that it is morally permissible for the United States (or China, or Germany, or . . .) to sell large numbers of military weapons to almost any developing nation because others will do so if the United States does not, also seems to be an invalid inference (the inference of a normative conclusion from a purely empirical premise). One might be tempted to think that if Hume is correct, there is no sense in which science can be a basis for ethics and there is no purely scientific ground for normative policy recommendations. Nevertheless, it is clear that empirical suppositions play a crucial role in moral argument. Let us explore why. Consider this argument:

(b) If the United States set off its stock of lethal nerve gas weapons, millions, if not billions, of human and other lives would be destroyed.

(c) Hence, the United States ought not to set off its stock of lethal nerve gas weapons.

The argument, as stated, is simply an invalid one.[16] The conclusion does not follow unless we supply a relevant normative assumption. In this particular case we may supply one that is not very controversial; for example, we ought not to do that which would cause the deaths of millions of humans and other beings on earth. As originally stated, the preceding argument violated Hume's stricture. Consider this argument:

(a) We ought not to do that which would cause the death of millions of human and other lives.

(c) Hence, the United States ought not to set off its stock of lethal nerve gas weapons.

This argument is also one in which the conclusion does not necessarily follow from the premises (and not even with any degree of probability). In brief, one could construct a valid and plausible argument in favor of the conclusion by assuming *a* and *b* and inferring *c*. Without the crucial empirical assumption, the argument is not valid. So, even if one cannot validly infer moral conclusions from purely empirical premises, empirical claims may still play a crucial role in moral arguments. Because we must often employ scientific inquiry to determine on which empirical assumptions we should rely, it follows that science and ethics are not divorced. Indeed, particular issues in applied ethics cannot be explored without some reliance on good science. Thus, many explorations in environmental ethics must make good use of the results of biology, botany, chemistry, geology, climatology, marine science, forestry, and so on (both basic, and derivative, and mixed fields). The twofold task is to determine which empirical assumptions to make and to determine which moral assumptions to make, that is, what empirical and moral beliefs we should accept or, to put the point another way, which ones are belief-worthy. In brief, systematic scientific inquiry and theorizing are necessary to achieve one of these goals, and systematic ethical inquiry and theorizing are necessary to achieve the other. But these tasks are not unusual, esoteric, or merely academic ones. For example, many have pondered the question of whether John F. Kennedy (or Martin Luther King, Jr., Prince Phillip, Lady Diana, or Eleanor Roosevelt, or . . .) engaged in extramarital affairs and, if so, whether he (or they) deserve serious blame for doing so. In other words, familiar discussions involve trying to determine facts and relevant normative principles.[17]

Sometimes that which seems elusive or controversial is the relevant moral principle or assumption. For example, there is much dispute over whether nonhuman animals have rights, and if so, which rights, and so on. We speak of moral rights that may or may not be embodied in the law.[18] Similarly, should we think that human fetuses, or adult humans in permanent vegetative states, have rights? Should we think that above all we should do what is "efficient" (for whom?)? Do we have duties to future generations—of humans, of sentient creatures, of the biota? Is it a wrong or a terrible wrong to *allow* a species (or a sub-species) to become extinct—or cause it to become extinct—even if it is the human immunodeficiency virus (HIV)? However, there is a great deal of exaggeration about how much distinctly "moral disagreement" there is. Further, we may question the pes-simistic assumption that such matters are unassessable, inscrutable, and so on.

In fact, much so-called moral disagree-ment derives from empirical or scientific dis-agreement. Consider some examples. In the mid-1980s some held the normative view that those with AIDS (actually only those HIV-infected) ought to be isolated (incarcerated) on islands or in camps (something like this was done in Cuba); others took the contrary view. In many cases, however, the parties agreed on the moral principle to be invoked; for example, we ought to do what is necessary to prevent the further spread of HIV infection. Some believed, though falsely, that HIV is an airborne virus that is spreadable by sneezing, and some correctly denied that empirical assumption. The basis of the specific, norma-tive disagreement was not disagreement over the moral principle but over the facts.

Consider another example. Should the United States spend $18 to $28 per barrel of crude oil imported from the Near East, as opposed to putting that sum into other energy sources? Suppose what seems reasonable—that we agree that the United States, in the absence of other, countervailing moral consid-erations, ought to purchase oil at the lowest price (this is the relevant normative principle). Suppose there is no competitive energy source in that price range. If (a big "if," of course) there are no countervailing considerations, then it seems that the United States should buy at that price. But some economists reject

that normative conclusion, because they reject the empirical assumption that the cost of Near Eastern oil is as we have represented it. They reason that the true cost of that oil ought to include the subsidies provided by the U.S. government to many Near Eastern countries and the tremendous investment in the U.S. military, much of which is aimed at ensuring favorable conditions for U.S. trade with such countries. Some economists estimate that if such costs were factored in, the true cost of that oil to the United States would be closer to $80 to $85 per barrel. There may be other sources of energy that are superior or compet-itive at that price. Again, we have normative or moral disagreement about what *ought* to be done, but it is rooted in empirical disagree-ment (over what is the case—pricewise).

Coming to understand just what the facts are can be absolutely transforming. It may provoke a change of attitude, perhaps by altering one's arguments, but sometimes a new perspective seems to occur in a flash, as if a blindfold were removed from one's eyes. For example, one consequence of clear-cutting forests, tropical or otherwise, is the erosion of topsoil. This result may be thought unfortu-nate, but when one realizes that it takes from 200 to 500 years for 1 inch of topsoil to accu-mulate, the severity and comparative irre-versibility of the effect strikes home. Similarly, when Michael Boskin, the head of the Council of Economic Advisers under former U.S. President Bush, was told that global warming might mean that the temperature would be, on average, 3 to 5 degrees Celsius warmer in northern latitudes, he supposedly replied that it often got that much warmer in Washington, DC, in a single morning.[19] This appears to be a casual discounting of a situation that, were it to occur, could involve millions of deaths. Why? First, it is important that the focus be on average global surface temperature and not a one-day, local variation. Second, during the last ice age, when the average temperature was that many degrees cooler, there were massive glaciers in the northern part of the United States, and New York City was underneath about a half mile of ice. So much for the significance of an alteration of a few degrees in the average global surface temperature. The significance of global warming or global cooling can be properly assessed only if one understands just what the facts are (both the harms and benefits that would occur if certain scenarios were to be realized as well as the probabilities of their occurrence). An increase of 3 to 5 degrees Celsius in average temperature would, due to the melting of ice and the consequent rise in ocean levels, put the entire Republic of Maldives under water. Imagine an economist (or anyone else) trying to do a cost-benefit analysis on such matters if she or he had no grasp of climatology and geology. So, in examining and constructing arguments for normative environmental policy conclusions, the facts are crucial.[20]

Deeply held preconceptions often *determine* what we *perceive* to be "the facts" or "the data." The latter do not just leap onto the table, so to speak, for our examination. For example, in 1985, when the hole in the ozone layer over the Antarctic was discovered, the data supporting such a conclusion were discarded as erroneous; the computer was programmed to disregard data that the programmers *assumed* to be incredible.[21] Today, philosophers have little influence compared to Aristotle, whose view that the planets were crystalline spheres was still accepted in 1609, when Galileo, looking at the moon through his telescope, declared the moon to be pockmarked. Galileo's assertion was regarded as incredible. Similarly, when scientist Louis Agassiz concluded in 1837 that rocks and boulders in Switzerland were not put there by a "Great Flood" but were put there by other causes, scientists wedded to the traditional view were furious.[22] The procedures of empirical science foster, but *do not guarantee*, the filtering out of *deep, a priori* (apart from all experience or evidence)

assumptions or those based on very limited experience or evidence?[23]

1.4 HARM AND BENEFIT

Most negative moral principles or judgments seem aimed at preventing harm to members of one species, *Homo sapiens*. Compare the following:

> It is wrong to kill.
>
> It is wrong to steal.
>
> It is wrong to break promises.
>
> One ought to get regular medical checkups.
>
> One ought not to smoke.
>
> One ought not to drive 85 miles per hour in school zones.

The point will be addressed further in the Preview to Part III, but almost all traditional moral outlooks and theories suppose that only harm or benefit to *humans* is morally significant—deserving weight in decisions about what ought or ought not to be done (moral or normative decision making). This point is widely taken for granted, but the presupposition is of enormous consequence. Basically, it has meant that we humans have always, with a few notable exceptions, thought and acted as if everything nonhuman, all other forms of life as well as inanimate matter, has no value except its utility to us as a means to an end. We have tended to divide the world into what is consumable (everything nonhuman) and what is not (other members of our species, though even here the lines are sometimes drawn more narrowly, such as between those in our nation, our tribe, or our family, and those outside). The assumption that all, and only, humans "count" or are valuable in themselves (not just as a means to an end of some other creature) is called *anthropocentrism* (a quasi-technical term in the literature of moral philosophy).[24]To state the anthropocentric view in a second useful manner, let us first

define another important term in the literature: To say that a being has *moral standing* is
to say that the well-being of that individual
(or ecosystem, habitat, or some other entity) is
morally relevant for its own sake and not just
because it is of value to another individual or
group of such. The anthropocentric view,
then, is just the view that all and only humans
have moral standing. Whether anthropocentrism is just a bald prejudice, or on a par with
racism or sexism, is examined in Part III. If it
is, traditional moral theories need to be
revised or rejected, along with other theories
that seem strongly anthropocentric, namely,
standard economic theory, in so far as the latter functions as a normative theory, as well as
a political philosophy.

Aside from the question of *whose* harm or
benefit is morally relevant, the notions of
harm and benefit need examining. The notion
of harm can be explicated as (1) premature
death (often premature, permanent cessation
of consciousness, whether or not accompanied by permanent cessation of all bodily
functions); (2) *pain* (ranging from agony to
frustration); and (3) *nonfulfillment of wants or
desires*. Those "states of affairs" that we call
"bad" or "undesirable" tend to involve one or
more of these three conditions. The expression
frustration of desire may refer to (2) or (3).
What's the difference? One can have one's
desires blocked and not fulfilled *without knowing* that this is the case; for example, one
wants to be loved by one's spouse but is not,
and is ignorant of the fact. In contrast, we
often experience unpleasant mental states
(depression, sorrow, anger, worry, or frustration) because we are aware that we did not get
what we wanted (the job, affection, a raise,
attention, recognition, a good grade). It is also
worth noting how this "pain" may be the by-
product of what we believe and hence it may
be rationally assessed; for example, his jealousy was foolish, because it was based on a
false belief. It is often said that "what people
don't know won't hurt them," but although it

may not hurt in sense (2) of "harm," it may
harm them in sense (3).

Is there a presumption against harming
whatever beings are capable of suffering
harm? A number of important matter must be
kept in mind. One is that there are different
forms and degrees of harm. It is one thing to
be vaccinated with a needle and another to be
burned alive. Second, it is one thing to discuss
whether harm is a bad state of affairs as such
and another to discuss the justification of
imposing harm on another individual (or collective entity, ecosystem, and so forth).

Special, morally significant considerations
arise when we focus on options or policy
alternatives that will, foreseeably, harm those
subject to them. For example, one may plausibly argue that there is some qualified right of
self-defense against individuals who in a
blameworthy manner initiate an attack on
innocent parties (our law tends to reflect this
moral judgment, but these matters are not as
simple as some think). Further, there may be
significant differences between individual and
collective defense. In short, considerations of
innocence and noninnocence may rightly
influence the answer to the question of when
it is justifiable to impose (redundantly, then
unconsented to) harm on another person.
Other morally relevant considerations may
also be involved. For example, many arguments about the justifiability of pollution concern whether or not people have consented to
it by, for instance, living in certain areas, taking certain high-risk jobs (say, handling pesticides), or accepting so-called compensating
wage differentials attached to their work. A
great deal of environmental ethics is concerned with the question of whether it is permissible to impose harm, or the risk of harm,
on entities in "the environment" or to what
extent we have a duty to avoid doing so.

Situations that are "morally difficult" tend
to be ones in which all the alternatives
(including doing nothing) involve causing, or
allowing, harm to someone. We might call

them "conflict situations," and it is often in this context that talk of "moral dilemmas" arises. The situation may be naturally describable as one in which the conflict concerns one harm versus another or, alternatively, a harm versus a benefit. Recall familiar alleged "tradeoffs": farming versus habitat preservation, industrial growth versus the halting of the buildup of greenhouse gases, use of the oceans as sinks for wastes and maintenance of coral reefs and sea life, use of the air as a sink and having air fit to breathe. Some of these conflicts pit human life against human life, human life now versus that of future (human) generations, or human life against that of non-human fauna or flora. Sometimes, in cases of conflicts of interest, the parties are readily identifiable, and the nature of the conflict is quite clear; for example, compare thieves and their victims, the killing of an elephant to obtain an ivory tusk, or the killing of a wildebeest to make a fly-swatter of its tail. We need to see what makes some environmental cases difficult to think about and resolve. Among the central cases of conflict of interest among humans (the cases we are accustomed to thinking about), we have (imagine a case of assault) two humans, a deliberate, single act causing a clear harm that rises above some threshold of significance, and agreement by all that the recipient possesses *moral standing* (recall the meaning: The well-being of this individual is morally relevant for its own sake and not just because it is of value to another individual).

In contrast, many environmental disputes are complex for a number of reasons: (1) the individuals affected are "nonstandard" (such as spotted owls, pandas, krill); (2) rather than individuals, the focus may be on, say, ecosystems; (3) the individuals may not exist (such as future generations); (4) the harm is the *cumulative* result of the acts of many individuals over a long period of time (compare forests dying from air pollution, rivers dying from agricultural runoffs of fertilizer, pesticides, or

dioxin from paper mills); and (5) the occurrence of actual harm is a matter of some probability. Consider harm resulting from the existence of stocks of nerve gas, stocks of deadly plutonium, the storage of other forms of toxic wastes, the effects of substantial global warming, and the likely dire consequences to be associated with a probable increase of the world's population to about 10 billion people in the twenty-first century.

The point of systematic thinking about ethical questions is to help us decide what to do in hard cases.[25] And many of the issues in environmental ethics are hard cases indeed for some of the reasons we just mentioned. The following, however, is not a difficult case. In the spring of 1992, in Durham, North Carolina, a 13-year-old boy brutally beat to death, in about 45 blows with a pipe, an innocent 90-year-old woman in order to get a car for the evening. The morality of that act is not in doubt; it was wrong if anything is. We are not helped in deciding the morality of such acts by ethical theories; rather, we insist that any acceptable theory must yield (imply) that moral judgment—barring some extraordinary showing to the contrary.

To emphasize our main point, however, there is a good deal of perplexity and dispute about certain environmental issues for the reasons we have begun to discuss and that we explore in this volume. In the ongoing, and not so easy, task of assessing, the small number of influential and competing ethical theories, it is reasonable to insist that any theory deserving acceptance should have, when combined with relevant, plausible empirical assumptions, a reasonably clear, precise set of implications for what we should do in the hard cases and a clear, coherent rationale as to why. Some philosophers would insist that this last claim is too strong and that all one can reasonably demand is that a theory explain the moral dimensions of why a particular case is, in fact, a morally difficult case to decide. We leave the question open. As a minimum, the systematic moral outlook or theory should (1) state whose life, well-being, or integrity morally counts and why; and (2) yield reasonably determinate implications for how the noted "conflict" situations ought to be handled and why. Traditional ethical theories have seemed dogmatic with respect to (1) namely because they are based on an anthropocentric view with little or no rationale for so being. Recent efforts to develop an "environmental ethic" tend to explicitly address (1) but often tend to be less than explicit about (2).

1.5 EVALUATING ETHICAL THEORIES

Arguably, the best *scientific* theory with respect to some set of phenomena is not one to which there are no tempting objections or one that offers no difficulty whatsoever in the "handling" of evidence to the contrary. Rather, it is one that is superior to all its competitors in a number of relevant respects. Something similar needs to be said about the concept of the best ethical theory. With embarrassing brevity, we will note some relevant criteria for choosing among competing ethical theories. We do not maintain that all these criteria are noncontroversial.

Any theory consists of a set of claims, claims thought to be belief-worthy. Ethical theories will involve one or more normative claims but, explicitly or not, will presuppose certain empirical claims as well, such as that human nature is like this or that, that there is or is not freedom of choice, that there is or is not an afterlife, or that some animals are or are not sentient. One criterion of assessment, then, for an ethical theory is simply whether its empirical assumptions are plausible. For example, certain socialist visions of the ideal society suppose the possibility of substantial sharing of resources or products without the use of serious market incentives. Such theories are often thought to be faulty because human beings are not capable of regular, thor-ough-going high levels of altruism toward strangers. In brief, if a normative theory presupposes empirically false assumptions, that seems sufficient reason to reject it. So here is a way in which even a normative theory may be said to be "testable" or "falsifiable." There is an old, not well-defined doctrine that "ought implies can." The slogan is often understood to mean that certain judgments about what people ought to do presuppose the existence of certain capacities (for example, to choose freely, to act altruistically). The judgment about what ought to be done is implausible if the capacities for doing it do not exist. Again, scientific inquiry may be required to determine whether the capacity exists.

A set of claims is said to be logically consistent if and only if they can all be true. If a set is inconsistent, the statements in the set cannot all be true, at least one will be false. We want any theory to be consistent; otherwise it will have at least one false assumption. A simple example is the set below, which is inconsistent:

The earth was created in 4004 B.C.E.

The earth was created 4.5 billion years ago.

Both statements cannot be true, although they might both be false. It seems reasonable to demand consistency in any theory, ethical or otherwise.

As noted earlier, because we want an ethical theory to guide our decision making in hard cases, we want it to yield reasonably determinate or precise judgments about what is permissible or what is obligatory. Normally a theory will not do this if its basic principle(s) are too vague. The following statements, however wholesome sounding, all seem excessively vague (without further supplementary guidelines):

Do the right thing.

Be good.

Love your neighbor.

Be kind.

Promote happiness.

Look out for number one.

Foster family values.

Do no harm.

Leave the world a better place than when you got here.

In contrast, "Maximize one's self-interest," "Maximize total net utility," and "Do whatever maximizes the gross national product of Japan" all seem more precise and can yield precise conclusions when combined with other relevant assumptions.

Consider next comprehensiveness of scope. Other things being equal, it would be nice to have an ethical theory that would provide guidance over a greater range of decision making. Thus we may prefer to have a theory about when it is all right to take any life and not merely a theory about when it is all right to use lethal force in self-defense. A theory about how we ought to live so as to have a just and sustainable mode of life on earth would be one of considerable breadth, one calling for consideration of a great variety of complex moral and scientific matters.

Another widely accepted criterion of the acceptability of a moral theory is whether the judgments it yields, when combined with suitable empirical assumptions, exhibit compatibility with our *deepest, pretheoretical moral convictions* (ones that are not psychologically suspect).[26] When a normative principle yields a conclusion that seems radically counterintuitive, two choices can be made (if the empirical premises are beyond criticism): reject the theory and adhere to one's convictions, or surrender one's convictions and accept the theory. Sometimes it seems reasonable to do the latter. A principle implying that the previously mentioned beating of the 90-year-old woman was all right is extremely uninviting, to put the point mildly. Sometimes principles have surprising implications. For example, "We

ought to minimize human suffering" would, if we could painlessly kill everyone instantaneously, imply that we have a duty to wipe out the human race. Further, as George Bernard Shaw pointed out, the implications of acting on the principle "Do unto others as you would have them do unto you" have rather harsh (read: counterintuitive) implications when combined with a statement by a sadomasochist of what he or she, the sadomasochist, wants. He or she may enjoy being whipped and. . . . The worry is about compatibility with one's deepest pretheoretical moral convictions (say, about the moral unacceptability of routine torture of children for purposes of constructing an interesting Saturday evening) and not one's conjectures about whether South American coffee-producing nations ought to pay an ongoing fee to Ethiopia, the country in which coffee originated. Still. one's deepest conviction may be the result of cultural indoctrination and rationally suspect. Aristotle (384–322 B.C.E.) believed that some people were slaves by nature. Many Christian churches in the nineteenth century defended human slavery as ordained by God; a good slave was thought to be like a good ox—a useful thing but lacking in rights. A sincere Nazi might have been shocked at the notion that Jews should not be exterminated. Still, our deepest convictions, perhaps especially those of well-informed psychologically healthy people, must be given weight, but must be continually *subjected to scrutiny*—lest we accept only those principles that are compatible with our deepest, perhaps irrational, prejudices.[27]

In summary, it is widely and plausibly held that the most acceptable moral outlook will be one that is clear, sufficiently precise, comprehensive, logically consistent, compatible with the best scientific theories and results, and compatible with our deepest, most prejudice-free, specific moral convictions about particular cases. We turn now to a succinct over-view of the leading theories.

2. INFLUENTIAL ETHICAL IDEAS AND THEORIES _____

2.1 FROM ETHICAL EGOISM TO SOCIAL DARWINISM

Two "egoisms" (two theses) are commonly distinguished: (1) Psychological Egoism, that every human act is motivated by a desire to promote one's self-interest, and (2) Ethical Egoism, that each person ought to act in such a manner as to promote (or maximize) her or his self-interest. Note that (1) seems to be an *empirical* thesis and a most sweeping one, namely about every human action, or rather, the motive behind every action. We will not review the arguments pro and con here except to say that defenders of psychological egoism do not deny that people donate blood anonymously, that soldiers jump on grenades to save their buddies, or that people spend years caring for children or for aging parents without overt compensation; rather, defenders try to find reasons to construe each and every one of these cases as involving a self-interested motive, such as hope of a reward in the next life. A different story, of course, must be told about atheists. To be less than neutral here, as the defender of the thesis tries to spin his or her web of interpretation about each purported counterexample, one begins to suspect that the thesis is not really an empirical one at all.[28] Still, if Psychological Egoism were true, that fact would be subversive of policy proposals that require for their success that people act altruistically; hence, its relevance to normative questions. We should note that one need not believe that people always act altruistically if one rejects Psychological Egoism; one should reject the thesis if one thinks altruistic acts occur, even if not routinely.

This matter, or at least the question of just how extensive our altruistic resources are, arises with regard to whether it is feasible to ask or expect people, or nations, to act altruistically to benefit other species, other nations, or future generations. For example,

many nations, such as those that are the habitats of many rare species of plants and animals, ask how they can be expected to function as custodians of those living creatures (and often thereby forgo, as a result, the rewards of other uses of these habitats) without receiving compensation. An alternative sometimes is to try to structure markets (for example, by allowing trading in pollution permits) in such a way that there are adequate incentives of self-interest ("market-based incentives") for nations or individuals to act in an environmentally friendly manner. It is worth observing that we do not *always* think it appropriate to provide market incentives, or payoffs of some kind, to get people to act in a certain manner; for example, we do not try to provide market-based incentives to get people to refrain from child abuse. Still, we sometimes hear "tough-minded" businesspeople insist that "environmentalists" must provide such incentives (as if that were the only possible and viable motivation).

Ethical Egoism is the thesis that each person ought to promote her or his own interest. It seems noncontroversial to say that we ought to do so—up to a point; after all, should not each person seek to feed herself or himself, alleviate or prevent illness to—himself or hers and so on? Often, promotion of one's own interest will require that one act so as to benefit others; for example, one might take care of one's children to maintain his or her reputation or to have extra farmhands. No one denies that many acts that benefit others proceed from actions aimed at promoting self-interest. Ethical Egoism, and similar variants such as those found in the (overly popular) writings of Ayn Rand, may have an understandable appeal to those (such as females or those raised in certain religious families) who have been subjected to messages throughout their lives that it is "selfish" to be concerned about one's own welfare or to fail to "stuff" (repress expression of) one's feelings in order to promote the ostensive well-being of some group, such as the family.

Still, the thesis is not merely that one should *sometimes* act in her or his self-interest. That is thin soup indeed. The main objection to the principle is that it is counterintuitive. It advocates placing noninstrumental value on only the well-being and aims of the agent, and in effect no value on anyone else's well-being or aims *except* in so far as promoting them is in the agent's interest (the latter is called placing *instrumental* value on another's well-being, as a slaveholder might value a slave's well-being). What could justify this discrimination between Self and Anyone Else? On the face of things, Ethical Egoism is radically at odds with our deepest convictions and with the view that other people (for starters) are not mere "commodities" or "resources" to be used or abused according to the agent's slightest whim. There is no evident basis for an environmental ethic emerging from Ethical Egoism except one that says that the universe is to be divided into the Agent and Everything Else, the latter being the environment for the agent, and that the Agent should do whatever he or she wishes to the latter in promoting his or her interest.

Ethical Egoism is not unrelated to what is usually called "Social Darwinism." The latter label has typically been used for the view that "the fittest *ought* to survive," and sometimes for the view that "the fittest *will* survive." The label has often been used to characterize a political viewpoint especially popular around the turn of this last century in the United States (with a certain revival in the 1980s as well). Generally, Social Darwinists seemed to appeal to the Darwinian notion that, in the struggle to survive only "the fittest" (in *some* elusive sense, we hasten to add) will survive. That's the empirical part. Further, this point was taken as a reason to draw the normative conclusion that it is *desirable* that the fittest

survive—and often that we have no duties to render aid to those who are less fit, those who have been losing out in the competitive struggle. Just as Calvinists had in earlier centuries taken existing wealth as a sign of virtue ("God helps those who help themselves"), these Social Darwinists believed that poverty was often a sign if not of vice then one of weakness, of being unfit, that is, not deserving of survival. So it was "nature's way," they claimed (and dubiously sought Darwin's authority), and we ought not interfere; better to stand aside. In the long run, rendering aid, feeding the poor, creating welfare programs was "unnatural." There are the strong and weak in the animal world; likewise in the human one. Thus, it was thought that social and economic inequalities are fitting and proper—and egalitarian ideals and programs are misguided. Such views may or may not be associated with further assumptions about one "race," or sex, and so on being naturally superior. The normative parts of Social Darwinism are not ones to which Charles Darwin himself would have subscribed.

In Social Darwinism we do not have the view that one ought to maximize one's own self-interest but something close to it, certainly an endorsement of the view that it is fitting to be indifferent to the interests of other human beings—and presumably the rest of the biosphere as well—except, of course, in so far as being indifferent does not adversely affect one's own well-being. Oddly, some people appeal to the mere *expression* "survival of the fittest" as if it was clear and obvious, and as a way of trying to justify indifference to nonhuman welfare—when the full doctrine seems as problematic as Ethical Egoism. Indeed, it seems to "prove too much," for it seems to imply the permissibility of the deeds of serial killers, when combined with suitable empirical assumptions. Why does not the principle that the fittest ought to survive not "justify" the acts of a serial killer like Jeffrey Dahmer? Or perhaps the doing away with one's grandparents after they become infirm? Why should anyone adopt a principle with such implications?

There is competition in nature, often of a lethal sort, but this fact does not obviously entail that we must refuse to help the helpless, babies, toddlers, the infirm, the retarded, the temporarily disabled, and so on. There is also cooperation in nature and, arguably, along with impulses toward pursuing our self-interest, we are also hard-wired to care about others, humans and nonhumans—and sometimes to risk our lives for them.

Briefly, we note the need to clarify the meaning of the term *fitness*.[29] Clearly it should not be taken to mean "physically strong" in the sense of well-muscled. Many kinds of fitness are *context relative*. The world class English physicist Stephen Hawking is physically disabled in a profound manner—"unfit," in some interpretations. He lives with the help of others. He would not long survive in the jungles of Borneo; nor would the editors of this book. Analogously, Michael Jordan is in some sense "more fit" in professional basketball than in professional baseball. The world would be much the poorer if others were indifferent to Hawking's well-being. Arguably, we should care about him not just for our sake but for his as well. We leave it to the reader to examine further the slippery claim that "the fittest survive." Even if it is true in some sense collectively and in the long run, Hume might observe that nothing whatever follows about how we *ought* to act—in the individual case—and perhaps in the case of families, nations, and corporations—food for thought for those who advocate a laissez-faire economic system but advocate something else within the family.

There are indeed deeper questions concerning the moral relevance of Charles Darwin's theory of evolution.[30] It is a little over 140 years ago that Darwin arguably opened the door to our seeing that we humans are products of the same extraordinary, slow, and unpredictable process as are all living crea-tures—that we are not unique in all the world in terms of our origins. We are still identifying and digesting the implications of this fact.

2.2 THE DIVINE COMMAND THEORY

A character in one of Dostoyevsky's novels proclaims that if there is no God, everything is permitted. The suggestion seems to be that there are no duties, no moral constraints at all if there is no God: One may murder, plunder, and make sandwiches of human babies if one wishes. Many think that morality must be "based on" religion, perhaps in the sense that what is right or wrong is, in fact, dependent on what God commands (that is, prescribes, not causes). The approach to moral decision making being proposed, then, involves at least the following assumptions:

1. There is a God.

2. God commands and forbids certain acts.

3. An act is right (or permissible) if and only if God commands it.

4. Humans can sometimes ascertain what it is that God commands or forbids.

Unless all these claims are deserving of our belief, this theory must be rejected; it is worth observing that scientific results have not been friendly to (1) and (2). And even if (1), (2) and (3) were acceptable, if (4) were false, then this theory would be entirely useless in the quest to figure out how we ought to live. If 1 through 4 were unproblematic, the next assumption needed to arrive at any specific moral conclusion would be one to the effect that God does command some specific act or omission. Many believe that some do know what God commands either through direct divine revelation or through reliable reports of such ("scriptures" of some sort).

There are problems here. There is disagreement about what the scriptures are. And even when there is agreement about what they are, there is disagreement over interpretation. Thomas Aquinas (1222—1274), the most influential writer in the history of the Roman Catholic church, was once asked whether it was all right to kill because, after all, the second commandment allegedly given to Moses by God was not to kill, but in Deuteronomy 22 it is reported that God commanded the Israelites to wipe out an entire tribe of people, including "women, children, and asses." The Thomistic solution was that it is a misunderstanding of Christian morality to think that a crucial part of it is an unqualified prohibition on killing (popular misconceptions to the contrary, including simplifications by those who describe themselves as "pro-life"), even the killing of innocent human beings. In other words, in this version of Christianity, *whether an act is right or not depends solely on whether God commands it.*

True believers often have great confidence that God would not command anything such as genocide or other acts that we may be sure would be rejected by any right-thinking person—although the ways of God are said to be mysterious and beyond human understanding. Nevertheless, the voice of God has often resembled the norms of the culture or subculture of those reporting it; for example, the "New Testament" urges that women be silent in the churches, slavery is taken for granted, and views are expressed that many today would describe as homophobic. The Hebrew scriptures in places condone war, animal sacrifice, slavery, and brutal punishment ("Whoever curses his father or his mother shall be put to death"; Exod. 21:17), and prohibits the taking of (monetary) interest (Deut. 23:19). A person who acted on many of these beliefs today would stand a good chance of being locked up—so great is the distance between a good deal of biblical prescription and ordinary notions of what is permissible and right. None of this is to deny that certain biblical stories hold out ideals that retain their pull, such as Jesus's pressing the issue of

"Who is your neighbor?" the Good Samaritan, and the emphasis on unpretentiousness. Perhaps the "intuitively good parts" make it difficult for many believers to recognize or acknowledge the morally counterintuitive parts, the parts that get ignored, or are claimed to be merely derivative, inessential, superseded, or misinterpretations.

There is another puzzle about the Divine Command Theory, arguably an even deeper one. It is identified in the question, Is an act right just because God commands it, or does God command it because it is (antecedently) right? If the answer is the former, then what is right seems dependent on the arbitrary will of God; if God were to command universal suicide, then it would be right! Is it plausible that such mayhem, or to consider another case, the gassing of Jews by the thousands in the ovens at Auschwitz, could be right if God prescribed it? Alternatively, if God commands acts *because* they *are right,* then they must be right independently of God's so commanding them; it must be *some other feature that makes right acts right.* But if so, perhaps we can figure that out (maybe it's respecting rights, or maximizing the opportunity for all sentient creatures to have a decent life in a manner that is indefinitely sustainable on our planet or . . .) independently of any reference to God's will or any commitment to the metaphysics of the Divine Command Theory.

These difficulties aside, it is clear that possibly billions of people are influenced by religious doctrine (we have focused on only theistic types), and in thinking about environmental issues we may ask whether the Divine Command Theory can be a rational basis for our moral beliefs (we editors cast a negative vote here). We may also ask whether its overall influence has been for evil or for good. The matter is controversial, and it is explored in more detail in Part II of this book.

It is evident, in a world with a human population of over 6 billion, that there is not, and never will be, unanimity on matters of moral principle or even basic science. The intellectual world of many people remains one in which the earth is only a few thousand years old, in which the continents have never moved, in which sinks (places to put what we think of as "waste") and resources are unlimited, in which human life did not evolve from more simple forms, and in which immortal souls have a wonderful life after death. But, fortunately, we need not agree about all those matters to agree about many important things. For example, people who hold wildly diverse views about scientific matters, religious questions, or basic moral principles may totally agree about the morality of certain specific acts, such as child abuse, rape, and murder; freedom of thought; and the value of knowledge. So, for example, an ethical egoist, a religious believer, a rights theorist, and a utilitarian, respectively, may agree that poisoning the local water supply is wrong, although they infer that conclusion from quite different principles. This convergence has its limits, of course. We should not assume that agreement of different parties is sufficient to conclude the moral justification of the policy to which there is agreement; for example, some historic defenders of rights and some Christians have denied that women have equal moral rights, and we may recall the agreement between Nazi Germany and the (then) Soviet Union to carve up Poland and other East European nations at the beginning of World War II.

2.3 RIGHTS THEORIES

In English-speaking and perhaps French-speaking nations, especially, we are used to thinking about moral questions in terms of who *has a right* and whether the right is being respected. We may tend to overlook that not all peoples at all times have thought this way (a defender of a rights theory may think, "Well, *too bad* for those who do not; there are also a lot of people who fail to realize that the

sun does not revolve around the earth, that humans could not long exist without invertebrates, or that smoking tobacco enhances the risk of cancer"). Indeed, it appears that a clear notion of "having a right" did not seem to emerge before the late medieval period; so the ethical views of Socrates (470–399 B.C.E.), Plato (427–347 B.C.E.), and Aristotle (384–322 B.C.E.) did not include the concept as we know it. Today, some ridicule talk of "turkey rights" or "the rights of rats," but the idea of "human rights" might have been ridiculed by the ancients. What is *meant* by "has a right"? Later we will consider possible *grounds for the possession* of rights. To say that an *act is* right and to say that *someone has* a right is to make two different, but not unrelated, claims. Often, to say that an act is right is merely to assert that someone has a duty to perform the act, but that is not an implication of saying that someone has a night to perform an act; for example, one might have a right to a slice of the "killer chocolate cake" but no duty to take it. We now offer one plausible (slightly fastidious, but not canonical) analysis of "having a right" and "having a duty." To say that

> *A has a right* against B (B may be another moral agent or many or all such agents) to do X (where X is some action, such as to speak), to enjoy some state (such as being in private, living), or to be the recipient of an act of another (such as to receive a wage, punitive damages, or attention; use the apartment; not to be coerced)

is to say that

1. It is permissible for A to so do, enjoy, or have these things.

and

2. It is impermissible for B to prevent, disrupt, or fail to provide these things.

We are trying briefly to offer some clarification of the idea of what it is to possess a right, the moral relation between the right's possessor (or bearer of the right) and others who may be moral agents and who, thus, can deliberately "respect" or "accord" the right. What is "owed" to the holder of the right will depend on the *content* of the right—what the right is a right to. We may think of some rights as "active rights," that is, rights to do things, such as use the library, drive the rental car, eat the meal, or take the sneakers from Wal-Mart (one acquired *the right* if he or she gave the store the right to some of his or her money); some are "passive rights" (such as to be left alone). We shall turn to the concept of a duty in a moment, but there is another important distinction to be made, that between negative and positive rights. A right is said to be *negative* if the agent respecting the right morally ought to refrain from acting in a certain manner toward the holder of the right, such as a right not to be noncasually touched without one's consent. A right is said to be *positive* if the respecter of the right must act in some positive fashion; for example, a child is often said to have a right to care (provision of food and shelter) from her or his parents.[31] The relations between friends, family members, and employees and employers, for example, are often spelled out at least partially in terms of rights (although loving relationships are commonly thought to require "going beyond" respecting rights, it does not follow that respect for rights is inessential; compare what goes wrong in cases of child abuse.)[32]

Many rights are often, arguably, *packages* of rights. In Section V.C, questions about property are explored. What is involved in having property in something, that is, a property right? First, it is often thought that the concept of a property right involves the right to use what is owned, to *exclude* others from so doing, to *transfer* the right to another (as a gift, or as part of an exchange—what we call trade, sale, or purchase), and sometimes, controver-

sially, to *destroy*.[33] Do people collectively own the earth? Do parents own "their" children? Do those with legal property rights to a wetland have a moral right to destroy it—even when to do so would be to wreak serious ecological damage to the surrounding ecosystem and virtually permanent losses to the chain of future generations? Who owns the oceans, the old-growth forests, or nonhuman animals?

It is commonplace to distinguish between moral and legal rights; indeed, slaves in the United States in the early nineteenth century had few legal rights and possessed many moral rights, which, in fact, were not embodied in the racist laws that prevailed. It is worth recalling that the revered "founding fathers" counted a black human being as three-fifths of a person for purposes of distributing electoral votes to the states. Until 1920, women in the United States lacked the legal right to vote (as remained the case in Swiss cantons until recent decades), but they surely had the moral right if men did. Given the legal/moral distinction, we may ask whether biotechnological creators of new life forms have special moral rights with respect to such forms and should be allowed to patent (have legal rights to) those forms. One notion is some sort of property rights (the standard kind of right that companies seek), but another might be the sort of rights possessed by guardians. On this issue the reader might consult Christopher Stone's "Should Trees Have Standing?" (Essay 23) in Section IV.A. In brief, many environmental issues, including absolutely fundamental ones, can be couched in terms of the existence of moral rights.

The distinctions we have noted can help us investigate many questions. For example, before deciding whether some entity (say, a human fetus, a comatose adult human, a Maine Coon cat, a Norwegian elkhound, an iguana, a giant Sequoia, a coral reef, a logger in the state of Washington, or a philosopher in Vancouver) has a right to life, we need to know exactly *what* the "right to life" is a right to. Perhaps "right to life" should be construed negatively, as a right not to be killed. If so, it may not be difficult for one to respect another's right to life; one only has to refrain from killing the other person. This may not be too demanding. Alternatively, if the "right to life" is to be construed positively, as a right to be supplied with whatever one needs to live, then it will be most burdensome for one to respect another's right to life, assuming that the latter is a creature in possession of such. Indeed, one may need a heart transplant; surely, another person does not owe his or hers, albeit the case that it would be quite hospitable of the person to give his or hers. So, it is counterintuitive to think that all people have a positive right to life (along the line of interpretation noted here). Whether we believe something has a right to life depends in part on what we mean by "right to life" (thus, the importance of conceptual analysis with complex matters—in moral philosophy, science, or some other area).

We also need some defensible conception of the *grounds for possession* of any particular kind of right. Some rights are thought to be possessed because of a prior act, such as a contract or a gift; for example, a person has a right to kiss another person because that person has agreed to it; otherwise, not. Some rights are thought to be possessed by certain entities just because the entities are of a certain kind, such as human, alive, sentient, or subjects of a life. Any adequate rights theory must address these matters and defend some set of grounds as necessary and/or sufficient for the possession of rights. There is, in fact, an extensive literature that does just this.

In this space it is impossible to convey much of the substance of any particular theory of rights. Historically, the works of Thomas Hobbes (1588–1679), John Locke (1632–1704), Jean-Jacques Rousseau (1712–1778), and Immanuel Kant (1724–1804) are important. Both Hobbes and Locke asserted that humans have certain basic rights in a "state of nature,"

that is, in a hypothetical state in which government and law are absent. Locke claimed that people have a right to life, liberty, and property. A central thrust of all rights theories is that bearers of rights have a certain moral standing and that they are owed at least certain forms of treatment. Thus, they are not to be viewed as "mere resources" or as entities whose use is entirely unconstrained by duty. Generally, such theories have a certain egalitarian thrust in that they maintain that all beings within a certain more or less "natural" kind have the same rights (for example, all persons, all men, all male property owners, all adult male property owners, or all sentient creatures). There is, however, one rub, so to speak. The rights theorists that we just mentioned all seemed to deny rights to any non-human; thus, the recent critique of *anthropocentrism* is a radical one, for it calls in question a fundamental assumption of all such theories. These matters receive attention in Parts II, III, and IV especially.

There is little reason to think that all humans, say, have all the same rights. First, if a ground for possessing a right to drive is that one can see, then not everybody can have that right. Second, a distinction is often made between certain *natural rights* (rights one has because one is of a certain natural kind: human, sentient, rational, or simply alive), such as a right to life or a right not to be tortured, and rights one may have because of some past action, such as a right to one's shirt because of a purchase or a gift (often labeled "acquired" or "artificial" rights). Likewise, even if some rights are possessed only by humans (say, a right to vote), it does not follow that all animals are entirely lacking in rights. Popular discussion to the contrary, acknowledgment that certain nonhumans, such as animals, ecosystems, or forests, have rights would not necessarily settle moral disputes. Consider a common distinction, namely the distinction between *absolute* and *presumptive* rights. If by "absolute right" one means a right on which it is always wrong to infringe, then it is doubtful that any rights (attributed to individuals) are "absolute." For example, we might not unreasonably conclude that it would be right to torture an innocent grandmother (or perhaps any editors) who possesses a right to life—if that were the *only* way to prevent nuclear war. If fairly serious rights can be justifiably overridden under certain circumstances, then the seeming great gap between rights theories and utilitarian modes of thinking fades seriously; the reader might "file" this basic point and consider it after the upcoming discussion of Utilitarianism.

Let's consider a brief comment on the concept of a duty. To say that

> *A* has a duty to *B* to do *X* (whether *X* is an act or an omission),

is to say (roughly) that

> it is impermissible for *A* not to do *X* on account of *B* (whether *X* is an act or an omission).

In our analysis of rights and duties in terms of permissibility, for each right there is one or more correlative duties. But some duties may exist without any particular individual possessing any corresponding rights. Perhaps we have, for example, a duty to be charitable even if no particular individual has a right to our charity. Something similar might be said about a duty of an existing person to help pass on a stock of environmental resources no smaller than that which was passed on to her or him. It was, in fact, the view of Jeremy Bentham, the famous British philosopher and exponent of Utilitarianism (1748–1832), that we have *only* certain duties and that talk about rights (moral, not legal) is "nonsense on stilts." We leave it an open question whether talk of rights is not more than rhetorically useful, and whether all that which we wish to say, morally, can be said in the language of duty.

Most rights theories are "individualistic" in their attribution of rights only to individuals, say humans or animals, but it is not obvious that the bearers of rights *must* be individuals; so those who value collectivities or communities may hope to revise the traditional rights framework. Legal rights are attributed to corporations, states, cities, and so forth. Nevertheless, some philosophers believe that the notion of species' rights is nonsense.[34] Further, rights theories are often criticized as being focused on a selfish stance, on what is mine as a matter of right, on violations of "my rights," and it is claimed that all this contributes to a complaining attitude and a litigious society. Many complaints are misguided; those who insist on respect of rights *need not* defend their own rights, but the rights of, say, sexually abused children, raped women, gay persons who have been discriminated against, blacks, or innocent whites who may have been unfairly treated (say, those poisoned to death in the 1990s by a North Carolina woman, Blanche Moore). These objections hardly exhaust the list of complaints made against rights theories.

A theory of rights should address the preceding and other objections. If it allows rights to be overridden under certain circumstances, its defense needs to show why it does not collapse into Utilitarianism or some other consequentialist theory. A rights theory should say what is to be done in the event that rights conflict with one another. It should, as noted, specify the grounds for the possession of rights. The theory should be reasonably clear in terms of its policy implications, and reasons should be given as to why the theory should be preferred over competing theories.

Probably the two most influential ethical outlooks among contemporary moral philosophers are rights theories on the one hand and versions of Utilitarianism on the other. We now turn to the latter. Because Utilitarianism has special importance in current environmental controversies and because, arguably, in its anthropocentric incarnation Utilitarianism underlies mainstream economic theory, we will spend some time examining it.

2.4 UTILITARIANISM

Although the writings of David Hume (1711–1776) and others were suggestive, it was the work of Jeremy Bentham, especially his *Introduction to the Principles of Morals and Legislation* (1789), that articulated the theory of Utilitarianism. His work and that of one of his disciples, John Stuart Mill (1806–1873), constitute the classic sources of this view. Bentham was a critic of British law and policy and believed that it was a hodgepodge, inconsistent and unprincipled. He sought to identify some rational, principled basis for deciding what should be a matter of law and policy. He reasoned that while many things are good as means to some ends, only one state of affairs can be said to be good for its own sake or intrinsically good, and that is the experience of pleasure or happiness. The opposite state is pain, which is intrinsically bad. Having formulated this "theory of the (nonmoral) good," the question "What should we do?" remains. The short answer is, Do whatever results in good or has good consequences. Because many acts bring pleasure for some and pain for others, we ought, Bentham thought, do that which will bring about the greatest balance of pleasure over pain, or utility over disutility; indeed, this constitutes the fundamental duty of all individuals and governments as well. Thus, we arrive at the famous *principle of utility;* our formulation here will be, What is right (or a duty) is whatever maximizes the total amount of net utility. The principle is sometimes referred to as the "greatest happiness principle."

Arguably, this view has revolutionary implications. First, normative theories that suppose that the rightness or wrongness of an act is entirely dependent on the kinds of consequences that an act has are called *consequen-* *tialist* theories, and Utilitarianism is a clear example (so is Ethical Egoism). Unlike the thesis of Ethical Egoism, Utilitarianism demands that the good and bad consequences for everyone affected by an action be taken into account and given due weight in determining whether the action, among all the alternatives available, will maximize total net utility (or, at least, result in as much net utility as any other available alternative) and, hence, be the right thing to do. So it is not merely the agent's well-being that is significant.

The emphasis on consequences is striking in that consideration of motives seems neglected, and the latter are often thought important. Jesus is alleged to have said that any man who has looked on a woman with lust in his heart has already sinned. A rather high standard, and one that former U.S. President Jimmy Carter confessed to not meeting. A utilitarian might insist that motives may be relevant to judgments of moral character but that they play no direct role in the assessment of actions.

It is tempting to translate talk of "benefit" as "utility" and "harm" or "cost" as "disutility."[35] So it looks as if the principle of utility approximates the principle that we should maximize benefits minus costs, though employers of *cost-benefit analysis* usually operate with "dollar" or monetary measures of cost and benefit. Because this procedure is widely used and recommended in deciding questions of public policy, indeed, environmental policy, assessing the adequacy of Utilitarianism is closely related to the task of assessing the cost-benefit approach. Both are consequentialist in outlook, and both are maximizing principles. These matters receive attention in Part V.

Although we have lived, in the last two decades, in an era in which appeals to rights are very popular (compare the movement for civil rights, women's rights, and so on), the Utilitarians can claim to have a method for deciding between competing policies, a method that is responsive to considerations of welfare and illfare. When it comes to formulating public policy, cost-benefit analysis is the prevalent approach. When it comes to deciding an array of legal questions, we tend to think often in terms of rights. Why this disparity exists is a question deserving consideration.

Utilitarianism is untraditional in that it promises to discard traditional moral rules that we learn, or are supposed to learn, as children, such as Tell the truth, Keep promises, Don't steal, Don't kill. This is so because there are cases in which violating these admonitions will maximize utility. For example, it might maximize utility to lie to an Uzi-toting maniac about the whereabouts of schoolchildren he or she wishes to harm—or to deceive potential terrorists. Indeed, utilitarians may say that this example illustrates the intuitive superiority of their theory because rigid adherence to traditional, specific rules leads to radically counterintuitive results. If their defender says, "Well, one must apply them judiciously," the utilitarian can insist that *that* suggestion is either urging arbitrariness or is sneaking utilitarian considerations in the back door after kicking them out the front door. Further, specific principles, such as "Keep promises" and "Help those in distress," can conflict; in contrast, the utilitarian theory avoids this problem of rule conflict because the theory contains only one rule: Maximize total net utility.

Whose utility or disutility, whose welfare or illfare must be taken into account? Surprisingly perhaps, given the virtual omnipresence of anthropocentrism, Bentham and Mill thought that pain and pleasure were an evil and a good, respectively, to *whomever* they occur. Because many animals evidently have both these capacities, it would be arbitrary for a moral agent not to take that into account in deciding which act will maximize utility. So the class of creatures to whom duties are owed is the class of all *sentient* creatures. The term *sentient* is used in philosophy to refer to any crea-

ture capable of experiencing suffering or satisfaction, in whatever forms they may take. Evidence of such capacities tends to be linguistic ("Stop, you're hurting me!"), nonlinguistic behavior (screams of pain, moaning, writhing), and the presence of physiological traits such as a central nervous system.[36] Which animals or humans are sentient is, thus, an empirical question and subject to scientific investigation. The implications of this theory for our treatment of animals are explored in Part III, especially by Peter Singer (Essay 15). What duties we have with respect to nonsentient life on earth is the focus of much of this book, but Part IV is especially relevant.

We need to consider a familiar misunderstanding of Utilitarianism and then turn to a leading objection to the theory. The Principle of Utility is normally understood as not being equivalent to a certain bastardized variant of it, namely, the view that what's right is what most people want (what some call "the principle of majority rule").[37] For the moment let us finesse a serious question, namely, whether utility and disutility can be adequately measured so as to have units that can be added or subtracted. Recall that when economists estimate the costs of a particular instance of pollution in terms of dollars, they are attempting to establish some measure of the magnitude of harm or disutility to humans. An agent, in applying the principle of utility, attempts to identify alternative actions, say, A, B, and C, next she or he will identify the likely relevant consequences (those involving utility or disutility) to all who will be affected by her or his choice of alternative. To simplify *enormously* and to speak most abstractly, suppose that doing A will involve five bad results (sooner or later; later might be in 50 or 500 years) and three good ones (benefits or utilities of some sort to a sentient creature). Suppose that these numbers represent the magnitude of the bad results: $-40, -80, -90, -25,$ and -70 (so, the sum of the disutilities is: -305). Suppose, too, that these numbers represent the magnitudes of the benefits of utilities: +83, +77, and +36 (so, the sum of the utilities is +196).[38] The projected total net utility (TNU), then, of the agent's performing alternative A is –109 (subtracting the smaller from the larger). Abstractly, that is how the calculation is to be done for each alternative. Suppose that the TNU of option B is +99 and that the TNU of C is +550.[39] Given these results, act C maximizes TNU, and the utilitarian argument for doing C takes this form:

a.   What is right is whatever maximizes TNU.

b. C maximizes TNU.

c. C is right.

Because the argument is valid, one who is skeptical of the conclusion can only question the calculation leading to (*b*) or find reason to reject the principle, (*a*).

Note that one of the bad consequences of doing C may be to cause serious harm to one person, say, giving over a known innocent person to terrorists who are certain to torture the individual. Because the utilitarian calculation allows *summing* the harms and benefits, the act that maximizes TNU may include what many of us may be sure is a terrible wrong. It is partly because of actual or hypothetical cases like this that many people find utilitarian, and other maximizing, consequentialist theories, radically counterintuitive. Utilitarianism involves other worries, too. Suppose that a rapist got so much pleasure from raping that his or her pleasure exceeded the sum of the disutilities resulting from the act (is this not *possible?*). If so, the raping might maximize utility. In brief, the very idea that we should count this pleasure as a good and/or assign it positive weight in a calculation of utility is preposterous to many. Perhaps what is morally right should not be thought of as identical with *whatever* maximizes utility.

Concerns about *justice* or fairness have to do with the acceptability of the *distribution* of benefits or burdens among a number of individuals.[40] In certain cases, such as a judge's choosing to mete out radically unequal punishments to two people equally responsible for the same kind of crime, there is, other things being equal, a clear case of injustice. One standard accusation is that the utilitarian theory ignores morally significant considerations having to do with the distribution of "goods" and "bads." In passing, we note that many environmental disputes concern the distribution of environmental benefits (say, from burning coal) and the distribution of environmental harms (say, pollution in the form of acid rain); one dispute concerns distribution between nations (for example, U.S. coal-burning plants versus forest damage in Canada); another concerns benefits to the current generation versus losses to later generations (or the reverse). This last matter is labeled a matter of "intergenerational equity." It receives attention in Parts V.E and VI.D.

Three further points regarding distributional issues. First, although Utilitarianism includes no principle of distribution as such, it may be that more or less egalitarian social arrangements (say, some limit on inequality of wealth but equality of basic legal rights) are more productive of happiness (at least human happiness) than the alternatives. In short, Utilitarianism conjoined with relevant empirical assumptions will have interesting and perhaps intuitively plausible *distributional implications*. This type of concern motivated much of the political efforts of the nineteenth-century "philosophical radicals" (Bentham, J. S. Mill, and others; in particular, Mill fought the milieu of his day in opposing the unequal treatment of women. On this topic, see his extraordinary little book *On the Subjection of Women*.).

Second, the *"principle" of declining marginal utility* seems to be a rough but plausible generalization; it says that "consumption" of further successive homogeneous units of certain goods (such as gin or ice cream) yields declining amounts of satisfaction or utility. More intelligibly, one's first ice cream serving is very satisfying, the second almost as satisfying, the third not bad, the fourth an effort, the fifth hard work, and the sixth nausea inducing. Perhaps something similar is true of one's first million dollars, and so on. Although it would involve making a much disputed judgment involving "interpersonal comparison of utility levels," it is credible that the disutility we might cause to Bill Gates (a billionaire) if we took a million dollars from him and gave it to a poor person would be much less than the increase in utility to that poor individual. If so, the transfer, the reduction in financial inequality, yields a net increase in total utility. Thus, taking into account the principle of declining marginal utility, a utilitarian argument exists in favor of limiting inequalities, even if we agree that the principle of utility is not itself a distributional principle.[41]

A third point regarding equality is that at the stage in which judgments of the amount of utility or disutility are involved in different consequences. Bentham insisted that "each is to count as one" and no one more than one. That is, like amounts of utility are to be counted equally whether the subjects of it are friends or foes, relatives or not, compatriots or not, indeed, fellow humans or not. This egalitarian streak is, nevertheless, compatible with the theory's condoning severe inequalities of treatment in the effort to maximize utility.

In view of the serious objections that have been made to the utilitarian theory, many are surprised that it is the preferred view of many professional moral philosophers (who would not be surprised by any objection noted here). In this short space, we can only observe that some difficulties confront all theories (no, we do *not* think that they are all equally serious). The main attraction of rights theories is that they tend to insist that there are moral limits of a rather urgent kind on what one can permissibly do to people (and perhaps other creatures as well); that is, they insist that an act that may, as a contingent matter of fact, maximize the sum of happiness in the world does not serve as a justification for doing some very nasty things to innocent, nonconsenting individuals in the process.[42] But the idea that *any means* leading to the greatest sum total of happiness is all right, much less a duty, seems to countenance many counterintuitive and radical inequalities. Still, rights theories may allow the overriding of rights in extreme cases, and when they do, then they may also condone, counterintuitively, some rather nasty acts. The utilitarian view avoids the rather generous metaphysical assumptions of the Divine Command Theory and its stringent requirement of knowing what God wills. Utilitarians also avoid the extraordinary understanding of moral relevance embodied in Ethical Egoism, namely, that the well-being of those other than the agent is important *only* in so far as it bears on the well-being of the agent.

We need to investigate theories that might suggest maximizing, or perhaps only optimizing, a good such as happiness or desire fulfillment *under constraints,* constraints that when respected ensure that the relevant individuals have decent lives, or at least the opportunity for such, given certain unalterable results of the natural lottery.

2.5 UTILITARIANISM AND ECONOMIC THEORY

For about 125 years, from the publication of *An Inquiry into the Causes of the Wealth of Nations* in 1776, there was a perceived closer connection between economics and moral philosophy. Adam Smith was a friend of David Hume, and taught moral philosophy at the University of Edinburgh in Scotland.[43] To be concerned about how to increase the wealth of individuals or nations is normally to be concerned about how to promote the opportunities and welfare of human beings, their utility. One mark of the work done by economists is their focus on specific empirical questions relevant to choice (exactly what are the effects of rent control, the effects of allowing a free market in drugs, or a 10 percent increase in the minimum wage?), while moral philosophers have had more general concerns and have not shied away from the exploration of explicitly normative questions (Mill in his *On the Subjection of Women*, 1869, argued that it was the unjust treatment of women that is the proper explanation of their seemingly less significant, intellectual and artistic contributions). It seems fair to say that late-nineteenth-century Western economic theory took a consequentialist, indeed utilitarian, view— that what ought to be done is whatever maximizes, or at least increases, human satisfaction or utility. Hence, the importance of choosing the most *efficient* policies and social/economic arrangements or institutions. This moral assumption, the principle of utility, has become largely covert as economists aspired to be scientists, something they often claim to be a "value free" discipline; hence, a certain embarrassment about saying in public that they thought efficiency *valuable,* or valuable *because* it is a means to promote total net utility and that that is what *ought* to be done (the recent posture has been that if you want to know which is the most efficient policy, we can tell you what it is). This adoption of a posture of moral neutrality, if not indifference, was due in part to their being somewhat intimidated (so it appears) by the challenge of the Logical Positivists, who implied that anyone making normative judgments was thinking or talking nonsense.[44] A similar effect of the positivists seemed to drive philosophers away from any serious examination of specific normative issues for about three decades (from the 1920s to the late 1950s). Since then both groups have been less reluctant to regard such matters as fit subjects of intellectual inquiry.

Economic theorizing has been relentlessly anthropocentric, and the deepest cleavage between it and some moral theories and some environmental critics derives from that source. In cost-benefit analysis, "cost" and "benefit" refer, ultimately, in studies by standard economists, to what harms or helps humans alone. As we noted earlier, there are two fundamentally different ways in which the term "utility" has been understood historically: as simple preference, or *want fulfillment* (whether or not accompanied by some pleasant mental or psychological state), or, alternatively, as a pleasing psychological state, that is, *pleasure*. Because pleasure (and pain) seem to come in amounts, one view is that we can ascertain when individuals experience such, and how much, and we can sum the utilities or disutilities to determine which act maximizes total net utility. Aside from one's own case, many economists and some philosophers became convinced that it is either logically impossible (but why?), or at least practically impossible, to ascertain how much pleasure or pain others experience or to make sensible judgments that compare the pains or pleasures of others to one another; if so, there can be no summing and rational selection of the option that maximizes utility. That path, it is claimed, is a dead end.

The other path that modern economists take is roughly the following one. Construe "utility" as (human) want fulfillment. Ignore questions about how wants arise and whether they have important cognitive components (consider: Why did Sirhan Sirhan want to shoot Robert F. Kennedy?). Make an extreme antipaternalistic assumption that each person (focus on competent adults, thus ignoring one or two billion people) knows better than anyone else what makes him or her better or worse off and chooses accordingly if apprised of relevant information.[45] Avoid as much as possible making choices for others (because it is not, as it is said, possible rationally to make interpersonal utility comparisons and, say, distribute things in a fashion that would maximize utility); let each person decide for himself or herself (by having a market) whether to keep what she or he has (time, money, leisure, and so on) or to make an exchange (purchase, sale).[46] Assume that no one will do so unless he or she will be better off (perhaps acknowledging that there will be rare, masochistic exceptions, and of course, occasional difficulties in gathering information).[47] Without our trying to state all the assumptions mainstream economists make, *under these conditions* with each exchange *at least someone will be better off and no one will be worse off* (at least if there are no "negative externalities," that is, cases in which there are harms caused to individuals not party to [consenting to] the exchange). Now if someone is better off and no one is worse off, we have an increase in total net utility; what has come to be called a "Pareto improvement" has occurred (after the Italian economist and sociologist Vilfredo Pareto [1848–1923]). The postexchange state of affairs is more efficient than the preexchange state (because at least one person is better off and no one is worse off than in the preexchange situation).

Several comments are in order. First, economists have adopted a definition of *efficiency* (or its cognates) that may only loosely connect with ordinary usage of the term *efficient*; compare "more efficient engine." Some situation, *A*, then, is said to be more *efficient* than another, *B*, if in *A* there is at least one person better off in his or her own estimation than in *B*, and no one is worse off in her or his own estimation. Why, then, is efficiency a good thing? The natural answer would seem to be because it increases utility. Note that there may be acts that increase utility but that fail to make Pareto improvements. For example, we might experiment on some unwilling people to find a cure for AIDS; perhaps the result would maximize total utility. Still, some people would be worse off (they may suffer and die prematurely). One serious objection to the

utilitarian view (as we noted earlier) is that it seems to condone doing nasty things to innocent, unconsenting individuals (keep in mind that a rights theory may also do so if it allows for cases of justified infringement of certain rights[48]). In contrast, if we only act according to what we shall dub the Normative Pareto Principle (make *only* Pareto improvements), then that possibly counterintuitive implication is avoided. So the Normative Pareto Principle has its attractions. Two difficulties of utilitarianism are avoided. First, no interpersonal comparisons of utility are made. Second, the principle does not sanction intuitively immoral actions. However, there is a severe difficulty with the notion that much of life could be organized along lines dictated by the Normative Pareto Principle, because almost any nontrivial proposal for change will make some parties worse off. The principle will support virtually no changes; it is a recipe for paralysis outside of certain highly limited contexts.[49] In the larger world, we morally must coerce from time to time, and we cannot do *only* those things that avoid making some worse off in their own estimation. It seems as if efficiency is a good thing if there are no countervailing considerations and if we have an appropriate conception of what counts as someone's being better off (surely identifying this with on-balance want fulfillment will not do) and a justifiable conception of whose well-being matters (surely the answer that it is only the well-being of humans is dubious). So in spite of support for the value of efficiency derivable from the utilitarian theory and partly because of some suspect aspects that the assumption of such value shares with that theory, it is morally problematic to assume that we ought to choose whichever policy is the most efficient one, or that we ought to maximize benefits minus costs, or that these principles should guide us as we try to formulate a sound basis for environmental decision making. Efficiency, like sex, is not nothing, but it is not everything either. These matters are very important, given the undue influence that such principles have had, overtly or covertly, and they will receive further exploration in this volume, especially in Sections V.A, V.B, and V.E. Our main aim here has been to lay out some of the basics of economic thinking, some connections to one influential ethical theory, to open the door to exploring relations to other moral points of view and, ultimately, to questions of environmental policy.

2.6 NATURAL LAW THEORY

"Natural law" theory is not a position as well defined as Utilitarianism. It is tempting to speak of this position as a tradition; those who are thought to be representative figures—the Stoics, Aristotle, Aquinas, Grotius (1588–1645), Suarez (1548–1617), and sometimes Kant—share some common features perhaps, but often they simply exhibit resemblances, in the way that members of a family might exhibit physical similarities. Hence, it is not surprising that one contemporary defender of this approach, Alan Donagan, responded to a critique of his view by saying, "What she says is natural law is not what natural law theorists say it is." His general characterization of the theory is that it is "a set of rules or precepts of conduct, constituting a divine law which is binding upon all rational creatures as such, and which in principle can be ascertained by human reason."[50] Except for the reference to divine law, this characterization fits almost any normative ethical theory (for example, Utilitarianism and Ethical Egoism) in that it only insists that there are normative principles that determine what we ought to do and that these are ascertainable by reason. This abstraction needs fleshing out by stating the specific "precepts of conduct."

Without further defense, we will suggest that there are a small number of features that have been characteristic of, and some arguably definitive of, what has been labeled the natural law tradition from the Stoics to Hugo Grotius and others. We have noted (1) the belief in objective, given norms or principles by which rational beings should guide their conduct. Thus, (2) a contrast is marked between what is merely a matter of convention (e.g., to queue up for a purchase in some cultures) and what is a matter of human law (often called "positive" law historically). There is, further, a "natural order of things." This last claim seems to be construed both as (3) an empirical claim about the regularity we find in the nexus of causal processes around us, and also as (4) a claim that what is good and right is a direct function of the way things are, in particular the way human beings are (focus on their natural capacities, tendencies, and desires). Given the latter, certain norms are to be found in nature. Indeed, we usually find the assumption that (5) the good of humans (perhaps other creatures as well) is constituted by the realization of these natural strivings or natural tendencies; the "perfection" of such capacities in humans constitutes human flourishing. The (6) discovery of the natural law is ascertainable by the use of reason. As noted, (7) the natural law is often claimed to be an expression of the divine will. A specific instance of this theory will include (8) a list of the natural tendencies, the fulfillment of which constitutes flourishing. Claims (1) through (3) do not much individuate this theory. Developed in one way, feature (7) may render this view a variant of the already discussed Divine Command Theory. If, however, the divine will prescribes conduct *because* human nature is as it is, then we have a view more deserving of the label "naturalistic ethic" or "ethic based on nature." But it is not obvious that *any* ethical theory allows no role for facts about human nature.

It is assumptions (4) and (5) that make this view distinctive. A central thrust of this theory, then, is that the world ought to be organized in such a fashion as to foster human flourishing; this feature is supportive, or reflective, of an anthropocentric view, although to the extent that value may be assigned to the fulfillment of *any* natural tendencies (not just human ones), one may find some basis for a biocentric outlook (here understood simply as the view that it is desirable that all living things flourish). Natural law theorists, however, do not seem to take this path. For an example of the biocentric outlook, see Essay 24, by Paul Taylor, in Section IV.A.

A serious problem with this view concerns whether we can ascertain natural tendencies. Of whom? The majority? Adult members of our species? Normal (statistically average?) adult members of our species? The need to sift out what is a result of cultural influence is a familiar, persistent difficulty. Suppose we can identify natural tendencies (perhaps by identifying what is statistically typical for adult members of the species, or appropriate subsets); must their fulfillment be assumed to constitute a good?[51] However, the tendency to act self-destructively seems rather natural, as does the tendency to act violently toward others. A defender of natural law might cry "foul" here. There is certainly a good deal of evidence that tendencies toward self- and other destructiveness, although very widespread, are a result of physical and/or emotional deprivation. Further, many evidently important sources of intense satisfaction are found in sexual relations, in challenging work, in intimate give-and-take with friends and family, and in the exercise of one's talents in various ways; all these activities seem in many ways natural, and one's capacities as a human play a central role in what results in what is, arguably, our good. Still, what follows by way of giving moral guidance to us is either not so obvious, or when implications have been drawn by natural law theorists, are problematic.

In its historical development of the natural law doctrine, going back to Aquinas, the Roman Catholic church has classified sexual relations not between male and female as unnatural and to be condemned. A partial by-product of this view is the legal prohibition on homosexual acts by consenting adults. Indeed, the view of the Roman Catholic church is even narrower; what is claimed to be natural is procreation and the desire to procreate. Thus, heterosexual relations not involving the *possibility* of procreation are condemned, for example, sexual acts not leading to the possibility of conception such as those employing artificial contraceptives, masturbation, or, for that matter, anal intercourse among heterosexuals. In view of the fact that some 10 to 20 million people have died from AIDS in the last two decades, one would think that the consequence *in part* of not using condoms would weigh heavily in the thinking of those who appeal to an ethic that waves the banner of human flourishing. Something similar might be said about the harmful effects of burgeoning human population—also a partial by-product of the unavailability of contraceptives and the opposition of powerful groups to their becoming more available, such as the Roman Catholic church. Indeed the tendency to ignore weighty, cosmic consequences constitutes an objection to certain familiar developments of natural law theory. A broader conception of the nature of human flourishing within the natural law framework would lead to a radically different set of moral precepts.[52]

One may object that, after all, natural law theory is not a consequentialist view, and one may insist that what one ought to do is what it is natural to do *regardless of the consequences.* Further, Aristotle and Aquinas tend to define "natural" in terms of the function of an object. When one has identified the function of an object *somehow* then one may assume that it is appropriate to assess the behavior of the entity in question according to whether or not it fulfills that function. Thus, if the function of an object is to hammer nails, we may label it "a hammer" and then evaluate it according to whether or not it performs that function or does so well. For it to be a "good hammer" is for it to so function. It is tempting to equate two different things: whether an entity is effective in fulfilling a certain function, and whether its so doing is morally good (or failing to do so is morally bad). One may be good at the function of assassinating and therefore be a good assassin, but not, as a result, be morally good. It is worth noting that it is not wrong to use a hammer as a doorstop, to not use an Uzi to kill, or to use one's mouth to kiss (though its "natural" function is, arguably, to eat with). Sexual activity in which procreation is possible may fulfill one function of sexual activity, but it does not follow that we ought to judge to be wrong or unnatural any activity that does not. From the fact that something *can* fulfill a certain function, it does not follow that it *ought* to do so. Even though a person might make a mighty fine slave, it does not follow that the individual is wrong not to fulfill that function or that his or her "deviating" from so doing is "unnatural" if the latter is construed to mean "wrongful."[53]

We do not wish to suggest that natural law theorists should be saddled with Aristotle's view that some people are "slaves by nature," but there is a question on this view of whether *kinds* of beings have certain identifiable natural ends. For example, in a famous passage, Aristotle said that

> Plants exist for the sake of animals. . . . All other animals exist for the sake of man, tame animals for the use he can make of them as well as for the food they provide; and as for the wild animals most though not all of these can be used for food or are useful in other ways; clothing and instruments can be made out of them. If we are right in believing that nature makes nothing without some end in view, nothing to no purpose, it must be that nature has made all things specifically for the sake of man.[54]

It is not obvious that the inference in the last sentence would be less invalid, in spite of Aristotle's extraordinary intellectual feats, if "man" were replaced by "the HIV." That

aside, can we defend a particular hierarchy of beings on the ground that one group is *useful* to another? Aren't humans quite *useful* to the human immunodeficiency virus? In effect, the virus makes homes out of us. See Pollan's Essay 69. Can we say, then, that the natural end of some species is to serve others? A similar problem arises with Aristotle's broader hierarchy; he said, "animals are to serve human ends, women are to serve the ends of men, and men are to serve the ends of God." This view has had enormous influence historically. It *need* not be part of a natural law theory, but it *has* been. The deeper question is whether living things should achieve their *natural ends* (a difficult concept to understand clearly, but one may consider those outcomes that a being has a natural tendency to achieve, if they have such). It is uncertain whether any of this provides the basis for a moral ideal attractive to rational persons. Behavior is often thought to be good or right because it is natural; but then devotees of this view ought to say what we should make of natural tendencies, for example, toward infanticide, which has been observed among various birds, rodents, lions, African wild dogs, and langurs (and not just among defective offspring). See the Sidelight in Section IV.B called "Do What's Natural, You Say?"[55]

We have called attention to some worries about whether one can *nonarbitrarily* determine from nature just what are natural tendencies ("find" them and elaborate good reasons for so doing) and, if so, whether one should assume that the good for humans (or others) is constituted by the fulfillment of these tendencies, and whether fulfillment of "unnatural" tendencies must be counted as an evil—something to be either voluntarily avoided, prevented, or punished by the coercive power of the law. Recall Hume's claim that one cannot validly infer normative conclusions from purely empirical premises. Further, one might accuse natural law theory of focusing *too little* on nature, and instead on *some* desires of *some* humans and weaving an ethic around the view that the world should be organized to promote fulfillment of those desires. No doubt we are too skeptical, and the curious should read those who are believers and who set out sophisticated versions of this view. After all, some worries stated here are only about certain ways of identifying just what are natural human tendencies, and some natural law theorists may draw quite different moral conclusions if they identify natural tendencies differently, or assign positive weight to the fulfillment of nonhuman natural tendencies. No one disputes that the realization of certain human tendencies is sometimes a good and sometimes ought to be fostered; the arguments begin there, not terminate.

2.7 THE INFLUENCE OF KANT

Our glimpse of influential theories is much like our view of icebergs; we look quickly and see only a small part.[56] A major implication of the moral view of Immanuel Kant (1724–1804) is that one cannot determine the moral value of an act solely by some sort of assessment of its consequences; that is, his view is anticonsequentialist. Kant labeled what he believed is the supreme principle of morality "the Categorical Imperative." It had two "versions," which Kant deemed equivalent. It is not obvious, however, that they are. The first version, in our terms, says that one should *act only on those maxims of one's actions that one can, as a rational being, will to be (or endorse as) a universal law, that is, obeyed by all moral agents.* Kant seems to give heavy weight to the idea of reciprocity and to the related notion that what is right or a duty for one is a duty for any other relevantly similar moral agent, and that moral principles are not custom designed for only certain agents. He reasoned that the maxim of one person's deciding not to help another who is in distress is "help others only if it is convenient," but that no rational agent could endorse everyone's acting on that prin-

ciple because the agent herself or himself might be in need of help on some occasion, thus involving himself or herself in a sort of "contradiction" of the will. We will not explore whether passing Kant's "test" for maxims is necessary, sufficient, or merely relevant to a maxim's being defensible. But suppose that a maxim is "Let generation X use up environmental resources and let generation Y bear the burden." With one further supposition, that the agent is not allowed to know into which generation he or she is born, an argument may be developed for a duty to use up resources only in sustainable ways or ways that make other generations no worse off.[57]

We have suggested a connection between Kant's theory and environmental questions about whether we have duties to future generations, if so, why, and just what they are. If Kant is right, then "Drive a car if it is convenient" might be indefensible because if all obeyed such a maxim (say, about 4 billion adults), the result would be environmental catastrophe (a scenario not "willable" by a rational person). Of course, one person's driving may have no noticeable effect, so from a consequentialist's point of view, there may be no objection to the maxim. It is of interest, however, that because no rational being could approve of everyone's acting on the rule in question, no one should act according to that rule. Hence, we seem to observe a difference between Kant's view and the approach of a consequentialist. This is food for thought about the environment.

Kant's other version of the Categorical Imperative is that we would *never treat a person as a mere means;* by "person" he seems to mean "rational creature." Indeed, there is great stress in Kant's writing on the value of rational beings, beings capable of reflecting on options, on principles, and autonomously deciding for themselves what duty demands. That is, this value is due, in his view, to the fact that people have the capacity to formulate goals, reflect on values, and so on. Thus, we as such agents owe them a certain respect; generally, for example, we must refrain from causing them harm by acting contrary to their wills. Having a servant need not involve treating the person as a mere means if, for example, the person consents and is compensated for his or her efforts. If we should never treat a person as a mere means (a most suggestive notion; but what is precluded here—bad argument, bribery, guilt tripping, browbeating, insulting, ridiculing, shaming—along with the usual "force and fraud"?), then we may not do so *even* if the result would be maximization of total net utility. On occasion Kant expresses his view in terms of respect for rights. Thus we note a major source of tension between the Kantian approach and the utilitarian approach to deciding moral questions.

Kant's strikingly different attitude toward treatment of those he took to be (all?) non-rational beings ("animals") is found in this passage:

> . . . so far as animals are concerned we have no direct duties. Animals are not self-conscious and are there merely as a means to an end. That end is man. . . . Our duties toward animals are merely indirect duties towards humanity. . . . If he is not to stifle his human feelings, he must practice kindness towards animals, for he who is cruel to animals becomes hard also in his dealings with men. . . . Vivisectionists . . . certainly act cruelly . . . and they can justify their cruelty, since animals must be regarded as man's instruments.[58]

In the same lecture, he claimed that a man who shoots his dog when the dog is no longer useful "does not fail in his duty to the dog," in brief, because there is no duty to the dog. One cannot *wrong* it even if one can *harm* it in Kant's view—for "it cannot judge."[59] Note the importance of cognitive capacities in Kant's view. The question arises as to whether it would then be all right to vivisect profoundly retarded humans—if, in fact, the presence of

the capacity to judge is a necessary condition for being owed any duties. Is there a justification for differential treatment of animals and humans when they are on a par with respect to mental capacities and sentience? It may be evident that Kant's thesis about the source of noninstrumental value implies that virtually nothing nonhuman has such value; perhaps strictly speaking Kant would, or should, deny that profoundly retarded humans or the severely senile are owed any direct duties either. If so, then he does not mark the boundary of those possessing moral standing (see the Preview to Part III) in a way coextensive with the bounds around our species. A powerful moral intuition is that there are relevant differences among rocks, cabbages, and giant pandas. With respect to their being owed direct duties, Kant says not. Many today insist that we should *not* treat sentient nonhumans, for example, as mere means—thus deploying Kant's conception in a way that he did not. Frequently, the term animal liberationists or "defender of animal rights" is used for those who take, roughly, this view (for example, Peter Singer and Tom Regan, Essays 15 and 16, respectively). Some philosophers and others hold that we have duties to all living things ("biocentrists," such as Paul Taylor, Essay 24) or to the earth itself (which some tend to view as itself alive, such as James Lovelock). The various viewpoints emerge with accompanying arguments, especially in Part III and Part IV.

2.8 ENVIRONMENTAL JUSTICE

Utilitarians are often criticized for urging that we simply maximize the total *amount* of utility or happiness on the planet, ignoring the important question of how happiness or unhappiness is distributed among the population of humans or even sentient beings. This matter of the *distribution* of benefits (and burdens) is important. Suppose that you and your classmate independently answer questions on a quiz in the same manner, but she gets an A and you receive a C. You may "feel" (= believe!) that this is unfair or *unjust*—a wrongful distribution among the two of you—in the absence of any *relevant difference* between your responses. It is tempting to think, as did Aristotle back in the fourth century B.C.E. that "equals should be treated equally." Thus, we might think that there is some important connection between justice and some kind of equality. Important questions arise: (1) What counts as being equal (or when are the individuals in question *relevantly similar*)? and (2) What counts as equal treatment? A "theory of justice" should give us reasoned answers to those questions. Aristotle broke ground by suggestively urging that justice required that we treat equals equally and unequals unequally (but he even thought some humans were unequal and were "slaves by nature").

One key question concerns this: Across what population of beings is it that considerations of justice arise? To whom could we be said to be unjust under certain circumstances? One's friend? One's mother? One's dog? A wolf? A coral reef? A mountain? The traditional view has been the anthropocentric one; we have simply tended to think in terms of members of *Homo sapiens*. The challenges to this view have been noted and receive considerable discussion in the readings. Is it unfair to dump a nonhuman family companion ("pet") just because one would find him or her inconvenient to take on a vacation, to kill greyhounds when they are no longer capable of competitive racing? Clearly one can *harm* a living thing such as a rat, but could one be said to be *unfair* to it? We need not generalize quickly here in our search for a principled answer.

So we have often thought in terms of what constitutes a just society (of human beings) and ignored other living things in so far as our understanding of justice goes. Clearly "environmental burdens" of various sorts do affect humans, and it is important to consider the way in which environmental burdens get distributed by *policies* that we consciously adopt (for example, to cooperate or not in collective efforts to reduce destruction of the ozone layer or efforts to reduce the risk of serious global, warming) or *processes* to which we individually contribute, (such as air pollution—especially by vehicles we use or rely on to haul our Ethiopian coffee, Canadian beer, New Zealand sweaters, or . . .) in affluent nations. Without begging the question of whether the evidence for heightened global warming is decisive, it is clear that if it does occur—be it in 2050, 2100, or 2250—the burdens and benefits will be uneven. Global warming might result in an increased capacity to grow certain crops in parts of Canada or Siberia; however, it would likely result in the destruction of the nation of Maldives, inundation of much of Florida, New Orleans, Venice, and the Netherlands, to start a long list. Consider something over which we have more control, and certainly do at a national level, namely the dispersal of toxic wastes. Suppose we decided to ship and bury all toxic wastes, including nuclear, west of the Mississippi to an already somewhat polluted area such as Nevada— and all the wastes east of the Mississippi to South Carolina, a state receiving nuclear materials from the Southeast for a number of years. The state in which we editors reside, North Carolina, has unofficially adopted the usual NIMBY viewpoint (Not In My Backyard), even though some years ago agreeing with other states to take its turn ("it's only fair") at being a recipient of such wastes. What does justice require in such cases? We do not suggest that there is any simple answer, but *it will depend in part on what principle of just distribution we accept*—and this is a matter of reasoned investigation. Often distributions, especially of harmful things such as toxic wastes, are determined by who can buy out whom (some African nations have agreed to be recipients of the wastes of affluent nations—for a price) or which group has the least economic and political clout. Wastes dumps are usually placed by legislatures or the executive branch in poor, often minority, neighborhoods (see Essay 81 by Karl Grossman in VI.D). One can raise the question of whether this a matter of "simple economics" (where the land is cheapest) or whether some form of racism is at work. It is not news that who gets the dirty work or the "dirt" has often been a matter of which groups are least favored in a particular society.

What can be said then about which principle or principles of justice should guide us—initially at the level of thinking about the distribution of basic goods, say, jobs, political and legal rights, access to health care, shelter, or opportunities to obtain such? Here we will only mention the important contribution philosopher John Rawls has made to formulating a reasoned answer to this monumental question, which any society must address. Rawls's view, and a conception of justice in general, no doubt has important implications to thinking through questions of environmental policy and in shaping the elusive notion of what a good planet, maybe even an ideal planet, would look like. We humans have only begun to address the question of environmental justice in the last fraction of a geological instant. The next generation, if anyone, will carry it further.

Some thinkers (John Locke and Thomas Hobbes in the seventeenth century) thought that what was just depended on what kind of contractual agreement members of society reached (whatever distribution was agreed to was just). A tempting notion—because whether an arrangement is fair often seems to be simply a matter of agreement between the parties. However, some parties cannot participate at all or in a reasonable way in such agreements, for example, young children and the profoundly retarded (not to mention nonhumans). In practice, in the time of Locke and Hobbes, the actual participants in many contracts were a restricted group, namely, white, male property owners. Thus many individuals significantly *affected by* a contract did not

agree to it. This latter point is a source of serious criticism of actual contract theories of justice. Rawls, in his influential 1971 study *A Theory of Justice,* suggested that justice may be usefully thought of in terms of the principles of distribution that would be agreed to by rational, self-interested people designing the kind of society they wished to live in. This exercise is a kind of grand thought experiment concerning what hypothetical contractors would agree to under imaginary circumstances. A key part of the experiment is that each participant (we imaginatively become the participants) must figuratively enter behind a "veil of ignorance"; that is, each is disallowed use of a certain knowledge we normally have in bargaining situations, namely, *the economic class of which one may be a member, what so-called race we are, our nationality, to what generation we belong,* and so on. Lacking this information we are not able to seek special advantage for our actual selves as we often do in "hard-nosed" bargaining. The basic principles of social design are agreed to in this manner; whatever is agreed to is what is just, Rawls claims. Notably, if we did not have knowledge about to which generation we belonged, as participants we would likely adopt policies that would distribute benefits more evenly over generations; thus, any given generation would have some duties, as a matter of justice, to *future generations*—of humans (to other beings also?). The nature and extent of our obligations to future generations, if any, is a fundamental question for any ethic seeking to provide guidance for environmental policy.

There is little direct reference to Rawls's theory in what follows, but the questions of environmental justice arise at numerous points, as suggested earlier. Rawls's theory may strike one as anthropocentric. He allows that it is designed such that only humans, or "persons with a sense of justice," can be participants in the thought experiment. But what if one were designing social and political structures for all sentient creatures, not just humans? What if the participants were also disallowed knowledge of the *species* to which they belonged? This interesting question aside, Rawls's theory, and consideration of questions about the distribution of benefits and burdens across and over generations, helps us break out of the microbubble of focusing on how we compare with our peers, such as who has the coolest shoes, jacket, CDs, or "do." In any case, distributive questions are unavoidable in discussions of environmental policy, and at a variety of levels—across existing persons, generations, nations, and species or habitats.

2.9 THE IDEA OF A UNIQUE ENVIRONMENTAL ETHIC

Can there be a distinctive "environmental ethic"? The question itself is not clear. If it concerns the possibility of an ethic with implications about how we treat the environment, then the answer is that all ethical theories have such implications. We may think the implications of some are intolerable, but that is another matter. Indeed, many have thought that the implications of most or all traditional ethical theories with regard to our dealings with the environment are unacceptable and have therefore called for a new, distinct environmental ethic. Whether the new theory will be a revision of some traditional theoretical framework (Australian philosopher John Passmore, in a pioneering work, has defended this possibility[60]) or one that involves a radical jettisoning of all traditional frameworks is an open question. It is difficult to imagine a theory that would not incorporate key features of traditional views; arguably, however, none has appeared. Some incorporate significantly new assumptions; see especially the views of Leopold, Callicott, and Taylor in Part IV.A, and Rolston in Part VI.A.

Serious questions have been raised in recent years about traditional views. The major issue is the attack on anthropocentrism: the assumption that it is the well-being of *all* and only human beings that counts (for its own sake and not merely instrumentally). This matter is explored in Part III and Part IV. Competing views extend moral standing, in various manners, to all sentient beings, to all "subjects of a life," or to all living individuals. A second challenging thesis of recent work is that not only individuals count, but entire ecosystems or biological processes or sets of such. Once one grants moral standing to entities other than humans, a third crucial, seemingly inscrutable, recalcitrant difficulty arises about how to articulate a reasonable, principled way to resolve conflicts between competing interests of very diverse beings or webs of life. Some essays in Parts IV.A, IV.B, and VI address this issue. Recent moral positions that urge an extension of moral standing to nonhumans, and especially to *collectivities* ("environmental holist" views as opposed to "individualist" views) of some sort, sometimes seem to offer little guidance about this issue; for example, they offer rather romantic nostrums about how we humans are one with nature or are mere nodes of consciousness in the sea of life. Analogous *intrahuman* conflict situations are extremely difficult to think through; to add nonhuman interests muddies the ethical waters; but something similar must have occurred to those who, in earlier times, came to the view that women counted, or that blacks counted. Sometimes simplicity is purchased at the price of reasonableness.

One might regard one's own skin as the line of division between oneself and "the environment," and this is just what the ethical egoist recommends. To call attention to this point is to remind oneself, or perhaps notice more vividly, that many of the environmental questions we face are largely (if not solely) questions of a more or less familiar type about how we may, and how we ought to, treat *human beings*. To suggest a crude taxonomy, many of the important questions concern the justification of restrictions on the liberty of persons (or governments, corporations, and the like), questions about justice, and questions about the defensibility of imposing risks on other persons. That is, they are the central questions of recent work in moral and political philosophy. Hence one point we urge is increased integration of environmental ethics and modern moral and political philosophy. For this to occur, people who work in these areas must pay attention to the explorations of others who have often worked in comparative isolation.

Consider some examples. Questions about the defensibility of pollution, or the desirability of auctioning off pollution rights, at once involve issues about the acceptability of imposing risks on others, typically those who have not given informed consent to the risk. Such actions evidently restrict the liberty of others. And the distribution of burdens may occur in such a manner that questions of fairness arise. Frequently spokespeople for the third world complain that countries such as Japan, the United States, and Germany generate extremely high rates of pollution per capita in comparison to third-world countries. Imagine the pollution we would see if a billion people in China owned one or more cars that ran on fossil fuels. Yet developed countries insist that nations such as Brazil abstain from cutting tropical forests in order to have more trees to recycle the great carbon output of heavily industrialized nations. Apologists for high-tech nations (including George W. Bush) have claimed in reply that many of their high-tech products benefit the world, including the less developed nations, thereby compensating them for being subjected to higher pollution rates. These matters raise familiar questions about the extent to which nations ought to respect the sovereignty of other nations. The United States invaded Panama to depose President Noriega; is it permissible for other nations to depose a U.S. President on the ground that he leads a country that is the major contributor to the production of plutonium, nerve gas, and carbon pollution? The question of how, and at what rate, any nation should be using up resources raises the question of what duties current generations have to future ones (see Section V.E). This, too, can be thought of as a question of fairness, in part, as well as a question about subjecting others to serious risks.

Complicating matters is an issue that thus far has received no comment herein. It is widely held that each nation should do only what will promote or maximize its own interests. Sometimes, instead of this broad doctrine, the view one finds in, say, the United States is that the United States ought to do whatever will promote its own interest. This view looks like Ethical Egoism on a national scale (we could call it National Ethical Egoism). This view is no obscure doctrine; it is the basis for much foreign policy—in many nations. It is often associated with the assumption that there are no moral relations between nations, no duties, no rights, and that rather the situation is one Hobbes described as a state of nature (the doctrine of so-called *political realism*). Addressing many of the planetary environmental issues is indeed difficult if this (we think absurd) doctrine is accepted. With respect to certain ecological advantages, it might well be better if the world were not organized into numerous nation–states in which national boundaries bear little or no relation to ecotones, the boundaries between roughly identifiable sets of ecosystems (or bioregions). Perhaps it would be easier under such circumstances to avoid habitat deterioration, the massive kill-off of species, the diminishment of biodiversity, population crashes, and decline in the quality of life for humans and others.

But we do not start with an undesigned planet, one consisting of raw material to be distributed, or one in which more than 6 billion people are to be assigned to spaces as on the first day of school. We are, for better or worse, up to our sometimes myopic, nationalistic eyeballs in existing political, religious, racial, and ethnic loyalties, with systems of property rights, traditions of sovereignty, and so on. These practices, norms, and institutions often deserve to be radically criticized and altered, but doing so could also be unjust in certain ways, and this fact must also be given weight in proposed solutions. For some otherwise desirable goals, we may not be able morally "to get there from here." But we do not wish to urge any presumption in favor of the status quo. We are suggesting that many traditional questions of *intranational* and *international* justice have important bearings on attempts to identify morally acceptable solutions to the problems we confront. Indeed, they also affect just how we define or identify those problems.

NOTES

1. Carl Sagan and Ann Druyan, *Shadows of Forgotten Ancestors* (New York: Random House, 1992), p. 3.

2. As quoted in William Irvine, *Apes, Angels, and Victorians* (London: Reader's Union, 1956), p. 49.

3. This is a loose and somewhat formal characterization that in the end will not do; intuitively "You ought to wear your purple tie" is not a moral claim. Likewise, neither is "If you are going to Montreal, you ought to brush up on your French."

4. A plausible, broader taxonomy might regard moral or normative claims as a subset of evaluative ones. Evaluative claims would be understood to include both moral claims but also nonmoral evaluative claims. The latter category would include evaluative claims about objects or states of affairs; for example, Mrs. Brown has got a lovely daughter, the Musee D'Orsay is exhilarating, Beethoven's *Fifth Symphony* is sublime, pleasure is good, Koko is one fine animal, or Lake Louise in British Columbia is a joy to the eyes. We will often use *normative* interchangeably with *moral* or *ethical* but it is frequently used by others as a more generic term such as *evaluative*.

5. A remark of Dorothy Parker in a book review.

6. This movement consisted largely of a group of philosophers and scientists who wished to rid the world of what they considered nonsense; it is associated with the Vienna Circle and A. J. Ayer, Moritz Schlick, and Rudolf Carnap, among others.

7. As reported by Plato in the *Republic*.

8. Tautologies and logical truths are statements that are true because of their form or simply in virtue of the meaning of the words used, such as bachelors are unmarried, everything that has shape has size, all purple things are colored, eye color is a heritable trait or it is not.

9. However, we note that there may be moral agents who are not humans and that not all humans are moral agents. One should compare, regardless of whether they exist, human infants, profoundly retarded humans, God, angels, E.T., or Koko the gorilla (who signed in American Sign Language "Me bite, bad" after biting her trainer one day).

10. If one is unfamiliar with certain basic standards used in assessing arguments, a logic course can be very helpful.

11. David Hume, from Book III, Part I, Section I of *A Treatise of Human Nature*, edited by L. A. Selby-Bigge (Oxford: Clarendon Press, 1965), p. 469.

12. We can validly infer "Hilary's car is colored" from the premise "Hilary's car is blue." However, it is invalid to infer that "Hilary's car is blue" from the premise "Hilary's car is colored"—even if it happens to be true that her car is blue. Valid arguments are "truth preserving" but may not start with true premises. The terms *valid* and *invalid* are technical terms as used here.

13. The fact that one cannot validly infer normative conclusions from purely empirical premises in the examples noted would not, of course, show that one can never do so. Many philosophers, "ethical naturalists," think otherwise. On this point one might consult the writings of Philippa Foot.

14. By design this test for toxicity of substances is not complete until at least half of the test animals die.

15. If "murder" is used to mean "unlawful killing," the sentence looks empirical, but if what is meant is "wrongful killing," the sentence is being used to make a moral claim.

16. As the term is used technically by mathematicians, philosophers, and logicians, *invalid* does not mean bad; and an invalid argument need not, but may, have a false conclusion. However, invalid arguments are commonly appraised as bad in one respect: Their premises fail to support their conclusions in the strongest possible manner. An argument that has this fault may nevertheless happen to have a true conclusion.

17. Compare the remark of Albert Einstein, no artsy antiscientific sort, "We should be on our guard not to overestimate science and scientific methods when it is a question of human problems; and we

should not assume that experts are the only ones who have a right to express themselves on questions affecting the organization of society." From *Ideas and Opinions by Albert Einstein* (New York: Crown, 1954), p. 152.

18. On the moral/legal distinction, recall the view that black persons had moral rights even when in the antebellum period in the United States few such rights were also legally institutionalized.

19. Paul and Anne Ehrlich, *Healing the Planet* (Reading, MA: Addison-Wesley, 1991), p. 85.

20. The best philosophy and the best science get the facts straight; even if that is done, reasoning about the facts is another matter. We leave it to a well-known scientist to express an opinion about the receptiveness of scientists to philosophical untangling of arguments. To quote Stephen Jay Gould "I deplore the unwillingness of scientists to explore seriously the logical structure of arguments." And further, "Scientists tend to ignore academic philosophy as an empty pursuit. Surely, any intelligent person can think straight by intuition." Evidently, Gould is speaking ironically in the last sentence. See Stephen Jay Gould, *Ever Since Darwin* (New York: Norton, 1977), p. 40.

21. Paul and Anne Ehrlich, *Healing the Planet*, p. 116.

22. For the Galileo example, see Jonathan Weiner, *Planet Earth* (Toronto: Bantam Books, 1986), p. 153. Concerning Agassiz, see p. 116.

23. The term *a priori* means "before or apart from" experience or empirical evidence. An *a priori* assumption may be true; whether it is belief-worthy is another matter.

24. By "anthropocentric grounds" or "anthropocentric values," some may mean simply "human ideals"; but among them may be the view, for example, that we ought not inflict pain or premature death on animals gratuitously, or even the view that species boundaries are morally without weight. But such a usage of "anthropocentrism " threatens to muddy the conceptual waters. Compare Bryan Norton's characterization and use of "weak anthropocentrism": Bryan Norton, *Why Preserve Natural Variety?* (Princeton, NJ: Princeton University Press, 1987), pp. 7, 12.

25. Strictly, philosophers normally divide "ethics" as a discipline into normative ethics and metaethics, and the attempt to figure out the most defensible moral principles, or specifically what we ought to do, is the focus of normative ethics. The focus of metaethics is more abstract; the questions are those *about* ethical claims. e.g., are they rationally decidable, does "right" refer to some natural property, and so on.

26. On this point one might consult Mary Midgley, "Duties Concerning Islands," reprinted in *People, Penguins, and Plastic Trees*. edited by Donald VanDeVeer and Christine Pierce (Belmont, CA: Wadsworth, 1986), pp. 156–164.

27. Richard Brandt suggests that it is those convictions surviving cognitive psychotherapy that deserve weight. See his *Theory of the Good and the Right* (New York: Oxford University Press, 1979). One critic has observed that we would regard as suspect any theory of psychotherapy unless it accorded with our deepest pretheoretical moral convictions; the reference has evaporated.

28. Rather what is said in defense of the claim seems to support only theses like all acts have motives, people always want to achieve whatever they desire to achieve, or all acts are acts of a self.

29. Saying that "fitness" means "reproductive fitness" does not do away with all the questions.

30. It was not Darwin but rather English social scientist philosopher Herbert Spencer who introduced the expression "survival of the fittest." Spencer is not well-known today but was widely read in the United States in the nineteenth century.

31. How to characterize the negative-positive distinction is not straightforward. Refraining from acting may be a kind of effortful action, such as braking a car to refrain from hitting another one.

32. See Susan Miller Okin, *Justice, Gender, and the Family* (New York: Basic Books, 1989).

33. We employ suggestions from Frank Stare, "The Concept of Property," *American Philosophical Quarterly 9*, 1972, 200–207.

34. See J. Baird Callicott, "On the Intrinsic Value of Non-Human Species," in *The Preservation of Species*, edited by Bryan Norton (Princeton, NJ: Princeton University Press, 1986), p. 144. Note also Norton's view that appeals to rights "provide no theoretically defensible basis for species preservation." Ibid., p. 275.

35. However, dying prematurely seems to count as a harm or a cost, and it may be painless. So one cannot classify painless dying as a form of disutility (understood as pain of some sort).

36. See Charles Darwin's *The Expression of Emotion in Man and Animals* (Chicago: University of Chicago Press, 1965) for Darwin's focus on bodily and facial expressions as compelling evidence of emotional states in humans and animals.

37. If the sum of the utilities of a majority's getting its wants fulfilled is more than offset by the sum of the disutilities of a minority's losing out, then what maximizes total net utility and what most people want may be contrary paths.

38. We note in passing that in his Introduction to the *Principles of Morals and Legislation* (1789), Bentham addressed the difficulty of measuring pleasure or pain and proposed that intensity, duration, fecundity (the tendency of the feeling to give rise to more of the same kind), and so on should be taken into account.

39. Predicting consequences may be very difficult (compare current worries over whether someone released from jail will steal again or whether global warming by the year 2050 will increase at least 4 degrees centigrade). Probabilities may need to be taken into account; so strictly the calculation is to determine total net expected utility.

40. In 1992 it was decided that the captain of the oil tanker *Exxon Valdez* was immune to prosecution for having allowed his ship to run aground. The law is that a captain is immune to prosecution once he reports the event. The rationale for the law is thus utilitarian or consequentialist in nature; it is to encourage captains to report such events, presumably thereby promoting the overall best results. Some utilitarians might draw a different conclusion. Defenders of a retributivist theory of justice may insist that the captain deserved a serious punishment and that it is wrongheaded to look forward to the consequences as a way of determining the correct policy. There are serious worries about fairness here; compare the severe penalties imposed on certain consenting adult homosexual behavior (up to 20 years in jail in North Carolina). In the days of David Hume (eighteenth century), in Great Britain one could be hung for simply disbelieving in the existence of God. This fact tended to discourage publication on certain issues.

41. Economists and philosophers agree, to our knowledge, that there are many Pareto-optimal states of affairs at which one might arrive depending on the initial distribution of goods. A Pareto-optimal situation is one in which it is impossible to rearrange things and make someone better off without also making someone worse off; in that respect it is one that is totally "efficient" as economists use that term. The initial or final distribution of goods may or may not be thought of as fair or just. Discerning whether a situation is Pareto-optimal or not, that is, efficient, does not then address the distributional problem. In an imaginary two-person community consisting of a slave and his "master," it might be impossible to make one better off without making the other worse off and, thus, the situation would be efficient; all this suggests, of course, is that efficiency is not everything. We believe that a theory of justice is required and that only within the constraints required by principles of justice (whatever those constraints might be) is it permissible to pursue efficiency. The principles of justice may, of course, allow an important role for moral rights. Such a theory of efficiency within justice may allow for cost-benefit analysis within the framework of a rights theory. These most succinct, if not obtuse, remarks are meant to be suggestive for further inquiry. The burden would seem to be on philosophers to try to supply the right theory of justice.

42. Maybe we should not go so far as Albert Schweitzer, who purportedly said "happiness is for pigs." No doubt this was Schweitzer's way of discounting the importance of human happiness, but Benthamite utilitarians might give it a different twist (we should care about the happiness of animals as well).

43. Although we would strongly discourage anyone from thinking that ethical issues have any necessary connection with religious ones, Malcolm Gillis cites an essay by E. Mason, who points out that the economics department at Harvard University was dominated by preachers until the 1880s. See Malcolm Gillis, "Economics, Ecology, and Ethics: Mending the Broken Circle of the Tropical Forests" in the excellent volume *The Broken Circle*, edited by F. H. Bormann and Stephen Kellert (New Haven, CT: Yale University Press, 1991), p. 155.

44. We rely here on one of many helpful comments by Talbot Page.

45. The term *paternalism* or *paternalistic interference* refers to interference with others in an effort to promote their own good, such as taking away car keys from a drunk. One question that arises is whether we can ever know better than the other what is for his or her own good and if so under what circumstances. On this topic see Joel Feinberg, *Harm to Self* (New York: Oxford University Press, 1986) or Donald VanDeVeer, *Paternalistic Intervention* (Princeton, NJ: Princeton University Press, 1986).

46. It is worth reminding ourselves of all the choices that routinely get made for others, such as children, the severely retarded, the senile, many medical patients, and animals. And those without funds cannot cast a "dollar vote" in the marketplace.

47. Something like the thesis of psychological egoism (each person always acts out of a desire to promote his or her own interest) usually seems to get assumed about here. Yet if being "better off" simply means getting one's desires satisfied on balance, then one might be "better off" if one commits suicide or is subjected to torture—if that is what one wanted, on balance.

48. Still, the rights theory may allow that infringements are justified only under certain rather limited

conditions. The utilitarian theory is committed to condoning any and all nasty acts if doing so would indeed maximize utility. A question for any rights theory allowing infringements is whether its grounds for doing so are nonarbitrary.

49. If potential gainers from a transaction compensated those who would otherwise be losers (and remained gainers), then interesting alternatives would arise. Generally, economists insist that moving to a situation in which such compensation could be made is an improvement (why? because there would be an increase in total net utility?) even if compensation is not actually paid. This "potential compensation" variant on the Pareto principle seems nontrivial partly because it seems to condone unjust redistributions (on balance the losers just appear to be wrongfully harmed), as does the principle of utility. So it seems to gain nontriviality at the cost of serious conflict with our pretheoretical convictions.

50. These comments were made at a meeting of the American Philosophical Association in Columbus, Ohio, April 29–May 1, 1982. The paper was entitled "Natural Law and Moral Rights: Comments on a Paper by Christine Pierce."

51. On this matter one might consult the essay by Christopher Boorse, "Concepts of Health," in *Health Care Ethics*, edited by Donald VanDeVeer and Tom Regan (Philadelphia: Temple University Press, 1987).

52. On this point one might examine the work of Joseph Raz or Germain Grisez.

53. It is crucial to notice the frequent slide from purely descriptive uses of *abnormal* and *unnatural* (for example, statistically unusual) to evaluative uses of the same terms.

54. There is no doubt that there are certain natural tendencies. Some hold that these are divinely implanted. Some hold that they are just there and offer no explanation. The prevailing scientific view is, of course, that there is an explanation and that it has to do with which behaviors were advantageous in the competitive process of natural selection. Male robber flies, for example, court female robber flies; this behavior, to which there is a natural tendency, seems to have the advantage of helping the female to recognize the male as something not to be eaten (at least not at that moment).

55. Arthur Fisher, "A New Synthesis Comes of Age," *Mosaic* 22(1) (Spring 1991), 13.

56. We speak of "influential theories." Perhaps no one has gone to war thinking that she or he is out to defend "a theory," but as we have used the term, the evaluative beliefs of the Nazis led them to war, the Crusades sought to spread a certain doctrine, and Columbus both wanted to find lots of gold for Spain and to Christianize "the natives" in the process. The gospel of free trade, of the classless society, of ethnic purity and certain Islamic ideals have led to enslavement and to wholesale destruction of species and ecosystems. Somewhere, John Stuart Mill noted that the logic of tyrants is, Since we are right, it is all right to persecute those who disagree. Prescriptions such as that of one of the church fathers, Tertullian, "Love God and do as you please," are recipes for God knows what, so to speak. Some theories explicitly prohibit the forcible spread of any doctrine, including their own. One might compare Kant's views and Utilitarianism in this respect. If it would maximize utility to forcibly spread the doctrine of Utilitarianism, why not do it—if one accepts the principle of utility? In contrast, the Kantian notion to never treat a person as a mere means would seem to prohibit the forcible spread of that very notion.

57. In passing, we note that a work of great importance and one with acknowledgment of Kant's influence, John Rawls's *A Theory of Justice,* makes important and inventive use of the idea that principles of justice plausibly may be thought of, in an elaborate thought experiment, as those principles that would be accepted by rational, "self-interested" persons seeking to determine those principles that would guide their own future interaction, including the design of basic institutions, the distribution of basic goods and opportunities—such deciders being subject to important informational constraints, namely, that they are not allowed to know or to use information by which everyday bargainers seek special advantage; that is, they are supposed to be ignorant of the generation into which they are born (see Chapter 3), their race, their nationality, and so on. In effect Kant says, pay attention only to what you can rationally endorse or will, not your actual wants. Similarly, Rawls constructs a decision scenario to give weight to people's impartial wants, not their actual, biased ones. See John Rawls, *A Theory of Justice* (Cambridge, MA: Belknap Press of Harvard University, 1971). It may be useful to take a course in moral philosophy first, or to take along one's personal philosopher for the trip.

58. Immanuel Kant, "Duties to Animals and Spirits," in *Lectures on Ethics* translated by Louis Infield (New York: Harper & Row, 1963), pp. 239–241.

59. Most wrongings involve harming, but arguably many do not. On this, see Joel Feinberg, *Harmless Wrongdoing.* (Oxford: Oxford University Press, 1988).

60. John Passmore, *Man's Responsibility for Nature* (New York: Scribner's 1974).

II

WESTERN RELIGIOUS AND CULTURAL PERSPECTIVES

3. PREVIEW

Whenever I injure life of any kind I must be quite clear as to whether this is necessary or not. I ought never to pass the limits of the unavoidable, even in apparently insignificant cases. The countryman who has mowed down a thousand blossoms in his meadow as fodder for his cows should take care that on the way home he does not, in wanton pastime, switch off the head of a single flower growing on the edge of the road, for in so doing he injures life without being forced to do so by necessity.[1]

Albert Schweitzer

Christ himself shows that to refrain from the killing of animals and the destroying of plants is the height of superstition for, judging that there are no common rights between us and the beasts and trees, he sent the devils into a herd of swine and with a curse withered the tree on which he found no fruit.[2]

Augustine

Many systems of ideas and bodies of doctrine have influenced our views on nature. Some are religious; some are secular. We will say a little about secular influences later. In this section we initially focus on the Judeo-Christian tradition.

When we speak, in particular of Christianity, it is important to distinguish between (1) the historical *institution* of the Christian church on the one hand, and (2) the logical implications of its *doctrine* on the other (especially those found in its chosen sacred

writings).[3] Historian Lynn White, Jr., in his famous 1967 essay "The Historic Roots of Our Ecologic Crisis" (Essay 4), discusses Christianity in the former sense, that is, as a historical institution in the Latin West, when he blames Christianity for the part it has played in fostering an attitude of human arrogance toward nature. White says, "No new set of values has been accepted in our society to displace those of Christianity. Hence we shall continue to have a worsening ecologic crisis until we reject the Christian axiom that nature has no reason for existence save to serve man."

White's focus is not on how one *ought to interpret* biblical texts, but rather on how biblical texts *have been interpreted* (historically) and how those interpretations have fit together with the emergence of a democratic culture and the growth of science and technology to produce ecologic crisis. The following is a striking example of his thesis: In antiquity, White reminds us, it was believed that "every tree, every spring, every stream, every hill had its own . . . guardian spirit." This belief is called animism. He observes that Christianity destroyed animism . . . and many forests. As he points out, "For nearly 2 millennia Christian missionaries have been chopping down sacred groves, which are idolatrous because they assume spirit in nature. Presumably, the actions of Christians are and were linked to their beliefs that 'man [sic] shares, in great measure, God's transcendence of nature.'" Spirit then, was thought to belong to humans only. By destroying pagan animism, White

43

asserts, "Christianity made it possible to exploit nature in a mood of indifference to the feelings of natural objects." He is saying that people's *beliefs have consequences*. Many beliefs that are destructive to the environment stem from what Latin Christians understood biblical doctrine to be. It could have been (or could be) otherwise. In "Continuing the Conversation," a paper White wrote in 1973 as a reply to his critics, he says, "Scattered through the Bible, but especially the Old Testament, there are passages that can be read as sustaining the notion of a spiritual democracy of all creatures."[4] His point is that historically they seem seldom or never to have been so interpreted. This should not inhibit anyone from taking a fresh look at them.

In "Continuing the Conversation," White says of his critics: "The most common charge was that I had ignorantly misunderstood the nature of 'man's dominion' and that it is not an arbitrary rule but rather a *stewardship* of our fellow creatures for which mankind is responsible to God."[5] The relevant biblical passage here is the creation story in Genesis 1:

> Then God said, "Let us make man in our image, after our likeness; and let them have dominion over the fish of the sea and over the birds of the air, and over the cattle, and over all the earth and over every creeping thing that creeps upon the earth.

> So God created man in his own image, in the image of God he created them; male and female he created them.

> And God blessed them, and God said to them, "Be fruitful and multiply, and fill the earth and subdue it; and have dominion over the fish of the sea and over the birds of the air, and over every living thing that moves upon the earth."

> And God said, "Behold I have given you every plant yielding seed which is upon the face of all the earth, and every tree with seed in its fruit; you shall have them for food."[6]

Like many of White's critics, environmental philosopher Robin Attfield sets about showing that *stewardship* is the only credible interpretation here and that other interpretations such as the *despotic* one are "distortions" and "rationalizations of exploitative practices." But White's thesis is not about what is the correct interpretation of the Bible; instead he maintains that biblical texts are often open to more than one interpretation and that, the "best one" aside, a particular reading unfavorable to the environment became dominant historically.

As White's discussion of St. Francis of Assisi (1181–1226) makes clear, there was some difference of opinion about what Christian doctrine was taken to be even in medieval times. Again, the historical point is that it was the views of thinkers such as Augustine (354–430) and St. Thomas Aquinas (1225–1274) that prevailed, not the views of St. Francis. As White puts it, "The prime miracle of St. Francis is the fact that he did not end up at the stake, as many of his left-wing followers did." White, also a self-acknowledged "churchman," is hopeful that Westerners will "find a new religion or rethink our old one."

The *stewardship* view is a fairly popular example of one rethinking. What exactly is this view? A. R. Peacocke gives the following characterization:

> Although "dominion" has [a] kingly reference, it is a caring "dominion" exercised under the authority of the Creator, and so it is a more accurate reflection of the meaning of the Genesis myth to say that it describes man as vice-regent, or steward, or manager, or trustee (as of a property, or a charity) as well as exercising the leadership of a king of creation. He is, in the myth, called to tend the earth and its creatures in responsibility to its Creator. He is accountable. He is responsible.[7]

According to the stewardship view, then, there is a God who expects us to exercise responsibility toward the earth. The earth belongs to God, and members of *Homo sapiens* are commanded to take care of it and the creatures that dwell therein. A stewardship interpretation may be committed to an acceptance of a traditional private property view. That is, it may assume that humans should not ruthlessly exploit the earth, because the earth belongs to God. If we ought to treat the earth in a responsible and virtuous way, it is not because the earth and its creatures have independent moral standing or inherent worth, but because they are God's property.[8] A "citizenship" interpretation, as J. Baird Callicott has called it, is possible here as well if the relevant parts of the Genesis story are read as a directive for humans to look after the welfare of the beings and things created by God not insofar as they are God's property, but insofar as they are inherently good themselves. For example, the text, "And God saw that [the creation] was good,"[9] may mean that God declared that the earth and the things and beings in it have intrinsic value, that is, a value of their own. Although Callicott and others see "stewardship" and "citizenship" as alternative interpretations, Attfield claims that "stewardship is best construed . . . as involving humble recognition of the intrinsic value of fellow-creatures."

"For God So Loved the World," Essay 5, is a sermon preached at Salisbury Cathedral by Andrew Linzey, a Senior Research Fellow, Mansfield College, Oxford, and Special Professor of Theology, University of Nottingham, England. Linzey substantially agrees with White about the actual role of Christian churches; he elaborates with examples from church history. Linzey, however, believes that there is a basis in the tradition for believers (and others) to be stewards of the environment.

One would think that the bottom line principle in Judaism, as with Christianity or Islam, would also be "whatever God commands or wills is right." Different conceptions of what that divine will is are then the source of divergent outlooks or policy views. The "sacred writings" to which Jews appeal are different (the Hebrew Bible, the Torah, etc.), as the ensuing discussion "Judaism and the Environment" by Robert Gordis (editor of the quarterly, *Judaism*) reflects. One finds an endorsement in Judaism of the view that people are stewards of God's creation that is similar to some Christian interpretations; once again there is some textual wrestling with the phrase "subdue the earth," a key fragment from Genesis 1:28. Gordis claims that the true genius of Judaism, however, is in "specifics." He mentions those strains in rabbinical law that prohibit causing certain kinds of pain to animals. Indeed, part of "keeping Kosher" is to use a sharp knife when slitting the throat of animals for food—lest they experience undue pain.

A second "basic Jewish concept" is said to be "do not destroy" (*bal tashchit*). Indeed, Gordis insists that ". . . any act of destruction is an offense against the property of God." One might wonder why such a prescription would not prohibit all killings of animals and plants or all killings in war; we let the question stand. Gordis observes how the principle was understood to prohibit using trees (while besieging a city), which might yield fruit; other trees were permissible to use. Such reasoning is often described as *moral casuistry*—an attempt to draw highly specific, detailed conclusions about how one ought to act. At one time it was prohibited to look in a mirror on the Sabbath—lest one might put a hair in place, a forbidden bit of labor on the Sabbath. A counterpart principle (more widely invoked and perhaps applicable) in Catholicism might be the use of the Doctrine of Double Effect[10] to justify the killing of a fetus if it is a *foreseen* effect but not an *intended* consequence of removing a cancerous uterus in a pregnant woman. A seeming attraction of such principles is the provision of detail for the by-itself-empty appeal to God's will. One might, however, consider the likelihood of logically extracting in some nonarbitrary way specific and useful policy guidance from a principle such as "do not destroy."

Traditionally, the Roman Catholic church has also adopted a stewardship view of what is seen as God's creation. It has seen itself as endorsing the value of *all* human life forms—notoriously being relentlessly opposed to abortion and recently the use of human stem cells for research. It opposes the pantheist notion that God is eminent in the material world, a "pagan" notion found among some "environmentalists." God is said to be "transcendent." While all creation is seen as good—in some sense—(instrumentally or intrinsically?), humans ("man" is a "little less than a god" as the Psalmist [Ps. 8:3–8] put it) —and they are at the summit of God's creation. There is then a clear emphasis on a *hierarchy* among God's creatures with humans having *the right and the duty* to govern nonhuman things. No biocentric egalitarianism here (see Part IV). But, it is claimed, humans must respect God's creation and God's purposes; what *moral constraints this places on human choices* is important and obscure. One Catholic source states that "tigers are marvelous creatures" but have also been the "bane of human existence." So "untamed nature would continue to inflict tremendous suffering on the human family."[11] It is tempting to say that the emphasis in this variant of Christianity is on human dominance—and on resisting the notion that human population should be constrained for the sake of protecting nonhuman life. Further, this view seems to be supportive of economic development, opposed to contraception, abortion, deliberately non-procreative sex, and perhaps limitations on family size.[12] Still, Pope John Paul II speaks of ". . . the [ecological question]—ranging from the preservation of the natural habitats of the different species of animals and of other forms of life to 'human ecology' properly speaking—which finds in the

Bible clear and strong ethical direction, leading to a solution which respects the great good of life, of every life."[13] Just where such a view might conflict with a straight up, secular, anthropocentric environmental ethic is a question we leave for investigation. What must we do when our growing population of 6 billion continues to bring about an orgy of extinction for animal and plant life?

Some people question not only whether mistakes in management are being made but whether stewardship is even a viable concept. For example, Christian environmentalist John Haught sees stewardship as "too managerial a concept to support the kind of ecological ethics we need today. Most ecologists would argue that the earth's life systems were a lot better off before we humans came along to manage them. In fact, it is almost an axiom of ecology that these systems would not be in such jeopardy if the human species had never appeared in evolution at all."[14] Peter Wenz adds to Haught's critique by noting that "history suggests that people lack the knowledge and wisdom needed to manage nature well. Any God who would appoint us stewards would let Dracula guard the blood bank."[15]

The stewardship approach, Haught continues, fails to accentuate that we belong to the earth much more than it belongs to us, that we are more dependent on it than it is on us."[16] Whether the concept of stewardship is sufficiently democratic to be the substitute for the animism White wants is an interesting question. Theologian Sallie McFague thinks we can do better. McFague, Professor of Theology and former Dean of Vanderbilt Divinity School, challenges both the patriarchal conception of God and the idea of God as a supreme being with a dependent realm. She rejects the model of God as lord, king, monarch, ruler, or patriarch. With the metaphor of the world as God's body, her aim is to bring God and the world closer together (unlike the pope) and to develop a notion of sin as against the world, i.e., our own species, other species, and nature rather than against God.

In explaining her "organic" model, McFague says, "The model of the world as God's body encourages us to dare to love bodies and find them valuable and wonderful—just that and nothing more. The 'God part' will take care of itself if we can love and value bodies. That is what an incarnational theology assures us: it is all right to have a nature spirituality. In fact we should have one."[17] It is probably claims like this one that lead critics like Andrew Linzey to say, "I judge that [Sallie McFague] has fundamentally deified nature."[18] But McFague would deny this claim. The theological challenge she takes on is to make sense of the idea that God is both transcendent and immanent, and such a view cannot result in a simple pantheism.

Like Jay McDaniel, McFague belongs to a group of contemporary theologians who value nature for its own sake and work comfortably with the theory of evolution. For example, when McFague speaks of "the common creation story," she means ". . . the story of everything that is, of how the universe began fifteen billion years ago and how it evolved into some hundred billion galaxies of which our Milky Way is one."[19] Thus, much of the assault on traditional views of God and the environment is coming from *within* contemporary Christian theology. One might argue that McFague and McDaniel are doing just what Lynn White, Jr., hoped for, finding an interpretation of existing religion that is environmentally responsible.

There is sometimes a striking lack of dialogue between those who work in different areas of inquiry (e.g., between theology and environmental ethics). A notable exception is the work of theologian Jay McDaniel. McDaniel in part puzzles over how to conceive of God, given the fact that a good deal of pain and premature death is built in to the natural order. His striking example is illustrated in the "backup chicks" of pelicans.

Pelicans lay two eggs; soon the older chick attacks the younger, often driving it out of the nest. The parents do not allow it to return (in this vein see the essay by Barash in this section). In spite of this, McDaniel believes that God (whom he is willing to conceive as a divine mother) loves the world. Indeed, he goes so far as to say that "even if there were no God, individual beings would deserve our respect; they would have rights." Here McDaniel enters a discussion of contemporary "environmental philosophy" and discussions of animal rights. In brief, he agrees that animals have "intrinsic value" and interests to be given weight in moral decision making, though, significantly, he insists that they have "different degrees of intrinsic value" (compare the discussions in Part III and Regan's and VanDeVeer's essays in particular). Note here that McDaniel has moved beyond the stewardship-versus-exploitation debate, vague admonitions about "the value of all life," or "loving our neighbors." Thus he begins to wrestle with the hard questions as to whether there are plausible, principled grounds for deciding hard questions about tradeoffs, ones where some lives (or the welfare of some) are sacrificed for the benefit of others—tradeoffs of an *inter*specific and not merely *intra*specific kind.[20] These are tough questions and matters of considerable dispute, ones that emerge when one gives up the assumption (much explored in the next section) that all *and only* humans, members of the species *Homo sapiens,* are valuable or have a right to life. A good question to consider as one explores environmental issues is whether or not a proposed "environmental ethic" *addresses* these issues in any serious manner. McDaniel's work does so, whatever further assessment is to be made of his views and arguments. Thus McDaniel's following remark is both a step away from traditional Christian environmental views and also a promissory note for further, specific discussion and argument: "For those interested in a biocentric Christianity, God must be conceived as loving all creatures on their own terms and for their own sakes; the living cell, the mosquito, the pelican, and the human being."

An even broader acquaintance with diverse cultural perspectives is afforded by the Nina Rosenstand essay (10), "Everyone Needs a Stone: Alternative Views of Nature." Rosenstand canvases some secular attitudes among the ancient Greeks, ones that contributed to prevailing Western indifference toward the nonhuman world. She also surveys attitudes and views of nature typical of the Romantic period in the nineteenth century, and earlier anticipations of Jean-Jacques Rousseau. Of special interest today are the traditional ideals and practices of American Indians who, contrary to the view that America was "empty" or "first settled" by Europeans, lived in America for centuries and, on the face of it, did not generate the sort of environmental destruction we see around us. We can ask why and, with Rosenstand, whether any of these traditions offer an inviting contribution to an environmental ethic.

As one looks about for "environmental wisdom," examining both secular and religious sources and traditions, one understandably is drawn to the views of those peoples who live close to the ground or water—those who survive by farming and hunting, and whose lives are not insulated from natural phenomena by steel vehicles, asphalt roads, and brick walls of an air-conditioned mall, those who instead walk among trees and rivers and do not just view them on the Nature channel, and those who see and hear real birds, and not just by means of their MP3 players. We have and do often dismiss the views of such people by regarding them as "primitive," "technologically backward," and "poor." Such terms say something about us, our views and attitudes, and sometimes our ignorance. It is clearer now that their knowledge of nature, of the use of plants in healing

for example, is often very sophisticated. Indeed, pharmaceutical companies spend millions to seek out this knowledge and sometimes to patent it. R. E. Johannes in "Traditional Ecological Knowledge" notes "that Palauan fishermen could describe lunar periodic spawning aggregations in their waters for more than twice as many species of fish as had been thus described in the scientific literature for the entire world.[21] This knowledge is indeed impressive, but Johannes remarks that, swinging to the opposite extreme, ". . . the notion of preternatural harmony with nature has metastasized through the media, and indigenous peoples are often now presented to us as environmentalist role models." However, it is dangerous to romanticize any people and uncritically to assume that they have some unerring access to wisdom in the manner of Rousseau's "noble savage." Johannes discusses the attractions *and* hazards of looking to the practices and judgments of those living in traditional "undeveloped" communities.

Most of the essays in this section make quite substantial assumptions that are not shared by a good portion of the world's population (Muslims, Christians, Jews, and so on), assumptions that there is a powerful person-like Being who has created and who sustains the world, that we and all living things are his creation, that he has a will [or prescribes] that we should behave in certain ways, that what is right is doing just that, and so on. Given those assumptions, an environmental ethic should be based on them. This is the fundamental approach of Linzey, Gordis, Attfield, and with qualifications, McDaniel. Secular dissenters (agnostics, atheists) may disagree for many different reasons. Some observe that the best evidence is that life on earth goes back about 3.6 billion years and that humans have only been around for 4 million or so; hence, we humans are latecomers and it is surpassingly strange to suggest that we are caretakers for the rest of the living world. For over 99 percent of the time life on earth has existed, the alleged "stewards" have not been around. Some suggest that what we now know of biological processes does not support over time any notion that humans are the "pinnacle" of creation or the highpoint of evolution (it is not unidirectional; later need not be better)—somehow the natural, predestined goal of the complex, very long-term process of natural selection. David Barash, professor of psychology at the University of Washington and author of *Revolutionary Biology,* discusses one prominent argument for the existence of God, an argument not unrelated to how we view life in the natural world and the place of humans in it. It is sometimes argued that the power, beauty, and complexity of the natural world [cf. the human brain] demonstrate God's existence. Barash notes that biologists today tend to take these traits as evidence of *natural selection* in the process of evolution. Because both groups appeal to "perfections" in nature, Barash suggests that the evidence of "imperfections" should not be ignored. What are they? As an example, one might wonder why the exit for the human fetus is through "the narrow confines of the pelvic bones." Childbirth is commonly painful and often lethal. What should we make of this? What is the explanation? Would an intelligent engineer have designed such a system from scratch? Given the Genesis story, Barash queries, if Eve had restrained herself, would not every woman have a vagina where the belly button is? Males have similar plumbing problems. What should we infer about our condition from these facts? In Barash's view, it is not a plausible answer that we are made in the image of God. If so, no one has *assigned* a stewardship role to humans. In spite of that, one might consider to what extent a person with theistic beliefs might agree with Barash's view that humans are not the endpoint of creation, or whether they might agree that nevertheless humans are fine, not always "well-designed," animals—talented ones if not always pleasant

or fair ones. And if, however, we are only late twigs on the bush of evolution, what should be our attitude about our own species, and our proper role on the planet? Can we not choose a steward-like role—just as we might choose to be good parents? Or choose to be caretaking children of parents?

We have so far largely neglected secular traditions, which contribute to contemporary environmental attitudes—sometimes in ways of which we are unaware. We turn briefly to such matters. In ancient Greece there arose a number of intellectual mavericks who refused simply to accept legends and stories of the gods being angry at each other as explanatory (for example, lightning was Zeus's hurling arrows of fire). These curiosity seekers, or intellectual nonconformists, were labeled "lovers of knowledge or wisdom" (from *philos* and *sophos* in the Greek), that is, "philosophers" (a label that also included those that today we label as scientists and mathematicians). Among them was Protagoras, who is famous for his remark, "Man is the measure of all things." With the tendency to reject the view that humans are merely the playthings of the gods, there came a focus on the natural powers and importance of human beings. There was certainly an interest in learning about the nonhuman parts of the natural world, but not a strong tendency to assign any particular noninstrumental value to it. As we noted in the Introduction, Aristotle (387–322 B.C.E.), whose views were enormously influential in the West for the next 2000 years, regarded nature as hierarchically arranged, with plants having the purpose of serving animals and animals having the purpose of serving people. This view looks like the kind of evaluative pyramid found in the Judeo-Christian tradition without an omniscient, omnipotent Being reigning at the top. Suffice it to say that these secular sources also tend to place the nonhuman at the bottom (or "off the chart") of a great chain of beings. Aristotle's teacher, Plato (427–347 B.C.E.), tended to find the Real (we speak vaguely) in the nonmaterial realm of the perfect forms, rather like the domain of the perfect figures of geometry, in the world of the unchangeable, not in the world of Appearances (that is, among the breathing, changing, copulating, fighting, excreting, decaying, growing creatures of the biosphere).

It was characteristic of the Stoics (fourth century B.C.E. and following) to conceive of the body as a tomb (*soma sema* in Greek), as inferior to the mind and a drag on achieving the good or ideal life. This view is, of course, paralleled by the Christian tendency to believe in the survival of a soul without a body, or the belief that one will get a new "spiritual" body in the afterlife, at which time one may be liberated from the "warring in one's members" (see Paul's remarks about this issue and his plea to be delivered from "the body of this death" in Romans 7:23–25), the lust of the flesh or the lack of voluntary control over his sexual organ, a phenomenon that enabled young Augustine to believe in the doctrine of the inheritance of original sin. In any case, this attitude of devaluation of the body, of the wild, of the organic can be found in nonreligious sources as well.

During the Renaissance, and the advent of the new sciences in the fourteenth to the seventeenth centuries especially, we find an emphasis on mind–body dualism (it and materialism can be found among the ancient philosophers). French philosopher and mathematician (recall "Cartesian coordinates") Rene Descartes (1596–1650) notoriously found animals lacking in minds. He claimed that in spite of "the astuteness and cunning of dogs and foxes," one could explain the acts of all of them "from the constitution of their organs."[22] In Descartes's influential view, all natural beings are mindless except for humans; this empirical claim is typically found in tandem today with the evaluative claim that only humans have any intrinsic value or inherent worth.

The rise of modern science tended to contribute to a kind of human euphoria. A new era

was at hand; humans could understand the world. Far from being a place filled with demons over which one might lack control, nature was intelligible, governed by natural laws accessible and discoverable in principle by human beings. Humans could overcome natural obstacles, "conquer nature," or later in the New World (after already existing "Americans" discovered Christopher Columbus and his men entering their shores) "win the West." Sometimes nature came to be thought of as more like a machine, something over which one could exert influence for one's own ends. Indeed, Descartes conceived of animals as being like clocks that emitted noises but that were merely automata. With understanding and the power to predict came the power to control, to manipulate, and to dominate. The later works of Galileo and Isaac Newton, for all their merits, certainly encouraged the view of the universe as matter in motion, functioning in ways describable by precise mathematical formulas; the full title of Newton's famous work of 1687 was *Mathematical Principles of Natural Philosophy.*[23] Some philosophers and scientists concluded that humans were no special exception to the rule in this huge, mechanistic, mindless, deterministic universe; they viewed humans as machines that also possessed the illusion of free choice. Generally, however, the view has been, especially to the period of Charles Darwin[24] (and even after), that humans are exceptions, that we are not really "animals" (people tend to reserve the term for nonhumans), not fully determined, and of special value—hence we have a right and perhaps a duty to manage the planet. Thus, religious traditions have no monopoly on this brand of anthropocentrism.[25]

The emergence of industrialization and development of market economies have greatly affected what people have done to the planet. They also have influenced attitudes about the planet and what is permissible to do to nonhumans. The influences run in both directions. Viewing nonhumans as simply a source of goods for human benefit or a sink for human wastes, obstacles to "development" and "growth" are not given any weight in decision making. We get used to the cornucopia of products and services that industrial production contributes and the market (or the state in "command" economies) distributes. It is in the self-interest of producers in market economies to generate a diverse and unending stream of desires for their products, even when those products generate social costs that exceed their social benefits. So, although it may be the bread maker's self-interest (and not his or her altruism) that gets us our bread, the so-called invisible hand of which Adam Smith spoke in 1776 will not, unaided by the right sorts of social structures, generate that which is beneficial on balance. The "free market" also supplies, if enough people are willing and able to pay for them, slaves, child prostitutes, assassinations, destructive drugs, enough nerve gas to destroy all the mammals on the earth, and exquisite devices of torture. The market shapes preferences, and it responds to virtually any existing ones; its role, therefore, in the use and abuse of the biosphere is hardly negligible, and the question about what constraints *should* be placed on it is a moral question.

The rise of industrial forces and the market system in the West brought both goods and bads. We are beginning to notice the bads and their magnitudes. Many of them are like a series of time bombs starting to go off, a few here and a few there: dying lakes and oceans, sick coral reefs, the loss of 70 percent of the world's forests, nuclear wastes for which there are no evident safe depositories, the cascade of extinctions occurring in life-forms whose lineage dates back 3.5 billion years, a hole in the ozone layer, the related and increasing risk of cancer as well as destruction of ocean life, and possibly vast devastation due to global warming in the next century. In the final analysis, we recall the line from Walt Kelly's *Pogo* cartoon: "We have met the enemy, and he is us."

NOTES

1. "The Ethic of Reverence for Life," from *Civilization and Ethics*, in *Animal Rights and Human Obligations*, edited by Tom Regan and Peter Singer (Englewood Cliffs, NJ: Prentice Hall, 1976), p. 137.

2. Robin Attfield, *The Ethics of Environmental Concern*, 2nd ed. (Athens: The University of Georgia Press, 1991), pp. 29–30. For relevant biblical passages, see Matt. 8:28 ff., Mark 5:1–20, Luke 8:26–39 (on swine), and Matt. 21:18–19, and Mark 11:12–14 (on the withered tree).

3. The interest in determining what the scriptures actually prescribe regarding treatment of the non-human environment is usually motivated by the belief that they provide a reliable guide to determining God's will; the latter is one of several assumptions that constitute, or supplement, the Divine Command Theory. For discussion, see Section 2.2.

4. Lynn White, Jr., "Continuing the Conversation," in *Western Man and Environmental Ethics*, edited by Ian Barbour (Reading, MA: Addison-Wesley, 1973), p. 61.

5. Ibid., p. 60.

6. Gen. 1:26 ff., Revised Standard Version.

7. A. R. Peacocke, *Creation and the World of Science* (Oxford: Oxford University Press, 1979), p. 283.

8. Compare Gordis's remarks reprinted here, Essay 6.

9. Gen. 1:11, Revised Standard Version.

10. A rough formulation of the *Doctrine of Double Effects* is the principle that when an act has a good effect (say, saving a woman's life) and a bad one (say, destroying a human fetus), one may perform the act (for example, removing the cancerous uterus—and killing the fetus) as long as one only foresees the bad effect and does not intend it. Many people would call this a kind of abortion, but not the Roman Catholic Church, for whom it is not a "direct killing." Hence, in their terms it is not "abortion." To be that it would have to be a direct killing, and for a killing to be direct it would have to be intended—according to the doctrine in question.

11. These last quotes are from "The Catholic Church and Stewardship of Creation," an online document of the Acton Institute on the Study of Religion and Liberty; it is found at http://www.acton.org/ppolicy/environment/theology/m_catholic.html.

12. Note, however, that Pope John Paul II in "Sollicitudo rei Socialis" said "the appropriateness of acquiring a growing awareness of the fact that one cannot use with impunity the different categories of beings, whether living or inanimate—

animals, plants, the natural elements—simply as one wishes, according to one's own economic needs. On the contrary, one must take into account the nature of each being and its mutual connection in an ordered system, which is precisely the cosmos. This remark is online at: http://www.vatican.va/holy_father/john_paul_ii/encyclicals/documents/hf_jp-ii_enc_30121987_sollicitudo-rei-socialis_en.html.

13. From the *Evangelium Vitae* March 25, 1995.

14. John Haught, "Christianity and Ecology" in Roger S. Gottlieb, ed., *This Sacred Earth: Religion, Nature, Environment* (New York: Routledge, 1996), p. 277.

15. Peter Wenz, *Environmental Ethics Today* (New York: Oxford University Press, 2001), p. 230.

16. Haught, p. 277.

17. Sallie McFague, *The Body of God: An Ecological Theology* (Minneapolis: Fortress Press, 1993), p. 211.

18. Andrew Linzey, *Animal Theology* (Urbana: University of Illinois Press, 1995), p. 190.

19. McFague, p. 27.

20. "Interspecific" means across species, and "Intraspecific" means within a single species.

21. From *Values at Sea: Ethics of the Marine Environment,* ed. by Dorinda G. Dallmeyer (Athens, GA: University of Georgia Press, 2003).

22. See the selection from Descartes in *Animal Rights and Human Obligations,* ed. by Tom Regan and Peter Singer (Englewood Cliffs, NJ: Prentice Hall, 1976), p. 65.

23. At least until the time of Newton, "scientists" were not called "scientists"; from about the medieval period they were called "natural philosophers," as Newton's title suggests. One would do well to keep this in mind. For a long time intellectual inquiry was not compartmentalized as it is in the contemporary university. Most sciences are less than a few hundred years old as distinct disciplines.

24. *On the Origin of Species* was published in 1859.

25. "Anthropocentrism" is used technically in moral philosophy to refer to the view that all and only members of *Homo sapiens* have moral standing.

4. The Historical Roots of Our Ecologic Crisis

Lynn White, Jr.

A conversation with Aldous Huxley not infrequently put one at the receiving end of an unforgettable monologue. About a year before his lamented death he was discoursing on a favorite topic: Man's unnatural treatment of nature and its sad results. To illustrate his point he told how, during the previous summer, he had returned to a little valley in England where he had spent many happy months as a child. Once it had been composed of delightful grassy glades; now it was becoming overgrown with unsightly brush because the rabbits that formerly kept such growth under control had largely succumbed to a disease, myxomatosis, that was deliberately introduced by the local farmers to reduce the rabbits' destruction of crops. Being something of a Philistine, I could be silent no longer, even in the interests of great rhetoric. I interrupted to point out that the rabbit itself had been brought as a domestic animal to England in 1176, presumably to improve the protein diet of the peasantry.

All forms of life modify their contexts. The most spectacular and benign instance is doubtless the coral polyp. By serving its own ends, it has created a vast undersea world favorable to thousands of other kinds of animals and plants. Ever since man became a numerous species he has affected his environment notably. The hypothesis that his fire-drive method of hunting created the world's great grasslands and helped to exterminate the monster mammals of the Pleistocene from much of the globe is plausible, if not proved. For 6 millennia at least, the banks of the lower Nile have been a human artifact rather than the swampy African jungle which nature, apart from man, would have made it. The Aswan Dam, flooding 5000 square miles, is only the latest stage in a long process. In many regions terracing or irrigation, overgrazing, the cutting of forests by Romans to build ships to fight Carthaginians or by Crusaders to solve the logistics problems of their expeditions, have profoundly changed ecologies. Observations that the French

Science, Vol. 155, No. 3767 (March 1967), pp. 1203–1207. ©1967 by the AAAS. Reprinted by permission.

landscape falls into two basic types, the open fields of the north and the *bocage* of the south and west, inspired Marc Bloch to undertake his classic study of medieval agricultural methods. Quite unintentionally, changes in human ways often affect nonhuman nature. It has been noted, for example, that the advent of the automobile eliminated huge flocks of sparrows that once fed on the horse manure littering every street.

The history of ecologic change is still so rudimentary that we know little about what really happened, or what the results were. The extinction of the European aurochs as late as 1627 would seem to have been a simple case of overenthusiastic hunting. On more intricate matters it often is impossible to find solid information. For a thousand years or more the Frisians and Hollanders have been pushing back the North Sea, and the process is culminating in our own time in the reclamation of the Zuider Zee. What, if any, species of animals, birds, fish, shore life, or plants have died out in the process? In their epic combat with Neptune have the Netherlanders overlooked ecological values in such a way that the quality of human life in the Netherlands has suffered? I cannot discover that the questions have ever been asked, much less answered.

People, then, have often been a dynamic element in their own environment, but in the present state of historical scholarship we usually do not know exactly when, where, or with what effects man-induced changes came. As we enter the last third of the 20th century, however, concern for the problem of ecologic backlash is mounting feverishly. Natural science, conceived as the effort to understand the nature of things, had flourished in several eras and among several peoples. Similarly there had been an age-old accumulation of technological skills, sometimes growing rapidly, sometimes slowly. But it was not until about four generations ago that Western Europe and North America arranged a marriage between science and technology, a union of the theoretical and the empirical approaches to our natural environment. The emergence in widespread practice of the Baconian creed that scientific knowledge means technological power over nature can scarcely be dated before about 1850, save in the chemical industries, where it is anticipated in the 18th century. Its acceptance as a normal pattern of action may mark the greatest event in human history

since the invention of agriculture, and perhaps in nonhuman terrestrial history as well.

Almost at once the new situation forced the crystallization of the novel concept of ecology; indeed, the word *ecology* first appeared in the English language in 1873. Today, less than a century later, the impact of our race upon the environment has so increased in force that it has changed in essence. When the first cannons were fired, in the early 14th century, they affected ecology by sending workers scrambling to the forests and mountains for more potash, sulfur, iron ore, and charcoal, with some resulting erosion and deforestation. Hydrogen bombs are of a different order: a war fought with them might alter the genetics of all life on this planet. By 1285 London had a smog problem arising from the burning of soft coal, but our present combustion of fossil fuels threatens to change the chemistry of the globe's atmosphere as a whole, with consequences which we are only beginning to guess. With the population explosion, the carcinoma of planless urbanism, the now geological deposits of sewage and garbage, surely no creature other than man has ever managed to foul its nest in such short order.

There are many calls to action, but specific proposals, however worthy as individual items, seem too partial, palliative, negative: ban the bomb, tear down the billboards, give the Hindus contraceptives and tell them to eat their sacred cows. The simplest solution to any suspect change is, of course, to stop it, or, better yet, to revert to a romanticized past: make those ugly gasoline stations look like Anne Hathaway's cottage or (in the Far West) like ghost-town saloons. The "wilderness area" mentality invariably advocates deep-freezing an ecology, whether San Gimignano or the High Sierra, as it was before the first Kleenex was dropped. But neither atavism nor prettification will cope with the ecologic crisis of our time.

What shall we do? No one yet knows. Unless we think about fundamentals, our specific measures may produce new backlashes more serious than those they are designed to remedy.

As a beginning we should try to clarify our thinking by looking, in some historical depth, at the presuppositions that underlie modern technology and science. Science was traditionally aristocratic, speculative, intellectual in intent; technology was lower-class, empirical, action-oriented. The quite sudden fusion of these two, towards the middle of the 19th century, is surely related to the slightly prior and contemporary democratic revolutions which, by reducing social barriers, tended to assert a functional unity of brain and hand. Our ecologic crisis is the product of an emerging, entirely novel, democratic culture. The issue is whether a democratized world can survive its own implications. Presumably we cannot unless we rethink our axioms.

The Western Traditions of Technology and Science

One thing is so certain that it seems stupid to verbalize it: both modern technology and modern science are distinctively *Occidental*. Our technology has absorbed elements from all over the world, notably from China; yet everywhere today, whether in Japan or in Nigeria, successful technology is Western. Our science is the heir to all the sciences of the past, especially perhaps to the work of the great Islamic scientists of the Middle Ages, who so often outdid the ancient Greeks in skill and perspicacity: al-Rāzī in medicine, for example; or ibn-al-Haytham in optics; or Omar Khay-yám in mathematics. Indeed, not a few works of such geniuses seem to have vanished in the original Arabic and to survive only in medieval Latin translations that helped to lay the foundations for later Western developments. Today, around the globe, all significant science is Western in style and method, whatever the pigmentation or language of the scientists.

A second pair of facts is less well recognized because they result from quite recent historical scholarship. The leadership of the West, both in technology and in science, is far older than the so-called Scientific Revolution of the 17th century or the so-called Industrial Revolution of the 18th century. These terms are in fact outmoded and obscure the true nature of what they try to describe—significant stages in two long and separate developments. By A.D. 1000 at the latest—and perhaps, feebly, as much as 200 years earlier—the West began to apply water power to industrial processes other than milling grain. This was followed in the late 12th century by the harnessing of wind power. From simple beginnings, but with remarkable consistency of style, the West rapidly expanded its skills in the development of power machinery, labor-saving devices, and automation. Those who

doubt should contemplate that most monumental achievement in the history of automation: the weight-driven mechanical clock, which appeared in two forms in the early 14th century. Not in craftsmanship but in basic technological capacity, the Latin West of the later Middle Ages far outstripped its elaborate, sophisticated, and esthetically magnificent sister cultures, Byzantium and Islam. In 1444 a great Greek ecclesiastic, Bessarion, who had gone to Italy, wrote a letter to a prince in Greece. He is amazed by the superiority of Western ships, arms, textiles, glass. But above all he is astonished by the spectacle of water-wheels sawing timbers and pumping the bellows of blast furnaces. Clearly, he had seen nothing of the sort in the Near East.

By the end of the 15th century the technological superiority of Europe was such that its small, mutually hostile nations could spill out over all the rest of the world, conquering, looting, and colonizing. The symbol of this technological superiority is the fact that Portugal, one of the weakest states of the Occident, was able to become, and to remain for a century, mistress of the East Indies. And we must remember that the technology of Vasco da Gama and Albuquerque was built by pure empiricism, drawing remarkably little support or inspiration from science.

In the present-day vernacular understanding, modern science is supposed to have begun in 1543, when both Copernicus and Vesalius published their great works. It is no derogation of their accomplishments, however, to point out that such structures as the *Fabrica* and the *De revolutionibus* do not appear overnight. The distinctive Western tradition of science, in fact, began in the late 11th century with a massive movement of translation of Arabic and Greek scientific works into Latin. A few notable books—Theophrastus, for example—escaped the West's avid new appetite for science, but within less than 200 years effectively the entire corpus of Greek and Muslim science was available in Latin, and was being eagerly read and criticized in the new European universities. Out of criticism arose new observation, speculation, and increasing distrust of ancient authorities. By the late 13th century Europe had seized global scientific leadership from the faltering hands of Islam. It would be as absurd to deny the profound originality of Newton, Galileo, or Copernicus as to deny that of the 14th century scholastic scientists like Buridan or Oresme on whose work they built. Before the 11th century, science scarcely existed in the Latin West, even in Roman times. From the 11th century onward, the scientific sector of Occidental culture has increased in a steady crescendo.

Since both our technological and our scientific movements got their start, acquired their character, and achieved world dominance in the Middle Ages, it would seem that we cannot understand their nature or their present impact upon ecology without examining fundamental medieval assumptions and developments.

Medieval View of Man and Nature

Until recently, agriculture has been the chief occupation even in "advanced" societies; hence, any change in methods of tillage has much importance. Early plows, drawn by two oxen, did not normally turn the sod but merely scratched it. Thus, cross-plowing was needed and fields tended to be squarish. In the fairly light soils and semiarid climates of the Near East and Mediterranean, this worked well. But such a plow was inappropriate to the wet climate and often sticky soils of northern Europe. By the latter part of the 7th century after Christ, however, following obscure beginnings, certain northern peasants were using an entirely new kind of plow, equipped with a vertical knife to cut the line of the furrow, a horizontal share to slice under the sod, and a moldboard to turn it over. The friction of this plow with the soil was so great that it normally required not two but eight oxen. It attacked the land with such violence that cross-plowing was not needed, and fields tended to be shaped in long strips.

In the days of the scratch-plow, fields were distributed generally in units capable of supporting a single family. Subsistence farming was the presupposition. But no peasant owned eight oxen: to use the new and more efficient plow, peasants pooled their oxen to form large plow-teams, originally receiving (it would appear) plowed strips in proportion to their contribution. Thus, distribution of land was based no longer on the needs of a family but, rather, on the capacity of a power machine to till the earth. Man's relation to the soil was profoundly changed. Formerly man had been part of nature; now he was the exploiter of nature. Nowhere else in the world did farmers develop any analogous agricultural implement. Is it coincidence

that modern technology, with its ruthlessness toward nature, has so largely been produced by descendants of these peasants of northern Europe?

This same exploitive attitude appears slightly before A.D. 830 in Western illustrated calendars. In older calendars the months were shown as passive personifications. The new Frankish calendars, which set the style for the Middle Ages, are very different: they show men coercing the world around them—plowing, harvesting, chopping trees, butchering pigs. Man and nature are two things, and man is master.

These novelties seem to be in harmony with larger intellectual patterns. What people do about their ecology depends on what they think about themselves in relation to things around them. Human ecology is deeply conditioned by beliefs about our nature and destiny—that is, by religion. To Western eyes this is very evident in, say, India or Ceylon. It is equally true of ourselves and of our medieval ancestors.

The victory of Christianity over paganism was the greatest psychic revolution in the history of our culture. It has become fashionable today to say that, for better or worse, we live in "the post-Christian age." Certainly the forms of our thinking and language have largely ceased to be Christian, but to my eye the substance often remains amazingly akin to that of the past. Our daily habits of action, for example, are dominated by an implicit faith in perpetual progress which was unknown either to Greco-Roman antiquity or to the Orient. It is rooted in, and is indefensible apart from, Judeo-Christian teleology. The fact that Communists share it merely helps to show what can be demonstrated on many other grounds: that Marxism, like Islam, is a Judeo-Christian heresy. We continue today to live, as we have lived for about 1700 years, very largely in the context of Christian axioms.

What did Christianity tell people about their relations with the environment?

While many of the world's mythologies provide stories of creation, Greco-Roman mythology was singularly incoherent in this respect. Like Aristotle, the intellectuals of the ancient West denied that the visible world had had a beginning. Indeed, the idea of a beginning was impossible in the framework of their cyclical notion of time. In sharp contrast, Christianity inherited from Judaism not only a concept of time as nonrepetitive and linear but also a striking story of creation. By gradual stages a loving and all-powerful God had created light and darkness, the heavenly bodies, the earth and all its plants, animals, birds, and fishes. Finally, God had created Adam and, as an afterthought, Eve to keep man from being lonely. Man named all the animals, thus establishing his dominance over them. God planned all of this explicitly for man's benefit and rule: no item in the physical creation had any purpose save to serve man's purposes. And, although man's body is made of clay, he is not simply part of nature: he is made in God's image.

Especially in its Western form, Christianity is the most anthropocentric religion the world has seen. As early as the 2nd century both Tertullian and Saint Irenaeus of Lyons were insisting that when God shaped Adam he was foreshadowing the image of the incarnate Christ, the Second Adam. Man shares, in great measure, God's transcendence of nature. Christianity, in absolute contrast to ancient paganism and Asia's religions (except, perhaps, Zoroastrianism), not only established a dualism of man and nature but also insisted that it is God's will that man exploit nature for his proper ends.

At the level of the common people, this worked out in an interesting way. In antiquity every tree, every spring, every stream, every hill had its own genius loci, its guardian spirit. These spirits were accessible to men, but were very unlike men; centaurs, fauns, and mermaids show their ambivalence. Before one cut a tree, mined a mountain, or dammed a brook, it was important to placate the spirit in charge of that particular situation, and to keep it placated. By destroying pagan animism, Christianity made it possible to exploit nature in a mood of indifference to the feelings of natural objects.

It is often said that for animism the Church substituted the cult of saints. True; but the cult of saints is functionally quite different from animism. The saint is not in natural objects; he may have special shrines, but his citizenship is in heaven. Moreover, a saint is entirely a man; he can be approached in human terms. In addition to saints, Christianity of course also has angels and demons inherited from Judaism and perhaps, at one remove, from Zoroastrianism. But these were all as mobile as the saints themselves. The spirits in natural objects, which formerly had protected nature from man, evaporated. Man's effective monopoly on spirit in this world was confirmed, and the old inhibitions to the exploitation of nature crumbled.

When one speaks in such sweeping terms, a note of caution is in order. Christianity is a complex faith, and its consequences differ in differing contexts. What I have said may well apply to the medieval West, where in fact technology made spectacular advances. But the Greek East, a highly civilized realm of equal Christian devotion, seems to have produced no marked technological innovation after the late 7th century, when Greek fire was invented. The key to the contrast may perhaps be found in a difference in the tonality of piety and thought which students of comparative theology find between the Greek and the Latin Churches. The Greeks believed that sin was intellectual blindness, and that salvation was found in illumination, orthodoxy—that is, clear thinking. The Latins, on the other hand, felt that sin was moral evil, and that salvation was to be found in right conduct. Eastern theology has been intellectualist. Western theology has been voluntarist. The Greek saint contemplates; the Western saint acts. The implications of Christianity for the conquest of nature would emerge more easily in the Western atmosphere.

The Christian dogma of creation, which is found in the first clause of all the Creeds, has another meaning for our comprehension of today's ecologic crisis. By revelation, God had given man the Bible, the Book of Scripture. But since God had made nature, nature also must reveal the divine mentality. The religious study of nature for the better understanding of God was known as natural theology. In the early Church, and always in the Greek East, nature was conceived primarily as a symbolic system through which God speaks to men: the ant is a sermon to sluggards; rising flames are the symbol of the soul's aspiration. This view of nature was essentially artistic rather than scientific. While Byzantium preserved and copied great numbers of ancient Greek scientific texts, science as we conceive it could scarcely flourish in such an ambience.

However, in the Latin West by the early 13th century natural theology was following a very different bent. It was ceasing to be the decoding of the physical symbols of God's communication with man and was becoming the effort to understand God's mind by discovering how his creation operates. The rainbow was no longer simply a symbol of hope first sent to Noah after the Deluge: Robert Grosseteste, Friar Roger Bacon, and Theodoric of Freiberg produced startlingly sophisticated work on the optics of the rainbow, but they did it as a venture in religious understanding. From the 13th century onward, up to and including Leibnitz and Newton, every major scientist, in effect, explained his motivations in religious terms. Indeed, if Galileo had not been so expert an amateur theologian he would have got into far less trouble: the professionals resented his intrusion. And Newton seems to have regarded himself more as a theologian than as a scientist. It was not until the late 18th century that the hypothesis of God became unnecessary to many scientists.

It is often hard for the historian to judge, when men explain why they are doing what they want to do, whether they are offering real reasons or merely culturally acceptable reasons. The consistency with which scientists during the long formative centuries of Western science said that the task and the reward of the scientist was "to think God's thoughts after him" leads one to believe that this was their real motivation. If so, then modern Western science was cast in a matrix of Christian theology. The dynamism of religious devotion, shaped by the Judeo-Christian dogma of creation, gave it impetus.

An Alternative Christian View

We would seem to be headed toward conclusions unpalatable to many Christians. Since both *science* and *technology* are blessed words in our contemporary vocabulary, some may be happy at the notions, first, that, viewed historically, modern science is an extrapolation of natural theology and, second, that modern technology is at least partly to be explained as an Occidental, voluntarist realization of the Christian dogma of man's transcendence of, and rightful mastery over, nature. But, as we now recognize, somewhat over a century ago science and technology—hitherto quite separate activities—joined to give mankind powers which, to judge by many of the ecologic effects, are out of control. If so, Christianity bears a huge burden of guilt.

I personally doubt that disastrous ecologic backlash can be avoided simply by applying to our problems more science and more technology. Our science and technology have grown out of Christian attitudes toward man's relation to nature which are almost universally held not only by Christians and neo-Christians but also by those who fondly regard themselves as post-Christians.

Despite Copernicus, all the cosmos rotates around our little globe. Despite Darwin, we are *not*, in our hearts, part of the natural process. We are superior to nature, contemptuous of it, willing to use it for our slightest whim. The newly elected Governor of California*, like myself a churchman but less troubled than I, spoke for the Christian tradition when he said (as is alleged), "when you've seen one redwood tree, you've seen them all. " To a Christian a tree can be no more than a physical fact. The whole concept of the sacred grove is alien to Christianity and to the ethos of the West. For nearly 2 millennia Christian missionaries have been chopping down sacred groves, which are idolatrous because they assume spirit in nature.

What we do about ecology depends on our ideas of the man–nature relationship. More science and more technology are not going to get us out of the present ecologic crisis until we find a new religion, or rethink our old one. The beatniks, who are the basic revolutionaries of our time, show a sound instinct in their affinity for Zen Buddhism, which conceives of the man–nature relationship as very nearly the mirror image of the Christian view. Zen, however, is as deeply conditioned by Asian history as Christianity is by the experience of the West, and I am dubious of its viability among us.

Possibly we should ponder the greatest radical in Christian history since Christ: Saint Francis of Assisi. The prime miracle of Saint Francis is the fact that he did not end at the stake, as many of his left-wing followers did. He was so clearly heretical that a General of the Franciscan Order, Saint Bonaventura, a great and perceptive Christian, tried to suppress the early accounts of Franciscanism. The key to an understanding of Francis is his belief in the virtue of humility—not merely for the individual but for man as a species. Francis tried to depose man from his monarchy over creation and set up a democracy of all God's creatures. With him the ant is no longer simply a homily for the lazy, flames a sign of the thrust of the soul toward union with God; now they are Brother Ant and Sister Fire, praising the Creator in their own ways as Brother Man does in his.

Later commentators have said that Francis preached to the birds as a rebuke to men who would not listen. The records do not read so: he urged the little birds to praise God, and in spiritual

*Former president Ronald Reagan

ecstasy they flapped their wings and chirped rejoicing. Legends of saints, especially the Irish saints, had long told of their dealings with animals but always, I believe, to show their human dominance over creatures. With Francis it is different. The land around Gubbio in the Apennines was being ravaged by a fierce wolf. Saint Francis, says the legend, talked to the wolf and persuaded him of the error of his ways. The wolf repented, died in the odor of sanctity, and was buried in consecrated ground.

What Sir Steven Ruciman calls "the Franciscan doctrine of the animal soul" was quickly stamped out. Quite possibly it was in part inspired, consciously or unconsciously, by the belief in reincarnation held by the Cathar heretics who at that time teemed in Italy and southern France, and who presumably had got it originally from India. It is significant that at just the same moment, about 1200, traces of metempsychosis are found also in western Judaism, in the Provençal *Cabbala*. But Francis held neither to transmigration of souls nor to pantheism. His view of nature and of man rested on a unique sort of pan-psychism of all things animate and inanimate, designed for the glorification of their transcendent Creator, who, in the ultimate gesture of cosmic humility, assumed flesh, lay helpless in a manger, and hung dying on a scaffold.

I am not suggesting that many contemporary Americans who are concerned about our ecologic crisis will be either able or willing to counsel with wolves or exhort birds. However, the present increasing disruption of the global environment is the product of a dynamic technology and science which were originating in the Western medieval world against which Saint Francis was rebelling in so original a way. Their growth cannot be understood historically apart from distinctive attitudes toward nature which are deeply grounded in Christian dogma. The fact that most people do not think of these attitudes as Christian is irrelevant. No new set of basic values has been accepted in our society to displace those of Christianity. Hence we shall continue to have a worsening ecologic crisis until we reject the Christian axiom that nature has no reason for existence save to serve man.

The greatest spiritual revolutionary in Western history, Saint Francis, proposed what he thought was an alternative Christian view of nature and man's relation to it: he tried to substitute the idea of the equality of all creatures, including man, for the idea of man's limitless rule of creation. He failed. Both our present science and our present technology are so tinctured with orthodox Christian arrogance toward nature that no solution for our ecologic crisis can be expected from them alone. Since the roots of our trouble are so largely religious, the remedy must also be essentially religious, whether we call it that or not. We must rethink and refeel our nature and destiny. The profoundly religious, but heretical, sense of the primitive Franciscans for the spiritual autonomy of all parts of nature may point a direction. I propose Francis as a patron saint for ecologists.

5. For God So Loved the World

The Reverend Dr. Andrew Linzey

Imagine a scene. The date is the 18th of April, 1499. The time is sometime in the afternoon. The place is the Abbey of Josaphat, near Chartres. Within this Abbey a trial is taking place. It is a criminal prosecution before the Bailiff of the Abbey. The defendant is charged with having killed an infant. The verdict is announced. The defendant is found guilty. The sentence of the ecclesiastical court is that the defendant should be hanged. Mercifully, unlike other defendants, the fate is only death and not torture or mangulation. And the defendant was hanged by its neck at a public hanging that day in the market square. The defendant, however, was not a human being, but a pig.

What is the point of recounting this grisly, surely altogether extraordinary episode from the 15th century, you may ask? The answer is this: grisly it certainly was, extraordinary it certainly was not. From the 9th to the 19th century we have over 200 written accounts of the criminal

Between the Species, Vol. 6, No. 1 (Winter 1990), pp. 12–16. Reprinted by permission.

prosecution and capital punishment of animals. These trials of animals, pigs, dogs, wolves, locusts, rats, termites, cows, horses and doves inflicted great and terrible suffering. And the important thing to appreciate is that these trials were mainly or wholly religious in character. They drew their inspiration from Christian doctrine, based on a silly biblical fundamentalism—a fundamentalism I'm distressed to say is still with us in some quarters of the Church today. In particular it was St. Thomas Aquinas in his *Summa Theologiae* who held that some animals were satellites of Satan: "instigated by the powers of hell and proper to be cursed?" St. Thomas added: "the anathema then is not to be pronounced against the animals as such, but should be hurled inferentially at the devil who makes use of irrational creatures to our detriment."

Armed with this awful dictum (however originally qualified by St. Thomas) Christians have spent more than 10 centuries anathematizing, cursing and reviling the animal world. The echoes of this violence are found today in our very language. The word "animal" is a term of abuse, not to mention "brute," "beast" or "bestial." How we have libelled the animal world. For myself I cannot but be bemused by the reference in the marriage service of the *Book of Common Prayer* to "brute beasts which hath no understanding." Who are these brute beasts? Most higher mammals seem to know more about life-long monogamy than many human beings.

This low, negative, even hating, attitude towards animals, regarding them as a source of evil, or as instruments of the devil, or regarding them as beings without any moral status, has, sad to say, been the dominant view within Christendom for the largest part of its history. In the 9th century, Pope Stephen IV prepared great quantities of holy water with which to anathematize hordes of locusts. In the 19th century, Pope Pius IX forbade the opening of an animal protection office in Rome on the grounds that humans had duties to other humans, but none to animals. For a clear run of at least 10 centuries the dominant ecclesiastical voice did not even regard animals as worthy of moral concern. We do well to remember that Catholic textbooks still regard animals as morally without status, save when they are deemed human property. Worse than that, they have been frequently classified as things without rights, to be used—as St. Thomas himself wrote—"in any way

whatever." If Jesus can weep over Jerusalem we have more than good reason to weep over the sins of Mother Church.

It seems to me that there is no use pretending that all has been well with the Church either in the past, or even now in the present. The very community which should be the cradle of the Gospel of God's Love for the world has only been too good at justifying violence and legitimizing hatred towards the world. Those like myself who have the temerity to preach to Christian and non-Christian alike, must be quite clear that the record of Christianity has been, and still is, on this issue as on many others, in many respects shameful and second rate. Christians are simply too good at forgetting how awful they have been. The fact is that Christians have had enormous difficulties in believing their own Gospel.

And what is this Gospel? It is nothing less than the conviction and experience that God loves the whole world. What we see in Jesus is the revelation of an inclusive, all-embracing, generous Loving. A Loving that washes the feet of the world. A Loving that heals individuals from oppression—physical and spiritual. A Loving that takes sides with the poor, vulnerable, diseased, hated, despised, and outcasts of his day. A Loving that is summed up in his absolute commitment to love at all costs even in extreme suffering and death. As that distinguished former Dean of Salisbury, Sydney Evans, once wrote: "What Jesus did on the Cross was to demonstrate the truth of what he had taught: he showed a quality of love—such that the worst that evil could do to such love was to give such love ever fresh opportunities for loving."

The world we live in is desperate for love. The whole world needs to be loved. When I was young I used to mock the notion of "Gentle Jesus, meek and mild." How wrong I was! For there is great power in humility, strength in gentleness, wisdom in forbearance. We need to listen again to Father Zossima's advice in Dostoyevsky's *The Brothers Karamazov*:

> Brothers, be not afraid of men's sins. Love man even in his sin, for that already bears the semblance of divine love and is the highest love on earth. Love all God's creation, the whole of it and every grain of sand. Love every leaf, every ray of God's light! Love the animals, love the plants, love everything. And if you love everything you will perceive the

divine mystery in things. And once you have perceived it, you will begin to comprehend it ceaselessly more and more every day. And you will at last come to love the whole world with an abiding, universal love.

Not all Christians have been happy with this Gospel. While God's love is free, generous and unlimited, we Christians have only been too good at placing limits on Divine Love. St. Thomas Aquinas was a great scholar and saint, but even he believed quite erroneously that God did not love animals for their own sakes, but only in so far as they were of use to human beings. We Christians have at various times made of this Revelation of Unlimited Love its precise opposite. We have conceived of this Revelation in exclusive terms, exclusive of one group or race: those who were non-Jews, those who are women, those who are coloured, and so on. Not all Christians have seen how the love of God gives each individual human being a unique and equal value. But at least we can say that these issues have been on the agenda of the Churches. Not so with other suffering non-human creatures. What has not been seen is that the love of God is inclusive not only of humans *but also all creatures*. It took Christians many years to realize that we cannot love God and keep humans as slaves. It has taken even longer for Christians to realize that we cannot love God and regard women as second class humans. Now is the time for Christians to realize that we cannot love God and hate his non-human creatures. Christians are people who need to be liberated by the Gospel they preach. Christians cannot love God and be free to hate.

For people, like myself, who are concerned for justice in our dealings with animals there are three things we must learn.

The first is that we must not hate even those who hate animals. "Do not be afraid of men's sins," writes Dostoyevsky. People who work for justice for animals are often disappointed, angry, unhappy people, and more often than not with just cause. It is incredible that we should treat God's creatures with so little love and respect; incredible that we should despoil animal life for fun and amusement; incredible that we should wantonly slaughter; incredible that we should make wild animals captive for entertainment; incredible that we should inflict suffering and pain on farm and laboratory animals. It is spiritually infantile that we should continue to look upon the world as "made for us"

and animals simply as means to human ends, as resources, as tools, as machines, indeed simply as things. And yet we must not hate those who hate God's world. By doing so we simply push them further into their own abyss and spiritual darkness. All of us need to be loved, all of us need interior resources to go on loving. And all this is very, very hard, especially when we see creatures treated so cruelly that their cause cries to heaven for justice. But we have one real and lasting weapon at our disposal: "Soul-force." As Dostoyevsky writes: "Loving humility is a terrible force, the strongest of all . . . (with it we shall) conquer the world." So I don't want to hate anybody, even vivisectors, butchers, trappers, factory farmers and bull-fighters. On the contrary I want to love them so much that they will not find time, or have the inclination, to hunt, and kill, and destroy and maim God's good creatures. I refuse to give those who exploit animals another good reason for not believing in a God of love.

Secondly, we must not hate, even the Church. I know that this is very difficult, not least of all because the Church has a lamentable record on animals and, what is more, is still a party to animal cruelty. I say now, and have said privately in the past, to the Church Commissioners that the time has come when in the name of God most loving they must stop allowing factory farming (and also hunting) on their owned lands. Christians, even Church Commissioners, must be signs of the Gospel for which all creatures long. I know that the Church is not always very lovable to say the least. But I also say to you that we shall not advance the cause of animals by hating the Church. On the contrary we must love it so much that it repents of its theological foolishness, its far too frequent humanist arrogance and its complicity in sins against animals. But I say to you that hatred is too great a burden to bear.

I want to give you one example that should give us hope. If we go back in history 200 years or so, we will find intelligent, respectable, conscientious Christians for whom slavery was not a moral issue. If pressed some might have defended slavery as "progress" as many thought it was. Some might even have taken the view of William Henry Holcombe writing in 1860 that slavery was a natural means of "the Christianization of the dark races." The quite staggering fact to grapple with is that this very same community which in some ways provided the major ideological impetus for the defence of slavery came within an historically short period, 100, perhaps only 50, years to change its mind. The same tradition which helped keep slavery alive was the same community that became by and large determined to end it. So successful has this change been that within this congregation today we shall have difficulty in finding one slave trader, even one individual Christian who thought that the practice was anything other than inimical to the moral demands of the Christian faith. In short, while it is true that Christian churches have been and frequently are awful on the subject of animals, it is just possible, even plausible that given say 50 or 100 years we shall witness among this same community amazing shifts of consciousness as we have witnessed on other moral issues, no less complex or controversial. Christian Churches then have been agents of oppression—that is commonplace—but they can also be agents of liberation.

We do well in this context to remember and honour all those courageous Christians: saints, and seers, theologians and poets, mystics and writers who have championed the cause of animals. The list must include almost two thirds of those canonized saints East and West, not only St. Francis but also St. Martin, Richard of Chichester, Chrysostom, Isaac the Syrian, Bonaventure, and countless others. Poets also like Rosetti, Browning, Carlyle, Longfellow, Hardy, Cowper, and the many others who have led the way in sensitivity to the animal world. And if we are to be grateful for these luminaries, then one name especially must be mentioned, namely Arthur Broome. Few people appreciate that it was this Anglican priest who founded the first animal welfare society in the world, the RSPCA, in 1824. Fewer people appreciate that this Society was the result of Christian inspiration and vision. Even fewer appreciate that this Society was founded specifically on "Christian Faith and Christian Principles." Broome's work was immensely sacrificial. He served the Society as its first secretary; he gave up his London living to work full-time for the Society, he suffered imprisonment for the Society's debts, and finally died in obscurity. The animal movement today would be nowhere if it was not for this one man's courage and Christian faith. Long may his name be honoured among those who work for the cause of animals.

And there are just one or two hints today that Christians are again waking up to the idea that

God's creation must not be reviled, anathematized, and treated as evil as in the past.

"[P]reoccupation with humanity will seem distinctly parochial . . . our theology . . . has been distorted by being too man-centered. We need to maintain the value, the preciousness of the human by maintaining the value, the preciousness of the non-human also." These words are not mine. They come from no less a person than the Archbishop of Canterbury, Robert Runcie, speaking in April of this year. He went on:

"For our concept of God forbids the idea of a cheap creation, of a throwaway universe in which everything is expendable save human existence. The whole universe is a work of love. And nothing which is made in love is cheap. The value, the worth of natural things is not found in Man's view of himself but in the goodness of God who made all things good and precious in his sight. . . ." As Barbara Ward used to say, "We have only one earth. Is it not worth our love?" These words may have cost our Archbishop more than we imagine. Let us congratulate him on his testimony and take heart.

The third thing we must learn is that we must not hate one another. It is no use people like me in the animal rights movement—complaining about animal abusers and the churches for their lack of love and compassion—when we so often show so little love and compassion to one another. I can give personal testimony here. I spent 4 years on the ruling council of one of the largest animal welfare societies in this country and 10 or more years later I am still trying to heal the wounds I suffered. The animal movement is the place where we can find as much if not more sin than anywhere else. Jealousy, rivalry, misquotation, guile, stupidity, and, worst of all, self-righteousness. We must not fall into this last trap especially. None of us is pure when it comes to animals. We are all involved in animal abuse either through the food we eat, the products we buy, or the taxes we pay. There is no pure land on earth. A clean conscience is a figment of the imagination. I spend some of my time counselling students who suffer from unrelieved feelings of guilt—often inculcated by the Churches. I have no desire to make anyone feel guilty. Guilt is a redundant emotion.

Christians in the animal movement have a unique opportunity. St. Paul speaks of the creation as in a state of childbirth awaiting a new age. Together we have a vision of a new age, a new world. A world at peace, a world in which we have begun to make peace with creation. A world in which the Love of God is claimed and championed and through whose Spirit new world possibilities are constantly being opened up for us. What a difference it would make if Christians began to practice the Gospel of Love they preach. At the very least what we need to do is to encourage and inspire people to live free of injury to animals. All of us, in addition to whatever social vision we may have, need a programme of personal disengagement from injury to animal life.

Let me be personal for a moment. I haven't always been an advocate of animal rights. By no means. When I was young I used to enjoy controlling animals and making them captive. I used to enjoy fishing. I used to eat animals. I had no problems about eating veal. My entry into the animal rights movement coincided with my entry into a slaughterhouse when I was 16 years old. The questions that it raised in my mind have been with me ever since. Recently, during my speaking tour of the United States, I visited another slaughterhouse in the State of Massachusetts. As I stood watching a young pig being slaughtered—"stuck" as they say in the US—I asked myself this question: "What has

changed in 26 years when animals are still treated as things?" And soon I had my answer: the owner of the slaughterhouse, despite the fact that I had asked permission in the usual way, turfed me out. I'm not used to being turfed out of places. It was a new experience and a valuable one. For I learnt this one thing: What is changing is that many people, even those intensely involved in the exploitation of animals, many people are not so sure as they once were that what they are doing is right. People are beginning to have a conscience even in the most unlikely places.

When I became intellectually convinced of the case for animal rights, I first thought it one of those important but comparatively minor questions in Christian ethics. I don't think that today. On the contrary, I think the question of how we treat animals one of the BIG questions confronting all humanity: if God loves and cares for this world, shall we learn to live at peace with one another and with this world? In short: Are we to hate the world or are we to love it? "We must love one another or die," wrote W. H. Auden. The truth we also have to learn is this: We must love the world, or we shall perish with it.

6. Judaism and the Environment

Robert Gordis

Judaism is the oldest living religion of the world. Pollution, the massive destruction of our environment, is perhaps the "youngest" problem that affects our world and every living thing in it. Pollution, of course, is not "new": technological progress—coupled with an unbridled struggle for material gain—has been with us for many decades. Only recently have we come to recognize the dangerous impact of modern industrial processes upon the environment. And only in the past few years have we given a name to the worldwide menace and begun to examine it seriously. Facing up to the facts of pollution and dealing with them will be painful and costly.

What, if anything, has Judaism to do with the universal problem of pollution? What is the authen-

tic teaching of Judaism about the relationship of humankind to nature? And how do Jews interpret the biblical phrase, "and subdue it [the earth]"? This phrase, which has been seen by some as giving people the license to use and abuse the natural world and its resources as they see fit, without limit or restriction, occurs in Genesis 1:28:

> And God blessed them [Adam and Eve]; and God said unto them: "Be fruitful and multiply, and replenish the earth, and subdue it and have dominion over the fish of the sea, and over the fowl of the air, and over every living thing that moves upon the earth."

The unsensational truth is that this passage in Genesis was never invoked in order to establish a principal of action by humankind vis-à-vis the

Congress Monthly, Vol. 57, No. 6 (Sept./Oct. 1990) pp. 7–10. Reprinted by permission.

environment. In fact, the Talmud, by a method of interpretation all its own, related "and subdue it" to the first part of the sentence, "Be fruitful and multiply." It then declared that since subduing enemies in war is primarily a male undertaking, the verb "subdue" teaches that the obligation to propagate the human race falls upon the male rather than the female (Yebamot 65b)!

Medieval Jewish commentators saw in the phrase "and subdue it" a reference to the biological and ecological fact that humans are the dominant species on this planet able to exercise their will upon other creatures (with the possible exception of insects and some rodents) and to modify the environment as they choose. Nachmanides explained the passage as follows: "He gave them law and dominion on the earth to act according to their wish with the animals and creeping things and to build and uproot plants and to mine copper out of the hills and carry on other similar activities." The Italian commentator Obadiah Sforno gave the phrase a more restricted meaning: "*And subdue it*—that you protect yourself with your reason and prevent the animals from entering within your boundaries and you rule over them."

These interpretations, however, are phrased in generalities. The true genius of Judaism has always lain in specifics. Thus, there is no passage in the Hebrew Bible, "Love your enemies." What we do find instead are concrete instructions for dealing with those we dislike. For instance, Proverbs 25:21 commands us: "If your enemy is hungry, give him bread to eat; and if he is thirsty, give him water to drink."

Similarly, Judaism's teachings about people's duties and rights vis-à-vis the natural habitat are not to be sought in high-sounding phrases which obligate them to nothing concrete; rather, they will be found in specific areas of Jewish law and practice. A wise Talmudic maxim declares: "The words of the Torah may be limited in their original passage, but they are amplified in another" (J. Rosh Hashanah 3:5). This maxim should warn us against the widespread practice of taking a phrase or a verse out of context without relating it to the larger whole of which it is a part.

If we apply this maxim to the passage we have been reviewing, we will notice that the opening chapter of Genesis, in which humankind is given the right to "subdue" the earth and to "have dominion" over all living things, does not even permit people to use animals for food. For the very next verse—Genesis 1:29—declares: ". . . I have given you every plant yielding seed which is upon the face of all the earth, and every tree with seed in its fruit you shall have them for food." This is surely a drastic limitation upon humankind's rights. Not until many centuries later, after the Flood, are people (in the person of Noah and his family) permitted to eat meat. And even then, all people are forbidden to eat the blood of the creatures they have used for food because the blood is the seat of life. Reverence for life dictates that the blood be poured out and not consumed. This ritual is a symbolic recognition that all life is sacred—all life, even the life of animals we kill for the sake of sustenance.

We need not resort to inference to arrive at the fundamental Jewish teaching on humankind's relationship to the environment. It is explicitly contained in two very broad and far-reaching ethical principles that are written large in our classic literature. The first principle governs humankind's treatment of the so-called "lower" animals; the second, their attitude toward inanimate nature. Both of these basic principles have numerous corollary teachings that are profoundly important in our lives; taken together, the two fundamental concepts direct and shape humankind's action, thinking, and outlook on their fellow creatures, their environment and their role on earth.

The first principle, relating to the treatment of the "lower" animals, is known by its beautiful rabbinic name, *tza'ar ba'alei chayim*—"the pain of living creatures." This principle has been extensively elaborated upon in rabbinic law; its roots are multiple and deep in the Bible. For example, the Fourth Commandment enjoins rest for one's ox, donkey, and every creature on the Sabbath day. Deuteronomy 22:10 forbids the farmer to plow with an ox and a donkey yoked together because the practice would obviously impose great hardship upon the weaker animal. Nor was one permitted to muzzle an ox during the threshing period so that he could not eat any of the grain (Deuteronomy 25:4).

Equally significant was the desire of the Torah to spare the feelings of living creatures and inculcate the spirit of mercy in human beings. Thus, it is forbidden in Leviticus 22:28 to slaughter an ox or a sheep together with its offspring on the same day. This twofold concern finds exquisite expression in the law in Deuteronomy 22:6–7:

If you chance to come upon a bird's nest in any tree or on the ground, with young ones or eggs, and the mother sitting upon the young or upon the eggs, you shall not take the mother with the young. You shall let the mother go, but the young you may take to yourself; that it may go well with you, and that you may live long.

The traditional laws of kosher slaughtering (*shechitah*) are designed to keep alive the sense of reverence for life by forbidding the eating of blood and by minimizing the pain of the animal when it is slaughtered.

Perhaps the most eloquent affirmation of Judaism's preoccupation with the welfare of all living things—eloquent precisely because it is so indirect and so seemingly unintentional—occurs in the noble climax of the Book of Jonah. The prophet Jonah feels himself aggrieved because his forecast that the sinful city of Nineveh will be destroyed has been averted—the people repented. Jonah then finds a measure of comfort in a gourd, a large-leafed plant which the Lord has created especially to shield him against the sun. The next night God destroys the gourd and Jonah becomes very angry. There then ensues this colloquy (it ends, be it noted, in characteristic Jewish fashion—with a question!):

God said to Jonah, "Are you very angry for the gourd?" And Jonah said, "I am very angry, angry enough to die." And the Lord said, "You pity the gourd, for which you did not labor, nor did you make it grow, which came into being in a night and perished in a night. And should I not pity Nineveh, that great city, in which there are more than a hundred and twenty thousand persons who do not know their right hand from their left, and also much cattle? (Jonah 4:9–11)

Love and pity for innocent children are equated with mercy for animals.

The second basic Jewish concept, which unfortunately is far too unfamiliar to most people, enunciates one of the most profound and civilized ideas in Jewish tradition. It concerns the attitude of man toward inanimate nature and is referred to in Talmudic and post-Talmudic literatures as *bal tashchit*, "do not destroy." The phrase is borrowed from a striking passage in Deuteronomy 20:19–20, concerning the laws of warfare:

When you besiege a city for a long time, making war against it in order to take it, you shall not destroy (*tashchit*) its trees by wielding an ax against them, but you shall not cut them down. Are the trees in the field men that they should be besieged by you? Only the trees which you know are not trees for food you may destroy and cut down, that you may build siege-works against the city that makes war with you, until it falls.

This injunction ran counter to accepted procedures in ancient war, procedures practiced for example by the Assyrians, who were particularly known for their ruthlessness. It has continued as a prime war tactic to this day. In the Vietnam conflict, for example, the term "defoliation" tries to cover up the horror of the total destruction of nature.

The Rabbis of the Talmud, moreover, went far beyond the letter of the law in Deuteronomy. With their genius for discerning a fundamental principle in a concrete law, they enunciated a universal doctrine under the rubric of *bal tashchit*. The biblical passage forbade "wielding an ax" against a tree. The rabbis extended the prohibition to any means of destruction, including shifting the course of a stream so that the tree would dry up (*Sifre Shofetim*, section 203). They forbade the killing of animals (B. Chullin 7b), or giving them possibly polluted water to drink (Tosafot Bava Kamma 115b based on Avodah Zarah 30b). Most important of all, they broadened the prohibition to apply not only to a state of siege, but also to all conditions, including peacetime.

The biblical passage dealt with a tree, which is an artifact of nature. The rabbis of the Talmud extended the principle to refer to *all* the artifacts of humankind: "Whoever breaks vessels, or tears garments, or destroys a building, or clogs up a fountain, or does away with food in a destructive manner, violates the prohibition of *bal tashchit* (Kiddushin 321). The general principle was clearly formulated: "It is forbidden to destroy or to injure (*hamekalkel*) anything capable of being useful to mankind (*lehanot bo bnei adam*)" (Shulchan Aruch of the Rav, Hilchot Shemirat Guf Vanefesh, section 14).

The principle of *bal tashchit* entered deep into Jewish consciousness, so that the aversion to vandalism became an almost psychological reflex and wanton destruction was viewed with loathing and horror by Jews for centuries.

The full dimension of this profound ethical principle needs to be appreciated. *Bal tashchit* has nothing in common with the sanctity of private property. One is forbidden to destroy not only the property of others, but also one's own. This principle derives in part from the recognition that what we are wont to call "our" property is really not our own, but God's. It is this principle that is invoked to validate the two great laws of social justice found in Leviticus: the laws of the Sabbatical Year and the Jubilee Year.

The Torah ordained that the farmer was permitted to plow, sow, and reap his harvest for six years. Each seventh year, however, is to be observed as "a Sabbath to the Lord." Neither the field nor the vineyard may be tended.

> What grows of itself in your harvest you shall not reap, and the grapes of your undressed vine you shall not gather; it shall be a year of solemn rest for the land. The sabbath of the land shall provide food for yourself, and for your male and female slaves and for your hired servant and the sojourners who live with you. (Leviticus 25:5–60)

The Sabbatical Year served several purposes. In the days before anyone knew about crop rotation or chemical treatment of the soil, the practice of letting the land lie fallow enabled it to regain its fertility. In addition, the poor and the stranger had the right to eat the produce that grew by itself during the seventh year, just as they had the right to eat the windfall and the unpicked harvest in the corners of the field in other years. This was an important element in the far-flung system of social legislation for the underprivileged in ancient Israel.

But even more fundamental than the above agricultural and social functions, the law reaffirmed a deep religious principle: God was dramatically reasserting His ownership of the land, of which humankind is only the temporary custodian.

After seven sabbatical years had passed, the 50th year was ushered in as the Jubilee Year. The law ordains that on the 50th year all property that had been sold during the preceding half-century be returned to its original owner without compensation. This radical step is justified by the basic legal principle: "The land shall not be sold in perpetuity, for the land is Mine; for you are strangers and sojourners with Me" (Leviticus 25:23). Psalm 24 gives this same principle beautiful poetic expression in cosmic terms:

> The earth is the Lord's and the fulness thereof,
> the world and those who dwell therein. . . .

From this basic concept of God's ownership of the earth and all of its natural resources, it follows that any act of destruction is an offense against the property of God.

The principle of *bal tashchit* contains still another religious insight: *the recognition that every natural object is an embodiment of the creative power of God and is therefore sacred*. That is not all. Whatever has been fashioned by human beings and is the product of their gifts and energies is equally *a manifestation of God's creative power*, one step removed, since humans with all their qualities are themselves the handiwork of God. Vandalism is, therefore, far more than an act of violence against property: it is rebellion against the cosmic order of the universe, which human beings may enjoy but dare not destroy!

To claim, as some do, that the Hebrew Bible somehow provides "justification" for the exploitation of the environment, leading to the poisoning of the atmosphere, the pollution of our water, and the spoliation of natural resources is thus a complete distortion of the truth.

The Hebrew Bible and the Jewish interpreters prohibit exploitation of the environment. Judaism goes much further and insists that human beings have an obligation not only to conserve the world of nature, but to enhance it because mankind is the "copartner of God in the work of creation" (B. Shabbat 10a). Indeed, quite in the spirit of the Jewish tradition, human beings are "junior partners" in the enterprise, who are dependent upon God for their well-being in the world which God "created not for chaos but for habitation" (Isaiah 45:18)—a world which they share with all living things as *beneficiaries, not as owners*. All animal life and all growing and life-giving things have rights in the cosmos that human beings must consider, even as they strive to ensure their own survival. The war against the spoliation of nature and the pollution of the environment is therefore the command of the hour and the call of the ages.

7. Stewardship Versus Exploitation*

Robin Attfield

Introduction

Christianity, despite well-publicized claims to the contrary, upholds the independent value of natural creatures, and is committed to an ethic of responsible care and stewardship of the natural world. These values were enshrined in the Old Testament, presupposed by Jesus Christ and assumed throughout the New Testament. They were sometimes forgotten or distorted, particularly in medieval and early modern times, but were never abandoned, and have continually been rediscovered, receiving renewed and widespread commitment in the late twentieth century.

Controversies surround the teaching, inherited from the Old Testament, that humanity has dominion or mastery over other creatures, and attach also to the desacralization of nature implicit in the adoption of the belief in nature as a creature of God, and not itself God. Yet dominion facilitates responsible stewardship and need not involve domination, recklessness, or ruthlessness: at the same time, belief in creation implies that the world does not belong to humanity, but is God's world, full of God's glory, and need not involve objectionable varieties of metaphysical dualism such as other-worldliness or contempt of nature or non-human species. Central Christian teachings turn out to encourage ecological sensitivity, despite episodes (and whole periods) in history which seem to suggest the contrary.

Controversies, however, surround not only what Christianity can or should say in the present, but also what was said or implied in the Bible, the patristic (age of the church fathers) and medieval periods, and in subsequent periods. . . .

Attitudes of Jesus and the Synoptic Gospels

To understand Jesus' teaching about nature, we have to bear in mind the Old Testament beliefs about creation and also the Jewish ethical and legal tradi-

tion which he and his hearers shared. . . . The assumptions of Jesus and the New Testament about creation and thus about nature have been characterized by John Muddiman (in a public lecture given in 1995) as including the following beliefs: the one true God made everything in the universe; the world was created for God's glory, and not for the exclusive benefit or convenience of any one species; God orders everything with divine wisdom and providence; the world is God's world and shares, as creation, in the good gifts of its Creator, including the gift of freedom; and God bestows a little of the divine creativity upon human beings, who are made in God's image, and calls them to cooperate with the Creator's purposes as the responsible holders of dominion over nature. These are largely unspoken beliefs, surfacing just occasionally, but implicit throughout the New Testament, including the teaching of Jesus (although sometimes recessive in subsequent Christian history).

The related belief is also present that God has established a covenant with humanity and (in some versions) with the animals too (Genesis 9:8–11). Old Testament ethics and law express the human part in this covenant. Thus when Jesus appealed to recognized exceptions to the prohibition of work on the sabbath, exceptions concerning acts of compassion to relieve the suffering of domestic animals (Matthew 12:11–12, Luke 13:15–16 and Luke 14:5), he assumed a responsibility for compassion toward domestic animals, and common practices embodying it. Such responsibility is commanded in passages such as Proverbs 12:10 ("A right-minded person cares for his beast") and implicitly in several more detailed passages of law in Exodus, Leviticus, and Deuteronomy (Exodus 23:19, 34:26; Leviticus 22:27ff; Deuteronomy 14:21, 22:10, 25:4), passages which Jesus' near-contemporary, Philo of Alexandria, expressly interpreted as motivated by compassion for animals (Bauckham 1998). Far from focusing on animals, Jesus was arguing that relieving the suffering of human beings on the sabbath

Reprinted from *A Companion to Environmental Philosophy*, edited by Dale Jamieson, Blackwell Publishers, 2001.
*[This piece was originally titled "Christianity," but has been renamed for this publication—Eds.]

(such as his own hearings) must all the more be lawful; but shared beliefs about considerate treatment of animals comprised the indispensable background of this argument.

These passing references of Jesus to animals already show that, like the Old Testament, the New Testament cannot be interpreted as authorizing a despotic attitude according to which humans may treat nature as they please. This despotic interpretation is ascribed to the Bible as a whole by Lynn White (1967), and allowed as a possible interpretation of at least the New Testament by John Passmore (1974, pp. 3–40); but neither the teaching of Jesus nor the Old Testament beliefs which it presupposes can be interpreted in this way without distortion. Despotic interpretations have time and again been read into the Jewish and Christian scriptures, and have often suited those who find them there; but this does not make them any more deserving of credibility.

When Jesus' teaching explicitly focused on birds and plants, it again presupposed Old Testament teaching. "Your heavenly father feeds the birds and clothes the lilies," he reminds his hearers, echoing the creation theology of the Psalms: "are you not of greater value than they?" (Matthew 6:29; Luke 12:24). Jesus' point here is God's provision for humans; but his conclusion depends, as Richard Bauckham (1998) shows, on shared beliefs in birds being fellow-creatures, and in God's providential care for the birds. It also presupposes God's bestowal on humanity of dominion over nature; but not an authorization of despotic or tyrannical rule.

Further sayings of Jesus stress God's concern for individual sparrows, despite their cheapness in the human valuation of his day (Matthew 6:26; 10:29–31; Luke 12:6–7; 12:24), and for individual sheep (Matthew 12:12). These passages, which also allude to Old Testament precedents, all argue that, because humans are of greater value, God is also concerned with each and every human. At the same time, they presuppose that individual animals too have intrinsic value in the eyes of God, albeit less than Jesus' individual human hearers; indeed, the saying about lilies implies the presence of such value in plant life as well (Matthew 6:28–30).

Thus the New Testament (like the Old) is irreconcilable both with an anthropocentric ontology and with anthropocentric accounts of value, in which nothing but humans and their interests have independent value. Also, the presupposition about the intrinsic value of individual animals conflicts with the view of some medieval Jewish and Christian writers that God's providence extends not to individual animals, but only to species (Bauckham 1998). This later, species-related, view coheres with belief in the Great Chain of Being, often adopted by Christians influenced by Plato and Aristotle, but not with the New Testament. . . . Yet it would be an artificial exercise to attempt to classify the Bible as biocentric, any more than anthropocentric or ecocentric, however much its value-theory may indicate such a label for its attitudes to creatures. For the Bible, all creatures derive their existence from God, and therewith the very possibility of having value in the actual world. If any "centrism" is found in the Bible, it is theocentrism, the belief that the world exists for God's glory.

As Bauckham adds, none of Jesus' teachings accept that animals have been created only to serve humans, an idea subsequently adopted by Rabbi Simeon ben Eleazar, but absent from Genesis, and inconsistent with Job 39 (and Psalm 104 too). As such, it is unlikely to be an assumption of Jesus or the New Testament writers. Such notions sometimes entered later Jewish and Christian thought from Aristotelian and Stoic sources, where it was often held that all non-human creatures exist for the sake of their usefulness to humanity (Bauckham 1998). Thus if the dominion over nature bestowed on humanity (according to Genesis 1 and Psalm 8) implies some kind of superiority for humans over animals, the context remains that humans and non-human animals are alike fellow-creatures, that animals are not to be regarded as merely of instrumental value, and that humans have responsibilities toward the animals that serve them.

This also clearly excludes the view of Augustine (354–430) that humans have no responsibilities toward animals. Augustine seems to have been influenced in an early work, *De Moribus Manichaeorum*, by the Stoic belief that humans are rational and animals irrational, and that therefore there can be no ties of justice in dealings with animals (Passmore 1975). But Jesus, who accepted human responsibilities toward domestic animals, would have rejected Augustine's view. Augustine was commenting on Jesus permitting the demons that he exorcized from the Gerasene demoniac to enter a herd of pigs, which then hurled themselves over a cliff. However, even if this narrative originated as an event (rather than as one of the parables which Jesus told), it does not show that he regarded pigs as valueless, unclean as they were held to be, but at most that he regarded a human being as of greater value than the pigs (Bauckham 1998).

Jesus' relation to animals and to nature figures more significantly in the prologue to Mark's gospel, which relates that after his baptism Jesus spent 40 days in the wilderness "with the wild beasts" (Mark 1:13). The language used (in the wilderness Jesus is also tempted by Satan and ministered to by angels, and a heavenly voice had just proclaimed him "my beloved Son") presents him as the Messiah, inaugurating the kingdom of God. In the prophecy of Isaiah, an age is proclaimed of peace between wild animals and humans, in a context that makes it the age of the coming of the Messiah (Isaiah 11:1–9). Against this background, Mark's phrase "he was with the wild animals" conveys that the Messianic age is dawning, in which relations of fear between humanity and wild nature will be overcome. However, the animals are not subdued or tamed (as in some contemporary Jewish portrayals of the restoration of paradise); Jesus' companionable presence with the animals affirmed their otherness and their independent value. As at other moments of his life and teaching, he thus enacted an anticipation of the forthcoming kingdom of God (a kingdom not confined to humanity), and of the relations that are to characterize it (Bauckham 1998).

Other New Testament Attitudes

Paul, despite his emphasis on sin and corruption, retained the Old Testament belief that the world is God's world, holding that God's creation is to be clearly discerned from the material universe (Romans 1:20). Here he was echoing a Jewish work of the recent past, the Wisdom of Solomon, which asserts that "the greatness and beauty of created things give us a corresponding idea of their creator" (Wisdom 13:1–5): Paul's claim was to prove an important bulwark against both other-worldliness and critics of natural theology in centuries to come. Terrestrial bodies of different kinds (humans, beasts, fishes, birds), he taught, have their own glory, comparable with but different from the glory

of celestial bodies (sun, moon, and stars) (1 Corinthians 15:39–41). Indeed, everything visible and invisible was created by and for God's Son, and is to be reconciled through him to God (Colossians 1:15–20).

Certainly, when discussing the Old Testament prohibition of muzzling the ox that treads the corn, Paul seems to forget these themes, and asks "Does God care for oxen?" (1 Corinthians 9:9ff), implying that the answer is "no," and claiming that this text is to be interpreted as concerning human laborers. But when concentrating on non-human nature he represents the whole creation as groaning in travail in expectation of release from corruption and of participation in the liberty of the children of God (Romans 8:19–22). For Paul, despite the effects of sin and of demonic influences, the entire created world forms part of God's redemptive plan and is destined to regain its proper glory.

The Johannine writings seek to counter tendencies (from within the Jewish and early Christian communities) to represent the world as a battleground between equal forces of good and evil, in which salvation requires rejection of the world of flesh (Gnosticism). John's prologue maintains that the bringer of salvation is also the *Logos*, God's agent in creation, who has also become flesh and dwelt amongst us (John 1:1–14). Among other themes present here, the value of the created world is reaffirmed. In another of the Johannine writings, the Book of Revelation, John's vision symbolically concerns the restoration of Eden and the tree of life, the leaves of which "were for the healing of nations" (Revelation 22:2).

Thus the cosmic visions of Paul and John cannot be regarded as instrumentalist or anthropocentric. Like Mark, and like the author of Hebrews (Hebrews 1:2ff), these writers appealed to Old Testament beliefs concerning creation, and represented salvation as not confined to humanity, but as a cosmic fulfillment of the Creator's plan.

While the biblical writers do not use the metaphor of stewardship with regard to the role of humanity in relation to the natural world, and while their view of the roles of both humanity and nature extends beyond stewardship, the model of humanity as God's steward is, as Clarence J. Glacken writes (1967, p. 168), an appropriate one. It fits the injunctions to till and to keep the garden (Genesis 2:15); the making of man and woman in the image of God (Genesis 1:27); Jesus' presuppositions about the value of non-human creatures (see above); the Old Testament teaching that the land belongs not to humans but to God (Leviticus 25:23, Psalm 24:1), and is only held conditionally (Leviticus 25:2–13); Jesus' parables about stewardship and accountability for the use of resources (Matthew 21:33–41; 24:45–51; 25:14–30; Mark 12:1–9; Luke 12:36–38; 19:12–27; 20:9–l6); and the teachings about responsibilities for compassion and consideration to non-humans which (as we have seen) pervade the Old and New Testaments. . . . It is noteworthy that the historian Keith Thomas (1983, p. 359) endorses, against John Passmore (1974, pp. 3–40), John Black's account (1970, pp. 44–57) of the biblical basis of belief in stewardship. While no anthropocentric interpretation is credible, and while stewardship has sometimes been charged, as by Clare Palmer (1992, pp. 69–82), with an anthropocentric tendency that treats nature as mere resources, an ethic of responsibility before God to work, cherish, and preserve the natural environment and respect the independent value (and the glory) of fellow-creatures, can fairly be recognized as immune from this charge, without ceasing to be one of stewardship. . . .

Overview

Besides the charges of other-worldliness and of disparagement of life on earth, the more widespread charges that Christianity teaches a despotic and anthropocentric attitude to nature turn out to be similarly misplaced, despite their relevance to some tracts of medieval and early modern history. Such charges are usually based on unreflective interpretations of the Judeo-Christian belief in human dominion over nature, which sounds as if it might support unqualified domination. But in view of the conditional and qualified understanding of all human authority in the Old Testament, and of explicit biblical teaching endorsing the independent value of natural creatures and recognizing the place of non-human nature in the scheme of salvation, such interpretations prove to have been no better than rationalizations of exploitative practices. Dominion over nature is rather to be construed as responsible stewardship, while, for Christians who are true to their scriptures, stewardship is best construed not anthropocentrically (as with Calvin), but as involving humble recognition of the intrinsic value of fellow-creatures.

Belief in stewardship is sometimes held to be actually inconsistent with belief in the independent value of natural creatures, or with God's immanent presence in creation, as it supposedly involves a managerial and instrumentalist attitude to the material order. But these claims of inconsistency are an illusion; for stewardship (as with Hale) need not involve an instrumentalist attitude, and need not be solely managerial (as even Calvin shows in teaching ethical limits to the treatment of animals). Further, belief in divine immanence in nature cannot preclude its use by humanity, or this belief would also have precluded using nature for food and shelter from earliest times.

Yet criticism of dualism continues, even after charges of other-worldliness and of arrogance and lack of humility have been discarded. Thus, Matthew Fox criticizes an ethic of care for the garden of creation as dualistic, since it distinguishes between God and the garden, instead of recognizing that God *is* the garden (Berry 1995). But if God *is* the garden, then the garden (and the rest of the material universe too) is not created, there is no Creator, there are no fellow-creatures to care for, and the world is not God's world. Short of some other basis, belief in the goodness of creation collapses too. Belief in the distinctness of God and creation is essential to theistic ethics, whether Christian, Jewish, or Islamic. . . . If this is dualism, then dualism (of this kind) is essential to theistic ethics, and to positions such as the panentheism of St. Francis too. But this kind of dualism in no way implies either a dualism of body and spirit or the dualism of other-worldliness.

However, it is sometimes claimed that belief in stewardship itself implies dualism in the form of an unacceptable relation between humanity and other species. For it implies that humanity is empowered to remold much of the natural world, despite the ethical constraints that attach to this power. This, it is suggested, too greatly privileges humanity; instead, humans should see themselves as simply one species among others, and humanity as a plain citizen in ecological society.

Now if this just means that equal interests should be given equal consideration, whichever creature has these interests, it can be accepted. But it also seems to imply that there is nothing distinctive about human agency and human moral responsibility; for it seems to imply that no higher priority should be accorded to developing, preserving, and respecting capacities for freedom of choice than to the interests of creatures which lack these capacities. This, however, cannot be reconciled with a recognition of distinctive human moral responsibilities, which cannot be significantly exercised unless the corresponding capacities are fostered and respected. Once human moral responsibility is recognized, humanity cannot be seen as simply one species among others; and the distinctive role of humanity as empowered to shape considerable tracts of the natural world has to be recognized as well. This makes it all the more important to stress the ethical constraints on this power, as belief in stewardship does, rather than to pretend that this power does not or should not exist, as egalitarians in matters of species relations seem to do. Thus the distinctive role which belief in stewardship assumes for humanity is not fundamentally objectionable, or therefore incompatible with the aims of clear-thinking environmentalists.

Yet there is a danger that the exercise of human power will too greatly erode both wilderness and other species, and that well before all the mountains are mined, all the oceans are fished, and all the forests are felled, we should plan to halt human expansion, and devise sustainable means of survival which preserve most remaining creatures and habitats, together with the systems on which they and we depend. The Christian vision of companionship with the wild creatures supports such limits as without them there will be no wild creatures to be companionable with, as opposed to domestic animals and parasite species. The claim that such limits should be endorsed is consistent with belief in stewardship, and can be argued to be mandated by that belief in the prevailing circumstances. Moreover, this claim is in any case supported by the biblical belief in the independent value of wild creatures. Hence, a range of Judaic and Christian teachings can be appealed to in its support.

Accordingly, despite ugly episodes and depressing periods in its history, Christianity turns out to encapsulate beliefs supportive of environmentally sensitive attitudes and policies, and can be appealed to as such. While this does not make Christian doctrines true, it means that no one need choose between Christianity and environmentalism, and that theistic belief in creation (whether Judaic, Islamic, or Christian) can inspire sustainable relations between humanity and the rest of the natural world.

References*

Attfield, Robin (1991) *The Ethics of Environmental Concern*, 2nd ed. (Athens, Ga., and London: University of Georgia Press).

——— (1993) *God and The Secular: A Philosophical Assessment of Secular Reasoning from Bacon to Kant*, 2nd ed. (Aldershot: Gregg Revivals).

Bauckham, Richard (1996) "The new age theology of Matthew Fox: a Christian theological response," *Anvil* 13, pp. 115–26.

——— (1998) "What was Jesus' attitude to animals?," in *Animals on the Agenda: Questions about Animals for Theology and Ethics*, ed. A. Linzey (London: SCM Press).

Berkhof, Hendrikus (1968) "Science and the biblical world view," in *Science and Religion*, ed. Ian G. Barbour (London: SCM), pp. 43–53.

Berry, R. J. (1995) "Creation and the environment," *Science and Christian Belief* 7 pp. 21–43.

Black, John (1970) *Man's Dominion: The Search for Ecological Responsibility* (Edinburgh: Edinburgh University Press).

Bratton, Susan Power (1988) "The original desert solitaire: early Christian monasticism and wilderness." *Environmental Ethics* 10, pp. 31–53.

Chadwick, Owen (1973) "Evolution and the churches," in *Science and Religious Belief*, ed. C. A. Russell (London: University of London Press), pp. 282–93.

Dubos, René (1973) "A theology of earth," in *Western Man and Environmental Ethics*, ed. Ian G. Barbour (Reading, Mass., and Don Mills, Ontario: Addison-Wesley), pp. 43–54.

Fox, Matthew (1983) *Original Blessing* (Santa Fe, NM: Bear).

Glacken, Clarence J. (1967) *Traces on the Rhodian Shore; Nature and Culture in Western Thought from Ancient Times to the End of the Eighteenth Century* (Berkeley: University of California Press).

Montefiore, Hugh, ed. (1975) *Man and Nature* (London: Collins).

Muddiman, John (1995; unpublished) "A New Testament basis for environmentalism?" Fourth Yvonne Workman Lecture, Mansfield College, Oxford (September).

Nash, Roderick (1989) *The Rights of Nature: A History of Environmental Ethics* (Madison, Wis.: University of Wisconsin Press).

Palmer, Clare (1992) "Stewardship: a case study in environmental ethics," in *The Earth Beneath: A Critical Guide*

*[References have been condensed and edited from original text.—Eds.]

to Green Theology, eds. Ian Ball. Margaret Goodall, Clare Palmer, and John Reader (London: SPCK Books), pp. 67–86.

Passmore, John (1974) Man's Responsibility for Nature (London: Duckworth).

——— (1975) "The treatment of animals," Journal of the History of Ideas 36, pp. 195–218.

Pelikan, Jaroslav (1993) Christianity and Classical Culture: The Metamorphosis of Natural Theology in the Christian Encounter with Hellenism (New Haven and London: Yale University Press).

Santmire, H. Paul (1985) The Travail of Nature: The Ambiguous Ecological Promise of Christian Theology (Philadelphia: Fortress Press).

Thomas, Keith (1983) Man and the Natural World: A History of the Modern Sensibility (New York: Pantheon Books).

Welbourn, F. B. (1975) "Man's dominion," Theology 78, pp. 561–8.

White, Jr., Lynn (1967) "The historical roots of our ecological crisis." Science 155.37, pp. 1203–7.

8. The World as God's Body

Sallie McFague

Major Models of God and the World

The First Vatican Council (1870) expressed a view of the relation of God and the world that is, with some variations, a common one in major creeds of various Christian churches since the Reformation:

"The Holy, Catholic, Apostolic, Roman Church believes and confesses that there is one true and living God, Creator and Lord of Heaven and earth, almighty, eternal, immense, incomprehensible, infinite in intelligence, in will, and in all perfection, who, as being one, sole, absolutely simple and immutable spiritual substance, is to be declared really and essentially distinct from the world, of supreme beatitude in and from himself, and ineffably exalted above all things beside himself which exist or are conceivable."[1]

What drives this statement is the passion to remove God from any real connection with the world—"really and essentially distinct from the world" sums it up. In fact, it is difficult to imagine how a God so described could have a genuine, significant relationship with anything outside the divine reality. And yet the Christian tradition has insisted that God not only created the world but admired it and loved at least its human creatures sufficiently so that when they "fell," God became one of them, suffering and dying to redeem them from their sins. The two images of God—one as the distant, all-powerful, perfect, immutable Lord existing in lonely isolation, and the other as the One who enters human flesh as a baby to eventually assume the alienation and oppression of all peoples in the world—do not fit together. Jesus as the immanent, loving image of God is a surd, an enigma, against the background of the distant, exalted, incomprehensible deity. In its creedal statements on God and Jesus the tradition attempts to express this view of radical transcendence and radical immanence: the totally distant, "other" God, exalted and perfect, entered into human flesh in Jesus of Nazareth, so that this one man is fully divine and fully human. In the worldview current in first-century Mediterranean times and operable through the Middle Ages, that way of radicalizing and relating transcendence and immanence had some credibility; but it does not in our time. This view seems neither sufficiently radical (God is transcendent only over our world and especially human beings and immanent only in one human being) nor believable (it assumes a dualistic view of reality with God dwelling somewhere external to and exalted above the world and yet entering it at one particular point).

What other options are there for relating God and the world?. . . First, the deistic model, the simplest and least satisfying one, arose during the sixteenth-century scientific revolution. It imagines God as a clockmaker who winds up the clock of the

From Sallie McFague, The World as God's Body (Minneapolis: Fortress Press, 1993), 136–141; 150; 99–129; 202–205, The Body of God, by Sallie McFague. © 1993 Augsburg Fortress. Reprinted by permission.

world by creating its laws and then leaves it to run by itself. The model has the advantage of freeing science to investigate the world apart from divine control but essentially banishes God from the world. It is, sadly, the view of many contemporary scientists as well as Christians, with the qualification that some Christians allow periodic, personal interventions of God in times of crisis such as natural disasters, accidents, and death. The view encourages an irresponsible, idolatrous attitude in the scientific community, allowing it to claim for itself sole rights both to interpret and to dispose of the world. On the part of Christians it encourages an interventionist, God-of-the-gaps view of divine activity.

The second view of God and the world, the dialogic one, has deep roots in both Hebrew and Christian traditions: God speaks and we respond. It has been a central view within Protestantism and was highlighted in twentieth-century existentialism. In its contemporary form the relation between God and the world is narrowed to God and the individual: the I-Thou relation between God and a human being. . . . God and the human being meet, not in the world, whether of nature or culture, but only in the inner, internal joy and pain of human experiences. . . .

The monarchical model, the relation of God and the world in which the divine, all-powerful king controls his subjects and they in turn offer him loyal obedience, is the oldest and still the most prevalent one. It is both a personal and a political model, correcting the impersonalism of the deistic model and the individualism of the dialogic. It also underscores the "goodness" of God, for the monarchical imagery calls forth awe and reverence, as well as vocational meaningfulness, since membership in the kingdom entails service to the divine Lord. But since all power is controlled by the king, issues of human freedom and theodicy are highly problematic. Moreover, and most critical for our concerns, the king is both distant from the natural world and indifferent to it, for as a political model it is limited to human beings.

The continuing power of this model in liturgical use is curious, since contemporary members of royalty scarcely call up responses of awe, reverence, and obedience, but its nostalgic appeal, as evidenced in the gusto with which we all sing Christmas carols that are rife with this imagery, cannot be underestimated. Any model that would

attempt to criticize or partially subvert it ought to look carefully at the main reason for its attraction: it is the only model that attempts to dramatize divine transcendence. Nonetheless, the model of God as king is domesticated transcendence, for a king rules only over human beings, a minute fraction of created reality. The king/realm model is neither genuinely transcendent (God is king over one species recently arrived on a minor planet in an ordinary galaxy) nor genuinely immanent (God as king is an external superperson, not the source, power, and goal of the entire universe).

A fourth model, the agential, also has strong backing in the Hebrew and Christian traditions. Here God is assumed to be an agent whose intentions and purposes are realized in history, especially human history. It has been revived during this century as a way of talking about divine purpose throughout the entire span of cosmic history. . . . The classic agential model, which is at heart personal (God as father, mother, lord, lover, king, friend), God as actor and doer, creating and redeeming the world, has profound ethical and liturgical dimensions. . . .

The agential model should, I believe, be joined with the fifth and final major model, the organic, for either alone is lacking . . . but together they suggest a more adequate model. The organic model is the one on which this essay is focused: the world or universe as God's body. However, alone, that is, apart from the agential model, which suggests a center of being not exhausted by or completely identified with the world or universe, the organic model is pantheistic. The world is, becomes, divine. Christian thinking, with its ancient commitment to a transcendent deity who created a world distinct from himself has had, as we have seen, a highly ambivalent relationship to the organic model. . . .

The agential model preserves transcendence, while the organic model underscores immanence. Alone, the agential model overemphasizes the transcendent power and freedom of God at the expense of the world. Alone, the organic model tends to collapse God and the world, denying the freedom and individuality of both. But if the model were that God is related to the world as spirit is to body, perhaps the values of both the agential and organic models could be preserved. . . .

To sum up: we have suggested that God as the embodied spirit of the universe is a personal/organic model that is compatible with interpretations of both Christian faith and contemporary science, although not demanded by either. It is a way of speaking of God's relation to all matter, all creation, that "makes sense" in terms of an incarnational understanding of Christianity and an organic interpretation of postmodern science. It helps us to be *whole* people within our faith and within our contemporary world. Moreover, the model does not reduce God to the world nor relegate God to another world; on the contrary, it radicalizes both divine immanence (God is the breath of each and every creature) and divine transcendence (God is the energy empowering the entire universe). Finally, it underscores our bodiliness, our concrete physical existence and experience that we share with all other creatures: it is a model on the side of the well-being of the planet, for it raises the issue of ethical regard toward *all* bodies as all are interrelated and interdependent. . . .

At Home on the Earth

An ecological theology based on the model of embodiment is a theology of space and place. It is a theology that begins with the body, each and every body, which is the most basic, primary notion of space: each life-form is a body that occupies and needs space. A theology of embodiment takes space seriously, for the first thing bodies need is space to obtain the necessities to exist—food, water, air. Space is not an empty notion from an ecological perspective ("empty space"), but a central one, for it means the basic world that each and every creature inhabits. Finding our niche, our space, which will provide the necessities for life, is the primary struggle of all life-forms, including human ones. Many cannot find the needed space or are edged out from occupying it by stronger individuals.

Space is an earthy, physical, lowly category unlike time, which is a peculiarly human, often mental, and sometimes grand notion. (To be sure, in postmodern physics space and time are on a continuum and must be considered together, but from an ecological perspective, our ordinary separation of the two is still a functional notion.) In Christian thought space has often been connected with "pagan" fertility, earthy religions that celebrate the rebirth of life in the spring after its wintry death. The eternal return of the earth's physical cycle is contrasted with the historical movement toward the eschatological fulfillment of creation in the

kingdom of God, a fulfillment beyond earthly joys. In space versus time, the old dichotomy of nature versus history is played out. The dichotomy is certainly not absolute, for history takes place in nature and nature itself has a history, as the common creation story clearly demonstrates, but for the past several hundred years at least, the focus and preference of Western thought his been on history to the detriment of nature. We can scarcely overstate the importance of time and history in relation to evolutionary development, both biological and cultural. We *are*, everything *is*, only as it has become and is becoming through the complex machinations of temporal development. However, since this essay deals with bodies and their most basic needs, it will focus on a neglected necessity for bodies: space. For us, now, space should become the primary category for thinking about ourselves and other life-forms. Let us look at a few reasons why this ought to be the case.

First, space is a levelling, democratic notion that places us on a par with all other life-forms. As the self-conscious, responsible form of life on our planet, we enjoy more than this status, but we need to begin our anthropology (who we are in the scheme of things) with the basics. The category of space reminds us not only that each and every life-form needs space for its own physical needs, but also that we all exist together in one space, our finite planet or, in terms of our model, within the nurturing matrix of God's body. We are all enclosed together in the womblike space of our circular planet, the indispensable space from which we derive all our nourishment. With the notion of space, the peculiar kind of differentiation and unity that characterizes contemporary science takes on new meaning and depth. Each and every life-form needs its own particular space and habitat in which to grow and flourish. This includes, of course, human beings who need not only food, water, and shelter, but loving families, education, medicine, meaningful work, and, some would include, music, art, and poetry. Spaces are specific and different for the billions of species on our planet; hence, the notion of space helps us to acknowledge both the basic necessity of all life-forms for space to satisfy their physical needs as well as the specific environments needed by each life-form, given their real differences. And yet, all these differences and special needs must be satisfied within one overarching space, the body of our planet. We are united to one another through complex networks of interrelationship and interdependence, so that when one species overreaches its habitat, encroaching on that of others, sucking the available resources out of others' space, diminishment and death must occur at some point. This process of natural selection has been going on since the beginning of the earth and has resulted in the rich, diverse planet we presently inhabit. The issue now, however, is whether one species, our own, has encroached so heavily on the space, the habitats of other species, that serious imbalance has occurred. As the dominant species for several hundred years, we have forgotten the primary reality of planetary space: it is limited and therefore attention to the primacy of space for other life-forms entails a levelling move toward egalitarianism. We need to remember that at a basic level all life-forms are the same: all need a space for the basics of life.

The second reason we need to turn from a historical (temporal) to a natural (spatial) perspective is because space highlights the relationship between ecological and justice issues. The crisis facing our planet is, in a sense, temporal: How much time do we have to preserve the possibility of life in community? But the reason that time matters is because we are misusing space. Theoretically, we have plenty of time, at least the five billion years of our sun's life, but we may only have a few hundred because of what we have done and continue to do to our plants, trees, water, and atmosphere. We are ruining the space, and when this occurs, justice issues emerge centrally and painfully. When good space—arable land with clean water and air, comfortable temperatures and shade trees—becomes scarce, turf wars are inevitable. Wars have usually, not just accidentally, been fought over land, for land is the bottom line. Without good land, none of the other goods of human existence is possible. Geography, often considered a trivial subject compared to the more splendid history (the feats of the forefathers), may well be *the* subject of the twenty-first century. Where is the best land and who controls it? How much good space is left and who is caring for it? Justice for those on the underside, whether these be human beings or other vulnerable species, has everything to do with space. In a theology of embodiment, space is the central category, for if justice is to be done to the many different kinds of bodies that comprise the planet, they must each have the space, the habitat, they need.

The third reason that we ought to focus on nature rather than history, on space rather than time, is that we need to realize that the earth is our home, that we belong here, that this is not only our space but our *place*. Christians have often not been allowed to feel at home on the earth, convinced after centuries of emphasis on otherworldliness that they belong somewhere else—in heaven or another world. That sojourner sensibility his faded with the rise of secularism, but it has not been replaced with a hearty embrace of the earth as our only and beloved home. Rather, many still feel, if not like aliens or tourists, at least like lords of the manor who inhabit the place but do not necessarily consider it their only, let alone beloved, home. Christian theologies as well as works of spirituality have not encouraged meditation on the beauty, preciousness, and vulnerability of the earth and its many creatures. The profound ascetic strain within the tradition that has feared too-close association with human bodies has extended this as well to other animals and the body of the earth. But what if we were not only allowed but encouraged to love the earth? What if we saw the earth as part of the body of God, not as separate from God (who dwells elsewhere) but as the visible reality of the invisible God? What if we also saw this body as overlain by the body of the cosmic Christ, so that wherever we looked we would see bodies that are incorporated into the liberating, healing, inclusive love of God? Would we not then feel obliged to love the earth and all its many bodies? Would it not be the first duty of those who not only belong to the earth but know we belong to it? If the earth is an aspect of God's body, and if the paradigmatic story of Christianity is that the Word became flesh to liberate, heal, and include all who are needy, then Christians have a mandate to *love* the earth. God, in the model of the universe as God's body, makes her home in the universe (and in our planet) and gives us, we believe, in the story of Jesus of Nazareth some clues as to how we should live in our home. The most basic clue is to *love it*, for that is what the liberating parables, the healing stories, and the eating practices in different ways suggest. We belong to the earth; it is not only our space, but our place, our beloved home.

But we are reaching beyond where we ought to begin. An embodiment anthropology must start with who we are as earthly, physical creatures who have evolved over billions of years as pictured by postmodern science. This is a modest, humble beginning but one with enormous consequences for how we view both our status and our responsibilities. Reflections on our place in the scheme of things will provide clues to where we belong, our proper place, and hence from the perspective of contemporary science, what improper behavior might be. Thus, this chapter will focus on fleshing out the place (space) of human beings, not primarily from a Christian or even a religious perspective, but from the broad parameters of evolutionary biology. This will be a mundane view, the earthly, physical, bodily view, which should be a significant element in any interpretation of the status of human beings as well as of our wrongdoing.

Our Place in the Scheme of Things

The first step in a theological anthropology for our time is not to follow the clues from the Christic paradigm or even from the model of the universe as God's body, but to step backward and ask, Who are we in the scheme of things as pictured by contemporary science? Who are we simply as creatures of planet earth, quite apart from our religious traditions? That is not a question Christians have usually asked, believing that theological anthropology had little relationship to so-called secular views of human nature. Failing to ask that question, however, has often meant that Christian reflection on human existence has been "docetic": human beings come off as a little lower than the angels—not fully human. We have not seen ourselves as mundane, as being of this world, of the earth, earthy. We have defined our duties primarily in relationship to God (First Great Commandment) and secondarily in relationship to other human beings (Second Great Commandment), but seldom in relationship to the earth, its creatures and its care. A first, sobering step, therefore, is to look at ourselves from the earth up, rather than from the sky down. The postmodern scientific picture of reality will by no means tell us all we need to know about ourselves, but it will give us a base in reality (as understood in our time), so that whatever else we say about ourselves from the perspective of belonging to the body of God, a body overlain by the cosmic Christ, will be grounded, literally rooted, in the earth.

As we begin this task, let us recall the central features of the contemporary scientific view of reality. At its heart is the common creation story. In broad strokes, the story emerging from the various sciences claims that some fifteen billion years ago the universe began with a big bang that was infinitely hot and infinitely concentrated. This explosion eventually created some hundred billion galaxies of which our galaxy, the Milky Way, is one, itself containing billions of stars, including our sun and its planets. From this beginning came all that followed, so that everything that is is related, woven into a seamless network, with life gradually emerging after billions of years on our planet (and probably on others as well), and evolving into the marvelously complex and beautiful earth that is our home. All things living and all things not living are the products of the same primal explosion and evolutionary history and hence interrelated in an internal way right from the beginning. We are distant cousins to the stars and near relations to the oceans, plants, and in other living creatures on our planet.

We need to highlight several features of this story as we consider how it might help reformulate a postmodern theological anthropology, that is, who we are in the scheme of things. First of all, the world here is the universe, beside which the traditional range of divine concern—mainly with human subjects—dwindles, to say the least. In this view, God would relate to the entire fifteen-billion-year history of the universe and all its entities and inhabitants, living and nonliving. On the universe's clock, human existence appears a *few seconds* before midnight. This suggests, surely, that the whole show could scarcely have been put on for our benefit; our natural anthropocentrism is sobered, to put it mildly. Nevertheless, since it took fifteen billion years to evolve creatures as complex as human beings, the question arises as to our peculiar role in this story, especially in relation to our planet.

A second feature of the new picture is its story character: it is a historical narrative with a beginning, middle, and presumed end, unlike the Newtonian universe, which was static and deterministic. It is not a realm belonging to a king or an artifact made by an artist, but a changing, living, evolving event (with billions of smaller events making up its history). In our new cosmic story, time is irreversible, genuine novelty results through the interplay of chance and law, and the future is open. This is an unfinished universe, a dynamic universe, still in process. Other cosmologies, including mythic ones such as Genesis and even earlier scientific ones, have not been historical, for in them creation was finished. At the very least, this suggests that in our current picture God would be understood as a continuing creator, but of equal importance, we human beings might be seen as partners in creation, as the self-conscious, reflexive part of the creation that could participate in furthering the process.

A third characteristic of the common creation story is the radical interrelatedness and interdependence of all aspects of it, a feature of utmost importance to the development of an ecological sensibility. It is one story, a common story, so that everything that is traces its ancestral roots within it, and the closer entities are in time and space, the closer they are related. The organic character of the universe in no sense, however, supports a levelling or simplifying direction, that is, a lack of individuation. Precisely the opposite is the case. Whether we turn to the macrocosm or the microcosm, what we see is an incredibly complex, highly individuated variety of things, both living and nonliving. No two things, whether they be two exploding stars or the stripes on two zebras, are the same; individuality is not just a human phenomenon—it is a cosmic one. At the same time, however, the exploding stars and the zebras are related through their common origin and history. The implications of this feature of the universe for theological anthropology are immense. The common character of the story undercuts notions of human existence as separate from the natural, physical world; or of human individuality as the only form of individuality; or of human individuals existing apart from radical interdependence and interrelatedness with others of our own species, with other species, and with the ecosystem. As physicist Brian Swimme puts it, "No tribal myth, no matter how wild, ever imagined a more profound relationship connecting all things in an internal way right from the beginning of time. All thinking must begin with this cosmic genetic relatedness."[2] Were this feature of the scientific picture to become a permanent and deep aspect of our sensibility, it would be the beginning of an evolutionary, ecological, theological anthropology that could have immense significance in transforming how we think about ourselves as well as our relations and responsibilities toward other human beings, other species, and our home, planet earth.

A fourth feature is the multilevelled character of the universe, from the flow of energy in subatomic reality to the incredibly complex set of levels that comprise a human being. One critical aspect of this complexification is increasing subjectivity or the ability to experience and feel. Whatever we might or might not want to say about subjectivity in atoms or rocks, it surely increases as we progress to animals and to its present culmination in human self-consciousness. On the one hand, this means that no absolute distinction exists between the living and the nonliving, for life is a type of organization, not an entity or substance. As Ian Barbour reminds us, the chemical elements in our hands and brains were forged in the furnaces of the stars. On the other hand, the higher levels should not be reduced to or understood entirely in terms of the lower levels, as reductionists claim. What is significant, however, for a theological anthropology is not only the continuity from the simplest events in the universe to the most complex, but also their inverse dependency, which undercuts any sense of absolute superiority. That is, the so-called higher levels depend on the lower ones rather than vice versa. This is obviously the case with human beings and plants; the plants can do very nicely without us, in fact, better, but we would quickly perish without them. But it is also the case with aspects of our earth that we have until recently taken for granted, such as clean air and water. This very important point needs to be underscored: *The higher and more complex the level, the more vulnerable it is and dependent upon the levels that support it.* For theological anthropology, this is a very sobering thought, especially for a tradition that has been accused of advising human beings to subdue and have dominion over all other created beings. It has profound implications for reconceiving the place of human beings in the scheme of things.

Finally, the common creation story is a public one, available to all who wish to learn about it. Other creation stories, the cosmogonies of the various world religions, are limited to the adherents of different religions. Our present one is not so limited, for any person on the planet has potential access to it and, as a human being, is included in it. This common story is available to be remythologized in different ways by any and every religious tradition, and hence is a place of meeting for the religions, whose conflicts in the past and present have often been the cause of immense suffering and bloodshed as belief is pitted against belief. Moreover, various ancient organic creation stories can enrich the common story. What this common story suggests is that our primary loyalty should not be to nation or religion, but to the earth and its creator (albeit we would understand that creator in different ways). We are members of the universe and citizens of planet earth. Again, were that reality to sink into human consciousness all over the world, not only war among human beings but ecological destruction would have little support in reality. This is not to say that they would disappear, but those who continue such practices would be living a lie, that is, living in a way not in keeping with reality as currently understood.

Who are we, then, according to the common creation story? According to the major characteristics of that story, human beings are radically other than what either the Christian tradition, especially since the Reformation, claims we are or what secular, modern culture allows. These two views differ in critical ways, with the religious picture focusing on the importance of human beings, especially those who accept Jesus Christ as savior, whereas the secular picture elevates individualism, consumerism, and technology. In both cases, however, the focus is on human beings and individual well-being. In light of the common creation story, however, this is a narrow vision indeed. Yet so profoundly does it reflect a part of the post-Enlightenment consciousness that we, for the most part, accept it as natural, that is, as the proper order of things.

But, according to contemporary science, the religious/secular/modern picture of human reality is a lie, a very large and dangerous lie. According to the common creation story, we are not the center of things by any stretch of the imagination, although in a curious reversal, we are increasingly very important. That is, even as the sense of our insignificance deepens when we see our place in an unimaginably old and immense universe, nonetheless, at least on our tiny planet at this time, because of the wedding of science and technology, we are in a critically important position. We have the knowledge and power to destroy ourselves as well as many species *and* we have the knowledge and the power to help the process of the ongoing creation continue. This means, in a way unprecedented in the past, that we are profoundly responsible.

The several characteristics of the common creation story we have highlighted suggest, then, a decentering and a recentering of human beings. From this story we learned that we are radically interrelated with and dependent on everything else in the universe and especially on our planet. We exist as individuals in a vast community of individuals within the ecosystem, each of which is related in intricate ways to all others in the community of life. We are especially dependent on the so-called lower forms of life. We exist with all other human beings from other nations and religions within a common creation story that each of us can know about and identify with. The creation of which we are a part is an ongoing, dynamic story that we alone (we believe) understand and hence have the potential to help continue and thrive or let deteriorate through our destructive, greedy ways. Our position in this story is radically different than it is, for instance, in the king/realm story, one of the major models in Western religion. We are decentered as the only subjects of the king and recentered as those responsible for both knowing the common creation story and helping it to flourish. In this story we feel profoundly connected with all other forms of life, not in a romantic but in a realistic way. We are so connected, and hence we had better live as if we were. We feel deeply related, especially, to all other human beings, our closest relatives, and realize that together we need to learn to live responsibly and appropriately in our common home.

In light of this story, the model of the human being seeking its own individual salvation, whether through spiritual or material means, is not only anachronistic to our current sense of reality but dangerous. We need to think holistically, and not just in terms of the well-being of human beings. We need to move beyond democracy to biocracy, seeing ourselves as one species among millions of other species on a planet that is our common home. That is not the only context in which we need to view ourselves, but it is an important, neglected perspective. Our loyalty needs to move beyond family, nation, and even our own species to identify, in the broadest possible horizon, with all life: we *are* citizens of planet earth.

Such identification is not sentimental; it does not emerge merely from a fondness for charming panda bears or baby seals. It is simply the truth about who we are according to the contemporary picture of reality. We are profoundly interrelated and interdependent with everything living and nonliving in the universe and especially on our planet, and our peculiar position here is that we are radically dependent on all that is, so to speak, "beneath" us (the plants on land and the microorganisms in the ocean as well as the air, water, and soil). At the same time we have become, like it or not, the guardians and caretakers of our tiny planet. In a universe characterized by complex individuality beyond our comprehension, our peculiar form of individuality *and* interdependence has developed into a special role for us. We are the responsible ones, responsible for all the rest upon which we are so profoundly dependent. No longer should we speak of ourselves as children, especially in a religious context, as the passive, needy children of a loving, all-powerful father who will take care of us and our planet. Nor can we continue to act like willful, brash adolescents out of control, as we have been doing in the modern story of scientism, militarism, individualism, and consumerism. We need to become who we really are, neither the possessor nor principal tenant of planet earth, but responsible adults, the only species on the planet that knows the common creation story and can assume our role as partners for its well-being. We no longer have an excuse, the excuse of ignorance, for the story unfolding before our eyes over the last hundred years has revealed our place in the whole. This proper place has decentered and recentered us: we are no longer the point of the whole show, as Western culture and the Christian tradition have often implied, but we have emerged as bearing heavy responsibilities for the well-being of the whole, responsibilities that will be difficult and painful to carry out.

Theological anthropologies emerging from this understanding of human being can and will vary greatly, given the tradition, social context, and kinds of oppression experienced by different communities and individuals. The context with which we are dealing is the broadest one possible—the human being as species. It is, nevertheless, but *one* context, not the only one. But were it to become a feature of theology for the planetary agenda, it would contribute some of the following notes: a focus on gratitude for the gift of life rather than a longing for eternal life; an end to dualistic hierarchies, including human beings over nature; an appreciation for the individuality of all things

rather than the glorification of human individualism; a sense of radical interrelatedness and interdependence with all that exists; the acceptance of responsibility for other forms of life and the ecosystem, as guardians and partners of the planet; the acknowledgment that salvation is physical as well as spiritual and hence, that sharing the basics of existence is a necessity; and, finally, the recognition that sin is the refusal to stay in our proper place—sin is, as it always has been understood in the Jewish and Christian traditions, living a lie.

We began our theological anthropology with the place of human beings as seen in the common creation story rather than as a reflection of divine reality, understood either from revelation or from fundamental theology. It is important to underscore that this is a modest thesis that is not directly concerned with the liberation and salvation of the outcast and the oppressed—in other words, with the heart of Christian faith, as I understand it. The focus has been on our empirical, cosmic setting as earthlings (although that setting has significant implications for understanding salvation in our time, as we have seen). This setting has been for the most part neglected in recent theology and needs to be recalled and reinterpreted. Christian theologians will want to say more and other things about who we are, but we need to begin with our planetary citizenship.

It is a modest thesis, but given the great differences between the understanding of our proper place in post-Reformation Christianity and the common creation story, theological reflection conducted in terms of the new story would have revolutionary results. Once the scales have fallen from our eyes, once we have seen and believed that reality is put together in such a fashion that we are profoundly united to and interdependent with all other beings, everything is changed. We see the world differently, not anthropocentrically, not in a utilitarian way, not in terms of dualistic hierarchies, not in parochial terms. We have a sense of belonging to the earth, of having a place in it, and of loving it more than we ever thought possible.

In conclusion, it is precisely this sense of belonging, of being at home, that is perhaps the heart of the matter. It is the heart of the matter because it is the case—we *do* belong. As philosopher Mary Midgley writes: "We are not tourists here. . . . We are at home in this world because we were made for it. We have developed here, on this planet, and we are adapted to life here. . . . We are not fit to live anywhere else."[3] Postmodern science allows us to regain what late medieval culture lost during the Reformation and during the rise of dualistic mechanism in the seventeenth century—a sense of the whole and where we fit in it. Medieval culture was organic, at least to the extent that it saw human beings, while still central, as embedded in nature and dependent upon God. For the last several centuries, for a variety of complex reasons, we have lost that sense of belonging. Protestant focus on the individual and otherworldly salvation, as well as Cartesian dualism of mind and body, divided what we are now trying to bring back together and what must be reintegrated if we and other beings are to survive and prosper. But now, once again, we know that we belong to the earth, and we know it more deeply and thoroughly than any other human beings have ever known it. The common creation story is more than a scientific affair; it is, implicitly, deeply moral, for it raises the question of the place of human beings in nature, and calls for a kind of praxis in which we see ourselves in proportion, in harmony, and in a fitting manner relating to all others that live and all the systems that support life.

To *feel* that we belong to the earth and to accept our proper place within it is the beginning of a natural piety, what Jonathan Edwards called "consent to being," consent to what is. It is the sense that we and all others belong together in a cosmos, related in an orderly fashion, one to the other. It is the sense that each and every being is valuable in and for itself, and that the whole forms a unity in which each being, including oneself, has a place. It involves an ethical response, for the sense of belonging, of being at home, only comes when we accept our proper piece and live in a fitting, appropriate way with all other beings. It is, finally, at a deep level, an aesthetic and religious sense, a response of wonder at and appreciation for the unbelievably vast, old, rich, diverse, and surprising cosmos, of which one's self is an infinitesimal but conscious part, the part able to sing its praises.

Sin: The Refusal to Accept Our Place

The common creation story gives us a functional, working cosmology. It gives us a way of understanding where we fit. It tells us that we

belong and where we belong: it is both a welcoming word celebrating our grandeur as the most developed, complex creatures on our planet to date and a cautionary word reminding us that we belong in a place, not all places, on the earth. In the words of James Gustafson, human beings are thus reminded of "their awesome possibilities and their inexorable limitations."[4] The Genesis myth no longer functions for most people as a working cosmology, as a framework providing a sense of both space and place, grandeur and groundedness, possibilities and limitations, for the conduct of daily living. The Genesis myth, rich and profound as it still can be shown to be, does not strike most people as a working model or construct within which the ordinary events and details of their lives can be understood. Moreover, the creation story that does function, at least implicitly, in Western culture is one heavy with otherworldly overtones, seeing human beings as resident aliens on the earth. But the common creation story has for many people immediate credibility upon first hearing. "So this is where I, we, fit, not as a little lower than the angels but as an inspirited body among other living bodies, one with some distinctive and marvelous characteristics and some genuine limitations. I am of the earth, a product of its ancient and awesome history, and I really and truly belong here. But I am only one among millions, now billions of other human beings, who have a place, a space, on the earth. I am also a member of one species among millions, perhaps billions, of other species that need places on the earth. We are all, human beings and other species, inhabitants of the same space, planet earth, and interdependent in intricate and inexorable ways. I feel a sense of comfort, of settledness, of belonging as I consider my place in this cosmology, but also a sense of responsibility, for I know that I am a citizen of the planet. I have an expanded horizon as I reflect on my place in the common creation story: I belong not only to my immediate family or country or even my species, but to the earth and all its life-forms. I *do* belong to this whole. I know this now. The question is, can I, will I, *live* as if I did? Will I accept my proper place in the scheme of things? Will *we*, the human beings of the planet, do so?"

This little meditation has led us into the second major contribution of the common creation story to a theological anthropology: not only does it give us a functional cosmology but also a grounded or earthly notion of sin. One of the advantages of starting our reflections on human existence with our possibilities and limitations as seen in light of the common creation story is that it keeps them from being overstated or spiritualized. In this story we are not a little lower than the angels, nor the only creatures made in the image of God: our particular form of grandeur is in relation to the earth and derived from it—we are the self-conscious, responsible creatures. Likewise, in the common creation story, we are not sinners because we rebel against God or are unable to be sufficiently spiritual: our particular failing (closely related to our peculiar form of grandeur) is our unwillingness to stay in our place, to accept our proper limits so that other individuals of our species as well as other species can also have needed space. From the perspective of the common creation story, we gain a sober, realistic, mundane picture of ourselves: our grandeur is our role as responsible partners helping our planet prosper, and our sin is plain old selfishness—wanting to have everything for ourselves.

We need to press more deeply into the issue of sin, both what we can learn about it from the common creation story and how this view is both like and unlike the classical understanding of sin in the Christian tradition. We need also to reflect on what an ecological view of sin means in a number of different contexts—in relation to other human beings (us versus us), other animals (us versus them), and nature (us versus it). But before delving into these matters, we need to ask why God has been left out of the contexts to be considered. Sin in the Christian tradition has usually been, first of all, against God; it is in our reflections also, for in the model of the universe (world) as God's body, sin against any part of the body *is* against God. Our model helps us to keep theology earthly; it helps us to avoid abstraction, generalization, and spiritualization. To anticipate what we will say in subsequent chapters, an incarnational theology always insists that both sin and salvation are earthly matters—fleshly, concrete, particular matters having to do with disproportion and well-being *in relation to* the forms of God's presence we encounter in our daily, ordinary lives: other bodies. Sin against the many different bodies—the bodies of other people, other animals, and nature—*is* sin against God in the model of the world as God's body.

What is the relation of an ecological view of sin with the classical Christian view? It deepens rather than contradicts it. The classical view can be summarized with the phrase "living a lie," living out of proper relations with God, self, and other beings. Sin, in the Hebrew and Christian traditions, is a relational notion, having to do with the perversion of fitting, appropriate attitudes and actions in relation to other beings and the source of all being. Sin is, therefore, thinking, feeling, and acting in ways contrary to reality, contrary to the proper, right relations among the beings and entities that constitute reality. Some interpretations of sin in Judaism and Christianity, such as legalism or personalism (sin as breaking God's law or offending the divine majesty), do not, I believe, point to what is most profound in these traditions. Sin is not just breaking divine laws or blaspheming God; rather, it is living falsely, living contrary to reality, to the way things are. (And yet, breaking divine laws and blaspheming God are *symptoms* of living falsely, of failing to accept one's place as limited. The limits of law and humility before the divine glory are signs pointing to our proper, realist place in the scheme of things.)

An autobiographical point might make the point clearer. When I was first introduced to Christian theology as a college student, I recall being deeply impressed with its view of sin—it struck a chord of authenticity in me—while I remained quite unmoved by the various traditional interpretations of redemption. The classical understanding of sin focuses on wanting to be the center of things, and I already knew deeply that longing. Augustine calls it "concupiscence," literally, insatiable sexual desire but, more broadly, wanting to have it all, whatever the all is. In other words, sin is limitless greed. As a privileged member of the world's elite, I was an easy target for this view of sin. While as a female in the American fifties I perhaps lacked an overbearing sense of my own self-worth—or sin understood as pride—yet by class and race I fit the pattern of the voracious Western appetite for more than my share: I was an "ecological" sinner. The Augustinian interpretation, in focusing on the bloated self, the self that wants it all, the self that refuses to share, highlights the ecological dimension of sin. From this perspective, selfishness is the one-word definition of sin—at least for us first-world types.

To say that sin has an ecological dimension means that we must view beings, organisms, in relation to their environment. The environment of all beings, according to our model of the universe as God's body, is the "divine *milieu*": we live and move and have our being, along with all other beings, in God. Therefore, sin or living a lie will be living disproportionately, falsely, inappropriately within this space, refusing to accept the limitations and responsibilities of our place. Moreover, this space, place, has been further defined and qualified for Christians by the cosmic Christ, the embodied life paradigmatically expressed in the liberating, healing, inclusive ministry of Jesus of Nazareth. But in order to ground living rightly in the earth, in our mundane relations, let us step back from the divine *milieu* as our environment and consider an ecological view of sin within a more lowly environment: our relations with other human beings, other animals, and the natural world.

Us versus Us: Living a Lie in Relation to Other Human Beings

This section need not be long because the evidence of disproportionate space and place of some human beings in contrast to others—the rich and poor within nations and between nations—is everywhere and growing. If the most basic meaning of justice is fairness, then from an ecological point of view, justice means sharing the limited resources of our common space. From the perspective of the one home we all share, injustice is living a lie, living contrary to reality, pretending that all the space or the best space belongs to some so that they can live in lavish comfort and affluence, while others are denied even the barest necessities for physical existence. The disproportion here, epitomized in the billionaires versus the homeless, the standard of living of the first-world versus third-world countries, the swollen stomachs of starving people versus obesity in others, forces us to think concretely and physically about sin. The common creation story deepens the classical view of right relations in regard to members of our own species: it suggests that loving our neighbor must be grounded in mundane issues of space, turf, habitat, land. Every human being needs an environment capable of supporting its sustenance and growth. While this might at first appear to be a minimalist view, reducing human beings to the physical (animal?!) level, it is precisely the minimum that those individuals and nations bloated with self, living the life of insatiable greed, refuse to recognize. It is far easier as well as less costly to one's own life-style to

offer spiritual rather than material goods to the poor. The ecological view of sin refuses to raise its eyes above the minimalist view, insisting that justice among human beings means first of all adequate space for basic needs. It also means, for some, staying in their own proper, limited place.

While our analysis of ecological sin will focus on the more neglected areas of our relations with other animals and nature, proper relations with our nearest and dearest kin, our own species, must be first in consideration and importance. Some environmentalists, most notably deep ecologists, claim that human beings as one species among many million, perhaps billion, are of no special importance. Their needs for space, for land, for nourishment should not take precedence over the needs of all other species. This radical egalitarianism gives the assumption of a split between ecological and justice issues a theoretical base. It is not simply that space on our planet is limited and we must share it; it is also the case, say some, that we do not deserve any special space or more space than, say, the polar bear or giant sequoia trees. Undoubtedly on some scales of reckoning, we do not deserve it, but try telling this to the parent of a starving child, and all we have done, in the minds of many, is widen the abyss separating justice and ecological issues.

The issue on which to focus when we consider justice versus ecological issues is not our species versus other species, but *some members* of our species versus other members. While it is certainly the case that the human population is too large and encroaches on the habitats of other species, lumping human beings all together as *the* ecological problem masks the profound justice issues within our population. Those to whom this essay is addressed—we well-off Westerners—need to admit that the first lie we live is in relation to others of our own kind. *The* ecological sin is the refusal of the haves to share space and land with the have nots. It has been shown that human populations stabilize when the standard of living improves; hence, it is not only our gross numbers encroaching on other species' populations that is the problem but the disproportionate way in which space is controlled by some humans to the disadvantage of others. Over the long haul, stabilizing the human population at a sustainable level is primarily a justice issue among human beings. Thus, justice issues *within* the human species have a direct effect on environmental issues between our species and other species. Simply put, we need to do some housecleaning as a first step. Until we rectify gross injustices among human beings, in other words, begin our ecological work at home, we will have little chance of success abroad, that is, in relation to other species and the planet as a whole.

Us versus Them: Living a Lie in Relation to Other Animals

The ecological view of sin deepens when we realize that other animals, beside human ones, must have space, and that they too have a place. The common creation story not only tells us that we are related to the physical bodies of all other animals but also gives detail and depth to this statement. While there are tens of billions of known kinds of organic molecules, only about fifty are used for the essential activities of life. Molecules are essentially identical in all plants and animals. "An oak tree and I are made of the same stuff. If you go back far enough, we have a common ancestor."[5] If some degree of intimacy is true of us and oak trees, it is astonishingly true of us and other animals. We not only *are* animals but we are genetically very similar to all other animals and only a fraction of difference away from those animals, the higher mammals, closest to us. And yet one would scarcely suspect this from the way animals are conventionally regarded as well as used in our culture. While most people now have or pretend to have a raised consciousness in regard to the needs of all human beings for the basic necessities of life, the same cannot be said for attitudes about other animals. This is not the place for a review of human use and misuse of animals as manifest in pleasure hunting, excessive meat eating, the fur trade, circuses and traditional zoos, vivisection, cosmetic animal testing, and so on. But even listing a few of our more callous practices in regard to animals illustrates our degree of insensitivity to their needs, wishes, and feelings. In fact, it is by suppressing any thought that they might have needs, wishes, or feelings, in other words, that they are *anything like us* (or we like them—the more valid evolutionary comparison) that we can continue such practices with good, or at least numbed, consciences.

What does it mean to live a lie in relation to other animals? What is ecological sin in regard to them? The common creation story helps us answer this question specifically by providing a realistic picture of who we are in relation to other animals,

both our profound intimacy with them and our important differences from them. We recall that one of the special features of this story is the way both unity and diversity are understood: the interrelationship and interdependence of all living things as well as the distinctive individuality and differences among living forms. Embodied knowing, paying attention to concrete differences, is a necessary step in embodied doing, behaving appropriately toward other life-forms, each of whom has special characteristics and needs. The common creation story helps us to move into a new paradigm for responding to our fellow animals, one in which we appreciate the network of our interdependence with them as well as their real differences from us. In the conventional model, the model that views them as resources or recreation, as something to serve us or amuse us, we can appreciate neither our profound closeness nor our genuine differences: they are simply "other." The new paradigm, however, presses us into a much more complex, highly nuanced relationship with other animals, one that refuses either a sentimental fusion or an absolute separation. In this paradigm we are neither "a species among species" nor "the crown of creation." Who, then, are we?

One way to answer this question is to focus on the characteristic that has usually separated us totally and irrevocably from all other animals: our intellect. We are rational, linguistic, logical beings and therefore unlike all other animals. Various studies of incipient language and reasoning powers in some higher mammals have questioned this assumption, so that few would any longer agree with Immanuel Kant's inflated view of man [sic]: "As the single being on earth that possesses understanding, he is certainly titular lord of nature, and, supposing that we regard nature as a teleological system, he is born to be its ultimate end."[6] Nonetheless, few probably agree either with philosopher Mary Midgley that mathematical rationality in human beings is not necessarily superior to practical reason in a mother elephant as she cannily maneuvers to protect her young.[7] While Kant saw a human being as a thinking thing with no relation to body, many of us still see other animals as bodily things with no mind or spirit. Our common creation story tells us that neither position is the case: We are on a continuum with them as they are with us; it is not us versus them but us *and* them, for the roots of human nature lie deep within those others we call animals.[8] Who we are, then, is in some sense who they are: whatever we are and have is based in and derived from those others. Nor is it self-evident that the characteristic we have chosen to distinguish ourselves from the other animals, namely rationality, is worthy of being elevated above all others. As Midgley comments, "Being clever is not obviously so much more important than being kind, brave, friendly, patient, and generous. . . ."[9] Dualism—separating reason and feeling—is part of the impasse to thinking in a connected, relational way about animals, because we lock animals into the feeling category. Rationality, however, is not just cleverness, and intelligence includes a structure of preferences, a priority system based on feeling. The higher animals have deep, lasting preferences, and hence a type of practical reason.

We are like other animals in complex ways; we are also different from them—and they from one another—in complex ways.[10] We have simplified our relationship with other animals by focusing on one human characteristic, a kind of rationality divorced from feeling, which has allowed us to put ourselves on top, with other animals as inferior to us and radically different from us. The operating model here is the ladder, with rationality at the top and ourselves as its sole possessor. Everything that does not possess rationality is alien, including our own feelings and bodies as well as other animals, plant life, and the earth. But what if the evolutionary model were the bush rather than the ladder, a model much closer to what the common creation story tells us. A bush does not have a main trunk, a dominant direction of growth, or a top. There is no privileged place on a bush; rather, what a bush suggests is *diversity* (while at the same time interconnectedness and interdependence, since all its parts are related and all are fed by a common root system). The bush model helps us to appreciate different kinds of excellence, each of which is an end in itself. In this model other animals are not defined by their *lack* of rationality. "Is there nothing to a giraffe except being a person *manqué*?"[11] Asked positively, would a dolphin think that we could swim, a dog be impressed with our sense of smell, or a migrating bird be awed by our sense of direction?[12] We are profoundly and complexly united with other animals as well as profoundly and complexly different from them and they from each other. The more we know in detail about other

species, the more this abstraction will take on reality and power. Even to learn about one other species, for instance, following the research of a naturalist who has devoted her life to studying the lowland gorillas or fruitbats or caterpillars, will raise consciousness regarding the deep as well as subtle ways that animals resemble and differ from one another.

What such study often does is return us to a state of wonder, curiosity, and affection that we as children had for other animals. Children often possess wide powers of sympathy for injured animals, demonstrating a natural affection for members of other species that we need to develop rather than squelch. The young of different species play together in a mixed community that, unfortunately, gets rather thoroughly sorted out by adulthood.[13] But we can make at least a partial return to this mixed community by way of a "second naïvete," a way that involves educating ourselves on our genuine, deep, and concrete forms of interrelatedness with other life-forms.[14]

The study of similarities and differences among animals (including ourselves) also presses us to refuse easy notions of egalitarianism between ourselves and other animals as a solution to our historic insensibility toward them.[15] If equality has proven to be problematic in valuing differences among human beings, tending toward universalism or essentialism in its integration of the minority into the majority's assumptions, it is even more questionable a category to help us live appropriately with other animals. "Speciesism" is not just a prejudice against other animals that can be rectified by treating them like human beings; rather, it is the refusal to appreciate them *in their difference,* their differences from us and from each other that require, for instance, special and particular habitats, food, privacy, and whatever else each species needs to flourish.

Who are we, then, in the scheme of things in relation to other animals? What does it mean to live a lie in relation to them? The common creation story tells us that we are like and unlike them; that special forms of similarity and difference unite and divide us from them and each of them from one another. We need to develop a sensibility that appreciates some of these most central ways in which we are united and different. Living a lie in relation to them means, the common creation story tells us, lumping the other animals all together in an inferior category judged by our own superior intellect; separating ourselves from them as alien creatures with whom we have no intrinsic relationships; and, most especially, numbing ourselves to their real needs, preferences, and ability to feel pain so that we can continue to use them for our own benefit.

Refusing to live this lie will not make life easier or better for us—at least not in the short run. It will complicate it. If the resources of our planet are already strained in dealing with the needs of the human population, a large proportion of whom go hungry daily, how, why should the rights of other animals be included? Again, the issue of space is central, for increasingly, it is not hunting that is decimating other animal species, but loss of habitats due to our excessive population and the voracious life-style of some of us. But the common creation story tells us that space must be shared. It tells us that life on our planet evolved together and is interdependent in complex ways beyond our imagining; it deepens our understanding of who "family" is and the needs of different family members. At the very least it tells us that we cannot live alone, that for utilitarian reasons we need to live truthfully, rightly, appropriately with our kin, the other animals. But the work of naturalists—as well as the wonder and pleasure we felt as children and our own children feel for other animals—makes us ask: Do we not also *want* them as our companions?[16] Do we not also delight in them and value them, not just for their usefulness to us, but in their differences as well? Is wonder at the sublimity of a whale or the intricacy of an ant colony a marginal, dispensable part of human existence that few of us care about?[17] It all depends on how you define our most distinctive characteristic, as rationality or wonder?

Wonder may well be what is special about us from the perspective of the common creation story. We are the creatures who *know* that we know. Many creatures know many things; intelligence is not limited to human beings. But the ability to step back, to reflect on *that* we know and *what* we know—in other words, self-consciousness—may well be our peculiar specialty. As Annie Dillard notes, "The point is that not only does time fly and . . . we die, but that in these reckless conditions we live at all, and are vouchsafed, for the duration of certain inexplicable moments, to know it."[18] To live at all and to know it: these are the roots of wonder. I was distinctly and

peculiarly human when, at age seven, I thought with terror and fascination that someday I would not "be" any longer. In that thought was contained not only consciousness of life but self-consciousness of it: it is a wonder to be alive but it is a deeper wonder to know it. Knowing that we know places special possibilities and responsibilities on us. Self-consciousness is the basis of free will, imagination, choice, or whatever one calls that dimension of human beings that makes us capable of changing ourselves and our world. The issues around this area in regard to limitations and possibilities are enormous and beyond dealing with in this essay. The point relevant to our concerns is that in relation to other animals, our ability to wonder, to step back and reflect on what we know, places us in a singular position: our place in the scheme of things may well be to exercise this ability. To be sure, the distance that self-consciousness gives us has many aspects. A technological, rational dimension, one that can be used both for the destruction and preservation of our planet and its creatures, allows us to assess the results of various kinds of knowledge. But we are more likely to put this knowledge to work on the side of the well-being of the planet if we are moved by a deeper dimension of self-consciousness. That dimension is one close to the root meaning of wonder as surprise, fascination, awe, astonishment, curiosity: we are the ones capable of being amazed by life. *It is a wonder.* The common creation story deepens that wonder in us, not only through knowing that it has occurred at all on this planet, but also by knowing the complex, diverse, intricate way it has developed, eventuating in the truly wonderfilled creatures that we are. It is indeed a "wonderful life." One of the most profound lessons we can learn from the common creation story is appreciation for life, not just our own, but that of all the other creatures in the family of life. We are the ones, the only ones on our planet, who know the story of life and the only ones who know that we know: the only ones capable of being filled with wonder, surprise, curiosity, and fascination by it. A first step, then, toward a healthy ecological sensibility may well be a return, via a second naïveté, to the wonder we as children had for the world, but a naïveté now informed by knowledge of and a sense of responsibility for our planet and its many life-forms. To know that we know places special burdens on us: it means being designated as God's partners. On our planet we are the self-conscious aspect of the body of God, the part of the divine body able to work with God, the spirit who creates and redeems us, to bring about the liberation and healing of the earth and all its creatures. We know that we know: we have a choice to act on behalf of the wonderful life that we are and that surrounds us.

Us Versus It: Living a Lie in Relation to Nature

John Muir, the eminent American naturalist, wrote at the end of his life: "I only went out for a walk and finally concluded to stay until sundown, for going out, I discovered, was actually going in."[19] This summarizes a life-long conversion to the earth, the realization that one *belongs* to the earth. It is not natural for most of us to believe, let alone feel, that we belong to nature, to realize that by going out we are actually going in. Susan Griffin, poet and ecofeminist, eloquently expresses our complex in-and-out relationship with nature: "We know ourselves to be made from this earth. We know this earth is made from our bodies. For we see ourselves. And we are nature. We are nature seeing nature. We are nature with a concept of nature. Nature weeping. Nature speaking of nature to nature."[20] We are the self-conscious ones who can think about, weep for, and speak of nature, but we are also one in flesh and bone with nature. It is this dual awareness of both our responsibility for nature and our profound and complex unity with it that is the heart of the appropriate, indeed necessary, sensibility that we need to develop.

The proper balance of this dual awareness in relation to nature, specifically in relation to the earth, the land, may be even more difficult than in relation to other people and other animals, for we have a clearer notion of the ways we are both united to and distinct from them than we do with such things as oceans, plants, and land. Most Westerners tend to objectify nature so totally that human beings are essentially distinct from it. But for the contemporary movement called deep ecology, bent on converting us from *ego*centricity to *eco*centricity, human beings are essentially one with nature. We see here two extremes.[21]

Nonetheless it is instructive, given how difficult it is for most of us to identify with nature, to listen to deep ecology remembering, once again, that the planetary agenda is a conversation of many voices. The limitations of any position should not blind us to its insights. The central insight of deep ecology is, as one of its founders Aldo Leopold puts it, that we are "fellow-voyagers with other creatures in the odyssey of evolution," just "plain citizens" of the biotic community.[22] We are not special: humanism is an error of egocentricity, for we live with other species in an "ecological egalitarianism," as one among many. But deep ecology presses us to acknowledge more than egalitarianism; it wants us to *feel* our deepest, physical connections with and dependence on the earth. This is its greatest asset as well as limitation, for in identifying us ever more deeply with nature, deep ecology tends to blend us into nature, which is problematic in a number of ways.

But first let us learn how this perspective can help us identify with the earth, with the land and especially its plants, waters, and atmosphere. The value of deep ecology is that it insists we are not merely connected to nature but that all its parts, including ourselves, intermingle and interpenetrate. The Amazon rainforest is not just important to our well-being; it is, literally, our external lungs without which we will not be able to breathe. Deep ecology assumes profound organicism, a reliance on the model of body absolutely and totally. This organic model is not distinguished by diversity but rather by the fusion of its many parts. The danger of a position based on this model may already be evident, but since the value of deep ecology is not, I believe, in its conceptual adequacy but in its poetic power to make us feel unity, let us listen to a few of its most able spokespersons.

Richard Nelson, anthropologist and essayist, writes of his experience on a remote Northwest island off the Pacific coast. "There is nothing in me that is not of earth, no split instant of separateness, no particle that disunites me from the surroundings. I am no less than the earth itself. The rivers run through my veins, the winds blow in and out with my breath, the soil makes my flesh, the sun's heat smolders inside me. A sickness or injury that befalls the earth befalls me. A fouled molecule that runs through the earth runs through me. Where the earth is cleansed and nourished, its purity infuses me. The life of the earth is my life. My eyes are the earth gazing at itself."[23]

Gary Snyder, poet and deep ecologist, comments on his poem, "Song of the Taste": "All of nature is a gift-exchange, a potluck banquet, and there is no death that is not somebody's food, no life that is not somebody's death . . . We all take life to live . . . The shimmering food-chain, food-web, is the scary, beautiful condition of the biosphere. . . . Eating is truly a sacrament."[24]

The following credo by poet Robinson Jeffers is often quoted by deep ecologists: "I believe the universe is one being, all its parts are different expressions of the same energy, and they are all in communication with each other, therefore parts of an organic whole. . . . It seems to me that this whole alone is worthy of the deeper love."[25]

Some may, however, object to the extreme fringe as expressed in a comment such as the following: "Deep ecology . . . requires openness to the black bear, becoming truly intimate with the black bear, so that honey dribbles down your fur as you catch the bus to work."[26]

At its best deep ecology helps us to enlarge our sense of self—that is, what we include in our definition of who we are. A narrow self-definition includes only one's nearest and dearest: family and friends, or at most, one's tribe or nation. A broader self-definition takes in not only all people but some of the higher or more interesting animals (at least the poster ones, such as dolphins or snow leopards). But a cosmological self-identification acknowledges that we are part and parcel of everything on the planet, or, as Alan Watts puts it, "the world is your body."[27] Only as we are able both to think and feel this enlarged definition of self will we be able to begin to respond appropriately and responsibly to the crises facing our planet. Deep ecology makes an important contribution, for it radicalizes us into a new way of looking at the earth in which we are decentered as masters, as crown, as goal, and begin to feel empathy in an *internal* way for the sufferings of other species. As Aldo Leopold comments, "For one species to mourn the death of another is a new thing under the sun."[28] It is indeed new and requires an expanded self-identification, a sense that I care about another species in a way analogous to the way I care about those near and dear to me. I do not merely regret the loss, but I feel it and weep for it. Can we also expand this sense of self to include ecosystems and even the planet? When we read of the pollution of the oceans or the destruction of rainforests, do we feel grief for the earth itself, for that beautiful blue-green living marvel of a planet spinning alone in space?

We are a part of the whole, deep ecology insists, and we need to internalize that insight as a first step toward living truthfully, living in reality. A question, however, that rises immediately is *which* part are we? just any part? no particular part? Deep ecology is based on the classic body model of a single organism, a model made more extreme by a view of ecological unity in which living things are so profoundly interrelated and interdependent that they are, in effect, one. The result is a merging of parts, "an oceanic fusion of feeling," that denies the diversity, individuality, and complexity of lifeforms that have emerged from evolutionary history, and is a weak basis for an environmental ethic. The organic model based on the common creation story does not fuse all the parts; difference and individuality are central ingredients of this picture. Ecofeminists have been especially concerned to deny fusion and insist that the "loving eye" pays attention to the independence and difference of the other.[29] It is a kind of knowing that acknowledges the others in the world "as being independent, different, perhaps even indifferent to humans. Humans *are* different from rocks in important ways, even if they are also both members of some ecological community."[30]

Unless this difference is acknowledged—including the *indifference*—and acknowledged in relation to the particularity and peculiarity of this and that species, this and that ecosystem, there is no solid basis for an environmental ethic. A statement by one deep ecologist indicates the problem with an ethic based on the fused self: "Just as we need no morals to make us breathe . . . [so] if your 'self' in the wide sense embraces another being, you need no moral exhortation to show care. . . ."[31] No "oughts" are necessary, for care flows "naturally" from the expanded self. The sentimentality and danger of this view are evident: Even parents and lovers, whose sense of self certainly does embrace the child or the beloved, can and do engage in outrageous acts of emotional and physical destruction toward the other. What is missing from deep ecology is a developed sense of *difference*. An environmental ethic in regard to nature—the land, ecosystems, the planet—must be based on knowledge of and appreciation for the intrinsic and particular differences of various species, biotic regions, oceanic ecosystems, and so on. We need to learn about these differences and make them central in our interaction with the environment. A sense of oneness with the planet and in its lifeforms is a necessary first step, but an *informed* sensibility is the prerequisite second step. Aldo Leopold, a deep ecologist who does not fall into the fusion trap, is on the right track when he tells us that we need a land ethic, an ethic toward the land that no longer sees it "like Odysseus' slave-girls" as still property, as "still strictly economic, entailing privileges but not obligations."[32] The intrinsic value and independence of the land, not our sense of oneness with it, is the basis of living rightly in relation to it. A land ethic that aims "to preserve the integrity, stability, and beauty of the biotic community" is in example of living appropriately on the land, refusing to live the lie that we are the conquerors, the possessors, the masters of the earth.[33] A land ethic deals with the issue of space—the prime issue for an environmental anthropology— in its broadest and deepest context. *The* space, the ultimate space, as it were, that we all share, is the land, oceans, and atmosphere that comprise the planet. The complex question that faces us is how to share this space with justice and care for our own species, other species, and the ecosystems that support us all. How can we live with the others that inhabit this space appropriately and justly, realizing we have a place, but not all places, that we need space but cannot have the whole space?

Our reflection on sin in three contexts—as living a lie in relation to other human beings, other animals, and nature—has highlighted space as a central category for an ecological anthropology. In each case we have insisted that the attention to difference, even though we acknowledge and feel profound unity with these others, is central. . . .

Ethics: A New Lens for Seeing

As we begin these reflections we need to recall that the principal task of all ecological theology, at least the one attempted in these pages, is not to decide the complex, specific issues facing us. Its main task is to change consciousness, to develop a new sensibility about who we are in the scheme of things so that when we deal with concrete issues we can do so differently than in the past. The focus of this essay is on *thinking differently* so that we might behave differently. The focus is a limited one that does not pretend to solve the intricate, complex dilemmas and issues that we face in every dimension of our personal, communal, and political lives. It will not, for instance, tell us what to do about the consumer-addicted life-style of the first

world or the destruction of rainforests; it will not formulate the specific economic, political, and social policies and laws needed to address these issues. But it does insist that we look at these and all other issues from the context of a different paradigm than the one that brought about these crises. It suggests a new vision, a new shape for humanity and for our world, a vision that changes the way we see everything and, hence, the way we decide any specific issue and concern.

This essay has been about ethics, that is, correct human conduct, from the very beginning. The constructs within which we live, such as the organic or machine models, imply a mode of conduct. Conduct is not an addendum or applied from a theory because each model contains within itself a way of being in the world. All the preceding chapters have been focused on unfolding the ecological, theological, and christological implications of the organic model for human behavior, that is, how we consider and comport ourselves in the world and in relation to other beings. Hence, in considering ethics at the close of this essay we mean a particular aspect of our conduct: the relationship of an ecological theology of embodiment to concrete, nitty-gritty decisions on all sorts of difficult issues in our personal and private lives. And there are a vast number of these, needless to say; in fact, there is scarcely any issue facing us in the political, economic, medical, technological, military, educational, or family arenas that lies outside the range of an ecological theology of embodiment. Difficult issues concerning the well-being of bodies, especially the most vulnerable ones, confront us wherever we look: prenatal and nutritional care of the young, experimental genetics, rape and sexual abuse, endangered species, AIDS, the homeless, clear-cut logging practices, affirmative action laws, taxation policies, pollution control and water rights, abortion and contraception availability, immigration laws, health insurance and care, educational costs and opportunities, and on and on. The range of ecotheological issues is endless, and the view from the body, especially the needy body, changes how we see *every* issue. To make things more complex, the rights of some needy bodies are often in competition with the rights of other needy bodies, as in the case of the livelihood of loggers versus the lives of nearly extinct animals or the allocation of scarce funds to meals for disadvantaged school children or for the housebound elderly.

Our new paradigm does help us, however, to ask some novel questions and see some new connections. For instance, we become aware of the deep as well as subtle relationships among issues that in the modern individualistic, anthropocentric paradigm are not connected, such as those involving economic priorities and environmental health. The unwillingness of the American government at the 1992 UN Conference on Environment and Development to support policies on biodiversity and carbon dioxide emissions is a case in point. President Bush claimed that such policies would have adverse effects on American business. From the perspective of the embodiment model that stresses the basic needs of all life-forms, as well as the long-term health of our planet, that claim is parochial and shortsighted. Or the current battle over the right to abortion in the United States, when seen in light of our new paradigm, becomes an issue not of the sacredness of every human embryo, as it is in the individualistic, anthropocentric point of view, but of two other broader and deeper bodily concerns: the right of each child born to be wanted and to have the essentials for a healthy, satisfying life as well as the right of women to control their own bodies. The new paradigm widens the perspective on abortion from a narrow, absolutist one of human embryonic rights to the well-being of those born in addition to the well-being of those who must care for those born.

The view from the body will not tell us precisely what to do about biodiversity, global warming, or abortion, but this paradigm does offer to these issues, as well as others, a way of reflecting upon them within a framework larger than individualistic anthropocentrism. It suggests that the many issues facing us be considered in light of these notes: the need of other life-forms (not just human ones) for the basic essentials; the admonition for humans to live appropriately, allowing space for other species; our vocation to help life continue on our planet and especially to side with the oppressed, which in our time must include the new poor, nature. A shift in paradigm from the modern construct to the organic one involves decentering our species individually and collectively in terms of both numbers and life-style and recentering us as the species responsible for helping the rich, varied, interdependent community of individuals of many species to continue.

Our model, as is true of all models, helps us to see issues through its own lens. It highlights a few insights and blocks out others; it does not give us the whole picture. The major issues before us are difficult, painful, and complex; the point is certainly not to claim our new vision has all the answers and pit it against other positions. Many factors, areas of expertise, personal stories, and values enter into responsible decision making at both the private and public level. Different models suggest different assumptions and sensibilities and provide different perspectives on the issues, whatever they are. Our model—the world as God's body, rooted in the common creation story and qualified by the Christic paradigm—helps us to think differently in a number of important ways about ourselves and where we fit in the world. To think differently in these ways is but one contribution to the planetary agenda, but it is, we have insisted, an essential and neglected different kind of thinking. . . .

Notes*

1. Vincent McNabb, ed., *The Decrees of the Vatican Council* (London, 1907) as quoted by Grace Jantzen, *God's World, God's Body* (Philadelphia: Westminster Press, 1984), 102.

2. Brian Swimme, "Science: A Partner in Creating the Vision," in *Thomas Berry and the New Cosmology*, eds. Anne Lonergan and Caroline Richards (Mystic, CT: Twenty-Third Publications, 1987), 87.

3. Mary Midgley, *Beast and Man: The Roots of Human Nature* (Ithaca, NY: Cornell University Press, 1978), 194–95.

4. James M. Gustafson, *Ethics from a Theocentric Perspective*, vol. 1, *Theology and Ethics* (Chicago: University of Chicago Press, 1981), 96–97.

5. Carl Sagan, *Cosmos* (New York: Random House, 1980), 34.

6. As quoted by Midgley, *Beast and Man*, 219.

7. See Midgley, *Beast and Man*, 206ff.; also Midgley, *Animals and Why They Matter* (Athens, GA: University of Georgia Press, 1983).

8. The "roots of human nature" as well as the analysis of this concept are from Midgley, *Beast and Man*. See also Ian Barbour's discussion of sentience and purpose in animals in *Religion in an Age of Science*, vol. 1 (New York: Harper and Row, 1990), 170–72.

9. Midgley, *Beast and Man*, 255–56.

10. Midgley, *Beast and Man*, 206.

11. Midgley, *Beast and Man*, 358.

12. Midgley, *Beast and Man*, 225ff.

*[Notes have been edited and renumbered.—Eds.]

13. For an interesting discussion of this phenomenon, see Midgley, *Animals and Why They Matter*, chap. 10. . . .

14. The phrase "second naïvete" is Paul Ricoeur's and refers to the possibility of returning to the most basic roots of our being by a conscious, informed route when the intuitive acceptance found in our own youth and the youth of the human community is no longer possible for us.

15. See Midgley's discussion of "the pathology of egalitarianism" in *Animals and Why They Matter*, 78.

16. One of the most delightful and consciousness-raising short pieces on our relationship with the other animals is "She Unnames Them," by Ursula K. LeGuin, originally published in *The New Yorker*, 21 January 1985. . . .

17. Midgley states the centrality of wonder in human experience with eloquence: "We are receptive, imaginative beings, adapted to celebrate and rejoice in the existence, quite independent of ourselves, of the other beings on this planet. Not only does our natural sympathy reach out easily beyond the barrier of species but we rejoice in the mere existence of plants and lifeless bodies—*not* regarding them just as furniture provided to stimulate our pampered imagination. . . . We need the vast world, and it must be a world that does not need us; a world constantly capable of surprising us, a world we did not program, since only such a world is the proper object of wonder" (*Beast and Man*, 361–62).

18. Annie Dillard, *Pilgrim at Tinker Creek: A Mystical Excursion into the Natural World* (New York: Bantam Books, 1974), 81.

19. As quoted by Bill Devall and George Sessions, *Deep Ecology: Living as if Nature Mattered* (Salt Lake City: Peregrine Smith Books, 1985), 205.

20. Susan Griffin, *Made from This Earth: An Anthology of Writings* (New York: Harper and Row, 1982), 343.

21. This distinction is from the introduction to *Dharma Gaia: A Harvest of Essays in Buddhism and Ecology*, ed. Allan Hunt Badiner (Berkeley, CA: Parallax Press, 1990), xiv. . . .

22. As quoted by Devall and Sessions, *Deep Ecology*, 85.

23. Richard Nelson, *The Island Within* (New York: Random House, 1989), 249.

24. As quoted by Devall and Sessions, *Deep Ecology*, 13.

25. As quoted by Marti Kheel, "Ecofeminism and Deep Ecology: Reflections on Identity and Difference," in *Reweaving the World: The Emergence of Ecofeminism*, eds. Irene Diamond and Gloria Orenstein (San Francisco: Sierra Club Books, 1990), 136.

26. Warwick Fox, *Toward a Transpersonal Ecology: Developing New Foundations for Environmentalism* (Boston: Shambhala Publications, 1990), 239.

27. As quoted in the introduction to *Nature in Asian Traditions of Thought: Essays in Environmental Philosophy*, ed. J. Baird Callicott and Robert Ames (Albany, NY: SUNY Press, 1989), 62.

28. Aldo Leopold, *A Sand County Almanac and Sketches Here and There* (New York: Oxford University Press, 1949), 110.

29. See Marilyn Frye, "In and Out of Harm's Way: Arrogance and Love," in *The Politics of Reality* (Trumansburg, NY: The Crossing Press, 1983), 66–72.

30. Karen J. Warren, "The Power and Promise of Ecological Feminism," *Environmental Ethics* 12 (Summer 1990): 138. . . .

31. Arne Naess as quoted by Fox, *Toward a Transpersonal Ecology*, 217.

32. Leopold, *A Sand County Almanac*, 203.

33. Leopold, *A Sand County Almanac*, 224–25.

9. Of God and Pelicans

Jay B. McDaniel

"If God watches the sparrow fall, God must do so from a very great distance (Rolston, 1987, 140). This observation is made by Holmes Rolston III, a North American environmental philosopher and Christian who wrestles with the fact that so many sentient creatures die violent and painful deaths before reaching maturity. How, he asks, is God related to such creatures and their suffering? Does God share in their suffering, or does God watch from a distance? Is God empathic, or cool and distant?

From Jay B. McDaniel, *Of God and Pelicans: A Theology of Reverence for Life* (Louisville, KY: Westminster/John Knox Press, 1989), 19–21, 148–9, 54ff. © 1989 Jay B. McDaniel. Reprinted by permission of Westminster John Knox Press.

As a case in point, Rolston considers the plight of newborn white pelicans. Female pelicans generally lay two eggs, the second two days after the first. Because few parents can raise two young, "the earlier hatched chick, more aggressive in grabbing food from its parent's pouch, becomes progressively larger, attacking the smaller sibling" (1987, 138). The second chick—whom we will imagine as male—is often driven out of his nest by the first chick. His return to the nest is prevented by the parents, lest they accidentally adopt an alien chick and waste precious parental energy. Nine times out of ten, he thrashes about in search of food and then dies of abuse or starvation.

Rolston points out that this mode of parenting has been very successful from an evolutionary perspective. It has led to the survival of generations of white pelicans for almost thirty million years. The second chick is an insurance policy in case the first chick runs into trouble. He is a "backup chick." Neither the parents nor the first chick should be condemned for their behavior. Both are genetically conditioned to behave as they do, and they have little if any capacity for moral responsibility in relation to the second chick. The treatment of the hapless chick is a "subroutine in a larger evolutionary process," a means to the end of species continuation (1987, 140).

From the backup chick's own perspective, however, this evolutionary analysis misses something. The analysis presents him from the outside rather than the inside. Viewed externally, he is indeed a cog in the evolutionary process: a mere backup. But from the inside, in terms of his own point of view, he is a sentient creature who suffers pain and enjoys pleasure, and who desires his own well-being, however trivial that well-being might be compared to our standards. Of course, the second chick probably does not "view himself" in the sense of objectifying himself as an "I" or "me." Such self-objectification involves conceptual and linguistic skills he undoubtedly lacks, as do human infants. His experience is prereflective and, analogous to our own experience in sleep, preconscious. But his behavior certainly suggests (1) that at least in a preconscious way he is aware of his own body and the surrounding environment, which is to say that he is sentient, and (2) that he has needs of his own, including the need to survive with some degree of satisfaction relative to the situation at hand. As a creature with sentience and with subjec-

tive needs, he is more than an object in the evolutionary process. Like a newborn human infant who has not yet acquired language, but who nevertheless has a perspective of his or her own, the second chick is a subject for himself.

As cognitive ethologists such as Donald Griffin point out (1984, 133–153), the recognition of sentience and internal needs in nonhuman organisms with nervous systems is not mere human projection. It is a sound inference from biological evidence. Analysis shows that birds such as pelicans have the nervous systems and the biochemical endowments to enjoy pleasure, to suffer pain, and to have interests in avoiding pain and preferring pleasure. Moreover, evolution itself posits a continuity between human mentality and nonhuman psychic life. As Bernard Rollin explains, "given that evolutionary theory is at the cornerstone of all modern biology, and evolutionary theory postulates continuity of all life," it is unlikely "that a creature that has a nervous system displaying biochemical processes that in us regulate consciousness, or that withdraws from the same noxious stimuli as we do, or from other dangers, and that has sense organs, does not enjoy a mental life" (1981, 41). It is more likely that the creature *does* have some kind of mental life.

And here lies the problem, at least for the chick. Because the chick is the second or backup chick, his yearning for satisfaction is frustrated and his life ends in pain. While the chick's brief existence may serve larger evolutionary ends, this fact is of no consolation to him. From his perspective, his life matters for its own sake. He is an end in himself.

How about from God's perspective? From the divine point or view, does the pelican chick matter for his own sake? Does God envision him as an end in himself, or merely as a means to other ends? This is the question that Rolston raises and one that any Christian interested in the relation between God and nature must address. It is the question that serves as the point of departure for this work. . . .

Christians such as Matthew Fox who employ the phrase "creation-centered" fittingly recognize that there is more to nature than what we call "life," at least inasmuch as "life" refers to the realms of plants and animals and perhaps also, as it does for me, to the living quality, the creativity, even within inorganic materials of the Earth. Nature also includes the cosmos, of whose evolutionary history we are a part. . . .

I choose to highlight the phrase "life-centered" over "God-centered" for two reasons. First, much more directly than "creation-centered," the phrase "God-centered" can suggest to the popular imagination—though for Gustafson it does not—fidelity to a vainglorious ruler who is cut off from the world, who arbitrarily demands worship and obedience for his own sake, and who is the sole possessor of value. The God whom I hope to describe is neither vain, nor arbitrarily demanding, nor the sole possessor of value. In choosing "life-centered" over "God-centered," I wish to avoid connotations of a patriarchal, monarchical God to whom Christians owe blind obedience.

Second, and in a more positive vein, the God whom I hope to describe is indeed living, the supreme instance of that creativity and sentience with which we associate the word "life." A Christianity that is centered in life can and should involve trust in an ultimate Life, God, who is on the side of each and every living being. I use the phrase "life-centered" because the phrase includes within its horizons each and every living being, on the one hand, and the divine Life on the other, each understood in intimate connection with the other.

. . . Of course, I am by no means the first to be interested in showing God's care for the whole of creation. All who are interested in doing so are deeply indebted to Irenaeus, the later Augustine, Francis of Assisi, John Wesley; to the Orthodox tradition with its sacramental approach to nature; to more recent life-centered theologies emerging in Africa and Asia; to emerging environmental theologies in North America; and . . . to feminist theologies. . . .

There are numerous resources from which Christians can draw as we seek to envision and embody a biocentric ethic. We can turn to neglected traditions within Judaism, Christianity, and Islam, both biblical and postbiblical, highlighting the motif of stewardship; we can turn to feminism and other world religions; and we can turn to contemporary developments in art and science (Joranson 1984). In addition, we can learn from a contemporary movement in philosophy called "environmental philosophy," which has a growing number of advocates in Western Europe, the United States, and Australia. In particular, Christians interested in biocentric ethics can benefit from reviewing two

developments in environmental philosophy: the "land ethics" movement and the "animal rights" tradition. . . .

As animal activists recognize, neither the instrumentality of an organism for other organisms nor the relationality of its own subjective existence belie the fact that is has intrinsic value, and hence that it is a moral patient. While there may be differences between human and nonhuman experiencers, no differences justify inclusion of the former and exclusion of the latter from moral considerability.

Does this mean, then, that animals have rights? If so, what about plants? And rocks? And mountains? And stars? In reconciling the concerns of animal rights activists with those of land ethicists, I believe it helpful at the outset to limit the use of the word "rights" to individual animals (1) who have discernible interests in living with some degree of satisfaction and (2) whose interests can be respected or violated by human moral agents. To say that these animals have rights is to say that we, as humans, have duties to respect their interests. . . .

Even if there were no God, individual living beings would deserve our respect; they would have rights. The role of God in a life-centered ethic is not to ground the rights of animals, as if their rights were assigned by God. Rather, the role of God is to beckon us into a respect for those rights, to lure us toward a care for animals that, in our own finite way, mirrors and internalizes God's own care.

In order to affirm this point, it can be helpful to imagine God on the analogy of a cosmic Parent. Imagine, for example, that the Psyche of the universe is in some way like a human mother, except that her love is utterly unfailing and unlimited. A human mother may in some sense create her children, but once the children are created, they have a goodness that is independent of her ascription. Even if she decides they are valueless, they nevertheless have value as living subjects with goals and needs of their own. Similarly, though God lures sentient beings into existence out of a primordial chaos, those sentient beings have a value that is independent of God's ascription. In Genesis, after creating the animals on the fifth day, God does not assign them their goodness, God *sees* that they are good (Gen. 1:21). God is "God" because she invites others to share in her wisdom. She beckons us, humans made in her own image, to recognize the intrinsic value that she herself sees.

Nonhuman animals have rights because they have intrinsic value. . . .

Furthermore, it is important to recognize, as will be argued in greater detail, that there can be degrees of moral patience, or moral considerability. The greater the intensity of a creature's interests, the greater our obligation to respect them. Simple plants, for example, have interests, at least insofar as the cells of which they are composed have aims and needs. Yet the intensity of a plant cell's aim to survive—much less to survive with satisfaction—does not seem to be as great as that of a porpoise's interest in surviving with satisfaction. Instrumental considerations being equal, it is more problematic to take the life of a porpoise than a simple plant, which is to say that the porpoise has a greater degree of moral patience than the plant. While every living being has moral patience of one sort or another, some have more than others. A speculative justification for this claim, hinging on a structural difference between plants and animals and a recognition of degrees of intrinsic value, is offered in the final section of this chapter.

Finally, it is important to recognize that the category of intrinsic value is itself more inclusive than that of moral patience. Rivers, rocks, and stars may have intrinsic value, even though they are not moral patients with discernible interests subject to human violation. Many more things have intrinsic value than have rights. Indeed, biocentric Christians can affirm that all existents—inorganic as well as organic—have intrinsic value.

The speculative foundations for expanding the notion or intrinsic value beyond animals to plants and even rocks will be suggested shortly. For now, however, let us assume that a biocentric ethic should respect the rights to life, liberty, and the pursuit of happiness of individual animals under human domestication and the rights to habitat protection of living beings in the wild. What would it mean, then, to live in light of such respect? It would mean both that we adopt certain biocentric practices and that we embody what might be called biocentric virtues. First, consider some of the practices.

Biocentric Practices

Given the manifold areas in which humans abuse domesticated animals, we must practice a respect for animal rights on a case-by-case basis. In general, the following principles of the Humane Society of the United States (Morris 1978, 236) can serve as guidelines for appropriate action:

> It is wrong to kill animals needlessly or for entertainment or to cause animals pain or torment.
>
> It is wrong to fail to provide adequate food, shelter, and care for animals for which humans have accepted responsibility.
>
> It is wrong to use animals for medical, educational, or commercial experimentation or research, unless absolute necessity can be demonstrated and unless such is done without causing the animals pain or torment.
>
> It is wrong to maintain animals that are to be used for food in such a manner that causes them discomfort or denies them an opportunity to develop and live in conditions that are reasonably natural for them.
>
> It is wrong for those who eat animals to kill them in any manner that does not result in instantaneous unconsciousness. Methods employed should cause no more than minimum apprehension.
>
> It is wrong to confine animals for display, impoundment, or as pets in conditions that are not comfortable or appropriate.
>
> It is wrong to permit domestic animals to propagate to an extent that leads to overpopulation or misery.

As Birch and Cobb point out (1981, 156), "the serious application of these principles would enormously reduce the suffering now inflicted by us on our fellow creatures."

It is noteworthy that the principles of the Humane Society do not prohibit the killing of animals for food. However, contrary to John Henry Cardinal Newman (1801–1890), who argued that the least human good compensates for any possible cost to animals, biocentric Christians recognize that "it requires a great human advantage to compensate for animal suffering and loss" (Birch and Cobb 1981, 161). Despite the possible justification of killing animals for food in certain circumstances, particularly if necessary for human survival, Christians in industrial societies whose lives do not depend on the eating of meat can and should choose vegetarianism. Given the appalling conditions under which most animals are raised for food and transported to slaughter, we are right to follow Peter Singer's advice and boycott the meat industry.

This is not to say that cows, sheep, chickens, and fish have an *inviolable* right to life. Rather, it is to say that they have interests in surviving with some degree of satisfaction and that as moral agents we humans must be as sensitive as we can to these interests. The needs of animals to avoid unnecessary pain and to pursue pleasure are persistently violated by factory farming techniques such as the debeaking of chickens and the immobilization of veal calves. If we want factory farming abuses to end, we ought to boycott meat industries. In so doing, we can simultaneously serve the interests of the human poor, for, as Singer has argued, the adoption of vegetarianism helps reduce the waste currently involved in feeding grain to animals and thus helps encourage the production of crops more suited to the world's hungry. Vegetarian diets are also salutary for health reasons, since they are low in cholesterol and fats (Robbins 1987, 148–348). And they can contribute to the well-being of the environment. The intensive rearing methods of modern agribusiness, which we support with meat buying, often have disastrous effects on the environment in terms of the waste products they release into rivers and streams; and the raising of animals for food in Central and South America, much of which meat is imported to supply Western tables, plays a considerable role in denuding the Earth of its tropical forests (Robbins 1987, 363–373). Here the World Council's interests in affirming human well-being and the integrity of nature can be jointly served by the adoption of a vegetarian diet.

As land ethicists in the tradition of Aldo Leopold rightly point out, however, an exclusive focus on the rights of individual animals under human domestication does not go far enough if we are to dwell as benevolently as possible with our kindred creatures. A concern for animal rights must be complemented by a concern for land ethics: that is, for the well-being of biotic communities that serve as habitats for living beings. Christians are reminded by land ethicists that the recognition of moral considerability of other animals must result in a concern for terrestrial ecosystems and for the countless species in the wild whose home is the Earth.

Endangered species are themselves collections of individual beings that, if subjects, have intrinsic value and moral patience. Whether plant or animal, each member of a species embodies a form of life—that is, a distinctive way of experiencing with qualities of its own and with distinctive needs—characteristic of the species as a whole.

Among these interests is usually an aim for reproductive success and hence for the survival of at least some members of its own species. This form of life can be made into an object of reflection in its own right: something on the analogy of a Platonic form. But most proponents of a land ethic are not Platonic. They recognize that the form's actuality—that is, its life and vitality—is to be found only in the individual creatures that embody it. Preservationists are not interested in preserving the abstract form for its own sake, which could be accomplished simply by describing the form in books, perhaps with accompanying illustrations or photographs. Rather, they are concerned with preserving at least some of the individual creatures who embody that form. Here, too, the concern is with the intrinsic value and hence the moral patience of individual creatures. Many of these species, which include plants as well as animals, are endangered by pollution and by habitat disruption, which is itself partly the result of overpopulation and partly the result of a misuse and exploitation of land by ruling classes.

As in the case of animal rights, a Christian concern for species protection can seek to unite concerns for social justice with those for ecological sustainability. In Latin America, for example, the rural poor are often forced to farm the less arable land of tropical rain forests because the more productive land is owned by large agribusiness concerns. These rain forests are the habitats for many endangered species of plants and animals. If the arable land is reclaimed by the poor, their own poverty will be lessened, and the rain forests can themselves be better protected. Moreover, the forms of agriculture and land management traditionally practiced by rural peasants are often more conducive to ecological sustainability than are those practiced by absentee landlords. Christians rightly hope that policies and practices that promote social justice can also promote a respect for the integrity of endangered species.

In addition to working for modes of social justice that reduce the destruction of habitats, Lee Durrell in *State of the Ark: An Atlas Conservation in Action* notes six practices many in industrial societies can adopt in order to help preserve habitats and the species threatened by their disruption. First, if we live in circumstances that allow, we can do our part to help minimize human overpopulation either by adopting children or by having children at replacement rate, two surviving children for every couple. Second, we can learn about the environments in which we live, trying both to understand the ecosystems of which we are a part and on which we depend and to advocate agricultural and industrial policies that are minimally destructive of those systems. Third, we can examine the consequences of our own professions and life-styles, adjusting our behavior where consequences are destructive of environmental well-being. Fourth, if we are among the affluent minority in the world, we can keep our consumption of new goods within reasonable levels, trying not to waste or overconsume water, energy, or food and learning to live more simply to allow for a more equitable distribution of the world's natural resources. Fifth, we can join environmental organizations oriented toward a protection of habitats and an ecologically sound use of resources. Sixth, if we are able, we can cast our votes for those legislators who promise to protect the environment and to respect the needs of individual animals under human subjugation (Durrell 1986, 215).

Moral Virtues

However, such practical steps are not enough if Christians are truly to overcome the anthropocentrism of our past. What is required, in addition to the taking of practical steps, is a conversion of sensibility and character. In general terms, to adopt a biocentric ethic is to be informed by three "moral virtues." Each of these virtues can be encouraged by local churches through education, liturgy, and worship, and each can be allowed to flourish in meditation and prayer.

The first moral virtue is reverence for life. This is to have all inward disposition that is respectful of, and caring for, other animals, plants, and the Earth and that refuses to draw a sharp dichotomy between human life and other forms of life. This reverence has been evident in primal traditions in Africa, Oceania, and the Americas, and in certain Asian religions such as Buddhism and Taoism. Christians in these nonwestern settings, as well as their sisters and brothers in the West, can well appreciate the fact that dialogues with other faiths can and should inform the development of a biocentric ethic.

The second moral virtue is *ahimsa*, or noninjury. This is to refrain as much as possible from the violation of other creatures' interests: for example, to refrain from inflicting pain when another creature has an interest in avoiding pain and to refrain from taking its life when it has an interest in surviving. The most dramatic example of this perspective as applied to nonhuman creatures is Jainism in India. The biocentric perspective developed by the World Council of Churches will not go as far as Jainism, but it can take this tradition as a welcome and ever-present challenge to the anthropocentrism that has prevailed in so much of Christianity.

The third moral virtue is the exercise of active goodwill. In relation to nonhuman creatures, this is not simply an avoidance of harm, it is the active fostering of opportunities for an animal to realize its interests. It is, for example, to protect and sometimes even to create habitats that are essential to the survival of a species and to provide individual animals under human domestication with adequate food and shelter.

For the Christian, each of these three virtues involves a generalization of the golden rule: an application of agape to neighbors who in many instances are nonhuman. The first of these three practices—reverence for life—is an art, not a science. In relation to nonhuman creatures, such reverence can and must be guided by factual information from biologists familiar with the anatomical and behavioral needs of the animal under consideration. But it also involves and requires imaginative empathy. Avoiding the extremes of anthropocentric projection on the one hand and an absolute denial of the sentience of other creatures on the other, one must imagine oneself inside the perspective of the creature at issue, experiencing the world from its perspective and in light of its interests. If this is impossible, as it is in many cases, one must at least imagine that the creature has an experiential perspective of its own informed by interests of its own. With regard to humans and nonhumans alike, imaginative empathy is an essential feature of a life-centered ethical perspective.

The second and third practices, noninjury and active goodwill, require capacities in addition to imaginative empathy: capacities of discernment and judgment. The kind of moral considerability appropriately given to a moral patient—human or nonhuman—depends at least in part on the kind of interests possessed by that patient. If an animal has an interest in being in a warm climate, that interest can and should be considered in one's treatment of it; if it has an interest in being in a cold climate, that interest should be taken into account. The interests to be considered by moral agents are those that are held by, or relevant to, the moral patient. Different patients have different interests.

Moreover, in a world where there are competing interests among moral patients, not all interests can be respected. We live in a world where life is robbery. For one creature to live, thus realizing its interests, others must die, thus having theirs frustrated. As humans, we too must choose between lives, violating the interests of some for the sake of respecting the interests of others. This fact becomes particularly relevant when we consider the intrinsic value—and hence the moral considerability—of nonhuman forms of life. Every time we wash our faces we kill millions of bacteria; every time we eat, we are accomplices in many deaths. As Gabriel Moran puts it, "To walk across the lawn, take a shower, or even to breathe is to assert that some human concerns outweigh some nonhuman concerns" (1987, 698). The discernment of interests involves and requires a recognition of competing interests and a ranking of interests. It requires judgment.

Degrees of Intrinsic Value

The need for judgment—preceded as it must be by the recognition that all living things have intrinsic value—requires that a biocentric ethic be accompanied by an adequate theology of nature. While the existence of intrinsic value in nonhuman creatures does not depend on such a theology, the sustained recognition of such value does, as does the ranking of interests once intrinsic value is recognized. Consider two inadequate theologies of nature from which, in principle, Christians might proceed: the first obstructs the recognition of intrinsic value; the second obstructs any capacity to rank interests.

Two Inadequate Theologies of Nature

First, Christians can approach other animals with a mechanistic theology of nature that stems from seventeenth-century science. Animals are viewed as complex instances of lifeless matter in motion, different in kind from humans, who alone are thought to possess souls. Here animals become mere instruments for human or divine purposes. "Stewardship" means no more than prudent management of nonhuman "resources." The goodness of the earth and its creatures—a goodness of which Genesis speaks and which can be understood as that of intrinsic value—is ignored.

On the other hand, those disillusioned with a mechanistic orientation can approach other animals through the lens of an egalitarian monism, such as one finds, for example, in Taoist points of view or in the contemporary movement of Deep Ecology (Devall 1985). Such perspectives are often emanationist in orientation, pointing toward an ultimate stuff—God or the Tao—of which all things are expressions and on the basis of which all things have equal intrinsic value. These perspectives are indeed advances over a mechanistic orientation. With their help, we can recognize that we have something in common with the rest of nature because we are all expressions of the same ultimate reality. But if we follow the lead of such perspectives alone, we are left with no basis— other than arbitrary whim—for the kind of discernment and ranking of interests that is so needed if a biocentric ethic is to be practiced. When, for example, we must choose between the life of a ringworm-causing fungus and the interests of a dog whose skin cells and hair shafts are invaded by this fungus, egalitarian monism offers us no help in making the decision, since fungi and animals have equal intrinsic value. We may decide to take the life of the fungus, but we have nothing to say to others who choose the contrary. Nor have we anything to say to those who argue that the AIDS virus has greater right to life than the humans infected by it. Arbitrary whim is the final arbiter.

What is needed, then, is an adequate theology of nature. To be adequate, it must accomplish three tasks. First, it must help us see the reality and nature of subjectivity, and hence intrinsic value, in human as well as nonhuman life and then guide us in discerning how far down and across the evolutionary chain such value extends. It must deal with the reality, nature, and the range of subjectivity. Second, it must help us distinguish types of organisms so that, among other things, we can deal with the world of plants as well as animals.

And third, it must help us distinguish degrees of intrinsic value. . . .

Distinguishing Degrees of Intrinsic Value

Intrinsic value is the experiential richness and self-concern of an organism. If some organisms have greater intrinsic value than others, it must be because their experiences are richer and their self-concern greater. *Do* some organisms have greater experiential richness and self-concern than others?

Any answer to this question will be speculative, and it must be posed in humility. Yet speculation is required if we are to rank competing interests. If choices must be made between the interests of fungal cells and those of the dogs on whom they feed, or between the interests of malarial mosquitoes and those of the humans on whom they feed, we must try to respect the interests of the organisms with the greatest degree of intrinsic value: that is, with the richest experience and the greatest self-concern.

The only example of degrees of intrinsic value to which we have immediate access are our own lives. We know (1) that some moments of our own experience have greater richness than others, (2) that at some moments we matter more to ourselves than at others, and (3) that, in general, the greater richness of experience we have, or believe we can have, the more we matter to ourselves. Experiential richness and self-concern seem directly proportional. If we are to speculate concerning the degrees of intrinsic value in nonhuman organisms, we must assume that, in other creatures as well, there is a direct correlation between degrees of experiential richness and self-concern, and hence that those creatures that have, or can have, greater degrees of experiential richness also have, or can have, greater self-concern. Then we must seek criteria by which to evaluate richness of experience. And here our only option is to generalize from criteria discovered in our own experience.

Is such generalization warranted? I believe that it is. Within Christianity the very notion of creation—and the attendant claim that we are, like other animals, creatures of this creation—offers one resource for generalization. Whether understood metaphorically or literally, the second creation story in Genesis suggests that we and other creatures are made from the same earth: "The LORD God formed man of dust from the ground" (Gen.

2:7) and "out of the ground the LORD God formed every beast of the field and every bird of the air" (Gen. 2:19). The idea that we come from a similar substance suggests that we share features in common, among which might be general possibilities for richness of experience.

Adding to biblical perspectives is evolutionary theory, with its suggestion that there is an ontological continuity among and between life forms. On these grounds we rightly surmise that our own lives are instances of, rather than exceptions to, the phenomenon of life as it is found in other creatures. Just as our lives consist of occasions of experience with varying degrees of richness, so must their lives. This is not to deny that there is something distinctively human about human experience, just as there is something distinctively canine about canine experience and distinctively cellular about cellular experience. But it is to say that human experience, canine experience, and cellular experience are instances of a similar kind of activity: that of consciously or subconsciously taking into account environmental influences in light of consciously or subconsciously felt interests. And it is to say that amid this activity there is some kind of qualitative enjoyment, some kind of richness. We rightly surmise that the general qualities we find rich are those which, in different ways relative to the species at issue, other organisms find rich.

Let us identify first, then, the qualities we find rich. They are harmony and intensity. Each are affective tones qualifying our act of experiencing—that is, taking into account—influences from other beings.

Harmony is a general feeling of attunement, balance, accord, and affinity. For us, harmony often includes the attunement of our psyches with our bodies, or physical health. Amid such harmony, the "other beings" in relation to which harmony is felt are cells, tissues, organs, and limbs. Whether or not we enjoy health, harmony in human life can also be sought and enjoyed in relations with other people, with kindred creatures, with the world of ideas, and with God. Compassion, understood as sharing in the joys and sufferings of others, is one of the highest forms of harmony enjoyed by humans: a harmony that Christians claim mirrors God's own.

Intensity is zest or energetic vitality in relation to other beings. It is exemplified in feelings of creativity, energy, strength, excitement, enthusiasm, vigor, passion, and potency. In human life intensity has at least two forms: the active vitality of creatively synthesizing environmental, social, and historical influences and the receptive vitality of allowing oneself to be strongly affected by such influences. Active vitality includes the joy of artistic creativity and the zest of physical exercise; receptive vitality includes the immediate physical pleasure and the meaning found in allowing oneself to share in the sufferings of others. As the latter example suggests, richness of experience need not be pleasurable in order to be meaningful. Pleasure is one form of richness, but not all richness is pleasurable.

Can these two forms of richness—harmony and intensity—serve as criteria by which we evaluate, albeit speculatively, the richness of experience of other creatures? If divorced from aspects and associations that are uniquely human, and if applied with imagination and tentativeness, they can.

The creatures most distant from us and concerning which our speculations will have to be the most tentative are those molecular, atomic, and subatomic energy pulsations composing inorganic matter. We cannot know with assurance, but we can at least speculate, that in being drawn toward stable configurations, energy events are drawn toward certain forms of subconscious, submicroscopic harmony. Perhaps stability as observed from the outside is harmony as lived from the inside. And again we cannot know, but we can at least conjecture, that these harmonies are imbued with powerful intensities, as is evident from the release of energy when stable energy configurations are disrupted. No doubt these forms of richness would be subconscious and quite different from anything we know. Nevertheless, they would be primitive instances of what, later, we call richness of experience.

If in fact even inorganic realities enjoy certain forms of harmony and intensity, the moral stakes of this fact are not high. There is no evidence that the interests of inorganic materials at a submicroscopic level can be violated by human manipulation. This means that, in making moral decisions, inorganic materials can be treated as instruments for the well-being of plants and animals, humans included. While we may appreciate their intrinsic value—as, for example, when we feel the awesomeness of a mountain or the freshness of clean air—our appreciation of their intrinsic value is aesthetic rather than moral. Moral issues emerge when we consider the living beings for whom they serve as habitats.

When making moral decisions, ecosystems too can be treated primarily as instruments for the well-being of the life forms they include. We respect the integrity, beauty, and stability of ecosystems not because these systems are agents or patients in their own right but, rather, because they include complex networks of living beings who are moral patients in their own right. The land ethic of which Aldo Leopold spoke, and which has fittingly captured the imaginations of so many in the environmental movement in the West, has its justification in a "life ethic," because land—understood broadly to include ocean and air as well as solid ground—is the habitat of life. We work to protect the Earth's lands, oceans, and atmosphere not because the interests of these inorganic materials can be violated but because living beings depend on them.

Though a land ethic has its value in serving a life ethic, speculations concerning the aliveness of "dead matter" are important because they help Christians affirm more deeply the goodness of the Earth, from which, after all, life itself emerged and on which life depends. Moreover, though the land and water masses composing the Earth may not command moral respect in the same way that, for example, other living beings command such respect, Christians can nevertheless enjoy religious awe in the presence of inorganic matter and its myriad forms, cognizant that we emerge out of matter's aliveness. From the living rock, after all, come the waters of spirit.

Somewhat closer to what we know as humans, but still requiring much tentativeness, are living cells existing in or outside the bodies of both plants and animals. Here the intuitions of a contemporary physician and writer such as Lewis Thomas in *The Lives of a Cell* can be helpful. Realizing that cells in our bodies have lives of their own, Thomas writes, "I like to think that they work in my interest, that each breath they draw for me, but perhaps it is they who walk through the local park in the early morning, sensing my senses, listening to my music, and thinking my thoughts" (1974, 2–3). Here Thomas, like many biologists, recognizes that living cells seem able to take into account influences from their environments and that, in so doing, they are drawn toward certain forms of energy exchange and balance. We cannot know, but we can at least speculate, that energy exchange and balance as observed from the outside are intensity and harmony as lived from the inside. As with the energy pulsations composing inorganic matter, the intensities and harmonies would be subconscious. And yet here, in contrast to energy pulsations, interests can indeed be violated. Cancer cells seem to have interests in surviving, and we violate these interests when we destroy the cells. The necessity of ranking interests among organisms becomes obvious.

Evolutionarily closer to our experience, and perhaps furthest from sheer speculation, are multi-celled animals with psyches, or monarchies. As indicated earlier, evidence from neurophysiology, biochemistry, anatomy, behavior, and evolutionary theory shows that such animals have experiences and interests. By the same token we can conjecture that such animals enjoy, and are drawn toward, their own forms of harmony and intensity, either consciously or subconsciously. It is not difficult to imagine, for example, that at least subconsciously a butterfly enjoys a harmony of hunger satiation when it sucks nectar with its proboscis, or that a snake feels a subconscious intensity of physical movement when it strikes at a prey. Nor is it difficult to imagine that nonhuman mammals feel and enjoy experiential richness: for example, that a cat feels intensity while playing with other cats, that a chimp feels harmony when nursing her young, that a deer feels intensity when running through a forest, or that a dog feels harmony when satisfied by a meal. There is no need to say that such harmonies and intensities entirely transcend genetic influence or that they are divorced from bodily needs. On the contrary, opportunities for experiential richness may well be conditioned by genes and meet physical needs. But such physical grounding does not obviate the fact that these qualities of experience are enjoyed by the animal from its own perspective. Physically based or not, harmony and intensity seem to be the qualities desired, not simply by us but by those creatures closest to us.

With these speculative assumptions concerning living cells and multicelled organisms, we approach a basis upon which we can distinguish degrees of intrinsic value. If we assume a direct correlation between experiential richness and self-concern, organisms that on balance can enjoy greater degrees of harmony and intensity than those with which they are being compared will have greater intrinsic value. When we must rank interests, we can do so on the basis of such differences.

But this, of course, is theoretical. How can we decide *in fact* which organisms have greater intrinsic value? Here again we must generalize from human experience. We know that we are psyches supported by bodies, that some or our own experiences are richer than others, and that complex nervous systems are required for at least the kinds of richness of experience that we find most valuable. While some may propose that energy quanta or living cells enjoy forms of harmony and intensity that are equally if not more valuable than our own, we have no evidence for or against the claim. Lacking such evidence, and given the need for judgment in deciding which lives must be respected in cases of incompatible interests, we must act on the basis of what we do know from human experience. We can make concrete decisions on the basis of two assumptions: (1) that animals with psyches, or monarchies, are able to enjoy greater degrees of experiential richness and self-concern than are organisms without psyches, or democracies, and (2) that monarchies with more complex nervous systems are able to enjoy greater degrees of experiential richness and self-concern than those with simpler nervous systems. The first assumption implies that a dog has greater intrinsic value than a fungus, the second that a dog has greater intrinsic value than a tick.

Concerning these conclusions, however, two words of caution are in order. First, all creatures, monarchies or democracies, organic or inorganic, have some degree of intrinsic value. In a biocentric ethic, the spirit of land, water, and air—and that of single-celled organisms and plants—should be respected. Focused as it is on living beings, a biocentric ethic can and should be informed by an appreciation of the goodness of all creation.

Second, even when living beings are ranked in terms of their intrinsic value, it should be recognized that, from the nonhuman creature's own point of view, its own value is not less than those of other creatures we deem more valuable. As the tick invades the dog, it does not deem itself less worthy of survival than the dog. While in fact its life may matter less to it than does that of the dog to the dog, and its subconscious experiences may be less rich than that of the dog, it does not know this. A tick does not rank itself.

This truth must itself be internalized if humans attempting to practice a biocentric ethic are to avoid arrogance as we rank interests. The need for judgment on the basis of degrees of value must be complemented by reverence for life, and this reverence must itself involve empathy for organisms on their own terms. The practice of empathy can be fostered if it is recognized that such empathy has a cosmic counterpart in God. This is to say that there is an ultimate point of view—a divine perspective—in which each creature is appreciated on its own terms and loved for its own sake. Creatures with lesser intrinsic value may or may not contribute less to the divine perspective than creatures with greater value; in any case they are not loved less. For those interested in a biocentric Christianity, God must be conceived as loving all creatures on their own terms and for their own sakes: the living cell, the mosquito, the pelican, and the human being.

References

Birch, Charles, and John B. Cobb, Jr. 1981. *The Liberation of Life: From Cell to Community.* Cambridge: Cambridge University Press.

Devall, Bill, and George Sessions. 1985. *Deep Ecology.* Layton, Utah: Peregrine Smith Books.

Durell, Lee. 1986. *State of the Ark: An Atlas of Conservation in Action.* New York: Doubleday & Co.

Griffin, Donald. 1984. *Animal Thinking.* Cambridge, Mass: Harvard University Press.

Joranson, Philip N., and Ken Butigan. 1984. *Cry of the Environment: Rebuilding the Christian Creation Tradition.* Sante Fe, N. Mex.: Bear & Co.

Moran, Gabriel. 1987. "Dominion Over the Earth." *Commonwealth* 114(21): 697–701.

Morris, Richard Knowles, and Michael W. Fox, eds. 1978. *On the Fifth Day: Animal Rights and Human Ethics.* Washington, D.C.: Acropolis Books.

Robbins, John. 1987. *Diet for a New America.* Walpole, N.H.: Stillpoint Publishing.

Rollin, Bernard E. 1981. *Animal Rights and Human Morality.* Buffalo, N.Y.: Prometheus Books.

Rolston, Homes, III. 1987. *Science and Religion: a Critical Survey.* New York: Random House.

Thomas, Lewis. 1974. *The Lives of a Cell: Notes of a Biology Watcher.* New York: Viking Press.

10. Everyone Needs a Stone: Alternative Views of Nature _____

Nina Rosenstand

In 1831 the French politician Alexis de Tocqueville visited the United States and expressed a wish to see the American wilderness all Europe was talking about, and it surprised him that few Americans seemed to care much about it. He wrote,

> They are insensitive to the wonders of inanimate nature and they may be said not to perceive the mighty forests that surround them till they fall beneath the hatchet. Their eyes are fixed upon another sight, the . . . march across these wilds, draining swamps, turning the course of rivers, peopling solitudes, and subduing nature.[1]

Although this is certainly not true of all Americans any longer, many people concerned with the state of the environment would say that the attitude still persists today. Here we will explore three different historical approaches to nature: (1) the one that Tocqueville found so appalling, and that I will be calling the "Western" tradition for the sake of convenience; (2) one that is an alternative view within the Western tradition: romantic primitivism; and finally (3) the Native American tradition.[2]

The Western Tradition Before Rousseau

In 1967 the historian Lynn White [Essay 4 in this book] wrote an important paper, "The Historical Roots of Our Ecologic Crisis." In his paper, White suggests that we take a critical look at the Judeo-Christian influence on Western attitudes toward the environment: The world is given to

Reprinted by permission of the author. This essay was written for this volume. Sections of this essay have previously been published in Nina Rosenstand, *The Moral of the Story: An Introduction to Questions of Ethics and Human Nature* (Mountain View, CA: Mayfield Publishing Company, 1994). These sections have been rewritten for this volume.

humans to improve—not for the sake of the world, but for the sake of human beings. Nature is not good in itself, but only good to the extent that it can serve as a tool for human self-improvement. White is not the only, or even the first, person to point this out, but his paper has influenced a great many readers.

To carry White's analysis further, the Judeo-Christian world view is based on the belief in a god who is outside the world, who is creating and affecting that world but not as a part of it—in other words, a god who transcends the world, is beyond it. This translates directly into a view of nature as being godless, empty, possibly just neutral and ready to be worked, or possibly even evil—something that must be subdued.

Is White correct that it is Christianity that is to blame for the attitude that nature is merely there to be used by humans, and has no value in itself? If we must "blame" somebody, we can point a finger at another, the Greek philosopher Plato (427–347 B.C.E.). In Plato's dialogue *Phaedrus,* Socrates him-self Plato's lifelong teacher, says to one of his friends that he never goes outside the city gates of Athens, because trees and countryside have noth-ing to teach him—only the men in the city do. Throughout Plato's writings we learn about the value of the intellect over the senses, and the pri-macy of the life of the soul over the life of the body. To many modern scholars it is partly due to Plato's influence that Christianity, in its early centuries, acquired a disdain for everything physical, both wild nature and human nature. The Greeks them-selves had a deep-rooted fear of their own wild countryside, which they populated with dangerous demons. So did the Romans, for that matter, as well as the Germanic tribes, the Scandinavians, and the English. The wilderness was thought full of spirits and goblins who were up to no good, ones that could rob people of their will to live through only one accidental encounter.

Toward the end of the Roman, and the begin-ning of the Christian, era, the philosopher Plotinus (205–270 C.E.), inspired by Plato, claimed that real-ity consists of the original Divinity spreading out, dividing itself into smaller parts. The smallest parts are individual human souls, but the material world (including nature) is simply nothing, since it con-tains no trace of the divine. The human task is to strive upward to the Divine to experience a total fusion with God, and to leave the evils of the phys-

ical world behind. This view reflects the metaphys-ical idea that evil is really just the absence (*privatio*) of goodness. Thus, the Judeo-Christian tradition is not the only source in the Western tradition for the attitude that nature is by definition an instrument for human use and improvement, and not intrinsi-cally valuable.

In Western art we find this metaphysical and moral view mirrored. Medieval art and lifestyle distinguished between the garden and the wilder-ness, a destination shaped on the model of Genesis. The original garden was the Garden of Eden, and Adam and Eve were banished to the Wilderness, so paradise and wilderness were from ancient times diametrically opposed. In medieval art the culti-vated, enclosed area is beautiful and serene; the lands outside are dangerous and chaotic (which indeed they were, to the traveler in those days). Renaissance art uses nature merely as a backdrop, usually as a symbolic comment to the personality of the person whose portrait is in the foreground. Painters of the seventeenth century begin to put humans in the landscape rather than the landscape behind a person, but with a few exceptions they are pastoral scenes, not scenes of uncultivated wilder-ness. The animals signify goodness and peace when they are depicted as domesticated, danger and temptation when depicted as wild. It is not until the late eighteenth and early nineteenth cen-tury that we see, in European and Euro-American art, depictions of humans dwarfed by a wilderness containing wild animals, as in the paintings of Albert Bierstadt and Thomas Moran.

A final factor needs to be mentioned: the flour-ishing of modern science. For Western science the natural world, including its nonhuman inhabitants, has primarily utilitarian value, and is viewed as a resource, for knowledge or for wealth. Is this per-spective exclusively a result of the historical factors we have discussed, or is there an additional source for this attitude? Today many Western scholars agree that the scientific approach to the environ-ment as a resource was fostered by the philosophy of René Descartes (1596–1650), commonly known as the founder of modern philosophy. Descartes believed that he established a firm ground (an undoubtable proposition) on which to build a new science, by pointing out that although all other things could be doubted, I can't doubt that I exist while I am doubting and thinking. He expressed this certitude in the statement, *Cogito, ergo sum* ("I think, therefore I am"). I can thus be certain that I have a mind that thinks—but only humans can have this certitude, as humans are the only beings endowed with minds, says Descartes. Animals may act as though they have minds, but he believed that they are nothing but automata, robotlike creatures without awareness. Because you need awareness to feel pain, according to Descartes, the conclusion is simple: Animals cannot feel pain. This conclusion, as preposterous as it may seem to modern readers, affected philosophy as well as concrete approaches toward animals and the environment until recent decades. Whereas the Judeo-Christian religious traditions taught that only humans have souls, the disciples of Descartes taught that only humans have minds, and that all other manifestations of nature are merely inert matter, to be used, formed, and developed.

If the traditional Western attitude is that nature is there to be controlled by humans, then it means that controlled nature is morally preferable, while uncontrolled nature is morally unacceptable. We can outline four major aspects of such an attitude.[3]

1. The first aspect is practical: It sees nature as the enemy that has to be conquered. This attitude is probably one of the most basic of all human experiences. It may be largely forgotten by city people over the last century, but it is a powerful experience that most human cultures share somewhere in their history: Nature is dangerous, and full of rocks, crevices, swamps, savage beasts, and outlaws.

2. The second aspect is religious: Humans are the rulers of creation, and their job is to pacify and order the wilderness. It presents a task and a challenge set by God, because before the wilderness acquires a shape given to it by humans, it is nothing, or perhaps even something evil and threatening—it becomes a "something," or something good, only through human control and intervention, through human development.[4]

3. The third is an economic aspect: Nature is valuable only if it can be used to increase aggregated wealth, or to serve humans in some other sense. This view is epitomized in a statement I heard a few years ago that a certain area of chaparral in San Diego ought to be developed because it was "just sitting there, doing nothing."

4. The fourth aspect is psychological: Just as controlled nature is preferable and chaotic nature is undesirable, so too are human passions good if they are controlled, and bad if they are not kept in check; this moral view of human desires is a direct legacy of Platonism, which taught that a good person is one who can control his or her desires. But it is also part of the Christian legacy, which teaches that human beings are good if they look toward God who has created them, and try to live by his rules. If they let themselves live according to their nature, however, then they are lost, because humans are born sinful and must overcome their frail, untrustworthy, lustful nature in order to be good. In today's terminology it translates into a warning against giving in to one's unconscious drives and letting one's feelings reign unchecked.

Rousseau and Romantic Primitivism

The British philosopher David Hume (1711–1776) described a ride through the countryside, quite comfortably within the old traditional view of nature: "The eye is pleased with the prospect of cornfields and loaded vineyards, horses grazing, and flocks pasturing, but files the view of briars and rambles, affording shelter to wolves and serpents."[5]

What fascinated Hume was that we seem to feel a natural attraction for things that are useful to us—we are happy to see the bountiful fields of grain promising good bread, beer, and fodder for animals, vineyards ripe with future bottles of wine, and animals for human use; for Hume (who, by the way, loved a good meal) there was nothing attractive about being reminded of the wilderness, of briars and brambles, of wolves and serpents—because to Hume they were not useful to humans, they had no utilitarian value.[6]

For Hume's colleague and friend, the Swiss philosopher Jean-Jacques Rousseau (1712–1778), nature had a different meaning. Although Rousseau also in his writings talked about the joy at seeing the bounty of the earth, and worshiped God as the creator of natural beauty, he added a new element: Nature is beautiful in its uncultivated form, left untouched since it was created. Rousseau loved to take walks in nature, and described his favorite types of trails: "It is already clear what I mean by fine country. Never does a plain, however beautiful it may be, seem so in my eyes. I need torrents, rocks, firs, dark woods, mountains, steep roads to climb or descend, abysses beside me to make me afraid."[7]

What we have here is an entirely new way of looking at nature—an enjoyment of the wilderness. And not only that: an enjoyment of the wild feelings it inspires. Rousseau actually enjoyed feeling afraid at the edge of a chasm. His precipitous walk in the mountains was thus a far cry from the orderly tour of the fields of grain so enjoyed by Hume.

This new approach toward the wilderness hardly implies that people didn't enjoy nature walks prior to Rousseau. The fourteenth-century Italian scholar Petrarch tells of hiking up a mountain and enjoying the beauty of the landscape before him, but his joy was cut short by his own conscience: In his pocket he carried a copy of St. Augustine's *Confessions,* and when opening the book at random he found himself admonished by the author not to let the contemplation of earthly beauty distract him from the true quest for salvation. So Petrarch immediately hastened to lower ground.[8] However, a traditional Western Christian would ordinarily be able to enjoy nature, but the enjoyment would usually come from seeing nature cultivated, a pastoral landscape, like Hume's joy at seeing the ripening fields. Hume's revulsion at the wilderness was the most common attitude, even in the eighteenth century where the increase in scientific knowledge about the world caused some scientists and others to believe that even uncultivated nature might be beautiful, because it was created by God. But here Rousseau adds that one can have intellectual and emotional enjoyment of the wilderness, partly because it may lead one to appreciate God, but even more because it makes one appreciate the original natural virtue of human beings. What is natural is now understood as something morally superior to what has been altered by humans, and Rousseau implies that humans can learn from the uncorrupted innocence of everything natural and regain some of their own lost innocence.

This view explains the origin of the term "back to nature." For Rousseau, it was an abstract ideal, because humans can't return to nature, or to their own natural past. The best we can do is try to become less cramped by civilization, more attuned to our natural feelings, and more aware of unspoiled nature present in children.

There had, in fact, been others before Rousseau who were interested in unspoiled nature and in those people who live in harmony with nature; this interest is known as "primitivism." Rousseau, however, became the most influential of European primitivists, perhaps because his love of nature was part of a comprehensive anthropological and political theory. Rousseau speculated—without much interest in gathering evidence, true to his time period—that humans originally lived in a paradise-like state of nature. In this state humans were in good health and lived in complete harmony with their environment, primarily because there was not much interaction between people. But eventually humans began to develop ideas about owning land, establishing commerce, and enslaving each other, and that was the beginning of civilization and the end of human bliss.

Rousseau himself was never very consistent about his visions of humans in nature. Sometimes we hear that the true golden age for humans was when they first gathered together in small communities. At other times we hear that the first community was also the first step on the downward slope of civilization. What does remain consistent is his skepticism about the splendors of civilization. A famous passage in an early work by Rousseau tells us that

> When I consider [man], in a word, as he must have left the hands of nature, I see an animal less strong than some, less agile than others; but, all in all, the most advantageously organized of all. I see him satisfying his hunger under an oak tree, quenching his thirst at the first stream, finding his bed at the foot of the same tree that supplied his meal; and thus all his needs are satisfied.[9]

This example of primitivism is also what we call a romantic view of humans in nature, but Rousseau expressed it a generation before Romanticism became popular in the Western world; Rousseau is one important source of inspiration for the Romantic movement of the early nineteenth century with its emphasis on examining one's emotions and displaying them in public.

One of the emotions Rousseau sees as part of the original human in the state of nature is compassion toward others. At this point, Rousseau's view of nature becomes not just a love of the wilderness, but a moral vision of the goodness of the natural and the uncorrupted, in contrast to the long Christian tradition of a belief in nature as neutral or evil, and belief in humans as inherently sinful.[10] For Rousseau humans are good and compassionate by nature, but civilization has corrupted us so we appear to be naturally selfish and easily tempted to do evil—a viewpoint that the British philosopher Thomas Hobbes had introduced to philosophy a century before Rousseau.[11]

This romantic attitude toward nature includes:

1. *The psychological factor:* Emotions are considered more natural than the control of reason and logic—a notion that carries over into the arts and has inspired countless books, paintings, and works of music in the late eighteenth and early nineteenth century.

2. *The ethical factor:* Nature represents moral goodness and innocence, and beings close to nature, such as pretechnological cultures, young children, and animals, become associated with the same sense of goodness and purity.

3. *The historical factor:* The early nineteenth century witnessed a rising European interest in the myths and legends of early European cultures, as well as a romantic admiration for peoples around the world who presumably were in closer proximity to their natural origin, such as the American Indians.

4. *The political factor:* Rousseau's view of nature promoted a theory of democracy based on the assumption that humans are good by nature, and thus can be trusted to govern themselves without having to give away their fundamental right to self-determination, provided that they are continually reminded that greed and selfishness is something added by culture and must be controlled.[12]

To this day, the influence of Rousseau is noticeable. Our preoccupation with everything natural, with products containing no artificial ingredients, and with the "natural look," reveals the legacy of romanticism. We may have modern, scientific reasons for preferring natural to artificial ingredients, for wanting to preserve the wilderness, for saving the earth from pollution, and for reintroducing the wolf in its former habitats, but we may also see these current trends as being part of the legacy left to us by Rousseau.[13]

We may be tempted to pronounce Rousseau "the first modern environmentalist." However, such labeling is acceptable only if we intend to use the term in its anthropocentric meaning.[14] Even though Rousseau affords a view of nature that is utterly opposed to the traditional Western view in many ways, his is not a holistic view,[15] and it is not a sentientist view.[16] In a sense his view is as anthropocentric as the view he opposes, because, in his view, the intrinsic goodness of nature is seen as a guiding light for humans to discover their own nature. Nature may be good in itself because it is untouched, but it is primarily good for humans as a source of emotional and intellectual inspiration for the improvement of humans. As different as Rousseau's primitivism is compared to the traditional Western disdain for, or fear of, nature, it still shares the viewpoint with the Western tradition that nature exists for the sake of humans: Humans are the primary inhabitants of the land, and the land is still a resource, albeit a spiritual one. In addition, the beneficiaries of his philosophy are humans, who are considered so good by nature that they can be allowed to take part in a democracy, provided that they focus on what is good for everybody rather than their own personal preferences.[17]

Metaphysically,[18] the traditional Western attitude, the attitude of romantic primitivism, and the Native American approach are all dualistic, although the traditional Western position gravitates toward a materialistic view. Even if they are all in some sense "dualistic," believing that the material world has a spiritual side to it, the difference lies in where they draw the line between mind and matter. Are humans the only ones endowed with mind, or spirit, or soul, as the Western tradition generally claims, or can there be a spiritual presence in nature also? In order to look at a philosophy of nature that sees nature as inspired, and that can be viewed as holistic, we will turn to the American Indian view.

A Holistic Alternative? The American Indian View of Nature

While Rousseau was developing his theories of natural goodness in Europe, the end of a cultural era was approaching in America—the era of the American Indian culture. As European attention was beginning to focus on the "noble red man" of Rousseau's state of nature, the people who were the focal points of this attention were fighting for their existence. The environmental values of American Indian tribes have themselves acquired a rather mythological status today; they have come to stand for ecological virtue, because it is commonly believed that these tribal people lived in harmony with nature, without abusing their own resources. The American Indian "land ethic" has for some acquired the status of a value system capable of teaching people of the twenty-first century to preserve their endangered environment.

What are the essential characteristics of this land ethic? A sense of kinship with the land and its lifeforms; a belief that spirits reside, not just in humans, or in animals, but in the entire ecosystem; a sense that nature as a whole is sacred, and cannot be regarded as property, or as a thing to be used merely for human purposes. This norm does not imply that the American Indian can't use his or her environment to survive, but it is essential that nature's cooperation is sought before using it: The hunter asks permission of his prey before killing it, and traditionally does not let any part of his kill go to waste. The gatherers and hunters understand about the seasons, and see the natural resources not as theirs by right, but as gifts that must be reciprocated—with other gifts, or with prayers. This approach toward nature can be described with a terminology borrowed from contemporary moral theory: It can be seen as a quest to develop a good character, to become a good member of the community, in other words, to develop a certain set of social and personal virtues. American Indian mythology abounds with stories teaching the people to become better persons, and to learn to respond responsibly to life's challenges, and to develop a sense of gratitude toward life. In these stories, the good person succeeds in the end, while the morally flawed person perishes, and most often the moral flaw shows itself not only in how someone treats another human being but how he or she treats nonhuman animals or spirits.

The American philosopher J. Baird Callicott, coeditor of several works on environmental ethics—including *Earth Summit* (1996)—makes the following comments about American Indian values and the environment: Although there is no unified American Indian belief system, their typical world view does include and support an environmental ethic, contrary to (what Callicott sees as) the exploitative European world view. This environmental ethic can be described as requiring a genuine respect for the welfare of other lifeforms.[19] In contrast to the Western view of nature, which considers earth, rocks, water, and wind to be inert, the American Indian world view sees them as "very much alive," as the Sioux Indian John Lame Deer said. "Every man needs a stone. . . . You ask stones for aid to find things which are lost or missing. Stones can give warning of an enemy, of approaching misfortune."[20] Not just stones, but small and large animals must be listened to, because "they have secrets to tell." Callicott interprets this aliveness of natural entities to mean that they have a share in the same consciousness that we do—not in the Western sense that animals have an instinct or some other form of consciousness that can't be compared with human self-awareness, but that they are of the same kind. How might American Indians reach such a conclusion? From analogy, says Callicott—if I have a body and a spirit, then I assume (because I can't know for certain) that other humans also have a spirit; the American Indian goes on to make the same assumption from analogy about other creatures with whom he or she sees a similarity to himself or herself. Arguments from analogy are notoriously inconclusive, but for many pretechnological cultures this is a common form of reasoning.

For Lame Deer, all creatures, indeed all things, are a part of the Great Spirit. The Great Spirit has split itself up into stones, trees, insects, and other animals, including people; and all flow back to their spiritual source. Contrary to the philosopher Plotinus who also thought the All-Soul had split itself up, the Great Spirit extends even to what Plotinus saw as inanimate matter. This makes a considerable difference, because it means that nature itself is endowed with spirit, and is not inert, empty, or "deprived," as in the traditional Western view. Thus we can label the American Indian approach to the environment holistic, in the sense that it is the balance of all elements in nature that is of importance. This does not preclude an interest in one's own affairs. You talk to the stone to find out things that are useful for you, and perhaps not for the stone. This outlook is holistic in the sense that it views all elements of the environment as irreplaceable parts of a great web that includes everything, rocks as well as humans.

Does this mean that American Indians are "environmentalists," though? Not to Callicott, because that would mean that they would focus on the needs of the environment for the sake of preserving its genetic characteristics. American Indians were not early environmentalists or conservationists, because they did not have that kind of conceptualization—in other words, they didn't think in scientific terms. However, since American Indian values included the world as inspirited, entities in nature were viewed as persons, as part of the social order and the moral community. In Callicott's view, conservation and ecological restraint thus become part of that package without it being a conscious goal.

It is a historical fact that American Indian tribes lived in a quite another relationship with their environment than the settler from Europe.[21] Does this mean that the American Indians were what Rousseau and other romantic primitivists thought they were, people living always in complete harmony with nature? Callicott says yes, in principle, but we can't expect that every individual always lived up to those principles. To the criticism that even among American Indians there have been ecological human-made problems Callicott responds that we should not judge a culture by the greed or ignorance of some individuals, but by the overall philosophy of the culture. Indian culture had an ideal of the elements of nature being interdependent, and ideally such an interdependency was to be respected. Because not everyone respected those ideals is not sufficient reason to denounce American Indian environmental values as fictional.

However, we should be careful not to plunge back into the "noble red man" mythology, because that would just be adding to the many misunderstandings over the years. If we want to truly understand American Indians and their relationship to their environment, we have to recognize that there has been occasional ecological mismanagement among American Indian tribes as well, and not merely the existence of a few selfish people breaking the rules, as Callicott seems to think. Scientists now speculate that part of early Native American history may have involved misuse of resources, such as in the case of the Anasazi tribe of Arizona and New Mexico who abandoned their cliff cities after centuries of occupation. These locations were in all likelihood hit by a severe drought, but there also seems to be evidence that the resources had been depleted, necessitating a move. Also, the hunting practices of the Plains Indians are well known for displaying environmental responsibility: The hunters would not hunt more animals than the tribe could use and process, and no part of the animal would go to waste. However, some scientists speculate that this ecological balance may have been partly due to the fact that the tribes were not very numerous. A larger number of hunters might have resulted in a decline in the animal population. It is now believed that early and well-organized hunting contributed to the extinction of the woolly mammoth in North America and in Eurasia.[22] A dramatic human impact on nature may not always have the traditional Western quest for power and wealth as its motivating force: Religious enthusiasm may also be a factor. The ecological disaster visited on the Pacific people of Easter Island, for example, was apparently brought about by religious fervor: The giant heads we now know as a hallmark of Easter Island may have cost the population their lives as well as their ecology. To transport the heads to their positions by the ocean, a large number of trees had to be cut. Eventually, this led to deforestation on a grand scale, and more: Without trees there were no more canoes for fishing, and without trees the topsoil eroded, agriculture declined, and eventually, with dwindling food resources, the population itself declined. It seems that any human population has the potential for abusing their environment as well as for caring for it and using it in a responsible manner.

Furthermore, just because everything carries a spark of spirit in the American Indian view, doesn't mean that everything in nature is good. It is a Western-style dualism to think of the world as split between good and evil, such as "Spirit is good, physical nature is evil." For the American Indian the spirits in nature have power, and this power can be used for evil as well as for good. If humans can be made friends or foes, so can animals and things. The environment and its inhabitants may indeed be viewed as a moral community, as Callicott claims, but one must remember that when the hunter asks the spirit of the bear for permission to kill it, he does so partly out of respect for the bear, but also because the spirit of a dead, angry bear is dangerous. In other words, you want to live in peace with your neighbors in a high-risk neighborhood. The Sioux Indian view of the cosmogony (creation of the world) involves Mother Earth and Father Sky, and all things are related as their children, but even among siblings there can be enmity. The traditional Navajo (Diné) Indians even today live in a universe of power where any mishap, any accident is not what a Westerner would call a "natural" occurrence, meaning accidental. For the Diné an accident or an illness, or even death is caused by a spirit with evil intent, and since spirits are part of nature, it is in some sense natural. It is a metaphysical dualism, but not like the traditional Western one in which nature consists of matter alone, and humans have spirit in conjunction with matter. For the American Indian everything has two sides to it, a matter side and a spirit side, and good and evil are both a part of the spirit world. The key word is power, not morals. The contemporary traditional Diné has a large number of taboos that he or she is supposed to uphold. The reasons behind the taboo is not always clear, and sometimes they seem to be added by later rationalizations, but these taboos reflect a fundamental sense of connectedness with the nonhuman world. A few examples will have to suffice:[23]

TABOO: Don't bother a coyote that takes the first-born goat or lamb.

EXPLANATION: It is his—keeps order in the world. If he is given the first-born freely, he hopefully will leave the rest in peace.

TABOO: Don't sleep on a piñon shell.

EXPLANATION: It will go into you—you aren't showing respect.

TABOO: Don't break a deer bone while you are eating.

EXPLANATION: You'll have a broken bone.

TABOO: Don't spit out deer meat once it is in your mouth.

EXPLANATION: Next time there won't be any deer.

TABOO: Don't throw deerskin or bones away.

EXPLANATION: They are sacred—you won't have any luck hunting.

TABOO: Don't hang rugs out in the sun.

EXPLANATION: The sun will take it as an insult.

And then there are the down-to-earth recommendations such as:

TABOO: Don't run around while eating corn.

EXPLANATION: It will choke you.

This short excerpt is not representative of Native American cultural taboos as such, nor does it tell us all we need to know about Diné life, but it does show two things of interest: (1) That contemporary Diné continue to have a sense of nature as inspirited, and (2) that while nature is recognized as having a moral standing, these rules are primarily rules of prudence: You ought to behave around powerful spirits, or else your callousness and selfishness will come back to haunt you. Although nature in the American Indian tradition is viewed as intrinsically valuable,[24] this does not preclude the existence of a strong element of human interest: Nature can also be of instrumental value, as long as it is not abused. Getting back to Lame Deer: If everyone needs a stone, it is not primarily for the stone's sake, but for the human's.

The Issue of Personhood

A final theme needs to be explored: Callicott's statement that the traditional American Indian viewed both human and nonhuman animals as persons. What does such a view entail? The question of what makes someone a person is becoming increasingly controversial in today's moral and political debates, because whatever answer we choose will have large-scale consequences. A person is generally supposed to be a human being, but legally, corporations and other groups are referred to as persons. When someone is referred to as a person, more than his or her biological status as a human is implied: What is implied is that someone has special moral status—that she or he counts, morally and legally. Classification as a person is thus not just a description, it is a prescription: It prescribes how someone ought to be treated; in this day and age, it means having inalienable rights. Historically, not all humans have been considered persons: Previous ages have excluded women, slaves, foreigners, people of races different from one's own, children, the infirm, the disabled, the aged—and even though we in the West pride ourselves that we consider all (neonatal) humans as persons with human rights, there are still human multitudes around the world (including Western countries) who, for various reasons, experience problems being recognized as persons.

The German philosopher Immanuel Kant (1724–1804) believed that the criterion for personhood is being rational. Rational beings must never be treated merely as a means to an end, he admonished, but always as ends in themselves.[25] This means that persons should never be treated merely as stepping stones for others' happiness or convenience. Since for Kant rationality is a hallmark of a human being, this criterion meant a dramatic expansion of the moral universe to include all humans regardless of status.[26] However, to a reader of today with an interest in environmental sentientism or holism, this expansion falls far short of what is needed. A wholly anthropocentric approach, Kant's theory leaves no room for nonhuman animals or the environment as such to have any moral standing. Some, like the animal rights activist Tom Regan, choose to expand Kant's concept of rights to include not merely rational beings, but any being who is the subject of a life. This view reflects concern for many animals, but not for the entire environment. Others, like Callicott, turn to the Native American tradition and its view of the environment as a moral community. But in what sense does the American Indian see the environment as a moral community of persons? Since everything is inspirited, personhood can be conferred on rocks, trees, and rivers as well as on coyotes, bears, and humans. And as we have already seen, the traditional Native American does not abstain from using his or her environment, or even from killing other members of the moral community—the deer, the bear, and the buffalo—and as such, the American Indian concept of personhood is rather different from the Kantian tradition. The latter concept of personhood entails a right not to be killed for someone else's purpose. Kant's concept of personhood provides the abstract groundwork for a moral and legal system of rights; the American Indian view of personhood is a concrete response to immediate human concerns. Within the American Indian holistic world view, there is no talk of inalienable rights not to be killed—not for animals, humans, or any other entities. But there is a strong message of respect for all elements of the environment. For those concerned with the environment who are looking for a view where humans have no exalted standing above all others, and where persons in nature must be treated with respect regardless of who or what they are, the American Indian tradition may provide such an alternative. We won't find direct prohibitions against using domesticated animals for food, clothing, and labor, or against hunting, or cutting trees, nor is there any Kantian prohibition against using human beings. However, perhaps the Native American view may not be as far removed from Kant's view as some would have it. Might this outlook not be interpreted as a deep, ancient, practical commitment never to use one another—the entire moral community of human and nonhuman persons—merely as a means to an end?

Notes

1. Alexis de Tocqueville, *Journey to America,* trans. George Lawrence, ed. J. P. Mayer (New Haven, CT: Yale University Press, 1960), p. 33.

2. I will be using not only the term Native American, but also the term American Indian, because I agree with the argument, presented by many people including American Indians, that anybody born in the United States can consider herself or himself a Native American. And since I don't belong to that privileged group myself, being born and raised in Europe, I find that the argument makes much sense.

3. See also: Nina Rosenstand, *The Moral of the Story: An Introduction to Questions of Ethics and Human Nature,* 1st edition (Mountain View, CA: Mayfield, 1994), pp. 387–392.

4. Many environmentally concerned Christians choose to view the theological relationship between humans and nonhuman animals not as a relationship of dominion, but of stewardship: The earth has been given to humans, not merely to be used, but to be cared for. In many ways this resembles the traditional Muslim approach to the environment as taught by the Qu'ran.

5. David Hume, *An Enquiry Concerning the Principles of Morals,* Section II, Part II (Oxford: Oxford Clarendon Press, 1957).

6. What Hume failed to foresee was that, for one thing, many people now feel a natural attraction toward those same briars and brambles, and toward the wolves and serpents evoking the idea of untouched wilderness—and for another, that we today are increasingly willing to acknowledge that briars and brambles, wolves and serpents may indeed have a utilitarian value—perhaps not directly to us, but definitely to the ecosystem.

7. Jean-Jacques Rousseau, *Confessions,* trans. J. M. Cohen (Baltimore: Penguin Books, 1954), p. 167.

8. Sir Kenneth Clark, *Landscape into Art* (New York: Harper & Row, 1979), p. 10.

9. Jean-Jacques Rousseau, *Discourse on the Origin of Inequality,* trans. by Donald A. Cress (Indianapolis: Hackett, 1983), p. 120.

10. This doesn't mean that Rousseau completely broke with the Christian tradition, by the way—he moved back and forth between Protestantism and Catholicism, but at least made the pretense of working within a general Christian framework.

11. For Hobbes humans are by nature focused on self-preservation, and humans living in the state of nature without a strong government to protect us from each other will experience lives that are, in the famous words of Hobbes, "solitary, poor, nasty, brutish, and short." Rousseau comments on Hobbes's negative view of the natural human being that what Hobbes believes to be humans in nature, warring against each other, is actually humans in the first, depressing stage of civilization.

12. See also Nina Rosenstand, *The Moral of the Story,* 1st ed., pp. 387–392.

13. See also Rosenstand, *The Moral of the Story,* 1st ed., p. 390.

14. The term *anthropocentrism* stands for the attitude that the environment has importance only in as much as it is important for human beings. An anthropocentric attitude may entail that one uses the environment without any regard for ecological balance or for the well-being of its nonhuman inhabitants, viewing it as a resource that need not be considered in itself; but it may also entail that one uses the environment with careful forethought for the sake of future generations who will need access to clean water, healthy livestock and disease-resistant plants, as well as access to nature for recreational purposes.

15. *Holism* is also sometimes referred to as biocentrism. A holist is concerned with the welfare and balance of the entire ecosystem—sometimes from the belief that it is somehow "alive," and at other times simply from a concern that living things can't thrive unless the entire environment is in balance.

16. The term *sentientism* means respecting all sentient beings, in other words, all beings who can feel pleasure and pain—who can thrive with a clean environment and who will suffer without it. Today sentience is often taken to mean the same as sapience, ability to think, but the original meaning is the ability to feel pain and pleasure.

17. Rousseau's world of democracy was a male world without room for women, though. Although others in the years before and during the French Revolution argued in favor of women's rights, Rousseau's opinion that men and women were best served by women remaining in the home became the adopted political view of postrevolution France.

18. *Metaphysics:* theory of the nature of being, or reality. We all have a metaphysical approach to reality, the question is just which one. Do we believe our reality, including the environment, just consists of things that can be measured and weighed, matter without any spiritual dimension? Then we are metaphysical materialists. If we think there must also be some kind of a spiritual side to reality, then we are dualists, believing that there is both mind and matter shaping the world we know. And if we think that the world is really an illusion, or can only be accessed as sense perception, or is perhaps one of God's dreams, then we are metaphysical idealists.

19. J. Baird Callicott, "Traditional American Indian and Western European Attitudes Towards Nature," *Environmental Ethics* 4(4) (Winter 1982), p. 294.

20. Ibid., p. 301.

21. Asian settlers actually had much more in common with the Indians, since Asian traditions generally agree that the natural world is populated with spirits, and that uncultivated nature can be the source of inspiration and insight.

22. See also Rosenstand, *The Moral of the Story,* 1st ed., p. 213; *The Moral of the Story: An Introduction to Ethics,* 2nd ed., p. 429.

23. The following taboos are quoted from Ernie Bulow, *Navajo Taboos* (Gallup: Buffalo Medicine Books, 1991). Bulow is not an American Indian, but he has lived among migrant Navajo families in Idaho, and has been a teacher at the Navajo High School at Fort Wingate, New Mexico. The taboos are collected from contemporary Diné students and friends of Bulow.

24. *Intrinsic value:* valuable for its own sake. Instrumental (extrinsic) value: valuable as a tool to achieve something else.

25. This does not imply that we can't use each others' services, as long as we maintain a respectful attitude toward one another.

26. Kant's critics frequently point out that there are severe shortcomings within Kant's concept of personhood, such as his reluctance to see women as fully rational beings, and his lack of provisions for those humans who are not rational. The latter criticism is in some sense met by Kant himself in *Metaphysics of Morals* (First Part, 2nd section, Appendix 2–3) where he introduces an intermediate stage between being a person and being a thing, reserved for humans who are not to be considered wholly autonomous: "Being a person akin to being a thing," such as children who are, in a sense, owned by their parents, and servants who are bound by their contract.

11. Traditional Ecological Knowledge

R. E. Johannes

. . . [U]nless the researcher's objectives are very narrowly defined, questionnaires are not a good tool for eliciting TEK [Traditional Ecological Knowledge—Eds.].

It is generally much more productive to use flexible, open-ended interviews where the informant is encouraged to lead the interviewer, not vice versa. Encouraging an elderly, illiterate fisher to lead the interviewer, as enormously instructive as it can be, is nevertheless not always palatable to, or even imaginable by university-educated fisheries researchers.

Idealizing TEK

As a growing number of researchers demonstrate the importance of TEK and traditional resource management, environmental and social activists have been quick to recognize the powerful rhetorical tool this concept provides. Unfortunately the resulting rhetoric is often misleading.

Activists often use the facts selectively, excluding those inconvenient to their causes. Acknowledging megafaunal overkill, for example, is not a preferred strategy for persuading North Americans to help Indians protect their natural resources. Mentioning Hawaiians' extermination of more than half of their indigenous bird species will not help predispose voters to support Hawaiian land rights.

Nature and religion are more intimately interfused in many indigenous cultures than in the West. Environmental activists often make a convenient but tenuous extrapolation from this by routinely referring to TEK and indigenous attitudes toward nature as "sacred." During (1992, 28–29), for example, says, "amid the endless variety of indigenous belief there is a striking unity on the sacredness of ecological systems." Suzuki and Knudtson (1992) talk about the "sacred ecology" of indigenous peoples. The reader is clearly meant to conflate sacredness here with profound ecological wisdom.

Because of such ploys, the notion of indigenous peoples as environmental paragons living in preternatural harmony with nature has metastasized through the media, and indigenous peoples are now often presented to us as environmentalist role models.

Some would justify this intellectual dishonesty as the lesser of two evils; "doesn't the pursuit of a fairer deal for indigenous peoples and better protection of their natural environments justify engaging in the selective use of information?" they might ask. My response is: arguably—provided you do not get caught—but sooner or later you probably will.

And when people discover that they are being duped in this manner, the damage that is done—the erosion of public trust—not only in the activists and their often worthy causes, but also in the indigenous peoples who have been falsely elevated—can easily outweigh any short-term benefits. In my opinion it is unethical to take that risk.

This urge to select and embellish the facts is not limited to Western environmental activists. Some indigenous people, observing the resonance of such environmental rhetoric among many Westerners today, have adopted it. And this has brought the inevitable temptation to use it to influence the outcomes of resource management or development initiatives so as to favor themselves. For example they may exaggerate the environmental significance of an area being considered for development in order to extract greater concessions from the government or developers.

One type of indigenous environmental embroidery is not so calculated, but it is no less troubling. Prone to embrace and propagate modern myths about themselves, some young urban islanders, remote from their own village-based TEK, earnestly repeat the inflated claims about their people's environmental wisdom promulgated by outside environmental activists.

When professional ecologists wear their environmental activist hats they do not always avoid such selective use of the facts either. And some of their graduate students don't realize how selective the material is with which they are, in some cases, presented.

Social scientists are not blameless either. I have been collaborating enthusiastically with them for two decades and arguing that their increased participation in fisheries research and management is critical. So what I am about to say should not be construed as reflecting any general lack of sympathy with them—quite the contrary.

But the fact remains that they, too, have their taboos. One such taboo prohibits many from acknowledging that there are traditional maladaptations in non-Western cultures—many, in fact. Perhaps in order to minimize the exploitation of their observations by racists—or to avoid being labeled racists themselves—many anthropologists, for example, maintain the fiction that all cultural practices are beyond censure (except Western cultural practices, which often seem to be ranked well beneath the rest).

This raises an especially vexing ethical issue: Should important judgements concerning human behavior be suppressed because they might inflame racism? That's not a subject with an easy answer and I won't even begin to try to address it here except to suggest that perhaps the answer is not generic, but dependent, rather, upon the specific circumstances.

A general respect for others' customs is the mark of a civilized society. But is *unlimited, uncritical* respect civilized? Widespread public discussion of certain clearly maladaptive cultural practices, such as *female genital mutilation,* would seem to have made cultural relativism increasingly less tenable in recent years. Yet it seems to have retained its currency among many anthropologists, including some who address environmental issues.

From the standpoint of environmental sustainability, some islanders' traditional environmental practices have been useless or worse. Prohibiting the hunting of certain species, which is assumed by some anthropologists to be an obvious conservation measure (see McDonald 1977 for examples), may, in fact, have the opposite effect—that is, to put increased pressure on some other, more easily depleted species. For example, as noted above Hawaiians (as well as some other Pacific islanders) prohibited tuna fishing periodically with the notion of protecting tuna stocks.

They thus closed off a functionally unlimited pelagic resource (unlimited, that is, when exploited by traditional means). This inevitably resulted in putting increased fishing pressure on much more vulnerable nearshore reef and lagoon resources.

Unsettling, also, is the uncritical manner with which some anthropologists assume that superstitions and myths concerning the environment embody functional environmental adaptations. Some probably do, but the generalized attribution of environmental utility to such beliefs does not deserve serious scrutiny. Moreover, locally prescribed methods for improving fishing or hunting that focused on propitiating spirits or counteracting the effects of sorcery can divert attention from the real, and sometimes correctable, causes.

Some islander elites have been quick to exploit the cultural relativist stance that they have picked up from anthropologists. They use it not only to warn off outside critics, but also to justify their exploitation to their own people (Lawson 1996). Serious environmental harm is being done in Oceania, most visibly in Melanesia, by island leaders who take advantage of their traditional environmental stewardship responsibilities and allow multinationals in to rip off their people's natural resources. This is best documented in connection with logging (e.g., Barrow and Windup 1998). Colchester (1993) says, for example, of some Papua New Guinea leaders:

> Whereas under traditional circumstances (Papua New Guinea village) leadership was openly accountable and, in the context of frequent inter-tribal war, dependent on the allegiance of clan members, this is no longer so true. Today community leaders are as likely to be in an office in the local administrative center as in the village men's house, and their wealth is more likely to be stashed in a bank in Port Moresby or Singapore than accumulated as pigs, wives, and cowries. As local leadership becomes less and less accountable and responsive to community needs and rights, opportunities for making land use decisions that increase personal gain at the expense of the social and environmental security of the community are widening.

In the same general fashion, fisheries resources in some Pacific Islands have been sacrificed to enrich leaders. For example, exporting live reef food fish to Southeast Asia has become a big industry in recent years. If allowed to proceed without proper controls, it results in severe fish stock depletion as well as other serious environmental and socioeconomic damage (Johannes and Reopen 1995; Johannes and Lam 1999). Cultural relativism impedes efforts to address such practices.

Emboldened indigenous politicians who despoil their islands' natural resource tell critics, "Stay out of this. You don't understand our culture; these actions are in accord with our traditional customs." Yet, as Lawson (1996) points out, members of Pacific Island elites are often among those islanders most out of touch with their own traditions.

Conclusions

I have gone to some lengths here to try to show that, although Pacific Islanders' marine environmental knowledge and practices can be exceptionally valuable, this is only to be expected of people who have depended so heavily for centuries on their marine resources. Moreover, islanders are not, and never were paragons of environmental wis-

dom and virtue. Some of their environmental practices were just as bad as anyone else's worst environmental blunders (provided, of course, that one factors out differences in technological power such that similar blunders in industrialized nations may have far greater environmental consequences). No culture is exempt from such human failings.

The task of those who are concerned with practical environmental issues among indigenous peoples is not to idealize TEK. Nor is it to hide, ignore, or distort it. Rather it is to encourage its possessors to capitalize on its strengths as well as to reduce the effects of its weaknesses. This means:

1. asking indigenous peoples to teach us about their knowledge and practices,

2. teaching them about environmental issues on which Western science throws some useful light, and

3. collaborating with them to combine the insights offered by both perspectives in order to develop better resource management than that based on either indigenous or Western knowledge and practices alone.

12. Why Bad Things Have Happened to Good Creatures _____

David P. Barash

In 1829, Francis Henry Egerton, the eighth Earl of Bridgewater, bequeathed £8,000 to the Royal Society of London to support the publication of works "On the Power, Wisdom, and Goodness of God, as Manifested in the Creation." The resulting Bridgewater Treatises, published from 1833 to 1840, were classic statements of "natural theology," seeking to demonstrate God's existence by examining the natural world's "perfection."

These days, biologists are often inclined, similarly, to cite the extraordinary complexity and near-perfection of living things, but as evidence of the power, wisdom, and the goodness of natural selection, as manifested in evolution. Such gestures are understandable and perhaps even laudable, contributing as they do to a healthy, "gee-whiz" appreciation of the Darwinian process and the organic world. But ironically, they are less useful than one

might think, especially in distinguishing natural selection from its premier alternative (at least among the biologically illiterate): special creation, or, in its barely disguised incarnation, "intelligent-design theory."

The problem is that those same wonders of perfection used by biologists to buttress their confidence in natural selection can also be used by believers in "intelligent design" as evidence for a divine designer. Fortunately, however, the two are in fact discriminable, and some of the most powerful distinctions are provided not by the perfection of living things, but by their imperfection. Thus, it is worth emphasizing that even though natural selection regularly produces marvels of improbability (a living thing is, above all else, tremendously nonrandom and low-entropy), it is necessarily a blundering, imperfect, and unintelligent engineer,

The Chronicle of Higher Education, August 17, 2001, p. B13. Reprinted by permission of the publisher.

as compared with any purportedly omniscient and omnipotent creator. Ironically, it is the stupidity and inefficiency of evolution—its manifold design flaws—that argue most strongly for its material and wholly earth-bound nature.

Natural selection is a mathematically precise process, whose outcome should be—and for the most part is—a remarkable array of "optimal" structures and systems. A naive view therefore assumes that the biological world is essentially perfect and certainly highly predictable, like a carefully orchestrated geometric proof. Or like a billiard game, in which a skilled player can be expected to employ the correct angles, inertia, force, and momentum. And in fact, living things reveal some pretty fancy shooting. Specialists no less than biologically literate amateurs are therefore inclined to applaud, and rightly so.

And so it was that even David Hume—materialist and atheist—marveled at how the parts of living things "are adjusted to each other with an accuracy which ravishes into admiration all men who have ever contemplated them."

But admiration is not always warranted. Gilbert and Sullivan's Mikado sings about "letting the punishment fit the crime," gleefully announcing, for example, that the billiard sharp will be condemned to play "on a cloth untrue, with a twisted cue, and elliptical billiard balls." To a degree not generally appreciated, the organic world contains all sorts of imperfections, and as a result, shots often go awry—not because the laws of physics and geometry aren't valid, or because the player isn't skillful, but because even Minnesota Fats was subject to the sting of reality.

Make no mistake, evolution—and thus nature—is wonderful. The smooth-running complexity of physiological systems, anatomical structures, ecological interactions, and behavioral adjustments are powerful testimony to the effectiveness of natural selection in generating highly nonrandom systems such as the incredible complexity of the human brain, the remarkable lock-and-key fit between organism and environment, the myriad interlocking details of how a cell reproduces itself, extracts energy from complex molecules, and so forth.

But imperfections intrude, and in many ways. For now, let's concentrate on just one dimension and, moreover, on just one species: *Homo sapiens.*

Among evolution's numerous constraints, one of the most vexing, and unavoidable, is history—

the simple fact that living things have not been created *de novo*, but rather have evolved from antecedents. If they were specially and intelligently designed in each case, there is no reason for the designer not to have chosen the optimal pattern in each case; insofar as they are constrained by their past, however, and the products of small incremental steps altogether lacking in foresight, living things are necessarily jury-rigged and more than a little ramshackle.

It might be optimal, for example, if elephants could fly. After all, because of local overpopulation in increasingly threatened game parks, many elephants are undernourished, even starving, but for some reason, they are unable to hover 30 feet above the ground and eat leaves currently beyond their reach. Walt Disney's Dumbo notwithstanding, the evolutionary past of today's pachyderms severely constrains their present and future.

But I promised some human examples.

Consider the human skeleton. Ask yourself, if you were designing the optimal exit for a fetus, would you engineer a route that passes through the narrow confines of the pelvic bones? Add to this the tragic reality that childbirth is not only painful in our species, but downright dangerous and sometimes lethal, owing to occasional cephalo-pelvic disproportion (literally, the baby's head is too large for the mother's birth canal), breech presentation, and so forth. This design flaw is all the more serious given that there is plenty of room for even the most stubbornly misoriented, large-brained fetus to be easily delivered, anywhere in that vast nonbony region below the ribs! And in fact, that is precisely what obstetricians do when they perform a Caesarean section. (This seemingly obvious point was first made, I believe, by George C. Williams, whose book *The Pony Fish's Glow* is a superb source for diverse insights into evolutionary theory, design flaws included.)

It is notable that evolution has altogether neglected the simple, straightforward solution, which would have been for the vagina to open anywhere in the lower abdomen. Instead, it stubbornly and stupidly insisted on threading its way through the ridiculously narrow pelvic ring.

Why? Because human beings are mammals, and therefore tetrapods by history. As such, our ancestors carried their spines parallel to the ground; it was only with our insistence on upright posture that the pelvic girdle had to be rotated, thereby making a tight fit out of what for other mammals is nearly always an easy passage. An engineer who designed such a system from scratch would get a failing grade, but evolution didn't have the luxury of intelligent design. It had to make do with the materials available. (Admittedly, it can be argued that the dangers and discomforts of childbirth were preplanned after all, since Genesis gives us God's judgement upon Eve, that as punishment for her disobedience in Eden, "in pain you shall bring forth children." Might this imply that if Eve had only restrained herself, her vagina would have been where every woman's belly-button currently resides?)

On to men. An especially awkward design flaw of the human body—male and female alike—results from the close anatomical association of the excretory and reproductive systems, a proximity attributable to a long-standing, primitive vertebrate connection, and one that is troubling, not only for those who are sexually fastidious. Thus, although there is no obvious downside to the deplorable fact that the male urethra does double duty, carrying both semen and urine, most elderly men have occasion to regret that the prostate gland is adjacent to the bladder, so that enlargement of the former impinges awkwardly on the latter.

In addition, as human testicles descended—both in evolution and in embryology—from their position inside the body cavity, the vas deferens (which connects the testes to the urethra) became looped around the ureter (which carries urine from the kidneys to the bladder), resulting in an altogether ridiculous arrangement that would never have occurred if evolution could have anticipated the problem and, like an even minimally competent structural engineer, designed male tubing to run in a direct line.

A final example, although plenty more are available: The primitive vertebrate system, still found among some of today's chordates, combined both feeding and respiration (just as excretion and reproduction used to overlap, and still do in many species). Water went in, food was filtered out, and passive diffusion sufficed for respiration. As body size increased, a separate respiratory system was added, but by piggybacking onto the pre-existing digestive plumbing. In consequence, air's access to what became the lungs was achieved only by sharing a common anteroom with incoming food. As a result, people are vulnerable to choking. The Heimlich maneuver is a wonderful innovation, but it would not be needed if evolution only had the foresight to design separate passages for food and air, instead of combining the two. But here as in other respects, natural selection operated by small, mindless increments, without the slightest attention to any bigger picture or anything approaching a wise, benevolent overview.

It must be emphasized that the preceding does *not* constitute an argument against evolution; in fact, quite the opposite! Thus, if living things (including human beings) were the products of special creation rather than of natural selection, then the flawed nature of biological systems, including ourselves, would pose some awkward questions, to say the least. If God created "man" in his image, does this imply that He, too, has comparably ill-constructed knee joints, a poorly engineered lower back, a dangerously narrow birth canal, and ridiculously ill-conceived urogenital plumbing? A novice engineer could have done better. The point is that those and other structural flaws are not "anti-evolutionary" arguments at all, but rather cogent statements of the contingent, unplanned, entirely natural nature of natural selection. Evolution has had to make do with an array of constraints, including—but not limited to—those of past history.

We are profoundly imperfect, deep in our nature. And in those imperfections reside some of the best arguments for our equally profound naturalness.

III

THE OTHER ANIMALS

13. PREVIEW

> The lion looked at Alice wearily, "Are you animal, vegetable, or mineral?" he said, yawning at every other word. "It's a fabulous monster!" the Unicorn cried out, before Alice could reply.
>
> *Lewis Carroll*

> Remote from universal nature, and living by complicated artifice, man in civilization surveys the creature through the glass of his knowledge and sees thereby a feather magnified and the whole image in distortion. We patronize them for their incompleteness, for their tragic fate of having taken form so far below ourselves. And therein we err. For the animal shall not be judged by man. In a world older than ours they move finished and complete, gifted with extensions of the senses we have lost or never attained, living by voices we shall never hear. They are not our brethren, they are not our underlings; they are other nations, caught with ourselves in the net of life and time, fellow prisoners of the splendour and travail of the earth.
>
> *Henry Beston*

> [T]he mental faculties of man and the lower animals do not differ in kind, although immensely in degree. A difference in degree, however great, does not justify placing man in a distinct kingdom.
>
> *Charles Darwin*

Immanual Kant thought that there is something very special about human beings, and that because of this they should never be treated as a mere means; in contrast, in his view it is permissible to so act toward nonhumans, the notable exception in his view probably being any divine being. Other things could be, as we put it today, of great instrumental value and we may have great duties regarding them (such as one's indirect duty not to destroy a sculpture by Rodin, for example). Are all nonhuman animals like that—only of instrumental value? Are they only of value if and when there is some human around who desires them for some reason or another? Or is it only a very deep-seated prejudice that we learn as children that we only have direct duties toward one species on the entire planet? And what would we think of such a claim if the word "species" was replaced with the word "race" or "sex" ("gender" if one prefers)? What is the great gulf that should be regarded as the morally relevant difference between humans and animals, especially between humans and those closest to us in terms of intelligence and psychological capacities? What is it by possession of which one has that special status of being owed a certain respect, or certain duties of nonharm? Surely these are among the most basic questions an environmental ethic must address. We will look carefully at some of the arguments, but first we must clarify some terminology so that we can frame a few central questions in a careful manner.

Let us turn to the concept of moral standing. Quite apart from the question of whether someone has "legal standing," we commonly think that the interest or well-being of certain things (normally, certain organisms) must be positively weighed in deciding what is permissible to do.[1] Thus, it is morally wrong to kill humans for food when one is hungry. Similarly, it seems wrong to cause premature death to young (human) children to achieve the same goal. (Compare a simple taxonomy of the world: division into edibles and inedibles.) However, most people have few reservations about causing premature death to young nonhuman offspring for culinary purposes. The different outlooks presupposed in these latter differential judgments may be couched in terms of *moral standing*. Let us stipulate for anything, *X*,

> *X* has moral standing if and only if the continued existence of *X* or its interests in well-being have positive moral weight.[2]

Explicitly or implicitly, one traditional view, often called the *"anthropocentric* paradigm," answers the basic question

> Which things have moral standing?

by proposing that

> All and only human beings have moral standing.

This latter view, in effect, assumes that the most defensible answer to another question,

> What is the appropriate criterion of moral standing?

Is

> Membership in *Homo sapiens*.

This proposed criterion has several virtues, one of which is reasonable clarity. However, there are hard cases: Does this include human fetal progeny; brain-dead, yet breathing, humans; recently dead humans; anencephalic babies? Also worrisome is what the anthropocentric criterion excludes; based on such a criterion, the well-being of nonhuman animals, nonhuman members or parts of the ecosystem, or even intelligent, "personable," alien beings do not, in themselves, count. If by "natural resource" we mean anything that is not a human being (or part of one), such

things are, based on the view under consideration, mere resources to be used to pursue human goals. This pervasive and traditional outlook has come under sharp attack in the last two decades—as the following essays demonstrate.

Shortly, we shall return to questions about (1) the implications of the anthropocentric criterion of moral standing, and (2) competing criteria. First, however, it is useful to reflect on the relation of duty to the issue of moral standing. If we could settle the issue of what is the appropriate criterion of moral standing, then, in principle, we could ascertain which things have moral standing (technically, the *extension* of "things with moral standing"). Suppose that these difficult problems were resolved. What would be the implications of recognizing that something has moral standing, that its continued existence or interest in well-being have positive moral weight? A plausible answer is that, if so, then we moral agents (those who have the freedom and rational capacities to be responsible for choices) have a presumptive duty not to terminate, or undermine the interest of, those entities with moral standing. If this is right, matters are clarified somewhat. However, most of the important questions are left to be resolved, for reasons that will become clearer as we proceed.

If something lacks moral standing, its well-being just does not morally count (by definition of "moral standing"). However, if something has moral standing, its well-being does count and is the basis of a presumptive duty to that thing. Presumptive duties, however, can be overridden under certain circumstances. Consider that most of us think that ordinary people have moral standing. Thus, we have a presumptive duty not to kill them—roughly, a duty not to kill them in the absence of morally compelling reasons for doing so. Most people, however, think that some killing in self-defense, or in defense of other innocents against aggressors, is morally justifiable. The contrary view, that we have an "absolute" or "categorical" duty never to kill people (those paradigmatic beings with moral standing) is held by few (not even those who talk of the sanctity or infinite value of life or all human life) and is hard to defend rationally. The appeal to what most people think is not a compelling consideration. The more basic point is that even with regard to those paradigms of beings with moral standing (people), there well may be important issues to be decided regarding legitimate treatment of such beings, even if we accept that such beings have moral standing. The moral of this story is twofold:

1. Whether we have a presumptive duty to some entity depends on our settling the dispute over whether it has moral standing.

2. However, even if we settle this dispute, there is still the issue of just what reasons would justify our thwarting the interests of a being with moral standing.

To stress a point, a *necessary* but not *sufficient* condition of formulating an adequate ethical theory (and, hence, an adequate environmental ethic) is determining the most defensible criterion of moral standing. Beyond that, there are other recalcitrant and challenging issues. The issue of moral standing, however, is more basic. Further, it is the one most neglected because, historically, very few writers have questioned the anthropocentric position. Like other deeply entrenched assumptions, it often has functioned as a pair of lenses through which we view and conceptualize the environment—and not as an object itself, something to be subjected to philosophical scrutiny. Let us reflect again on the implications of the anthropocentric viewpoint—and the assumption that all, and only, humans have moral standing. For one with such a view, only the well-being or the lives of humans count. Does this mean that it is all right to burn cats for recreational purposes? Or poison one's pri-

vately owned lake? Or blow up a small planet to entertain those with astronomical curiosities? Or fertilize our gardens with the cadavers of those who died natural deaths (and, perhaps, earlier voiced no objection)? Or, if I knew that I was the last person on earth, would it be all right for me to trigger (if I could) all the nuclear weapons already in place—when I was ready to say "farewell," of course? After all, according to one view the well-being of all, and only, humans count. The answer to these questions (except perhaps the last one), according to the anthropocentric view, surely is: not necessarily.

To explain, or call to mind, why not, it is useful to consider further the distinction between (1) duties to something, and (2) duties regarding something. If a person has moral standing, then one has a presumptive duty not to harm that person. Suppose that nonliving things lack moral standing—as the anthropocentric paradigm implies. Then a car lacks moral standing. One cannot have duties to it, since one can have (direct) duties only to (or toward) entities with moral standing. Still, the anthropocentric view reasonably can account for why it is wrong to destroy another's car without that individual's consent. Were one to do so, it would damage the legitimate interests of a being with moral standing, namely, the owner. Hence, one has duties regarding another's car (for example, not to destroy it) even though its well-being in itself does not count; that is, it lacks moral standing. In principle, then, even though the anthropocentric criterion of moral standing excludes everything nonhuman (mountains, penguins, real or plastic trees, blue whales, and so on) from possessing such standing, humans have certain duties to protect or not harm the nonhuman "furniture of the earth." A key feature, of course, is that according to this view any such duties will obtain only if they are derivative from duties we have toward human beings. Some writers make this (or a similar) point in terms of *intrinsic* versus *extrinsic* value. Certain things, human beings (their existence or their well-being), for example, are thought to be valuable in themselves, or intrinsically valuable; hence, certain duties are owed to them. In contrast, other things are thought to lack intrinsic value, and if valuable at all, they are valuable only if valued by beings that are intrinsically valuable. According to such views, duties regarding certain things, or values being assigned to them, are contingent on their being valued by, or being objects whose existence is in the legitimate interest of, beings with moral standing. That certain animals, for example, are extrinsically valuable (so are humans) is noncontroversial. That no duties are owed to animals, that they lack intrinsic value, is not noncontroversial. Similar points may be proposed about mountains, oceans, redwood trees, and marshes. Such claims are among the central sources of contention in environmental ethics.

So far, we have focused on only one proposed criterion of moral standing, albeit a pervasive and influential one: membership in *Homo sapiens*. As several of the selections to follow make clear, other views have been proposed as more defensible. A list of some of the leading views among them would include the following (or some combination):

1. Personhood

2. Potential personhood

3. Rationality

4. Linguistic capacity

5. Sentience

6. Being alive

7. Being an integral part of an ecosystem

8. Being an ecosystem

Generally, the different criteria will select out different sets of beings (or entities) as possessing moral standing; some of the criteria clearly are more inclusive than others. Those who, like Albert Schweitzer (twentieth-century Christian physician and talented

organist), would try to maneuver a housefly outside rather than kill it may be committed to, or presuppose, criterion 6. Criterion 7 promises to be even more inclusive since, according to this view, even things that are not alive (for example, a mountain) may be part of an ecosystem. Some people, of course, are inclined toward vitalism, which we understand as asserting that all things are, in some sense, alive. Others would insist that at least the earth's surface and atmosphere, the biosphere, should be thought of as a dynamic, living system—even like a gigantic, somewhat diffuse organism. In recent years, atmospheric chemist James Lovelock, in his book *Gaia*, has argued that the earth's biosphere behaves like "a single organism, even a living creature." This view revives, after a fashion, the predominant ancient conception of the earth as a goddess, as alive and a fitting referent of the expressions "sister" or "earth mother," used by both Plato and St. Francis of Assisi.

Some contemporary environmentalists think it no small matter, and indeed of the greatest consequence, that a shift occurred (about the time of Descartes and Newton) in the seventeenth and eighteenth centuries from the concept of the earth as alive, as a generous parent, to the concept of its being an object, a wound-up clock to be tinkered with instead of affectionately tended by humans. Evidently, the implications of being alive as the criterion of moral standing will vary depending on what is viewed as being alive. In contrast, as we noted earlier, the famous English utilitarian Jeremy Bentham defended sentience as the criterion of moral standing. Thus, in his view the central question is whether a being can suffer or experience satisfaction—is it sentient? (criterion 5)—not whether it can reason (criterion 3), can use language (criterion 4), or is simply alive (criterion 6). In a possibly ambiguous passage, the famous seventeenth-century French philosopher and mathematician René Descartes seems to have taken the view that nonhuman animals lack linguistic capacity and, therefore, lack a mental-psychological life. Thus, animals are not sentient. If so, of course, they cannot be caused pain—appearances to the contrary. Hence, there could be no duty not to cause them pain. In Cartesian language they are mere automata; in modern language they are like programmed robots. Thus, if Descartes is right—even if sentience is the most defensible criterion of moral standing—then nonhuman animals cannot have such standing. Some people may side with Descartes in his denial of sentience to (any) animals, but his view seems indefensible. Many animals, after all, exhibit physiological and behavioral responses similar to those of humans and possess developed central nervous systems whose presence is normally sufficient for us to infer the presence of pain and pleasure in others. Darwin considered Cartesian skepticism on this issue irrational.

It is worth noting that the criterion of sentience would not only include certain animals (those that are sentient; contrary to Descartes, we assume many are) but also exclude non-sentient humans. But which humans are not sentient? Possibly the irreversibly comatose, some anencephalic (brainless or partly brainless) babies, first-trimester fetuses, and perhaps those of later fetal stages as well. In any case, the class of sentient creatures certainly does not coincide with the class of members of *Homo sapiens*. At least three reasons may be offered for accepting sentience, as opposed to membership in our species, as the most defensible criterion of moral standing: (1) drawing the line around our own species is entirely arbitrary—much like what, in effect, the racist or sexist does in favoring his or her own race or gender; (2) it is implausible that some humans, for example, the irreversibly comatose, have moral standing; and (3) if suffering is an evil that, in the absence of other morally relevant considerations, ought to be prevented, it is arbitrary to regard only human suffering as an evil. These points are some-

what controversial; we note them here merely to hint at some of the debates that are part of the current reassessment of our dealings with animals. They are discussed in later essays.

Criterion 4, linguistic capacity, finds few defenders today. Even if it were the most defensible criterion of moral standing, two implications are of interest. First, it would imply that certain very seriously retarded humans lack moral standing. That we have no presumptive duties to such beings is a view many find repugnant. Second, a plausible case can be made that some nonhuman primates (at least) satisfy this condition—given the success in teaching Ameslan (American Sign Language) to certain gorillas and chimpanzees. Whether certain animals possess linguistic competence is a matter of current dispute, mainly because of conceptual disagreement over what counts as "possessing a language."

Criterion 3 is somewhat obscure also. What counts as being rational? If rationality is construed in a nonstringent fashion, it is likely that many animals will satisfy the condition (though not rocks, rivers, coral reefs, or ecosystems). If the concept of rationality is construed stringently, although it *may* exclude all animals it is likely to exclude certain humans as well, for example, the severely retarded. Those who accept the sentience criterion or the anthropocentric one will find this an intolerable implication. Some philosophers who regard rationality as the proper criterion (as do some who accept sentience) do not hesitate to conclude that some members of *Homo sapiens* lack moral standing. Others, finding this implication repugnant, seek to avoid it by defending other proposals. According to one view, if something is a member of a species whose paradigm members (for example, normal adult members) are rational, then any member is classifiable as a rational creature. Thus, although no one would say of a human zygote (fertilized egg) that it can reason, in the 1980s, Alan Donagan, for example, viewed it as a rational creature, and, hence, deserving of the respect owed to rational creatures. According to this view, of course, it is clear that actual possession of the (allegedly) crucial trait, rationality, is not judged necessary for moral standing.

Donagan's view, for a reason to be noted, should be contrasted with various "potentiality principles." Suppose, for example, one were to propose that "actual rationality or potential rationality" (either trait or both) is the proper criterion of moral standing. On this criterion, normal persons, infants, and embryos (maybe zygotes too) have moral standing. Embryos would have it, of course, because of their potential to become actually rational. On this criterion, however, an anencephalic infant is not potentially rational, and thus lacks moral standing. On Donagan's criterion, in contrast, it (probably) possesses moral standing. So, Donagan's extension of moral standing (although he does not employ this terminology) to "marginal members" of *Homo sapiens* diverges from potentiality principles.

It is tempting to think that, although neonates or fetuses lack rationality or certain other complex psychological characteristics, they (or most of them) directly are owed some duties, and, hence, to presuppose that they possess moral standing. Further, it is tempting to think that such standing is possessed because of their prospect of developing into beings who uncontroversially are agreed to have standing, namely, normal persons. Some claim that although certain adult primates may exhibit "more personality" or have capacities for rational choice not possessed by neonatal humans, a reason for attributing moral standing to such humans but not to such primates is that the former have a unique potential that the latter do not. According to this line of thought, it may not be thought that membership in *Homo sapiens* as such is the proper criterion of moral standing; rather, it is actual or potential personhood (or rationality

according to a variant view). This criterion tends to include virtually all humans (though not the most severely retarded, anencephalic infants, or those in persistent vegetative states) but probably no animals—at least if the facts support the claim that no animals are rational or none exhibit the requisites of personhood. Such a view contrasts with the anthropocentric criterion; it also allows the possibility that nonhumans (for example, possible alien creatures; consider "E.T.") possess moral standing.

In spite of the intuitive appeal of regarding a creature's potentiality as morally significant, some deny its relevance. We note one objection here. Suppose that a *sufficient* condition for possessing moral standing is that an entity, X, possesses a certain trait (P), that is, is a person. Let MS stand for "moral standing." Then the supposition is that

1. For any X, if X has P, X has MS.

Defenders of the importance of potential personhood seem to assume that

2. For any X, if X potentially has P, X has MS.

Opponents of (2) wonder why we should accept (2). Claim (2) does not follow from (1). Nor does (2) follow from the weaker claim (3):

3. For any X, if X potentially has P, X potentially has MS.

To be less formal, consider some related examples. Although an acorn potentially is an adult oak tree, and adult oak trees are large, acorns are not large. Normal adult persons, it is commonly held (at least in the Western world), have a right to decide whom to vote for; human zygotes are (generally) potential normal adults, but they, arguably, lack the right in question. Even though we may agree that a certain morally important trait (for example, having certain rights) is possessed by an entity in virtue of its having certain actual properties (for example, being an adult person), why think that an entity that only has the potential for these properties has the relevant trait? To press the point, infants are potentially adults. Actual adults (normally) have a right to vote. Why attribute such a right to the infant? Its potential adulthood does not seem a good reason. In short, there is a puzzle as to why potential possession of relevant properties is morally significant as opposed to actual possession. Getting clear about these matters is no easy task; here we call attention only to one source of contention. Further inquiry is in order.

Another perspective is worth noting here. One might think that the most stringent duties of all are directly owed to persons (in the psychological as opposed to the biological interpretation) and yet other entities, say the merely sentient ones, also possess moral standing. Thus, one might think that there is a sort of moral hierarchy of entities; for example, all and only sentient creatures have moral standing but among those with such standing, the well-being or lives of some morally count more heavily than others. Thus, although there is a presumption against destroying or causing pain to any sentient creature, in certain conflicts of interest between persons and the merely sentient it is all right (or obligatory) to sacrifice the interest of the latter. If a baboon heart or liver can be transplanted to a human to save the latter's life (but the baboon will die), it is, according to this view, proper that the transplant be carried out. Even some staunch advocates of animal liberation or animal rights (for example, Peter Singer or Tom Regan) seem to accept this judgment. Why it should be accepted is, however, a matter of considerable controversy. If one is to include both persons and others (say, the merely sentient) within the moral community but one views some as, in some sense, second-class citizens, serious perplexities arise. Is there a nonarbitrary basis for such differentiations within the set of beings possessing moral standing? If so, what is it? And if rationality, for example, is invoked, will that not suggest that we can, or ought to, discriminate (differentiate) among humans—according to possession (or not) of rationality (or even degrees of rationality)? Further, does such a view open the door to, or commit one to, a policy of invidious discrimination? If not, why not?

In discussing the question of what sorts of entities have moral standing we have focused on individuals. Some think that the real locus of value is in ecosystems or networks of life and that at the very least the focus on lives of individuals is misplaced and wrongheaded. The view of "holists" on this matter does not seem entirely clear, but one possible interpretation (call it *Extreme Holism*) is that the value of individuals is derivative from and dependent on its value to some larger network. Thus individuals seem replaceable and perhaps only of instrumental value; there is a similar worry about the value of individuals in the view of utilitarians in that the principle of utility would require the elimination of individuals if they can be replaced by others whose existence would contribute more to the total sum of utility. Another possible form of holism (call it *Moderate Holism*) would hold that both the relevant individuals and the relevant systems possess moral standing; with this latter view the value of the individuals would not be merely derivative.[3]

In the twenty-first century, it is astonishing that there is such wide range of disagreement about whether nonhuman animals have mental capacities, whether any are sentient or act purposively, or any possess a language. The first selection in this part, Essay 14, by Frans de Waal, "Good Natured," provides us with some results of recent scientific studies of animal behavior. Various issues arise here: our similarities to certain animals, animal capacities for sympathy, the origins of altruism and morality—indeed matters that fundamentally affect our understanding of ourselves as a species on this planet, human origins, and just what is a scientifically informed view of nature and other living creatures. Then we turn to the famous essay (15) "Animal Liberation," by Peter Singer (his later well-known book has the same title) in which he sketches out the utilitarian based case for the view that we have duties at least to all sentient creatures and we are, therefore, unjust in much of our treatment of animals, especially in our imposition of pain (as opposed to death) on them in the context of our use of them both in scientific experiments and in their plight on factory farms.[4] Singer has little to say (and did not intend to) in that essay about how we should think about ecosystems or questions of preserving biodiversity. From the standpoint of some advocates of an environmental ethic, there is an important distinction to be made between domestic and wild animals. For example, philosopher J. Baird Callicott has claimed that "From the perspective of the land ethic a herd of cattle, sheep, or pigs is as much or more a ruinous blight on the landscape as a fleet of four-wheel-drive off-road vehicles."[5] In contrast, the wild—domestic distinction is not regarded as having any particular significance in the position of Singer, or in that of Tom Regan.

Regan, in "The Case for Animal Rights" (Essay 16) sets out a case for the view that we must radically alter our treatment of animals and that the appropriate view of things is one in which we recognize that (many) animals have rights. In this respect he rejects the assumption that the utilitarian theory provides an acceptable approach to deciding how we ought to treat animals. He calls for a complete halt to scientific experimentation on animals.

In "Interspecific Justice" (Essay 17), Donald VanDeVeer argues that it is fruitful to recognize diverse sorts of conflicts of interest that may exist between humans and animals, and a key task is to figure just what are permissible or obligatory ways of resolving such conflicts of interest. It is one thing to consider killing an elephant to make ivory piano keys, and another to experiment on a limited number of primates to find a cure for AIDS; his essay is critical at points of the positions of both Singer and Regan. In some contrast, Gary Varner's recent essay (18), "The Prospect for Consensus and Convergence in the Animal Rights Debate," searches for, and finds, some common ground among nonanthropocentric philosophical disputants over the status of animals.

The main focus of many "animal liberationists" is on sentient animals; hence it is useful to think about the little, probably nonsentient, creatures that we so often ignore, ones that have at least an enormously instrumental value to the ongoing dynamic of life on earth. Edward O. Wilson in Essay 19, "The Little Things That Run the World," explains why. Should we think of them as beyond the moral pale—in the sense that they should be judged as lacking moral standing—even if they have enormous value as parts of ecosystems? The following "Sidelight" suggests that thinking about classes of living things in isolation from one another is seriously myopic and is conducive to foolish public policy.

NOTES

1. Some people in a country (for example, illegal aliens) may have no legal standing as citizens; that is, they may enjoy none (or few) of the constitutional protections guaranteed to those who enjoy the status of citizens. For certain purposes, at least, they are not owed certain legal duties, and they lack certain legal rights. To have the legal standing of being a citizen, then, is to be regarded as a being whose interests must be positively weighed in governmental decisions about what may be done. The state is thought to have at least a presumptive duty not to disregard or subvert the basic interests (say, in continued life, bodily integrity, or freedom of movement) of one who possesses legal standing. That these interests must be given positive weight in the decision making of others is a point usually implicit in claims that such interest bearers have rights or that we owe them certain duties.

2. To give positive moral weight to the interests of the being is, roughly, to give those interests favorable and proper weight in one's deciding what one ought to do.

3. We are indebted to one of our reviewers for suggesting this useful distinction.

4. In an analytic fashion, Mary Midgley, in *Animals: Why They Matter*, calls attention to the fact of our living in communities of mixed species and that for many the presence of animals is like that of kin; we have ongoing relationships with animals. They have names. It is contrary to much of our experience to think of (many of) them as men: commodities, or "crops" to be harvested.

5. J. Baird Callicott, "Animal Liberation: A Triangular Affair," *Environmental Ethics* 2(4) (Winter 1980), 311–338.

14. Good Natured—The Origins of Right and Wrong in Humans and Other Animals

Frans de Waal

In addition to being human, we pride ourselves on being *humane*. What a brilliant way of establishing morality as the hallmark of human nature—by adopting our species name for charitable tendencies! Animals obviously cannot be human; could they ever by humane?

If this seems an almost-rhetorical question, consider the dilemma for biologists—or anyone else adopting an evolutionary perspective. They would argue that there must at some level be continuity between the behavior of humans and that of other primates. No domain, not even our celebrated morality, can be excluded from this assumption.

Not that biologists have an easy time explaining morality. Actually, there are so many problems with it that many would not go near the subject, and I may be considered foolish for stepping into this morass. For one thing, inasmuch as moral rule represents the power of the community over the individual, it poses a profound challenge to evolutionary theory. Darwinism tells us that traits evolve because their bearers are better off with them than without them. Why, then, are collective interests and self-sacrifice valued so highly in our moral systems?

Debate of this issue dates back a hundred years, to 1893 when Thomas Henry Huxley gave a lecture on "Evolution and Ethics" to a packed auditorium in Oxford, England. Viewing nature as nasty and indifferent, he depicted morality as the sword forged by *Homo sapiens* to slay the dragon of its animal past. Even if the laws of the physical world—the cosmic process—are unalterable, their impact on human existence can be softened and modified. "The ethical progress of society depends, not on imitating the cosmic process, still less in running away from it, but in combating it."[1]

By viewing morality as the antithesis of human nature, Huxley deftly pushed the question of its origin outside the biological realm. After all, if moral conduct is a human invention—a veneer beneath which we have remained as amoral or immoral as any other form of life—there is little need for an evolutionary account. That this position is still very much with us is illustrated by the startling statement of George Williams, a contemporary evolutionary biologist: "I account for morality as an accidental capability produced, in its boundless stupidity, by a biological process that is normally opposed to the expression of such a capability."[2]

In this view, human kindness is not really part of the larger scheme of nature: it is either a cultural counterforce or a dumb mistake of Mother Nature. Needless to say, this view is extraordinarily pessimistic, enough to give goose bumps to anyone with faith in the depth of our moral sense. It also leaves unexplained where the human species can possibly find the strength and ingenuity to battle an enemy as formidable as its own nature.

Several years after Huxley's lecture, the American philosopher John Dewey wrote a little-known critical rejoinder. Huxley had compared the relation between ethics and human nature to that between gardener and garden, where the gardener struggles continuously to keep things in order. Dewey turned the metaphor around, saying that gardeners work as much with nature as against it. Whereas Huxley's gardener seeks to be in control and root out whatever he dislikes, Dewey's is what we would today call an organic grower. The successful gardener, Dewey pointed out, creates conditions and introduces plant species that may not be normal for this particular plot of land "but fall within the wont and use of nature as a whole."[3]

I come down firmly on Dewey's side. Given the universality of moral systems, the tendency to develop and enforce them must be an integral part of human nature. A society lacking notions of right and wrong is about the worst thing we can imagine—if we can imagine it at all. Since we are moral beings to the core, any theory of human behavior that does not take morality 100 percent seriously is bound to fall by the wayside. Unwilling to accept this fate for evolutionary theory, I have set myself the task of seeing if some of the building blocks of morality are recognizable in other animals.

Although I share the curiosity of evolutionary biologists about *how* morality might have evolved, the chief question that will occupy us here is *whence* it came. . . . Do animals show behavior that parallels the benevolence as well as the rules and regulations of human moral conduct? If so, what motivates them to act this way? And do they realize how their behavior affects others? With questions such as these, the book carries the stamp of the growing field of *cognitive ethology:* It looks at animals as knowing, wanting, and calculating beings. . . .

Biologicizing Morality

Social inclusion is absolutely central to human morality, commonly cast in terms of how we should or should not behave in order to be valued as members of society. Immoral conduct makes us outcasts, either here and now or—in the beliefs of some people—when we are turned away from the gates of heaven. Universally, human communities are moral communities; a morally neutral existence is as impossible for us as a completely solitary existence. As summed up by Mary Midgley, a philosopher, "Getting right outside morality would be rather like getting outside the atmosphere."[4] Human morality may indeed be an extension of general primate patterns of social integration, and of the adjustment required of each member in order to fit in. If so, the broadest definition of this book's theme would be as an investigation into how the social environment shapes and constrains individual behavior.

No doubt some philosophers regard morality as entirely theirs. The claim may be justifiable with regard to the "high end" of morality: abstract moral rules can be studied and debated like mathematics, almost divorced from their application in the real world. According to child psychologists, however, moral reasoning is constructed upon much simpler foundations, such as fear of punishment and a desire to conform. In general, human moral development moves from the social to the personal, from a concern about one's standing in the group to an autonomous conscience. While the early stages hardly seem out of reach of nonhuman animals, it is impossible to determine how close they get to the more rational, Kantian levels. Reliable nonverbal signs of thought in humans do not exist, and the indicators that we sometimes do use (staring into the distance, scratching the head, resting the chin on a fist) are commonly observed in anthropoids. Would an extraterrestrial observer ever be able to discern that humans ponder moral dilemmas, and if so, what would keep that observer from arriving at the same conclusion for apes?

Biologists take the back door to the same building that social scientists and philosophers, with their fondness for high-flung notions, enter through the front door. When the Harvard sociobiologist E. O. Wilson twenty years ago proclaimed that "the time has come for ethics to be removed temporarily from the hands of the philosophers and biologicized,"[5] he formulated the same idea a bit more provocatively. My own feeling is that instead of complete reliance on biology, the best way to generate fresh air is simultaneously to open both front and back doors. Biologists look at things in a rather functional light; we always wonder about the utility of a trait, on the assumption that it would not be there if it did not serve some purpose. Successful traits contribute to "fitness," a term that expresses how well adapted (fitted) an individual is to its environment. Still, emphasis on fitness has its limitations. These are easily recognized when

Figure 1 Evolutionary tree showing the main branches of the primate order: the New World monkeys, the Old World monkeys, and the hominoid lineage that produced our own species. This diagram reflects recent advances in DNA analysis that place the African apes (gorillas, chimpanzees, and bonobos) much closer to humans than previously thought.

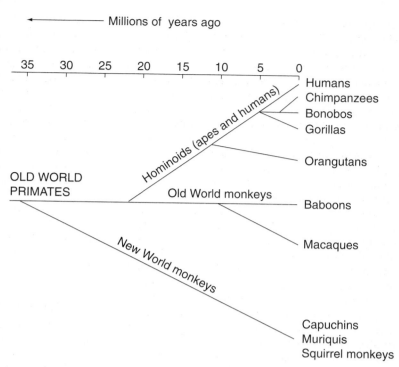

paleontologists hold up the fossil remains of an ancestor who could barely walk, declaring it a defining moment in human prehistory when the unfit began to survive.

To understand the depth of these limitations, one need only realize the influence of Thomas Malthus' essay on population growth that appeared at the beginning of the nineteenth century. His thesis was that populations tend to outgrow their food supply and are cut back automatically by increased mortality. The idea of competition within the *same* species over the *same* resources had immediate appeal to Charles Darwin, who read Malthus; it helped bring his Struggle for Existence principle into focus.

Sadly, with these valuable insights came the burden of Malthus' political views. Any help one gives the poor permits them to survive and propagate, hence negates the natural process according to which these unfortunates are supposed to die off. Malthus went so far as to claim that if there is one right that man clearly does *not* possess, it is the right to subsistence that he himself is unable to purchase with his labor.[6]

Although Darwin appears to have struggled more with the moral implications of these ideas than most of his contemporaries, he could not prevent his theory from being incorporated into a closed system of thought in which there was little room for compassion. It was taken to its extreme by Herbert Spencer in a grand synthesis of sociology, political economy, and biology, according to which the pursuit of self-interest, the lifeblood of society, creates progress for the strong at the expense of the inferior. This convenient justification of disproportionate wealth in the hands of a happy few was successfully exported to the New World, where it led John D. Rockefeller to portray the expansion of a large business as "merely the working-out of a law of nature and a law of God."[7]

Given the popular use and abuse of evolutionary theory (comparing Wall Street to a Darwinian jungle, for example), it is not surprising that in the minds of many people natural selection has become synonymous with open, unrestricted competition. How could such a harsh principle ever explain the concern for others and the benevolence encountered in our species? That a reason for such behavior does not follow readily from Darwin's theory should not be held against it. In the same way that birds and airplanes appear to defy the law of gravity yet are fully subjected to it, moral decency may appear to fly in the face of natural selection yet still be one of its many products.

Altruism is not limited to our species. Indeed, its presence in other species, and the theoretical challenge this represents, is what gave rise to *sociobiology*—the contemporary study of animal (including human) behavior from an evolutionary perspective. Aiding others at a cost or risk to oneself is widespread in the animal world. The warning calls of birds allow other birds to escape a predator's talons, but attract attention to the caller. Sterile castes in social insects do little else than serve food to the larvae of their queen or sacrifice themselves in defense of their colony. Assistance by relatives enables a breeding pair of jays to fill more hungry mouths and thus raise more offspring than otherwise possible. Dolphins support injured companions close to the surface in order to keep them from drowning. And so on.

Should not a tendency to endanger one's life for someone else be quickly weeded out by natural selection? It was only in the 1960s and 1970s that satisfactory explanations were proposed. According to one theory, known as *kin selection*, a helping tendency may spread if the help results in increased survival and reproduction of kin. From a genetic perspective it does not really matter whether genes are multiplied through the helper's own reproduction or that of relatives. The second explanation is known as *reciprocal altruism*; that is, helpful acts that are costly in the short run may produce long-term benefits if recipients return the favor. If I rescue a friend who almost drowns, and he rescues me under similar circumstances, both of us are better off than without mutual aid.

Wilson's *Sociobiology: The New Synthesis* summarized the new developments. It is an influential and impressive book predicting that all other behavioral sciences will one day see the light and convert to the creed of sociobiology. Confidence in this future was depicted in an amoebic drawing with pseudopods reaching out to devour other disciplines. Understandably, nonbiologists were piqued by what they saw as an arrogant attempt at annexation; but also within biology, Wilson's book provoked battles. Should Harvard be allowed to lay claim to an entire field? Some scientists preferred to be known as behavioral ecologists rather than sociobiologists, even though their theories were essentially the same. Moreover, like children ashamed of their old folks, sociobiologists were quick to categorize earlier studies of animal behavior as "classical ethology." That way everyone could be sure that ethology was dead and that we were onto something totally new.

Sociobiology represents a giant stride forward; it has forever changed the way biologists think about animal behavior. Precisely because of their power and elegance, however, the new theories have lured some scientists into a gross simplification of genetic effects. Behavior that at first sight does not conform to the framework is regarded as an oddity, even a mistake. This is best illustrated by a single branch of sociobiology, which has gotten so caught up in the Malthusian dog-eat-dog view of the world that it sees no room for moral behavior. Following Huxley, it regards morality as a counterforce, a rebellion against our brutish makeup, rather than as an integrated part of human nature.[8]

Calvinist Sociobiology

At the Yerkes Regional Primate Research Center, one chimpanzee has been named Atlanta and another Georgia. It is impossible for me to forget where I am, as I see both individuals on a daily basis. I moved to the Star of the South, as the city likes to call itself, to resume my study of the species that surpasses every other when it comes to similarity to our own. My tower office has a large window that overlooks the outdoor enclosure of twenty chimpanzees. The group is as close-knit as any family can be; they are together day and night, and several of the adults were born into the colony. One of these is Georgia, the rascal of the group. Robert Yerkes, a founder of primatology, once declared it "a securely established fact that the chimpanzee is not necessarily utterly selfish."[9] From everything I know about Georgia, she is not the sort of character Yerkes had in mind when he made that declaration six decades ago.

When we provision the colony with freshly cut branches and leaves from the forest around the field station, Georgia is often the first to grab one of the large bundles, and one of the last to share it with anybody else. Even her daughter, Kate, and younger sister, Rita, have trouble getting food. They may roll over the ground, screaming in a pitiful tantrum, but to no avail.

No, Yerkes must have thought of individuals such as Mai, an older high-ranking female, who shares quite readily not only with her children but also with nonrelatives, young and old. Or he may have thought of adult male chimpanzees, most of whom are remarkably generous when it comes to food distribution.

While a distinction between sharing and keeping means a lot in human society, it is sometimes lost in the language of a particular brand of sociobiology that takes the gene as absolute king. Gene-centric sociobiology has managed to reach a wide audience with its message that humans and other animals are entirely selfish. From this standpoint, the only difference between Mai and Georgia is in the *way* they pursue self-interest; whereas Georgia is just plain greedy, Mai shares food so as to make friends or receive return favors in the future. Both think only of themselves. In human terms, this interpretation amounts to the claim that Mother Teresa follows the same basic instinct as any inside trader or thief. A more cynical outlook is hard to come by.

Gene-centric sociobiology looks at survival and reproduction from the point of view of the gene, not the individual. A gene for bringing home food for one's children, for example, will ensure the survival of individuals likely to carry the same gene.[10] As a result, that gene will spread. Taken to its logical extreme, genes favor their own replication; a gene is successful if it produces a trait that in turn promotes the gene (sometimes summed up as "a chicken is an egg's way of making other eggs"). To describe such genetic self-promotion, Richard Dawkins introduced a psychological term in the title of his book, *The Selfish Gene.* Accordingly, what may be a generous act in common language, such as bringing home food, may be selfish from the gene's perspective. With time, the important addition "from the gene's perspective" was often forgotten and was eventually left out. All behavior was selfish, period.

Since genes have neither a self nor the emotions to make them selfish, one would think this phrase is just a metaphor. True, but when repeated often enough, metaphors tend to assume an aura of literal truth. Even though Dawkins cautioned against his own anthropomorphism of the gene, with the passage of time, carriers of selfish genes became selfish by association. Statements such as "we are born selfish" show how some sociobiologists have made the nonexistent emotions of genes into the archetype of true emotional nature. A critical article by Mary Midgley compared the socio-

biologists' warnings against their own metaphor to the paternosters of the Mafiosi.

Pushed into a corner by a witty philosopher, Dawkins defended his metaphor by arguing that it was *not* a metaphor. He really meant that genes are selfish, and claimed the right to define selfishness any way he wanted. Still, he borrowed a term from one domain, redefined it in a very narrow sense, then applied it in another domain to which it is completely alien. Such a procedure would be acceptable if the two meanings were kept separate at all times; unfortunately, they merge to the extent that some authors of this genre now imply that if people occasionally think of themselves as unselfish, the poor souls must be deceiving themselves.

It is important to clear up this confusion, and to emphasize once and for all that the selfish gene metaphor says nothing, either directly or indirectly, about motivation, emotion, or intention. Elliott Sober, another philosopher interested in the semantic trappings of sociobiology, proposes a distinction between *vernacular egoism,* our everyday usage of the term, and *evolutionary egoism,* which deals exclusively with genetic self-promotion. A plant, for example, is able to further its genetic interests yet cannot possibly be selfish in the vernacular sense. A chimpanzee or person who shares food with others acts altruistically in the vernacular sense, yet we assume that the behavior came into existence because it served survival and reproduction, hence that it is self-serving in an evolutionary sense.[11]

There is almost no point in discussing the evolution of morality if we let the vernacular sense of our terminology be overshadowed by the evolutionary sense. Human moral judgment always looks for the intention behind behavior. If I lean out of a window on the fifth floor and unknowingly nudge a flowerpot, thereby killing a pedestrian on the sidewalk below, I might be judged awkward or irresponsible, but not murderous. The latter accusation would surely be heard, however, had someone watched me grab the pot and throw it at the person. The effect is the same, but the motives are absolutely crucial. Jury and judge would want to know which emotions I showed, the degree of planning involved, my relationship with the target, and so on. In short, they would want to fathom the psychology behind the act.

These distinctions are largely irrelevant within a sociobiology exclusively interested in the effects of behavior. In such a framework, no different values are attached to intended versus unintended results, self-serving versus other-serving behavior, what we say versus what we mean, or an honest versus a dishonest mistake. Having thus denied themselves the single most important handle on ethical issues, some sociobiologists have given up on explaining morality. . . .

Whereas de Mandeville provided a mere satire, the idea of public blessings derived from the pursuit of self-interest gained respectability when the father of economics, Adam Smith, pronounced self-interest society's guiding principle. In a passage from the *Wealth of Nations*, first published in 1776, Smith saw each individual as being "led by an invisible hand to promote an end which was no part of his intention. Nor is it always the worse for society that it was no part of it. By pursuing his own interest he frequently promotes that of the society more effectually than when he really intends to promote it."[12]

The crux of Smith's famous invisible hand metaphor is that of a gap between intention and consequence; our actions may mean something entirely different in the bigger scheme of things than they do to us individually. Thus, life in the city depends on the professional services of bakers, mechanics, and storekeepers, whereas these people are only carving out a living for themselves and unknowingly are driven to serve the larger whole. To this day, the metaphor is popular with economists: a recent *New Yorker* cartoon showed a gathering of economists kneeling in the grass, hoping for a huge invisible hand to appear in the sky.

Smith's views were complex, however. As a moral philosopher, he knew full well that it would be hard to hold a society together purely on the basis of egoism. Like Huxley, Smith mellowed with age; he consecrated the final years of his life to a revision of *A Theory of Moral Sentiments,* expanding on his earlier belief in unselfish motives. Throughout this work Smith rejected the self-love thesis of de Mandeville, observing in the very first sentence that man possesses capacities "which interest him in the fortune of others, and render their happiness necessary to him, though he derives nothing from it, except the pleasure of seeing it."[13] This passage still stands as one of the most succinct and elegant definitions of human sympathy, a tendency Smith believed present in even the staunchest ruffian.

What makes the invisible hand metaphor so powerful is the idea of simultaneous micro and macro realities: the reality in the mind of each individual is not the same as the reality that emerges when many individuals interact. At one level we do A for reason B, while at another level A serves purpose C. Biologists are familiar with such multilevel thinking. For example, sex serves reproduction, yet animals engage in it without the slightest notion of its function; they are not driven by any desire to reproduce, only by sexual urges (as are humans most of the time). Similarly, members of a species do not need to have the benefits of mutual aid in mind when they help one another; these benefits may be so indirect and delayed in time that they matter only on an evolutionary timescale.

Imagine that you and I are sitting in individual boats adrift in the large swimming pool of an immense cruise ship. The ship has a slow and steady course to the north, but we care only about the direction of our little boats and cannot see beyond the body of water within which we are maneuvering. Even though I decide to head west and you to head south, to the outside observer both of us wind up going north. Since our experiences do not match our eventual destination, we live in separate proximate and ultimate realities.[14]

Intention and consequence need not be independent, however, particularly in our species. Often we have a reasonable understanding of the effects of our actions, especially when these effects are immediately obvious. Thus, it cannot escape us that one function of cooperative behavior is what appears to be its antipode: competition. Is not cooperative competition what team sport and party politics are all about?

In the primate order, the most widespread and best-developed collaboration is alliance formation, defined as two or more individuals banding together to defeat a third. For example, two male chimpanzees team up in order to overthrow the established ruler. The two challengers will swagger shoulder to shoulder in an intimidating manner, with their hair on end, often embracing or mounting each other directly in front of their rival, and of course supporting each other if it comes to an actual confrontation. By doing so for weeks or months on end, they wage a veritable war of nerves that may force the other male out of power. This is one of the most committed forms of animal cooperation that I know, one in which lives are literally at stake. Alpha males rarely go down without a fight.

Idealists such as Kropotkin tend to focus entirely on the agreeable side of cooperation, such as loyalty, trust, and camaraderie, while ignoring the competitive side. Although the Russian naturalist did refer to the role of a common enemy in fostering mutual aid, he conveniently ignored the possibility that the enemy might belong to one's own species. In *The Biology of Moral Systems* the biologist Richard Alexander presents our violent history of group against group and nation against nation as the ultimate reason why we attach so much value to the common good and to ethical conduct.

Alexander points out, however, that conflict between groups cannot be the whole explanation. Ants, for example, engage in terrible warfare on a massive scale, yet no one would argue that they have anything resembling a moral system. Thousands of them may be locked in deadly combat carried out in broad daylight on the sidewalks of our cities, while thousands more are recruited to join the massacre. Within each colony, however, harmony reigns. Ants form colonies of millions of individuals produced by and reproducing through a single female, the queen. With such overlapping reproductive interests, why should they compete with their own colony mates? And without conflicts of interest to be settled, what good would a moral system do?

The second condition for the evolution of morality, then, is conflict *within* the group. Moral systems are produced by tension between individual and collective interests, particularly when entire collectivities compete against one another.

If the need to get along and treat each other decently is indeed rooted in the need to stick together in the face of external threats, it would explain why one of Christianity's most heralded moral principles, the sanctity of life, is interpreted so flexibly, depending on which group, race, or nation the life belongs to. As recently as 1991, a war was declared "clean" and said to have been conducted with "clinical precision" despite the loss of more than a hundred thousand lives! Because the overwhelming majority of the dead in the Gulf War had fallen on the other side, Western media and politicians saw no need to burden our consciences.

Human history furnishes ample evidence that moral principles are oriented to one's own group,

and only reluctantly (and never evenhandedly) applied to the outside world. Standing on the medieval walls of a European city, we can readily imagine how tightly life within the walls was regulated and organized, whereas outsiders were only important enough to be doused with boiling oil. There is of course great irony in Alexander's suggestion that the moral underpinnings of the community, on the one hand, and warfare and ethnic strife, on the other, are two sides of the very same coin. In modern times we highly value the first, yet feel embarrassed by the stubborn persistence of the second.

Both conditions for the evolution of morality apply to monkeys and apes. First, many species engage in intergroup conflict, mostly at low intensity but sometimes with extreme brutality. Wild male chimpanzees, for example, may take over a neighboring territory by systematically killing off the males of the other community. Second, while there is no lack of strife and competition within groups, we also know that primates have ways of resolving conflict nonaggressively. . . .

It is simply unimaginable that fish would come to the rescue of an unlucky pond mate who is jerked out of the water, that they would bite the angler's line, or butt their heads against his boat in protest. We also do not expect them to miss their mate, search around, stop eating, and waste away. Fish are, well, cold to each other. They neither groom one another like primates, nor do they mutually lick, nibble, preen, or chat. I say this without any antifish bias. As a lifelong aquarium enthusiast, I can watch these animals for hours, yet I would never recommend them to someone in need of affection.

How different from the warm-blooded animals that took to the sea eighty million years ago!

Warm Blood in Cold Waters

Reports of leviathan care and assistance go back to the ancient Greeks. Dolphins are said to save companions by biting through harpoon lines or by hauling them out of nets in which they have gotten entangled. Whales may interpose themselves between a hunter's boat and an injured conspecific or capsize the boat. In fact, their tendency to come to the defense of victims is so predictable that whalers take advantage of it. Once a pod of sperm whales is sighted, the gunner need only strike one among them. When other pod members encircle the ship, splashing the water with their flukes, or surround the injured whale in a flower-like formation known as the marguerite, the gunner has no trouble picking them off one by one. Such "sympathy entrapment" would be effective with few other animals.

But am I justified in using the term "sympathy," which after all is a venerated human concept with very special connotations? Let us for the moment simply speak of *succorant behavior*, defined as helping, caregiving, or providing relief to distressed or endangered individuals other than progeny. Thus, the dog staying protectively close to a crying child shows succorance, whereas the same dog responding to the yelps of her puppies shows nurturance. In reviewing the succorant behavior of animals we will pay special attention to characteristics it might share with human sympathy, the most important being empathy—that is, the ability to be vicariously affected by someone else's feelings and situation. Psychologists and philosophers consider this capacity so central that "empathy" has gradually replaced "sympathy," "compassion," "sorrow," and "pity" in much of their writings (I have even seen the famous Stones' song . . . paraphrased as "Empathy for the Devil").

This blurring is unfortunate, for it ignores the distinction between the ability to recognize someone else's pain and the impulse to do something about it. Administering electrical shocks to someone else's genitals or pouring bleach in open wounds, as done by the torturers of our fine race, involves the very same ability of knowing what makes others suffer, yet it is quite the opposite of sympathy. What sets sympathy apart from cruelty, sadism, or plain indifference is that sensitivity to the other's situation goes together with *concern* about him or her. As neatly summed up by the psychologist Lauren Wispé: "The object of empathy is understanding. The object of sympathy is the other person's well-being."[15]

Whether based on empathy or not, animal succorance is the functional equivalent of human sympathy, expected only in species that know strong attachment. I am not speaking here of anonymous aggregations of fish or butterflies, but the individualized bonding, affection, and fellowship of many mammals and birds.

There certainly is no shortage of attachment among whales and dolphins, which may beach themselves collectively because of their reluctance to abandon a distressed group mate, including a disoriented one. Whereas this action is often fatal to an entire herd, James Porter, an American oceanographer, describes a fascinating exception. When in 1976 thirty pseudorcas (false killer whales) had stranded on an island off the coast of Florida, they remained together in shallow water for three entire days until the largest one had died. The twenty-nine healthy whales would have been unable to return to the ocean (hence would have perished with their apparent leader) under normal tidal conditions. But the tidal range happened to be minimal, so that most of the time the whales did have the option of leaving. "Stranding" is the wrong word, therefore; the whales stayed close to shore of their own accord.

With blood exuding from his right ear, the sick male was flanked and protected by fourteen or fifteen whales in a wedge-shaped configuration. The group was noisy, producing an incredible variety of chirps and squeaks. "With some trepidation, but no common sense," as he commented afterward, Porter entered the water to snorkel toward the group. The outermost individual responded by breaking loose and heading menacingly toward him. Instead of attacking, however, the whale lowered its head and slid underneath the scientist, lifting him out of the water and carrying him to the beach. This procedure was repeated three times, after which Porter tried his luck on the other side. There, too, the outermost whale carried him back to land several times. Porter noted that the whales lost interest in him as soon as he took off his snorkel, suggesting that they were showing a rescue response to sounds that perhaps resembled those of a clogged blowhole.[16]

The U.S. Coast Guard was unable to break up the formation or push the pseudorcas offshore: "If separated from the pack a whale would become highly agitated, and no amount of human effort could restrain its returning to the group. As soon as the whales touched each other, however, they became docile and could easily be nudged into deeper water."[17] (The calming effect of body contact extended to humans who, in a typical act of cross-species sympathy, applied suntan oil to whale backs exposed to sun and air.)

Once the large male had died, the formation around him loosened. Breaking ranks, the whales headed for deeper water while uttering high-pitched descending whistles. Autopsy revealed that the male, 6 meters long, had a massive worm infection in his ear. It is possible that parasitic worms impair a whale's echolocation system, hence its feeding efficiency: the victim's stomach proved empty.

While this account by no means solves the mystery of whale strandings, it gives an idea of how extraordinarily attached to each other these creatures are. If attachment and bonding are at the root of succorant behavior, parental care must be its ultimate evolutionary source. As explained by Lauren Eibl-Eibesfeldt, with the evolution of parental care in birds and mammals came feeding, warming, cleaning, alleviation of distress, and grooming of the young, which in turn led to the development of infantile appeals to trigger these activities. Once tender exchanges between parent and offspring had evolved—with the one asking for and the other providing care—they could be extended to all sorts of other relationships, including those among unrelated adults. Thus, in many birds, the female begs for food from her mate with the same gaping mouth and wing shaking as that of a hungry fledgling, while the male demonstrates his caretaking abilities by providing her with a nice tidbit.

Absorption of parental care into adult human relationships is evident from the widespread use of infantile names (such as "baby") for mates and lovers, and the special high-pitched voice that we reserve for both young children and intimate partners. In this context, Eibl-Eibesfeldt mentions the kiss, which probably derives from mouth-to-mouth feeding of masticated food. Kissing without any transfer of food is an almost universal human expression of love and affection, which, according to the ethologist, resembles kiss-feeding "with one partner playing the accepting part by opening the mouth in a babyish fashion and the other partner performing tongue movements as if to pass food."[18] Significantly, chimpanzees both kiss-feed their young and kiss between adults. A close relative of the chimpanzee, the bonobo, even tongue-kisses. . . .

Having Broad Nails

For decades students of animal behavior considered it wrong and naive to speak of animals as wanting, intending, feeling, thinking, or expecting beings. Animals just behave; that is all we know, and all we will *ever* know about them.

Curiously, the key to behavior was sought not within but outside the individual. The individual was merely a passive instrument of the environment. Psychologists studied how responses to stimuli increase if rewarded, and biologists analyzed how behavior spreads if it promotes reproduction. The first is a learning process, the second natural selection; the timescales are of course vastly different, yet the role of the environment as final arbiter of the suitability of behavior was the same. With biologists and psychologists quibbling endlessly over whose discipline offered the better explanation, it is hard to believe that they shared so much common ground.

The critical insights of both disciplines steered attention away from the acting agents themselves. If the environment controls behavior, why do we need the individual? Psychologists came up with their infamous black box, which mediates between stimulus and response, yet remains inaccessible to science. Biologists described animals as survival machines and preprogrammed robots, another way of saying that we should not worry too much about what goes on in their heads. The final presentation of the late B. F. Skinner, who firmly kept the lid on the black box, therefore could hardly have been accidental. Addressing fellow psychologists, he compared cognitive psychologists to creationists, thus throwing together the enemies of behaviorism and Darwinism![19]

When evaluating the succorant behavior of animals, we face already so many obstacles relative to the scarcity of data and the design of experiments that we do not need the additional burden of a narrow-minded rejection of the entire problem of cognition. Some biologists will point out that most of the accounts of caregiving discussed earlier—certainly the more striking ones—concern kin. Why not simply view these instances as investments of genetic relatives in one another, and leave them at that? While perfectly valid when it comes to evolutionary explanations, this point has absolutely no bearing on the question at hand. We are concerned here with motivations and intentions. Regardless of how care is being allotted, the caregiver must be sensitive to the situation of the other, feel an urge to assist, and determine which actions are most appropriate under the circumstances.

If Tallulah stuffs grass into the mouth of a dying herd member, if a chimpanzee goes to hug another who has just been beaten up, or if the top male of a monkey group fails to punish a brain-damaged infant for bothering him, we want to know what makes these animals react in this way. How do they perceive the distress or special circumstances of the other? Do they have any idea of how their behavior will affect the other? These questions remain exactly the same whether or not the other is a relative.

Times are changing. Interest in the mental life of animals is regaining respectability. Whereas some scientists propose a gradual shift in this direction, depending on evidence along the way, others are less patient. Believing it unfair to hold a new perspective hostage to the availability of final answers, they advocate a clean break with the Cartesian view of animals as automatons.

This is not to say that all we need to do is "feel as one" with animals without some critical distance, without putting ideas to the test, and without choosing our words carefully. Discussions about animal behavior often boil down to discussions about language. The ethologist inevitably borrows concepts from common language, which is primarily designed for communication about people. Yet the familiarity of these concepts by no means absolves us from the obligation to be specific about what they mean when applied to animals. Anthropomorphism can never replace science.

Take "reconciliation" and "consolation," two blatantly anthropomorphic terms applied to primate behavior. They refer to circumscribed encounters and come with a set of predictions that, if contradicted, should spell the end of their use. For example, reconciliation is defined as a reunion between former opponents shortly after an aggressive conflict between them. If it were found that reconciliations thus defined do not occur, or do nothing to reduce renewed hostility, it would be time to rethink the label. The same argument applies to older, more widely accepted terms, such as "threat," "greeting," "courtship," and "dominance," which have already gone through a process of fine-tuning and critical evaluation, but can still be questioned at any moment.[20]

It is this use of anthropomorphism as a *means* to get at the truth, rather than as an end in itself, that sets its use in science apart from use by the layperson. The ultimate goal of the scientist is emphatically *not* to arrive at the most satisfactory projection of human feelings onto the animal, but rather at testable ideas and replicable observations. Thus, anthropomorphism serves the same exploratory function as that of intuition in all science, from mathematics to medicine. As advocated by Gordon Burghardt:

> What I am calling for is a critical anthropomorphism, and predictive inference that encourages the use of data from many sources (prior experiments, anecdotes, publications, one's thoughts and feelings, neuroscience, imagining being the animal, naturalistic observations ... et cetera). But however eclectic in origin, the product must be an inference that can be tested or, failing that, can lead to predictions supportable by public data.[21]

But what about the cherished principle of parsimony—the one great bulwark against all liberal thinking? The problem is that insofar as monkeys and apes are concerned, a profound conflict exists between *two* kinds of parsimony. The first is the traditional canon that tells us not to invoke higher capacities if the phenomenon can be explained with lower ones. This favors simple explanations, such as learned adjustment, over more complex ones, such as cognitive empathy.

The second form of parsimony considers the shared evolutionary background of humans and other primates. It posits that if closely related species act the same, the underlying process probably is the same too. The alternative would be to assume the evolution of divergent processes for similar behavior; a highly uneconomic assumption for organisms with only a few million years of separate evolution. If we normally do not propose different causes for the same behavior in, say, tigers and lions, there is no good reason to do so for humans and chimpanzees, which are genetically as close or closer.

In short, the principle of parsimony has two faces. At the same time that we are supposed to favor low-level over high-level cognitive explanations, we also should not create a double standard according to which shared human and ape behavior is explained differently. Such "evolutionary parsimony" is a factor especially when both humans and apes exhibit traits not seen in monkeys, and two explanations are proposed where one may do. If accounts of human behavior commonly invoke complex cognitive abilities—and they certainly do—we must carefully consider whether these abilities are perhaps also present in apes. We do not need to jump to conclusions, but the possibility should at least be allowed on the table.

Behind the debate about parsimony towers the much larger issue of humanity's place in nature. To this day, those who see our species as part of the animal kingdom continue to lock horns with those who see us as separate. Even authors with a distinctly evolutionary perspective often cannot resist searching for the one big difference, the one trait that sets us apart—whether it is opposable thumbs, tool-making, cooperative hunting, humor, pure altruism, sexual orgasm, the incest taboo, language, or the anatomy of the larynx. Countless book titles reflect this search: *Man the Tool-Maker, Man the Hunter, The Ethical Animal, Uniquely Human,* and so on.

Claims of human uniqueness go back to the debate between Plato and Diogenes about the most succinct definition of the human species. Plato proposed that humans were the only creatures at once naked and walking on two legs. This definition proved flawed, however, when Diogenes brought a plucked fowl to the lecture room, setting it loose with the words, "Here is Plato's man." From then on the definition included "having broad nails."[22]

In 1784 Johann Wolfgang von Goethe triumphantly announced that he had discovered the cornerstone of humanity: a tiny piece of bone in the human upper jaw known as the *os intermaxillare.* The bone, though present in other mammals including apes, had long been thought absent in us and had therefore been labeled a "primitive" trait by a Dutch anatomist, Petrus Camper. Goethe's bone, as it became known, confirmed our continuity with nature long before Darwin formulated his theory of evolution. It was a slap in the face—the first of many—to people postulating human uniqueness.

Do claims of uniqueness in any way advance science? Are they even scientifically motivated? Until now, all of these claims have either been forgotten, like Camper's, or required qualification, like Plato's. As a separate species, humans do possess distinct traits, yet the overwhelming majority of our anatomical, physiological, and psychological characteristics are part of an ancient heritage. Holding the magnifying glass over a few beauty spots (our distinct traits are invariably judged advanced and superior) is a much less exciting enterprise, it seems to me, than trying to get a good look at the human animal as a whole.

In this broader perspective, peculiarly human traits are juxtaposed with the obvious continuity with the rest of nature. Included are both our most noble traits and the ones of which we are less proud, such as our genocidal and destructive tendencies. Even if we like to blame the latter on our progenitors (as soon as people hack each other to pieces they are said to be "acting like animals") and claim the former for ourselves, it is safe to assume that both run in our extended family.

There is no need to launch probes into space in order to compare ourselves with other intelligent life: there is plenty of intelligent life down here. It is infinitely more suitable to elucidate the working of our minds than those of whatever extraterrestrial forms might exist. In order to explore earthly intelligences, we need breathing room in the study of animal cognition: freedom from traditional constraints that tell us that nothing is there, or that *if* anything is there, we will never be able to catch even a glimpse.

Critics say there is no way to see what goes on inside an animal's head. That is, of course, not literally what cognitive ethologists are trying to do. Rather, they seek to *reconstruct* mental processes in much the way the nuclear physicist "looks inside" the atom by testing predictions based on a model of its structure. Admittedly, the use of anthropomorphism and anecdotal evidence, along with reservations about the principle of parsimony, have created uncertainty and confusion—as well as lively debate.[23] Yet these are only the delivery pains of a much-needed change in the study of animal behavior. . . .

Human ethics everywhere urge us to adopt someone else's perspective and look at the world through the eyes of others, as in the Golden Rule: *do unto others as you would have them do unto you.* Perhaps the evolution of role-taking, which is a very special capacity indeed, began with rather simple forms. For example, monkeys seem perfectly capable of identification with another monkey. If Azalea's sister interrupts hair plucking of her retarded sibling by another monkey, even though Azalea herself does nothing to draw attention, or if a mother monkey hurries over to stop an approach by her child toward an ill-tempered individual well before anything happens, these actions suggest great sensitivity to potential harm involving others.

It is not hard to see why monkeys would want to avoid harm to themselves, but why would harm to another bother them? Probably they see certain others as extensions of themselves, and the distress of those resonates within them. Known as *emotional contagion*,[24] this mechanism initially operates indiscriminately, yet becomes more selective with age. Monkeys learn to recognize subtle signs of distress, even situations in which distress is merely imminent. They follow closely what happens around them, especially if it involves friends and relatives.

Full-blown role-taking involves quite a bit more, however. The other is recognized not just as an extension of the self, but as a separate entity. Cognitive empathy is the ability to put oneself in the "shoes" of this other entity without losing the distinction between self and other. The American psychologist Martin Hoffman believes that this remarkable capacity grows out of emotional contagion. Being vicariously affected by others may make the child curious about their internal state, and stimulate him to search for cues about the others' feelings. Out of this challenge grows an increased awareness of the self in relation to others.

The same challenge may have occurred in the course of evolution. Perhaps some species evolved social organizations in which it became particularly advantageous to appreciate how companions were doing—not just at an emotional level, but also by imagining their situation. Sharper awareness of the other entailed increased self-awareness. If the mirror test somehow taps into this ability, as Gallup suggests, higher levels of empathy may be limited to humans and apes.

One indication of a relation between the two is that the first signs of cognitive empathy in children appear at about the same time as mirror self-recognition.[25] Another sign is that consolation occurs in a self-recognizing species, the chimpanzee, but apparently not in macaques. Do macaques rarely reassure victims of aggression because they lack the required ability to trade places mentally with them? Signs of distress in others do affect them, but once the fight is over and these indications subside, macaques quickly lose interest.[26]

As so often with regard to gradual processes, the tension between continuity and discontinuity cannot easily be resolved. Even if temperatures change steadily, there is an abrupt change in properties when water turns into ice or steam. Both the gradualist and the believer in fundamental distinc-

tions have a point when considering the evolution of empathy and sympathy. Yes, apes do share our capability for self-recognition in a mirror, but no, this capability does not necessarily mean that humans and apes are the only animals conscious of themselves. And yes, apes do show remarkable empathy, but no, they are not the only animals sensitive to the needs of others. We only need think of the incredible assistance elephants, dolphins, and lemurs offer each other to realize how widespread and well developed these tendencies are. Caring responses go back much further in evolutionary history than the ape–human lineage.

Notes

1. Huxley, 1989 (1894), p. 83.

2. Williams, 1988, p. 438.

3. Dewey, 1993 (1898), p. 98.

4. Midgley, 1991, p. 8.

5. Wilson, 1975, p. 562.

6. According to Kenneth Lux, opposition to welfare assistance (the so-called Poor Laws) was most evident in the second edition of Malthus' *Essay on the Principle of Population* and was expunged from subsequent editions: "A man who is born into a world . . . if he cannot get subsistence from his parents on whom he has a just demand and if the society does not want his labour, has no claim of right to the smallest portion of food, and, in fact, has no business to be where he is. At nature's mighty feast there is no vacant cover for him. She tells him to be gone, and will quickly execute her own orders, if he does not work upon the compassion of some of her guests. If these guests get up and make room for him, other intruders immediately appear demanding the same favour" (quoted in Lux, 1990, pp. 34–35).

7. Rockefeller quoted in Lux, 1990, p. 148.

8. History is not as simple as presented here. Charles Darwin, Alfred Russell Wallace, Thomas Henry Huxley, and Herbert Spencer each took a different position with regard to the (im)possibility of an evolved morality. Well-documented accounts of this early debate may be found in Richards (1987) and Cronin (1991).

9. Yerkes and Yerkes, 1935, p. 1024.

10. Gene-centric sociobiologists often speak of "a gene for behavior *x*," regardless of what is known about the heritability of behavior *x* (usually, little or nothing). In reality, each gene acts in conjunction with hundreds of others. So every behavior is likely to depend on a wide range of genetic factors. Even if

we grant gene-centric sociobiologists that their one-gene–one-behavior scheme is not to be taken literally—that it is a mere shorthand for discussion—it is advisable to balance it with another generalization, one that is at least as close to the truth: "Every character of an organism is affected by all genes and every gene affects all characters" (Mayr, 1963, p. 164).

11. Apparently Dawkins is not convinced that we are born selfish, in the vernacular sense. In response to Midgley (1979) he admits that selfish-gene rhetoric may well be out of touch with actual human motives: "To the extent that I know about human psychology (a rather small extent), I doubt if our emotional nature is, as a matter of fact, fundamentally selfish" (Dawkins, 1981, p. 558).

This is a message to bear in mind, for it certainly is not evident in the author's writings. A general problem with pop sociobiology is that complex issues are compressed to such a degree that even if the author is fully aware of what is left out, the reader has no way of knowing. The simplifications are then perpetuated ad nauseam by less-informed writers until they haunt the field in general and must be countered as if they represented serious ideas (Kitcher, 1985).

In *The Ethical Primate,* Midgley (1994, p. 17) has reiterated her views on the pitfalls and illusions of reductionist science, giving scathing attention to sociobiology's forays into the psychological domain: "Darwinism is often seen—and indeed is often presented—not as a wide-ranging set of useful suggestions about our mysterious history, but as a slick, reductive ideology, requiring us, in fact, to dismiss as illusions matters which our experience shows to be real and serious."

12. Smith, 1982 (1776), bk. 3, p. 423.

13. Smith, 1937 (1759), p. 9.

14. Ethologists distinguish sharply between proximate and ultimate causes. *Proximate causes* concern learning, experience, and the direct circumstances and motivations underlying behavior. *Ultimate causes* promoted a behavior in the course of evolution. If a behavior assists survival and reproduction, for example because it repels predators or attracts mates, this is the ultimate reason for its existence. Since evolution takes place on a timescale that escapes perception, only proximate causes exist in the minds of animals and most humans. Students of evolutionary biology are unique in that they care about ultimate causes.

Unfortunately, proximate and ultimate levels are frequently confused, particularly when the function of a behavior seems so obvious that it is hard to imagine that the actors are oblivious to it. Popular nature documentaries contribute to the mixup by describing animal behavior in ultimate terms. They will explain that two male walruses fight over the right to impregnate the female, whereas these males neither know nor care about what happens in the female's womb after they have mated.

15. Wispé, 1991, p. 80.

16. On the basis of this incident, Porter (1977, p. 10) comments that he would not automatically discount the numerous reports of people who claim to have been saved by porpoises or some of the smaller whales. Accounts of Cetacea helping humans generally describe one of the following: (a) a drowning person is lifted to the surface; (b) a boat or ship is guided to safety (around submerged rocks, out of a storm); or (c) a swimmer is protected against sharks by a dolphin cordon. Reviews of both interspecific and intraspecific succorant behavior of Cetacea may be found in Caldwell and Caldwell (1966), Connor and Norris (1982), and Pilleri (1984).

17. Porter, 1977, pp. 10, 13.

18. Eibl-Eibesfeldt, 1990, p. 156.

19. Skinner (1990) saw both cognitive psychology and creationism as heavily influenced by religion. This element is obvious enough with regard to creationism, sometimes mislabeled creation science ("mislabeled" because creationists work with a single hypothesis, determined a priori to be true, whereas science tries to choose among alternative hypotheses). The effect of religion on cognitive psychology may be less evident—hidden as it is by centuries of sophisticated philosophizing, it is revealed in the persistent mind/body and human/animal dualisms. These dualisms lack a factual basis, and psychology would be much better off without them (Gibson, 1994).

20. Most readers would long ago have laid aside this book if I had limited myself to purely descriptive, technical language. There is a fine but important line between the use of anthropomorphism for communicatory purposes or as a heuristic device, and gratuitous anthropomorphism that projects human emotions and intentions onto animals without justification, explication, or critical investigation. Strong opinions about the use and abuse of anthropomorphism can be found in Kennedy (1992), Marshall Thomas (1993), Masson and McCarthy (1995), and in Mitchell, Thompson, and Miles (forthcoming).

21. Burghardt, 1985, p. 917.

22. Diogenes Laertius, quoted in Menzel, 1986, p. 167.

23. Promises and problems of the cognitive approach to animal behavior have been extensively debated among ethologists. See Kummer (1982), Kummer,

Dasser, and Hoyningen-Huene (1990), de Waal (1982, 1991a), and Cheney and Seyfarth (1990).

24. Hatfield, Cacioppo, and Rapson (1993, p. 96) define emotional contagion as "the tendency to automatically mimic and synchronize expressions, vocalizations, postures, and movements with those of another person and, consequently, to converge emotionally."

25. This correlation was reported by Johnson (1982) and Bischof-Köhler (1988). According to the latter study, the link between mirror self-recognition and the emergence of cognitive empathy holds up even after correction for age.

26. The main alternative to a cognitive explanation of the absence of consolation in macaques is the so-called constraints hypothesis. It posits that macaques run serious risks in associating with an individual who has just been attacked. With their more tolerant and flexible relationships, chimpanzees may not be operating under the same constraints. We plan to conduct experiments to eliminate the risk of approaching a victim of aggression. If macaques still fail to contact distressed group members under these circumstances, the social constraints hypothesis would be weakened (de Waal and Aureli, forthcoming).

15. Animal Liberation[1]

Peter Singer

I

We are familiar with Black Liberation, Gay Liberation, and a variety of other movements. With Women's Liberation some thought we had come to the end of the road. Discrimination on the basis of sex, it has been said, is the last form of discrimination that is universally accepted and practiced without pretense, even in those liberal circles which have long prided themselves on their freedom from racial discrimination. But one should always be wary of talking of "the last remaining form of discrimination." If we have learned anything from the liberation movements, we should have learned how difficult it is to be aware of the ways in which we discriminate until they are forcefully pointed out to us. A liberation movement demands an expansion of our moral horizons, so that practices that were previously regarded as natural and inevitable are now seen as intolerable.

Animals, Men and Morals is a manifesto for an Animals Liberation movement. The contributers to the book may not all see the issue this way. They are a varied group. Philosophers, ranging from professors to graduate students, make up the largest contingent. There are five of them, including the three editors, and there is also an extract from the unjustly neglected German philosopher with an English name, Leonard Nelson, who died in 1927. There are

essays by two novelist/critics, Brigid Brophy and Maureen Duffy, and another by Muriel the Lady Dowding, widow of Dowding of Battle of Britain fame and the founder of "Beauty without Cruelty," a movement that campaigns against the use of animals for furs and cosmetics. The other pieces are by a psychologist, a botanist, a sociologist, and Ruth Harrison, who is probably best described as a professional campaigner for animal welfare.

Whether or not these people, as individuals, would all agree that they are launching a liberation movement for animals, the book as a whole amounts to no less. It is a demand for a complete change in our attitudes to nonhumans. It is a demand that we cease to regard the exploitation of other species as natural and inevitable, and that, instead, we see it as a continuing moral outrage. Patrick Corbett, Professor of Philosophy at Sussex University, captures the spirit of the book in his closing words:

> . . . we require now to extend the great principles of liberty, equality and fraternity over the lives of animals. Let animal slavery join human slavery in the graveyard of the past.

The reader is likely to be skeptical. "Animal Liberation" sounds more like a parody of liberation movements than a serious objective. The reader may think: We support the claims of blacks and women for equality because blacks and women really are equal to whites and males—equal in intelligence and in abilities, capacity for leadership, rationality, and so on. Humans and nonhumans obviously are not equal in these respects. Since justice demands only that we treat equals equally, unequal treatment of humans and nonhumans cannot be an injustice.

This is a tempting reply, but a dangerous one. It commits the non-racist and non-sexist to a dogmatic belief that blacks and women really are just as intelligent, able, etc., as whites and males—and no more. Quite possibly this happens to be the case. Certainly attempts to prove that racial or sexual differences in these respects have a genetic origin have not been conclusive. But do we really want to stake our demand for equality on the assumption that there are no genetic differences of this kind between the different races or sexes? Surely the appropriate response to those who claim to have found evidence for such genetic differences is not to stick to the belief that there are no differences, whatever the evidence to the contrary; rather one should be clear that the claim to equality does not depend on IQ. Moral equality is distinct from factual equality. Otherwise it would be nonsense to talk of the equality of human beings, since humans, as individuals, obviously differ in intelligence and almost any ability one cares to name. If possessing greater intelligence does not entitle one human to exploit another, why should it entitle humans to exploit nonhumans?

Jeremy Bentham expressed the essential basis of equality in his famous formula: "Each to count for one and none for more than one." In other words, the interests of every being that has interests are to be taken into account and treated equally with the like interest of any other being. Other moral philosophers, before and after Bentham, have made the same point in different ways. Our concern for others must not depend on whether they possess certain characteristics, though just what that concern involves may, of course, vary according to such characteristics.

Bentham, incidentally, was well aware that the logic of the demand for racial equality did not stop at the equality of humans. He wrote:

> The day may come when the rest of the animal creation may acquire those rights which never could have been withholden from them but by the hand of tyranny. The French have already discovered that the blackness of the skin is no reason why a human being should be abandoned without redress to the caprice of a tormentor. It may one day come to be recognized that the number of the legs, the villosity of the skin, or the termination of the *os sacrum*, are reasons equally insufficient for abandoning a sensitive being to the same fate. What else is it that should trace the insuperable line? Is it the faculty of reason, or perhaps the faculty of discourse? But a full-grown horse or dog is beyond comparison a more rational, as well as more conversable animal, than an infant of a day, or a week, or even a month old. But suppose they were otherwise, what would it avail? The question is not, Can they *reason?* nor Can they *talk?* but, Can they *suffer?*[2]

Surely Bentham was right. If a being suffers, there can be no moral justification for refusing to take that suffering into consideration, and, indeed, to count it equally with the like suffering (if rough comparisons can be made) of any other being.

So the only question is: do animals other than man suffer? Most people agree unhesitatingly that animals like cats and dogs can and do suffer, and this seems also to be assumed by those laws that prohibit wanton cruelty to such animals. Personally, I have no doubt at all about this and find it hard to take seriously the doubts that a few people apparently do have. The editors and contributors of *Animals, Men and Morals* seem to feel the same way, for although the question is raised more than once, doubts are quickly dismissed each time. Nevertheless, because this is such a fundamental point, it is worth asking what grounds we have for attributing suffering to other animals.

It is best to begin by asking what grounds any individual human has for supposing that other humans feel pain. Since pain is a state of consciousness, a "mental event," it can never be directly observed. No observations, whether behavioral signs such as writhing or screaming or physiological or neurological recordings, are observations of pain itself. Pain is something one feels and one can only infer that others are feeling it from various external indications. The fact that only philosophers are ever skeptical about whether other humans feel pain shows that we regard such inference as justifiable in the case of humans.

Is there any reason why the same inference should be unjustifiable for other animals? Nearly all the external signs which lead us to infer pain in other humans can be seen in other species, especially "higher" animals such as mammals and birds. Behavioral signs—writhing, yelping, or other forms of calling, attempts to avoid the source of pain, and many others—are present. We know, too, that these animals are biologically similar in the relevant respects, having nervous systems like ours which can be observed to function as ours do.

So the grounds for inferring that these animals can feel pain are nearly as good as the grounds for inferring other humans do. Only nearly, for there is one behavioral sign that humans have but nonhumans, with the exception of one or two specially raised chimpanzees, do not have. This, of course, is a developed language. As the quotation from Bentham indicates, this has long been regarded as an important distinction between man and other animals. Other animals may communicate with each other, but not in the way we do. Following Chomsky, many people now mark this distinction by saying that only humans communicate in a form that is governed by rules of syntax. (For the purposes of this argument, linguists allow those chimpanzees who have learned a syntactic sign language to rank as honorary humans.) Nevertheless, as Bentham pointed out, this distinction is not relevant to the question of how animals ought to be treated, unless it can be linked to the issue of whether animals suffer.

This link may be attempted in two ways. First, there is a hazy line of philosophical thought, stemming perhaps from some doctrines associated with Wittgenstein, which maintains that we cannot meaningfully attribute states of consciousness to beings without language. I have not seen this argument made explicit in print, though I have come across it in conversation. This position seems to me very implausible, and I doubt that it would be held at all if it were not thought to be a consequence of a broader view of the significance of language. It may be that the use of a public, rule-governed language is a precondition of conceptual thought. It may even be, although personally I doubt it, that we cannot meaningfully speak of a creature having an intention unless that creature can use a language. But states like pain, surely, are more primitive than either of these, and seem to have nothing to do with language.

Indeed, as Jane Goodall points out in her study of chimpanzees, when it comes to the expression of feelings and emotions, humans tend to fall back on nonlinguistic modes of communication which are often found among apes, such as a cheering pat on the back, an exuberant embrace, a clasp of hands, and so on.[3] Michael Peters makes a similar point in his contribution to *Animals, Men and Morals* when he notes that the basic signals we use to convey pain, fear, sexual arousal, and so on are not specific to our species. So there seems to be no reason at all to believe that a creature without language cannot suffer.

The second, and more easily appreciated way of linking language and the existence of pain is to say that the best evidence that we can have that another creature is in pain is when he tells us that he is. This is a distinct line of argument, for it is not being denied that a non-language-user conceivably could suffer, but only that we could know that he is suffering. Still, this line of argument seems to me to fail, and for reasons similar to those just given. "I am in pain" is not the best possible evidence that the speaker is in pain (he might be lying) and it is certainly not the only possible evidence. Behavioral signs and knowledge of the animals' biological similarity to ourselves together provide adequate evidence that animals do suffer. After all, we would not accept linguistic evidence if it contradicted the rest of the evidence. If a man was severely burned, and behaved as if he were in pain, writhing, groaning, being very careful not to let his burned skin touch anything, and so on, but later said he had not been in pain at all, we would be more likely to conclude that he was lying or suffering from amnesia than that he had not been in pain.

Even if there were stronger grounds for refusing to attribute pain to those who do not have a language, the consequences of this refusal might lead us to examine these grounds unusually critically. Human infants, as well as some adults, are unable to use language. Are we to deny that a year-old infant can suffer? If not, how can language be crucial? Of course, most parents can understand the responses of even very young infants better than they understand the responses of other animals, and sometimes infant responses can be understood in the light of later development.

This, however, is just a fact about the relative knowledge we have of our own species and other species, and most of this knowledge is simply derived from closer contact. Those who have studied the behavior of other animals soon learn to understand their responses at least as well as we understand those of an infant. (I am not just referring to Jane Goodall's and other well-known studies of apes. Consider, for example, the degree of understanding achieved by Tinbergen from watching herring gulls.)[4] Just as we can understand infant human behavior in the light of adult human behavior, so we can understand the behavior of other species in the light of our own behavior (and sometimes we can understand our own behavior better in the light of the behavior of other species).

The grounds we have for believing that other mammals and birds suffer are, then, closely analogous to the grounds we have for believing that other humans suffer. It remains to consider how far down the evolutionary scale this analogy holds. Obviously it becomes poorer when we get further away from man. To be more precise would require a detailed examination of all that we know about other forms of life. With fish, reptiles, and other vertebrates the analogy still seems strong, with molluscs like oysters it is much weaker. Insects are more difficult, and it may be that in our present state of knowledge we must be agnostic about whether they are capable of suffering.

If there is no moral justification for ignoring suffering when it occurs, and it does occur in other species, what are we to say of our attitudes toward these other species? Richard Ryder, one of the contributors of *Animals, Men and Morals,* uses the term "speciesism" to describe the belief that we are entitled to treat members of other species in a way in which it would be wrong to treat members of our own species. The term is not euphonious, but it neatly makes the analogy with racism. The nonracist would do well to bear the analogy in mind when he is inclined to defend human behavior toward nonhumans. "Shouldn't we worry about improving the lot of our own species before we concern ourselves with other species?" he may ask. If we substitute "race" for "species" we shall see that the question is better not asked. "Is a vegetarian diet nutritionally adequate?" resembles the slaveowner's claim that he and the whole economy of the South would be ruined without slave labor. There is even a parallel with skeptical doubts about whether animals suffer, for some defenders of slavery professed to doubt whether blacks really suffer in the way that whites do.

I do not want to give the impression, however, that the case for Animal Liberation is based on the analogy with racism and no more. On the contrary, *Animals, Men and Morals* describes the various ways in which humans exploit nonhumans, and several contributors consider the defenses that have been offered, including the defense of meat-eating mentioned in the last paragraph. Sometimes the rebuttals are scornfully dismissive, rather than carefully designed to convince the detached critic. This may be a fault, but it is a fault that is inevitable, given the kind of book this is. The issue is not one on which one can remain detached. As the editors state in their Introduction:

> Once the full force of moral assessment has been made explicit there can be no rational excuse left for killing animals, be they killed for food, science, or sheer personal indulgence. We have not assembled this book to provide the reader with yet another manual on how to make brutalities less brutal. Compromise, in the traditional sense of the term, is simple unthinking weakness when one considers the actual reasons for our crude relationships with the other animals.

The point is that on this issue there are few critics who are genuinely detached. People who eat pieces of slaughtered nonhumans every day find it hard to believe that they are doing wrong; and they also find it hard to imagine what else they could eat. So for those who do not place nonhumans beyond the pale of morality, there comes a stage when further argument seems pointless, a stage at which one can only accuse one's opponent of hypocrisy and reach for the sort of sociological account of our practices and the way we defend them that is attempted by David Wood in his contribution to this book. On the other hand, to those unconvinced by the arguments, and unable to accept that they are rationalizing their dietary preferences and their fear of being thought peculiar, such sociological explanations can only seem insultingly arrogant.

II

The logic of speciesism is most apparent in the practice of experimenting on nonhumans in order to benefit humans. This is because the issue is rarely obscured by allegations that nonhumans are so different from humans that we cannot know anything about whether they suffer. The defender of vivisection cannot use this argument because he needs to stress the similarities between man and other animals in order to justify the usefulness to the former of experiments on the latter. The researcher who makes rats choose between starvation and electric shocks to see if they develop ulcers (they do) does so because he knows that the rat has a nervous system very similar to man's, and presumably feels an electric shock in a similar way.

Richard Ryder's restrained account of experiments on animals made me angrier with my fellow men than anything else in this book. Ryder, a clinical psychologist by profession, himself experimented on animals before he came to hold the view he puts forward in his essay. Experimenting on animals is now a large industry, both academic and commercial. In 1969, more than 5 million experiments were performed in Britain, the vast majority without anesthetic (though how many of these involved pain is not known). There are no accurate US figures, since there is no federal law on the subject, and in many cases no state law either. Estimates vary from 20 million to 200 million. Ryder suggests that 80 million may be the best guess. We tend to think that this is all for vital medical research, but of course it is not. Huge numbers of animals are used in university departments from Forestry to Psychology, and even more are used for commercial purposes, to test whether cosmetics can cause skin damage, or shampoos eye damage, or to test food additives or laxatives or sleeping pills or anything else.

A standard test for foodstuffs is the "LD50." The object of this test is to find the dosage level at which 50 percent of the test animals will die. This means that nearly all of them will become very sick before finally succumbing or surviving. When the substance is a harmless one, it may be necessary to force huge doses down the animals, until in some cases sheer volume or concentration causes death.

Ryder gives a selection of experiments, taken from recent scientific journals. I will quote two, not for the sake of indulging in gory details, but in order to give an idea of what normal researchers think they may legitimately do to other species. The point is not that the individual researchers are cruel men, but that they are behaving in a way that is allowed by our speciesist attitudes. As Ryder points out, even if only 1 percent of the experiments involve severe pain, that is 50,000 experiments in Britain each year, or nearly 150 every day (and about fifteen times as many in the United States, if Ryder's guess is right). Here then are two experiments:

> O. S. Ray and R. J. Barrett of Pittsburgh gave electric shocks to the feet of 1,042 mice. They then caused convulsions by giving more intense shocks through cup-shaped electrodes applied to the animals' eyes or through pressure spring clips attached to their ears. Unfortunately some of the mice who "successfully completed Day One training were found sick or dead prior to testing on Day Two." [*Journal of Comparative and Physiological Psychology*, 1969, Vol. 67, pp. 110–116]

> At the National Institute for Medical Research, Mill Hill, London, W. Feldberg and S. L. Sherwood injected chemicals into the brains of cats—"with a number of widely different substances, recurrent patterns of reaction were obtained. Retching, vomiting, defaecation, increased salivation and greatly accelerated respiration leading to panting were common features."...
>
> The injection into the brain of a large dose of Tubocuraine caused the cat to jump "from the table to the floor and then straight into its cage, where it started calling more and more noisily whilst moving about restlessly and jerkily . . . finally the cat fell with legs and neck flexed, jerking in rapid clonic movements, the condition being that of a major [epileptic] convulsion . . . within a few seconds the cat got up, ran for a few yards at high speed and fell in another fit. The whole process was repeated several times within the next ten minutes, during which the cat lost faeces and foamed at the mouth."
>
> This animal finally died thirty-five minutes after the brain injection. [*Journal of Physiology*, 1954, Vol. 123, pp. 148–167]

There is nothing secret about these experiments. One has only to open any recent volume of a learned journal, such as the *Journal of Comparative and Physiological Psychology*, to find full descriptions of experiments of this sort, together with the results obtained—results that are frequently trivial and obvious. The experiments are often supported by public funds.

It is a significant indication of the level of acceptability of these practices that, although these experiments are taking place at this moment on university campuses throughout the country, there has, so far as I know, not been the slightest protest from the student movement. Students have been rightly concerned that their universities should not discriminate on grounds of race or sex, and that they should not serve the purposes of the military or big business. Speciesism continues undisturbed, and many students participate in it. There may be a few qualms at first, but since everyone regards it as normal, and it may even be a required part of a course, the student soon becomes hardened and, dismissing his earlier feelings as "mere sentiment," comes to regard animals as statistics rather than sentient beings with interests that warrant consideration.

Argument about vivisection has often missed the point because it has been put in absolutist terms: would the abolitionist be prepared to let thousands die if they could be saved by experimenting on a single animal? The way to reply to this purely hypothetical question is to pose another: Would the experimenter be prepared to experiment on a human orphan under six months old, if it were the only way to save many lives? (I say "orphan" to avoid the complication of parental feelings, although in doing so I am being overfair to the experimenter, since the nonhuman subjects of experiments are not orphans.) A negative answer to this question indicates that the experimenter's readiness to use nonhumans is simple discrimination, for adult apes, cats, mice, and other mammals are more conscious of what is happening to them, more self-directing, and, so far as we can tell, just as sensitive to pain as a human infant. There is no characteristic that human infants possess that adult mammals do not have to the same or a higher degree.

(It might be possible to hold that what makes it wrong to experiment on a human infant is that the infant will in time develop into more than the nonhuman, but one would then, to be consistent, have to oppose abortion, and perhaps contraception, too, for the fetus and the egg and sperm have the same potential as the infant. Moreover, one would still have no reason for experimenting on a nonhuman rather than a human with brain damage severe enough to make it impossible for him to rise above infant level.)

The experimenter, then, shows a bias for his own species whenever he carries out an experiment on a nonhuman for a purpose that he would not think justified him in using a human being at an equal or lower level of sentience, awareness, ability

to be self-directing, etc. No one familiar with the kind of results yielded by these experiments can have the slightest doubt that if this bias were eliminated the number of experiments performed would be zero or very close to it.

III

If it is vivisection that shows the logic of speciesism most clearly, it is the use of other species for food that is at the heart of our attitudes toward them. Most of *Animals, Men and Morals* is an attack on meat-eating—an attack which is based solely on concern for nonhumans, without reference to arguments derived from considerations of ecology, macrobiotics, health, or religion.

The idea that nonhumans are utilities, means to our ends, pervades our thought. Even conservationists who are concerned about the slaughter of wild fowl but not about the vastly greater slaughter of chickens for our tables are thinking in this way—they are worried about what we would lose if there were less wildlife. Stanley Godlovitch, pursuing the Marxist idea that our thinking is formed by the activities we undertake in satisfying our needs, suggests that man's first classification of his environment was into Edibles and Inedibles. Most animals came into the first category, and there they have remained.

Man may always have killed other species for food, but he has never exploited them so ruthlessly as he does today. Farming has succumbed to business methods, the objective being to get the highest possible ratio of output (meat, eggs, milk) to input (fodder, labor costs, etc.). Ruth Harrison's essay "On Factory Farming" gives an account of some aspects of modern methods, and of the unsuccessful British campaign for effective controls, a campaign which was sparked off by her *Animal Machines* (Stuart: London, 1964).

Her article is in no way a substitute for her earlier book. This is a pity since, as she says "Farm produce is still associated with mental pictures of animals browsing in the fields, . . . of hens having a last forage before going to roost. . . ." Yet neither in her article nor elsewhere in *Animals, Men and Morals* is this false image replaced by a clear idea of the nature and extent of factory farming. We learn of this only indirectly, when we hear of the code of reform proposed by an advisory committee set up by the British government.

Among the proposals, which the government refused to implement on the grounds that they were too idealistic, were: "*Any animal should at least have room to turn around freely.*"

Factory farm animals need liberation in the most literal sense. Veal calves are kept in stalls five feet by two feet. They are usually slaughtered when about four months old, and have been too big to turn in their stalls for at least a month. Intensive beef herds, kept in stalls only proportionately larger for much longer periods, account for a growing percentage of beef production. Sows are often similarly confined when pregnant, which, because of artificial methods of increasing fertility, can be most of the time. Animals confined in this way do not waste food by exercising, nor do they develop unpalatable muscle.

"*A dry bedded area should be provided for all stock.*" Intensively kept animals usually have to stand and sleep on slatted floors without straw, because this makes cleaning easier.

"*Palatable roughage must be readily available to all calves after one week of age.*" In order to produce the pale veal housewives are said to prefer, calves are fed on an all-liquid diet until slaughter, even though they are long past the age at which they would normally eat grass. They develop a craving for roughage, evidenced by attempts to gnaw wood from their stalls. (For the same reason, their diet is deficient in iron.)

"*Battery cages for poultry should be large enough for a bird to be able to stretch one wing at a time.*" Under current British practice, a cage for four or five laying hens has a floor area of twenty inches by eighteen inches, scarcely larger than a double page of the *New York Review of Books*. In this space, on a sloping wire floor (sloping so the eggs roll down, wire so the dung drops through) the birds live for a year or eighteen months while artificial lighting and temperature conditions combine with drugs in their food to squeeze the maximum number of eggs out of them. Table birds are also sometimes kept in cages. More often they are reared in sheds, no less crowded. Under these conditions all the birds' natural activities are frustrated, and they develop "vices" such as pecking each other to death. To prevent this, beaks are often cut off, and the sheds kept dark.

How many of those who support factory farming by buying its produce know anything about the way it is produced? How many have heard something about it, but are reluctant to check up for fear that it will make them uncomfortable? To non-speciesists, the typical consumer's mixture of ignorance, reluctance to find out the truth, and vague belief that nothing really bad could be allowed seems analogous to the attitudes of "decent Germans" to the death camps.

There are, of course, some defenders of factory farming. Their arguments are considered, though again rather sketchily, by John Harris. Among the most common: "Since they have never known anything else, they don't suffer." This argument will not be put by anyone who knows anything about animal behavior, since he will know that not all behavior has to be learned. Chickens attempt to stretch wings, walk around, scratch, and even dustbathe or build a nest, even though they have never lived under conditions that allowed these activities. Calves can suffer from maternal deprivation no matter at what age they were taken from their mothers. "We need these intensive methods to provide protein for a growing population." As ecologists and famine relief organizations know, we can produce far more protein per acre if we grow the right vegetable crop, soy beans for instance, than if we use the land to grow crops to be converted into protein by animals who use nearly 90 percent of the protein themselves, even when unable to exercise.

There will be many readers of this book who will agree that factory farming involves an unjustifiable degree of exploitation of sentient creatures, and yet will want to say that there is nothing wrong with rearing animals for food, provided it is done "humanely." These people are saying, in effect, that although we should not cause animals to suffer, there is nothing wrong with killing them.

There are two possible replies to this view. One is to attempt to show that this combination of attitudes is absurd. Roslind Godlovitch takes this course in her essay, which is an examination of some common attitudes to animals. She argues that from the combination of "animal suffering is to be avoided" and "there is nothing wrong with killing animals" it follows that all animal life ought to be exterminated (since all sentient creatures will suffer to some degree at some point in their lives). Euthanasia is a contentious issue only because we place some value on living. If we did not, the least amount of suffering would justify it. Accordingly, if we deny that we have a duty to exterminate all animal life, we must concede that we are placing some value on animal life.

This argument seems to me valid, although one could still reply that the value of animal life is to be derived from the pleasures that life can have for them, so that, provided their lives have a balance of pleasure over pain, we are justified in rearing them. But this would imply that we ought to produce animals and let them live as pleasantly as possible, without suffering.

At this point, one can make the second of the two possible replies to the view that rearing and killing animals for food is all right so long as it is done humanely. This second reply is that so long as we think that a nonhuman may be killed simply so that a human can satisfy his taste for meat, we are still thinking of nonhumans as means rather than as ends in themselves. The factory farm is nothing more than the application of technology to this concept. Even traditional methods involve castration, the separation of mothers and their young, the breaking up of herds, branding or ear-punching, and of course transportation to the abattoirs and the final moments of terror when the animal smells blood and senses danger. If we were to try rearing animals so that they lived and died without suffering, we should find that to do so on anything like the scale of today's meat industry would be a sheer impossibility. Meat would become the prerogative of the rich.

I have been able to discuss only some of the contributions to this book, saying nothing about, for instance, the essays on killing for furs and for sport. Nor have I considered all the detailed questions that need to be asked once we start thinking about other species in the radically different way presented by this book. What, for instance, are we to do about genuine conflicts of interest like rats biting slum children? I am not sure of the answer, but the essential point is just that we *do* see this as a conflict of interests, that we recognize that rats have interests too. Then we may begin to think about other ways of resolving the conflict—perhaps by leaving out rat baits that sterilize the rats instead of killing them.

I have not discussed such problems because they are side issues compared with the exploitation of other species for food and for experimental purposes. On these central matters, I hope that I have said enough to show that this book, despite its flaws, is a challenge to every human to recognize his attitudes to nonhumans as a form of prejudice no less objectionable than racism or sexism. It is a challenge that demands not just a change of attitudes, but a change in our way of life, for it requires us to become vegetarians.

Can a purely moral demand of this kind succeed? The odds are certainly against it. The book holds out no inducements. It does not tell us that we will become healthier, or enjoy life more, if we cease exploiting animals. Animal Liberation will require greater altruism on the part of mankind than any other liberation movement, since animals are incapable of demanding it for themselves, or of protesting against their exploitation by votes, demonstrations, or bombs. Is man capable of such genuine altruism? Who knows? If this book does have a significant effect, however, it will be a vindication of all those who have believed that man has within himself the potential for more than cruelty and selfishness.

Notes

1. This article originally appeared as a book review of *Animals, Men and Morals,* edited by Stanley and Roslind Godlovitch and John Harris.

2. *The Principles of Morals and Legislation,* Ch. XVII, Sec. 1, footnote to paragraph 4. (Italics in original.)

3. Jane van Lawick-Goodall, *In the Shadow of Man* ([Boston:] Houghton Mifflin, 1971), p. 225.

4. N. Tinbergen, *The Herring Gull's World* (New York: Basic Books, 1961).

16. The Case for Animal Rights

Tom Regan

I regard myself as an advocate of animal rights—as a part of the animal rights movement. That movement, as I conceive it, is committed to a number of goals, including:

1. the total abolition of the use of animals in science

2. the total dissolution of commercial animal agriculture

3. and the total elimination of commercial and sport hunting and trapping.

There are, I know, people who profess to believe in animal rights who do not avow these goals. Factory farming, they say, is wrong—violates animals' rights—but traditional animal agriculture is all right. Toxicity tests of cosmetics on animals violates their rights; but not important medical research—cancer research, for example. The clubbing of baby seals is abhorrent; but not the harvesting of adult seals. I used to think I understood this reasoning. Not any more. You don't change unjust institutions by tidying them up.

What's wrong—what's fundamentally wrong—with the way animals are treated isn't the details that vary from case to case. It's the whole system. The forlornness of the veal calf is pathetic—heart wrenching; the pulsing pain of the chimp with electrodes planted deep in her brain is repulsive; the slow, torturous death of the raccoon caught in the leg hold trap, agonizing. But what is fundamentally wrong isn't the pain, isn't the suffering, isn't the deprivation. These compound what's wrong. Sometimes—often—they make it much worse. But they are not the fundamental wrong.

The fundamental wrong is the system that allows us to view animals as *our resources,* here for us—to be eaten, or surgically manipulated, or put in our cross hairs for sport or money. Once we accept this view of animals—as our resources—the rest is as predictable as it is regrettable. Why worry about their loneliness, their pain, their death? Since animals exist for us, here to benefit us in one way or another, what harms them really doesn't matter—or matters only if it starts to bother us, makes us feel a trifle uneasy when we eat our veal scampi, for example. So, yes, let us get veal calves out of solitary confinement, give them more space, a little straw, a few companions. But let us keep our veal scampi.

But a little straw, more space, and a few companions don't eliminate—don't even touch—the fundamental wrong, the wrong that attaches to our viewing and treating these animals as our resources. A veal calf killed to be eaten after living in close confinement is viewed and treated in this way: but so, too, is another who is raised (as they say) "more humanely." To right the fundamental wrong of our treatment of farm animals requires more than making rearing methods "more human"—requires something quite different—requires the total dissolution of commercial animal agriculture.

How we do this—whether we do this, or as in the case of animals in science, whether and how we abolish their use—these are to a large extent political questions. People must change their beliefs before they change their habits. Enough people, especially those elected to public office, must believe in change—must want it—before we will have laws that protect the rights of animals. This process of change is very complicated, very demanding, very exhausting, calling for the efforts of many hands—in education, publicity, political organization and activity, down to the licking of envelopes and stamps. As a trained and practicing philosopher the sort of contribution I can make is limited, but, I like to think important. The currency of philosophy is ideas—their meaning and rational foundation—not the nuts and bolts of the legislative process, say, or the mechanics of community organization. That's what I have been exploring over the past ten years or so in my essays and talks and, more recently, in my book, *The Case for Animal Rights.*[1] I believe the major conclusions I reach in that book are true because they are supported by

In Defense of Animals, edited by Peter Singer (Oxford: Basil Blackwell, Inc., 1985), pp. 13–26. Reprinted by permission.

the weight of the best arguments. I believe the idea of animal rights has reason, not just emotion, on its side.

In the space I have at my disposal here I can only sketch, in the barest outlines, some of the main features of the book. Its main themes—and we should not be surprised by this—involve asking and answering deep foundational moral questions, questions about what morality is, how it should be understood, what is the best moral theory all considered. I hope I can convey something of the shape I think this theory is. The attempt to do this will be—to use a word a friendly critic once used to describe my work—cerebral. In fact I was told by this person that my work is "too cerebral." But this is misleading. My feelings about how animals sometimes are treated are just as deep and just as strong as those of my more volatile compatriots. Philosophers do—to use the jargon of the day—have a right side to their brains. If it's the left side we contribute—or mainly should—that's because what talents we have reside there.

How to proceed? We begin by asking how the moral status of animals has been understood by thinkers who deny that animals have rights. Then we test the mettle of their ideas by seeing how well they stand up under the heat of fair criticism. If we start our thinking in this way we soon find that some people believe that we have no duties directly to animals—that we owe nothing *to them*—that we can do nothing that *wrongs them.* Rather, we can do wrong acts that involve animals, and so we have duties regarding them, though none to them. Such views may be called indirect duty views. By way of illustration:

Suppose your neighbor kicks your dog. Then your neighbor has done something wrong. But not to your dog. The wrong that has been done is a wrong to you. After all, it is wrong to upset people, and your neighbor's kicking your dog upsets you. So you are the one who is wronged, not your dog. Or again: by kicking your dog your neighbor damages your property. And since it is wrong to damage another person's property, your neighbor has done something wrong—to you, of course, not to your dog. Your neighbor no more wrongs your dog than your car would be wronged if the windshield were smashed. Your neighbor's duties involving your dog are indirect duties to you. More generally, all of our duties regarding animals are indirect duties to one another—to humanity.

How could someone try to justify such a view? One could say that your dog doesn't feel anything and so isn't hurt by your neighbor's kick, doesn't care about the pain since none is felt, is as unaware of anything as your windshield. Someone could say this but no rational person will since, among other considerations, such a view will commit one who holds it to the position that no human being feels pain either—that human beings also don't care about what happens to them. A second possibility is that though both humans and your dog are hurt when kicked, it is only human pain that matters. But, again, no rational person can believe this. Pain is pain wheresoever it occurs. If your neighbor's causing you pain is wrong because of the pain that is caused, we cannot rationally ignore or dismiss the moral relevance of the pain your dog feels.

Philosophers who hold indirect duty views—and many still do—have come to understand that they must avoid the two defects just noted—avoid, that is, both the view that animals don't feel anything as well as the idea that only human pain can be morally relevant. Among such thinkers the sort of view now favored is one or another form of what is called *contractarianism.*

Here, very crudely, is the root idea: morality consists of a set of rules that individuals voluntarily agree to abide by—as we do when we sign a contract (hence the name: contractarianism). Those who understand and accept the terms of the contract are covered directly—have rights created by, and recognized and protected in, the contract. And these contractors can also have protection spelled out for others who, though they lack the ability to understand morality and so cannot sign the contract themselves, are loved or cherished by those who can. Thus young children, for example, are unable to sign and lack rights. But they are protected by the contract nonetheless because of the sentimental interests of others, most notably their parents. So we have, then, duties involving these children, duties regarding them, but no duties to them. Our duties in their case are indirect duties to other human beings, usually their parents.

As for animals, since they cannot understand the contract, they obviously cannot sign; and since they cannot sign, they have no rights. Like children, however, some animals are the objects of the sentimental interest of others. You, for example, love your dog . . . or cat. So these animals—those enough people care about: companion animals, whales, baby seals, the American bald eagle—these animals, though they lack rights themselves, will be protected because of the sentimental interests of people. I have, then, according to contractarianism, no duty directly to your dog or any other animal, not even the duty not to cause them pain or suffering; my duty not to hurt them is a duty I have to those people who care about what happens to them. As for other animals, where no or little sentimental interest is present—farm animals, for example, or laboratory rats—what duties we have grow weaker and weaker, perhaps to the vanishing point. The pain and death they endure, though real, are not wrong if no one cares about them.

Contractarianism could be a hard view to refute when it comes to the moral status of animals if it was an adequate theoretical approach to the moral status of human beings. It is not adequate in this latter respect, however, which makes the question of its adequacy in the former—regarding animals—utterly moot. For consider: morality, according to the (crude) contractarian position before us, consists of rules people agree to abide by. What people? Well, enough to make a difference—enough, that is, so that collectively they have the power to enforce the rules that are drawn up in the contract. That is very well and good for the signatories—but not so good for anyone who is not asked to sign. And there is nothing in contractarianism of the sort we are discussing that guarantees or requires that everyone will have a chance to participate equitably in framing the rules of morality. The result is that this approach to ethics could sanction the most blatant forms of social, economic, moral, and political injustice, ranging from a repressive caste system to systematic racial or sexual discrimination. Might, on this theory, does make right. Let those who are the victims of injustice suffer as they will. It matters not so long as no one else—no contractor, or too few of them—cares about it. Such a theory takes one's moral breath away . . . as if, for example, there is nothing wrong with apartheid in South Africa if too few white South Africans are upset by it. A theory with so little to recommend it at the level of the ethics of our treatment of our fellow humans cannot have anything more to recommend it when it comes to the ethics of how we treat our fellow animals.

The version of contractarianism just examined is, as I have noted, a crude variety, and in fairness to those of a contractarian persuasion it must be noted that much more refined, subtle, and ingenious varieties are possible. For example, John Rawls, in his *A Theory of Justice*, sets forth a version of contractarianism that forces the contractors to ignore the accidental features of being a human being—for example, whether one is white or black, male or female, a genius or of modest intellect. Only by ignoring such features, Rawls believes, can we insure that the principles of justice contractors would agree upon are not based on bias or prejudice. Despite the improvement a view such as Rawls's shows over the cruder forms of contractarianism, it remains deficient: it systematically denies that we have direct duties to those human beings who do not have a sense of justice—young children, for instance, and many mentally retarded humans. And yet it seems reasonably certain that, were we to torture a young child or a retarded elder, we would be doing something that wrongs them, not something that is wrong if (and only if) other humans with a sense of justice are upset. And since this is true in the case of these humans, we cannot rationally deny the same in the case of animals.

Indirect duty views, then, including the best among them, fail to command our rational assent. Whatever ethical theory we rationally should accept, therefore, it must at least recognize that we have some duties directly to animals, just as we have some duties directly to each other. The next two theories I'll sketch attempt to meet this requirement.

The first I call the cruelty–kindness view. Simply stated, this view says that we have a direct duty to be kind to animals and a direct duty not to be cruel to them. Despite the familiar, reassuring ring of these ideas, I do not believe this view offers an adequate theory. To make this clearer, consider kindness. A kind person acts from a certain kind of motive—compassion or concern, for example. And that is a virtue. But there is no guarantee that a kind act is a right act. If I am a generous racist, for example, I will be inclined to act kindly toward members of my own race, favoring their interests above others. My kindness would be real and, so far as it goes, good. But I trust it is too obvious to require comment that my kind acts may not be above moral reproach—may, in fact, be positively wrong because rooted in injustice. So kindness, not withstanding its status as a virtue to be encouraged, simply will not cancel the weight of a theory of right action.

Cruelty fares no better. People or their acts are cruel if they display either a lack of sympathy for or, worse, the presence of enjoyment in, seeing another suffer. Cruelty in all its guises *is* a bad thing—is a tragic human failing. But just as a person's being motivated by kindness does not guarantee that they do what is right, so the absence of cruelty does not assure that they avoid doing what is wrong. Many people who perform abortions, for example, are not cruel, sadistic people. But that fact about their character and motivation does not settle the terribly difficult question about the morality of abortion. The case is no different when we examine the ethics of our treatment of animals. So, yes, let us be for kindness and against cruelty. But let us not suppose that being for the one and against the other answers questions about moral right and wrong.

Some people think the theory we are looking for is utilitarianism. A utilitarian accepts two moral principles. The first is a principle of equality: everyone's interests count, and similar interests must be counted as having similar weight or importance. White or black, male or female, American or Iranian, human or animal: everyone's pain or frustration matter and matter equally with the like pain or frustration of anyone else. The second principle a utilitarian accepts is the principle of utility: do that act that will bring about the best balance of satisfaction over frustration for everyone affected by the outcome.

As a utilitarian, then, here is how I am to approach the task of deciding what I morally ought to do: I must ask who will be affected if I choose to do one thing rather than another, how much each individual will be affected, and where the best results are most likely to lie—which option, in other words, is most likely to bring about the best results, the best balance of satisfaction over frustration. That option, whatever it may be, is the one I ought to choose. That is where my moral duty lies.

The great appeal of utilitarianism rests with its uncompromising *egalitarianism:* everyone's interests count and count equally with the like interests of everyone else. The kind of odious discrimination some forms of contractarianism can justify—discrimination based on race or sex, for example—seems disallowed in principle by utilitarianism, as is speciesism—systematic discrimination based on species membership.

The sort of equality we find in utilitarianism, however, is not the sort an advocate of animal or human rights should have in mind. Utilitarianism has no room for the equal moral rights of different individuals because it has no room for their equal inherent value or worth. What has value for the utilitarian is the satisfaction of an individual's interests, not the individual whose interests they are. A universe in which you satisfy your desire for water, food, and warmth, is, other things being equal, better than a universe in which these desires are frustrated. And the same is true in the case of an animal with similar desires. But neither you nor the animal have any value in your own right. Only your feelings do.

Here is an analogy to help make the philosophical point clearer: a cup contains different liquids—sometimes sweet, sometimes bitter, sometimes a mix of the two. What has value are the liquids: the sweeter the better, the bitter the worse. The cup—the container—has no value. It's what goes into it, not what they go into, that has value. For the utilitarian, you and I are like the cup; we have no value as individuals and thus no equal value. What has value is what goes into us, what we serve as receptacles for; our feelings of satisfaction have positive value, our feelings of frustration have negative value.

Serious problems arise for utilitarianism when we remind ourselves that it enjoins us to bring about the best consequences. What does this mean? It doesn't mean the best consequences for me alone, or for my family or friends, or any other person taken individually. No, what we must do is, roughly, as follows: we must add up—somehow! —the separate satisfactions and frustrations of everyone likely to be affected by our choice, the satisfactions in one column, the frustrations in the other. We must total each column for each of the options before us. That is what it means to say the theory is aggregative. And then we must choose that option which is most likely to bring about the best balance of totaled satisfactions over totaled frustrations. Whatever act would lead to this outcome is the one we morally ought to perform—is where our moral duty lies. And that act quite clearly might not be the same one that would bring about the best results for me personally, or my family or friends, or a lab animal. The best aggregated consequences for everyone concerned are not necessarily the best for each individual.

That utilitarianism is an aggregative theory—that different individual's satisfactions or frustrations are added, or summed, or totaled—is the key objection to this theory. My Aunt Bea is old, inactive, a cranky, sour person, though not physically ill. She prefers to go on living. She is also rather rich. I could make a fortune if I could get my hands on her money, money she intends to give me in any event, after she dies, but which she refuses to give me now. In order to avoid a huge tax bite, I plan to donate a handsome sum of my profits to a local children's hospital. Many, many children will benefit from my generosity, and much joy will be brought to their parents, relatives, and friends. If I don't get the money rather soon, all these ambitions will come to naught. The once-in-a-lifetime opportunity to make a real killing will be gone. Why, then, not really kill my Aunt Bea? Oh, of course I *might* get caught. But I'm no fool and, besides, her doctor can be counted on to cooperate (he has an eye for the same investment and I happen to know a good deal about his shady past). The deed can be done . . . professionally, shall we say. There is *very* little chance of getting caught. And as for my conscience being guilt ridden, I am a resourceful sort of fellow and will take more than sufficient comfort—as I lie on the beach at Acapulco—in contemplating the joy and health I have brought to so many others.

Suppose Aunt Bea is killed and the rest of the story comes out as told. Would I have done anything wrong? Anything immoral? One would have thought that I had. But not according to utilitarianism. Since what I did brought about the best balance of totaled satisfaction over frustration for all those affected by the outcome, what I did was not wrong. Indeed, in killing Aunt Bea the physician and I did what duty required.

This same kind of argument can be repeated in all sorts of cases, illustrating, time after time, how the utilitarian's position leads to results that impartial people find morally callous. It *is* wrong to kill my Aunt Bea in the name of bringing about the best results for others. A good end does not justify an evil means. Any adequate moral theory will have to explain why this is so. Utilitarianism fails in this respect and so cannot be the theory we seek.

What to do? Where to begin anew? The place to begin, I think, is with the utilitarian's view of the value of the individual—or, rather, lack of value. In its place suppose we consider that you and I, for example, do have value as individuals—what we'll call *inherent value*. To say we have such value is to say that we are something more than, something different from, mere receptacles. Moreover, to insure that we do not pave the way for such injustices as slavery or sexual discrimination, we must believe that all who have inherent value have it equally, regardless of their sex, race, religion, birthplace, and so on. Similarly to be discarded as irrelevant are one's talents or skills, intelligence and wealth, personality or pathology, whether one is loved and admired—or despised and loathed. The genius and the retarded child, the prince and the pauper, the brain surgeon and the fruit vendor, Mother Teresa and the most unscrupulous used car salesman—all have inherent value, all possess it equally, and all have an equal right to be treated with respect, to be treated in ways that do not reduce them to the status of things, as if they exist as resources for others. My value as an individual is independent of my usefulness to you. Yours is not dependent on your usefulness to me. For either of us to treat the other in ways that fail to show respect for the other's independent value is to act immorally—is to violate the individual's rights.

Some of the rational virtues of this view— what I call the rights view—should be evident. Unlike (crude) contractarianism, for example, the rights view *in principle* denies the moral tolerability of any and all forms of racial, sexual, or social discrimination; and unlike utilitarianism, this view *in principle* denies that we can justify good results by using evil means that violate an individual's rights—denies, for example, that it would be moral to kill my Aunt Bea to harvest beneficial consequences for others. That would be to sanction the disrespectful treatment of the individual in the name of the social good, something the rights view will not—categorically will not—ever allow.

The rights view—or so I believe—is rationally the most satisfactory moral theory. It surpasses all other theories in the degree to which it illuminates and explains the foundation of our duties to one another—the domain of human morality. On this score, it has the best reasons, the best arguments, on its side. Of course, if it were possible to show that only human beings are included within its scope, then a person like myself, who believes in animal rights, would be obliged to look elsewhere than to the rights view.

But attempts to limit its scope to humans only can be shown to be rationally defective. Animals, it is true, lack many of the abilities humans possess. They can't read, do higher mathematics, build a bookcase, or make *baba ghanoush*. Neither can many human beings, however, and yet we don't say—

and shouldn't say—that they (these humans) therefore have less inherent value, less of a right to be treated with respect, than do others. It is the *similarities* between those human beings who most clearly, most noncontroversially have such value—the people reading this, for example—it is our similarities, not our differences that matter most. And the really crucial, the basic similarity is simply this; we are each of us the experiencing subject of a life, each of us a conscious creature having an individual welfare that has importance to us whatever our usefulness to others. We want and prefer things; believe and feel things; recall and expect things. And all these dimensions of our life, including our pleasure and pain, our enjoyment and suffering, our satisfaction and frustration, our continued existence or our untimely death—all make a difference to the quality of our life as lived, as experienced by us as individuals. As the same is true of those animals who concern us (those who are eaten and trapped, for example), they, too, must be viewed as the experiencing subjects of a life with inherent value of their own.

There are some who resist the idea that animals have inherent value. "Only humans have such value," they profess. How might this narrow view be defended? Shall we say that only humans have the requisite intelligence, or autonomy, or reason? But there are many, many humans who will fail to meet these standards and yet who are reasonably viewed as having value above and beyond their usefulness to others. Shall we claim that only humans belong to the right species—the species *Homo sapiens?* But this is blatant speciesism. Will it be said, then, that all—and only—humans have immortal souls? Then our opponents more than have their work cut out for them. I am myself not ill-disposed to there being immortal souls. Personally, I profoundly hope I have one. But I would not want to rest my position on a controversial ethical issue on the even more controversial question about who or what has an immortal soul. That is to dig one's hole deeper, not climb out. Rationally, it is better to resolve moral issues without making more controversial assumptions than are needed. The question of who has inherent value is such a question, one that is more rationally resolved without the introduction of the idea of immortal souls than by its use.

Well, perhaps some will say that animals have some inherent value, only *less* than we do. Once

again, however, attempts to defend this view can be shown to lack rational justification. What could be the basis of our having more inherent value than animals? Will it be their lack of reason, or autonomy, or intellect? Only if we are willing to make the same judgment in the case of humans who are similarly deficient. But it is not true that such humans—the retarded child, for example, or the mentally deranged—have less inherent value than you or I. Neither, then, can we rationally sustain the view that animals like them in being the experiencing subjects of a life have less inherent value. *All* who have inherent value have it *equally,* whether they be human animals or not.

Inherent value, then, belongs equally to those who are the experiencing subjects of a life. Whether it belongs to others—to rocks and rivers, trees and glaciers, for example—we do not know. And may never know. But neither do we need to know, if we are to make the case for animal rights. We do not need to know how many people, for example, are eligible to vote in the next presidential election before we can know whether I am. Similarly, we do not need to know *how many* individuals have inherent value before we can know that some do. When it comes to the case for animal rights, then what we need to know is whether the animals who, in our culture are routinely eaten, hunted, and used in our laboratories, for example, are like us in being subjects of a life. And we *do* know this. We do *know* that many—literally, billions and billions—of these animals are the subjects of a life in the sense explained and so have inherent value if we do. And since, in order to have the best theory of our duties to one another, we must recognize our equal inherent value, as individuals, reason—not sentiment, not emotion—reason compels us to recognize the equal inherent value of these animals. And, with this, their equal right to be treated with respect.

That, *very* roughly, is the shape and feel of the case for animal rights. Most of the details of the supporting argument are missing. They are to be found in the book I alluded to earlier. Here, the details go begging and I must, in closing, limit myself to four final points.

The first is how the theory that underlies the case for animal rights shows that the animal rights movement is a part of, not antagonistic to, the human rights movement. The theory that rationally grounds the rights of animals also grounds the rights of humans. Thus are those involved in the animal rights movement partners in the struggle to secure respect for human rights—the rights of women, for example, or minorities and workers. The animal rights movement is cut from the same moral cloth as these.

Second, having set out the broad outlines of the rights view, I can now say why its implications for farming and science, for example, are both clear and uncompromising. In the case of using animals in science, the rights view is categorically abolitionist. Lab animals are not our tasters; we are not their kings. Because these animals are treated—routinely, systematically—as if their value is reducible to their usefulness to others, they are routinely, systematically treated with a lack of respect, and thus are their rights routinely, systematically violated. This is just as true when they are used in trivial, duplicative, unnecessary or unwise research as it is when they are used in studies that hold out real promise of human benefits. We can't justify harming or killing a human being (my Aunt Bea, for example) just for these sorts of reasons. Neither can we do so even in the case of so lowly a creature as a laboratory rat. It is not just refinement or reduction that are called for, not just larger, cleaner cages, not just more generous use of anaesthetic or the elimination of multiple surgery, not just tidying up the system. It is replacement—completely. The best we can do when it comes to using animals in science is—not to use them. That is where our duty lies, according to the rights view.

As for commercial animal agriculture, the rights view takes a similar abolitionist position. The fundamental moral wrong here is not that animals are kept in stressful close confinement, or in isolation, or that they have their pain and suffering, their needs and preferences ignored or discounted. *All* these *are* wrong, of course, but they are not the fundamental wrong. They are symptoms and effects of the deeper, systematic wrong that allows these animals to be viewed and treated as lacking independent value, as resources for us—as, indeed, a renewable resource.

Giving farm animals more space, more natural environments, more companions does not right the fundamental wrong, any more than giving lab animals more anaesthesia or bigger, cleaner cages would right the fundamental wrong in their case. Nothing less than the total dissolution of commercial animal agriculture will do this, just as, for similar reasons I won't develop at length here, morality requires nothing less than the total elimination of commercial and sport hunting and trapping. The rights view's implications, then, as I have said, are clear—and are uncompromising.

My last two points are about philosophy—my profession. It is most obviously, no substitute for political action. The words I have written here and in other places by themselves don't change a thing. It is what we do with the thoughts the words express—our acts, our deeds—that change things. All that philosophy can do, and all I have attempted, is to offer a vision of what our deeds could aim at. And the why. But not the how.

Finally, I am reminded of my thoughtful critic, the one I mentioned earlier, who chastised me for being "too cerebral." Well, cerebral I have been: indirect duty views, utilitarianism, contractarianism—hardly the stuff deep passions are made of. I am also reminded, however, of the image another friend once set before me—the image of the ballerina as expressive of disciplined passion. Long hours of sweat and toil, of loneliness and practice, of doubt and fatigue; that is the discipline of her craft. But the passion is there, too; the fierce drive to excel, to speak through her body, to do it right, to pierce our minds. That is the image of philosophy I would leave with you; not "too cerebral," but *disciplined passion*. Of the discipline, enough has been seen. As for the passion:

There are times, and these are not infrequent, when tears come to my eyes when I see, or read, or hear of the wretched plight of animals in the hands of humans. Their pain, their suffering, their loneliness, their innocence, their death. Anger. Rage. Pity. Sorrow. Disgust. The whole creation groans under the weight of the evil we humans visit upon these mute, powerless creatures. It is our heart, not just our head, that calls for an end, that demands of us that we overcome, for them, the habits and forces behind their systematic oppression. All great movements, it is written, go through three stages: ridicule, discussion, adoption. It is the realization of this third stage—adoption—that demands both our passion and our discipline, our heart and our head. The fate of animals is in our hands. God grant we are equal to the task.

Note

1. Tom Regan, *The Case for Animal Rights* (Berkeley: University of California Press, 1983).

17. Interspecific Justice

Donald VanDeVeer

I have never committed an axe-murder, bludg-eoned fellow-humans to death, nor eaten any of their babies. Even though I would not think of set-ting fire to cats (though I am not at all fond of them), I have most of my adult life paid people to axe-murder and bludgeon to death a considerable variety of creatures, some of whom were babies, so that I might eat them; they were, in fact, tasty. That this description applied to my actions or that there were moral questions about these practices is some-thing to which I was largely oblivious until reading Peter Singer's essay "Animal Liberation" several years ago.[1]

The effect of Singer's early essay was some-times—and in my case—to shake one from his "dogmatic slumbers." However, before the uptake could secure itself, Singer lost some hard-won cred-ibility near the end of his essay by stating:

> What, for instance, are we to do about genuine conflicts of interest like rats biting slum chil-dren? I am not sure of the answer, but the essential point is just that we *do* see this as a conflict of interests, that we recognize that rats have interests too.[2]

To be fair, Singer does *not* say or suggest that the interests of rats ought to be weighed equally, but his willingness to consider that there might be a serious moral question here no doubt struck some readers as a *reductio* of his position. A further factor in such a reaction may be that there is naturally a powerful *desire* to believe that one is not party to morally outrageous practices and that arguments that suggest as much "must" be fallacious. This less than reflective reaction may have occurred, I specu-late, with many initial encounters with Singer's essay.

In that essay and more explicitly in Singer's book by the same title, there is a simple, tempting argument in favor of the view that humans have some duties toward animals; one possible recon-struction is this:

1. All or virtually all human beings are sentient creatures.

2. Many animals are sentient creatures.

3. Moral agents have a duty not to cause suffer-ing to sentient creatures.

4. So, moral agents have a duty to refrain from causing suffering to (sentient) humans and (sentient) animals.

5. The interests of *all* sentient creatures (in not suffering) must be given equal consideration.

6. So, the imposition of suffering on animals (an overriding of the duty mentioned in [4]) would have to be justified by grounds of the same moral weight as those which would be neces-sary to justify the imposition of suffering on humans.[3]

The argument seems plausible, and some of its premises are incontrovertible. Singer's strong and specific admonitions (e.g., to become a vegetarian) in his radical critique of almost universal current practices affecting animals appeal to this argument and to further assumptions about (a) the actual effects of existing practices on animals (e.g., experi-mentation, raising animals for food and other prod-ucts), (b) judgments about the painfulness or disability of these practices for the animals involved, and (c) the falsity of the claim that certain human satisfactions are obtainable only by harming or killing animals. The first four claims of my recon-struction of Singer's argument are reasonable. What is meant, in (5), by giving the interests of all sentient creatures "equal consideration" is less clear. Does it mean "taking into account" all such interests? Does this mean giving *equal* moral *weight* to like interests? If not, will (6) follow? Further, since killing may be performed painlessly the constraint on causing ani-mals suffering (even if [6] is conceded) cannot yield an adequate basis for deciding on the legitimacy of killing animals if it is done painlessly. It is not my purpose to dwell on Singer's argument in any direct way, although I shall survey some principles that proffer answers to some of the above questions. Of the views to be considered, one emerges that is rea-sonable and in some important ways stands in

Inquiry, Vol. 22, No. 1-2 (Summer 1979), 55–70. Reprinted by permission of the publisher.

agreement with *Animal Liberation*. At points, however, it delineates a competing view on the question of how we may legitimately treat animals. While I shall allude on occasion to the views of those who have taken a stand on these matters in recent literature, e.g., Peter Singer and Tom Regan, I conceive my task as a more constructive than critical one, and I shall try to sketch some of the features that I think must be incorporated in an adequate theory. Since I will focus on conflicts of interests between humans and animals and the question of a just resolution of competing morally relevant claims, one might describe what is needed as a theory of interspecific justice.[4] Questions about the treatment of animals, like questions about nonparadigm humans (e.g., *Homo sapiens* fetuses) are hard cases, and even if the suggestions posed here are correct, they will fall short of a fully adequate account. Indeed, it seems to me that the formulation of an adequate theoretical basis for the legitimate treatment of animals is no simple task and cannot be done simply by extending, in any straightforward way, principles widely accepted or thought to be uncontroversial. It is not surprising that some of the recalcitrant problems confronting the formulation of an adequate theory of justice with regard to humans have parallels in attempts to formulate an adequate theory of interspecific justice.

I. Interests and Conflicts of Interests

Of those animals capable of suffering we may assume that they have at least one interest, namely, in not suffering. By this assumption I do not mean that they are interested in not suffering (though they may be) but, roughly, that it is *in their interest* not to suffer. This last claim means that it is not conducive to an animal's well-being to suffer—whether or not the animal is capable of "consciously" wanting not to suffer. Further, the claim that it is not in the interest of an animal to suffer is, I think, a strong presumptive one. While pain *per se* is undesirable, it may be in the interest of animals to suffer *on balance* for the sake of a certain beneficial result—as in the painful removal of a gangrenous leg by surgery—as it is also for human beings. While the concept of an action's being in the interest of a creature is not transparently clear, it is contingently and commonly in the interest of a being not to suffer, although there are exceptions

when it is in its over-all interest to do so. Since it is possible to cause death painlessly, an animal in whose interest it is not to suffer *may* not be such that it is in its interest not to die. However, I shall simply assume that *generally* when it is in some creature's interest not to suffer it is also in its interest not to die (and, hence, not to be killed). Let us assume, then—somewhat more strongly than our earlier (3)—that moral agents have a duty, *ceteris paribus,* not to cause suffering to those animals that can suffer and a duty, *ceteris paribus,* not to cause animals to die. On this view there are many common practices that are not in the interests of many animals, and there is a presumptive duty not to engage in certain practices, namely, any that cause suffering or death to *those* animals in whose interest it is not to suffer or not to die. The troublesome and difficult question that arises, once one is convinced that both human beings (or many) and animals (or many) have at least some morally relevant interests, concerns how to *weigh* their respective interests in general and how to adjudicate *conflicts of interest* that arise between humans and animals. What we crucially need, to advance the current reconsideration of our treatment of animals, is an identification and assessment of principles that provide a basis for comparatively weighing such interests. We may be guided here by the standard method of testing principles by checking their implications against our deepest and strongest pretheoretical convictions about specific cases ("intuitions" in *one* sense of the term), and also by how well such principles cohere with other defensible principles, in particular, how well principles advocating interspecific discriminations (weightings of respective interests) seem to be consistent with parallel and defensible intraspecific discriminations.[5]

II. Principles of Adjudicating Conflicts of Interests

Singer characterizes views that advocate a certain preferential weighing of human interests over that of animals as "speciesist."[6] He claims:

> If a being suffers there can be no moral justification for refusing to take that suffering into consideration. No matter what the nature of the being, the principle of equality requires that its suffering be counted equally with the like suffering—in so far as rough comparisons can be made—of any other being.

The racist violates the principle of equality by giving greater weight to the interests of members of his own race when there is a clash between their interests and the interests of those of another race. The sexist violates the principle of equality by favoring the interests of his own sex. Similarly the speciesist allows the interests of his own species to override the greater interests of members of other species. The pattern is identical in each case.[7]

The quoted passage does not distinguish some relevantly different principles that may be aptly classified as speciesist views and not all of which are equally tempting. I shall identify three forms of speciesism and two nonspeciesist views, which I shall dub Two Factor Egalitarianism and Species Egalitarianism respectively; the first three principles may be entitled "speciesist" because they all advocate a heavier weighting of human interests over that of animals or do not concede that animals have any interests at all. The fourth principle also weights human interests more heavily but only when certain contingent conditions are satisfied; for reasons mentioned later, it would be misleading to label it a speciesist view. I list the names of the principles here, and consider each in turn:

1. Radical Speciesism
2. Extreme Speciesism
3. Interest Sensitive Speciesism
4. Two Factor Egalitarianism
5. Species Egalitarianism

In turning to Radical Speciesism we consider the only one of the five principles to be identified that in fact is incompatible with the premises of the mentioned argument appealing to animal suffering.

Radical Speciesism

Radical Speciesism is the view that

It is morally permissible, *ceteris paribus*, to treat animals in any fashion one chooses.

One ground for this claim is the view that there is no *intrinsic* feature of any animal *per se* in virtue of which there is any moral constraint on how it may be treated. I speak of "intrinsic feature" because the radical speciesist may allow that a given animal ought not to be harmed because of its relational trait, e.g., it is Smith's pet. This view is similar to the by now familiar view of Descartes's that animals were mere automata, extended things that neither think nor are sentient. With the further assumption that only thinking or sentient things are such that something may be in their interests, it follows that animals have no interests. So, it could not be the case that the interest of any animal outweighs that of any human being. There seem to be no premises that are both strong enough to entail Radical Speciesism (RS) and plausible. The Cartesian assumption is a strong one but not at all tempting. I shall not explore it. That many animals can and do suffer intensely is quite obvious. The anti-Cartesian arguments may be found elsewhere; in general, they are the arguments against extreme scepticism about Other Minds. Since many animals can suffer, the Cartesian assumption is evidently an untenable view. I include it for purposes of contrast and completeness. The reader may wish to examine the more patient discussions in Singer's book.[8]

What are the moral implications of Radical Speciesism? On RS there is no presumption at all, based on the effects *on the animal,* against putting live puppies in one's oven, and heating them in order to watch them squirm or convulse or fall over; the reader can imagine other "perverse" experiments. The important issue here is simply put. Can animals (some) suffer? If so, it is, in general, in their interest not to suffer and moral agents have a presumptive duty to avoid causing such suffering. Hence, we must judge, if we acknowledge that animals suffer, that RS is mistaken or that the *ceteris paribus* clause is rarely satisfied.

It may be noted that Singer characterizes the "speciesist" as allowing "the interests of his own species to override the greater interests of members of other species" (see earlier quotation). While such unequal weighting of interests seems to be an objectionable feature of other principles that I have dubbed speciesist, it is worth observing that the Cartesian elaboration that may be associated with Radical Speciesism (as part of the ground for the latter) is not speciesist on Singer's criterion, for RS in its Cartesian elaboration does not weigh interests *unequally;* it simply concedes no interests at all to animals.

Those forms of speciesism that allow that animals have interests and that are compatible with the statements constituting the Suffering Argument are those remaining to be considered. They may all be regarded as principles purporting to guide action in cases of *conflicts of interests*. In examining such cases it is desirable to focus, when possible, on cases where the existence of animals is no threat to humans (e.g., not on cases of animals attacking humans) and, when possible, on "normal" before extreme or bizarre situations.

Extreme Speciesism

To distinguish two further forms of speciesism we must suppose that there is a difference between the basic and peripheral interests of a being. It would be difficult to elaborate such a distinction in a precise manner or offer a full-fledged defense of it. It is clear, however, that in the absence of certain sorts of goods many creatures cannot function in ways common to their species; they do not function in a "minimally adequate" way, for example, in the absence of food, water, oxygen or the presence of prolonged, intense pain. We may say that it is in a creature's *basic* interest to have (not have) such things. In contrast there are goods such that in their absence it is true only that the creature does not thrive and that are, then, not in its basic interest (e.g., toys for my dog). This distinction is admittedly vague but it is not empty. Its application must, in part, depend on contextual matters. Given such a distinction, Extreme Speciesism is the view that

When there is a conflict of interests between an animal and a human being, it is morally permissible, *ceteris paribus*, so to act that a basic interest of the animal is subordinated for the sake of promoting even a peripheral interest of a human being.

Extreme Speciesism (ES) proffers a different theoretical basis for actions affecting animals from Radical Speciesism when RS is linked to Cartesian assumptions, but, as stated, RS and ES will, in practice, sanction the same policies when there is, in fact, a requisite conflict of interests. When there is not, ES allows (is compatible with) acting to promote an animal interest, e.g., the interest in not suffering. As stated, however, ES would not prohibit puppy cooking and cat torturing as long as such acts promote some peripheral (or basic) human interest. In the end, perhaps, much may depend on *how* peripheral the human interest one is considering is or further discriminations of that sort. Nevertheless, unless we wish to defend the moral permissibility of recreational puppy cooking and

like acts, ES must be rejected as well as RS. On ES the kind or level of animal interest involved in a conflict of interests is, in effect, unimportant and need not be considered; this is not true of the next form of speciesism to be considered.

Interest Sensitive Speciesism

Interest Sensitive Speciesism (ISS) is the view that

When there is a conflict of interests between an animal and a human being, it is morally permissible, *ceteris paribus*, so to act that an interest of the animal is subordinated for the sake of promoting a *like* interest of a human being (or a more basic one) but one may not subordinate a *basic* interest of an animal for the sake of promoting a *peripheral* human interest.

On this principle what is permissible depends importantly on whether or not the conflicting interests are basic or not; it is, thus, "interest sensitive." This principle sanctions a wide range of treatment preferential to human beings. For example, in a life raft case where the raft is overloaded and about to go under and either I or my dog will die (not both) before rescue, ISS permits me to sacrifice my dog if I so choose. In cases of conflict of *like* interests it is permissible, *ceteris paribus*, to subordinate that of the animal. Anti-speciesist principles that do *not* yield this result are hard to defend. Unlike RS and ES, which also yield this result, ISS does *not* permit puppy cooking or cat torturing for the pleasure of watching them squirm. This fact immediately makes ISS a more viable contender for the appellation, "justifiable form of speciesism."

While ISS clearly permits an evident discrimination in favor of human interests while not, in effect, assigning infinite weight to the latter, it will strike many as giving *insufficient* weight to human interests. For, on ISS, if it is in a bird's interest not to be incarcerated (as in a cage) and this interest is more basic than a hedonistic interest of a human owner in keeping it there, then such acts are impermissible since they would subordinate a basic animal interest in order to promote a peripheral human one. Suppose that having musk perfume, leather wearing apparel or luggage, fur rugs, ivory piano keys, or animal-derived glue are not necessary to promote basic human interests. If so, then ISS would entail that killing animals for these purposes would (supposing that doing so violates a basic interest of these animals in continuing to live), *ceteris paribus,* be impermissible. Given the mentioned suppositions some would judge ISS as "too strong" even though it plausibly prohibits cat torturing to promote sadistic pleasure. I leave the question of whether ISS is "too strong" or "too weak" open here. There is a more basic objection to ISS, namely, that it omits consideration of another factor that is morally relevant in adjudicating conflicts of interests.

The objection calls attention, in part, to the enormous diversity *among* animals whose basic interest may conflict with some human interest. In this regard, the use of the expression "speciesism" tends to suggest, perhaps, that we are only dealing with two groups and, hence, encourages formulating principles that suggest the permissibility of some sort of subordination of the interests of members of one group to the interests of members of the other.[9] This perspective reflects our tendency, Jonathan Swift to the contrary, to divide the animal world into the human and nonhuman or, analogously, into the inedible and the edible.[10] We ought not to forget that there are estimated to be about 1.5 million species and about 10,000 new ones discovered each year.[11] Significant differences *among* nonhuman species may become ignored with Interest Sensitive Speciesism. If it is in the interest of both an oyster and a chimpanzee not to be killed, ISS only requires that one consider the fact that the interest is in each case a basic and not a peripheral one. However, it is most tempting to think that while both interests are basic, the interest of the chimpanzee is of greater moral weight than that of the oyster, a judgment analogous to the one about the same-level or "like" interests of my dog and myself in my life raft case. If so, then a principle purporting to be a reasonable guide to weighting the interests of members of different species must take account of something other than whether the interests in question are "like" or "unlike." Such a consideration provides a basis for another principle, one to which we may now turn.

Two Factor Egalitarianism

It is necessary, to formulate our next principle, to recognize interests that are not basic in the sense suggested earlier yet not frivolous. I shall call such interests "serious interests." A rough criterion for serious interests would be that something is in a

being's serious interest if and only if, though it can survive without it, it is difficult or costly (to its well-being) to do so. Hence, it may be in the serious interest of a lonely child to have a pet or in the serious interest of an eagle to be able to fly. Serious interests are not *as* peripheral as Jones's interest in watching cockfights. It would be less messy if interests did not exhibit degrees of importance to their possessors; unfortunately, they do. This is also true of the other factor considered by the next principle, the factor of psychological capacities.

Two Factor Egalitarianism can now be formulated; it holds that

When there is an interspecies conflict of interests between two beings, A and B, it is morally permissible, *ceteris paribus:*

1. to sacrifice the interest of A to promote a like interest of B if A lacks significant psychological capacities possessed by B,

2. to sacrifice a basic interest of A to promote a serious interest of B if A substantially lacks significant psychological capacities possessed by B,

3. to sacrifice the peripheral interest to promote the more basic interest if the beings are similar with respect to psychological capacity (regardless of who possesses the interests).[12]

On TFE the subordination of basic animal interests (say, in living or not suffering) may be subordinated if the animal is (significantly) psychologically "inferior" to the human in question. "Psychological" is intended to include the "mental." Let us conjecture about the implications of TFE; I leave certain assumptions tacit. On TFE killing oysters or (most kinds of) fish for food for human survival would be permissible; killing them only for the human pleasure of doing so would not be. On this view *certain* forms of hunting (recreational killing) would seem to be immoral. Similarly certain rodeo activities and bull-fighting would not be justified. The killing of seals for food by an Eskimo would be justified; the killing (and radical deprivation and suffering) of veal calves by people in agriculturally affluent areas may be wrong.[13] TFE allows the sacrifice of my dog in our life raft case. Many of these implications are plausible. In general, TFE permits scientific experiments on animals where the promised utility for humans and/or animals is very considerable but not otherwise; recent criticisms suggest that a small proportion of the millions of experiments regularly performed can be so categorized.[14] It appears, then, on TFE as well as with some other speciesist principles, that fairly *simple generalizations* about the morality of hunting, killing animals for food, and experiments on animals are unreasonable. This feature of course parallels the difficulties with familiar simple generalizations about when it is permissible to kill or experiment on humans; this consideration is not unfavorable to TFE.

So far I have neglected what will strike the traditionally minded as an unfortunate and "radical" implication of TFE. On TFE if there is a conflict of interests between a human permanently and (seriously) psychologically incapacitated by illness, injury, or senility and, on the other hand, an animal with similar or superior psychological capacities (self-awareness, capacity for purposive action, diverse emotions, affection, devotion, and so on), then the more peripheral interest must be subordinated, and the peripheral interest *may* be that of the human being. If the animal is sufficiently developed psychologically, then even a serious interest of a no more capacitated human should not take precedence over the basic interests of the animal. An example where an "under-capacity" human is involved might be this. Suppose, contrary to fact, that an infant with Tay-Sachs disease could be saved from imminent death by a kidney transplant from a healthy chimpanzee at the expense of the chimpanzee's life; TFE prohibits this way of adjudicating the conflict of interests.[15] This case would be, at best, a statistically unusual one, and is mentioned in the attempt to get clearer about principles which have implications concerning other almost universal practices, e.g., raising and killing animals for certain human purposes. An important general characteristic of TFE is that not *any* interest of *any* human morally outweighs *any* interest of *any* animal, such a consideration seems a desideratum of any acceptable principle. TFE attempts to take into account both the kind of interests at stake and also psychological traits of the beings in question.

If the core of speciesism is the belief that it is permissible to give preferential treatment to humans over animals *just because* the former are human beings, then TFE is not a speciesist view. Being a member of *Homo sapiens per se* is not assumed to justify preferential treatment of humans over animals. It is a matter of fact as to whether a given human being will match or exceed a given animal in terms of psychological capacity; usually humans will. However, TFE allows that if there were, for example, beings physiologically like apes except for large brains and more complicated central nervous systems who had intellectual and emotional lives more developed than mature humans, then in a conflict of *like* interests the interests of these ape-looking persons should take precedence.[16]

We shall return (in Section IV) to further examination of TFE. First, I shall describe a final principle purporting to adjudicate interspecific conflicts of interest. Then I shall turn to the challenge posed by those who are sharply opposed to much of our preferential treatment of humans, with the larger aim of seeing whether any principle proposed here meets the challenge and provides a satisfactory basis for justifying certain preferential treatment of humans over animals.

Species Egalitarianism

In contrast to principles that permit the subordination of animal interests in *a priori* fashion (radical speciesism) or do so in practice even when like interests are being considered (extreme speciesism), is a view that is distinctly anti-speciesist, one I label Species Egalitarianism:

When there is a conflict of interests between an animal and a human being it is morally permissible, *ceteris paribus,* to subordinate the more peripheral to the more basic interest and not otherwise; facts not relevant to how basic the interests are, are not morally relevant to resolving this conflict.

SE is a one factor (level of interests) principle in contrast to TFE. Like TFE it plausibly denies that any interest of any human outweighs any interest of any animal. In fact it suggests, in a radical way, that species identification of the possessors of the interests is irrelevant except in so far as this might bear on a nonevaluative description of the interests in question.

It is tempting to call this view "radical egalitarianism" because it allows, like Interest Sensitive Speciesism, no weight to the many impressive and (seemingly) morally relevant psychological differences among species. On this view it is not "where you are on the evolutionary scale" or what psychological capacities you have but only how fundamental your interest is that counts. This view is unacceptable. That we should, for example, equally weigh the interest in not being killed of an oyster, earthworm, or fruitfly with that of a like interest of a human being, is an implication in virtue of which we can summarily judge, I submit, that SE indeed reduces to an absurdity. While Radical and Extreme Speciesism both give undue weight to human interests over that of animals, Species Egalitarianism swings to the opposite error of giving too little. Part of the attraction of the former views may in fact derive from the blatant ignoring of relevant differences that occurs with SE and the assumption that there are no plausible alternative positions. In view of reasons discussed to this point the least counterintuitive principle appears to be Two Factor Egalitarianism, or possibly some variant of it. Before elaborating on such a view and considering objections to it, it will be useful to consider more thoroughly the challenge posed by those who are critical of current policies toward radically differential treatment of animals and humans. After doing so we will be in a better position to determine whether TFE is acceptable as it is, whether it requires revision, or whether it should be relegated to the wasteland of tempting but, in the end, irrational proposals.

III. The Challenge of the Critics

It has been argued by Tom Regan that the radically differential treatment that we extend toward animals as opposed to human beings cannot be justified unless "we are given some morally relevant difference that characterizes all humans, but no animals"—one that would, in other words, justify the different sorts of duties and/or rights that we commonly assume we have toward the two groups, or attribute to the two groups, respectively.[17] It is tempting to believe (as Regan allows), however, that not all animals have interests, e.g., protozoa. While protozoa, I shall assume, are not *sentient*, perhaps we should allow, to the contrary, that even for protozoa something may be in their interest, e.g., conducive to their well-being. If so, possession of some (at least one) interest will not serve as a difference, possibly a morally relevant one, between all human beings on the one hand and all animals on the other. A feature that *is* possessed by humans but not, however, by all animals is sentience. This

feature, since it *is* possessed by many animals, will not, however, satisfy Regan's requirement that we be given "some morally relevant difference that characterizes all humans, but no animals" (my italics). Such a feature will not, then, serve as a justification, or part of a justification, for radically differential treatment of all humans on the one hand and *all* animals on the other. The presence or absence of sentience is, however, a morally relevant trait, and it *will* serve to justify, or as part of a justification of, differential treatment of sentient creatures on the one hand and nonsentient creatures on the other, e.g., the subordination of certain animals (nonsentient ones) for the sake of the well-being of others (sentient humans and sentient nonhumans). Hence, *some* differential treatment of humans on the one hand and *some* animals on the other is, *ceteris paribus*, justifiable, I believe, without satisfying the stringent requirement that there is "some morally relevant difference that characterizes all humans, but no animals." This conclusion serves to undermine certain arguments prohibiting radically differential treatment of nonsentient animals. The conclusion is, however, a very weak one. For most differential treatment of humans and animals that is controversial involves differential treatment *within* the class of sentient creatures. The challenge posed by critics of established practices toward animals, such as Tom Regan and, possibly, Peter Singer, is more reasonably posed in the following way: to justify radically differential treatment of creatures *all of whom are sentient* it is necessary to identify a morally relevant difference between those who receive preferential treatment and those who do not. Further, any such morally relevant difference must be sufficiently significant to justify the specific differential treatment in question.[18] Of the views previously considered the only one not subject to decisive objections (considered to this point) that also proposes a basis for subordinating the interests of animals when there is a conflict of like interests between humans and sentient animals, is Two Factor Egalitarianism. It, thus, *purports* to provide the requisite morally relevant difference that would serve to justify some, at least, of the radically differential treatment of humans and animals, treatment that is not merely the kind involved in extending preferential treatment to humans over *nonsentient* animals. TFE is, then, of special interest and, in view of current disputes, not uncontroversial. Let us examine it in more detail.

IV. Two Factor Egalitarianism Explored

Two Factor Egalitarianism assumes the relevance of two matters: (1) level or importance of interests to each being in a conflict of interests, and (2) the psychological capacities of the parties whose interests conflict. It is worth considering further the rationale for assuming their relevance. First, consider the importance of the respective interests. In familiar infelicitous situations where a conflict of interests can be resolved only by sacrificing the interest of one party, a plausible principle would seem to be that there is a *presumption* in favor of maximizing utility or at least choosing an alternative that will minimize net disutility.[19] Given our initial crude distinction between basic and peripheral interests we can classify four basic types of conflicts of interests between, to oversimplify, a human and an animal:

	Human interest	Animal interest
1.	basic	basic
2.	basic	peripheral
3.	peripheral	basic
4.	peripheral	peripheral

The following examples illustrate (roughly) the above conflicts, e.g., (1) my life versus my dog's in the life raft case, (2) giving up my career to move to a climate where my dog will be happier, (3) my obtaining a new flyswatter by killing a wildebeest (for its tail), (4) my spending for a new wallet for myself or spending for a toy for my dog. If we suppose that the nonsatisfaction of a basic interest yields a greater disutility than the nonsatisfaction of a peripheral interest and if the conflict of interests in (2) and (3) is resolved by sacrificing the basic to the peripheral interest, it is tempting to suppose that there is a net loss of aggregate utility. Giving the interests of the animal no weight in calculating utilities in (2) or (3) is speciesism with a vengeance. That tack is an obvious target of current critics of many standard ways in which animals are treated and ways in which their interests are evaluated (if indeed recognized at all). For an example of the latter, to the criticism that DDT usage damages penguins, one writer states:

> My criteria are oriented to people, not penguins. Damage to penguins . . . is . . . simply irrelevant. . . . Penguins are important because people enjoy seeing them walk about rocks . . . I have no interest in preserving penguins for their own sake . . . it is the only tenable starting place for analysis. . . . First, no other position corresponds to the way most people really think and act.[20]

On the principle that utility ought to be maximized in adjudicating conflicts of interests, peripheral interests ought to be subordinated to basic ones. Such a principle seems to underlie Interest Sensitive Speciesism. For reasons mentioned earlier such a view is problematic, e.g., if it is in any animal's basic interest to live then killing cockroaches for the sake of a certain convenience to humans would be prohibited. On the assumption that satisfaction (or nonsatisfaction) of like interests involves promotion (or nonattainment) of like utilities and the assumption that we should maximize aggregate utility, it is not clear how to resolve conflicts of types (1) and (4). Recall the case of my dog and myself in the overloaded life raft. The conflict is between basic interests; one has to go overboard (assume drowning is then inevitable) so that the other may live. If promoting my dog's interest will promote the same utility as promoting my own, the principle of maximizing utility will fail to require what, intuitively, seems permissible, namely, that I sadly do away with my canine friend.[21]

It is reasonable to believe, however, that in the life raft example the disutilities of my dying and my dog's dying are not really equal, even though the case seems correctly describable as one where a *basic* interest of mine is in conflict with an *equally basic* interest of my dog. But would not the assignment of different utilities to *like interests* be arbitrary—a giving of greater *weight* to interests of my own species over like interests of members of other species—and, hence, in some sense, "speciesist"? The more important question, labels aside, is whether a case can be made for giving *greater weight* to my own interest in such a case as opposed to my dog's.[22] In general, is there a justification for weighting human interests more heavily than *comparable* or *like* interests of animals in cases of conflicts of interests and, thus, justifying the extension of differential treatment toward animals in certain cases where it would not be justified if extended to (most) other humans (e.g., it may be worth comparing a life raft case like the one discussed except that the conflict is between the reader and myself)?[23] Two Factor Egalitarianism assumes an affirmative answer to this question. The basis for doing so is not simply that human interests are, after all, *human interests* and necessarily deserving of more weight than comparable or like interests of animals. The ground is rather that the interests of beings with more complex psychological capacities deserve greater weight than those with lesser capacities—up to a point. Let us call this the Weighting Principle.[24] What may be said in defense of the Weighting Principle? I am not sure that an adequate defense can be proposed, but let us consider some possible attempts. It might be proposed that humans are typically subject to certain kinds of suffering that animals are not. For example, humans are typically capable of suffering from the dread of impending disaster (e.g., death from terminal cancer) in a way that animals are not (e.g., a turkey will not be wary of impending Thanksgiving events). This fact, however, may only show that a given type of act (e.g., death sentence) may cause unequal disutilities to an animal and a human. However, the *same amount* of suffering may be imposed on a human and an animal on a given occasion. Would there be any reason for assigning different disutilities to the two acts respectively? There may be if we take into account not just the comparative amounts of suffering on *that* occasion but consequent suffering over time, a factor affected by life span and the capacity to remember. Suppose it were true that the pain experienced by a steer upon being castrated and the pain experienced by a woman who was raped were of the "same amount."[25] The steer would not suffer from the memory of such an experience in the way that women continue to suffer from the trauma of rape, e.g., "reliving" of the experience in dreams, and so on. What such an example suggests is that in cases where a basic interest (e.g., an interest in not being subjected to serious bodily harm) is violated, the different disutilities to the animal and human may be obscured by focusing on the fact that a "basic interest" was violated in *both* cases. The long-term disutilities of each individual may be radically different, and whether this is so is very much a function of the psychological capacities of the beings involved. That the *interests* of a human and an animal are "like or comparable" seems no sure guide to the comparative amounts of harm done in such cases. Hence, in conflicts of *like* interests between humans and animals (basic–basic, or peripheral–peripheral) it may be important to focus on the less

obvious and long-term disutilities that may accrue in not promoting the interest; focusing on "levels of interest" may fail to take into account matters of importance.

Another and, I believe, overlooked consideration that may be used in defense of the Weighting Principle concerns the economist's notion of "opportunity cost." Generally, in employing one's capital or one's efforts in achieving one goal, the cost of doing so can be thought of as the opportunities thereby forgone, goods and satisfactions that may not be obtained but that could have been if one's capital or efforts were employed in other ways. Most of my examples have focused on cases of inflicting pain or deprivation rather than death. The notion of opportunity cost is a useful one in trying to assign some weight to the imposition of death upon a human or an animal—as well as to weighting the imposition of pain or deprivation upon an animal or a human. Suppose that a group of rabbits is used in testing possibly toxic drugs and that the test is of the LD-50 type, where it is built into the experimental design that the experiment is complete only when fifty percent of the rabbits die (thus, Lethal Dosage—fifty percent).[26] Imagine a comparable test on a group of retarded human beings. Why are we inclined to think that if either experiment (but not both) is justified it must be the one involving rabbits? It need not be, I believe, because we think the suffering of rabbits has no weight. Neither must it be because we would deny that like interests are involved in the two cases. The psychological capabilities of even retarded human beings, such as those suffering from Down syndrome, are, however, far greater than those of rabbits. Even with the predictable shorter than normal life span for Down syndrome persons, the opportunities for a satisfying life for the retarded that would be forgone in the event of death are enormously greater than those of rabbits—or even, to take a "less favorable" case—those of typical nonhuman primates. Generally, though not necessarily nor in every case, the prospects of satisfaction are qualitatively and quantitatively greater for human beings than for animals. And this fact, this morally relevant fact, is a function of the psychological complexity of the beings in question. Further, it is clear that membership in the species *Homo sapiens* is no *a priori* guarantee of the existence of greater psychological capacity to experience satisfaction than that which may be possessed by beings of other species. The more basic point is that, generally, the opportunity cost of dying for humans and for animals at comparable ages, barring abnormalities, is vastly greater for the former. The harm, then, of killing in the former case is much greater than in the latter. From the fact, *if it were a fact*, that nothing could be more important to a given human than preservation of his life and that nothing could be more important to a given animal than preservation of its life, it does not follow that the disvalue of the loss of life in the two cases is equal.[27] For reasons mentioned, the discounting of the value of the preservation of the lives of many animals seems reasonable. A principle such as Two Factor Egalitarianism, based in part, then, on the Weighting Principle, is not unreasonable, and need not appeal to species membership *per se* as a basis for assigning unequal weights to like interests of animals and humans, respectively.

The extent of discounting the interests of a being, or more generally—weighting its interests—will, on this view, depend on the psychological complexities of the being in question. There is no reason, except to have practical presumptions, to make, *a priori*, generalizations about the capacities of all humans, all animals, all primates, or all chimpanzees. Nontrivial variations in capacity occur in any such group.

The importance of forgone satisfactions, as I have observed in passing, is a function not only of psychological capacity but of life span. The fact that the merciful letting die of quite aged humans with terminal diseases seems more acceptable than failure to extend analogous life preserving treatment to young adult humans, may reflect an implicit acceptance of the view that the opportunity cost of death is morally relevant and, in fact, a relevant difference in the two cases just mentioned.[28] In that respect, more familiar judgments about the comparative value of preserving human lives suggest that the emphasis here on opportunity cost accords with reflective moral judgments that are made with regard to differential treatment among human beings. Similarly, the general acceptance of allowing seriously defective infants to expire may assume the plausibility of attending to psychological capacity as part of the determination of the value of promoting or sacrificing a basic interest—such as the interest in the preservation of life.

If Two Factor Egalitarianism is correct, and for the reasons mentioned, it will *sometimes* be permissible to do what Singer regards as an arbitrary prejudice, namely, for the speciesist (or any human) to "allow the interests of his own species to override the greater interests of members of other species." The unfortunate implication of Singer's claim that this is impermissible is that it prohibits killing a minimally sentient nonhuman creature for the sake of a "lesser human interest" in cases where the human's psychological capacities are distinctly more complex. TFE is not anthropocentric in the way that a view is if it regards species membership in *Homo sapiens* as relevant *per se*. The latter assumption is what Singer takes to be invidious and arbitrary about views he labels speciesist. On this point Singer is right. If Singer, or others, were to claim that TFE is also invidious and arbitrary in its "psychocentric" emphasis, reasons need to be stated other than that it takes species membership *per se* as relevant; for it does not.

V. Some Persistent Difficulties

To this point I have argued that among the widely divergent proposals considered (Radical Speciesism, etc.), Two Factor Egalitarianism best accords with both matters of fact and considered and not unreasonable pre-theoretical convictions about how we ought to resolve conflicts of interests between humans and animals. Thus, it seems the most plausible among the five positions considered. I have further suggested an answer (or part of one) to the basic challenge posed by critics of our treatment of animals (as I would pose it): to justify radically differential treatment of creatures all of whom are sentient it is necessary to identify a morally relevant difference between those who receive preferential treatment and those who do not. The difference proposed is psychological complexity in so far as that bears on the capacity of the entity to live a satisfying life; further, to the extent that the entity lacks capacities necessary for such, it is reasonable to discount its interests. The thorny question of what counts as a reasonable discounting I have not tried to settle. I have further argued that TFE avoids the counter-intuitive implications of Singer's principle of equality that requires (of *any* being) "that its suffering be counted equally with the like suffering—in so far as rough comparisons can be made—of any other being." As I understand the principle it focuses on actual suffering and not also on forgone satisfactions. Further, TFE avoids the charge of taking species membership *per se* as a morally relevant difference serving to justify interspecific differential treatment. If the argument so far is correct (perhaps even, approximately correct), TFE stands as the most reasonable approach.

Nevertheless, TFE is subject to a number of objections not yet considered, some of which are obvious and some of which are not. Most evident, the principle is vague. There is no precise way of determining which interests are basic, which serious, and which are more peripheral or how to rank interests precisely. Similarly, no adequate account has been offered of how to determine levels of psychological complexity. I will not dwell on these problems. If they are relevant (I believe they are) we must do the best we can; perhaps these difficulties are no *more* difficult than those faced in analogous problems of intraspecies conflicts of interests. These difficulties do not strike me as *decisive* ones; in any case I do not pursue them here.

TFE is, I believe, more troubling in another respect. In regarding level of psychological complexity as morally important (rather than, say, possession or lack of fur, feathers, a tail, or claws) it may require or allow that the interests of human beings need not be assigned equal weight where it is the case that there are significant empirical differences among humans in terms of psychological capacity. If an implication exists that the interests of dull, psychologically less complicated humans (the retarded? the senile? the brain damaged?) need not be counted as much as that of other humans (in the process of coming to some all-things-considered moral judgment about acts affecting them and perhaps others), it will be tempting to judge that accepting TFE would commit one to sanctioning intraspecific injustices—perhaps on the conviction that "all human beings are of equal intrinsic worth" or convictions that appear to demand that the like interests of all human beings must be assigned equal moral weight initially regardless of final specific moral judgments. The worry is, generally, that a tempting basis for making *interspecific discrimination* entails possibly counter-intuitive results with regard to *intraspecific* discriminations.

Is there any way of reasonably weighting interests based on the psychological capacities of interest holders that will not commit one who does so to policies of intraspecific (human) discrimination of an objectionable sort? A simple principle—

give greater weight to the interests of a being with greater psychological capacity than one with less, proportionately—may indeed lead to objectionable discrimination. But a plausible weighting principle need not look like this. We may well regard it as an arbitrary and unjustified extension of differential treatment to offer, other things being equal, to finance the college education of one of our children with an "I.Q." of 140 but to refuse to do so for another with an "I.Q." of 120. Possession of a capacity beyond a certain degree may not count as a morally relevant difference. Beyond a certain threshold point it may. It might not be unjustified to refuse such support for a Down syndrome child. Suppose we adopt a bright chimpanzee and a quite retarded Down syndrome child. Would it be permissible to torture either? Intuitively: no. Would it be permissible to extend differential treatment to them regarding the provision of educational opportunities? Intuitively, one would think so. My more general point is that differences in psychological capacity may, up to a point, not justify differential treatment. Beyond a certain point they may, and whether they do may depend in part on the kind of differential treatment we are considering and what difference it might make to the prospective satisfactions or dissatisfactions of the beings considered. For example, virtually all human beings are capable of understanding promises and forming expectations of their being kept. Wide variations in psychological capacity exist alongside this particular capacity. These variations may provide no reason for justifying differing presumptions about the importance of promise-keeping for these humans. It is not evident that any nonhuman is capable of understanding promises, although some certainly seem to form expectations.[29]

To clarify, a weighting principle may recognize threshold points. Possession of certain capacities (e.g., intelligence) above a certain point may preclude certain forms of differential treatment. Below a certain point it may not. These assumptions may justify certain forms of interspecific discrimination. They also may serve to justify *certain* forms of intraspecific discrimination (among humans), e.g., treating differently an anencephalic infant, a Down syndrome infant, and a normal infant.[30] Because of the recognition of the importance of threshold considerations it is not obvious that a weighting principle, if applied, would lead to *objectionable* forms of intraspecific discrimination. So, the genuine worry about such a consequence does not evidently disqualify TFE (or some variant on it), which presupposes a weighting principle, from consideration. If so, more needs to be said, but I shall make no attempt to say it here (at least partly because it is beyond *my* capacity).

For the reasons discussed TFE seems more adequate than other proposals about how we ought to treat animals—in spite of its deficiencies. Some of its deficiencies may be remedied by a more specific, determinate statement of a variant on TFE. Further, supplementary principles are needed to elaborate and defend distinctions among levels of interests, as well as an elaboration of which psychological capacities are relevant or which sets of such capacities are relevant (and relevant to different forms of proposed differential treatment). That such supplementary assumptions are necessary complicates what may be called, appropriately, a theory of interspecific justice. That such a theory would be complicated may be disappointing; most of us hope for and value simplicity in a theory. TFE is not itself complicated, from one standpoint. It explicitly recognizes only two considerations as morally relevant in adjudicating interspecific conflicts of interests (levels of interests and psychological complexity of the beings). As noted, however, these considerations need more complicated elaboration and defense. Given the difficulties commonly acknowledged today in formulating and defending principles of justice for human interaction, it should not be surprising that plausible principles for just interspecific interactions turn out to be not readily or easily formulated.

In testing the proposed principles I have depended considerably on what I take to be thoughtful pre-theoretic convictions about how specific conflicts ought to be or may permissibly be resolved. Some may claim that this approach is wrong-headed at the outset, but I will leave it to others to say why. More likely, some will claim that the convictions invoked are a by-product of prejudice or are uniquely mine. I do not find this obvious, and I have tried to show that distinctions among levels of interests are supposed by those who take a somewhat different view of these matters, e.g., Peter Singer. I have also indicated how some limited weighting of interests is presupposed in what appears to be reasonable albeit differential treatment of human beings. If the admittedly incomplete account presented here is approximately correct, then certain general criteria are available for assessing which sorts of subordination of animal interests are justifiable and which are not. That some subordination of animal interests is, in general, acceptable and that some is not is evident. The important and more practical task of ascertaining which is which remains. In general, the implications of the position defended here will, I think, neither sanction many common dealings with animals nor lend support to some of the sweeping condemnations of preferential treatment set out by recent critics. But a more moderate position on the proper treatment of animals must, I think, side with recent critics in judging much of the prevailing wholesale disregard of the basic interests of higher animals as unconscionable.[31]

Notes

1. Peter Singer's essay "Animal Liberation" appeared in *The New York Review of Books* (April 5, 1973), pp. 10–15.

2. Ibid., p. 15.

3. Later references will be to Singer's book, *Animal Liberation*. Avon Books, New York 1977. In that book Singer emphasizes that his primary moral assumption is "the principle of equality," which does not require identical treatment of but "equal consideration" of beings with interests (pp. 3, 6). Further, beings with interests are only those with a capacity for suffering and enjoyment (p. 8). Recognizing complexities about killing, as opposed to the imposition of pain, he claims that "the conclusions that are argued for in this book flow from the principle of minimizing suffering alone" (p. 22). Given this last emphasis and Singer's rejection of any necessity to couch his position in terms of animal rights (see Peter Singer, "The Fable of the Fox and the Unliberated Animals," *Ethics*, Vol. 88, No. 2 [January 1978], p. 122), I have chosen to reconstruct his argument as above.

4. The parallel with current theories of justice "for" human beings, theories that attempt to adjudicate conflicting interests, is evident.

5. Of course, the radical subordination of certain *human* interests (those of "natural slaves") seemed intuitively innocent and natural to Aristotle, and, as J. S. Mill noted in *The Subjection of Women*, it is a standard mark of a deeply held prejudice that it seem perfectly *natural* to the one who holds it.

There is always the danger of accepting only those principles that are compatible with our prejudices.

6. For aesthetic reasons I would prefer use of "specieism," but to avoid multiplication of variants I adhere to the current use of "speciesism."

7. Singer, op. cit., pp. 8–9.

8. Ibid., pp. 9–15.

9. It is worth noting a dissimilarity between racism or sexism on the one hand and speciesism on the other, namely, that in the former cases those whose interests are subordinated are biologically "homogeneous" with their subordinators but not in the latter case.

10. See Stanley Godlovitch, "Utilities" in *Animals, Men, and Morals*, Taplinger Publishing Company, New York 1972, p. 181.

11. A. J. Cain, *Animal Species and Their Evolution*, Harper & Row, New York 1960.

12. It would be plausible to add: (4) to use a fair (e.g., random) procedure to decide whose interest should be sacrificed if the beings are psychologically similar and the interests are like. But see the (here unincorporated) consideration in Note 19.

13. See Singer, op. cit., pp. 122–8.

14. Ibid., Ch. 2.

15. The Tay-Sachs infant will die "soon" anyway, typically by the age of five or six years and will suffer in the interim. Its interest in continuing to exist may, then, be less basic than that of the healthy chimpanzee in continuing to live. The capacities of the infant may not exceed those of the chimpanzee at the time supposed.

16. See the intriguing fictionalized thought-experiment in Desmond Stewart's "The Limits of Trooghaft" in Tom Regan and Peter Singer (Eds.), *Animal Rights and Human Obligations*, Prentice Hall, Englewood Cliffs, New Jersey 1976, pp. 238–45.

17. Tom Regan, "The Moral Basis of Vegetarianism," *Canadian Journal of Philosophy*, Vol. 5, No. 2 (October 1975), pp. 181–214.

18. Without this qualification (sufficiently . . .), someone might argue that since there is a morally relevant difference between those who commit traffic violations and those who do not, it is justified to extend capital punishment to the former but not the latter.

19. I have so far deliberately ignored a complicating factor that seems relevant, namely, how a conflict of interest arises. A fuller account of things should consider this; I make no such attempt here. To elaborate, however, conflicts of interests sometimes arise only because one party *wants* what another has, and resolution of such a conflict *may not* be a matter of balancing legitimate claims. There may be a conflict of interests between my neighbor and myself since I want his new car, or between a rapist and his victim. Many of the conflicts of interests between humans and animals are generated by human desires to do what is harmful to animals; we eat them more than they eat us.

20. William F. Baxter, *People or Penguins: The Case for Optimal Pollution*, Columbia University Press, New York 1974, p. 5.

21. Considering utilities or disutilities to others would likely weight the case in favor of my preservation—solely on grounds of maximizing aggregate utility. But we can imagine cases where this would not be so; in any case I exclude such considerations above by assumption.

22. The relation between having rights and having interests is not clear. It is doubtful that having interests is sufficient for having rights (on this see the discussions by myself and James Rachels in Tom Regan and Peter Singer's anthology, *Animal Rights and Human Obligations*, Prentice Hall, Englewood Cliffs, New Jersey 1976, pp. 205–32). More plausible is the claim that any entity having rights must also have interests. If so, at least many entities having interests also have rights. If the interests of rightholders are regarded as very important, according those interests may be thought to be sufficiently important to override the *interests* of others—or, and this seems not insignificant—the *rights* of others (who have not only interests but rights). For example, Lawrence Haworth, who defends the view that some nonhumans have rights, maintains that when the latter rights conflict with "worthy human interests . . . then it is in general reasonable to give preference to these human concerns and violate . . . the rights of nonhumans." See Lawrence Haworth, "Rights, Wrongs, and Animals," *Ethics*, Vol. 88, No. 2 (January 1978), p. 100.

So *even if* it is allowed that some animals have *rights*, the *weightings* of the respective interests in interspecific conflicts of interests are important and may affect our ultimate "on balance" judgments concerning justified violations (or justified infringements) of rights. Hence, my aims in the text are not, I think, irrelevant *even if* it is shown that animals have rights (short of being unqualifiedly "absolute").

23. Again, I simplify. Assume that neither of us owns the boat, has a special duty to sacrifice for the other, consents to die, or agrees to "draw straws."

24. The notion of psychological complexity needs further elaboration. I do have in mind complexity bearing on capacity to experience satisfaction and dissatisfaction. After all there might be a type of

psychological complexity *not* conducive to a greater capacity to experience satisfaction. Suppose a microcomputer could be implanted in a turkey so that it became an excellent chess player but in other respects remained turkey-like, e.g., still did not worry about the prospect of Thanksgiving rituals.

25. I am, of course, bypassing all sorts of difficulties about the possibility of having a cardinal measure of utility and making "interbeing" comparisons of utilities.

26. On this type of test, see Peter Singer, op. cit., p. 48.

27. While the death of an animal or a human results in its forgoing *all* the potential satisfactions either could have, still the quantity of such satisfactions would typically be different for each. Hence it is reasonable to conclude that the disvalue of the death of a normal animal is less than the disvalue of the death of a normal human (at similar stages in typical life spans) even though the death of each involves a total loss of their respective potential satisfactions. The difference in disvalues is partly a function of whatever differences there are in respective psychological capacities.

28. Compare the absence of capacities in aged humans due to their waning, their absence in defective humans, and their absence in young normal animals. Absence of capacities may be a result of natural decline, injury, disease, or one's genetic lot.

29. Who would not feel some sense of betrayal when an aged dog eagerly gets in the car for a ride but does not know that it is being taken to be put to death (commonly: "to sleep")? Further, it will not surprise me if communications with nonhuman primates, in Ameslan, provide evidence of a capacity for understanding promises or, indeed, a sense of regret or remorse.

30. It does not seem to me that one should shrink from the view that *some* weighting of human interests and, hence, *some* differential treatment of humans is justified. There is great danger that I shall be misunderstood here—as approving in some degree the sorts of unequal consideration intrinsic to repulsive doctrines commonly labeled racist, sexist, or Nazilike. Respect for persons requires respecting their interests but not, I think, giving equal weight to them.

31. With regard to various facets of this essay I have benefited from discussions with my colleagues, W. R. Carter, Robert Hoffman, Harold Levin, Tom Regan, and Alan Sparer—as well as the writings of both Tom Regan and Peter Singer. Any or all are, of course, entitled to complain that I did not benefit enough.

18. The Prospects for Consensus and Convergence in the Animal Rights Debate

Gary E. Varner

Controversies over the use of nonhuman animals (henceforth animals) for science, nutrition, and recreation are often presented as clear-cut stand-offs, with little or no common ground between opposing factions and, consequently, with little or no possibility for consensus-formation. As a philosopher studying these controversies, my sense is that the apparent intransigence of opposing parties is more a function of political posturing than theoretical necessity, and that continuing to paint the situation as a clear-cut standoff serves the interests of neither side. A critical look at the philosophical bases of the animal rights movement reveals surprising potential for *convergence* (agreement at the level of policy despite disagreement at the level

of moral theory) and, in some cases, *consensus* (agreement at both levels).[1] Recognizing this should make defenders of animal research take animal rights views more seriously and could refocus the animal rights debate in a constructive way.

In response to the growth of the animal rights movement, animal researchers have begun to distinguish between animal rights views and animal welfare views, but they have not drawn the distinction the way a philosopher would. Researchers typically stress two differences between animal welfarists and animal rightists. First, welfarists argue for reforms in research involving animals, whereas rightists argue for the total abolition of such research. Second, welfarists work within the system, whereas rightists advocate using theft, sabotage, or even violence to achieve their ends. A more philosophical account of the animal rights/animal welfare distinction cuts the pie very differently, revealing that many researchers agree with some animal rights advocates at the level of moral theory, and that, even where they differ dramatically at the level of moral theory, there is some potential for convergence at the level of policy.

Animal Welfare: The Prospects for Consensus

Peter Singer's *Animal Liberation* is the acknowledged Bible of the animal rights movement. Literally millions of people have been moved to vegetarianism or animal activism as a result of reading this book. PETA (People for the Ethical Treatment of Animals) distributed the first edition of the book as a membership premium, and the number of copies in print has been cited as a measure of growth in the animal rights movement. However, Singer wrote *Animal Liberation* for popular consumption, and in it he intentionally avoided discussion of complex philosophical issues.[2] In particular, he avoided analyzing the concepts of 'rights' and 'harm,' and these concepts are crucial to drawing the animal rights/animal welfare distinction in philosophical terms.

In *Animal Liberation,* Singer spoke loosely of animals having moral "rights," but all that he intended by this was that animals (at least some of them) have some basic moral standing and that there are right and wrong ways of treating them. In later, more philosophically rigorous work—summarized in his *Practical Ethics,* a second edition of which has just been issued[3]—he explicitly eschews the term *rights,* noting that, as a thoroughgoing utilitarian, he must deny not only that animals have moral rights, but also that human beings do.

When moral philosophers speak of an individual "having moral rights," they mean something much more specific than that the individual has some basic moral standing and that there are right and wrong ways of treating him or her. Although there is much controversy as to the specifics, there is general agreement on this: to attribute moral rights to an individual is to assert that the individual has some kind of special moral dignity, the cash value of which is that certain things cannot justifiably be done to him or her (or it) for the sake of

benefit to others. For this reason, moral rights have been characterized as "trump cards" against utilitarian arguments. Utilitarian arguments are based on aggregate benefits and aggregate harms. Specifically, utilitarianism is the view that right actions maximize aggregate happiness. In principle, nothing is inherently or intrinsically wrong, according to a utilitarian; any action could be justified under some possible circumstances. One way of characterizing rights views in ethics, by contrast, is that there are some things which, regardless of the consequences, it is simply wrong to do to individuals, and that moral rights single out these things.

Although a technical and stipulative definition of 'rights,' this philosophical usage reflects a familiar concept. In day-to-day discussions, appeals to individuals' rights are used to assert, in effect, that there is a limit to what individuals can be forced to do, or to the harm that may be inflicted upon them, for the benefit of others. So the philosophical usage of rights talk reflects the common-sense view that there are limits to what we can justifiably do to an individual for the benefit of society.

To defend the moral rights of animals would be to claim that certain ways of treating animals cannot be justified on utilitarian grounds. But in *Practical Ethics* Peter Singer explicitly adopts a utilitarian stance for dealing with our treatment of nonhuman animals. So the author of "the Bible of the animal rights movement" is not an animal *rights* theorist at all, and the self-proclaimed advocates of animal welfare are appealing to precisely the same tradition in ethics as is Singer. Both believe that it is permissible to sacrifice (even involuntarily) the life of one individual for the benefit of others, where the aggregated benefits to others clearly outweigh the costs to that individual. (At least they agree on this as far as animals are concerned. Singer is a thoroughgoing utilitarian, whereas my sense is that most animal researchers are utilitarians when it comes to animals, but rights theorists when it comes to humans.)

Many researchers also conceive of harm to animals very similarly to Singer, at least where nonmammalian animals are concerned. In *Animal Liberation,* Singer employs a strongly hedonistic conception of harm. He admits that the morality of killing is more complicated than that of inflicting pain (p.17) and that although pain is pain wherever it occurs, this "does not imply that all lives are of equal worth" (p. 20). This should be stressed, because researchers commonly say that according to animal rights philosophies, of which Singer's is their paradigm, all animals' lives are of equal value. No fair reading of Singer's *Animal Liberation* would yield this conclusion, let alone any fair reading of *Practical Ethics*, where he devotes four chapters to the question of killing.

The morality of killing is complicated by competing conceptions of harm. In *Animal Liberation*, Singer leaves the question of killing in the background and uses a strongly hedonistic conception of animal welfare. He argues that the conclusions reached in the book, including the duty to refrain from eating animals, "flow from the principle of minimizing suffering alone" (p. 21). To conceive of harm hedonistically is to say that harm consists in felt pain or lost opportunities for pleasure. For a utilitarian employing a hedonistic conception of harm, individuals are replaceable in the following sense. If an individual lives a pleasant life, dies a painless death, and is replaced by an individual leading a similarly pleasant life, there is no loss of value in the world. Agriculturalists appear to be thinking like hedonistic utilitarians when they defend humane slaughter in similar terms. Researchers employ a similarly hedonistic conception of harm when they argue that if all pain is eliminated from an experimental protocol then, ethically speaking, there is nothing left to be concerned about.

Singer conceives of harm to "lower" animals in hedonistic terms and thus agrees with these researchers and agriculturalists. He even acknowledges that the replaceability thesis could be used to defend some forms of animal agriculture, although not intensive poultry systems, where the birds hardly live happy lives or die painless deaths. However, Singer argues that it is implausible to conceive of harm in hedonistic terms when it comes to "self-conscious individuals, leading their own lives and wanting to go on living" (p. 125), and he argues that all mammals are self-conscious in this sense.

Singer equates being self-conscious with having forward-looking desires, especially the desire to go on living. He argues that such self-conscious individuals are not replaceable, because when an individual with forward-looking desires dies, those desires go unsatisfied even if another individual is born and has similar desires satisfied. With regard

to self-conscious individuals, Singer is still a utilitarian, but he is a *preference* utilitarian rather than a *hedonistic* utilitarian. Singer cites evidence to demonstrate that the great apes are self-conscious in his sense (pp. 11–16) and states, without saying what specific research leads him to this conclusion, that neither fish nor chickens are (pp. 95, 133), but that "a case can be made, though with varying degrees of confidence," that all mammals are self-conscious (p. 132).

It is easy to disagree with Singer about the range of self-consciousness, as he conceives of it, in the animal kingdom.[4] Probably most mammals have forward-looking desires, but the future to which they look is doubtless a very near one. Cats probably think about what to do in the next moment to achieve a desired result, but I doubt that they have projects (long-term, complicated desires) of the kind suggested by saying that they are "leading their own lives and wanting to go on living."

However, even if we grant Singer the claim that all mammals have projects, so long as we remain utilitarians this just means that research on mammals carries a higher burden of justification than does research on "lower" animals like reptiles or insects, a point many researchers would readily grant. A preference utilitarian is still a utilitarian, and in at least some cases, a utilitarian must agree that experimentation is justified.

In the following passage from *Practical Ethics*, Singer stresses just this point:

> In the past, argument about animal experimentation has often . . . been put in absolutist terms: would the opponent of experimentation be prepared to let thousands die from a terrible disease that could be cured by experimenting on one animal? This is a purely hypothetical question, since experiments do not have such dramatic results, but as long as its hypothetical nature is clear, I think the question should be answered affirmatively—in other words, if one, or even a dozen animals had to suffer experiments in order to save thousands, I would think it right and in accordance with equal consideration of interests that they should do so. This, at any rate, is the answer a utilitarian must give. (p. 67)

Singer doubts that most experiments are justified, not because he believes experimentation is wrong *simpliciter*, but because he doubts that the benefits to humans significantly outweigh the costs to the animals. In the pages preceding the passage just quoted, Singer cites examples of experiments he thinks cannot plausibly be said "to serve vital medical purposes": testing of new shampoos and food colorings, armed forces experiments on the effects of radiation on combat performance, and H. F. Harlow's maternal deprivation experiments. "In these cases, and many others like them," he says, "the benefits to humans are either nonexistent or uncertain, while the losses to members of other species are certain and real" (p. 66).

So the disagreement between Singer and the research establishment is largely empirical, about how likely various kinds of research are to lead to important human benefits. Researchers often argue that we cannot be expected to know ahead of time which lines of research will yield dramatic benefits. Critics respond that these same scientists serve on grant review boards, whose function is to permit funding agencies to make such decisions all the time. Here I want only to emphasize that this is an empirical dispute that cannot be settled *a priori* or as a matter of moral theory. One of the limitations of utilitarianism is that its application requires very detailed knowledge about the effects of various actions or policies. When it comes to utilitarian justifications for animal research, the probability—and Singer is correct that it is never a certainty—that various lines of research will save or significantly improve human lives must be known or estimated before anything meaningful can be said. Singer is convinced that most research will not meet this burden of proof; most researchers are convinced of just the opposite.

Animal Rights: The Prospects for Convergence

Most animal researchers agree to a surprising extent with the Moses of the animal rights movement. Their basic ethical principles are the same (at least where nonhuman animals are concerned), and they apply to all animals the same conception of harm which Singer applies to all animals except mammals. Where they disagree with Singer is at the level of policy; they see the same ethical theory implying different things in practice. Dramatic disagreement at the level of moral theory emerges only when we turn to the views of Tom Regan, whose ethical principles and conception of harm are dramatically different from Singer's and the researchers'.

Regan's *The Case for Animal Rights*[5] is a lengthy and rigorous defense of a true animal rights position. It is impossible to do justice to the argument of a 400-page book in a few paragraphs, so here I will simply state the basic destination Regan reaches, in order to examine its implications for animal research.

For Regan, there is basically one moral right: the right not to be harmed on the grounds that doing so benefits others, and all individuals who can be harmed in the relevant way have this basic right. Regan conceives of harm as a diminution in the capacity to form and satisfy desires, and he argues that all animals who are capable of having desires have this basic moral right not to be harmed. On Regan's construal, losing an arm is more of a harm than stubbing one's toe (because it frustrates more of one's desires), but death is always the worst harm an individual can suffer because it completely destroys one's capacity to form and satisfy desires. As to which animals have desires, Regan explicitly defends only the claim that all mentally normal mammals of a year or more have desires, but he says that he does this to avoid the controversy over "line drawing," that is, saying precisely how far down the phylogenetic scale one must go to find animals that are incapable of having desires. Regan is confident that at least all mammals and birds have desires, but acknowledges that the analogical evidence for possession of desires becomes progressively weaker as we turn to herpetofauna (reptiles and amphibians), fish, and then invertebrates.[6]

Regan defends two principles to use in deciding whom to harm where it is impossible not to harm someone who has moral rights: the miniride and worse-off principles. The *worse-off principle* applies where *noncomparable* harms are involved, and it requires us to avoid harming the worse-off individual. Regan's discussion of this principle makes it clear that for him, harm is measured in absolute, rather than relative terms. If harm were measured relative to the individual's original capacity to form and satisfy desires, rather than in absolute terms, then death would be uniformly catastrophic wherever it occurs. But Regan reasons that although death is always the greatest harm which any individual can suffer (because it forecloses all of that individual's opportunities for desire formation and satisfaction), death to a normal human being is noncomparably worse than death to any nonhuman animal, because a normal human being's capacity to form and satisfy desires is so much greater. To illustrate the use of the worse-off principle, Regan imagines that five individuals, four humans and a dog, are in a lifeboat that can support only four of them. Since death to any of the human beings would be noncomparably worse than death to the dog, the worse-off principle applies, and it requires us to avoid harming the human beings, who stand to lose the most.

The *miniride principle* applies to cases where *comparable* harms are involved, and it requires us to harm the few rather than the many. Regan admits that, where it applies, this principle yields the same conclusion as the principle of utility, but he emphasizes that the reasoning is nonutilitarian. The focus, he says, is on individuals rather than the aggregate. What the miniride principle instructs us to do is minimize the overriding of individuals' rights, rather than to maximize aggregate happiness. To illustrate the miniride principle's application, Regan imagines that a runaway mine train must be sent down one of two shafts, and that fifty miners would be killed by sending it down the first shaft but only one by sending it down the second. Since the harms that the various individuals in the example would suffer are comparable (only humans are involved, and all are faced with death), the miniride principle applies, and we are obligated to send the runaway train down the second shaft.

Regan argues that the rights view (as he labels his position) calls for the total abolition of animal research. In terms of the basic contrast drawn above between rights views and utilitarianism, it is easy to see why one would think this. The fundamental tenet of rights views is opposition to utilitarian justifications for harming individuals, and as we saw above, researchers' justifications for animal research is utilitarian. They argue that by causing a relatively small number of individuals to suffer and die, a relatively large number of individuals can live or have their lives significantly improved.

However, Regan's worse-off principle, coupled with his conception of harm, would seem to imply that at least *some* research is not only permissible but required, even on a true animal rights view. For as we just saw, Regan believes that death for a normal human is noncomparably worse than death for any nonhuman animal. So if we knew that by performing fatal research on a given number of nonhuman animals we could save even one

human life, the worse-off principle would apply, and it would require us to perform the research. In the lifeboat case referred to above, Regan emphasizes that where the worse-off principle applies, the numbers do not matter. He says:

> Let the number of dogs be as large as one likes; suppose they number a million; and suppose the lifeboat will support only four survivors. Then the rights view still implies that, special considerations apart, the million dogs should be thrown overboard and the four humans saved. To attempt to reach a contrary judgment will inevitably involve one in aggregative [i.e., utilitarian] considerations. (p. 325)

The same reasoning, in a hypothetical case like that described by Singer (where we *know*, with absolute certainty, that one experiment will save human lives), would imply that the experiment should be performed.

One complication is that the empirical dispute over the likelihood of significant human benefits emerging from various lines of research, which makes utilitarian justifications of experimentation so complex, will reappear here. Having admitted that some research is justified, animal rights advocates would doubtless continue to disagree with researchers over which research this is. Nevertheless, the foregoing discussion illustrates how the implications of a true animal rights view can converge with those of researchers' animal welfare philosophy. Even someone who attributes moral rights in the philosophical sense to animals, and whose ethical theory thus differs dramatically from most animal researchers', could think that some medical research is justified. This warrants stressing, because researchers commonly say things like, "According to animal rightists, 'a rat is a pig is a dog is a boy,'" and, "Animal rightists want to do away with all uses of animals, including life-saving medical research." However, no fair reading of either Singer or Regan would yield the conclusion that they believe that a rat's or a pig's life is equal to a normal human's. And, consequently, it is possible for someone thinking with Singer's or Regan's principles to accept research that actually saves human lives.

It is *possible*, but Regan himself continues to oppose all animal research to benefit humans. His basis is not the worse-off principle, but that the principle applies, "special considerations apart."

One of those considerations is that "risks are not morally transferrable to those who do not voluntarily choose to take them," and this, he claims, blocks application of the worse-off principle to the case of medical experimentation (p. 377). For example, subjects used to screen a new vaccine run higher risks of contracting the disease when researchers intentionally expose them to it. Humans can voluntarily accept these risks, but animals cannot. Consequently, the only kind of research on "higher" animals (roughly, vertebrates) that Regan will accept is that which tests a potential cure for a currently incurable disease on animals that have already acquired the disease of their own accord.

However, most people believe that in at least some cases, we can justifiably transfer risks without first securing the agreement of those to whom the risks are transferred. For instance, modifying price supports can redistribute the financial risks involved in farming, and changing draft board policies in time of war can redistribute the risk of being killed in defense of one's country. Yet most people believe such transfers are justifiable even if involuntary. In these cases, however, the individuals among whom risks are redistributed are all members of a *polis* through which, arguably, they give implicit consent to the policies in question. Still, in some cases there cannot plausibly be said to be even implicit consent. When we go to war, for instance, we impose dramatic risks on thousands or even millions of people who have no political influence in our country. But if the war is justified, so too, presumably, are the involuntarily imposed risks.

The Prospects for Conversation

It has not been my purpose in this paper to decide which particular forms of experimentation are morally justifiable, so I will not further pursue a response to Regan's abolitionist argument. My goal has been to refocus the animal rights debate by emphasizing its philosophical complexity. The question is far more complicated than is suggested by simplistic portrayals by many researchers and in the popular media.

According to the common stereotype, an animal rights advocate wants to eliminate all animal research and is a vegetarian who even avoids wearing leather. But the first "serious attempt . . . to assess the accuracy of this stereotype, a survey of about 600 animal activists attending the June 1990 "March for Animal Rights" in Washington, D.C., found that: nearly half of all activists believe the animal rights movement should not focus on animal research as its top priority; over a third eat red meat, poultry, or seafood; and 40 percent wear leather.[7] I have often heard agriculturalists and scientists say that it is hypocritical for an animal rights advocate to eat any kind of meat, wear leather, or use medicines that have been developed using animal models. But it would only be hypocritical if there were a single, monolithic animal rights philosophy that unambiguously ruled them all out.

In this essay, I have stressed the philosophical diversity underlying the animal rights movement. The "animal rights philosophies" of which many researchers are so contemptuous run the philosophical gamut from a utilitarianism very similar to their own to a true animal rights view that is quite different from their own. On some of these views, certain kinds of animal agriculture are permissible, but even on a true animal rights view like Regan's, it is possible to endorse some uses of animals, including experimentation that is meaningfully tied to saving human lives.

Continuing to paint all advocates of animal rights as unreasoning, antiscience lunatics will not make that movement go away, any more than painting all scientists who use animal models as Nazis bent on torturing the innocent will make animal research go away. Animal protection movements have surfaced and then disappeared in the past, but today's animal rights movement is squarely grounded in two major traditions in moral philosophy and, amid the stable affluence of a modern, industrialized nation like the United States, cannot be expected to go away. By the same token, twentieth-century medical research has dramatically proven its capacity to save lives and to improve the quality of human life, and it cannot be expected to go away either. So the reality is going to involve some level of some uses of animals, including some kinds of medical research.

A more philosophical understanding of the animal welfare/animal rights distinction can help replace the current politics of confrontation with a genuine conversation. Researchers who understand the philosophical bases of the animal rights movement will recognize similarities with their own views and can rest assured that genuinely important research will not be opposed by most advocates of animal rights. In the last analysis, what animal rights views do is increase the burden of proof the defenders of research must meet, and this is as it should be. Too often, pain and suffering have been understood to be "necessary" whenever a desired benefit could not be achieved without them, without regard to how important the benefit in question was.[8]

When it comes to research on animals, "academic freedom" cannot mean freedom to pursue any line of research one pleases, even in the arena of medical research. In most areas of research, someone who spends her career doing trivial work wastes only the taxpayers' money. But a scientist who spends his career doing trivial experiments on animals can waste the lives of hundreds or even thousands of sentient creatures. There will be increasing public oversight of laboratory research on animals, because major traditions in Western ethical theory support at least basic moral consideration for all sentient creatures. Researchers who react by adopting a siege mentality, refusing to disclose information on research and refusing to talk to advocates of animal rights, only reinforce the impression that they have something to hide.

Notes

1. I owe this account of the consensus/convergence distinction to Bryan G. Norton, *Toward Unity among Environmentalists* (New York: Oxford University Press, 1991), pp. 237–43.

2. Peter Singer, *Animal Liberation*, 2nd ed. ([New York:] Avon Books, 1990), pp. x–xi.

3. Peter Singer, *Practical Ethics*, 2nd ed. (New York: Cambridge University Press, 1993).

4. In any case, as Raymond Frey has pointed out, it is not clear that having forward-looking desires is a necessary condition for being self-conscious. R. G. Frey, *Rights, Killing, and Suffering: Moral Vegetarianism and Applied Ethics* (Oxford: Basil Blackwell, 1983), p. 163.

5. Tom Regan, *The Case for Animal Rights* (Berkeley and Los Angeles: University of California Press, 1983).

6. This evidence is reviewed in Chapter two of my *In Nature's Interests: Interests, Animal Rights, and Environmental Ethics* (Oxford University Press, 1998).

7. S. Plous, "An Attitude Survey of Animal Rights Activists," *Psychological Science* 2 (May 1991): 194–96.

8. Susan Finsen, "On Moderation," in *Interpretation and Explanation in the Study of Animal Behavior*, ed. Marc Bekoff and Dale Jamieson, vol. 2 (Boulder: Westview Press, 1990), pp. 394–419.

19. The Little Things That Run the World

Edward O. Wilson

On the occasion of the opening of the remarkable new invertebrate exhibit of the National Zoological Park, let me say a word on behalf of these little things that run the world. To start, there are vastly more kinds of invertebrates than of vertebrates. At the present time, on the basis of the tabulation that I have just completed (from the literature and with the help of specialists), I estimate that a total of 42,580 vertebrate species have been described, of which 6,300 are reptiles, 9,040 are birds, and 4,000 are mammals. In contrast, 990,000 species of invertebrates have been described, of which 290,000 alone are beetles—seven times the number of all the vertebrates together. Recent estimates have placed the number of invertebrates on the earth as high as 30 million, again mostly beetles—although many other taxonomically comparable groups of insects and other invertebrates also greatly outnumber vertebrates.

We don't know with certainty why invertebrates are so diverse, but a commonly held opinion is that the key trait is their small size. Their

Address given at the opening of the invertebrate exhibit, National Zoological Park, Washington, D.C., on May 7, 1987.
Conservation Biology, Vol. 1, No. 4 (December 1987), pp. 344–346. Reprinted by permission of Blackwell Scientific Publications, Inc., and the Society for Conservation Biology.

niches are correspondingly small, and they can therefore divide up the environment into many more little domains where specialists can coexist. One of my favorite examples of such specialists living in microniches are the mites that live on the bodies of army ants: one kind is found only on the mandibles of the soldier caste, where it sits and feeds from the mouth of its host; another kind is found only on the hind foot of the soldier caste, where it sucks blood for a living; and so on through various bizarre configurations.

Another possible cause of invertebrate diversity is the greater antiquity of these little animals, giving them more time to explore and fill the environment. The first invertebrates appeared well back into Precambrian times, at least 600 million years ago. Most invertebrate phyla were flourishing before the vertebrates arrived on the scene, some 500 million years ago.

Invertebrates also rule the earth by virtue of sheer body mass. For example, in tropical rain forest near Manaus, in the Brazilian Amazon, each hectare (or 2.5 acres) contains a few dozen birds and mammals but well over one billion invertebrates, of which the vast majority are not beetles this time but mites and springtails. There are about 200 kilograms dry weight of animal tissue in a hectare, of which 93 percent consists of invertebrates. The ants and termites alone compose one-third of this biomass. So when you walk through a tropical forest, or most other terrestrial habitats for that matter, or snorkel above a coral reef or some other marine or aquatic environment, vertebrates may catch your eye most of the time—biologists would say that your search image is for large animals—but you are visiting a primarily invertebrate world.

It is a common misconception that vertebrates are the movers and shakers of the world, tearing the vegetation down, cutting paths through the forest, and consuming most of the energy. That may be true in a few ecosystems such as the grasslands of Africa with their great herds of herbivorous mammals. It has certainly become true in the last few centuries in the case of our own species, which now appropriates in one form or other as much as 50 percent of the solar energy captured by plants. That circumstance is what makes us so dangerous to the fragile environment of the world. But it is otherwise more nearly true in most parts of the world of the invertebrates rather than the nonhuman verte-

brates. The leafcutter ants, for example, rather than deer, or rodents, or birds, are the principal consumers of vegetation in Central and South America. A single colony contains over two million workers. It sends out columns of foragers a hundred meters or more in all directions to cut forest leaves, flower parts, and succulent stems. Each day a typical mature colony collects about 50 kilograms of this fresh vegetation, more than the average cow. Inside the nest, the ants shape the material into intricate sponge-like bodies on which they grow a symbiotic fungus. The fungus thrives as it breaks down and consumes the cellulose, while the ants thrive by eating the fungus.

The leafcutting ants excavate vertical galleries and living chambers as deep as 5 meters into the soil. They and other kinds of ants, as well as bacteria, fungi, termites, and mites, process most of the dead vegetation and return its nutrients to the plants to keep the great tropical forests alive.

Much the same situation exists in other parts of the world. The coral reefs are built out of the bodies of coelenterates. The most abundant animals of the open sea are copepods, tiny crustaceans forming part of the plankton. The mud of the deep sea is home to a vast array of mollusks, crustaceans, and other small creatures that subsist on the fragments of wood and dead animals that drift down from the lighted areas above, and on each other.

The truth is that we need invertebrates but they don't need us. If human beings were to disappear tomorrow, the world would go on with little change. Gaia, the totality of life on earth, would set about healing itself and return to the rich environmental states of a few thousand years ago. But if invertebrates were to disappear, I doubt that the human species could last more than a few months. Most of the fishes, amphibians, birds, and mammals would crash to extinction about the same time. Next would go the bulk of the flowering plants and with them the physical structure of the majority of the forests and other terrestrial habitats of the world. The earth would rot. As dead vegetation piled up and dried out, narrowing and closing the channels of the nutrient cycles, other complex forms of vegetation would die off, and with them the last remnants of the vertebrates. The remaining fungi, after enjoying a population explosion of stupendous proportions, would also perish. Within a few decades the world would return to the state of a billion years ago, composed primarily of bacteria, algae, and a few other very simple multicellular plants.

If humanity depends so completely on these little creatures that run the earth, they also provide us with an endless source of scientific exploration and naturalistic wonder. When you scoop up a double handful of earth almost anywhere except the most barren deserts, you will find thousands of invertebrate animals, ranging in size from clearly visible to microscopic, from ants and springtails to tardigrades and rotifers. The biology of most of the species you hold is unknown: we have only the vaguest idea of what they eat, what eats them, and the details of their life cycle, and probably nothing at all about their biochemistry and genetics. Some of the species might even lack scientific names. We have little concept of how important any of them are to our existence. Their study would certainly teach us new principles of science to the benefit of humanity. Each one is fascinating in its own right. If human beings were not so impressed by size alone, they would consider an ant more wonderful than a rhinoceros.

New emphasis should be placed on the conservation of invertebrates. Their staggering abundance and diversity should not lead us to think that they are indestructible. On the contrary, their species are just as subject to extinction due to human interference as are those of birds and mammals. When a valley in Peru or an island in the Pacific is stripped of the last of its native vegetation, the result is likely to be the extinction of several kinds of birds and some dozen of plant species. Of that tragedy we are painfully aware, but what is not perceived is that hundreds of invertebrate species will also vanish.

The conservation movement is at last beginning to take recognition of the potential loss of invertebrate diversity. The International Union for the Conservation of Nature has an ongoing invertebrate program that has already published a Red Data Book of threatened and endangered species—although this catalog is obviously still woefully incomplete. The Xerces Society, named after an extinct California butterfly, was created in 1971 to further the protection of butterflies and other invertebrates. These two programs are designed to complement the much larger organized efforts of other organizations on behalf of vertebrates and plants. They will help to expand programs to encompass entire ecosystems instead of just selected star species. The new invertebrate exhibition of the National Zoological Park is one of the most promising means for raising public appreciation of invertebrates, and I hope such exhibits will come routinely to include rare and endangered species identified prominently as such.

Several themes can be profitably pursued in the new field of invertebrate conservation:

- It needs to be repeatedly stressed that invertebrates as a whole are even more important in the maintenance of ecosystems than are vertebrates.

- Reserves for invertebrate conservation are practicable and relatively inexpensive. Many species can be maintained in large, breeding populations in areas too small to sustain viable populations of vertebrates. A 10-ha plot is likely to be enough to sustain a butterfly or crustacean species indefinitely. The same is true for at least some plant species. Consequently, even if just a tiny remnant of natural habitat exists, and its native vertebrates have vanished, it is still worth setting aside for the plants and invertebrates it will save.

- The *ex situ* preservation of invertebrate species is also very cost-effective. A single pair of rare mammals typically costs hundreds or thousands of dollars yearly to maintain in a zoo (and worth every penny!). At the same time, large numbers of beautiful tree snails, butterflies, and other endangered invertebrates can be cultured in the laboratory, often in conjunction with public exhibits and educational programs, for the same price.

- It will be useful to concentrate biological research and public education on star species when these are available in threatened habitats, in the manner that has proved so successful in vertebrate conservation. Examples of such species include the tree snails of Moorea, Hawaii, and the Florida Keys; the Prairie sphinx moth of the Central States; the birdwing butterflies of New Guinea; and the metallic blue and golden ants of Cuba.

- We need to launch a major effort to measure biodiversity, to create a complete inventory of all the species of organisms on Earth, and to assess their importance for the environment and humanity. Our museums, zoological parks, and arboreta deserve far more support than they are getting—for the future of our children.

A hundred years ago few people thought of saving any kind of animal or plant. The circle of concern has expanded steadily since, and it is just now beginning to encompass the invertebrates. For reasons that have to do with almost every facet of human welfare, we should welcome this new development.

20. SIDELIGHT: Parachuting Cats and Interconnectedness _____

One need not believe that we are "all one," or that there are not significant differences between people and their environments, to recognize the incredible mutual interdependence among many living creatures or between systems of life. Indeed, much contemporary discussion is flawed by the tacit assumption that there is much less dependence than, in fact, exists.

It is frequently tempting to ask, "What does that have to do with me?" "So what; what difference does that make?" Paul and Anne Ehrlich tell of the spraying of DDT in Borneo in order to kill houseflies. Someone must have thought that the costs and benefits made doing so worthwhile. Leading animal rights theorists do not attribute rights to houseflies.[1] The gecko lizards ate the houseflies and died. Then house cats ate the dying lizards, and there were fewer house cats. Rats found the situation more agreeable, but they brought bubonic plague. And humans did not find this situation at all agreeable. In short, the houseflies were part of a food chain and the disturbance of that chain had a profound impact on some members of *Homo sapiens*. To try to remedy the problem, the government of Borneo parachuted cats into the area. We often leap at technological solutions without careful estimation of the long-term, possible unknown, effects of their adoption. There is no need for one to be either protechnology or antitechnology. Some innovations are wonderful, as far as we can tell, but some turn out to be a witches' brew. In many cases there is certainly no evil intent on the part of the inventors or developers of technology. In the best of cases, a scientist wishes to make life better for all; the worst cases are marked by recklessness or out and out indifference to the well-being of others, mixed perhaps with a measure of self-deception. In many cases what generated risky or extremely risky consequences were the collective actions of millions of people who sought to carry on, or achieve, a happy existence. The creation of CFCs (chlorofluorocarbons), for example, was part of an effort to find effective means of cooling, and their use in refrigerators and automobile air-conditioning systems improved the lives of millions. The goal was admirable. The means seemed perfectly innocent, indeed a brilliant solution and another occasion to salute the "wonders" of modern science. And the developers could make a profit. The situation seemed, like many others, to involve no losers. But then we began to learn the effects of CFCs on the ozone layer. This layer of ozone is about 12 to 20 miles up in the stratosphere and protects life from the harmful effects of certain ultraviolet rays of the sun (the UV-B rays). Aside from their capacity to alter genetic material deep within human cells and cause skin cancer (in Australia, with greater exposure to these rays, two out of three people get some form of this cancer) these rays seem to have harmful effects on phytoplankton, tiny creatures that tend to inhabit the upper few feet of the ocean. It is just here that one tends to engage in the knee-jerk reaction "So what?" or "Who cares?" We must think about the fact that small fish survive on a diet of phytoplankton, and larger fish and other forms of sea life survive by eating the smaller ones. We make no final estimate of the prospective danger that we and other forms of life may face, but millions and millions of people depend on the existence of sea creatures. Nevertheless, the introduction of CFCs (whose effects in eroding the ozone layer will be felt throughout the twenty-first century even if their production was phased out by 1995) may have catastrophic consequences beyond those associated with cancer and cataracts—largely because of our ignorance, our lack of caution, and our bravado in our ability to manipulate nature.

Similarly, we produced dangerous amounts of nuclear wastes on the assumption that our political leaders and world-class scientists would devise a means of dealing with them at some point. In poker they say that one should not bid to an inside straight.

Note

1. For example, Tom Regan in *The Case for Animal Rights* holds that at least animals that are "subjects of a life" have rights (for starters, mammals over one year of age). He leaves it an open question whether other creatures do.

CONSTRUCTING AN ENVIRONMENTAL ETHIC

IV.A THE BROADER BIOTIC COMMUNITY

21. PREVIEW

> On reflection, I find it as odd to think that the plants have value only for the happiness of the dusky-footed wood-rats as to think that the dusky-footed wood-rats have value only for the happiness of humans.[1]
>
> *John Rodman*

Cows scream louder than carrots.[2]

> *Alan Watts (explaining why he is a vegetarian)*

We begin with a discussion of the nineteenth-century environmental movements in the United States called conservationism and preservationism. These movements were influential in the thinking of major environmental writers such as Aldo Leopold. Moreover, contemporary philosophers such as J. Baird Callicott, Bryan G. Norton, and Anthony Weston employ the terms *conservationism* and *preservationism* in their work. To understand what they are talking about, we need some historical background.

In the context of developing appropriate attitudes toward the earth, Anthony Weston says,

> We need to think of the earth itself in a different way: not as an infinite waste sink, and not as a collection of resources fortuitously provided for our use, but as a complex system with its own integrity and dynamics, far more intricate than we understand or perhaps *can* understand, but still the system within which we live and on which we necessarily and utterly depend. We must learn a new kind of respect.[3]

If being more mindful of, and attentive to, the way we interact with and depend on nature is, as Weston claims, the minimum required by an environmental ethic, what else is required? For answers, we examine "the land ethic," Deep Ecology, social ecology, and ecofeminism. In this larger discussion in Section IV.A, we read works by legal theorist Christopher Stone, philosophers Kenneth Goodpaster and Paul Taylor, and the originator of the land ethic, Aldo Leopold (Essays 22, 23, 24, and 25). They raise such questions as the following: Is sentience the correct standard for determining who or what has moral standing or inherent value? Do trees have rights? Do wildflowers have inherent value? Are ecosystems, rather than the individuals who make up such systems, the real sources of inherent value? Even though Leopold is chronologically earlier than Goodpaster, Stone, and Taylor, some believe his ideas are a more radical departure from traditional humanistic ethics than those of Goodpaster, Stone, and Taylor.[4] So our classification in this part is based on the logical progression of ideas rather than historical order.

HISTORICAL MOVEMENTS

The conservation movement had scientific roots. Some of its leaders, such as Gifford Pinchot (1865–1914), came from different fields of study, such as forestry. The emphasis of the movement was on wise management of resources over a long period of time.

Pinchot favored commercial development of the U.S. forest reserves for present and future American citizens. In his book, *The Fight for Conservation*, he maintained the following:

> The first great fact about conservation is that it stands for development. There has been a fundamental misconception that conservation means nothing but the husbanding of resources for future generations. There could be no more serious mistake. Conservation does mean provision for the future, but it means also and first of all the recognition of the right of the present generation to the fullest necessary use of all the resources with which this country is so abundantly blessed. Conservation demands the welfare of this generation first, and afterward the welfare of the generations to follow. The first principle of conservation is development, the use of the natural resources now existing on this continent for the benefit of the people who live here now.[5]

Pinchot further emphasized that forest resources should not fall into the hands of the powerful few, corporations, for example, but should be used to make homes for all American citizens. Pinchot, who in 1905 became head of the newly established U.S. Forest Service, once told the Society of American Foresters, "The object of our forest policy is not to preserve the forests because they are beautiful . . . or because they are refuges for the wild creatures of the wilderness . . . but . . . the making of prosperous homes."[6] As a spokesperson for the conservationist movement and a supporter of Theodore Roosevelt's policies, he said, "If we succeed, there will exist upon this continent a sane, strong people, living through the centuries in a land sub-dued and controlled for the service of the people, its rightful masters, owned by the many and not by the few."[7]

Pinchot was opposed by the preservationist movement, headed by John Muir (1838–1914), the founder of the Sierra Club. Muir wanted to preserve the wilderness for aesthetic and spiritual reasons.

> Watch the sunbeams over the forest awakening the flowers, feeding them every one, warming, reviving the myriads of the air, setting countless wings in motion—making diamonds of dewdrops, lakes, painting the spray of falls in rainbow colors. Enjoy the great night like a day, hinting the eternal and imperishable in nature amid the transient and material.[8]

For Muir, nature provides an experience of the sacred or holy. The experience is not simply one of inspiration, but one of recognition of the divine in nature. As Muir once reported his experience of a stroll in the woods: "How beautiful and fresh and Godful the world began to appear."[9]

One famous example of the opposition between the conservationists and the preservationists is the controversy over the Hetch Hetchy Valley in California. Muir and his followers fought for the protection of the Hetch Hetchy Valley in Yosemite National Park. The city of San Francisco wanted to dam the area, thus flooding the park, and construct a reservoir. Pinchot, whose colleagues contemptuously referred to the preservationists as "nature lovers," threw his support behind James R. Garfield, Secretary of the Interior, who approved the city's request to build a dam. Both Pinchot and Muir brought pressure to bear on President Theodore Roosevelt, who in the end supported Pinchot.

Despite their difference, it can be argued that both traditions, conservationism and preservationism, were anthropocentric. If so, whether Hetch Hetchy Valley is used as a water supply for human beings or as a source of peak experiences for humans, its value lies in human use.[10] Nonetheless, one can find in the writings of John Muir the idea that nature has value independent of human beings: "Rocks have a kind of life not so different from ours as we imagine. Anyhow their material beauty is only a veil covering spiritual beauty—a divine incarnation—instonation."[11] Although this independent value may not be independent of a pantheistic view of nature, it is nevertheless independent of human beings.[12] As such, Muir and his followers influenced Aldo Leopold and later advocates of the land ethic such as J. Baird Callicott and advocates of the rights of trees such as Christopher Stone. Callicott claims that nature has value in itself or for its own sake, that we should value nature in much the same way as parents value their children. Stone argues that trees and streams should be able to sue in court (or have guardians sue on their behalf) for their own injuries. One task of this section is to investigate the various grounds for attempting to establish the independent value of nature.

THE CONTEMPORARY DISCUSSION

Christopher Stone, a law professor at the University of Southern California, wrote an important treatise entitled *Should Trees Have Standing?* (Essay 23). Stone sees the history of moral development as an extension of the scope of our moral concern to more and more beings and entities as we progressively are able to identify or empathize with them. Originally, according to Stone, "each man had regard only for himself and those of a very narrow circle around him."[13] As we have seen, the circle that Aristotle drew was very small indeed. What we have done, says Stone, is to view many beings and entities in the world as less than persons, and indeed as objects or things in the world exist only for the use of people. Our law increasingly has reflected a shift from this view by "making persons of children . . . prisoners, aliens, women (especially of the married variety), the insane,

Blacks, foetuses, and Indians."[14] Many authors in this book argue against the notion that nature exists solely for the use of human beings. Some believe that such a denial points the way to expanding the circle of right-holders to include environmental "objects" such as trees and streams.

Stone suggests that as we become more sensitive, we add more and more previously rightless entities to the list of persons. His remarks on sensitivity and empathy raise questions about the role of rational argument in ethics. On what basis is the law "making persons"? In Stone's view, it is only when we perceive nature as like us that we will be able to generate the love and empathy for the environment that in turn will enable us to attribute rights to it. Does such a thesis imply that rights should be attributed to all things cute and cuddly? Suppose we identify with human fetuses. Do they have rights on that account? Must E.T. be rightless if we do not empathize with him (it)? Is there anything in the universe we will not add to the list of persons assuming we can empathize with it? Should our capacities for empathy be a determining factor in ascertaining what sorts of things possess rights? Suppose some cannot identify with Jews, gypsies, or people of another color?

Justice William O. Douglas, in the U.S. Supreme Court case *Sierra v. Morton*, 1972, cited Stone's book in support of his dissenting opinion that "Contemporary public concern for protecting nature's ecological equilibrium should lead to the conferral of standing upon environmental objects to sue for their own preservation."[15] In this landmark case, the Sierra Club tried to prevent Walt Disney Enterprises from building a ski resort in the Mineral King Valley adjacent to Sequoia National Park. The case was not decided on the relative merits of ski resorts versus natural beauty. Rather, it was decided on the issue of standing to sue. "Whether a party has a sufficient stake in an otherwise justiciable controversy to obtain judicial resolution of that controversy is what traditionally has been referred to as the question of standing to sue."[16] The law requires that the party seeking review must itself have suffered an injury or itself have been adversely affected. The Court decided in favor of Disney and against the Sierra Club. After all, it is hard to say that the Sierra Club's members suffered an injury simply because others like to ski. Mineral King Valley might have received legal consideration if trees and streams had standing to sue for their own preservation and/or injury. Much of Stone's essay is a plea for a liberalized domain of *legal* standing. Because trees cannot initiate proceedings on their own behalf, Stone recommends a guardianship approach similar to the one we have now with respect to incompetent human beings, such as the profoundly retarded and young children. Incompetent humans have legal rights even if they are unable to claim them for themselves, such as rights to proper medical treatment.

As recently as June 12, 1992, in *Lujan v. Defenders of Wildlife*, the U.S. Supreme Court decided an important environmental case on the basis of the standing-to-sue doctrine articulated in *Sierra v. Morton*. As a result, the Court did not address substantive environmental issues such as alleged violations of the Endangered Species Act of 1973 by U.S.-agency-funded projects in foreign countries and whether the Endangered Species Act applies only within the borders of the United States.

In 1978, the Carter administration issued a regulation saying that the Endangered Species Act did apply to American projects abroad. In 1983, Ronald Reagan's Secretary of the Interior, James Watt, reversed that policy. Several environmental groups sought to challenge the policy continued by George Bush's Secretary of the Interior, Manual Lujan. Two members of the Defenders of Wildlife, Joyce Kelly and Amy Skilbred, submitted affidavits claiming that certain federally supported projects threatened an endangered Egyptian crocodile and the Asian elephant and leopard in Sri Lanka. The information in the affidavits was based on Kelly and Skilbred's professional interest in the areas and their visits to the sites of the federal projects.

The Court said, "We shall assume for the sake of argument that these affidavits contain facts showing that certain agency-funded projects threatened listed species. . . . They plainly contain no facts, however, showing how damage to the species will produce 'imminent' injury to Mss. Kelly and Skilbred."[17] In making their case that Kelly and Skilbred were not injured, the Court weighed heavily the fact that the environmentalists were unable to say exactly when they would return to the areas. Despite the fact that a civil war was going on in Sri Lanka, thus hampering one plaintiff's ability to be precise about her future plans to return to the area, the Court demanded detail on future conduct.

In *Lujan*, the Court admitted that "when the plaintiff is not himself the object of the government action or inaction he challenges, standing is not precluded, but it is ordinarily 'substantially more difficult' to establish."[18] In Stone's view, the crocodiles, elephants, and leopards should have been the plaintiffs in this case, but, of course, they do not have standing to sue. In our efforts to think hard about how to achieve better environmental policies in the United States, we need to consider whether changing the standing-to-sue doctrine will bring about significant gains.

In a move similar to Peter Singer's claim that species membership as such is irrelevant to moral standing, Kenneth Goodpaster rejects sentience as the criterion that must be met in order for a being (or entity) to count for something, morally speaking. Singer believes that the species one happens to be, like the race or the sex one happens to be, is an arbitrary characteristic that has no moral significance. What matters, in his view, is whether a being can suffer. But Goodpaster, like the Deep Ecologists, and others such as Paul Taylor, thinks that seeing sentience as all important is as arbitrary as claiming the same for membership in *Homo sapiens*. Goodpaster says, "Nothing short of the condition of *being alive* seems to me to be a plausible and non-arbitrary criterion [of moral considerability]."[19] He adds, "This criterion, if taken seriously, could admit of application to . . . the biosystem itself."[20] In making this claim, Goodpaster seems to be moving in the direction of what is called ethical holism.

Roughly speaking, *holism* is the view that the biosphere as an interconnected whole has moral standing. Such a view is often attributed to Aldo Leopold and is explicitly endorsed by his intellectual descendant, J. Baird Callicott. Paul Taylor's views must be distinguished from those of the holists. Taylor describes his view as *biocentric egalitarianism*. According to Taylor, all living beings have equal inherent worth in that each living being is a goal-directed system pursuing its own good.[21] Respect for nature is respect for these pursuits. However, Taylor's biocentric ethic, in contrast to Callicott, is individualistic and not holistic. In Taylor's view, according to reviewer T.L.S. Sprigge, "Total eco-systems only matter because individuals find their good within them; there is no over-all value of the whole, since the whole (it is claimed) is pursuing no good of its own."[22]

Taylor, as Sprigge points out, is prepared to push his individualistic biocentrism pretty far. For example, it is just as important that nonconscious individuals such as plants achieve their goals as it is that a conscious individual should.[23] Plants do not have to be conscious to be valued for their own sake or to be as valuable as human beings. Taylor says, "[t]he killing of a wildflower, then, when taken in and of itself, is just as wrong, other-things-being-equal, as the killing of a human."[24]

Aldo Leopold (1887–1948) is a major figure in the emergence of contemporary ecological/environmental ethics. His ethical views, often referred to as "the land ethic," are found mainly in his book *A Sand County Almanac*. In this influential work, Leopold tells the story of Odysseus, who, after returning from the wars of Troy, hanged a dozen female slaves whom he suspected of misconduct. Because Odysseus thought of slaves as mere property, his concept of ethical obligation did not extend to them. He felt that he could dispose of them as he wished. Leopold draws an analogy between the former status of slaves and the current status of land. Land, Leopold argues, should not be viewed as property. His "land ethic" extends moral concern to "soils, waters, plants, and animals, or collectively: the land."[25] Land in Leopold's view is not a commodity that belongs to us, but a community to which we belong.[26] Elsewhere, Leopold refers to the land as an "organism." As might be expected, some expositors of Leopold have emphasized the "community" model and others the "organism" model.

A study of Leopold's work raises a host of important questions. Leopold advocated a harmonious relationship with the land. The land ethic, he said, "changes the role of *Homo sapiens* from conqueror of the land-community to plain member and citizen of it. It implies respect for his fellow-members, and also respect for the community as such."[27] But what does this respect entail? Respect for land, in his view, does not mean leaving it alone, because Leopold believed that we can alter if for the better. "The swampy forest of Caesar's Gaul were utterly changed by human use—for the better. Moses' land of milk and honey was utterly changed—for the worse."[28] In Leopold's view, a harmonious, as opposed to an exploitative, relationship with nature does not imply that humans should refrain from killing animals. As John Rodman characterizes Leopold's view, "it would be pretentious to talk of a land ethic until we have . . . shot a wolf (once) and looked into its eyes as it died."[29]

One famous remark by Aldo Leopold is "think like a mountain." We are urged to take a different perspective—to view ourselves as "fellow-citizens" with other beings on this planet, not appointed lords of creation. Leopold's emphasis on a *land* ethic and the comparative invisibility of life in the rivers, lakes and oceans—waters covering 70% of the earth's crust—may contribute to our academic and nonacademic blindness to the importance of marine life. There is an appalling loss of life in our oceans, rivers, bays, and estuaries. Many areas are fished out, e.g., cod off the Northeast coast and the oyster population in the Chesapeake Bay. Part of the problem is human pollution—oil spills, the runoff of nitrogen from fertilizer usage, and so on. Elliot Norse in "Marine Environmental Ethics" discusses a number of the sharp contrasts between the way we think and act with regard to the land versus the seas. He notes that "someone who dumped vast amounts of sewage on public lands would be arrested, but we routinely do the same into our streams and rivers, which empty into our estuaries, coastal waters, and oceans, as if the act of flushing made wastes go away, vanishing without a trace." On land, bald eagles, for example, have protection; there is little analogous protection with regard to marine life. Norse notes that there is a dead zone the size of New Jersey off the mouth of the Mississippi—a zone in which life requiring oxygen disappears from the ocean floor. The further contrasts can be eye opening. Reacting to such matters, Bryan Norton suggests that we should "think like an ocean." What is happening to the oceans is partly a by-product of the absence of established property rights—or some form of social control of the private exploitation of the oceans, a matter central to Garrett Hardin's essay "The Tragedy of the Commons" [found in V.C]. Partly we have viewed marine life as lacking moral standing. Partly we have accepted the unfounded by self-serving belief that the oceans or rivers "renew themselves" after a number of decades.

Callicott, in his essay "The Conceptual Foundations of the Land Ethic" (Essay 26), reads Leopold as intending to extend moral standing to things that are not themselves individual humans or animals. This, according to Callicott, is what is new and radical about Leopold's land ethic. "[The] standard modern model of ethical theory provides no possibility whatever for the moral consideration of wholes—of threatened *populations* of animals and plants, or of endemic, rare, or endangered *species*, or of biotic *communities*, or most expansively, of the *biosphere* in its totality."[30] Callicott emphasizes Leopold's call for "respect for the community as such" in the famous characterization of the land ethic (quoted earlier) where human beings are said to be plain members and citizens of the earth.

Not everyone agrees with Callicott that Leopold intended to attribute moral standing to the biosphere as a whole. Bryan Norton, for example, says the following: "That Leopold saw new and grave responsibilities limiting human activities in the modern world of bulldozers and concrete is without question. But whether he saw these obligations as deriving from sources outside of, and independent of, human affairs seems to me doubtful."[31] Although both Callicott and Norton characterize Leopold's view as "holistic," the two could not be further apart on the issue of whether the biosphere as a whole has moral standing or intrinsic value and whether Leopold claimed that it does. The difference is this: By "holism," Norton means "the interests of the human species interpenetrate those of the living Earth."[32]

It might be helpful to contrast Norton's view of holism with our earlier characterization. Earlier, we said that holism is the view that the biosphere as an interconnected whole has moral standing. For Norton, holism is the view that the biosphere is an interconnected whole. As individuals we are part of a larger system and we should value the system, but we value the system from the viewpoint of individuals rather than claiming that the system is the source of independent value.[33] Norton rejects the following dilemma: "either nature is saved for future consumptive purposes or it is saved for itself . . . this reasoning ignores human, nonconsumptive motives for protecting natural ecosystems."[34]

Calling Leopold an "uncompromising preservationist," Norton goes on to claim that preservationism is characterized by "the exclusion of disruptive human activities from specified areas"[35] for the purpose of preventing overexploitation and in turn ecological breakdown. "On the grandest scale, [preservationists] pursue . . . the setting aside of large, pristine tracts where the struggle to survive can continue untrammeled by human interference, or as nearly so as possible."[36] In Norton's view, whether preservationists are motivated by anthropocentrism or nonanthropocentrism matters little. Nonanthropocentrism, Norton says, "is sufficient, but not necessary, to support preservationism. The preservationist perspective requires no more than a concern for long-term effects of pervasive management on biological diversity."[37]

The disagreement between the integrator of perspectives, Bryan Norton, on the one hand, and Callicott and his followers, on the other, runs deep. Norton is a pragmatist and would probably agree with the following assessment of Leopold's work by Anthony Weston: Leopold is "not offering an ethical *theory*, [but] only a provisional statement of *some* of the values that ought to find their place in an ecologically intelligent land-use policy."[38] The values to which Weston refers are integrity, stability, and beauty—the ones expressed in Leopold's famous maxim "A thing is right when it tends to preserve the integrity, stability, and beauty of the biotic community. It is wrong when it tends otherwise."[39] Callicott characterizes Leopold's maxim as the "'summary moral maxim' of the land ethic."[40] For Callicott, Leopold is not simply suggesting some intelligent land-use values; he is asserting a fundamental, if not ultimate, ethical principle that is part of a larger ethical theory, the land ethic.

Callicott's approach to the land ethic has developed over a long period of time. In 1980, he wrote his provocative "Animal Liberation: A Triangular Affair," in which he argued that animal liberation with its emphasis of the importance of individuals and environmental ethics with its holistic emphasis are based on incompatible philosophies. In the article, he referred to Leopold's maxim as "the categorical imperative or principle precept of the land ethic."[41] It expresses "the idea that the good of the biotic community is the ultimate measure of the moral value, the rightness or wrongness of actions."[42] Callicott interpreted Leopold's maxim as implying that concern for the biotic system should take precedence over a more traditional concern for individuals. "The land ethic manifestly does not accord equal moral worth to each and every member of the biotic community; the moral worth of individuals (including, *N.B.*, human individuals) is relative, to be assessed in accordance with the particular relation of each to the collective entity which Leopold called 'land.'"[43]

Claims such as the one just given that seem to imply that individual animals may be sacrificed for ecological reasons or that humans might be killed for obstructing a sustainable future, prompted Tom Regan to accuse advocates of the land ethic of environmental fascism—a charge Callicott alludes to in "The Conceptual Foundations of the Land Ethic."

> The implications of [Leopold's maxim] include the clear prospect that the individual may be sacrificed for the greater biotic good. . . . It is difficult to see how the notion of rights of the individual could find a home within a view that . . . might be fairly dubbed "environmental fascism." . . . The rights view cannot abide this position . . . because it denies the propriety of deciding what should be done to individuals who have rights by appeal to aggregative consideration, including, therefore, computations about what will or will not maximally "contribute to the integrity, stability, and beauty of the biotic community." Individual rights are not to be outweighed by such considerations. . . . Environmental fascism and the rights view are like oil and water: they don't mix.[44]

Callicott now repudiates many of the views he expressed in "Animal Liberation: A Triangular Affair." His article "Animal Liberation and Environmental Ethics: Back Together Again"[45] is his major effort at reconciliation; however, some such effort can be seen in the essay reprinted herein, "The Conceptual Foundations of the Land Ethic" (Essay 26). Following Mary Midgley, Callicott talks about ever-widening circles of kinship that eventually embrace the land. However, "the land ethic . . . neither replaces nor overrides previous accretions [inner social circles to which we belong]."[46] In fact, "as a general rule, the duties correlative to the inner social circles to which we belong eclipse those correlative to the rings farther from the heartwood when conflicts arise."[47]

Norton, in his article reprinted here (Essay 28), says the following of Callicott's journey: "[T]he upshot is that Callicott advocates allegiance to monistic inherentism in theory, but recognizes that the more intimate obligations of kinship and culture will usually outrank obligations to protect species and ecosystems. If this seems a capitulation to business as usual in environmental ethics, with inherent value reduced to a meaningless slogan, it must in fairness be said that Callicott faces a difficult and apparently destructive theoretical dilemma"[48]: Maximize inherent value and be accused of fascism, or find a way to argue that our obligations to persons as owners of inherent value override our obligations to ecosystems as owners of inherent value.

In "Holistic Environmental Ethics and the Problem of Ecofascism," an essay published in his 1999 *Beyond the Land Ethic: More Essays in Environmental Philosophy*, Callicott claims to "dispel the pseudoproblem of ecofascism that has bedeviled holistic environmental ethics for more than fifteen years—at least, hopefully, once and for all."[49] He argues here that when there are conflicts between communities—the human community, the nonhuman community, the land which is also a community—we should prioritize our duties by using two second-order principles. The first such principle is the one discussed above: "our more venerable and intimate community memberships are the more primitive and urgent."[50] Using this principle alone, Callicott concedes, would seem to result in almost always putting human interests first. However, using this principle in conjunction with a second principle which "requires an agent to give priority to the stronger interests at issue"[51] will result in subordinating weak human interests to stronger environmental ones. "We have a much stronger obligation to save endangered species from extinction, for instance, than we have to raise the Dow Jones Industrial Average by a percentage point or two."[52]

As a pragmatist in the tradition of Peirce and Dewey, Norton's method of dealing with issues in environmental ethics is to recognize that multiple values are at stake (rejecting monism) and to try to integrate these values to design a workable environmental policy. It is probably not an exaggeration to suggest that pragmatists view philosophical discussions about intrinsic value or inherent value to be a waste of time. Certainly Anthony Weston suggests that philosophical disputes about intrinsic value might better be replaced by an understanding that the earth is valuable because it is our home.[53] In reply to the pragmatists, Callicott argues that one's theoretical beliefs matter. It is not enough to simply seek common ground, policy consensus, and workable solutions. Environmental philosophers are needed, he argues, to help "reconfigure the prevailing cultural world view and thus [help] to push general practice in the direction of environmental responsibility."[54]

NOTES

1. John Rodman, "The Liberation of Nature," *Inquiry* 20 (Spring 1977), 84.

2. Bryan G. Norton, *Toward Unity Among Environmentalists* (New York: Oxford University Press, 1991), p. 224.

3. Anthony Weston, *Toward Better Problems: New Perspectives on Abortion, Animal Rights, the*

Environment, and Justice (Philadelphia: Temple University Press, 1992), p. 105.

4. J. Baird Callicott, in correspondence.

5. Gifford Pinchot, *The Fight for Conservation* (Seattle: University of Washington Press, 1910), pp. 42-43.

6. Samuel P. Hays, *Conservation and the Gospel of Efficiency: The Progressive Conservation Movement*, 1890–1920 (Cambridge, MA: Harvard University Press, 1959), pp. 41–42.

7. Gifford Pinchot, *The Fight for Conservation*, p. 27.

8. John Muir, *To Yosemite and Beyond, Writings from the Years 1863–1875*, edited by Robert Engberg and Donald Wesling (Madison: University of Wisconsin Press, 1980), p. 113.

9. Ibid., p. 27.

10. Samuel Hays makes a similar point when he says that the crux of the controversy was over two public uses of the area: water supply and recreation. *Conservation and the Gospel of Efficiency*, p. 193.

11. John Muir, *To Yosemite and Beyond*, p. 113.

12. John Rodman suggests this in "Four Forms of Ecological Consciousness," *Ethics and the Environment*, edited by Donald Scherer and Thomas Attig (Englewood Cliffs, NJ: Prentice Hall, 1983), p. 85.

13. Christopher Stone, *Should Trees Have Standing? Toward Legal Rights for Natural Objects* (Los Altos, CA: William Kaufmann, 1974), p. 3.

14. Ibid., p. 4.

15. *Sierra v. Morton*, April 19, 1972, pp. 70–34. Reprinted in Stone (ibid.).

16. *Sierra v. Morton*, quoted in Stone, p. 62.

17. *Lujan, Secretary of the Interior, Petitioner v. Defenders of Wildlife, et al.* 504 U.S. 555, 564 (1992).

18. 504 U.S. 555, 562 (1992).

19. Kenneth E. Goodpaster, "On Being Morally Considerable," *Ethics and the Environment*, edited by Donald Scherer and Thomas Attig (Englewood Cliffs, NJ: Prentice Hall, 1983), p. 31.

20. Ibid.

21. Tom Regan challenges Taylor's species egalitarianism by arguing that Taylor has made an improper inference from the "equal *independence* of the good of individual living beings" to the "equal *inherent* worth" of such beings. Tom Regan, "Less Is More: Some Remarks on Paul Taylor's *Respect for Nature*," unpublished paper presented at Brooklyn College, 1987, p. 13.

22. T.L.S. Sprigge, "Some Recent Positions in Environmental Ethics Examined," *Inquiry* 34(1) (March 1991), p. 117.

23. This remark is a paraphrase of a point made by Sprigge in "Some Recent Positions in Environmental Ethics Examined," p. 116.

24. Paul Taylor, "In Defense of Biocentrism," *Environmental Ethics* 5 (1983), p. 242, quoted in Sprigge, p. 116.

25. Aldo Leopold, *A Sand County Almanac* (New York: Ballantine Books, 1970) p. 239.

26. Ibid., p. xxviii.

27. Ibid., p. 240.

28. Aldo Leopold, "The Conservation Ethic," *Journal of Forestry* 31(1939), 636.

29. John Rodman, "The Liberation of Nature," p. 110.

30. J. Baird Callicott, "The Conceptual Foundations of the Land Ethic," *Companion to A Sand County Almanac: Interpretive and Critical Essays*, edited by J. Baird Callicott (Madison: University of Wisconsin Press, 1987), pp. 197–198.

31. Bryan G. Norton, *Toward Unity Among Environmentalists*, p. 57.

32. Bryan G. Norton, "Conservation and Preservation: A Conceptual Rehabilitation," *Environmental Ethics* 8 (Fall 1986), 220.

33. This point is a paraphrase of a remark made by Norton in a review of J. Baird Callicott's *In Defense of the Land Ethic: Essays in Environmental Philosophy*, *Environmental Ethics* 13(2) (Summer 1991), p. 182.

34. Bryan G. Norton, "Conservation and Preservation," p. 208.

35. Ibid., p. 201.

36. Ibid., p. 218.

37. Ibid., p. 214.

38. Anthony Weston, *Toward Better Problems*, p. 121.

39. Aldo Leopold, *A Sand County Almanac*, p. 262. For a criticism of "stability" as incompatible with contemporary ecology, see James Sterba "A Biocentrist Strikes Back" in *Earth Ethics: Introductory Readings on Animal Rights and Environmental Ethics*, 2nd ed., edited by James P. Sterba (Upper Saddle River, NJ: Prentice Hall, 2000).

40. J. Baird Callicott, "Conceptual Foundations of the Land Ethic," p. 196.

41. J. Baird Callicott, "Animal Liberation: A Triangular Affair," *People, Penguins, and Plastic Trees*, 2nd ed., edited by Christine Pierce and Donald VanDeVeer (Belmont, CA: Wadsworth, 1995), p. 241.

42. Ibid.

43. Ibid., p. 244.

44. Tom Regan, *The Case for Animal Rights* (Berkeley: University of California Press, 1983), pp. 361–362.

45. J. Baird Callicott, ed., *In Defense of the Land Ethic: Essays in Environmental Philosophy* (Albany, NY: State University of New York Press, 1989).

46. J. Baird Callicott, "The Conceptual Foundations of the Land Ethic," pp. 207, 208.

47. Ibid., p. 208.

48. Bryan G. Norton, "Integration or Reduction: Two Approaches to Environmental Values," *Environmental Pragmatism*, edited by Andrew Light and Eric Katz (New York: Routledge, 1996), p. 114.

49. J. Baird Callicott, "Holistic Environmental Ethics and the Problem of Ecofascism," *Beyond the Land Ethic: More Essays in Environmental Philosophy* (Albany, NY: State University of New York Press, 1999) p. 7.

50. Ibid., p. 14.

51. Ibid., p. 76.

52. Ibid., p. 14.

53. See Anthony Weston, *Toward Better Problems*, pp. 110–117.

54. J. Baird Callicott, "Environmental Philosophy Is Environmental Activism: The Most Radical and Effective Kind," *Environmental Philosophy and Environmental Activism*, edited by Don E. Marietta, Jr., and Lester Embree (Lanham, MD: Rowman & Littlefield, 1995), p. 34.

22. On Being Morally Considerable

Kenneth E. Goodpaster

> A thing is right when it tends to preserve the integrity, stability, and beauty of the biotic community. It is wrong when it tends otherwise.
>
> *-Aldo Leopold*

What follows is a preliminary inquiry into a question which needs more elaborate treatment than an essay can provide. The question can be and has been addressed in different rhetorical formats, but perhaps G. J. Warnock's formulation of it[1] is the best to start with:

> Let us consider the question to whom principles of morality apply from, so to speak, the other end—from the standpoint not of the agent, but of the "patient." What, we may ask here, is the condition of moral *relevance*? What is the condition of having a claim to be *considered*, by rational agents to whom moral principles apply? (148)

Modern moral philosophy has taken ethical egoism as its principal foil for developing what can fairly be called a *humanistic* perspective on value and obligation. That is, both Kantian and Humean approaches to ethics tend to view the philosophical challenge as that of providing an epistemological and motivational generalization of an agent's natural self-interested concern. Because of this preoccupation with moral "take-off," however, too little critical thought has been devoted to the flight and its destination. One result might be a certain feeling of impotence in the minds of many moral philosophers when faced with the sorts of issues . . . that question the breadth of the moral enterprise more than its departure point. To be sure, questions of conservation, preservation of the environment, and technology assessment *can* be approached simply as application questions, e.g., "How shall we evaluate the alternatives available to us instrumentally in relation to humanistic satisfactions?" But there is something distressingly uncritical in this way of framing such issues—distressingly uncritical in the way that deciding foreign policy solely in terms of "the national interest" is uncritical. Or at least, so I think.

It seems to me that we should not only wonder about, but actually follow "the road not taken into the wood." Neither rationality nor the capacity to experience pleasure and pain seem to me necessary (even though they may be sufficient) conditions on moral considerability. And only our hedonistic and concentric forms of ethical reflection keep us from acknowledging this fact. Nothing short of the condition of *being alive* seems to me to be a plausible and nonarbitrary criterion. What is more, this criterion, if taken seriously, could admit of application to entities and systems of entities heretofore unimagined as claimants on our moral attention (such as the biosystem itself). Some may be inclined to take such implications as a *reductio* of the move "beyond humanism." I am beginning to be persuaded, however, that such implications may provide both a meaningful ethical vision and the hope of a more adequate action guide for the long-term future. Paradigms are crucial components in knowledge—but they can conceal as much as they reveal. Our paradigms of moral considerability are

Kenneth E. Goodpaster in *The Journal of Philosophy*, Vol. LXXV, No. 6 (June 1978), pp. 308–325 (with deletions). Reprinted by permission.

individual persons and their joys and sorrows. I want to venture the belief that the universe of moral consideration is more complex than these paradigms allow.

My strategy, now that my cards are on the table, will be to spell out a few rules of the game . . . and then to examine the "hands" of several respected philosophers whose arguments seem to count against casting the moral net as widely as I am inclined to. . . . In concluding . . . I will discuss several objections and touch on further questions needing attention.

The first (of four) distinctions that must be kept clear in addressing our question has already been alluded to. It is that between moral *rights* and moral *considerability.* My inclination is to construe the notion of rights as more specific than that of considerability, largely to avoid what seem to be unnecessary complications over the requirements for something's being an appropriate "bearer of rights." The concept of rights is used in wider and narrower senses, of course. Some authors (indeed, one whom we shall consider later in this paper) use it as roughly synonymous with Warnock's notion of "moral relevance." Others believe that being a bearer of rights involves the satisfaction of much more demanding requirements. The sentiments of John Passmore[2] are probably typical of this narrower view:

> The idea of "rights" is simply not applicable to what is non-human. . . . It is one thing to say that it is wrong to treat animals cruelly, quite another to say that animals have rights. (116/7)

I doubt whether it is so clear that the class of rights-bearers is or ought to be restricted to human beings, but I propose to suspend this question entirely by framing the discussion in terms of the notion of moral considerability (following Warnock), except in contexts where there is reason to think the widest sense of "rights" is at work. Whether beings who deserve moral consideration in themselves, not simply by reason of their utility to human beings, also possess moral *rights* in some narrow sense is a question which will, therefore, remain open here—and it is a question the answer to which need not be determined in advance.

A second distinction is that between what might be called a *criterion of moral considerability* and a *criterion of moral significance.* The former represents the central quarry here, while the latter, which might easily get confused with the former, aims at governing *comparative* judgments of moral "weight" in cases of conflict. Whether a tree, say, deserves any moral consideration is a question that must be kept separate from the question of whether trees deserve more or less consideration than dogs, or dogs than human persons. We should not expect that the criterion for having "moral standing" at all will be the same as the criterion for adjudicating competing claims to priority among beings that merit that standing. In fact, it may well be an insufficient appreciation of this distinction which leads some to a preoccupation with rights in dealing with morality. I suspect that the real force of attributions of "rights" derives from comparative contexts, contexts in which moral considerability is presupposed and the issue of strength is crucial. Eventually, of course, the priority issues have to be dealt with for an operational ethical account—this much I have already acknowledged—but in the interests of clarity, I set them aside for now.

Another important distinction, the third, turns on the difference between questions of intelligibility and questions of normative substance. An adequate treatment of this difficult and complicated division would take us far afield,[3] but a few remarks are in order. It is tempting to assume, with Joel Feinberg,[4] that we can neatly separate such questions as

1.   What sorts of beings can (logically) be *said* to deserve moral consideration?

from questions like

2.   What sorts of beings do, as a matter of "ethical fact" deserve moral consideration?

But our confidence in the separation here wanes (perhaps more quickly than in other philosophical contexts where the conceptual/substantive distinction arises) when we reflect upon the apparent *flexibility* of our metamoral beliefs. One might argue plausibly, for example, that there were times and societies in which the moral standing of blacks was, as a matter of *conceptual analysis,* deniable. Examples could be multiplied to include women, children, fetuses, and various other instances of what might be called "metamoral disenfranchisement." I suspect that the lesson to be learned here is that, as William Frankena has pointed out,[5] metaethics is, and has always been, a partially normative discipline. Whether we are to take this to mean that it is really impossible ever to engage in morally neutral conceptual analysis in ethics is, of course, another question. In any case, it appears that, with respect to the issue at hand, keeping (1) and (2) apart will be difficult. At the very least, I think, we must be wary of arguments that purport to answer (2) *solely* on the basis of "ordinary language"–style answers to (1).

Though the focus of the present inquiry is more normative than conceptual [hence aimed more at (2) than at (1)], it remains what I called a "framework" inquiry nonetheless, since it prescinds from the question of relative weights (moral significance) of moral considerability claims.

Moreover—and this brings us to the fourth and last distinction—there is another respect in which the present inquiry involves framework questions rather than questions of application. There is clearly a sense in which we are subject to *thresholds* of moral sensitivity just as we are subject to thresholds of cognitive or perceptual sensitivity. Beyond such thresholds we are "morally blind" or suffer disintegrative consequences analogous to "information overload" in a computer. . . . Let us, then, say that the moral considerability of X is *operative* for an agent A if and only if the thorough acknowledgment of X by A is psychologically (and in general, causally) possible for A. If the moral considerability of X is defensible on all grounds independent of operativity, we shall say that it is *regulative.* An agent may, for example, have an obligation to grant regulative considerability to all living things, but be able psychologically and in terms of his own nutrition to grant operative consideration to a much smaller class of things (though note that capacities in this regard differ among persons and change over time).

Using all these distinctions, and the rough and ready terminology that they yield, we can now state the issue in (1) as a concern for a relatively substantive (vs. purely logical) criterion of moral considerability (vs. moral significance) of a regulative (vs. operative) sort. As far as I can see, X's being a living thing is both necessary and sufficient for moral considerability so understood, whatever may be the case for the moral *rights* that rational agents should acknowledge. Let us begin with Warnock's own answer to the question, now that the question has been clarified somewhat. In setting out his answer, Warnock argues (in my view, persuasively) against two more restrictive candidates. The first, what might be called the *Kantian principle,* amounts to little more than a reflection of the requirements of moral *agency* onto those of moral considerability:

3.   For X to deserve moral consideration from A, X must be a rational human person.

Observing that such a criterion of considerability eliminates children and mentally handicapped adults, among others, Warnock dismisses it as intolerably narrow.

The second candidate, actually a more generous variant of the first, sets the limits of moral considerability by disjoining "potentiality":

4.   For all A, X deserves moral consideration from A if and only if X is a rational human person or is a potential rational human person.

Warnock's reply to this suggestion is also persuasive. Infants and imbeciles are no doubt potentially rational, but this does not appear to be the reason why we should not maltreat them. And we would not say that an imbecile reasonably judged to be incurable would thereby reasonably be taken to have no moral claims (151). In short, it seems arbitrary to draw the boundary of moral *considerability* around rational human beings (actual or potential), however plausible it might be to draw the boundary of moral *responsibility* there.[6]

Warnock then settles upon his own solution. The basis of moral claims, he says, may be put as follows:

> . . . just as liability to be judged as a moral agent follows from one's general capability of alleviating, by moral action, the ills of the predicament, and is for that reason confined to rational beings, so the condition of being a proper "beneficiary" of moral action is the capability of *suffering* the ills of the predicament—and for that reason is not confined to rational beings, nor even to potential members of that class. (151)

The criterion of moral considerability then, is located in the *capacity to suffer:*

5.   For all A, X deserves moral consideration from A if and only if X is capable of suffering pain (or experiencing enjoyment).

And the defense involves appeal to what Warnock considers to be (analytically) the *object* of the moral enterprise: amelioration of "the predicament."

W. K. Frankena, in a recent paper,[7] joins forces:

> Like Warnock, I believe that there are right
> and wrong ways to treat infants, animals,
> imbeciles, and idiots even if or even though
> (as the case may be) they are not persons or
> human beings—just because they are capable
> of pleasure and suffering, and not just because
> their lives happen to have some value to or for
> those who clearly are persons or human
> beings.

And Peter Singer[8] writes:

> If a being is not capable of suffering, or of
> experiencing enjoyment or happiness, there is
> nothing to be taken into account. This is why
> the limit of sentience (using the term as a con-
> venient, if not strictly accurate, shorthand for
> the capacity to suffer or experience enjoyment
> or happiness) is the only defensible boundary
> of concern for the interests of others. (154)

. . . Although I acknowledge and even applaud
the conviction expressed by these philosophers that
the capacity to suffer (or perhaps better, *sentience*) is
sufficient for moral considerability, I fail to understand their reasons for thinking such a criterion necessary. To be sure, there are hints at reasons in each
case. Warnock implies that nonsentient beings could
not be proper "beneficiaries" of moral action. Singer
seems to think that beyond sentience "there is nothing to take into account." And Frankena suggests
that nonsentient beings simply do not provide us
with moral reasons for respecting them unless it be
potentiality for sentience.[9] Yet it is so clear that there
is something to take into account, something that is
not merely "potential sentience" and which surely
does qualify beings as beneficiaries and capable of
harm—namely, *life*—that the hints provided seem to
me to fall short of good reasons.

Biologically, it appears that sentience is an
adaptive characteristic of living organisms that
provides them with a better capacity to anticipate,
and so avoid, threats to life. This at least suggests,
though of course it does not prove, that the capacities to suffer and to enjoy are ancillary to something
more important rather than tickets to considerability in their own right. In the words of one perceptive scientific observer:

> If we view pleasure as rooted in our sensory
> physiology, it is not difficult to see that our
> neurophysiological equipment must have
> evolved via variation and selective retention in

such a way as to record a positive signal to
adaptationally satisfactory conditions. . . . The
pleasure signal is only an evolutionarily
derived indicator, not the goal itself. It is the
applause which signals a job well done, but
not the actual completion of the job.[10]

Nor is it absurd to imagine that evolution might
have resulted (indeed might still result?) in beings
whose capacities to maintain, protect, and advance
their lives did not depend upon mechanisms of
pain and pleasure at all.

Joel Feinberg (51) offers what may be the clearest and most explicit case for a restrictive criterion
on moral considerability (restrictive with respect to
life). . . .

The central thesis defended by Feinberg is that
a being cannot intelligibly be said to possess moral
rights (read: deserve moral consideration) unless
that being satisfies the "interest principle," and that
only the subclass of humans and higher animals
among living beings satisfies this principle:

> . . . the sorts of beings who can have rights are
> precisely those who have (or can have) inter-
> ests. I have come to this tentative conclusion for
> two reasons: (1) because a right-holder must be
> capable of being represented and it is impossi-
> ble to represent a being that has no interests,
> and (2) because a right-holder must be capable
> of being a beneficiary in his own person, and a
> being without interests is a being that is inca-
> pable of being harmed or benefited, having no
> good or "sake" of its own. (51)

Implicit in this passage are the following two arguments, interpreted in terms of moral considerability:

(A1) Only beings who can be represented can
deserve moral consideration.

Only beings who have (or can have) interests
can be represented.

Therefore, only beings who have (or can have)
interests can deserve moral consideration.

(A2) Only beings capable of being beneficiaries
can deserve moral consideration.

Only beings who have (or can have) interests
are capable of being beneficiaries.

Therefore, only beings who have (or can have)
interests can deserve moral consideration.

I suspect that these two arguments are at work between the lines in Warnock, Frankena, and Singer, though of course one can never be sure. In any case, I propose to consider them as the best defense of the sentience criterion in recent literature.

I am prepared to grant, with some reservations, the first premises in each of these obviously valid arguments. The second premises, though, are *both* importantly equivocal. To claim that only beings who have (or can have) interests can be represented might mean that "mere things" cannot be represented because they have nothing to represent, no "interests" as opposed to "usefulness" to defend or protect. Similarly, to claim that only beings who have (or can have) interests are capable of being beneficiaries might mean that "mere things" are incapable of being benefited or harmed—they have no "well-being" to be sought or acknowledged by rational moral agents. So construed, Feinberg seems to be right; but he also seems to be committed to allowing any *living* thing the status of moral considerability. For as he himself admits, even plants

> . . . are not "mere things"; they are vital objects with inherited biological propensities determining their natural growth. Moreover we do say that certain conditions are "good" or "bad" for plants, thereby suggesting that plants, unlike rocks, are capable of having a "good." (51)

But Feinberg pretty clearly wants to draw the nets tighter than this—and he does so by interpreting the notion of "interests" in the two second premises more narrowly. The contrast term he favors is not "mere things" but "mindless creatures." And he makes this move by insisting that "interests" logically presuppose *desires* or *wants* or *aims*, the equipment for which is not possessed by plants (nor, we might add, by many animals or even some humans?).

But why should we accept this shift in strength of the criterion? In doing so, we clearly abandon one sense in which living organisms like plants do have interests that can be represented. There is no absurdity in imagining the representation of the needs of a tree for sun and water in the face of a proposal to cut it down or pave its immediate radius for a parking lot. We might of course, on reflection, decide to go ahead and cut it down or do the paving, but there is hardly an intelligibility problem about representing the tree's interest in

our deciding not to. In the face of their obvious dencies to maintain and heal themselves, it is difficult to reject the idea of interests on the part of trees (and plants generally) in remaining alive.[11]

Nor will it do to suggest, as Feinberg does, that the needs (interests) of living things like trees are not really their own but implicitly *ours*: "Plants may need things in order to discharge their functions, but their functions are assigned by human interests, not their own." (54) As if it were human interests that assigned to trees the tasks of growth or maintenance! The interests at stake are clearly those of the living things themselves, not simply those of the owners or users or other human persons involved. Indeed, there is a suggestion in this passage that, to be capable of being represented, an organism must *matter* to human beings somehow— a suggestion whose implications for human rights (disenfranchisement) let alone the rights of animals (inconsistently for Feinberg, I think) —are grim.

The truth seems to be that the "interests" that nonsentient beings share with sentient beings (over and against "mere things") are far more plausible as criteria of *considerability* than the "interests" that sentient beings share (over and against "mindless creatures"). This is not to say that interests construed in the latter way are morally irrelevant—for they may play a role as criteria of moral *significance*—but it is to say that psychological or hedonic capacities seem unnecessarily sophisticated when it comes to locating the minimal conditions for something's deserving to be valued for its own sake. Surprisingly, Feinberg's own reflections on "mere things" appear to support this very point:

> . . . mere things have no conative life: no conscious wishes, desires, and hopes; or urges and impulses; or unconscious drives, aims, and goals; or latent tendencies, direction of growth, and natural fulfillments. Interests must be compounded somehow out of conations; hence mere things have no interests. (49)

Together with the acknowledgment, quoted earlier, that plants, for example, are not "mere things," such observations seem to undermine the interest principle in its more restrictive form. I conclude, with appropriate caution, that the interest principle either grows to fit what we might call a "life principle" or requires an arbitrary stipulation of psychological capacities (for desires, wants, etc.) which are neither warranted by (A1) and (A2) nor independently plausible.

Let us now turn to several objections that might be thought to render a "life principle" of moral considerability untenable quite independently of the adequacy or inadequacy of the sentience or interest principle.

(O1) Consideration of life can serve as a criterion only to the degree that life itself can be given a precise definition; and it can't.

(R1) I fail to see why a criterion of moral considerability must be strictly decidable in order to be tenable. Surely rationality, potential rationality, sentience, and the capacity for or possession of interests fare no better here. Moreover, there do seem to be empirically respectable accounts of the nature of living beings available which are not intolerably vague or open-textured:

> The typifying mark of a living system . . . appears to be its persistent state of low entropy, sustained by metabolic processes for accumulating energy, and maintained in equilibrium with its environment by homeostatic feedback processes.[12]

Granting the need for certain further qualifications, a definition such as this strikes me as not only plausible in its own right, but ethically illuminating, since it suggests that the core of moral concern lies in respect for self-sustaining organization and integration in the face of pressures toward high entropy.

(O2) If life, as understood in the previous response, is really taken as the key to moral considerability, then it is possible that larger systems besides our ordinarily understood "linear" extrapolations from human beings (e.g., animals, plants, etc.) might satisfy the conditions, such as the biosystem as a whole. This surely would be a *reductio* of the life principle.

(R2) At best, it would be a *reductio* of the life principle in this form or without qualification. But it seems to me that such (perhaps surprising) implications, if true, should be taken seriously. There is some evidence that the biosystem as a whole exhibits behavior approximating to the definition sketched above,[13] and I see no reason to deny it moral considerability on that account. Why should the universe of moral considerability map neatly onto our medium-sized framework of organisms?

(O3) There are severe epistemological problems about imputing interests, benefits, harms, etc., to nonsentient beings. What is it for a tree to have needs?

(R3) I am not convinced that the epistemological problems are more severe in this context than they would be in numerous others which the objector would probably not find problematic. Christopher Stone has put this point nicely:

> I am sure I can judge with more certainty and meaningfulness whether and when my lawn wants (needs) water than the Attorney General can judge whether and when the United States wants (needs) to take an appeal from an adverse judgment by a lower court. The lawn tells me that it wants water by a certain dryness of the blades and soil—immediately obvious to the touch—the appearance of bald spots, yellowing, and a lack of springiness after being walked on; how does "the United States" communicate to the Attorney General? (24)

We make decisions in the interests of others or on behalf of others every day—"others" whose wants are far less verifiable than those of most living creatures.

(O4) Whatever the force of the previous objections, the clearest and most decisive refutation of the principle of respect for life is that one cannot *live* according to it, nor is there any indication in nature that we were intended to. We must eat, experiment to gain knowledge, protect ourselves from predation (macroscopic and microscopic), and in general deal with the overwhelming complexities of the moral life while remaining psychologically intact. To take seriously the criterion of considerability being defended, all these things must be seen as somehow morally wrong.

(R4) This objection . . . can be met, I think, by recalling the distinction made earlier between regulative and operative moral consideration. It seems to me that there clearly are limits to the operational character of respect for living things. We must eat, and usually this involves killing (though not always). We must have knowledge, and sometimes this involves experimentation with living things and killing (though not always). We must protect ourselves from predation and disease, and sometimes this involves killing (though not always). The regulative character of the moral consideration due to all living things asks, as far as I can see, for sensitivity and awareness, not for suicide (psychic or otherwise). But it is not vacuous, in that it does provide a *ceteris paribus* encouragement in the direction of nutritional, scientific, and medical practices of a genuinely life-respecting sort.

As for the implicit claim, in the objection, that since nature doesn't respect life, we needn't, there are two rejoinders. The first is that the premise is not so clearly true. Gratuitous killing in nature is rare indeed. The second, and more important, response is that the issue at hand has to do with the appropriate moral demands to be made on rational moral agents, not on beings who are not rational moral agents. Besides, this objection would tell equally against *any* criterion of moral considerability so far as I can see, if the suggestion is that nature is amoral.

Notes

1. *The Object of Morality* (New York: Methuen, 1971); parenthetical page references to Warnock will be to this book.

2. *Man's Responsibility for Nature* (New York: Scribner's, 1974).

3. Cf. R. M. Hare, "The Argument from Received Opinion," in *Essays on Philosophical Method* (New York: Macmillan, 1971), p. 117.

4. "The Rights of Animals and Unborn Generations," in Blackstone, *Philosophy and Environmental Crisis* (Athens: University of Georgia, 1974), p. 43; parenthetical page references to Feinberg will be to this paper.

5. "On Saying the Ethical Thing," in Goodpaster, ed., *Perspectives on Morality* (Notre Dame, IN: Notre Dame University Press, 1976), pp. 107–24.

6. Actually, it seems to me that we ought not to draw the boundary of moral responsibility just here. See my "Morality and Organizations," in *Proceedings of the Second National Conference on Business Ethics* (Waltham, MA: Bentley College, 1978).

7. "Ethics and the Environment," in K. E. Goodpaster and K. M. Sayre eds., *Ethics and Problems of the 21st Century* (Notre Dame, IN: Notre Dame University Press, 1978).

8. "All Animals Are Equal," in Tom Regan and Peter Singer, *Animal Rights and Human Obligations* (Englewood Cliffs, NJ: Prentice-Hall, 1976), p. 316.

9. "I can see no reason, from the moral point of view, why we should respect something that is alive but has no conscious sentiency and so can experience no pleasure or pain, joy or suffering, unless perhaps it is potentially a consciously sentient being, as in the case of a fetus. Why, if leaves and trees have no capacity to feel pleasure or to suffer, should I tear no leaf from a tree? Why should I respect its location any more than that of a stone in my driveway, if no benefit or harm comes to any person or sentient being by my moving it?" ("Ethics and the Environment").

10. Mark W. Lipsey, "Value Science and Developing Society," paper delivered to the Society for Religion in Higher Education, Institute on Society, Technology and Values (July 15–August 4,1973), p. 11.

11. See Albert Szent-Gyorgyi, *The Living State* (New York: Academic Press, 1972), esp. chap. VI, "Vegetable Defense Systems."

12. K. M. Sayre, *Cybernetics and the Philosophy of Mind* (New York: Humanities, 1976), p. 91.

13. See J. Lovelock and S. Epton, "The Quest for Gaia," *The New Scientist,* 65:935 (February 6, 1975): 304–09.

23. Should Trees Have Standing?—Toward Legal Rights for Natural Objects

Christopher D. Stone

Introduction: The Unthinkable

In *Descent of Man*, Darwin observes that the history of man's moral development has been a continual extension in the objects of his "social instincts and sympathies." Originally each man had regard only for himself and those of a very narrow circle about him; later, he came to regard more and more "not only the welfare, but the happiness of all his fellow-men"; then "his sympathies became more tender and widely diffused, extending to men of all races, to the imbecile, maimed, and other useless members of society, and finally to the lower animals."[1]

The history of the law suggests a parallel development. Perhaps there never was a pure Hobbesian state of nature, in which no "rights" existed except in the vacant sense of each man's "right to self-defense." But it is not unlikely that so far as the earliest "families" (including extended kinship groups and clans) were concerned, everyone outside the family was suspect, alien, rightless.[2] And even

Should Trees Have Standing?—Toward Legal Rights for Natural Objects, by Christopher D. Stone (Portola Valley, CA: Tioga Publishing Company, 1974), pp. 3–18, 24, 27–33, 45–46, 48–54. Reprinted by permission.

within the family, persons we presently regard as the natural holders of at least some rights had none. Take, for example, children. We know something of the early rights-status of children from the widespread practice of infanticide—especially of the deformed and female.[3] (Senicide[4] as among the North American Indians, was the corresponding rightlessness of the aged.)[5] Maine tells us that as late as the Patria Potestas of the Romans, the father had *jus vitae necisque*—the power of life and death—over his children. A fortiori, Maine writes, he had power of "uncontrolled corporal chastisement; he can modify their personal condition at pleasure; he can give a wife to his son; he can give his daughter in marriage; he can divorce his children of either sex; he can transfer them to another family by adoption; and he can sell them." The child was less than a person: an object, a thing.[6]

The legal rights of children have long since been recognized in principle, and are still expanding in practice. Witness, just within recent time, *In re Gault*,[7] guaranteeing basic constitutional protections to juvenile defendants, and the Voting Rights Act of 1970.[8] We have been making persons of children although they were not, in law, always so. And we have done the same, albeit imperfectly some would say, with prisoners,[9] aliens, women (especially of the married variety), the insane,[10] Blacks, foetuses,[11] and Indians.

Nor is it only matter in human form that has come to be recognized as the possessor of rights. The world of the lawyer is peopled with inanimate rightholders: trusts, corporations, joint ventures, municipalities, Subchapter R partnerships,[12] and nationstates, to mention just a few. Ships, still referred to by courts in the feminine gender, have long had an independent jural life, often with striking consequences.[13] We have become so accustomed to the idea of a corporation having "its" own rights, and being a "person" and "citizen" for so many statutory and constitutional purposes, that we forget how jarring the notion was to early jurists. "That invisible, intangible and artificial being, that mere legal entity" Chief Justice Marshall wrote of the corporation in *Bank of the United States v. Deveaux*[14]—could a suit be brought in its name? Ten years later, in the *Dartmouth College* case,[15] he was still refusing to let pass unnoticed the wonder of an entity "existing only in contemplation of law."[16] Yet, long before Marshall worried over the personifying of the modern corporation, the best

medieval legal scholars had spent hundreds of years struggling with the notion of the legal nature of those great public "corporate bodies," the Church and the State. How could they exist in law, as entities transcending the living Pope and King? It was clear how a king could bind *himself*—on his honor—by a treaty. But when the king died, what was it that was burdened with the obligations of, and claimed the rights under, the treaty *his* tangible hand had signed? The medieval mind saw (what we have lost our capacity to see)[17] how *unthinkable* it was, and worked out the most elaborate conceits and fallacies to serve as anthropomorphic flesh for the Universal Church and the Universal Empire.[18]

It is this note of the *unthinkable* that I want to dwell upon for a moment. Throughout legal history, each successive extension of rights to some new entity has been, theretofore, a bit unthinkable. We are inclined to suppose the rightlessness of rightless "things" to be a decree of Nature, not a legal convention acting in support of some status quo. It is thus that we defer considering the choices involved in all their moral, social, and economic dimensions. And so the United States Supreme Court could straightfacedly tell us in *Dred Scott* that Blacks had been denied the rights of citizenship "as a subordinate and inferior class of beings, who had been subjugated by the dominant race. . . ."[19] In the nineteenth century, the highest court in California explained that Chinese had not the right to testify against white men in criminal matters because they were "a race of people whom nature has marked as inferior, and who are incapable of progress or intellectual development beyond a certain point . . . between whom and ourselves nature has placed an impassable difference."[20] The popular conception of the Jew in the 13th Century contributed to a law which treated them as "men *ferae naturae,* protected by a quasi-forest law. Like the roe and the deer, they form an order apart."[21] Recall, too, that it was not so long ago that the foetus was "like the roe and the deer." In an early suit attempting to establish a wrongful death action on behalf of a negligently killed foetus (now widely accepted practice), Holmes, then on the Massachusetts Supreme Court, seems to have thought it simply inconceivable "that a man might owe a civil duty and incur a conditional prospective liability in tort to one not yet in being."[22] The first woman in Wisconsin who thought she might have a right to practice law was told that she did not, in the following terms:

The law of nature destines and qualifies the female sex for the bearing and nurture of the children of our race and for the custody of the homes of the world. . . . [A]ll life-long callings of women, inconsistent with these radical and sacred duties of their sex, as is the profession of the law, are departures from the order of nature; and when voluntary, treason against it. . . . The peculiar qualities of womanhood, its gentle graces, its quick sensibility, its tender susceptibility, its purity, its delicacy, its emotional impulses, its subordination of hard reason to sympathetic feeling, are surely not qualifications for forensic strife. Nature has tempered woman as little for the juridical conflicts of the court room, as for the physical conflicts of the battle field. . . .[24]

The fact is, . . . each time there is a movement to confer rights onto some new "entity," the proposal is bound to sound odd or frightening or laughable. This is partly because until the rightless thing receives its rights, we cannot see it as anything but a *thing* for the use of "us"—those who are holding rights at the time.[24] In this vein, what is striking about the Wisconsin case above is that the court, for all its talk about women, so clearly was never able to see women as they are (and might become). All it could see was the popular "idealized" version of *an object it needed.* Such is the way the slave South looked upon the Black.[25] There is something of a seamless web involved: there will be resistance to giving the thing "rights" until it can be seen and valued for itself; yet, it is hard to see it and value it for itself until we can bring ourselves to give it "rights"—which is almost inevitably going to sound inconceivable to a large group of people.

The reason for this little discourse on the unthinkable, the reader must know by now, if only from the title of the paper. I am quite seriously proposing that we give legal rights to forests, oceans, rivers and other so-called "natural objects" in the environment—indeed, to the natural environment as a whole.

As strange as such a notion may sound, it is neither fanciful nor devoid of operational content. In fact, I do not think it would be a misdescription of recent developments in the law to say that we are already on the verge of assigning some such rights, although we have not faced up to what we are doing in those particular terms.[26] We should do so now, and begin to explore the implications such a notion would hold.

Toward Rights for the Environment

Now, to say that the natural environment should have rights is not to say anything as silly as that no one should be allowed to cut down a tree. We say human beings have rights, but—at least as of the time of this writing—they can be executed. Corporations have rights, but they cannot plead the fifth amendment; *In re Gault* gave 15-year-olds certain rights in juvenile proceedings, but it did not give them the right to vote. Thus, to say that the environment should have rights is not to say that it should have every right we can imagine, or even the same body of rights as human beings have. Nor is it to say that everything in the environment should have the same rights as every other thing in the environment.

What the granting of rights does involve has two sides to it. The first involves what might be called the legal-operational aspects; the second, the psychic and socio-psychic aspects. I shall deal with these aspects in turn.

The Legal-Operational Aspects
What It Means to Be a Holder of Legal Rights

There is, so far as I know, no generally accepted standard for how one ought to use the term "legal rights." Let me indicate how I shall be using it in this piece.

First and most obviously, if the term is to have any content at all, an entity cannot be said to hold a legal right unless and until *some public authoritative body* is prepared to give *some amount of review* to actions that are colorably inconsistent with that "right." For example, if a student can be expelled from a university and cannot get any public official, even a judge or administrative agent at the lowest level, either (i) to require the university to justify its actions (if only to the extent of filling out an affidavit alleging that the expulsion "was not wholly arbitrary and capricious") or (ii) to compel the university to accord the student some procedural safeguards (a hearing, right to counsel, right to have notice of charges), then the minimum requirements for saying that the student has a legal right to his education do not exist.[27]

But for a thing to be *a holder of legal rights,* something more is needed than that some authoritative body will review the actions and processes of those who threaten it. As I shall use the term, "holder of legal rights," each of three additional criteria must be satisfied. All three, one will observe, go towards making a thing *count* jurally—to have a legally recognized worth and dignity in its own right, and not merely to serve as a means to benefit "us" (whoever the contemporary group of rights-holders may be). They are, first, that the thing can institute legal actions *at its behest*, second, that in determining the granting of legal relief, the court must take *injury to it* into account; and, third, that relief must run to the *benefit of it*. . . .

The Rightlessness of Natural Objects at Common Law

Consider, for example, the common law's posture toward the pollution of a stream. True, courts have always been able, in some circumstances, to issue orders that will stop the pollution. . . . But the stream itself is fundamentally rightless, with implications that deserve careful reconsideration.

The first sense in which the stream is not a rights-holder has to do with standing. The stream itself has none. So far as the common law is concerned, there is in general no way to challenge the polluter's actions save at the behest of a lower riparian—another human being—able to show an invasion of *his* rights. This conception of the riparian as the holder of the right to bring suit has more than theoretical interest. The lower riparians may simply not care about the pollution. They themselves may be polluting, and not wish to stir up legal waters. They may be economically dependent on their polluting neighbor. And, of course, when they discount the value of winning by the costs of bringing suit and the chances of success, the action may not seem worth undertaking. Consider, for example, that while the polluter might be injuring 100 downstream riparians $10,000 a year *in the aggregate*, each riparian separately might be suffering injury only to the extent of $100—possibly not enough for any one of them to want to press suit by himself, or even to go to the trouble and cost of securing co-plaintiffs to make it worth everyone's while. This hesitance will be especially likely when the potential plaintiffs consider the burdens the law puts in their way:[28] proving, e.g., specific damages, the "unreasonableness" of defendant's use of the water, the fact that practicable means of abatement exist, and overcoming difficulties raised by issues such as joint causality, right to pollute by prescription, and so forth. Even in states which, like California, sought to overcome these difficulties by empowering the attorney general to sue for abatement of pollution in limited instances, the power has been sparingly invoked and, when invoked, narrowly construed by the courts.[29]

The second sense in which the common law denies "rights" to natural objects has to do with the way in which the merits are decided in those cases in which someone is competent and willing to establish standing. At its more primitive levels, the system protected the "rights" of the property-owning human with minimal weighing of any values: *"Cujus est solum, ejus est usque ad coelum et ad infernos."*[30] Today we have come more and more to make balances—but only such as will adjust the economic best interests of identifiable humans. For example, continuing with the case of streams, there are commentators who speak of a "general rule" that "a riparian owner is legally entitled to have the stream flow by his land with its quality unimpaired" and observe that "an upper owner has, prima facie, no right to pollute the water."[31] Such a doctrine, if strictly invoked, would protect the stream absolutely whenever a suit was brought; but obviously, to look around us, the law does not work that way. Almost everywhere there are doctrinal qualifications on riparian "rights" to an unpolluted stream.[32] Although these rules vary from jurisdiction to jurisdiction, and upon whether one is suing for an equitable injunction or for damages, what they all have in common is some sort of balancing. Whether under language of "reasonable use," "reasonable methods of use," "balance of convenience" or "the public interest doctrine," what the courts are balancing, with varying degrees of directness, are the economic hardships on the upper riparian (or dependent community) of abating the pollution vis-à-vis the economic hardships of continued pollution on the lower riparians. What does not weigh in the balance is the damage to the stream, its fish and turtles and "lower" life. So long as the natural environment itself is rightless, these are not matters for judicial cognizance. Thus, we find the highest court of Pennsylvania refusing to stop a coal company from discharging polluted mine water into a tributary of the Lackawanna River because a plaintiff's "grievance is for a mere personal inconvenience; and . . . mere private personal inconveniences . . . must yield to the necessities of a great public industry, which although in the hands of a private corporation, subserves a great public interest."[33] The stream itself is lost sight of in "a quantitative compromise between *two* conflicting interests."[34]

The third way in which the common law makes natural objects rightless has to do with who is regarded as the beneficiary of a favorable judgment. Here, too, it makes a considerable difference that it is not the natural object that counts in its own right. To illustrate this point, let me begin by observing that it makes perfectly good sense to speak of, and ascertain, the legal damage to a natural object, if only in the sense of "making it whole" with respect to the most obvious factors. The costs of making a forest whole, for example, would include the costs of reseeding, repairing watersheds, restocking wildlife—the sorts of costs the Forest Service undergoes after a fire. Making a polluted stream whole would include the costs of restocking with fish, water-fowl, and other animal and vegetable life, dredging, washing out impurities, establishing natural and/or artificial aerating agents, and so forth. Now, what is important to note is that, under our present system, even if a plaintiff riparian wins a water pollution suit for damages, no money goes to the benefit of the stream itself to repair *its* damages. This omission has the further effect that, at most, the law confronts a polluter with what it takes to make the plaintiff riparians whole; this may be far less than the damages to the stream, but not so much so as to force the polluter to desist. For example, it is easy to imagine a polluter whose activities damage a stream to the extent of $10,000 annually, although the aggregate damage to all the riparian plaintiffs who come into the suit is only $3000. If $3000 is less than the cost to the polluter of shutting down, or making the requisite technological changes, he might prefer to pay off the damages (i.e., the legally cognizable damages) and continue to pollute the stream. Similarly, even if the jurisdiction issues an injunction at the plaintiffs' behest (rather than to order payment of damages), there is nothing to stop the plaintiffs from "selling out" the stream, i.e., agreeing to dissolve or not enforce the injunction at some price (in the example above, somewhere between plaintiffs' damages—$3000—and defendants' next best economic alternative). Indeed, I take it this is exactly what Learned Hand had in mind in an opinion in which, after issuing an anti-pollution injunction, he suggests that the defendant "make its peace with the plaintiff as best it can."[35] What is meant is a peace between *them*, and not amongst them and the river.

I ought to make clear at this point that the common law as it affects streams and rivers, which I have been using as an example so far, is not exactly the same as the law affecting other environmental objects. Indeed, one would be hard pressed to say that there was a "typical" environmental object, so far as its treatment at the hands of the law is concerned. There are some differences in the law applicable to all the various resources that are held in common: rivers, lakes, oceans, dunes, air, streams (surface and subterranean), beaches, and so forth. And there is an even greater difference as between these traditional communal resources on the one hand, and natural objects on traditionally private land, e.g., the pond on the farmer's field, or the stand of trees on the suburbanite's lawn.

On the other hand, although there be these differences which would make it fatuous to generalize about a law of the natural environment, most of these differences simply underscore the points made in the instance of rivers and streams. None of the natural objects, whether held in common or situated on private land, has any of the three criteria of a rights-holder. They have no standing in their own right; their unique damages do not count in determining outcome; and they are not the beneficiaries of awards. In such fashion, these objects have traditionally been regarded by the common law, and even by all but the most recent legislation, as objects for man to conquer and master and use—in such a way as the law once looked upon "man's" relationships to African Negroes. Even where special measures have been taken to conserve them, as by seasons on game and limits on timber cutting, the dominant motive has been to conserve them *for us*—for the greatest good of the greatest number of human beings. Conservationists, so far as I am aware, are generally reluctant to maintain otherwise.[36] As the name implies, they want to conserve and guarantee *our* consumption and *our* enjoyment of these other living things. In their own right, natural objects have counted for little, in law as in popular movements.

As I mentioned at the outset, however, the rightlessness of the natural environment can and should change; it already shows some signs of doing so.

Toward Having Standing in Its Own Right

It is not inevitable, nor is it wise, that natural objects should have no rights to seek redress in their own behalf. It is no answer to say that streams and forests cannot have standing because streams and forests cannot speak. Corporations cannot speak either; nor can states, estates, infants, incompetents, municipalities or universities. Lawyers speak for them, as they customarily do for the ordinary citizen with legal problems. One ought, I think, to handle the legal problems of natural objects as one does the problems of legal incompetents—human beings who have become vegetable. If a human being shows signs of becoming senile and has affairs that he is *de jure* incompetent to manage, those concerned with his well-being make such a showing to the court, and someone is designated by the court with the authority to manage the incompetent's affairs. The guardian (or "conservator" or "committee"—the terminology varies) then represents the incompetent in his legal affairs. Courts make similar appointments when a corporation has become "incompetent"—they appoint a trustee in bankruptcy or reorganization to oversee its affairs and speak for it in court when that becomes necessary.

On a parity of reasoning, we should have a system in which, when a friend of a natural object perceives it to be endangered, he can apply to a court for the creation of a guardianship. Perhaps we already have the machinery to do so. California law, for example, defines an incompetent as "any person, whether insane or not, who by reason of old age, disease, weakness of mind, or other cause, is unable, unassisted, properly to manage and take care of himself or his property, and by reason thereof is likely to be deceived or imposed upon by artful or designing persons."[37] Of course, to urge a court that an endangered river is "a person" under this provision will call for lawyers as bold and imaginative as those who convinced the Supreme Court that a railroad corporation was a "person" under the fourteenth amendment, a constitutional provision theretofore generally thought of as designed to secure the rights of freedmen.[38] . . .

The guardianship approach, however, is apt to raise . . . [the following objection]: a committee or guardian could not judge the needs of the river or forest in its charge; indeed, the very concept of "needs," it might be said, could be used here only in the most metaphorical way. . . .

. . . Natural objects *can* communicate their wants (needs) to us, and in ways that are not terribly ambiguous. I am sure I can judge with more certainty and meaningfulness whether and when my lawn wants (needs) water, than the Attorney General can judge whether and when the United States wants (needs) to take an appeal from an adverse judgment by a lower court. The lawn tells me that it wants water by a certain dryness of the blades and soil—immediately obvious to the touch—the appearance of bald spots, yellowing, and a lack of springiness after being walked on; how does "the United States" communicate to the Attorney General? For similar reasons, the guardian-attorney for a smog-endangered stand of pines could venture with more confidence that his client wants the smog stopped, than the directors of a corporation can assert that "the corporation" wants dividends declared. We make decisions on behalf of, and in the purported interests of, others every day; these "others" are often creatures whose wants are far less verifiable, and even far more metaphysical in conception, than the wants of rivers, trees, and land. . . .

The argument for "personifying" the environment, from the point of damage calculations, can best be demonstrated from the welfare economics position. Every well-working legal-economic system should be so structured as to confront each of us with the full costs that our activities are imposing on society. Ideally, a paper mill, in deciding what to produce—and where, and by what methods—ought to be forced to take into account not only the lumber, acid, and labor that its production "takes" from other uses in the society, but also what costs alternative production plans will impose on society through pollution. The legal system, through the law of contracts and the criminal law, for example, makes the mill confront the costs of the first group of demands. When, for example, the company's purchasing agent orders 1000 drums of acid from the Z Company, the Z Company can bind the mill to pay for them, and thereby reimburse the society for what the mill is removing from alternative uses.

Unfortunately, so far as the pollution costs are concerned, the allocative ideal begins to break down, because the traditional legal institutions have a more difficult time "catching" and confronting us with the full social costs of our activities. In the lakeside mill example, major riparian interests might bring an action, forcing a court to weigh *their* aggregate losses against the costs to the mill of installing the anti-pollution device. But many other interests—and I am speaking for the moment of recognized homocentric interests—are too fragmented and perhaps "too remote" causally to warrant securing representation and pressing for recovery: the people who own summer homes and motels, the man who sells fishing tackle and bait, the man who rents rowboats. There is no reason not to allow the lake to prove damages to them as the prima facie measure of damages to it. *By doing so, we in effect make the natural object, through its guardian, a jural entity competent to gather up these fragmented and otherwise unrepresented damage claims, and press them before the court even where, for legal or practical reasons, they are not going to be pressed by traditional class action plaintiffs.* Indeed, one way—the homocentric way—to view what I am proposing so far, is to view the guardian of the natural object as the guardian of unborn generations, as well as of the otherwise unrepresented, but distantly injured, contemporary humans.[39] By making the lake itself the focus of these damages, and "incorporating" it so to speak, the legal system can effectively take proof upon, and confront the mill with, a larger and more representative measure of the damages its pollution causes.

So far, I do not suppose that my economist friends (unremittant human chauvinists, every one of them!) will have any large quarrel in principle with the concept. Many will view it as a *trompe l'oeil* that comes down, at best, to effectuate the goals of the paragon class action, or the paragon water pollution control district. Where we are apt to part company is here—I propose going beyond gathering up the loose ends of what most people would presently recognize as economically valid damages. The guardian would urge before the court injuries not presently cognizable—the death of eagles and inedible crabs, the suffering of sea lions, the loss from the face of the earth of species of commercially valueless birds, the disappearance of a wilderness area. One might, of course, speak of the damages involved as "damages" to us humans, and indeed, the widespread growth of environmental groups shows that human beings do feel these losses. But they are not, at present, economically measurable losses: how can they have a monetary value for the guardian to prove in court?

The answer for me is simple. Wherever it carves out "property" rights, the legal system is engaged in the process of *creating* monetary worth. One's literary works would have minimal monetary value if anyone could copy them at will. Their economic value to the author is a product of the law of copyright; the person who copies a copyrighted book has to bear a cost to the copyright-holder because the law says he must. Similarly, it is through the law of torts that we have made a "right" of—and guaranteed an economically meaningful value to—privacy. (The value we place on gold—a yellow inanimate dirt—is not simply a function of supply and demand—wilderness areas are scarce and pretty too—but results from the actions of the legal systems of the world, which have institutionalized that value; they have even done a remarkable job of stabilizing the price). I am proposing we do the same with eagles and wilderness areas as we do with copyrighted works, patented inventions, and privacy: *make* the violation of rights in them to be a cost by declaring the "pirating" of them to be the invasion of a property interest.[40] If we do so, the net social costs the polluter would be confronted with would include not only the extended homocentric costs of his pollution (explained above) but also costs to the environment *per se.*

How, though, would these costs be calculated? When we protect an invention, we can at least speak of a fair market value for it, by reference to which damages can be computed. But the lost environmental "values" of which we are now speaking are by definition over and above those that the market is prepared to bid for: they are priceless.

One possible measure of damages, suggested earlier, would be the cost of making the environment whole, just as, when a man is injured in an automobile accident, we impose upon the responsible party the injured man's medical expenses. Comparable expenses to a polluted river would be the costs of dredging, restocking with fish, and so forth. It is on the basis of such costs as these, I assume, that we get the figure of $1 billion as the cost of saving Lake Erie.[41] As an ideal, I think this is a good guide applicable in many environmental situations. It is by no means free from difficulties, however.

One problem with computing damages on the basis of making the environment whole is that, if understood most literally, it is tantamount to asking for a "freeze" on environmental quality, even at the costs (and there will be costs) of preserving "useless" objects. Such a "freeze" is not inconceivable to me as a general goal, especially considering that, even by the most immediately discernible homocentric interests, in so many areas we ought to be cleaning up and not merely preserving the environmental status quo. In fact, there is presently strong sentiment in the Congress for a total elimination of all river pollutants by 1985,[42] notwithstanding that such a decision would impose quite large direct and indirect costs on us all. Here one is inclined to recall the instructions of Judge Hays, in remanding Consolidated Edison's Storm King application to the Federal Power Commission in *Scenic Hudson*:

> The Commissions renewed proceedings must include as a basic concern the preservation of natural beauty and of natural historic shrines, keeping in mind that, in our affluent society, the cost of a project is only one of several factors to be considered.[43]

Nevertheless, whatever the merits of such a goal in principle, there are many cases in which the social price tag of putting it into effect are going to seem too high to accept. Consider, for example, an oceanside nuclear generator that could produce low cost electricity for a million homes at a savings of $1 a year per home, spare us the air pollution that comes of burning fossil fuels, but which through a slight heating effect threatened to kill off a rare species of temperature-sensitive sea urchins; suppose further that technological improvements adequate to reduce the temperature to present environmental quality would expend the entire one million dollars in anticipated fuel savings. Are we prepared to tax ourselves $1,000,000 a year on behalf of the sea urchins? In comparable problems under the present law of damages, we work out practicable compromises by abandoning restoration costs and calling upon fair market value. For example, if an automobile is so severely damaged that the cost of bringing the car to its original state by repair is greater than the fair market value, we would allow the responsible tortfeasor to pay the fair market value only. Or if a human being suffers the loss of an arm (as we might conceive of the ocean having irreparably lost the sea urchins), we can fall back on the capitalization of reduced earning power (and pain and suffering) to measure the damages. But what is the fair market value of sea urchins? How can we capitalize their loss to the

ocean, independent of any commercial value they may have to someone else?

One answer is that the problem can sometimes be sidestepped quite satisfactorily. In the sea urchin example, one compromise solution would be to impose on the nuclear generator the costs of making the ocean whole somewhere else, in some other way, e.g., reestablishing a sea urchin colony elsewhere, or making a somehow comparable contribution.[44] In the debate over the laying of the trans-Alaskan pipeline, the builders are apparently prepared to meet conservationists' objections halfway by reestablishing wildlife away from the pipeline, so far as is feasible.[45]

But even if damage calculations have to be made, one ought to recognize that the measurement of damages is rarely a simple report of economic facts about "the market," whether we are valuing the loss of a foot, a foetus, or a work of fine art. Decisions of this sort are always hard, but not impossible. We have increasingly taken (human) pain and suffering into account in reckoning damages, not because we think we can ascertain them as objective "facts" about the universe, but because, even in view of all the room for disagreement, we come up with a better society by making rude estimates of them than by ignoring them.[46] We can make such estimates in regard to environmental losses fully aware that what we are really doing is making implicit normative judgments (as with pain and suffering)—laying down rules as to what the society is going to "value" rather than reporting market evaluations. In making such normative estimates decision-makers would not go wrong if they estimated on the "high side," putting the burden of trimming the figure down on the immediate human interests present. All burdens of proof should reflect common experience; our experience in environmental matters has been a continual discovery that our acts have caused more long-range damage than we were able to appreciate at the outset.

To what extent the decision-maker should factor in costs such as the pain and suffering of animals and other sentient natural objects, I cannot say; although I am prepared to do so in principle.[47] Given the conjectural nature of the "estimates" in all events, and the roughness of the "balance of conveniences" procedure where that is involved, the practice would be of more interest from the socio-psychic point of view, discussed below, than from the legal-operational.

The Psychic and Socio-Psychic Aspects

. . . The strongest case can be made from the perspective of human advantage for conferring rights on the environment. Scientists have been warning of the crises the earth and all humans on it face if we do not change our ways—radically—and these crises make the lost "recreational use" of rivers seem absolutely trivial. The earth's very atmosphere is threatened with frightening possibilities: absorption of sunlight, upon which the entire life cycle depends, may be diminished; the oceans may warm (increasing the "greenhouse effect" of the atmosphere), melting the polar ice caps, and destroying our great coastal cities; the portion of the atmosphere that shields us from dangerous radiation may be destroyed. Testifying before Congress, sea explorer Jacques Cousteau predicted that the oceans (to which we dreamily look to feed our booming populations) are headed toward their own death: "The cycle of life is intricately tied up with the cycle of water . . . the water system has to remain alive if we are to remain alive on earth."[48] We are depleting our energy and our food sources at a rate that takes little account of the needs even of humans now living.

These problems will not be solved easily; they very likely can be solved, if at all, only through a willingness to suspend the rate of increase in the standard of living (by present values) of the earth's "advanced" nations, and by stabilizing the total human population. For some of us this will involve forfeiting material comforts; for others it will involve abandoning the hope someday to obtain comforts long envied. For all of us it will involve giving up the right to have as many offspring as we might wish. Such a program is not impossible of realization, however. Many of our so-called "material comforts" are not only in excess of, but are probably in opposition to, basic biological needs. Further, the "costs" to the advanced nations is not as large as would appear from Gross National Product figures. G.N.P. reflects social gain (of a sort) without discounting for the social *cost* of that gain, e.g., the losses through depletion of resources, pollution, and so forth. As has well been shown, as societies become more and more "advanced," their real marginal gains become less and less for each additional dollar of G.N.P.[49] Thus, to give up "human progress" would not be as costly as might appear on first blush.

Nonetheless, such far-reaching social changes are going to involve us in a serious reconsideration of our consciousness toward the environment. . . .

A radical new conception of man's relationship to the rest of nature would not only be a step toward solving the material planetary problems; there are strong reasons for such a changed consciousness from the point of making us far better humans. If we only stop for a moment and look at the underlying human qualities that our present attitudes toward property and nature draw upon and reinforce, we have to be struck by how stultifying of our own personal growth and satisfaction they can become when they take rein of us. Hegel, in "justifying" private property, unwittingly reflects the tone and quality of some of the needs that are played upon:

> A person has as his substantive end the right of putting his will into any and every thing and thereby making it his, because it has no such end in itself and derives its destiny and soul from his will. This is the absolute right of appropriation which man has over all "things."[50]

What is it within us that gives us this need not just to satisfy basic biological wants, but to extend our wills over things, to objectify them, to make them ours, to manipulate them, to keep them at a psychic distance? Can it all be explained on "rational" bases? Should we not be suspect of such needs within us, cautious as to why we wish to gratify them? When I first read that passage of Hegel, I immediately thought not only of the emotional contrast with Spinoza, but of the passage in Carson McCullers' *A Tree, A Rock, A Cloud,* in which an old derelict has collared a twelve-year-old boy in a streetcar cafe. The old man asks whether the boy knows "how love should be begun?"

The old man leaned closer and whispered:

"A tree. A rock. A cloud."

. . .

"The weather was like this in Portland," he said. "At the time my science was begun. I meditated and I started very cautious. I would pick up something from the street and take it home with me. I bought a goldfish and I concentrated on the goldfish and I loved it. I graduated from one thing to another. Day by day I was getting this technique. . . .

. . .

. . . "For six years now I have gone around by myself and built up my science. And now I am a master. Son. I can love anything. No longer do I have to think about it even. I see a street full of people and a beautiful light comes in me. I watch a bird in the sky. Or I meet a traveler on the road. Everything, Son. And anybody. All stranger and all loved! Do you realize what a science like mine can mean?"[51]

To be able to get away from the view that Nature is a collection of useful senseless objects is, as McCullers' "madman" suggests, deeply involved in the development of our abilities to love—or, if that is putting it too strongly, to be able to reach a heightened awareness of our own, and others' capacities in their mutual interplay. To do so, we have to give up some psychic investment in our sense of separateness and specialness in the universe. And this, in turn, is hard giving indeed, because it involves us in a flight backwards, into earlier stages of civilization and childhood in which we had to trust (and perhaps fear) our environment, for we had not then the power to master it. Yet, in doing so, we—as persons—gradually free ourselves of needs for supportive illusions. Is not this one of the triumphs for "us" of our giving legal rights to (or acknowledging the legal rights of) the Blacks and women? . . .

. . . A few years ago the pollution of streams was thought of only as a problem of smelly, unsightly, unpotable water i.e., to us. Now we are beginning to discover that pollution is a process that destroys wonderously subtle balances of life within the water, and as between the water and its banks. This heightened awareness enlarges our sense of the dangers to us. But it also enlarges our empathy. We are not only developing the scientific capacity, but we are cultivating the personal capacities *within us* to recognize more and more the ways in which nature—like the woman, the Black, the Indian and the Alien—is like us (and we will also become more able realistically to define, confront, live with, and admire the ways in which we are all different).

The time may be on hand when these sentiments, and the early stirrings of the laws, can be coalesced into radical new theory or myth—felt as well as intellectualized—of man's relationships to the rest of nature. I do not mean "myth" in a demeaning sense of the term, but in the sense in which, at different times in history, our social "facts" and relationships have been comprehended and integrated by reference to the "myths" that we

are cosigners of a social contract, that the Pope is God's agent, and that all men are created equal. Pantheism, Shinto and Tao all have myths to offer. But they are all, each in its own fashion, quaint, primitive and archaic. What is needed is a myth that can fit our growing body of knowledge of geophysics, biology and the cosmos. In this vein, I do not think it too remote that we may come to regard the Earth, as some have suggested, as one organism, of which Mankind is a functional part—the mind, perhaps: different from the rest of nature, but different as a man's brain is from his lungs.

. . . As I see it, the Earth is only one organized "field" of activities—and so is the *human person*—but these activities take place at various levels, in different "spheres" of being and realms of consciousness. The lithosphere is not the biosphere, and the latter not the . . . ionosphere. The Earth is not *only* a material mass. Consciousness is not only "human"; it exists at animal and vegetable levels, and most likely must be latent, or operating in some form, in the molecule and the atom; and all these diverse and in a sense hierarchical modes of activity and consciousness should be seen integrated in and perhaps transcended by an all-encompassing and "eonic " planetary Consciousness.

. . .

Mankind's function within the Earth-organism is to extract from the activities of all other operative systems within this organism the type of consciousness which we call "reflective" or "self" consciousness—or, we may also say to *mentalize* and give meaning, value, and "name" to all that takes place anywhere within the Earth-field. . . .[52]

As radical as such a consciousness may sound today, all the dominant changes we see about us point in its direction. Consider just the impact of space travel, of world-wide mass media, of increasing scientific discoveries about the interrelatedness of all life processes. Is it any wonder that the term "spaceship earth" has so captured the popular imagination? The problems we have to confront are increasingly the world-wide crises of a global organism: not pollution of a stream, but pollution of the atmosphere and of the ocean. Increasingly, the death that occupies each human's imagination is not his own, but that of the entire life cycle of the planet earth, to which each of us is as but a cell to a body.

To shift from such a lofty fancy as the planetarization of consciousness to the operation of our municipal legal system is to come down to earth hard. Before the forces that are at work, our highest court is but a frail and feeble—a distinctly human—institution. Yet, the Court may be at its best not in its work of handing down decrees, but at the very task that is called for: of summoning up from the human spirit the kindest and most generous and worthy ideas that abound there, giving them shape and reality and legitimacy. Witness the School Desegregation Cases which, more importantly than to integrate the schools (assuming they did), awakened us to moral needs which, when made visible, could not be denied. And so here, too, in the case of the environment, the Supreme Court may find itself in a position to award "rights" in a way that will contribute to a change in popular consciousness. It would be a modest move, to be sure, but one in furtherance of a large goal: the future of the planet as we know it.

How far we are from such a state of affairs, where the law treats "environmental objects" as holders of legal rights, I cannot say. But there is certainly intriguing language in one of Justice Black's last dissents, regarding the Texas Highway Department's plan to run a six-lane expressway through a San Antonio Park.[53] Complaining of the Court's refusal to stay the plan, Black observed that "after today's decision, the people of San Antonio and the birds and animals that make their home in the park will share their quiet retreat with an ugly, smelly stream of traffic. . . . Trees, shrubs, and flowers will be mowed down."[54] Elsewhere he speaks of the "burial of public parks," of segments of a highway which "devour parkland," and of the park's heartland.[55] Was he, at the end of his great career, on the verge of saying—just saying—that "nature has 'rights' on its own account"? Would it be so hard to do?

Notes

1. C. Darwin, *Descent of Man*, 119,120–21 (2d ed. 1874). *See also* R. Waelder, *Progress and Revolution* 39 et seq. (1967).

2. *See* Darwin, *supra* note 1, at 113–14.

3. *See* Darwin, *supra* note 1, at 113. *See also* E. Westermarck,1 *The Origin and Development of the Moral Ideas* 406–12 (1912).

4. There does not appear to be a word "gericide" or "geronticide" to designate the killing of the aged. "Senicide" is as close as the *Oxford English*

Dictionary comes, although, as it indicates, the word is rare. 9 *Oxford English Dictionary*, 454 (1933).

5. *See* Darwin, *supra* note 1, at 386–93. Westermarck, *supra* note 3, at 387–89, observes that where the killing of the aged and infirm is practiced, it is often supported by humanitarian justification; this, however, is a far cry from saying that the killing is *requested* by the victim as his right.

6. H. Maine, *Ancient Law* 153 (Pollock ed. 1930).

7. 387 U.S. 1 (1967).

8. 42 U.S.C. §§ 1973 et seq. (1970).

9. *See Landman v. Royster*, 40 U.S.L.W. 2256 (E.D. Va., Oct. 30,1971).

10. *But See* T. Szasz, *Law, Liberty and Psychiatry* (1963).

11. *See* note 22. The trend toward liberalized abortion can be seen either as a legislative tendency back in the direction of rightlessness for the foetus—or toward increasing rights of women. This inconsistency is not unique in the law of course; it is simply support for Hohfeld's scheme that the "jural opposite" of someone's right is someone else's "no-right." W. Hohfeld, *Fundamental Legal Conceptions* (1923) . . .

12. In. Rev. Code of 1954, § 1361 (repealed by Pub. L. No. 89-389, effective Jan. 1, 1969).

13. For example, *see United States v. Cargo of the Brig Malek Adhel*, 43 U.S. (2 How.) 210 (1844). There, a ship had been seized and used by pirates. All this was done without the knowledge or consent of the owners of the ship. After the ship had been captured, the United States condemned and sold the "offending vessel." The owners objected. In denying release to the owners, Justice Story cited Chief Justice Marshall from an earlier case: "This is not a proceeding against the owner; it is a proceeding against the vessel for an offense committed by the vessel; which is not the less an offense . . . because it was committed without the authority and against the will of the owner." 43 U.S. at 234, quoting from *United States v. Schooner Little Charles*, 26 F. Cas. 979 (No. 15,612) (C.C.D. Va.1818).

14. 9 U.S. (5 Cranch) 61, 86 (1809).

15. *Trustees of Dartmouth College v. Woodward*, 17 U.S. (4 Wheat.) 518 (1819).

16. *Id.* at 636.

17. Consider, for example, that the claim of the United States to the naval station at Guantanamo Bay, at $2000-a-year rental, is based upon a treaty signed in 1903 by José Montes for the President of Cuba and a minister representing Theodore Roosevelt; it was subsequently ratified by two-thirds of a Senate no member of which is living today. Lease [from Cuba] of Certain Areas for Naval or Coaling Stations, July 2, 1903, T.S. No. 426; C. Bevans, 6 *Treaties and Other International Agreements of the United States* 1776 –1949, at 1120 (U.S. Dept. of State Pub. 8549,1971).

18. O. Gierke, *Political Theories of the Middle Age* (Maitland transl. 1927), especially at 22–30. . . .

19. *Dred Scott v. Sandford*, 60 U.S. (19 How.) 396, 404–05 (1856). . . .

20. *People v. Hall*, 4 Cal. 399, 405 (1854). . . .

21. Schechter, *The Rightlessness of Mediaeval English Jewry*, 45 Jewish Q. Rev. 121, 135 (1954) quoting from M. Bateson, *Medieval England* 139 (1904). . . .

22. *Dietrich v. Inhabitants of Northampton*, 138 Mass. 14, 16 (1884).

23. *In re Goddell*, 39 Wisc. 232, 245 (1875). The court continued with the following "clincher":

> And when counsel was arguing for this lady that the word, person, in sec. 32, ch. 119 [respecting those qualified to practice law], necessarily includes females, her presence made it impossible to suggest to him as *reductio ad absurdum* of his position, that the same construction of the same word . . . would subject woman to prosecution for the paternity of a bastard, and . . . prosecution for rape.

Id. at 246.

The relationship between our attitudes toward woman, on the one hand, and, on the other, the more central concern of this article—land—is captured in an unguarded aside of our colleague, Curt Berger: ". . . after all, land, like woman, was meant to be possessed. . . ." *Land Ownership and Use*, 139 (1968).

24. Thus it was that the Founding Fathers could speak of the inalienable rights of all men, and yet maintain a society that was, by modern standards, without the most basic rights for Blacks, Indians, children and women. There was no hypocrisy; emotionally, no one *felt* that these other things were men.

25. The second thought streaming from . . . the older South [is] the sincere and passionate belief that somewhere between men and cattle, God created a *tertium quid*, and called it a Negro—a clownish, simple creature, at times even lovable within its limitations, but straitly foreordained to walk within the Veil. W. E. B. DuBois, *The Souls of Black Folk* 89 (1924).

26. The statement in text is not quite true; *cf.* Murphy, *Has Nature Any Right to Life?* 22 Hast. L. J. 467 (1971). An Irish court, passing upon the validity of a testamentary trust to the benefit of someone's dogs, observed in dictum that "'lives' means lives of human beings, not of animals or trees in California." *Kelly v. Dillon*, 1932 Ir. R. 255, 261. (The intended gift over on the death of the last surviving dog was held void for remoteness, the court refusing "to enter into the question of a dog's expectation of life," although prepared to observe that "in point of fact neighbor's [sic] dogs and cats are unpleasantly longlived. . . . *Id.* at 260–61).

27. *See Dixon v. Alabama State Bd. of Educ.*, 294 F.2d 150 (5th Cir.), *cert. denied*, 368 U.S. 930 (1961).

28. The law in a suit for injunctive relief is commonly easier on the plaintiff than in a suit for damages. *See* J. Gould, *Law of Waters* § 206 (1883).

29. However, in 1970 California amended its Water Quality Act to make it easier for the Attorney General to obtain relief, e.g., one must no longer allege irreparable injury in a suit for an injunction. Cal. Water Code § 13350(b) (West 1971).

30. To whomsoever the soil belongs, he owns also to the sky and to the depths. *See* W. Blackstone, 2 Commentaries *18.

31. *See* Note, *Statutory Treatment of Industrial Stream Pollution*, 24 Geo. Wash. L. Rev. 302, 306 (1955); H. Farnham, 2 Law of Waters and Water Rights § 461 (1904); Gould, *supra* note 32, at § 204.

32. For example, courts have upheld a right to pollute by prescription, *Mississippi Mills Co. v. Smith*, 69 Miss. 299, 11 So. 26 (1882), and by easement, *Luama v. Bunker Hill & Sullivan Mining & Concentrating Co.*, 41 F.2d 358 (9th Cir. 1930).

33. *Pennsylvania Coal Co. v. Sanderson*, 113 Pa. 126,149, 6 A. 453, 459 (1886).

34. Hand, J. in *Smith v. Staso Milling Co.*, 18 F.2d 736, 738 (2d Cir. 1927) (emphasis added). *See also Harrisonville v. Dickey Clay Co.*, 289 U.S. 334 (1933) (Brandeis, J.).

35. *Smith v. Staso*, 18 F.2d 736, 738 (2d Cir. 1927).

36. By contrast, for example, with humane societies.

37. Cal. Prob. Code § 1460 (West Supp. 1971). . . .

38. *Santa Clara County v. Southern Pac. RR*, 118 US. 394 (1886).

39. *Cf.* Golding, *Ethical Issues in Biological Engineering*, 15 U.C.L.A. L. Rev. 443, 451–63 (1968).

40. Of course, in the instance of copyright and patent protection, the creation of the "property right" can be more directly justified on homocentric grounds.

41. *See* Schrag, *Life on a Dying Lake*, in The Politics of Neglect 167, at 173 (R. Meek & J. Straayer eds. 1971).

42. On November 2, 1971, the Senate, by a vote of 86–0, passed and sent to the House the proposed Federal Water Pollution Control Act Amendments of 1971, 117 Cong. Rec. S17464 (daily ed. Nov. 2, 1971). Sections 101 (a) and (a)(1) of the bill declare it to be "national policy that, consistent with the provisions of this Act—(1) the discharge of pollutants into the navigable waters be eliminated by 1985." S.2770, 92d Cong., 1st Sess., 117 Cong. Rec. S17464 (daily ed. Nov. 2, 1971).

43. 354 F.2d 608, 624 (2d Cir. 1965).

44. Again, there is a problem involving what we conceive to be the injured entity.

45. *New York Times,* Jan. 14, 1971, § 1, col. 2, and at 74, col. 7.

46. Courts have not been reluctant to award damages for the destruction of heirlooms, literary manuscripts or other property having no ascertainable market value. In *Willard v. Valley Gas Fuel Co.,* 171 Cal. 9, 151 Pac. 286 (1915), it was held that the measure of damages for the negligent destruction of a rare old book written by one of plaintiff's ancestors was the amount which would compensate the owner for all detriment including sentimental loss proximately caused by such destruction. . . .

47. It is not easy to dismiss the idea of "lower" life having consciousness and feeling pain, especially since it is so difficult to know what these terms mean even as applied to humans. *See* Austin, *Other Minds,* in *Logic and Language* 342 (S. Flew ed.1965); Schopenhauer, *On the Will in Nature,* in *Two Essays by Arthur Schopenhauer* 193, 281–304 (1889). Some

experiments on plant sensitivity—of varying degrees of extravagance in their claims—include Lawrence, *Plants Have Feelings, Too. . . ,* Organic Gardening & Farming 64 (April 1971); Woodlief, Royster & Huang, *Effect of Random Noise on Plant Growth,* 46. *J. Acoustical Soc. Am.* 481 (1969); Backster, *Evidence of a Primary Perception in Plant Life,* 10 Int'l J. Parapsychology 250 (1968).

48. Cousteau, *The Oceans: No Time to Lose,* L.A. Times, Oct. 24, 1971, § (opinion), at 1, col. 4.

49. *See* J. Harte & R. Socolow, Patient Earth (1971).

50. G. Hegel, *Hegel's Philosophy of Right,* 41 (T. Knox transl. 1945).

51. C. McCullers, *The Ballad of the Sad Cafe and Other Stories* 150–51 (1958).

52. D. Rudhyar, Directives for New Life 21–23 (1971).

53. 136. *San Antonio Conservation Soc'y v. Texas Highway Dep't, cert. denied,* 400 U.S. 968 (1970) (Black, J. dissenting to denial of certiorari).

54. *Id.* at 969.

55. *Id.* at 971.

24. The Ethics of Respect for Nature

Paul W. Taylor

I. Human-Centered and Life-Centered Systems of Environmental Ethics

In this paper I show how the taking of a certain ultimate moral attitude toward nature, which I call "respect for nature," has a central place in the foundations of a life-centered system of environmental ethics. I hold that a set of moral norms (both standards of character and rules of conduct) governing human treatment of the natural world is a rationally grounded set if and only if, first, commitment to those norms is a practical entailment of adopting the attitude of respect for nature as an ultimate moral attitude, and second, the adopting of that attitude on the part of all rational agents can itself be justified. When the basic characteristics of the attitude of respect for nature are made clear, it will be seen that a life-centered system of environmental ethics need not be holistic or organicist in its conception of the kinds of entities that are deemed the appropriate objects of moral concern and consideration. Nor does such a system require that the concepts of ecological homeostasis, equilibrium, and integrity provide us with normative principles from which could be derived (with the addition of factual knowledge) our obligations with regard to natural ecosystems. The "balance of nature" is not itself a moral norm, however important may be the role it plays in our general outlook on the natural world that underlies the attitude of respect for nature. I argue that finally it is the good (well-being, welfare) of individual organisms, considered as entities having inherent worth, that determines our moral relations with the Earth's wild communities of life.

In designating the theory to be set forth as life-centered, I intend to contrast it with all anthropocentric views. According to the latter, human actions affecting the natural environment and its

Environmental Ethics, Vol. 3 (Fall 1981), pp. 197–218. Reprinted by permission.

nonhuman inhabitants are right (or wrong) by either of two criteria: they have consequences which are favorable (or unfavorable) to human well-being, or they are consistent (or inconsistent) with the system of norms that protect and implement human rights. From this human-centered standpoint it is to humans and only to humans that all duties are ultimately owed. We may have responsibilities *with regard to* the natural ecosystems and biotic communities of our planet, but these responsibilities are in every case based on the contingent fact that our treatment of those ecosystems and communities of life can further the realization of human values and/or human rights. We have no obligation to promote or protect the good of nonhuman living things, independently of this contingent fact.

A life-centered system of environmental ethics is opposed to human-centered ones precisely on this point. From the perspective of a life-centered theory, we have prima facie moral obligations that are owed to wild plants and animals themselves as members of the Earth's biotic community. We are morally bound (other things being equal) to protect or promote their good for *their* sake. Our duties to respect the integrity of natural ecosystems, to preserve endangered species, and to avoid environmental pollution stem from the fact that these are ways in which we can help make it possible for wild species populations to achieve and maintain a healthy existence in a natural state. Such obligations are due those living things out of recognition of their inherent worth. They are entirely additional to and independent of the obligations we owe to our fellow humans. Although many of the actions that fulfill one set of obligations will also fulfill the other, two different grounds of obligation are involved. Their well-being, as well as human well-being, is something to be realized *as an end in itself.*

If we were to accept a life-centered theory of environmental ethics, a profound reordering of our moral universe would take place. We would begin to look at the whole of the Earth's biosphere in a new light. Our duties with respect to the "world" of nature would be seen as making prima facie claims upon us to be balanced against our duties with respect to the "world" of human civilization. We could no longer simply take the human point of view and consider the effects of our actions exclusively from the perspective of our own good.

II. The Good of a Being and the Concept of Inherent Worth

What would justify acceptance of a life-centered system of ethical principles? In order to answer this it is first necessary to make clear the fundamental moral attitude that underlies and makes intelligible the commitment to live by such a system. It is then necessary to examine the considerations that would justify any rational agent's adopting that moral attitude.

Two concepts are essential to the taking of a moral attitude of the sort in question. A being which does not "have" these concepts, that is, which is unable to grasp their meaning and conditions of applicability, cannot be said to have the attitude as part of its moral outlook. These concepts are, first, that of the good (well-being, welfare) of a living thing, and second, the idea of an entity possessing inherent worth. I examine each concept in turn.

1. Every organism, species population, and community of life has a good of its own which moral agents can intentionally further or damage by their actions. To say that an entity has a good of its own is simply to say that, without reference to any *other* entity, it can be benefited or harmed. One can act in its overall interest, and environmental conditions can be good for it (advantageous to it) or bad for it (disadvantageous to it). What is good for an entity is what "does it good" in the sense of enhancing or preserving its life and well-being. What is bad for an entity is something that is detrimental to its life and well-being.[1]

We can think of the good of an individual nonhuman organism as consisting in the full development of its biological powers. Its good is realized to the extent that it is strong and healthy. It possesses whatever capacities it needs for successfully coping with its environment and so preserving its existence throughout the various stages of the normal life cycle of its species. The good of a population or community of such individuals consists in the population or community maintaining itself from generation to generation as a coherent system of genetically and ecologically related organisms whose average good is at an optimum level for the given environment. (Here *average good* means that the degree of realization of the good of *individual organisms* in the population or community is, on average, greater than would be the case under any other ecologically functioning order of interrelations among those species populations in the given ecosystem.)

The idea of a being having a good of its own, as I understand it, does not entail that the being must have interests or take an interest in what affects its life for better or for worse. We can act in a being's interest or contrary to its interest without its being interested in what we are doing to it in the sense of wanting or not wanting us to do it. It may, indeed, be wholly unaware that favorable and unfavorable events are taking place in its life. I take it that trees, for example, have no knowledge or desires or feelings. Yet it is undoubtedly the case that trees can be harmed or benefited by our actions. We can crush their roots by running a bulldozer too close to them. We can see to it that they get adequate nourishment and moisture by fertilizing and watering the soil around them. Thus we can help or hinder them in the realization of their good. It is the good of trees themselves that is thereby affected. We can similarly act so as to further the good of an entire tree population of a certain species (say, all the redwood trees in a California valley) or the good of a whole community of plant life in a given wilderness area, just as we can do harm to such a population or community.

When construed in this way, the concept of a being's good is not coextensive with sentience or the capacity for feeling pain. William Frankena has argued for a general theory of environmental ethics in which the ground of a creature's being worthy of moral consideration is its sentience. I have offered some criticisms of this view elsewhere, but the full refutation of such a position, it seems to me, finally depends on the positive reasons for accepting a life-centered theory of the kind I am defending in this essay.[2]

It should be noted further that I am leaving open the question of whether machines—in particular, those which are not only goal-directed, but also self-regulating—can properly be said to have a good of their own.[3] Since I am concerned only with human treatment of wild organisms, species populations, and communities of life as they occur in our planet's natural ecosystems, it is to those entities alone that the concept "having a good of its own" will here be applied. I am not denying that other living things, whose genetic origin and environmental conditions have been produced, controlled, and manipulated by humans for human ends, do have a good of their own in the same sense as do wild plants and animals. It is not my purpose in this essay, however, to set out or defend the principles that should guide our conduct with regard to their good. It is only insofar as their production and use by humans have good or ill effects upon natural ecosystems and their wild inhabitants that the ethics of respect for nature comes into play.

2. The second concept essential to the moral attitude of respect for nature is the idea of inherent worth. We take that attitude toward wild living things (individuals, species populations, or whole biotic communities) when and only when we regard them as entities possessing inherent worth. Indeed, it is only because they are conceived in this way that moral agents can think of themselves as having validly binding duties, obligations, and responsibilities that are *owed* to them as their *due*. I am not at this juncture arguing why they *should* be so regarded; I consider it at length below. But so regarding them is a presupposition of our taking the attitude of respect toward them and accordingly understanding ourselves as bearing certain moral relations to them. This can be shown as follows:

What does it mean to regard an entity that has a good of its own as possessing inherent worth? Two general principles are involved: the principle of moral consideration and the principle of intrinsic value.

According to the principle of moral consideration, wild living things are deserving of the concern and consideration of all moral agents simply in virtue of their being members of the Earth's community of life. From the moral point of view their good must be taken into account whenever it is affected for better or worse by the conduct of rational agents. This holds no matter what species the creature belongs to. The good of each is to be accorded some value and so acknowledged as having some weight in the deliberations of all rational agents. Of course, it may be necessary for such agents to act in ways contrary to the good of this or that particular organism or group of organisms in order to further the good of others, including the good of humans. But the principle of moral consideration prescribes that, with respect to each being an entity having its own good, every individual is deserving of consideration.

The principle of intrinsic value states that, regardless of what kind of entity it is in other respects, if it is a member of the Earth's community of life, the realization of its good is something *intrinsically* valuable. This means that its good is prima facie worthy of being preserved or promoted as an end in itself and for the sake of the entity whose good it is. Insofar as we regard any organism, species population, or life community as an entity having inherent worth, we believe that it must never be treated as if it were a mere object or thing whose entire value lies in being instrumental to the good of some other entity. The well-being of each is judged to have value in and of itself.

Combining these two principles, we can now define what it means for a living thing or group of living things to possess inherent worth. To say that it possesses inherent worth is to say that its good is deserving of the concern and consideration of all moral agents, and that the realization of its good has intrinsic value, to be pursued as an end in itself and for the sake of the entity whose good it is.

The duties owed to wild organisms, species populations, and communities of life in the Earth's natural ecosystems are grounded on their inherent worth. When rational, autonomous agents regard such entities as possessing inherent worth, they place intrinsic value on the realization of their good and so hold themselves responsible for performing actions that will have this effect and for refraining from actions having the contrary effect.

III. The Attitude of Respect for Nature

Why should moral agents regard wild living things in the natural world as possessing inherent worth? To answer this question we must first take into account the fact that, when rational, autonomous agents subscribe to the principles of moral consideration and intrinsic value and so conceive of wild living things as having that kind of worth, such agents are *adopting a certain ultimate moral attitude toward the natural world*. This is the attitude I call "respect for nature." It parallels the attitude of respect for persons in human ethics. When we adopt the attitude of respect for persons as the proper (fitting, appropriate) attitude to take toward all persons as persons, we consider the fulfillment of the basic interests of each individual to have intrinsic value. We thereby make a moral commitment to live a certain kind of life in relation to other persons. We place ourselves under the

direction of a system of standards and rules that we consider validly binding on all moral agents as such.[4]

Similarly, when we adopt the attitude of respect for nature as an ultimate moral attitude we make a commitment to live by certain normative principles. These principles constitute the rules of conduct and standards of character that are to govern our treatment of the natural world. This is, first, an *ultimate* commitment because it is not derived from any higher norm. The attitude of respect for nature is not grounded on some other, more general, or more fundamental attitude. It sets the total framework for our responsibilities toward the natural world. It can be justified, as I show below, but its justification cannot consist in referring to a more general attitude or a more basic normative principle.

Second, the commitment is a *moral* one because it is understood to be a disinterested matter of principle. It is this feature that distinguishes the attitude of respect for nature from the set of feelings and dispositions that comprise the love of nature. The latter stems from one's personal interest in and response to the natural world. Like the affectionate feelings we have toward certain individual human beings, one's love of nature is nothing more than the particular way one feels about the natural environment and its wild inhabitants. And just as our love for an individual person differs from our respect for all persons as such (whether we happen to love them or not), so love of nature differs from respect for nature. Respect for nature is an attitude we believe all moral agents ought to have simply as moral agents, regardless of whether or not they also love nature. Indeed, we have not truly taken the attitude of respect for nature ourselves unless we believe this. To put it in a Kantian way, to adopt the attitude of respect for nature is to take a stance that one wills it to be a universal law for all rational beings. It is to hold that stance categorically, as being validly applicable to every moral agent without exception, irrespective of whatever personal feelings toward nature such an agent might have or might lack.

Although the attitude of respect for nature is in this case a disinterested and universalizable attitude, anyone who does adopt it has certain steady, more or less permanent dispositions. These dispositions, which are themselves to be considered disinterested and universalizable, comprise three interlocking sets: dispositions to seek certain ends, dispositions to carry on one's practical reasoning and deliberation in a certain way, and dispositions to have certain feelings. We may accordingly analyze the attitude of respect for nature into the following components. (a) The disposition to aim at, and to take steps to bring about, as final and disinterested ends, the promoting and protecting of the good of organisms, species populations, and life communities in natural ecosystems. (These ends are "final" in not being pursued as means to further ends. They are "disinterested" in being independent of the self-interest of the agent.) (b) The disposition to consider actions that tend to realize those ends to be prima facie obligatory *because* they have that tendency. (c) The disposition to experience positive and negative feelings toward states of affairs in the world *because* they are favorable or unfavorable to the good of organisms, species populations, and life communities in natural ecosystems.

The logical connection between the attitude of respect for nature and the duties of a life-centered system of environmental ethics can now be made clear. Insofar as one sincerely takes that attitude and so has the three sets of dispositions, one will at the same time be disposed to comply with certain rules of duty (such as nonmaleficence and noninterference) and with standards of character (such as fairness and benevolence) that determine the obligations and virtues of moral agents with regard to the Earth's wild living things. We can say that the actions one performs and the character traits one develops in fulfilling these moral requirements are the way one expresses or embodies the attitude in one's conduct and character. In his famous essay, "Justice as Fairness," John Rawls describes the rules of the duties of human morality (such as fidelity, gratitude, honesty, and justice) as "forms of conduct in which recognition of others as persons is manifested."[5] I hold that the rules of duty governing our treatment of the natural world and its inhabitants are forms of conduct in which the attitude of respect for nature is manifested.

IV. The Justifiability of the Attitude of Respect for Nature

I return to the question posed earlier, which has not yet been answered: why *should* moral agents regard wild living things as possessing inherent worth? I now argue that the only way we can answer this question is by showing how adopting the attitude of respect for nature is justified for all moral agents. Let us suppose that we were able to establish that there are good reasons for adopting the attitude, reasons which are intersubjectively valid for every rational agent. If there are such reasons, they would justify anyone's having the three sets of dispositions mentioned above as constituting what it means to have the attitude. Since these include the disposition to promote or protect the good of wild living things as a disinterested and ultimate end, as well as the disposition to perform actions for the reason that they tend to realize that end, we see that such dispositions commit a person to the principles of moral consideration and intrinsic value. To be disposed to further, as an end in itself, the good of any entity in nature just because it is that kind of entity, is to be disposed to give consideration to *every* such entity and to place intrinsic value on the realization of its good. Insofar as we subscribe to these two principles we regard living things as possessing inherent worth. Subscribing to the principle is what it *means* to so regard them. To justify the attitude of respect for nature, then, is to justify commitment to these principles and thereby to justify regarding wild creatures as possessing inherent worth.

We must keep in mind that inherent worth is not some mysterious sort of objective property belonging to living things that can be discovered by empirical observation or scientific investigation. To ascribe inherent worth to an entity is not to describe it by citing some feature discernible by sense perception or inferable by inductive reasoning. Nor is there a logically necessary connection between the concept of a being having a good of its own and the concept of inherent worth. We do not contradict ourselves by asserting that an entity that has a good of its own lacks inherent worth. In order to show that such an entity "has" inherent worth we must give good reasons for ascribing that kind of value to it (placing that kind of value upon it, conceiving of it to be valuable in that way). Although it is humans (persons, valuers) who must do the valuing, for the ethics of respect for nature, the value so ascribed is not a human value. That is to say, it is not a value derived from considerations regarding human wellbeing or human rights. It is a value that is ascribed to nonhuman animals and plants themselves, independently of their relationship to what humans judge to be conducive to their own good.

Whatever reasons, then, justify our taking the attitude of respect for nature as defined above are also reasons that show why we *should* regard the living things of the natural world as possessing inherent worth. We saw earlier that, since the attitude is an ultimate one, it cannot be derived from a more fundamental attitude nor shown to be a special case of a more general one. On what sort of grounds, then, can it be established?

The attitude we take toward living things in the natural world depends on the way we look at them, on what kind of beings we conceive them to be, and on how we understand the relations we bear to them. Underlying and supporting our attitude is a certain *belief system* that constitutes a particular world view or outlook on nature and the place of human life in it. To give good reasons for adopting the attitude of respect for nature, then, we must first articulate the belief system which underlies and supports that attitude. If it appears that the belief system is internally coherent and well-ordered, and if, as far as we can now tell, it is consistent with all known scientific truths relevant to our knowledge of the object of the attitude (which in this case includes the whole set of the Earth's natural ecosystems and their communities of life), then there remains the task of indicating why scientifically informed and rational thinkers with a developed capacity of reality awareness can find it acceptable as a way of conceiving of the natural world and our place in it. To the extent we can do this we provide at least a reasonable argument for accepting the belief system and the ultimate moral attitude it supports.

I do not hold that such a belief system can be *proven* to be true, either inductively or deductively. As we shall see, not all of its components can be stated in the form of empirically verifiable propositions. Nor is its internal order governed by purely logical relationships. But the system as a whole, I contend, constitutes a coherent, unified, and rationally acceptable "picture" or "map" of a total world. By examining each of its main components and seeing how they fit together, we obtain a scientifically informed and well-ordered conception of nature and the place of humans in it.

This belief system underlying the attitude of respect for nature I call (for want of a better name) "the biocentric outlook on nature." Since it is not wholly analyzable into empirically confirmable assertions, it should not be thought of as simply a compendium of the biological sciences concerning our planet's ecosystems. It might best be described as a philosophical world view, to distinguish it from a scientific theory or explanatory system. However, one of its major tenets is the great lesson we have learned from the science of ecology: the interdependence of all living things in an organically unified order whose balance and stability are necessary conditions for the realization of the good of its constituent biotic communities.

Before turning to an account of the main components of the biocentric outlook, it is convenient here to set forth the overall structure of my theory of environmental ethics as it has now emerged. The ethics of respect for nature is made up of three basic elements: a belief system, an ultimate moral attitude, and a set of rules of duty and standards of character. These elements are connected with each other in the following manner. The belief system provides a certain outlook on nature which supports and makes intelligible an autonomous agent's adopting, as an ultimate moral attitude, the attitude of respect for nature. It supports and makes intelligible the attitude in the sense that, when an autonomous agent understands its moral relations to the natural world in terms of this outlook, it recognizes the attitude of respect to be the only *suitable* or *fitting* attitude to take toward all wild forms of life in the Earth's biosphere. Living things are now viewed as *the appropriate objects of the attitude of respect* and are accordingly regarded as entities possessing inherent worth. One then places intrinsic value on the promotion and protection of their good. As a consequence of this, one makes a moral commitment to abide by a set of rules of duty and to fulfill (as far as one can by one's own efforts) certain standards of good character. Given one's adoption of the attitude of respect, one makes that moral commitment because one considers those rules and standards to be validly binding on all moral agents. They are seen as embodying forms of conduct and character structures in which the attitude of respect for nature is manifested.

This three-part complex which internally orders the ethics of respect for nature is symmetrical with a theory of human ethics grounded on respect for persons. Such a theory includes, first, a conception of oneself and others as persons, that is, as centers of autonomous choice. Second, there is the attitude of respect for persons as persons. When this is adopted as an ultimate moral attitude it involves the disposition to treat every person as having inherent worth or "human dignity." Every human being, just in virtue of her or his humanity, is understood to be worthy of moral consideration, and intrinsic value is placed on the autonomy and well-being of each. This is what Kant meant by conceiving of persons as ends in themselves. Third, there is an ethical system of duties which are acknowledged to be owed by everyone to everyone. These duties are forms of conduct in which public recognition is given to each individual's inherent worth as a person.

This structural framework for a theory of human ethics is meant to leave open the issue of consequentialism (utilitarianism) versus non-consequentialism (deontology). That issue concerns the particular kind of system of rules defining the duties of moral agents toward persons. Similarly, I am leaving open in this paper the question of what particular kind of system of rules defines our duties with respect to the natural world.

V. The Biocentric Outlook on Nature

The biocentric outlook on nature has four main components. (1) Humans are thought of as members of the Earth's community of life, holding that membership on the same terms as apply to all the nonhuman members. (2) The Earth's natural ecosystems as a totality are seen as a complex web of interconnected elements, with the sound biological functioning of each being dependent on the sound biological functioning of the others. (This is the component referred to above as the great lesson that the science of ecology has taught us.) (3) Each individual organism is conceived of as a teleological center of life, pursuing its own good in its own way. (4) Whether we are concerned with standards of merit or with the concept of inherent worth, the claim that humans by their very nature are superior to other species is a groundless claim and, in the light of elements (1), (2), and (3) above, must be rejected as nothing more than an irrational bias in our own favor.

The conjunction of these four ideas constitutes the biocentric outlook on nature. In the remainder of this paper I give a brief account of the first three components, followed by a more detailed analysis of the fourth. I then conclude by indicating how this outlook provides a way of justifying the attitude of respect for nature.

VI. Humans as Members of the Earth's Community of Life

We share with other species a common relationship to the Earth. In accepting the biocentric outlook we take the fact of our being an animal species to be a fundamental feature of our existence. We consider it an essential aspect of "the human condition." We do not deny the differences between ourselves and other species, but we keep in the forefront of our consciousness the fact that in relation to our planet's natural ecosystems we are but one species population among many. Thus we acknowledge our origin in the very same evolutionary process that gave rise to all other species and we recognize ourselves to be confronted with similar environmental challenges to those that confront them. The laws of genetics, of natural selection, and of adaptation apply equally to all of us as biological creatures. In this light we consider ourselves as one with them, not set apart from them. We, as well as they, must face certain basic conditions of existence that impose requirements on us for our survival and well-being. Each animal and plant is like us in having a good of its own. Although our human good (what is of true value in human life, including the exercise of individual autonomy in choosing our own particular value systems) is not like the good of a nonhuman animal or plant, it can no more be realized than their good can without the biological necessities for survival and physical health.

When we look at ourselves from the evolutionary point of view, we see that not only are we very recent arrivals on Earth, but that our emergence as a new species on the planet was originally an event of no particular importance to the entire scheme of things. The Earth was teeming with life long before we appeared. Putting the point metaphorically, we are relative newcomers, entering a home that has been the residence of others for hundreds of millions of years, a home that must now be shared by all of us together.

The comparative brevity of human life on Earth may be vividly depicted by imagining the geological time scale in spatial terms. Suppose we start with algae, which have been around for at least 600 million years. (The earliest protozoa actually predated this by several *billion* years.) If the time that algae have been here were represented by the length of a football field (300 feet), then the period during which sharks have been swimming in the world's oceans and spiders have been spinning their webs would occupy three quarters of the length of the field; reptiles would show up at about the center of the field; mammals would cover the last third of the field; hominids (mammals of the family *Hominidae*) the last two feet; and the species *Homo sapiens* the last six inches.

Whether this newcomer is able to survive as long as other species remains to be seen. But there is surely something presumptuous about the way humans look down on the "lower" animals, especially those that have become extinct. We consider the dinosaurs, for example, to be biological failures, though they existed on our planet for 65 million years. One writer has made the point with beautiful simplicity:

> We sometimes speak of the dinosaurs as failures; there will be time enough for that judgment when we have lasted even for one tenth as long. . . .[6]

The possibility of the extinction of the human species, a possibility which starkly confronts us in the contemporary world, makes us aware of another respect in which we should not consider ourselves privileged beings in relation to other species. This is the fact that the well-being of humans is dependent upon the ecological soundness and health of many plant and animal communities, while their soundness and health does not in the least depend upon human well-being. Indeed, from their standpoint the very existence of humans is quite unnecessary. Every last man, woman, and child could disappear from the face of the Earth without any significant detrimental consequence for the good of wild animals and plants. On the contrary, many of them would be greatly benefited. The destruction of their habitats by human "developments" would cease. The poisoning and polluting of their environment would come to an end. The Earth's land, air, and water would no longer be subject to the degradation they are now undergoing as the result of large-scale technology and uncontrolled population growth. Life communities in natural ecosystems would gradually return to their former healthy state. Tropical forests, for example, would again be able to make their full

contribution to a life-sustaining atmosphere for the whole planet. The rivers, lakes, and oceans of the world would (perhaps) eventually become clean again. Spilled oil, plastic trash, and even radioactive waste might finally, after many centuries, cease doing their terrible work. Ecosystems would return to their proper balance, suffering only the disruptions of natural events such as volcanic eruptions and glaciation. From these the community of life could recover, as it has so often done in the past. But the ecological disasters now perpetrated on it by humans—disasters from which it might never recover—these it would no longer have to endure.

If, then, the total, final, absolute extermination of our species (by our own hands?) should take place and if we should not carry all the others with us into oblivion, not only would the Earth's community of life continue to exist, but in all probability its wellbeing would be enhanced. Our presence, in short, is not needed. If we were to take the standpoint of the community and give voice to its true interest, the ending of our 6-inch epoch would most likely be greeted with a hearty "Good riddance!"

VII. The Natural World as an Organic System

To accept the biocentric outlook and regard ourselves and our place in the world from its perspective is to see the whole natural order of the Earth's biosphere as a complex but unified web of interconnected organisms, objects, and events. The ecological relationships between any community of living things and their environment form an organic whole of functionally independent parts. Each ecosystem is a small universe itself in which the interactions of its various species populations comprise an intricately woven network of cause–effect relations. Such dynamic but at the same time relatively stable structures as food chains, predator–prey relations, and plant succession in a forest are self-regulating, energy-recycling mechanisms that preserve the equilibrium of the whole.

As far as the well-being of wild animals and plants is concerned, this ecological equilibrium must not be destroyed. The same holds true of the well-being of humans. When one views the realm of nature from the perspective of the biocentric outlook, one never forgets that in the long run the integrity of the entire biosphere of our planet is essential to the realization of the good of its constituent communities of life, both human and non-human.

Although the importance of this idea cannot be overemphasized, it is by now so familiar and so widely acknowledged that I shall not further elaborate on it here. However, I do wish to point out that this "holistic" view of the Earth's ecological systems does not itself constitute a moral norm. It is a factual aspect of biological reality, to be understood as a set of causal connections in ordinary empirical terms. Its significance for humans is the same as its significance for nonhumans, namely, in setting basic conditions for the realization of the good of living things. Its ethical implications for our treatment of the natural environment lie entirely in the fact that our *knowledge* of these causal connections is an essential *means* to fulfilling the aims we set for ourselves in adopting the attitude of respect for nature. In addition, its theoretical implications for the ethics of respect for nature lie in the fact that it (along with the other elements of the biocentric outlook) makes the adopting of that attitude a rational and intelligible thing to do.

VIII. Individual Organisms as Teleological Centers of Life

As our knowledge of living things increases, as we come to a deeper understanding of their life cycles, their interactions with other organisms, and the manifold ways in which they adjust to the environment, we become more fully aware of how each of them is carrying out its biological functions according to the laws of its species-specific nature. But besides this, our increasing knowledge and understanding also develop in us a sharpened awareness of the uniqueness of each individual organism. Scientists who have made careful studies of particular plants and animals, whether in the field or in laboratories, have often acquired a knowledge of their subjects as identifiable individuals. Close observation over extended periods of time has led them to an appreciation of the unique "personalities" of their subjects. Sometimes a scientist may come to take a special interest in a particular animal or plant, all the while remaining strictly objective in the gathering and recording of data. Nonscientists may likewise experience this development of interest when, as amateur naturalists,

they make accurate observations over sustained periods of close acquaintance with an individual organism. As one becomes more and more familiar with the organism and its behavior, one becomes fully sensitive to the particular way it is living out its life cycle. One may become fascinated by it and even experience some involvement with its good and bad fortunes (that is, with the occurrence of environmental conditions favorable or unfavorable to the realization of its good). The organism comes to mean something to one as a unique, irreplaceable individual. The final culmination of this process is the achievement of a genuine understanding of its point of view and, with that understanding, an ability to "take" that point of view. *Conceiving of it as a center of life, one is able to look at the world from its perspective.*

This development from objective knowledge to the recognition of individuality, and from the recognition of individuality to full awareness of an organism's standpoint, is a process of heightening our consciousness of what it means to be an individual living thing. We grasp the particularity of the organism as a teleological center of life, striving to preserve itself and to realize its own good in its own unique way.

It is to be noted that we need not be falsely anthropomorphizing when we conceive of individual plants and animals in this manner. Understanding them as teleological centers of life does not necessitate "reading into" them human characteristics. We need not, for example, consider them to have consciousness. Some of them may be aware of the world around them and others may not. Nor need we deny that different kinds and levels of awareness are exemplified when consciousness in some form is present. But conscious or not, all are equally teleological centers of life in the sense that each is a unified system of goal-oriented activities directed toward their preservation and well-being.

When considered from an ethical point of view, a teleological center of life is an entity whose "world" can be viewed from the perspective of *its* life. In looking at the world from that perspective we recognize objects and events occurring in its life as being beneficent, maleficent, or indifferent. The first are occurrences which increase its powers to preserve its existence and realize its good. The second decrease or destroy those powers. The third have neither of these effects on the entity. With regard to our human role as moral agents, we can conceive of a teleological center of life as a being whose standpoint we can take in making judgments about what events in the world are good or evil, desirable or undesirable. In making those judgments it is what promotes or protects the being's own good, not what benefits moral agents themselves, that sets the standard of evaluation. Such judgments can be made about anything that happens to the entity which is favorable or unfavorable in relation to its good. As was pointed out earlier, the entity itself need not have any (conscious) *interest* in what is happening to it for such judgments to be meaningful and true.

It is precisely judgments of this sort that we are disposed to make when we take the attitude of respect for nature. In adopting that attitude those judgments are given weight as reasons for action in our practical deliberation. They become morally relevant facts in the guidance of our conduct.

IX. The Denial of Human Superiority

This fourth component of the biocentric outlook on nature is the single most important idea in establishing the justifiability of the attitude of respect for nature. Its central role is due to the special relationship it bears to the first three components of the outlook. This relationship will be brought out after the concept of human superiority is examined and analyzed.[7]

In what sense are humans alleged to be superior to other animals? We are different from them in having certain capacities that they lack. But why should these capacities be a mark of superiority? From what point of view are they judged to be signs of superiority and what sense of superiority is meant? After all, various nonhuman species have capacities that humans lack. There is the speed of a cheetah, the vision of an eagle, the agility of a monkey. Why should not these be taken as signs of *their* superiority over humans?

One answer that comes immediately to mind is that these capacities are not as *valuable* as the human capacities that are claimed to make us superior. Such uniquely human characteristics as rational thought, aesthetic creativity, autonomy and self-determination, and moral freedom, it might be held, have a higher value than the capac-

ities found in other species. Yet we must ask: valuable to whom, and on what grounds?

The human characteristics mentioned are all valuable to humans. They are essential to the preservation and enrichment of our civilization and culture. Clearly it is from the human standpoint that they are being judged to be desirable and good. It is not difficult here to recognize a begging of the question. Humans are claiming human superiority from a strictly human point of view, that is, from a point of view in which the good of humans is taken as the standard of judgment. All we need to do is to look at the capacities of nonhuman animals (or plants, for that matter) from the standpoint of *their* good to find a contrary judgment of superiority. The speed of the cheetah, for example, is a sign of its superiority to humans when considered from the standpoint of the good of its species. If it were as slow a runner as a human, it would not be able to survive. And so for all the other abilities of nonhumans which further their good but which are lacking in humans. In each case the claim to human superiority would be rejected from a nonhuman standpoint.

When superiority assertions are interpreted in this way, they are based on judgments of *merit*. To judge the merits of a person or an organism one must apply grading or ranking standards to it. (As I show below, this distinguishes judgments of merit from judgments of inherent worth.) Empirical investigation then determines whether it has the "good-making properties" (merits) in virtue of which it fulfills the standards being applied. In the case of humans, merits may be either moral or nonmoral. We can judge one person to be better than (superior to) another from the moral point of view by applying certain standards to their character and conduct. Similarly, we can appeal to nonmoral criteria in judging someone to be an excellent piano player, a fair cook, a poor tennis player, and so on. Different social purposes and roles are implicit in the making of such judgments, providing the frame of reference for the choice of standards by which the nonmoral merits of people are determined. Ultimately such purposes and roles stem from a society's way of life as a whole. Now a society's way of life may be thought of as the cultural form given to the realization of human values. Whether moral or nonmoral standards are being applied, then, all judgments of people's merits finally depend on human values. All are made from an exclusively human standpoint.

The question that naturally arises at this juncture is: why should standards that are based on human values be assumed to be the only valid criteria of merit and hence the only true signs of superiority? This question is especially pressing when humans are being judged superior in merit to nonhumans. It is true that a human being may be a better mathematician than a monkey, but the monkey may be a better tree climber than a human being. If we humans value mathematics more than tree climbing, that is because our conception of civilized life makes the development of mathematical ability more desirable than the ability to climb trees. But is it not unreasonable to judge nonhumans by the values of human civilization, rather than by values connected with what it is for a member of *that* species to live a good life? If all living things have a good of their own, it at least makes sense to judge the merits of nonhumans by standards derived from *their* good. To use only standards based on human values is already to commit oneself to holding that humans are superior to nonhumans, which is the point in question.

A further logical flaw arises in connection with the widely held conviction that humans are *morally* superior beings because they possess, while others lack, the capacities of a moral agent (free will, accountability, deliberation, judgment, practical reason). This view rests on a conceptual confusion. As far as moral standards are concerned, only beings that have the capacities of a moral agent can properly be judged to be *either* moral (morally good) *or* immoral (morally deficient). Moral standards are simply not applicable to beings that lack such capacities. Animals and plants cannot therefore be said to be morally inferior in merit to humans. Since the only beings that can have moral merits *or be deficient in such merits* are moral agents, it is conceptually incoherent to judge humans as superior to nonhumans on the ground that humans have moral capacities while nonhumans don't.

Up to this point I have been interpreting the claim that humans are superior to other living things as a grading or ranking judgment regarding their comparative merits. There is, however, another way of understanding the idea of human superiority. According to this interpretation, humans are superior to nonhumans not as regards their merits but as regards their inherent worth. Thus the claim of human superiority is to be understood as asserting that all humans, simply in virtue of their humanity, have *a greater inherent worth* than other living things.

The inherent worth of an entity does not depend on its merits.[8] To consider something as possessing inherent worth, we have seen, is to place intrinsic value on the realization of its good. This is done regardless of whatever particular merits it might have or might lack, as judged by a set of grading or ranking standards. In human affairs, we are all familiar with the principle that one's worth as a person does not vary with one's merits or lack of merits. The same can hold true of animals and plants. To regard such entities as possessing inherent worth entails disregarding their merits and deficiencies, whether they are being judged from a human standpoint or from the standpoint of their own species.

The idea of one entity having more merit than another, and so being superior to it in merit, makes perfectly good sense. Merit is a grading or ranking concept, and judgments of comparative merit are based on the different degrees to which things satisfy a given standard. But what can it mean to talk about one thing being superior to another in inherent worth? In order to get at what is being asserted in such a claim it is helpful first to look at the social origin of the concept of degrees of inherent worth.

The idea that humans can possess different degrees of inherent worth originated in societies having rigid class structures. Before the rise of modern democracies with their egalitarian outlook, one's membership in a hereditary class determined one's social status. People in the upper classes were looked up to, while those in the lower classes were looked down upon. In such a society one's social superiors and social inferiors were clearly defined and easily recognized.

Two aspects of these class-structured societies are especially relevant to the idea of degrees of inherent worth. First, those born into the upper classes were deemed more worthy of respect than those born into the lower orders. Second, the superior worth of upper class people had nothing to do with their merits nor did the inferior worth of those in the lower classes rest on their lack of merits. One's superiority or inferiority entirely derived from a social position one was born into. The modern concept of a meritocracy simply did not apply. One could not advance into a higher class by any sort of moral or nonmoral achievement. Similarly, an aristocrat held his title and all the privileges that went with it just because he was the eldest son of a titled nobleman. Unlike the bestowing of knighthood in contemporary Great Britain, one did not earn membership in the nobility by meritorious conduct.

We who live in modern democracies no longer believe in such hereditary social distinctions. Indeed, we would wholeheartedly condemn them on moral grounds as being fundamentally unjust. We have come to think of class systems as a paradigm of social injustice, it being a central principle of the democratic way of life that among humans there are no superiors and no inferiors. Thus we have rejected the whole conceptual framework in which people are judged to have different degrees of inherent worth. That idea is incompatible with our notion of human equality based on the doctrine that all humans, simply in virtue of their humanity, have the same inherent worth. (The belief in universal human rights is one form that this egalitarianism takes.)

The vast majority of people in modern democracies, however, do not maintain an egalitarian outlook when it comes to comparing human beings with other living things. Most people consider our own species to be superior to all other species and this superiority is understood to be a matter of inherent worth, not merit. There may exist thoroughly vicious and depraved humans who lack all merit. Yet because they are human they are thought to belong to a higher class of entities than any plant or animal. That one is born into the species *Homo sapiens* entitles one to have lordship over those who are one's inferiors, namely, those born into other species. The parallel with hereditary social classes is very close. Implicit in this view is a hierarchical conception of nature according to which an organism has a position of superiority or inferiority in the Earth's community of life simply on the basis of its genetic background. The "lower" orders of life are looked down upon and it is considered perfectly proper that they serve the interests of those belonging to the highest order, namely humans. The intrinsic value we place on the well-being of our fellow humans reflects our recognition of their rightful position as our equals. No such intrinsic value is to be placed on the good of other animals,

unless we choose to do so out of fondness or affection for them. But their well-being imposes no moral requirement on us. In this respect there is an absolute difference in moral status between ourselves and them.

This is the structure of concepts and beliefs that people are committed to insofar as they regard humans to be superior in inherent worth to all other species. I now wish to argue that this structure of concepts and beliefs is completely groundless. If we accept the first three components of the biocentric outlook and from that perspective look at the major philosophical traditions which have supported that structure, we find it to be at bottom nothing more than the expression of an irrational bias in our own favor. The philosophical traditions themselves rest on very questionable assumptions or else simply beg the question. I briefly consider three of the main traditions to substantiate the point. These are classical Greek humanism, Cartesian dualism, and the Judeo-Christian concept of the Great Chain of Being.

The inherent superiority of humans over other species was implicit in the Greek definition of man as a rational animal. Our animal nature was identified with "brute" desires that need the order and restraint of reason to rule them (just as reason is the special virtue of those who rule in the ideal state). Rationality was then seen to be the key to our superiority over animals. It enables us to live on a higher plane and endows us with a nobility and worth that other creatures lack. This familiar way of comparing humans with other species is deeply ingrained in our Western philosophical outlook. The point to consider here is that this view does not actually provide an argument *for* human superiority but rather makes explicit the framework of thought that is implicitly used by those who think of humans as inherently superior to nonhumans. The Greeks who held that humans, in virtue of their rational capacities, have a kind of worth greater than that of any nonrational being, never looked at rationality as but one capacity of living things among many others. But when we consider rationality from the standpoint of the first three elements of the ecological outlook, we see that its value lies in its importance for *human* life. Other creatures achieve their species-specific good without the need of rationality, although they often make use of capacities that humans lack. So the humanistic outlook of classical Greek thought does not give us a neutral (nonquestion-begging) ground on which to construct a scale of degrees of inherent worth possessed by different species of living things.

The second tradition, centering on the Cartesian dualism of soul and body, also fails to justify the claim to human superiority. That superiority is supposed to derive from the fact that we have souls while animals do not. Animals are mere automata and lack the divine element that makes us spiritual beings. I won't go into the now familiar criticisms of this two-substance view. I only add the point that, even if humans are composed of an immaterial, unextended soul and a material, extended body, this in itself is not a reason to deem them of greater worth than entities that are only bodies. Why is a soul substance a thing that adds value to its possessor? Unless some theological reasoning is offered here (which many, including myself, would find unacceptable on epistemological grounds), no logical connection is evident. An immaterial something which thinks is better than a material something which does not think only if thinking itself has value, either intrinsically or instrumentally. Now it is intrinsically valuable to humans alone, who value it as an end in itself, and it is instrumentally valuable to those who benefit from it, namely humans.

For animals that neither enjoy thinking for its own sake nor need it for living the kind of life for which they are best adapted, it has no value. Even if "thinking" is broadened to include all forms of consciousness, there are still many living things that can do without it and yet live what is for their species a good life. The anthropocentricity underlying the claim to human superiority runs throughout Cartesian dualism.

A third major source of the idea of human superiority is the Judeo-Christian concept of the Great Chain of Being. Humans are superior to animals and plants because their Creator has given them a higher place on the chain. It begins with God at the top, and then moves to the angels, who are lower than God but higher than humans, then to humans, positioned between the angels and the beasts (partaking of the nature of both), and then on down to the lower levels occupied by nonhuman animals, plants, and finally inanimate objects. Humans, being "made in God's image," are inherently superior to animals and plants by virtue of their being closer (in their essential nature) to God.

The metaphysical and epistemological difficulties with this conception of a hierarchy of entities are, in my mind, insuperable. Without entering into this matter here, I only point out that if we are unwilling to accept the metaphysics of traditional Judaism and Christianity, we are again left without good reasons for holding to the claim of inherent human superiority.

The foregoing considerations (and others like them) leave us with but one ground for the assertion that a human being, regardless of merit, is a higher kind of entity than any other living thing. This is the mere fact of the genetic makeup of the species *Homo sapiens*. But this is surely irrational and arbitrary. Why should the arrangement of genes of a certain type be a mark of superior value, especially when this fact about an organism is taken by itself, unrelated to any other aspect of its life? We might just as well refer to any other genetic makeup as a ground of superior value. Clearly we are confronted here with a wholly arbitrary claim that can only be explained as an irrational bias in our own favor.

That the claim is nothing more than a deep-seated prejudice is brought home to us when we look at our relation to other species in the light of the first three elements of biocentric outlook. Those elements taken conjointly give us a certain overall view of the natural world and of the place of humans in it. When we take this view we come to understand other living things, their environmental conditions, and their ecological relationships in such a way as to awake in us a deep sense of our kinship with them as fellow members of the Earth's community of life. Humans and nonhumans alike are viewed together as integral parts of one unified whole in which all living things are functionally interrelated. Finally, when our awareness focuses on the individual lives of plants and animals, each is seen to share with us the characteristic of being a teleological center of life striving to realize its own good in its own unique way.

As this entire belief system becomes part of the conceptual framework through which we understand and perceive the world, we come to see ourselves as bearing a certain moral relation to nonhuman forms of life. Our ethical role in nature takes on a new significance. We begin to look at other species as we look at ourselves, seeing them as beings which have a good they are striving to realize just as we have a good we are striving to realize. We accordingly develop the disposition to view the world from the standpoint of their good as well as from the standpoint of our own good. Now if the groundlessness of the claim that humans are inherently superior to other species were brought clearly before our minds, we would not remain intellectually neutral toward that claim but would reject it as being fundamentally at variance with our total world outlook. In the absence of any good reasons for holding it, the assertion of human superiority would then appear simply as the expression of an irrational and self-serving prejudice that favors one particular species over several million others.

Rejecting the notion of human superiority entails its positive counterpart: the doctrine of species impartiality. One who accepts that doctrine regards all living things as possessing inherent worth—the *same* inherent worth, since no one species has been shown to be either "higher" or "lower" than any other. Now we saw earlier that, insofar as one thinks of a living thing as possessing inherent worth, one considers it to be the appropriate object of the attitude of respect and believes that attitude to be the only fitting or suitable one for all moral agents to take toward it.

Here, then, is the key to understanding how the attitude of respect is rooted in the biocentric outlook on nature. The basic connection is made through the denial of human superiority. Once we reject the claim that humans are superior either in merit or in worth to other living things, we are ready to adopt the attitude of respect. The denial of human superiority is itself the result of taking the perspective on nature built into the first three elements of the biocentric outlook.

Now the first three elements of the biocentric outlook, it seems clear, would be found acceptable to any rational and scientifically informed thinker who is fully "open" to the reality of the lives of nonhuman organisms. Without denying our distinctively human characteristics, such a thinker can acknowledge the fundamental respects in which we are members of the Earth's community of life and in which the biological conditions necessary for the realization of our human values are inextricably linked with the whole system of nature. In addition, the conception of individual living things as teleological centers of life simply articulates how a scientifically informed thinker comes to understand them as the result of increasingly careful and detailed observations. Thus, the biocentric outlook recommends itself as an acceptable system of concepts and beliefs to anyone who is clear-minded, unbiased, and factually enlightened, and who has a developed capacity of reality awareness with regard to the lives of individual organisms. This, I submit, is as good a reason for making the moral commitment involved in adopting the attitude of respect for nature as any theory of environmental ethics could possibly have.

X. Moral Rights and the Matter of Competing Claims

I have not asserted anywhere in the foregoing account that animals or plants have moral rights. This omission was deliberate. I do not think that the reference class of the concept, bearer of moral rights, should be extended to include nonhuman living things. My reasons for taking this position, however, go beyond the scope of this paper. I believe I have been able to accomplish many of the same ends which those who ascribe rights to animals or plants wish to accomplish. There is no reason, moreover, why plants and animals, including whole species populations and life communities, cannot be accorded *legal* rights under my theory. To grant them legal protection could be interpreted as giving them legal entitlement to be protected, and this, in fact, would be a means by which a society that subscribed to the ethics of respect for nature could give public recognition to their inherent worth.

There remains the problem of competing claims, even when wild plants and animals are not thought of as bearers of moral rights. If we accept the biocentric outlook and accordingly adopt the attitude of respect for nature as our ultimate moral attitude, how do we resolve conflicts that arise from our respect for persons in the domain of human ethics and our respect for nature in the domain of environmental ethics? This is a question that cannot adequately be dealt with here. My main purpose in this paper has been to try to establish a base point from which we can start working toward a solution to the problem. I have shown why we cannot just begin with an initial presumption in favor of the interests of our own species. It is after all within our power as moral beings to place limits on human population and technology with the deliberate intention of sharing the Earth's bounty with other species. That such sharing is an ideal difficult to realize even in an approximate way does not take away its claim to our deepest moral commitment.

Notes

1. The conceptual links between an entity *having* a good, something being good *for* it, and events doing good *to* it are examined by G. H. Von Wright in *The Varieties of Goodness* (New York: Humanities Press, 1963), chaps. 3 and 5.

2. See W. K. Frankena, "Ethics and the Environment," in K. E. Goodpaster and K. M. Sayre, eds., *Ethics and Problems of the 21st Century* (Notre Dame, IN: University of Notre Dame Press, 1979), pp. 3–20. I critically examine Frankena's views in "Frankena on Environmental Ethics," *The Monist,* Volume 64, number 3, July 1981, pp. 313–324.

3. In the light of considerations set forth in Daniel Dennett's *Brainstorms: Philosophical Essays on Mind and Psychology* (Montgomery, VT: Bradford Books, 1978), it is advisable to leave this question unsettled at this time. When machines are developed that function in the way our brains do, we may well come to deem them proper subjects of moral consideration.

4. I have analyzed the nature of this commitment of human ethics in "On Taking the Moral Point of View," *Midwest Studies in Philosophy,* Vol. 3, *Studies in Ethical Theory* (1978), pp. 35–61.

5. John Rawls, "Justice as Fairness," *Philosophical Review* 67 (1958):183.

6. Stephen R. L. Clark, *The Moral Status of Animals* (Oxford: Clarendon Press, 1977), p.112.

7. My criticisms of the dogma of human superiority gain independent support from a carefully reasoned essay by R. and V. Routley showing the many logical weaknesses in arguments for human-centered theories of environmental ethics. R. and V. Routley, "Against the Inevitability of Human Chauvinism," in K. E. Goodpaster and K. M. Sayre, eds, *Ethics and Problems of the 21st Century* (Notre Dame, IN: University of Notre Dame Press, 1979), pp. 36–59.

8. For this way of distinguishing between merit and inherent worth, I am indebted to Gregory Vlastos, "Justice and Equality," in R. Brandt, ed., *Social Justice* (Englewood Cliffs, NJ: Prentice-Hall, 1962), pp. 31–72.

25. The Land Ethic

Aldo Leopold

When godlike Odysseus returned from the wars in Troy, he hanged all on one rope a dozen slave-girls of his household whom he suspected of misbehavior during his absence.

This hanging involved no question of propriety. The girls were property. The disposal of property was then, as now, a matter of expediency, not of right and wrong.

Concepts of right and wrong were not lacking from Odysseus' Greece: witness the fidelity of his wife through the long years before at last his black-prowed galleys clove the wine-dark seas for home. The ethical structure of that day covered wives, but had not yet been extended to human chattels. During the three thousand years which have since elapsed, ethical criteria have been extended to many fields of conduct, with corresponding shrinkages in those judged by expediency only.

The Ethical Sequence

This extension of ethics, so far studied only by philosophers, is actually a process in ecological evolution. Its sequences may be described in ecological as well as in philosophical terms. An ethic, ecologically, is a limitation on freedom of action in the struggle for existence. An ethic, philosophically, is a differentiation of social from antisocial conduct. These are two definitions of one thing. The thing has its origin in the tendency of interdependent individuals or groups to evolve modes of cooperation. The ecologist calls these symbioses. Politics and economics are advanced symbioses in which the original free-for-all competition has been replaced, in part, by cooperative mechanisms with an ethical content.

The complexity of cooperative mechanisms has increased with population density, and with the efficiency of tools. It was simpler, for example, to define the anti-social uses of sticks and stones in the days of the mastodons than of bullets and billboards in the age of motors.

The first ethics dealt with the relation between individuals; the Mosaic Decalogue is an example. Later accretions dealt with the relation between the individual and society. The Golden Rule tries to integrate the individual to society; democracy to integrate social organization to the individual.

There is as yet no ethic dealing with man's relation to land and to the animals and plants which grow upon it. Land, like Odysseus' slave-girls, is still property. The land-relation is still strictly economic, entailing privileges but not obligations.

The extension of ethics to this third element in human environment is, if I read the evidence correctly, an evolutionary possibility and an ecological necessity. It is the third step in a sequence. The first two have already been taken. Individual thinkers since the days of Ezekiel and Isaiah have asserted that the despoliation of land is not only inexpedient but wrong. Society, however, has not yet affirmed their belief. I regard the present conservation movement as the embryo of such an affirmation.

An ethic may be regarded as a mode of guidance for meeting ecological situations so new or intricate, or involving such deferred reactions, that the path of social expediency is not discernible to the average individual. Animal instincts are modes of guidance for the individual in meeting such situations. Ethics are possibly a kind of community instinct in-the-making.

The Community Concept

All ethics so far evolved rest upon a single premise: that the individual is a member of a community of interdependent parts. His instincts prompt him to compete for his place in the community, but his ethics prompt him also to cooperate (perhaps in order that there may be a place to compete for).

The land ethic simply enlarges the boundaries of the community to include soils, waters, plants, and animals, or collectively: the land.

This sounds simple: do we not already sing our love for and obligation to the land of the free and the home of the brave? Yes, but just what and whom do we love? Certainly not the soil, which we are sending helter-skelter downriver. Certainly not the waters, which we assume have no function except to turn turbines, float barges, and carry off sewage. Certainly not the plants, of which we exterminate whole communities without batting an eye. Certainly not the animals, of which we have already extirpated many of the largest and most beautiful species. A land ethic of course cannot prevent the alteration, management, and use of these "resources," but it does affirm their right to continued existence, and, at least in spots, their continued existence in a natural state.

In short, a land ethic changes the role of *Homo sapiens* from conqueror of the land-community to plain member and citizen of it. It implies respect for his fellow-members, and also respect for the community as such.

In human history, we have learned (I hope) that the conqueror role is eventually self-defeating. Why? Because it is implicit in such a role that the conqueror knows, *ex cathedra*, just what makes the community clock tick, and just what and who is valuable, and what and who is worthless, in community life. It always turns out that he knows neither, and this is why his conquests eventually defeat themselves.

In the biotic community, a parallel situation exists. Abraham knew exactly what the land was for: it was to drip milk and honey into Abraham's mouth. At the present moment, the assurance with which we regard this assumption is inverse to the degree of our education.

The ordinary citizen today assumes that science knows what makes the community clock tick; the scientist is equally sure that he does not. He knows that the biotic mechanism is so complex that its workings may never be fully understood.

That man is, in fact, only a member of a biotic team is shown by an ecological interpretation of history. Many historical events, hitherto explained solely in terms of human enterprise, were actually biotic interactions between people and land. The characteristics of the land determined the facts quite as potently as the characteristics of the men who lived on it.

Consider, for example, the settlement of the Mississippi valley. In the years following the

Revolution, three groups were contending for its control: the native Indian, the French and English traders, and the American settlers. Historians wonder what would have happened if the English at Detroit had thrown a little more weight into the Indian side of those tipsy scales which decided the outcome of the colonial migration into the cane-lands of Kentucky. It is time now to ponder the fact that the cane-lands, when subjected to the particular mixture of forces represented by the cow, plow, fire, and axe of the pioneer, became bluegrass. What if the plant succession inherent in this dark and bloody ground had, under the impact of these forces, given us some worthless sedge, shrub, or weed? Would Boone and Kenton have held out? Would there have been any overflow into Ohio, Indiana, Illinois, and Missouri? Any Louisiana Purchase? Any transcontinental union of new states? Any Civil War?

Kentucky was one sentence in the drama of history. We are commonly told what the human actors in this drama tried to do, but we are seldom told that their success, or the lack of it, hung in large degree on the reaction of particular soils to the impact of the particular forces exerted by their occupancy. In the case of Kentucky, we do not even know where the bluegrass came from—whether it is a native species, or a stowaway from Europe.

Contrast the cane-lands with what hindsight tells us about the Southwest, where the pioneers were equally brave, resourceful, and persevering. The impact of the occupancy here brought no bluegrass, or other plant fitted to withstand the bumps and buffetings of hard use. This region, when grazed by livestock, reverted through a series of more and more worthless grasses, shrubs, and weeds to a condition of unstable equilibrium. Each recession of plant types bred erosion; each increment to erosion bred a further recession of plants. The result today is a progressive and mutual deterioration, not only of plants and soils, but of the animal community subsisting thereon. The early settlers did not expect this: on the ciénegas of New Mexico some even cut ditches to hasten it. So subtle has been its progress that few residents of the region are aware of it. It is quite invisible to the tourist who finds this wrecked landscape colorful and charming (as indeed it is, but it bears scant resemblance to what it was in 1848).

This same landscape was "developed" once before, but with quite different results. The Pueblo Indians settled the Southwest in pre-Columbian times, but they happened *not* to be equipped with range livestock. Their civilization expired, but not because their land expired.

In India, regions devoid of any sod-forming grass have been settled, apparently without wrecking the land, by the simple expedient of carrying the grass to the cow, rather than vice versa. (Was this the result of some deep wisdom, or was it just good luck? I do not know.)

In short, the plant succession steered the course of history; the pioneer simply demonstrated, for good or ill, what successions inhered in the land. Is history taught in this spirit? It will be, once the concept of land as a community really penetrates our intellectual life.

The Ecological Conscience

Conservation is a state of harmony between men and land. Despite nearly a century of propaganda, conservation still proceeds at a snail's pace; progress still consists largely of letterhead pieties and convention oratory. On the back forty we still slip two steps backward for each forward stride.

The usual answer to this dilemma is "more conservation education." No one will debate this, but is it certain that only the *volume* of education needs stepping up? Is something lacking in the *content* as well?

It is difficult to give a fair summary of its content in brief form, but as I understand it, the content is substantially this: obey the law, vote right, join some organizations, and practice what conservation is profitable on your own land; the government will do the rest.

Is not this formula too easy to accomplish anything worthwhile? It defines no right or wrong, assigns no obligation, calls for no sacrifice, implies no change in the current philosophy of values. In respect of land-use, it urges only enlightened self-interest. Just how far will such education take us? An example will perhaps yield a partial answer.

By 1930 it had become clear to all except the ecologically blind that southwestern Wisconsin's topsoil was slipping seaward. In 1933 the farmers were told that if they would adopt certain remedial practices for five years, the public would donate CCC labor to install them, plus the necessary machinery and materials. The offer was widely accepted, but the practices were widely forgotten when the five-year contract period was up. The farmers continued only those practices that yielded an immediate and visible economic gain for themselves.

This led to the idea that maybe farmers would learn more quickly if they themselves wrote the rules. Accordingly the Wisconsin Legislature in 1937 passed the Soil Conservation District Law. This said to farmers, in effect: *We, the public, will furnish you free technical service and loan you specialized machinery, if you will write your own rules for land-use. Each county may write its own rules, and these will have the force of law.* Nearly all the counties promptly organized to accept the proffered help, but after a decade of operation, *no county has yet written a single rule.* There has been visible progress in such practices as stripcropping, pasture renovation, and soil liming, but none in fencing woodlots against grazing, and none in excluding plow and cow from steep slopes. The farmers, in short, have selected those remedial practices which were profitable anyhow, and ignored those which were profitable to the community, but not clearly profitable to themselves.

When one asks why no rules have been written, one is told that the community is not yet ready to support them; education must precede rules. But the education actually in progress makes no mention of obligations to land over and above those dictated by self-interest. The net result is that we have more education but less soil, fewer healthy woods, and as many floods as in 1937.

The puzzling aspect of such situations is that the existence of obligations over and above self-interest is taken for granted in such rural community enterprise as the betterment of roads, schools, churches, and baseball teams. Their existence is not taken for granted, nor as yet seriously discussed, in bettering the behavior of the water that falls on the land, or in the preserving of the beauty or diversity of the farm landscape. Land-use ethics are still governed wholly by economic self-interest, just as social ethics were a century ago.

To sum up: we asked the farmer to do what he conveniently could to save his soil, and he has done just that, and only that. The farmer who clears the woods off a 75 per cent slope, turns his cows into the clearing, and dumps its rainfall, rocks, and soil into the community creek, is still (if otherwise decent) a respected member of society. If he puts lime on his fields and plants his crops on contour, he is still entitled to all the privileges and emoluments of his Soil Conservation District. The District is a beautiful piece of social machinery, but it is coughing along on two cylinders because we have been too timid, and too anxious for quick success, to tell the farmer the true magnitude of his obligations. Obligations have no meaning without conscience, and the problem we face is the extension of the social conscience from people to land.

No important change in ethics was ever accomplished without an internal change in our intellectual emphasis, loyalties, affections, and convictions. The proof that conservation has not yet touched these foundations of conduct lies in the fact that philosophy and religion have not yet heard of it. In our attempt to make conservation easy, we have made it trivial.

Substitutes for a Land Ethic

When the logic of history hungers for bread and we hand out a stone, we are at pains to explain how much the stone resembles bread. I now describe some of the stones which serve in lieu of a land ethic.

One basic weakness in a conservation system based wholly on economic motives is that most members of the land community have no economic value. Wildflowers and songbirds are examples. Of the 22,000 higher plants and animals native to Wisconsin, it is doubtful whether more than 5 percent can be sold, fed, eaten, or otherwise put to economic use. Yet these creatures are members of the biotic community, and if (as I believe) its stability depends on its integrity, they are entitled to continuance.

When one of these non-economic categories is threatened, and if we happen to love it, we invent subterfuges to give it economic importance. At the beginning of the century songbirds were supposed to be disappearing. Ornithologists jumped to the rescue with some distinctly shaky evidence to the effect that insects would eat us up if birds failed to control them. The evidence had to be economic in order to be valid.

It is painful to read these circumlocutions today. We have no land ethic yet, but we have at least drawn nearer the point of admitting that birds should continue as a matter of biotic right, regardless of the presence or absence of economic advantage to us.

A parallel situation exists in respect of predatory mammals, raptorial birds, and fish-eating birds. Time was when biologists somewhat overworked the evidence that these creatures preserve the health of game by killing weaklings, or that they control rodents for the farmer, or that they prey only on "worthless" species. Here again, the evidence had to be economic in order to be valid. It is only in recent years that we hear the more honest argument that predators are members of the community, and that no special interest has the right to exterminate them for the sake of a benefit, real or fancied, to itself. Unfortunately this enlightened view is still in the talk stage. In the field the extermination of predators goes merrily on: witness the impending erasure of the timber wolf by fiat of Congress, the Conservation Bureaus, and many state legislatures.

Some species of trees have been "read out of the party" by economics-minded foresters because they grow too slowly, or have too low a sale value to pay as timber crops: white cedar, tamarack, cypress, beech, and hemlock are examples. In Europe, where forestry is ecologically more advanced, the non-commercial tree species are recognized as members of the native forest community, to be preserved as such, within reason. Moreover some (like beech) have been found to have a valuable function in building up soil fertility. The interdependence of the forest and its constituent tree species, ground flora, and fauna is taken for granted.

Lack of economic value is sometimes a character not only of species or groups, but of entire biotic communities: marshes, bogs, dunes, and "deserts" are examples. Our formula in such cases is to relegate their conservation to government as refuges, monuments, or parks. The difficulty is that these communities are usually interspersed with more valuable private lands; the government cannot possibly own or control such scattered parcels. The net effect is that we have relegated some of them to ultimate extinction over large areas. If the private owner were ecologically minded, he would be proud to be the custodian of a reasonable proportion of such areas, which add diversity and beauty to his farm and to his community.

In some instances, the assumed lack of profit in these "waste" areas has proved to be wrong, but only after most of them had been done away with. The present scramble to reflood muskrat marshes is a case in point.

There is a clear tendency in American conservation to relegate to government all necessary jobs that private landowners fail to perform. Government ownership, operation, subsidy, or regulation is now widely prevalent in forestry, range management, soil and watershed management, park and wilderness conservation, fisheries management, and migratory bird management, with more to come. Most of this growth in governmental conservation is proper and logical, some of it is inevitable. That I imply no disapproval of it is implicit in the fact that I have spent most of my life working for it. Nevertheless the question arises: What is the ultimate magnitude of the enterprise? Will the tax base carry its eventual ramifications? At what point will governmental conservation, like the mastodon, become handicapped by its own dimensions? The answer, if there is any, seems to be in a land ethic, or some other force which assigns more obligation to the private landowner.

Industrial landowners and users, especially lumbermen and stockmen, are inclined to wail long and loudly about the extension of government ownership and regulation to land, but (with notable exceptions) they show little disposition to develop the only visible alternative: the voluntary practice of conservation on their own lands.

When the private landowner is asked to perform some unprofitable act for the good of the community, he today assents only with outstretched palm. If the act costs him cash this is fair and proper, but when it costs only forethought, open-mindedness, or time, the issue is at least debatable. The overwhelming growth of land-use subsidies in recent years must be ascribed, in large part, to the government's own agencies for conservation education: the land bureaus, the agricultural colleges, and the extension services. As far as I can detect, no ethical obligation toward land is taught in these institutions.

To sum up: a system of conservation based solely on economic self-interest is hopelessly lopsided. It tends to ignore, and thus eventually to eliminate, many elements in the land community that lack commercial value, but that are (as far as we know) essential to its healthy functioning. It assumes, falsely, I think, that the economic parts of the biotic clock will function without the uneconomic parts. It tends to relegate to government many functions eventually too large, too complex, or too widely dispersed to be performed by government.

An ethical obligation on the part of the private owner is the only visible remedy for these situations.

The Land Pyramid

An ethic to supplement and guide the economic relation to land presupposes the existence of some mental image of land as a biotic mechanism. We can be ethical only in relation to something we can see, feel, understand, love, or otherwise have faith in. The image commonly employed in conservation education is "the balance of nature." For reasons too lengthy to detail here, this figure of speech fails to describe accurately what little we know about the land mechanism. A much truer image is the one employed in ecology: the biotic pyramid. I shall first sketch the pyramid as a symbol of land, and later develop some of its implications in terms of land-use.

Plants absorb energy from the sun. This energy flows through a circuit called the biota, which may be represented by a pyramid consisting of layers. The bottom layer is the soil. A plant layer rests on the soil, an insect layer on the plants, a bird and rodent layer on the insects, and so on up through various animal groups to the apex layer, which consists of the larger carnivores.

The species of a layer are alike not in where they came from, or in what they look like, but rather in what they eat. Each successive layer depends on those below it for food and often for other services, and each in turn furnishes food and services to those above. Proceeding upward, each successive layer decreases in numerical abundance. Thus, for every carnivore there are hundreds of his prey, thousands of their prey, millions of insects, uncountable plants. The pyramidal form of the system reflects this numerical progression from apex to base. Man shares an intermediate layer with the bears, raccoons, and squirrels which eat both meat and vegetables.

The lines of dependency for food and other services are called food chains. Thus soil-oak-deer-Indian is a chain that has now been largely converted to soil-corn-cow-farmer. Each species, including ourselves, is a link in many chains. The deer eats a hundred plants other than oak, and the cow a hundred plants other than corn. Both, then, are links in a hundred chains. The pyramid is a tangle of chains so complex as to seem disorderly, yet the stability of the system proves it to be a highly organized structure. Its functioning depends on the cooperation and competition of its diverse parts.

In the beginning the pyramid of life was low and squat; the food chains short and simple. Evolution has added layer after layer, link after link. Man is one of thousands of accretions to the height and complexity of the pyramid. Science has given us many doubts, but it has given us at least one certainty: the trend of evolution is to elaborate and diversify the biota.

Land, then, is not merely soil; it is a fountain of energy flowing through a circuit of soils, plants, and animals. Food chains are the living channels which conduct energy upward; death and decay return it to the soil. The circuit is not closed; some energy is dissipated in decay, some is added by absorption from the air, some is stored in soils, peats, and long-lived forests; but it is a sustained circuit, like a slowly augmented revolving fund of life. There is always a net loss by downhill wash, but this is normally small and offset by the decay of rocks. It is deposited in the ocean and, in the course of geological time, raised to form new lands and new pyramids.

The velocity and character of the upward flow of energy depend on the complex structure of the plant and animal community, much as the upward flow of sap in a tree depends on its complex cellular organization. Without this complexity, normal circulation would presumably not occur. Structure means the characteristic numbers, as well as the characteristic kinds and functions, of the component species. This interdependence between the complex structure of the land and its smooth functioning as an energy unit is one of its basic attributes.

When a change occurs in one part of the circuit, many other parts must adjust themselves to it. Change does not necessarily obstruct or divert the flow of energy; evolution is a long series of self-induced changes, the net result of which has been to elaborate the flow mechanism and to lengthen the circuit. Evolutionary changes, however, are usually slow and local. Man's invention of tools has enabled him to make changes of unprecedented violence, rapidity, and scope.

One change is in the composition of floras and faunas. The larger predators are lopped off the apex of the pyramid; food chains, for the first time in history, become shorter rather than longer. Domesticated species from other lands are substituted for wild ones, and wild ones are moved to new habitats. In this worldwide pooling of faunas and floras, some species get out of bounds as pests and diseases, others are extinguished. Such effects are seldom intended or foreseen; they represent unpredicted and often untraceable readjustments in the structure. Agricultural science is largely a race between the emergence of new pests and the emergence of new techniques for their control.

Another change touches the flow of energy through plants and animals and its return to the soil. Fertility is the ability of soil to receive, store, and release energy. Agriculture, by overdrafts on the soil, or by too radical a substitution of domestic for native species in the superstructure, may derange the channels of flow or deplete storage. Soils depleted of their storage, or of the organic matter which anchors it, wash away faster than they form. This is erosion.

Waters, like soil, are part of the energy circuit. Industry, by polluting waters or obstructing them with dams, may exclude the plants and animals necessary to keep energy in circulation.

Transportation brings about another basic change: the plants or animals grown in one region are now consumed and returned to the soil in another. Transportation taps the energy stored in rocks, and in the air, and uses it elsewhere; thus we fertilize the garden with nitrogen gleaned by the guano birds from the fishes of seas on the other side of the Equator. Thus the formerly localized and self-contained circuits are pooled on a world-wide scale.

The process of altering the pyramid for human occupation releases stored energy, and this often gives rise, during the pioneering period, to a deceptive exuberance of plant and animal life, both wild and tame. These releases of biotic capital tend to becloud or postpone the penalties of violence.

This thumbnail sketch of land as an energy circuit conveys three basic ideas:

1. That land is not merely soil.

2. That the native plants and animals kept the energy circuit open; others may or may not.

3. That man-made changes are of a different order than evolutionary changes, and have effects more comprehensive than is intended or foreseen.

These ideas, collectively, raise two basic issues: Can the land adjust itself to the new order? Can the desired alterations be accomplished with less violence?

Biotas seem to differ in their capacity to sustain violent conversion. Western Europe, for example, carries a far different pyramid than Caesar found there. Some large animals are lost; swampy forests have become meadows or plowland; many new plants and animals are introduced, some of which escape as pests; the remaining natives are greatly changed in distribution and abundance. Yet the soil is still there and, with the help of imported nutrients, still fertile; the waters flow normally; the new structure seems to function and to persist. There is no visible stoppage or derangement of the circuit.

Western Europe, then, has a resistant biota. Its inner processes are tough, elastic, resistant to strain. No matter how violent the alterations, the pyramid, so far, has developed some new *modus vivendi* which preserves its habitability for man, and for most of the other natives.

Japan seems to present another instance of radical conversion without disorganization.

Most other civilized regions, and some as yet barely touched by civilization, display various stages of disorganization, varying from initial symptoms to advanced wastage. In Asia Minor and North Africa diagnosis is confused by climatic changes, which may have been either the cause or the effect of advanced wastage. In the United States the degree of disorganization varies locally; it is worst in the Southwest, the Ozarks, and parts of the South, and least in New England and the Northwest. Better land-uses may still arrest it in the less advanced regions. In parts of Mexico, South America, South Africa, and Australia a violent and accelerating wastage is in progress, but I cannot assess the prospects.

This almost world-wide display of disorganization in the land seems to be similar to disease in an animal, except that it never culminates in complete disorganization or death. The land recovers, but at some reduced level of complexity, and with a reduced carrying capacity for people, plants, and animals. Many biotas currently regarded as "lands of opportunity" are in fact already subsisting on exploitative agriculture, i.e., they have already exceeded their sustained carrying capacity. Most of South America is overpopulated in this sense.

In arid regions we attempt to offset the process of wastage by reclamation, but it is only too evident that the prospective longevity of reclamation projects is often short. In our own West, the best of them may not last a century.

The combined evidence of history and ecology seems to support one general deduction: the less violent the man-made changes, the greater the probability of successful readjustment in the pyramid. Violence, in turn, varies with human population density; a dense population requires a more violent conversion. In this respect, North America has a better chance for permanence than Europe, if she can contrive to limit her density.

This deduction runs counter to our current philosophy, which assumes that because a small increase in density enriched human life, that an indefinite increase will enrich it indefinitely. Ecology knows of no density relationship that holds for indefinitely wide limits. All gains from density are subject to a law of diminishing returns.

Whatever may be the equation for men and land, it is improbable that we as yet know all its terms. Recent discoveries in mineral and vitamin nutrition reveal unsuspected dependencies in the up-circuit: incredibly minute quantities of certain substances determine the value of soils to plants, of plants to animals. What of the down-circuit? What of the vanishing species, the preservation of which we now regard as an esthetic luxury? They helped build the soil; in what unsuspected ways may they be essential to its maintenance? Professor Weaver proposes that we use prairie flowers to reflocculate the wasting soils of the dust bowl; who knows for what purpose cranes and condors, otters and grizzlies may some day be used?

Land Health and the A–B Cleavage

A land ethic, then, reflects the existence of an ecological conscience, and this in turn reflects a conviction of individual responsibility for the health of the land. Health is the capacity of the land for self-renewal. Conservation is our effort to understand and preserve this capacity.

Conservationists are notorious for their dissensions. Superficially these seem to add up to mere confusion, but a more careful scrutiny reveals a single plane of cleavage common to many specialized fields. In each field one group (A) regards the land as soil, and its function as commodity-production; another group (B) regards the land as a biota, and its function as something

broader. How much broader is admittedly in a state of doubt and confusion.

In my own field, forestry, group A is quite content to grow trees like cabbages, with cellulose as the basic forest commodity. It feels no inhibition against violence; its ideology is agronomic. Group B, on the other hand, sees forestry as fundamentally different from agronomy because it employs natural species, and manages a natural environment rather than creating an artificial one. Group B prefers natural reproduction on principle. It worries on biotic as well as economic grounds about the loss of species like chestnut, and the threatened loss of the white pines. It worries about a whole series of secondary forest functions: wildlife, recreation, watersheds, wilderness areas. To my mind, Group B feels the stirrings of an ecological conscience.

In the wildlife field, a parallel cleavage exists. For Group A the basic commodities are sport and meat; the yardsticks of production are ciphers of take in pheasants and trout. Artificial propagation is acceptable as a permanent as well as a temporary recourse—if its unit costs permit. Group B, on the other hand, worries about a whole series of biotic side-issues. What is the cost in predators of producing a game crop? Should we have further recourse to exotics? How can management restore the shrinking species, like prairie grouse, already hopeless as shootable game? How can management restore the threatened rarities, like trumpeter swan and whooping crane? Can management principles be extended to wildflowers? Here again it is clear to me that we have the same A–B cleavage as in forestry.

In the larger field of agriculture I am less competent to speak, but there seem to be somewhat parallel cleavages. Scientific agriculture was actively developing before ecology was born, hence a slower penetration of ecological concepts might be expected. Moreover the farmer, by the very nature of his techniques, must modify the biota more radically than the forester or the wildlife manager. Nevertheless, there are many discontents in agriculture which seem to add up to a new vision of "biotic farming."

Perhaps the most important of these is the new evidence that poundage or tonnage is no measure of the food-value of farm crops; the products of fertile soil may be qualitatively as well as quantitatively superior. We can bolster poundage from depleted soils by pouring on imported fertility, but we are not necessarily bolstering food-value. The possible ultimate ramifications of this idea are so immense that I must leave their exposition to abler pens.

The discontent that labels itself "organic farming," while bearing some of the earmarks of a cult, is nevertheless biotic in its direction, particularly in its insistence on the importance of soil flora and fauna.

The ecological fundamentals of agriculture are just as poorly known to the public as in other fields of land-use. For example, few educated people realize that the marvelous advances in technique made during recent decades are improvements in the pump, rather than the well. Acre for acre, they have barely sufficed to offset the sinking level of fertility.

In all of these cleavages, we see repeated the same basic paradoxes: man the conqueror *versus* man the biotic citizen; science the sharpener of his sword *versus* science the searchlight on his universe; land the slave and servant *versus* land the collective organism. Robinson's injunction to Tristram may well be applied, at this juncture, to *Homo sapiens* as a species in geological time:

> Whether you will or not
> You are a King, Tristram, for you are one
> Of the time-tested few that leave the world,
> When they are gone, not the same place it was.
> Mark what you leave.

The Outlook

It is inconceivable to me that an ethical relation to land can exist without love, respect, and admiration for land, and a high regard for its value. By value, I of course mean something far broader than mere economic value; I mean value in the philosophical sense.

Perhaps the most serious obstacle impeding the evolution of a land ethic is the fact that our educational and economic system is headed away from, rather than toward, an intense consciousness of land. Your true modern is separated from the land by many middlemen, and by innumerable physical gadgets. He has no vital relation to it; to him it is the space between cities on which crops grow. Turn him loose for a day on the land, and if the spot does not happen to be a golf links or a "scenic" area, he is bored stiff. If crops could be

raised by hydroponics instead of farming, it would suit him very well. Synthetic substitutes for wood, leather, wool, and other natural land products suit him better than the originals. In short, land is something he has "outgrown."

Almost equally serious as an obstacle to a land ethic is the attitude of the farmer for whom the land is still an adversary, or a taskmaster that keeps him in slavery. Theoretically, the mechanization of farming ought to cut the farmer's chains, but whether it really does is debatable.

One of the requisites for an ecological comprehension of land is an understanding of ecology, and this is by no means co-extensive with "education"; in fact, much higher education seems deliberately to avoid ecological concepts. An understanding of ecology does not necessarily originate in courses bearing ecological labels; it is quite as likely to be labeled geography, botany, agronomy, history, or economics. This is as it should be, but whatever the label, ecological training is scarce.

The case for a land ethic would appear hopeless but for the minority which is in obvious revolt against these "modern" trends.

The "key-log" which must be moved to release the evolutionary process for an ethic is simply this: quit thinking about decent land-use as solely an economic problem. Examine each question in terms of what is ethically and esthetically right, as well as what is economically expedient. A thing is right when it tends to preserve the integrity, stability, and beauty of the biotic community. It is wrong when it tends otherwise.

It of course goes without saying that economic feasibility limits the tether of what can or cannot be done for land. It always has and it always will. The fallacy the economic determinists have tied around our collective neck, and which we now need to cast off, is the belief that economics determines all land-use. This is simply not true. An innumerable host of actions and attitudes, comprising perhaps the bulk of all land relations, is determined by the land-user's tastes and predilections, rather than by his purse. The bulk of all land relations hinges on investments of time, forethought, skill, and faith rather than on investments of cash. As a land-user thinketh, so is he.

I have purposely presented the land ethic as a product of social evolution because nothing so important as an ethic is ever "written." Only the most superficial student of history supposes that

Moses "wrote" the Decalogue; it evolved in the minds of a thinking community, and Moses wrote a tentative summary of it for a "seminar." I say tentative because evolution never stops.

The evolution of a land ethic is an intellectual as well as emotional process. Conservation is paved with good intentions which prove to be futile, or even dangerous, because they are devoid of critical understanding either of the land, or of economic land-use. I think it is a truism that as the ethical frontier advances from the individual to the community, its intellectual content increases.

The mechanism of operation is the same for any ethic: social approbation for right actions: social disapproval for wrong actions.

By and large, our present problem is one of attitudes and implements. We are remodeling the Alhambra with a steam-shovel, and we are proud of our yardage. We shall hardly relinquish the shovel, which after all has many good points, but we are in need of gentler and more objective criteria for its successful use.

26. The Conceptual Foundations of the Land Ethic

J. Baird Callicott

As Wallace Stegner observes, *A Sand County Almanac* is considered "almost a holy book in conservation circles," and Aldo Leopold a prophet, "an American Isaiah." And as Curt Meine points out, "The Land Ethic" is the climactic essay of *Sand County*, "the upshot of 'The Upshot,'"[1] One might, therefore, fairly say that the recommendation and justification of moral obligations on the part of people to nature is what the prophetic *A Sand County Almanac* is all about. . . .

Here I first examine and elaborate the compactly expressed abstract elements of the land ethic and expose the "logic" which binds them into a proper, but revolutionary, moral theory. I then discuss the controversial features of the land ethic and defend them against actual and potential criticism. I hope to show that the land ethic cannot be ignored as merely the groundless emotive exhortations of a moonstruck conservationist or dismissed as entailing wildly untoward practical consequences. It poses, rather, a serious intellectual challenge to business-as-usual moral philosophy.

"The Land Ethic" opens with a charming and poetic evocation of Homer's Greece, the point of which is to suggest that today land is just as routinely and remorsely enslaved as human beings then were. A panoramic glance backward to our most distant cultural origins, Leopold suggests, reveals a slow but steady moral development over

three millennia. More of our relationships and activities ("fields of conduct") have fallen under the aegis of moral principles ("ethical criteria") as civilization has grown and matured. If moral growth and development continue, as not only a synoptic review of history, but recent past experience suggests that it will, future generations will censure today's casual and universal environmental bondage as today we censure the casual and universal human bondage of three thousand years ago.

A cynically inclined critic might scoff at Leopold's sanguine portrayal of human history. Slavery survived as an institution in the "civilized" West, more particularly in the morally self-congratulatory United States, until a mere generation before Leopold's own birth. And Western history from imperial Athens and Rome to the Spanish Inquisition and the Third Reich has been a disgraceful series of wars, persecutions, tyrannies, pogroms, and other atrocities.

The history of moral practice, however, is not identical with the history of moral consciousness. Morality is not descriptive; it is prescriptive or normative. In light of this distinction, it is clear that today, despite rising rates of violent crime in the United States and institutional abuses of human rights in Iran, Chile, Ethiopia, Guatemala, South Africa, and many other places, and despite persistent organized social injustice and oppression in still

Companion to *A Sand County Almanac: Interpretive and Critical Essays,* edited by J. Baird Callicott. Madison: University of Wisconsin Press, 1987, pp. 186–214. Reprinted by permission.

others, moral consciousness is expanding more rapidly now than ever before. Civil rights, human rights, women's liberation, children's liberation, animal liberation, etc., all indicate, as expressions of newly emergent moral ideals, that ethical consciousness (as distinct from practice) has if anything recently accelerated—thus confirming Leopold's historical observation.

Leopold next points out that "this extension of ethics, so far studied only by philosophers"—and, therefore, the implication is clear, not very satisfactorily studied—"is actually a process in ecological evolution" (202).* What Leopold is saying here, simply, is that we may understand the history of ethics, fancifully alluded to by means of the Odysseus vignette, in biological as well as philosophical terms. From a biological point of view, an ethic is "a limitation on freedom of action in the struggle for existence" (202).

I had this passage in mind when I remarked that Leopold manages to convey a whole network of ideas in a couple of phrases. The phrase "struggle for existence" unmistakably calls to mind Darwinian evolution as the conceptual context in which a biological account of the origin and development of ethics must ultimately be located. And at once it points up a paradox: Given the unremitting competitive "struggle for existence" how could "limitations on freedom of action" ever have been conserved and spread through a population of *Homo sapiens* or their evolutionary progenitors?

For a biological account of ethics, as Harvard social entomologist Edward O. Wilson has recently written, "the central theoretical problem . . . [is] how can altruism [elaborately articulated as morality or ethics in the human species], which by definition reduces personal fitness, possibly evolve by natural selection?"[2] According to modern sociobiology, the answer lies in kinship. But according to Darwin—who had tackled this problem himself "exclusively from the side of natural history" in *The Descent of Man*—the answer lies in society.[3] And it was Darwin's classical account (and its divers variations), from the side of natural history, which informed Leopold's thinking in the late 1940s.

*Page references are to Aldo Leopold's *A Sand County Almanac with Sketches Here and There* (New York: Oxford University Press, 1949).

Let me put the problem in perspective. How, we are asking, did ethics originate and, once in existence, grow in scope and complexity?

The oldest answer in living human memory is theological. God (or the gods) imposes morality on people. And God (or the gods) sanctions it. A most vivid and graphic example of this kind of account occurs in the Bible when Moses goes up on Mount Sinai to receive the Ten Commandments directly from God. That text also clearly illustrates the divine sanctions (plagues, pestilences, droughts, military defeats, etc.) for moral disobedience. Ongoing revelation of the divine will, of course, as handily and as simply explains subsequent moral growth and development.

Western philosophy, on the other hand, is almost unanimous in the opinion that the origin of ethics in human experience has somehow to do with human reason. Reason figures centrally and pivotally in the "social contract theory" of the origin and nature of morals in all its ancient, modern, and contemporary expressions from Protagoras, to Hobbes, to Rawls. Reason is the wellspring of virtue, according to both Plato and Aristotle, and of categorical imperatives, according to Kant. In short, the weight of Western philosophy inclines to the view that we are moral beings because we are rational beings. The ongoing sophistication of reason and the progressive illumination it sheds upon the good and the right explain "the ethical sequence," the historical growth and development of morality, noticed by Leopold.

An evolutionary natural historian, however, cannot be satisfied with either of these general accounts of the origin and development of ethics. The idea that God gave morals to man is ruled out in principle—as any supernatural explanation of a natural phenomenon is ruled out in principle in natural science. And while morality might *in principle* be a function of human reason (as, say, mathematical calculation clearly is), to suppose that it is so *in fact* would be to put the cart before the horse. Reason appears to be a delicate, variable, and recently emerged faculty. It cannot, under any circumstances, be supposed to have evolved in the absence of complex linguistic capabilities which depend, in turn, for their evolution upon a highly developed social matrix. But we cannot have become social beings unless we assumed limitations on freedom of action in the struggle for existence. Hence we must have become ethical before we became rational.

Darwin, probably in consequence of reflections somewhat like these, turned to a minority tradition of modern philosophy for a moral psychology consistent with and useful to a general evolutionary account of ethical phenomena. A century earlier, Scottish philosophers David Hume and Adam Smith had argued that ethics rest upon feelings or "sentiments"—which, to be sure, may be both amplified and informed by reason.[4] And since in the animal kingdom feelings or sentiments are arguably far more common or widespread than reason, they would be a far more likely starting point for an evolutionary account of the origin and growth of ethics.

Darwin's account, to which Leopold unmistakably (if elliptically) alludes in "The Land Ethic," begins with the parental and filial affections common, perhaps, to all mammals.[5] Bonds of affection and sympathy between parents and offspring permitted the formation of small, closely kin social groups, Darwin argued. Should the parental and filial affections bonding family members chance to extend to less closely related individuals, that would permit an enlargement of the family group. And should the newly extended community more successfully defend itself and/or more efficiently provision itself, the inclusive fitness of its members severally would be increased, Darwin reasoned. Thus, the more diffuse familial affections, which Darwin (echoing Hume and Smith) calls the "social sentiments," would be spread throughout a population.[6]

Morality, properly speaking—i.e., morality as opposed to mere altruistic instinct—requires, in Darwin's terms, "intellectual powers" sufficient to recall the past and imagine the future, "the power of language" sufficient to express "common opinion," and "habituation" to patterns of behavior deemed, by common opinion, to be socially acceptable and beneficial.[7] Even so, ethics proper, in Darwin's account, remains firmly rooted in moral feelings or social sentiments which were—no less than physical faculties, he expressly avers—naturally selected, by the advantages for survival and especially for successful reproduction, afforded by society.[8]

The protosociobiological perspective on ethical phenomena, to which Leopold as a natural historian was heir, leads him to a generalization which is remarkably explicit in his condensed and often merely resonant rendering of Darwin's more deliberate and extended paradigm: Since "the thing [ethics] has its origin in the tendency of interdependent individuals or groups to evolve modes of co-operation, . . . all ethics so far evolved rest upon a single premise: that the individual is a member of a community of interdependent parts" (202–3).

Hence, we may expect to find that the scope and specific content of ethics will reflect both the perceived boundaries and actual structure or organization of a cooperative community or society. *Ethics and society or community are correlative.* This single, simple principle constitutes a powerful tool for the analysis of moral natural history, for the anticipation of future moral development (including, ultimately, the land ethic), and for systematically deriving the specific precepts, the prescriptions and proscriptions, of an emergent and culturally unprecedented ethic like a land or environmental ethic.

Anthropological studies of ethics reveal that, in fact, the boundaries of the moral community are generally coextensive with the perceived boundaries of society.[9] And the peculiar (and, from the urbane point of view, sometimes inverted) representation of virtue and vice in tribal society—the virtue, for example, of sharing to the point of personal destitution and the vice of privacy and private property—reflects and fosters the life way of tribal peoples.[10] Darwin, in his leisurely, anecdotal discussion, paints a vivid picture of the intensity, peculiarity, and sharp circumscription of "savage" mores: "A savage will risk his life to save that of a member of the same community, but will be wholly indifferent about a stranger."[11] As Darwin portrays them, tribes-people are at once paragons of virtue "within the limits of the same tribe" and enthusiastic thieves, manslaughterers, and torturers without.[12]

For purposes of more effective defense against common enemies, or because of increased population density, or in response to innovations in subsistence methods and technologies, or for some mix of these or other forces, human societies have grown in extent or scope and changed in form or structure. Nations—like the Iroquois nation or the Sioux nation—came into being upon the merger of previously separate and mutually hostile tribes. Animals and plants were domesticated and erstwhile hunter-gatherers became herders and farmers. Permanent habitations were established. Trade, craft, and (later) industry flourished. With each change in society came corresponding and correlative changes in ethics. The moral community expanded to become coextensive with the newly drawn boundaries of societies and the representation of virtue and vice, right and wrong, good and evil, changed to accommodate, foster, and preserve the economic and institutional organization of emergent social orders.

Today we are witnessing the painful birth of a human super-community, global in scope. Modern transportation and communication technologies, international economic interdependencies, international economic entities, and nuclear arms have brought into being a "global village." It has not yet become fully formed and it is at tension—a very dangerous tension—with its predecessor, the nation-state. Its eventual institutional structure, a global federalism or whatever it may turn out to be, is, at this point, completely unpredictable. Interestingly, however, a corresponding global human ethic—the "human rights" ethic, as it is popularly called—has been more definitely articulated.

Most educated people today pay lip service at least to the ethical precept that all members of the human species, regardless of race, creed, or national origin, are endowed with certain fundamental rights which it is wrong not to respect. According to the evolutionary scenario set out by Darwin, the contemporary moral ideal of human rights is a response to a perception—however vague and indefinite—that mankind worldwide is united into one society, one community—however indeterminate or yet institutionally unorganized. As Darwin presciently wrote:

> As man advances in civilization, and small tribes are united into larger communities, the simplest reason would tell each individual that he ought to extend his social instincts and sympathies to all the members of the same nation, though personally unknown to him. This point being once reached, there is only an artificial barrier to prevent his sympathies extending to the men of all nations and races. If, indeed, such men are separated from him by great differences of appearance or habits, experience unfortunately shows us how long it is, before we look at them as our fellow-creatures.[13]

According to Leopold, the next step in this sequence beyond the still incomplete ethic of uni-

versal humanity, a step that is clearly discernible on the horizon, is the land ethic. The "community concept" has, so far, propelled the development of ethics from the savage clan to the family of man. "The land ethic simply enlarges the boundary of the community to include soils, waters, plants, and animals, or collectively: the land" (204).

As the foreword to *Sand County* makes plain, the overarching thematic principle of the book is the inculcation of the idea—through narrative description, discursive exposition, abstractive generalization, and occasional preachment—"that land is a community" (viii). The community concept is "the basic concept of ecology" (viii). Once land is popularly perceived as a biotic community—as it is professionally perceived in ecology—a correlative land ethic will emerge in the collective cultural consciousness.

Although anticipated as far back as the mid-eighteenth century—in the notion of an "economy of nature"—the concept of the biotic community was more fully and deliberately developed as a working model or paradigm for ecology by Charles Elton in the 1920s.[14] The natural world is organized as an intricate corporate society in which plants and animals occupy "niches," or as Elton alternatively called them, "roles" or "professions," in the economy of nature.[15] As in a feudal community, little or no socioeconomic mobility (upward or otherwise) exists in the biotic community. One is born to one's trade.

Human society, Leopold argues, is founded, in large part, upon mutual security and economic interdependency and preserved only by limitations on freedom of action in the struggle for existence—that is, by ethical constraints. Since the biotic community exhibits, as modern ecology reveals, an analogous structure, it too can be preserved, given the newly amplified impact of "mechanized man," only by analogous limitations on freedom of action—that is, by a land ethic (viii). A land ethic, furthermore, is not only "an ecological necessity," but an "evolutionary possibility" because a moral response to the natural environment—Darwin's social sympathies, sentiments, and instincts translated and codified into a body of principles and precepts—would be automatically triggered in human beings by ecology's social representation of nature (203).

Therefore, the key to the emergence of a land ethic is, simply, universal ecological literacy.

The land ethic rests upon three scientific cornerstones: (1) evolutionary and (2) ecological biology set in a background of (3) Copernican astronomy. Evolutionary theory provides the conceptual link between ethics and social organization and development. It provides a sense of "kinship with fellow-creatures" as well, "fellow-voyagers" with us in the "odyssey of evolution" (109). It establishes a diachronic link between people and nonhuman nature.

Ecological theory provides a synchronic link—the community concept—a sense of social integration of human and nonhuman nature. Human beings, plants, animals, soils, and waters are "all interlocked in one humming community of cooperations and competitions, one biota."[16] The simplest reason, to paraphrase Darwin, should, therefore, tell each individual that he or she ought to extend his or her social instincts and sympathies to all the members of the biotic community though different from him or her in appearance or habits.

And although Leopold never directly mentions it in *A Sand County Almanac*, the Copernican perspective, the perception of the Earth as "a small planet" in an immense and utterly hostile universe beyond, contributes, perhaps subconsciously, but nevertheless very powerfully, to our sense of kinship, community, and interdependence with fellow denizens of the Earth household. It scales the Earth down to something like a cozy island paradise in a desert ocean.

Here in outline, then, are the conceptual and logical foundations of the land ethic: Its conceptual elements are a Copernican cosmology, a Darwinian protosociobiological natural history of ethics, Darwinian ties of kinship among all forms of life on Earth, and an Eltonian model of the structure of biocenoses all overlaid on a Humean-Smithian moral psychology. Its logic is that natural selection has endowed human beings with an affective moral response to perceived bonds of kinship and community membership and identity; that today the natural environment, the land, is represented as a community, the biotic community; and that, therefore, an environmental or land ethic is both possible—the biopsychological and cognitive conditions are in place—and necessary, since human beings collectively have acquired the power to destroy the integrity, diversity, and stability of the environing and supporting economy of nature. In the remainder of this essay I discuss special fea-

tures and problems of the land ethic germane to moral philosophy.

The most salient feature of Leopold's land ethic is its provision of what Kenneth Goodpaster has carefully called "moral considerability" for the biotic community per se, not just for fellow members of the biotic community:[17]

> In short, a land ethic changes the role of *Homo sapiens* from conquerer of the land-community to plain member and citizen of it. It implies respect for his fellow-members, *and also respect for the community as such.* (204, emphasis added)

The land ethic, thus, has a holistic as well as an individualistic cast.

Indeed, as "The Land Ethic" develops, the focus of moral concern shifts gradually away from plants, animals, soils, and waters severally to the biotic community collectively. Toward the middle, in the subsection called Substitutes for a Land Ethic, Leopold invokes the "biotic rights" of *species*—as the context indicates—of wildflowers, songbirds, and predators. In The Outlook, the climatic section of "The Land Ethic," nonhuman natural entities, first appearing as fellow members, then considered in profile as species, are not so much as mentioned in what might be called the "summary moral maxim" of the land ethic: "A thing is right when it tends to preserve the integrity, stability, and beauty of the biotic community. It is wrong when it tends otherwise" (224–25).

By this measure of right and wrong, not only would it be wrong for a farmer, in the interest of higher profits, to clear the woods off a 75 percent slope, turn his cows into the clearing, and dump its rainfall, rocks, and soil into the community creek, it would also be wrong for the federal fish and wildlife agency, in the interest of individual animal welfare, to permit populations of deer, rabbits, feral burros, or whatever to increase unchecked and, thus to threaten the integrity, stability, and beauty of the biotic communities of which they are members. The land ethic not only provides moral considerability for the biotic community per se, but ethical consideration of its individual members is preempted by concern for the preservation of the integrity, stability, and beauty of the biotic community. The land ethic, thus, not only has a holistic aspect; it is holistic with a vengeance.

The holism of the land ethic, more than any other feature, sets it apart from the predominant paradigm of modern moral philosophy. It is, therefore, the feature of the land ethic which requires the most patient theoretical analysis and the most sensitive practical interpretation.

As Kenneth Goodpaster pointed out, mainstream modern ethical philosophy has taken egoism as its point of departure and reached a wider circle of moral entitlement by a process of generalization:[18] I am sure that *I*, the enveloped ego, am intrinsically or inherently valuable and thus that *my* interests ought to be considered, taken into account, by "others" when their actions may substantively affect *me*. My own claim to moral consideration, according to the conventional wisdom, ultimately rests upon a psychological capacity—rationality or sentiency were the classical candidates of Kant and Bentham, respectively—which is arguably valuable in itself and which thus qualifies *me* for moral standing.[19] However, then I am forced grudgingly to grant the same moral consideration I demand from others, on this basis, to those others who can also claim to possess the same general psychological characteristic.

A *criterion* of moral value and consideration is thus identified. Goodpaster convincingly argues that mainstream modern moral theory is based, when all the learned dust has settled, on this simple paradigm of ethical justification and logic exemplified by the Benthamic and Kantian prototypes.[20] If the criterion of moral value and consideration is pushed low enough—as it is in Bentham's criterion of sentiency—a wide variety of animals are admitted to moral entitlement.[21] If the criterion of moral value and consideration is pushed lower still—as it is in Albert Schweitzer's reverence-for-life ethic—all minimally conative things (plants as well as animals) would be extended moral consideration.[22] The contemporary animal liberation/rights, and reverence-for-life/life-principle ethics are, at bottom, simply direct applications of the modern classical paradigm of moral argument. But this standard modern model of ethical theory provides no possibility whatever for the moral consideration of wholes—of threatened *populations* of animals and plants, or of endemic, rare, or endangered *species,* or of biotic *communities,* or most expansively, of the *biosphere* in its totality—since wholes per se have no psychological experience of any kind.[23] Because mainstream modern moral theory has been "psychocentric, " it has been radically and intractably individualistic or "atomistic" in its fundamental theoretical orientation.

Hume, Smith, and Darwin diverged from the prevailing theoretical model by recognizing that altruism is as fundamental and autochthonous in human nature as is egoism. According to their analysis, moral value is not identified with a natural quality objectively present in morally considerable beings—as reason and/or sentiency is objectively present in people and/or animals—it is, as it were, projected by valuing subjects.[24]

Hume and Darwin, furthermore, recognize inborn moral sentiments which have society as such as their natural object. Hume insists that "we must renounce the theory which accounts for every moral sentiment by the principle of self-love. We must adopt a more *public affection* and allow that the *interests of society* are not, *even on their own account,* entirely indifferent to us."[25] And Darwin, somewhat ironically (since "Darwinian evolution" very often means natural selection operating exclusively with respect to individuals), sometimes writes as if morality had no other object than the commonweal, the welfare of the community as a corporate entity:

> We have now seen that actions are regarded by savages, and were probably so regarded by primeval man, as good or bad, solely as they obviously affect the welfare of the tribe, —not that of the species, nor that of individual members of the tribe. This conclusion agrees well with the belief that the so-called moral sense is aboriginally derived from social instincts, for both relate at first exclusively to the community.[26]

Theoretically then, the biotic community owns what Leopold, in the lead paragraph of The Outlook, calls "value in the philosophical sense"—i.e., direct moral considerability—because it is a newly discovered proper object of a specially evolved "public affection" or "moral sense" which all psychologically normal human beings have inherited from a long line of ancestral social primates (223).[27]

In the land ethic, as in all earlier stages of social-ethical evolution, there exists a tension between the good of the community as a whole and the "rights" of its individual members considered severally. While The Ethical Sequence section of

"The Land Ethic" clearly evokes Darwin's classical biosocial account of the origin and extension of morals, Leopold is actually more explicitly concerned, in that section, with the interplay between the holistic and individualistic moral sentiments—sympathy and fellow-feeling on the one hand, and public affection for the commonweal on the other:

> The first ethics dealt with the relation between individuals; the Mosaic Decalogue is an example. Later accretions dealt with the relation between the individual and society. The Golden Rule tries to integrate the individual to society; democracy to integrate social organization to the individual. (202–3)

Actually, it is doubtful that the first ethics dealt with the relation between individuals and not at all with the relation between the individual and society. (This, along with the remark that ethics replaced an "original free-for-all competition," suggests that Leopold's Darwinian line of thought has been uncritically tainted with Hobbesean elements [202]. Of course, Hobbes's "state of nature," in which there prevailed a war of each against all, is absurd from an evolutionary point of view.) A century of ethnographic studies seems to confirm, rather, Darwin's conjecture that the relative weight of the holistic component is greater in tribal ethics—the tribal ethic of the Hebrews recorded in the Old Testament constitutes a vivid case in point—than in more recent accretions. The Golden Rule, on the other hand, does not mention, in any of its formulations, society per se. Rather, its primary concern seems to be "others," i.e., other human individuals. Democracy, with its stress on individual liberties and rights, seems to further rather than countervail the individualistic thrust of the Golden Rule.

In any case, the conceptual foundations of the land ethic provide a well-formed, self-consistent theoretical basis for including both fellow members of the biotic community and the biotic community itself (considered as a corporate entity) within the purview of morals. The preemptive emphasis, however, on the welfare of the community as a whole, in Leopold's articulation of the land ethic, while certainly *consistent* with its Humean-Darwinian theoretical foundations, is not *determined* by them alone. The overriding holism of the land ethic results, rather, more from the way our moral sensibilities are informed by ecology.

Ecological thought, historically, has tended to be holistic in outlook.[28] Ecology is the study of the *relationships* of organisms to one another and to the elemental environment. These relationships bind the *relata*—plants, animals, soils, and waters—into a seamless fabric. The ontological primacy of objects and the ontological subordination of relationships, characteristic of classical Western science, is, in fact, reversed in ecology.[29] Ecological relationships determine the nature of organisms rather than the other way around. A species is what it is because it has adapted to a niche in the ecosystem. The whole, the system itself, thus, literally and quite straightforwardly shapes and forms its component parts.

Antedating Charles Elton's community model of ecology was F. E. Clements' and S. A. Forbes' organism model.[30] Plants and animals, soils and waters, according to this paradigm, are integrated into one superorganism. Species are, as it were, its organs; specimens its cells. Although Elton's community paradigm (later modified, as we shall see, by Arthur Tansley's ecosystem idea) is the principal and morally fertile ecological concept of "The Land Ethic," the more radically holistic superorganism paradigm of Clements and Forbes resonates in "The Land Ethic" as an audible overtone. In the peroration of Land Health and the A–B Cleavage, for example, which immediately precedes The Outlook, Leopold insists that

> in all of these cleavages, we see repeated the same basic paradoxes: man the conqueror *versus* man the biotic citizen; science the sharpener of his sword *versus* science the searchlight on his universe; land the slave and servant *versus* land the collective organism. (223)

And on more than one occasion Leopold, in the latter quarter of "The Land Ethic," talks about the "health" and "disease" of the land—terms which are at once descriptive and normative and which, taken literally, characterize only organisms proper.

In an early essay, "Some Fundamentals of Conservation in the Southwest," Leopold speculatively flirted with the intensely holistic superorganism model of the environment as a paradigm pregnant with moral implications:

> It is at least not impossible to regard the earth's parts—soil, mountains, rivers, atmosphere, etc. —as organs or parts of organs, of *a coordinated whole,* each part with a definite function. And if we could see *this whole, as a*

whole, through a great period of time, we might perceive not only organs with coordinated functions, but possibly also that process of consumption and replacement which in biology we call metabolism, or growth. In such a case we would have all the visible attributes of a living thing, which we do not realize to be such because it is too big, and its life processes too slow. And there would also follow that invisible attribute—a soul or consciousness—which . . . many philosophers of all ages ascribe to all living things and aggregates thereof, including the "dead" earth.

Possibly in our intuitive perceptions, which may be truer than our science and less impeded by words than our philosophies, we realize the indivisibility of the earth—its soil, mountains, rivers, forests, climate, plants, and animals—and *respect it collectively* not only as a useful servant but as a living being, vastly less alive than ourselves, but vastly greater than ourselves in time and space. . . . Philosophy, then, suggests one reason why we cannot destroy the earth with moral impunity; namely, that the "dead" earth is an organism possessing a certain kind and degree of life, which we intuitively respect as such.[31]

Had Leopold retained this overall theoretical approach in "The Land Ethic," the land ethic would doubtless have enjoyed more critical attention from philosophers. The moral foundations of a land or, as he might then have called it, "earth" ethic, would rest upon the hypothesis that the Earth is alive and ensouled—possessing inherent psychological characteristics, logically parallel to reason and sentiency. This notion of a conative whole Earth could plausibly have served as a general criterion of intrinsic worth and moral considerability, in the familiar format of mainstream moral thought.

Part of the reason, therefore, that "The Land Ethic" emphasizes more and more the integrity, stability, and beauty of the environment as a whole, and less and less the "biotic right" of individual plants and animals to life, liberty, and the pursuit of happiness, is that the superorganism ecological paradigm invites one, much more than does the community paradigm, to hypostatize, to reify the whole, and to subordinate its individual members.

In any case, as we see, rereading "The Land Ethic" in light of "Some Fundamentals," the whole Earth organism image of nature is vestigially present in Leopold's later thinking. Leopold may have abandoned the "earth ethic" because ecology had abandoned the organism analogy, in favor of the community analogy, as a working theoretical paradigm. And the community model was more suitably given moral implications by the social/sentimental ethical natural history of Hume and Darwin.

Meanwhile, the biotic community ecological paradigm itself had acquired, by the late thirties and forties, a more holistic cast of its own. In 1935 British ecologist Arthur Tansley pointed out that from the perspective of physics the "currency" of the "economy of nature" is energy.[32] Tansley suggested that Elton's qualitative and descriptive food chains, food webs, trophic niches, and biosocial professions could be quantitatively expressed by means of a thermodynamic flow model. It is Tansley's state-of-the-art thermodynamic paradigm of the environment that Leopold explicitly sets out as a "mental image of land" in relation to which "we can be ethical" (214). And it is the ecosystemic model of land which informs the cardinal practical precepts of the land ethic.

The Land Pyramid is the pivotal section of "The Land Ethic"—the section which effects a complete transition from concern for "fellow-members" to the "community as such." It is also its longest and most technical section. A description of the "ecosystem" (Tansley's deliberately nonmetaphorical term) begins with the sun. Solar energy "flows through a circuit called the biota" (215). It enters the biota through the leaves of green plants and courses through plant-eating animals, and then on to omnivores and carnivores. At last the tiny fraction of solar energy converted to biomass by green plants remaining in the corpse of a predator, animal feces, plant detritus, or other dead organic material is garnered by decomposers—worms, fungi, and bacteria. They recycle the participating elements and degrade into entropic equilibrium any remaining energy. According to this paradigm

> land, then, is not merely soil; it is a fountain of energy flowing through a circuit of soils, plants, and animals. Food chains are the living channels which conduct energy upward; death and decay return it to the soil. The circuit is not closed; . . . but it is a sustained circuit, like a slowly augmented revolving fund of life. (216)

In this exceedingly abstract (albeit poetically expressed) model of nature, process precedes substance and energy is more fundamental than matter. Individual plants and animals become less autonomous beings than ephemeral structures in a patterned flux of energy. According to Yale biophysicist Harold Morowitz,

> viewed from the point of view of modern [ecology], each living thing . . . is a dissipative structure, that is, it does not endure in and of itself but only as a result of the continual flow of energy in the system. An example might be instructive. Consider a vortex in a stream of flowing water. The vortex is a structure made of an ever-changing group of water molecules. It does not exist as an entity in the classical Western sense; it exists only because of the flow of water through the stream. In the same sense, the structures out of which biological entities are made are transient, unstable entities with constantly changing molecules, dependent on a constant flow of energy from food in order to maintain form and structure. . . . From this point of view the reality of individuals is problematic because they do not exist per se but only as local perturbations in this universal energy flow.[33]

Though less bluntly stated and made more palatable by the unfailing charm of his prose, Leopold's proffered mental image of land is just as expansive, systemic, and distanced as Morowitz'. The maintenance of "the complex structure of the land and its smooth functioning as an energy unit" emerges in The Land Pyramid as the *summum bonum* of the land ethic (216).

From this good Leopold derives several practical principles slightly less general, and therefore more substantive, than the summary moral maxim of the land ethic distilled in The Outlook. "The trend of evolution [not its "goal," since evolution is ateleological] is to elaborate and diversify the biota" (216). Hence, among our cardinal duties is the duty to preserve what species we can, especially those at the apex of the pyramid—the top carnivores. "In the beginning, the pyramid of life was low and squat; the food chains short and simple. Evolution has added layer after layer, link after link" (215–16). Human activities today, especially those, like systematic deforestation in the tropics, resulting in abrupt massive extinctions of species, are in effect "devolutionary"; they flatten the biotic pyramid; they choke off some of the channels and gorge others (those which terminate in our own species).[34]

The land ethic does not enshrine the ecological status quo and devalue the dynamic dimension of nature. Leopold explains that "evolution is a long series of self-induced changes, the net result of which has been to elaborate the flow mechanism and to lengthen the circuit. Evolutionary changes, however, are usually slow and local. Man's invention of tools has enabled him to make changes of unprecedented violence, rapidity, and scope" (216–17). "Natural" species extinction, i.e., species extinction in the normal course of evolution, occurs when a species is replaced by competitive exclusion or evolves into another form.[35] Normally speciation outpaces extinction. Mankind inherited a richer, more diverse world than had ever existed before in the 3.5 billion-year odyssey of life on Earth.[36] What is wrong with anthropogenic species extirpation and extinction is the *rate* at which it is occurring and the *result:* biological impoverishment instead of enrichment.

Leopold goes on here to condemn, in terms of its impact on the ecosystem, "the world-wide pooling of faunas and floras," i.e., the indiscriminate introduction of exotic and domestic species and the dislocation of native and endemic species; mining the soil for its stored biotic energy, leading ultimately to diminished fertility and to erosion; and polluting and damming water courses (217).

According to the land ethic, therefore: Thou shalt not extirpate or render species extinct; thou shalt exercise great caution in introducing exotic and domestic species into local ecosystems, in extracting energy from the soil and releasing it into the biota, and in damming or polluting water courses; and thou shalt be especially solicitous of predatory birds and mammals. Here in brief are the express moral precepts of the land ethic. They are all explicitly informed—not to say derived—from the energy circuit model of the environment.

The living channels—"food chains"—through which energy courses are composed of individual plants and animals. A central, stark fact lies at the heart of ecological processes: Energy, the currency of the economy nature, passes from one organism to another, not from hand to hand, like coined money, but, so to speak, from stomach to stomach. Eating *and being eaten,* living *and dying* are what make the biotic community hum.

The precepts of the land ethic, like those of all previous accretions, reflect and reinforce the structure of the community to which it is correlative. Trophic asymmetries constitute the kernel of the biotic community. It seems unjust, unfair. But that is how the economy of nature is organized (and has been for thousands of millions of years). The land ethic, thus, affirms as good, and strives to preserve, the very inequities in nature whose social counterparts in human communities are condemned as bad and would be eradicated by familiar social ethics, especially by the more recent Christian and secular egalitarian exemplars. A "right to life" for individual members is not consistent with the structure of the biotic community and hence is not mandated by the land ethic. This disparity between the land ethic and its more familiar social precedents contributes to the apparent devaluation of individual *members* of the biotic community and augments and reinforces the tendency of the land ethic, driven by the systemic vision of ecology, toward a more holistic or community-per-se orientation.

Of the few moral philosophers who have given the land ethic a moment's serious thought, most have regarded it with horror because of its emphasis on the good of the community and its deemphasis on the welfare of individual members of the community. Not only are other sentient creatures members of the biotic community and subordinate to its integrity, beauty, and stability; so are *we*. Thus, if it is not only morally permissible, from the point of view of the land ethic, but morally required, that members of certain species be abandoned to predation and other vicissitudes of wild life or even deliberately culled (as in the case of alert and sentient whitetail deer) for the sake of the integrity, stability, and beauty of the biotic community, how can we consistently exempt ourselves from a similar draconian regime? We too are only "plain members and citizens" of the biotic community. And our global population is growing unchecked. According to William Aiken, from the point of view of the land ethic, therefore, "massive human diebacks would be good. It is our duty to cause them. It is our species' duty, relative to the whole, to eliminate 90 percent of our numbers." Thus, according to Tom Regan, the land ethic is a clear case of "environmental fascism."[37]

Of course Leopold never intended the land ethic to have either inhumane or antihumanitarian implications or consequences. But whether he intended them or not, a logically consistent deduction from the theoretical premises of the land ethic might force such untoward conclusions. And given their magnitude and monstrosity, these derivations would constitute a *reductio ad absurdum* of the whole land ethic enterprise and entrench and reinforce our current human chauvinism and moral alienation from nature. If this is what membership in the biotic community entails, then all but the most radical misanthropes would surely want to opt out.

The land ethic, happily, implies neither inhumane nor inhuman consequences. That some philosophers think it must follows more from their own theoretical presuppositions than from the theoretical elements of the land ethic itself. Conventional modern ethical theory rests moral entitlement, as I earlier pointed out, on a criterion or qualification. If a candidate meets the criterion—rationality or sentiency are the most commonly posited—he, she, or it is entitled to equal moral standing with others who possess the same qualification in equal degree. Hence, reasoning in this philosophically orthodox way, and forcing Leopold's theory to conform: If human beings are, with other animals, plants, soils, and waters, equally members of the biotic community, and if community membership is the criterion of equal moral consideration, then not only do animals, plants, soils, and waters have equal (highly attenuated) "rights," but human beings are equally subject to the same subordination of individual welfare and rights in respect to the good of the community as a whole.

But the land ethic, as I have been at pains to point out, is heir to a line of moral analysis different from that institutionalized in contemporary moral philosophy. From the biosocial evolutionary analysis of ethics upon which Leopold builds the land ethic, it (the land ethic) neither replaces nor overrides previous accretions. Prior moral sensibilities and obligations attendant upon and correlative to prior strata of social involvement remain operative and preemptive.

Being citizens of the United States, or the United Kingdom, or the Soviet Union, or Venezuela, or some other nation-state, and therefore having national obligations and patriotic duties, does not mean that we are not also members of smaller communities or social groups—cities or townships, neighborhoods, and families—or that we are relieved of the peculiar moral responsibilities attendant upon and correlative to these memberships as well. Similarly, our recognition of the biotic community and our immersion in it does not imply that we do not also remain members of the human community—the "family of man" or "global village"—or that we are relieved of the attendant and correlative moral responsibilities of that membership, among them to respect universal human rights and uphold the principles of individual human worth and dignity. The biosocial development of morality does not grow in extent like an expanding balloon, leaving no trace of its previous boundaries, so much as like the circumference of a tree.[38] Each emergent, and larger, social unit is layered over the more primitive, and intimate, ones.

Moreover, as a general rule, the duties correlative to the inner social circles to which we belong eclipse those correlative to the rings farther from the heartwood when conflicts arise. Consider our moral revulsion when zealous ideological nationalists encourage children to turn their parents in to the authorities if their parents should dissent from the political or economic doctrines of the ruling party. A zealous environmentalist who advocated visiting war, famine, or pestilence on human populations (those existing somewhere else, of course) in the name of the integrity, beauty, and stability of the biotic community would be similarly perverse. Family obligations in general come before nationalistic duties and humanitarian obligations in general come before environmental duties. The land ethic, therefore, is not draconian or fascist. It does not cancel human morality. The land ethic may, however, as with any new accretion, demand choices which affect, in turn, the demands of the more interior social-ethical circles. Taxes and the military draft may conflict with family-level obligations. While the land ethic, certainly, does not cancel human morality, neither does it leave it unaffected.

Nor is the land ethic inhumane. Nonhuman fellow members of the biotic community have no "human rights," because they are not, by definition, members of the human community. As fellow members of the biotic community, however, they deserve respect.

How exactly to express or manifest respect, while at the same time abandoning our fellow members of the biotic community to their several fates or even actively consuming them for our own needs (and wants), or deliberately making them casualties of wildlife management for ecological integrity, is a difficult and delicate question.

Fortunately, American Indian and other traditional patterns of human-nature interaction provide rich and detailed models. Algonkian woodland peoples, for instance, represented animals, plants, birds, waters, and minerals as other-than-human persons engaged in reciprocal, mutually beneficial socioeconomic intercourse with human beings.[39] Tokens of payment, together with expressions of apology, were routinely offered to the beings whom it was necessary for these Indians to exploit. Care not to waste the usable parts, and care in the disposal of unusable animal and plant remains, were also an aspect of the respectful, albeit necessarily consumptive, Algonkian relationship with fellow members of the land community. As I have more fully argued elsewhere, the Algonkian portrayal of human–nature relationships is, indeed, although certainly different in specifics, identical in abstract form to that recommended by Leopold in the land ethic.[40] . . .

Today, two processes internal to civilization are bringing us to a recognition that our renunciation of our biotic citizenship was a mistaken self-deception. Evolutionary science and ecological science, which certainly are products of modern civilization now supplanting the anthropomorphic and anthropocentric myths of earlier civilized generations, have rediscovered our integration with the biotic community. And the negative feedback received from modern civilization's technological impact upon nature—pollution, biological impoverishment, etc.—forcefully reminds us that mankind never really has, despite past assumptions to the contrary, existed apart from the environing biotic community.

This reminder of our recent rediscovery of our biotic citizenship brings us face to face with the paradox posed by Peter Fritzell.[41] Either we are plain members and citizens of the biotic community, on a par with other creatures, or we are not. If we are, then we have no moral obligations to our fellow members or to the community per se because, as understood from a modern scientific perspective, nature and natural phenomena are amoral. Wolves and alligators do no wrong in killing and eating deer and dogs (respectively). Elephants cannot be blamed for bulldozing acacia trees and generally wreaking havoc in their natural habitats. If human beings are natural beings, then human behavior, however destructive, is natural behavior and is as blameless, from a natural point of view, as any other behavioral phenomenon exhibited by other natural beings. On the other hand, we are moral beings, the implication seems clear, precisely to the extent that we are civilized, that we have removed ourselves from nature. We are more than natural beings; we are metanatural—not to say, "supernatural"—beings. But then our moral community is limited to only those beings who share our transcendence of nature, i.e., to human beings (and perhaps to pets who have joined our civilized community as surrogate persons) and to the human community. Hence, have it either way—we are members of the biotic community or we are not—a land or environmental ethic is aborted by either choice.

But nature is *not* amoral. The tacit assumption that we are deliberating, choice-making ethical beings only to the extent that we are metanatural, civilized beings, generates this dilemma. The biosocial analysis of human moral behavior, in which the land ethic is grounded, is designed precisely to show that in fact intelligent moral behavior *is* natural behavior. Hence, we are moral beings not in spite of, but in accordance with, nature. To the extent that nature has produced at least one ethical species, *Homo sapiens,* nature is not amoral.

Alligators, wolves, and elephants are not subject to reciprocal interspecies duties or land ethical obligations themselves because they are incapable of conceiving and/or assuming them. Alligators, as mostly solitary, entrepreneurial reptiles, have no apparent moral sentiments or social instincts whatever. And while wolves and elephants certainly do have social instincts and at least protomoral sentiments, as their social behavior amply indicates, their conception or imagination of community appears to be less culturally plastic than ours and less amenable to cognitive information. Thus, while we might regard them as ethical beings, they are not able, as we are, to form the concept of a universal biotic community, and hence conceive an all-inclusive, holistic land ethic.

The paradox of the land ethic, elaborately noticed by Fritzell, may be cast more generally still in more conventional philosophical terms: Is the land ethic prudential or deontological? Is the land ethic, in other words, a matter of enlightened (collective, human) self-interest, or does it genuinely admit nonhuman natural entities and nature as a whole to true moral standing?

The conceptual foundations of the land ethic, as I have here set them out, and much of Leopold's hortatory rhetoric, would certainly indicate that the land ethic is deontological (or duty oriented) rather than prudential. In the section significantly titled The Ecological Conscience, Leopold complains that the then-current conservation philosophy is inadequate because "it defines no right or wrong, assigns no obligations, calls for no sacrifice, implies no change in the current philosophy of values. In respect of land-use, it urges *only* enlightened self-interest" (207–8, emphasis added). Clearly, Leopold himself thinks that the land ethic goes beyond prudence. In this section he disparages mere "self-interest" two more times, and concludes that "obligations have no meaning without conscience, and the problem we face is the extension of the social conscience from people to land" (209).

In the next section, Substitutes for a Land Ethic, he mentions rights twice—the "biotic right" of birds to continuance and the absence of a right on the part of human special interest to exterminate predators.

Finally, the first sentences of The Outlook read: "It is inconceivable to me that an ethical relation to land can exist without love, respect, and admiration for land, and a high regard for its value. By value, I of course mean something far broader than mere economic value; I mean value in the philosophical sense" (223). By "value in the philosophical sense," Leopold can only mean what philosophers more technically call "intrinsic value" or "inherent worth."[42] Something that has intrinsic value or inherent worth is valuable in and of itself, not because of what it can do for us. "Obligation," "sacrifice," "conscience," "respect," the ascription of rights, and intrinsic value—all of these are consistently opposed to self-interest and seem to indicate decisively that the land ethic is of the deontological type.

Some philosophers, however, have seen it differently. Scott Lehmann, for example, writes,

> Although Leopold claims for communities of plants and animals a "right to continued existence," his argument is homocentric, appealing to the human stake in preservation. Basically it is an argument from enlightened self-interest, where the self in question is not an individual human being but humanity—present and future—as a whole. . . .[43]

Lehmann's claim has some merits, even though it flies in the face of Leopold's express commitments. Leopold does frequently lapse into the language of (collective, long-range, human) self-interest. Early on, for example, he remarks, "in human history, we have learned (I hope) that the conqueror role is eventually *self*-defeating" (204, emphasis added). And later, of the 95 percent of Wisconsin's species which cannot be "sold, fed, eaten, or otherwise put to economic use," Leopold reminds us that "these creatures are members of the biotic community, and if (as I believe) its stability depends on its integrity, they are entitled to continuance" (210). The implication is clear: The economic 5 percent cannot survive if a significant portion of the uneconomic 95 percent are extirpated; nor may *we*, it goes without saying, survive without these "resources."

Leopold, in fact, seems to be consciously aware of this moral paradox. Consistent with the biosocial foundations of his theory, he expresses it in sociological terms:

> An ethic may be regarded as a mode of guidance for meeting ecological situations so new or intricate, or involving such deferred reactions, that the path of social expediency is not discernible to the average individual. Animal instincts are modes of guidance for the individual in meeting such situations. Ethics are possibly a kind of community instinct in-the-making. (203)

From an objective, descriptive sociological point of view, ethics evolve because they contribute to the inclusive fitness of their carriers (or, more reductively still, to the multiplication of their carriers' genes); they are expedient. However, the path to self-interest (or to the self-interest of the selfish gene) is not discernible to the participating individuals (nor, certainly, to their genes). Hence, ethics are grounded in instinctive feeling—love, sympathy, respect—not in self-conscious calculating intelligence. Somewhat like the paradox of hedonism—the notion that one cannot achieve happiness if one directly pursues happiness per se and not other things—one can only secure self-interest by putting the interests of others on a par with one's own (in this case long-range collective human self-interest and the interest of other forms of life and of the biotic community per se).

So, is the land ethic deontological or prudential, after all? It is both—self-consistently both—depending upon point of view. From the inside, from the lived, felt point of view of the community member with evolved moral sensibilities, it is deontological. It involves an affective-cognitive posture of genuine love, respect, admiration, obligation, self-sacrifice, conscience, duty, and the ascription of intrinsic value and biotic rights. From the outside, from the objective and analytic scientific point of view, it is prudential. "There is no other way for land to survive the impact of mechanized man," nor, therefore, for mechanized man to survive his own impact upon the land (viii).

Notes

1. Wallace Stegner, "The Legacy of Aldo Leopold"; Curt Meine, "Building 'The Land Ethic.'"; both in this volume. The oft-repeated characterization of Leopold as a prophet appears traceable to Roberts Mann, "Aldo Leopold: Priest and Prophet," *American Forests* 60, no. 8 (August 1954): 23, 42–43; it was picked up, apparently, by Ernest Swift, "Aldo Leopold: Wisconsin's Conservationist Prophet," *Wisconsin Tales and Trails* 2, no. 2 (September 1961): 2–5; Roderick Nash institutionalized it in his chapter, "Aldo Leopold: Prophet," in *Wilderness and the American Mind* (New Haven: Yale University Press, 1967; revised edition, 1982).

2. Edward O. Wilson, *Sociobiology: The New Synthesis* (Cambridge: Harvard University Press, 1975), 3. See also W. D. Hamilton, "The Genetical Theory of Social Behavior," *Journal of Theoretical Biology* 7 (1964): 1–52.

3. Charles R. Darwin, *The Descent of Man and Selection in Relation to Sex.* (New York: J. A. Hill and Company, 1904). The quoted phrase occurs on p. 97.

4. See Adam Smith, *Theory of the Moral Sentiments* (London and Edinburgh: A. Millar, A. Kinkaid, and J. Bell, 1759) and David Hume, *An Enquiry Concerning the Principles of Morals* (Oxford: The Clarendon Press, 1777; first published in 1751). Darwin cites both works in the key fourth chapter of *Descent* (pp. 106 and 109, respectively).

5. Darwin, *Descent*, p. 98 ff.

6. Ibid., p. 105 f.

7. Ibid., p. 113 ff.

8. Ibid., p. 105.

9. See, for example, Elman R. Service, *Primitive Social Organization: An Evolutionary Perspective* (New York: Random House, 1962).

10. See Marshall Sahlins, *Stone Age Economics* (Chicago: Aldine Atherton, 1972).

11. Darwin, *Descent*, p. III.

12. Ibid., p. 117 ff. The quoted phrase occurs on p. 118.

13. Ibid., p. 124.

14. See Donald Worster, *Nature's Economy: The Roots of Ecology* (San Francisco: Sierra Club Books, 1977).

15. Charles Elton, *Animal Ecology* (New York: Macmillan, 1927).

16. Aldo Leopold, *Round River* (New York: Oxford University Press, 1953), 148.

17. Kenneth Goodpaster, "On Being Morally Considerable," *Journal of Philosophy* 22 (1978): 308–25. Goodpaster wisely avoids the term *rights*, defined so strictly albeit so variously by philosophers, and used so loosely by nonphilosophers.

18. Kenneth Goodpaster, "From Egoism to Environmentalism" in *Ethics and Problems of the 21st Century*, ed. K. E. Goodpaster and K. M. Sayre (Notre Dame, IN: University of Notre Dame Press, 1979), pp. 21–35.

19. See Immanuel Kant, *Foundations of the Metaphysics of Morals* (New York: Bobbs-Merrill,1959; first published in 1785); and Jeremy Bentham, *An Introduction to the Principles of Morals and Legislation*, new edition (Oxford: The Clarendon Press, 1823).

20. Goodpaster, "Egoism to Environmentalism." Actually Goodpaster regards Hume and Kant as the co-fountainheads of this sort of moral philosophy. But Hume does not reason in this way. For Hume, the other-oriented sentiments are as primitive as self-love.

21. See Peter Singer, *Animal Liberation: A New Ethics for Our Treatment of Animals* (New York: Avon Books, 1975) for animal liberation; and see Tom Regan, *All That Dwell Therein: Animal Rights and Environmental Ethics* (Berkeley: University of California Press, 1982) for animal rights.

22. See Albert Schweitzer, *Philosophy of Civilization: Civilization and Ethics*, trans. John Naish (London: A. & C. Black, 1923). For a fuller discussion, see J. Baird Callicott, "On the Intrinsic Value of Non-human Species," in *The Preservation of Species*, ed. Bryan Norton (Princeton: Princeton University Press, 1986), pp. 138–72.

23. Peter Singer and Tom Regan are both proud of this circumstance and consider it a virtue. See Peter Singer, "Not for Humans Only: The Place of Nonhumans in Environmental Issues" in *Ethics and Problems of the 21st Century*, pp. 191–206; and Tom Regan, "Ethical Vegetarianism and Commercial Animal Farming" in *Contemporary Moral Problems*, ed. James E. White (St. Paul, MN: West Publishing Co., 1985), pp. 279–94.

24. See J. Baird Callicott, "Hume's Is/Ought Dichotomy and the Relation of Ecology to Leopold's Land Ethic," *Environmental Ethics* 4 (1982): 163–74, and "Non-anthropocentric Value Theory and Environmental Ethics," *American Philosophical Quarterly* 21 (1984): 299–309, for an elaboration.

25. Hume, *Enquiry,* p. 219.

26. Darwin, *Descent*, p. 120.

27. I have elsewhere argued that "value in the philosophical sense" means "intrinsic" or "inherent" value. See J. Baird Callicott, "The Philosophical Value of Wildlife," in *Valuing Wildlife: Economic and Social Values of Wildlife,* ed. Daniel J. Decker and Gary Goff (Boulder, CO: Westview Press, 1986), pp. 214–221.

28. See Worster, *Nature's Economy.*

29. See J. Baird Callicott, "The Metaphysical Implications of Ecology," *Environmental Ethics* 8 (1986):300–315, for an elaboration of this point.

30. Robert P. McIntosh, *The Background of Ecology: Concept and Theory* (Cambridge: Cambridge University Press, 1985).

31. Aldo Leopold, "Some Fundamentals of Conservation in the Southwest," *Environmental Ethics* 1 (1979):139–40, emphasis added.

32. Arthur Tansley, "The Use and Abuse of Vegetational Concepts and Terms," *Ecology* 16 (1935): 292–303.

33. Harold J. Morowitz, "Biology as a Cosmological Science," *Main Currents in Modern Thought* 28 (1972): 156.

34. I borrow the term "devolution" from Austin Meredith, "Devolution," *Journal of Theoretical Biology* 96 (1982):49–65.

35. Holmes Rolston III, "Duties to Endangered Species," *Bioscience* 35 (1985): 718–26. See also Geerat Vermeij, "The Biology of Human-Caused Extinction," in Norton, *Preservation of Species*, pp. 28–49.

36. See D. M. Raup and J. J. Sepkoski, Jr., "Mass Extinctions in the Marine Fossil Record," *Science* 215 (1982):1501–3.

37. William Aiken, "Ethical Issues in Agriculture," in *Earthbound: New Introductory Essays in Environmental Ethics,* ed. Tom Regan (New York: Random House, 1984), p. 269. Tom Regan, *The Case for Animal Rights* (Berkeley: University of California Press, 1983) p. 262, and "Ethical Vegetarianism," 291. See also Eliott Sober, "Philosophical Problems for Environmentalism," in Norton, *Preservation of Species*, pp. 173–94.

38. I owe the tree-ring analogy to Richard and Val Routley (now Sylvan and Plumwood, respectively), "Human Chauvinism and Environmental Ethics," in *Environmental Philosophy*, ed. D. Mannison, M. McRobbie, and R. Routley (Canberra: Department of Philosophy, Research School of the Social Sciences, Australian National University, 1980), pp. 96–189. A good illustration of the balloon analogy

may be found in Peter Singer, *The Expanding Circle: Ethics and Sociobiology* (New York: Farrar, Straus and Giroux, 1983).

39. For an elaboration see Thomas W. Overholt and J. Baird Callicott, *Clothed-in-Fur and Other Tales: An Introduction to an Ojibwa World View* (Washington, DC: University Press of America, 1982).

40. J. Baird Callicott, "Traditional American Indian and Western European Attitudes Toward Nature: An Overview," *Environmental Ethics* 4 (1982):163–74.

41. Peter Fritzell, "The Conflicts of Ecological Conscience," in *Companion to A Sand County Almanac*, ed. J. Baird Callicott (Madison: University of Wisconsin Press, 1987).

42. See Worster, *Nature's Economy*.

43. Scott Lehmann, "Do Wildernesses Have Rights?" *Environmental Ethics* 3 (1981), 131.

27. Marine Environmental Ethics

Elliot Norse

. . . [A] number of lines of evidence show that our marine environment ethics are less advanced than those we have on land. Here are some examples.

On land, someone who dumped vast amounts of sewage on public lands would be arrested, but we routinely do the same into our streams and rivers, which empty into our estuaries, coastal waters, and oceans, as if the act of flushing made wastes go away, vanishing without a trace.

But in a growing list of places, phytoplankton, tiny drifting marine plant-like cells, are stimulated by the nutrients from sewage and have population explosions. Some kinds become so abundant that, when they die, their decomposition depletes vast areas of oxygen.

The largest of these "dead zones" where oxygen-breathing life on the sea floor disappears is an area the size of the state of New Jersey off the mouth of the Mississippi on the Louisiana continental shelf.

And more and more of these population explosions, called phytoplankton blooms, are blooms of toxic phytoplankton species, ones whose cells produce poisons that kill other marine wildlife and can sicken people as well.

I suspect that you have heard about *Pfiesteria piscicida*, the species that attacks fishes by the millions and the nervous systems of fishermen, a species whose increase has been linked to the overloading of estuaries with hog and chicken wastes from intensive livestock operations.

My guess is that states would act to clean up these massive sewage sources much faster if these harmful algal blooms were happening on land. We have a long tradition of using our waters as toilets, a tradition that springs from our underdeveloped marine ethics.

On land the vast majority of food humans take is from species that we breed for desired traits and for which we provide nutrients before we harvest them. In many cases we work hard to eliminate their parasites, competitors, and predators.

In the sea, the vast majority of food humans take is from wild species that we don't breed, feed, or protect. We do, however, delude ourselves by using the same term for this catch of marine wildlife: we call it "harvest."

On land, people have to be licensed to hunt for large animals. Indeed, licenses for killing some species on federal lands, such as bighorn sheep, can run thousands of dollars. This provides money for habitat improvement for these species.

But in the sea, people view killing wildlife as a right, not a privilege. The commercial and sport-fishing industries have succeeded in preventing licensing for the killing of wildlife in areas under federal jurisdiction. What we prohibit or strictly regulate on land, we allow in the sea. Clearly this comes from different values we put on life on land and in the sea.

Where governments once encouraged killing of "vermin" because they sometimes kill "good"

From *Values at Sea: Ethics for the Marine Environment*, ed. Dorinda G. Dallmeyer, University of Georgia Press, 2003.

species such as deer and livestock, the growing recognition that predators play crucial roles in their ecosystems and that they are especially vulnerable because of their inherent rarity and slow reproduction, has led to protection for most species of large predators, from wolves to mountain lions and bald eagles.

You have probably seen old photos of proud men with big rifles with a foot on the head of a grizzly or a tiger. Notice I said old because you don't see such photos being taken now on land. But in the sea, the large predators—sharks, big tunas, swordfish, and marlin—are still eagerly sought by commercial and sportfishers as food and trophies.

You can see recent photos of men with big rods with a foot on the head of a giant bluefin tuna or tiger shark. You don't see many mounted cougar heads in homes and restaurants anymore, but mounted sailfishes are common. That difference comes from our different ethics.

On land, the federal government's USDA Forest Service permits clear-cut logging only in certain places under certain conditions, and charges loggers for doing so. But in the sea, the Department of Commerce's National Marine Fisheries Service allows fishers to trawl or dredge for fishes, scallops, and shrimp, an activity very similar in its effects on structure-forming species on the sea floor.

They can do it virtually anywhere they wish, and they don't have to compensate the taxpayers; it's absolutely free. Although the United States has complete regulatory control over economic activities such as fishing between the three-mile limit of state waters and the 200-mile limit of the Exclusive Economic Zone, far less than one percent of these submerged federal lands are off limits to the undersea equivalent of clear-cutting. Why is there such a marked difference?

Our National Parks and National Forests are the gems of the American landscape and the safest places we have for protecting our wealth of biological diversity. The closest analogue in the sea, our National Marine Sanctuaries, are far less numerous, cover a far smaller area, and are even more starved for funds.

In the 1998 federal budget request, the administration asked for 121 times more money for our National Parks and 235 times more money for our National Forests than for our National Marine

Sanctuaries. If, indeed, we are "putting our money where our mouth is," then the sea is being short-changed. That, in turn, comes from an environmental ethic that fails to consider the sea.

On land, the Endangered Species Act has protected a fraction of the thousands of species that we have put at high risk of extinction. America still has bald eagles, whooping cranes, gray wolves, and American alligators because of the Endangered Species Act.

But marine fishes, invertebrates, and plants have been given almost no such protection. No truly marine U.S. fish or invertebrate species has ever been listed under the Endangered Species Act, although a number, such as white and green abalone in California, are gravely endangered. We just assume that the sea is huge and invulnerable, and marine life can withstand whatever we throw at them.

Here's another. You probably know that there are now strict regulations that prevent people from introducing alien species into our country, lest we loose still another kudzu. Indeed, when you fly into the United States, you have to declare whether you have any plants, seeds, or even soil in your luggage; if you fail, you will be arrested and fined severely.

But ships routinely come from other countries to the United States with ballast tanks filled with millions of gallons of seawater containing vast numbers of adult and larval stages of marine organisms that are not native to our estuaries and coastal waters. They discharge this water when they enter port, introducing a huge inoculum of alien species. And this is entirely legal.

The result is a growing list of alien species in our ports, species that can wreak havoc with native marine species. In the state of Washington where I live, the European green crab arrived in 1998, after having established itself in San Francisco Bay in 1990. It is expected to devastate the oyster farming industry and other aquaculture operations.

One last one: over the last two decades, the young science of conservation biology has been making major contributions to resolving conservation fights on land.

In the Pacific northwest, experts on forest ecology, landscape ecology, ecosystem ecology, community dynamics, population demography, and genetics all made major contributions to slowing the logging of the last ancient forests that was fast eliminating spotted owls and a whole host of other species.

Scientists working together across the usual disciplinary lines helped to resolve this situation. But I had a strong suspicion that there wasn't anything like a comparable effort being devoted to marine conservation biology.

So I looked at papers published in the leading scientific journal in this field, *Conservation Biology*, and found that terrestrial papers outnumber marine papers 13 to 1. The scientific community had not yet awakened to the opportunities for research in marine conservation biology. Its marine environmental ethic hasn't been well developed.

My point with all these cases is not to say that our land ethic is good. It is not nearly strong enough. But I am saying that society's prevailing marine environmental ethic is even weaker than its land ethic.

By many measures, we are destroying our nation's marine environment even faster than we are destroying our land, and have far fewer measures for protecting life in the sea.

How can we change this? Where lies the root of change? It all starts with our ethics. If we see the sea as an inexhaustible cornucopia, or as a toilet with infinite assimilative capacity, we will continue on our current course.

One of the reasons why people hold these erroneous beliefs is that we barely started to examine the sea's vulnerability and resilience. To me, an obvious solution is to encourage the growth of a new science of marine conservation biology as a means of generating the information that will raise awareness of the finiteness and fragility of the sea among decision makers and the general public.

Ignorance is the worst enemy of marine conservation. Knowing is essential to the evolution of a viable marine environmental ethic. Perhaps the clearest and most powerful statement of this is from the Senegalese ecologist Baba Dioum, who said in 1968: "In the end we will conserve only what we love; we will love only what we understand; and we will understand only what we are taught."

The odds against saving the living sea might seem impossible to many people. But what's at stake is so great that I believe it is worth every bit of money and every erg of effort we can devote to generate the understanding necessary to establish a deeper, more enduring marine environmental ethic, one that calls on people to live as integral part[s] of a diverse, functioning biosphere instead of destroying it.

28. Integration or Reduction: Two Approaches to Environmental Values

Bryan G. Norton

Introduction: The Role of Environmental Ethicists in Policy Process

Environmental ethics has been dominated in its first twenty years by questions of axiology, as practitioners have mainly searched for a small set of coherent principles to guide environmental action. In axiological studies, a premium is placed on the systematization of moral intuitions, which is achieved when all moral judgments are shown to be derivable from a few central principles. The goal of these studies is to propose and defend a set of first principles that is (1) *complete* in the sense that this small set of principles can generate a single correct answer for every moral quandary and (2) *jointly justifiable* in the sense that, once the principles are warranted, then every particular moral directive derived from the principles must also be warranted.

Reprinted by permission of Routledge Ltd. from Bryan G. Norton, "Integration or Reduction: Two Approaches to Environmental Values," in *Environmental Pragmatism*, edited by Andrew Light and Eric Katz, 1996, pp. 105–38.

The limiting case of axiological simplification is *moral monism,* the view that a single principle suffices to support a uniquely correct moral judgment in every situation.[1] Monism represents to some philosophers an ideal because, provided the adopted principle is self-consistent, problems of coherence and consistency are resolved once and for all—there is no need to worry about what to do if two principles imply differing actions in a given situation, no worry that there will be irresoluble conflicts among competing and equally worthy moral claims. This reasoning motivates the drive towards unification.[2] The goal of environmental ethics as a discipline, in keeping with this ideal, has most centrally been to offer a unified and monistic account of our moral obligations. The adoption of this goal is what has given environmental ethics its axiological character.

What is curious is that this axiological approach rests on an assumption that is common to both sides in what has become a polarized debate: both neoclassical welfare economists—who believe that all value is expressible in units of individual, human welfare—and advocates of attributing inherent value to non-humans—who argue that the moral force of environmental principles derive from the moral considerability of natural objects—are unyieldingly monistic in their approaches. The adoption of the monistic viewpoint and the associated goal of developing a universal moral theory are applicable in all cases is inevitably "reductionistic." Because all values, which are experienced in multiple modes and contexts, must on the monistic approach be accounted for under a single theory, the basic strategy must be to reduce all moral concerns to a unified analytic vernacular in which solutions to specific moral quandaries are generated, by unavoidable inferences, from a single theory.

This shared assumption of monism has, I believe, locked environmental ethicists into a paralyzing dilemma, a dilemma that lies at the heart of most discussions of environmental values. Most participants in these discussions have subscribed to a crucial alternation in the theory of environmental valuation: either the value of nature is entirely instrumental to human objectives, or elements of nature have a "good of their own"—value not dependent on human valuations.[3] Could it be that the polarized thinking that paralyzes environmental policy today results from false alternatives forced upon us by the assumption, unquestioned by neoclassical economists and by most of their opponents among environmental ethicists alike, that whatever the units of environmental value turn out to be, there will be only one kind of them?

The thesis of this paper is that the goal of seeking a unified, monistic theory of environmental ethics represents a misguided mission, a mission that was formulated under a set of epistemological and moral assumptions that harks back to Descartes and Newton. An assessment of the contribution of environmental ethics to environmental policy in its first two decades is accordingly bleak. The search for a "Holy Grail" of unified theory in environmental values has not progressed towards any consensus regarding what inherent value in nature is, what objects have it, or what it means to have such value. Nor have environmental ethicists been able to offer useful practical advice by providing clear management directives regarding difficult and controversial problems in environmental planning and management.[4] One very practical effect of the monistic assumption is that the range of topics open for discussion in environmental ethics has been narrowed, and opportunities for building bridges with other, more practice-oriented disciplines have been lost. Another effect has been to define an often unhelpful role for environmental ethicists in environmental policy debates.

In order to emphasize these practical implications of the issues raised in this paper, I complete this introduction by drawing a distinction between "applied" and "practical" philosophy as representing two somewhat different roles for environmental policy. After this practice-oriented introduction, the remainder of the paper falls into two parts, one destructive and critical, and the other positive and speculative. Part 1 illustrates the problems of formulating a monistic environmental ethic by exploring the evolution of the monistic, ecocentric theory of J. Baird Callicott. This retrospective of Callicott's position, and a criticism of his current position, provide reasons to be very skeptical both of Callicott's specific monistic theory and also of his mission as he understands it.[5] As counterpoint to this negative argument, I briefly present a pluralist conception of the role and possible content of an environmental ethic in Part 2. Influenced by a pragmatist attitude towards social problems, I will sketch an environmental ethic that applies multiple principles, but one which seeks integration of these principles in a way that is sensitive to place orientation and to temporal and spatial scales.

Let me explain my basic methodology and advocate the importance of practice by reference to a distinction between two kinds of non-theoretical philosophy: I call them "applied" philosophy and "practical" philosophy, despite the fact that these terms are sometimes used interchangeably. I use them here to correspond to two somewhat different roles for philosophers in the process of public policy formation. Applied philosophy refers to the application of general philosophical principles in adjudications among policy goals and options. Applied philosophy's method is usually to develop very general and abstract principles and then to illustrate their use by discussing a few, carefully circumscribed hypothetical cases. This conception of the role of environmental ethicists has encouraged the confinement of philosophers, in their day-to-day work, within their traditional academic roles of teaching and writing. The actual applications of these principles is usually left to others such as environmental managers or environmental groups.[6] Moral monism and applied philosophy are naturally complementary—a single principle agreed on by all disputants provides just the sort of moral guidance that applied philosophers would like to give. They want to furnish a universal principle from which actual decision-makers can derive moral directives and then apply them to the cases they encounter in the day-to-day process of setting policy. Since the universal principle functions as an essential premise in an argument that one or another policy is justified, agreement on a policy option will emerge only if the general principle is accepted by all parties to the dispute.[7] Philosophers' contributions, given the role envisaged by applied philosophers, can only be as strong and decisive as the case for one universal principle. If some disputants do not accept the unitary moral principle proposed by applied philosophers, or if applied philosophers cannot agree among themselves regarding the formulation of the universal principle, they must retreat to theoretical arguments and attempt to establish more definitively the universal, monistic principle/premise before returning to applications. I therefore turn to a discussion of the assumptions that shape environmental ethicists' view of what they can offer in the policy process.

Practical philosophy, as I am defining it here in contrast to applied philosophy, is more problem-oriented; its chief characteristic is an emphasis on theories as tools of the understanding, tools that are developed to resolve specific policy controversies. It shares with applied philosophy the goal of contributing to problem solution; but practical philosophy does not assume that useful theoretical principles will be developed and established independent of the policy process and then applied within that process. It works towards theoretical principles by struggling with real cases, appealing to less sweeping rules of thumb that can be argued to be appropriate in a particular context, rather than establishing a universal theory and "applying" it to real cases. Practice is prior to theory in the sense that principles are ultimately generated from practice, not vice versa.

I do not mean to claim that theorizing is worthless; on the contrary, theory-building that addresses real-world problems, in the spirit of John Dewey and Aldo Leopold—the forester-philosopher—is absolutely essential if the environmental movement is to develop a vision for the future.[8] In the meantime, however, theoretical differences often need not impede progress in developing current policy; if all disputants agree on central management principles, even without agreeing on ultimate values, management can proceed on these principles.[9] And philosophers have a lot to offer policy-makers in specific, complex situations in which they face many conflicting moral directives, even though it has proved impossible for them to deliver the Holy Grail of monism as promised.

What sets practical philosophy in contrast to applied philosophy is the differing practices and impacts they envision for philosophers in the processes of policy articulation, evaluation and implementation. Not surprisingly, such deep differences in conceiving the role of environmental ethics are associated with differences of philosophical theory. This paper explores the philosophical beliefs and assumptions that shape the thinking of avowed applied philosophers.

Part 1: Monism and the Mission of Environmental Ethics

Having noted that moral monism and applied philosophy tend to go together, I now explain the reasons that have convinced me that the search for a monistic ethic is intellectually, as well as practically, misguided in a profound sense. Monists are not simply wrong in that they have not yet proposed the correct universal principle, or because they have not quite successfully specified the precise boundaries of moral considerability in nature. No, I believe that the entire project of shoehorning all of our obligations regarding other humans and nature into a "monistic" system of analysis is the wrong strategy at the wrong time, given that it allows decisive intervention in public policy formation only after a single, unified moral principle is articulated and agreed upon, an outcome that seems unlikely in the foreseeable future.

As noted above, monism is embraced by both environmental ethicists and economic theorists—both are equally "reductionistic" in this sense. In this paper I will focus on the dominant form of monism in environmental ethics—the large and diverse collection of theories that assert nature has value independent of humans in some sense.[10] It may not at first be clear how such theories achieve monism, so I begin by tracing briefly the development of the idea of human-independent value in the writings of J. Baird Callicott. Callicott provides an excellent case study for several reasons. First, his position claims less than other non-anthropocentric theories in the sense that Callicott does not assert that human-independent values in nature are independent of human consciousness; he claims only that value in nature is independent of human *valuations*. So criticisms of this moderate view may apply equally to theorists who defend a more radical independence of values in nature.[11] Second, Callicott has experimented with several different versions, or at least formulations, over the past fifteen years, and has readily noted shifts in his own thinking. By tracing Callicott's changing formulations of inherent value we can better understand the dynamic of a complex argument. Finally, Callicott has explicitly embraced monism, explained explicitly the sense in which he considers himself a monist and criticized pluralistic alternatives, providing us with greater insight into the nature and implications of monism as a moral mission.[12]

As a preliminary to this brief historical examination, it must be noted that Callicott and his monistic colleagues never question an underlying conceptual assumption, an assumption that lies at the heart of the assumed mission of applied environmental ethics: success in the axiology of environmental ethics must include as a centerpiece an answer to the question of *moral standing:* "What

beings are morally considerable?" Given the project of applied philosophy, it is not surprising that non-anthropocentrists believe that, whatever monistic principle or theory turns out to be the correct one, this principle will fulfill two conditions: (1) The principle/theory must specify what objects in nature are morally considerable. Interestingly, success in this specification has been identified with the task of identifying which objects in nature "own" their own inherent worth, of which more below. (2) The principle/theory must also provide some *motivation* for moral beings to protect natural objects. The universal, underlying principle is that moral individuals act to protect inherent value, wherever it is determined to reside. Condition (1) ensures environmental activists can identify which objects deserve moral consideration in any given situation. Condition (2) ensure[s] that goals to protect inherent value are invested with moral gravity.[13] Any morally committed environmentalist ought always to act so as to maximize the protection of inherent value, wherever it occurs. Monistic, non-anthropocentric theory can on these conditions rival economists in universalism. This monistic principle is attractive to philosophers who hope to resolve environmental problems by throwing fully formed, general principles over the edge of the ivory tower, to be used as intellectual armaments by the currently outgunned environmental activists, to aid them against the economic philistines in the political street wars that determine the fate of natural environments.

Callicott's Dilemma

This heroic version of applied philosophy's role in the policy process can be realized if environmental ethicists, laboring in the tower, can agree on which principles to throw down to the street-fighters. And, if these principles are to exert moral force to protect the environment, they must be "objectively" supportable.

The measure of objectivity, on Callicott's view, is the extent to which the central theory of environmental values succeeds in attributing human-independent value to natural objects themselves. In the words of Callicott, the blue whale and the Bridger wilderness "may therefore, be said in a quite definite, straightforward sense to own inherent value, that is to be valued *for themselves.*" Callicott goes on in the same paragraph to state that the institution of a "genuine" environmental ethic—one that recognizes inherent value in nature—provides the only defensible basis for the environmentalists' platform of social reforms: "Environmental policy decisions, because they may thus be based upon a genuine environmental ethic, may thus be rescued from reduction to cost–benefit analyses in which valued natural aesthetic, religious, and epistemic experiences are shadow priced and weighed against the usually overwhelming material and economic benefits of development and exploitation."[14] In this passage, Callicott commits himself to a good, old-fashioned realist interpretation of the problem of objectivity: "the very sense of the hypothesis that inherent or intrinsic value [sic: exists?] in nature seems to be that value *inheres* in natural objects as an intrinsic characteristic. To assert that something is inherently or intrinsically valuable seems, indeed, to entail that its value is objective."[15] What is interesting is that Callicott, having formulated the problem of objectivity in terms of representational realism, immediately retreats from asserting an objectivist solution. Instead he argues that his own Humean subjectivist solution asserts as much objectivity for claims that objects in nature own their inherent values as exists for scientific claims. So, Callicott's "ownership" theory of inherent value, which attributes to ecosystems their own inherent value, is offered to environmental activists as the fruits of his search for the Holy Grail of monistic ecocentrism.

Three comments are necessary. First, the general principle of "ecocentrism," so defined, hardly resolves the question of what beings in nature are proper owners of inherent value. The Bridger Wilderness and the blue whale are given as examples, but they themselves represent different scales on the biological hierarchy, and Callicott owes his readers an account of the breadth to which he would generalize these examples. Second, as long as the first comment remains unanswered, Callicott cannot claim to have provided any definitive policy direction to activists because they can only know what they are obliged under the universal principles of non-anthropocentrism to protect after they know what particular entities in nature have inherent value. Third, Callicott, who wishes to interpret the land ethic as a moral theory, betrays an underlying commitment to moral individualism. He interprets Leopold's holism as attributing inherent value to ecosystems *as individuals* who can "own"

their own goodness. But this conclusion only brings us to the heart of the matter—Callicott's original assumption that the land ethic is to be interpreted as monistic and holistic. It will therefore be necessary to look briefly at Callicott's changing definitions of ecocentric holism, and to question whether they express the kernel ideas of Leopold's land ethic.

In an important 1980 article, Callicott established himself as the leading interpreter and proponent of Aldo Leopold's land ethic, and also caused an important alteration in the intellectual terrain on which the principles of environmental ethics were to be debated in the subsequent decade.[16] Callicott showed that, if one took Leopold's holistic pronouncements and arguments seriously, the land ethic was logically incompatible with extensionist ethics of animal rights advocates whose individualistic ethics are based in utilitarianism or rights theory.

Callicott's initial interpretation of Leopold's land ethic was therefore boldly holistic and strongly non-anthropocentric. He argued that ecological communities, not individuals, are the real locus of values in nature (as we have learned by drawing out the metaphysical implications of ecology) and that individuals have value in so far as they contribute to ecosystematic processes that support the community, leaving the clear implication that protecting inherent value in nature might involve sacrificing individual specimens of *any* species—including, presumably, human individuals—if those individuals threaten "ecological integrity" of the biotic community. Not surprisingly, his position was attacked as brutal towards individual animals and apparently misanthropic. In particular, it was pointed out by critics that this reduction of all individual value to functional value in a larger whole smacks of fascism.[17]

Subsequently, admitting that he had left his holism unqualified in order to be provocative, Callicott offered a much more conventional view of our moral obligations to human individuals, other species, and ecosystems.[18] But Callicott revised the apparent implications of the bold holism of the 1980 paper without so much as questioning his earlier conclusions that the land ethic establishes the whole biotic community as a morally considerable being. What Callicott did instead was simply to specify how we should rank our obligations to various objects that have inherent value, theoretically and practically, in accord with the "communitarian" principles of the land ethic, taking communitarianism to imply that humans and other elements of nature make up one moral community among others. Nonhuman elements of nature, including species and biotic communities, have inherent value because they are morally considerable "owners" of their own value as members, along with humans, in the land community. He therefore explains why we may give precedence to obligations to family members or our human community over obligations to ecosystems: "we are members of nested communities each of which has a different structure and therefore different moral requirements . . . I have obligations to my fellow citizens which I do not have to human beings in general *and* I have obligations to human beings in general which I do not have towards animals in general."[19] Building on this graduation of obligations, Callicott extricates himself from charges of fascism thus: "our holistic environmental obligations are not preemptive. We are still subject to all the other more particular and individually oriented duties to the members of our various more circumscribed and intimate communities. And since they are closer to home, they come first."[20]

It is significant that Callicott shifts the grounds of the debate over fascism from obligations flowing from attributions of inherent value—the central source of normative obligation in his monistic theory—to the origins of special obligations that emerge in specific communities in biology, culture and ecology; he differentiates the obligations according to the intimacy of the community. There can be multiple criteria of right action—one stringent criterion of protectionism applicable in cases of parents to children, and a less stringent moral criterion of protectionism that applies to the broader, ecological community. The commitment to moral monism recedes into the theoretical background as these special, community-based (and presumably not universal) obligations do the hard work of resolving conflicts that were introduced by generalizations of inherent value to species and ecosystems as well as individuals in human communities.

Callicott's 1980 formulation, which alarmed readers who wondered if persons and individual animals would be sacrificed to a single principle that apparently followed from his theory that all value originates in ecosystems, has given way

more recently to an endorsement of theoretical monism rather than a monism of principles (as explained in note 1). Callicott therefore adopted a qualified version of holism that recognizes a plurality of rules applicable according to specific circumstances, explaining that pluralism on the level of principles of action is not consistent with monism on a more general, theoretical level in which various practical rules are unified and related to a single moral ontology.

Callicott's version of monism allows, he thinks, *both* unification under a single theory of value *and* flexibility in the formulation of rules. He claims a unified theory because he relates all obligations to a moral ontology in inherent value. Recognizing the subjective source of inherent value in human consciousness and in cultural ideas and institutions, however, the theory can nevertheless be elaborated in ways that are appropriate, depending on the special circumstances of the communities in which the obligations arose. But this solution to the charge of fascism—and one assumes Callicott must answer this charge if his theory is to be taken seriously—surely taxes the semantic elasticity of the concept of "inherent" value. Inherent value of natural objects, on this account, is due to "virtual" characteristics of objects of value, even though the specific, practical implications of the evaluations of these characteristics is ultimately determined by individual actors, according to the moral sensibilities of particular, independent, moral communities.

Ignoring these semantic difficulties, the upshot is that Callicott advocates allegiance to monistic inherentism in theory, but recognizes that the more intimate obligations of kinship and culture will usually outrank obligations to protect species and ecosystems. If this seems a capitulation to business as usual in environmental affairs, with inherent value reduced to a meaningless slogan, it must in fairness be said that Callicott faces a difficult and apparently destructive theoretical dilemma, for which he has thus far offered no resolution.[21] If moral inherentism is to provide the unified foundation for an environmental ethic, inherent value must be protected wherever it occurs. This apparently implies that any conflicts between a person's obligations to protect her children, for example, and her obligations to protect some inherently valuable biotic community, should strictly be determined by the obligation to maximize the protection of inherent value. But this would leave the theory open to charges of fascism, unless Callicott can prove that our obligations to persons could never, in principle, conflict with our obligations to ecosystems. Such a proof seems highly unlikely, so he chooses the other horn of the dilemma. While we have obligations to ecosystems as owners of inherent value and obligations to persons as owners of inherent value, the latter can override the former because of the special circumstances of the moral agent within the specific community in which those obligations arose.

But what are we to make of these auxiliary rules that resolve disputes when the interests of inherently valuable and morally considerable entities conflict? Can they, or can they not, be derived from the central, monistic theory of ecocentrism? If they can, it would seem that inherent value must come in grades, providing objective resolution of conflicts in interest among inherently valuable entities. But Callicott has never, to my knowledge, offered even a sketch of the required theory of gradations of inherent value or an explanation of how such gradations should inform our choices of what protectionist goals to give priority in action. If, on the other hand, these auxiliary rules cannot be derived from the central theory, we apparently have uncovered a most important class of moral quandaries that require we step outside Callicott's complete and unified theory, negating any claim to monism and universality. Until this dilemma has been resolved, it appears that Callicott's modified monistic ecocentrism can tell us nothing about what we are morally obligated to protect.

While this criticism of Callicott's adventures in ecocentric holism has proceeded on a theoretical level, it is important to note that Callicott's decision to interpret the land ethic as monistic and ecocentric has had at least two important practical consequences for the development of environmental ethics. Callicott's early comments on the land ethic as the standard interpretation of Leopold's mature thought. The criterion has not, accordingly, been operationalized because, on this standard interpretation it embodies all of the ambiguities of non-anthropocentrism, as just listed; worse, the criterion has been used as a shibboleth by one side in the polarized situation described above, rather than as the powerful practical guide it could be, because this interpretation identifies the criterion with the idiosyncratic views of a small subset of scientists and the public. Second, Callicott and other non-anthropocentrists have used this interpretation to support a highly tendentious, and narrowing, definition of the field of study of environmental ethics. These two issues are discussed in the following two subsections.

Non-Anthropocentrism and the Land Ethic

Callicott has interpreted what is perhaps the most important passage in the history of conservation thought, Leopold's famous "criterion" of right management, as monistic, holistic and non-anthropocentric in its philosophical commitments. Leopold said: "A thing is right when it tends to preserve the integrity, stability and beauty of the biotic community. It is wrong when it tends otherwise."[22] Callicott and the Deep Ecologists have taken the two sentences of Leopold's criterion to imply that the community or ecosystem is the *object of value* which conservationists should be attempting to protect. They have assumed, accordingly, that the ecosystem/community must, for Leopold, be *an object of value independent of human values*. This passage is read as an endorsement of the view that the ecological community has "integrity" understood as wholeness, *and therefore that ecosystems are moral subjects*. To be a moral patient, however, requires, given the objectivity requirement, non-human ownership. And ownership requires a moral subject. Under the influence of his commitment to ownership as the basis of moral considerability, and implicitly unliberated from the subject–object dichotomies of Cartesian dualism, Callicott reifies biotic communities as "moral subjects" who can own human-independent value. Callicott and his followers therefore interpret this passage as Leopold's definitive statement that communities themselves are loci of inherent, human-independent value that can be considered in competition with human values. To the extent that this has become the standard interpretation of Leopold's land ethic, environmental ethicists have encouraged environmentalists to understand this passage as an assertion of non-anthropocentrism.[23]

While I agree with Callicott's identification of "integrity" as the key concept of environmental ethics and management, we nevertheless differ strongly regarding how to interpret this conceptual centerpiece of the land ethic. Callicott believes that, by attributing integrity to the biotic community, *taken as a whole,* Leopold stepped across the line to non-anthropocentrism and declared his moral allegiance to the hypothesis that nature has inherent value. Our obligations to protect this integrity are "objective" in the sense that they originate in the integrity of whole agent/object which are morally considerable owners of their own value. Being constantly tempted to think of ecosystems as persons by the requirement that they are "owners" of their own value, it is natural also to think of them as objects capable of strategizing and having "interests" and "strategies" of their own.[24] Philosophers and ecologists, under the influence of this misguided, morally driven holism, have unfortunately failed to confront another ancient philosophical problem—how an organ can behave relatively independently, as an object in its own right, while at the same time being an organ that functions as a part of a larger organism. In philosophy, it can be called the problem of parts and wholes. In ecology, it can be called the problem of scalar dynamics. It is a problem that cannot get a hearing on the current assumption that the objects of moral attention in nature are necessarily "wholes."

Consider an alternative interpretation of Leopold's famous remark; consider it as a *practical* remark on the *proper focus of conservation management,* not as a philosophical statement of what objects in nature are of ultimate value. On this view, Leopold is in this passage summarizing his wisdom, drawing a broad, inductive generalization from the experiences of his long and varied career in environmental management, rather than asserting a moral, "first principle." On this reading Leopold was making the ontologically less committed, but none the less insightful point that, because of the complexity of the interrelationships in nature, and because there are so many different values exemplified in nature, the only way to manage to protect *all* of these diverse and pluralistic values is to protect the integrity of community processes (which supports and sustains the individuals and species of which it is composed). The latter two guidelines—stability and beauty—are then interpreted as glosses on, or specific criteria to employ— in our search for the sometimes elusive analogy of integrity. On this interpretation Leopold is not telling us *what to value* in nature, but rather telling us *what to protect* in our practical environmental management (given the diversity of values and scales involved).

On this view, then, Leopold is proposing an approach to management: he is defining right action in environmental use and management, rather than addressing the problem of standing. Further, he is strongly endorsing an integrative, systems approach to environmental management as the only way to encompass multifarious human goals as we manage a many-level, complex system which is our habitat. An advantage of this interpretation is that it unites the land ethic with Leopold's seminal managerial metaphor of "thinking like a mountain."[25] As I have argued elsewhere, the key idea behind the admonition to think like a mountain is the recognition of multiscalar relationships in time and space and a prescription that citizens and environmental managers in a technological age must pay attention to longer-scale values embodied in the structure and processes of slow-changing systems, as well as the immediate and short-term values of economics.[26] But on my interpretation of Leopold, he is emphatically *not* committing himself to a moral ontology of inherent value; nor is he expressing fealty to a single, monistic principle or theory of value. I see Leopold as a moral pluralist who was struggling to integrate multiple values rather than as an axiomatic deducer of applications from some universal theory.

My interpretation, it can be argued, fits much better into the context in which the criterion is found in the essay, "The Land Ethic." In the section immediately preceding the one in which the criterion is stated, Leopold outlined a systematic practical difference, cutting across all fields of resource management, between Group A and Group B conservationists.[27] Group A conservationists are primarily concerned with commodity production, whereas Group B conservationists, among whom Leopold counted himself, regard "the land as a biota, and its function as something broader. How much broader is admittedly in a state of doubt and confusion." Now Leopold often used the term "broader" to apply to the philosophical aspects of a problem, so I interpret this passage as explicitly choosing *not* to embrace any particular moral ideology. Leopold confidently made the separation between the two activist groups but, faced with the opportunity to make a pronouncement on the philosophical principles of the Group B movement, Leopold deferred and turned humble, admitting the question of what their principles meant philosophically is "in a state of doubt and confusion." It would be rather odd, would it not, if he had changed moods in the very next section of the essay and explicitly endorsed a full-blown theory of inherent moral goodness which implies that ecological communities are morally considerable beings who own their own good?

The Scope of Environmental Ethics

Non-anthropocentrists such as Callicott and Tom Regan, though they disagree strongly on what non-anthropocentric principle to apply, and which beings/subjects have it, agree that, if environmental ethics is to have a distinctive subject matter, the field must embrace some form of non-anthropocentrism. Regan asserts that, lacking a commitment to biocentrism, environmental ethics "collapses into an ethic for managing the environment [for human purposes]."[28] Remarkably, this definition excludes problems of environmental justice within generations and problems of intergenerational fairness from the discipline of environmental ethics. Callicott nevertheless quotes Regan approvingly and, seeing non-anthropocentrism as the only route to rationally defensible values, he accepts Regan's tendentious definition of environmental ethics as the search for a non-anthropocentric ethic.[29] One suspects that Callicott's belief that the land ethic is non-anthropocentric must be at work in predisposing him to accept Regan's otherwise implausible definitional narrowing; one also suspects that this definition is encouraged by the unquestioned goal of monistic theory-building and by the mission of applied philosophy as it is understood by Callicott and other monists. Non-anthropocentrism is not, apparently, an empirical hypothesis; it is a principle that is established "philosophically"—independent of experience, because that is what is required if philosophers are to operate independently of real environmental problems and constraints to establish moral principles independent of management science.

Ontology and Epistemology

Having examined a number of characteristics of applied philosophy by examining the ideas and practices of a leading proponent of that approach, and generalizing from them, I conclude this first part with one last look at the standard problematic of environmental ethics since its beginning as a recognized sub-discipline having a "distinctive" sub-ject matter. Because of his prior commitment to monism, Callicott assumed that the discipline of environmental ethics must achieve two goals with a single theory. There is, of course, the problem of determining who, or what, has *moral standing*, as noted above. And there is the quite distinct problem of the *warranted assertibility* of environmentalists' pronouncements that certain policies should be instituted because they are morally required and trump mere preferences of consumers. His solution is to provide a realistic moral ontology in which there exist moral objects in nature as well as among human individuals, subjects capable of "owning" inherent value. But whereas the first problem might (although I doubt it) be usefully addressed by an ontological theory of moral monism, the second problem is essentially a question of warranted assertibility of environmentalists' claims to priority in certain cases. This is an *epistemological* problem; we require no *ontological* solution to it. Once we avoid Callicott's conflation and problematize monism, there is no reason to consider it obligatory that our theory of value will be (1) realistic and (2) designed to provide *both* a theory of value *and* an epistemological warrant for assertions of priority.

The single ontological solution to two distinct problems seems plausible to Callicott, I submit, because he is operating on a fundamentally Cartesian conception of knowledge and reality, a conception in which epistemological justification requires location of a causal antecedent of perception and knowledge that can be located in reality, independent of human perception. He accordingly attempts to establish independent existence of environmental values by reifying ecosystems and making them owners of values. His single solution to the two problems is to recognize Cartesian moral subjects in nature as the owners of objective moral characteristics.

It is especially puzzling that Callicott attempts to reify ecosystems in this way, given that he clearly rejects the description of ecosystems as tending towards an inevitable and stable context. Callicott brilliantly shows that the lesson from ecology is that ecosystems are multilayered, dynamic processes, not self-like, organismic wholes that seek a stable equilibrium.[30] Is it even plausible to say that multilayered dynamic processes are owners of inherent value?

We can now see why Callicott's ontological, monistic interpretation of the integrity criterion and of the land ethic has led to ambiguities and paralysis. If the land ethic must be morally monistic, then to fulfill its unifying role in the non-anthropocentrists' moral ontology, it must consider ecosystems analogous to human organisms or at least Cartesian subjects who can "own" inherent value. But to answer the epistemological demand of activists for warranted assertibility, Callicott must claim that these owned values must have their existence independently of human valuation—they must be "objective" and exist independently of human evaluations. The theoretical dragon, "inherent value in nature," is necessarily two-headed, because it was created to slay two logically distinct monsters: ontological pluralism in value theory and moral skepticism. But the ontological solution of positing independent moral subjects in nature has unfortunately encouraged the organicist interpretation of ecological assemblages and led to the fascist tendencies of reified holism.

The difficulty in all of this, of course, is that organicism does have an important point to make. Organicists are correct that mechanistic models do not explain the ability of ecological processes to create, sustain and to heal themselves. Ecological management requires that we accept two elements of organicism—the idea that the whole is more than the sum of its parts and the related idea that relationships among multi-scalar processes—not the static characteristics of objects—provide the key to understanding ecosystems. The problem is to express this idea in a way that does not carry us all the way to teleology and personalism. We must emphasize the creative nature of environmental processes and the key role of energy flows in those processes, without personalizing them.[31]

My concern in this paper is not so much with epistemology[32] as with the ontology that should unify the underlying theory of environmental ethics. Callicott's overall position represents a curious mixture of Cartesian modernism and postmodernism. He attributes to Leopold, and seems to accept himself, a Darwinian, dynamic, particularistic and postmodern viewpoint in *ethics*, while at the same time addressing the problem of warranted assertibility within a distinctly modern epistemology. Despite direct evidence that Leopold employed a pragmatist theory of truth,[33] Callicott

assumes Leopold would have given a *realist* answer to the question: how can we justify our pursuit of environmental protection? I, on the other hand, see Leopold's many cautions about specifying the *purposes* behind creation and his numerous remarks that the exact interpretation of reality is "beyond language" as indicating that Leopold had at least the glimmerings of a postmodern conception of knowledge and objectivity, as well as morals.[34] Had Callicott placed Leopold's remarks regarding good environmental management in the context of Darwinian epistemology as well as Darwinian ethics, he would have conceived the "objectivity" problem very differently.[35]

If we focus for a moment on the problem of warranted assertibility of environmentalists' goals, it seems likely that environmentalists will achieve more by appealing to the relatively noncontroversial and intuitive idea that the use of natural resources implies an obligation to protect them for future users[36]—a sustainability theory based in intergenerational equity—rather than exotic appeals to hitherto unnoticed inherent values in nature. Callicott argues it is an advantage of intrinsic value in nature that, if it can be shown to exist, then it would shift the burden of proof in environmental arguments from environmental protectors to the despoilers.[37] But from the fact that such value might be *sufficient* to shift the burden of proof, it does not follow that it is the only, nor the best, means available to environmentalists to shift the burden.

The epistemological problem is that environmentalists need to be able to enter the public arena armed with genuine and defensible moral principles so that they can assert the priority of their goals over the mere preferences of the consumer society. As long as we can assert *other* morally binding obligations—such as an obligation to sustain the integrity and health of the ecological systems we are now damaging so that future generations can enjoy the bounties of intact ecological communities—we have a basis warrantedly to assert obligations to protect biodiversity over many generations. But these obligations are anthropocentric and cannot, apparently, be comprehended in a monistic non-anthropocentrism, even though abiding by these less controversial obligations would lead to most of the environmental protections favored by inherent value theorists.

Part 2: An Alternative to Ontology

In our search for an environmental ethic we will never, I submit, find any environmental values or goals more defensible than the sustainability principle, which asserts that each generation has an obligation to protect productive ecological and physical processes necessary to support options necessary for future human freedom and welfare. The normative force supporting the protection of the environment for future generations should be based on a commitment to building just, well-adapted and sustainable human communities. Accepting responsibility for our expanding numbers and for the power of our technologies follows simply from the recognition that we now affect the productivity of the human habitat and the very survival of the human community. This responsibility becomes less and less escapable as we learn the many consequences, expected and unexpected, of our increasingly violent and pervasive alteration of natural systems.[38] This principle is consistent with a Darwinian emphasis on survival and complements a pragmatic conception of truth. The acceptance of both the facts of human impacts and the associated *moral responsibility* to protect the integrity of ecological communities as repositories of many human options and values in the future is destined, in the terms of Peirce, to be adopted as the conclusion of all rational inquirers, as they struggle through many experiments to make coherent sense of human experience. I believe that *both* the descriptive problem of understanding the impacts of our actions on future generations *and* our resulting responsibilities as moral beings must be addressed within processes of inquiry constitutive of the Peircean community of inquirers/actors. For example, considering species threatened with extinction to represent "books" of information—information that may be essential to future generations in their struggle to understand and act within a changing environment—seems to entail that the obligation to contribute to the process of inquiry requires protection of the sources of information and knowledge for future inquirers.

While the sustainability principle can give a certain unity to environmental action, this unity represents an open-ended direction, an appeal to learning and small-scale adaption, community-building, and experimentation, not a slavish commitment to a priori principles of value such as monism and anthropocentrism. Thus this principle is unifying without being monistic—it sees the task of living sustainably as a problem of social learning, guided by a method that is socially open and scientifically experimental. This means that diverse stakeholder groups will be encouraged to assert and defend their own values and interests and to participate in social experiments in search of solutions that allow diverse users to fulfill their diverse needs with minimal disruption of the interests of other groups. The goal of value and policy discussions in democracy should be inclusive, recognizing that the diversity of values humans and communities find in nature is only the first step towards an integrative policy that preserves differences; in this sense it differs from monisms, which demand that diverse groups formulate their values in a single vernacular or have their considerations excluded from discussion and possible consensus.

I propose a new beginning for environmental philosophy—both for environmental ethics and environmental epistemology—a beginning based broadly in the pragmatic epistemology of Charles Sanders Peirce, who replaced the failed project of representational and foundational realism with a constructivist method that recognizes that the correctibility of scientific inquiry must be fully characterized within human experience, not by reference to "external objects" that exist beyond experience.[39] Truth and objectivity must be sought in the specific characteristics of specific situations in which action is required. If environmental values can justifiably be asserted to have priority in some situations, the mark of this will be their eventual emergence in a complex process of inquiry, including diverse groups with diverse interests and viewpoints, that will submit both values and scientific hypotheses to discussion and testing. The relevant intellectual community is not philosophers with a distinctive subject matter, but the activist community that is committed to human survival and improvement. Knowledge and moral discussion must be understood as a part of the struggle to determine adaptable policies, rather than a distinct "field" of theoretical morality. The inclusion of values as well as information in the process of inquiry can be traced to the experimental approach to social activism of John Dewey, who clearly rejected as folly the search for certainty and deductivism in moral and social matters.[40]

1 therefore place my work in the tradition of "adaptive management,"[41] first introduced by C. S. Holling and developed by his colleagues in the Pacific Northwest and in Northern Canada. Adaptive management has recently been given a political formulation by Kai Lee, who explicitly and concretely bases his political analysis in the philosophy of John Dewey.[42] Lee also shows that the Deweyan approach is usefully complemented by the creative work of policy analysts on "bounded rationality," who have recognized that arriving at improved policies is often a matter of "muddling through" rather than a matter of establishing idealistic goals and instituting decisive and abrupt changes to achieve those goals.[43] The pragmatic approach recognizes that there is great uncertainty in both human knowledge and human valuations and attempts to nurture processes and institutions that seek compromise and incremental change and improvement of understanding and goals. In the process, both information and values will be adjusted to become more appropriate and adaptive to particular situations.

Nature as a Multi-Scalar, Open System

Modeling a natural system is not a simple matter of choosing the hierarchy which best represents natural processes because, for any given ecological system, there are many—no doubt an infinite number—of models which will correctly *describe* some aspect of ecosystem functioning.[44] Further, because ecological systems are irreducibly complex, it follows that these models are not reducible to a single model without loss of descriptive content. I represent this essential complexity by using *hierarchy theory* (HT)—a theoretical approach to multi-scalar systems of analysis developed by theoretical ecologists such as Holling, T. F. H. Allen, and Robert O'Neill. Hierarchy theory represents a scalar application of general systems theory.[45] Systems are best understood as open, multi-scaled processes in which each system is viewed also as a subsystem on a more encompassing level of the system. Multi-scalar analysis has just as important a positive role in understanding environmental value and management goals as it does in describing natural systems; it is the scientific cornerstone of the adaptive management approach. Multi-scalar analysis is based on the neutral, model-constituting assumption that smaller sub-systems function on faster dynamics, and that all models that capture the

multi-scaled nature of ecological and physical systems should embody this spatio-temporal correlation between greater extent in physical space and slower dynamics of change. The central idea of a multi-scalar, contextual approach to analysis and management is therefore the very simple idea that human activities, economic and otherwise, take place within, and affect, larger systems that should be interpreted as multi-scaled ecological processes. As noted above and elsewhere, this multiscalar approach represents a more precise and operational formalization of Aldo Leopold's insight that we must learn to "think like a mountain," and therefore provides both a connection backward to Leopold's seminal managerial insights and also points forward to new directions for scientific and policy research that proceed by organizing information and value studies into a spatio-temporally structured system of analysis.[46]

Most uses of HT so far have been purely descriptive. T. F. H. Allen and his co-authors, for example, argue that the only type of reason that can be advanced to prefer on scalar model of an ecological phenomenon over another is that the preferred model *enhances our understanding of the system* more extensively than do less preferred models. While they refer to this justification as "utilitarian," it is clear from the context that utility is understood by Allen and Starr as "scientific" or methodological utility, not general social utility.[47] By contrast, I also apply a normative filter of *usefulness in understanding and protecting social values* as well as a descriptive filter, reducing drastically the class of descriptive models that must be considered as relevant to policy. The goal should be to develop scalar models that improve our understanding in the specific sense that they illuminate environmental problems and allow us to focus on those natural dynamics that are causally related to important social values. Hopefully, these models also help us to define our management goals clearly and to measure success and failure in attempts to achieve those goals.

Conservation biology—and also the "pure" disciplines of zoology, botany, etc.—must adopt the twin goals of understanding *and protecting* ecological systems just as human and veterinary medicine have adopted the twin, descriptive-and-normative goals of understanding *and healing* their patients. Commitment to the Peircean ideal of eventually understanding nature apparently carries with it the obligation to protect the sources of biological knowledge, living organisms, especially from irreversible losses such as species extinctions. The descriptive models chosen in normative sciences must therefore pass a double criterion. They must help us to understand nature, but they must also encourage us to understand nature in a way that will help us to formulate and measure environmental goals effectively and to propose and implement policies to achieve those goals. The problem in linking biological science, social science and value theory into an adequate plan for environmental management is to choose from among this multitude of *descriptively* adequate models a few models that truly help us to understand *and to integrate* human activities into the landscape.

This *multi-scalar and biogeographic* approach to environmental values assumes at the outset that management will proceed from a human perspective and also, that human values quite legitimately shape the modeling decisions of ecological and physical scientists. This latter point is deserving of further explanation: the decisions of biological and physical scientists have an unavoidable normative component. The point is not to *purge* science of those values, which is both impossible and undesirable, the point is to *understand and justify* those values in specific contexts requiring action, and to attempt to adjust them through public discussion and education when they become maladaptive.

A successful integrative ethic for the environment must be morally pluralistic, but it must also be contextual, rather than either objectivist or subjectivist. Good environmental decisions are ones that take into account likely impacts on a number of spatio-temporal scales in specific contexts. As the world becomes more full of humans and as technology becomes more powerful, there will be more and more cases in which there will be spill-over impacts from one level of hierarchical organization to another, especially from our expanding economic and social systems to the natural systems that form their ecological context. Environmental policy and action must do more than enhance values in one dynamic, such as the dynamic driving the economic decision of individual farmers; it is necessary also to examine the impacts on the larger- and usually slower-changing dynamic that determines the structure and diversity of the landscape. Here the focus of moral analysis turns to multiple generations and to the landscape scale.

The goal of an integrative ethic should be to sort the many and various values that humans derive from their environment and to associate these variables with real dynamic processes unfolding on the various levels and scales of the physical and ecological context of our activities. Environmental problems are in this sense essentially scalar problems and I seek to define models that illuminate the dynamics which support human values.

A Tri-Scalar Model

Since the practical philosopher and the adaptive manager set as a goal of all model-building that the models inform environmental decision-making, and since we firmly believe that environmental decision-making must be democratic, any model for this purpose must be fairly simple in structure. The model must be a simple enough representation of multi-scaled natural processes to serve as an aid in public discussion of the goals of a forest management plan or a plan for ecological restoration of a river system. Prescriptive, multi-scalar models must therefore provide a publicly useful vocabulary for discussing environmental goals; they must shape our models of management by associating them with the temporal and spatial scales of the natural dynamics that generate the values guiding our choice of goals. The goal is to develop a spatio-temporally organized and ecologically informed phenomenology of the moral space in which individuals formulate and pursue personal and environmental values.[48] The problem, on this pragmatic approach, is to characterize and categorize pluralistic values in a way that is sensitive to spatio-temporal features—what I call the "scale"—of human interactions with nature. It is to design a method of inquiry, which includes both a descriptive and evaluative component so organized as to increase the likelihood of both achieving truth (defined in a broadly Darwinian sense) and sustainability of fair and equitable communities, and of traditional values and cultural diversity for the benefit of humans today and in the future.

To initiate discussion, let me suggest three basic scales, each of which corresponds a temporally distinct *policy* horizon:

1. Locally developed values that express the preference of individuals, given the established limits and "rules"—laws, physical laws,

governmental laws, and market conditions, for example—within which individual transactions take place;

2. A longer and larger community-oriented scale on which we hope to protect and contribute to our community which might be taken to include the entire *ecological* community;

3. A global scale with essentially indefinite time scales on which humans express a hope that their own species, even beyond current cultures, will survive and thrive. (See Figure 1.)

On the first scale, which unfolds in the relatively short term and local space in which individuals make economic choices, an economics of cost–benefit, if supplemented with a sense of individual justice and equity, can provide useful decision models. The middle scale, on which we feel concern for our cultural connection to the past and future, is especially important for two reasons. Viewed socially, this multiple-generational level is the one on which we protect, develop and nurture our sense of who we are as a culture. It is on this level that we "decide" what kind of society we want to be. These "decisions" are expressed in our art, in our religion and spirituality, and in our governing political institutions such as the constitution. It is on this scale that we feel concern about the culture's interaction with the ecological communities that form its context. This second scale is doubly important because it corresponds roughly to the ecological time scale on which multiple generations of human individuals, organized into communities, must relate to populations of other species that share their habitat. Thinking intergenerationally apparently requires that we pay special attention to large-scale aspects of the landscape.

Modern ecological knowledge has forced upon us the conclusion that we must act as members of the natural as well as the human social community; it follows also that we must pay attention to the context in which our values are formulated and acted upon, and that context is the interaction between a culture and its habitat that is described in the "natural history" of a place. That natural history must reach back in time, and protect itself in a creative way into the future.[49] According to the multi-scalar, contextual view, humans necessarily understand their world from a given local perspective. A preference for localism is really a preference over preferences—a favoring of values that emerge from experience of one's home place. This home place locates the perspective from which one understands and values elements and processes in the natural context of our actions. Localism is represented in the proposed theory of environmental values by an endorsement of the importance of *sense of place values*. I therefore advocate many different locally originating sustainability ethics, each of which is anchored to a particular place by a strong sense of the history and the future of the place. In particular, a sense of place manifests itself, for example, in the defense of local determination and in an inclination of citizens to fight and defeat solutions imposed by centralized and authoritarian institutions.[50]

But a full-blown sense of place must include a sense of the space around that place.[51] And here we

Figure 1 Correlation of human concerns and natural system dynamics at different temporal scales

Temporal Horizon of Human Concern	Time Scales	Temporal Dynamics in Nature
Individual/economic	0–5 years	Human economies
Community, intergenerational bequests	Up to 200 years	Ecological dynamics/ Interaction of species in communities
Species survival and our genetic successors	Indefinite time	Global physical systems

invoke our multi-scalar phenomenology of environmental concerns as the evaluative space in which each citizen, as an individual, as a member of an ongoing, cultural community, and as a member of the global community, must seek local solutions which reduce impacts on larger systems.

We can represent action–decision aspects of the phenomenological models I am describing as in Figure 2. Imagine, conceptually, that the surface of the earth is represented as many points, or individual perspectives, each of which is tied by a cultural history to a human community and by a "natural" history to the land community. These individuals are understood as representative individuals who live in a community—their personal identity is therefore associated with that community. They are therefore not selfish only—they seek to project their culture by affecting future generations, though they unavoidably conceive the world from their own, local perspective. On these assumptions, our individuals must view themselves also as members of a community of plants and animals, as well as a community of humans. They therefore experience, articulate and defend environmental values from a local perspective and from the present point in time. But impacts on the larger and long-term, intergenerational scale can also impact local and personal values if the ecological context changes so rapidly that traditional values and practices become meaningless in a few years. While individuals perceive values from a local perspective, those values are also shaped within a larger space in which there can be impacts on larger, physical systems, which in turn constrain future choices. Note that greater population density and expansions in the scale of a community increase the likelihood of impacts from one community to another horizontally, across communities, and also vertically, across generations.

An implication of the multi-scalar approach outlined here is that the search for an acceptable environmental policy will not be a search for the policy that maximizes benefits to costs as measured in present dollars. A good environmental policy will be one that has positive implications for values associated with the various scales on which humans *are in fact* concerned, and also on the scales on which environmentalists think we *should* be concerned if we accept responsibility for the impacts of our current activities on the life prospects and options—the "freedom" of future generations.[52]

In a situation that recognizes multiple human values and associates these with various dynamics, it is possible to conceive, describe and seek policies that will protect or even enhance the processes maintaining ecological structure and processes that are crucial in future interactions of human and natural communities. The goal of policy is not to analyze and rank various policies with respect to how well they score on a single criterion, but rather to

Figure 2 Multi-scalar relationship of individual, community and global scales

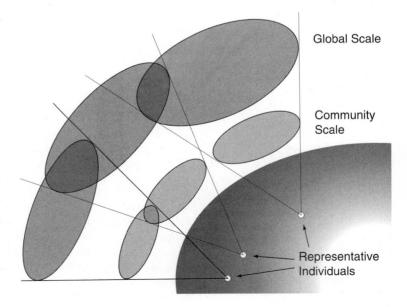

Global Scale

Community Scale

Representative Individuals

devise win–win policies that are robust enough to score highly on a number of relevant criteria of good management. Win–win policies, on the approach proposed here, are policies that have positive (or, failing that, neutral) results on all three "scales" of human concern—the individual welfare level, the community level and on the emerging values of the global community.

Consider an example which fulfills this robustness condition. In many deforested developing countries poor families must expend considerable effort to gather firewood for cooking and heating as the scarcity of firewood can cause extended searches consuming many person-days per week per household. In such areas a creative environmental policy would institute many locally based tree-planting programs. Successful programs begin with small loans to private entrepreneurs who use the loan to purchase seedlings and for other start-up costs. Full payment to the entrepreneurs will occur when the trees reach a certain age or height, encouraging the entrepreneurs' clan to protect the trees so that they can reach the pay-off goal. If the trees are planted close together, they will provide increases to economic welfare within a few years as culled trees provide firewood nearer home. Meanwhile, local ecological processes should become more healthy as eroding land is replaced by forests, or at least small and diverse tree farms improving water retention and improving streamwater quality. Finally, on the largest scale, the impact on current choices on the functioning of global physical systems, we can expect that birth rates will be reduced because peasant families will have less incentive to have children to help with household chores.

Figure 2 helps us to conceptualize a new criterion for acceptable and appropriate environmental action. I refer to the proposed criterion as advocating actions and policies that conform to the *scalar Pareto criterion*. The scalar Pareto criterion represents a multi-scalar application of the Pareto optimality criterion, which was originally stated on the individual level as the requirement that all actions have a positive impact on some individuals and negative impacts on nobody. The scalar application of the Pareto criterion is stated as follows: choose policies that, from the viewpoint of a representative individual in each community, the policy will have positive (or at least non-negative) impacts on goals formulated by that person on the individual level,

on the community level, and on the global level. While the scalar Pareto approach retains an individualist perspective (it is human individuals who formulate, discuss and defend values on all levels), it does not seek reduction of all values to economic preferences or to some generic form of "inherent value." It is *pluralistic* in the sense that the value of ecosystems is understood on a community, not an individual, scale and no reduction of community-level values to individual values is attempted. But the pluralistic ethic is also *integrative* in the sense that we seek actions that will have positive (or at least non-negative) impacts on the relatively distinct dynamics that produce and support human values that are expressed on multiple scales (here hypothesized as three).

Conclusion

Thus ends my explanation of, and plea for, a practical environmental ethic that seeks to *integrate* pluralistic principles across multiple levels/dynamics. Rather than *reducing* pluralistic principles by relating them to an underlying value theory that recognizes only economic preferences or "inherent" value as the ontological stuff that unifies all moral judgments, I have sought integration of multiple value on three irreducible scales of human concern and valuation, choosing pluralism over monism, and attempting to integrate values within an ecologically informed, multi-scalar model of human habitat. I believe that the non-ontological, pluralistic approach to values can better express the inductively based values and management approach of Leopold's land ethic, which can be seen as a precursor to the tradition of adaptive management. And, if the problem of environmentalism is the need to support rationally the goals of environmental protection—the problem Callicott misconceived as the need for a realist moral ontology to establish the "objectivity" of environmental goals—then I endorse the broadly Darwinian approach to both epistemology and morals proposed by the American pragmatists. The environmental community *is* the community of inquirers; it is the community of inquirers that, for better or worse, must struggle, immediately as individuals and indefinitely as a community, both to survive and to know. In this struggle useful knowledge will be information about how to survive in a rapidly evolving culture and habitat. It is in this sense that human actors are a part of multi-layered scales. We humans will understand our moral responsibilities only if we understand the consequences of our actions as they unfold on multiple scales; and the human community will only survive to further evolve and adapt if we learn to achieve individual welfare and justice in the present in ways that are less disruptive of the processes, evolving on larger spatio-temporal scales, essential to human and ecological communities.[53]

Acknowledgment

A slightly altered version of the first part of this paper appears in *Environmental Ethics* Vol. 17, under the title "Why I Am Not a Nonanthropocentrist."

Notes

1. It is interesting, and perhaps not accidental, that the power and importance of the assumption that environmental ethics should be monistic in form was pointed out not by an environmental ethicist or philosopher, but by a legal scholar. See Christopher Stone, *Earth and Other Ethics* (New York: Harper & Row, 1987). Environmental ethicists, who responded directly to the charge by historian Lynn White, Jr., that Western thought has led to environmental degradation because it is anthropocentric, have for the most part never questioned that anthropocentrism must be replaced with a non-anthropocentric form of monism. White's argument appeared in *Science* 155 (1967): 1203–1207.

    More recently, it has been noted that monisms come in several versions. See Peter Wenz, "Minimal, Moderate, and Extreme Moral Pluralism," *Environmental Ethics* 15 (1993): 61–74. Following J. Baird Callicott, I will restrict my discussion to "principles monism" and "theoretical monism," as explained in Callicott's "The Case Against Moral Pluralism," *Environmental Ethics* 12 (1990): 99–124. According to principles monism, there is a single principle that covers all moral quandaries, with principle understood as a moral standard sufficiently practical to imply a single correct action in every situation. Theoretical monism, by contrast, might employ more than one principle in different situations, but achieves monism on a theoretical level by providing an over-arching theory that explains and unifies the use of divergent principles in terms of a monistic theory. It seems reasonable to consider principles monism to be a special case of theoretical monism because, as in the case of some simple versions of utilitarianism, a single theory of

value justifies a single principle applicable to all cases. This paper is directed at both principle and theoretical versions because of the reductionistic tendencies they share. For simplicity, I will refer only to the general form, theoretical monism, because arguments applicable to it will apply also to the special case of principles monism as well.

2. See Callicott, "The Case Against Moral Pluralism," op. cit., for a discussion of the strengths of monism as opposed to pluralism in environmental ethics.

3. I have discussed the "environmentalists' dilemma" in detail in *Toward Unity Among Environmentalists* (New York: Oxford University Press, 1991).

4. See B. Norton, "Applied Philosophy vs. Practical Philosophy: Toward an Environmental Policy Integrated According to Scale," in Donald Marietta and Lester Embree, eds, *Environmental Philosophy and Environmental Activism* (Lanham, MD: Rowman & Littlefield, 1995, pp. 125–148), for a more detailed discussion of the failure of non-anthropocentrism to address real management problems.

5. It should be noted that Callicott has on occasion suggested an alternative. See note 53.

6. See J. Baird Callicott, "Environmental Philosophy *Is* Environmental Activism: The Most Radical and Effective Kind," in Marietta and Embree, *Environmental Philosophy and Environmental Activism*, for a brief exposition and aggressive defense of applied philosophy and the role he sees for it.

7. Interestingly, Callicott asserts (ibid., p. 25) that applied philosophy does "rather little deducing of specific rules of conduct." Rather, he sees the role of philosophy as one of "articulating and thus helping to effect . . . a radical change in outlook. The specific ethical norms of environmental conduct remain for the most part implicit—a project postponed to the future or something left for ecologically informed people to work out for themselves." Despite this well-placed skepticism regarding whether environmental ethicists can get much mileage out of abstract, philosophical theories, Callicott never doubts that his monistic theories of value are important in effecting a change in consciousness of citizens and capable of bringing about a new, environmental era: "Therefore, since human actions are carried out and find their meaning and significance in a cultural ambience of ideas, we speculative environmental philosophers are inescapably environmental activists" (p. 25). So, whether deduction is involved or not, the applied philosopher's contribution is to provide thoughtful persons with reasons or some form of motivation to adopt a new "cultural ambience," which includes his, particular, monistic principle. Only after

persons (at some time in the future) agree on the existence and meaning of non-anthropocentric monistic value can the principle begin to provide guidance in specific situations.

8. This point shows how badly Callicott misunderstands the anti-monistic position, which he refers to as "anti-philosophical." "Environmental Philosophy Is Environmental Activism" (p. 5). I, at least, am not anti-philosophical; I am against philosophical theory which is developed independently of real-world problems and I reject the role for theory assumed by Callicott and other monists and applied philosophers. Callicott mistakes an attack on *outmoded, modernist theory* for an attack on all theorizing.

9. See Bryan G. Norton, *Toward Unity Among Environmentalists* (New York: Oxford University Press, 1991).

10. See Bryan G. Norton, "Evaluating Ecosystem States: Two Competing Paradigms," *Ecological Economics* (1995, forthcoming); "Economists' Preferences and the Preferences of Economists," *Environmental Values* 3 (1994): 311–332; and "Thoreau's Insect Analogies: Or, Why Environmentalists Hate Mainstream Economists," *Environmental Ethics* 13 (1991): 235–261 for criticisms of welfare economics as a similarly inadequate monistic theory of environmental valuation.

11. Such as Holmes Rolston, III, *Environmental Ethics: Duties to and Values in the Natural World* (Philadelphia: Temple University Press, 1988) and Paul Taylor, *Respect for Nature* (Princeton, NJ: Princeton University Press, 1986).

12. Mainly in "The Case Against Moral Pluralism" and "Moral Monism in Environmental Ethics Defended," *Journal of Philosophical Research* XIX (1994): 51–60.

13. I use this vague phrase, "moral gravity," because Callicott has recently admitted that, because of the subjectivist foundations of his philosophy in David Hume, he cannot claim to offer a theory that exerts "moral force" (the more usual formulation), but only a "moral dimension." See "Can a Theory of Moral Sentiments Support a Genuinely Normative Environmental Ethic?" *Inquiry* 35 (1992): 183–198.

14. J. Baird Callicott, *In Defense of the Land Ethic* (Albany, NY: State University of New York Press, 1989), p. 163.

15. Ibid., p. 160.

16. J. Baird Callicott, "Animal Liberation: A Triangular Affair," *Environmental Ethics* 2 (1980): 311–338. Reprinted in Callicott, *In Defense.*

17. Tom Regan, *The Case for Animal Rights* (Berkeley, CA: University of California Press, 1983), p. 362.

18. Callicott, *In Defense,* pp. 55–59, 93–94.

19. Ibid., pp. 55–56.

20. Ibid., p. 58.

21. I first pointed out the difficulty of this dilemma in "Review of *In Defense of the Land Ethic,*" *Environmental Ethics* 13 (1991): 185. As far as I know, Callicott has not responded in print or verbally to this dilemma, which apparently requires some response if we are to understand what is meant by monistic inherentism.

22. Aldo Leopold, *A Sand County Almanac and Sketches Here and There* (London: Oxford University Press, 1949), pp. 224–225.

23. There have, however, been dissenting opinions regarding the non-anthropocentrism of the land ethic. See Scott Lehmann, "Do Wildernesses Have Rights?" *Environmental Ethics* 3 (1981): 129–146; Bryan G. Norton, "The Constancy of Leopold's Land Ethic," *Conservation Biology* 2 (1988): 93–102 . . . and Norton, *Toward Unity.*

24. See, for example, Eugene Odum, "The Strategy of Ecosystem Development," *Science* 164 (1969): 262–270. I have criticized this form of strong organicism in "Should Environmentalists Be Organicists?" *Topoi* 12 (1991): 21–30.

25. Leopold, *A Sand County Almanac,* pp. 129–133.

26. See Bryan G. Norton, "Context and Hierarchy in Aldo Leopold's Theory of Environmental Management" *Ecological Economics* 2 (1990): 11–127; Norton, *Toward Unity.*

27. Leopold, *A Sand County Almanac,* pp. 221–222.

28. Tom Regan, "The Nature and Possibility of an Environmental Ethic," *Environmental Ethics* 3 (1981): 20.

29. Callicott, *In Defense,* p. 157; J. Baird Callicott, "Rolston on Intrinsic Value: A Deconstruction," *Environmental Ethics* 14 (1992): 130–131.

30. Ibid., pp. 107–112.

31. See Norton, "Should Environmentalists Be Organicists?"

32. See Norton, "Epistemology and Environmental Values," *Monist* 75 (1992): 208–226, for a detailed criticism of the epistemology of intrinsic value theory.

33. See Norton, "The Constancy of Aldo Leopold's Land Ethic" (Andrew Light, Eric Katz, eds. *Environmental Pragmatism,* NY: Routledge, 1996).

34. See A. Leopold, "Some Fundamentals of Conservation in the Southwest," *Environmental Ethics* 1 (1979): 131–141; also see Norton, "The Constancy of Leopold's Land Ethic." (Andrew Light, Eric Katz, eds. *Environmental Pragmatism.*)

35. See Michael Ruse, *Taking Darwin Seriously: A Naturalist Approach to Philosophy* (Oxford: Blackwell,

1987), for a survey and convincing defense of Darwinian epistemology.

36. See E. B. Weiss, *In Fairness to Future Generations* (Tokyo, Japan, and Dobbs Ferry, NY: The United Nations University and Transnational Publishers, Inc., 1989). Weiss shows that every major world religion, and many minor ones as well, assert that the use of resources obligates current generations to an obligation to pass the resources on to future generations.

37. Callicott, "Environmental Philosophy Is Environmental Activism."

38. See A. Leopold, "A Biotic View of Land," *Journal of Forestry* 37 (1939): 727–730.

39. C. S. Peirce, *The Philosophical Writings of Peirce* (New York: Dover, 1955), especially pp. 21, 39.

40. See, especially, John Dewey, *The Public and Its Problems*, in *John Dewey: The Later Works, Volume 2: 1925–1927*, edited by Jo Ann Boydston (Carbondale, IL: Southern Illinois University Press, 1984), pp. 235–372.

41. The adaptive management approach was introduced by C. S. Holling, ed. *Adaptive Environmental Assessment and Management* (New York: John Wiley & Sons, 1978). Also see Carl J. Walters, *Adaptive Management of Renewable Resources* (New York: Macmillan, 1986) and, especially, Kai N. Lee, *Compass and Gyroscope: Integrating Science and Politics for the Environment* (Covelo, CA: Island Press, 1993).

42. Lee, *Compass and Gyroscope*, pp. 91–115.

43. Herbert Simon, *Administrative Behavior* (New York: Macmillan, 1954), and Charles Lindblom, "The Science of Muddling Through," *Public Administration Review* (1959): 79–88. The present volume at last provides a discussion of the philosophical principles of pragmatism in connection with environmental policies and values.

44. See Simon Levin, "The Problem of Pattern and Scale in Ecology," *Ecology* 73(6): pp. 1943–1967 for the scientific argument for this conclusion.

45. T. F. H. Allen and T. B. Starr, *Hierarchy: Perspectives for Ecological Complexity* (Chicago: University of Chicago Press, 1982); and R. V. O'Neill, D. L. DeAngelis, J. B. Waide and T. F. H. Allen, *A Hierarchial Concept of Ecosystems* (Princeton, NJ: Princeton University Press, 1986).

Despite connotations sometimes associated with the term "hierarchy," it is important to understand that there is no implication that higher levels of the system dominate, or should dominate, lower levels. In fact, the processes described in hierarchical systems analysis exhibit communication both upward and downward through the hierarchy, and for this reason we prefer the more neutral terminology, "multi-scalar analysis."

46. This use of hierarchy theory differs dramatically from recent applications of the theory by environmental ethicists Cheney and Warren, who have used the theory negatively to attack Callicott's uses of ecological theory. They argue that, because hierarchy theory does not claim ontological priority for any of the hierarchical models it proposes, the efforts of Callicott and others to use ecological theories to support "moral ontologies" is a doomed project. See Karen J. Warren and Jim Cheney, "Ecosystem Ecology and Metaphysical Ecology: A Case Study," *Environmental Ethics* 15 (1993): 99–116. But I believe hierarchy has much stronger potential as a useful method for dealing with troubling scalar issues in the discussion of environmental information, values and goals positively. See Norton,"Scale and Hierarchy in Aldo Leopold's Land Ethic."

47. See T. F. H. Allen and T. B. Starr, *Hierarchy: Perspectives for Ecological Complexity* op. cit., p. 6. See also T. F. H. Allen and Thomas W. Hoekstra, *Toward a Unified Ecology* (New York: Columbia University Press, 1992), pp. 31–35.

48. Bryan G. Norton and Bruce Hannon, "Environmental Values: A Place-Based Theory," *Environmental Ethics* 19 (Fall 1997), pp. 553–568.

49. Holmes Rolston, III, *Environmental Ethics*.

50. Bryan G. Norton and Bruce Hannon, "Democracy and Sense of Place Values in Environmental Policy," *Philosophy and Geography* 3 (1998), pp. 119–146.

51. Yi-Fu Tuan, *Space and Place: The Perspective of Experience* (Minneapolis, MN: University of Minnesota Press, 1977): Tuan, "Man and Nature," Commission on College Geography, Resource Paper 10, Association of American Geographers, Washington, DC, 1971; and Norton and Hannon, "Democracy and Sense of Place Values."

52. See T. F. H. Allen and T. B. Starr, *Hierarchy: Perspectives for Ecological Complexity* op. cit., p. 15, for definition of "freedom" in this sense, a sense that can be understood within hierarchical models.

53. I gratefully acknowledge that my understanding of these problems has been improved by countless discussions, in formal and informal situations, with Baird Callicott. I have learned much from our discussions, and have concluded that Callicott and I agree on most practical issues of management, but that we cannot agree regarding the theoretical foundations of environmental ethics. I do not, of course, expect that Callicott will agree with my arguments or my approach, but I hope this opposing viewpoint will carry forward the discussion of the

proper role and mission of environmental ethics into the larger community of scholars.

It should also be said that Calhcott has, on occasion, recognized the insidious associations of monistic inherentism when associated with a modernist conception of scientific objectivity with Cartesianism and he has even suggested that achievement of a truly adequate, postmodern conceptualization of nature and value would require a different formulation. If I understand this postmodern version of Callicott's philosophy, it still includes a central role for inherent value. See *In Defense*, especially pp. 165–174 for a tentative trying-out of this alternative position. The arguments of this paper, however, have not been directed at the postmodern, non-Cartesian version of inherent value, but at the version defended in the vast majority of Callicott's published writings.

IV.B DEEP ECOLOGY AND SOCIAL ECOLOGY

29. PREVIEW

Now I see the secret of the making of the best persons. It is to grow in the open air, and then to eat and sleep with the earth.

Walt Whitman, Leaves of Grass

I think it pisses God off it you walk by the color purple in a field and don't notice it.[1]

Alice Walker

The term *Deep Ecology* was coined by the Norwegian philosopher Arne Naess in his "The Shallow and the Deep, Long-Range Ecology Movement: A Summary."[2] Deep Ecology, in what Warwick Fox calls the "formal" sense, refers to a level of questioning that is fundamental. In an interview with Bill Devall and George Sessions, Naess states, "The essence of deep ecology is to ask deeper questions. The adjective 'deep' stresses that we ask why and how, where others do not."[3] Again, he maintains, "the deep ecological movement tries to clarify the fundamental presuppositions underlying our economic approach in terms of value priorities, philosophy, religion. In the shallow movement, argument comes to halt long before this."[4] The deep-shallow distinction has come under fire as "pejorative . . . smug, self-congratulatory, self-righteous, or holier-than-thou . . . [and] patronizing."[5] Nevertheless, neither Naess nor his followers (for the most part) have abandoned the phrase.

Presumably, Fox labels this construal of "Deep Ecology"—asking deeper questions as "formal" because it refers only to a depth of questioning and not to the content of any answers to these questions. However, Deep Ecology must mean more than this if only because those who call themselves Deep Ecologists typically do have substantive views that can be characterized as nonanthropocentric or ecocentric. The eight-point program arrived at by Naess and Sessions in 1984 and delineated by Devall and Sessions in this section (Essay 30) is a representative list of such substantive claims. Moreover, according to Devall and Sessions, Deep Ecology subscribes to two fundamental or ultimate norms: biocentric egalitarianism and self-realization. Fox singles out the idea of self-realization as central to his views and renames his development of the idea "transpersonal ecology."

Biocentric egalitarianism is the claim that all living things are of equal moral worth or equal intrinsic value. It is important to recognize that "life" here is being used in a very broad sense to include, for example, "rivers (watersheds), landscapes, ecosystems."[6] A central idea here is that human are in nature. Humans are not "above or outside of nature."[7] Deep Ecology challenges the human centeredness of the dominant Western world view.

Arne Naess has the following to say about biocentric egalitarianism:

The ecological field-worker acquires a deep-seated respect . . . for ways and forms of life. He reaches . . . a kind of understanding that others reserve for fellow men and for a narrow section of ways and forms of life. To the ecological fieldworker, the equal right to live and blossom is an intuitively clear and obvious value axiom. Its restriction to humans is an anthropocentrism with detrimental effects upon the life quality of humans themselves. This quality depends in part upon the deep pleasure and satisfaction we receive from close partnership with other forms of life. The attempt to ignore our dependence and to establish a master–slave role has contributed to the alienation of man from himself.[8]

Carolyn Merchant, in her discussion of Deep Ecology, suggests that there is a connection between our world view and our attitude toward the earth. Of the Deep Ecologists, she says, "Modesty and humility and an awe of evolution take precedence over an assertion of power over the biosphere."[9] Changing our attitude toward nature, according to some, is mainly what Deep Ecology is about. For example, Eric Katz says, "Deep Ecology, its advocates argue, is not an attempt to discover 'intrinsic value' or to develop universal moral rules, but a re-shaping and re-direction of human consciousness."[10] In a review of Devall and Sessions's *Deep Ecology: Living as if Nature Mattered*, Evelyn M. Hurwich expresses pleasure at the prospect that such concepts as "biocentric equality" and "self-realization" "may serve to develop ecological consciousness . . . an experiential and uniquely personal process of discovery." But she is frustrated because these phrases and concepts do "not help move us forward as a global society faced by critical issues that require choices made between varying and often conflicting . . . values."[11] Hurwich continues, "Until an ecological basis is articulated by which competing vital interests can be weighed and evaluated, it cannot be expected that any meaningful decision-making process will evolve out of the

deep ecology movement."[12] It may be true that Deep Ecologists do not formulate specific tradeoff principles of the type Hurwich and others desire; nonetheless, in fairness to Naess, he addresses questions about conflict.

In "Self-Realization in Mixed Communities of Humans, Bears, Sheep, and Wolves," Naess says, "the interaction between the members of the community is not systematically codified."[13] He calls his approach "a posteriori."[14] A posteriori is a Latin phrase used especially by philosophers when they refer to knowledge obtained by experience rather than by reason alone. So Naess means here that the way to achieve the well-being of the members of the community is not by applying previously adopted rules established by reason, but by experiencing the problems and character of individual bears. In listening to Arne Naess talk about bears, it seems as if the bears are "Fred" and "Esther"—folks we know:

> Bears and humans live in overlapping territories in southern Norway. Conflicts arise because some bears develop a habit of killing sheep. No sheep-owner thinks that all bears in his area should be killed. The cultural pattern is such that bears are considered to have a right to live and flourish. They are considered to have a value in themselves. The problem is one of co-existence with humans and with sheep.
>
> When sheep are killed in southern Norway and a bear seems to have been responsible, an expert is called in. He investigates closely the way the sheep has been killed and notes all the signs of the presence of the bear. Knowing the various habits of practically all the bears in the area—even if he has not actually seen them—he is generally able to tell not only whether a bear has been there, but also which bear.
>
> The sheep-owner is paid an indemnity if the expert arrives at the conclusion that a bear is responsible. If that bear has been guilty of similar "crimes," a verdict may

be reached that it has forfeited its rights to existence. An expert bear-hunter is given license to kill it, but if he does not succeed, a whole team of hunters is mobilized. (Somewhat inexplicably, bears are able under such circumstances to hide for years, which is deeply embarrassing as well as mystifying for the hunters.)

Many factors are considered before a bear is condemned to death. What is his or her total record of misdeeds? How many sheep have been killed? Does he or she mainly kill to eat, or does he or she maim or hurt sheep without eating? Is particular cruelty shown? Is it a bear mother who will probably influence her cubs in a bad way? Did the sheep enter the heart of the bear area or did the bear stray far into established sheep territory?[15]

Whatever guidelines Naess uses emerge from the situation in which bears, wolves, sheep, and people find themselves.

Self-realization is the remaining ultimate norm of Deep Ecology to be considered. "We underestimate ourselves," says Naess, if we "confuse [self] with the narrow ego."[16] In a fairly sophisticated summary of the notion, Naess says that self-realization "in its absolute maximum is . . . the mature experience of oneness in diversity. . . . The minimum is the self-realization by more or less consistent egoism —by the narrowest experience of what constitutes one's self and a maximum of alienation. As empirical beings we dwell somewhere in between, but increased maturity involves increase of the wideness of the self."[17] We develop a wider self, according to Naess, by a process of identification. Sometimes, Naess talks as though identification is a psychological process, something like empathy or solidarity, by which we establish connection with other life-forms. For example, he says, "Identification is a spontaneous, nonrational, but not irrational, process in which the interest or interests of another being are reacted to as our own interest or interests."[18] At other times, when speaking of identification, he seems to

be talking about what is real (metaphysics or ontology) or what we can know (epistemology). For example, Naess says, "In the shallow ecological movement, intense and wide identification is described and explained psychologically. In the deep movement [mysticism] is at least taken seriously: reality consists of wholes which we cut down rather than of isolated items which we put together."[19] Eric Katz maintains that in "the most complete expression of the philosophy of deep ecology, [Naess] makes clear that deep ecology is much less a theory of ethics than a theory of ontology and epistemology."[20] Naess leans heavily on Hindu metaphysics. Note that in the selection reprinted here he says, "As a student and admirer since 1930 of Gandhi's nonviolent direct action, I am inevitably influenced by his metaphysics."[21] However, it is also true that Naess's view has implications for ethics even if his "Deep Ecology" ("ecosophy," as he would prefer) is not, in his view, properly called ethics.

We note one ethical implication of the self-realization doctrine: the expansion of self is motivated by self-interest. As Warwick Fox puts it, "ecological resistance is simply another name for self-defense."[22] These consequences for ethics are also apparent in the following remark by Naess: "If your self in the wide sense embraces another being, you need no moral exhortation to show care. You care for yourself without feeling any moral pressure to do it—unless you have succumbed to a neurosis of some kind, developed self-destructive tendencies, or hate yourself."[23] Another commentator's remarks are also illustrative here:

> Indeed, I consider that this shift [to an emphasis on our "capacity to identify with the larger collective of all beings"] is essential to our survival at this point in history precisely because it can serve in lieu of morality and because moralizing is so ineffective. . . . If would not occur to me, for example, to exhort you to refrain from cutting off your leg. That wouldn't

occur to me or to you, because your leg is part of you. Well, so are the trees in the Amazon Basin; they are our external lungs. We are gradually discovering that we are our world.[24]

"[I]n environmental affairs," Naess says, "we should primarily try to influence people toward beautiful acts by finding ways to work on their inclinations rather than their morals."[25] Naess borrows the phrase "beautiful action" from philosopher Immanuel Kant. Naess notes in the selection reprinted here that for Kant, a moral act is one done out of duty, not inclination. Indeed, acts done from inclination, according to Kant, are suspect from a moral point of view even if we do the right thing. Doing the right thing from inclination Naess calls—and claims that Kant does too—a beautiful action. Naess wants to dispense with moral actions in favor of beautiful ones. Recall what he said earlier about "no moral exhortation," no "moral pressure." Bill Devall talks about not "imposing environmental ethics"; instead, "we will naturally respect, love, honor, and protect that which is our self."[26] Still, it is worth observing how many people are "naturally" self-destructive! Elsewhere, Arne Naess has said, "The history of cruelty [inflicted] in the name of morals has convinced me that increase in identification might achieve what moralizing cannot: beautiful actions."[27]

Murray Bookchin, a severe and irreverent critic of Deep Ecology once said that Deep Ecology "parachuted into our midst . . . from the sunbelt's bizarre mix of Hollywood and Disneyland."[28] This, of course, is untrue, insofar as Deep Ecology comes from Norway. In a serious vein, Bookchin has for many years asserted that Deep Ecologists care only about wilderness preservation and little or nothing about social justice.

When Bookchin speaks of "biocentrism," he is talking about the views of Deep Ecologists. Human beings, Bookchin argues, are products of natural evolution; they are also unique as thinking beings. Bookchin rejects both strong anthropocentrism, that "confers on the privileged few the right to plunder the world of life, including human life," and biocentricity, which "denies or degrades the uniqueness of human beings, human subjectivity, rationality, aesthetic sensibility, and the ethical potential of humanity."[29] In Essay 32 reprinted here, others beside Deep Ecologists are criticized by Bookchin. "Gaian consciousness" and "eco-theology" are grouped together with Deep Ecology because all these movements are, he claims, mystical or antirational movements, and all are antihuman or antihumanist. These "antihuman" movements, Bookchin says, "exculpate the present society for its role in famines, epidemics, poverty, and hunger."[30] Bookchin claims, "The ecology movement is too important to allow itself to be taken over by airy mystics and reactionary misanthropes."[31]

NOTES

1. Alice Walker, *The Color Purple* (New York: Pocket Books, 1982), p. 203.

2. Arne Naess, "The Shadow and the Deep, Long-Range Ecology Movement: A Summary," *Inquiry* 16(1) (Spring 1973). This piece is a summary of an introductory lecture at the third World Future Research Conference, Bucharest, September 3–10, 1972.

3. Arne Naess, "Interview with Naess," in *Deep Ecology: Living as if Nature Mattered,* by Bill Devall and George Sessions (Salt Lake: Peregrine Smith Books, 1985), p. 74.

4. Arne Naess, "The Deep Ecological Movement: Some Philosophical Aspects," *Philosophical Inquiry* 8(1–2) (1986), p. 22.

5. Warwick Fox, *Toward a Transpersonal Ecology* (Boston: Shambhala, 1990), pp. 112–123.

6. Bill Devall and George Sessions, *Deep Ecology: Living as if Nature Mattered* (Salt Lake City: Peregrine Smith Books, 1985), p. 71.

7. Bill Devall, "The Deep Ecology Movement," *Natural Resources Journal* 20(2) (April 1980), p. 303.

8. Arne Naess, "The Shallow and the Deep, Long-Range Ecology Movement, A Summary," pp. 95–96.

9. Carolyn Merchant, *Radical Ecology: The Search for a Livable World* (New York: Routledge, 1992), p. 87.

10. Eric Katz, "Ethics and Philosophy of the Environment: A Brief Review of the Major Literature," *Environmental History Review* 15(2) (1991), p. 84. See also Bill Devall, "The Deep Long-Range Ecology Movement: 1960–2000—A Review" *Ethics and the Environment* 6(1) (Spring 2001).

11. Evelyn M. Hurwich, Review of *Deep Ecology: Living as if Nature Mattered*, edited by Bill Devall and George Sessions, cited in Note 3, in *Ecology Law Quarterly* 13 (1986), pp. 770–771.

12. Ibid., p. 771.

13. Arne Naess, "Self-Realization in Mixed Communities of Human, Bears, Sheep, and Wolves," *Inquiry* 22(1–2) (Summer 1979), p. 238.

14. Ibid.

15. Ibid., p. 237.

16. Arne Naess, "Self-Realization: An Ecological Approach to Being in the World," in *Thinking Like a Mountain: Towards a Council of All Beings*, edited by John Seed, Joanna Macy, Pat Fleming, and Arne Naess (Philadelphia: New Society Publishers, 1988). p. 19.

17. Arne Naess, "Identification as a Source of Deep Ecological Attitudes," in *Radical Environmentalism: Philosophy and Tactics*, edited by Peter C. List (Belmont, CA: Wadsworth, 1993), p. 28.

18. Ibid., p. 29.

19. Ibid., p. 30.

20. Eric Katz, "Ethics and Philosophy of the Environment: A Brief Review of the Literature,"

p. 85. Katz means by "most complete expression" Naess's *Ecology, Community and Lifestyle* (New York: Cambridge University Press, 1989).

21. Arne Naess, "Self-Realization: An Ecological Approach to Being in the World," p. 24.

22. See Warwick Fox, "Approaching Deep Ecology: A Response to Richard Sylvan's Critique of Deep Ecology," *Environmental Studies Occasional Paper* 20 (Hobart: University of Tasmania Centre for Environmental Studies, 1986).

23. Arne Naess, "Self-Realization: An Ecological Approach to Being in the World," pp. 26–27.

24. Joanna Macy in *Toward a Transpersonal Ecology* by Warwick Fox, p. 229.

25. Arne Naess, "Self-Realization: An Ecological Approach to Being in the World, p. 28.

26. Bill Devall, *Simple in Means, Rich in Ends: Practicing Deep Ecology* (Salt Lake City: Peregrine Smith Books, 1988), p. 43.

27. Arne Naess, "Identification as a Source of Deep Ecological Attitudes," in *Radical Environmentalism*, p. 32.

28. Murray Bookchin, "Social Ecology and Deep Ecology," *Socialist Review* 88(3) (1988), p. 13.

29. Ibid., p. 27.

30. Murray Bookchin, "Will Ecology Become 'The Dismal Science?' " in *Which Way for the Ecology Movement?* (San Francisco: AK Press, 1994), p. 29.

31. Ibid., p. 28.

30. Deep Ecology

Bill Devall and George Sessions

The term *deep ecology* was coined by Arne Naess in his 1973 article, "The Shallow and the Deep, Long-Range Ecology Movements."[1] Naess was attempting to describe the deeper, more spiritual approach to nature exemplified in the writings of Aldo Leopold and Rachel Carson. He thought that this deeper approach resulted from a more sensitive openness to ourselves and nonhuman life around us. The essence of deep ecology is to keep asking more searching questions about human life, society, and Nature as in the Western philosophical tradition of Socrates. As examples of this deep questioning, Naess points out "that we ask why and how, where others do not. For instance, ecology as a science does not ask what kind of a society would be the best for maintaining a particular ecosystem— that is considered a question for value theory, for politics, for ethics." Thus deep ecology goes beyond the so-called factual scientific level to the level of self and Earth wisdom.

Deep Ecology: Living as if Nature Mattered, by Bill Devall and George Sessions (Salt Lake City: Peregrine Smith Books, 1985), pp. 65–73. Reprinted by permission of the publisher.

Deep ecology goes beyond a limited piecemeal shallow approach to environmental problems and attempts to articulate a comprehensive religious and philosophical worldview. The foundations of deep ecology are the basic intuitions and experiencing of ourselves and Nature which comprise ecological consciousness. Certain outlooks on politics and public policy flow naturally from this consciousness. And in the context of this book, we discuss the minority tradition as the type of community most conducive both to cultivating ecological consciousness and to asking the basic questions of values and ethics addressed in these pages.

Many of these questions are perennial philosophical and religious questions faced by humans in all cultures over the ages. What does it mean to be a unique human individual? How can the individual self maintain and increase its uniqueness while also being an inseparable aspect of the whole system wherein there are no sharp breaks between self and the *other*? An ecological perspective, in this deeper sense, results in what Theodore Roszak calls "an awakening of wholes greater than the sum of their parts. In spirit, the discipline is contemplative and therapeutic."[2]

Ecological consciousness and deep ecology are in sharp contrast with the dominant worldview of technocratic-industrial societies which regards humans as isolated and fundamentally separate from the rest of Nature, as superior to, and in charge of, the rest of creation. But the view of humans as separate and superior to the rest of Nature is only part of larger cultural patterns. For thousands of years, Western culture has become increasingly obsessed with the idea of *dominance:* with dominance of humans over nonhuman Nature, masculine over the feminine, wealthy and powerful over the poor, with the dominance of the West over non-Western cultures. Deep ecological consciousness allows us to see through these erroneous and dangerous illusions.

For deep ecology, the study of our place in the Earth household includes the study of ourselves as part of the organic whole. Going beyond a narrowly materialist scientific understanding of reality, the spiritual and the material aspects of reality fuse together. While the leading intellectuals of the dominant worldview have tended to view religion as "just superstition," and have looked upon ancient spiritual practice and enlightenment, such as found in Zen Buddhism, as essentially subjec-

tive, the search for deep ecological consciousness is the search for a more objective consciousness and state of being through an active deep questioning and meditative process and way of life.

Many people have asked these deeper questions and cultivated ecological consciousness within the context of different spiritual traditions—Christianity, Taoism, Buddhism, and Native American rituals, for example. While differing greatly in other regards, many in these traditions agree with the basic principles of deep ecology.

Warwick Fox, an Australian philosopher, has succinctly expressed the central intuition of deep ecology: "It is the idea that we can make no firm ontological divide in the field of existence: That there is no bifurcation in reality between the human and the non-human realms . . . to the extent that we perceive boundaries, we fall short of deep ecological consciousness."[3]

From this most basic insight or characteristic of deep ecological consciousness, Arne Naess has developed two *ultimate norms* or intuitions which are themselves not derivable from other principles or intuitions. They are arrived at by the deep-questioning process and reveal the importance of moving to the philosophical and religious level of wisdom. They cannot be validated, of course, by the methodology of modern science based on its usual mechanistic assumptions and its very narrow definition of data. These ultimate norms are *self-realization* and *biocentric equality.*

1. Self-Realization

In keeping with the spiritual traditions of many of the world's religions, the deep ecology norm of self-realization goes beyond the modern Western *self* which is defined as an isolated ego striving primarily for hedonistic gratification or for a narrow sense of individual salvation in this life or the next. This socially programmed sense of the narrow self or social self dislocates us, and leaves us prey to whatever fad or fashion is prevalent in our society or social reference group. We are thus robbed of beginning the search for our unique spiritual/biological personhood. Spiritual growth, or unfolding, begins when we cease to understand or see ourselves as isolated and narrow competing egos and begin to identify with other humans from our family and friends to, eventually, our species. But the deep ecology sense of self requires a further maturity and growth, an identification which goes beyond humanity to include the nonhuman world. We must see beyond our narrow contemporary cultural assumptions and values, and the conventional wisdom of our time and place, and this is best achieved by the meditative deep-questioning process. Only in this way can we hope to attain full mature personhood and uniqueness.

A nurturing nondominating society can help in the "real work" of becoming a whole person. The "real work" can be summarized symbolically as the realization of "self-in-Self" where "Self" stands for organic wholeness. This process of the full unfolding of the self can also be summarized by the phrase, "No one is saved until we are all saved," where the phrase "one" includes not only me, an individual human, but all humans, whales, grizzly bears, whole rain forest ecosystems, mountains and rivers, the tiniest microbes in the soil, and so on.

II. Biocentric Equality

The intuition of biocentric equality is that all things in the biosphere have an equal right to live and blossom and to reach their own individual forms of unfolding and self-realization within the larger Self-realization. This basic intuition is that all organisms and entities in the ecosphere, as parts of the interrelated whole, are equal in intrinsic worth. Naess suggests that biocentric equality as an intuition is true in principle, although in the process of living, all species use each other as food, shelter, etc. Mutual predation is a biological fact of life, and many of the world's religions have struggled with the spiritual implications of this. Some animal liberationists who attempt to sidestep this problem by advocating vegetarianism are forced to say that the entire plant kingdom including rain forests have no right to their own existence. This evasion flies in the face of the basic intuition of equality.[4] Aldo Leopold expressed this intuition when he said humans are "plain citizens" of the biotic community, not lord and master over all other species.

Biocentric equality is intimately related to the all-inclusive Self-realization in the sense that if we harm the rest of Nature then we are harming ourselves. There are no boundaries and everything is interrelated. But insofar as we perceive things as individual organisms or entities, the insight draws us to respect all human and non-human individuals in their own right as parts of the whole without feeling the need to set up hierarchies of species with humans at the top.

The practical implications of this intuition or norm suggest that we should live with minimum rather than maximum impact on other species and on the Earth in general. Thus we see another aspect of our guiding principle: "simple in means, rich in ends." . . .

A fuller discussion of the biocentric norm as it unfolds itself in practice begins with the realization that we, as individual humans, and as communities of humans, have vital needs which go beyond such basics as food, water, and shelter to include love, play, creative expression, intimate relationships with a particular landscape (or Nature taken in its entirety) as well as intimate relationships with other humans, and the vital need for spiritual growth, for becoming a mature human being.

Our vital material needs are probably more simple than many realize. In technocratic-industrial societies there is overwhelming propaganda and advertising which encourages false needs and destructive desires designed to foster increased production and consumption of goods. Most of this actually diverts us from facing reality in an objective way and from beginning the "real work" of spiritual growth and maturity.

Many people who do not see themselves as supporters of deep ecology nevertheless recognize an overriding vital human need for a healthy and high-quality natural environment for humans, if not for all life, with minimum intrusion of toxic waste, nuclear radiation from human enterprises, minimum acid rain and smog, and enough free flowing wilderness so humans can get in touch with their sources, the natural rhythms and the flow of time and place.

Drawing from the minority tradition and from the wisdom of many who have offered the insight of interconnectedness, we recognize that deep ecologists can offer suggestions for gaining maturity and encouraging the processes of harmony with nature, but that there is no grand solution which is guaranteed to save us from ourselves.

The ultimate norms of deep ecology suggest a view of the nature of reality and our place as an individual (many in the one) in the larger scheme of things. They cannot be fully grasped intellectually but are ultimately experiential. . . .

Dominant Worldview	Deep Ecology
Dominance over Nature	Harmony with Nature
Natural environment as resource for humans	All nature has intrinsic worth/biospecies equality
Material/economic growth for growing human population	Elegantly simple material needs (material goals serving the larger goal of self-realization)
Belief in ample resource reserves	Earth "supplies" limited
High technological progress and solutions	Appropriate technology; nondominating science
Consumerism	Doing with enough/recycling
National/centralized community	Minority tradition/bioregion

Figure 1 The contrast between the dominant worldview and Deep Ecology

As a brief summary of our position thus far, Figure 1 summarizes the contrast between the dominant worldview and deep ecology.

III. Basic Principles of Deep Ecology

In April 1984, during the advent of spring and John Muir's birthday, George Sessions and Arne Naess summarized fifteen years of thinking on the principles of deep ecology while camping in Death Valley, California. In this great and special place, they articulated these principles in a literal, somewhat neutral way, hoping that they would be understood and accepted by persons coming from different philosophical and religious positions.

Readers are encouraged to elaborate their own versions of deep ecology, clarify key concepts and think through the consequences of acting from these principles.

Basic Principles

1. The well-being and flourishing of human and nonhuman life on earth have value in themselves (synonyms: intrinsic value, inherent value). These values are independent of the usefulness of the nonhuman world for human purposes.

2. Richness and diversity of life forms contribute to the realization of these values and are also values in themselves.

3. Humans have no right to reduce this richness and diversity except to satisfy *vital* needs.

4. The flourishing of human life and cultures is compatible with a substantial decrease of the human population. The flourishing of nonhuman life requires such a decrease.

5. Present human interference with the nonhuman world is excessive, and the situation is rapidly worsening.

6. Policies must therefore be changed. These policies affect basic economic, technological, and ideological structures. The resulting state of affairs will be deeply different from the present.

7. The ideological change is mainly that of appreciating *life quality* (dwelling in situations of inherent value) rather than adhering to an increasingly higher standard of living. There will be a profound awareness of the difference between big and great.

8. Those who subscribe to the foregoing points have an obligation directly or indirectly to try to implement the necessary changes.

Naess and Sessions Provide Comments on the Basic Principles

RE (1). This formulation refers to the biosphere, or more accurately, to the ecosphere as a whole. This includes individuals, species, populations, habitat, as well as human and nonhuman cultures. From our current knowledge of all-pervasive intimate relationships, this implies a fundamental deep concern and respect. Ecological processes of the planet should, on the whole, remain intact. "The world environment should remain 'natural'" (Gary Snyder).

The term "life" is used here in a more comprehensive nontechnical way to refer also to what biologists classify as "nonliving"; rivers (watersheds), landscapes, ecosystems. For supporters of deep ecology, slogans such as "Let the river live" illustrate this broader usage so common in most cultures.

Inherent value as used in (1) is common in deep ecology literature. ("The presence of inherent value in a natural object is independent of any awareness, interest, or appreciation of it by a conscious being.")[5]

RE (2). More technically, this is a formulation concerning diversity and complexity. From an ecological standpoint, complexity and symbiosis are conditions for maximizing diversity. So-called simple, lower, or primitive species of plants and animals contribute essentially to the richness and diversity of life. They have value in themselves and are not merely steps toward the so-called higher or rational life forms. The second principle presupposes that life itself, as a process over evolutionary time, implies an increase of diversity and richness. The refusal to acknowledge that some life forms have greater or lesser intrinsic value than others (see points 1 and 2) runs counter to the formulations of some ecological philosophers and New Age writers.

Complexity, as referred to here, is different from complication. Urban life may be more complicated than life in a natural setting without being more complex in the sense of multifaceted quality.

RE (3). The term "vital need" is left deliberately vague to allow for considerable latitude in judgment. Differences in climate and related factors, together with differences in the structures of societies as they now exist, need to be considered (for some Eskimos, snow-mobiles are necessary today to satisfy vital needs).

People in the materially richest countries cannot be expected to reduce their excessive interference with the nonhuman world to a moderate level overnight. The stabilization and reduction of the human population will take time. Interim strategies need to be developed. But this in no way excuses the present complacency—the extreme seriousness of our current situation must first be realized. But the longer we wait the more drastic will be the measures needed. Until deep changes are made, substantial decreases in richness and diversity are liable to occur: the rate of extinction of species will be ten to one hundred times greater than any other period of earth history.

RE (4). The United Nations Fund for Population Activities in their State of World Population Report (1984) said that high human population growth rates (over 2.0 percent annum) in many developing countries "were diminishing the quality of life for many millions of people." During the decade 1974–1984, the world population grew by nearly 800 million—more than the size of India. "And we will be adding about one Bangladesh (population 93 million) per annum between now and the year 2000."

The report noted that "The growth rate of the human population has declined for the first time in human history. But at the same time, the number of people being added to the human population is bigger than at any time in history because the population base is larger."

Most of the nations in the developing world (including India and China) have as their official government policy the goal of reducing the rate of human population increase, but there are debates over the types of measures to take (contraception, abortion, etc.) consistent with human rights and feasibility.

The report concludes that if all governments set specific population targets as public policy to help alleviate poverty and advance the quality of life, the current situation could be improved.

As many ecologists have pointed out, it is also absolutely crucial to curb population growth in the so-called developed (i.e., overdeveloped) industrial societies. Given the tremendous rate of consumption and waste production of individuals in these societies, they represent a much greater threat and impact on the biosphere per capita than individuals in Second and Third World countries.

RE (5). This formulation is mild. For a realistic assessment of the situation, see the unabbreviated version of the IUCN's World Conservation Strategy. There are other works to be highly recommended, such as Gerald Barney's Global 2000 Report to the President of the United States.

The slogan of "noninterference" does not imply that humans should not modify some ecosystems as do other species. Humans have modified the earth and will probably continue to do so. At issue is the nature and extent of such interference.

The fight to preserve and extend areas of wilderness or near-wilderness should continue and should focus on the general ecological functions of these areas (one such function: large wilderness areas are required in the biosphere to allow for continued evolutionary speciation of animals and plants). Most present designated wilderness areas and game preserves are not large enough to allow for such speciation.

RE (6). Economic growth as conceived and implemented today by the industrial states is incompatible with (1)–(5). There is only a faint resemblance between ideal sustainable forms of economic growth and present policies of the industrial societies. And "sustainable" still means "sustainable in relation to humans."

Present ideology tends to value things because they are scarce and because they have a commodity value. There is prestige in vast consumption and waste (to mention only several relevant factors).

Whereas "self-determination," "local community," and "think globally, act locally," will remain key terms in the ecology of human societies, nevertheless the implementation of deep changes requires increasingly global action—action across borders.

Governments in Third World countries (with the exception of Costa Rica and a few others) are uninterested in deep ecological issues. When the governments of industrial societies try to promote ecological measures through Third World governments, practically nothing is accomplished (e.g, with problems of desertification). Given this situation, support for global action through nongovernmental international organizations becomes increasingly important. Many of these organizations are able to act globally "from grassroots to grassroots," thus avoiding negative governmental interference.

Cultural diversity today requires advanced technology, that is, techniques that advance the basic goals of each culture. So-called soft, intermediate, and alternative technologies are steps in this direction.

RE (7). Some economists criticize the term "quality of life" because it is supposed to be vague.

But on closer inspection, what they consider to be vague is actually the nonquantitative nature of the term. One cannot quantify adequately what is important for the quality of life as discussed here, and there is no need to do so.

RE (8). There is ample room for different opinions about priorities: what should be done first, what next? What is most urgent? What is clearly necessary as opposed to what is highly desirable but not absolutely pressing?

Notes

1. Arne Naess, "The Shallow and the Deep, Long-Range Ecology Movements: A Summary," *Inquiry 16* (Oslo, 1973), pp. 95–100.

2. Theodore Roszak, *Where the Wasteland Ends* (New York: Anchor, 1972).

3. Warwick Fox, "The Intuition of Deep Ecology" (Paper presented at the Ecology and Philosophy Conference, Australian National University, September, 1983). To appear in *The Ecologist* (England, Fall 1984).

4. Tom Regan, *The Case for Animal Rights* (New York: Random House, 1983). For excellent critiques of the animal rights movement, see John Rodman, "The Liberation of Nature?" *Inquiry 20* (Oslo, 1977). J. Baird Callicott, "Animal Liberation," *Environmental Ethics 2, 4* (1980); see also John Rodman, "Four Forms of Ecological Consciousness Reconsidered" in T. Attig and D. Scherer, eds., *Ethics and the Environment* (Englewood Cliffs, NJ: Prentice-Hall, 1983).

5. Tom Regan, "The Nature and Possibility of an Environmental Ethic," *Environmental Ethics 3* (1981), pp. 19–34.

31. Self-Realization: An Ecological Approach to Being in the World

Arne Naess

For at least 2500 years, humankind has struggled with basic questions about who we are, what we are heading for, what kind of reality we are part of. Two thousand five hundred years is a short period in the lifetime of a species, and still less in the life-time of the Earth, on whose surface we belong as mobile parts.

What I am going to say more or less in my own way, may roughly be condensed into the following six points:

Thinking Like a Mountain: Towards a Council of All Beings, by John Seed, Joanna Macy, Pat Fleming, and Arne Naess (Philadelphia: New Society Publishers, 1988), pp. 19–30. Reprinted by permission of the publisher.

1. We underestimate ourselves. I emphasize *self*. We tend to confuse it with the narrow ego.

2. Human nature is such that with sufficient all-sided maturity we cannot avoid "identifying" ourselves with all living beings, beautiful or ugly, big or small, sentient or not. I will elucidate my concept of identifying later.

3. Traditionally, the *maturity of the self* develops through three stages—from ego to social self, and from social self to metaphysical self. In this conception of the process nature—our home, our immediate environment, where we belong as children, and our identification with living human beings—is largely ignored. I therefore tentatively introduce the concept of an *ecological self*. We may be in, of and for nature from our very beginning. Society and human relations are important, but our self is richer in its constitutive relations. These relations are not only relations we have with humans and the human community, but with the larger community of all living beings.

4. The joy and meaning of life is enhanced through increased self-realization, through the fulfillment of each being's potential. Whatever the differences between beings, increased self-realization implies broadening and deepening of the *self*.

5. Because of an inescapable process of identification with others, with growing maturity, the self is widened and deepened. We "see ourself in others." Self-realization is hindered if the self-realization of others, with whom we identify, is hindered. Love of ourself will labor to overcome this obstacle by assisting in the self-realization of others according to the formula "live and let live." Thus, all that can be achieved by altruism—the dutiful, *moral* consideration of others—can be achieved—and much more—through widening and deepening ourself. Following Immanuel Kant's critique, we then act *beautifully* but neither morally nor immorally.

6. The challenge of today is to save the planet from further devastation which violates both the enlightened self-interest of humans and nonhumans, and decreases the potential of joyful existence for all.

The simplest answer to who or what I am is to point to my body, using my finger. But clearly I cannot identify my self or even my ego with my body. For example, compare:

I know Mr. Smith.	with	My body knows Mr. Smith.
I like poetry.		My body likes poetry.
The only difference between us is that you are Presbyterian and I am a Baptist.		The only difference between our bodies is that your body is Presbyterian whereas mine is Baptist.

In the above sentences we cannot substitute "my body" for "I" nor can we substitute "my mind" or "my mind and body" for "I." But this of course does not tell us what the ego or self is.

Several thousand years of philosophical, psychological and social-psychological discourse has not brought us any stable conception of the "I," ego, or the self. In modern psychotherapy these notions play an indispensable role, but the practical goal of therapy does not necessitate philosophical clarification of the terms. For our purposes, it is important to remind ourselves what strange and marvelous phenomena we are dealing with. They are extremely close to each of us. Perhaps the very nearness of these objects of reflection and discourse adds to our difficulties. I shall only offer a single sentence resembling a definition of the ecological self. The ecological self of a person is that with which this person identifies.

This key sentence (rather than definition) about the self, shifts the burden of clarification from the term *self* to that of *identification* or more accurately, the *process of identification*.

What would be a paradigmatic situation of identification? It is a situation in which identification elicits intense empathy. My standard example has to do with a nonhuman being I met 40 years ago. I looked through an old-fashioned microscope at the dramatic meeting of two drops of different chemicals. A flea jumped from a lemming strolling along the table and landed in the middle of the acid chemicals. To save it was impossible. It took many minutes for the flea to die. Its movements were dreadfully expressive. What I felt was, naturally, a painful compassion and empathy. But the empathy was *not* basic. What *was* basic was the process of identification, that "I see myself in the flea." If I was alienated from the flea, not seeing intuitively anything resembling myself, the death struggle would have left me indifferent. So there must be identification in order for there to be compassion and, among humans, solidarity.

One of the authors contributing admirably to clarification of the study of self is Erich Fromm:

> The doctrine that love for oneself is identical with *selfishness* and an alternative to love for others has pervaded theology, philosophy, and popular thought; the same doctrine has been rationalized in scientific language in Freud's theory of narcissism. Freud's concept presupposes a fixed amount of libido. In the infant, all of the libido has the child's own person as its objective, the stage of *primary narcissism* as Freud calls it. During the individual's development, the libido is shifted from one's own person toward other objects. If a person is blocked in his *object-relationships* the libido is withdrawn from the objects and returned to his or her own person; this is called *secondary narcissism*. According to Freud, the more love I turn toward the outside world the less love is left for myself, and vice versa. He thus describes the phenomenon of love as an impoverishment of one's self-love because all libido is turned to an object outside oneself.[1]

Fromm, however, disagrees with Freud's analysis. He concerned himself solely with love of humans, but as "ecosophers" we find the notions of "care, respect, responsibility, knowledge" applicable to living beings in the wide sense.

> Love of others and love of ourselves are not alternatives. On the contrary, an attitude of love toward themselves will be found in all those who are capable of loving others. Love, in principle, is indivisible as far as the connection between *objects* and one's own self is concerned. Genuine love is an expression of productiveness and implies care, respect responsibility, and knowledge. It is not an *effect* in the sense of being effected by somebody, but an active striving for the growth and happiness of the loved person, rooted in one's own capacity to love.[2]

Fromm is very instructive about unselfishness—diametrically opposite to selfishness, but still based upon alienation and a narrow perception of self. What he says applies also to persons experiencing sacrifice of themselves.

The nature of unselfishness becomes particularly apparent in its effect on others and most frequently, in our culture, in the effect the "unselfish" mother has on her children. She believes that by her unselfishness her children will experience what it means to be loved and in turn to learn what it means to love. The effect of her unselfishness, however, does not at all correspond to her expectations. The children do not show the happiness of persons who are convinced that they are loved; they are anxious, tense, afraid of the mother's disapproval, and anxious to live up to her expectations. Usually, they are affected by their mother's hidden hostility against life, which they sense rather than recognize, and eventually become imbued with it themselves:

> If one has a chance to study the effect of a mother with genuine self-love, one can see that there is nothing more conducive to giving a child the experience of what love, joy, and happiness are than being loved by a mother who loves herself.[3]

From the viewpoint of ecophilosophy, the point is this: We need environmental ethics, but when people feel they unselfishly give up, even sacrifice, their interest in order to show love for nature, this is probably in the long run a treacherous basis for ecology. Through broader identification, they may come to see their own interest served by environmental protection, through genuine self-love, love of a widened and deepened self.

*

As a student and admirer since 1930 of Gandhi's nonviolent direct action, I am inevitably influenced by his metaphysics which furnished him tremendously powerful motivation to keep on going until his death. His supreme aim, as he saw it, was not only India's *political* liberation. He led crusades against extreme poverty, caste suppression, and against terror in the name of religion. These crusades were necessary, but the liberation of the individual human being was his highest end. Hearing Gandhi's description of his ultimate goal may sound strange to many of us.

> What I want to achieve—what I have been striving and pining to achieve these thirty years—is self-realization, to see God face to face, to attain *Moksha* (Liberation). I live and move and have my being in pursuit of that goal. All that I do by way of speaking and writing, and all my ventures in the political field, are directed to this same end.[4]

This sounds individualistic to the Western mind, a common misunderstanding. If the self Gandhi is speaking about were the ego or the "narrow" self (*jiva*) of egocentric interest, of narrow ego gratifications, why then work for the poor? For him it is the supreme or universal Self—the *atman*—that is to be realized. Paradoxically, it seems, he tries to reach self-realization through *selfless action*, that is, through reduction of the dominance of the narrow self or ego. Through the wider Self every living being is connected intimately, and from this intimacy follows the capacity of *identification* and as its natural consequences, the practice of nonviolence. No moralizing is necessary, just as we do not require moralizing to make us breathe. We need to cultivate our insight, to quote Gandhi again: "The rock-bottom foundation of the technique for achieving the power of nonviolence is belief in the essential oneness of all life."

Historically we have seen how ecological preservation is nonviolent at its very core. Gandhi notes:

> I believe in *advaita* (non-duality), I believe in the essential unity of man and, for that matter, of all that lives. Therefore I believe that if one man gains spirituality, the whole world gains with him and, if one man fails, the whole world fails to that extent.[5]

Some people might consider Gandhi extreme in his personal consideration for the self-realization of living beings other than humans. He traveled with a goat to satisfy his need for milk. This was part of a nonviolent witness against certain cruel features in the Hindu way of milking cows. Furthermore, some European companions who lived with Gandhi in his ashram were taken aback that he let snakes, scorpions and spiders move unhindered into their bedrooms—animals fulfilling their lives. He even prohibited people from having a stock of medicines against poisonous bites. He believed in the possibility of satisfactory coexistence and he proved right. There were no accidents. Ashram people would naturally look into their shoes for scorpions before putting them on. Even when moving over the floor in darkness one could easily avoid trampling on one's fellow beings. Thus, Gandhi recognized a basic, common right to live and blossom, to self-realization applicable to any being having interests or needs. Gandhi made manifest the internal relation between self-realization, nonviolence and what is sometimes called biospherical egalitarianism.

In the environment in which I grew up, I heard that what is important in life is to *be* somebody—usually implying to outdo others, to be victorious in comparison of abilities. This conception of the meaning and goal of life is especially dangerous today in the context of vast international economic competition. The law of supply and demand of separate, isolatable "goods and services" independent of real needs, must not be made to reign over increasing areas of our lives. The ability to cooperate, to work with people, to make them feel good *pays* of course in a fiercely individualist society, and high positions may require it. These virtues are often subordinated to the career, to the basic norms of narrow ego fulfillment, not to a self-realization worth the name. To identify self-realization with ego indicates a vast underestimation of the human self.

According to a usual translation of Pali or Sanskrit, Buddha taught his disciples that the human *mind* should embrace all living things as a mother cares for her son, her only son. For some it is not meaningful or possible for a human *self* to embrace all living things, then the usual translation can remain. We ask only that your *mind* embrace all living beings, and that you maintain an intention to care, feel and act with compassion.

If the Sanskrit word *atman* is translated into English, it is instructive to note that this term has the basic meaning of *self* rather than *mind* or *spirit*, as you see in translations. The superiority of the translation using the word *self* stems from the consideration that *if* your *self* in the wide sense embraces another being, you need no moral exhortation to show care. You care for yourself without feeling any moral pressure to do it—unless you have succumbed to a neurosis of some kind, developed self-destructive tendencies, or hate yourself.

The Australian ecological feminist Patsy Hallen uses a formula close to that of Buddha: "we are here to embrace rather than conquer the world." Notice that the term *world* is used here rather than *living beings*. I suspect that our thinking need not proceed from the notion of living being to that of the world. If we can conceive of reality or the world we live in as alive in a wide, not easily defined sense then there will be no non-living beings to care for!

If "self-realization" today is associated with life-long narrow ego gratification, isn't it inaccurate to use this term for self-realization in the widely different sense of Gandhi, or less religiously loaded, as a term for the widening and deepening of the self so it embraces all life forms? Perhaps it is. But I think the very popularity of the term makes people listen for a moment and feel safe. In that moment the notion of a greater Self can be introduced, contending that if people equate self-realization with narrow ego fulfillment, they seriously *underestimate* themselves. We are much greater, deeper, more generous and capable of dignity and joy than we think! A wealth of non-competitive joys is open to us!

I have another important reason for inviting people to think in terms of deepening and widening their selves, starting with narrow ego gratification as the crudest, but inescapable starting point. It has to do with the notion usually placed as the opposite of egoism, namely the notion of *altruism*. The Latin term *ego* has as its opposite the *alter*. Altruism implies that *ego* sacrifices its interest in favour of the other, the *alter*. The motivation is primarily that of duty; it is said that we *ought* to love others as strongly as we love ourself.

What humankind is capable of loving from mere duty or more generally from moral exhortation is, unfortunately, very limited. From the Renaissance to the Second World War about four hundred cruel wars have been fought by Christian nations, usually for the flimsiest of reasons. It seems to me that in the future more emphasis has to be given to the conditions which naturally widen and deepen our self. With a sufficiently wide and deep sense of self, ego and alter as opposites are eliminated stage by stage as the distinctions are transcended.

Early in life, the social *self* is sufficiently developed so that we do not prefer to eat a big cake alone. We share the cake with our family and friends. We identify with these people sufficiently to see our joy in their joy, and to see our disappointment in theirs. Now is the time to share with all life on our maltreated earth by deepening our identification with all life-forms, with the ecosystems, and with Gaia, this fabulous, old planet of ours.

The philosopher Immanuel Kant introduced a pair of contrasting concepts which deserve extensive use in our effort to live harmoniously in, for, and of nature: the concept of *moral* act and that of *beautiful* act. Moral acts are acts motivated by the intention to follow moral laws, at whatever cost, that is, to do our moral duty solely out of respect for that duty. Therefore, the supreme indication of our success in performing a pure, moral act is that we do it completely against our inclination, that we hate to do it, but are compelled by our respect for

moral law. Kant was deeply awed by two phenomena, "the heaven with its stars above me and the moral law within me."

If we do something we should because of a moral law, but do it out of inclination and with pleasure—what then? If we do what is right because of positive inclination, then, according to Kant, we perform a *beautiful* act. My point is that in environmental affairs we should primarily try to influence people toward beautiful acts by finding ways to work on their inclinations rather than their morals. Unhappily, the extensive moralizing within the ecological movement has given the public the false impression that they are primarily asked to sacrifice, to show more responsibility, more concern, and better morals. As I see it we need the immense variety of sources of joy opened through increased sensitivity toward the richness and diversity of life, through the profound cherishing of free natural landscapes. We all can contribute to this individually, and it is also a question of politics, local and global. Part of the joy stems from the consciousness of our intimate relation to something bigger than our own ego, something which has endured for millions of years and is worth continued life for millions of years. The requisite care flows naturally if the self is widened and deepened so that protection of free nature is felt and conceived of as protection of our very selves.

What I am suggesting is the supremacy of ecological ontology and a higher realism over environmental ethics as a means of invigorating the ecology movement in the years to come. If reality is experienced by the ecological Self, our behavior *naturally* and beautifully follows norms of strict environmental ethics. We certainly need to hear about our ethical shortcomings from time to time, but we change more easily through encouragement and a deepened perception of reality and our own *self*, that is, through a deepened realism. How that is to be brought about is too large a question for me to deal with here. But it will clearly be more a question of community therapy than community science: we must find and develop therapies which heal our relations with the widest community, that of all living beings.

Notes

1.   Erich Fromm, "Selfishness, Self-Love, and Self-interest," in *The Self: Explorations in Personal Growth*,

edited by Clark E. Moustakas (New York: Harper, 1956), p. 58.

2. Ibid., p. 59.

3. Gandhi quotations are taken from Arne Naess, *Gandhi and Group Conflict* (Oslo, Norway:

Universitetsforlaget, 1974), p. 35 where the metaphysics of self-realization are treated more thoroughly in that work.

4. Ibid.

5. Ibid.

32. Will Ecology Become "The Dismal Science"?

Murray Bookchin

Almost a century and a half ago, Thomas Carlyle described economics as "the dismal science." The phrase was to stick, especially as it applied to economics premised on a supposedly unavoidable conflict between "insatiable needs" and "scarce natural resources." In this economics, the limited bounty provided by a supposedly "stingy nature" doomed humanity to economic slumps, misery, civil strife, and hunger.

Today, the phrase "dismal science" appropriately describes certain trends in the ecology movement—trends that seem to be riding on an overwhelming tide of religious revivalism and mysticism. I refer not to the large number of highly motivated, well-intentioned, and often radical environmentalists who are making earnest efforts to arrest the ecological crisis, but rather to exotic tendencies that espouse deep ecology, biocentrism, Gaian consciousness, and eco-theology, to cite the main cults that celebrate a quasi-religious "reverence" for "Nature" with what is often a simultaneous denigration of human beings and their traits.

Mystical ecologists, like many of today's religious revivalists, view reason with suspicion and emphasize the importance of irrational and intuitive approaches to ecological issues. For the Reverend Thomas Berry, whom many regard as the foremost eco-theologian of our day, the "very rational process that we exalt as the only true way to understanding is by a certain irony discovered to be itself a mythic imaginative dream experience. The difficulty of our times is our inability to awaken out of this cultural pathology."

One does not have to be a member of the clergy to utter such atavistic notions. In a more secular vein, Bill Devall and George Sessions, professors of sociology and philosophy, respectively, who wrote *Deep Ecology,* one of the most widely read books in mystical ecology, offer a message of "self-realization" through an immersion of the personal self in a hazy "Cosmic Self," or, as they put it, a "'self-in-Self' where 'Self' stands for organic wholeness."

The language of *Deep Ecology* is distinctly salvational: "This process of the full unfolding of the self can also be summarized in the phrase: 'No one is saved until we are all saved,' where the phrase 'one' includes not only me, an individual human, but all humans, whales, grizzly bears, whole rainforest ecosystems mountains and rivers, the tiniest microbes in the soil, and so on." The words "and so on" omit the need to deal with pathogenic microbes, animal vectors of lethal diseases, earthquakes, and typhoons, to cite less aesthetically satisfying beings and phenomena than whales, grizzly bears, wolves, and mountains. This selective view of "Mother Nature's" biotic and physiographic inventory has raised some stormy problems for mystical ecology's message of universal salvation.

Mystical ecologists tend to downgrade social issues by reducing human problems (a generally distasteful subject to them) to a "species" level—to matters of genetics. In the words of Pastor Berry, humanity must be "reinvented on the species level" by going "beyond our cultural coding, to our genetic coding, to ask for guidance." The rhetoric that follows this passage in *The Dream of the Earth* verges on the mythopoeic, in which our "genetic coding" binds us "with the larger dimensions of the universe"—a universe that "carries the deep mysteries of our existence within itself." Berry's

From *Which Way for the Ecology Movement? Essays by Murray Bookchin* (San Francisco, CA: AK Press, 1994), pp. 21–29. Reprinted by permission.

exhortations enjoy great popularity these days, and have been quoted with approval even in the conventional environmental literature, not to speak of the mystical variety.

Such cosmological evangelism, clothed in ecological verbiage, deprecates humanity. When human beings are woven into the "web of life" as nothing more than one of "Mother Nature's" innumerable species, they lose their unique place in natural evolution as rational creatures of potentially unsurpassed qualities, endowed with a deeply social nature, creativity, and the capacity to function as moral agents.

Anthropocentrism, the quasi-theological notion that the world exists for human use, is derided by mystical ecologists in favor of the equally quasi-theological notion of biocentricity, namely, that all life-forms are morally interchangeable with one another in terms of their "intrinsic worth." In their maudlin *Gaia Mediations,* two mystical ecologists, John Seed and Joanna Macy, enjoin us human mortals to "think to your next death. Will your flesh and bones back into the cycle. Surrender. Love the plump worms you will become. Launder your weary being through the fountain of life." In the mystically over-baked world of the American Sunbelt, such drivel tends to descend to the level of bumper-sticker slogans or is evoked in poetic recitations at various ashrams in Anglo-American cities and towns.

Taken as a whole, the crude reduction of the ecological crisis to biological and psychological sources has produced an equally reductionist body of "correctives" that makes the dismal economics of an earlier time seem almost optimistic by comparison. For many, perhaps most, mystical ecologists, the standard recipe for a "sustainable" future involves a lifestyle based on harsh austerity—basically, a rustic discipline marked by dietary simplicity, hard work, the use of "natural resources" only to meet survival needs and a theistic primitivism that draws its inspiration from an alleged Pleistocene or Neolithic "spirituality" rather than from Renaissance or Enlightenment rationality.

Spirituality and rationality, which mystical ecologies invariably perceive in crassly reductionist and simplistic terms, are pitted against each other as angels and demons. The mystics usually regard technology, science, and reason as the basic sources of the ecological crisis and contend these should be contained or even replaced by toil, divination, and intuition. What is even more troubling is that many mystical ecologists are neo-Malthusians, whose more rambunctious elements regard famine and disease as necessary and even desirable to reduce human population.

The grim future evoked by mystical ecologists is by no means characteristic of the vision the ecology movement projected a generation ago. To the contrary, radical ecologists of the 1960s celebrated the prospect of a satisfying life, freed from material insecurity, toil and the self-denial produced by the market and bureaucratic capitalism.

This utopian vision, advanced primarily by social ecology in 1964 and 1965, was not antitechnological, antirational or antiscientific. It expressed for the first time in the merging ecology movement the prospect of a new social, technological, and spiritual dispensation. Social ecology claimed that the idea of dominating nature stemmed from the domination of human by human, in the form not only of class exploitation but of hierarchical domination. Capitalism—not technology, reason, or science as such—produced an economy that was systematically anti-ecological. Guided by the competitive marketplace maxim "grow or die," it would literally devour the biosphere, turning forests into lumber and soil into sand.

Accordingly, the key to resolving the ecological crisis was not only a change in spirituality—and not a regression to prehistoric religiosity—but a sweeping change in society. Social ecology offered the vision of a nonhierarchical, communitarian society that would be based on directly democratic confederal communities with technologies structured around solar, wind, and renewable sources of energy; food cultivation by organic methods; and a combined use of crafts and highly versatile, automatic, and sophisticated machinery to reduce human toil and free people to develop themselves as fully informed and creative citizens.

The disappearance of the utopian 1960s into the reactionary 1970s saw a steady retreat by millions of people into a spiritualistic inwardness that had already been latent in the counterculture of the previous decade. As possibilities for social change began to wane, people sought a surrogate reality to veil the ills of the prevailing society and the difficulty of removing them. Apart from a brief interlude of environmental resistance to the construction of nuclear power plants, large parts of the ecology movement began to withdraw from social concerns to spiritual ones, many of which were crassly mystical and theistic.

In the universities, Lynn White, Jr., whose advocacy of religious explanations for the ecological crisis began to give it an otherworldly character, initiated this withdrawal. Around the same time, Garrett Hardin's *Tragedy of the Commons* brought Malthus's ghost into ecological discourse in the academy, further deflecting the social thrust of the 1960s ecology movement into a demographic numbers game. Both of these academicians had advanced their views largely in *Science* magazine, which has only limited public outreach, so it fell to a California entomologist, Paul Ehrlich, to divert the ecological concerns of the early 1970s from the social domain to the single issue of population growth in a hysterical paperback, *The Population Bomb*, that went through numerous editions and reached millions of readers.

Writing like an SS officer touring the Warsaw ghetto, Ehrlich in the opening pages of his tract saw nothing but "People! People!"—failing to notice a vicious society that had degraded human lives. The slender thread that united White and, more firmly, Hardin and Ehrlich was the nonsocial interpretation they gave to ecological problems, not any shared ecological overview.

Arne Naess, a Norwegian academic and mountain-climber, provided such an overview in 1973. He coined the term "deep ecology" and nurtured it as an ecological philosophy or sensibility that asks "deep questions" in contrast to "shallow ecology." Recycled into a form of California spiritualism by Devall and Sessions with a bizarre mix of Buddhism, Taoism, Native American beliefs, Heidegger, and Spinoza, among others, mystical ecology was now ready to take off as a new "Earth Wisdom."

What catapulted this confused sensibility from the campus into newspaper headlines, however, was a wilderness movement, Earth First!, that began to take dramatic direct actions against the lumbering of old-growth forests and similar indecencies inflicted on wild areas by corporate America.

Earth First!'s founders, particularly David Foreman, had been conservationists who were weary of the ineffectual lobbying tactics of Washington-based conservation organizations. Inspired by Edward Abbey, the author of the highly popular novel *The Monkey Wrench Gang,* whose avowedly misanthropic views bordered on racism with its accolades to America's "northern European culture," Earth First!'s leaders began to seize upon deep ecology as a philosophy.

This is not to say that most Earth First!ers knew anything about "deep ecology" other than its claim to be "deep." But Devall and Sessions had placed Malthus in its pantheon of prophets and described "industrial society"—not capitalism—as the embodiment of the ills that mystical ecologists generally deride. Indeed, their book was distinctly wilderness-oriented, expressly "biocentric," and seemed to make short shrift of humanity's place in the cosmos.

Consistency has never been the strong point of any antirational movement, so it is not surprising that while Devall and Sessions piously extolled a "self-in-Self," a caring form of pantheism or hylozoism, Foreman did not hesitate to describe human beings as a "cancer" in the natural world, and quite surprisingly, Gary Snyder, the poet-laureate of the deep ecology movement, described humans as "locust-like."

Mystical ecology as a dismal science is, in fact, antihuman. Despite his gentle piety, Pastor Berry, for example, becomes positively ferocious in his treatment of human beings, describing them as "the most pernicious mode of earthly being." Indeed, "We are the termination, not the fulfillment, of the Earth process. If there were a parliament of creatures, its first decision might well be to vote the humans out of the community, too deadly a presence to tolerate any further. We are an affliction of the world, its demonic presence. We are the violation of Earth's most sacred aspects."

Clerical vitriol has often been more selective. In the best of cases, it has targeted the rich, not the poor; the oppressor, not the oppressed; the ruler, not the downtrodden. But mystical ecology tends to be more all-embracing. Berry's ecumenical "we," like his treatment of "human beings" as a species rather than as beings who are divided by the oppressions of race, sex, material means of life, culture, and the like, tends to permeate mystical ecology.

"We are all capitalists at heart," declares a well-intentioned Norwegian writer, Erik Dammann, whose *The Future in Our Hands* has been touted by Arne Naess as a virtual manifesto for social improvement. The homeless in American cities, the

AIDS victims who have been left to die in Zurich's notorious needle park, the overworked people in the First World's mines and factories—none of these count for much in Dammann's plea that "we" in America and Europe reduce our consumption of goods in behalf of the Third World's poor.

Laudable as the goal of reduced consumption may seem, it is an ineffectual exercise in charity, not social mobilization; in humanitarianism, not social change. It is also an exercise in a superficial form of social analysis that grossly underplays the profoundly systemic factors that have produced overfed elites in all parts of the world and masses of underfed underlings. Nearly all we learn from Dammann's liberal good intentions is that an ecumenical "we" must be faulted for the ills of the world—a mystical "consumer" who greedily demands goodies that "our" overworked corporations are compelled to produce.

Despite the radical rhetoric to which Devall and Sessions resort, the principal *practical* recipe for social change they have to offer "us" in *Deep Ecology* is little more than a naive prayer. "Our first principle," they write, "is to encourage agencies, legislators, property owners and managers to consider flowing with rather than forcing natural processes." We should "act through the political process to inform managers and government agencies of the principles of deep ecology," to achieve "some significant changes in the direction of wise long-range management policies."

The watered-down liberalism of Devall and Sessions is echoed more explicitly in Paul and Anne Ehrlich's latest book, *Healing the Planet*, in which the authors declare their adherence to deep ecology, a "quasi-religious movement" (to use their own words) that "recognizes that a successful new philosophy cannot be based on scientific nonsense." Such denigration of science hardly befits writers whose reputation is based on their scientific credentials, with or without the vague use of the word "nonsense" to qualify their remarks.

More guarded these days than in their earlier, somewhat hysterical tracts, the Ehrlichs offer something for everyone in a rather bewildering number of scenarios which show concern for the poor as well as the rich, the Third World as well as the First, even Marxists as well as avowed conservatives. But almost every important passage in the book repeats the refrain that marks their earlier works: "Controlling population growth is critical."

The Ehrlichs' treatment of fundamental social issues, however, reveals the extent to which they come to terms with the status quo. Our democratic "market-based economies [are] so far the most successful political and economic systems human beings have ever devised." That there is a systemic relationship between "market-based" economy and the ruthless plundering of the planet hardly appears on the Ehrlichs' social horizon.

Naess is equally troubling in his solutions. As he weighs such alternative political philosophies as communism and anarchism, the father of deep ecology asserts, in his recently translated *Ecology, Community, and Lifestyle*, that deep ecology has an affinity with "contemporary nonviolent anarchism." But the reader stunned by this commitment to a libertarian alternative quickly learns that "with the enormous and exponentially increasing human population pressure and war or warlike conditions in many places, it seems inevitable to maintain some fairly strong central institutions"—or, put less obliquely than deep ecologists are wont to do, a "fairly strong" centralized state. Here, in fact, Naess's neo-Malthusianism and his pessimistic view of the human condition reinforce elitist beliefs in the ecology movement for state centralization and the use of coercion. The views of such deep ecologists as Christopher Manes, whose own colleagues regard him as an extremist, barely deserve serious discussion. Manes has welcomed the AIDS epidemic as a means of population control. Many mystical ecology writers echo his claim that "wilderness and not civilization is the real world."

One of the most strident condemnations of human beings as the source of the ecological crisis comes from James Lovelock, the architect of the "Gaia hypothesis," a mythopoeic notion that the Earth, personified as "Gaia" (the Greek goddess of our planet), is literally a living organism. In this theology, "we," needless to say, are not merely trivial and expendable but, as some Gaians have put it, parasitic "intelligent fleas" on the planet. For Lovelock, the word "we" replaces all distinctions between elites and their victims in a shared responsibility for present-day ecological ills.

"Our humanist concerns about the poor of the inner cities or the Third World," Lovelock declaims, "and our near-obscene obsession with death, suffering, and pain as if these were evils in themselves—these thoughts divert the mind from our gross and excessive domination of the natural world. Poverty and suffering are not sent; they are the consequences of what we do."

It is "when we drive our cars and listen to the radio bringing news of acid rain [that] we need to remind ourselves that we, personally, are the polluters." Accordingly, "we are therefore accountable, personally, for the destruction of the trees by photochemical smog and acid rain." The lowly consumer is seen as the real source of the ecological crisis, not the producers who orchestrate public tastes through the mass media and the corporations who own and ravage Lovelock's divine Gaia.

The ecology movement is too important to allow itself to be taken over by airy mystics and reactionary misanthropes. The traditional labor movement, on which so many radicals placed their hopes for creating a new society, has withered, and in the United States the old-time populist movements have died with the agrarian strata that provided them with sizable followings. Rooseveltian liberalism's future hangs in the balance as a result of the Reagan-Bush assault on New Deal reforms. The cooptation of nearly every worthwhile cause, including conventional environmentalism itself, is symbolized by the ease with which corporations tout the slogan "Every Day is Earth Day!"

But the natural world itself is not cooptable. The complexity of organic and climatic processes still defies scientific control, just as the marketplace's drive to expand still defies social control. The conflict between the natural world and the present society has intensified over the past two decades. Ecological dislocations of massive proportions may well begin to overshadow the more sensational issues that make headlines today.

A decisive collision looms: On one side is the "grow-or-die" economy, lurching out of control. On the other, the fragile conditions necessary to the maintenance of advanced life-forms on this planet. This collision, in fact, confronts humanity itself with sharp alternatives: an ecological society structured around social ecology's ideal of a confederal, directly democratic, and ecologically oriented network of communities, or an authoritarian society in which humanity's interactions with the natural world will be structured around a command economics and politics. The third prospect, of course, is the immolation of humanity in a series of ecological and irreversible disasters.

For the ecology movement to become frivolous and allow itself to be guided by various sorts of mystics would be unpardonable—a tragedy of enormous proportions. Despite the dystopian atmosphere that seems to pervade much of the movement, its utopian vision of a democratic, rational, and ecological society is as viable today as it was a generation ago.

The misanthropic strain that runs through the movement in the name of biocentrism, antihumanism, Gaian consciousness, and neo-Malthusianism threatens to make ecology, in the broad sense of the term, the best candidate we have for a "dismal science." The attempt of many mystical ecologists to exculpate the present society for its role in famines, epidemics, poverty, and hunger serves the world's power elites as the most effective ideological defense for the extremes of wealth on the one side and poverty on the other.

It is not only the great mass of people who must make hard choices about humanity's future in a period of growing ecological dislocation; it is the ecology movement itself that must make hard choices about its sense of direction in a time of growing mystification.

33. SIDELIGHT: Do What's Natural, You Say?

We live in an age in which some marketing specialists exploit a certain revulsion against the plastic, that is, what is quintessentially artificial, a matter of artifice, or human-made. Correlatively there is a certain desire to live more naturally. "Natural" fibers and "all-natural" food are increasingly in demand. Indeed, the term *natural* seems honorific; conversely, the term *unnatural* is frequently used pejoratively, that is, implying that the thing so labeled is bad or wrong. Is there any rational basis for associating the natural with the right and the unnatural with the wrong? In particular, should we scan the processes of nature to find normative models, that is, types of behavior that we should emulate? There are indeed subtleties to this topic, which we shall address briefly.

There is a broad sense of 'natural' in which anything that happens in part of the nature of the world as we know it. In this sense any action is natural, so none is unnatural. Thus, Jeffrey Dahmer's cannibalizing was natural, as was the mass destruction of Jews and Gypsies by the Nazis, or the mass killing of hundreds of thousands of Japanese by the American bombing of Hiroshima and Nagasaki.

Typically, however, we identify certain actions or events, from the set of all actions or events, by using labels such as *natural* or *unnatural*; that is, we contrast some events with others when we say only of some that they are natural or of others that they are unnatural. Thus, by 'natural' we do not normally mean "whatever happens." Although we humans are without question a part of nature, by 'natural' we often mean that which occurs without deliberate human intervention or a by-product of such. Hence, the mass extinction of 65 million years ago, the glaciations of the last Ice Age, the tides, the ocean currents, the revolution of the earth about the sun, volcanic eruptions, typhoons, photosynthesis, or even the striking of the earth by a meteor are, or would be, natural occurrences. Some of these events may be tragic, but there is no obvious connection between the fact that they are natural and their assessment as good or bad. Natural processes are extremely wasteful of life and potential life; in the ejaculation of a male human, enough sperm are produced to inseminate several hundred million eggs; of the offspring produced by a single member of some species only a tiny fraction can survive. This is not what one would expect of a world guided by the Protestant God of "waste not, want not."[1]

Among "unnatural" events, that is, those resulting from human action, are a wildly diverse lot: the expected leaking of plutonium into arctic waters above Norway from a deteriorating, sunken Russian submarine (not to worry: it will cease to be radioactive by the year 26000), the selling of children into prostitution, destruction of 70 percent of the world's forests, the rescue of millions of people from the ravages of disease and injury, the heroic resistance against Nazi and fascist movements, the music of Mozart, the paintings of Seurat, Matisse, or van Gogh, and so on. All such behavior is unnatural if by the term one means involving human action or the result of such.

May we turn to animal behavior for inspiration as to how to live (as if we are not animals and as if we are not part of nature)? Let us consider some interesting examples revealed by recent studies of "animal behavior" (some not to be read just before meals perhaps). Among nonhuman animals are many examples of wonderfully cooperative behavior. We find the analogue of monogamy among geese, swans, angelfish, beavers, and soldier beetles. Among owl monkeys males rear the offspring and females search for food.[2] We focus elsewhere. Burying beetle couples prepare the corpses of small animals for their young to eat. When the young are born, the parents eat the numbers down to a size that the food supply can support (perhaps they have read Garrett Hardin on "carrying capacity"); thus, cannibalism gives the surviving youngsters a "head start" so to speak. Or would you rather be a shark, specifically a tiger shark? Of the 100 eggs formed by the shark after mating, the first one to reach the uterus survives by eating all the other embryos and unfertilized eggs as they are released.[3] So among sharks it is perfectly natural to kill of one's "unborn siblings." Are all mothers nourishing? Not among the emu; they abandon their offspring at the slightest sign of danger.[4]

Some other examples. Two woodpeckers often share a nest, but when one lays an egg the other destroys it (perhaps to destroy the advantage the first one has). This continues until both lay an egg at the same time. A female praying mantis may start chewing off her partner's head while he is still mating. Among Australian red-backed spiders, the male, halfway through the mating process, will jump into the female's jaws and allow himself to be eaten a bit; when he is finished mating, he surrenders for the last time to her waiting fangs. For the Australian red-backed spider, this is doing what comes naturally. The female Ormia fly can detect a male cricket's sounds, drop down on it, and deposit on it a squirming maggot that bores into the cricket and eats it. The mother fly may have an extra incentive to succeed: if she fails, the hungry maggots begin to devour her from the inside out. So, perhaps nature won't do as a guide to family values.

Sometimes, it seems, we ought to be unnatural. We note in passing that in the Roman Catholic tradition, homosexuality, masturbation, contracepted heterosexual sex, and in vitro fertilization (to name a few) are unnatural, and hence, it is implied, morally wrong (recall the discussion of natural law in the Introduction to Ethical Theory). In this regard various instances of same-sex "courtship, affectionate, sexual, pair-bonding and/or parenting" behaviors can be found among nonhuman creatures—for example, ostriches, dolphins, sheep, lizards, and lions.[5] A comment by Alfred Kinsey and his co-workers is of interest: "... The sexual acts which are demonstrably part of the phylogenetic heritage of any species cannot be classified as acts contrary to nature, biologically unnatural, abnormal, or perverse."[6]

We encounter appeals to the assumption that what is natural is right and the claim that what is unnatural is wrong with regard to questions of sexual behavior, who should be dominant, the acceptability of biotechnology, debates over vegetarianism, and so on. Perhaps enough has been said to discourage ready acceptance of the key normative, often tacit, assumptions noted.

Notes

1. The apt expression is due to David Hull in his introduction to Lamarck's philosophy.

2. Facts about monogamy are derived from a column by June Reinisch entitled "The Kinsey Report," in the *News and Observer* (Raleigh, North Carolina), September 10, 1987.

3. For this discussion we drew on an article by Carol Kaesuk Yoon, "In Some Species, Eating Your Own Is Good Sense," *New York Times,* September 29, 1992.

4. See the review by Rona Cherry of *Females of the Species* by Bettyann Kevles (Cambridge: Harvard University Press), in the *New York Times Book Review,* October 5, 1986.

5. Biologist Bruce Bagemihl defines *homosexuality* as the activities listed above when they occur in animals of the same sex, whereas *heterosexuality* is defined as these same behaviors when they occur in animals of the opposite sex. Bruce Bagemihl, *Biological Exuberance: Animal Homosexuality and Natural Diversity* (New York: St. Martin's Press, 1999), p. 12. See also Simon LeVay, *Queer Science: The Use and Abuse of Research into Homosexuality* (Cambridge, MA: The MIT Press, 1996).

6. James Weinrich, "Is Homosexuality Biologically Natural?" in *Homosexuality: Social, Psychological, and Biological Issues,* edited by William Paul et al. (Beverly Hills, CA: Sage Publications, 1982), p. 204.

IV.C Ecofeminism

34. PREVIEW

[Ecofeminism] has asked important questions no one else has thought to pose.

Jan Clausen[1]

There is now a growing awareness that the Western philosophical tradition which has identified, on the one hand, maleness with the sphere of rationality, and on the other hand, femaleness with the sphere of nature, has provided one of the main intellectual bases for the domination of women in Western culture.

Val Plumwood[2]

Ecological feminism, says Karen J. Warren (Essay 35), "is the position that there are important connections—historical, symbolic, theoretical—between the domination of women and the domination of nonhuman nature."[3] Warren argues that "the conceptual connections between the dual dominations of women and nature are located in an oppressive patriarchal conceptual framework characterized by a logic of domination."[4] Warren implies, by her claim that there is a logic of domination that extends to both women and nature, that feminism needs to become ecological feminism and environmental ethics need to become distinctively feminist. Warren concludes, "A reconceiving and re-visioning of both feminism and environmental ethics is, I think, the power and the promise of ecofeminism."[5]

Crucial to the logic of domination is the assumption that in situations of diversity, differences (real or alleged) such as those between humans and rocks or men and women, are interpreted as moral hierarchies. For example, it is thought that humans are better than rocks and that men are better than women in some moral sense of "better." This assumption, plus the further assumption that moral superiority justifies subordination, transforms talk about diversity—or, for that matter, superiority or hierarchies—into a logic of domination. As Warren puts it so nicely, "without a logic of domination, a description of similarities and differences would be just that—a description of similarities and differences." In a very important observation, she says, "Contrary to what many feminists and ecofeminists have said or suggested, there may be nothing inherently problematic about 'hierarchical thinking' or even 'value hierarchical thinking' in contexts other than contexts of oppression." Warren ties her insights regarding diversity to Marilyn Frye's distinction between "arrogant perception" and "loving perception"[6] in a way that further illuminates Frye's original creative discussion.

In a collection on ecofeminism,[7] Greta Gaard is critical of Warren's omission of concern for animals in (Warren's) "The Power and the Promise of Ecological Feminism." Gaard says Warren "leaves no space for addressing animals and how humans should interact with them. In fact, . . . [her] conclusion romanticizes the slaughter of an animal."[8] Gaard seems to take the position that the narrative in question can be used to justify deer slaying in the Lakota culture, but not to justify factory farming and meat eating in America. However, the narrative seems open to criticism regardless of cultural context for reasons stated by Gaard herself, namely, that the four-legged can hardly be said to have offered itself to the humans given that it was shot in the hindquarters. Although it seems doubtful that Warren intends to justify meat eating in the United States via this narrative, speciesism is conspicuously absent from her list of systems of oppression, which includes sexism, racism, classism, ageism, and heterosexism.[9] Warren's view that the oppressions of women and nature are connected is shared by Vandana Shiva and Victoria Davion (Essays 36 and 37)—the other authors represented in this section.

More specifically, Victoria Davion argues that "a truly feminist perspective cannot embrace either the feminine or the masculine uncritically, as a truly feminist perspective requires a critique of gender roles, and this critique must include masculinity *and* femininity." Davion renames as ecofeminine a number of purported ecofeminist views that critique masculinity, but fail to do the same in the case of femininity. To push the point, ecofeminine views see the problem as the devaluation of the feminine role, whereas Davion says that feminists should be highly critical and suspicious of the feminine role in part because the feminine role is both inextricable from, and senseless without, its counterpart, the masculine role. So it would be unlikely that the one role would have damaging effects for those who play it, but the other role would not. Moreover, says Davion, "A vital tradition in feminist critique has long argued that gender roles cannot exist without domination and subordination." In sum, feminists, according to Davion, see gender roles as the problem, not the undervaluing of the feminine role.

Vandana Shiva's work, equally at home here or under the category of economics, analyzes and makes explicit certain value commitments underlying a number of important Western economic notions such as development, productivity, and poverty. As an ecofeminist, Shiva comes under fire from Victoria Davion for suggesting that "what is missing from the western patriarchal perspective is the 'feminine principle.'" Davion, however, finds Shiva's arguments on development and poverty convincing, talk about femininity and gender complementarity aside.

Western development in third-world countries, according to Shiva, "destroys wholesome and sustainable lifestyles and creates real material poverty, or misery, by the denial of survival needs themselves through the diversion of resources to resource intensive commodity production." The point is that the resources needed to produce commodities such as cash crops for a market economy are resources that are *already being used* by third-world people for purposes of sustenance. As Shiva says, "The needs of the Amazonian tribes are more than satisfied by the rich rainforest; their poverty begins with its destruction." Although third-world men as well as women suffer from the devastation of their environment, women are more the losers because they, as the primary producers of food, water, and fuel, have lost their livelihood; their knowledge and practices have been undermined. Moreover, unsurprisingly, they have virtually no access, and certainly less access than do men, to land ownership, technology, employment for wages, and small business loans should they have any desire to convert to a Western lifestyle. The frustration over the loss of forests can be heard in the voice of Hima Devi, a member of the women-led Chipko ("tree-hugging") movement when she says to her audiences:

> My sisters are busy harvesting the Kharif crop. They are busy winnowing. I have come to you with their message. Stop cutting trees. There are no trees even for birds to perch on. Birds flock to our crops and eat them. What will we eat? The firewood is disappearing: how will we cook?[10]

Shiva calls Western-type development "maldevelopment" because it results in real poverty (the denial of survival needs) while, ironically, trying to eliminate culturally perceived poverty. By describing subsistence economies as situations of *poverty*, those who favor market economies can present themselves as rescuing third-world countries from poverty. In so doing, Shiva says, they mask the

need to argue the case that market economies are superior to subsistence economies. Indeed, the Western ploy is to deny that subsistence economies count as economies at all. The work done for the sake of sustenance is not "productive." And if the work done by many women in the Western world is not considered "productive," or worth anything from an economic point of view, it is easy to see how woman-based subsistence economies can be viewed as not "productive." Shiva sums it up in one of her apt subtitles: "development as a new project of Western patriarchy."

NOTES

1. Jan Clausen, "Rethinking the World," *The Nation,* September 23, 1991, p. 346.
2. Val Plumwood, "Women, Humanity and Nature," *Radical Philosophy 48* (Spring 1988), p. 16.
3. Karen J. Warren, "Abstract: The Power and the Promise of Ecological Feminism," *Environmental Ethics 12*(2) (Summer 1990), p. 125.
4. Ibid.
5. Ibid.
6. Marilyn Frye, *The Politics of Reality* (Trumansburg, NY: The Crossing Press, 1983), pp. 66–72.
7. *Ecofeminism: Women, Animals, Nature,* edited by Greta Gaard (Philadelphia: Temple University Press, 1992).
8. Greta Gaard, "Ecofeminism and Native American Cultures: Pushing the Limits of Cultural Imperialism?" in *Ecofeminism: Women, Animals, Nature,* edited by Greta Gaard (Philadelphia: Temple University Press, 1992), p. 296.
9. Warren does include "naturism," that is, the oppression of nature, in her discussion. She may mean to include animals.
10. Vandana Shiva, "Development, Ecology and Women," in *Staying Alive: Women, Ecology, and Development* (London: Zed Books, 1998) pp. 74–75.

35. The Power and the Promise of Ecological Feminism

Karen J. Warren

Introduction

Ecological feminism (ecofeminism) has begun to receive a fair amount of attention lately as an alternative feminism and environmental ethic.[1] Since Francoise d'Eaubonne introduced the term *ecofeminisme* in 1974 to bring attention to women's potential for bringing about an ecological revolution,[2] the term has been used in a variety of ways. As I use the term in this paper, ecological feminism is the position that there are important connections—historical, experiential, symbolic, theoretical—between the domination of women and the domination of nature, an understanding of which is crucial to both feminism and environmental ethics. I argue that the promise and power of ecological feminism is that *it provides a distinctive framework both for reconceiving feminism and for developing an environmental ethic which takes seriously connections between the domination of women and the domination of nature.* I do so by discussing the nature of a feminist ethic and the ways in which ecofeminism provides a feminist and environmental ethic. I conclude that any feminist theory *and* any environmental ethic which fails to take seriously the twin and interconnected dominations of women and nature is at best incomplete and at worst simply inadequate.

Feminism, Ecological Feminism, and Conceptual Frameworks

Whatever else it is, feminism is at least the movement to end sexist oppression. It involves the elimination of any and all factors that contribute to the continued and systematic domination or subordination of women. While feminists disagree about the nature of and solutions to the subordination of women, all feminists agree that sexist oppression exists, is wrong, and must be abolished.

A "feminist issue" is any issue that contributes in some way to understanding the oppression of women. Equal rights, comparable pay for comparable work, and food production are feminist issues wherever and whenever an understanding of them contributes to an understanding of the continued exploitation or subjugation of women. Carrying water and searching for firewood are feminist issues wherever and whenever women's primary responsibility for these tasks contributes to their lack of full participation in decision making, income producing, or high status positions engaged in by men. What counts as a feminist issue, then, depends largely on context, particularly the historical and material conditions of women's lives.

Environmental degradation and exploitation are feminist issues because an understanding of them contributes to an understanding of the oppression of women. In India, for example, both deforestation and reforestation through the introduction of a monoculture species tree (e.g., eucalyptus) intended for commercial production are feminist issues because the loss of indigenous forests and multiple species of trees has drastically affected rural Indian women's ability to maintain a subsistence household. Indigenous forests provide a variety of trees for food, fuel, fodder, household utensils, dyes, medicines, and income-generating uses, while monoculture species forests do not.[3] Although I do not argue for this claim here, a look at the global impact of environmental degradation

Environmental Ethics, Vol. 12, No. 2 (Summer 1990), 125–146. Reprinted by permission of the author and publisher.

Earlier versions of this paper were presented at the American Philosophical Association Meeting in New York City, December 1987, and at the University of Massachusetts, April 1988. The author wishes to thank the following people for their helpful comments and support: Bob Ackerman, Kim Brown, Jim Cheney, Mahmoud El-Kati, Eric Katz, Michael Keenan, Ruthanne Kurth-Schai, Greta Gaard, Roxanne Gudeman, Alison Jaggar, H. Warren Jones, Gareth Matthews, Michael McCall, Patrick Murphy, Bruce Nordstrom, Nancy Shea, Nancy·Tuana, Bob Weinstock-Collins, Henry West, and the anonymous referees of *Environmental Ethics.*

on women's lives suggests important respects in which environmental degradation is a feminist issue.

Feminist philosophers claim that some of the most important feminist issues are *conceptual* ones: these issues concern how one conceptualizes such mainstay philosophical notions as reason and rationality, ethics, and what it is to be human. Ecofeminists extend this feminist philosophical concern to nature. They argue that, ultimately, some of the most important connections between the domination of women and the domination of nature are conceptual. To see this, consider the nature of conceptual frameworks.

A *conceptual framework* is a set of *basic* beliefs, values, attitudes, and assumptions which shape and reflect how one views oneself and one's world. It is a socially constructed lens through which we perceive ourselves and others. It is affected by such factors as gender, race, class, age, affectional orientation, nationality, and religious background.

Some conceptual frameworks are oppressive. An *oppressive conceptual framework* is one that explains, justifies, and maintains relationships of domination and subordination. When an oppressive conceptual framework is *patriarchal*, it explains, justifies, and maintains the subordination of women by men.

I have argued elsewhere that there are three significant features of oppressive conceptual frameworks: (1) value-hierarchical thinking, i.e., "up-down" thinking which places higher value, status, or prestige on what is "up" rather than on what is "down"; (2) value dualisms, i.e., disjunctive pairs in which the disjuncts are seen as oppositional (rather than as complementary) and exclusive (rather than as inclusive), and which place higher value (status, prestige) on one disjunct rather than the other (e.g., dualisms which give higher value or status to that which has historically been identified as "mind," "reason," and "male" than to that which has historically been identified as "body," "emotion," and "female"); and (3) logic of domination, i.e., a structure of argumentation which leads to a justification of subordination.[4]

The third feature of oppressive conceptual frameworks is the most significant. A logic of domination is not *just* a logical structure. It also involves a substantive value system, since an ethical premise is needed to permit or sanction the "just" subordination of that which is subordinate. This justification typically is given on grounds of some alleged characteristic (e.g., rationality) which the dominant (e.g., men) have and the subordinate (e.g., women) lack.

Contrary to what many feminists and ecofeminists have said or suggested, there may be nothing *inherently* problematic about "hierarchical thinking" or even "value-hierarchical thinking" in contexts other than contexts of oppression. Hierarchical thinking is important in daily living for classifying data, comparing information, and organizing material. Taxonomies (e.g., plant taxonomies) and biological nomenclature seem to require *some* form of "hierarchical thinking." Even "value-hierarchical thinking" may be quite acceptable in certain contexts. (The same may be said of "value dualisms" in nonoppressive contexts.) For example, suppose it is true that what is unique about humans is our conscious capacity to radically reshape our social environments (or "societies"), as Murray Bookchin suggests.[5] Then one could truthfully say that humans are better equipped to radically reshape their environments than are rocks or plants—a "value-hierarchical" way of speaking.

The problem is not simply *that* value-hierarchical thinking and value dualisms are used, but *the way* in which each has been used in *oppressive conceptual frameworks*[6] to establish inferiority and to justify subordination. It is the logic of domination, *coupled with* value-hierarchical thinking and value dualisms, which "justifies" subordination. What is explanatorily basic, then, about the nature of oppressive conceptual frameworks is the logic of domination.

For ecofeminism, that a logic of domination is explanatorily basic is important for at least three reasons. First, without a logic of domination, a description of similarities and differences would be just that—a description of similarities and differences. Consider the claim, "Humans are different from plants and rocks in that humans can (and plants and rocks cannot) consciously and radically reshape the communities in which they live; humans are similar to plants and rocks in that they are both members of an ecological community." Even if humans are "better" than plants and rocks with respect to the conscious ability of humans to radically transform communities, one does not *thereby* get any *morally* relevant distinction between humans and nonhumans, or an argument for the domination of plants and rocks by humans. To get *those* conclusions one needs to add at least two powerful assumptions, viz., (A2) and (A4) in argument A below:

(A1)   Humans do, and plants and rocks do not, have the capacity to consciously and radically change the community in which they live.

(A2)   Whatever has the capacity to consciously and radically change the community in which it lives is morally superior to whatever lacks this capacity.

(A3)   Thus, humans are morally superior to plants and rocks.

(A4)   For any X and Y, if X is morally superior to Y, then X is morally justified in subordinating Y.

(A5)   Thus, humans are morally justified in subordinating plants and rocks.

Without the two assumptions that *humans are morally superior* to (at least some) nonhumans, (A2), and that *superiority justifies subordination,* (A4), all one has is some difference between humans and some nonhumans. This is true *even if* that difference is given in terms of superiority. Thus, it is the logic of domination, (A4), which is the bottom line in ecofeminist discussions of oppression.

Second, ecofeminists argue that, at least in Western societies, the oppressive conceptual framework which sanctions the twin dominations of women and nature is a patriarchal one characterized by all three features of an oppressive conceptual framework. Many ecofeminists claim that, historically, within at least the dominant Western culture, a patriarchal conceptual framework has sanctioned the following argument B:

(B1)   Women are identified with nature and the realm of the physical; men are identified with the "human" and the realm of the mental.

(B2)   Whatever is identified with nature and the realm of the physical is inferior to ("below") whatever is identified with the "human" and the realm of the mental; or, conversely, the latter is superior to ("above") the former.

(B3)   Thus, women are inferior to ("below") men; or, conversely, men are superior to ("above") women.

(B4)   For any X and Y, if X is superior to Y, then X is justified in subordinating Y.

(B5)   Thus, men are justified in subordinating women.

If sound, argument B establishes *patriarchy,* i.e., the conclusion given at (B5) that the systematic domination of women by men is justified. But according to ecofeminists, (B5) is justified by just those three features of an oppressive conceptual framework identified earlier: value-hierarchical thinking, the assumption at (B2); value dualisms, the assumed dualism of the mental and the physical at (B1) and the assumed inferiority of the physical vis-à-vis the mental at (B2); and a logic of domination, the assumption at (B4), the same as the previous premise (A4). Hence, according to ecofeminists, insofar as an oppressive patriarchal conceptual framework has functioned historically (within at least dominant Western culture) to sanction the twin dominations of women and nature (argument B), both argument B and the patriarchal conceptual framework, from whence it comes, ought to be rejected.

Of course, the preceding does not identify which premises of B are false. What is the status of premises (B1) and (B2)? Most, if not all, feminists claim that (B1), and many ecofeminists claim that (B2), have been assumed or asserted within the dominant Western philosophical and intellectual tradition.[7] As such, these feminists assert, as a matter of historical fact, that the dominant Western philosophical tradition has assumed the truth of (B1) and (B2). Ecofeminists, however, either deny (B2) or do not affirm (B2). Furthermore, because some ecofeminists are anxious to deny any ahistorical identification of women with nature, some ecofeminists deny (B1) when (B1) is used to support anything other than a strictly historical claim about what has been asserted or assumed to be true within patriarchal culture—e.g., when (B1) is used to assert that women properly are identified with the realm of nature and the physical.[8] Thus, from an ecofeminist perspective, (B1) and (B2) are properly viewed as problematic though historically sanctioned claims: they are problematic precisely because of the way they have functioned historically in a patriarchal conceptual framework and culture to sanction the dominations of women and nature.

What *all* ecofeminists agree about, then, is the way in which *the logic of domination* has functioned historically within patriarchy to sustain and justify the twin dominations of women and nature.[9] Since *all* feminists (and not just ecofeminists) oppose patriarchy, the conclusion given at (B5), all feminists (including ecofeminists) must oppose at least the logic of domination, premise (B4), on which argument B rests—whatever the truth-value status of (B1) and (B2) *outside of* a patriarchal context.

That *all* feminists must oppose the logic of domination shows the breadth and depth of the ecofeminist critique of B: it is a critique not only of the three assumptions on which this argument for the domination of women and nature rests, viz., the assumptions at (B1), (B2), and (B4); it is also a critique of patriarchal conceptual frameworks generally, i.e., of those oppressive conceptual frameworks which put men "up" and women "down," allege some way in which women are morally inferior to men, and use that alleged difference to justify the subordination of women by men. Therefore, ecofeminism is necessary to *any* feminist critique of patriarchy, and, hence, necessary to feminism (a point I discuss again later).

Third, ecofeminism clarifies why the logic of domination, and any conceptual framework which gives rise to it, must be abolished in order both to make possible a meaningful notion of difference which does not breed domination and to prevent feminism from becoming a "support" movement based primarily on shared experiences. In contemporary society, there is no one "woman's voice," no *woman (or human) simpliciter:* every woman (or human) is a woman (or human) of some race, class, age, affectional orientation, marital status, regional or national background, and so forth. Because there are no "monolithic experiences" that all women share, feminism must be a "solidarity movement" based on shared beliefs and interests rather than a "unity in sameness" movement based on shared experiences and shared victimization.[10] In the words of Maria Lugones, "Unity—not to be confused with solidarity—is understood as conceptually tied to domination."[11]

Ecofeminists insist that the sort of logic of domination used to justify the domination of humans by gender, racial or ethnic, or class status is also used to justify the domination of nature. Because eliminating a logic of domination is part of a feminist critique—whether a critique of patriarchy, white supremacist culture, or imperialism—ecofeminists insist that *naturism* is properly viewed as an integral part of any feminist solidarity move-

ment to end sexist oppression and the logic of domination which conceptually grounds it.

Ecofeminism Reconceives Feminism

The discussion so far has focused on some of the oppressive conceptual features of patriarchy. As I use the phrase, the "logic of traditional feminism" refers to the location of the conceptual roots of sexist oppression, at least in Western societies, in an oppressive patriarchal conceptual framework characterized by a logic of domination. Insofar as other systems of oppression (e.g., racism, classism, ageism, heterosexism) are also conceptually maintained by a logic of domination, appeal to the logic of traditional feminism ultimately locates the basic conceptual interconnections among *all* systems of oppression in the logic of domination. It thereby explains at a *conceptual* level why the eradication of sexist oppression requires the eradication of the other forms of oppression.[12] It is by clarifying this conceptual connection between systems of oppression that a movement to end sexist oppression—traditionally the special turf of feminist theory and practice—leads to a reconceiving of feminism as *a movement to end all forms of oppression.*

Suppose one agrees that the logic of traditional feminism requires the expansion of feminism to include other social systems of domination (e.g., racism and classism). What warrants the inclusion of nature in these "social systems of domination"? Why must the logic of traditional feminism include the abolition of "naturism" (i.e., the domination or oppression of nonhuman nature) among the "isms" feminism must confront? The conceptual justification for expanding feminism to include ecofeminism is twofold. One basis has already been suggested: by showing that the conceptual connections between the dual dominations of women and nature are located in an oppressive and, at least in Western societies, patriarchal conceptual framework characterized by a logic of domination, ecofeminism explains how and why feminism, conceived as a movement to end sexist oppression, must be expanded and reconceived as also a movement to end naturism. This is made explicit by the following argument C:

(C1)   Feminism is a movement to end sexism.

(C2)   But Sexism is conceptually linked with naturism (through an oppressive conceptual framework characterized by a logic of domination).

(C3)   Thus, Feminism is (also) a movement to end naturism.

Because, ultimately, these connections between sexism and naturism are conceptual—embedded in an oppressive conceptual framework—the logic of traditional feminism leads to the embrace of ecological feminism.[13]

The other justification for reconceiving feminism to include ecofeminism has to do with the concepts of gender and nature. Just as conceptions of gender are socially constructed, so are conceptions of nature. Of course, the claim that women and nature are social constructions does not require anyone to deny that there are actual humans and actual trees, rivers, and plants. It simply implies that *how* women and nature are conceived is a matter of historical and social reality. These conceptions vary cross-culturally and by historical time period. As a result, any discussion of the "oppression or domination of nature" involves reference to historically specific forms of social domination of nonhuman nature by humans, just as discussion of the "domination of women" refers to historically specific forms of social domination of women by men. Although I do not argue for it here, an ecofeminist defense of the historical connections between the dominations of women and of nature, claims (B1) and (B2) in argument B, involves showing that within patriarchy the feminization of nature and the naturalization of women have been crucial to the historically successful subordinations of both.[14]

If ecofeminism promises to reconceive traditional feminism in ways which include naturism as a legitimate feminist issue, does ecofeminism also promise to reconceive environmental ethics in ways which are feminist? I think so. This is the subject of the remainder of the paper.

Climbing from Ecofeminism to Environmental Ethics

Many feminists and some environmental ethicists have begun to explore the use of first-person narrative as a way of raising philosophically germane issues in ethics often lost or underplayed in mainstream philosophical ethics. Why is this so?

What is it about narrative which makes it a significant resource for theory and practice in feminism and environmental ethics? Even if appeal to first-person narrative is a helpful literary device for describing ineffable experience or a legitimate social science methodology for documenting personal and social history, how is first-person narrative a valuable vehicle of argumentation for ethical decision making and theory building? One fruitful way to begin answering these questions is to ask them of a particular first-person narrative.

Consider the following first-person narrative about rock climbing:

> For my very first rock climbing experience, I chose a somewhat private spot, away from other climbers and on-lookers. After studying "the chimney," I focused all my energy on making it to the top. I climbed with intense determination, using whatever strength and skills I had to accomplish this challenging feat. By midway I was exhausted and anxious. I couldn't see what to do next—where to put my hands or feet. Growing increasingly more weary as I clung somewhat desperately to the rock, I made a move. It didn't work. I fell. There I was, dangling midair above the rocky ground below, frightened but terribly relieved that the belay rope had held me. I knew I was safe. I took a look up at the climb that remained. I was determined to make it to the top. With renewed confidence and concentration, I finished the climb to the top.
>
> On my second day of climbing, I rappelled down about 200 feet from the top of the Palisades at Lake Superior to just a few feet above the water level. I could see no one—not my belayer, not the other climbers, no one. I unhooked slowly from the rappel rope and took a deep cleansing breath. I looked all around me—really looked—and listened. I heard a cacophony of voices—birds, trickles of water on the rock before me, waves lapping against the rocks below. I closed my eyes and began to feel the rock with my hands—the cracks and crannies, the raised lichen and mosses, the almost imperceptible nubs that might provide a resting place for my fingers and toes when I began to climb. At that moment I was bathed in serenity. I began to talk to the rock in an almost inaudible, child-like way, as if the rock were my friend. I felt an overwhelming sense of gratitude for what it offered me—a chance to know myself and the rock differently, to appreciate unforeseen

miracles like the tiny flowers growing in the even tinier cracks in the rock's surface, and to come to know a sense of *being in relationship* with the natural environment. It felt as if the rock and I were silent conversational partners in a longstanding friendship. I realized then that I had come to care about this cliff which was so different from me, so unmovable and invincible, independent and seemingly indifferent to my presence. I wanted to be with the rock as I climbed. Gone was the determination to conquer the rock, to forcefully impose my will on it; I wanted simply to work respectfully with the rock as I climbed. And as I climbed, that is what I felt. I felt myself *caring* for this rock and feeling thankful that climbing provided the opportunity for me to know it and myself in this new way.

There are at least four reasons why use of such a first-person narrative is important to feminism and environmental ethics. First, such a narrative gives voice to a felt sensitivity often lacking in traditional analytical ethical discourse, viz., a sensitivity to conceiving of oneself as fundamentally "in relationship with" others, including the nonhuman environment. It is a modality which *takes relationships themselves seriously.* It thereby stands in contrast to a strictly reductionist modality that takes relationships seriously only or primarily because of the nature of the *relators* or parties to those relationships (e.g., relators conceived as moral agents, right holders, interest carriers, or sentient beings). In the rock-climbing narrative above, it is the climber's relationship with the rock she climbs which takes on special significance—which is itself a locus of value—in addition to whatever moral status or moral considerability she or the rock or any other parties to the relationship may also have.[15]

Second, such a first-person narrative gives expression to a variety of ethical attitudes and behaviors often overlooked or underplayed in mainstream Western ethics, e.g., the difference in attitudes and behaviors toward a rock when one is "making it to the top" and when one thinks of oneself as "friends with" or "caring about" the rock one climbs.[16] These different attitudes and behaviors suggest an ethically germane contrast between two different types of relationships humans or climbers may have toward a rock: an imposed conqueror-type relationship, and an emergent caring-type relationship. This contrast grows out of, and is faithful to, felt, lived experience.

The difference between conquering and caring attitudes and behaviors in relation to the natural environment provides a third reason why the use of first-person narrative is important to feminism and environmental ethics: it provides a way of conceiving of ethics and ethical meaning as *emerging out of* particular situations moral agents find themselves in, rather than as being *imposed on* those situations (e.g., as a derivation or instantiation of some predetermined abstract principle or rule). This emergent feature of narrative centralizes the importance of *voice*. When a multiplicity of cross-cultural *voices* are centralized, narrative is able to give expression to a range of attitudes, values, beliefs, and behaviors which may be overlooked or silenced by imposed ethical meaning and theory. As a reflection of and on felt, lived experiences, the use of narrative in ethics provides a stance from which ethical discourse can be held accountable to the historical, material, and social realities in which moral subjects find themselves.

Lastly, and for our purposes perhaps most importantly, the use of narrative has argumentative significance. Jim Cheney calls attention to this feature of narrative when he claims, "To contextualize ethical deliberation is, in some sense, to provide a narrative or story, from which the solution to the ethical dilemma emerges as the fitting conclusion."[17] Narrative has argumentative force by suggesting *what counts* as an appropriate conclusion to an ethical situation. One ethical conclusion suggested by the climbing narrative is that what counts as a proper ethical attitude toward mountains and rocks is an attitude of respect and care (whatever that turns out to be or involve), not one of domination and conquest.

In an essay entitled "In and Out of Harm's Way: Arrogance and Love," feminist philosopher Marilyn Frye distinguishes between "arrogant" and "loving" perception as one way of getting at this difference in the ethical attitudes of care and conquests.[18] Frye writes:

> The loving eye is a contrary of the arrogant eye.
> The loving eye knows the independence of the other. It is the eye of a seer who knows that nature is indifferent. It is the eye of one who knows that to know the seen, one must consult something other than one's own will and interests and fears and imagination. One must look at the thing. One must look and listen and check and question.

> The loving eye is one that pays a certain sort of attention. This attention can require a discipline but *not* a self-denial. The discipline is one of self-knowledge, knowledge of the scope and boundary of the self. . . . In particular, it is a matter of being able to tell one's own interests from those of others and of knowing where one's self leaves off and another begins. . . .
>
> The loving eye does not make the object of perception into something edible, does not try to assimilate it, does not reduce it to the size of the seer's desire, fear and imagination, and hence does not have to simplify. It knows the complexity of the other as something which will forever present new things to be known. The science of the loving eye would favor The Complexity Theory of Truth [in contrast to The Simplicity Theory of Truth] and presuppose The Endless Interestingness of the Universe.[19]

According to Frye, the loving eye is not an invasive, coercive eye which annexes others to itself, but one which "knows the complexity of the other as something which will forever present new things to be known."

When one climbs a rock as a conqueror, one climbs with an arrogant eye. When one climbs with a loving eye, one constantly "must look and listen and check and question." One recognizes the rock as something very different, something perhaps totally indifferent to one's own presence, and finds in that difference joyous occasion for celebration. One knows "the boundary of the self," where the self—the "I," the climber—leaves off and the rock begins. There is no fusion of two into one, but a complement of two entities *acknowledged* as separate, different, independent, *yet in relationship;* they are in relationship *if only* because the loving eye is perceiving it, responding to it, noticing it, attending to it.

An ecofeminist perspective about both women and nature involves this shift in attitude from "arrogant perception" to "loving perception" of the nonhuman world. Arrogant perception of nonhumans by humans presupposes and maintains *sameness* in such a way that it expands the moral community to those beings who are thought to resemble (be like, similar to, or the same as) humans in some morally significant way. Any environmental movement or ethic based on arrogant perception builds a moral hierarchy of beings and assumes some common denominator of moral considerability in virtue of which like beings deserve

similar treatment or moral consideration and unlike beings do not. Such environmental ethics are or generate a "unity in sameness." In contrast, "loving perception" presupposes and maintains *difference*—a distinction between the self and other, between human and at least some nonhumans—in such a way that perception of the other as other *is* an expression of love for one who/which is recognized at the outset as independent, dissimilar, different. As Maria Lugones says, in loving perception, "Love is seen not as fusion and erasure of difference but as incompatible with them."[20] "Unity in sameness" alone is an *erasure of difference.*

"Loving perception" of the nonhuman natural world is an attempt to understand what it means *for humans* to care about the nonhuman world, a world *acknowledged* as being independent, different, perhaps even indifferent to humans. Humans *are* different from rocks in important ways, even if they are also both members of some ecological community. A moral community based on loving perception of oneself *in relationship with* a rock, or with the natural environment as a whole, is one which acknowledges and respects difference, whatever "sameness" also exists.[21] The limits of loving perception are determined only by the limits of one's (e.g., a person's, a community's) ability to respond lovingly (or with appropriate care, trust, or friendship)—whether it is to other humans or to the nonhuman world and elements of it.[22]

If what I have said so far is correct, then there are very different ways to climb a mountain and *how* one climbs it and *how* one narrates the experience of climbing it matter ethically. If one climbs with "arrogant perception," with an attitude of "conquer and control," one keeps intact the very sorts of thinking that characterize a logic of domination and an oppressive conceptual framework. Since the oppressive conceptual framework which sanctions the domination of nature is a patriarchal one, one also thereby keeps intact, even if unwittingly, a patriarchal conceptual framework. Because the dismantling of patriarchal conceptual frameworks is a feminist issue, *how* one climbs a mountain and *how* one narrates—or tells the story—about the experience of climbing also are *feminist issues.* In this way, ecofeminism makes visible why, at a conceptual level, environmental ethics is a feminist issue. I turn now to a consideration of ecofeminism as a distinctively feminist and environmental ethic.

Ecofeminism as a Feminist and Environmental Ethic

A feminist ethic involves a twofold commitment to critique male bias in ethics wherever it occurs, and to develop ethics which are not male-biased. Sometimes this involves articulation of values (e.g., values of care, appropriate trust, kinship, friendship) often lost or underplayed in mainstream ethics.[23] Sometimes it involves engaging in theory building by pioneering in new directions or by revamping old theories in gender sensitive ways. What makes the critiques of old theories or conceptualizations of new ones "feminist" is that they emerge out of sex-gender analyses and reflect whatever those analyses reveal about gendered experience and gendered social reality.

As I conceive feminist ethics in the pre-feminist present, it rejects attempts to conceive of ethical theory in terms of necessary and sufficient conditions, because it assumes that there is no essence (in the sense of some transhistorical, universal, absolute abstraction) of feminist ethics. While attempts to formulate joint necessary and sufficient conditions of a feminist ethic are unfruitful, nonetheless, there are some necessary conditions, what I prefer to call "boundary conditions," of a feminist ethic. These boundary conditions clarify some of the minimal conditions of a feminist ethic without suggesting that feminist ethics has some ahistorical essence. They are like the boundaries of a quilt or collage. They delimit the territory of the piece without dictating what the interior, the design, the actual pattern of the piece looks like. Because the actual design of the quilt emerges from the multiplicity of voices of women in a cross-cultural context, the design will change over time. It is not something static.

What are some of the boundary conditions of a feminist ethic? First, nothing can become part of a feminist ethic—can be part of the quilt—that promotes sexism, racism, classism, or any other "isms" of social domination. Of course, people may disagree about what counts as a sexist act, racist attitude, classist behavior. What counts as sexism, racism, or classism may vary cross-culturally. Still, because a feminist ethic aims at eliminating sexism and sexist bias, and (as I have already shown) sexism is intimately connected in conceptualization and in practice to racism, classism, and naturism, a feminist ethic must be anti-sexist, anti-racist, anti-classist, anti-naturist and opposed to any "ism" which presupposes or advances a logic of domination.

Second, a feminist ethic is a *contextualist* ethic. A contextualist ethic is one which sees ethical discourse and practice as emerging from the voices of people located in different historical circumstances. A contextualist ethic is properly viewed as a *collage* or *mosaic*, a *tapestry* of voices that emerges out of felt experiences. Like any collage or mosaic, the point is not to have *one picture* based on a unity of voices, but a *pattern* which emerges out of the very different voices of people located in different circumstances. When a contextualist ethic is *feminist*, it gives central place to the voices of women.

Third, since a feminist ethic gives central significance to the diversity of women's voices, a feminist ethic must be structurally pluralistic rather than unitary or reductionistic. It rejects the assumption that there is "one voice" in terms of which ethical values, beliefs, attitudes, and conduct can be assessed.

Fourth, a feminist ethic reconceives ethical theory as theory in process which will change over time. Like all theory, a feminist ethic is based on some generalizations.[24] Nevertheless, the generalizations associated with it are themselves a pattern of voices within which the different voices emerging out of concrete and alternative descriptions of ethical situations have meaning. The coherence of a feminist theory so conceived is given within a historical and conceptual context, i.e., within a set of historical, socioeconomic circumstances (including circumstances of race, class, age, and affectional orientation) and within a set of basic beliefs, values, attitudes, and assumptions about the world.

Fifth, because a feminist ethic is contextualist, structurally pluralistic, and "in-process," one way to evaluate the claims of a feminist ethic is in terms of their *inclusiveness:* those claims (voices, patterns of voices) are morally and epistemologically favored (preferred, better, less partial, less biased) which are more inclusive of the felt experiences and perspectives of oppressed persons. The condition of inclusiveness requires and ensures that the diverse voices of women (as oppressed persons) will be given legitimacy in ethical theory building. It thereby helps to minimize empirical bias, e.g., bias rising from faulty or false generalizations based on stereotyping, too small a sample size, or a skewed sample. It does so by ensuring that any generalizations which are made about ethics and ethical decision making include—indeed cohere with—the patterned voices of women.[25]

Sixth, a feminist ethic makes no attempt to provide an "objective" point of view, since it assumes that in contemporary culture there really is no such point of view. As such, it does not claim to be "unbiased" in the sense of "value-neutral" or "objective." However, it does assume that whatever bias it has as an ethic centralizing the voices of oppressed persons is a *better bias*—"better" because it is more inclusive and therefore less partial—than those which exclude those voices.[26]

Seventh, a feminist ethic provides a central place for values typically unnoticed, underplayed, or misrepresented in traditional ethics, e.g., values of care, love, friendship, and appropriate trust.[27] Again, it need not do this at the exclusion of considerations of rights, rules, or utility. There may be many contexts in which talk of rights or of utility is useful or appropriate. For instance, in contracts or property relationships, talk of rights may be useful and appropriate. In deciding what is cost-effective or advantageous to the most people, talk of utility may be useful and appropriate. In a feminist *qua* contextualist ethic, whether or not such talk is useful or appropriate depends on the context; *other values* (e.g., values of care, trust, friendship) are *not* viewed as reducible to or captured solely in terms of such talk.[28]

Eighth, a feminist ethic also involves a reconception of what it is to be human and what it is for humans to engage in ethical decision making, since it rejects as either meaningless or currently untenable any gender-free or gender-neutral description of humans, ethics, and ethical decision making. It thereby rejects what Alison Jaggar calls "abstract individualism," i.e., the position that it is possible to identify a human essence or human nature that exists independently of any particular historical context.[29] Humans and human moral conduct are properly understood essentially (and not merely accidentally) in terms of networks or webs of historical and concrete relationships.

All the props are now in place for seeing how ecofeminism provides the framework for a distinctively feminist and environmental ethic. It is a feminism that critiques male bias wherever it occurs in ethics (including environmental ethics) and aims at providing an ethic (including an environmental ethic) which is not male biased—and it does so in a way that satisfies the preliminary boundary conditions of a feminist ethic.

First, ecofeminism is quintessentially anti-naturist. Its anti-naturism consists in the rejection of any way of thinking about or acting toward non-human nature that reflects a logic, values, or attitude of domination. Its anti-naturist, anti-sexist, anti-racist, anti-classist (and so forth, for all other "isms" of social domination) stance forms the outer boundary of the quilt: nothing gets on the quilt which is naturist, sexist, racist, classist, and so forth.

Second, ecofeminism is a contextualist ethic. It involves a shift *from* a conception of ethics as primarily a matter of rights, rules, or principles predetermined and applied in specific cases to entities viewed as competitors in the contest of moral standing, *to* a conception of ethics as growing out of what Jim Cheney calls "defining relationships," i.e., relationships conceived in some sense as defining who one is.[30] As a contextualist ethic, it is not that rights, or rules, or principles are *not* relevant or important. Clearly they are in certain contexts and for certain purposes.[31] It is just that what *makes* them relevant or important is that those to whom they apply are entities *in relationship with* others.

Ecofeminism also involves an ethical shift *from* granting moral consideration to nonhumans *exclusively* on the grounds of some similarity they share with humans (e.g., rationality, interests, moral agency, sentiency, right-holder status) *to* "a highly contextual account to see clearly what a human being is and what the nonhuman world might be, morally speaking, *for* human beings."[32] For an ecofeminist, *how* a moral agent is in relationship to another becomes of central significance, not simply *that* a moral agent is a moral agent or is bound by rights, duties, virtue, or utility to act in a certain way.

Third, ecofeminism is structurally pluralistic in that it presupposes and maintains difference—difference among humans as well as between humans and at least some elements of nonhuman nature. Thus, while ecofeminism denies the "nature/culture" split, it affirms that humans are both members of an ecological community (in some respects) and different from it (in other respects). Ecofeminism's attention to relationships and community is not, therefore, an erasure of difference but a respectful acknowledgement of it.

Fourth, ecofeminism reconceives theory as theory in process. It focuses on patterns of meaning which emerge, for instance, from the story-telling and first-person narratives of women (and others) who deplore the twin dominations of women and nature. The use of narrative is one way to ensure that the content of the ethic—the pattern of the quilt—may/will change over time, as the historical and material realities of women's lives change and as more is learned about women–nature connections and the destruction of the nonhuman world.[33]

Fifth, ecofeminism is inclusivist. It emerges from the voices of women who experience the harmful domination of nature and the way that domination is tied to their domination as women. It emerges from listening to the voices of indigenous peoples such as Native Americans who have been dislocated from their land and have witnessed the attendant undermining of such values as appropriate reciprocity, sharing, and kinship that characterize traditional Indian culture. It emerges from listening to voices of those who, like Nathan Hare, critique traditional approaches to environmental ethics as white and bourgeois, and as failing to address issues of "black ecology" and the "ecology" of the inner city and urban spaces.[34] It also emerges out of the voices of Chipko women who see the destruction of "earth, soil, and water" as intimately connected with their own inability to survive economically.[35] With its emphasis on inclusivity and difference, ecofeminism provides a framework for recognizing that what counts as ecology and what counts as appropriate conduct toward both human and nonhuman environments is largely a matter of context.

Sixth, as a feminism, ecofeminism makes no attempt to provide an "objective" point of view. It is a social ecology. It recognizes the twin dominations of women and nature as social problems rooted both in very concrete, historical, socioeconomic circumstances and in oppressive patriarchal conceptual frameworks which maintain and sanction these circumstances.

Seventh, ecofeminism makes a central place for values of care, love, friendship, trust, and appropriate reciprocity—values that presuppose that our relationships to others are central to our understanding of who we are.[36] It thereby gives voice to the sensitivity that in climbing a mountain, one is doing something in relationship with an "other," an "other" whom one can come to care about and treat respectfully.

Lastly, an ecofeminist ethic involves a reconception of what it means to be human, and in what human ethical behavior consists. Ecofeminism denies abstract individualism. Humans are who we are in large part by virtue of the historical and social contexts and the relationships we are in, including our relationships with nonhuman nature. Relationships are not something extrinsic to who we are, not an "add on" feature of human nature; they play an essential role in shaping what it is to be human. Relationships of humans to the nonhuman environment are, in part, constitutive of what it is to be a human.

By making visible the interconnections among the dominations of women and nature, ecofeminism shows that both are feminist issues and that explicit acknowledgment of both is vital to any responsible environmental ethic. Feminism *must* embrace ecological feminism if it is to end the domination of women because the domination of women is tied conceptually and historically to the domination of nature.

A responsible environmental ethic also *must* embrace feminism. Otherwise, even the seemingly most revolutionary, liberational, and holistic ecological ethic will fail to take seriously the interconnected dominations of nature and women that are so much a part of the historical legacy and conceptual framework that sanctions the exploitation of nonhuman nature. Failure to make visible these interconnected, twin dominations results in an inaccurate account of how it is that nature has been and continues to be dominated and exploited and produces an environmental ethic that lacks the depth necessary to be truly *inclusive* of the realities of persons who at least in dominant Western culture have been intimately tied with that exploitation, viz., women. Whatever else can be said in favor of such holistic ethics, a failure to make visible ecofeminist insights into the common denominators of the twin oppressions of women and nature is to perpetuate, rather than overcome, the source of that oppression.

This last point deserves further attention. It may be objected that as long as the end result is "the same"—the development of an environmental ethic which does not emerge out of or reinforce an oppressive conceptual framework—it does not matter whether that ethic (or the ethic endorsed in getting there) is feminist or not. Hence, it simply is *not* the case that any adequate environmental ethic must be feminist. My argument, in contrast, has been that it *does* matter, and for three important reasons. First, there is the scholarly issue of accurately representing historical reality, and that, ecofeminists claim, requires acknowledging the historical feminization of nature and naturalization of women as part of the exploitation of nature. Second, I have shown that the conceptual connections between the domination of women and the domination of nature are located in an oppressive and, at least in Western societies, patriarchal conceptual framework characterized by a logic of domination. Thus, I have shown that failure to notice the nature of this connection leaves at best an incomplete, inaccurate, and partial account of what is required of a conceptually adequate environmental ethic. An ethic which *does not* acknowledge this is simply *not* the same as one that does, whatever else the similarities between them. Third, the claim that, in contemporary culture, one can have an adequate environmental ethic which is *not* feminist assumes that, in contemporary culture, the label *feminist* does not add anything crucial to the nature or description of environmental ethics. I have shown that at least in contemporary culture this is false, for the word *feminist* currently helps to clarify just *how* the domination of nature is conceptually linked to patriarchy and, hence, how the liberation of nature is conceptually linked to the termination of patriarchy. Thus, because it has critical bite in contemporary culture, it serves as an important reminder that in contemporary sex-gendered, raced, classed, and naturist culture, an unlabeled position functions as a privileged and "unmarked" position. That is, without the addition of the word *feminist*, one presents environmental ethics as if it has no bias, including male-gender bias, which is just what ecofeminists deny: failure to notice the connections between the twin oppressions of women and nature *is* male-gender bias.

One of the goals of feminism is the eradication of all oppressive sex-gender (and related race, class, age, affectional preference) categories and the creation of a world in which *difference does not breed domination*—say, the world of 4001. If in 4001 an "adequate environmental ethic" is a "feminist environmental ethic," the word *feminist* may then be redundant and unnecessary. However, this is not 4001, and in terms of the current historical and conceptual reality the dominations of nature and of

women are intimately connected. Failure to notice or make visible that connection in 1990 perpetuates the mistaken (and privileged) view that "environmental ethics" is *not* a feminist issue, and that *feminist* adds nothing to environmental ethics.[37]

Conclusion

I have argued in this paper that ecofeminism provides a framework for a distinctively feminist and environmental ethic. Ecofeminism grows out of the felt and theorized about connections between the domination of women and the domination of nature. As a contextualist ethic, ecofeminism refocuses environmental ethics on what nature might mean, morally speaking, *for* humans, and on how the relational attitudes of humans to others—humans as well as nonhumans—sculpt both what it is to be human and the nature and ground of human responsibilities to the nonhuman environment. Part of what this refocusing does is to take seriously the voices of women and other oppressed persons in the construction of that ethic.

A Sioux elder once told me a story about his son. He sent his seven-year-old son to live with the child's grandparents on a Sioux reservation so that he could "learn the Indian ways." Part of what the grandparents taught the son was how to hunt the four-leggeds of the forest. As I heard the story, the boy was taught, "to shoot your four-legged brother in his hind area, slowing it down but not killing it. Then, take the four-legged's head in your hands, and look into his eyes. The eyes are where all the suffering is. Look into your brother's eyes and feel his pain. Then, take your knife and cut the four-legged under his chin, here, on his neck, so that he dies quickly. And as you do, ask your brother, the four-legged, for forgiveness for what you do. Offer also a prayer of thanks to your four-legged kin for offering his body to you just now, when you need food to eat and clothing to wear. And promise the four-legged that you will put yourself back into the earth when you die, to become nourishment for the earth, and for the sister flowers, and for the brother deer. It is appropriate that you should offer this blessing for the four-legged and, in due time, reciprocate in turn with your body in this way, as the four-legged gives life to you for your survival." As I reflect upon that story, I am struck by the power of the environmental ethic that grows out of and takes seriously narrative, context, and such values and relational attitudes as care, loving perception, and appropriate reciprocity, and doing what is appropriate in a given situation—however that notion of appropriateness eventually gets filled out. I am also struck by what one is able to see, once one begins to explore some of the historical and conceptual connections between the dominations of women and of nature. A *re-conceiving* and *re-visioning* of both feminism and environmental ethics, is, I think, the power and promise of ecofeminism.

Notes

1. Explicit ecological feminist literature includes works from a variety of scholarly perspectives and sources. Some of these works are Leonie Caldecott and Stephanie Leland, eds., *Reclaim the Earth: Women Speak Out for Life on Earth* (London: The Women's Press, 1983); Jim Cheney, "Eco-Feninism and Deep Ecology," *Environmental Ethics* 9 (1987): 11–45; Andrée Collard with Joyce Contrucci, *Rape of the Wild: Man's Violence against Animals and the Earth* (Bloomington: Indiana University Press, 1988); Katherine Davies, "Historical Associations: Women and the Natural World," *Women & Environments* 9, no. 2 (Spring 1987): 4–6; Sharon Doubiago, "Deeper Than Deep Ecology: Men Must Become Feminists," in *The New Catalyst Quarterly*, no. 10 (Winter 1987/88): 10–11; Brian Easlea, *Science and Sexual Oppression: Patriarchy's Confrontation with Women and Nature* (London: Weidenfeld & Nicholson, 1981); Elizabeth Dodson Gray, *Green Paradise Lost* (Wellesley, MA: Roundtable Press, 1979); Susan Griffin, *Women and Nature: The Roaring Inside Her* (San Francisco: Harper & Row, 1978); Joan L. Griscom, "On Healing the Nature/History Split in Feminist Thought," in *Heresies #13: Feminism and Ecology* 4, no. 1 (1981): 4–9; Ynestra King, "The Ecology of Feminism and the Feminism of Ecology," in *Healing Our Wounds: The Power of Ecological Feminism*, ed. Judith Plant (Boston: New Society Publishers, 1989), pp. 18–28; "The Eco-Feminist Imperative," in *Reclaim the Earth*, ed. Caldecott and Leland (London: The Women's Press, 1983), pp. 12–16; "Feminism and the Revolt of Nature," in *Heresies #13: Feminism and Ecology* 4, no. 1 (1981), 12–16, and "What Is Ecofeminism?" *The Nation*, 12 December 1987; Marti Kheel, "Animal Liberation Is a Feminist Issue," *The New Catalyst Quarterly*, no. 10 (Winter 1987–88): 8–9; Carolyn Merchant, *The Death of Nature: Women, Ecology and the Scientific Revolution* (San Francisco:

Harper & Row, 1980); Patrick Murphy, ed., "Feminism, Ecology, and the Future of the Humanities," special issue of *Studies in the Humanities* 15, no. 2 (December 1988); Abby Peterson and Carolyn Merchant, "Peace with the Earth: Women and the Environmental Movement in Sweden," *Women's Studies International Forum* 9, no. 5–6 (1986): 465–79; Judith Plant, "Searching for Common Ground: Ecofeminism and Bioregionalism," in *The New Catalyst Quarterly*, no. 10 (Winter 1987/88): 6–7; Judith Plant, ed., *Healing Our Wounds: The Power of Ecological Feminism* (Boston: New Society Publishers, 1989); Val Plumwood, "Ecofeminism: An Overview and Discussion of Positions and Arguments," *Australasian Journal of Philosophy*, Supplement to vol. 64 (June 1986): 120–37; Rosemary Radford Ruether, *New Woman/New Earth: Sexist Ideologies & Human Liberation* (New York: Seabury Press, 1975); Kirkpatrick Sale, "Ecofeminism—A New Perspective," *The Nation*, 26 September 1987, 302–05; Ariel Kay Salleh, "Deeper Than Deep Ecology: The Eco-Feminist Connection," *Environmental Ethics* 6 (1984): 339–45, and "Epistemology and the Metaphors of Production: An Eco-Feminist Reading of Critical Theory," in *Studies in the Humanities* 15 (1988): 130–39; Vandana Shiva, *Staying Alive: Women, Ecology and Development* (London: Zed Books, 1988); Charlene Spretnak, "Ecofeminism: Our Roots and Flowering," *The Elmswood Newsletter*, Winter Solstice 1988; Karen J. Warren, "Feminism and Ecology: Making Connections," *Environmental Ethics* 9 (1987): 3–21; "Toward an Ecofeminist Ethic," *Studies in the Humanities* 15 (1988): 140–156; Miriam Wyman, "Explorations of Ecofeminism," *Women & Environments* (Spring 1987): 6–7; Iris Young, " 'Feminism and Ecology' and 'Women and Life on Earth: Eco-Feminism in the 80s,' " *Environmental Ethics* 5 (1983): 173–80; Michael Zimmerman, "Feminism, Deep Ecology, and Environmental Ethics," *Environmental Ethics* 9 (1987): 21–44.

2. Françoise d'Eaubonne, *Le Feminisme ou la Mort* (Paris: Pierre Horay, 1974), pp. 213–52.

3. I discuss this in my paper, "Toward an Ecofeminist Ethic."

4. The account offered here is a revision of the account given earlier in my paper "Feminism and Ecology: Making Connections." I have changed the account to be about "oppressive" rather than strictly "patriarchal" conceptual frameworks in order to leave open the possibility that there may be some patriarchal conceptual frameworks (e.g., in non-Western cultures) which are *not* properly characterized as based on value dualisms.

5. Murray Bookchin, "Social Ecology Versus 'Deep Ecology,'" in *Green Perspectives: Newsletter of the Green Program Project*, no. 4–5 (Summer 1987): 9.

6. It may be that in contemporary Western society, which is so thoroughly structured by categories of gender, race, class, age, and affectional orientation, that there simply is no meaningful notion of "value-hierarchical thinking" which does not function in an oppressive context. For purposes of this paper, I leave that question open.

7. Many feminists who argue for the historical point that claims (B1) and (B2) have been asserted or assumed to be true within the dominant Western philosophical tradition do so by discussion of that tradition's conceptions of reason, rationality, and science. For a sampling of the sorts of claims made within that context, see "Reason, Rationality, and Gender," ed. Nancy Tuana and Karen J. Warren, a special issue of the American Philosophical Association's *Newsletter on Feminism and Philosophy* 88, no. 2 (March 1989): 1–71. Ecofeminists who claim that (B2) has been assumed to be true within the dominant Western philosophical tradition include Gray, *Green Paradise Lost*; Griffin, *Woman and Nature: The Roaring Inside Her*; Merchant, *The Death of Nature*, Ruether, *New Woman/New Earth*. For a discussion of some of these ecofeminist historical accounts, see Plumwood, "Ecofeminism." While I agree that the historical connections between the domination of women and the domination of nature is a crucial one, I do not argue for that claim here.

8. Ecofeminists who deny (B1) when (B1) is offered as anything other than a true, descriptive, historical claim about patriarchal culture often do so on grounds that an objectionable sort of biological determinism, or at least harmful female sex-gender stereotypes, underlie (B1). For a discussion of this "split" among those ecofeminists ("nature feminists") who assert and those ecofeminists ("social feminists") who deny (B1) as anything other than a true historical claim about how women are described in patriarchal culture, see Griscom, "On Healing the Nature/History Split."

9. I make no attempt here to defend the historically sanctioned truth of these premises.

10. See, e.g., bell hooks, *Feminist Theory: From Margin to Center* (Boston: South End Press, 1984), pp. 51–52.

11. Maria Lugones, "Playfulness, 'World-Travelling,' and Loving Perception," *Hypatia* 2, no. 2 (Summer 1987): 3.

12. At an *experiential* level, some women are "women of color," poor, old, lesbian, Jewish, and physically challenged. Thus, if feminism is going to liberate these women, it also needs to end the racism, classism, heterosexism, anti-Semitism, and discrimination against the handicapped that is constitutive of their oppression as black, or Latina, or poor, or older, or lesbian, or Jewish, or physically challenged women.

13. This same sort of reasoning shows that feminism is also a movement to end racism, classism, ageism, heterosexism and other "isms" which are based in oppressive conceptual frameworks characterized by a logic of domination. However, there is an important caveat: ecofeminsm is *not* compatible with all feminisms and all environmentalisms. For a discussion of this point, see my article, "Feminism and Ecology: Making Connections." What it *is* compatible with is the minimal condition characterization of feminism as a movement to end sexism that is accepted by all contemporary feminisms (liberal, traditional Marxist, radical, socialist, Blacks and non-Western).

14. See, e.g., Gray, *Green Paradise Lost*; Griffin, *Women and Nature*; Merchant, *The Death of Nature*; and Ruether, *New Woman/New Earth*.

15. Suppose, as I think is the case, that a necessary condition for the existence of a moral relationship is that at least one party to the relationship is a moral being (leaving open for our purposes what counts as a "moral being"). If this is so, then the *Mona Lisa* cannot properly be said to have or stand in a moral relationship with the wall on which she hangs, and a wolf cannot have or properly be said to have or stand in a moral relationship with a moose. Such a necessary-condition account leaves open the question whether *both* parties to the relationship must be moral beings. My point here is simply that however one resolves *that* question, recognition of the relationships themselves as a locus of value is a recognition of a source of value that is different from and not reducible to the values of the "moral beings" in those relationships.

16. It is interesting to note that the image of being friends with the Earth is one which cytogeneticist Barbara McClintock uses when she describes the importance of having "a feeling for the organism," "listening to the material [in this case the corn plant]," in one's work as a scientist. See Evelyn Fox Keller, "Women, Science, and Popular Mythology," in *Machina Ex Dea: Feminist Perspectives on Technology*, ed. Joan Rothschild (New York: Pergamon Press, 1983), and Evelyn Fox Keller, *A Feeling for the Organism: The Life and Work of Barbara McClintock* (San Francisco: W. H. Freeman, 1983).

17. Cheney, "Eco-Feminism and Deep Ecology," 144.

18. Marilyn Frye, "In and Out of Harm's Way: Arrogance and Love," *The Politics of Reality*

(Trumansburg, New York: The Crossing Press, 1983), pp. 66–72.

19. Ibid., pp. 75–76.

20. Maria Lugones, "Playfulness," p. 3.

21. Cheney makes a similar point in "Eco-Feminism and Deep Ecology," p. 140.

22. Ibid., p. 138.

23. This account of a feminist ethic draws on my paper "Toward an Ecofeminist Ethic."

24. Marilyn Frye makes this point in her illuminating paper, "The Possibility of Feminist Theory," read at the American Philosophical Association Central Division Meetings in Chicago, 29 April–1 May 1986. My discussion of feminist theory is inspired largely by that paper and by Kathryn Addelson's paper "Moral Revolution," in *Women and Values: Reading in Recent Feminist Philosophy*, ed. Marilyn Pearsall (Belmont, CA: Wadsworth Publishing Co., 1986) pp. 291–309.

25. Notice that the standard of inclusiveness does not exclude the voices of men. It is just that those voices must cohere with the voices of women.

26. For a more in-depth discussion of the notions of impartiality and bias, see my paper, "Critical Thinking and Feminism," *Informal Logic* 10, no. 1 (Winter 1988): 31–44.

27. The burgeoning literature on these values is noteworthy. See, e.g., Carol Gilligan, *In a Different Voice: Psychological Theories and Women's Development* (Cambridge: Harvard University Press, 1982); *Mapping the Domain: A Contribution of Women's Thinking to Psychological Theory and Education*, ed. Carol Gilligan, Janie Victoria Ward, and Jill McLean Taylor, with Betty Bardige (Cambridge: Harvard University Press, 1988); Nel Noddings, *Caring: A Feminine Approach to Ethics and Moral Education* (Berkeley: University of California Press, 1984); Maria Lugones and Elizabeth V. Spelman, "Have We Got a Theory for You! Feminist Theory, Cultural Imperialism, and the Women's Voice," *Women's Studies International Forum* 6 (1983): 573–81; Maria Lugones, "Playfulness"; Annette C. Baier, "What Do Women Want in a Moral Theory?" *Nous* 19 (1985): 53–63.

28. Jim Cheney would claim that our fundamental relationships to one another as moral agents are not as moral agents to rights-holders, and that whatever rights a person properly may be said to have are relationally defined rights, not rights possessed by atomistic individuals conceived as Robinson Crusoes who do not exist essentially in relation to others. On this view, even rights talk itself is properly conceived as growing out of a relational ethic, not vice versa.

29. Alison Jaggar, *Feminist Politics and Human Nature* (Totowa, NJ: Rowman & Allanheld, 1980), pp. 42–44.

30. Henry West has pointed out that the expression "defining relations" is ambiguous. According to West, "the 'defining' as Cheney uses it is an adjective, not a principle—it is not that ethics defines relationships; it is that ethics grows out of conceiving of the relationships that one is in as defining what the individual is."

31. For example, in relationships involving contracts or promises, those relationships might be correctly described as that of moral agent to rights holders. In relationships involving mere property, those relationships might be correctly described as that of moral agent to objects having only instrumental value, "relationships of instrumentality." In comments on an earlier draft of this paper, West suggested that possessive individualism, for instance, might be recast in such a way that an individual is defined by his or her property relationships.

32. Cheney, "Eco-Feminism and Deep Ecology," p. 144.

33. One might object that such permission for change opens the door for environmental exploitation: This is not the case. An ecofeminist ethic is anti-naturist. Hence, the unjust domination and exploitation of nature is a "boundary condition" of the ethic; no such actions are sanctioned or justified on ecofeminist grounds. What it *does* leave open is some leeway about what counts as domination and exploitation. This, I think, is a strength of the ethic, not a weakness, since it acknowledges that *that* issue cannot be resolved in any practical way in the abstract, independent of a historical and social context.

34. Nathan Hare, "Black Ecology," in *Environmental Ethics*, ed. K. S. Shrader-Fréchette (Pacific Grove, CA: Boxwood Press, 1981), pp. 229–36.

35. For an ecofeminist discussion of the Chipko movement, see my "Toward an Ecofeminist Ethic," and Shiva's *Staying Alive*.

36. See Cheney, "Eco-Feminism and Deep Ecology," p. 122.

37. I offer the same sort of reply to critics of ecofeminism such as Warwick Fox who suggest that for the sort of ecofeminism I defend, the word *feminist* does not add anything significant to environmental ethics and, consequently, that an ecofeminist like myself might as well call herself a deep ecologist. He asks: "Why doesn't she just call it [i.e., Warren's vision of a transformative feminism] deep ecology? Why specifically attach the label *feminist* to it . . . ?" (Warwick Fox, "The Deep Ecology-Ecofeminism Debate and Its Parallels," *Environmental Ethics* 11, no. 1 [1989]: 14, n.22). Whatever the important similarities between deep ecology and ecofeminism (or,

specifically, my verson of ecofeminism)—and, indeed, there are many—it is precisely my point here that the word *feminist* does add something significant to the conception of environmental ethics, and that any environmental ethic (including deep ecology) that fails to make explicit the different kinds of interconnections among the domination of nature and the domination of women will be, from a feminist (and ecofeminist) perspective such as mine, inadequate.

36. Development, Ecology, and Women

Vandana Shiva

Development as a New Project of Western Patriarchy

"Development" was to have been a post-colonial project, a choice for accepting a model of progress in which the entire world remade itself on the model of the colonising modern west, without having to undergo the subjugation and exploitation that colonialism entailed. The assumption was that western style progress was possible for all. Development, as the improved well-being of all, was thus equated with the westernisation of economic categories—of needs, of productivity, of growth. Concepts and categories about economic development and natural resource utilisation that had emerged in the specific context of industrialisation and capitalist growth in a centre of colonial power, were raised to the level of universal assumptions and applicability in the entirely different context of basic needs satisfaction for the people of the newly independent Third World countries. Yet, as Rosa Luxemberg has pointed out, early industrial development in western Europe necessitated the permanent occupation of the colonies by the colonial powers and the destruction of the local "natural economy."[1] According to her, colonialism is a constant necessary condition for capitalist growth: without colonies, capital accumulation would grind to a halt. "Development" as capital accumulation and the commercialisation of the economy for the generation of "surplus" and profits thus involved the reproduction not merely of a particular form of creation of wealth, but also of the associated creation of poverty and dispossession. A replication of economic development based on commercialisation of resource use for commodity production in the newly independent countries created the internal colonies.[2] Development was thus reduced to a continuation of the process of colonisation; it became an extension of the project of wealth creation in modern western patriarchy's economic vision, which was based on the exploitation or exclusion of women (of the west and non-west), on the exploitation and degradation of nature, and on the exploitation and erosion of other cultures. "Development" could not but entail destruction for women, nature and subjugated cultures, which is why, throughout the Third World, women, peasants and tribals are struggling for liberation from "development" just as they earlier struggled for liberation from colonialism.

The UN Decade for Women was based on the assumption that the improvement of women's economic position would automatically flow from an expansion and diffusion of the development process. Yet, by the end of the Decade, it was becoming clear that development itself was the problem. Insufficient and inadequate 'participation' in 'development' was not the cause for women's increasing underdevelopment; it was, rather, their enforced by asymmetric participation in it, by which they bore the costs but were excluded from the benefits, that was responsible. Development exclusivity and dispossession aggravated and deepened the colonial processes of ecological degradation and the loss of political control over nature's sustenance base. Economic growth was a new colonialism, draining resources away from those who needed them most. The discontinuity lay in the fact that it was now new national elites, not colonial powers, that masterminded the exploitation on grounds of 'national interest' and

Staying Alive, by Vandana Shiva (London: Zed Books Ltd., 1988), pp. 1–13. Reprinted by permission of the publisher.

growing GNPs, and it was accomplished with more powerful technologies of appropriation and destruction.

Ester Boserup[3] has documented how women's impoverishment increased during colonial rule; those rulers who had spent a few centuries in subjugating and crippling their own women into de-skilled, de-intellectualised appendages, disfavoured the women of the colonies on matters of access to land, technology and employment. The economic and political processes of colonial underdevelopment bore the clear mark of modern western patriarchy, and while large numbers of women and men were impoverished by these processes, women tended to lose more. The privatisation of land for revenue generation displaced women more critically, eroding their traditional land-use rights. The expansion of cash crops undermined food production, and women were often left with meagre resources to feed and care for children, the aged and the infirm, when men migrated or were conscripted into forced labour by the colonisers. As a collective document by women activists, organisers and researchers stated at the end of the UN Decade for Women, "The almost uniform conclusion of the Decade's research is that with a few exceptions, women's relative access to economic resources, incomes and employment has worsened, their burden of work has increased, and their relative and even absolute health, nutritional and educational status has declined."[4]

The displacement of women from productive activity by the expansion of development was rooted largely in the manner in which development projects appropriated or destroyed the natural resource base for the production of sustenance and survival. It destroyed women's productivity both by removing land, water, and forests from their management and control, as well as through the ecological destruction of soil, water and vegetation systems so that nature's productivity and renewability were impaired. While gender subordination and patriarchy are the oldest of oppressions, they have taken on new and more violent forms through the project of development. Patriarchal categories which understand destruction as "production" and regeneration of life as "passivity" have generated a crisis of survival. Passivity, as an assumed category of the "nature" of nature and of women, denies the activity of nature and life. Fragmentation and uniformity as assumed categories of progress and development destroy the living forces which arise from relationships within the "web of life" and the diversity in the elements and patterns of these relationships.

The economic biases and values against nature, women and indigenous peoples are captured in this typical analysis of the "unproductiveness" of traditional natural societies:

> Production is achieved through human and animal, rather than mechanical, power. Most agriculture is unproductive; human or animal manure may be used but chemical fertilisers and pesticides are unknown. . . . For the masses, these conditions mean poverty.[5]

The assumptions are evident: nature is unproductive; organic agriculture based on nature's cycles of renewability spells poverty; women and tribal and peasant societies embedded in nature are similarly unproductive, not because it has been demonstrated that in cooperation they produce *less* goods and services for needs, but because it is assumed that "production" takes place only when mediated by technologies for commodity production, even when such technologies destroy life. A stable and clean river is not a productive resource in this view: it needs to be "developed" with dams in order to become so. Women, sharing the river as a commons to satisfy the water needs of their families and society are not involved in productive labour: when substituted by the engineering man, water management and water use become productive activities. Natural forests remain unproductive till they are developed into monoculture plantations of commercial species. Development thus, is equivalent to maldevelopment, a development bereft of the feminine, the conservation, the ecological principle. The neglect of nature's work in renewing herself, and women's work in producing sustenance in the form of basic, vital needs is an essential part of the paradigm of maldevelopment, which sees all work that does not produce profits and capital as non or unproductive work. As Maria Mies[6] has pointed out, this concept of surplus has a patriarchal bias because, from the point of view of nature and women, it is not based on material surplus produced *over and above* the requirements of the community: it is stolen and appropriated through violent modes from nature (who needs a share of her produce to reproduce herself) and from women (who need a share of nature's produce to produce sustenance and ensure survival).

From the perspective of Third World women, productivity is a measure of producing life and sustenance; that this kind of productivity has been rendered invisible does not reduce its centrality to survival—it merely reflects the domination of modern patriarchal economic categories which see only profits, not life.

Maldevelopment as the Death of the Feminine Principle

In this analysis, maldevelopment becomes a new source of male–female inequality. "Modernisation" has been associated with the introduction of new forms of dominance. Alice Schlegel[7] has shown that under conditions of subsistence, the interdependence and complementarity of the separate male and female domains of work is the characteristic mode, based on diversity, not inequality. Maldevelopment militates against this equality in diversity, and superimposes the ideologically constructed category of western technological man as a uniform measure of the worth of classes, cultures and genders. Dominant modes of perception based on reductionism, duality and linearity are unable to cope with equality in diversity, with forms and activities that are significant and valid, even though different. The reductionist mind superimposes the roles and forms of power of western male-oriented concepts on women, all non-western peoples and even on nature, rendering all three "deficient," and in need of "development." Diversity, and unity and harmony in diversity, become epistemologically unattainable in the context of maldevelopment, which then becomes synonymous with women's underdevelopment (increasing sexist domination), and nature's depletion (deepening ecological crises). Commodities have grown, but nature has shrunk. The poverty crisis of the South arises from the growing scarcity of water, food, fodder, and fuel, associated with increasing maldevelopment and ecological destruction. This poverty crisis touches women most severely, first because they are the poorest among the poor, and then because, with nature, they are the primary sustainers of society.

Maldevelopment is the violation of the integrity of organic, interconnected and interdependent systems, that sets in motion a process of exploitation, inequality, injustice and violence. It is blind to the fact that a recognition of nature's harmony and action to maintain it are preconditions for distributive justice. This is why Mahatma Gandhi said, "There is enough in the world for everyone's need, but not for some people's greed."

Maldevelopment is maldevelopment in thought and action. In practice, this fragmented, reductionist, dualist perspective violates the integrity and harmony of man in nature, and the harmony between men and women. It ruptures the cooperative unity of masculine and feminine, and places man, shorn of the feminine principle, above nature and women, and separated from both. The violence to nature as symptomatised by the ecological crisis, and the violence to women, as symptomatised by their subjugation and exploitation, arise from this subjugation of the feminine principle. I want to argue that what is currently called development is essentially maldevelopment, based on the introduction or accentuation of the domination of man over nature and women. In it both are viewed as the "other," the passive nonself. Activity, productivity, creativity which were associated with the feminine principle are expropriated as qualities of nature and women, and transformed into the exclusive qualities of man. Nature and women are turned into passive objects, to be used and exploited for the uncontrolled and uncontrollable desires of alienated man. From being the creators and sustainers of life, nature and women are reduced to being "resources" in the fragmented, anti-life model of maldevelopment.

Two Kinds of Growth, Two Kinds of Productivity

Maldevelopment is usually called "economic growth," measured by the Gross National Product. Porritt, a leading ecologist, has this to say of GNP:

> *Gross* National Product—for once a word is being used correctly. Even conventional economists admit that the hey-day of GNP is over, for the simple reason that as a measure of progress, it's more or less useless. GNP measures the lot, all the goods and services produced in the money economy. Many of these goods and services are not beneficial to people, but rather a measure of just how much is going wrong; increased spending on crime, on pollution, on the many human casualties of our society, increased spending because of waste or planned obsolescence, increased spending because of growing bureaucracies: it's all counted.[8]

The problem with GNP is that it measures some costs as benefits (e.g., pollution control) and fails to measure other costs completely. Among these hidden costs are the new burdens created by ecological devastation, costs that are invariably heavier for women, both in the North and South. It is hardly surprising, therefore, that as GNP rises, it does not necessarily mean that either wealth or welfare increase proportionately. I would argue that GNP is becoming, increasingly, a measure of how real wealth—the wealth of nature and that produced by women for sustaining life—is rapidly decreasing. When commodity production as the prime economic activity is introduced as development, it destroys the potential of nature and women to produce life and goods and services for basic needs. More commodities and more cash mean less life— in nature (through ecological destruction) and in society (through denial of basic needs). Women are devalued first, because their work cooperates with nature's processes, and second, because work which satisfies needs and ensures sustenance is devalued in general. Precisely because more growth in maldevelopment has meant less sustenance of life and life-support systems, it is now imperative to recover the feminine principle as the basis for development which conserves and is ecological. Feminism as ecology, and ecology as the revival of Prakriti, the source of all life, become the decentred powers of political and economic transformation and restructuring.

This involves, first, a recognition that categories of "productivity" and growth which have been taken to be positive, progressive and universal are, in reality, restricted patriarchal categories. When viewed from the point of view of nature's productivity and growth, and women's production of sustenance, they are found to be ecologically destructive and a source of gender inequality. It is no accident that the modern, efficient and productive technologies created within the context of growth in market economic terms are associated with heavy ecological costs, borne largely by women. The resource and energy intensive production processes they give rise to demand ever increasing resource withdrawals from the ecosystem. These withdrawals disrupt essential ecological processes and convert renewable resources into nonrenewable ones. A forest, for example, provides inexhaustible supplies of diverse biomass over time if its capital stock is maintained and it is har-

vested on a sustained yield basis. The heavy and uncontrolled demand for industrial and commercial wood, however, requires the continuous overfelling of trees which exceeds the regenerative capacity of the forest ecosystem, and eventually converts the forests into nonrenewable resources. Women's work in the collection of water, fodder and fuel is thus rendered more energy and time-consuming. (In Garhwal, for example, I have seen women who originally collected fodder and fuel in a few hours, now travelling long distances by truck to collect grass and leaves in a task that might take up to two days.) Sometimes the damage to nature's intrinsic regenerative capacity is impaired not by over-exploitation of a particular resource but, indirectly, by damage caused to other related natural resources through ecological processes. Thus, the excessive overfelling of trees in the catchment areas of streams and rivers destroys not only forest resources, but also renewable supplies of water, through hydrological destabilisation. Resource-intensive industries disrupt essential ecological processes not only by their excessive demands for raw material, but by their pollution of air and water and soil. Often such destruction is caused by the resource demands of non-vital industrial products. In spite of severe ecological crises, this paradigm continues to operate because for the North and for the elites of the South, resources continue to be available, even now. The lack of recognition of nature's processes for survival *as factors in the process of economic development* shrouds the political issues arising from resource transfer and resource destruction, and creates an ideological weapon for increased control over natural resources in the conventionally employed notion of productivity. All other costs of the economic process consequently become invisible. The forces which contribute to the increased "productivity" of a modern farmer or factory worker, for instance, come from the increased use of natural resources. Lovins has described this as the amount of "slave" labour presently at work in the world.[9] According to him each person on earth, on an average, possesses the equivalent of about 50 slaves, each working a 40 hour week. Man's global energy conversion from all sources (wood, fossil fuel, hydroelectric power, nuclear) is currently approximately 8×10^{12} watts. This is more than 20 times the energy content of the food necessary to feed the present world population at the FAO standard diet of 3,600 cal/ day. The "productivity" of the western male compared to women or Third World peasants is not intrinsically superior; it is based on inequalities in the distribution of this "slave" labour. The average inhabitant of the USA for example has 250 times more "slaves" than the average Nigerian. "If Americans were short of 249 of those 250 'slaves,' one wonders how efficient they would prove themselves to be?"

It is these resource and energy intensive processes of production which divert resources away from survival, and hence from women. What patriarchy sees as productive work is, in ecological terms, highly destructive production. The second law of thermodynamics predicts that resource intensive and resource wasteful economic development must become a threat to the survival of the human species in the long run. Political struggles based on ecology in industrially advanced countries are rooted in this conflict between *long term survival options* and *short term over-production and over-consumption*. Political struggles of women, peasants and tribals based on ecology in countries like India are far more acute and urgent since they are rooted in the *immediate threat to the options for survival* for the vast majority of the people, *posed by resource intensive and resource wasteful economic growth* for the benefit of a minority.

In the market economy, the organising principle for natural resource use is the maximisation of profits and capital accumulation. Nature and human needs are managed through market mechanisms. Demands for natural resources are restricted to those demands registering on the market; the ideology of development is in large part based on a vision of bringing all natural resources into the market economy for commodity production. When these resources are already being used by nature to maintain her production of renewable resources and by women for sustenance and livelihood, their diversion to the market economy generates a scarcity condition for ecological stability and creates new forms of poverty for women.

Two Kinds of Poverty

In a book entitled *Poverty: The Wealth of the People*[10] an African writer draws a distinction between poverty as subsistence, and misery as deprivation. It is useful to separate a cultural conception of subsistence living as poverty from the material experience of poverty that is a result of dispossession and deprivation. Culturally per-

ceived poverty need not be real material poverty: subsistence economies which satisfy basic needs through self-provisioning are not poor in the sense of being deprived. Yet the ideology of development declares them so because they do not participate overwhelmingly in the market economy, and do not consume commodities produced for and distributed through the market *even though they might be satisfying those needs through self-provisioning mechanisms*. People are perceived as poor if they eat millets (grown by women) rather than commercially produced and distributed processed foods sold by global agri-business. They are seen as poor if they live in self-built housing made from natural material like bamboo and mud rather than in cement houses. They are seen as poor if they wear handmade garments of natural fibre rather than synthetics. Subsistence, as culturally perceived poverty, does not necessarily imply a low physical quality of life. On the contrary, millets are nutritionally far superior to processed foods, houses built with local materials are far superior, being better adapted to the local climate and ecology, natural fibres are preferable to man-made fibres in most cases, and certainly more affordable. This cultural perception of prudent subsistence living as poverty has provided the legitimisation for the development process as a poverty removal project. As a culturally biased project it destroys wholesome and sustainable lifestyles and creates real material poverty, or misery, by the denial of survival needs themselves, through the diversion of resources to resource intensive commodity production. Cash crop production and food processing take land and water resources away from sustenance needs, and exclude increasingly large numbers of people from their entitlements to food. "The inexorable processes of agriculture-industrialisation and internationalisation are probably responsible for more hungry people than either cruel or unusual whims of nature. There are several reasons why the high-technology export-crop model increases hunger. Scarce land, credit, water, and technology are preempted for the export market. Most hungry people are not affected by the market at all. . . . The profits flow to corporations that have no interest in feeding hungry people without money."[11]

The Ethiopian famine is in part an example of the creation of real poverty by development aimed at removing culturally perceived poverty. The displacement of nomadic Afars from their traditional pastureland in Awash Valley by commercial agriculture (financed by foreign companies) led to their struggle for survival in the fragile uplands which degraded the ecosystem and led to the starvation of cattle and the nomads.[12] The market economy conflicted with the survival economy in the Valley, thus creating a conflict between the survival economy and nature's economy in the uplands. At no point has the global marketing of agricultural commodities been assessed against the background of the new conditions of scarcity and poverty that it has induced. This new poverty moreover, is no longer cultural and relative: it is absolute, threatening the very survival of millions on this planet.

The economic system based on the patriarchal concept of productivity was created for the very specific historical and political phenomenon of colonialism. In it, the input for which efficiency of use had to be maximised in the production centres of Europe, was industrial labour. For colonial interest therefore, it was rational to improve the labour resource *even at the cost of wasteful use of nature's wealth*. This rationalisation has, however, been illegitimately universalised to all contexts and interest groups and, on the plea of increasing productivity, labour reducing technologies have been introduced in situations where labour is abundant and cheap, and resource demanding technologies have been introduced where resources are scarce and already fully utilised for the production of sustenance. Traditional economies with a stable ecology have shared with industrially advanced affluent economies the ability to use natural resources to satisfy basic vital needs. The former differ from the latter in two essential ways: first, the same needs are satisfied in industrial societies through longer technological chains requiring higher energy and resource inputs and excluding large numbers without purchasing power; and second, affluence generates new and artificial needs requiring the increased production of industrial goods and services. Traditional economies are not advanced in the matter of non-vital needs satisfaction, but as far as the satisfaction of basic and vital needs is concerned, they are often what Marshall Sahlins has called "the original affluent society." The needs of the Amazonian tribes are more than satisfied by the rich rainforest; their poverty begins with its destruction. The story is the same for the Gonds of Bastar in India or the Penans of Sarawak in Malaysia.

Thus are economies based on indigenous technologies viewed as "backward" and "unproductive." Poverty, as the denial of basic needs, is not necessarily associated with the existence of traditional technologies, and its removal is not necessarily an outcome of the growth of modern ones. On the contrary, the destruction of ecologically sound traditional technologies, often created and used by women, along with the destruction of their material base, is generally believed to be responsible for the "feminisation" of poverty in societies which have had to bear the costs of resource destruction.

The contemporary poverty of the Afar nomad is not rooted in the inadequacies of traditional nomadic life, but in the *diversion of the productive pastureland of the Awash Valley*. The erosion of the resource base for survival is increasingly being caused by the demand for resources by the market economy, dominated by global forces. The creation of inequality through economic activity which is ecologically disruptive arises in two ways: first, inequalities in the distribution of privileges make for unequal access to natural resources—these include privileges of both a political and economic nature. Second, resource intensive production processes have access to subsidized raw material on which a substantial number of people, especially from the less privileged economic groups, depend for their survival. The consumption of such industrial raw material is determined purely by market forces, and not by considerations of the social or ecological requirements placed on them. The costs of resource destruction are externalized and unequally divided among various economic groups in society, but are borne largely by women and those who satisfy their basic material needs directly from nature, simply because they have no purchasing power to register their demands on the goods and services provided by the modern production system. Gustavo Esteva has called development a permanent war waged by its promoters and suffered by its victims.[13]

The paradox and crisis of development arises from the mistaken identification of culturally perceived poverty with real material poverty, and the mistaken identification of the growth of commodity production as better satisfaction of basic needs. In actual fact, there is less water, less fertile soil, less genetic wealth as a result of the development process. Since these natural resources are the basis of nature's economy and women's survival economy, their scarcity is impoverishing women and marginalized peoples in an unprecedented manner. Their new impoverishment lies in the fact that resources which supported their survival were absorbed into the market economy while they themselves were excluded and displaced by it.

The old assumption that with the development process the availability of goods and services will automatically be increased and poverty will be removed, is now under serious challenge from women's ecology movements in the Third World, even while it continues to guide development thinking in centers of patriarchal power. Survival is based on the assumption of the sanctity of life; maldevelopment is based on the assumption of the sacredness of "development." Gustavo Esteva asserts that the sacredness of development has to be refuted because it threatens survival itself. "My people are tired of development," he says, "they just want to live."[14]

The recovery of the feminine principle allows a transcendence and transformation of these patriarchal foundations of maldevelopment. It allows a redefinition of growth and productivity as categories linked to the production, not the destruction, of life. It is thus simultaneously an ecological and a feminist political project which legitimises the way of knowing and being that create wealth by enhancing life and diversity, and which delegitimises the knowledge and practice of a culture of death as the basis for capital accumulation.

Notes

1. Rosa Luxemberg, *The Accumulation of Capital*, London: Routledge and Kegan Paul, 1951.

2. An elaboration of how "development" transfers resources from the poor to the well-endowed is contained in J. Bandyopadhyay and V. Shiva, "Political Economy of Technological Polarisations" in *Economic and Political Weekly*, Vol. XVIIL 1982, pp. 1827–32; and J. Bandyopadhyay and V. Shiva, "Political Economy of Ecology Movements," in *Economic and Political Weekly*, forthcoming.

3. Ester Boserup, *Women's Role in Economic Development*, London: Allen and Unwin, 1970.

4. *Development Crisis and Alternative Visions: Third World Women's Perspectives*, Bergen: Christian Michelsen Institute, 1985, p. 21.

5. M. George Foster, *Traditional Societies and Technological Change*, Delhi: Allied Publishers, 1973.

6. Maria Mies, *Patriarchy and Accumulation on a World Scale*, London: Zed Books, 1986.

7. Alice Schlegel (ed.), *Sexual Stratification: A Cross-Cultural Study*, New York: Columbia University Press, 1977.

8. Jonathan Porritt, *Seeing Green*, Oxford: Blackwell, 1984.

9. A. Lovins, cited in S. R. Eyre, *The Real Wealth of Nations*, London: Edward Arnold, 1978.

10. R. Bahro, *From Red to Green*, London: Verso, 1984, p. 211.

11. R. J. Barnet, *The Lean Years*, London: Abacus, 1981, p. 171.

12. U. P. Koehn, "African Approaches to Environmental Stress: A Focus on Ethiopia and Nigeria," in R. N. Barrett (ed.), *International Dimensions of the Environmental Crisis*. Boulder, CO: Westview, 1982, pp. 253–89.

13. Gustavo Esteva, "Regenerating Peoples Space," in S. N. Mendlowitz and R. B. J. Walker, *Towards a Just World Peace: Perspectives from Social Movements*. London: Butterworths and Committee for a Just World Peace, 1987.

14. G. Esteva, Remarks made at a conference of the Society for International Development, Rome, 1985.

37. How Feminist Is Ecofeminism?

Victoria Davion

I. Introduction

This paper explores some doubts I have regarding ecofeminism, a relatively new movement attempting to bring feminist insights to environmental ethics.[1] Although there are a variety of different ecofeminist positions, ecofeminists agree that there is an important link between the domination of women and the domination of nature, and that an understanding of one is aided by an understanding of the other. Ecofeminists argue that any environmental ethic that fails to recognize important conceptual ties between the domination of women and the domination of nature cannot provide an adequate understanding of either.[2] Therefore, ecofeminists argue that a feminist perspective contributes to a fuller understanding of the domination of nature by human beings, and is necessary for the generation of a deeper environmental ethic.

My project is not to question this thesis; I agree with it. My project is to explore whether much of what is currently called "ecofeminist" is actually feminist. I will argue that at least some of the ideas coming from thinkers identifying themselves as ecofeminists are, in very important ways, *not* feminist. Because these ideas are not feminist, they cannot be ecofeminist. The ideas I shall explore glorify the feminine uncritically and suggest that embracing a feminine perspective will help humans solve the ecological crisis. I will argue that a truly feminist perspective cannot embrace either the feminine or the masculine uncritically, as a truly feminist perspective requires a critique of gender roles, and this critique must include masculinity *and* femininity. While the views I have in mind critique masculinity, they fail to do the same in the case of femininity. I shall, therefore, argue that these views are better understood as *ecofeminine*, as they do not embrace a feminist perspective.[3] Before turning to this task, I shall argue that views which *uncritically* embrace masculinity or femininity are, in crucial ways, not feminist. With this conceptual framework in place, I shall discuss five *ecofeminine* views in section IV. Finally, I shall suggest some positive directions for ecofeminism in the concluding section.

II. Important Ecofeminist Insights

Ecofeminists agree that the domination of nature by human beings comes from a patriarchal world view, the same world view that justifies the domination of women. Because both dominations come from the same world view, the movement to stop devaluing nature should, in consistency, include a movement against the domination of women, i.e., should incorporate a feminist perspective.

In her recent article, "The Power and the Promise of Ecological Feminism," Karen Warren explores some major conceptual connections between the domination of women by men and the domination of nature by humans. She argues that both depend on the "logic of domination." This logic makes use of premises about differences between human beings and the rest of nature, along with a premise that asserts that these differences allow human beings to dominate non-humans. She offers the following example:

(A1) Humans do, . . . plants do not, have the capacity to consciously . . . change the community in which they live.

(A2) Whatever has [this] capacity . . . is morally superior to whatever [doesn't have] it.

Ecological Feminism, edited by Karen J. Warren. New York: Routledge, Chapman & Hall, Inc., 1994. Reprinted by permission of the author.

I owe special thanks to Karen J. Warren, whose help in reading ealier drafts of this work has resulted in substantive conceptual changes that have improved the piece greatly, and have also contributed to my understanding of the complexity and importance of various ecofeminist perspectives. An updated version of this piece appears in *Ecological Feminist Philosophies*, edited by Karen Warren, Routledge and Chapman Hall, Spring 1994. I would also like to thank Chris Cuomo and Claudia Card for their helpful suggestions.

(A3) . . . Humans are morally superior to plants and rocks.

(A4) For any X and Y, if X is morally superior to Y, then X is morally justified in subordinating Y.

(A5) . . . Humans are morally justified in subordinating plants and rocks.[4]

This argument incorporates what Warren refers to as an oppressive conceptual framework. Features of such a framework include hierarchical thinking, value dualisms, and the logic of domination. Such a framework includes the idea that particular characteristics of individuals place them either above or below each other in moral hierarchies, and the assumption that whatever is above something else in the hierarchy has the moral right to dominate that which is below it. These features combine to create a world view that offers a justification for human domination of nature. Thus, Warren shows how a particular logic is involved in justifying the domination of nature by humans, and makes explicit just what that logic is.

Warren maintains that the same logic allows for the sexist domination of women under patriarchy by way of the association of women with nature. She sketches the argument as follows:

(B1) Women are identified with nature and the realm of the physical; men are identified with the "human" and the realm of the mental.

(B2) Whatever is identified with nature and the realm of the physical is inferior to ("below") whatever is identified with the "human" and the realm of the mental. . . .

(B3) Thus, women are inferior to . . . men. . . .

(B4) For any X and Y, if X is superior to Y, then X is justified in subordinating Y.

(B5) . . . Men are justified in subordinating women.[5]

As I said earlier, I agree with the ecofeminist argument that there are links between the domination of women under patriarchy and the domination of nature. Noticing these links allows us to recognize that the domination of nature by humans and the sexist domination of women by men rely on the same general framework. Thus, the overthrowing of this framework is fundamental to both projects and, therefore, the projects are conceptually linked. This important insight shows that environmentalists and feminists should be allies, and makes explicit what it is we must work against. It represents a very important ecofeminist contribution to both movements. If one grants conceptual links between the domination of nature and the domination of women, it follows that a movement that is not feminist will yield at best a superficial understanding of the domination of nature.

III. Feminism

Feminism pays attention to women. Although there are many different kinds of feminism, virtually all feminists agree that sexist oppression is wrong, and therefore seek to overthrow patriarchy in its various forms. Thus, for an analysis to be feminist, it must include an analysis of sex and gender. It must look for the various ways that sexist oppression damages women, and seek alternatives to them. In looking at *how* patriarchy damages women, a feminist analysis must look closely at the roles women play in various patriarchies, the *feminine* roles. In so far as these roles are damaging (to those who play them), they must be viewed with suspicion. If feminists fail to assert that at least some of the roles assigned to women under patriarchy are damaging, we fail to assert the very premise that makes feminism, the overthrowing of patriarchy, important. For, if sexist oppression is not damaging to women, women have no reason to resist it. If it does cause damage, we should expect to see this damage in feminine roles. Thus, ecofeminist solutions which assert that feminine roles can provide an answer to the ecological crisis, without first examining how these roles are damaging to those who play them, lose the conceptual underpinnings of feminism in this assertion.

Before continuing, I want to be clear about what it is I am *not* doing here. I am *not* claiming that there can be only one truly feminist perspective. There are many different kinds of feminism, including radical feminism, marxist feminism, cultural feminism, and so forth. I am not attempting to distinguish between these approaches here. In my view, all of these can be feminist approaches as long as they have a critical analysis of sex and gender. It is the *uncritical* acceptance of various aspects of sex and gender that concerns me.

In what follows I will examine five ecofeminist views which fail to critically examine femininity in its various forms. Each of them suggests that a more "feminine" perspective on the environment will help solve the ecological crisis. Some suggest that we can overthrow patriarchy by having men become more "feminine," without considering that femininity may be a product of patriarchy itself. Because they all fail to consider that feminine perspectives are most likely damaged, and fail to explore just what this damage might be, they fail to explore the possible negative aspects of bringing more "feminine" perspectives to environmental ethics. In addition, several of these views imply that there is something that is THE feminine role, that the feminine perspective is a unified perspective. However, if feminism is to be understood as a movement for the liberation of all women, we must understand that there is no one feminine voice. Rather, there are many different feminine voices, many "feminine" perspectives. Therefore, views which uncritically embrace feminine sides of gender dichotomies are not feminist, and when these views are linked with ecological perspectives they are better understood as *ecofeminine*. They are, in fact, dangerous views from a genuinely feminist perspective.

IV. Five Ecofeminine Views

Although there are significant differences in each of the five views I will discuss, each glorifies the feminine uncritically, and therefore none are truly feminist on my understanding of feminism as committed to a critique of gender reality.

The first position I shall examine is presented by Ariel Kay Salleh in "Deeper Than Deep Ecology: The Ecofeminist Connection." She says the following about women's lived experience under patriarchy:

> . . . if women's lived experience were recognized as meaningful and were given legitimation in our culture, it would provide an immediate "living" social basis for alternative consciousness which the deep ecologist is trying to formulate and introduce as an abstract ethical construct. Women already, to borrow Devall's turn of phrase, "flow with the system of nature."[6]

According to Salleh, we do not need abstract ethical constructs to help create a consciousness of our connection with the rest of nature; women

already have it. What we need to do is to recognize the value of women's experiences, something which patriarchal societies fail to do.

Salleh claims that while the masculine sense of self-worth in our culture has become entrenched in scientific habits of thought:

> Women, on the other hand, socialized as they are for a multiplicity of contingent tasks and practical labor functions in the home and out, do not experience the inhibiting constraints of status validation to the same extent. The traditional feminine role runs counter to the exploitative technical rationality which currently is the requisite masculine norm. In place of the disdain that the feminine role receives from all quarters, "the separate reality" of this role could well be taken seriously by ecologists and reexamined as a legitimate source of alternative values. As Snyder suggests, men should try out roles which are not highly valued in society, and one might add, particularly this one, for herein lies the basis of a genuinely grounded and nurturant environmentalism.[7]

Thus, the problem, according to Salleh, is that "the traditional feminine role" is devalued. Salleh does not tell us exactly what "the traditional feminine role" is. However, she does imply that women under patriarchy are socialized into it. It is a woman's role under conditions of sexual oppression. She suggests that this role can provide the basis for a genuinely grounded and nurturant environmental ethic. However, the arguments supplied to back this up leave out some important facts about domination and submission that feminists must attend to. According to Salleh, because of the way women are socialized, we ". . . do not experience the inhibiting constraints of status validation to the same extent." However, in many contemporary societies the particular ways in which women seek validation are part of the feminine role. Validation-seeking is often bound up with physical attractiveness. It is shown in contemporary American society by such things as the cosmetic industry, the increasing number of women opting for "elective" cosmetic surgery, and by the number of women with eating disorders. Women may demonstrate the quest for social validation differently both from men and from each other, but it is certainly a part of many feminine roles. And the industries supported by women playing out feminine roles are often responsible for gross environmental damage. The damage to the ozone layer that is done by aerosol cans used to package hairsprays is one example, the cruel testing of cosmetics on animals is another. Finally, we must never forget the extent to which women have dominated other women and men through assertion of status conferred by other things such as race and class. Thus, I think it is false to say that women, in our playing out feminine roles, do not seek status validation, and are more concerned with the environment.

I find the reference to "the separate reality" of women disturbing as well. First, this implies that all women share the same reality. However, an important part of the history of feminist thought has been the lessons white middle class feminists have learned from being called on our racism and classism as we attempted to speak for all women. Because of this, sensitivity to such differences has come to be central to feminist projects. Many feminists now realize that if we want feminism to be more than just a movement for the liberation of a particular group of women, if we wish it to be a movement for the liberation of all women, we must accept and address that there may be no unified experience of femininity or womanhood. There are very deep differences among us. The assumption that there is a separate reality occupied by all women must be examined and argued for, rather than simply assumed.

Another aspect of the "separate reality" claim I find troubling involves the idea that women's reality is separate from men's. In some very important ways, women don't live in a reality separate from men's. Men and women living under conditions of sexist oppression live in a world inhabited by oppressors as well as by the oppressed. The reality of oppressed women is intimately connected to that of the oppressors. Women oppressed under a particular patriarchy may share experiences as members of the same group. However, to say that these experiences constitute a separate reality is not only to ignore some of the differences that other aspects of oppression may bring to the situation (such as race or class oppression), but also to ignore the connections *to* oppressors that make women's oppression possible. Femininity makes sense only in relation to masculinity and vice versa. In an important sense there is no separate reality because patriarchy *is* part of reality, and this is the problem.

The idea that men could adopt the feminine role as a start to changing their attitude implies that the feminine role can be understood without its masculine counterpart. However, because the traditional feminine role is the role of the dominated under conditions of sexist oppression, it makes no sense for it to exist independently of the masculine role. The role of the dominated requires that of the dominator. And, if we must seek a society without domination and subordination as part of the solution to the present ecological crisis, this idea cannot be part of that solution.

These considerations lead me to the conclusion that "the feminine role" is unlikely to provide genuine grounding for anything other than the oppression of women. However, even if this role can provide something more, before we assume that it can, it is important to think about the origins of this role, the possible damaging effects of playing it, and whether it makes sense to abstract it from patriarchy in the first place. We must look critically at femininity in its various forms.

A second so-called "ecofeminist" approach glorifies the feminine as a *principle* rather than a *gender role*. In *Development as a New Project of Western Patriarchy*, Vandana Shiva discusses the concept of "development" from the perspective of western patriarchy. She concludes that this so-called "development" actually breeds poverty in the areas that are "developed," and, therefore, it is really maldevelopment. Her argument for this is convincing. However, her discussion of the problem includes the idea of gender complementarity as a good thing and the idea that what is missing from the western patriarchal perspective is the "feminine principle." The following quotation is taken from her article:

> The western development model based on the neglect of nature's work and women's work has become a source of deprivation of basic needs.
>
> In practice this reductionist, dualist perspective gives rise to the violation of the integrity and harmony between men and women. It ruptures the cooperative unity of the masculine and feminine, and puts men, deprived of the feminine principle above and thus separated from nature and women. The violence to nature as symptomized by the current ecological crisis, and the violence to women as symptomized by women's subjugation and

exploitation arise from the subjugation of the feminine principle.[8]

Shiva doesn't supply a definition of the feminine principle. However, she associates it with conservation and nurturing. She states of the western patriarchal concept of development, "Such development becomes maldevelopment—deprived of the feminine, the conserving, the ecological principle."[9]

This analysis implies several things which I believe must be questioned. One is natural gender complementarity. The suggestion is that gender roles aren't the problem, but that rather, the devaluation of the feminine role causes trouble. However, this must be shown rather than assumed. A vital tradition in feminist critique has long argued that gender roles cannot exist without domination and subordination. It is dangerous for feminists to assume that there is something "natural" or good in gender complementarity. References to the integrity and harmony between men and women, the idea that the western patriarchal concept of development ". . . ruptures the cooperative unity between the masculine and the feminine" presuppose that there is some "natural" way for the sexes to relate to each other, that there is a "natural" division of labor, and that problems emerge from the devaluation of the feminine side. To simply accept gender complementarity without exploring questions it raises is to ignore feminist literature claiming that gender roles are part of *the means of* domination and subordination in patriarchy. It thus ignores questions of gender central to feminist analysis.

Shiva refers to the feminist principle as if there is *a* principle that is feminine. It isn't clear what is meant by this. However, as in Salleh's analysis discussed previously, there is an assumption that the feminine is one thing, and that it has something to offer in solving the ecological crisis. Again my response is that we must remember that the feminine may be shaped by patriarchy, that it is not necessarily an independent category but may be a cluster of various traits emerging out of oppression. There is great danger in abstracting it from patriarchy, and a great danger in assuming it is one thing, given the importance of differences among women.

A third approach within ecofeminist literature which I believe is ecofeminine rather than ecofeminist assumes women have some special understanding of nature but is not clear about the source of this special understanding. Thus far, I have discussed only the views of *women* ecofeminists. However, a number of men also are now identifying with ecofeminism. In "How to Cure a Frontal Lobotomy" Brian Swimme says the following in praise of women's intuition, using Starhawk as an example:

> Starhawk intuits effortlessly what remained beyond the group of the scientists. Our universe is quite clearly a great swelling and birthing event, but why was this hidden from the very discoverers of the primeval birth? The further truth of the universe was closed to them because central regions of the mind were closed. . . . This sentience is awake in Starhawk because of her life as a woman, as one who has the power to give birth herself, and because of her work as a scholar. . . . Women are beings who know from the inside out what it is like to weave the earth into a new human being. Given that experience and the congruent sensitivities seething within body and mind, it would be utterly shocking if ecofeminists did not bring forth meanings to the scientific data that were hidden from the scientists themselves.[10]

Swimme claims that there is some truth to the idea that the earth is a birthing process, but that this truth can only be seen, in fact, effortlessly intuited by women. Swimme seems unsure whether this epistemic privilege is the result of biology, socialization, or both. He refers both to Starhawk's life as a woman, and to the fact that she is a being who can give birth. Perhaps Swimme wants to deny any distinction between biology and socialization as an untenable dualism. However, if Swimme has reasons for leaving the source of this epistemic privilege vague, he doesn't state them. The source of this so-called privilege is of vital importance to any feminist analysis. If this special understanding is the result of oppression, we should expect it to be skewed. Even if it is not skewed, we must ask whether there are other ways to get it. This is a crucial question because if there is no other way to get it, we risk saying that women's oppression is necessary to create the opportunity to gain knowledge needed to solve the ecological crisis. Once again, crucial questions concerning sex and gender are left vague, and women's roles under patriarchy are glorified.[11]

Along with literature assuming that the feminine offers an understanding of human connection to the earth comes literature praising Goddess worship. Much of this literature suggests that cultures that worshipped the Goddess instead of God, cultures in which the feminine was valued, were *peaceful* cultures in which human connection to non-human nature was understood. The next position I shall discuss is an example of this. In "The Gaia Tradition and the Partnership Future" Riane Eisler discusses societies that worshipped the Goddess and argues that they were more like the kind of society we need today to solve the ecological crisis. She says:

> Prehistoric societies worshipped the Goddess of nature and spirituality, our great Mother, the giver of life and creator of us all. But even more fascinating is that these ancient societies were structured very much like the more peaceful and just society we are now trying to construct.
>
> In short, they were societies which had what we today call an ecological consciousness: the awareness that the Earth must be treated with reverence and respect. And this reverence for life-giving and life-sustained powers of the Earth was rooted in a social structure where women and "feminine" values such as caring, compassion, and non-violence were not subordinate to men and the so-called masculine values of conquest and domination. Rather, the life-giving powers incarnated in women's bodies were given the highest social value.[12]

Eisler calls upon us to value these so-called "feminine values" once more:

> Let us reaffirm our ancient covenant, our sacred bond with our Mother, the Goddess of nature and spirituality. Let us renounce the worship of angry gods wielding thunderbolts or swords. Let us once again honor the chalice, the ancient symbol of the power to create and enhance life—and let us understand that this power is not woman's alone but also man's.[13]

Thus, Eisler, like several others discussed here, claims that the problem lies in the devaluing of what she calls "feminine values." By reaffirming such values we can better form the ecological conscience needed to deal with our destructive tendencies.

There is nothing problematic in examining history for ideas to help solve current problems. Eisler's work is interesting and instructive. However, once again I have problems with the use of the gender terms "masculine" and "feminine" in her analysis. My worries in this case stem from the context within which this work is written: this sort of historical work can easily be taken as a glorification of the feminine.

Eisler uses the terms *masculine* and *feminine* to refer to kinds of values in her analysis. She maintains that traits now associated with the term 'feminine' were highly valued during the time period she discusses. However, whether we should refer to these values as feminine is problematic. If patriarchy is necessary for femininity as we now understand it, then if these ancient cultures were not patriarchal or descended from patriarchies, they could not have feminine gender roles. It may be true that some of the respected values in those cultures are devalued in our culture, and that they are considered feminine now. This is very different from asserting that there was anything "feminine" that was respected. Eisler, however, refers to "feminine" values without questioning what it means to call anything "feminine" in a nonpatriarchal culture. Thus, she implies that femininity can exist without patriarchy, a dangerous assumption indeed.

The final view I shall discuss is offered by Marti Kheel in "Ecofeminism and Deep Ecology," and discusses the importance of connection. Kheel argues that ecofeminists and deep ecologists have very different perspectives regarding the kinds of connection to be endorsed in an ecological ethic. Many deep ecologists support developing a sense of oneself that is expanded to include all of nature.[14] They argue that the concept of the self as a static individual with clear ego boundaries is a major factor in the ecological crisis. However, many deep ecologists believe that this sense of self can be developed through activities that involve killing. Hunting is often praised in the literature. Kheel quotes philosopher/biologist Randall Eaton to exemplify this way of thinking.

> To hunt is to experience extreme oneness with nature. . . . The hunter imitates his prey to the point of identity . . . hunting connects a man completely with the earth more deeply and profoundly than any other human enterprise.[15]

This experience of connection is not the type that ecofeminists should support, according to Kheel. She suggests that the way women feel a sense of connection is very different.

It is out of women's unique, felt sense of connection to the natural world that an ecofeminist philosophy must be forged. Identification may, in fact, enter into this philosophy, but only to the extent that it flows from an *existing* connection with individual lives. Individual beings must not be used in a kind of psychological instrumentalism to help establish a *feeling* of connection that in fact does not exist. Our sense of oneness with nature must be connected with concrete, loving actions.[16]

If Kheel is right, much more needs to be said. Not all women feel connected to nature. Some men may feel this more than many women. More importantly, in order to decide what kinds of connections are valuable, and in order to distinguish real connection from a feeling of connection that does not exist, we need to examine various kinds of connection. We should not assume that (a) all women feel this connection with nature or (b) that the connections women do feel are healthy. In doing this, we fail once again to recognize important differences between women, and uncritically glorify women's experiences without critically examining them.

V. Conclusion

Ecofeminism raises interesting questions in spite of the failure of some ecofeminists to critically examine gender roles before incorporating them wholesale as part of solutions to the environmental crisis. Ecofeminists such as Karen Warren have shown how the logic of domination is at work in both the domination of nature by humans, and the domination of women by men under various forms of patriarchy. In so doing, they have shown that the fights to end both are linked conceptually and therefore politically. This insight helps us to see that feminists and environmentalists are allies in a greater fight to end the logic of domination. Hence, I believe the next important task facing ecofeminists is that of generating alternative ways of thinking, ways that are not contaminated by the logic of domination. An understanding of how the logic of domination works on the conceptual level places ecofeminists in an excellent position to do this.

Notes

1. This term was first used by Françoise d'Eaubonne in "Feminism or Death," in *New French Feminisms:*
An Anthology, edited by Elaine Marks and Isabelle de Courtivron (Amherst: University of Massachusetts Press, 1980). For a useful overview of ecofeminist philosophy, see Karen J. Warren, "Feminism and the Environment: An Overview of the Issues," APA Newsletter on *Feminism and Philosophy* (Fall 1991). Also, for another critique of ecofeminism see Janet Biehl, *Rethinking Ecofeminist Politics* (Boston: South End Press, 1991). Although Biehl makes some similar criticisms in this work, she does not examine the work of individual ecofeminists in detail.

2. This position is explicitly argued in Karen J. Warren, "The Power and the Promise of Ecological Feminism." *Environmental Ethics* 12 (2) (1990), pp. 125–146.

3. The term *ecofeminine* was suggested to me by Lorena Sax. My argument will not presuppose that there is only one way that ideas can be feminist, or that there is only one type of feminism. There are many. Thus, for example, I am not distinguishing between radical feminism and marxist feminism here. Rather, I am making a general claim that all types of feminism *must* include a critical look at gender.

4. Warren, 129. Please note, Warren does not support this argument, and does not argue that (A1) is true. This is merely an example of how the logic of domination works.

5. Warren, 130. Again, it is important to note that Warren does not support this argument, and does not argue in favor of any of its premises. Instead, she uses it as an example of the logic of domination at work.

6. Ariel Kay Salleh, "Deeper Than Deep Ecology: The Ecofeminist Connection," *Environmental Ethics* (6) 1 (1984), p. 340.

7. Salleh, p. 342.

8. Vandana Shiva, "Development as a New Project of Western Patriarchy," in *Reweaving the World: The Emergence of Ecofeminism,* edited by Irene Diamond and Gloria Feman Orenstein (San Francisco: Sierra Club Books, 1990), p. 193.

9. Shiva, p. 191. The word *development* appears in quotation marks to indicate Shiva's position that what is called development is in reality not development at all.

10. Brian Swimme, "How to Cure a Frontal Lobotomy," in *Reweaving the World: The Emergence of Ecofeminism,* p. 19.

11. For an interesting discussion of epistemic privilege, see Uma Narayan, "Working Together Across Difference: Some Considerations on Emotions and

Political Practice," *Hypatia: A Journal of Feminist Philosophy* (3) 2 (1988), pp. 31–47.

12. Riane Eisler, "The Gaia Tradition and the Partnership Future," in *Reweaving the World: The Emergence of Ecofeminism*, pp. 23–24.

13. Eisler, p. 34.

14. For an excellent critique of this position see Val Plumwood, "Nature, Self, and Gender: Feminism, Environmental Philosophy, and the Critique of Rationalism," *Hypatia: A Journal of Feminist Philosophy* (6) 1 (1991), 3–27.

15. Marti Kheel, "Ecofeminism and Deep Ecology," in *Reweaving the World: The Emergence of Ecofeminism*, p. 131.

16. Kheel, p. 137.

ECONOMICS, ETHICS, AND ECOLOGY

V.A LETTING THE MARKET DECIDE

38. PREVIEW

> The way to make money is to buy when blood is running in the streets.
>
> *John D. Rockefeller*

> Darwin's theory of the struggle for existence . . . has . . . been cited as authorization of the encouragement of the spirit of competition. Some people also in such a way have tried to prove pseudo-scientifically the necessity of the destructive economic struggle of competition among individuals. But this is wrong.
>
> *Albert Einstein*

Many people probably share the sentiments of two writers who, in commenting on the despoliation of "our natural heritage" and the poisoning of the environment with the use of pesticides, stated that "although it is obvious that what we are doing is wrong, it is by no means obvious what would be right."[1] Indeed, the perplexities are deep. There is disagreement about whether certain practices are wrong, what proper policies would be, and, importantly, the grounds for deciding such matters. As noted in the "Introduction to Ethical Theory" and in Part III, one source of dispute concerns what sorts of things have moral standing. Even if that difficult question were resolved, there are other sources of perplexity. Although the following suggestion deserves critical reflection and continued reassessment, one way of categorizing competing approaches to deciding an important range of environmental disputes is to divide them crudely into (1) those which assume that the mechanism of the marketplace is the proper means of determining both the allocation of resources to different productive uses and the distribution of benefits and burdens across the relevant populations, and (2) those which assume that these matters should not be left much, or at all, to the contingencies of the marketplace (that is, certain matters should be decided politically and certain protections or constraints on the market must be politically enforced to avoid failure or abuses to which unconstrained markets lead).

We need to think about the effects of the market mechanism on the environment and assess the arguments for claiming that the environmental effects of the market mechanism are tolerable or desirable. Markets, of course, existed long before economists or ecologists did. A major source of defense of the desirability of the market mechanism comes, however, from economists. For this reason and because economists, more than any other group of social scientists, have explored environmental issues in considerable detail, it is important to identify and examine some fundamental strands in economic theory and also to see how economists tend to approach particular current problems, such as pollution, species extinction, or the question of whether we should save for the sake of future generations. "Economic reasoning"—indeed, the

311

economic point of view—is extremely influential in policymaking and, for a number of reasons, inviting. Shortly we shall note a number of objections to orthodox economic theory; first, however, we should make it quite clear that economists deserve special praise for paying careful attention to consequences and to related trade-offs. In short, the "economic approach" is sensitive to particular facts, it is specific, and it suggests a method for resolving questions of trade-offs between competing and valued ends. The economic approach seems, then, "practical," "hard-nosed," and "realistic," and its use of precise, formal modes of quantification and calculation is alluring.

In recent years there has developed a more concentrated effort to identify the points of agreement and disagreement between economic theory, ethical theory, and the outlooks of ecologists. This effort (of which some essays in this book are examples) promises to be an important and revealing one for developing an adequate view of our environment and a reasonable approach to setting policy on environmental matters. Here we have room to touch on only a few central matters.

On the one hand, markets seem terribly useful. They provide us (or many of us) with all sorts of goods, including decent shelter, nutrition, medical care, and transportation—some "items" that few fail to value. In a decentralized fashion, without the (maligned) "government bureaucrats" deciding for the rest of us, the market allocates resources to myriad productive functions and provides a mode for distributing benefits (as well as the burdens of work, risk taking, and so on). That the market mechanism produces all sorts of wonderful results is not subverted by the disdain we may rightly feel for certain insipid, tasteless, or defective products that it also generates. Sometimes one person's junk is another's treasure; sometimes it is just another's junk as well.

The main defense of the market mechanism appeals to the value of efficiency; it can be characterized as follows. In the best, perhaps idealized, case, two parties, for example, are mature, have settled preferences, are well informed, and with no undue pressure or misrepresentation agree to exchange goods or services. Perhaps one agrees to paint the other's house in exchange for an old car. One values the car more than the labor effort one must make, and the other values having her house painted more than the car. After the exchange, both are better off. Other things being equal, the welfare of each is enhanced, and their respective utility levels are raised. Thus, the sum of (their) utilities is increased; alternatively, even if utilities cannot be summed (there is a dispute about this issue, and many economists since the 1930s "ordinalist" revolution deny the possibility), we may conclude that overall utility has increased if the judgment of all the affected parties is affirmative (and credible). The pretrade situation was one in which at least one of the two could be better off and no one worse off. It was, in the technical sense in which economists use the term, an *inefficient situation*. The posttrade situation is more efficient. Someone has become better off, and no one is worse off. Is efficiency valuable in itself? The answer from orthodox economic theory is no; rather, moving toward more efficient arrangements is viewed as desirable because to do so is to increase the total utility or welfare (to take a step toward "maximization of total net expected utility," to put matters more carefully). To understand the argument for adopting or perpetuating the use of the market mechanism, it is crucial to note these assumptions—ones that too often are in the background and that, hence, frequently escape scrutiny and moral appraisal.

To highlight some crucial assumptions and to emphasize which values or principles are being treated as basic, or alternatively, as derivative ones, it is useful to set out certain elements of economic reasoning more explicitly and systematically. Typically, what is implicit is the anthropocentric view that all and only humans morally count; thus, only benefits (utilities) or harms (disutilities) to humans have weight in evaluating actions or policies. For example, consider this representative remark: "To assert that there is a pollution problem or an environmental problem is to assert, at least implicitly, that one or more resources is not being used so as to maximize human satisfactions."[12] Thus, what is conceptually to count (for example) as pollution, directly or indirectly, must involve harm to humans; if penguins are poisoned by an industrial chemical but no humans (now or in the future?) are affected, that is not "pollution" (or, at least, morally significant pollution). Somewhat representative of this view are the remarks of economist William Baxter:

> My criteria are oriented to people, not penguins. Damage to penguins, or sugar pines, or geological marvels is, without more, simply irrelevant. One must . . . say: Penguins are important because people enjoy seeing them walk about rocks. . . . I reject the proposition that we ought to respect the "balance of nature" or to "preserve the environment" unless the reason for doing so, express or implied, is the benefit of man. Every man is entitled to his own definition of Walden Pond, but there is no definition that has any moral superiority over another, except by reference to the selfish needs of the human race.[3]

To make an important point briefly, if the anthropocentric assumption embodied in traditional economic theory is indefensible, then the theory as it stands is unacceptable—as would be a theory that regarded only benefits and harms to white people as having moral significance. A theory that is not anthropocentric will be a theoretically more complex one. But simplicity is not the sole determinant of rationality.

The modern economic approach also assumes and accepts (however inexplicitly) a distribution of legally protected property rights. Often there are further implicit assumptions. For example, human beings can be owners but cannot be owned. Any non-human can be owned. This view reflects the anthropocentric criterion of moral standing. Legal property in an object X is best understood as possession of a package of rights over what is owned, often a right to use X, to exclude others from doing so, to authorize others to use X, to be compensated for unauthorized uses, and, sometimes, to destroy X if one wishes. There is a moral question whether anyone should have a legal right to kill (or torture) animals. The "It's my property to do with as I please" mentality implies an affirmative answer. The main point here, however, is just that orthodox economists typically assume the moral legitimacy of some set of well defined property rights. (On these matters see Section V.C, "From the Commons to Property.") Further, it is assumed that these rights will foster certain sorts of exchanges, for example, voluntary, nonfraudulent ones between competent persons. Thus, the core of the market mechanism, exchanges of goods or services (actually rights to such), is understood to occur against the background of morally acceptable norms and institutions; the latter constitute "the rules of the game" as it were.

Many economists often insist that they engage in value-free inquiry, that they are impotent (as economists) to say whether the rules are good or right. Some deny that evaluative claims are rationally decidable or are any more than expressions of emotion. For example, McKenzie and Tullock claim that "the approach of the economist is amoral" and that "as economists we cannot say what is 'just' or 'fair.'"[4] Paul Heyne and Thomas Johnson maintain that "we do not have any (means) of resolving ethical disagreements, they are ultimately judgments of value . . . and cannot finally be proved or disproved."[5] These stances are questionable (and have been explored systematically and in detail in the philosophical literature for years), but many economists seem oblivious to this fact, and to the fact that their own implicit or explicit commitment to the value of the market mechanism or to efficiency or to maximizing utility (or aggregate human want satisfaction) suggests, to the contrary, that the discipline of economics (insofar as it purports not merely to explain or predict human behavior) rests, in part, on evaluative assumptions.[6] One who thought that only benefits or harms to penguins were significant would be making an important evaluative assumption. So also does one who says, "Aryans count; Jews do not." The question, rather, would seem to be which view is rationally superior; we simply cannot avoid evaluations.

The concept of efficiency, and its assumed high value (or possibly, overriding, value), is so central in economic approaches to environmental matters that we should dissect it more thoroughly. To do so requires a bit of technical terminology; one would be helpless in trying to assess the economic approach without mastery of a few concepts.

In ordinary (nontechnical) talk, there is a tendency to use *efficient* as an honorific term; thus, if X if efficient, X is thought to be good (in a respect). Conversely, if X is inefficient, X is thought to be bad (in a respect). *Given* such usage, it seems perverse to question or oppose the efficient course, and unobjectionable or "nice" to urge efficient policies. All this can mislead us, however. The term *efficient* has a technical sense in economics; further, we should distinguish (1) what it *means* to say that some state of affairs is efficient, and (2) whether efficiency is a valuable goal that we ought to pursue. And importantly, is efficiency valuable in itself or only as a means? First, we have noted, in so many words, that a standard implicit assumption is, not surprisingly, that efficiency is understood as efficiency for humans. Modern factory farms that raise veal calves may be quite efficient for

humans, but hardly so, let us assume, for the calves.[7] Let us return to (1). The standard criterion of efficiency that is employed is called the *Pareto criterion* (after the early twentieth-century economist-sociologist Vilfredo Pareto). If a situation in which parties possess various goods is such that at least one party could be better off (in that party's own estimation) *without* making anyone worse off, the situation is said to be inefficient (or not maximally efficient). A *"Pareto improvement"* could be made; that is, at least one party could be better off without worsening another's situation.[8] In our earlier tale, in which one individual got another's car and the other got her house painted, a Pareto improvement was made. Voluntary exchanges are thought to generate Pareto improvements—that is, to increase efficiency. If a situation is one in which it is not possible for anyone to become better off without worsening another's circumstance, it is said to be *Pareto optimal* (or maximally efficient).[9] As noted before, the core idea is that in a more efficient situation the total welfare of the relevant parties is greater than in the less efficient one even if one is not able to say by how much. Moving toward more efficient circumstances *seems* desirable because it moves things closer to maximum utility. If, in fact, the sketched mechanism is the best means of maximizing welfares or achieving ever-increasing improvements, that fact seems to be a strong reason to employ it. Thus, the market is often defended on grounds that it best maximizes utility (quite apart from, or in addition to, appeals to implementation of, or respecting, some sort of human right to choose). Although we may give three cheers for markets as we commonly encounter them, critical reflection may make us wonder whether they deserve three, or even two. Much depends on how much we should value utility maximization, or efficiency as a means of fostering it—whether voluntary exchanges invariably or usually increase efficiency, and to what extent exchanges really are voluntary when elements of misrepresentation are often present.[10]

It is easy to overlook some crucial points. We may have serious moral reservations about even maximally efficient situations. For example, suppose that X is a master and Y is X's slave. There may be no way to alter this arrangement so that one can be better off and no one worse off. That is, it may be Pareto optimal or maximally efficient. The criterion focuses on a given situation and prospective departures from it, not on how it came about. As noted, a distribution of goods between master and slave may be Pareto optimal or maximally efficient (in the Paretian sense), but morally indefensible. In short, it seems absurd to believe that whatever is efficient is right or permissible. If so, then we must conclude that although efficiency is desirable, it only is desirable *other things being equal.*

In the exchange of an old car for the painting of a house, there was a gain from trade—both parties were better off, and aggregate welfare increased. In applying the Pareto criterion, economists typically assume that the proper way of determining whether the parties to the transaction are better off is to solicit the judgments of the parties themselves (usually posttrade). Several comments are relevant here, and all of them may reduce one's enthusiasm for thinking that the market is invariably the proper vehicle (or an effective one) to enhance social (human) welfare. First, in idealized models, the traders may possess "complete information." In fact, actual traders are ignorant to a degree (sometimes victimized by self-interested, or profit-maximizing, individuals or corporations). We may believe, prior to trading, that acquiring a widget (a product often discussed in economics texts, but hard to find) and forgoing some money may improve our lot. On getting the widget, the car, the meal, or the compact disc, we often regard ourselves as worse off. In fact, voluntary exchanges do not always (often?) yield a Pareto improvement over the preexchange situation, because one party is worse off postexchange. This point tends to be overlooked or discounted by some ostensibly empirical scientists.

To avoid, so it would seem, this awkward result of observing what actually happens with some actual transactions, some economists seem to stipulatively define *voluntary exchange* as one an individual would engage in if and only if beneficial to that individual. Thus, with this conceptual sleight of hand, it becomes analytically true (roughly, true by definition) that "all voluntary exchanges benefit the parties who engage in them." But then this use of *voluntary exchange* does not mean what most of us mean by the expression.

A brief comment may provide food for thought. We desire things *under-a-description* (at least often). Thus, Oedipus wanted to marry Jocasta. He got "what he wanted." Was he better off? He did not want to marry his mother, but because Jocasta was his mother, he also got what, in one sense, he did *not* want. The economists' model of human psychology and choice seems too simple in not attending sufficiently to complexities that result from the existence of multiple true descriptions of what one wants, self-deception, ambivalence, weakness of will, subconscious motivation, and so on.

Another feature of the market mechanism concerns *who* participates in market transactions, either small or large. It is worth observing that only those who are *willing and able* to pay have access to markets—that is, can participate in market transactions. It may not be far wrong to estimate that of the world's 6 billion members of *Homo sapiens*, at least a billion or so are unable to cast, or are radically hindered from casting, an effective vote in the economic marketplace, such as the extremely poor, the very young, the severely retarded, the seriously (mentally) disturbed. Nonhumans are not the only ones who have no say about the distribution of benefits and burdens generated by market transactions; a large number of existing humans are also voiceless in this way—not to mention future generations.

For the reasons mentioned, it is doubtful that voluntary, "informed" exchanges invariably benefit existing human participants in those exchanges. Even if they did, much of the world's population effectively is excluded from participation in market transactions. In spite of the incautious praise heaped on capitalism by some ideologues, the proper assessment of markets (and especially commercial practices and environmental effects) must involve consideration of the alternatives to a given market system. Large questions of political philosophy and economics arise that cannot be explored here. However, there are two basic alternatives to a comparatively unconstrained market system. If a given system seems intolerable in some respect, it may be possible to add a new constraint to it in order to remedy the problem. This is the alternative of setting appropriate constraints on the market. Thus, if we judge that blood (or bodily parts, or babies) ought not to be bought and sold (to the highest bidder?), we can legally prohibit the practice—and let the distribution be determined by nonmarket procedures. Similarly, if we judge that a corporation's self-interest in a good reputation is not an adequate safeguard to prevent if from selling defective products or polluting the environment, we can require governmental testing and set stringent liability rules that function as disincentives to corporate distribution of dangerous products or polluting. Defenders of the market are fond of pointing out that it is not the baker's altruism but his self-interest that makes bread available for purchase. This is no doubt true, but this same motive also can lead to industrial spying, theft of trade secrets, corporate bribery, and "cover-ups" of dangerous products.

We have noted some important criticisms of letting the market mechanism determine allocation and distribution questions. The alleged efficiency of the market process seems a means to maximizing utility. Utility maximization is hardly an uncontroversial goal. There are powerful philosophical arguments in favor of the view that maximizing utility allows or *requires* unjust distributions of benefits and burdens. As we have noted, to assume the value of maximizing only human utility is to beg the question against antianthropocentric counterarguments. Further, even if those difficulties were not serious, there are reasons (as noted) to doubt that all (most?) voluntary participants in market exchanges are better off as a result. If they are not, there may be no net increase in efficiency or total utility. We have observed also that much of the world's population is disenfranchised from casting an effective monetary vote in the market decision process.

In this brief survey of moral and other worries about the market, we have omitted a concern that economists rightly and increasingly have stressed in recent decades: that many parties who are not participants to voluntary, informed exchanges are made worse off as a result of the exchanges. These are what are called *negative externalities*. The focus here is on the generations of unconsented-to harms to some individuals, "costs" generated for which compensation is not paid. Thus, much pollution of the air or water is a prime example of negative externalities. Because only some of the costs to all parties are borne by the "private parties," the "social costs" exceed the "private costs." It is commonly held that if external costs only could be "internalized" (borne by those who seek to benefit from activities that generate them), there would be no problem (no moral complaint?). Thus, it is claimed that we *ought* to prevent or minimize externalities (some economists might be uncomfortable with this blatantly normative mode of speaking). How can we do that? To oversimplify, three basic alternatives present themselves: (1) persuade people or corporations or nations not to generate externalities, that is, appeal to voluntary self-restraint;

(2) coerce by attaching criminal penalties to violations of publicly set standards; or (3a) coerce by attaching "taxes" or charges to each additional unit of pollution emitted beyond a certain amount—or (3b) coerce by requiring possession of legal rights to pollute and possibly allowing trading in such rights. Many economists have a sufficiently low estimate of human nature so as to dismiss (1) rather quickly. A less than rosy estimate is surely correct even if one regards the picture of people embodied in *Homo economicus* (roughly the assumption of psychological egoism and the earlier mentioned simplifications regarding motives) as a nontrivial misrepresentation of human nature.

The debate between defenders of (2) and (3) is important, intriguing, and embodies noteworthy psychological and moral assumptions. Once more, the focus on unconsented-to harm to others is viewed anthropocentrically. Only harms to humans count. The English hunter W. D. M. Bell is reported to have killed 1,011 elephants in his lifetime.[11] This slaughter, if involving no unconsented-to harm to humans, fails to count as an externality needing any internalizing—according to the orthodox economic view. The term *social costs* means costs to human society. An obvious question is whether a cost-benefit accounting can be thought thorough when "costs to non-humans" are either tacitly treated as nonsensical or recognized but treated as irrelevant. These matters are taken up in the next section.

It should not go unnoticed that many economists would object to labeling negative externalities as "instances of market failure." Instead, they would maintain that unconsented-to harms ("negative externalities," "overexploitation of resources," "pollution," and so on) result from the failure to have a market. As some have argued, the solution is to allow property rights in "resources." The "tragedy of the commons" is that "goods" that are unowned (except "owned by all") get misused in one fashion or another. Because "chunks" of air of water rarely can be partitioned off so that particular individuals have a right to them, such persons may have little (self-interest) incentive to preserve, respect, or ration consumption of such things. According to the view being considered, it is better to allow the market to operate more broadly (by creating a more extensive distribution of property rights) than to restrict the market's scope of operation. Having been somewhat negative about much in economic theory in these introductory remarks, we leave it to the reader to critically appraise this proposal—as well as the criticism we have set forth.

The earlier quote from William Baxter expresses, in no uncertain terms, an anthropocentric approach to environmental trade-offs. One might question whether "maximize human satisfaction" underlies his economic viewpoint. A more qualified and cautious effort at setting out fundamental, theoretic assumptions of modern economic doctrine (such as Pareto considerations) and applying them to environmental questions (for example, what to do about pollution) is found in A. Myrick Freeman's "The Ethical Basis of the Economic View of the Environment" (Essay 39). It is not easy reading, but it is a rich summary and deserves careful study. That approach is often one that conflicts with alternative views; this kind of disagreement occurs in the dispute over sustainability, a matter discussed in Section V.E.

Part of the critique of "the economic viewpoint" (*actually* traditional, neoclassical economic doctrine) is set out in Mark Sagoff's "At the Shrine of Our Lady of Fatima, or Why Political Questions Are Not All Economic" (Essay 40). Sagoff calls attention to where market decision making (or "the cult of Pareto optimality") has led us. He is not enamored of the resulting gas stations, tract developments, strip mines, pizza stands, beach condos, and snowmobiles in the mountains. Importantly, he questions the tendency of economists to view citizens' expressions of *ideals* (such as "we ought to preserve dolphins") as just another consumer *preference or desire*—as just another consumer vote in the economic marketplace—to be taken seriously only if backed by the willingness and ability to pay.

NOTES

1. Robert and Nancy Dorfman, eds. *Economics and the Environment* (New York: Norton & Company, 1972), p. XIX.

2. William Baxter, *People or Penguins: The Case for Optimal Pollution* (New York: Columbia University Press, 1974) p. 17.

3. William Baxter, *People or Penguins*, p. 5.

4. Richard B. McKenzie and Gordon Tullock, *The New World of Economics* (Homewood, IL: Irwin, 1978), p. 7.

5. Paul Heyne and Thomas Johnson, *Toward Economic Understanding* (Chicago: Science Research Associates, 1976), p. 767.

6. It is worth noting that moral and political philosophers and those who work in environmental ethics in particular, have some things to learn from economists in game theory, decision theory, and examination of slippery issues surrounding the notions of efficiency and utility that are of importance to virtu-ally any environmental policy question. For example, the important idea of choosing behind a veil of ignorance, one that has been put to such creative use by John Rawls in his *A Theory of Justice*, could have been found in the work of economist John Harsanyi in the early 1950s; we do not know whether Rawls was, in fact, influenced by Harsanyi on this point.

7. See Peter Singer, *Animal Liberation* (New York: Avon Books, 1975).

8. To emphasize a point "another" is usually understood *not* to include future persons and not to consider nonhuman living creatures. Thus evaluative assumptions get made here. The desirability of efficiency so understood is hardly self-evident, but this point often goes undiscussed and undefended.

9. There may be *many* Pareto-optimal situations, and some may be, on the face of things, unjust and have been arrived at in an unjust manner.

10. For example, General Electric has offered an electric light bulb advertised as replacing a 100-watt bulb and saving money; the deal sounds attractive until one examines the fine print and learns that the "replacement" is simply a 90-watt bulb that yields less light.

11. Bell's act is reported in Cleveland Armory, *Man Kind?* (New York: Dell, 1974), p. 30.

39. The Ethical Basis of the Economic View of the Environment

A. Myrick Freeman III

I. Introduction

At least in some circles, economists' recommendations for a policy concerning pollution and other environmental problems are regarded with a good deal of skepticism and perhaps even distrust.[1] For example, when we suggest that economic factors such as cost should be taken into account in setting ambient air quality standards, we are told that it is wrong to put a price on human life or beauty. And when we argue that placing a tax or charge on the emissions of pollutants would be more effective than the present regulatory approach, we are told that this would simply create "licenses to pollute" and pollution is wrong.

I am not sure how much of this type of reaction stems from a misunderstanding or lack of familiarity with the arguments for the economists' policy recommendations, and how much is due to a rejection of the premises, analysis, and value judgments on which these recommendations are based. And I will not attempt to answer this question here. Rather, I will limit myself to making clear the

Center for the Study of Values and Social Policy at the University of Colorado at Boulder (1983). Reprinted by permission of the author.

rationale for some of our recommendations concerning policy and the value judgments on which they are based.

To the economist, the environment is a scarce resource which contributes to human welfare. The economic problem of the environment is a small part of the overall economic problem: how to manage our activities so as to meet our material needs and wants in the face of scarcity. The economists' recommendations concerning the environment flow out of our analysis of the overall economic problem. It will be useful to begin with a brief review of the principal conclusions of economic reasoning concerning the allocation of scarce resources to essentially unlimited needs and wants. After reviewing some basic economic principles and the criteria that economists have used in the evaluation of alternative economic outcomes, I will explain the economic view of the environment and some of the major policy recommendations which follow from that view. I will conclude by identifying some of the major questions and possible sources of disagreement about the validity and usefulness of economic reasoning as a way of looking at environmental problems.

II. Some Basic Economics

We begin with the basic premises that the purpose of economic activity is to increase the well-being of the individuals who make up the society, and that each individual is the best judge of how well off he or she is in a given situation. To give this premise some operational content, we assume that each individual has preferences over alternative bundles of economic goods and services. In other words, the individual can rank all of the alternative combinations of goods and services he can consume from most preferred to least preferred. Of course there may be ties in this ranking.[2] We assume that individuals act so as to obtain the most preferred (to them) bundles given the constraints imposed by technology and the availability of the means of production.

These preferences of individuals are assumed to have two properties which are important for our purposes: substitutability among the components of bundles, and the absence of limits on wants. Substitutability simply means that preferences are not lexicographic. Consider a consumption bundle labeled A with specified quantities of food, cloth-

ing, shelter, and so forth. Now consider alternative bundle B which contains 10 percent less clothing and the same quantities of all other goods. Since B contains less clothing, it is less desirable to the individual. In other words, bundle A is preferred to bundle B. But substitutability means that it is possible to alter the composition of bundle B by increasing the quantities of one or more of the other goods in the bundle to the point where the individual will consider A and B as equally preferred. That is to say, the individual can be compensated for the loss of some quantity of one good by increases in the quantities of one or more of the other goods. The value of the lost clothing to this individual can be expressed in terms of the quantities of the other goods which must be added to the bundle to substitute for it. This principle is the basis of the economic theory of value. In a market economy where all goods and services can be bought and sold at given prices in markets, the necessary amount of substitution can be expressed in money terms.

The significance of the substitution principle for the economic view of the environment should be apparent. If the substitution principle applies to good things that are derived from a clean environment, then it is possible to put a price on those things. The price is the money value of the quantities of other goods that must be substituted to compensate for the loss of the environmental good. Whether the substitution principle applies to those things derived from the environment is essentially an empirical question about human behavior. It is possible to think of examples that violate the substitution principle. The slogan printed on all license plates issued in New Hampshire ("Live Free or Die") shows a lexicographic preference for freedom. If the statement is believed, there is no quantity of material goods that can compensate for the loss of freedom. It is not clear that all individuals have lexicographic preferences for freedom. And the question for our purpose is whether there are similar examples in the realm of environmental goods.

By unlimited wants, I mean that for any conceivable bundle A, it is possible to describe another bundle B with larger quantities of one or more goods such that an individual would prefer B to A. Is this property plausible? It is possible to imagine some upper limit on the gross consumption of food as measured by calories or weight. But quality and variety are also goods over which individuals have preferences. And it may always be possible to conceive of a bundle containing a more exotic dish or one with more careful preparation with higher quality ingredients. Again, whether this property is plausible is an empirical question about human behavior. But its significance for anti-growth arguments is apparent.

Much of economic theory is concerned with understanding how individuals with given preferences interact as they seek to attain the highest level of satisfaction. Many societies have developed systems of markets for guiding this interaction; and historically the bulk of economists' effort has gone to the study of market systems. In part this can be explained by the historic fact that economics as a separate discipline emerged during a period of rapid industrialization, economic change, and growth in the extent of the market system. But it is also true that as early as Adam Smith's time, it was recognized that a freely functioning market system had significant advantages over alternative means of organizing and coordinating economic activity. Even in more primitive societies, markets facilitate exchange whereby an individual can attain a more preferred bundle by giving up less preferred goods in exchange for more preferred goods. And in more developed economies, markets also facilitate the specialization of productive activities and the realization of economies of scale in production.

A market system can be said to have advantages only in terms of some criterion and in comparison with some alternative set of economic institutions. It is time now to make the criterion explicit. The criterion is economic efficiency, or after the man who first developed the concept in formal terms, Pareto Optimality. An economy has reached a state of economic efficiency if it is not possible to rearrange production and consumption activity so as to make at least one person better off except by making one or more other individuals worse off. To put it differently, an economy is in an inefficient position if it is possible to raise at least one individual to a more preferred consumption bundle while hurting no one. If an economy is in an inefficient position, it is possible to achieve a sort of "free lunch" in the form of an improvement for at least one individual *at no cost* to anyone.

One of the fundamental conclusions of economic reasoning is that given certain conditions a market system will always reach a position of economic efficiency. The conditions are that: (*a*) all goods that matter to individuals (that is, all goods over which individuals have preference orderings) must be capable of being bought and sold in markets; and (*b*) all such markets must be perfectly competitive in the sense that there are large numbers of both buyers and sellers no one of which has any influence over market price.[3] The extensiveness and competitiveness of markets are sufficient to assure that economic efficiency in the allocation of resources will be achieved. This conclusion provides much of the intellectual rationale for *laissez faire* capitalism as well as the justification for many forms of government intervention in the market, for example, anti-monopoly policies, the regulation of the prices charged by monopolies such as electric utilities, and, as we shall see, the control of pollution.

The ideal of efficiency and the perfectly competitive market economy which guarantees its attainment acts as a yardstick by which the performance of real world economies can be measured. If there is monopoly power in a market, the yardstick shows that there is a shortfall in the performance of the economy. It would be possible by eliminating monopoly and restoring perfect competition to the market to increase output in such a way that no one would be made worse off and at least one person would be made better off. How monopoly power is to be eliminated without making at least the monopolist worse off is a difficult question in practice. But I will return to this point below.

The ideal of perfect competition and economic efficiency is a powerful one. But it is not without its limitations. Perhaps the most important of these is that there is no single, unique Pareto Optimum position. Rather there is an infinite number of alternative Pareto Optimums, each different from the others in the way in which it distributes economic well-being among the members of the society.

A society in which one individual owned all of the capital, land, and resources could achieve a Pareto Optimum position. It would likely be one in which all but one of the individuals lived in relative poverty. But it would not be possible to make any of the workers better off without making the rich person worse off. This Pareto Optimum position would be quite different from the Pareto Optimum which would be achieved by an economy in which each individual owned equal shares of the land, capital, and so forth. Which Pareto

Optimum position is attained by an economy depends upon the initial distribution of the entitlements to receive income from the ownership of factor inputs such as land and capital. Each conceivable distribution of rights of ownership has associated with it a different Pareto Optimum. And each Pareto Optimum position represents the best that can be done for the members of society *conditioned* upon acceptance of the initial distribution of entitlements. Since the ranking of different Pareto Optimums requires the comparison of alternative distributions of well-being, it is inherently an ethical question. There is nothing more that economic reasoning can contribute to this issue.

III. Policy Evaluation

Given the fact that the real world economy is characterized by many market imperfections and failures and that for a variety of reasons it is not possible to create the perfect, all encompassing market system of the Pareto ideal, we must consider piecemeal efforts to make things better at the margin. The question is: what criterion should be used to evaluate policy proposals which would alter the outcomes of existing market processes?

The Pareto Criterion says to accept only those policies that benefit some people while harming no one. In other words, this criterion rules out any policy which imposes costs on any individual, no matter how small the cost and no matter how large the benefits to any other members of the society. This is a very stringent criterion in practice. There are very few policy proposals which do not impose some costs on some members of the society. For example, a policy to curb pollution reduces the incomes and welfares of those who find it more profitable to pollute than to control their waste. The Pareto Criterion is not widely accepted by economists as a guide to policy. And it plays no role in what might be called "mainstream" environmental economics.[4]

The most widely accepted criterion asks whether the aggregate of the gains to those made better off measured in money terms is greater than the money value of the losses of those made worse off. If the gains exceed the losses, the policy is accepted by this criterion. The gains and losses are to be measured in terms of each individual's willingness-to-pay to receive the gains or to prevent the policy-imposed losses. Thus this criterion draws on the substitutability principle discussed earlier. If

the gains or losses came in the form of goods over which individuals have lexicographic preferences, this criterion could not be utilized.

This criterion is justified on ethical grounds by observing that if the gains outweigh the losses, it would be possible for the gainers to compensate fully the losers with money payments and still themselves be better off with the policy. Thus if the compensation were actually paid, there would be no losers, only gainers. This criterion is sometimes referred to as the potential compensation criterion. This criterion is the basis of the benefit–cost analysis of public policy. Benefits are the money values of the gains to individuals and costs are the money values of the losses to individuals. If benefits exceed costs, the gainers could potentially compensate the losers.

There are two observations concerning the potential compensation criterion. First, the criterion is silent on the question of whether compensation should be paid or not. If society decides that compensation shall always be paid, compensation becomes a mechanism for assuring that there are never any losers and that all adopted policies pass the Pareto Criterion. On the other hand, if society decides that compensation should never be paid, the potential compensation criterion becomes a modern form of utilitarianism in which the aggregate of utilities is measured by the sum of the money values of all goods consumed by all individuals. Finally, society may decide that whether compensation should be paid or not depends upon the identity and relative deservingness of the gainers and losers. If this is the case, then society must adopt some basis for determining relative deservingness, that is, some ethical rule concerning the justness of creating gains and imposing losses on individuals.

The second observation concerns the measurement of gains and losses in money terms. Willingness to pay for a good is constrained by ability to pay. Economic theory shows that an individual's willingness to pay for a good depends on his income and that for most goods, higher income means higher willingness to pay, other things equal. As a consequence, the potential compensation criterion has a tendency to give greater weight to the preferences of those individuals with higher incomes. As a practical matter there are reasons to doubt that this bias is quantitatively significant in most cases. But the question is often raised when benefit–cost analysis is applied to environmental goods. And it is well to keep this point in mind.

IV. Environmental Economics

The environment is a resource which yields a variety of valuable services to individuals in their roles as consumers and producers. The environment is the source of the basic means of life support—clean air and clean water. It provides the means for growing food. It is a source of minerals and other raw materials. It can be used for recreation. It is the source of visual amenities. And it can be used as a place to deposit the wastes from production and consumption activities. The economic problem of the environment is that it is a scarce resource. It cannot be called upon to provide all of the desired quantities of all of the services at the same time. Greater use of one type of environmental service usually means that less of some other type of service is available. Thus the use of the environment involves trade-offs. And the environment must be managed as an economic resource. But unlike other resources such as land, labor, or capital, the market does not perform well in allocating the environment to its highest valued uses. This is primarily because individuals do not have effective property rights in units of the environment.

For example, if a firm wishes to use one hour of labor time in production, it must find an individual who is willing to provide one hour of labor and it must pay that individual an amount at least equal to the value to the individual of that time in an alternative use. If a voluntary exchange of labor for money takes place, it is presumed that neither party is made worse off, and it is likely that both parties benefit from the exchange. Otherwise they would not have agreed to it. But if a firm wishes to dump a ton of sulfur dioxide into the atmosphere, it is under no obligation to determine whose health or whose view might be impaired by this use of the environment and to obtain their voluntary agreement through the payment of money. Thus firms need not take into account the costs imposed on others by their uses of the environment. Because there is no market for environmental services, the decentralized decision making of individuals and firms will result in a misallocation of environmental resources. The market fails. And the economy does not achieve a Pareto Optimum allocation.

Where markets have failed, economists have made two kinds of suggestions for dealing with market failure. The first is to see if markets can be established through the creation of legally transferable property rights in certain environmental services. If such property rights can be created, then markets can assume their proper role in achieving an efficient allocation of environmental services. Because of the indivisible nature of many aspects of the environment, for example, the urban air shed, there is limited scope for this solution. The second approach is to use various forms of government regulations, taxes, and subsidies to create incentives which replicate the incentives and outcomes that a perfectly functioning market would produce. Activities under this approach could include the setting of ambient air quality standards, placing limits on discharges from individual polluters, imposing taxes on pollution, and so forth. In the next section, I take up several specific applications of this approach to dealing with the environment in an economically rational manner.

V. Applications

Environment Quality Standards

An environmental quality standard is a legally established minimum level of cleanliness or maximum level of pollution in some part of the environment, for example, an urban air shed or a specific portion of a river. A standard, once established, can be the basis for enforcement actions against a polluter whose discharges cause the standard to be violated. The principle of Pareto Optimality provides a basis for determining at what level an environmental quality standard should be set. In general, Pareto Optimality requires that each good be provided at the level for which the marginal willingness to pay for the good (the maximum amount that an individual would be willing to give up to get one more unit of the good) is just equal to the cost of providing one more unit of the good (its marginal cost).

Consider for example an environment which is badly polluted because of existing industrial activity. Consider making successive one-unit improvements in some measure of environment quality. For the first unit, individuals' marginal willingnesses to pay for a small improvement are likely to be high. The cost of the first unit of clean-up is likely to be low. The difference between them is a net benefit.

Further increases in cleanliness bring further net benefits as long as the marginal willingness to pay is greater than the marginal cost. But as the environment gets cleaner, the willingness to pay for additional units of cleanliness decreases, while the additional cost of further cleanliness rises. At that point where the marginal willingness to pay just equals the marginal cost, the net benefit of further cleanliness is zero, and the total benefits of environmental improvement are at a maximum. This is the point at which the environmental quality standard should be set, if economic reasoning is followed.

There are two points to make about this approach to standard setting. First, an environmental quality standard set by this rule will almost never call for complete elimination of pollution. As the worst of the pollution is cleaned up, the willingness to pay for additional cleanliness will be decreasing, while the extra cost of further clean-up will be increasing. The extra cost of going from 95 percent clean-up to 100 percent clean-up may often be several times larger than the total cost of obtaining the first 95 percent clean-up. And it will seldom be worth it in terms of willingness to pay. Several economists have argued that the air quality standards for ozone that were first established in 1971 were too stringent in terms of the relationship between benefits and costs. If this is true, then the resources devoted to controlling ozone could be put to better use in some other economic activity. Many economists have urged Congress to require that costs be compared with benefits in the setting of ambient air quality standards.

The second point is that the logic of benefit-cost analysis does not require that those who benefit pay for those benefits or that those who ultimately bear the cost of meeting a standard be compensated for those costs. It is true that if standards are set so as to maximize the net benefits, then the gainers could fully compensate the losers and still come out ahead. But when beneficiaries do not compensate losers, there is a political asymmetry. Those who benefit call for ever more strict standards and clean-up, because they obtain the gross benefits and bear none of the costs, while those who must control pollution call for less strict standards.

Charging for Pollution

One way to explain the existence of pollution is in terms of the incentives faced by firms and others whose activities generate waste products. Each unit of pollution discharged imposes costs or damages on other individuals. But typically the dischargers are not required to compensate the losers for these costs. Thus there is no economic incentive for the discharger to take those costs into account. This is the essence of the market failure argument.

If it is impractical to establish a private market in rights to clean air, it may be possible to create a pseudo-market by government regulation. Suppose that the government imposed a charge or tax on each unit of pollution discharged and set the tax equal to the money value of the damage that pollution caused to others. Then each discharger would compare the tax cost of discharging a unit of pollution with the cost of controlling or preventing that discharge. As long as the cost of control were less than the tax or charge, the firm would prevent the discharge. In fact it would control pollution back to the point where its marginal cost of control was just equal to the marginal tax and by indirection equal to the marginal damage the pollution would cause. The properly set tax or charge would cause the firm to undertake on its own accord the optimum amount of pollution control. By replicating a market incentive, the government regulation would bring about an efficient allocation of resources.

Since the firm would likely find that some level of discharges would be more preferred to a zero discharge level, it would be paying taxes to the government equal to the damages caused by the remaining discharges. In principle, the government could use the tax revenues to compensate those who are damaged by the remaining discharges.

Risk and the Value of Life

Because some forms of pollution are harmful to human health and may increase mortality, economists have had to confront the question of the economic value of life. It turns out that the "value of life" is an unfortunate phrase which does not really reflect the true nature of the question at hand. This is because pollutants do not single out and kill readily identifiable people. Rather, they result in usually small increases in the *probability* of death to exposed *groups* of individuals. So what is really at issue is the economic value of reductions in the risk of death. This is a manageable question and one on which we have some evidence.

People in their daily lives make a variety of choices that involve trading off changes in the risk of death with other economic goods whose values we can measure in money terms. For example, some people travel to work in cars rather than by bus or by walking because of the increased convenience and lower travel time, even though they increase the risk of dying prematurely. Also, some people accept jobs with known higher risks of accidental death because those jobs pay higher wages. The "value" of saving a life can be calculated from information on individuals' trade-offs between risk and money.

Suppose there were a thousand people each of whom has a probability of .004 of dying during this next year. Suppose an environmental change would reduce that probability to .003, a change of .001. Let us ask each individual to state his or her maximum willingness to pay for that reduction in risk. Suppose for simplicity that each person states the same willingness to pay, $100. The total willingness to pay of the group is $100,000. If the policy is adopted, there will on average be one less death during this next year (.001 × 1000). The total willingness to pay for a change that results in one fewer deaths is $100,000. This is the "value of life" that is revealed from individual preferences. Efforts to estimate the value of life from data on wage premiums for risky jobs have led to values in the range of $500,000 to $5 million.

If an economic approach is to be used in setting standards for toxic chemicals, hazardous air pollutants, and so forth, then some measure of the value of reductions in risk must be the basis for computing the benefits of pollution control. There are immense practical difficulties in providing accurate, refined estimates of this value. But these are not my concern here. Rather I am concerned with the ethical issues of even attempting to employ this approach to environmental decision making.

I think that the principal ethical issue here is compensation. Suppose that a standard has been set for an air pollutant such that even with the standard being met the population has a higher probability of death than if the pollutant were fully controlled. The standard was presumably set at this level because the cost of eliminating the remaining risk exceeded the individuals' willingness to pay to eliminate the risk. Many people would argue that the risk should be reduced to zero regardless of

cost. After all, some people are being placed at risk while others are benefiting by avoiding the cost of controlling pollution. But suppose the population is compensated for bearing this risk with money from, for example, a charge on the polluting substance. Is there then any reason to argue for reducing pollution to zero? If the pollution were reduced to zero and the compensation withdrawn, the people at risk would be no better off in their own eyes than they are with the pollution and compensation. But some people would be made worse off because of the additional costs of eliminating the pollution.[5]

Future Generations

Some environmental decisions impose risks on future generations in order to achieve present benefits. In standard benefit–cost analysis based on the economic efficiency criterion, a social rate of discount is used to weight benefits and costs occurring at different points in time.[6] There have been long debates about the appropriateness of applying a discount rate to effects on future generations. It is argued that ethically unacceptable damage imposed on future generations may be made to appear acceptably small, from today's perspective, by discounting.

Consider the case where this generation wishes to do something which will yield benefits today worth $B. This act will also set in motion some physical process which will cause $D of damages 100,000 years from now. Assume that the events are certain and that the values of benefits and damages based on individual preferences can be accurately measured.

In brief, the argument against discounting is: at any reasonable (nonzero) discount rate, r, the present value of damages

$$\$P = \frac{\$D}{(1+r)^{100,000}}$$

will be trivial and almost certainly will be outweighed by present benefits. The implication of discounting is that we care virtually nothing about the damages that we inflict on future generations provided that they are postponed sufficiently far into the future. Therefore, the argument goes, we should discard the discounting procedure. Instead, since the real issue is intergenerational equity, a zero discount rate should be used. This would represent the most appropriate value judgment about the relative weights to be attached to the consumption of present and future generations.

I believe this argument is confused. Certainly, the problem is equity; but that has nothing to do with discounting. Rather, the equity question revolves around the distinction between actual and potential compensation.

In order to separate the compensation and discounting issues, consider a project for which both benefits and costs are realized today. Whenever benefits are greater than costs, the efficiency criterion says that the project should be undertaken, even if the benefits and costs accrue to different groups. This is because there is at least the *possibility* of compensation. Whether compensation should be paid or not is a value judgment hinging on equity considerations.

Now consider the intergenerational case. If $B is greater than $P (the discounted present value of future damages), the project is worthwhile and should be undertaken if the objective is economic efficiency. If the trivial sum of $P is set aside now at interest, it will grow to

$$_{(1+r)}100{,}000_{\$P}$$

which of course is the same as $D and therefore by definition will just compensate the future generation for the damages our actions will have imposed on them. If actual compensation is provided for, no one, present or future, will be made worse off, and some will benefit.

Some may wish to adhere to the principle that compensation should *always* be paid. The principle would apply to losers in the present as well as future generations. The discount rate would help them to calculate the amount to be set aside for future payment. Others may wish to say that whether compensation should be paid or not depends on the relative positions of potential gainers and losers. Finally some will choose to ignore the compensation question entirely. But no matter how they resolve the compensation question, they should discount future damages.

Ecological Effects

Suppose that an accidental spill of a toxic chemical or crude oil wipes out the population of some marine organism in a certain area. What is the economic value of this damage? If the organism is a fish that is sought by sports or commercial fishermen, then there are standard economic techniques for determining the willingness to pay for or value of fish in the water. If the organism is part of the food chain which supports a commercially valuable fishery, then it is also possible, at least conceptually, to establish the biological link between the organism and the economic system. The value of the organism is based on its contribution to maintaining the stock of the commercially valued fish. But if there is no link between the organism and human production or consumption activity, there is no basis for establishing an economic value. Those species that lie completely outside of the economic system also are beyond the reach of the economic rubric for establishing value.

Some people have suggested alternative bases for establishing values, for example, cost of replacing the organisms, or cost of replacing biological functions such as photosynthesis and nitrogen fixation. But if those functions have no economic value to man, for example, because there are substitute organisms to perform them, then we would not be willing to pay the full cost of replacement. And this signifies that the economic value is less, perhaps much less, than replacement cost.

Rather than introduce some arbitrary or biased method for imputing a value to such organisms, I prefer to be honest about the limitations of the economic approach to determining values. This means that we should acknowledge that certain ecological effects are not commensurable with economic effects measured in dollars. Where trade-offs between noncommensurable magnitudes are involved, choices must be made through the political system.

VI. Conclusions

The argument for the adoption of the economists' point of view concerning environmental policy can be summarized as follows. Given the premises about individual preferences and the value judgment that satisfying these preferences should be the objective of policy, the adoption of the economists' recommendations concerning environmental policy will always lead to a potential Pareto improvement, that is, it will always be possible through taxes and compensating payments to make sure that at least some people are better off and that no one loses. Society could choose not to make these compensating payments; but this choice should be on the basis of some ethical judgment concerning the deservingness of the gainers and losers from the policy.

It might be helpful at this point to review and summarize these premises and value judgments so that they might be in the focus of discussion:

1. Should individual preferences matter? If not individual preferences, then whose preferences should matter? What about ecological effects that have no perceptible effect on human welfare, that is, that lie outside of the set of things over which individuals have preferences?

2. Does the substitution principle hold for environmental services? Or are individuals' preferences for environmental goods lexicographic? This is an empirical question. Economists have developed a substantial body of evidence that people are willing to make trade-offs between environmental goods such as recreation, visual amenities, and healthful air and other economic goods.

3. Are preferences characterized by unlimited wants? This is also an empirical question. But I think that most economists would agree that if there are such limits, we have not begun to approach them for the vast bulk of the citizens of this world. A related question is whether it should be the objective of economic activity to satisfy wants without limits? But this question is more closely related to question (1) concerning the role of individual preferences.

4. Is achieving an efficient allocation of resources that important? Or, as Kelman (1981) has argued, should we be willing to accept less economic efficiency in order to preserve the idea that environmental values are in some sense superior to economic values? An affirmative answer to the latter question implies a lexicographic preference system and a rejection of the substitution principle for environmental goods.

5. Should compensation always be paid? Paid sometimes? Never? This is an ethical question. But as I have indicated, I think it plays a central role in judging the ethical implications of economists'

environmental policy recommendations. Not only is there the question of whether compensation should be paid, but also the question of who should be compensated. For example, should compensation be paid to those who are damaged by the optimal level of pollution? Or should compensation be paid to those who lose because of the imposition of pollution control requirements?

Notes

1. For some empirical evidence in support of this assertion, see Kelman (1981).
2. This is equivalent to saying that the individual has a utility function which assigns utility numbers to all possible consumption bundles. More preferred bundles have higher utility numbers.
3. There are other more technical conditions which need not concern us here.
4. For a different view of the Pareto Criterion and public policy, see Peacock and Rowley (1975).
5. In discussions of the use of risk–benefit analysis in policy making, the distinction is sometimes made between voluntary and involuntary risk. The argument being made is that involuntary risks are somehow worse. But I think that this misses the point. The real distinction is between compensated and uncompensated risk. A compensated risk is one, by the definition of compensation, that the individual would bear voluntarily.
6. The following argument is based on Freeman (1977).

References

Freeman, A. Myrick, III. "Equity, Efficiency, and Discounting: The Reasons for Discounting Intergenerational Effects," *Futures* (October, 1977), 375–376.

Kelman, Steven. "Economists and the Environmental Muddle," *The Public Interest* 641 (Summer, 1981), 106–123.

Peacock, Alan T., and Charles K. Rowley. *Welfare Economics: A Liberal Restatement,* London, M. Robertson, 1975.

40. At the Shrine of Our Lady of Fàtima, or Why Political Questions Are Not All Economic

Mark Sagoff

Lewiston, New York, a well-to-do community near Buffalo, is the site of the Lake Ontario Ordinance Works, where the federal government, years ago, disposed of the residues of the Manhattan Project. These radioactive wastes are buried but are not forgotten by the residents, who say that when the wind is southerly radon gas blows through the town. Several parents at a recent conference I attended there described their terror on learning that cases of leukemia had been found among area children. They feared for their own lives as well. At the other sides of the table, officials from New York State and from local corporations replied that these fears were ungrounded. People who smoke, they said, take greater risks than people who live close to waste disposal sites. One speaker talked in terms of "rational methodologies of decisionmaking." This aggravated the parents' rage and frustration.

The speaker suggested that the townspeople, were they to make their decision in a free market, would choose to live near the hazardous waste facility, if they knew the scientific facts. He told me later they were irrational—he said, "neurotic"—because they refused to recognize or to act upon their own interests. The residents of Lewiston were unimpressed with his analysis of their "willingness to pay" to avoid this risk or that. They did not see what risk–benefit analysis had to do with the issues they raised.

If you take the Military Highway (as I did) from Buffalo to Lewiston, you will pass through a formidable wasteland. Landfills stretch in all directions, where enormous trucks—tiny in that landscape—incessantly deposit sludge which great bulldozers, like yellow ants, then push into the ground. These machines are the only signs of life, for in the miasma that hangs in the air, no birds, not even scavengers, are seen. Along colossal power lines which crisscross this dismal land, the dynamos at Niagara send electric power south, where factories have fled, leaving their remains to decay. To drive along this road is to feel, oddly, the mystery and awe one experiences in the presence of so much power and decadence.

Henry Adams had a similar response to the dynamos on display at the Paris Exposition of 1900. To him "the dynamo became a symbol of infinity."[1] To Adams, the dynamo functioned as the modern equivalent of the Virgin, that is, as the center and focus of power. "Before the end, one began to pray to it; inherited instinct taught the natural expression of man before silent and infinite force."[2]

Adams asks in his essay "The Dynamo and the Virgin" how the products of modern industrial civilization will compare with those of the religious culture of the Middle Ages. If he could see the landfills and hazardous waste facilities bordering the power stations and honeymoon hotels of Niagara Falls he would know the answer. He would understand what happens when efficiency replaces infinity as the central conception of value. The dynamos at Niagara will not produce another Mont-Saint-Michel. "All the steam in the world," Adams wrote, "could not, like the Virgin, build Chartres."[3]

At the Shrine of Our Lady of Fàtima, on a plateau north of the Military Highway, a larger than life sculpture of Mary looks into the chemical air. The original of this shrine stands in central Portugal, where in May, 1917, three children said they saw a Lady, brighter than the sun, raised on a cloud in an evergreen tree.[4] Five months later, on a wet and chilly October day, the Lady again appeared, this time before a large crowd. Some who were skeptical did not see the miracle. Others in the crowd reported, however, that "the sun appeared and seemed to tremble, rotate violently and fall, dancing over the heads of the throng. . . ."[5]

The Shrine was empty when I visited it. The cult of Our Lady of Fàtima, I imagine, has only a few devotees. The cult of Pareto optimality, however, has many. Where some people see only environmental devastation, its devotees perceive efficiency, utility, and the maximization of wealth. They see the satisfaction of wants. They envision the good life. As I looked over the smudged and ruined terrain I tried to share that vision. I hoped that Our Lady of Fàtima, worker of miracles, might serve, at least for the moment, as the Patroness of cost–benefit analysis. I thought of all the wants and needs that are satisfied in a landscape of honeymoon cottages, commercial strips, and dumps for hazardous waste. I saw the miracle of efficiency. The prospect, however, looked only darker in that light.

I

This essay concerns the economic decisions we make about the environment. It also concerns our political decisions about the environment. Some people have suggested that ideally these should be the same, that all environmental problems are problems in distribution. According to this view there is an environmental problem only when some resource is not allocated in equitable and efficient ways.[6]

This approach to environmental policy is pitched entirely at the level of the consumer. It is his or her values that count, and the measure of these values is the individual's willingness to pay. The problem of justice or fairness in society becomes, then, the problem of distributing goods and services so that more people get more of what they want to buy. A condo on the beach. A snowmobile for the mountains. A tank full of gas. A day of labor. The only values we have, on this view, are those which a market can price.[7]

How much do you value open space, a stand of trees, an "unspoiled" landscape? Fifty dollars? A hundred? A thousand? This is one way to measure value. You could compare the amount consumers would pay for a townhouse or coal or a landfill and the amount they would pay to preserve an area in its "natural" state. If users would pay more for the land with the house, the coal mine, or the landfill, than without—less construction and other costs of development—then the efficient thing to do is to improve the land and thus increase its value. That is why we have so many tract developments. And pizza stands. And gas stations. And strip mines. And landfills. How much did you spend last year to preserve open space? How much for pizza and gas? "In principle, the ultimate measure of environmental quality," as one basic text assures us, "is

the value people place on these . . . services or their willingness to pay."[8]

Willingness to pay. What is wrong with that? The rub is this: not all of us think of ourselves simply as *consumers*. Many of us regard ourselves *as citizens* as well. We act as consumers to get what we want *for ourselves*. We act as citizens to achieve what we think is right or best *for the community*. The question arises, then, whether what we want for ourselves individually as consumers is consistent with the goals we would set for ourselves collectively as citizens. Would I vote for the sort of things I shop for? Are my preferences as a consumer consistent with my judgments as a citizen?

They are not. I am schizophrenic. Last year, I fixed a couple of tickets and was happy to do so since I saved fifty dollars. Yet, at election time, I helped to vote the corrupt judge out of office. I speed on the highway; yet I want the police to enforce laws against speeding. I used to buy mixers in returnable bottles—but who can bother to return them? I buy only disposables now, but, to soothe my conscience, I urge my state senator to outlaw one-way containers. I love my car; I hate the bus. Yet I vote for candidates who promise to tax gasoline to pay for public transportation. I send my dues to the Sierra Club to protect areas in Alaska I shall never visit. And I support the work of the American League to Abolish Capital Punishment although, personally, I have nothing to gain one way or the other. (When I hang, I will hang myself.) And of course I applaud the Endangered Species Act, although I have no earthly use for the Colorado squawfish or the Indiana bat. I support almost any political cause that I think will defeat my consumer interests. This is because I have contempt for—although I act upon—those interests. I have an "Ecology Now" sticker on a car that leaks oil everywhere it's parked.

The distinction between consumer and citizen preferences has long vexed the theory of public finance. Should the public economy serve the same goals as the household economy? May it serve, instead, goals emerging from our association as citizens? The question asks if we may collectively strive for and achieve only those items we individually compete for and consume. Should we aspire, instead, to public goals we may legislate as a nation?

The problem, insofar as it concerns public finance, is stated as follows by R. A. Musgrave, who reports a conversation he had with Gerhard Colm.

He [Colm] holds that the individual voter dealing with political issues has a frame of reference quite distinct from that which underlies his allocation of income as a consumer. In the latter situation the voter acts as a private individual determined by self-interest and deals with his personal wants; in the former, he acts as a political being guided by his image of a good society. The two, Colm holds, are different things.[9]

Are these two different things? Stephen Marglin suggests that they are. He writes:

The preferences that govern one's unilateral market actions no longer govern his actions when the form of reference is shifted from the market to the political arena. The Economic Man and the Citizen are for all intents and purposes two different individuals. It is not a question, therefore, of rejecting individual . . . preference maps; it is, rather, that market and political preference maps are inconsistent.[10]

Marglin observes that if this is true, social choices optimal under one set of preferences will not be optimal under another. What, then, is the meaning of "optimality"? He notices that if we take a person's true preferences to be those expressed in the market, we may, then, neglect or reject the preferences that person reveals in advocating a political cause or position. "One might argue on welfare grounds," Marglin speculates, "for authoritarian rejection of individuals' politically revealed preferences in favor of their market-revealed preferences!"

II

On February 19, 1981, President Reagan published Executive Order 12,291 requiring all administrative agencies and departments to support every new major regulation with a cost-benefit analysis establishing that the benefits of the regulation to society outweigh its costs.[11] The Order directs the Office of Management and Budget (OMB) to review every such regulation on the basis of the adequacy of the cost-benefit analysis supporting it. This is a departure from tradition. Traditionally, regulations have been reviewed not by OMB but by the courts on the basis of their relation not to cost-benefit analysis but to authorizing legislation.

A month earlier, in January 1981, the Supreme Court heard lawyers for the American Textile Manufacturers Institute argue against a proposed Occupational Safety and Health Administration (OSHA) regulation which would have severely restricted the acceptable levels of cotton dust in textile plants.[12] The lawyers for industry argued that the benefits of the regulation would not equal the costs. The lawyers for the government contended that the law required the tough standard. OSHA, acting consistently with Executive Order 12,291, asked the Court not to decide the cotton dust case, in order to give the agency time to complete the cost-benefit analysis required by the textile industry. The Court declined to accept OSHA's request and handed down its opinion on June 17, 1981.[13]

The Supreme Court, in a 5-3 decision, found that the actions of regulatory agencies which conform to the OSHA law need not be supported by cost-benefit analysis. In addition, the Court asserted that Congress in writing a statute, rather than the agencies in applying it, has the primary responsibility for balancing benefits and costs. The Court said:

When Congress passed the Occupational Health and Safety Act in 1970, it chose to place preeminent value on assuring employees a safe and healthful working environment, limited only by the feasibility of achieving such an environment. We must measure the validity of the Secretary's actions against the requirements of that Act.[14]

The opinion upheld the finding of the Appeals Court that "Congress itself struck the balance between costs and benefits in the mandate to the agency."[15]

The Appeals Court opinion in *American Textile Manufacturers vs. Donovan* supports the principle that legislatures are not necessarily bound to a particular conception of regulatory policy. Agencies that apply the law, therefore, may not need to justify on cost-benefit grounds the standards they set. These standards may conflict with the goal of efficiency and still express our political will as a nation. That is, they may reflect not the personal choices of self-interested individuals, but the collective judgments we make on historical, cultural, aesthetic, moral, and ideological grounds.

The appeal of the Reagan Administration to cost-benefit analysis, however, may arise more from political than economic considerations. The intention, seen in the most favorable light, may not be to replace political or ideological goals with economic ones but to make economic goals more apparent in regulation. This is not to say that Congress should function to reveal a collective willingness-to-pay just as markets reveal an individual willingness-to-pay. It is to suggest that Congress should do more to balance economic with ideological, aesthetic, and moral goals. To think that environmental or worker safety policy can be based exclusively on aspiration for a "natural" and "safe" world is as foolish as to hold that environmental law can be reduced to cost-benefit accounting. The more we move to one extreme, as I found in Lewiston, the more likely we are to hear from the other.

III

The labor unions won an important political victory when Congress passed the Occupational Safety and Health Act of 1970.[16] That Act, among other things, severely restricts worker exposure to toxic substances. It instructs the Secretary of Labor to set "the standard which most adequately assures, to the extent feasible . . . that no employee will suffer material impairment of health or functional capacity even if such employee has regular exposure to the hazard . . . for the period of his working life."[17]

Pursuant to this law, the Secretary of Labor, in 1977, reduced from ten to one part per million (ppm) the permissible ambient exposure level for benzene, a carcinogen for which no safe threshold is known. The American Petroleum Institute thereupon challenged the new standard in court.[18] It argued, with much evidence in its favor, that the benefits (to workers) of the one ppm standard did not equal the costs (to industry). The standard, therefore, did not appear to be a rational response to a market failure in that it did not strike an efficient balance between the interests of workers in safety and the interests of industry and consumers in keeping prices down.

The Secretary of Labor defended the tough safety standard on the ground that the law demanded it. An efficient standard might have required safety until it cost industry more to prevent a risk than it cost workers to accept it. Had Congress adopted this vision of public policy—one which can be found in many economics texts[19]—it would have treated workers not as ends-in-themselves but as means for the production of overall utility. And this, as the Secretary saw it, was what Congress refused to do.

The United States Court of Appeals for the Fifth Circuit agreed with the American Petroleum Institute and invalidated the one ppm benzene standard.[20] On July 2, 1980, the Supreme Court affirmed remanding the benzene standard back to OSHA for revision.[21] The narrowly based Supreme Court decision was divided over the role economic considerations should play in judicial review. Justice Marshall, joined in dissent by three other justices, argued that the Court had undone on the basis of its own theory of regulatory policy an act of Congress inconsistent with that theory. He concluded that the plurality decision of the Court "requires the American worker to return to the political arena to win a victory that he won before in 1970."[22]

To reject cost-benefit analysis, as Justice Marshall would, as a basis for public policymaking is not necessarily to reject cost-effectiveness analysis, which is an altogether different thing. "*Cost–benefit analysis*," one commentator points out, "is used by the decision maker to establish societal goals as well as the means for achieving these goals, whereas *cost-effectiveness analysis* only compares alternative means for achieving 'given' goals."[23] Justice Marshall's dissent objects to those who would make efficiency the goal of public policy. It does not necessarily object to those who would accomplish as efficiently as possible the goals Congress sets.[24]

IV

When efficiency is the criterion of public safety and health, one tends to conceive of social relations on the model of a market, ignoring competing visions of what we as a society should be like. Yet it is obvious that there are competing conceptions of how we should relate to one another. There are some who believe, on principle, that worker safety and environmental quality ought to be protected only insofar as the benefits of protection balance the costs. On the other hand, people argue, also on principle, that neither worker safety nor environmental quality should be treated merely as a commodity, to be traded at the margin for other commodities, but should be valued for its own sake. The conflict between these two principles is logical or moral, to be resolved by argument or debate. The question whether cost–benefit analysis should play a decisive role in policymaking is not to be decided by cost–benefit analysis. A contradiction between principles—between contending visions of the good society—cannot be settled by asking how much partisans are willing to pay for their beliefs.

The role of the *legislator*, the political role, may be more important to the individual than the role of *consumer*. The person, in other words, is not to be treated as merely a bundle of preferences to be juggled in cost–benefit analyses. The individual is to be respected as an advocate of ideas which are to be judged in relation to the reasons for them. If health and environmental statutes reflect a vision of society as something other than a market by requiring protections beyond what are efficient, then this may express not legislative ineptitude but legislative responsiveness to public values. To deny this vision because it is economically inefficient is simply to replace it with another vision. It is to insist that the ideas of the citizen be sacrificed to the psychology of the consumer.

We hear on all sides that government is routinized, mechanical, entrenched, and bureaucratized; the jargon alone is enough to dissuade the most mettlesome meddler. Who can make a difference? It is plain that for many of us the idea of a national political community has an abstract and suppositious quality. We have only our private conceptions of the good, if no way exists to arrive at a public one. This is only to note the continuation, in our time, of the trend Benjamin Constant described in the essay *De la Liberté des Anciens Comparee a Celle des Modernes.*[25] Constant observes that the modern world, as opposed to the ancient, emphasizes civil over political liberties, the rights of privacy and property over those of community and participation. "Lost in the multitude," Constant writes, "the individual rarely perceives the influence that he exercises," and, therefore, must be content with "the peaceful enjoyment of private independence."[26] The individual asks only to be protected by laws common to all in his pursuit of his own self-interest. The citizen has been replaced by the consumer; the tradition of Rousseau has been supplanted by that of Locke and Mill.

Nowhere are the rights of the moderns, particularly the rights of privacy and property, less helpful than in the area of the natural environment.

Here the values we wish to protect—cultural, historical, aesthetic, and moral—are public values; they depend not so much upon what each person wants individually as upon what he or she believes we stand for collectively. We refuse to regard worker health and safety as commodities; we regulate hazards as a matter of right. Likewise, we refuse to treat environmental resources simply as public goods in the economist's sense. Instead, we prevent significant deterioration of air quality not only as a matter of individual self-interest but also as a matter of collective self-respect. How shall we balance efficiency against moral, cultural, and aesthetic values in policy for the workplace and the environment? No better way has been devised to do this than by legislative debate ending in a vote. This is not the same thing as a cost–benefit analysis terminating in a bottom line.

V

It is the characteristic of cost–benefit analysis that it treats all value judgments other than those made on its behalf as nothing but statements of preference, attitude, or emotion, insofar as they are value judgments. The cost–benefit analyst regards as true the judgment that we should maximize efficiency or wealth. The analyst believes that this view can be backed by reasons.[27] The analyst does not regard it as a preference or want for which he or she must be willing to pay. The cost–benefit analyst, however, tends to treat all other normative views and recommendations as if they were nothing but subjective reports of mental states. The analyst supposes in all such cases that "this is right" and "this is what we ought to do" are equivalent to "I want this" and "this is what I prefer." Value judgments are beyond criticism if, indeed, they are nothing but expressions of personal preference; they are incorrigible since every person is in the best position to know what he or she wants. All valuation, according to this approach, happens *in foro interno*; debate *in foro publico* has no point. On this approach, the reasons that people give for their views, unless these people are welfare economists, do not count; what counts is how much they are willing to pay to satisfy their wants. Those who are willing to pay the most, for all intents and purposes, have the right view; theirs is the more informed opinion, the better aesthetic judgment, and the deeper moral insight.

The assumption that valuation is subjective, that judgments of good and evil are nothing but expressions of desire and aversion, is not unique to economic theory.[28] There are psychotherapists—Carl Rogers is an example—who likewise deny the objectivity or cognitivity of valuation.[29] For Rogers, there is only one criterion of worth: it lies in "the subjective world of the individual. Only he knows it fully."[30] The therapist shows his or her client that a "value system is not necessarily something imposed from without, but is something experienced."[31] Therapy succeeds when the client "perceives himself in such a way that no self-experience can be discriminated as more or less worthy of positive self-regard than any other. . . ."[32] The client then "tends to place the basis of standards within himself, recognizing that the 'goodness' or 'badness' of any experience or perceptual object is not something inherent in that object, but is a value placed in it by himself."[33]

Rogers points out that "some clients make strenuous efforts to have the therapist exercise the valuing function, so as to provide them with guides for action."[34] The therapist, however, "consistently keeps the locus of evaluation with the client."[35] As long as the therapist refuses to "exercise the valuing function" and as long as he or she practices an "unconditional positive regard"[36] for all the affective states of the client, then the therapist remains neutral among the client's values or "sensory and visceral experiences."[37] The role of the therapist is legitimate, Rogers suggests, because of this value neutrality. The therapist accepts all felt preferences as valid and imposes none on the client.

Economists likewise argue that their role as policymakers is legitimate because they are neutral among competing values in the client society. The political economist, according to James Buchanan, "is or should be ethically neutral: the indicated results are influenced by his own value scale only insofar as this reflects his membership in a larger group."[38] The economist might be most confident of the impartiality of his or her policy recommendations if he or she could derive them formally or mathematically from individual preferences. If theoretical difficulties make such a social welfare function impossible,[39] however, the next best thing, to preserve neutrality, is to let markets function to transform individual preference orderings into a collective ordering of social states. The analyst is able then to base policy on preferences that exist in society and are not necessarily his own.

Economists have used this impartial approach to offer solutions to many outstanding social problems, for example, the controversy over abortion. An economist argues that "there is an optimal number of abortions, just as there is an optimal level of pollution, or purity. . . . Those who oppose abortion could eliminate it entirely, if their intensity of feeling were so strong as to lead to payments that were greater at the margin than the price anyone would pay to have an abortion."[40] Likewise economists, in order to determine whether the war in Vietnam was justified, have estimated the willingness to pay of those who demonstrated against it.[41] Likewise it should be possible, following the same line of reasoning, to decide whether Creationism should be taught in the public schools, whether black and white people should be segregated, whether the death penalty should be enforced, and whether the square root of six is three. All of these questions depend upon how much people are willing to pay for their subjective preferences or wants—or none of them do. This is the beauty of cost–benefit analysis: no matter how relevant or irrelevant, wise or stupid, informed or uninformed, responsible or silly, defensible or indefensible wants may be, the analyst is able to derive a policy from them—a policy which is legitimate because, in theory, it treats all of these preferences as equally valid and good.

VI

Consider, by way of contrast, a Kantian conception of value.[42] The individual, for Kant, is a judge of values, not a mere haver of wants, and the individual judges not for himself or herself merely, but as a member of a relevant community or group. The central idea in a Kantian approach to ethics is that some values are more reasonable than others and therefore have a better claim upon the assent of members of the community as such.[43] The world of obligation, like the world of mathematics or the world of empirical fact, is intersubjective, it is public not private, so that objective standards of argument and criticism apply. Kant recognizes that values, like beliefs, are subjective states of mind, but he points out that like beliefs they have an objective content as well; therefore they are either correct or mistaken. Thus Kant discusses valuation in the context not of psychology but of cognition. He believes that a person who makes a value judgment—or a policy recommendation—claims to know what is *right* and not just what is *preferred*. A value judgment is like an empirical or theoretical judgment in that it claims to be *true*, not merely to be *felt*.

We have, then, two approaches to public policy before us. The first, the approach associated with normative versions of welfare economics, asserts that the only policy recommendation that can or need be defended on objective grounds is efficiency or wealth-maximization. Every policy decision after that depends only on the preponderance of feeling or preference, as expressed in willingness to pay. The Kantian approach, on the other hand, assumes that many policy recommendations other than that one may be justified or refuted on objective grounds. It would concede that the approach of welfare economics applies adequately to some questions, e.g., those which ordinary consumer markets typically settle. How many yo-yos should be produced as compared to how many frisbees? Shall pens have black ink or blue? Matters such as these are so trivial it is plain that markets should handle them. It does not follow, however, that we should adopt a market or quasi-market approach to every public question.

A market or quasi-market approach to arithmetic, for example, is plainly inadequate. No matter how much people are willing to pay, three will never be the square root of six. Similarly, segregation is a national curse and the fact that we are willing to pay for it does not make it better but only makes us worse. Similarly, the case for abortion must stand on the merits; it cannot be priced at the margin. Similarly, the war in Vietnam was a moral debacle and this can be determined without shadow-pricing the willingness to pay of those who demonstrated against it. Similarly, we do not decide to execute murderers by asking how much bleeding hearts are willing to pay to see a person pardoned and how much hard hearts are willing to pay to see him hanged. Our failures to make the right decisions in these matters are failures in arithmetic, failures in wisdom, failures in taste, failures in morality—but not market failures. There are no relevant markets to have failed. What separates these questions from those for which markets are appropriate is this. They involve matters of knowledge, wisdom, morality, and taste that admit of bet-

ter or worse, right or wrong, true or false—and these concepts differ from that of economic optimality. Surely environmental questions—the protection of wilderness, habitats, water, land, and air as well as policy toward environmental safety and health—involve moral and aesthetic principles and not just economic ones. This is consistent, of course, with cost-effectiveness and with a sensible recognition of economic constraints.

The neutrality of the economist, like the neutrality of Rogers' therapist, is legitimate if private preferences or subjective wants are the only values in question. A person should be left free to choose the color of his or her necktie or necklace—but we cannot justify a theory of public policy or private therapy on that basis. If the patient seeks moral advice or tries to find reasons to justify a choice, the therapist, according to Rogers' model, would remind him or her to trust his visceral and sensory experiences. The result of this is to deny the individual status as a cognitive being capable of responding intelligently to reasons; it reduces him or her to a bundle of affective states. What Rogers' therapist does to the patient the cost–benefit analyst does to society as a whole. The analyst is neutral among our "values"—having first imposed a theory of what value is. This is a theory that is impartial among values and for that reason fails to treat the persons who have them with respect or concern. It does not treat them even as persons but only as locations at which wants may be found. And thus we may conclude that the neutrality of economics is not a basis for its legitimacy. We recognize it as an indifference toward value—an indifference so deep, so studied, and so assured that at first one hesitates to call it by its right name.

VII

The residents of Lewiston at the conference I attended demanded to know the truth about the dangers that confronted them and the reasons for these dangers. They wanted to be convinced that the sacrifice asked of them was legitimate even if it served interests other than their own. One official from a large chemical company dumping wastes in the area told them, in reply, that corporations were people and that people could talk to people about their feelings, interests, and needs. This sent a shiver through the audience. Like Joseph K. in *The Trial*,[44] the residents of Lewiston asked for an explanation, justice, and truth, and they were told that their wants would be taken care of. They demanded to know the reasons for what was continually happening to them. They were given a personalized response instead.

This response, that corporations are "just people serving people" is consistent with a particular view of power. This is the view that identified power with the ability to get what one wants as an individual, that is, to satisfy one's personal preferences. When people in official positions in corporations or in the government put aside their personal interests, it would follow that they put aside their power as well. Their neutrality then justifies them in directing the resources of society in ways they determine to be best. This managerial role serves not their own interests but those of their clients. Cost–benefit analysis may be seen as a pervasive form of this paternalism. Behind this paternalism, as William Simon observes of the lawyer–client relationship, lies a theory of value that tends to personalize power. "It resists understanding power as a product of class, property, or institutions and collapses power into the personal needs and dispositions of the individuals who command and obey."[45] Once the economist, the therapist, the lawyer, or the manager abjures his own interests and acts wholly on behalf of client individuals, he appears to have no power of his own and thus justifiably manipulates and controls everything. "From this perspective it becomes difficult to distinguish the powerful from the powerless. In every case, both the exercise of power and submission to it are portrayed as a matter of personal accommodation and adjustment."[46]

The key to the personal interest or emotive theory of value, as one commentator has rightly said, "is the fact that emotivism entails the obliteration of any genuine distinction between manipulative and nonmanipulative social relations."[47] The reason is that once the effective self is made the source of all value, the public self cannot participate in the exercise of power. As Philip Reiff remarks, "the public world is constituted as one vast stranger who appears at inconvenient times and makes demands viewed as purely external and therefore with no power to elicit a moral response."[48] There is no way to distinguish tyranny from the legitimate authority that public values and public law create.[49]

"At the rate of progress since 1900," Henry Adams speculates in his *Education*, "every American who lived into the year 2000 would know how to control unlimited power."[50] Adams thought that the Dynamo would organize and release as much energy as the Virgin. Yet in the 1980s, the citizens of Lewiston, surrounded by dynamos, high tension lines, and nuclear wastes, are powerless. They do not know how to criticize power, resist power, or justify power—for to do so depends on making distinctions between good and evil, right and wrong, innocence and guilt, justice and injustice, truth and lies. These distinctions cannot be made out and have no significance within an emotive or psychological theory of value. To adopt this theory is to imagine society as a market in which individuals trade voluntarily and without coercion. No individual, no belief, no faith has authority over them. To have power to act as a nation, however, we must be able to act, at least at times, on a public philosophy, conviction, or faith. We cannot replace with economic analysis the moral function of public law. The antinomianism of cost–benefit analysis is not enough.

Notes

1. H. Adams, *The Education of Henry Adams* 380 (1970, 1961).

2. *Id*.

3. *Id*. at 388.

4. For an account, see J. Pelletier, *The Sun Danced at Fàtima* (1951).

5. *New Catholic Encyclopedia* 856 (1967).

6. See, e.g., W. Baxter, *People or Penguins: The Case for Optimal Pollution*, chap. 1 (1974). See generally A. Freeman III, R. Haveman, and A. Kneese, *The Economics of Environmental Policy* (1973).

7. R. Posner puts this point well in discussing wealth maximization as an ethical concept. "The only kind of preference that counts in a system of wealth-maximization," he writes, "is . . . one that is backed up by money—in other words, that is registered in a market." Posner, "Utilitarianism, Economics, and Legal Theory," 8 *J. Legal Stud.* 119 (1979).

8. Freeman et al., note 6 *supra* at 23.

9. R. Musgrave, *The Theory of Public Finance* 87–88 (1959).

10. Marglin, "The Social Rate of Discount and the Optimal Rate of Investment," 77 *Q. J. of Econ.* 98 (1963).

11. See 46 *Fed. Reg. 13193* (February 19, 1981). The Order specifies that the cost–benefit requirement shall apply "to the extent permitted by law."

12. *American Textile Mfgrs. Inst. v. Bingham*, 617 F.2d 636 (D.C. Cir. 1979) *cert.* granted *sub nom.* [1980]; *American Textile Mfgrs. v. Marshall*, 49 U.S.L.W. 3208.

13. *Textile Mfgrs. v. Donovan*, 101 S.Ct. 2478 (1981).

14. *Id.* U.S.L.W. (1981), 4733–34.

15. *Ibid.*, 4726–29.

16. Pub. L. No. 91-596, 84 Stat. 1596 (codified at 29 U.S.C. 651-78) (1970).

17. 29 U.S.C., 655(b) (5).

18. *American Petroleum Institute v. Marshall*, 581 F.2d 493 (1978) (5th Cir.), aff'd 100 S. Ct. 2844 (1980).

19. See, e.g., R. Posner, *Economic Analysis of Law*, parts I, II (1972, 1973). In *The Costs of Accidents* (1970), G. Calabresi argues that accident law balances two goals, "efficiency" and "equality" or "justice."

20. 581 F.2d 493 (1978).

21. 100 S.Ct. 2844 (1980).

22. *Id.* at 2903.

23. M. Baram, "Cost–Benefit Analysis: An Inadequate Basis for Health, Safety and Environmental Regulatory Decision Making," 8 *Ecological Law Quarterly* 473 (1980).

24. See 49 U.S.L.W. 4724–29 for this reasoning applied in the cotton dust case.

25. *De la Liberté des Anciens Comparee a Celle des Modernes* (1819).

26. *Oeuvres Politiques de Benjamin Constant*, ed. C. Luandre 269 (Paris, 1874); quoted in S. Wolin, *Politics and Vision* 281 (1960).

27. There are arguments that whatever reasons may be given are no good. See, e.g., Dworkin, "Why Efficiency?" 8 *Hofstra L. Rev.* 563 (1980); Dworkin, "Is Wealth a Value?" 9 *J. Legal Stud.* 191 (1980); Kennedy, "Cost-Benefit Analysis of Entitlement Problems: A Critique" 33 *Stan L. Rev.* 387 (1980); Rizzo, "The Mirage of Efficiency" 8 *Hofstra L. Rev.* 641 (1980); Sagoff, "Economic Theory and Environmental Law" 79 *Mich L. Rev.* 1393 (1981).

28. This is the emotive theory of value. For the classic statement, see C. Stevenson, *Ethics and Language*, chaps. 1, 2 (1944). For criticism, see Blanshard, "The New Subjectivism in Ethics" 9 *Philosophy and Phenomenological Research* 504 (1949). For a statement of the related interest theory of value, see E. Westermarck, *Ethical Relativity* chaps. 3, 4, 5 (1932); R. Perry, *General Theory of Value* (1926). For criticisms of subjectivism in ethics and a case for the objective theory presupposed here, see generally, P. Edwards, *The Logic of Moral Discourse* (1955) and W. Ross, *The Right and the Good* (1930).

29. My account is based on C. Rogers, *On Becoming a Person* (1961); C. Rogers, *Client Centered Therapy* (1965); and Rogers, "A Theory of Therapy, Personality, and Interpersonal Relationships, as Developed in the Client Centered Framework" 3 *Psychology: A Study of a Science* 184 (S. Koch ed., 1959). For a similar account used as a critique of the lawyer–client relation, see Simon, "Homo Psychologious: Notes on a New Legal Formalism" 32 *Stan. L. Rev.* 487 (1980).

30. Rogers, note 29 *supra* at 210.

31. C. Rogers, *Client Centered Therapy* 150 (1965).

32. Rogers, note 29 *supra* at 208.

33. Rogers, note 31 *supra* at 139.

34. *Id.* at 150.

35. *Id.*

36. Rogers, note 29 *supra* at 208.

37. *Id.* at 523–24.

38. Buchanan, "Positive Economics, Welfare Economics, and Political Economy" 2 *J. L. and Econ.* 124, 127 (1959).

39. K. Arrow, *Social Choice and Individual Values* i–v (2d ed., 1963).

40. H. Macaulay and B. Yandle, *Environmental Use and the Market* 120–21 (1978).

41. Cicchetti, Freeman, Haveman, and Knetsch, "On the Economics of Mass Demonstrations: A Case Study of the November 1969 March on Washington," 61 *Am. Econ. Rev.* 719 (1971).

42. I. Kant, *Foundations of the Metaphysics of Morals* (R. Wolff, ed., L. Beck trans., 1969). I follow the interpretation of Kantian ethics of W. Sellars, *Science and Metaphysics*, chap. VII (1968) and Sellars, "On Reasoning about Values" 17 *Am. Phil. Q.* 81 (1980).

43. See A. Macintyre, *After Virtue* 22 (1981).

44. F. Kafka, *The Trial* (rev. ed. trans. 1957). Simon (note 29 supra) at 524 applies this analogy to the lawyer–client relationship.

45. Simon, note 29 *supra* at 495.

46. *Id.*

47. Macintyre, note 43 *supra* at 22.

48. P. Reiff, *The Triumph of the Therapeutic: Uses of Faith after Freud* 52 (1966).

49. That public law regimes inevitably lead to tyranny seems to be the conclusion of H. Arendt, *The Human Condition* (1958); K. Popper, *The Open Society and Its Enemies* (1966); L. Strauss, *Natural Right and History* (1953). For an important criticism of this conclusion in these authors, see Holmes, "Aristippus in and out of Athens" 73 *Am. Pol. Sci. Rev.* 113 (1979).

50. H. Adams, note 1 *supra* at 476.

V.B Cost–Benefit Analysis _____

41. PREVIEW

[W]e should be on our guard not to overestimate science and scientific methods when it is a question of human problems; and we should not assume that experts are the only ones who have a right to express themselves on questions affecting the organization of society.

Albert Einstein

As noted earlier, it is widely agreed that markets as they exist are thought to fail in various respects. Unowned, or "commonly held," resources are overused or "exploited" (this issue is explored in detail in the next section). Some goods, such as fossil fuels, clean air, or water, are thought to be used up too quickly or in the wrong manner. Burdens are imposed on parties who do not consent to them (hence, "negative externalities"). It is often held that government intervention in certain cases is appropriate—for example, prohibiting certain activities by regulation (and perhaps criminal penalties) or placing charges on certain activities (such as through licensing or effluent charges). In some cases a government agency decides whether to undertake a project such as building a dam. If the aggregate costs were to exceed the aggregate benefit, it would be foolish to proceed. It is reasonable to claim that (1) if a policy is adopted, then the costs must not exceed the benefits. We should distinguish this claim and the following two claims from one another: (2) if a policy, *P*, ought to be carried out for whatever are the relevant reasons, *P* should be carried out in the way that maximizes benefits-minus-costs, and (3) if a policy, *P*, maximizes benefits-minus-costs, then *P* ought to be carried out (call this the *maximization principle*). The major controversy surrounds (3). Specifically, those who argue for the adoption of a particular policy (such as flooding a valley and building a dam) may do so as follows:

1. We (or a governmental agency) ought to do whatever maximizes benefits-minus-costs.

2. Policy *P* maximizes benefits-minus-costs. Hence,

3. We ought to carry out P.

Two basic questions are (1) why should we do whatever maximizes benefits-minus-costs, and (2) is it ever possible to know or reasonably believe of some (or any) policy that it maximizes benefits-minus-costs.

In late 1996 the U.S. government was deciding (Russia has a similar problem) what to do with 52 metric tons of plutonium in the next decades; it will be highly radioactive for *thousands* of years. What is the cost of our having produced it? Can we ascertain that even now? Was it ever calculated? Do we know how in principle? Further, in a given case is it reasonable to believe that a particular policy maximizes benefits-minus-costs? The essays that follow explore these matters (for example, the proper way to think about, and deal with, pollution) and in some cases how they bear on a particular dispute.

Here we begin to lay out the Pandora's box of puzzles that arise when one sets out to identify and reassess what is presupposed by the sort of normative cost–benefit approach identified earlier—whose core is (3) that the policy that maximizes benefits-minus-costs is right and, therefore, ought to be adopted. What seems at first only a simple truism like "don't be wasteful" is not so at all; rather, the presuppositions are many, hard to unearth, entrenched, and extremely influential. The concepts of cost and benefit are not as straightforward as is often implied. What is to count as a cost? A number of possibilities come to mind: premature death, injury, pain, (felt) frustration of preferences, or nonfulfillment of preferences—or *risk* of these occurring. Such suggestions may focus only on costs to humans. There are reasons to reject such anthropocentrism. Should we not include what economists (and many others) almost invariably exclude, such as pain or premature death to animals, or destruction of a river or forest if there is no nontrivial loss to humans? Analogously, what is to count as a benefit? Is pure life prolongation of humans a benefit (eternal life *as such* might be boring!)? Are all instances of human preferences satisfaction to be weighed positively in a cost–benefit calculation? There is a tendency to equate "benefit," "good," "welfare," "satisfaction," "utility," and "preference fulfillment," but should we regard the fulfillment of "antisocial preferences" (such as sadistic, envious, jealous ones) as a benefit? As noted earlier, should not preferences be "laundered"?[1]

Orthodox economists, perhaps in an excess of antipaternalism, antimoralism, or uncritical acceptance of moral subjectivism (an instance of egalitarianism run amok), tend not to pass judgment on existing preferences—acting as if all preferences had an equal right to be fulfilled (but consider a hunter's intense preference to maximize his or her kill of baby seals or whales, a soldier's desire to rape women, or a heterosexual soldier's desire to bash a gay comrade). If one says that some preferences do not *deserve* satisfaction (or that their fulfillment has no positive moral weight), then evaluation enters at a fundamental level, and it is inappropriate to proclaim value neutrality for any such economic theory (even if it does not insist on cardinal measures of utility). However, any theory advocating unqualified want fulfillment seems morally problematic for the reasons discussed.

Similarly, in many cases little is said about the *relation between beliefs and preferences* (as if preferences were like itches unconnected with cognition). However, it is clear that one's preferences are heavily dependent (sometimes causally and sometimes conceptually) on one's beliefs. Compare preferences for and against slavery, polygamy, the use of DDT, the killing of whales, or Oedipus's preference for Jocasta when he believed, and when he did not believe, Jocasta to be his mother. If preferences (such as for destroying all Jews, keeping women barefoot and pregnant, "nuking" the latest enemy) are based on irrational beliefs (Jews are vermin; women rightly are property of males—God's designated "helpmates" for men; retaliation by the enemy would be minor), it is not at all clear why satisfaction of such preferences is a benefit to be weighed positively in some cost–benefit calculations. Thus, aside from the fact that only effects on humans are given weight in the calculations, it seems doubtful that all instances of preference fulfillment should be conceptualized as benefits. If so, why maximize them? Further, it is not obvious that all harms to humans ("costs") can be viewed as frustration of wants. When urban children suffer brain damage (and consequent retardation) from exposure to lead (from our use of leaded gasoline), what preference of the child is frustrated? Suppose the child is only a year old. If acid rain destroys many of our forests, is there no cost if people do not care, and we come to prefer plastic trees (as a result of indoctrination or not missing what we never experienced)?

A different, competing analysis of welfare–illfare, benefit-cost, gain-loss is presented in terms of promoting or subverting the *interests* of a person or other organism—in terms of what is *in the interest* of, or subversive of, a being. When one takes into account children, the comatose, or the severely retarded—as philosophers and social theorists sometimes forget to do, it is especially clear that *what people want* and *what is in their interest* only overlap. Those who identify benefit with want satisfaction need to give reasons for rejecting a competing analysis of benefit. The person on the street probably believes that cost–benefit techniques are aimed at promoting welfare, but arguably want satisfaction and the promotion of welfare are not the same thing.

Even if it were unproblematic that benefit equals want satisfaction, it is questionable whether all benefits (so understood) can be identified and measured. There is no established market in some goods. Thus, economists infer by indirect means how much people ("consumers") "value" a good or a service (*value* in economics often means *prefer* in English). There are two main approaches to determining value: (1) determine which packages of goods people are willing and able to pay for if there is a market for them, and (2) ask people direct or indirect questions. Consider (1) first. What people are *willing* to pay is, in part, a function of how much they are *able* to pay. If willingness to pay for safety devices in a car is the criterion, then one may believe that the rich value their lives more than the poor value theirs. Should we believe as much? Suppose Jones is out of work and starving on Monday and then takes a highly risky job on Tuesday (washing windows on the fifth floor). He may "demand" only a modest premium to compensate for the extra risk to his life (suppose he could have had the first-floor job for a slightly smaller salary). Should we infer that the value of Jones's life is smaller—or that he does not value it much? According to another approach, the value (or "economic value"?) of a person's life is equivalent to his or her forgone earnings. Perhaps that is a suitable criterion for determining how much compensation should be made to a person's estate when that person is wrongfully killed. As a measure of the value of that person's life or the amount of money that should be spent to prevent premature death, a monetary measure seems dubious. Happenstance affects earnings (as do preferences for leisure time and moral convictions). Would Shaquille O'Neal's life be worth less if there were no market for basketball players—or that of Tiger Woods if people watched golf no more than they watched checkers? Is a ditchdigger's life at age 21 worth less than that of a 21-year-old physicist?

Years ago the Ford Motor Company did a cost-benefit analysis on the policy of adding certain devices to its cars to prevent the gas tanks from rupturing. One of the prospective benefits was saving a certain number of lives. How valuable is one life? Can a life rationally be assigned a monetary value? Ford figured $200,000 (for 1971!) as the cost of a death. Presumably, this figure largely reflects costs to others; only $10,000 of the amount was designated as the cost (value?) of the victim's pain and suffering. Why not $50,000 or $100,000? Is the benefit of preserving a life equal to avoiding the death (which is assumed to be a function of wages forgone)? Of course, the figure that is assigned here directly affects the outcome of the cost–benefit calculation and the ultimate policy determination. We note here the obvious questions that arise about the reasonableness of assigning monetary values to certain "goods and bads." There are important questions about the way "cost" and "benefit" are conceptualized, problems in attempting to identify all the costs and benefits, and difficulties in rationally assigning a monetary measure to many costs and benefits—even when one takes an anthropocentric approach. Avoiding complexities, however, can have a high price. Our cost–benefit calculations would be comparatively simpler if we did not count the well-being of children or the severely retarded.

THE MATTER OF CONSENT

In law and in common sense, whether another (voluntarily and knowingly) consents to the imposition of a "harm" is thought morally significant in deciding on the permissibility or desirability of generating the harm. The surgeon and the mugger may make similar "incisions," perhaps with similar results, but we view the unconsented-to cutting as wrong, and the one to which there is consent as acceptable. It is striking that, in some discussions defending cost–benefit analysis (in contrast, see Leonard and Zeckhauser, Essay 43), little attention is paid to whether those who are harmed, or subjected to risks, consent or not. It is clear that (more or less) voluntary smoking results in great harms (on average and in the aggregate) to smokers. A cost–benefit analysis of smoking (or alcohol usage) might (we conjecture) suggest strongly that the practice fails to maximize benefits-minus-costs. It is natural to wonder, however, whether the burdens on the smokers (aside from associated "indirect" burdens on non-smokers) should be counted as a cost in a cost–benefit calculation. At the least, we raise the question of whether *imposed* costs and *voluntarily absorbed* costs should be viewed similarly. As the issue is often discussed elsewhere, this distinction tends to be ignored.

THE MAXIMIZATION PRINCIPLE

Although an analyst may purport to identify only costs and benefits (and, thus, remain "untainted" by ethical commitments) and not subscribe to the maximization principle (we ought to do whatever maximizes benefits-costs), further questions arise for anyone who accepts the (normative) maximization principle. If the prior difficulties cannot be overcome, the principle may be inapplicable. Also, the principle seems subject to the well-known difficulties with the principle of utility; on one construal, "maximize benefits-minus-costs" is just the principle of utility. (Except that the classic utilitarians Jeremy Bentham and John Stuart Mill were not anthropocentric in their conception of "cost" and "benefit." Both explicitly maintained that the suffering of animals must be given weight in deciding what to do.) The main objection to be noted here concerns whether a policy of maximizing the balance of benefits over costs is defensible when it gives no direct weight to how those benefits and costs are distributed among the relevant population.

The policy that maximizes benefits-minus-costs may make some individuals worse off. Thus, adopting the policy may not be an efficient step in the sense of making a Pareto improvement (see the preceding Preview for an explanation). The gains to the "winners," however, may outweigh the losses to the losers. If so, it would be possible in principle for the gainers to *compensate* the losers—thus, making the latter "nonlosers" (no worse off). The costs of making the transfer (information costs, and so on) may make full compensation impossible. If, however, full compensation were made, a Pareto improvement would occur, there would be no losers on balance, and an injustice could not be claimed—namely, that some suffered an unconsented to, on balance, harm. (Note, however, that some might be relatively, if not absolutely, worse off—on one "objective" measure, at least.) Some economists and others, however, believe a "potential compensation principle" (or potential Pareto criterion) is satisfactory: The results of a policy must make full compensation *possible*, but the compensation need not be paid. This view is puzzling. To accept the potential compensation principle is to set aside an intuitively attractive feature of the strict Pareto principle (that no one will lose), one that sidesteps important moral objections based on considerations of justice. If salesperson A "steals" salesperson B's $5,000 car, and as a result earns an extra $50,000 a year, perhaps A could compensate B for his or her losses. If A does not, B has ground for serious moral complaint. We do not pursue the point here, but there may be ground for complaint *even if* compensation is made (assuming it can be).

To maximize benefits-minus-costs without compensating losers looks suspiciously like merely maximizing total net utility. Uncompensated losses look like "market failures" or negative externalities. A supposed attraction of cost–benefit analysis is that is helps to eliminate or reduce such externalities. Pure maximization policies (regardless of what is to be maximized, such as GNP, utility, wealth, or benefits-minus-costs) seem to give no direct weight to concerns about how benefits and costs are distributed. This seems morally intolerable.

Perhaps, however, a coupling (somehow) of cost–benefit analysis and principles of just distribution may be more attractive. If so, one may have to surrender the unqualified maximization principle. Further, one may have to drop the pervasive meta-ethical assumption seemingly made by many environmental economists that "the proper use of environmental resources is more a matter of economics than of morals."[2] This last assumption is plausible only if one accepts the maximization principle and the assumption that one can measure all the relevant benefits and costs. These claims cannot, however, be decided without careful inquiry.

Matters are not all this simple, of course. The claims that some "environmentalists," philosophers, and scientists have proposed as guidelines for use in making environmental decisions (maxims such as "Nature knows best," "A thing is right when it tends to preserve the integrity, stability, and beauty of the biotic community," "Maximize utility" [again], "Preserve endangered species," "Everything has a right to exist") seem to be too vague and indeterminate to be analytic truisms, or otherwise objectionable. The essays that follow address the attractions of efficiency and cost–benefit considerations—as well as the persistent reservations about their use (especially as grounds for policy *selection—as opposed* to their use to foster cheap implementation of an already selected policy such as cost-effectiveness).

To speak at length of these matters is not to talk directly of rain forests, blue whales, acid rain, marshlands, or estuaries; rather, it is to explore grounds for choices that will determine the destiny of such entities as well as that of humans. If one is concerned with the fate of our planet, to ignore such matters is to choose to be a naïve environmentalist.

In the first selection that follows (Essay 42), by Steven Kelman, "Cost-Benefit Analysis: An Ethical Critique," apart from considering questions about the anthropocentric nature of cost–benefit analysis, the author argues that a policy might be right even if it does *not* maximize benefits-minus-costs. Further, he questions the attempt to assign monetary values to nonmarketed benefits and costs. In short, Kelman's critique is important and provocative. Herman Leonard and Richard Zeckhauser in "Cost–Benefit Analysis Defended" then respond (Essay 43) to some of the current criticisms of cost–benefit analysis. In particular, they argue that such analysis is sensitive to distributional effects and need not be arbitrary in the assignment of monetary values. Their conflict with Kelman's view is not always direct, but the two essays are instructive.

An important and instructive case in point with regard to the determination of cost and benefits, and the practical use made of such procedures is found in the manner in which nations standardly make judgments about their own economic well-being. To those who are unaware of the extent to which our standard indexes of economic health or improvement fail to register serious environmental degradation, Robert Repetto's investigation "Earth in the Balance Sheet" (Essay 45) may have the impact of a cold shower. The brighter side is that with the development of more appropriate measure, nations may become more aware of "what on earth they are doing," develop new measures, and cease training the nonhuman world as being of little consequence, a mere static backdrop to human activities.

NOTES

1. We note the troubling fact that the desirability of efficiency is thought to derive from the fact it is a means to increasing human want fulfillment. The desirability of the latter in all cases is hardly

obvious because (1) it ignores the well-being of all other species (except derivatively), and (2) wants may be, arguably, irrational, such as the desire to torture for the fun of it. So, Nobel Prizes aside, why worry about the difficulty of formulating a feasible

social welfare function based solely on human wants? And why be tempted by the notion that whatever is efficient is right?

2. Robert and Nancy Dorfman, eds., *Economics of the Environment* (New York: Norton, 1972), p. XL.

42. Cost–Benefit Analysis: An Ethical Critique

Steven Kelman

At the broadest and vaguest level, cost–benefit analysis may be regarded simply as systematic thinking about decision-making. Who can oppose, economists sometimes ask, efforts to think in a systematic way about the consequences of different courses of action? The alternative, it would appear, is unexamined decision-making. But defining cost–benefit analysis so simply leaves it with few implications for actual regulatory decision-making. Presumably, therefore, those who urge regulators to make greater use of the technique have a more extensive prescription in mind. I assume here that their prescription includes the following views:

1. There exists a strong presumption that an act should not be undertaken unless its benefits outweigh its costs.

2. In order to determine whether benefits outweigh costs, it is desirable to attempt to express all benefits and costs in a common scale or denominator, so that they can be compared with each other, even when some benefits and costs are not traded on markets and hence have no established dollar values.

3. Getting decision-makers to make more use of cost–benefit techniques is important enough to warrant both the expense required to gather the data for improved cost–benefit estimation and the political efforts needed to give the activity higher priority compared to other activities, also valuable in and of themselves.

My focus is on cost–benefit analysis as applied to environmental, safety, and health regulation. In that context, I examine each of the above proposi-

tions from the perspective of formal ethical theory, that is, the study of what actions it is morally right to undertake. My conclusions are:

1. In areas of environmental, safety, and health regulation, there may be many instances where a certain decision might be right even though its benefits do not outweigh its costs.

2. There are good reasons to oppose efforts to put dollar values on nonmarketed benefits and costs.

3. Given the relative frequency of occasions in the areas of environmental, safety, and health regulation where one would not wish to use a benefits-outweigh-costs test as a decision rule, and given the reasons to oppose the monetizing of nonmarketed benefits or costs that is a prerequisite for cost–benefit analysis, it is not justifiable to devote major resources to the generation of data for cost–benefit calculations or to undertake efforts to "spread the gospel" of cost–benefit analysis further.

I

How do we decide whether a given action is morally right or wrong and hence, assuming the desire to act morally, why it should be undertaken or refrained from? Like the Molière character who spoke prose without knowing it, economists who advocate use of cost–benefit analysis for public decisions are philosophers without knowing it: the answer given by cost–benefit analysis, that actions should be undertaken so as to maximize net benefits, represents one of the classic answers given

Regulation (Jan., Feb. 1981), pp. 74–82. Reprinted by permission of the American Enterprise Institute for Public Policy Research, Washington, DC

by moral philosophers—that given by utilitarians. To determine whether an action is right or wrong, utilitarians tote up all the positive consequences of the action in terms of human satisfaction. The act that maximizes attainment of satisfaction under the circumstances is the right act. That the economists' answer is also the answer of one school of philosophers should not be surprising. Early on, economics was a branch of moral philosophy, and only later did it become an independent discipline.

Before proceeding further, the subtlety of the utilitarian position should be noted. The positive and negative consequences of an act for satisfaction may go beyond the act's immediate consequences. A facile version of utilitarianism would give moral sanction to a lie, for instance, if the satisfaction of an individual attained by telling the lie was greater than the suffering imposed on the lie's victim. Few utilitarians would agree. Most of them would add to the list of negative consequences the effect of the one lie on the tendency of the person who lies to tell other lies, even in instances when the lying produced less satisfaction for him than dissatisfaction for others. They would also add the negative effects of the lie on the general level of social regard for truth-telling, which has many consequences for future utility. A further consequence may be added as well. It is sometimes said that we should include in a utilitarian calculation the feeling of dissatisfaction produced in the liar (and perhaps in others) because, by telling a lie, one has "done the wrong thing." Correspondingly, in this view, among the positive consequences to be weighed into a utilitarian calculation of truth-telling is satisfaction arising from "doing the right thing." This view rests on an error, however, because it *assumes* what it is the purpose of the calculation to *determine*—that telling the truth in the instance in question is indeed the right thing to do. Economists are likely to object to this point, arguing that no feeling ought "arbitrarily" to be excluded from a complete cost–benefit calculation, including a feeling of dissatisfaction at doing the wrong thing. Indeed, the economists' cost–benefit calculations would, at least ideally, include such feelings. Note the difference between the economist's and the philosopher's cost–benefit calculations, however. The economist may choose to include feelings of dissatisfaction in his cost–benefit calculation, but what happens if somebody asks the economist, "Why is it right to evaluate an action on the basis of a cost–benefit test?" If

an answer is to be given to that question (which does not normally preoccupy economists but which does concern both philosophers and the rest of us who need to be persuaded that cost–benefit analysis is right), then the circularity problem reemerges. And there is also another difficulty with counting feelings of dissatisfaction at doing the wrong thing in a cost–benefit calculation. It leads to the perverse result that under certain circumstances a lie, for example, might be morally right if the individual contemplating the lie felt no compunction about lying and morally wrong only if the individual felt such a compunction!

This error is revealing, however, because it begins to suggest a critique of utilitarianism. Utilitarianism is an important and powerful moral doctrine. But it is probably a minority position among contemporary moral philosophers. It is amazing that economists can proceed in unanimous endorsement of cost–benefit analysis as if unaware that their conceptual framework is highly controversial in the discipline from which it arose—moral philosophy.

Let us explore the critique of utilitarianism. The logical error discussed before appears to suggest that we have a notion of certain things being right or wrong that *predates* our calculation of costs and benefits. Imagine the case of an old man in Nazi Germany who is hostile to the regime. He is wondering whether he should speak out against Hitler. If he speaks out, he will lose his pension. And his action will have done nothing to increase the chances that the Nazi regime will be overthrown: he is regarded as somewhat eccentric by those around him, and nobody has ever consulted his views on political questions. Recall that one cannot add to the benefits of speaking out any satisfaction from doing "the right thing," because the purpose of the exercise is to determine whether speaking out *is* the right thing. How would the utilitarian calculation go? The benefits of the old man's speaking out would, as the example is presented, be nil, while the costs would be his loss of his pension. So the costs of the action would outweigh the benefits. By the utilitarians' cost–benefit calculation, it would be *morally wrong* for the man to speak out.

To those who believe that it would not be morally wrong for the old man to speak out in Nazi Germany, utilitarianism is insufficient as a moral view. We believe that some acts whose costs are greater than their benefits may be morally right and, contrariwise, some acts whose benefits are greater than their costs may be morally wrong.

This does not mean that the question whether benefits are greater than costs is morally irrelevant. Few would claim such. Indeed, for a broad range of individual and social decisions, whether an act's benefits outweigh its costs is a sufficient question to ask. But not for all such decisions. These may involve situations where certain duties—duties not to lie, break promises, or kill, for example—make an act wrong, even if it would result in an excess of benefits over costs. Or they may involve instances where people's rights are at stake. We would not permit rape even if it could be demonstrated that the rapist derived enormous happiness from his act, while the victim experienced only minor displeasure. We do not do cost–benefit analyses of freedom of speech or trial by jury. The Bill of Rights was not RARGed.[1] As the United Steelworkers noted in a comment on the Occupational Safety and Health Administration's economic analysis of its proposed rule to reduce worker exposure to carcinogenic coke-oven emissions, the Emancipation Proclamation was not subjected to an inflationary impact statement. The notion of human rights involves the idea that people may make certain claims to be allowed to act in certain ways or to be treated in certain ways, even if the sum of benefits achieved thereby does not outweigh the sum of costs. It is this view that underlies the statement that "workers have a right to a safe and healthy work place" and the expectation that OSHA's decisions will reflect that judgment.

In the most convincing versions of nonutilitarian ethics, various duties or rights are not absolute. But each has a *prima facie* moral validity so that, if duties or rights do not conflict, the morally right act is the act that reflects a duty or respects a right. If duties or rights do conflict, a moral judgment, based on conscious deliberation, must be made. Since one of the duties non-utilitarian philosophers enumerate is the duty of beneficence (the duty to maximize happiness), which in effect incorporates all of utilitarianism by reference, a non-utilitarian who is faced with conflicts between the results of cost–benefit analysis and non-utility-based considerations will need to undertake such deliberation. But in that deliberation, additional elements, which cannot be reduced to a question of whether benefits outweigh costs, have been introduced. Indeed,

depending on the moral importance we attach to the right or duty involved, cost–benefit questions may, within wide ranges, become irrelevant to the outcome of the moral judgment.

In addition to questions involving duties and rights, there is a final sort of question where, in my view, the issue of whether benefits outweigh costs should not govern moral judgment. I noted earlier that, for the common run of questions facing individuals and societies, it is possible to begin and end our judgment simply by finding out if the benefits of the contemplated act outweigh the costs. This very fact means that one way to show the great importance, or value, attached to an area is to say that decisions involving the area should not be determined by cost–benefit calculations. This applies, I think, to the view many environmentalists have of decisions involving our natural environment. When officials are deciding what level of pollution will harm certain vulnerable people—such as asthmatics or the elderly—while not harming others, one issue involved may be the right of those people not to be sacrificed on the altar of somewhat higher living standards for the rest of us. But more broadly than this, many environmentalists fear that subjecting decisions about clean air or water to the cost–benefit tests that determine the general run of decisions removes those matters from the realm of specially valued things.

II

In order for cost–benefit calculations to be performed the way they are supposed to be, all costs and benefits must be expressed in a common measure, typically dollars, including things not normally bought and sold on markets, and to which dollar prices are therefore not attached. The most dramatic example of such things is human life itself; but many of the other benefits achieved or preserved by environmental policy—such as peace and quiet, fresh-smelling air, swimmable rivers, spectacular vistas—are not traded on markets either.

Economists who do cost–benefit analysis regard the quest after dollar values for non-market things as a difficult challenge—but one to be met with relish. They have tried to develop methods for imputing a person's "willingness to pay" for such things, their approach generally involving a search for bundled goods that *are* traded on markets and that vary as to whether they include a feature that is, *by itself,* not marketed. Thus, fresh air is not marketed, but houses in different parts of Los Angeles that are similar except for the degree of smog are. Peace and quiet is not marketed, but similar houses inside and outside airport flight paths are. The risk of death is not marketed, but similar jobs that have different levels of risk are. Economists have produced many often ingenious efforts to impute dollar prices to non-marketed things by observing the premiums accorded homes in clean air areas over similar homes in dirty areas or the premiums paid for risky jobs over similar nonrisky jobs.

These ingenious efforts are subject to criticism on a number of technical grounds. It may be difficult to control for all the dimensions of quality other than the presence or absence of the non-marketed thing. More important, in a world where people have different preferences and are subject to different constraints as they make their choices, the dollar value imputed to the non-market things that most people would wish to avoid will be lower than otherwise, because people with unusually weak aversion to those things or unusually strong constraints on their choices will be willing to take the bundled good in question at less of a discount than the average person. Thus, to use the property value discount of homes near airports as a measure of people's willingness to pay for quiet means to accept as a proxy for the rest of us the behavior of those least sensitive to noise, of airport employees (who value the convenience of a near-airport location) or of others who are susceptible to an agent's assurances that "it's not so bad." To use the wage premiums accorded hazardous work as a measure of the value of life means to accept as proxies for the rest of us the choices of people who do not have many choices or who are exceptional risk-seekers.

A second problem is that the attempts of economists to measure people's willingness to pay for non-marketed things assume that there is no difference between the price a person would require for *giving up* something to which he has a preexisting right and the price he would pay to *gain* something to which he enjoys no right. Thus, the analysis assumes no difference between how much a homeowner would need to be paid in order to give up an unobstructed mountain view that he already enjoys and how much he would be willing to pay to get an obstruction moved once it is already in place. Available evidence suggests that most people

would insist on being paid far more to assent to a worsening of their situation than they would be willing to pay to improve their situation. The difference arises from such factors as being accustomed to and psychologically attached to that which one believes one enjoys by right. But this creates a circularity problem for any attempt to use cost–benefit analysis to determine *whether* to assign to, say, the homeowner the right to an unobstructed mountain view. For willingness to pay will be different depending on whether the right is assigned initially or not. The value judgment about whether to assign the right must, thus, be made first. (In order to set an upper bound on the value of the benefit one might hypothetically assign the right to the person and determine how much he would need to be paid to give it up.)

Third, the efforts of economists to impute willingness to pay invariably involve bundled goods exchanged in *private* transactions. Those who use figures garnered from such analysis to provide guidance for *public* decisions assume no difference between how people value certain things in private individual transactions and how they would wish those same things to be valued in public collective decisions. In making such assumptions, economists insidiously slip into their analysis an important and controversial value judgment, growing naturally out of the highly individualistic microeconomic tradition—namely, the view that there should be no difference between private behavior and the behavior we display in public social life. An alternative view—one that enjoys, I would suggest, wide resonance among citizens—would be that public, social decisions provide an opportunity to give certain things a higher valuation than we choose, for one reason or another, to give them in our private activities.

Thus, opponents of stricter regulation of health risks often argue that we show by our daily risk-taking behavior that we do not value life infinitely, and therefore our public decisions should not reflect the high value of life that proponents of strict regulation propose. However, an alternative view is equally plausible. Precisely because we fail, for whatever reasons, to give life-saving the value in everyday personal decisions that we in some general terms believe we should give it, we may wish our social decisions to provide us the occasion to display the reverence for life that we espouse but do not always show. By this view, people do not have fixed unambiguous "preferences" to which they give expression through private activities and which therefore should be given expression in public decisions. Rather, they may have what they themselves regard as "higher" and "lower" preferences. The latter may come to the fore in private decisions, but people may want the former to come to the fore in public decisions. They may sometimes display racial prejudice, but support antidiscrimination laws. They may buy a certain product after seeing a seductive ad, but be skeptical enough of advertising to want the government to keep a close eye on it. In such cases, the use of private behavior to impute the values that should be entered for public decisions, as is done by using willingness to pay in private transactions, commits grievous offense against a view of the behavior of the citizen that is deeply engrained in our democratic tradition. It is a view that denudes politics of any independent role in society, reducing it to a mechanistic, mimicking recalculation based on private behavior.

Finally, one may oppose the effort to place prices on a non-market thing and hence in effect incorporate it into the market system out of a fear that the very act of doing so will reduce the thing's perceived value. To place a price on the benefit may, in other words, reduce the value of that benefit. Cost–benefit analysis thus may be like the thermometer that, when placed in a liquid to be measured, itself changes the liquid's temperature.

Examples of the perceived cheapening of a thing's value by the very act of buying and selling it abound in everyday life and language. The disgust that accompanies the idea of buying and selling human beings is based on the sense that this would dramatically diminish human worth. Epithets such as "he prostituted himself," applied as linguistic analogies to people who have sold something, reflect the view that certain things should not be sold because doing so diminishes their value. Praise that is bought is worth little, even to the person buying it. A true anecdote is told of an economist who retired to another university community and complained that he was having difficulty making friends. The laconic response of a critical colleague—"If you want a friend why don't you buy yourself one"—illustrates in a pithy way the intuition that, for some things, the very act of placing a price on them reduces their perceived value.

The first reason that pricing something decreases its perceived value is that, in many circumstances, non-market exchange is associated with the production of certain values not associated with market exchange. These may include spontaneity and various other feelings that come from personal relationships. If a good becomes less associated with the production of positively valued feelings because of market exchange, the perceived value of the good declines to the extent that those feelings are valued. This can be seen clearly in instances where a thing may be transferred both by market and by non-market mechanisms. The willingness to pay for sex bought from a prostitute is less than the perceived value of the sex consummating love. (Imagine the reaction if a practitioner of cost–benefit analysis computed the benefits of sex based on the price of prostitute services.)

Furthermore, if one values in a general sense the existence of a non-market sector because of its connection with the production of certain valued feelings, then one ascribes added value to any non-marketed good simply as a repository of values represented by the non-market sector one wishes to preserve. This seems certainly to be the case for things in nature, such as pristine streams or undisturbed forests: for many people who value them, part of their value comes from their position as repositories of values the non-market sector represents.

The second way in which placing a market price on a thing decreases its perceived value is by removing the possibility of proclaiming that the thing is "not for sale," since things on the market by definition are for sale. The very statement that something is not for sale affirms, enhances, and protects a thing's value in a number of ways. To begin with, the statement is a way of showing that a thing is valued for its own sake, whereas selling a thing for money demonstrates that it was valued only instrumentally. Furthermore, to say that something cannot be transferred in that way places it in the exceptional category—which requires the person interested in obtaining that thing to be able to offer something else that is exceptional, rather than allowing him the easier alternative of obtaining the thing for money that could have been obtained in an infinity of ways. This enhances its value. If I am willing to say "You're a really kind person" to whoever pays me to do so, my praise loses the value that attaches to it from being exchangeable only for an act of kindness.

In addition, if we have already decided we value something highly, one way of stamping it with a cachet affirming its high value is to announce that it is "not for sale." Such an announcement does more, however, than just reflect a preexisting high valuation. It signals a thing's distinctive value to others and helps us persuade them to value the thing more highly than they otherwise might. It also expresses our resolution to safeguard that distinctive value. To state that something is not for sale is thus also a source of value for that thing, since if a thing's value is easy to affirm or protect, it will be worth more than an otherwise similar thing without such attributes.

If we proclaim that something is not for sale, we make a once-and-for-all judgment of its special value. When something is priced, the issue of its perceived value is constantly coming up, as a standing invitation to reconsider that original judgment. Were people constantly faced with questions such as "how much money could get you to give up your freedom of speech?" or "how much would you sell your vote for if you could?", the perceived value of the freedom to speak or the right to vote would soon become devastated as, in moments of weakness, people started saying "maybe it's not worth *so much* after all." Better not to be faced with the constant questioning in the first place. Something similar did in fact occur when the slogan "better red than dead" was launched by some pacifists during the Cold War. Critics pointed out that the very posing of this stark choice—in effect, "would you *really* be willing to give up your life in exchange for not living under communism?"—reduced the value people attached to freedom and thus diminished resistance to attacks on freedom.

Finally, of some things valued very highly it is stated that they are "priceless" or that they have "infinite value." Such expressions are reserved for a subset of things not for sale, such as life or health. Economists tend to scoff at talk of pricelessness. For them, saying that something is priceless is to state a willingness to trade off an infinite quantity of all other goods for one unit of the priceless good, a situation that empirically appears highly unlikely. For most people, however, the word "priceless" is pregnant with meaning. Its value-affirming and value-protecting functions cannot be bestowed on expressions that merely denote a determinate,

albeit high, valuation. John Kennedy in his inaugural address proclaimed that the nation was ready to "pay any price [and] bear any burden . . . to assure the survival and the success of liberty." Had he said instead that we were willing to "pay a high price" or "bear a large burden" for liberty, the statement would have rung hollow.

III

An objection that advocates of cost–benefit analysis might well make to the preceding argument should be considered. I noted earlier that, in cases where various non-utility-based duties or rights conflict with the maximization of utility, it is necessary to make a deliberative judgment about what act is finally right. I also argued earlier that the search for commensurability might not always be a desirable one, that the attempt to go beyond expressing benefits in terms of (say) lives saved and costs in terms of dollars is not something devoutly to be wished.

In situations involving things that are not expressed in a common measure, advocates of cost–benefit analysis argue that people making judgments "in effect" perform cost–benefit calculations anyway. If government regulators promulgate a regulation that saves 100 lives at a cost of $1 billion, they are "in effect" valuing a life at (a minimum of) $10 million, whether or not they say that they are willing to place a dollar value on a human life. Since, in this view, cost–benefit analysis "in effect" is inevitable, it might as well be made specific.

This argument misconstrues the real difference in the reasoning processes involved. In cost–benefit analysis, equivalencies are established *in advance* as one of the raw materials for the calculation. One determines costs and benefits, one determines equivalencies (to be able to put various costs and benefits into a common measure), and then one sets to totting things up—waiting, as it were, with bated breath for the results of the calculation to come out. The outcome is determined by the arithmetic; if the outcome is a close call or if one is not good at long division, one does not know how it will turn out until the calculation is finished. In the kind of deliberative judgment that is performed without a common measure, no establishment of equivalencies occurs in advance. Equivalencies are not aids to the decision process. In fact, the decision-maker might not even be aware of what the "in effect" equivalencies were, at least before they are revealed to him afterwards by someone pointing out what he had "in effect" done. The decision-maker would see himself as simply having made a deliberative judgment; the "in effect" equivalency number did not play a causal role in the decision but at most merely reflects it. Given this, the argument against making the process explicit is the one discussed earlier in the discussion of problems with putting specific values on things that are not normally quantified—that the very act of doing so may serve to reduce the value of those things.

My own judgment is that modest efforts to assess levels of benefits and costs are justified, although I do not believe that government agencies ought to sponsor efforts to put dollar prices on non-market things. I also do not believe that the cry for more cost–benefit analysis in regulation is, on the whole, justified. If regulatory officials were so insensitive about regulatory costs that they did not provide acceptable raw material for deliberative judgments (even if not of a strictly cost–benefit nature), my conclusion might be different. But a good deal of research into costs and benefits already occurs—actually, far more in the U.S. regulatory process than in that of any other industrial society. The danger now would seem to come more from the other side.

Note

1. The Regulatory Analysis Review Group (RARG) was created by President Carter to improve the cost–benefit analysis of regulatory policy. It was subsequently disbanded by President Reagan. (editors' note)

43. Cost–Benefit Analysis Defended

Herman B. Leonard and Richard J. Zeckhauser

Cost–benefit analysis, particularly as applied to public decisions involving risks to life and health, has not been notably popular. A number of setbacks—Three Mile Island is perhaps the most memorable—have called into question the reliability of analytic approaches to risk issues. We believe that the current low reputation of cost–benefit analysis is unjustified, and that a close examination of the objections most frequently raised against the method will show that it deserves wider public support.

Society does not and indeed could not require the explicit consent of every affected individual in order to implement public decisions that impose costs or risks. The transaction costs of assembling unanimous consent would be prohibitive, leading to paralysis in the status quo. Moreover, any system that required unanimous consent would create incentives for individuals to misrepresent their beliefs so as to secure compensation or to prevent the imposition of relatively small costs on them even if the benefits to others might be great.

If actual individual consent is an impractically strong standard to require of centralized decisions, how should such decisions be made? Our test for a proposed public decision is whether the net benefits of the action are positive. The same criterion is frequently phrased: Will those favored by the decision gain enough that they would have a net benefit even if they fully compensated those hurt by the decision? Applying this criterion to all possible actions, we discover that the chosen alternative should be the one for which benefits most exceed costs. We believe that the benefit–cost criterion is a useful way of defining "hypothetical consent" for centralized decisions affecting individuals with widely divergent interests: hypothetically, if compensation could be paid, all would agree to the decision offering the highest net benefits. We turn now to objections commonly raised against this approach.

Compensation and Hypothetical Consent

An immediate problem with the pure cost–benefit criterion is that it does not require the actual payment of compensation to those on whom a given

The newsletter, *QQ: Report from the Center for Philosophy and Public Policy* at the University of Maryland at College Park, Maryland, Vol. 3, No. 3 (Summer 1983), pp. 6–9. Reprinted by permission.

decision imposes net costs. Our standard for public decision-making does not require that losers be compensated, but only that they *could* be if a perfect system of transfers existed. But unless those harmed by a decision are *actually* compensated, they will get little solace from the fact that someone is reaping a surplus in which they could have shared.

To this we make two replies. First, it is typically infeasible to design a compensation system that ensures that all individuals will be net winners. The transactions costs involved in such a system would often be so high as to make the project as a whole a net loss. But it may not even be desirable to construct full compensation systems, since losers will generally have an incentive under such systems to overstate their anticipated losses in order to secure greater compensation.

Second, the problem of compensation is probably smaller in practice than in principle. Society tends to compensate large losses where possible or to avoid imposing large losses when adequate compensation is not practical. Moreover, compensation is sometimes overpaid; having made allowances *ex ante* for imposing risks, society still chooses sometimes to pay additional compensation *ex post* to those who actually suffer losses.

Libertarians raise one additional argument about the ethical basis of a system that does not require full compensation to losers. They argue that a public decision process that imposes uncompensated losses constitutes an illegal taking of property by the state and should not be tolerated. This objection, however strongly grounded ethically, would lead to an untenable position for society by unduly constraining public decisions to rest with the status quo.

Attention to Distribution

Two distinct types of distributional issue are relevant in cost–benefit analysis. First, we can be concerned about the losers in a particular decision, whoever they may be. Second, we can be concerned with the transfers between income classes (or other defined groups) engendered by a given project. If costs are imposed differentially on groups that are generally disadvantaged, should the decision criterion include special consideration of their interests? This question is closely intertwined with the issue of compensation, because it is often alleged that the uncompensated costs of projects evaluated by cost–benefit criteria frequently fall on those who are disadvantaged to start with.

These objections have little to do with cost–benefit analysis as a method. We see no reason why any widely agreed upon notion of equity, or weighting of different individuals' interests, cannot in principle be built into the cost–benefit decision framework. It is merely a matter of defining carefully what is meant by a benefit or a cost. If, in society's view, benefits (or costs) to some individuals are more valuable (costly) than those to others, this can be reflected in the construction of the decision criterion.

But although distribution concerns could be systematically included in cost–benefit analyses, it is not always—or even generally—a good idea to do so. Taxes and direct expenditures represent a far more efficient means of effecting redistribution than virtually any other public program; we would strongly prefer to rely on one consistent comprehensive tax and expenditure package for redistribution than on attempts to redistribute within every project.

First, if distributional issues are considered everywhere, they will probably not be adequately, carefully, and correctly treated anywhere. Many critics of cost–benefit analysis believe that project-based distributional analysis would create a net addition to society's total redistributive effort; we suggest that is likely, instead, to be only an inefficient substitution.

Second, treating distributional concerns within each project can only lead to transfers within the group affected by a project, often only a small subset of the community. For example, unisex rating of auto insurance redistributes only among drivers. Cross-subsidization of medical costs affects only those who need medical services. Why should not the larger society share the burden of redistribution?

Third, the view that distributional considerations should be treated project-by-project reflects a presumption that on average they do not balance out—that is, that some groups systematically lose more often than others. If it were found that some groups were severely and systematically disadvantaged by the application of cost–benefit analyses that ignore distributional concerns, we would favor redressing the balance. We do not believe this is generally the case.

Sensitive Social Values

Cost–benefit analysis, it is frequently alleged, does a disservice to society because it cannot treat important social values with appropriate sensitivity. We believe that this view does a disservice to society by unduly constraining the use of a reasonable and helpful method for organizing the debate about public decisions. We are not claiming that every important social value can be represented effectively within the confines of cost–benefit analysis. Some values will never fit in a cost–benefit framework and will have to be treated as "additional considerations" in coming to a final decision. Some, such as the inviolability of human life, may simply be binding constraints that cannot be traded off to obtain other gains. Nor can we carry out a cost–benefit analysis to decide which values should be included and which treated separately—this decision will always have to be made in some other manner.

These considerations do not invalidate cost–benefit analysis, but merely illustrate that more is at stake than just dollar measures of costs and benefits. We would, however, make two observations. First, we must be very careful that only genuinely important and relevant social values be permitted to outweigh the findings of an analysis. Second, social values that frequently stand in the way of important efficiency gains have a way of breaking down and being replaced over time, so that in the long run society manages to accommodate itself to some form of cost–benefit criterion. If nuclear power were 1000 times more dangerous for its employees but 10 times less expensive than it is, we might feel that ethical considerations were respected and the national interest well served if we had rotating cadres of nuclear power employees serving short terms in high-risk positions, much as members of the armed services do. In like fashion, we have fire-fighters risk their lives; universal sprinkler systems would be less dangerous, but more costly. Such policies reflect an accommodation to the costs as a recognition of the benefits.

Measurability

Another objection frequently raised against cost–benefit analysis is that some costs and benefits tend to be ignored because they are much more difficult to measure than others. The long-term environmental impacts of large projects are frequently cited as an example. Cost–benefit analysis is charged with being systematically biased toward consideration of the quantifiable aspects of decisions.

This is unquestionably true: cost–benefit analysis is *designed* as a method of quantification, so it surely is better able to deal with more quantifiable aspects of the issues it confronts. But this limi-

tation is in itself ethically neutral unless it can be shown that the quantifiable considerations systematically push decisions in a particular direction. Its detractors must show that the errors of cost–benefit analysis are systematically unjust or inefficient— for example, that it frequently helps the rich at the expense of the poor, or despoils the environment to the benefit of industry, or vice versa. We have not seen any carefully researched evidence to support such assertions.

We take some comfort in the fact that cost–benefit analysis is sometimes accused of being biased toward development projects and sometimes of being biased against them. Cost–benefit analyses have foiled conservation efforts in national forests— perhaps they systematically weight the future too little. But they have also squelched clearly silly projects designed to bring "economic development" to Alaska—and the developers argued that the analysis gave insufficient weight to the "unquantifiable" value of future industrialization.

In our experience, cost–benefit analysis is often a tool of the "outs"—those not currently in control of the political process. Those who have the political power to back the projects they support often have little need of analyses. By contrast, analysis can be an effective tool for those who are otherwise not strongly empowered politically.

Analyzing Risks

Even those who accept the ethical propriety of cost–benefit analysis of decisions involving transfers of money or other tangible economic costs and benefits sometimes feel that the principles do not extend to analyzing decisions involving the imposition of risks. We believe that such applications constitute a *particularly* important area in which cost–benefit analysis can be of value. The very difficulties of reaching appropriate decisions where risks are involved make it all the more vital to employ the soundest methods available, both ethically and practically.

Historically, cost–benefit analysis has been applied widely to the imposition and regulation of risks, in particular to risks of health loss or bodily harm. The cost–benefit approach is particularly valuable here, for several reasons. Few health risks can be exchanged on a voluntary basis. Their magnitude is difficult to measure. Even if they could be accurately measured, individuals have difficulty interpreting probabilities or gauging how they would feel should the harm eventuate.

Compounding these problems of valuation are difficulties in contract, since risks are rarely conveyed singly between one individual and another.

The problem of risks conveyed in the absence of contractual approval has been addressed for centuries through the law of torts, which is designed to provide compensation after a harm has been received. If only a low-probability risk is involved, it is often efficient to wait to see whether a harm occurs, for in the overwhelming majority of circumstances transactions costs will be avoided. This approach also limits debate over the magnitude of a potential harm that has not yet eventuated. The creator of the risk has the incentive to gauge accurately, for he is the one who must pay if harm does occur.

While in principle it provides efficient results, the torts approach encounters at least four difficulties when applied to many of the risks that are encountered in a modern technological society. The option of declaring bankruptcy allows the responsible party to avoid paying and so to impose risks that it should not impose. Causality is often difficult to assign for misfortunes that may have alternative or multiple (and synergistically related) causes. Did the individual contract lung cancer from air pollution or from his own smoking, or both? Furthermore, the traditional torts requirement that individuals be made whole cannot be met in many instances (death, loss of a limb). Finally, paying compensation after the fact may also produce inappropriate incentives, and hence

be inefficient. Workers who can be more or less careful around dangerous machinery, for example, are likely to be more careful if they will not be compensated for losing an appendage.

Our normal market and legal system tends to break down when substantial health risks are imposed on a relatively large population. These are, therefore, precisely the situations in which the cost–benefit approach is and should be called into play. Cost–benefit analysis is typically used in just those situations where our normal risk decision processes run into difficulty. We should therefore not expect it to lead to outcomes that are as satisfactory as those that evolve when ordinary market and private contractual trade are employed. But we should be able to expect better outcomes than we would achieve by muddling through unsystematically.

We have defended cost–benefit analysis as the most practical of ethically defensible methods and the most ethical of practically usable methods for conducting public decision-making. It cannot substitute for—nor can it adequately encompass, analyze, or consider—the sensitive application of social values. Thus it cannot be made the final arbiter of public decisions. But it does add a useful structure to public debate, and it does enable us to quantify some of the quantifiable aspects of public decisions. Our defense parallels Winston Churchill's argument for democracy: it is not perfect, but it is better than the alternatives.

44. SIDELIGHT: Cost–Benefit Analysis: Tool for All Seasons? _____

Although the White House taping system installed by former president Richard Nixon was dismantled in July 1973 after its existence became publicly known, most offices in the White House still have their own tape machines used for a variety of purposes. Quite by accident in March 1980, one of these machines was left on "Record" and picked up a conversation that was recently transcribed. A reliable source forwarded a copy of that transcript to Alan B. Morrison, director of the Public Citizen Litigation Group in Washington, D.C., who has provided *Legal Times* with the following account.

To get his mind off his work, a tired Zbigniew Brzezinski strolled into the office of Charles Schultze, chairman of President Carter's Council of Economic Advisors. Schultze was out, but one of his deputies, Gary Greene Eyeshades was there. Brzezinski flopped down and began to talk.

"This Iranian situation is driving me crazy. No one's in charge. They tell you one thing one day, another the next, and a third the day after. The Revolutionary Council contradicts Ghotbzadeh, Bani-Sadr is countered by the students, and no one knows what Khomeini is thinking. How did we ever get into this mess?"

"The problem," responded Eyeshades, "is that your analysis at the beginning was faulty. Everyone was talking about politics, foreign relations, national defense, and oil. Those considerations are marginal. What you needed was a good cost–benefit analysis."

"What does that have to do with anything," snapped the national security advisor. "You economists think you have the answers to everything. This is diplomacy, power politics. It doesn't have anything to do with a cost–benefit analysis. If those things are useful at all, they only work for a few special kinds of problems."

"Not so," rejoined Eyeshades, sensing that he had Brzezinski's attention. "Defense has been using these since MacNamara's days to decide on weapons systems. Business uses them to buy new equipment, and we have been urging EPA to use them on toxic substances, DOT on highway safety, and HEW on regs to make life easier for the handicapped. The principle is well established; it would just have to be modified a little here."

Now Brzezinski's interest was perked. "OK, Mr. Economist. Let's see how you would have gone about it last November."

"It's really rather simple," said Eyeshades, taking out his yellow pad, drawing a line down the middle, and labeling one side "costs" and the other "benefits." "What we do is assign dollar figures to each variable and then see where the arithmetic leaves us. In this case, the only benefit we really want is to get back the hostages, putting us back to where we started. What we do here is compare the costs associated with each option and then pick the least expensive.

"The first option was to try a raid like the Israelis did at Entebbe, or Ford with the Mayaguez. I've been talking to people at DOD, and they say they could do it with 250 troops, four airplanes, some bombs, etc. In short, not a big operation. Now assuming the worst case and we lose all 250 men plus the hostages, what has it cost us?"

"Wait a minute, you can't do that. Those are American lives."

"Why not, we do it all the time. Seat belts and air bags save 10,000 lives a year, but we decided that question largely on cost. Coal mine accidents kill thousands a year, and we decided how much safety we can afford. Even controls on air pollution or cancerous chemicals in the workplace are determined by cost–benefit analyses. Why should this be any different?"

"How do you decide how to value human life?" queried Brzezinski.

"That's a cinch. Lawyers have figured a way in wrongful death cases. It's based primarily on earnings and life expectancy. And besides, in most cases, there will be no survivors, so there won't be any pain and suffering, which can really run up the cost.

"And another thing, how do you suppose businesses decide whether to take a defective product off the market. They use a cost–benefit analysis."

"What about other costs?" retorted Brzezinski. the ayatollah may throw us out, cut off our oil, deny us defense outposts. What do you say to that?"

"Well, we'll factor them in, too. I don't deny they are somewhat harder to calculate, but it's not impossible. After all, assigning dollars to antidiscrimination policies hasn't stood in the way of applying a cost–benefit analysis there, has it?"

Now Brzezinski was getting a little troubled. "The whole idea makes me nervous, deciding to sacrifice people just because of numbers."

Eyeshades quickly countered with two points. "First, let me say if you find our numbers on the value of Iran as an ally, for example, to be too low, you can simply change them."

"Hold on," interrupted Brzezinski. "How can you change the numbers? I thought this was supposed to be a precise, scientific way to solve the insoluble."

"Why not? We do it all the time. The cost–benefit analysis is only a tool in the hands of the decision-maker, not the answer to his prayers."

"But that's not the way you economists advertise it," replied Brzezinski. "You talk about cost–benefit analyses as though they were the answer to every question every bureaucrat has ever had."

"You don't expect us to downplay our own expertise, do you? Besides, a little puffing never hurt anyone."

"What's your second point?" queried Brzezinski.

"We haven't started figuring out the cost of the other options. You can't make up your mind about policy choices until we add up the costs of the alternatives, like loss of U.S. prestige, added defense cost to make us appear tough, the time the president and the senior staff spend worrying about Iran, all the travel of Secretary Vance, and lots of other things.

"Take my word for it. Cost–benefit analysis takes the agony out of decision-making. Now, you just make yourself comfortable while I get out my calculator. We should have this problem licked in no time. While we're at it, anything else been bothering you?"

"Well," said Brzezinski, "we're having a devil of a time with the manpower levels for the army, navy, and air force for the next five years. . . ."

45. Earth in the Balance Sheet

Robert Repetto

Whatever their shortcomings, the national income accounting systems used by governments to assess macroeconomic performance are undoubtedly one of the 20th century's most significant social inventions. Their political and economic impacts can scarcely be overestimated. However inappropriately, they serve to divide the world into "developed" and "developing" countries. In the developed countries, whenever the quarterly gross domestic product (GDP) figures emerge, policymakers stir. Should the latest figure be lower, even marginally, than those of the preceding three months, a recession is declared, the strategies and competence of the federal administration are impugned, and public political debate ensues. In the developing countries, the rate of growth of GDP is the principal measure of economic progress and transformation.

National income accounts have become so much a part of society that it is hard to remember that they have been in use for only 50 years: They were first published in the United States in 1942. It is no coincidence that, during the last half century, governments have taken responsibility for the growth and stability of their economies and have invested enormous amounts of talent and energy in understanding how economies can be better managed.

The aim of national income accounting is to provide an information framework suitable for analyzing the performance of a country's economic system. The current System of National Accounts promoted by the United Nations is a historical artifact, heavily influenced by the theories of the British economist John Maynard Keynes in the 1930s.[1] The system reflects the economic preoccupations of that time: the business cycle and persistent unemployment in industrial economies. Because raw material prices were at an all-time low in the 1930s, Keynesian economists paid little attention to the possibility of natural resource scarcities. Consequently, even today, the contribution that natural resources make to production and economic welfare is hardly acknowledged in national income accounts. Capital formation is assigned a central role in economic growth theories, but natural resources are not treated like other tangible assets in the System of National Accounts.

The result is a dangerous asymmetry in the way people measure and, hence, the way they think about the value of natural resources (see Figure 1). Manmade assets, such as buildings and equipment, are valued as productive capital and are written off against the value of production as they depreciate. Natural resource assets are not so valued: A country could exhaust its mineral resources, cut down its forests, erode its soils, pollute its aquifers, and hunt its wildlife and fisheries to extinction without affecting its measured national income. It is a bitter irony that the low-income countries most dependent on natural resources for employment, revenues, and foreign exchange earnings are instructed to use a system for national accounting and macroeconomic analysis that almost completely ignores their principal assets.

Environment, Vol. 34, No. 7 (September 1992), 13–18, 43–45. Reprinted with permission of the Helen Dwight Reid Educational Foundation. Published by Heldref Publications, 1319 Eighteenth St., N.W., Washington, DC 20036–1802. Copyright ©1992.

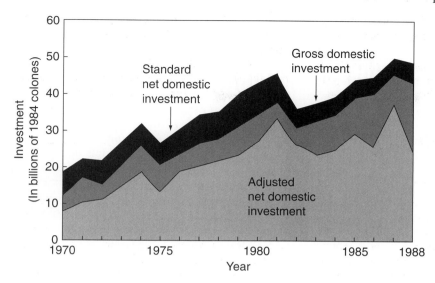

Figure 1 Gross domestic investment and net investment after depreciation of natural and manmade resources.

Shortcomings of the System

The System of National Accounts (SNA) published by the United Nations Statistical Office provides a standard, internationally accepted framework for setting up national income accounts.[2] SNA includes stock accounts that identify assets and liabilities at particular points in time and flow accounts that keep track of transactions during intervals of time. Flow accounts include all transactions of final goods that determine the level of national income, or GDP, including capital formation and depreciation, purchases of goods and services, payments to wage and profit earners, and import payments and export revenues for goods and services. Flows and stocks are linked, in that flows are equal to differences between stocks and stocks are equal to accumulated past flows. With a few specific exceptions, only goods and services exchanged in the market economy are included in national income accounts. This is so because market prices offer a ready way to establish value.

National income accounts have become the basis for almost all macroeconomic analysis, planning, and evaluation. SNA is supposed to be an integrated, comprehensive, and consistent accounting framework; unfortunately, however, it is not. SNA gives inconsistent treatment to the consumption of capital goods and natural resources. The value of capital goods, such as buildings and equipment, declines with use because of physical wear and obsolescence. This gradual decrease in the

future production potential of capital stocks is directly integrated into national flow accounts by a depreciation allowance that amortizes the asset's value over its useful lifetime. (Depreciation is the decline in the present value of a future income flow because of an asset's decay or obsolescence.) Depreciation of tangible, reproducible capital is subtracted from GDP in calculations of net domestic product. This subtraction reflects the fact that a nation must invest enough in new capital goods to offset the depreciation of existing assets if the future income-producing ability of the entire capital stock is to be preserved.

The United Nations recommends that countries create balance sheet accounts that include some natural resources, such as tree plantations, and nonrenewable resources, such as agricultural land and subsoil minerals, along with financial assets and stocks of capital goods.[3] Rather than integrate changes in natural resource stocks directly into national flow accounts, however, the United Nations recommends that stock accounts of natural resources flow through separate "satellite" or "reconciliation" accounts.[4]

Logically, if a country's national balance sheets indicate at two points in time that a natural resource, such as the forest, has been depleted, the flow accounts for the intervening years should show a capital consumption or depreciation allowance. If the forests have expanded, the accounts should show a corresponding amount of capital formation. This change would reflect perhaps the most basic identity[5] in all of accounting—namely, that the difference in stocks between two points of time equals the net flow in the intervening period. SNA violates this basic accounting identity.

Reconciliation accounts, or accounts that reconcile apparent differences or discrepancies in other accounts, are, however, a poor substitute solution. They provide a means of recording changes in the value of net assets between successive measurement dates without having to show any effect on the income of the intervening period.[6] Recording these changes in reconciliation accounts is likely to minimize their consideration in national policy analysis.

Ironically, SNA does classify as gross capital formation those expenses incurred in "improving" land for pastures, developing or extending timber-producing areas, or creating infrastructure for the fishing industry. SNA records such actions as contributing to recorded income and investment even though they sometimes destroy the income-producing potential of natural resources through deforestation, soil erosion, and overfishing. This loss of capital—as natural resources are used beyond their capacity to recover—is not recorded in national income and investment accounts. The national accounts thereby create the illusion of income development when, in fact, national wealth is being destroyed. Thus, economic disaster masquerades as progress.

Several misunderstandings underlie this anomalous treatment of natural resources. First, it is a misconception that natural resources are so abundant that they have no marginal value. Whether or not they enter the marketplace directly, natural resources make important contributions to long-term economic productivity and so, strictly speaking, are economic assets. Another misunderstanding underlies the contention that natural resources are free gifts of nature, so that there are no investment costs to be written off. The value of an asset is not its investment cost but, rather, the capitalized present value of its income potential. Many companies valued by the stock market to be worth many billions of dollars have as their principal assets the brilliant ideas and inventions of their founders. The Polaroid camera, the Apple computer, and the Lotus spreadsheet are good examples. These inspired inventions are worth vastly more than any measurable cost their inventors

incurred in developing them and, as the products of genius, could also be regarded as free gifts of nature.

The UN Statistical Office justifies its treatment of natural resources on the grounds that natural resources are nonmarketed goods and that their economic values cannot be readily established.[7] This notion also is wrong. Indeed, the United Nations itself provides guidelines for valuing natural resource assets in the stock accounts that could be applied just as well to the flow accounts: The assets' market values are to be used if available; if not, the discounted present value of the stream of rents or net revenues from the asset is to be used instead.[8]

The Scope of Natural Resource Accounting

A growing number of experts have recognized the need to correct SNA's environmental blind spots. Several member nations of the Organization for Economic Cooperation and Development, including Canada, France, the Netherlands, Japan, Norway, and the United States, have proposed or established systems of environmental accounts.[9] Although natural resources take priority in the Norwegian and French systems, the U.S. and Japanese systems have focused on pollution and environmental quality. Canada and the Netherlands have combined elements of both approaches.

Norway and France have established extensive resource-accounting systems to supplement their national income accounts. The Norwegian system includes accounts for such material resources as fossil fuels and other minerals, such biotic resources as forests and fisheries, and such environmental resources as land, water, and air.[10] The accounts are compiled in physical units of measurement, such as cubic meters or tons, and are not integrated with the national income accounts. However, resource accounts, especially those for petroleum and gas, have been expressed in monetary terms for use in macroeconomic planning.

The French natural patrimony accounts are intended as a comprehensive statistical framework to provide authorities with the data they need to monitor changes in "that subsystem of the terrestrial ecosphere that can be quantitatively and qualitatively altered by human activity."[11] Like their Norwegian counterparts, these accounts cover nonrenewable resources, the physical environment, and living organisms. Because material and energy flows to and from economic activities form only a subset of these accounts, they are conceptually much broader than the national income accounts.

Compiling such environmental statistics may well encourage decision makers to consider the impacts of specific policies on national stocks of natural resources. Physical accounting by itself has considerable shortcomings, however. For instance, it does not lend itself to useful aggregation: Aggregating wood from various tree species into a single number of cubic meters obscures wide differences in the economic value of different species. Aggregating mineral reserves into a single number of tons obscures vast differences—caused by grade and recovery costs—in the value of deposits. Yet, maintaining separate physical accounts for particular species or deposits yields a mountain of statistics that is not easily summarized or used. A further problem with physical accounting is that such accounts do not enable economic planners to understand the impact of economic policies on natural resources or, thereby, to integrate resource considerations into economic decisions, which presumably is the main point of the exercise. There is, however, no conflict between accounting in physical and economic units because physical accounts are necessary prerequisites to economic accounts. If measurement of economic depreciation is extended to cover natural resources, physical accounts are inevitable by-products.

The limits to monetary valuation of natural resources are set mainly by the remoteness of the resource in question from the market economy. Some resources, such as minerals, enter the marketplace directly. Others, such as groundwater, contribute to market production and can readily be assigned a monetary value even though they are rarely bought or sold. Still others, such as noncommercial wild species, are quite remote from the marketplace in that they do not contribute directly to production and can be assigned a monetary value only through quite roundabout methods involving many questionable assumptions. Although research into the economic value of resources that are remote from the market is to be encouraged, common sense suggests that highly speculative values should not be included in official accounts.

In industrial countries, where pollution and congestion are mounting while economies are becoming less dependent on agriculture, mining, and other forms of primary production, economists have proposed systems of environmental accounting that go well beyond the scope of natural resource accounting. One approach considers how GDP might be modified by the costs and benefits associated with pollution and its abatement.[12] Other economists have proposed general systems to account for the impacts of economic activities on the environment broadly defined to include all land, water, and atmospheric resources.[13]

To see, for example, how industrial countries are affected by the bizarre anomalies in the current SNA, consider how SNA treats toxic wastes. If toxic substances leak from a dump and pollute soils and aquifers, measured income does not fall despite the possibly severe impairment of vital natural resources. If the government spends millions of dollars to clean up the mess, however, measured income rises (other things being equal) because such government expenditures are considered to be purchases of final goods and services. If industry itself undertakes the cleanup, even under a court order, income does not rise because the same expenditures are considered to be intermediate production costs when they are made by enterprises. If the site is not cleaned up and nearby residents suffer increased medical expenses, measured income again rises because household medical expenses are also defined as final consumption expenditures in the national income accounts.

Clearly, environmental factors should be accounted for more completely. One aspect of environmental accounting—natural resource accounting—attempts to inject some environmental realities into national income accounting, but it excludes transitory environmental externalities, such as air pollution. There are good reasons to focus rather narrowly on accounting for renewable natural resources: The principal natural resources, such as land, timber, and minerals, are already listed under SNA as economic assets, although they are not treated like other tangible capital, and their physical and economic values can be readily established. Demonstrating the enormous costs of natural resource degradation to a national economy is an important first step in establishing the need for revamping national policy. It also helps people recognize the need for further developing environmental accounting methodologies.

Developing countries whose economies are dependent on natural resources are becoming particularly interested in developing an accounting framework that accounts for these assets more adequately. Work is already under way in the Philippines, China, India, Brazil, Chile, Colombia, El Salvador, and other developing countries.[14]

A Case Study of Costa Rica

The debate over natural resource accounting is not academic. Performance evaluations of resource-based economies are often seriously distorted by their failure to account for natural resource depreciation. Building on an earlier study of Indonesia,[15] the World Resources Institute in Washington, D.C., and the Tropical Science Center in San José, Costa Rica, recently completed a study that shows that the depletion of natural resources in Costa Rica threatens the country's long-term economic prospects.[16] The results of this study should demonstrate the feasibility of incorporating depreciation of natural resources into national income accounts.

In Costa Rica, as in many other developing countries, natural resources are the most important economic asset. If sustainably managed, they can generate a perpetual stream of diverse and important economic benefits. Forests, fisheries, agriculture, and mines directly contribute 17 percent of the national income, 28 percent of employment, and 55 percent of export earnings.[17] Yet, the SNA recommended by the United Nations not only ignores the importance of these assets but also treats their destruction as an increase in national income instead of as a loss of wealth. This distortion conceals from the public and policymakers alike the gravity of the economy's deteriorating resource base.

That Costa Rica's natural resources have deteriorated seriously is indisputable. But the loss is not reflected in the national accounts. On the contrary, the net revenues from overexploiting forest, soil, fishery, and water resources are treated by the national accounts as factor income, not as capital consumption. Furthermore, the accounting system defines as a capital investment the conversion of land suitable only for forests into cattle pastures even if cattle ruin the soil and the livestock enterprise is neither ecologically nor economically viable.

More than 60 percent of Costa Rica's territory is suitable only for forests.[18] Everywhere, the slopes are too steep, the rainfall is too heavy, or the soils are too poor for more intensive uses. Yet, at most, only 40 percent of the land remains under forest cover.[19] In contrast, cattle pasture has spread over 35 percent of the land, although only 8 percent of it is suitable for this use.[20] This expansion of the livestock frontier is squandering the country's natural resources and is draining its financial resources as well. Banks are losing 17 billion colones (about $382 million) annually in uncollectible loans to the cattle industry.[21]

If this trend continues, Costa Rica's commercial forests will be exhausted within the next five years, and the country will be forced to import forest products.[22] Thousands of jobs will be lost, and a source of valuable fuelwood, as well as nonwood products and wildlife habitat, will disappear.[23] Meanwhile, where forests once stood, tons of soil wash away every year from dry, stripped, overgrazed pastures.

The current national accounting system for Costa Rica is poor because it does not reflect the economic value of lost natural resources (see Figure 1). The system classifies clearing forests for pasture as investment and simply ignores the loss of forest capital. Like the national accounts, society and even forest owners have not recognized that the destruction of a forest today begets a loss of income tomorrow. The results are devastating. Investments in unproductive pasture land are actively promoted by government planners, while the loss of forest capital is shrugged off. If the loss of potential forest income were taken into account, the true net value of conversion would often be negative—a decline in the value of the nation's assets.

The inconsistency is highly misleading. Had the Costa Rican government constructed national balance sheets in 1970 and again in 1989, the calculations would have shown that natural resource assets valued at more than one year's worth of GDP had disappeared during those 20 years.[24] However, in not one of those 20 years did the annual accounts of national income, expenditure, savings, and capital formation reflect that ongoing loss. Instead, the accounts showed only continuing growth in national income and a high rate of capital formation until the economy crashed in the 1980s. The national accounts gave no warning that the basis for continuing growth was being destroyed.

Even after the economic crisis struck, economists labeled it a debt crisis, rather than an environmental crisis. The International Monetary Fund rushed in with programs to stabilize the monetary situation, but nobody spoke of stabilizing the natural resource base.[25] Yet, throughout the previous decade, the depreciation of natural resource assets, as an annual percentage of GDP, dwarfed the balance-of-payments deficit.[26] The difference was that the balance-of-payments deficit and the accumulation of external liabilities was recorded, obvious, and scrutinized, whereas the loss of domestic assets went unrecorded, unnoticed, and uncorrected. . . .

Recommendations

Natural resources are disappearing with increasing speed, but national policymakers are not yet considering the implications for future economic productivity. The situation can be reversed if corrective environmental and economic policies are adopted. This is unlikely to happen unless leaders are provided with information that genuinely reflects the relationship between economic development and the natural environment and shows how the abuse of natural resources impoverishes the country. Costa Rica's wealth lies in its people, its land, its forests, and the surrounding seas. This study shows that the economic "development" programs carried out to date have sacrificed the last three of these resources to the harm of the first.

The idea of sustainable development, which the World Commission on Environment and Development labored to promote, is undermined by SNA. According to the commission's definition, sustainable development meets the current generation's needs without depriving future generations. Thus, current consumption must match current earnings without depleting a country's productive assets for generating future income. The definition of income commonly recognized by economists encompasses the notion of sustainability. In the standard Hicksian definition, income is the maximum consumption possible in the present period that does not reduce future consumption possibilities. This definition encompasses not only current earnings but also changes in asset positions: Capital gains are a source of income, and capital losses are a reduction in income. The depreciation accounts reflect the fact that, unless the capital stock is maintained and replaced, future consumption possibilities will inevitably decline.

Treating the depletion of natural resource capital as current income, as SNA does, is inconsistent with the Hicksian definition of income and incompatible with sustainable development. Moreover, such treatment gives false signals to policymakers that a dichotomy exists between the economy and the environment and thus leads policymakers to destroy the latter in the name of economic development. It also confuses the depletion of valuable assets with the generation of income and thereby helps validate the idea that rapid economic growth can be achieved and sustained by exploiting the natural resource base. The result can be illusory gains in income and permanent losses in wealth.

A number of steps are warranted to integrate natural resource consumption into the national income accounts. First, in Costa Rica and other resource-dependent developing countries, national accounting systems must be changed so that economic policymakers no longer make misguided decisions based on inadequate and distorted information. Past failures to prevent natural resource degradation have already undermined efforts to develop economies and alleviate poverty. This effect still is not fully recognized by policymakers, however, who act as if natural resources were limitless or as if technology could always replace exhausted or degraded resources. Closer dialogue between policymakers and scientists can help dispel this simplistic view of the natural environment. An economic accounting system that reflects the true condition of natural resources would provide an essential tool for the integrated analysis of environmental and economic policies in every sector of government.

Introducing such an accounting system will require that key international economic institutions—such as the World Bank, the other multilateral development banks, the International Monetary Fund, and the Organization for Economic Cooperation and Development—begin to compile, use, and publish revised estimates of net national product and national income. All such institutions should ready themselves to provide technical assistance to the growing number of national statistical offices that wish to adopt these changes and make such estimates for themselves.

Finally, the United Nations should announce that the distortions in the treatment of natural resources will be removed in the ongoing revisions to SNA. This would be a timely and feasible way to ensure that the process begun at the UN Conference on Environment and Development in Rio de Janeiro in June goes forward with all deliberate speed in coming years. No other single action would go further to raise consciousness about the link between economic growth and the wise use of natural resources.

Notes

1. J. M. Keynes, *General Theory of Employment, Interest, and Money* (New York: Harcourt Brace, 1965). See, also, R. Lekachman, *The Age of Keynes* (New York: Random House, 1966).

2. Readers interested in SNA's evolution might consult the following studies: United Nations, Department of Economic and Social Affairs, "A System of National Accounts," Statistical Papers, series F, no. 2, rev. 3 (New York: United Nations, 1968); UN Statistical Office, "Future Directions for Work on the System of National Accounts" (New York: United Nations, 1975); UN Department of Economic and Social Affairs, "Provisional International Guidelines on the National and Sectoral Balance-Sheet and Reconciliation Accounts of the System of National Accounts," Statistical Papers, series M, no. 60 (New York: United Nations, 1977); UN Statistical Office, "Future Directions for Work on the System of National Accounts," (New York: United Nations, 1979); UN Economic and Social Council, Statistical Commission, "Future Directions for Work on the System of National Accounts" (New York: United Nations, 1980).

3. UN Department of Economic and Social Affairs, 1977, note 2 above.

4. Ibid.

5. *Identity* is a term used in economics to mean a relationship that is, by definition, true and is described in mathematical terms.

6. UN Department of Economic and Social Affairs, 1977, note 2 above.

7. UN Statistical Office, 1975, note 2 above.

8. UN Department of Economic and Social Affairs, 1977, note 2 above.

9. For evaluation of these systems, see O. Lone, *Natural Resource Accounting and Budgeting: A Short History of and Some Critical Reflections on the Norwegian Experience 1975–1987* (Paris: Organization for Economic Cooperation and Development, Environmental Directorate, 1987); A. Friend, "Natural Resource Accounting: International Experience" (Paper presented at the Consultative Meeting of the United Nations Environment Programme in Geneva, 23–25 February 1983); and E. Weiller, "The Use of Environmental Accounting for Development Planning" (New York: UNEP, January 1983).

10. For further information, see K. H. Alfsen, T. Bye, and L. Lorentsen, "Natural Resource Accounting and Analysis: The Norwegian Experience 1978–86" (Oslo: Central Bureau of Statistics of Norway, 1987); P. A. Garnasjordet and H. V. Saebo, "A System of Natural Resource Accounts in Norway," in *Information and Natural Resources* (Paris: Organization for Economic Cooperation and Development, 1986); P. Corniere, "Natural Resource Accounts in France: An Example—Inland Water," in *Information and Natural Resources* (Paris: OECD, 1986); Commission Interministerielle des Comptes du Patrimoine Naturel, *Les Comptes du Patrimoine Naturel* (Paris: Institut National de la Statistique et des Études Economiques, 1983); and J. L. Weber, "The French Natural Patrimony Accounts," *Statistical Journal of the United Nations* (ECI 1):419–44.

11. Corniere, note 10 above.

12. O. C. Herfindahl and A. Y. Kneese, "Measuring Social and Economic Change: Benefits and Costs of Environmental Pollution," in M. Moss, ed., *The Measurement of Economic and Social Performance: Studies in Income and Wealth*, no. 38 (New York: National Bureau of Economic Research, 1973); and K.-G. Mäler, "National Accounts and Environmental Resources," *Environmental and Resource Economics* 1, no.1 (1991):1–16.

13. See R. Eisner, "Extended Accounts for National Income and Product," *Journal of Economic Literature* 26, no. 4 (December 1988):1611–84, for an excellent survey of the approaches taken by Herfindahl and Kneese (see note 12 above) and by others in such works as H. E. Daly, "On Sustainable Development and National Accounts," in D. Collard, D. Pearce, and D. Ulph, eds., *Economics and Sustainable Environments: Essays in Honour of Richard Lecomber* (New York: Macmillan, 1986); R. Hueting, *New Scarcity and Economic Growth* (Amsterdam: North-Holland Publishing Company, 1980); R. Hueting, "Economic Aspects of Environmental Accounting" (Paper prepared for the Environmental Accounting Workshop organized by UNEP and hosted by the World Bank in Washington, D.C., 5–8 November 1984); H. M. Peskin and J. Peskin, "The Valuation of

Nonmarket Activities in Income Accounting," *Review of Income and Wealth* 24 (March 1989): 41–70; and H. M. Peskin, "A National Accounting Framework for Environmental Assets," *Journal of Environmental Economics and Management* 2 (1976): 255–62.

14. Information provided at an international workshop on natural resource accounting organized in Vancouver, British Columbia, 5–6 March 1991, by the World Resources Institute.

15. R. Repetto et al., *Wasting Assets: Natural Resources in the National Income Accounts* (Washington, D.C.: World Resources Institute, 1989).

16. R. Repetto et al., *Accounts Overdue: Natural Resource Depreciation in Costa Rica* (Washington, D.C.: World Resources Institute, 1991).

17. Ibid., 2. Values for both income and export earnings are for 1989. Employment values are from 1987.

18. J. A. Tosi, Jr., *Manual para la Determinación de la Capacidad de Uso de las Tierras de Costa Rica* (San José, Costa Rica: Tropical Science Center, 1985).

19. Repetto et al., note 16 above.

20. Suitability in this context implies neither overuse nor underuse of the land, as defined by the land-use capacity system described in Tosi, note 18 above.

21. All economic values that follow are 1984 colones at the exchange rate of 44.53 colones = U.S. $1.00. Banco Central de Costa Rica, *Estadisticas 1950–1985: División Económica* (San José, Costa Rica: BCCR, 1986).

22. Repetto et al., note 16 above.

23. J. F. Rodas, *Diagnostico del Sector Industrial Forestal* (San José, Costa Rica: Editorial Universidad Estato a Distancia,1985).

24. Repetto et al., note 16 above.

25. Ibid.

26. Ibid. The balance of payments deficit is here defined as the "basic" balance on current account, direct investment, and other long-term capital. The depreciation of natural resource assets is quantified as an annual percentage of GDP.

V.C FROM THE COMMONS TO PROPERTY

46. PREVIEW

"I wish you wouldn't squeeze so," said the Dormouse, who was sitting next to her. . . . "I can't help it," said Alice very meekly . . . "I'm growing." "You've no right to grow here," said the Dormouse. "Don't talk nonsense," said Alice. . . . "Yes, but I grow at a reasonable pace," said the Dormouse.

Lewis Carroll

Qu'est-ce que la proprieté?[1]

Proudhon

There are several key questions to be answered about property rights. The importance of these matters derives in large part from the fact that many people or corporations assert that environmental goals, or constraints advocated in the name of environmental goals, unjustifiably infringe their property rights. Whether this is true depends in part on the nature of property rights, what constitutes them, and a series of other philosophical and legal issues. The deeper questions are about how things ought to be and, hence, are more about moral rights than legal rights (recall Christopher Stone's Essay 23 in Section IV.A). Here is a list of some key questions:

1. What does it mean to say that someone, *A*, has a property right in something, *X*? If having a property right in something is having a certain set of rights over something, what are those specific rights?

2. In hard cases, how can we determine whether someone has a property right in something?

3. Related to (2), under what conditions does anything change in status from being unowned to being property? That is, how does something become property?

4. Related to (3), what sorts of things is it morally impermissible to own or have

property rights in? An anthropocentric answer to this question is that all and only humans cannot be owned.

5. In regard to respecting someone's rights, what is permissible or impermissible,[2] how do we appropriately weigh the property right in question? Alternatively, what is owed the right-bearer?

As we noted earlier, the concept of having property in something may be understood to mean having some combination of rights with respect to that thing—for example, a right to use it, a right to exclude others from doing so, a right to transfer what is owned (and the property right), a right to be compensated for its use by others (barring the right-bearer's consent to uncompensated use), and, in some cases, a right to destroy (compare: "consume") the thing in question.

Debates about whether someone owns, or ought to be able to own, something may be muddled by a failure to clarify which moral and/or legal rights may be at stake. The right to destroy something and the right to use it indefinitely may be excluded. Consider the rental of a tuxedo or a car. The legal rights inherent in owning a house do not include the right to use it as a brothel, as a laboratory for the manufacture of illegal drugs, or as a place to perform torturous experiments on children.

Sometimes the words *my* or *mine* express an ownership relation between owners and their property, and at other times express other relations. Compare "my watch," "my country," "my grandfather." Although many countries have recognized legal property rights in human beings, it seems difficult to believe that one could have moral rights of ownership in another human being. Many of us have probably seen a parent out of control and slapping a small child in a supermarket; it seems more than a conceptual confusion for parents to defend themselves with the claim, "but she's *my* child." The extraordinary and self-righteous indignation of such parents

when challenged about their behavior seems to suggest that they literally believe that they have the right to do whatever (destructive) thing they believe is necessary (or at least some very destructive actions). When one speaks of "my thumb," she or he may simply be indicating that a certain thumb bears a special relation (such as is a part of) to him or her or to "her or his body." The individual may also be suggesting that she or he has the right to decide how (and whether) to use it—for example, as a bookmark, to plug a hole in the dike, or in an Aztec recipe. Various moral theories suggest a sharp distinction between owners and what is owned or what may be owned.

To claim that something has moral standing is to suggest that it is not the sort of thing that can be owned in any full-blown sense, including the right to destroy it for any reason.[3] We may want to insist that among things possessing moral standing, there are further important distinctions to be made; we may conclude that it is all right to impose a risk of death on certain creatures but not on others—for example, lab mice as opposed to chimpanzees or gorillas. That is, we may hold that certain rights can be held over some creatures with moral standing, but these matters require some principled criteria that may not be easy to articulate. For example, it seems reasonable to believe that the property rights one could have over what is owned cannot include the prerogative to do anything with or to that entity that would violate one's basic duties to it, duties that may be correlative to the rights possessed by that entity. All this seems truistic, but perhaps a useful truism reminds us that the question of what can be owned, or what sort of ownership rights exist, is a function of the entity's moral standing (or, further, what rights it possesses or what duties it is owed).[4] Our laws reflect only a limited deviation from anthropocentrism here. They have not granted moral standing to all humans, and they usually do not grant any standing to nonhumans. We should recall once more that sometimes property in women or in "non-Caucasians" has been allowed; one strand of the Hebrew and Christian scriptures permits certain forms of slavery but says that slaves are not to be mistreated.[5] For example, Exodus 21:2 states, "When you buy a Hebrew slave, he shall serve six years, and in the seventh he shall go free, for nothing." Laws against cruelty to animals are a clear recognition of, shall we say, moral limits on the scope of actions compatible with humans having property rights in the animals in question.

In his famous "The Tragedy of the Commons" (Essay 47) Garrett Hardin maintains that a great deal of environmental harm has occurred because much that is valuable in the natural world has been held in common. In such cases there often are few effective restraints, or no restraints, on usage of what is held in common. Unrestrained access to the commons often leads to "exploitation" or "overuse" because individuals have little or no incentive to withdraw benefits (consume, destroy, and so on) and pass on costs to others.

A dramatic case in point, one that appears to confirm Hardin's view, concerns cod fishing off the North American coast. In 1980 Massachusetts fishermen pulled in 99 million pounds of cod; in 1994 the catch was down to 27 million pounds. This kind of story is happening all over the world. One report maintains that the fishing industry is spending $124 billion a year to catch $70 billion worth of fish; the difference is, revealingly, made up by government subsidies. All this is relevant to whether the world will be able to feed itself twenty-five years hence.[6]

Thus, one might conclude that the way to conserve or preserve nature's goods, or perhaps to use them in a more equitable and sustainable way, is to privatize them. Questions arise at different levels. One that is usually ignored: Is it permissible to grant property rights in ecosystems, or in which entities may be thought to have moral standing? Once

again, are we speaking of the sort of "property" that is thought to include a right to destroy? Is there any way of distributing private rights to such goods so that as much and as good is left for others? How adjudicate competing claims to shares of what may be divided? Indeed is there any effective and fair way of distributing property rights over all the many different sorts of commons that may be at issue (oceans, air, views, outer space, and so on)? What about shares for future generations?

A key feature of the existence of individual property rights is that the owner usually has a cluster of rights, namely the right to use, exclude others from using, to transfer that which is owned.[7] This cluster allows the right to control what is owned. Control can limit or regulate access and prevent overuse.[8] The frequent advantage of limiting access is the avoidance of overuse, Hardin's "tragedy of the commons." There are two important questions to ask. First, to what extent can we have effective limitation on usage without the institution of individual property rights? That is, can we have the apparent regulatory or rationing benefit of property rights without having that institution? Second, we should ask: Are there serious disadvantages to that institution (Karl Marx as well as the early Christians certainly thought so [see the Christian scripture: Acts 2:44–45], but one need not be a Marxist, or a Christian, to think so) that we might avoid by some other practice?

The study of other cultures is revealing, and George Monbiot in his Essay 49 reprinted here, "The Tragedy of Enclosure," examines the historically successful regulation of the use of acacia trees by the Turkana people in Kenya (their goats eat the pods of the acacia). There is a great contrast between something such as the oceans and the acacia trees because in the latter case, there is "ownership" of a sort; however, it is not of the "individual property rights" sort. Monbiot's essay urges that there are lessons to be learned concerning the difference between the totally unregulated oceans and regulated areas or items, and lessons concerning what happens when governments attempt to privatize *seeming* commons such as the acacia trees. The consequences have a bearing on our willingness to trust in privatization as a solution to, or prophylactic against overuse problems, and the question of whether the so-called invisible hand of the market will be benign. He suggests, in the final analysis, that we should recognize the tragedy of the disappearance of the commons. The reader can investigate the compatibility of Hardin's views and those of Monbiot, as well as the implications for policy formation.

The proper assessment of Hardin's privatization proposal (or at least some coercive scheme of constraints on usage) also depends on certain judgments we make about what counts, or may count, as property, what rights are included in property, and what arguments may be made in favor of adopting that or some alternative scheme of things. It is worth observing that defenders of one institution for exchanging already existing property rights, the marketplace, in fact presuppose certain answers to the above questions. In this respect the market is parasitic on some other more basic institution (a system for recognizing the creation of property rights) and answers to more basic questions of an evaluative nature.

With a useful working definition of the concept of property, one may ask how anything becomes property (morally, not legally) in the first place (question 3)? That is, how does anything come to be something over which some individuals come initially to have some set of property rights? John Locke (1632–1704) held the view (expressed in an excerpt that follows—Essay 49) that one may make something unowned his or her property by mixing his or her labor with it (a view that influenced Karl Marx's argument about capitalists' stealing value from the workers). So, in Locke's example, if one tills land unused by others and grows crops, the fruit of one's labor belongs by right to that person. Locke also added another condition (often called "the Lockean proviso"): One must "leave as much and as good for others." What counts as "as much and as good" we leave an open question; recall the discussion of sustainability in Part V. Intuitively, Locke has plausibly insisted on a *fairness condition*; one cannot just take as much as one wants. It is worth considering the reasonableness of the "fairness rider," and especially its implications for questions about what we owe future generations. If we owe them as much capital or environmental stock as has been available to us, it would seem to follow that we have serious duties not to destroy access to clean air, not to kill lakes, not to create a mass of toxic wastes (in short, not to diminish the quality and quantity of the sources and sinks that have benefited us), and so on.

In view of important contemporary disputes about the permissibility of "taking" someone's property without consent (for example, Do certain limitations on the use of property that diminish its market value to the owner constitute an unjustifiable taking of someone's property? Sometimes or always?), we comment here on some much-discussed and employed distinctions in contemporary moral philosophy. An "absolute" right may be defined as one that it is always wrong to infringe or override—that is, depriving the right-holder of that to which he or she has a right. If there are such rights, it would be wrong to infringe them—ever. But, in brief, it is not obvious that any right is absolute. It does not follow, however, that there is no presumption against infringing rights even if no right is absolute (reflect, for example, on a presumed right to life or right not be tortured). Nonabsolute rights are sometimes called presumptive, but, to emphasize a point, a presumptive right may be one that deserves great moral weight and may be the compelling factor in deciding what ought to be done. So, it is important to decide whether someone has a relevant right of some sort and precisely what the *content* of that right is. Still, if a right is not absolute, then infringing it may be all right. Or it may not. If it is, then the bearer of that right may be owed some compensation for the loss resulting from an infringement.

The excerpt from Essay 50 by Kristin Shrader-Frechette examines the implications of taking Locke's labor-mixing theory seriously. One worry concerns the number of property rights claims that can be sustained by appeal to it; for example, there are claims to portions of the oceans, the air, and large portions of the land where no serious claim can be made that anyone mixed her or his labor with them. And far from improving their value, claimants have often lessened it; for example, Italy and Greece are said to dump over 90 percent of their wastes into the Mediterranean. Many more infringements on property rights may deserve rectification than is often admitted by those who take a Lockean view. For example, "acid rain" is a violation of a wide range of property rights; it causes losses of $5 billion a year to the timber industry in Germany alone.[9] And if many Native American peoples mixed their labor appropriately with the land, then there is something amiss in speaking of America as a place of justice for all. Historically, then, what is now *de facto* property has been acquired by various means: via one's labor, getting there first, usurpation (involving force or fraud), and so on.

In recent years a number of economists have pressed for an economic approach to the analysis of legal questions. They have argued that the ways in which governmental decisions reduce the value of private property must include not only cases in which property owners are literally stripped of their property (as in the case of eminent domain) but also cases in which their property is subjected to regulatory restrictions that may reduce its economic value. A governmental restraint may be placed on the use of property in the name of promoting some public, and perhaps environmental, good—for example, the preservation of a wetland by not allowing it to be drained for purposes of erecting a condominium development. The imposition of such duties on property owners has been condemned by some on both moral and legal grounds. The legal issue concerns whether such regulation constitutes a violation of the Fifth Amendment of the U.S. Constitution, which provides that "private property [shall not] be taken for public use, without just compensation." An important practical question is whether governments must pay large amounts of compensation to landowners when they "take" property to pursue public, possibly environmental, goods. Mark Sagoff, in "Takings, Just Compensation, and the Environment" (Essay 51), defends the view that compensation need not attend regulation unless it also burdens individuals *unfairly;* hence, questions about "takings" involve not just matters of property rights but also questions of social justice more broadly conceived.

Garrett Hardin pointed out some of the drawbacks of *not* having property rights in certain goods. We have tried to indicate some of the drawbacks of having such systems, or at least the systems that we often encounter. A major question is whether we can find a system that protects the autonomy of right-bearers (such as property holders) as well as such other values as respect for what has intrinsic value, sustainability, the preservation of biodiversity, and fairness to current and future generations. There is no short *and* intelligent answer to this or other questions we have noted. A good deal of intellectual work has been done on many of these matters, and the curious reader may wish to investigate them further.[10]

NOTES

1. Translation: "What is property?"
2. For "permissible act" one may read "an act one has no duty not to do," and for "impermissible" one may read "an act one has a duty not to do."

3. In regard to attitudes toward what is legally own-able and the question of what has moral standing, we cannot resist repeating a story told by philoso-pher J. Baird Callicott. Callicott managed to disturb the dean of a Canadian university's college of agri-culture by making remarks critical of industrial approaches to agriculture. The dean replied that he and his fellow "animal scientists" did not consider factory farm animals to be Cartesian automata, but rather "production units." Enough said. See J. Baird Callicott, "La Nature est morte, vive la nature!" in the *Hastings Center Report* 22(5), 21.

4. In our view, if an entity is owed duties directly or is a possessor of moral rights, then it has moral stand-ing, but an entity may have moral standing without being a possessor of moral rights.

5. See Willie Lee Rose, "On the Killing of Nath," in *A Documentary History of Slavery in North America,* edited by Willie Lee Rose (New York: Oxford University Press, 1976), pp. 213–219. On the mixed views of the churches in the nineteenth century in the United States, see William Goodell, *Slavery and Anti-Slavery* (New York: Negro Universities Press, 1968).

6. See "Global Pool of Fish Is Shrinking, Now What?" *The News & Observer* (Raleigh, NC (December 1, 1996), p. 26A.

7. It is worth noting that the notion of rights is not universal, and it appears to have arisen in the late Middle Ages, or the Renaissance period. Of course the notion of a duty to respect others precedes it, and is arguably universal. We do not suggest that the notion of rights is an item that is inessential to the most defensible moral outlook.

8. Individual control can also lead to destruction, but because that may be the fulfillment of the owner's want, that result counts as an increase in utility in standard economic theory (*note:* Utility just is iden-tified with want fulfillment or an increase in "con-sumer satisfaction"—or "welfare" in that way of thinking).

9. Paul Elkins, *Green Economics* (New York: Doubleday, 1992), p.15.

10. We mention a few sources: Judith Thomson, *The Realm of Rights* (Cambridge, MA: Harvard University Press, 1990); Lawrence Becker, *Property Rights: Philosophic Foundations* (London: Routledge and Kegan Paul, 1977); Jeremy Waldron, *The Right to Private Property:* Richard Epstein, *Takings: Private Property and the Power of Eminent Domain* (Cambridge, MA: Harvard University Press, 1985); Ellen Frankel Paul, *Property Rights and Eminent Domain* (New Brunswick, NJ: Transaction Books, 1987).

47. The Tragedy of the Commons

Garrett Hardin

At the end of a thoughtful article on the future of nuclear war, Wiesner and York[1] concluded that: "Both sides in the arms race are . . . confronted by the dilemma of steadily increasing military power and steadily decreasing national security. *It is our considered professional judgment that this dilemma has no technical solution.* If the great powers continue to look for solutions in the area of science and tech-nology only, the result will be to worsen the situa-tion."

I would like to focus your attention not on the subject of the article (national security in a nuclear world) but on the kind of conclusion they reached, namely that there is no technical solution to the problem. An implicit and almost universal assump-tion of discussions published in professional and semipopular scientific journals is that the problem under discussion has a technical solution. A techni-cal solution may be defined as one that requires a change only in the techniques of the natural sci-ences, demanding little or nothing in the way of change in human values or ideas of morality.

In our day (though not in earlier times) technical solutions are always welcome. Because of previous failures in prophecy, it takes courage to assert that a desired technical solution is not possible. Wiesner

The author is professor of biology, University of California, Santa Barbara. This article is based on a presidential address presented before the meeting of the Pacific Division of the American Association for the Advancement of Science at Utah State University, Logan, 25 June 1968.
Science, Vol. 162, No. 3858 (December 1968), 1243–48. Copyright 1968 by the American Association for the Advancement of Science. Reprinted by permission.

and York exhibited this courage; publishing in a science journal, they insisted that the solution to the problem was not to be found in the natural sciences. They cautiously qualified their statement with the phrase, "It is our considered professional judgment. . . ." Whether they were right or not is not the concern of the present article. Rather, the concern here is with the important concept of a class of human problems which can be called "no technical solution problems," and, more specifically, with the identification and discussion of one of these.

It is easy to show that the class is not a null class. Recall the game of tick-tack-toe. Consider the problem, "How can I win the game of tick-tack-toe?" It is well known that I cannot, if I assume (in keeping with the conventions of game theory) that my opponent understands the game perfectly. Put another way, there is no "technical solution" to the problem. I can win only by giving a radical meaning to the word "win." I can hit my opponent over the head; or I can drug him; or I can falsify the records. Every way in which I "win" involves, in some sense, an abandonment of the game, as we intuitively understand it. (I can also, of course, openly abandon the game—refuse to play it. This is what most adults do.)

The class of "no technical solution problems" has members. My thesis is that the "population problem," as conventionally conceived, is a member of this class. How it is conventionally conceived needs some comment. It is fair to say that most people who anguish over the population problem are trying to find a way to avoid the evils of overpopulation without relinquishing any of the privileges they now enjoy. They think that farming the seas or developing new strains of wheat will solve the problem—technologically. I try to show here that the solution they seek cannot be found. The population problem cannot be solved in a technical way, any more than can the problem of winning the game of tick-tack-toe.

What Shall We Maximize?

Population, as Malthus said, naturally tends to grow "geometrically," or, as we would now say, exponentially. In a finite world this means that the per capita share of the world's goods must steadily decrease. Is ours a finite world?

A fair defense can be put forward for the view that the world is infinite; or that we do not know

that it is not. But, in terms of the practical problems that we must face in the next few generations with the foreseeable technology, it is clear that we will greatly increase human misery if we do not, during the immediate future, assume that the world available to the terrestrial human population is finite. "Space" is no escape.[2]

A finite world can support only a finite population; therefore, population growth must eventually equal zero. (The case of perpetual wide fluctuations above and below zero is a trivial variant that need not be discussed.) When this condition is met, what will be the situation of mankind? Specifically, can Bentham's goal of "the greatest good for the greatest number" be realized?

No—for two reasons, each sufficient by itself. The first is a theoretical one. It is not mathematically possible to maximize for two (or more) variables at the same time. This was clearly stated by von Neumann and Morgenstern,[3] but the principle is implicit in the theory of partial differential equations, dating back at least to D'Alembert (1717–1783).

The second reason springs directly from biological facts. To live, any organism must have a source of energy (for example, food). This energy is utilized for two purposes: mere maintenance and work. For man, maintenance of life requires about 1600 kilocalories a day ("maintenance calories"). Anything that he does over and above merely staying alive will be defined as work, and is supported by "work calories" which he takes in. Work calories are used not only for what we call work in common speech; they are also required for all forms of enjoyment, from swimming and automobile racing to playing music and writing poetry. If our goal is to maximize population it is obvious what we must do: We must make the work calories per person approach as close to zero as possible. No gourmet meals, no vacations, no sports, no music, no literature, no art. . . . I think that everyone will grant, without argument or proof, that maximizing population does not maximize goods. Bentham's goal is impossible.

In reaching this conclusion, I have made the usual assumption that it is the acquisition of energy that is the problem. The appearance of atomic energy has led some to question this assumption. However, given an infinite source of energy, population growth still produces an inescapable problem. The problem of the acquisition of energy is replaced by the problem of its dissipation, as J. H. Fremlin has so wittily shown.[4] The arithmetic signs in the analysis are, as it were, reversed; but Bentham's goal is still unobtainable.

The optimum population is, then, less than the maximum. The difficulty of defining the optimum is enormous; so far as I know, no one has seriously tackled this problem. Reaching an acceptable and stable solution will surely require more than one generation of hard analytical work—and much persuasion.

We want the maximum good per person; but what is good? To one person it is wilderness, to another it is ski lodges for thousands. To one it is estuaries to nourish ducks for hunters to shoot; to another it is factory land. Comparing one good with another is, we usually say, impossible because goods are incommensurable. Incommensurables cannot be compared.

Theoretically this may be true; but in real life incommensurables *are* commensurable. Only a criterion of judgment and a system of weighting are needed. In nature the criterion is survival. Is it better for a species to be small and hideable, or large and powerful? Natural selection commensurates the incommensurables. The compromise achieved depends on a natural weighting of the values of the variables.

Man must imitate this process. There is no doubt that in fact he already does, but unconsciously. It is when the hidden decisions are made explicit that the arguments begin. The problem for the years ahead is to work out an acceptable theory of weighting. Synergistic effects, nonlinear variation, and difficulties in discounting the future make the intellectual problem difficult, but not (in principle) insoluble.

Has any cultural group solved this practical problem at the present time, even on an intuitive level? One simple fact proves that none has: there is no prosperous population in the world today that has, and has had for some time, a growth rate of zero. Any people that has intuitively identified its optimum point will soon reach it, after which its growth rate becomes and remains zero.

Of course, a positive growth rate might be taken as evidence that a population is below its optimum. However, by any reasonable standards, the most rapidly growing populations on earth today are (in general) the most miserable. This association (which need not be invariable) casts doubt on the optimistic assumption that the positive growth rate of a population is evidence that it has yet to reach its optimum.

We can make little progress in working toward optimum population size until we explicitly exorcize the spirit of Adam Smith in the field of practical demography. In economic affairs, the *Wealth of Nations* (1776) popularized the "invisible hand," the idea that an individual who "intends only his own gain," is, as it were, "led by an invisible hand to promote . . . the public interest."[5] Adam Smith did not assert that this was invariably true, and perhaps neither did any of his followers. But he contributed to a dominant tendency of thought that has ever since interfered with positive action based on rational analysis, namely, the tendency to assume that decisions reached individually will, in fact, be the best decisions for an entire society. If this assumption is correct, it justifies the continuance of our present policy of laissez-faire in reproduction. If it is correct, we can assume that men will control their individual fecundity so as to produce the optimum population. If the assumption is not correct, we need to reexamine our individual freedoms to see which ones are defensible.

Tragedy of Freedom in a Commons

The rebuttal to the invisible hand in population control is to be found in a scenario first sketched in a little-known pamphlet[6] in 1833 by a mathematical amateur named William Forster Lloyd (1794–1852). We may well call it "the tragedy of the commons," using the word "tragedy" as the philosopher Whitehead used it[7]: "The essence of dramatic tragedy is not unhappiness. It resides in the solemnity of the remorseless working of things." He then goes on to say, "This inevitableness of destiny can only be illustrated in terms of human life by incidents which in fact involve unhappiness. For it is only by them that the futility of escape can be made evident in the drama."

The tragedy of the commons develops in this way. Picture a pasture open to all. It is to be expected that each herdsman will try to keep as many cattle as possible on the commons. Such an arrangement may work reasonably satisfactorily for centuries because tribal wars, poaching, and disease keep the numbers of both man and beast well below the carrying capacity of the land. Finally, however, comes the day of reckoning, that is, the day when the long-desired goal of social stability becomes a reality. At this point, the inherent logic of the commons remorselessly generates tragedy.

As a rational being, each herdsman seeks to maximize his gain. Explicitly or implicitly, more or less consciously, he asks, "What is the utility *to me* of adding one more animal to my herd?" This utility has one negative and one positive component.

1. The positive component is a function of the increment of one animal. Since the herdsman receives all the proceeds from the sale of the additional animal, the positive utility is nearly +1.

2. The negative component is a function of the additional overgrazing created by one more animal. Since, however, the effects of overgrazing are shared by all the herdsmen, the negative utility for any particular decision-making herdsman is only a fraction of –1.

Adding together the component partial utilities, the rational herdsman concludes that the only sensible course for him to pursue is to add another animal to his herd. And another; and another. . . . But this is the conclusion reached by each and every rational herdsman sharing a commons. Therein is the tragedy. Each man is locked into a system that compels him to increase his herd without limit—in a world that is limited. Ruin is the destination toward which all men rush, each pursuing his own best interest in a society that believes in the freedom of the commons. Freedom in a commons brings ruin to all.

Some would say that this is a platitude. Would that it were! In a sense, it was learned thousands of years ago, but natural selection favors the forces of psychological denial.[8] The individual benefits as an individual from his ability to deny the truth even though society as a whole, of which he is a part, suffers.

Education can counteract the natural tendency to do the wrong thing, but the inexorable succession of generations requires that the basis for this knowledge be constantly refreshed.

A simple incident that occurred a few years ago in Leominster, Massachusetts, shows how per-

ishable the knowledge is. During the Christmas shopping season the parking meters downtown were covered with plastic bags that bore tags reading: "Do not open until after Christmas. Free parking courtesy of the mayor and city council." In other words, facing the prospect of an increased demand for already scarce space, the city fathers reinstituted the system of the commons. (Cynically, we suspect that they gained more votes than they lost by this retrogressive act.)

In an approximate way, the logic of the commons has been understood for a long time, perhaps since the discovery of agriculture or the invention of private property in real estate. But it is understood mostly only in special cases which are not sufficiently generalized. Even at this late date, cattlemen leasing national land on the western ranges demonstrate no more than an ambivalent understanding, in constantly pressuring federal authorities to increase the head count to the point where overgrazing produces erosion and weed-dominance. Likewise, the oceans of the world continue to suffer from the survival of the philosophy of the commons. Maritime nations still respond automatically to the shibboleth of the "freedom of the seas." Professing to believe in the "inexhaustible resources of the oceans," they bring species after species of fish and whales closer to extinction.[9]

The National Parks present another instance of the working out of the tragedy of the commons. At present they are open to all, without limit. The parks themselves are limited in extent—there is only one Yosemite Valley—whereas population seems to grow without limit. The values that visitors seek in the parks are steadily eroded. Plainly, we must soon cease to treat the parks as commons or they will be of no value to anyone.

What shall we do? We have several options. We might sell them off as private property. We might keep them as public property, but allocate the right to enter them. The allocation might be on the basis of wealth, by the use of an auction system. It might be on the basis of merit, as defined by some agreed upon standards. It might be by lottery. Or it might be on a first-come, first-served basis, administered to long queues. These, I think, are all the reasonable possibilities. They are all objectionable. But we must choose—or acquiesce in the destruction of the commons that we call our National Parks.

Pollution

In a reverse way, the tragedy of the commons reappears in problems of pollution. Here it is not a question of taking something out of the commons, but of putting something in—sewage, or chemical, radioactive, and heat wastes into water; noxious and dangerous fumes into the air; and distracting and unpleasant advertising signs into the line of sight. The calculations of utility are much the same as before. The rational man finds that his share of the cost of the wastes he discharges into the commons is less than the cost of purifying his wastes before releasing them. Since this is true for everyone, we are locked into a system of "fouling our own nest," so long as we behave only as independent, rational, free-enterprisers.

The tragedy of the commons as a food basket is averted by private property, or something formally like it. But the air and waters surrounding us cannot readily be fenced, and so the tragedy of the commons as a cesspool must be prevented by different means, by coercive laws or taxing devices that make it cheaper for the polluter to treat his pollutants than to discharge them untreated. We have not progressed as far with the solution of this problem as we have with the first. Indeed, our particular concept of private property, which deters us from exhausting the positive resources of the earth, favors pollution. The owner of a factory on the bank of a stream—whose property extends to the middle of the stream—often has difficulty seeing why it is not his natural right to muddy the waters flowing past his door. The law, always behind the times, requires elaborate stitching and fitting to adapt it to this newly perceived aspect of the commons.

The pollution problem is a consequence of population. It did not much matter how a lonely American frontiersman disposed of his waste. "Flowing water purifies itself every 10 miles," my grandfather used to say, and the myth was near enough to the truth when he was a boy, for there were not too many people. But as population became denser, the natural chemical and biological recycling processes became overloaded, calling for a redefinition of property rights.

How to Legislate Temperance?

Analysis of the pollution problem as a function of population density uncovers a not generally recognized principle of morality, namely: *the morality of an act is a function of the state of the system at the time it is performed.*[10] Using the commons as a cesspool does not harm the general public under frontier conditions, because there is no public; the same behavior in a metropolis is unbearable. A hundred and fifty years ago a plainsman could kill an American bison, cut out only the tongue for his dinner, and discard the rest of the animal. He was not in any important sense being wasteful. Today, with only a few thousand bison left, we would be appalled at such behavior.

In passing, it is worth noting that the morality of an act cannot be determined from a photograph. One does not know whether a man killing an elephant or setting fire to the grassland is harming others until one knows the total system in which his act appears. "One picture is worth a thousand words," said an ancient Chinese; but it may take 10,000 words to validate it. It is as tempting to ecologists as it is to reformers in general to try to persuade others by way of the photographic shortcut. But the essence of an argument cannot be photographed: it must be presented rationally—in words.

That morality is system-sensitive escaped the attention of most codifiers of ethics in the past. "Thou shalt not . . ." is the form of traditional ethical directives which make no allowance for particular circumstances. The laws of our society follow the pattern of ancient ethics, and therefore are poorly suited to governing a complex, crowded, changeable world. Our epicyclic solution is to augment statutory law with administrative law. Since it is practically impossible to spell out all the conditions under which it is safe to burn trash in the back yard or to run an automobile without smog-control, by law we delegate the details to bureaus. The result is administrative law, which is rightly feared for an ancient reason—*Quis custodiet ipsos custodes?*—"Who shall watch the watchers themselves?" John Adams said that we must have "a government of laws and not men." Bureau administrators, trying to evaluate the morality of acts in the total system, are singularly liable to corruption, producing a government by men, not laws.

Prohibition is easy to legislate (though not necessarily to enforce); but how do we legislate temperance? Experience indicates that it can be accomplished best through the mediation of administrative law. We limit possibilities unnecessarily if we suppose that the sentiment of *Quis custodiet* denies us the use of administrative law. We should rather retain the phrase as a perpetual reminder of fearful dangers we cannot avoid. The great challenge facing us now is to invent the corrective feedbacks that are needed to keep custodians honest. We must find ways to legitimate the needed authority of both the custodians and the corrective feedbacks.

Freedom to Breed Is Intolerable

The tragedy of the commons is involved in population problems in another way. In a world governed solely by the principle of "dog eat dog"— if indeed there ever was such a world—how many children a family had would not be a matter of public concern. Parents who bred too exuberantly would leave fewer descendants, not more, because they would be unable to care adequately for their children. David Lack and others have found that such a negative feedback demonstrably controls the fecundity of birds.[11] But men are not birds, and have not acted like them for millenniums, at least.

If each human family were dependent only on its own resources; *if* the children of improvident parents starved to death; *if*, thus, overbreeding brought its own "punishment" to the germ line— *then* there would be no public interest in controlling the breeding of families. But our society is deeply committed to the welfare state,[12] and, hence, is confronted with another aspect of the tragedy of the commons.

In a welfare state, how shall we deal with the family, the religion, the race, or the class (or indeed any distinguishable and cohesive group) that adopts overbreeding as a policy to secure its own aggrandizement?[13] To couple the concept of freedom to breed with the belief that everyone born has an equal right to the commons is to lock the world into a tragic course of action.

Unfortunately this is just the course of action that is being pursued by the United Nations. In late 1967, some 30 nations agreed to the following:

> The Universal Declaration of Human Rights describes the family as the natural and fundamental unit of society. It follows that any choice and decision with regard to the size of the family must irrevocably rest with the family itself, and cannot be made by anyone else.[14]

It is painful to have to deny categorically the validity of this right; denying it, one feels as uncomfortable as a resident of Salem, Massachusetts, who denied the reality of witches in the 17th century. At the present time, in liberal quarters, something like a taboo acts to inhibit criticism of the United Nations. There is a feeling that the United Nations is "our last and best hope," that we shouldn't find fault with it; we shouldn't play into the hands of the archconservatives. However, let us not forget what Robert Louis Stevenson said: "The truth that is suppressed by friends is the readiest weapon of the enemy." If we love the truth we must openly deny the validity of the Universal Declaration of Human Rights, even though it is promoted by the United Nations. We should also join with Kingsley Davis[15] in attempting to get Planned Parenthood-World Population to see the error of its ways in embracing the same tragic ideal.

Conscience Is Self-Eliminating

It is a mistake to think that we can control the breeding of mankind in the long run by an appeal to conscience. Charles Galton Darwin made this point when he spoke on the centennial of the publication of his grandfather's great book. The argument is straightforward and Darwinian.

People vary. Confronted with appeals to limit breeding, some people will undoubtedly respond to the plea more than others. Those who have more children will produce a larger fraction of the next generation than those with more susceptible consciences. The difference will be accentuated, generation by generation.

In C. G. Darwin's words: "It may well be that it would take hundreds of generations for the progenitive instinct to develop in this way, but if it should do so, nature would have taken her revenge, and the variety *Homo contracipiens* would become extinct and would be replaced by the variety *Homo progenitivus*."[16]

The argument assumes that conscience or the desire for children (no matter which) is hereditary—but hereditary only in the most general formal sense. The result will be the same whether the attitude is transmitted through germ cells, or exosomatically, to use A. J. Lotka's term. (If one denies the latter possibility as well as the former, then what's the point of education?) The argument has here been stated in the context of the population problem, but it applies equally well to any instance in which society appeals to an individual exploiting a commons to restrain himself for the general good—by means of his conscience. To make such an appeal is to set up a selective system that works toward the elimination of conscience from the race.

Pathogenic Effects of Conscience

The long-term disadvantage of an appeal to conscience should be enough to condemn it; but [it] has serious short-term disadvantages as well. If we ask a man who is exploiting a commons to desist "in the name of conscience," what are we saying to him? What does he hear?—not only at the moment but also in the wee small hours of the night when, half asleep, he remembers not merely the words we used but also the nonverbal communication cues we gave him unawares? Sooner or later, consciously or subconsciously, he senses that he has received two communications, and that they are contradictory: (i) (intended communication) "If you don't do as we ask, we will openly condemn you for not acting like a responsible citizen"; (ii) (the unintended communication) "If you do behave as we ask, we will secretly condemn you for a simpleton who can be shamed into standing aside while the rest of us exploit the commons."

Everyman then is caught in what Bateson has called a "double bind." Bateson and his co-workers have made a plausible case for viewing the double bind as an important causative factor in the genesis of schizophrenia.[17] The double bind may not always be so damaging, but it always endangers the mental health of anyone to whom it is applied. "A bad conscience," said Nietzsche, "is a kind of illness."

To conjure up a conscience in others is tempting to anyone who wishes to extend his control beyond the legal limits. Leaders at the highest level succumb to this temptation. Has any President during the past generation failed to call on labor unions to moderate voluntarily their demands for higher wages, or to steel companies to honor voluntary guidelines on prices? I can recall none. The rhetoric used on such occasions is designed to produce feelings of guilt in noncooperators.

For centuries it was assumed without proof that guilt was a valuable, perhaps even an indispensable, ingredient of the civilized life. Now, in this post-Freudian world, we doubt it.

Paul Goodman speaks from the modern point of view when he says: "No good has ever come

from feeling guilty, neither intelligence, policy, nor compassion. The guilty do not pay attention to the object but only to themselves, and not even to their own interests, which might make sense, but to their anxieties."[18]

One does not have to be a professional psychiatrist to see the consequences of anxiety. We in the Western world are just emerging from a dreadful two-centuries-long Dark Ages of Eros that was sustained partly by prohibition laws, but perhaps more effectively by the anxiety-generating mechanisms of education. Alex Comfort has told the story well in *The Anxiety Makers*[19]; it is not a pretty one.

Since proof is difficult, we may even concede that the results of anxiety may sometimes, from certain points of view, be desirable. The larger question we should ask is whether, as a matter of policy, we should ever encourage the use of a technique the tendency (if not the intention) of which is psychologically pathogenic. We hear much talk these days of responsible parenthood; the coupled words are incorporated into the titles of some organizations devoted to birth control. Some people have proposed massive propaganda campaigns to instill responsibility into the nation's (or the world's) breeders. But what is the meaning of the word *responsibility* in this context? Is it not merely a synonym for the word conscience? When we use the word responsibility in the absence of substantial sanctions, are we not trying to browbeat a free man in a commons into acting against his own interest? Responsibility is a verbal counterfeit for a substantial *quid pro quo*. It is an attempt to get something for nothing.

If the word *responsibility* is to be used at all, I suggest that it be in the sense Charles Frankel uses it.[20] "Responsibility," says this philosopher, "is the product of definite social arrangements." Notice that Frankel calls for social arrangements—not propaganda.

Mutual Coercion Mutually Agreed Upon

The social arrangements that produce responsibility are arrangements that create coercion, of some sort. Consider bank-robbing. The man who takes money from a bank acts as if the bank were a commons. How do we prevent such action? Certainly not by trying to control his behavior solely by a verbal appeal to his sense of responsibility. Rather than rely on propaganda, we follow Frankel's lead and insist that a bank is not a commons; we seek the definite social arrangements that will keep it from becoming a commons. That we thereby infringe on the freedom of would-be robbers we neither deny nor regret.

The morality of bank-robbing is particularly easy to understand because we accept complete prohibition of this activity. We are willing to say, "Thou shalt not rob banks," without providing for exceptions. But temperance also can be created by coercion. Taxing is a good coercive device. To keep downtown shoppers temperate in their use of parking space, we introduce parking meters for short periods, and traffic fines for longer ones. We need not actually forbid a citizen to park as long as he wants to; we need merely make it increasingly expensive for him to do so. Not prohibition, but carefully biased options are what we offer him. A Madison Avenue man might call this persuasion; I prefer the greater candor of the word coercion.

Coercion is a dirty word to most liberals now, but it need not forever be so. As with the four-letter words, its dirtiness can be cleansed away by exposure to the light, by saying it over and over without apology or embarrassment. To many, the word coercion implies arbitrary decisions of distant and irresponsible bureaucrats; but this is not a necessary part of its meaning. The only kind of coercion I recommend is mutual coercion, mutually agreed upon by the majority of the people affected.

To say that we mutually agree to coercion is not to say that we are required to enjoy it, or even to pretend we enjoy it. Who enjoys taxes? We all grumble about them. But we accept compulsory taxes because we recognize that voluntary taxes would favor the conscienceless. We institute and (grumblingly) support taxes and other coercive devices to escape the horror of the commons.

An alternative to the commons need not be perfectly just to be preferable. With real estate and other material goods, the alternative we have chosen is the institution of private property coupled with legal inheritance. Is this system perfectly just? As a genetically trained biologist I deny that it is. It seems to me that, if there are to be differences in individual inheritance, legal possession should be perfectly correlated with biological inheritance—that those who are biologically more fit to be the custodians of property and power should legally inherit more. But genetic recombination continually makes a mockery of the doctrine of "like father, like son" implicit in our laws of legal inheritance. An idiot can inherit millions, and a trust fund can keep his estate intact.

We must admit that our legal system of private property plus inheritance is unjust—but we put up with it because we are not convinced, at the moment, that anyone has invented a better system. The alternative of the commons is too horrifying to contemplate. Injustice is preferable to total ruin.

It is one of the peculiarities of the warfare between reform and the status quo that it is thoughtlessly governed by a double standard. Whenever a reform measure is proposed it is often defeated when its opponents triumphantly discover a flaw in it. As Kingsley Davis has pointed out,[21] worshippers of the status quo sometimes imply that no reform is possible without unanimous agreement, an implication contrary to historical fact. As nearly as I can make out, automatic rejection of proposed reforms is based on one of two unconscious assumptions: (i) that the status quo is perfect; or (ii) that the choice we face is between reform and no action; if the proposed reform is imperfect, we presumably should take no action at all, while we wait for a perfect proposal.

But we can never do nothing. That which we have done for thousands of years is also action. It also produces evils. Once we are aware that the status quo is action, we can then compare its discoverable advantages and disadvantages with the predicted advantages and disadvantages of the proposed reform, discounting as best we can for our lack of experience. On the basis of such a comparison, we can make a rational decision which will not involve the unworkable assumption that only perfect systems are tolerable.

Recognition of Necessity

Perhaps the simplest summary of this analysis of man's population problems is this: the commons, if justifiable at all, is justifiable only under conditions of low population density. As the human population has increased, the commons has had to be abandoned in one aspect after another.

First we abandoned the commons in food gathering, enclosing farm land and restricting pastures and hunting and fishing areas. These restrictions are still not complete throughout the world.

Somewhat later we saw that the commons as a place for waste disposal would also have to be abandoned. Restrictions on the disposal of domestic sewage are widely accepted in the Western world; we are still struggling to close the commons to pollution by automobiles, factories, insecticide sprayers, fertilizing operations, and atomic energy installations.

In a still more embryonic state is our recognition of the evils of the commons in matters of pleasure. There is almost no restriction on the propagation of sound waves in the public medium. The shopping public is assaulted with mindless music, without its consent. Our government is paying out billions of dollars to create a supersonic transport which will disturb 50,000 people for every one person who is whisked from coast to coast three hours faster. Advertisers muddy the airwaves of radio and television and pollute the view of travelers. We are a long way from outlawing the commons in matters of pleasure. Is this because our Puritan inheritance makes us view pleasure as something of a sin, and pain (that is, the pollution of advertising) as the sign of virtue?

Every new enclosure of the commons involves the infringement of somebody's personal liberty. Infringements made in the distant past are accepted because no contemporary complains of a loss. It is the newly proposed infringements that we vigorously oppose; cries of "rights" and "freedom" fill the air. But what does "freedom" mean? When men mutually agreed to pass laws against robbing, mankind became more free, not less so. Individuals locked into the logic of the commons are free only to bring on universal ruin; once they see the necessity of mutual coercion, they become free to pursue other goals. I believe it was Hegel who said, "Freedom is the recognition of necessity."

The most important aspect of necessity that we must now recognize is the necessity of abandoning the commons in breeding. No technical solution can rescue us from the misery of overpopulation. Freedom to breed will bring ruin to all. At the moment, to avoid hard decisions many of us are tempted to propagandize for conscience and responsible parenthood. The temptation must be resisted, because an appeal to independently acting consciences selects for the disappearance of all conscience in the long run, and an increase in anxiety in the short.

The only way we can preserve and nurture other and more precious freedoms is by relinquishing the freedom to breed, and that very soon. "Freedom is the recognition of necessity"—and it is the role of education to reveal to all the necessity of abandoning the freedom to breed. Only so, can we put an end to this aspect of the tragedy of the commons.

References

1. J. B. Wiesner and H. F. York, *Sci. Amer.* 211 (No. 4), 27 (1964).

2. G. Hardin, *J. Hered.* 50, 68 (1959); S. von Hoernor, *Science* 137, 18 (1962).

3. J. von Neumann and O. Morgenstern, *Theory of Games and Economic Behavior* (Princeton Univ. Press, Princeton, N.J., 1947), p. 11.

4. J. H. Fremlin, *New Sci.*, No. 415 (1964), p. 285.

5. A. Smith, the *Wealth of Nations* (Modern Library, New York, 1937), p. 423.

6. W. F. Lloyd, *Two Lectures on the Checks to Population* (Oxford Univ. Press, Oxford, England, 1833), reprinted (in part) in *Population, Evolution, and Birth Control*, G. Hardin, Ed. (Freeman, San Francisco, 1964), p. 37.

7. A. N. Whitehead, *Science and The Modern World* (Mentor, New York, 1948), p. 17.

8. G. Hardin, Ed. *Population, Evolution, and Birth Control* (Freeman, San Francisco, 1964), p. 56.

9. S. McVay, *Sci. Amer.* 216 (No. 8), 13 (1966).

10. J. Fletcher, *Situation Ethics* (Westminster, Philadelphia, 1966).

11. D. Lack, *The Natural Regulation of Animal Numbers* (Clarendon Press, Oxford, 1954).

12. H. Girvetz, *From Wealth to Welfare* (Stanford Univ. Press, Stanford, Calif., 1950).

13. G. Hardin, *Perspec. Biol. Med.* 6, 366 (1963).

14. U Thant, *Int. Planned Parenthood News*, No. 168 (February 1968), p. 3.

15. K. Davis, *Science* 158, 730 (1967).

16. S. Tax, Ed., *Evolution after Darwin* (Univ. of Chicago Press, Chicago, 1960), vol. 2, p. 469.

17. G. Bateson, D. D. Jackson, J. Haley, J. Weakland, *Behav. Sci.* 1, 251 (1956).

18. P. Goodman, *New York Rev. Books* 10(8), 22 (23 May 1968).

19. A. Comfort, *The Anxiety Makers* (Nelson, London, 1967).

20. C. Frankel, *The Case for Modern Man* (Harper, New York, 1955), p. 203.

21. J. D. Roslansky, *Genetics and the Future of Man* (Appleton-Century-Crofts, New York, 1966), p. 177.

48. The Tragedy of Enclosure

George Monbiot

During the dry seasons in the far northwest of Kenya, the people of the Turkwel River keep themselves alive by feeding their goats on the pods of the acacia trees growing on the river's banks. Every clump of trees is controlled by a committee of elders, who decide who should be allowed to use them and for how long.

Anyone coming into the area who wants to feed his goats on the pods has to negotiate with the elders. Depending on the size of the pod crop, they will allow him in or tell him to move on. If anyone tries to browse his animals without negotiating first, he will be driven off with sticks; if he does it repeatedly, he may be killed. The acacia woods are a common: a resource owned by many families. Like all the commons of the Turkana people, they are controlled with fierce determination.

In the 1960s and 1970s the Turkana were battered by a combination of drought and raiding by enemy tribes. Many people came close to starvation, and the Kenyan government, the United Nations Development Program and the U.N.'s Food and Agriculture Organization decided that something had to be done to help them. The authorities knew nothing of how the Turkana regulated access to their commons. What they saw was a succession of unrelated people moving in, taking as much as they wanted, then moving out again. It looked like a free-for-all, and the experts blamed the lack of regulation for the disappearance of the vegetation. This was, in fact, caused not by people but by drought.

The authorities decided that the only way to stop the people from overusing their resources was to settle them down, get rid of most of their animals and encourage them to farm. On the banks of the Turkwel River they started a series of irrigation schemes, where the ex-nomads could own a patch of land and grow grain. People flocked in. With the first drought the irrigation scheme collapsed. The immigrants reverted to the only certain means of keeping themselves alive in the savannas: herding animals. They spread along the banks and into the acacia woods.

Overwhelmed by their numbers, the elders could do nothing to keep the outsiders away from the trees. The pods and surrounding grazing land were swiftly exhausted, and people started to starve. The commons had become a free-for-all. The authorities had achieved exactly what they set out to prevent.

The overriding of commoners' rights has been taking place, often with similarly disastrous consequences, for centuries, all around the world. But in the past two decades it has greatly accelerated. The impetus for much of this change came from a paper published some 25 years ago, whose title has become a catch phrase among developers.

In "The Tragedy of the Commons," the American biologist Garrett Hardin argued that common property will always be destroyed because the gain that individuals make by overexploiting it will outweigh the loss they suffer as a result of its overexploitation. He used the example of a herdsman who keeps his cattle on a common pasture. With every cow the man added to his herds, he would gain more than he lost: he would be one cow richer, and the community as a whole would bear the cost of the extra cow. He suggested that the way to prevent this tragedy was to privatize or nationalize common land.

The paper, published in *Science* in December 1968, had an enormous impact. It neatly encapsulated a prevailing trend of thought and appeared to provide some answers to the growing problem of how to prevent starvation. For authorities such as the World Bank and Western governments, it offered a rational basis for the privatization of land. In Africa, among newly independent governments looking for dramatic change, it encouraged the massive transfer of land from tribal peoples to the state or to individuals.

But Hardin's paper had one critical flaw. He had assumed that individuals can be as selfish as they like in a commons because no one stops them. In reality, traditional commons are closely regulated by the people who live there. Common property has two elements: common and property. A common is the property of a particular community that, like the Turkana of the Turkwel River, decides who is allowed to use it and to what extent.

Hardin's thesis works only where no ownership exists. The oceans, possessed by no one and poorly regulated, are overfished and polluted. Every user tries to get as much out of them as possible, and the cost of their exploitation is borne by the world as a whole. These are not commons but free-for-alls.

The effects of dismantling the commons to prevent Hardin's presumed tragedy can scarcely be overstated. While their impact has been felt by traditional peoples throughout the less developed world, no group has suffered more than those singled out by his paper: the traditional herders of animals, or pastoralists. In Kenya, the Masai have been cajoled into privatizing their commons: in some parts, every family now owns a small ranch. This has undercut the very basis of their survival.

In the varied and changeable savannas, the only way a herder can survive is by moving. The Masai followed the rain across their lands, leaving an area before its resources were exhausted and returning only when it recovered. Now, confined to a single plot, they have no alternative but to graze it until drought or overuse brings the vegetation to an end. When their herd dies, entrepreneurs move in, buy up their lands for a song and either plow them for wheat and barley, exhausting the soil within a few years, or use them as collateral for securing business loans.

Around the world, changes in the ownership of land lie at the heart of our environmental crisis. Traditional rural communities use their commons to supply most of their needs. To keep themselves alive, they have to maintain a diversity of habitats, and within these habitats they need to protect a wide range of species. But when the commons are privatized, they pass into the hands of people who[se] priority is to make money. The most efficient means of making it is to select the most profitable product and concentrate on producing that. As the land is no longer the sole means of survival but an investment that can be exchanged, the new owners can, if necessary, overexploit it and reinvest elsewhere.

The diverse environments protected by the commoners are replaced with uniform fields of grain or livestock. The displaced people move either to the overloaded cities or into new habitats, becoming poorer as they go, threatening the places they move to, sometimes dispossessing other commoners in turn. For human beings, as for the biosphere, the tragedy of the commons is not the tragedy of their existence but the tragedy of their disappearance.

49. The Creation of Property

John Locke

Whether we consider natural reason, which tells us that men being once born have a right to their preservation, and consequently to meat and drink and such other things as nature affords for their subsistence; or revelation, which gives us an account of those grants God made of the world to Adam, and to Noah and his sons, 'tis very clear that God, as King David says, Psalm cxv.16, "has given the earth to the children of men," given it to mankind in common. But this being supposed, it seems to some a very great difficulty how anyone should ever come to have a property in anything. I will not content myself to answer that if it be difficult to make out property upon a supposition that God gave the world to Adam and his posterity in common, it is impossible that any man but one universal monarch should have any property upon a supposition that God gave the world to Adam and his heirs in succession, exclusive of all the rest of his posterity. But I shall endeavor to show how men might come to have a property in several parts of that which God gave to mankind in common, and that without any express compact of all the commoners.

God, who hath given the world to men in common, hath also given them reason to make use of it to the best advantage of life and convenience. The earth and all that is therein is given to men for the support and comfort of their being. And though all

John Locke, from the second of his two *Treatises of Civil Government.*

the fruits it naturally produces, and beasts it feeds, belong to mankind in common, as they are produced by the spontaneous hand of nature; and nobody has originally a private dominion exclusive of the rest of mankind in any of them as they are thus in their natural state; yet being given for the use of men, there must of necessity be a means to appropriate them some way or other before they can be of any use or at all beneficial to any particular man. The fruit or venison which nourishes the wild Indian, who knows no enclosure, and is still a tenant in common, must be his, and so his, i.e., a part of him, that another can no longer have any right to it, before it can do any good for the support of his life.

Though the earth and all inferior creatures be common to all men, yet every man has a property in his own person; this nobody has any right to but himself. The labor of his body and the work of his hands we may say are properly his. Whatsoever, then, he removes out of the state that nature hath provided and left it in, he hath mixed his labor with, and joined it to something that is his own, and thereby makes it his property. It being by him removed from the common state nature placed it in, hath by this labor something annexed to it that excludes the common right of other men. For this labor being the unquestionable property of the laborer, no man but he can have a right to what that is once joined to, at least where there is enough, and as good left in common for others.

He that is nourished by the acorns he picked up under an oak, or the apples he gathered from the trees in the wood, has certainly appropriated them to himself. Nobody can deny but the nourishment is his. I ask, then, When did they begin to be his—when he digested, or when he ate, or when he boiled, or when he brought them home, or when he picked them up? And 'tis plain if the first gathering made them not his, nothing else could. That labor put a distinction between them and common; that added something to them more than nature, the common mother of all, had done, and so they became his private right. And will anyone say he had no right to those acorns or apples he thus appropriated, because he had not the consent of all mankind to make them his? Was it a robbery thus to assume to himself what belonged to all in common? If such a consent as that was necessary, man had starved, notwithstanding the plenty God had given him. We see in commons which remain so by

compact that 'tis the taking any part of what is common and removing it out of the state nature leaves it in, which begins the property; without which the common is of no use. And the taking of this or that part does not depend on the express consent of all the commoners. Thus the grass my horse has bit, the turfs my servant has cut, and the ore I have dug in any place where I have a right to them in common with others, become my property without the assignation or consent of anybody. The labor that was mine removing them out of that common state they were in, hath fixed my property in them.

By making an explicit consent of every commoner necessary to anyone's appropriating to himself any part of what is given in common. Children or servants could not cut the meat which their father or master had provided for them in common without assigning to everyone his peculiar part. Though the water running in the fountain be everyone's, yet who can doubt but that in the pitcher is his only who drew it out? His labor hath taken it out of the hands of Nature where it was common, and belonged equally to all her children, and hath thereby appropriated it to himself.

Thus this law of reason makes the deer that Indian's who hath killed it; it is allowed to be his goods who hath bestowed his labor upon it, though, before, it was the common right of everyone. And amongst those who are counted the civilized part of mankind, who have made and multiplied positive laws to determine property, this original law of nature for the beginning of property, in what was before common, still takes place, and by virtue thereof, what fish anyone catches in the ocean, that great and still remaining common of mankind; or what ambergris anyone takes up here is by the labor that removes it out of that common state nature left it in, made his property who takes that pains about it. And even amongst us, the hare that anyone is hunting is thought his who pursues her during the chase. For being a beast that is still looked upon as common, and no man's private possession, whoever has employed so much labor about any of that kind as to find and pursue her has thereby removed her from the state of nature wherein she was common, and hath began a property.

It will perhaps be objected to this, that if gathering the acorns, or other fruits of the earth, etc., makes a right to them, then anyone may engross as much as he will. To which I answer, Not so. The same law of nature that does by this means give us property, does also bound that property too. "God has given us all things richly" (1 Tim. vi. 17), is the voice of reason confirmed by inspiration. But how far has He given it us? To enjoy. As much as anyone can make use of to any advantage of life before it spoils, so much he may by his labor fix a property in; whatever is beyond this, is more than his share, and belongs to others. Nothing was made by God for man to spoil or destroy. And thus considering the plenty of natural provisions there was a long time in the world, and the few spenders, and to how small a part of that provision the industry of one man could extend itself, and engross it to the prejudice of others—especially keeping within the bounds, set by reason, of what might serve for his use—there could be then little room for quarrels or contentions about property so established.

But the chief matter of property being now not the fruits of the earth, and the beasts that subsist on it, but the earth itself, as that which takes in and carries with it all the rest, I think it is plain that property in that, too, is acquired as the former. As much land as a man tills, plants, improves, cultivates, and can use the product of, so much is his property. He by his labor does as it were enclose it from the common. Nor will it invalidate his right to say, everybody else has an equal title to it; and therefore he cannot appropriate, he cannot enclose, without the consent of all his fellow-commoners, all mankind. God, when He gave the world in common to all mankind, commanded man also to labor, and the penury of his condition required it of him. God and his reason commanded him to subdue the earth, i.e., improve it for the benefit of life, and therein lay out something upon it that was his own, his labor. He that, in obedience to this command of God, subdued, tilled, and sowed any part of it, thereby annexed to it something that was his property, which another had no title to, nor could without injury take from him.

Nor was this appropriation of any parcel of land, by improving it, any prejudice to any other man, since there was still enough and as good left, and more than the yet unprovided could use. So that in effect there was never the less left for others because of his enclosure for himself. For he that leaves as much as another can make use of, does as good as take nothing at all. Nobody could think himself injured by the drinking of another man, though he took a good draught, who had a whole

river of the same water left him to quench his thirst; and the case of land and water, where there is enough of both, is perfectly the same.

God gave the world to men in common; but since He gave it them for their benefit and the greatest conveniences of life they were capable to draw from it, it cannot be supposed He meant that it should always remain common and uncultivated. He gave it to the use of the industrious and rational (and labor was to be his title to it), not to the fancy or covetousness of the quarrelsome and contentious. He that had as good left for his improvement as was already taken up, needed not complain, ought not to meddle with what was already improved by another's labor; if he did, it is plain he desired the benefit of another's pains, which he had no right to, and not the ground which God had given him in common with others to labor on, and whereof there was as good left as that already possessed, and more than he knew what to do with, or his industry could reach to.

It is true, in land that is common in England, or any other country where there is plenty of people under Government, who have money and commerce, no one can enclose or appropriate any part without the consent of all, his fellow-commoners: because this is left common by compact, i.e., by the law of the land, which is not to be violated. And though it be common in respect of some men, it is not so to all mankind: but is the joint property of this country, or this parish. Besides, the remainder, after such enclosure, would not be as good to the rest of the commoners as the whole was, when they could all make use of the whole; whereas in the beginning and first peopling of the great common of the world it was quite otherwise. The law man was under was rather for appropriating. God commanded, and his wants forced him, to labor. That was his property, which could not be taken from him wherever he had fixed it. And hence subduing or cultivating the earth, and having dominion, we see are joined together. The one gave title to the other. So that God, by commanding to subdue, gave authority so far to appropriate. And the condition of human life, which requires labor and materials to work on, necessarily introduces private possessions.

The measure of property nature has well set by the extent of men's labor and the conveniency of life. No man's labor could subdue or appropriate all, nor could his enjoyment consume more than a small part; so that it was impossible for any man, this way, to entrench upon the right of another or acquire to himself a property to the prejudice of his neighbor, who would still have room for as good and as large a possession (after the other had taken out his) as before it was appropriated. Which measure did confine every mans possession to a very modest proportion, and such as might appropriate to himself without injury to anybody in the first ages of the world, when men were more in danger to be lost, by wandering from their company, in the then vast wilderness of the earth than to be straitened for want of room to plant in.

The same measure may be allowed still, without prejudice to anybody, full as the world seems. For, supposing a man or family, in the state they were at first, peopling of the world by the children of Adam or Noah, let him plant in some inland vacant places of America. We shall find that the possessions he could make himself, upon the measures we have given, would not be very large, nor, even to this day, prejudice the rest of mankind or give them reason to complain or think themselves injured by this man's encroachment, though the race of men have now spread themselves to all the corners of the world, and do infinitely exceed the small number was at the beginning. Nay, the extent of ground is of so little value without labor that I have heard it affirmed that in Spain itself a man may be permitted to plough, sow, and reap, without being disturbed, upon land he has no other title to, but only his making use of it. But, on the contrary, the inhabitants think themselves beholden to him who, by his industry on neglected, and consequently waste land, has increased the stock of corn, which they wanted. But be this as it will, which I lay no stress on, this I dare boldly affirm, that the same rule of propriety—viz., that every man should have as much as he could make use of, would hold still in the world, without straitening anybody, since there is land enough in the world to suffice double the inhabitants, had not the invention of money, and the tacit agreement of men to put a value on it, introduced (by consent) larger possessions and a right to them; which, how it has done, I shall by and by show more at large. . . .

50. Property Rights in Natural Resources

Kristin Shrader-Fréchette

Even in terms of classical anthropocentric ethics, our environmental actions are highly questionable. Further, good act-utilitarians, bent on ignoring distributive equity but maximizing the well-being of all persons of all generations, would have to admit that present policies of pollution and resource depletion cannot possibly be justified on the grounds that they optimize the welfare of all persons, especially members of future generations. Similarly, our current views of property rights, allegedly derived from the views of John Locke, are woefully inconsistent with classical criteria for generating and transferring ownership. In fact if we really accepted some of the claims made by Locke, we would see that it is ethically impossible at the present time to accord humans property rights in natural resources such as land or minerals. Why is this so?

Locke had a labor theory of property. He maintained that whatever a person takes out of the state of nature and mixes his labor with, he makes his own property. He held, further, that people have property rights as much as they "can make use of to any advantage of life before it spoils," but that "whatever is beyond this, is more than his share and belongs to others."[1] The one proviso that Locke made is that there be "as much and as good left in common for others."[2] Locke believed that this proviso could easily be fulfilled, since there were vast lands in the world and relatively few inhabitants,[3] and since he held that labor "puts the greatest part of value upon land, without which it would scarcely be worth anything."[4]

Of course, the crucial point in Locke's theory is whether appropriation of property such as land worsens the situation of others.[5] As long as global

The Global Possible: Resources, Development, and the New Century, edited by Robert Repetto (New Haven: Yale University Press, 1985), pp. 115–116. Reprinted by permission of the publisher.

population was small and unexplored lands extensive, there was likely to be "enough and as good left in common for others." But it is doubtful that contemporary theorists are correct if they defend Locke's theory of property rights and argue that his proviso can be met. How can one own and use vast amounts of land, oil, or coal, for example, and yet claim that "as much and as good" is left for others?

The whole point of Locke's reasoning is that the earth is given in common to all people, past, present, and future, and that people deserve to have property rights in what has been created by their labor. To the extent that contemporary theorists fail to recognize that one cannot have property rights in what one's labor does not create and in resources when one's ownership does not leave "as much and as good" for others, then to that degree are their allegedly Lockean justifications of private property in natural resources inconsistent with current patterns of ownership. Hence, even on traditional anthropocentric grounds it is not clear that it is ethical for humans to claim to have Lockean property rights over land, water, air, minerals, and other natural resources[6] when enough and as good will not be left for those to come. But if so, then many of our global problems arise not because our anthropocentric ethics errs but because we do not practice the Lockean ethics we preach. . . .[7]

Notes

1. John Locke, *Second Treatise of Government*, paragraphs 25–31.

2. Ibid., para. 27.

3. Ibid., para. 36.

4. Ibid., para. 43.

5. Robert Nozick, *Anarchy, State, and Utopia* (New York: Basic Books, 1974), pp. 174–76.

6. L. C. Becker, *Property Rights* (London: Routledge and Kegan Paul, 1977), p. 109, presents a similar argument.

7. See John Passmore, *Man's Responsibility for Nature* (New York: Charles Scribner's Sons, 1974), also W. K. Frankena, "Ethics and the Environment," in *Ethics and Problems of the 21st Century*, ed. K. E. Goodpaster and K. M. Sayre (Notre Dame, Ind.: University of Notre Dame Press, 1979), pp. 3–4.

   For Schrader-Fréchette's views, see Kristin Schrader-Fréchette, "Locke and Limits on Land Ownership," *Journal of the History of Ideas*, v. 54, n. 2 (April 1993), 201–219.

51. Takings, Just Compensation, and the Environment

Mark Sagoff

"The power vested in the American courts of justice of pronouncing a statute to be unconstitutional," Alexis de Tocqueville wrote, "forms one of the most powerful barriers that have ever been devised against the tyranny of political assemblies."[1] Judges apply this power to environmental law in many ways, but especially when they review zoning ordinances and statutes that restrict the uses of property.

Everyone who owns property has the duty, of course, to exercise his or her property rights in ways that respect the similar rights of others. In addition to this basic duty, political assemblies have gone far—perhaps too far—in obliging landowners, for example, to maintain the integrity of landmarks and scenic areas,[2] to refrain from filling wetlands,[3] to preserve open space,[4] to restore mined land to its original contours,[5] to maintain habitat for endangered species,[6] to allow public access to waterways and beaches,[7] to leave minerals in place to support surface structures,[8] and so on.[9] Landowners often ask judges to review these statutes on constitutional grounds.[10]

State and local governments, in general, impose these duties on landowners by regulation rather than by exercising eminent domain. States prefer regulation to condemnation so that they do not have to compensate landowners for the substantial losses in market value that often accompany the duties and restrictions statutes place on them. Governments may attempt to dedicate property to public use, then, not by taking property

Upstream/Downstream: Issues in Environmental Ethics, edited by Donald Scherer (Philadelphia: Temple University Press, 1990), pp. 158–79. ©1990 by Temple University Press. Reprinted by permission.

rights through eminent domain, but by regulating those rights away and, therefore, without compensating owners for the market value of those rights.

Courts are then called on to decide whether a statute that imposes public-spirited duties on property owners complies with the Fifth Amendment of the Constitution, which provides that "private property [shall not] be taken for public use, without just compensation."[11] When courts sustain these statutes and ordinances on constitutional grounds, as they frequently do,[12] local governments gain an important legal weapon for protecting the aesthetic, cultural, historical, and ecological values that often attract people and, therefore, subdividers and developers to a region. If the courts sheathe this legal weapon, however, society may have to kiss these values good-bye, since it can neither afford to exercise eminent domain to purchase the property in question nor can it depend, except in a limited way, on private action in common-law courts to protect these values.

When does a regulatory "taking" of property require the state to pay compensation, and when not? Justice Oliver Wendell Holmes, in a leading case decided in 1922, asserted that "this is a question of degree—and therefore cannot be disposed of by general propositions."[13] The absence of such propositions, that is, the lack of a theory on which to decide cases, has characterized "just compensation" jurisprudence for more than half a century. Commentators generally describe this area of law as a "muddle,"[14] a "crazy quilt,"[15] "unilluminating,"[16] "ad hoc,"[17] "confused,"[18] "baffling,"[19] "mystifying,"[20] and "chaotic."[21] In 1987, Justice John Paul Stevens summarized: "Even the wisest lawyers would have to acknowledge great uncertainty about the scope of this Court's takings jurisprudence."[22]

In recent years, several academic lawyers have analyzed takings law to try to define a theory on which future jurisprudence might be based.[23] Such an analysis could succeed, I think, if it (1) rests on acceptable normative and constitutional principles, and (2) is not so inconsistent with existing case law that it requires a dramatic recission of environmental statutes and ordinances now generally thought to be constitutionally sound.

In this [article], I want to suggest a line of analysis that will satisfy these conditions. I argue that compensation need not attend a regulation that takes property rights unless it also burdens some individuals unfairly to benefit other individuals or the public as a whole. The "takings" question, in other words, may not depend fundamentally on an analysis of property rights; instead, it may depend on a conception of justice.

Pragmatic Versus Theoretical Decision Making

Zoning is ubiquitous. Every state restricts the ways in which property owners can develop their land, especially in sensitive areas such as in flood plains, coastal zones, and agricultural districts. When such a restriction causes the market value of parcels of land to fall, the owners may believe that their land is being dedicated to a public use, for which the public ought to pay. They may then go to court to seek damages under the Fifth Amendment of the Constitution.

In one such case, *Just v. Marinette County*, the Supreme Court of Wisconsin upheld a zoning ordinance that prevented owners of a coastal marsh from using landfill on their property and thus from developing it for commercial purposes. The court held that the "takings" clause of the Constitution does not protect an interest, however profitable, in "destroying the natural character of a swamp or a wetland so as to make that location available for human habitation."[24] Citizens have no claim for compensation, the court reasoned, when an ordinance restricts their use of their land "to prevent a harm from the change in the natural character of the citizens' property."[25]

Ellen Frankel Paul, in her timely and well-argued book *Property Rights and Eminent Domain*,[26] points out that decisions such as *Just* strike "at the very heart of the property rights conception—that what is mine may be used by me as I see fit provided only that I not use it in a manner that violates the like right of other owners" (p. 138). Paul notes that by filling in his wetland, Mr. Just did not threaten the rights of others; he merely set about improving the economic utility of his land, just as many others had done up and down the coast.

Paul accepts common law, particularly tort, as the test for determining when a person uses his or her property in a way consistent with the rights of others. As she says, the concept of harm to others that limits the rights of landowners "would have to be comparable to a harm recognized in the tort law" (p. 139). Would filling the wetland cause an injury to anyone sufficient to give him or her standing to sue in common law? What sort of right could anyone assert as a matter of common law to enjoin Mr. Just from filling in his marsh?

Paul argues that nothing in nuisance, tort, or anywhere in common law suggests a basis for such an injunction. For more than a century, the public, for aesthetic, sanitary, economic, and other reasons, encouraged landowners to fill in swamps. Now, the public (for the same reasons) wants to keep remaining wetlands wet. This may be a valid objective; the public may legitimately change its values. Society may correctly believe that it now benefits many localities more from scenic and open space than from condominiums and commercial strips.

The question is whether the state may legitimately force Mr. Just and others like him to provide *gratis* the scenic, ecological, and perhaps moral benefits the public gains from the presence of open and undeveloped land. Should the state instead compensate Mr. Just for his financial loss or, if the government cannot afford to pay, allow him peacefully to develop his wetland?

Richard Epstein, in *Takings: Private Property and the Power of Eminent Domain*,[27] analyzes this case in the same way. He observes that the plaintiff, by filling in his wetland, might pollute his own property, but he threatens others with no harm cognizable in common law. Epstein argues that "the normal bundle of property rights contains no priority for land in its natural condition; it regards use, including development, as one of the standard incidents of ownership."

By building on their marsh, the plaintiffs do only what their neighbors had already done; no one would have a case against them in common law. Epstein concludes: "Stripped of its rhetoric, *Just* is a condemnation of these property rights, and compensation is thus required."

Ellen Paul's *Property Rights and Eminent Domain* and Richard Epstein's *Takings* endorse a theory of natural property rights, at the heart of which is the principle that people may use their property as they see fit as long as they respect the same rights and liberties of others. Both authors deplore the legal doctrine dominant in "takings" cases for 60 years, since it fails to recognize the existence of "natural" property rights; in fact, it rejects that theory out of hand. In place of this theory, the dominant doctrine, formulated by Justice Holmes, has called for ad hoc, case-by-case decision making,

an approach that attempts to determine a fair or just outcome in the circumstances of each suit, without relying or even speculating on a general theory or conception of property rights.

So both Paul and Epstein confront and oppose the pragmatic, case-by-case approach taken by the U.S. Supreme Court and many state courts. They are outraged that these courts routinely uphold legislation that plainly contravenes the theory of natural property rights they espouse. They argue that these courts should overturn their precedents to give legal force to that theory, especially the "core" freedom to do as one wishes with one's property as long as one remains within the constraints of common law. And they find thoroughly offensive the courts' refusal to advance a theory or conception of property—*any* theory—in cases brought under the Fifth Amendment of the Constitution.

Two questions arise, then, that Paul and Epstein must answer. First, is the pragmatic, case-by-case approach unworkable, unfair, or otherwise flawed in itself? In other words, does Paul or Epstein offer telling arguments against current practice per se and, thus, show that it must change to base itself on some theory of property? Or do they condemn it only because it does not accommodate the theory of "natural" property rights they believe to be correct?

Second, let us suppose that the courts reach principled and equitable, if pragmatic, resolutions of "takings" cases. Let us suppose that the principles on which the courts rely, while not unjust or unworkable in themselves, do not recognize but implicitly reject the theory of natural property rights Paul and Epstein espouse. Has this theory such a deep philosophical and constitutional basis that courts should adopt it, even if the pragmatic approach works well enough? The importance of these two books depends on how well they respond to these questions.

What Is Wrong with Current Practice?

The courts now follow a reasonably predictable course in "takings" jurisprudence—although not the one Paul and Epstein recommend. Courts at present view justice in this area as a privative virtue, which is to say, they overturn legislation only if it commits one of a list of specific injustices—for example, if it is intended (or plainly functions) to exclude racial groups from particular localities. Courts ask a series of ad hoc questions: Does the regulation physically remove the owner from the land? or deprive the owner of substantially all reasonable use of it?

Does the regulation fail to advance a legitimate public interest in a way rationally and closely related to the proscribed use? Does the restriction work unfairly to burden a few landowners to benefit a few others? Was the owner prevented from representing his or her interests in the political process? Has the government, through zoning, merely attempted to lower the market value of the land to make it cheaper to condemn?

Courts address "takings" cases with an ad hoc, pragmatic checklist of questions such as these—all of which are well known—reflecting a variety of moral, policy, and equity considerations. These questions go to the fairness and legitimacy of the statutes landowners challenge, but they pay little or no attention to any theory of property rights.

Courts rely on well-known ad hoc principles or rules of thumb, such as those these questions suggest, to determine whether the interests of the property owner have received a fair shake. The courts also take notice of the political and civil rights of various parties affected by a statute (e.g., the rights of minorities to live where they wish, the rights of individuals to political representation). In "takings" cases, courts mull over questions involving fairness, justice, and personal, civil, and political rights before making their decisions. But in answering these questions, the courts do not address or appear to want or need to address a theory of property rights.

Since lawyers know the kinds of questions the courts will ask—for example, whether a statute is "exclusionary," "extortionary," or "confiscatory"— they nearly always formulate zoning ordinances to survive this kind of review. As a result the outcome of "takings" or "inverse condemnation" proceedings is generally predictable. Absent some special infirmity in the law (e.g., it may be plainly extortionary), the decisions will go against the plaintiff.

Jurisdictions, then, through zoning and other ordinances, routinely succeed in vastly restricting the otherwise permissible ways landowners might use their land. And a good lawyer will tell aggrieved landowners not to bother to challenge a properly drafted statute because the courts will routinely and predictably uphold it, even though it

makes a mockery out of the notion of natural property rights.

As Paul notes, "takings" jurisprudence, which routinely upholds zoning regulations in this way, strikes "at the very heart of the property rights conception." She is right. Should judges take the theory of natural property rights seriously? May they instead properly remain indifferent to that theory and, indeed, to all theorizing about property and property rights?

Professor Paul proposes that the case-by-case, pragmatic, ad hoc decision making that characterizes "takings" jurisprudence "has simply not worked" (p. 188). She offers three arguments to support this contention.

First, Paul proposes that current jurisprudence puts too much power in the hands of politicians, who may next decide, for example, where each citizen will live. "The slippery slope is real, and it is alarming" (p. 192). Paul relies on this "slippery slope" appeal to dispatch what she sees, correctly, as her main opponent, namely, pragmatic modern liberalism. "If liberals are absolutists about any political value, it is certainly not property." Paul adds: "Modern liberalism . . . holds that civil rights can be separated from property rights. For modern liberals like John Dewey, property rights are relatively unimportant. A democratic society can flourish by protecting civil rights while not unduly concerning itself with property rights" (p. 190). Paul fails to provide, however, a single example of the reality of this slippery slope—an instance in which a judge or other public official moved in practice from "takings" precedents to a denial of civil, political, or personal rights. On the contrary, while the U.S. Supreme Court in its "takings" jurisprudence, over the last 60 years, may have kicked property rights into a cocked hat, the same Court has greatly advanced political, civil, and personal rights and liberties against the government. Perhaps Paul believes that the latter rights are connected, logically or empirically, with rights, for example, to develop one's marsh for commercial use. But no argument in her book, or anywhere else, as far as I know, demonstrates such a connection.

The second argument appeals to authority: "Virtually everyone admits that this area of the law is in a chaotic state" (p. 188). The third argument asserts that the pragmatic approach fails "to develop a sound theoretical underpinning for property rights" (p. 185).

These last two arguments are correct as far as they go. Commentators on "takings" jurisprudence, including Supreme Court justices, describe it as chaotic. Yet "takings" doctrine has given predictable results: The property owner will lose unless some special injustice, from an ad hoc but well-known list, has been done. If it is predictable and consistent, how, then, has it failed? People describe it as chaotic—but why should they?

The principal reason Paul, Epstein, and others believe that pragmatic, ad hoc jurisprudence is chaotic, as far as I can tell, is that it is ad hoc and pragmatic. They think it is bad for an important area of constitutional property law to fail to develop a sound theoretical underpinning for property rights. But why? If "takings" jurisprudence relies on an ad hoc, pragmatic list of reasonable concerns, why do judges need to indulge in theorizing? Academics theorize as a condition of getting tenure, of course, but justices already have lifetime terms.

The answer to the question whether the pragmatic, case-by-case approach fails may depend on the answer to the second question, namely, whether a different basis—one residing in deep philosophical principles—can and should be found. "I will argue that natural rights provides a consistent theory of property rights," Paul says, "and that a theory of property rights is essential for extricating ourselves from this impasse" (p. 188).

Paul Versus Epstein

I want to mention here reasons I believe Paul's *Property Rights and Eminent Domain* is not only an excellent book but is also better argued than Epstein's *Takings*. First, Epstein makes no attempt whatever to show that current jurisprudence has failed in its own terms, that is, failed to provide a workable, predictable resolution of controversies arising under the Fifth Amendment. Instead, Epstein merely reviews a large number of legal decisions, shows that they make mincemeat of the theory of natural property rights, and then rebukes the judges for being such jerks. If you, poor reader, are among the damned who have not seen the divine light of natural property rights theory Epstein regards you—along with Congress, the courts, state legislatures, municipal authorities, and other sinners—with contempt. Contempt, however, is not argument, and that is the problem with Epstein's treatise.

Paul, on the contrary, does not preach only to the saved. She recognizes that her opponents may favor current jurisprudence for initially plausible reasons, for example, to prevent "irreversible loss of agricultural land, estuaries, wetlands, and open space, and the wasteful consumption of energy" (p. 192). Paul believes that it may be more important for the law to protect natural property rights than to protect nature beyond the limits of tort. Unlike Epstein, she recognizes, however, that the truth of this belief is not self-evident.

Second, Paul clearly recognizes what Epstein only occasionally glimpses, namely, the strict incompatibility and antagonism between utilitarian and libertarian approaches to property rights. The old utilitarians, such as Jeremy Bentham, thought that governments create and protect property rights for purposes of utility maximization; Bentham described talk of natural rights as "nonsense on stilts." When property rights get in the way of the aggregate public interest (as they presumably do in "takings" cases), then it is property rights rather than the general welfare that must give way. Any intellectually honest utilitarian or utility maximizer must agree with Bentham on this point.

Chicago School utilitarians, who would maximize a form of utility Richard Posner calls "wealth," are driven to Bentham's conclusion. They would defend property rights, not as a matter of principle or of basic justice (as Paul would), but only insofar as that policy might promote the efficient allocation of resources. Owing to market failures, bargaining costs, holdouts, and everything else, however, governments may generally achieve greater efficiency through cost–benefit planning than by allowing free exchange. Paul notes correctly that the "wealth-maximization" or "efficiency" view presupposes the communistic fiction that everyone wants the same thing, namely, efficient allocation, and thus it encourages experts to override individual rights to provide it. "It is ironic that a view that sincerely intends to be supportive of individualism and property rights, is actually collectivist, and just as aggregative as utilitarianism" (p. 217).

Paul has replied to Epstein in other places, showing that utilitarian goals, such as wealth maximization, conflict just as thoroughly as any other centralized statist program with a regime of natural property rights.[28] Her discussion of this issue (pp. 212-24), which includes a devastating reply to Posner's conception of *ex ante* compensation, may be the best in the literature.

Epstein, after a wave of the hand to Locke, assumes that every well-socialized individual knows that property rights are natural rights—and he is off and running. Paul, in contrast, recognizes that "the advocates of natural rights did fail to provide a logical, internally consistent, deductive defense of these rights. Bentham certainly has his point" (p. 188). Thus, Paul attempts to argue for the fundamental thesis that Epstein merely assumes, namely, that property rights are natural rights.

She attempts "to supply the natural rights theory of property with such a deductive defense," which, she hopes, will be persuasive to those, like Bentham, "who are highly skeptical of 'metaphysical rights'" (p. 188). How successful, then, is her argument for natural property rights?

The Argument for Natural Property Rights

Paul's argument for natural property rights, although at times hard to follow, seems to depend on two plausible principles. First, following Locke, she reasons that every human being has a natural right to acquire from the commons such commodities as are necessary to his or her survival. "Man must labor," Paul points out, "in order to attain the rudiments necessary for his survival" (p. 226). Second, following Locke, Paul argues that everyone has a fundamental property right to anything useful that person creates through his or her labor and ingenuity. She asserts "that the person who creates X ought to own X" (p. 232).

While both principles are familiar and plausible, they do not entail anything about compensation in "takings" cases. How does Professor Paul get from a natural right to own what one creates and/or needs for survival to a doctrine about just compensation in "takings" cases? Let us grant that individuals have a natural right to the products they create and/or need in order to survive. How does this show that the government should compensate Mr. Just when an ordinance against certain kinds of development lowers the market value of his land?

While the answer to this question is by no means evident, Paul introduces two further premises. First, she rejects as "artificial" any "distinction between necessities and luxuries" (p. 236). "After all, who is to judge which are goods necessary for survival and which are luxuries?" Paul asks. "Such a task would entail the existence of a godlike omniscience, or else the moral system would hinge on caprice" (p. 234).

Second, Paul emphasizes this principle: "All value is the artifact of some purposive activity on the part of the individual." She continues: "What I am arguing goes one step beyond Locke, who contended, alternately, that nine-tenths or ninety-nine hundredths of the value of any commodity was the handiwork of man rather than nature. *I maintain that 100 percent of the value of a good is the work of human activity*" (p. 230).

Any real estate agent will tell you that there are three determinants of the market value of real property: location, location, and location. None of these depends on the labor, ingenuity, or creativity of the property owner. Henry George adopted his radical views about land tenure in part because he saw the price of property go up tenfold overnight when the government announced its plan to extend the railroad to a section of California. The lucky owners, far from laboring for their survival, were asleep at the time. They woke up to find that the government, by creating a railroad, highway, park, or whatever, had instantly multiplied the price at which they might sell their land.

Paul counters such an objection in advance by writing: "I am not talking about market value (or price) and how it is determined on a free market" (p. 231). She adds, in words that might warm the heart of any defender of current "takings" practice:

> Each person has a perpetual property right in that which he or she has created, that is, in the values produced. Your right, then, is to the object or process itself, and not to the market value or price, which is nothing more than the appraisal in the minds of others, at the margin, of the value to them of your good. The preference orders are beyond your control, and form no part of your entitlement (p. 234).

If Paul is not concerned with market value, then, it seems, she would have little to say on behalf of Mr. Just, who sued for the difference between the price he could get for his land before and after the zoning ordinance. He had made no use of his land—he had invested no labor or ingenuity in processing it—and he still possessed the object itself. The entire value of the land that Mr. Just sued to recover was market value: the value the land would have, as a matter of speculation, if it could be developed for commercial or residential purposes. On Paul's account, then, Mr. Just would have no entitlement to this value, since it is the creation not necessarily of his own action, but of the preferences of others.

All or nearly all zoning ordinances maintain the kind of property right that Paul defends. Statutes and regulations uniformly "grandfather" every existing use that cannot be construed as creating a nuisance. Current "takings" jurisprudence respects the sort of property right a person has to the products of his or her own labor—or at least Paul provides no evidence to the contrary. Accordingly, Paul's interesting defense of property rights seems to support, or at least not to undermine, current pragmatic, ad hoc, case-by-case approaches to "just" compensation under the Fifth Amendment of the Constitution.

Does the Right to Develop Imply a Right to Destroy?

As we have seen, Professor Paul distinguishes between "use value (i.e., the utility of a thing) and market value (or price)" (p. 230). While Paul does not develop this distinction, there are familiar examples of it. Water and air, for example, have high use values, since life cannot go on without them. Yet air and water are so plentiful in most localities that they have a low market value or price.

Land also has value both as an object of use and an object of exchange and speculation. The use value of a wetland consists, for example, in the many services and benefits it provides to the public. These include its function in the tertiary treatment of wastes, in the control of floods, in providing habitat for fish and wildlife, and so on. Wetlands tend also to be beautiful ecosystems delighting those who experience intelligently the play of natural history, scenic landscapes, and open space.

The market value of a wetland, like that of any real estate, depends principally on its location. In a coastal area, a wetland, once filled in, may provide the site for profitable enterprises, especially if, as in Atlantic City, gambling casinos, massage parlors, bars, and discos can be built. Everyone knows what happened to land values in and around Atlantic City when the government allowed gambling. That is what the market value or price of land is all about.

Now, policy problems arise when the use value of a wetland conflicts with its market value. In order to preserve the uses of the wetland—the ecological and aesthetic values associated with it—we should have to forbid certain kinds of development. In order to maximize the market value of the wetland, however, we should have to develop it in ways that destroy the use value. This is essentially the choice that confronted the *Just* court.

The court may have framed this question in terms of another: Did the owner's destruction of the use value of the wetland—for example, its value as a habitat, aquifer, or whatever—constitute a "noxious" activity that the legislature may prohibit without paying compensation, even though that sort of destruction would not be recognized as a tort in private law? In other words, if legislatures, rather than common-law courts, become the arbiters of what counts as a "nuisance" for purposes of "takings" jurisprudence, the Wisconsin zoning ordinance was perfectly constitutional. If the notion of a nuisance, and therefore the extent of property rights, depend on what may be enjoined at private law, however, the ordinance would not be constitutional. And so the question might amount to this: May legislatures identify and prohibit public nuisances that extend beyond activities that would contravene private rights and therefore be enjoined in common-law courts?

The courts have held that state governments will not run afoul of the Fifth Amendment when they enact measures to protect the public from injurious uses of private property, even when the injuries in question are not cognizable in tort. For example, the U.S. Supreme Court in *Mugler* v. *Kansas* 1887, its first full consideration of regulatory takings, found against the plaintiff, a brewery owner, the value of whose property had been severely diminished when the Kansas legislature prohibited the sale of alcoholic beverages in the state. Justice John Harlan wrote:

> The power which the states have of prohibiting such use by individuals of their property as will be prejudicial to the health, the morals, or the safety of the public, is not . . . burdened with the condition that the state must compensate such individual owners for pecuniary losses they may sustain, by reason of their not

being permitted, by a noxious use of their property, to inflict injury upon the community.[29]

It is clear in Harlan's majority opinion that the legislature has the power to declare as "noxious" or "injurious" uses that would not be identified as torts under common law.[30] Although the Supreme Court has held that "the legislature has no right to declare that to be a nuisance which is clearly not so,"[31] it has deferred to legislative findings as long as they met procedural due process requirements. Thus, when states justify regulations on the basis of a colorable "noxious use," the Fifth Amendment has no force beyond what the Fourteenth Amendment also guarantees, namely, that a person shall not be deprived of property without due process of law.[32]

One may surely argue, however, that the legislature should not be the judge of its own case, that is, that some "substantive due process" review is required to determine that the "noxious" use in question does involve a threat to the public health, safety, or welfare. How would this work out with respect to the Wisconsin ordinance? Does the ordinance simply benefit the public at the expense of the landowner? Or does it function to prevent the landowner from enriching himself at the expense of the public?

While it is notoriously hard to identify general principles by which to answer this question, courts have found that restrictions are not compensable when they stop a landowner from "engaging in conduct he ought, as a well-socialized adult, to have recognized as unduly harmful to others."[33] The conception of "undue harm" at work here is drawn not from common law alone but from the wider social and cultural standards of the community.[34] Since these standards change and evolve, "definition and redefinition of the institution of private property is always at stake."[35]

The decision in *Just* builds on this rationale, as one commentator writes, by denying that expectations of profit are legitimate if they "are inconsistent with widely prevailing standards of society."[36] To assume that one has an inherent right to develop one's land (e.g., to fill a marsh) "ignores or distorts an obvious relationship between such activity and interests of the public that have long existed, but that until recently have been taken for granted."[37]

This argument stands on the premise that the central incidents of property—the right to use, to

exclude, and to alienate[38]—do not include the right to destroy.[39] Professor Paul correctly attributes this point to Locke. She writes that appropriation from the common is limited by two conditions: "that as much and as good remain in common for the like appropriation of others, and that spoilage must not occur. Indeed, Locke maintains that one's right to land extends not beyond what one can use, so that one does not possess a right to waste" (p. 204).

It is easy to show that a right to use property does not entail a right to destroy it. The right to use a car one has borrowed or hired, for example, does not involve a right to destroy it; similarly, the right to use by consuming food does not entail a right to waste or spoil it. Locke reasons that a person can "heap up" as many resources as he can use or cause to be used economically—"the *exceeding of the bounds of his just property* not lying in the largeness of his possession, but in the perishing of anything uselessly in it."[40]

One might reply that the right to use consumables, such as food or fuel, implies a right to "destroy" them, for to use is to consume these things. This reply, however, shows only that the right to use entails a right to use up—not necessarily a right to destroy. The difference between using up provisions and destroying them is too obvious to require examples. Environmental resources of the sort that wetland regulations protect, moreover, are generally not consumable goods but "renewable" services. They are not consumed but conserved through proper use.

Similarly, the right to transfer property does not on its face entail a right to destroy it. Thus the auctioneer has a right to transfer property to the highest bidder, but this does not give him a right to destroy it, even if it is not sold. To be sure, if an item is worthless, the possessor may have a right to toss it out. But the right to destroy does not attach, for that reason, to property that has a high use value. For this reason, courts sometimes impose a "law of waste" to prevent property owners from destroying scarce resources that are of great usefulness to others.[41]

Mr. Just has no valid claim to compensation, according to this argument, because he has no right or entitlement to destroy resources that have become scarce and are of great importance to society. The decision in *Just* is correct, on this view, because a regulation that prevents a landowner from destroying resources by filling a marsh does not take a right from him. He has no right to destroy those resources.

This result seems entirely consistent with a Lockean theory of property rights, which limits property not only to that which can be possessed without waste, as we have seen, but also to that which may be acquired from a commons without creating scarcity. As Locke puts this thought, a person can rightfully acquire an unowned resource from the commons only if there is "enough and as good left in common for others."[42]

The *Just* court argued that an owner may not validly claim compensation when he or she is prevented from "destroying the natural character of a swamp or a wetland . . . when the new use . . . causes a harm to the general public."[43] The contention may be that the prohibited development would destroy resources that the public owns in common, owing to "the interrelationship of the wetlands, the swamps and the natural environment of shorelands to the purity of the water and to such natural resources as navigation, fishing, and scenic beauty."[44] In the past, an individual may have been free to appropriate these resources without depleting the common unduly, but those times are gone. Mr. Just has come too late to the commons; there is no longer as much and as good for others.

One might argue that this famous Lockean proviso[45] covers aesthetic and ecological resources that belong as organic parts (or even as emergent properties) to larger systems and are destroyed when land is removed from its natural condition. Those who come to the commons early may legitimately appropriate these resources by consuming or destroying them; but when a common resource, such as natural beauty, becomes critically scarce, society may rule against further appropriations because they significantly worsen the social situation from that which would obtain if the proposed "improvements" were not made. As Professor Paul rightly concludes in another place, a natural rights theory that "embraces the Lockean proviso can be utilized to validate environmentalist land use legislation . . . without such regulations constituting a compensable takings."[46]

Conclusion

Courts should uphold environmental regulations, such as the Wisconsin ordinance, that prevent landowners from destroying natural resources the public has long enjoyed and in which it has a legitimate interest. The incidents of property include the rights to use, exclude, and transfer, but not the right to destroy. Destruction of resources that implicitly belong to the common, then, constitute a "noxious" use, which is not protected by the Constitution. This approach may leave landowners little protection in the Fifth Amendment that they do not find in the Fourteenth and in the larger, ad hoc, pragmatic approach to "takings" jurisprudence such as we have described. Absent a persuasive theory of natural property rights, however, this may be the most reasonable approach that does not squander use values for the sake of market value—that does not ruin the environment to make speculators rich.

Notes

Acknowledgements: This essay is a revised version of a paper read at a conference, "Upstream/Downstream: Issues in Environmental Ethics," at Bowling Green State University, Bowling Green, Ohio, September 10, 1988. Portions of the paper will also appear in a book review of *Private Property and Eminent Domain* to be published in *Environmental Ethics.*

1. Alexis de Tocqueville, *Democracy in America* (New York: Random House, 1981), chap. 6.

2. See, e.g., *Penn Central Transportation Co.* v. *New York City*, 438 U.S. 104, 107 (1978) (holding that the city could operate a "comprehensive program to preserve historic landmarks" without "effecting a 'taking' requiring the payment of 'just compensation'"); *Steel Hill Developers, Inc.,* v. *Town of Sanbornton*, 469 F.2d 956, 959 (1st Cir. 1972) ("preserving [the] 'charm [of] a New England small town'"); and *County Commissioners* v. *Miles*, 246 Md. 355, 372, 228, A.2d 450, 459 (1967) (allowing "the preservation, in some manner, of existing conditions").

3. *Just* v. *Marinette County*, 56 Wis. 2d 7,201 N.W.2d, 761 (1972); *Sibson* v. *State of New Hampshire*, 115 N.H. 124, 336 A.2d 239 (1975). In dozens of similar court challenges to state prohibitions on filling or otherwise changing wetland and coastal environments, plaintiffs generally succeed in winning compensation under the "takings" clause of the Fifth Amendment (or under analogous provisions in state constitutions) only if they are able to show that they are deprived of all reasonable and viable economic use of their land. For an exhaustive survey showing a "trend" toward upholding the validity of wetland regulations, see Daniel R. Mandeleker, "Land Use Takings, the Compensation Issue," *Hastings Constitutional Law Quarterly* 8

(1981): 491, esp. 495–502; and Sarah E. Redfield, *Vanishing Farmland: A Legal Solution for the States* (Lexington, MA: D. C. Heath, 1984), chap. 2.

4. *Agins* v. *City of Tiburon*, 447 U.S. 255, 261 (quoting from the Cal. Gov't. Code Ann. sec. 65561 (b) (West, 1983) (recognizing the legitimacy of open space plans to "discourage the 'premature and unnecessary conversion of open-space land to urban uses'").

5. *Hodel* v. *Virginia Surface Mining and Reclamation Association*, 452 U.S. 264 (1981) (sustaining the Surface Mining Control and Reclamation Act).

6. The Endangered Species Act of 1973 (16 U.S.C. secs. 1531–43) (1976 & Supp. I 1977 & Supp. II 1978 & Supp. III 1979) requires (sec. 1536) that all federal departments and agencies "insure that actions authorized, funded, or carried out by them do not jeopardize the continued existence of such endangered species." The act effectively makes the preservation of habitat a condition of any federal permit for development.

7. For discussion of litigation concerning ordinances expanding public access to waterfront property, see Carol Rose, "The Comedy of the Commons: Custom, Commerce, and Inherently Public Property," *University of Chicago Law Review* 53 (1986): 711, 713–23.

8. *Keystone Bituminous Coal Association* v. *DeBenedictus*, 55 LW 4326 (March 9,1987).

9. For a discussion of environmental zoning for ecological purposes in the context of the "takings" problem see "Developments in the Law: Zoning," *Harvard Law Review* 91 (1978), 1427, 1618–24.

10. A landowner who proceeds against the government in this way is said to assert a theory of "inverse condemnation" of his land because he, rather than the government, initiates the action. See *San Diego Gas and Electric Co.* v. *City of San Diego*, 450 U.S. 621, 638 n. 2 (1981) (Brennan, J., dissenting).

11. The Fifth Amendment to the Constitution of the United States. This provision is now applicable to the states through the Fourteenth Amendment. *Chicago, B. & O. R.R.* v. *City of Chicago*, 166 U.S. 226, 235–41 (1897). Almost all the states have analogous clauses in their constitutions. For documentation, see "Developments in the Law," 1463.

12. Thus, in the leading case, *Pennsylvania Coal Co.* v. *Mahon* (260 U.S. 393, 415), Justice Holmes stated "that while property may be regulated to a certain extent, if regulation goes too far it will be considered as a taking." It is difficult to predict how a "taking" will be decided. Ackerman notes that "recent wetlands regulation cases have divided approximately evenly on the issue of compensa-

tion." Bruce Ackerman, *Private Property and the Constitution* (New Haven: Yale University Press, 1977), 191 n. 7 and 217 n. 54.

13. *Pennsylvania Coal*, 260 U.S. 416.

14. Carol M. Rose, "*Mahon* Reconstructed: Why the Takings Issue Is Still a Muddle," *Southern California Law Review* 57 (1984): 561.

15. Allison Dunham, "*Griggs* v. *Allegheny County* in Perspective: Thirty Years of Supreme Court Expropriation Law," *Supreme Court Review* 63 (1962): 105.

16. S. Van Alstyne, "Taking or Damaging by Police Power: The Search for Inverse Condemnation Criteria," *Southern California Law Review* 44 (1971): 1, 39. ("The judicial calculus involved in the balancing process is described in a variety of unilluminating ways.")

17. W. Oakes, "'Property Rights' in Constitutional Analysis Today," *Washington Law Review* 56 (1981): 583, 602–3 (characterizing takings decisions as "ad hoc line drawing").

18. W. B. Stoebuck, "Police Power, Takings, and Due Process," *Washington and Lee Law Review* 37 (1980): 1057, 1062–63 (referring to "extreme confusion about police power takings").

19. Comment, "Regulation of Land Use: From Magna Carta to a *Just* Formulation," *UCLA Law Review* 23 (1976): 904, 904–5 (takings decisions are "bafflingly" inconsistent).

20. Thomas Hippler, "Reexamining 100 Years of Supreme Court Regulatory Taking Doctrine: The Principles of 'Noxious Use,' 'Average Reciprocity of Advantage,' and 'Bundle of Rights,' from *Mugler* to *Keystone Bituminous Coal*," *Environmental Affairs* 14 (1987): 633–725 (describing "the rather mystifying nature of regulatory takings jurisprudence").

21. Fred Bosselman, David Callies, and John Banta, *The Taking Issue* (Washington, DC: Council on Environmental Quality, GPO, 1973), 322.

22. *Nollan* v. *California Coastal Commission*, 55 LW 5145, 5156 (Stevens, J., dissenting). Here Justice Stevens echoes Justice Brennan in Penn Central Transportation Co. (428 U.S. 123, 124) (stating that the question "of what constitutes a 'taking' for purposes of the Fifth Amendment has proved to be a problem of considerable difficulty" susceptible to no "set formula"). Cf. Joseph Sax, "Takings and the Police Power," *Yale Law Journal* 74 (1964): 36, 37 ("the predominant characteristic of this area of law is a welter of confusing and apparently incompatible results"). Cf. *Goldblatt* v. *Town of Hempstead*, 369 U.S. 590, 594 (1962). ("There is no set formula to determine where regulation ends and taking begins.")

23. See, e.g., Ackerman, *Private Property*; Frank Michelman, "Property, Utility, and Fairness: Comments of the Ethical Foundations of 'Just Compensation' Law," *Harvard Law Review* 80 (1968), 1165–1258; and Joseph Sax, "Takings, Private Property and Public Rights," *Yale Law Journal* 81 (1971), 149–86.

24. *Just* v. *Marinette Co.,* 56 Wis. 2d 7, 201 N.W.2d 761, 768 (1972).

25. Ibid., 767.

26. Ellen Frankel Paul, *Property Rights and Eminent Domain* (New Brunswick, NJ: Transaction Books, 1987), 138. Unless otherwise noted, all quotations attributed to Paul in this article are taken from this work.

27. Richard Epstein, *Takings: Private Property and the Power of Eminent Domain* (Cambridge: Harvard University Press, 1985), 123.

28. See, for example, Paul's comments in "A Reflection on Epstein and His Critics," *Miami Law Review* 41 (1986): 235.

29. 123 U.S. 623, 669 (1887).

30. Ibid., 671–672.

31. *Lawton* v. *Steele,* 152 U.S. 133, 140 (1894).

32. See, for example, *Powell* v. *Pennsylvania,* 127 U.S. 678 (1888).

33. Ackerman, *Private Property,* 102.

34. Courts may meet their constitutional obligation as long as they apply these standards consistently in all cases. For discussion of this point, see ibid., 14.

35. C. Haar, *Land-Use Planning* (Boston: Little, Brown, 1959), 410. Justice Holmes may have had the centrality of evolving community standards in mind when he said in *Mahon* that "this is a question of degree—and therefore cannot be disposed of by general propositions." This seems to be consistent with the view sometimes attributed to Holmes that judges apply standards of good taste and reasonableness and not simply formal legal prescriptions.

36. P. Soper, "The Constitutional Framework of Environmental Law," in his *Federal Environmental Law* (St. Paul, MN: West, 1974), 67.

37. Ibid.

38. Epstein, *Takings,* 20, endorses this analysis of property rights, citing W. Blackstone, *Commentaries* (1765), 2. Robert Goodin cites Frank Snare, "The Concept of Property," *American Philosophical Quarterly* 9 (1972), 200–206; and C. B. Macpherson, "Human Rights as Property Rights," *Dissent* 24 (1977): 72–77.

39. Robert Goodin puts the point as follows: "The right to destroy is usually not part and parcel of the central incidents of the right to property, as ordinarily understood." Robert Goodin, "Property Rights and Preservationist Duties," paper presented at the Conference Group on Political Economy, American Political Science Association Annual Conference, Chicago, September 1987, 3.

40. John Locke, *Second Treatise of Government,* chap. 5, sec. 46.

41. For discussion, see William Rogers, "Bringing People Back: Toward a Comprehensive Theory of Taking in Natural Resources Law," *Ecology Law Quarterly* 10 (1982): 205, 248–51. Rogers cites about 20 relevant cases at 2.49 nn. 214–16.

42. Locke, *Second Treatise,* chap. 5, sec. 27.

43. 56 Wis. 2d 18, 201 NW.2d 768.

44. Ibid., 17.

45. For a discussion of the "Lockean Proviso," see Robert Nozick, *Anarchy, State, and Utopia* (New York: Basic Books, 1974), 174–82.

46. Ellen Frankel Paul, "The Just Takings Issue," *Environmental Ethics* 3 (1981): 309, 320.

V.D HUMAN POPULATION AND PRESSURE ON "RESOURCES"

52. PREVIEW

The Aswan Dam in Egypt was built to irrigate enough farm land to feed four million people. By the time they finished it, Egypt had ten million more people than when they started. Twenty years from now, our tiny planet will have enough new people to make four new Europes or seven more Russias. Now we'd better act fast or the world's stability is in serious danger.

Leslie Nielsen

It is now quite lawful for a Catholic woman to avoid pregnancy by resort to mathematics, though she is still forbidden to resort to physics and chemistry.

H. L. Mencken

About 10,000 years ago there were approximately 5 million human beings on the earth, less than the current population of Rio de Janeiro. By the year 1850 the number was about *1 billion*. A few years after World War II, global population had increased to 2.5 billion. In a predecessor of this book, published in 1986, we spoke of a population of between 4 and 5 billion.[1] When a few of today's university students have their first grandchildren, there will likely be about 8 billion (near the year 2020 or so). Today's total of over 6 billion may reach to 10 billion by 2050 if the current annual rate of increase of 1.7 percent remains constant. Currently, 5 million humans are born every twenty days, about 1 million every four days.[2]

Unlike many animals, we humans so far have few successful nonhuman predators. A massive nuclear war could be devastating, as could biological or chemical warfare. The spread of AIDS caused the premature death of 22 million humans by 2001. Even though in recent decades there has been an increase in the gross national product of many nations and a significant increase in the total accessible supply of food, the GNP and the amount of food per person have shrunk, the latter due in large part to the rapid increases in population. So even extraordinary technological "advances" have not offset the increased demand for resources. We put "advances" in scare quotes to note that some so-called advances have been, in fact, purchased at a high price to the environment, one that cannot obviously be paid on a sustained basis (on this controversial matter, see Section V.E on questions of sustainability). Hence, some "advances" may have, to put an edge on the matter, simply taken food and water out of the mouths of our grandchildren or perhaps their grandchildren.

Starvation is not always, and may not even usually be, a by-product of a lack of food on the planet; it is often due to the skewed distribution of food and the radically unequal distribution of wealth or income that makes those who are hungry unable to call forth a response from a market ready to supply those who are willing and able to pay for food.[3]

In 1798 Thomas Malthus, a clergyman, published his now-famous *An Essay on the Principles of Population*, a book that was to have its influence both on Charles Darwin in the 1830s and today in continued debates about the relation of population and resources. Malthus argued, as our selection makes clear, that under certain conditions the increase in human population would increase exponentially, whereas the increase in food supply was likely to be only arithmetic. Thus, tragedy in terms of famine and premature death is in the cards. "Neo-Malthusians" today are, interestingly, criticized from both the political left and the political right. From the left because they are claimed to support genocidal programs to deal with overpopulation (or support infringement of "a right to procreate") and from the right because they are claimed to be technological pessimists, and to underestimate the capacity of the planet to support larger populations of humans. Some defenses of a neo-Malthusian view assert that on the matter of what the facts are, over the long run Malthus was basically right. Further, a morally defensible view of the value of the nonhuman environment tends to support Malthusian concern about the overall rapid increase in the size of the human population. Once more: We have increased from 1 billion in the early 1800s to over 6 billion today. Doubling times have been under fifty years recently. Can the earth hold 12 billion, or 24 billion people with the usual destruction of animal and plant habitats that this entails, and the apparent overuse of sources and sinks we find today?

Even if current resources were more equally distributed, the prospect of the planet's adding another 6 billion humans in the next century would seem to render dim the hope of relieving absolute destitution and lessening the gap between the nations of the northern hemisphere and the southern. One question, then, concerns what to do about the desperate plight of millions of current and future humans who are, or will be, on a path to premature death and the misery of hunger and nutrition-related diseases.[4] There are difficulties. If global population does not flatten out, will there not be tragedy for all? After all, particular resources such as copper or oil are not infinite—conceding the fact that predictions of disaster have often been wrong. Of course, the "boy who cried wolf" often said what was false—but then—at last, there was a wolf. If all the world began to look like the streets of Dacca in Bangladesh (or any area of extreme poverty and high population density), is that the inevitable outcome of food sharing and no halt to the increase in global population? So there are some questions:

1. What must we do about the current burgeoning human population?

2. Are resources in fact limited?

3. What must we do about the large number of human beings who are in fact starving to death?

4. In what ways must we think differently about these questions when we consider the well-being of future generations of humans?

5. In what ways must we think differently about these questions if we do not think that the well-being of all and only human beings is important?

6. What is an optimal population for the planet, all morally relevant matters considered?

7. What must we do to limit population size?

In the selections that follow, most of these questions are explored.

Biologist Garrett Hardin, in a famous essay entitled "The Tragedy of the Commons" (found earlier in Section V.C, Essay 47) has argued that resources (such as the oceans) that are "held in common," and thus not divided up according to some scheme of property rights, will be "overused" or wrongly exploited. Consider what has happened historically to what is thought of as "unowned" or sometimes "public" property, such as the air, many rivers, lakes, the oceans, and outer space. A free good is likely to become an overused good. Without the discipline of having some cost as a means of rationing the use of scarce resources, they will be used inefficiently. On this view it would be a great mistake to supply food at no cost to those nations in which there are a large number of starving people.

Indeed, in Hardin's view, doing so would lead to an even greater tragedy (such as a larger population crash) later. So, on this view it is not heroic and not even permissible to supply food; rather we have a duty not to do so (note the consequentialist train of thought). Surprising to many, Hardin spells out this view in Essay 55, "Lifeboat Ethics," in this section. An important part off Hardin's argument is that a given nation has a certain "carrying capacity," that is, an ability to support a human population up to a certain point, given its endowment of natural resources, ingenuity, and so on. If a nation exceeds its capacity for very long, there will be a significant gap between the needs of its population and the available resources and, barring an influx of aid, it will suffer from a population dieback. Thus, in his view an even worse harm will occur. However, the judgment that a nation has a fixed carrying capacity of a certain level may not be the straightforward empirical judgment that it appears to be.[5]

According to some philosophers, the lifeboat model provokes us to think of the famine situation as a competitive one in which our choices are severely limited, as one in which we can only think in terms of a simplified and tragic "us and them" model.[6] We need not be driven by this picture of things. We might consider whether we morally ought to take the view of an impartial moral spectator or whether "special relations" deserve weight in the question of who should receive aid (for example, relationships with friends, relatives, allies), and, indeed, should aid always go to those who are members of our species? In recent years criticism has been leveled at *impartialist* theories, Utilitarianism being a prime example, on the ground that they do not give appropriate moral weight to the significance of existing loyalties (to friends, family, and so on) in that they require that moral agents be "radically egalitarian" and "treat each equally." A possible upshot is that one ought to give food to (or throw the life raft to, and the like) that individual whose reception of it would maximize utility—even if that means letting the friend die. Some critics believe that any theory with such implications should not be taken seriously. Hardin's view looks to be basically utilitarian in outlook. In thinking about lifeboat situations, we need to remind ourselves that the world is one in which competition and cooperation charac-

terize relations between humans and also human–animal interactions. To be fair to Hardin, he holds out the hope of "mutual coercion mutually agreed upon," and this is a form it high-level cooperation.

The extremely important issue of human starvation can be, and commonly has been, discussed independently of attention to the enormous impact human proliferation has had, and is having, on the nonhuman biota of the planet. In a remarkable turn of political events, the Earth Summit that met in Rio de Janeiro in 1992 managed not to have any discussion of human population issues on its official agenda. We are tempted to say that this is a bit like discussing the "greenhouse effect" without discussing carbon emissions, but we shall refrain. From the outset, 77 developing countries wanted to focus on issues other than population increases, for obvious reasons. Without question, a major cause of pollution, the using up of "sources" (fresh water, clean air, a third of the world's forests, other fossil fuels, and so on) and the elimination of "sinks" (places to put wastes), is the leap from I billion humans in 1850 to over 6 billion today. However, the heavy human hand on the nonhuman environment is also a function of the degree of resource consumption per person. In the United States and many other "first world" or developed nations, the population is highly stable. It is not unusual for such developed nations to view with alarm the rate of population growth in certain less developed nations in which population often doubles in only 20 years.[7] This rate cannot be sustained for long without catastrophe. It is tempting to lay blame here and to conclude that the heaviest impact on the planet's environment is generated by the increased numbers of humans in such countries. Once again, things are not so simple. Once again, laying blame at the feet of others appeals to the desire to be thought innocent and to walk away with "clean hands." However, the environmental impact of one American (on the available sources and sinks) is fifty times that of one citizen of Bangladesh.[8] The amount of carbon emitted into the environment by the activity of the average American is five times the global average.[9] The environmental impact of the average person in other developed countries such as Japan, France, or Canada is very large. Political crosscurrents related to the dual emphasis on population size (and rate of growth) and consumption per person led to an impasse at the Earth Summit in 1992. The final outcome of the negotiations in Brazil is described by one observer in this fashion:

> When, in the final negotiating session, the United States moved to delete all references to consumption in the North, the G-77 retaliated by deleting references to the urgency of slowing population growth. That opened the way for extremely effective lobbying by the Holy See. The fate of the population language was sealed, ironically, by representatives of women. Feminist health groups, along with some women's groups in developing countries and representatives of minority women in the United States have long been antagonistic to population control because they believe it jeopardizes women's health, is disguised genocide or places blame on women.[10]

The expression "population control" is one, of course, of which we should be wary; it can be used to refer to coercive methods of a more or less extreme sort, ranging from Hitler's "population control" of the Jews and Gypsies, to the massacres of Croats by the Serbs, or to policies of mandatory abortion or mandatory pregnancy. In India in the 1970s thousands of people (males and females) were coercively sterilized.[11] The plight of women in many countries is that of working as day laborers for the family; they are uneducated and do not understand the nature and function of contraceptives or are not given access to such. Often they are oppressed by men, who do not allow their comparatively power-less wives to learn about or use contraception. In many cultures, including our own, a great deal of shame and guilt has been induced over even talking about, not to mention using, contraceptives; often Roman Catholic leaders tell those who wish to do so that they are "closing themselves off from God," perhaps dooming themselves to eternal suffering as a result.[12] Dissuading people from using "artificial" contraceptives, or preventing access to them, is, of course, viewed as a "moral victory" by such "leaders." In India one-fourth of the women are so badly off that they die by the time that they are 15 years of age. The low status of those who survive makes it difficult for them to have a voice, to get an education, to gain some autonomy, and exercise deliberate choice over their own reproductive capacities. In India some families have to choose between spending money on their daughter's education and spending it on her dowry. If the husband's family believes the wife's dowry is too small, they sometimes engage in the notorious practice of bride burning, although it is illegal. Under such enormous pressures and frequently taught by her parents to acquiesce to the wishes of her husband for the sake of a "peaceful" or "happy" marriage, she lives as a passive, powerless, laboring baby producer—with little hope and with little control. When many children die young, the parents often decide that it is necessary to have many children ("gifts of God"), because it is not certain that many will live. The ideology that male babies are more valuable than females affects the attitudes of men and women. Mothers are often deeply troubled if they have produced only females; the overwhelming majority of abortions in India are of female babies, a form of what some have called "gendercide." Thus, a nasty mixture of poverty, entrenched patriarchal attitudes, ignorance, passivity, prejudice, shame, and institutionalized barriers, sometimes expressive of cultural and religious ideologies, is at the root of the population excess in many poor nations;

population control, abstractly speaking, is desirable, but it must address these mentioned difficulties and do so in a just manner.[13] Doing so may require something falling short of "respecting other cultures" (or our own). The related issues here include, then, earth-wide environmental deterioration, sustainability, the availability of birth control and abortion, and others.

Human exploitation of the earth is so distressing to many people that occasional elements of misanthropic attitudes appear. For example, rare "environmentalist" voices express skepticism that AIDS or starvation or war is in fact tragic.[14] Such remarks are spotlighted for political purposes, understandably, by very-free-market, anthropocentric, jingoistic members of the so-called Wise Use movements[15] who attack "environmentalists" in a wholesale manner, with virtually no distinctions, as people who dismiss the value of human beings, as tree-hugging Bambi lovers indifferent to human property rights and to the plight of those who are (claimed to be) losing their jobs because of environmental restrictions (who "put birds, rats, and insects ahead of families and jobs," as Republican candidate for U.S. President Patrick Buchanan said in 1992).[16] Strange to say, but one is reminded of Mao Ze-Dong's call for a "war on nature."[17] What to do about the genuine conflicts between legitimate interests is an important and difficult matter. It is addressed in various parts of this book, especially in Sections IV.A, V.B, and V.C. What we believe about what sorts of things possess moral standing will, as discussed earlier in Parts III and IV, directly and profoundly affect the question of which things are possessors of legitimate interests and, hence, how we articulate the nature of the conflict of interests.

Even if one believes that duties are owed only to humans, do we have any duties to future generations of humans? One commentator, with rhetorical cleverness, asserted that we do not since, "after all . . . what have they ever done for us?"[18] But not all duties seem to arise as a matter of reciprocity toward those who have benefited us. For example, we normally believe that we have duties not to harm perfect strangers who have in no way benefited us, not to mention parental duties toward children from whom parents may never benefit. It is worth noting a distinction made by one philosopher between merely *possible people* who might exist and those who will exist; call the latter *future people*.[19] Are the latter not owed a fair share of the earth's resources and a fair share of the capital stock, comparable in some sense to the share that was part of the world into which we were born? Consider an analogy. Would it be fair for a sibling to take all of a parent's estate and pass on all the debt to his or her sibling? Would it be fair for the prior generation to virtually exhaust most of the planet's sources and sinks and leave the present generation with only the crumbs, so to speak? Could it be all right for us to do so to the next generation? These issues are explored more fully in Section V.E, "Future Generations and Sustainability Questions."

But is there really a serious problem of declining or disappearing resources? Can we find alternative materials when existing sources run out? Can we indefinitely find a technological fix for our problems? Some argue that all the worries (or most) about resources drying up are a grand miscalculation, if not a grand hoax. Indeed, such is the view of "technological optimists" or "cornucopians" such as Herman Kahn and economist Julian Simon (Simon denies that he deserves the label "cornucopian"). In Essay 56 in this section, Simon defends the view that the supply of natural resources is infinite. Given this view it is intelligible that Simon holds that "almost equally beyond any doubt, however, an additional person is also a boon."[20] After all, he says, each will pay taxes "and make efforts to beautify the environment."[21] Further, "enabling a potential human being to come into life and to enjoy life is a good thing."[22] It is at this point that Simon may commit the fallacy of inferring that more is better from the assumption that human life is good.[23] Alternatively, he may be claiming, more radically, that all potential human life ought to become actual. Because about one-third of pregnancies spontaneously abort, one wonders whether Simon regrets that the global population is not vastly larger. It is not clear why he accuses those arguing in favor of a smaller human population, such as Paul Ehrlich, as having an absence of respect for human life.[24] Should the same be said of couples who choose to have two children instead of ten?

Some predictions of famine and death by Ehrlich and others have been exaggerated. Ehrlich predicted in 1968 in *The Population Bomb* that "The battle to feed all of humanity is now over. In the 1970s and 1980s hundreds of millions of people will starve to death."[25] Others were more extreme. In 1991 Ehrlich claimed that about 200 million people *have* died of starvation or hunger-related diseases in the last couple of decades.[26] Should we say that the warnings of Ehrlich and others were irrational and to be dismissed because they overestimated the numbers? In comparatively evaluating the magnitude of the human tragedy involved, it is worth recalling the Holocaust, an event that by most accounts involved the deaths of 6 to 15 million people. Still, Simon was correct to insist that technology would allow greater food production than that which many, including Ehrlich, had estimated. Nevertheless, it seems absurdly myopic to focus only on predictions of supply and need over a period of a few decades, although that is expansive compared to the purview of the typical American politician, namely, 4 to 8 years.

Were it true that resources are infinite, it would considerably lessen worries about burgeoning population and sustainability of current patterns of consumption. Were it true, the question of fair distribution or equity might loom as the one important moral issue. There is, admittedly, no doubt that we will continue to discover ways of substituting one material for another as one becomes scarce and costly, such as the use of fiber optic cables in place of copper wire, The belief that this will *always* occur without enormous cost to humans or others seems firmly anchored in wish fulfillment and is largely an article of faith. In contrast, some prospects, such as for developing virtually unlimited supplies of energy, are supportable by good reasons. We need not generalize about all resources, and we need not succumb to the psychologically seductive voices that say, "Don't worry; be happy, and there will be a technological fix in due time." The important substitutivity issue is explored in Section V.E in connection with disputes over sustainability.

Partha S. Dasgupta, educated in India and England and professor of economics at the University of Cambridge, prods us to think about how matters work "closer to the ground." In Essay 57, Population, Poverty, and the Local Environment" Dasgupta asserts that recent studies of particular local communities show, contrary to simpler hypotheses, that three important factors, population growth, poverty, and environmental degradation, influence each other in complex, indirect ways. In studying the way in which family planning decisions get made within households in developing countries, Dasgupta finds a disparity among family members in the capacity to influence these decisions, one that cuts along lines of both gender and age. Generally, those who are old or female have less influence. There is also a correlative disparity in the kind and degree of burdens born within the family. In sub-Sahara Africa, for example, a typical woman spends half of her adult life either pregnant or breastfeeding a child, setting aside miscarriages. The women may spend several hours a day just obtaining water for the family. The more burdens, the more "hands" (such as children), therefore, are needed. Similarly, in this same area the rate of deaths of women is one per 50 births, in contrast to a rate of one per 20,000 in Scandinavia. The cost of procreation is thus both high and disproportionate. Dasgupta traces the related effects on education levels. The cultural milieu, including religious beliefs and norms, in which people live has a powerful effect on the kinds of motives they have with respect to decisions to bear children. People are reluctant to be nonconformists on these matters. Further, to the extent that the costs of raising children can get passed on, a problem of "the commons" arises again (see Section V.C, especially Essays 47 to 49). Dasgupta examines how communities have dealt with this problem, and the effects of economic development (see the discussion of *growth* in V.E, especially in Essays 60 to 62) on traditional community controls. It is worth examining how, in Dasgupta's view, the complex set of incentives for bearing children tends to result in an escalating spiral—with increasing poverty and inequality; bad outcomes lead to worse ones. Understanding this existing incentive structure may provide us with the keys to breaking this destructive spiral.

Shifting back to an even more global and abstract question, what is an ideal population size for planet Earth? The question should be addressed in connection with another question explored in this book: What size human population is sustainable indefinitely? Most people agree, as do we, that the existence of human life is good and that human life is valuable. Some enigmatically say that human life is *infinitely* valuable. But even if it is very valuable, it does not follow that the more, the better. This fact is overlooked in many discussions. Certain Roman Catholic bishops have asserted that the earth could support a population of 40 billion. Given the current human predation of the planet, we wonder what transformations of human nature would be required for this scenario to be realistic. What

argument can be given for urging this or that population size? It is tempting to believe that, given current problems and the "stealing" from the future that is already under way, we need to scale down the existing population size in permissible ways or at least curtail growth in permissible ways.

Let us take flight once more, and consider a very abstract question. There is a perplexity here over the implications of the principle of utility. We comment succinctly. Given the standard view that we ought to maximize *total* net utility (see Section 2.4), it seems that we ought to try to add any probably-happy-on balance human being. There are worries here about this "total view." Is it plausible that we have a duty to continue adding people who are just barely content on balance until their continued addition would somehow reduce total utility? Could we adopt a policy whereby we could be confident that this is the likely outcome? It seems doubtful. Further, this kind of discussion, typically carried on by philosophers, is admittedly almost always of the sort that is based on the view that only humans matter, and with no explicit consideration of ecological balance or sustainability. It is tempting to think that the principle "maximize average utility" is more reasonable than "maximize total utility." However, this principle seems to imply that we ought to eliminate those who are dragging down the average (even if it does not require us to add anyone whose utility level would have that undesired effect). One might murder homeless people in their sleep to achieve this end, but surely no utilitarian would, or should, accept this notion. It seems that utilitarians ought to explain why their position does not imply this. If it does not, it may be because the principle of utility has been augmented by other principles, but then it may not be obvious that the resulting view should be thought of as Utiltarianism[27] We have here another instance in which it is tempting to say that we ought to foster human (and other) well-being but only in certain ways (nonutilitarian philosophers sometimes say that the right precedes the good—that is, one cannot determine the right as whatever maximizes the good)—ways that are simply not indicated by a simple principle urging utility maximization. In general, discussion of what should be the optimal human population size seems a bit like contemplating exactly where to land when one's parachute has failed to open. The basic need is simply to regain control. A fundamental question is whether we should not attempt to promote well-being within certain constraints without trying simply to maximize it. Aside from the question of the implications of the principle of utility for population policy, it is clear that any adequate view will have to take into account the consequences of alternative policies. To that extent no theory can afford to ignore questions about consequences. So rights theories must do so as well.

NOTES

1. Donald VanDeVeer and Christine Pierce, eds., *People, Penguins, and Plastic Trees* (Belmont, CA: Wadsworth, 1986).

2. Paul and Anne Ehrlich, *Healing the Planet* (Reading, MA: Addison-Wesley, 1991), pp. 72–73.

3. Amartya Sen has pointed out that lack of access to food among many starving peoples is often a function of their lack of money; when money is supplied, market forces respond with food.

4. In the fall of 1992 some food was being airlifted to Somalia, but matters were so desperate that people there were eating animal skins to survive. Civil war and drought have combined to make one-fifth of its population face imminent starvation; over half suffer from malnutrition. A major airlift began at the end of that year. See "Starving Somalis Eat Animal Skins," in *News and Observer* (Raleigh, NC) August 20, 1992.

5. We refer the reader to the essay by William Aiken. "The 'Carrying Capacity' Equivocation" in *Social Theory and Practice* 6(l) (Spring 1980), 1–11.

6. See Mary Midgley, in *Animals and Why They Matter* (Harmondsworth, England: Penguin, 1983).

7. In thinking about doubling times, or for that matter mortgage rates or automobile loans, it is useful to know "the rule of 72." The rate of increase divided

into 72 will be the time span it will take for the entity in question to double. So if a population is growing at 2 percent annually, it will double in 36 years. The current rate of increase of the global population is lower than a decade or so ago; it is now about 1.7 percent. Hence, at this rate the doubling time is just over 42 years. A population of 500 million growing at a rate of 4 percent a year would double every 18 years and, hence, quadruple in less than 100 years, and become 2 billion in less than a century.

8. Paul and Anne Ehrlich, *Healing the Planet*, p. 8.

9. Jonathan Weiner, *The Next One Hundred Years* (New York: Bantam Books, 1991), p. 41.

10. Jessica Matthews, "Rift Is Hampering Real Work on Population Issue," *News and Observer* (Raleigh, NC) April 15 1990, p. 13A.

11. Some were offered inducements, but the promised benefits were often not delivered.

12. In 1992 a popular singer, Sinead O'Connor, on American television, tore up a picture of the Pope. This event offended many and some suggested she needed "spiritual counseling," but this reaction reveals in part a lack of understanding on the part of many as to why the Pope is often not viewed as a source of moral wisdom but a major contributor to environmental tragedy, and hence a source of morally evil advice.

13. A powerful film called *The People Bomb*, one that has influenced this paragraph is available from the television network CNN.

14. Murray Bookchin cites poet Gary Snyder assaying, "Mankind is a locust-blight on the planet" and has cited another environmental writer, under the pseudonym of "Miss Ann Thropy," as welcoming the AIDS epidemic as "a necessary solution" to the "population problem." See *Defending the Earth*, edited by Steve Chase (Boston: South End Press, 199 1), p. 123.

15. This movement, a backlash to the "environmental" movement, has Ron Arnold as one spokesman. The movement is supported mostly by those who are bitter about environmental restrictions on their "property rights," restrictions on the "free market," ranchers, various corporate interests, logging companies, and so on. Its views tend to be totally anthropocentric, oriented toward short-term human interests, indeed the interests of some rural Americans and those corporate backers who find common cause.

16. The remark was made at the Republican presidential nominating convention on August 17, 1992.

17. See Ian Barbour, *Technology, Environment and Human Values* (New York: Praeger Publishing), 1980, p. 19.

18. The reference to the author of the remark quoted is lost; however, this sort of position has been expressed by Thomas Schwartz who has said, "We've no obligation extending indefinitely or even terribly far into the future to provide any wide-spread, continuing benefits to our descendants." See Thomas Schwartz, "Obligations to Posterity" in *Obligations to Future Generations*, edited by R. I. Sikora and Brian Barry (Philadelphia: Temple University Press, 1978), p. 3.

19. The distinction is due to Mary Anne Warren in "Do Potential People Have Rights?" in Sikora and Barry, p. 28.

20. Julian Simon, *The Ultimate Resource* (Princeton: Princeton University Press, 1981), p. 4.

21. Ibid.

22. Ibid., p. 10.

23. It is worth noting that Simon allows himself various valuative judgments because his official (positivistic) view is that science cannot show that a population size is too large or too small because such judgments depend upon our values, a matter about which science is silent." See Chapter 23 of his book. It is astonishing how many professionals who are trained in a field commonly labeled a "science"

take this positivistic view but go on to defend to the death numerous normative judgments, all the while not admitting it or not ceasing to insist that their view is something more than a preference.

24. Ibid., p. 10. Simon expresses surprise that "Some people even impute feelings to nature, to trees or to animals" (see p. 153). This remark is symptomatic of much economic and philosophical doctrine, which until the last decade or so has been oblivious to the compelling arguments in favor of regarding many animals as sentient, and hence questioning the purely anthropocentric moral position such doctrine presupposes. In a related manner, he holds that resources are valuable only when found by humans gathered and "harnessed for human needs" (see p. 346). And some of us make the mistake of appreciating (hence, valuing) the sunshine, fresh air, and babbling brooks!

25. Ibid., pp. 54–16.

26. Paul and Anne Ehrlich, *Healing the Planet*, p. 5.

27. For a defense of the utilitarian view against these sorts of objections, see the fine book by Robin Attfield, *The Ethics of Environmental Concern* (New York: Columbia University Press, 1983), Chapter 6.

53. An Essay on the Principle of Population

Thomas Robert Malthus

. . .

I have read some of the speculations on the perfectibility of man and of society with great pleasure. I have been warmed and delighted with the enchanting picture which they hold forth. I ardently wish for such happy improvements. But I see great, and, to my understanding, unconquerable difficulties in the way to them. These difficulties it is my present purpose to state, declaring, at the same time, that so far from exulting in them, as a cause of triumph over the friends of innovation, nothing would give me greater pleasure than to see them completely removed.

The most important argument that I shall adduce is certainly not new. The principles on which it depends have been explained in part by Hume, and more at large by Dr. Adam Smith. It has

been advanced and applied to the present subject, though not with its proper weight, or in the most forcible point of view, by Mr. Wallace, and it may probably have been stated by many writers that I have never met with. I should certainly therefore not think of advancing it again, though I mean to place it in a point of view in some degree different from any that I have hitherto seen, if it had ever been fairly and satisfactorily answered.

. . .

I think I may fairly make two postulata.

First, That food is necessary to the existence of man.

Secondly, That the passion between the sexes is necessary and will remain nearly in its present state. These two laws, ever since we have had any

From Thomas Malthus, "An Essay on the Principle of Population," in *Population, Evolution and Birth Control: A College of Controversial Ideas,* 2nd ed., edited by Garrett Hardin (San Francisco: W. H. Freeman, 1969), pp. 4–10, 12, 13, 15, 16.

knowledge of mankind, appear to have been fixed laws of our nature, and, as we have not hitherto seen any alteration in them, we have no right to conclude that they will ever cease to be what they now are, without an immediate act of power in that Being who first arranged the system of the universe, and for the advantage of his creatures, still executes, according to fixed laws, all its various operations.

I do not know that any writer has supposed that on this earth man will ultimately be able to live without food. But Mr. Godwin has conjectured that the passion between the sexes may in time be extinguished. As, however, he calls this part of his work a deviation into the land of conjecture, I will not dwell longer upon it at present than to say that the best arguments for the perfectibility of man are drawn from a contemplation of the great progress that he has already made from the savage state and the difficulty of saying where he is to stop. But towards the extinction of the passion between sexes, no progress whatever has hitherto been made. It appears to exist in as much force at present as it did two thousand or four thousand years ago. There are individual exceptions now as there always have been. But, as these exceptions do not appear to increase in number, it would surely be a very unphilosophical mode of arguing, to infer merely from the existence of an exception that the exception would, in time, become the rule, and the rule the exception.

Assuming then, my postulata as granted, I say, that the power of population is indefinitely greater than the power in the earth to produce subsistence for man.

Population, when unchecked, increases in a geometrical ratio. Subsistence increases only in an arithmetical ratio. A slight acquaintance with numbers will show the immensity of the first power in comparison of the second.

By that law of our nature which makes food necessary to the life of man, the effects of these two unequal powers must be kept equal.

This implies a strong and constantly operating check on population from the difficulty of subsistence. This difficulty must fall some where and must necessarily be severely felt by a large portion of mankind.

Through the animal and vegetable kingdoms, nature has scattered the seeds of life abroad with the most profuse and liberal hand. She has been comparatively sparing in the room and the nourishment necessary to rear them. The germs of existence contained in this spot of earth, with ample food, and ample room to expand in, would fill millions of worlds in the course of a few thousand years. Necessity, that imperious all pervading law of nature, restrains them within the prescribed bounds. The race of plants, and race of animals shrink under this great restrictive law. And the race of man cannot, by any efforts of reason, escape from it. Among plants and animals its effects are waste of seed, sickness, and premature death. Among mankind, misery and vice. The former, misery, is an absolutely necessary consequence of it. Vice is a highly probable consequence, and we therefore see it abundantly prevail, but it ought not, perhaps, to be called an absolutely necessary consequence. The ordeal of virtue is to resist all temptation to evil.

This natural inequality of the two powers of population and of production in the earth and that great law of our nature which must constantly keep their effects equal form the great difficulty that to me appears insurmountable in the way to the perfectibility of society. All other arguments are of slight and subordinate consideration in comparison of this. I see no way by which man can escape from the weight of this law which pervades all animated nature. No fancied equality, no agrarian regulations in their utmost extent, could remove the pressure of it even for a single century. And it appears, therefore, to be decisive against the possible existence of a society, all the members of which should live in ease, happiness, and comparative leisure; and feel no anxiety about providing the means of subsistence for themselves and families.

Consequently, if the premises are just, the argument is conclusive against the perfectibility of the mass of mankind.

I have thus sketched the general outline of the argument, but I will examine it more particularly, and I think it will be found that experience, the true source and foundation of all knowledge, invariably confirms its truth.

. . .

I said that population, when unchecked, increased in a geometrical ratio, and subsistence for man in an arithmetical ratio.

Let us examine whether this position be just.

I think it will be allowed, that no state has hitherto existed (at least that we have any account of) where the manners were so pure and simple, and the means of subsistence so abundant, that no check whatever has existed to early marriages among the lower classes, from a fear of not providing well for their families, or among the higher classes, from a fear of lowering their condition in life. Consequently in no state that we have yet known has the power of population been left to exert itself with perfect freedom.

Let us now take any spot on earth, this Island for instance, and see in what ratio the subsistence it affords can be supposed to increase. We will begin with it under its present state of cultivation.

If I allow that by the best possible policy, by breaking up more land and by great encouragements to agriculture, the produce of this Island may be doubled in the first twenty-five years, I think it will be allowing as much as any person can well demand.

In the next twenty-five years, it is impossible to suppose that the produce could be quadrupled. It would be contrary to all our knowledge of the qualities of land. The very utmost that we can conceive, is, that the increase in the second twenty-five years might equal the present produce. Let us then take this for our rule, though certainly far beyond the truth, and allow that by great exertion, the whole produce of the Island might be increased every twenty-five years, by a quantity of subsistence equal to what it at present produces. The most enthusiastic speculator cannot suppose a greater increase than this. In a few centuries it would make every acre of land in the Island like a garden.

Yet this ratio of increase is evidently arithmetical.

It may be fairly said, therefore, that the means of subsistence increase in an arithmetical ratio. Let us now bring the effects of these two ratios together.

The population of the Island is computed to be about seven millions, and we will suppose the present produce equal to the support of such a number. In the first twenty-five years the population would be fourteen millions, and the food being also doubled, the means of subsistence would be equal to this increase. In the next twenty-five years the population would be twenty-eight millions, and the means of subsistence only equal to the support of twenty-one millions. In the next period, the population would be fifty-six millions, and the means of subsistence just sufficient for half that number. And

at the conclusion of the first century the population would be one hundred and twelve millions and the means of subsistence only equal to the support of thirty-five millions, which would leave a population of seventy-seven millions totally unprovided for.

A great emigration necessarily implies unhappiness of some kind or other in the country that is deserted. For few persons will leave their families, connections, friends, and native land, to seek a settlement in untried foreign climes, without some strong subsisting causes of uneasiness where they are, or the hope of some great advantages in the place to which they are going.

But to make the argument more general and less interrupted by the partial view of emigration, let us take the whole earth, instead of one spot, and suppose that the restraints to population were universally removed. If the subsistence for man that the earth affords was to be increased every twenty-five years by a quantity equal to what the whole world at present produces, this would allow the power of production in the earth to be absolutely unlimited, and its ratio of increase much greater than we can conceive that any possible exertions of mankind could make it.

Taking the population of the world at any number, a thousand millions, for instance, the human species would increase in the ratio of—1, 2, 4, 8, 16, 32, 64, 128, 256, 512, &c. and subsistence as—1, 2, 3, 4, 5, 6, 7, 8, 9, 10, &c. In two centuries and a quarter, the population would be to the means of subsistence as 512 to 10; in three centuries at 4096 to 13, and in two thousand years the difference would be almost incalculable, though the produce in that time would have increased to an immense extent.

No limits whatever are placed to the productions of the earth; they may increase for ever and be greater than any assignable quantity; yet still the power of population being a power of a superior order, the increase of the human species can only be kept commensurate to the increase of the means of subsistence, by the constant operation of the strong law of necessity acting as a check upon the greater power.

. . .

The situation of the labourer being then again tolerably comfortable, the restraints to population are in some degree loosened, and the same retrograde and progressive movements with respect to happiness are repeated.

This sort of oscillation will not be remarked by superficial observers, and it may be difficult even for the most penetrating mind to calculate its periods. Yet that in all old states some such vibration does exist, though from various transverse causes, in a much less marked, and in a much more irregular manner and I have described it, no reflecting man who considers the subject deeply can well doubt.

Many reasons occur why this oscillation has been less obvious, and less decidedly confirmed by experience, than might naturally be expected.

One principal reason is that the histories of mankind that we possess are histories only of the higher classes. We have but few accounts that can be depended upon of the manners and customs of that part of mankind, where these retrograde and progressive movements chiefly take place. A satisfactory history of this kind, of one people, and of one period, would require the constant and minute attention of an observing mind during a long life. Some of the objects of enquiry would be, in what proportion to the number of adults was the number of marriages, to what extent vicious customs prevailed in consequence of the restrains upon matrimony, what was the comparative mortality among the children of the most distressed part of the community and those who lived rather more at their ease, what were the variations in the real price of labour, and what were the observable differences in the state of the lower classes of society with respect to ease and happiness, at different times during a certain period.

Such a history would tend greatly to elucidate the manner in which the constant check upon population acts and would probably prove the existence of the retrograde and progressive movements that have been mentioned, though the times of their vibration must necessarily be rendered irregular, from the operation of many interrupting causes, such as the introduction or failure of certain manufactures, a greater or less prevalent spirit of agricultural enterprize, years of plenty, or years of scarcity, wars and pestilence, poor laws, the invention of processes for shortening labour without the proportional extension of the market for the commodity, and, particularly, the difference between the nominal and real price of labour, a circumstance which has perhaps more than any other contributed to conceal this oscillation from common view.

It very rarely happens that the nominal price of labour universally falls, but we well know that it frequently remains the same, while the nominal price of provisions has been gradually increasing. This is, in effect, a real fall in the price of labour, and during this period the condition of the lower orders of the community must gradually grow worse and worse. But the farmers and capitalists are growing rich from the real cheapness of labour.

. . .

The theory on which the truth of this position depends appears to me so extremely clear that I feel at a loss to conjecture what part of it can be denied.

That population cannot increase without the means of subsistence is a proposition so evident that it needs no illustration.

That population does invariably increase where there are the means of subsistence, the history of every people that have ever existed will abundantly prove.

And that the superior power of population cannot be checked without producing misery or vice, the ample portion of these too bitter ingredients in the cup of human life and continuance of the physical causes that seem to have produced them bear too convincing a testimony.

. . .

The only true criterion of a real and permanent increase in the population of any country is the increase of the means of subsistence. . . .

The happiness of a country does not depend, absolutely, upon its poverty or its riches, upon its youth or its age, upon its being thinly or fully inhabited, but upon the rapidity with which it is increasing, upon the degree in which the yearly increase of food approaches to the yearly increase of an unrestricted population. This approximation is always the nearest in new colonies, where the knowledge and industry of an old State, operate on the fertile unappropriated land of a new one. In other cases, the youth or the age of a State is not in this respect of very great importance. It is probable, that the food of Great Britain is divided in as great plenty to the inhabitants, at the present period, as it was two thousand, three thousand, or four thousand years ago. And there is reason to believe that the poor and thinly inhabited tracts of the Scotch Highlands, are as much distressed by an overcharged population, as the rich and populous province of Flanders. . . .

Famine seems to be the last, the most dreadful resource of nature. The power of population is so superior to the power in the earth to produce subsistence for man, that premature death must in some shape or other visit the human race. The vices of mankind are active and able ministers of depopulation. They are the precursors in the great army of destruction; and often finish the dreadful work themselves. But should they fail in this war of extermination, sickly seasons, epidemics, pestilence, and plague, advance in terrific array, and sweep off their thousands and ten thousands. Should success be still incomplete, gigantic inevitable famine stalks in the rear, and with one mighty blow, levels the population with the food of the world.

54. SIDELIGHT: If Earth Could Speak

It surprises me no end that you members of *Homo sapiens* can get so fascinated with your own family histories and yet tend to remain so abysmally ignorant of Me, the Home Planet, the sustainer of life; after all, to quote some human, your time living on my surface doesn't amount to a hill of beans. Lend me your 12 billion ears for a minute.

You finally came to recognize that I am not flat and that I do not have four corners. You came to understand rather noteworthy events such as continental drift only in the last forty years. Now virtually all of you have learned that I am a little older than 4004 B.C.E. If you wish to be "geologically correct" I am about 4.5 billion years old, and I am using "billion" as the Americans do to mean "1,000 million." So, you hominids have only been around, as some of you say, for a "twinkling of the geological eye," namely about 5 million years. Life itself took quite a while to get up and running, about one and a half-billion years since my birthday; that is, it began quite simply in my oceans about 3.6 billion years ago, as your scientists, in the 1950s, inferred from the stromatolite fossils found on one of my favorite continents, Australia. You "hyper-recent types"—that is, members of the species *Homo sapiens sapiens*—have been stirring things up for about 50,000 to 100,000 years. Of course your records only tend to go back about 5,000 years at best; you've really got to learn how to take care of your past better, and I'm not even going to mention the future you seem to be, rather literally, cooking up—what some of you used to call a "witches' brew," I believe. You are causing things to get out of hand, and even beyond my attempts to balance things out. That newcomer you call Aristotle was on to something when be said "moderation in all things." You were not such a problem when there were only a half-billion of you back about 1650, or when there were a billion of you back about 1800 or so, but you are about as bad as the rabbits; you're over 6 billion and now doubling in number in forty years or so. Do you not see the collision course that you are on, or is it that you just do not give a damn about your grandchildren? You finally invented a means of preventing conception and yet many of you prefer to ravage each other and use up my resources rather than use one of your more intelligent devices. Some of you still treat every fertilized human egg as if it were a rare phenomenon. Let me tell you something; eggs are cheap and human sperm are in plentiful supply. The average male's ejaculation could quickly repopulate the planet. What is not in plentiful supply, what is not so readily replaceable is the delicate balance of clean air, unfouled water (why do you keep moving humongous quantities of my oil through my nice oceans in gigantic single-hulled supertankers?), the balance of ecosystems, the protection of my ozone layer, and those factors that keep the climate in such gradual flux as to keep morbidity and premature mortality within the limits that allow for a healthy and biodiverse, sustainable planet.

Unlike some of my more successful species, such as the dinosaurs, who lasted over 150 million years, the "smart money" among planetary gamblers is that you people will not be around for a fraction of the time; was it not that foolish philosopher Protagoras who said that "man is the measure of all things"? And your "economists" and "utilitarians" seem to keep recommending ways to maximize fulfillment of the desires (however silly and contrary to my maintaining a healthy biosphere) of just one of millions of the species to whom I offer sustenance.

Of course, not all the hard times are to be blamed on your "high-rolling" practices. I must admit that a while back, about 245 million years ago, my Siberian volcanoes acted up considerably and about 95 percent of all species came to a bad end. I believe your scientists speak of it as the "great dying" or the Permian extinction. Most tragic. For your records, it was much worse than the other four Big Ones (namely, the Ordivician, 440 million years ago; the Late Devonian, 365 million years ago; the Late Triassic, 210 million years ago; or the one most familiar to you, the Final Cretaceous, 66 million years ago). Indeed, I much prefer having lively and biodiverse, ongoing (sustainable) activity.

Furthermore, some of you have ridiculous appetites—including many of your thinner members. For example, the average American is using 40 times as much energy as an average person in developing countries. Do you have any idea how many millions of years it took Me to store up those fossil fuels? You Americans seem to think that you are smart to charge a pittance for gasoline when other nations ration it out at $4 a gallon. Do you know that one of your "solutions," namely, nuclear power, yields deadly radioactivity for thousands of years, not long to me, of course, but perilous to human life and many other forms?

By the way, the next Ice Age is only about 10 years from now. Do you know that I have had many others during my history? I remember the last one, a real doozy—back around 20,000 B.C.E.—why, it seems like only yesterday! The average temperature on my surface was only about 1.5 to 2 degrees Celsius cooler than today, but the ice over that "beehive" of humans that you call New York City was about a half-mile high, of little interest to Me, of course, but more than a little trouble for you. Of course, it might put a needed dent in your numbers. Or are you rehearsing for that by overheating everything in the meantime? It's "no skin off my surface," so to speak, but you have warmed the surface about one-half a degree Celsius in the last moment, I mean what you call "a century," with all your carbon dioxide and other emissions. If you double those CO_2 levels again, the average temperature on my surface is going to be hotter than it has been in a *million* years (about 4 degrees Fahrenheit). Do you Youngsters on my surface really think that you can survive beyond the next century without catastrophe when, of course, you members of *Homo sapiens sapiens* have been around, I note once more, only about 50,000 years? I suppose that you have figured out what happens to my glaciers when you do that, and you might surmise where all that water goes, and what then happens to my land surface that is only a few feet above sea level—and what happens to large numbers of members of your species when you are under water for very long.

55. Lifeboat Ethics

Garrett Hardin

Environmentalists use the metaphor of the earth as a "spaceship" in trying to persuade countries, industries, and people to stop wasting and polluting our natural resources. Since we all share life on this planet, they argue, no single person or institution has the right to destroy, waste, or use more than a fair share of its resources.

But does everyone on earth have an equal right to an equal share of its resources? The spaceship metaphor can be dangerous when used by misguided idealists to justify suicidal policies for sharing our resources through uncontrolled immigration and foreign aid. In their enthusiastic but unrealistic generosity, they confuse the ethics of a spaceship with those of a lifeboat.

A true spaceship would have to be under the control of a captain, since no ship could possibly survive if its course were determined by committee. Spaceship Earth certainly has no captain; the United Nations is merely a toothless tiger, with little power to enforce any policy upon its bickering members.

If we divide the world crudely into rich nations and poor nations, two-thirds of them are desperately poor, and only one third comparatively rich, with the United States the wealthiest of all. Metaphorically, each rich nation can be seen as a lifeboat full of comparatively rich people. In the ocean outside each lifeboat swim the poor of the world, who would like to get in, or at least to share some of the wealth. What should the lifeboat passengers do?

First, we must recognize the limited capacity of any lifeboat. For example, a nation's land has a limited capacity to support a population and as the current energy crisis has shown us, in some ways we have already exceeded the carrying capacity of our land.

Adrift in a Moral Sea

So here we sit, say 50 people in our lifeboat. To be generous, let us assume it has room for 10 more, making a total capacity of 60. Suppose the 50 of us in the lifeboat see 100 others swimming in the water outside, begging for admission to our boat or for handouts. We have several options: we may be tempted to try to live by the Christian ideal of being "our brother's keeper," or by the Marxist ideal of "to each according to his needs." Since the needs of all in the water are the same, and since they can all be seen as "our brothers," we could take them all into our boat, making a total of 150 in a boat designed for 60. The boat swamps, everyone drowns. Complete justice, complete catastrophe.

Since the boat has an unused excess capacity of 10 more passengers, we could admit just 10 more to it. But which 10 do we let in? How do we choose? Do we pick the best 10, the neediest 10, "first come, first served"? And what do we say to the 90 we exclude? If we do let an extra 10 into our lifeboat, we will have lost our "safety factor," an engineering principle of critical importance. For example, if we don't leave room for excess capacity as a safety factor in our country's agriculture, a new plant disease or a bad change in the weather could have disastrous consequences.

Suppose we decide to preserve our small safety factor and admit no more to the lifeboat. Our survival is then possible, although we shall have to be constantly on guard against boarding parties.

While this last solution clearly offers the only means of our survival, it is morally abhorrent to many people. Some say they feel guilty about their good luck. My reply is simple: "Get out and yield your place to others." This may solve the problem of the guilt-ridden person's conscience, but it does not change the ethics of the lifeboat. The needy person to whom the guilt-ridden person yields his place will not himself feel guilty about his good luck. If he did, he would not climb aboard. The net result of conscience-stricken people giving up their unjustly held seats is the elimination of that sort of conscience from the lifeboat.

This is the basic metaphor within which we must work out our solutions. Let us now enrich the image, step by step, with substantive additions from the real world, a world that must solve real and pressing problems of overpopulation and hunger.

The harsh ethics of the lifeboat become even harsher when we consider the reproductive differences between the rich nations and the poor nations. The people inside the lifeboats are doubling in numbers every 87 years; those swimming around outside are doubling, on the average, every 35 years, more than twice as fast as the rich. And since the world's resources are dwindling, the difference in prosperity between the rich and the poor can only increase.

As of 1973, the U.S. had a population of 210 million people, who were increasing by 0.8 percent per year. Outside our lifeboat, let us imagine another 210 million people (say the combined populations of Colombia, Ecuador, Venezuela, Morocco, Pakistan, Thailand, and the Philippines) who are increasing at a rate of 3.3 percent per year. Put differently, the doubling time for this aggregate population is 21 years, compared to 87 years for the U.S.

Multiplying the Rich and the Poor

Now suppose the U.S. agreed to pool its resources with those seven countries, with everyone receiving an equal share. Initially, the ratio of Americans to non-Americans in this model would be one-to-one. But consider what the ratio would be after 87 years, by which time the Americans would have doubled to a population of 420 million. By then, doubling every 21 years, the other group would have swollen to 354 billion. Each American would have to share the available resources with more than eight people.

But, one could argue, this discussion assumes that current population trends will continue, and they may not. Quite so. Most likely the rate of population increase will decline much faster in the U.S. than it will in the other countries, and there does not seem to be much we can do about it. In sharing with "each according to his needs," we must recognize that needs are determined by population size, which is determined by the rate of reproduction, which at present is regarded as a sovereign right of every nation, poor or not. This being so, the philanthropic load created by the sharing ethic of the spaceship can only increase.

The Tragedy of the Commons

The fundamental error of spaceship ethics, and the sharing it requires, is that it leads to what I call "the tragedy of the commons." Under a system of private property, the men who own property recognize their responsibility to care for it, for if they don't they will eventually suffer. A farmer, for instance, will allow no more cattle in a pasture than its carrying capacity justifies. If he overloads it, erosion sets in, weeds take over, and he loses the use of the pasture.

If a pasture becomes a commons open to all, the right of each to use it may not be matched by a corresponding responsibility to protect it. Asking everyone to use it with discretion will hardly do, for the considerate herdsman who refrains from overloading the commons suffers more than a selfish one who says his needs are greater. If everyone would restrain himself, all would be well; but it takes only one less than everyone to ruin a system of voluntary restraint. In a crowded world of less than perfect human beings, mutual ruin is inevitable if there are no controls. This is the tragedy of the commons.

One of the major tasks of education today should be the creation of such an acute awareness of the dangers of the commons that people will recognize its many varieties. For example, the air and water have become polluted because they are treated as commons. Further growth in the population or per-capita conversion of natural resources into pollutants will only make the problem worse. The same holds true for the fish of the oceans. Fishing fleets have nearly disappeared in many parts of the world, technological improvements in the art of fishing are hastening the day of complete ruin. Only the replacement of the system of the commons with a responsible system of control will save the land, air, water and oceanic fisheries.

The World Food Bank

In recent years there has been a push to create a new commons called a World Food Bank, an international depository of food reserves to which nations would contribute according to their abilities and from which they would draw according to their needs. This humanitarian proposal has received support from many liberal international groups, and from such prominent citizens as Margaret Mead, U.N. Secretary General Kurt Waldheim, and Senators Edward Kennedy and George McGovern.

A world food bank appeals powerfully to our humanitarian impulses. But before we rush ahead with such a plan, let us recognize where the greatest political push comes from, lest we be disillusioned later. Our experience with the "Food for Peace program," or Public Law 480, gives us the answer. This program moved billions of dollars worth of U.S. surplus grain to food-short, population-long countries during the past two decades. But when P.L. 480 first became law, a headline in the business magazine *Forbes* revealed the real power behind it: "Feeding the World's Hungry Millions: How It Will Mean Billions for U.S. Business."

And indeed it did. In the years 1960 to 1970, U.S. taxpayers spent a total of $7.9 billion on the Food for Peace program. Between 1948 and 1970, they also paid an additional $50 billion for other economic-aid programs, some of which went for food and food-producing machinery and technology. Though all U.S. taxpayers were forced to contribute to the cost of P.L. 480, certain special interest groups gained handsomely under the program. Farmers did not have to contribute the grain; the Government, or rather the taxpayers, bought it from them at full market prices. The increased demand raised prices of farm products generally. The manufacturers of farm machinery, fertilizers and pesticides benefited by the farmers' extra efforts to grow more food. Grain elevators profited from storing the surplus until it could be shipped. Railroads made money hauling it to ports, and shipping lines profited from carrying it overseas.

The implementation of P.L. 480 required the creation of a vast Government bureaucracy, which then acquired its own vested interest in continuing the program regardless of its merits.

Extracting Dollars

Those who proposed and defended the Food for Peace program in public rarely mentioned its importance to any of these special interests. The public emphasis was always on its humanitarian effects. The combination of silent selfish interests and highly vocal humanitarian apologists made a powerful and successful lobby for extracting money from taxpayers. We can expect the same lobby to push now for the creation of a World Food Bank.

However great the potential benefit to selfish interests, it should not be a decisive argument against a truly humanitarian program. We must ask if such a program would actually do more good than harm, not only momentarily but also in the long run. Those who propose the food bank usually refer to a current "emergency" or "crisis" in terms of world food supply. But what is an emergency? Although they may be infrequent and sudden, everyone knows that emergencies will occur from time to time. A well-run family, company, organization or country prepares for the likelihood of accidents and emergencies. It expects them, it budgets for them, it saves for them.

Learning the Hard Way

What happens if some organizations or countries budget for accidents and others do not? If each country is solely responsible for its own well-being, poorly managed ones will suffer. But they can learn from experience. They may mend their ways, and learn to budget for infrequent but certain emergencies. For example, the weather varies from year to year, and periodic crop failures are certain. A wise and competent government saves out of the production of the good years in anticipation of bad years to come. Joseph taught this policy to Pharaoh in Egypt more than 2,000 years ago. Yet the great majority of the governments in the world today do not follow such a policy. They lack either the wisdom or the competence, or both. Should those nations that do manage to put something aside be forced to come to the rescue each time an emergency occurs among the poor nations?

"But it isn't their fault!" Some kind-hearted liberals argue. "How can we blame the poor people who are caught in an emergency? Why must they suffer for the sins of their governments?" The concept of blame is simply not relevant here. The real question is, what are the operational consequences of establishing a world food bank? If it is open to every country every time a need develops, slovenly rulers will not be motivated to take Joseph's advice. Someone will always come to their aid. Some countries will deposit food in the world food bank, and others will withdraw it. There will be almost no overlap. As a result of such solutions to food shortage emergencies, the poor countries will not learn to mend their ways, and will suffer progressively greater emergencies as their populations grow.

Population Control the Crude Way

On the average, poor countries undergo a 2.5 percent increase in population each year; rich countries, about 0.8 percent. Only rich countries have anything in the way of food reserves set aside, and even they do not have as much as they should. Poor countries have none. If poor countries received no food from the outside, the rate of their population growth would be periodically checked by crop failures and famines. But if they can always draw on a world food bank in time of need, their population can continue to grow unchecked, and so will their "need" for aid. In the short run, a world food bank may diminish that need, but in the long run it actually increases the need without limit.

Without some system of worldwide food sharing, the proportion of people in the rich and poor nations might eventually stabilize. The overpopulated poor countries would decrease in numbers, while the rich countries that had room for more people would increase. But with a well-meaning system of sharing, such as a world food bank, the growth differential between the rich and the poor countries will not only persist, it will increase. Because of the higher rate of population growth in the poor countries of the world, 88 percent of today's children are born poor, and only 12 percent rich. Year by year the ratio becomes worse, as the fast-reproducing poor outnumber the slow-reproducing rich.

A world food bank is thus a commons in disguise. People will have more motivation to draw from it than to add to any common store. The less provident and less able will multiply at the expense of the abler and more provident, bringing eventual ruin upon all who share in the commons. Besides, any system of "sharing" that amounts to foreign aid from the rich nations to the poor nations will carry the taint of charity, which will contribute little to the world peace so devoutly desired by those who support the idea of a world food bank.

As past U.S. foreign-aid programs have amply and depressingly demonstrated, international charity frequently inspires mistrust and antagonism rather than gratitude on the part of the recipient nation [see "What Other Nations Hear When the Eagle Screams," by Kenneth J. and Mary M. Gergen, PT, June].

Chinese Fish and Miracle Rice

The modern approach to foreign aid stresses the export of technology and advice, rather than money and food. As an ancient Chinese proverb goes: "Give a man a fish and he will eat for a day; teach him how to fish and he will eat for the rest of his days." Acting on this advice, the Rockefeller and Ford Foundations have financed a number of programs for improving agriculture in the hungry nations. Known as the "Green Revolution," these programs have led to the development of "miracle rice" and "miracle wheat," new strains that offer bigger harvests and greater resistance to crop damage. Norman Borlaug, the Nobel Prize winning agronomist who, supported by the Rockefeller Foundation, developed "miracle wheat," is one of the most prominent advocates of a world food bank.

Whether or not the Green Revolution can increase food production as much as its champions claim is a debatable but possibly irrelevant point: Those who support this well-intended humanitarian effort should first consider some of the fundamentals of human ecology. Ironically, one man who did was the late Alan Gregg, a vice president of the Rockefeller Foundation. Two decades ago he expressed strong doubts about the wisdom of such attempts to increase food production. He likened the growth and spread of humanity over the surface of the earth to the spread of cancer in the human body, remarking that "cancerous growths demand food; but, as far as I know, they have never been cured by getting it."

Overloading the Environment

Every human born constitutes a draft on all aspects of the environment: food, air, water, forests, beaches, wildlife, scenery, and solitude. Food can, perhaps, be significantly increased to meet a growing demand. But what about clean beaches, unspoiled forests, and solitude? If we satisfy a growing population's need for food, we necessarily decrease its per capita supply of the other resources needed by men.

India, for example, now has a population of 600 million, which increases by 15 million each year. This population already puts a huge load on a relatively impoverished environment. The country's forests are now only a small fraction of what they were three centuries ago, and floods and erosion continually destroy the insufficient farmland that remains. Every one of the 15 million new lives added to India's population puts an additional burden on the environment, and increases the economic and social costs of crowding. However humanitarian our intent, every Indian life saved through medical or nutritional assistance from abroad diminishes the quality of life for those who remain, and for subsequent generations. If rich countries make it possible, through foreign aid, for 600 million Indians to swell to 1.2 billion in a mere 28 years, as their current growth rate threatens, will future generations of Indians thank us for hastening the destruction of their environment? Will our good intentions be sufficient excuse for the consequences of our actions?

My final example of a commons in action is one for which the public has the least desire for rational discussion—immigration. Anyone who publicly questions the wisdom of current U.S. immigration policy is promptly charged with bigotry, prejudice, ethnocentrism, chauvinism, isolationism or selfishness. Rather than encounter such accusations, one would rather talk about other matters, leaving immigration policy to wallow in the crosscurrents of special interests that take no account of the good of the whole, or the interests of posterity.

Perhaps we still feel guilty about things we said in the past. Two generations ago the popular press frequently referred to Dagos, Wops, Polacks, Chinks and Krauts, in articles about how America was being "overrun" by foreigners of supposedly inferior genetic stock [see "The Politics of Genetic

Engineering: Who Decides Who's Defective?" PT, June]. But because the implied inferiority of foreigners was used then as justification for keeping them out, people now assume that restrictive policies could only be based on such misguided notions. There are other grounds.

A Nation of Immigrants

Just consider the numbers involved. Our Government acknowledges a net inflow of 400,000 immigrants a year. While we have no hard data on the extent of illegal entries, educated guesses put the figure at about 600,000 a year. Since the natural increase (excess of births over deaths) of the resident population now runs about 1.7 million per year, the yearly gain from immigration amounts to at least 19 percent of the total annual increase, and may be as much as 37 percent if we include the estimate for illegal immigrants. Considering the growing use of birth-control devices, the potential effect of educational campaigns by such organizations as Planned Parenthood Federation of America and Zero Population Growth, and the influence of inflation and the housing shortage, the fertility rate of American women may decline so much that immigration could account for all the yearly increase in population. Should we not at least ask if that is what we want?

For the sake of those who worry about whether the "quality" of the average immigrant compares favorably with the quality of the average resident, let us assume that immigrants and native-born citizens are of exactly equal quality, however one defines that term. We will focus here only on quantity; and since our conclusions will depend on nothing else, all charges of bigotry and chauvinism become irrelevant.

Immigration vs. Food Supply

World food banks *move food to the people*, hastening the exhaustion of the environment of the poor countries. Unrestricted immigration, on the other hand, *moves people to the food*, thus speeding up the destruction of the environment of the rich countries. We can easily understand why poor people should want to make this latter transfer, but why should rich hosts encourage it?

As in the case of foreign-aid programs, immigration receives support from selfish interests and humanitarian impulses. The primary selfish interest in unimpeded immigration is the desire of employers for cheap labor, particularly in industries and trades that offer degrading work. In the past, one wave of foreigners after another was brought into the U.S. to work at wretched jobs for wretched wages. In recent years the Cubans, Puerto Ricans, and Mexicans have had this dubious honor. The interests of the employers of cheap labor mesh well with the guilty silence of the country's liberal intelligentsia. White Anglo-Saxon Protestants are particularly reluctant to call for a closing of the doors to immigration for fear of being called bigots.

But not all countries have such reluctant leadership. Most educated Hawaiians, for example, are keenly aware of the limits of their environment, particularly in terms of population growth. There is only so much room on the islands, and the islanders know it. To Hawaiians, immigrants from the other 49 states present as great a threat as those from other nations. At a recent meeting of Hawaiian government officials in Honolulu, I had the ironic delight of hearing a speaker, who like most of his audience was of Japanese ancestry, ask how the country might practically and constitutionally close its doors to further immigration. One member of the audience countered: "How can we shut the doors now? We have many friends and relatives in Japan that we'd like to bring here some day so that they can enjoy Hawaii too." The Japanese-American speaker smiled sympathetically and answered: "Yes, but we have children now, and someday we'll have grandchildren too. We can bring more people here from Japan only by giving away some of the land that we hope to pass on to our grandchildren some day. What right do we have to do that?"

At this point, I can hear U.S. liberals asking: "How can you justify slamming the door once you're inside? You say that immigrants should be kept out. But aren't we all immigrants, or the descendants of immigrants? If we insist on staying, must we not admit all others?" Our craving for intellectual order leads us to seek and prefer symmetrical rules and morals: a single rule for me and everybody else; the same rule yesterday, today and tomorrow. Justice, we feel, should not change with time and place.

We Americans of non-Indian ancestry can look upon ourselves as the descendants of thieves who are guilty morally, if not legally, of stealing this land from its Indian owners. Should we then give back the land to the now living American descendants of those Indians? However morally or logically sound this proposal may be, I, for one, am unwilling to live by it and I know no one else who is. Besides, the logical consequence would be absurd. Suppose that, intoxicated with a sense of pure justice, we should decide to turn our land over to the Indians. Since all our other wealth has also been derived from the land, wouldn't we be morally obliged to give that back to the Indians too?

Pure Justice vs. Reality

Clearly, the concept of pure justice produces an infinite regression to absurdity. Centuries ago, wise men invented statutes of limitations to justify the rejection of such pure justice, in the interest of preventing continual disorder. The law zealously defends property rights, but only relatively recent property rights. Drawing a line after an arbitrary time has elapsed may be unjust, but the alternatives are worse.

We are all the descendants of thieves, and the world's resources are inequitably distributed. But we must begin the journey to tomorrow from the point where we are today. We cannot remake the past. We cannot safely divide the wealth equitably among all peoples so long as people reproduce at different rates. To do so would guarantee that our grandchildren, and everyone else's grandchildren, would have only a ruined world to inhabit.

To be generous with one's own possessions is quite different from being generous with those of posterity. We should call this point to the attention of those who, from a commendable love of justice and equality, would institute a system of the commons, either in the form of a world food bank, or of unrestricted immigration. We must convince them if we wish to save at least some parts of the world from environmental ruin.

Without a true world government to control reproduction and the use of available resources, the sharing ethic of the spaceship is impossible. For the foreseeable future, our survival demands that we govern our actions by the ethics of a lifeboat, harsh though they may be. Posterity will be satisfied with nothing less.

56. Can the Supply of Natural Resources Really Be Infinite? Yes!

Julian Simon

Natural resources are not finite. Yes, you read correctly. This [essay] shows that the supply of natural resources is not finite in any economic sense, which is why their cost can continue to fall in the future.

On the face of it, even to inquire whether natural resources are finite seems like nonsense. Everyone "knows" that resources are finite, from C. P. Snow to Isaac Asimov to as many other persons as you have time to read about in the newspaper. And this belief has led many persons to draw far-reaching conclusions about the future of our world economy and civilization. A prominent example is the *Limits to Growth* group, who open the preface to their 1974 book, a sequel to the *Limits,* as follows.

Most people acknowledge that the earth is finite. . . . Policy makers generally assume that growth will provide them tomorrow with the resources required to deal with today's problems. . . . Recently, however, concern about the consequences of population growth, increased environmental pollution, and the depletion of fossil fuels has cast doubt upon the belief that continuous growth is either possible or a panacea.[1]

(Note the rhetorical device embedded in the term "acknowledge" in the first sentence of the quotation. That word suggests that the statement is a fact, and that anyone who does not "acknowledge" it is simply refusing to accept or admit it.)

The idea that resources are finite in supply is so pervasive and influential that the President's 1972 Commission on Population Growth and the American Future based its policy recommendations squarely upon this assumption. Right at the beginning of its report the commission asked, "What does this nation stand for and where is it going? At some point in the future, the finite earth will not satisfactorily accommodate more human beings—nor will the United States. . . . It is both proper and in our best interest to participate fully in the worldwide search for the good life, which must include the eventual stabilization of our numbers."[2]

The assumption of finiteness is responsible for misleading many scientific forecasters because their conclusions follow inexorably from that assumption. From the *Limits to Growth* team again, this time on food: "The world model is based on the fundamental assumption that there is an upper limit to the total amount of food that can be produced annually by the world's agricultural system."[3]

The Theory of Decreasing Natural-Resource Scarcity

We shall begin with a far-out example to see what contrasting possibilities there are. (Such an analysis of far-out examples is a useful and favorite trick of economists and mathematicians.) If there is just one person, Alpha Crusoe, on an island, with a single copper mine on his island, it will be harder to get raw copper next year if Alpha makes a lot of copper pots and bronze tools this year. And if he continues to use his mine, his son Beta Crusoe will have a tougher time getting copper than did his daddy.

Recycling could change the outcome. If Alpha decides in the second year to make new tools to replace the old tools he made in the first year, it will be easier for him to get the necessary copper than it was the first year because he can reuse the copper from the old tools without much new mining. And if Alpha adds fewer new pots and tools from year to year, the proportion of copper that can come from recycling can rise year by year. This could mean a progressive decrease in the cost of obtaining copper with each successive year for this reason alone, even while the total amount of copper in pots and tools increases.

But let us be "conservative" for the moment and ignore the possibility of recycling. Another scenario: If there are two people on the island, Alpha Crusoe and Gamma Defoe, copper will be more scarce for each of them this year than if Alpha lived there alone, unless by cooperative efforts they can devise a more complex but more efficient mining operation—say, one man on the surface and one in the shaft. Or, if there are two fellows this year instead of one, and if copper is therefore harder to get and more scarce, both Alpha and Gamma may spend considerable time looking for new lodes of copper. And they are likely to be successful in their search. This discovery may lower the cost of copper to them somewhat, but on the average the cost will still be higher than if Alpha lived alone on the island.

Alpha and Gamma may follow still other courses of action. Perhaps they will invent better ways of obtaining copper from a given lode, say a better digging tool, or they may develop new materials to substitute for copper, perhaps iron.

The cause of these new discoveries, or the cause of applying ideas that were discovered earlier, is the "shortage" of copper—that is, the increased cost of getting copper. So a "shortage" of copper causes the creation of its own remedy. This has been the key process in the supply and use of natural resources throughout history.

Discovery of an improved mining method or of a substitute product differs, in a manner that affects future generations, from the discovery of a new lode. Even after the discovery of a new lode, on the average it will still be more costly to obtain copper, that is, more costly than if copper had never been used enough to lead to a "shortage." But discoveries of improved mining methods and of substitute products, caused by the shortage of copper, can lead to lower costs of the services people seek from copper. Let's see how.

The key point is that a discovery of a substitute process or product by Alpha or Gamma can benefit innumerable future generations. Alpha and Gamma cannot themselves extract nearly the full benefit from their discovery of iron. (You and I still benefit from the discoveries of the uses of iron and methods of processing it that our ancestors made thousands of years ago.) This benefit to later generations is an example of what economists call an "externality" due to Alpha and Gamma's activities, that is, a result of their discovery that does not affect them directly.

So, if the cost of copper to Alpha and Gamma does not increase, they may not be impelled to develop improved methods and substitutes. If the cost of getting copper does rise for them, however, they may then bestir themselves to make a new discovery. The discovery may not immediately lower the cost of copper dramatically, and Alpha and Gamma may still not be as well off as if the cost had never risen. But subsequent generations may be better off because their ancestors suffered from increasing cost and "scarcity."

This sequence of events explains how it can be that people have been using cooking pots for thousands of years, as well as using copper for many other purposes, and yet the cost of a pot today is vastly cheaper by any measure than it was 100 or 1,000 or 10,000 years ago.

It is all-important to recognize that discoveries of improved methods and of substitute products are not just luck. They happen in response to "scarcity"—an increase in cost. Even after a discovery is made, there is a good chance that it will not be put into operation until there is need for it due to rising cost. This point is important: Scarcity and technological advance are not two unrelated competitors in a race; rather, each influences the other.

The last major U.S. governmental inquiry into raw materials was the 1952 President's Materials Policy Commission (Paley Commission), organized in response to fears of raw-material shortages during and just after World War II. The Paley Commission's report is distinguished by having some of the right logic, but exactly the wrong . . . forecast[s].

> There is no completely satisfactory way to measure the real costs of materials over the long sweep of our history. But clearly the man-hours required per unit of output declined heavily from 1900 to 1940, thanks especially to improvements in production technology and the heavier use of energy and capital equipment per worker. This long-term decline in real costs is reflected in the downward drift of prices of various groups of materials in relation to the general level of prices in the economy.
>
> [But since 1940 the trend has been] soaring demands, shrinking resources, the consequences pressure toward rising real costs, the risk of wartime shortages, the strong possibility of an arrest or decline in the standard of living we cherish and hope to share.[4]

For the quarter century for which the commission predicted, however, costs declined rather than rose.

The two reasons why the Paley Commission's cost predictions were topsy-turvy should help keep us from making the same mistakes. First, the commission reasoned from the notion of finiteness and from a static technological analysis.

> A hundred years ago resources seemed limitless and the struggle upward from meager conditions of life was the struggle to create the means and methods of getting those materials into use. In this struggle we have by now succeeded all too well. . . . The nature of the problem can perhaps be successfully over-simplified by saying that the consumption of almost all materials is expanding at compound rates and is thus pressing harder and harder against resources which whatever else they may be doing are not similarly expanding.[5]

The second reason the Paley Commission went wrong is that it looked at the wrong facts. Its report gave too much emphasis to the trends of costs over the short period from 1940 to 1950, which included World War II and therefore was almost inevitably a period of rising costs, instead of examining the longer period from 1900 to 1940, during which the commission knew that "the man-hours required per unit of output declined heavily."[6]

We must not repeat the same mistakes. We should look at cost trends for the longest possible period, rather than focus on a historical blip; the OPEC-led price rise in all resources after 1973 is for us as the temporary 1940–50 wartime reversal was for the Paley Commission. And the long-run trends make it very clear that the costs of materials, and their scarcity, continuously decline with the growth of income and technology.

Resources as Services

As economists or as consumers, we are interested in the particular services that resources yield, not in the resources themselves. Examples of such services are an ability to conduct electricity, an ability to support weight, energy to fuel autos, energy to fuel electrical generators, and food calories.

The supply of a service will depend upon (a) which raw materials can supply that service with the present technology; (b) the availabilities of these materials at various qualities; (c) the costs of extracting and processing them; (d) the amounts needed at the present level of technology to supply the services that we want; (e) the extent to which the previously extracted materials can be recycled; (f) the cost of recycling; (g) the cost of transporting the raw materials and services; and (h) the social and institutional arrangements in force. What is relevant to us is not whether we can find any lead in existing lead mines but whether we can have the services of lead batteries at a reasonable price; it does not matter to us whether this is accomplished by recycling lead, by making batteries last forever, or by replacing lead batteries with another contraption. Similarly, we want intercontinental telephone and television communication, and, as long as we get it, we do not care whether this requires 100,000 tons of copper for cables or just a single quarter-ton communications satellite in space that uses no copper at all.[7]

Let us see how this concept of services is crucial to our understanding of natural resources and the economy. To return to Crusoe's cooking pot, we are interested in a utensil that we can put over the fire and cook with. After iron and aluminum were discovered, quite satisfactory cooking pots, perhaps even better than pots of copper, could be made of these materials. The cost that interests us is the cost of providing the cooking service rather than the cost of copper. If we suppose that copper is used only for pots and that iron is quite satisfactory for the same purpose, as long as we have cheap iron it does not matter if the cost of copper rises sky high. (But in fact that has not happened. As we have seen, the prices of the minerals themselves, as well as the prices of the services they perform, have fallen over the years.)

Are Natural Resources Finite?

Incredible as it may seem at first, the term "finite" is not only inappropriate but is downright misleading when applied to natural resources, from both the practical and philosophical points of view. As with many of the important arguments in this world, the one about "finiteness" is "just semantic." Yet the semantics of resource scarcity muddle public discussion and bring about wrongheaded policy decisions.

The word "finite" originates in mathematics, in which context we all learn it as schoolchildren. But even in mathematics the word's meaning is far from unambiguous. It can have two principal

meanings, sometimes with an apparent contradiction between them.[8] For example, the length of a one-inch line is finite in the sense that it is bounded at both ends. But the line within the endpoints contains an infinite number of points; these points cannot be counted, because they have no defined size. Therefore the number of points in that one-inch segment is not finite. Similarly, the quantity of copper that will ever be available to us is not finite, because there is no method (even in principle) of making an appropriate count of it, given the problem of the economic definition of "copper," the possibility of creating copper or its economic equivalent from other materials, and thus the lack of boundaries to the sources from which copper might be drawn.

Consider this quote about potential oil and gas from Sheldon Lambert, an energy forecaster. He begins, "It's like trying to guess the number of beans in a jar without knowing how big the jar is." So far so good. But then he adds, "God is the only one who knows—and even He may not be sure."[9] Of course Lambert is speaking lightly. But the notion that some mind might know the "actual" size of the jar is misleading, because it implies that there is a fixed quantity of standard-sized beans. The quantity of a natural resource that might be available to us—and even more important the quantity of the services that can eventually be rendered to us by that natural resource—can never be known even in principle, just as the number of points in a one-inch line can never be counted even in principle. Even if the "jar" were fixed in size, it might yield ever more "beans." Hence resources are not "finite" in any meaningful sense.

To restate: A satisfactory *operational* definition of the quantity of a natural resource, or of the services we now get from it, is the only sort of definition that is of any use in policy decisions. The definition must tell us about the quantities of a resource (or of a particular service) that we can expect to receive in any particular year to come, at each particular price, conditional on other events that we might reasonably expect to know (such as use of the resource in prior years). And there is no reason to believe that at any given moment in the future the available quantity of any natural resource or service at present prices will be much smaller than it is now, or nonexistent. Only such one-of-a-kind resources as an Arthur Rubenstein concert or a Julius Erving basketball game, for which there are no close replacements, will disappear in the future and hence are finite in quantity.

Why do we become hypnotized by the word "finite"? That is an interesting question in psychology, education, and philosophy. A first likely reason is that the word "finite" seems to have a precise and unambiguous meaning in any context, even though it does not. Second, we learn the word in the context of mathematics, where all propositions are tautologous definitions and hence can be shown logically to be true or false (at least in principle). But scientific subjects are empirical rather than definitional, as twentieth-century philosophers have been at great pains to emphasize. Mathematics is not a science in the ordinary sense because it does not deal with facts other than the stuff of mathematics itself, and hence such terms as "finite" do not have the same meaning elsewhere that they do in mathematics.

Third, much of our daily life about which we need to make decisions is countable and finite—our weekly or monthly salaries, the number of gallons of gas in a full tank, the width of the backyard, the number of greeting cards you sent out last year, or those you will send out next year. Since these quantities are finite, why shouldn't the world's total possible salary in the future, or the gasoline in the possible tanks in the future, or the number of cards you ought to send out, also be finite? Though the analogy is appealing, it is not sound. And it is in making this incorrect analogy that we go astray in using the term "finite."

A fourth reason that the term "finite" is not meaningful is that we cannot say with any practical surety where the bounds of a relevant resource system lie, or even if there are any bounds. The bounds for the Crusoes are the shores of their island, and so it was for early man. But then the Crusoes found other islands. Mankind traveled farther and farther in search of resources—finally to the bounds of continents, and then to other continents. When America was opened up, the world, which for Europeans had been bounded by Europe and perhaps by Asia too, was suddenly expanded. Each epoch has seen a shift in the bounds of the relevant resource system. Each time, the old ideas about "limits," and the calculations of "finite resources" within those bounds, were thereby falsified. Now we have begun to explore the sea, which contains amounts of metallic and other resources that dwarf any deposits we know about on land. And we have begun to explore the moon. Why shouldn't the boundaries of the system from which we derive resources continue to expand in such directions, just as they have expanded in the past? This is one more reason not to regard resources as "finite" in principle.

You may wonder, however, whether "nonrenewable" energy resources such as oil, coal, and natural gas differ from the recyclable minerals in such a fashion that the foregoing arguments do not apply. Energy is particularly important because it is the "master resource"; energy is the key constraint on the availability of all other resources. Even so, our energy supply is non-finite, and oil is an important example. (1) The oil potential of a particular well may be measured, and hence is limited (though it is interesting and relevant that as we develop new ways of extracting hard-to-get oil, the economic capacity of a well increases). But the number of wells that will eventually produce oil, and in what quantities, is not known or measurable at present and probably never will be, and hence is not meaningfully finite. (2) Even if we make the unrealistic assumption that the number of potential wells in the earth might be surveyed completely and that we could arrive at a reasonable estimate of the oil that might be obtained with present technology (or even with technology that will be developed in the next 100 years), we still would have to reckon the future possibilities of shale oil and tar sands—a difficult task. (3) But let us assume that we could reckon the oil potential of shale and tar sands. We would then have to reckon the conversion of coal to oil. That, too, might be done; yet we still could not consider the resulting quantity to be "finite" and "limited." (4) Then there is the oil that we might produce not from fossils but from new crops—palm oil, soybean oil, and so on. Clearly, there is no meaningful limit to this source except the sun's energy. The notion of finiteness does not make sense here, either. (5) If we allow for the substitution of nuclear and solar power for oil, since what we really want are the services of oil, not necessarily oil itself, the notion of a limit makes even less sense. (6) Of course the sun may eventually run down. But even if our sun were not as vast as it is, there may well be other suns elsewhere.

About energy from the sun: The assertion that our resources are ultimately finite seems most relevant to energy but yet is actually more misleading with respect to energy than with respect to other resources. When people say that mineral resources are "finite" they are invariably referring to the earth as a boundary, the "spaceship earth," to which we are apparently confined just as astronauts are confined to their spaceship. But the main source of our energy even now is the sun, no matter how you think of the matter. This goes far beyond the fact that the sun was the prior source of the energy locked into the oil and coal we use. The sun is also the source of the energy in the food we eat, and in the trees that we use for many purposes. In coming years, solar energy may be used to heat homes and water in many parts of the world. (Much of Israel's hot water has been heated by solar devices for years, even when the price of oil was much lower than it is now.) And if the prices of conventional energy supplies were to rise considerably higher than they now are, solar energy could be called on for much more of our needs, though this price rise seems unlikely given present technology. And even if the earth were sometime to run out of sources of energy for nuclear processes—a prospect so distant that it is a waste of time to talk about it—there are energy sources on other planets. Hence the notion that the supply of energy is finite because the earth's fossil fuels or even its nuclear fuels are limited is sheer nonsense.

Whether there is an "ultimate" end to all this—that is, whether the energy supply really is "finite" after the sun and all the other planets have been exhausted—is a question so hypothetical that it should be compared with other metaphysical entertainments such as calculating the number of angels that can dance on the head of a pin. As long as we continue to draw energy from the sun, any conclusion about whether energy is "ultimately finite" or not has no bearing upon present policy decisions. . . .

Summary

A conceptual quantity is not finite or infinite in itself. Rather, it is finite or infinite if you make it so—by your own definitions. If you define the subject of discussion suitably, and sufficiently closely so that it can be counted, then it is finite—for example, the money in your wallet or the socks in your top drawer. But without sufficient definition the subject is not finite—for example, the thoughts in your head, the strength of your wish to go to Turkey, your dog's love for you, the number of points in a one-inch line. You can, of course, develop definitions that will make these quantities finite; but that makes it clear that the finiteness inheres in you and in your definitions rather than in the money, love, or one-inch line themselves. There is no necessity either in logic or in historical trends to suggest that the supply of any given resource is "finite."

Notes

1. Meadows, Dennis L., William W. Behrens III, Donella H. Meadows, Roger F. Naill, Jorgen Randers, and Erich K. O. Zahn. *Dynamics of Growth in a Finite World* (Cambridge, MA: Wright-Allen, 1974), p. vii.

2. U.S., The White House. *Population and the American Future* (New York: Signet, 1972), pp. 2–3.

3. Meadows et al., p. 265.

4. U.S., The White House. *Resources for the Future.* Four volumes. The President's Materials Policy Commission (Washington, DC: GPO, June, 1952).

5. Ibid., p. 2.

6. Ibid., p. 1.

7. Fuller, Buckminster. *Utopia or Oblivion* (New York: Bantam Press, 1977), p. 45.

8. I appreciate a discussion of this point with Alvin Roth.

9. Sheldon Lambert, quoted in *Newsweek* (June 27, 1977), 71.

57. Population, Poverty and the Local Environment _____

Partha S. Dasgupta

As with politics, we all have widely differing opinions about population. Some would point to population growth as the cause of poverty and environmental degradation. Others would permute the elements of this causal chain, arguing, for example, that poverty is the cause rather than the consequence of increasing numbers. Yet even when studying the semiarid regions of sub-Saharan Africa and the Indian subcontinent, economists have typically not regarded poverty, population growth and the local environment as interconnected. Inquiry into each factor has in large measure gone along its own narrow route, with discussion of their interactions dominated by popular writings—which, although often illuminating, are in the main descriptive and not analytical.

Over the past several years, though, a few investigators have studied the relations between these ingredients more closely. Our approach fuses theoretical modeling with empirical findings drawn from a number of disciplines, such as anthropology, demography, ecology, economics, nutrition and political science. Focusing on the vast numbers of small, rural communities in the poorest regions of the world, the work has identified circumstances in which population growth, poverty and degradation of local resources often fuel one another. The collected research has shown that none of the three elements directly causes the other two; rather each influences, and is in turn influenced by, the others. This new perspective has significant implications for policies aimed at improving life for some of the world's most impoverished inhabitants.

In contrast with this new perspective with its focus on local experience, popular tracts on the environment and population growth have usually taken a global view. They have emphasized the deleterious effects that a large population would have on our planet in the distant future. Although that slant has its uses, it has drawn attention away from the economic misery endemic today. Disaster is not something the poorest have to wait for: it is occurring even now. Besides, in developing countries, decisions on whether to have a child and on how to share education, food, work, health care and local resources are in large measure made within small entities such as households. So it makes sense to study the link between poverty, population growth and the environment from a myriad of local, even individual, viewpoints.

The household assumes various guises in different parts of the world. Some years ago Gary S. Becker of the University of Chicago was the first investigator to grapple with this difficulty. He used an idealized version of the concept to explore how choices made within a household would respond to changes in the outside world, such as employment opportunities and availability of credit, insurance, health care and education.

One problem with his method, as I saw it when I began my own work some five years ago, was that it studied households in isolation; it did not investigate the dynamics between interacting units. In addition to understanding the forces that encouraged couples to favor large families, I wanted to understand the ways in which a reasoned decision to have children, made by each household, could end up being detrimental to all households.

In studying how such choices are made, I found a second problem with the early approach: by assuming that decision making was shared equally by adults, investigators had taken an altogether too benign view of the process. Control over a family's choices is, after all, often held unequally. If I wanted to understand how decisions were made, I would have to know who was doing the deciding.

Power and Gender

Those who enjoy the greatest power within a family can often be identified by the way the household's resources are divided. Judith Bruce of the Population Council, Mayra Buvinic of the International Center for Research of the International Center on Women, Lincoln C. Chen and Amartya Sen of Harvard University and others have observed that the sharing of resources within a household is often unequal even when differences in needs are taken into account. In poor households in the Indian subcontinent, for example, men and boys usually get more sustenance than do women and girls, and the elderly get less than the young.

Such inequities prevail over fertility choices as well. Here also men wield more influence, even though women typically bear the greater cost. To grasp how great the burden can be, consider the number of live babies a woman would normally have if she managed to survive through her child-bearing years. This number, called the total fertility rate, is between six and eight in sub-Saharan Africa. Each successful birth there involves at least a year and a half of pregnancy and breast-feeding. So in a society where female life expectancy at birth is 50 years and the fertility rate is, say, seven, nearly half of a woman's adult life is spent either carrying a child in her womb or breast-feeding it. And this calculation does not allow for unsuccessful pregnancies.

Another indicator of the price that women pay is maternal mortality. In most poor countries, complications related to pregnancy constitute the largest single cause of death of women in their reproductive years. In some parts of sub-Saharan Africa as many as one woman dies for every 50 live births. (The rate in Scandinavia today is one per 20,000.) At a total fertility rate of seven or more, the chance that a woman entering her reproductive years will not live through them is about one in six. Producing children therefore involves playing a kind of Russian roulette.

Given such a high cost of procreation, one expects that women, given a choice, would opt for fewer children. But are birth rates in fact highest in societies where women have the least power within the family? Data on the status of women from 79 so-called Third World countries display an unmistakable pattern: high fertility, high rates of illiteracy, low share of paid employment and a high percentage working at home for no pay—they all hang together. From the statistics alone it is difficult to discern which of these factors are causing, and which are merely correlated with, high fertility. But the findings are consistent with the possibility that lack of paid employment and education limits a woman's ability to make decisions and therefore promotes population growth.

There is also good reason to think that lack of income-generating employment reduces women's power more directly than does lack of education. Such an insight has implications for policy. It is all well and good, for example, to urge governments in poor countries to invest in literacy programs. But the results could be disappointing. Many factors militate against poor households' taking advantage of subsidized education. If children are needed to work inside and outside the home, then keeping them in school (even a cheap one) is costly. In patrilineal societies, educated girls can also be perceived as less pliable and harder to marry off. Indeed, the benefits of subsidies to even primary education are reaped disproportionately by families that are better off.

In contrast, policies aimed at increasing women's productivity at home and improving their earnings in the marketplace would directly empower them, especially within the family. Greater earning power for women would also raise for men the implicit costs of procreation (which keeps women from bringing in cash income). This is not to deny the value of public investment in primary and secondary education in developing countries. It is only to say we should be wary of claims that such investment is a panacea for the population problem.

The importance of gender inequality to overpopulation in poor nations is fortunately gaining international recognition. Indeed, the United Nations Conference on Population and Development held in Cairo in September 1994 emphasized women's reproductive rights and the means by which they could be protected and promoted. But there is more to the population problem than gender inequalities. Even when both parents participate in the decision to have a child, there are several pathways through which the choice becomes harmful to the community. These routes have been uncovered by inquiring into the various motives for procreation.

Little Hands Help . . .

One motive, common to humankind, relates to children as ends in themselves. It ranges from the desire to have children because they are playful and enjoyable, to the desire to obey the dictates of tradition and religion. One such injunction emanates from the cult of the ancestor, which,

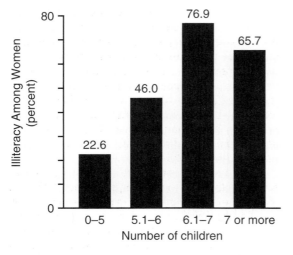

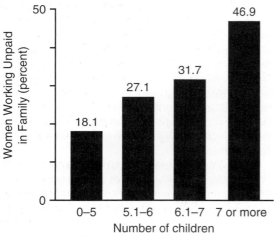

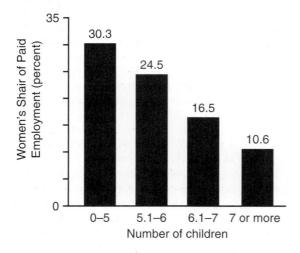

taking religion to be the act of reproducing the lineage, requires women to bear many children [see "High Fertility in Sub-Saharan Africa," by John C. Caldwell and Pat Caldwell; *Scientific American*, May 1990].

Such traditions are often perpetuated by imitative behavior. Procreation in closely knit communities is not only a private matter; it is also a social activity, influenced by the cultural milieu. Often there are norms encouraging high fertility rates that no household desires unilaterally to break. (These norms may well have outlasted any rationale they had in the past.) Consequently, so long as all others aim at large families, no household on its own will wish to deviate. Thus, a society can get stuck at a self-sustaining mode of behavior that is characterized by high fertility and low educational attainment.

This does not mean that society will live with it forever. As always, people differ in the extent to which they adhere to tradition. Inevitably some, for one reason or another, will experiment, take risks and refrain from joining the crowd. They are the nonconformists, and they help to lead the way. An increase in female literacy could well trigger such a process.

Still other motives for procreation involve viewing children as productive assets. In a rural economy where avenues for saving are highly restricted, parents value children as a source of security in their old age. Mead Cain, previously at the Population Council, studied this aspect extensively. Less discussed, at least until recently, is another kind of motivation, explored by John C. Caldwell of the Australian National University, Marc L. Nerlove of the University of Maryland and Anke S. Meyer of the World Bank and by Karl-Göran Mäler of the Beijer International Institute of Ecological Economics in Stockholm and me. It

Figure 1 Total fertility rate around the world (the average number of children a woman produces) generally increases with the percentage of women in a country who are illiterate (*top*) or work unpaid in the family (*middle*). Fertility decreases when a larger share of the paid employment belongs to women (*bottom*). Bringing in a cash income may empower a woman in making decisions within her family, allowing her to resist pressure to bear more children.

stems from children's being valuable to their parents not only for future income but also as a source of current income.

Third World countries are, for the most part, subsistence economies. The rural folk eke out a living by using products gleaned directly from plants and animals. Much labor is needed even for simple tasks. In addition, poor rural households do not have access to modern sources of domestic energy or tap water. In semiarid and arid regions the water supply may not even be nearby. Nor is fuelwood at hand when the forests recede. In addition to cultivating crops, caring for livestock, cooking food and producing simple marketable products, members of a household may have to spend as much as five to six hours a day fetching water and collecting fodder and wood.

Children, then, are needed as workers even when their parents are in their prime. Small households are simply not viable; each one needs many hands. In parts of India, children between 10 and 15 years have been observed to work as much as one and a half times the number of hours that adult males do. By the age of six, children in rural India tend domestic animals and care for younger siblings, fetch water and collect firewood, dung and fodder. It may well be that the usefulness of each extra hand increases with declining availability of resources, as measured by, say, the distance to sources of fuel and water.

. . . But at a Hidden Cost

The need for many hands can lead to a destructive situation, especially when parents do not have to pay the full price of rearing their children but share those costs with the community. In recent years, mores that once regulated the use of local resources have changed. Since time immemorial, rural assets such as village ponds and water holes, threshing grounds, grazing fields, and local forests have been owned communally. This form of control enabled households in semiarid regions to pool their risks. Elinor Ostrom of Indiana University and others have shown that communities have protected such local commons against overexploitation by invoking norms, imposing fines for deviant behavior and so forth.

But the very process of economic development can erode traditional methods of control. Increased urbanization and mobility can do so as well. Social rules are also endangered by civil strife and by the takeover of resources by landowners or the state. As norms degrade, parents pass some of the costs of children on to the community by overexploiting the commons. If access to shared resources continues, parents produce too many children, which leads to greater crowding and susceptibility to disease as well as to more pressure on environmental resources. But no household, on its own, takes into account the harm it inflicts on others when bringing forth another child.

Parental costs of procreation are also lower when relatives provide a helping hand. Although the price of carrying a child is paid by the mother, the cost of rearing the child is often shared among the kinship. Caroline H. Bledsoe of Northwestern University and others have observed that in much of sub-Saharan Africa fosterage is commonplace, affording a form of insurance protection in semiarid regions. In parts of West Africa about a third of the children have been found to be living with their kin at any given time. Nephews and nieces have the same rights of accommodation and support as do biological offspring. In recent work I have shown that this arrangement encourages couples to have too many offspring if the parent's share of the benefits from having children exceeds their share of the costs.

In addition, where conjugal bonds are weak, as they are in sub-Saharan Africa, fathers often do not bear the costs of siring a child. Historical demographers, such as E. A. Wrigley of the University of Cambridge, have noted a significant difference between western Europe in the 18th century and modern preindustrial societies. In the former, marriage normally meant establishing a new household. This requirement led to late marriages; it also meant that parents bore the cost of rearing their children. Indeed, fertility rates in France dropped before mortality rates registered a decline, before modern family-planning techniques became available and before women became literate.

The perception of both the low costs and high benefits of procreation induces households to produce too many children. In certain circumstances a disastrous process can begin. As the community's resources are depleted, more hands are needed to gather fuel and water for daily use. More children are then produced, further damaging the local environment and in turn providing the household with an incentive to enlarge. When this happens,

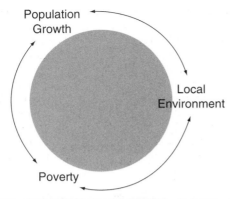

REGION	TOTAL FERTILITY RATE
Sub-Saharan Africa	6 to 8
India	4
China	2.3
Japan and Western Industrial Democracies	1.5 to 1.9

Figure 2   Poverty, population growth and environmental degradation interact in a cyclic pattern (*top*). The chart (*bottom*) shows that fertility is higher in countries that are poorer.

fertility and environmental degradation reinforce each other in an escalating spiral. By the time some countervailing set of factors—whether public policy or diminished benefits from having additional children—stops the spiral, millions of lives may have suffered through worsening poverty.

Recent findings by the World Bank on sub-Saharan Africa have revealed positive correlations among poverty, fertility and deterioration of the local environment. Such data cannot reveal causal connections, but they do support the idea of a positive-feedback process such as I have described. Over time, the effect of this spiral can be large, as manifested by battles for resources [see "Environmental Change and Violent Conflict," by T. F. Homer Dixon, J. H. Boutwell and G. W. Rathjens: *Scientific American*, February 1993].

The victims hit hardest among those who survive are society's outcasts—the migrants and the dispossessed, some of whom in the course of time become the emaciated beggars seen on the streets of large towns and cities in underdeveloped countries. Historical studies by Robert W. Fogel of the University of Chicago and theoretical explorations by Debraj Ray of Boston University and me, when taken together, show that the spiral I have outlined here is one way in which destitutes are created. Emaciated beggars are not lazy; they have to husband their precarious hold on energy. Having suffered from malnutrition, they cease to be marketable.

Families with greater access to resources are, however, in a position to limit their size and propel themselves into still higher income levels. It is my impression that among the urban middle classes in northern India, the transition to a lower fertility rate has already been achieved. India provides an example of how the vicious cycle I have described can enable extreme poverty to persist amid a growth in well-being in the rest of society. The Matthew effect—"Unto every one that hath shall be given, and he shall have abundance: but from him that hath not shall be taken away even that which he hath"—works relentlessly in impoverished countries.

Breaking Free

This analysis suggests that the way to reduce fertility is to break the destructive spiral. Parental demand for children rather than an unmet need for contraceptives in large measure explains reproductive behavior in developing countries. We should therefore try to identify policies that will change the options available to men and women so that couples choose to limit the number of offspring they produce.

In this regard, civil liberties, as opposed to coercion, play a particular role. Some years ago my colleague Martin R. Weale and I showed through statistical analysis that even in poor countries political and civil liberties go together with improvements in other aspects of life, such as income per person, life expectancy at birth and infant survival rate. Thus, there are now reasons for thinking that such liberties are not only desirable in themselves but also empower people to flourish economically. Recently Adam Przeworski of the University of Chicago demonstrated that fertility, as well, is lower in countries where citizens enjoy more civil and political freedom. (An exception is China, which represents only one country out of many in this analysis.)

The most potent solution in semiarid regions of sub-Saharan Africa and the Indian subcontinent is to deploy a number of policies simultaneously. Family-planning services, especially when allied with health services, and measures that empower women are certainly helpful. As societal norms break down and traditional support systems falter, those women who choose to change their behavior become financially and socially more vulnerable. So a literacy and employment drive for women is essential to smooth the transition to having fewer children.

But improving social coordination and directly increasing the economic security of the poor are also essential. Providing cheap fuel and potable water will reduce the usefulness of extra hands. When a child becomes perceived as expensive, we may finally have a hope of dislodging the rapacious hold of high fertility rates.

Each of the prescriptions suggested by our new perspective on the links between population, poverty and environmental degradation is desirable by itself, not just when we have those problems in mind. It seems to me that this consonance of means and ends is a most agreeable fact in what is otherwise a depressing field of study.

V.E FUTURE GENERATIONS AND SUSTAINABILITY QUESTIONS

58. PREVIEW

[F]uture people . . . we don't know what they will do, what they will like, what they will want. And to be honest, it is none of out business.[1]

Robert Solow, Nobel laureate in Economics

Take therefore no thought for the morrow: for the morrow shall take thought for the things of itself. Sufficient unto the day is the evil thereof.

Matthew 6:34

[E]very deliberation we make must be in consideration of the impact on the seventh generation from now.

American Indian principle

In 1987 the Brundtland Commission defined "sustainable development" as that that "meets the needs of the present without compromising the ability of future generations to meet their own needs."[2] There has been a growing consensus, especially since this "Brundtland report"[3] (entitled *Our Common Good*), that various commercial and governmental practices cannot be sustained, and that if these practices are continued we fare a wide range of catastrophes—not just for members of our species but for life on this planet. The admittedly vague but intuitively attractive proposal that all nations (or societies) need to adopt sustainable practices presupposes, as a "bottom line," that much is going on now that cannot continue indefinitely without the occurrence of catastrophe, that is, the occurrence of events that are intolerably costly—events involving widespread suffering, premature death to living creatures, and destruction of the wellsprings of life and biodiversity themselves.[4] That these practices—typically defended in the name of economic growth, or that to which growth allegedly leads, must be altered and constrained—is a point around which much controversy swirls.[5]

Here we will speak favorably of the notion of sustainability and of the view that those who invoke the notion are "on to something" important, but we observe straight off that there are thoroughgoing sophisticated skeptics on this matter, ones who speak of sustainability as "the fashionable concept in environmental discourse," as a concept that "only muddles the issues," and who claim that the concept has been defined in such a way as to be either morally repugnant or logically redundant."[6] Others refer to *sustainability* as a vague term that further has become a "buzzword"—thus inviting us to dismiss certain proposals.[7] Hence, a number of thoughtful professionals are much divided on this matter, and there is an important theoretical and practical challenge to adjudicate this disagreement about the appropriate ground for decision making.

Objections to proposals to adopt sustainable practices derive from a number of sources. One is disagreement over which empirical views are best supported by science. For example, there is some controversy over whether heightened global warming due to greenhouse effects is occurring (on this see Section V.E). Because the costs of reducing carbon dioxide emissions pose a threat to numerous business interests, at least in the short run, it is in the economic interest of such groups to cast doubt on such scientific reports. In some cases companies financially support "think tanks" or institutes that generate studies favorable to their interests, and castigate opposition (often labeled "activist" or "environmental") groups as relying on "bad science." Rachel Carson's pathbreaking book *A Silent Spring* (1962) was ruthlessly attacked in this manner, because of the threat it posed to certain chemical companies. Not only was her science attacked by representatives of these companies; arguments questioning her character and motivation were adduced in the familiar American mud-throwing style. In this David-versus-Goliath-like conflict, time has vindicated Carson.[8] It is, of course, possible that irrational attacks motivated by the desire to ward off threats to one's economic interests—"self-interested" in that sense—also may be defensible by good reasons and, indeed, correct, even if some actual instances of defense of the view are, as we say, "ill motivated." It is crucial to assess critically the rational merits of the views of all sides.

It is also worth recalling the prior efforts of the tobacco companies to question the scientific data that have supported the belief in a causal link between tobacco smoking and lung cancer. Sometimes they used the strategy of invoking a very narrow conception of proof in claiming that because we have not photographed or literally seen molecules of tobacco tar transforming some human gene that, in turn, allows cancerous growth, that there is, then, "no proof" of a causal connection. Of course, there is, to the contrary, very powerful evidence of an epidemiological nature. Indeed, the kind of evidence that exists is just the sort that persuades rational people to believe in causal connections in a variety of other cases.[9]

One further, major source of disagreement about sustainability concerns the desirability of growth. Those who resist proposals for ostensibly sustainable practices (and we have yet to press the question of what "sustainability" precisely means) appeal to the claim that the only way to improve the plight of many of the desperately poor on the planet is to "grow the economy," or to increase the gross national product of less developed countries.[10] The familiar proposed picture is that in any economy with significant economic inequalities (some individuals will have much larger pieces of the economic pie than others), the best way to improve the situation of the least advantaged is to increase the overall size of the pie. With a larger pie even the smaller pieces will be, it is maintained, larger. This hopeful by-product of economic growth is an attractive feature, other things being equal. After all, even if it does not reduce comparative inequality, it allegedly both does not make the best off worse off, and it improves the situation of the desperately poor.[11] Some would say that this result tends to remedy unjust inequalities. Thus, frequent recommendations from northern industrialized countries of the world to poorer southern hemisphere neighbors are to expand trade, sell natural resources to their more affluent neighbors, and thereby increase the gross national product of the less industrialized nation. Given this view, many nations have turned away from authoritarian or more centralized socialist economies in recent decades.

Initially, it seems hard to question the desirability of "growth" or "development." Indeed, the terms "growth" and "development" seem to connote something good so that the term *good growth* may seem redundant, and *bad growth* contradictory. However, in investigating these disputes it is important to explore exactly what is meant by key terms. Consider the phenomena of the "growth" of cancer, rape, or war. Growth of something, its literally getting bigger, is not necessarily a desirable thing. The *concept* of growth does not preclude the possibility of the growth being disastrous.

We thus need to reflect on whether "economic growth," as standardly understood, is always, or usually, or in a specific case, a good thing. Something similar might be said about the notion of "development." However, we note immediately that some writers wish to distinguish the concepts of "growth" and "development." As measured in the United States, the gross domestic product (GDP)[12] is increased if a hurricane makes things much worse off for people and various market-recognized reparative efforts ensue that make people almost as well off as prior to the hurricane. Intuitively, people may be genuinely worse off on average, but "growth" has increased in the sense that there has been an increase in the flow of market-recognized goods and services. This perhaps puzzling result, at least for those of us weaned on the syllogism that an increase in GNP is growth and that "growth is good," is generated before one even begins to engage in considerations about the improvement or decline of the well-being of nonhuman species or the

process that itself generates biodiversity. Although the concept of the gross national product was not introduced to measure national well-being, it seems clear that many people think of it in those terms—that is, as a good measure of economic well-being, and therefore the best measure of national well-being.[13] Initial intentions to the contrary, many economists speak and make policy recommendations as if increases in GNP (or GDP) are an appropriate measure of national well-being; further, politicians and citizens ("the enemy is us") seem routinely to fail to question this assumption. Many ecological economists (often labeled "fringe" economists and not part of "mainstream economics" by many economists; note the evaluation here) are devising new measures of well-being (see Essay 45, by Robert Repetto, in this book, and the use of a new measure, net domestic product). Indices that measure well-being over indefinite periods of time (not just for "our" generation, not just for Canadians, or Americans, and so forth, and perhaps someday not simply for our species) and give negative weight to losses of exhaustible natural "resources" hold out the attraction of being new steps in the right direction. We leave it an open question here as to whether existing measures do that job. One dissenting economist, Neva Goodwin, notes,

> The failure of economists to elevate the concept of *well-being* to an importance equal to that given to *wealth* is related to the loss (from most important writings in economics since the time of Alfred Marshall) of an appreciation of the salience of *moral issues* to economic behavior. It may be said that the basis of human morality is human values—our identification of *what matters.* In the mainstream, neoclassical economics paradigm the single value admitted to was efficiency. Efficiency however is only a means. When pressed to name the end to which efficiency is a means,

neoclassical economists offer the maximization of utility.[14]

Goodwin observes that because utility is difficult to measure, economists almost always use instead the goal of maximization of consumption (see GNP/GDP) as a proxy. Part of the argument in favor of limiting growth is that, as "it" is measured now increases in GNP do not always result in an increase in total net utility or satisfaction for humans.[15] Some of what we do is use up finite stocks—eat our own seed corn, so to speak—and even if improving our situation in terms of current consumption, we may make ourselves, this generation, worse off on balance. We do this in part because we assume that many of the functions performed by nature are free and their loss (recycling carbon dioxide by forests or the protection from harmful rays of the sun by the ozone layer) is not assigned an appropriate weight in a weighing up of costs and benefits. To put matters a bit differently, we start using up our capital instead of living off the interest. At some point there is no more interest if there is no more capital. If not for our generation, then for a later one. Analogously, the temporary advantages of overfishing (or overuse of pesticides, and so on) in the short run leads to ruin in the long run for fishermen (and others); the practice is not sustainable. The so-called invisible hand of the market does not obviously prevent this result; we see it all around us. Of course, we do not notice it so much if we do not fish, and if those who fish deliver some other fish (to those of us who are not vegetarians).

The hope of the optimists is that this process of finding substitutes for no longer existent natural stocks can go on forever (arguably, the prospect of unlimited substitutability is a key part of the doctrine of neoclassical economics).[16] A rather pure example of this view is found in Essay 56 in this book by Julian Simon, who holds that there is no limit to the supply of natural resources—pre-sumably because, in his view, there is no limit to substitutability. The fact that such substitutions can be, and often have been made (such as making fiber optic cable to replace copper wire), that they may continue to be made in a wide range of cases, and that human genius in this respect has often been underestimated—none of this entails the conclusion that the process can be endlessly sustained (so we need not accept this form of technological optimism—or the opposite extreme—call it technological pessimism—that we will never find substitutes).[17] Unless a better argument can be produced for technological optimism, this hopefulness appears to be like that of snake handlers who assume that they will be protected and that, because they have not yet been bitten they never will. There is always considerable danger in lacking skepticism about those claims that we earnestly *want* to believe—because believing them is comforting or flattering. The now familiar metaphor of earth as a spaceship supposes that many of our "resources" are indeed finite and irreplaceable.[18] The famous pictures of the earth taken from outer space are a further dramatic reminder. We earthlings have one major natural resource from outer space that is virtually inexhaustible, namely, solar energy—barring a *deus ex machina*.[19] A main point is that if the technological optimists are right, much of the worry over sustainability is misplaced, because growth can proceed without the constraints of living within finite limits inherent in the ecosystems in which we live. If they are wrong, then the familiar advocacy of unconstrained growth is a recipe for long-term, if not short-term, disaster.

Critics may object that the view just expressed rests on a serious confusion. It is not denied that there are finite amounts of natural stocks, such as copper or oil. They maintain that so long as other materials may be found or created that perform the same function for us as the nonrenewable material, then there is no need to worry over the fact that materials are of finite quantity on our planet. Can any materials be replaced in principle? Are there not some things that are "irreplaceable"? Important conceptual issues arise here. Much of the discussion in the following essay by Robert Goodin pursues these key points. If materials are replaceable without serious limit, then the desirability of sustainability may be undercut.

Time frames are important here. Those who are moderate technological pessimists about the next 100 years *may* be dead wrong, and the technological optimists dead right. However, the situation may be just the opposite if technological improvements peter out in the century after that. If we want to prevent massive worldwide devastation (it is now so easy for those of us who live in peaceful, affluent nations [the United States until September 11, 2001] to ignore the current starvation, disease, and desperation of war that is deep and widespread; the scale of harm done by the "Unabomber" in the United States in the mid-1990s or even the IRA in Britain pales in comparison), it may not be so important whether it is postponed 100 or 200 or 400 years; the ideal is permanent prevention. The optimist who has fallen from a tall mountain may note, after having fallen 4000 feet, "so far, so good" and she will be right at one level of comparison—for now and in the very near future. Some would say that there is no reason even to say "so far, so good" given our current obliteration of species and habitats, the very sources of human survival (see Sections VI.A on biodiversity and VI.C on forests), and widespread human starvation.[20]

We note a further link between the concept of sustainability and another concept discussed in Section V.C, namely that of the commons.[21] The problem of the commons (such as grazing land in Hardin's famous example) is that sources (or sinks—repositories for our unwanted stuff, "trash") held in common (not divvied up and not subject to property rights) are overused. One way of

interpreting the concept of "overuse" is that something is overused if it is treated in such a manner that its use cannot be sustained indefinitely. But this is roughly another way of saying that the practice is not sustainable; thus, the worry about what happens to commonly controlled sources and sinks is that they will be dealt with in a manner that is not sustainable. The numerous tragedies of the commons (and not all tragedies are) are failures resulting from unsustainable practices. One proposed solution to commons problems is the institution of property rights. Hence this is also a proposed solution to the sustainability problem. At least three evident difficulties face the privatization proposal: (1) how could items such as the ocean or the atmosphere be divided up, that is, be something over which property rights get distributed? and (2) when common items are divisible, on what basis could this be done fairly? and (3) does privatization really provide a motivation to care not just for short-term profit maximization rather than long-term sustainability (and thus promotion/preservation of the well-being of future generations)?

Much can be privately owned, and people are commonly motivated by the desire for gain when it can be secured by means of property rights. Without this, productivity might be severely subverted. Productivity is indeed desirable to a point—unless the resulting growth is unsustainable. However, we want to foster a number of things: a satisfactory level of human well-being, justice, sustainability, and a certain kind of efficiency. Without trying to be precise about it, one version of the tough emerging question is whether we can alter our practices in such a manner as to foster these socially desirable outcomes among others, such as preservation of biodiversity, and so on. Indeed, part of our problem is theoretical and conceptual; it is not crystal clear how the desirable goals are related (independent or derivative, and so on). For example, if a "need" of future generations is the continued existence of the process of speciation and a high degree of biodiversity, then the goal of sustainability may include certain goals that could be listed independently of goals concerning the welfare of future members of one species, namely, ours.[22]

The ranking or ordering of these goals is not something solvable by sheer stipulative definition. Agreement about what is desirable involves agreement about the relative importance of achieving certain end results, as well as what constraints ought to be followed in the process. If we have obligations to future generations and if nonhumans of some kind have moral standing, then the way we ought to unpack the notion of sustainability and seek to promote it is going to look quite different from the way it would otherwise (questions of interspecific justice arise).

How we think about the practice of "discounting" future costs and benefits may be quite different as well.[23] To this point some will say, "Aha, so the notion of sustainability is not purely empirical after all"—as if this is a serious and unique problem. But then the notion that growth is good, or that we ought to maximize it, or maximize efficiency are hardly value-free notions—many positivistic pretenses to the contrary. Indeed, with respect to the practice of discounting, some economists and philosophers argue that it is not a requirement of rationality (as perhaps most economists maintain) but, rather, that it is "a numerical way to operationalize the value judgment that (1) the near future is worth more than the distant future, and (2) beyond some point the worth of the future is negligible." If so, these evaluative or moral judgments need defense.[24] In some contrast, we note the striking proposal by certain American Indians (a term we often use, because, in one sense, anyone born in Canada or the United States is a "native American") that there be an amendment to the Constitution to the effect that "every deliberation we make must be in con-

sideration of the impact on the seventh generation from now."[25]

If the notion of sustainability is unpacked in substantial part, or in its entirety, in terms of practices that *can* be sustained indefinitely, as opposed to those that *ought* to be sustained indefinitely, then it appears that we must distinguish between asserting the claim that (1) what is sustainable is what we ought to do, and (2) what we ought to do is what is sustainable. Arguably, the practices of slavery, or perhaps cannibalism, are sustainable practices, but we need not be tempted by the view that the sustainability of a practice is sufficient to make the practice morally justifiable.[26] Further, no doubt some acts are permissible but not indefinitely repeatable.

We need further clarity about what is to count as a relevant "practice," that is, the range of things (if any) that reasonably ought to satisfy the sustainability requirement. Succinctly, the relevant level of description may be crucial. Compare the descriptions (1) "mining site 123 at Silverton, Colorado, for silver," (2) "mining for silver," (3) "mining," (4) "unearthing a metal with certain properties," (5) "making use of a substance with certain properties," and so on. We cannot carry on (1) indefinitely, but we could carry on something describable by description (5) for a very long period. Further, if a practice can go on for a million years, perhaps we need not reject it just because it could not go on "forever." Arguably, we need to identify practices that are both just *and* sustainable—and possess certain other virtues as well.

One could, then, characterize a sustainable ecosystem as one whose essential practices can be carried on indefinitely while maintaining its populations of living species at a certain level of well-being. This ideal of sustainability reflects a desire for the welfare and preservation of future generations. Here we encounter a problem of motivation that runs through many issues in environmental ethics such as reducing pollution and population, avoiding increased global warming, preserving biodiversity and old growth forests and so on. We are asked to care enough about generations living in the distant future to alter our behavior now. Advocates of sustainability predict that catastrophic costs lie down the road if we do not adopt sustainable practices now. However, most or all of these recommended alterations to save the future would impose significant cost on some group or other today. This situation is sometimes called the "motivation problem," a problem addressed by Ernest Partridge in his essay (59), "Future Generations." Partridge also discusses the moral status of future persons and the policy implications of our normative conclusions about such persons. His discussion of the former examines many of the ethical views explained in the Introduction to Ethical Theory.

Another fundamental issue to consider is this: In practice much policy recommendation has been guided by the assumption that all nations should increase or maximize national economic growth or national wealth. Call this the Maximizing Assumption. There are then a series of criticisms of reliance on this assumption. First, it is said to ignore ecological limits on what we can continue for an indefinite period because it treats certain goods as free (such as clean air), and thus their use is not rationed by the price mechanism of the marketplace. Vandana Shiva has argued not merely for tensions between the market system and the achievement of genuine sustainability but for their incompatibility. Advocacy of maximizing growth is also said to ignore ecological limits by assuming infinite or virtually infinite substitutability; thus, it assumes that "resources" (in one sense) are unlimited. Use of the Maximizing Assumption is further criticized for ignoring, or (as noted earlier) overly discounting, the well-being of future generations of human beings. It further is said to make some existing people worse off on balance, through the allied use of misguided

and inappropriate measures of national well-being. Finally, the Maximizing Assumption as typically construed is anthropocentric; zero or little (noninstrumental) weight is assigned to the well-being of other species—or to the very process that itself generates biodiversity.

Widely read writer Stephen Covey tells a story to illustrate the differences among managers, producers, and leaders, a story we use here for a different purpose. The producers are cutting their way through a jungle with machetes. The managers are just behind, sharpening machetes, holding muscle development programs, and bringing in improved technologies for the machete wielders. The leader, in contrast, is the one who says, "Wrong jungle!" Covey observes that the managers often respond by saying, "Shut up! We're making progress."[27] Today, the advocates of sustainable practices are saying we are in the wrong jungle; again, many voices respond by saying, "Shut up, we're making progress"—or perhaps, growth (welfare maximization—and seeking is all we need to do. So, who is correct here? Can we have growth indefinitely, should we aim for that, or must we significantly newly conceive and articulate the grounds for fundamental economic and political policy decisions? If so, there are pervasive and difficult questions about how to design the appropriate social, political and economic institutions—questions not much pursued here that are tied to classic issues of political philosophy concerning liberty, justice, authority, and so on.

The essays that follow explore the questions of whether or to what extent we have obligations to future generations. Others examine the slippery notion of sustainability, the concept of substitutivity, the relation of sustainability to the key concepts of growth or development, questions of justice, questions about natural limits to growth, and alternative ways of envisioning a viable and desirable future. These matters are of literally cosmic importance for life on this planet.

NOTES

1. From Robert Solow's essay, "Sustainability: An Economist's Perspective," reprinted herein as Essay 61.

2. World Commission on Environment and Development, *Our Common Future* (Oxford: Oxford University Press, 1987), p. ix. Reasons for criticizing the Brundtland Commission's evident focus on the needs of humans alone are found earlier in this book. A view similar to that of Brundtland, much publicized, was expressed earlier in *Limits to Growth* in 1972, a document produced by various scientists and industrialists known as the Club of Rome. On this see Andrew Dobson's *Green Political Thought*, 2nd ed.

3. Named after Grø Brundtland, prime minister of Norway.

4. Thomas Malthus's worry in his "An Essay on the Principle of Population" (see Essay 53), that human growth will vastly outstrip food supply, as well as John Stuart Mill's famous chapter on the desirability of a "stationary state" economy in his *Principles of Political Economy* in 1848, are expressions of the kind of concern voiced today with reference to "sustainability."

5. Highly relevant to this section is Essay 89, by Robert Goodland, "The Case That the World Has Reached Limits," which we have included in Section VI.E, "Sliding to Global Catastrophe."

6. See Wilfred Beckerman, "Sustainable Development," in *Environmental Values*, Vol. 3 (Cambridge, UK: White Horse Press, 1994), pp. 191–209.

7. See Robert Sollow, Essay 61.

8. See J. E. de Steiguer, *Age of Environmentalism* (New York: McGraw-Hill, 1997), pp. 39–41.

9. A related implied assumption has been that it is reasonable to believe only in what is proven. This also seems false; for example, if one has a clear memory of having dreamed of his or her uncle last night then it seems reasonable to believe that one did, even though one does not have something readily classifiable as a "proof," no intersubjectively testable data, no repeatable experiment, and so on. Because it takes some degree of analytical skill or sophistication to see through these shoddy arguments, no doubt the attempts at obfuscation succeed in many cases.

10. Multinational corporations, it is worth noting, can threaten to withdraw or withhold seductive sounding investments in any particular country, and thus by a combination of bribelike and threatlike maneuvers they can seek to avoid the constraints any nation poses to their freedom to proceed as they choose.

11. One skeptic refers to this hope as advocacy of "indiscriminate growth and trickle-down someday." See F. E. Trainer, "Environmental Significance of Development Theory," originally in *Ecological Economics* 2 (December 1990), 277, 86, and quoted in *A Survey of Ecological Economics,* edited by Rajaram Krishnan, Jonathan M. Harris, and Neva Goodwin (Washington, DC: Island Press, 1995), p. 47. Trainer also suggests that what many tend to see as a solution for inequality and poverty, namely growth (market-based GNP increases), is often the cause of such problems; ibid., p. 47.

12. Use of the measure labeled the gross national product was instituted in the United States about 1946, and in the 1990s a slightly different measure, gross domestic product, is used. On this see de Steiguer, pp. 66–67.

13. An important question: Why think that the *nation* is the appropriate level of analysis? What assumptions does this reflect? Can we do better?

14. See Neva Goodwin, "Series Introduction," in *A Survey of Ecological Economics* (Washington, DC: Island Press, 1995), p. xvii.

15. We emphasize that many of the key concepts that are relevant here—growth, measures of welfare, and so on—are ones that have received much investigation over the last century by economists, and it is naive to overlook these valuable explorations. Still there is room to critically reappraise; for example, if anthropocentrism is to be rejected, then the usual measures of welfare endorsed by economists for over a hundred years or so may need rejection or revision. So, we need to steer a course between reinventing the wheel, on the one hand, and uncritical acceptance of received opinion in modern Western economic theory. Useful, readable background on relevant economic thought can be found in the previously mentioned *Age of Environmentalism* by de Steiguer.

16. Neoclassical economics is a late nineteenth-century phenomenon best represented by the work of Alfred Marshall.

17. Clearly there are lots of possible views between these extremes, and one might be a pessimist about what is happening to the oceans and air but an optimist about harnessing new sources of energy.

18. The metaphor was made famous in the 1960s by economist Kenneth Boulding in an essay entitled "The Economics of Spaceship Earth," edited by A. C. Enthoven and A. M. Freeman III (New York: Norton, 1973).

19. It is of some interest that those who believe "God will provide," and thus we need not worry about the damage we do, ally themselves with the technological optimists just mentioned. Some of the faithful, however, assume God will vent his wrath given the diverse damage we do and thus disaster is in the works—at least for those not favored; some, it is said, will be caught up in a rapturous moment and delivered from this rotting sepulcher—mainly a view of some, but hardly all, Christians.

20. In a notice concerning a book entitled *Green Colored Glasses: Environmentalism Reconsidered* by Wilfred Beckerman, emeritus fellow at Balliol College, Oxford, the Cato Policy Report (a very conservative think tank), describes the view of "many environmentalists"—based on Beckerman's arguments—as one in which "the Western world would have to sacrifice economic growth and material prosperity for decades to come" and further, that thus future generations would "be born into a world with a pristine environment." Lamentably, the notice ignores questions about the desirability of growth as usually defined, and attributes a view to "many environmentalists" that, arguably, *no* environmentalist holds, namely, that even with sacrifices "future generations would be born into a pristine environment." Those "think tanks" that wish to promote rational thought might consider exploring or at least mentioning objections fairly, and avoiding distortions, and not mindlessly jumping on the antienvironmentalist bandwagon. See "A Fresh Look at the Environment" *Cato Policy Report* (September-October, 1996), p. 15. See also the essay by Partha Dasgupta, selection 57.

21. We have reprinted Hardin's famous essay in this book (Essay 47), but the problem of the commons was noted by economists back in the 1950s. On this, see J. E. de Steiguer, "Three Theories from Economics About the Environment," *Bioscience* 45(8) (September, 1995), 555.

22. This fact suggests the need for greater integration of work in political philosophy, ecological economics, environmental ethics, and conservation biology than we have seen (often because academic professions and universities reward specialization but not so much the efforts to acquire the skills and understanding necessary to work across disciplines in a nonsuperficial manner). The best training seems to be to start in one discipline and then to work up to a level of competence or better in another—as opposed to pursuing certain programs that are said to cross disciplines, and do, but do not require mastery of a genuine discipline with its special tools of inquiry and a genuine intellectual tradition. Specialization can foster a smug indifference about the need to search out the best in other disciplines. Specialization seems a necessary initial step but one not sufficient to address certain urgent category transgressing environmental problems. At some point focus on problems that need solving is crucial, not just on those problems for which one's discipline generates effective tools. That is, let the problems dictate what one does, not one's best tools.

23. Discounting assumes that future benefits and harms deserve less weight than those in the present. Tyler Cowen and Derek Parfit observe that according to a social discount rate of 1 percent the value of a present life may be more valuable than 1 million future lives if the latter are 1,400 years in the future—or more valuable than a million lives 145 years in the future if the discount rate is 10 percent. The moral questions of what obligations we have to future generations and the permissibility of discounting will much affect how we think about environmental policy. See Tyler Cowen and Derek Parfit, "Against the Social Discount Rate" in Peter Laslett and James S. Fishkin, eds., *Justice Between Age Groups and Generations* (New Haven, CT: Yale University Press, 1992), pp. 141–61.

24. The point is made by Robert Costanza and Herman E. Daly, in "Toward an Ecological Economics," *Ecological Modeling 38* (1987), 1.

25. See Winona LaDuke, "The Growing Strength of Native Environmentalism," *Sierra* (November–December 1996), p. 45.

26. This point is made by Robin Attfield and Barry Wilkins in "Sustainability," *Environmental Values* 3 (1994), 155–158.

27. Stephen R. Covey, *The Seven Habits of Highly Effective People* (New York: Simon & Schuster, 1989), p. 101.

28. There is insightful, detailed discussion of these matters, and bibliographical help, in Andrew Dobson's *Green Political Thought* (mentioned earlier).

59. Future Generations

Ernest Partridge

> We cannot escape history. We . . . will be
> remembered in spite of ourselves. No per-
> sonal significance or insignificance can
> spare one or another of us. The fiery trial
> through which we pass will light us down
> in honor or dishonor to the latest genera-
> tions. . . . We . . . hold the power and bear
> the responsibility.
>
> *Abraham Lincoln*

"Future generations" and "posterity" are terms that
are frequently encountered in popular journalism,
in political rhetoric, not to mention significant historical documents and literary works. For example,
the Preamble to the US Constitution cites as one of
its purposes, to "secure the Blessings of Liberty to
ourselves and our Posterity." Scarcely a week goes
by that one does not hear of "future generations" or
"posterity" in the popular media.

And yet, serious philosophical attention to the
issue of moral responsibility to future generations
is quite recent. Of the approximately one million
doctoral   dissertations   presently   listed   in
Dissertation Abstracts, the first to contain either the
term "future generations" or "posterity" in its title
was completed in 1976: "Rawls and the duty to posterity" (by this writer). Since then, 19 dissertations
have been completed which fit that description.
The Philosophers' Index lists 134 items under
"future generations" and "posterity." Of these, all
but three have been published since the first Earth
Day, April 22, 1970.

Why this apparent neglect until very recently,
by moral philosophers of an issue of such manifest
interest to the general public?

The answer might be found in an analysis of
the concept of moral responsibility. To say that a
moral agent or a corporate body is morally responsible for his or her actions would seem to entail at
the very least that the agent: (a) has, or is capable of
having, knowledge of the consequences of those
actions; (b) has the capacity to bring about these
consequences; (c) has the choice to do otherwise;
and (d) that these consequences have value signifi-

cance. The second and third conditions reiterate the
common meta-ethical insight that the realm of
morality is found between the extremes of the
impossible and the inevitable—or, to quote and
then extend the maxim of the eighteenth-century
philosopher, Immanuel Kant: *"ought* implies *can"*—
and yet might not.

If this analysis of the concept of responsibility
is accurate, then the reason for the emergence of
the posterity problem becomes clear: the issue has
arisen with the extraordinary advances in science
(knowledge) and *technology* (capacity). Before the
mid-twentieth century, the very idea that human
activities might seriously and permanently affect
the global atmosphere and oceans, or the gene
pool or our species and others, seemed preposterous. We were just too puny, we believed, and the
planet too vast for such consequences. Now the
sciences have disabused us of such assurances, as
technology has produced chemicals and radioactive substances unknown to nature, and as evidence proliferates of permanent anthropogenic
effects upon the seas, atmosphere, and the global
ecosystem. Furthermore, such consequences of
industrial civilization as ozone depletion, global
warming, the contamination of aquifers, and the
deposition of radwaste, while the by-products of
benefits to the present generation exact postponed
costs to remote generations.

Not coincidentally, the posterity question arose
alongside the emergence of the environmental
movement. While not all posterity issues are necessarily environmental in nature (the preservation of
landmark buildings and works of art come to mind
as exceptions), the preservation of the natural environment is clearly the public and moral issue with
the longest time entailments. And so, when in 1962
Rachel Carson's *Silent Spring* alerted the public to
the moral implications of bioscientific knowledge
and argo-industrial technology, and when, during
the same decade, the Sierra Club and other organizations decried the loss of *wilderness*, the consequences of these crises to future generations could

Reprinted from *A Companion to Environmental Philosophy*, ed. Dale Jamieson (Oxford, U.K.: Blackwell
Publishers, 2001). Reprinted with permission.

not be ignored. Accordingly, the emergence of the posterity issue during "the environmental decade" of the 1970s was virtually assured.

In short, the accelerating advances of science and technology have made it compellingly clear that future generations are vulnerable to our acts and policies. Furthermore, through science we have come to understand the long-term consequences of these policies, and, through technology, we have acquired the capacity to affect these consequences, if only through forbearance. In our hands lies the fate, for better or worse, of future persons whose lives we will never share. This is a burden of responsibility that we cannot escape, so long as we willingly accept the enlightenment of science and the capacities of our technology. "To do nothing, is to do something": namely, to assent to existing trends and entailments.

The Moral Status of Future Persons

At first glance, the posterity issue may appear to involve nothing more than a simple extension of our "moral community" to include, in addition to family, compatriots, distant contemporary victims of misfortune, and even *animals* and ecosystems, yet another category: persons who will be born after we have departed. By this superficial account, our responsibilities to future persons would not be significantly different in kind from our responsibilities to these contemporary "others." Put simply, it would seem that given our knowledge and capacities, future persons have the right to our responsible care and forbearance in their behalf.

A closer look reveals that the ontological and epistemological status of future persons raises numerous unique and extraordinary moral and meta-ethical problems. Among them:

- Most fundamentally, future persons, qua future, do not exist now, when alleged burdens of responsibility fall upon the living. Thus the question arises: can we have duties to non-existent beings? Still worse, what sense can be made of attributing rights to those who do not exist?

- Still more perplexing is the fact that by initiating a policy to improve the lives of future persons, we will be causing different individuals to be born in the future. But if so, then we can in no sense be said to be "improving the lives" of particular future persons, who, but for our provision (or neglect) would not exist (Parfit 1984).

- We cannot know future people as individuals. Instead, "posterity"' is an abstract category containing unnumbered and undifferentiated members. And yet, much moral theory is based upon the principle of "respect for autonomous individuals."

- Our relationship with future persons is unidirectional and non-reciprocal. Future persons will be unable to reward or punish us, as the case may be, for our provision for their lives.

- How can we tell with any confidence just what might benefit future persons—i.e., what will or will not be "goods" to them?

- Who is entitled to act in behalf of future persons?

Clearly, by assigning moral significance to those not yet born, we are introducing problems that are unique to the history of moral philosophy.

What then, is the moral status of future persons? Just how much claim do they have upon us to make provision for them or, at the very least, to forbear from causing future harm? The responses of contemporary moral philosophers cover a broad scope of the moral spectrum. To some, the contingency and non-actuality of future persons virtually excludes them from moral consideration. If any attempt to improve the lot of future persons results in a population of different individuals, then, so the argument goes, no particular lives can be "improved" by present policies.

Other responses include:

Libertarianism Some libertarians insist that with the privatization of all resources, future generations will be well cared for—as a beneficent "by-product" of rational, self-serving behavior. Because, they argue, no rational property owner will deliberately degrade the value of his property, private individuals are, in effect, suitable surrogates of the interests of future generations. Accordingly, writes Martino,

> it is quite possible to take the needs of the future into account by permitting the establishment of markets in which assets with future values can be bought and sold . . .

[S]peculation in resources with an expected large future demand automatically results in conservation. Thus the interests of the people who will live in the future are actively protected. (1982, p. 33)

It follows that the libertarian society will leave "as much and as good" for successor generations, with little need for individuals. and much less for governments, to concern themselves about the fate of remote posterity. As for resources, optimistic economists such as Julian Simon argue that so long as human ingenuity is mixed with the profit motive, suitable resources for an abundant life will be found, developed, and utilized, as they are needed at the time.

Critics reply that this account disregards, first, the diminution of economic value through time (i.e., "the discount rate"), and second, that these optimistic forecasts favor abstract economic models over fundamental scientific facts and principles, most notably ecosystemic complexity and the laws of thermodynamics. . . .

Utilitarianism   Though future individuals are implicitly factored into Bentham's "hedonic calculus" (in particular, through the criterion of "social extent"), considerable difficulties in the utilitarian approach to the posterity issue have only recently entered into philosophical debate.

First, how far into the future does our provision for posterity extend? Do we "discount" the future, or are the interests and preferences of furthest generations to count equally to those of our own children and grandchildren? Both alternatives present difficulties. If all future generations count, then equal distributive shares with this indefinite but enormously large number leaves us with virtually nothing for ourselves. And yet as Derek Parfit (1984) and others have pointed out, there seems to be no moral justification for a "pure time preference" for nearer over further generations.

Second, how can we calculate the "utility" of our provision for future individuals whose tastes, preferences, and needs we do not and cannot know?

Third, among the decisions that we make regarding future persons is the very size of that future population. Do we harm "might-have-beens" by denying them existence by adopting stringent population control policies? And most profoundly, what do the utilitarians propose to maximize: the average utility of future persons or the total utility, in a future population? This issue of average versus total utility, absent in utilitarian calculations regarding populations of fixed numbers (such as the present generation), arises with the question of population policy—i.e., how many future persons should we cause to exist? Full commitment to either average or total utility leads to counter-intuitive "repugnant conclusions." According to the average utility principle, Adam and Eve, before the fall, lived in a "better" world than a hypothetically later world of thousands or millions of individuals who, though quite happy on average, were slightly less so than the original couple. On the other hand, the total utility principle requires fertile couples to produce children whose lives will be on balance slightly happier than unhappy—an obligation which applies even in an overcrowded world. The average versus total utility dilemma leads to a question which lies at the very foundations of utilitarian philosophy: are we obliged to create people for happiness (total utility), or should we create happiness for people (average utility) (Warren, 1977; Sikora and Barry 1978. . . .)?

Communitarianism   Avner de-Shalit (1995) argues that we are morally bound to future generations through shared membership in a "community." This might appear to be an unpromising approach, for reasons now familiar to us: namely, that the present generation and its successors cannot interact—that their relationship is non-personal and non-reciprocal. Well aware of this difficulty, de-Shalit stipulates that just "one of three main conditions must be met in order for a group of people to count as a community: . . . interaction between people in daily life, cultural interaction, and moral similarity" (ibid, p. 22). Clearly, the first condition is not applicable between non-concurrent lives. But, de-Shalit contends, in a figurative and restricted, yet significant, sense, the second condition, "cultural interaction," is applicable, as is the third condition, "moral similarity." These two conditions bind us with future generations into a "community."

De-Shalit explains that while we do not "converse" with non-concurrent generations, we do have "cultural interaction" with them. To understand this concept, consider the U.S. Constitutional Convention in Philadelphia in 1787. As the

Preamble states, the document was enacted "for ourselves and our posterity," and thus it is clear that the framers of that document understood that they were affecting the life conditions of future generations. Reciprocally, every case that is heard before the Supreme Court today is responsive to this document, which was framed by our predecessors. Similarly, as we make provision for the remote future, we fully expect that future generations will be mindful of and responsive to these (then past) provisions.

"Moral similarity," de-Shalit's third condition, does not mean full agreement among generations of all moral precepts; indeed, rational moral debate along with moral adaptation and evolution is essential to a vital transgenerational community. Consider once again the example of the U.S. Constitution. That document was hotly debated and framed in the context of received moral and political presuppositions—a "frame of reference" or "form of life" (to use the twentieth-century philosopher Ludwig Wittgenstein's useful concept). It is within this context of agreement that moral debate takes place (or, to continue with our example, the Constitution is interpreted and occasionally amended). So long as this context of moral debate and interpretation remains essentially intact, de-Shalit argues, a "transgenerational community" can exist and continue. However, this concept carries with it the implication that this community across generations is time-contingent, and thus, as the moral "frame of reference"" itself evolves, "the time will come when it becomes questionable whether [remotely] future generations will still speak of the same transgenerational community" (Ibid, p. 47).

De-Shalit's book contains a sensitive and astute analysis of moral psychology—in particular an examination of the "time-binding" and "projective" aspect of human thought, action, and evaluation that is reminiscent of the twentieth-century philosopher, Martin Heidegger. Human life and experience, he argues, is incomprehensible without an awareness of the fact that we all, in an inescapable sense, live both in the present and the future, including a future that extends far beyond the span of our own lives. . . .

Deontological Views These focus on the moral status of future persons and the moral categories that apply to them, in particular, the issue of the putative rights of and duties to the not-yet-actual. Can we, in fact, be said to "have duties toward" non-actual future persons? If so, do these duties correlate with the rights of these future persons? The answer to that question may bear upon the moral urgency of our responsibility toward the future. "Uncorrelated" duties (also called "imperfect duties") may have less priority than those duties which correlate with the rights of others. Richard deGeorge is among those who recognize "duties toward" future persons, but deny that these duties correlate with the rights, now, of future persons. On the contrary, he insists, future generations "cannot now . . . be the present bearer or subject of anything, including rights. . . . [They] should correctly be said to have a right only to what is available when they come into existence" (deGeorge 1979, pp. 95–6).

Partridge (1990) replies that this argument succeeds in denying only one category of rights to future persons: what Feinberg and others call "active rights"—i.e., rights "to do such and such." However, "passive rights" (e.g., the right not to be deprived of opportunities, or not to be harmed, etc.), are quite applicable to future persons before they become actual. This is so, since, unlike "active rights," the option to honor or to violate passive rights falls upon the correlative "duty bearer"—in this case, the present generation.

John Rawls and the "Hypothetical Contract" One of the most influential and provocative treatments of the posterity issue appears in John Rawls's *A Theory of Justice* (1971), where Rawls proposes a "contractarian" approach to the question of what he calls "justice between generations." At first, a contractarian approach to the issue seems unpromising, for the very same reasons that it is troublesome for the communitarians: namely, that the "contractors," having non-concurrent lives, are incapable of bargaining and arriving at reciprocal agreements.

Fully aware of this difficulty, Rawls concedes at the outset that fundamental principles of justice cannot be arrived at through actual contract negotiations. Instead, the "contract" must be "hypothetical" and constructed through an elaborate thought-experiment which he calls "the original position." While we cannot describe here the details of Rawls's theory, suffice to say for our purposes that the "contractors," in drawing out the rules of "justice between generations," are denied knowledge of which generation in human history they belong to. Thus, the rules of intergenerational justice are devised in the original position to apply to all generations. Accordingly, the parties in the original position do not know whether, in the conditions of their actual lives, the rules of "just savings" will turn out to be a burden or a benefit. All they know is that, in either case, due to the conditions of "the original position," the rules will be "fair."

As a result of these deliberations in the original position (more traditionally, one might say, "from the moral point of view"), Rawls believes that the following rules of "just savings" would be adopted: "[1] preserve the gains of culture and civilization. . . . [2] maintain intact those just institutions that have been established [and 3], put aside in each period of time a suitable amount of real capital accumulation." He adds that "this saving may take various forms from net investment in machinery and other means of production to investment in learning and education" (1971, p. 285).

Conspicuously absent from this list is any direct reference to the conservation of natural resources or the preservation of the natural environment (though such considerations are not specifically excluded, and are arguably implicit in these principles). This omission is remedied by Edith Brown Weiss (1989), who stipulates as a fundamental "principle of intergenerational equity" that each generation leave to its successor a planet in at least as good a condition as that generation received it. Like Rawls, Weiss believes that principles of intergenerational justice should be drawn behind a "veil of ignorance"—without knowledge of which generation in the span of history is one's own. However, unlike Rawls, Weiss is attempting to derive principles that apply, not within a national entity, but to all nations—which is to say, will serve as a foundation of international law.

The Motivation Problem

Are human beings, either individually or communally, capable of making just provision for remotely future persons who they will never know and who cannot reciprocally reward or punish those of the present generation? While this question may seem to be more psychological and socio-logical than philosophical, it nonetheless is of profound concern to the moral philosopher.

Recall that one of the criteria of moral responsibility is capacity. While we earlier identified this as "technological capacity" to bring about or prevent foreseeable long-term consequences of our actions, "capacity" can also refer to psychological conditions. Rawls recognizes this issue as he asserts that moral principles, if they are to be valid, must be such that human beings are able to abide by them—they must, in Rawls's words, be capable of withstanding "the strains of commitment."

In an important paper, Norman Care presents doubts regarding "our ability to solve the motivation problem relative to what morality requires on behalf of future generations" (1982, p. 195). He argues that: (a) we can have no bonds of love or concern for indefinite future persons: "their interests cannot interest us"; (b) we have no "community bond" with future persons—no "sense of belonging to some joint enterprise"; and finally (c) we feel no "extended or unbounded shared-fate motivation," no "sense of common humanity" (ibid., pp. 207–9). Consequently, Care concludes:

> certain familiar sorts of motivation are not available to support policies demanding serious sacrifice for the sake of future generations, and we may well be discouraged by the further apparent fact that the cultivation of a form of motivation directly supportive of such policies might require something close to an overhaul of main elements in the makeup of our society which influence the moral psychology of citizens. (ibid., p. 213)

However, this conclusion does not completely close the door to a just provision for the remote future. Care does, after all, concede the possibility of a "moral overhaul" in society. Not only that, but the mere possibility of appropriate sacrifice for the sake of posterity is exemplified in the supererogatory acts of saints and heros.

Garrett Hardin, who largely shares Care's pessimism, nevertheless recounts two examples of extraordinary sacrifice in behalf of the future, both from the Soviet Union (1977, p. 78–9). In the first, during the 1921 famine, peasants in a starving village on the Volga refused to eat the seed grain stacked in an adjacent field. "We do not steal from the future," they said. In the second case, during the 900-day siege of Leningrad, while nearly a million residents starved, large stores of edible seeds in an agricultural research institute were untouched. Still, the essential question remains: notwithstanding known cases of extraordinary sacrifice in behalf of the remote future, can people in general and their established governments be persuaded to submit to "ordinary" constraints in order to make fair provision for posterity?

Rawls believes that to assure "just savings" for the future, the parties of his original position must understand themselves to be "heads of families," with parental ties and concerns for the immediately succeeding generation or two (1971, pp. 128–9). Provision for remote generations is thus accomplished through a "chain linking" of one generation to the next. This proposal immediately suggests two problems: first, it implies that childless individuals are incapable of caring for future generations, and thus are excused from making just provision. Second, Rawls's "heads of families" condition presents a "discounting" problem even more severe than that of the economists, for a parent's love and concern for a child is generally greater than for a grandchild, and so on, diminishing to insignificance within a very few generations.

A more positive account of the motivation question has been offered by Partridge (1981). Not only is significant "self-transcendent" concern for the remote future possible, he argues, it is in fact healthy—the result of normal processes of maturation and socialization. A "self-transcending concern" for persons, communities, locations, causes, artifacts, institutions, ideals, etc., arises from (a) the social origins of the self concept, (b) from the "objectification of values" (i.e., the perception of values as being "in" the valued objects), and (c) the universal awareness of one's mortality. All this leads to an interest in believing that these entities will continue to flourish beyond the span of one's lifetime. As further evidence of the claim that "self-transcendent concern" is healthy, Partridge points out that a lack thereof, described by clinical psychologists as "alienation" and "narcissism," is an unenviable condition (1981, p. 204).

In this account of self-transcendent concern we find an echo of an ancient yet timely moral insight, known as "the moral paradox": namely, that it is in one's own best interest not to seek deliberately one's own best interest—that the most fulfilling life is realized in outwardly directed activity and concern. If this condition is true of human nature, and if a widespread real-ization of self-transcending concern is available through educational and institutional reform, then the means of accomplishing Norman Care's "moral overhaul" may be at hand. Such an accomplishment may be difficult and even highly improbable given contemporary social conditions. However, mere possibility may suffice to prompt moral concern and involvement. Recall that capacity is a condition of moral responsibility, and that the arena of moral activity is found between the extremes of impossibility and inevitability.

Policy Implications

We have explored the meta-ethical issue of whether future generations can be said to have rights, and have reviewed a variety of normative approaches to the posterity issue. Now we turn to the practical question of just what we might do to best fulfill our responsibilities to the remote future.

To begin, we should turn an acute critical eye toward the "business as usual" of public policy-making: "cost-benefit analysis"—an approach promoted by economists, widely endorsed by legislatures and administrators, and enshrined in methodology of environmental impact analysis. . . . There are many criticisms of cost-benefit analysis. The most prominent among them are the following:

- By commensurating all values into cash (a non-moral value), morality is "factored out" of policy considerations.

- Cost-benefit analysis measures aggregated consumer preferences to the exclusion of community/citizen values.

- Economic analysis is descriptive—indicating what a consumer-public in fact values (economically), rather than prescribing what they should value (normatively). To put the matter bluntly, the economist asks: "What is the value? Tell me what are you willing to pay." The moral philosopher replies: "What am I willing to pay? First I must determine, independently, what is its value." This is a response that the economist cannot touch within the bounds of his discipline.

- Finally, and most significantly for the posterity issue, by measuring value in terms of cash, the future is discounted. Thus the costs and benefits to persons just a few generations into the future count for virtually nothing in economically based policy analyses.

The Ignorance Excuse   Before we proceed with policy recommendations, one more objection to provision for the remote future must be addressed. It is based upon the "knowledge criterion" of responsibility, and claims that we do not and in principle cannot, know what future generations will need or value, and thus can make no provision for them. How, for example, could previous generations have known of our need for rare semiconducting elements such as germanium? And conversely, what if they had needlessly sacrificed by storing up vast quantities of whale oil, with no anticipation of the coming ages of petroleum and electricity? When we examine the predictions of 50 and 100 years ago, regarding life at the close of the twentieth century, how can we with any confidence forecast conditions of life in the remote future?

Granting all this, there are, nonetheless, some fundamental facts that we can know about future generations:

1. First, they will be humans, with well-known biotic requirements necessary to sustain their health.

2. Second, future persons for whom we are responsible will be moral agents, which means that they will be sentient and self-conscious, having a sense of themselves and other persons as continuing beings with the capacity to choose among alternative futures, and with the capacity to reason abstractly and thus to act on principle. All this entails that these future persons will be bound by familiar moral categories of rights, responsibilities, and the demands of justice.

3. Third, if these future persons are to live and flourish, they must be sustained by a functioning ecosystem.

4. And finally, they will require stable social institutions and a body of knowledge and skills that will allow them to meet and overcome cultural and natural crises that may occur during their lifetimes. (Partridge 1994)

Assuming then that we know enough about the welfare of future persons to act responsibly in their behalf, what guidelines might direct our policies toward future generations? Prominent among those proposed by philosophers and others, are the following:

"First of All, Do No Harm"   Because "the ignorance excuse" is not without some merit, an insight from the utilitarians would be very helpful to the policy-makers: namely, we should favor policies that mitigate evil over policies that promote good. This precept is supported by common-sense considerations. First, avoidable or treatable pain demands the moral attention of everyone, while "the pursuit of happiness" is the appropriate concern of the individual. Furthermore, it is much easier to identify and address the causes of misery than it is to promote the well-springs of happiness. This is especially so with regard to the future. The pains and tribulations of future persons, like those of ourselves, can often be traced to disruptions in the fundamental biotic, ecosystemic, psychological, and institutional conditions listed above. Their pleasures and satisfactions will come from a future evolution of culture, taste and technology that we cannot even imagine.

The "Critical Lockean Proviso"   According to John Locke (1632–1704), it is morally permissible to "take from nature," mix one's labor with the taking, and claim the result as one's private property, so long as one leaves "as much and as good for others." While this may have been true in a world of frontiers and homesteads, it is no longer possible. Once a barrel of petroleum is extracted from the earth and consumed, there is no longer "as much and as good" remaining for our successors. But if we were to share equally our petroleum resources with all generations far into the future, we would be allocated a cupful each. So we must, instead, adopt a "critical Lockean proviso," whereby we leave for the future, not the very resource that we deplete, but the opportunity to obtain whatever it was for which the original resource was utilized. Thus while future generations may not need petroleum (just as we no longer need whale oil), they will need what petroleum provides, namely energy. Thus it is our responsibility to find a replacement. The proviso also entails that we utilize recycling technologies and "interest-bearing" (i.e., renewable) resources, such as sustained yield forestry and fisheries. And this in turn validates the need to preserve natural ecosystems.

Preserve the Options   This rule is clearly entailed by the previous two. While we cannot predict the technological solutions to future resource scarcity, we owe future generations a full range of options and opportunities for research and development of these technologies. This in turn entails a continuing investment in scientific and technical education and research. Happily, such an investment benefits our own generation and that of our immediate successors, as it also benefits the remote future.

Anticipation and Prevention is Preferable to Cure
We should therefore keep an informed eye on impending impacts upon the future. "Earlier" is easier and cheaper than "later." Accordingly, our responsibility to future generations must include technological and environmental impact studies which will foresee, and expand the capacity to foresee, developing crises and the consequences of our projects and policies far into the remote future. Obvious examples of this "duty of anticipation" include studies of stratospheric ozone depletion, global warming, chemical hormone disruption, and nuclear waste disposal.

Just Forbearance   This dimension of the duty to posterity clearly follows from the previous: for once we have determined, through scientific research, how our actions might affect the remote future, we may face a clear duty to forgo advantages for the sake of future generations. To cite our examples once again, studies of atmospheric physics and chemistry may determine that we face a choice between having our grandchildren protected from ultraviolet radiation or having our generation enjoy the convenience of aerosol sprays and supersonic aircraft. Similarly, due to the so-called "Greenhouse effect," our voracious appetite for fossil fuel energy may be inconsistent with a tolerable *climate* for our successors. Accordingly, a decision to favor future generations would, in these instances, require just forbearances on the part of those now living. A policy of "just forbearance" is a conservative approach to provision for the future, which is often favored by environmentalists. The ecosystem, they argue, is a network of complex and subtle interrelationships, the intricacies and ramifications of which we can never fully comprehend. Rather than carelessly toss aside components of this system (e.g., species and nutrients), we should

approach the planetary life community with humility and care. If our information is incomplete, it is better to postpone, or even to abandon, projects that threaten the integrity of the system.

Doing Well by Doing Good   We should favor policies that work to the advantage of both us and the future—and which, other factors being roughly equal, are least burdensome to the present generation. This rule is responsive to the constant political problem of convincing the public to accept sacrifices now to bring about benefits that they will never see. On reflection, it seems that a significant number of our "duties to the future" also benefit us and those we directly care about—our children and grandchildren. Among these benefits are the control of pollution, population, and global warming.

Educational Implications   None of the above will be accomplished unless succeeding generations acquire the moral stamina to face up to and carry out their moral responsibilities. This can only be accomplished through a carefully devised and generously funded program of environmental and moral education. Such a program would include the teaching of critical thinking, history, ecological principles, and a respect for free institutions.

The moral education here proposed is one, not of content but of process—not of answers, but of the skills to find the answers for oneself. As such, this approach prizes above all else the dignity and autonomy of the individual—qualities assaulted and threatened by our mass culture. Be that as it may, let us acknowledge that the youth will be "morally educated" somehow, if only by default. That is to say, they will have some set of values, for better or worse. Better that we assume the task deliberately, and do a good job of it.

Guardian for Future Generations   Such an arrangement should be established by the international community—preferably under the sanction of international law, but, failing that, with the widespread support of non-governmental organizations (Stone 1996; Weiss 1989). Christopher Stone suggests that such a guardian

> might be authorized: (1) to appear before the legislatures and administrative agencies of states considering actions with pronounced, long-term implications; (2) to appear as a special intervener-counsel in a variety of bilateral

and multi-lateral disputes, and, (3) perhaps most important, even to initiate legal and diplomatic action on the future's behalf in appropriate situations (1989, pp. 71–2).

As we noted at the outset, the posterity issue is new to the literature and debates of moral philosophy. But now, having made its appearance, the question of our responsibility to future Generations cannot be returned to obscurity. For if our analysis of "moral responsibility" (as knowledge, capacity, choice, and value significance) is correct, the only plausible escape from this responsibility would be a disavowal of the knowledge provided by our sciences, and an abandonment of the capacity and choice bestowed by our technology. Few seem willing to pay that price to avoid the moral burden of our duty to posterity. If, on the other hand, we continue to support the advancement of science and technology, and yet ignore the long-term consequences thereof, we will not avoid our moral responsibility—we will be in default thereof, and will be properly condemned by the generations that succeed us.

References

Care, N. (1982) "Future generations, public policy, and the motivation problem." *Environmental Ethics* (Fall).

de George, R. (1979) "The environment, rights and future generations." in *Ethics and Problems of the 21st Century*, ed. K. Goodpaster and K. Sayre (Notre Dame: University of Notre Dame Press).

de-Shalit, A. (1995) *Why Posterity Matters* (London: Routledge).

Hardin, G. (1977) *The Limits of Altruism* (Indiana: Indiana University Press).

Martino, J. P. (1982) "Inheriting the earth," *Reason* (November).

Parfit, D. (1984) *Reasons and Persons* (Oxford: Clarendon Press).

Partridge, E. (1981) "Why care about the future?," in *Responsibilities to Future Generations*, ed. E. Partridge (Buffalo: Prometheus).

——— (1990) "On the rights of future generations." in *Upstream/Downstream: Issues in Environmental Ethics*, ed. Donald Scherer (Philadelphia: Temple University Press).

——— (1994) "Posterity and the 'strains of commitment.'" in *Creating a New History for Future Generations*, ed. T. Kim. and J. Dator (Kyoto: Institute for the Integrated Study of Future Generations).

Rawls, J. (1971) *A Theory of Justice* (Cambridge: Harvard).

Sikora, R. and Barry, B. eds. (1978) *Obligations to Future Generations* (Philadelphia: Temple University Press).

Stone, C. (1996) "Should we establish a guardian for future generations?," in *Should Trees Have Standing? And Other Essays on Law, Morals and the Environment* (Dobbs Ferry, NY: Oceana).

Warren, M. (1977) "Do potential people have rights?" *Canadian Journal of Philosophy* (June).

Weiss, E. (1989) *In Fairness to Future Generations: International Law, Common Patrimony, and Intergenerational Equity* (New York: Transnational Publication and the United Nations University).

60. SIDELIGHT: The Nuclear Train to the Future[1]

Richard (Routley) Sylvan and Val (Routley) Plumwood

A long distance country train has just pulled out. The train, which is crowded, carries both passengers and freight. At an early stop in the journey, someone consigns as freight, to a far distant destination, a package which contains a highly toxic and explosive gas. This is packed in a very thin container which, as the consigner is aware, may well not contain the gas for the full distance for which it is consigned, and certainly will not do so if the train should strike any real trouble, for example, if the train should be derailed or involved in a collision, or if some passenger should interfere inadvertently or deliberately with the freight, perhaps trying to steal some of it. All of these sorts of things have happened on some previous journeys. If the container should break the resulting disaster would probably kill at least some of the people on the train in adjacent carriages, while others could be maimed or poisoned or sooner or later incur serious diseases.

And Justice for All: New Introductory Essays in Ethics and Public Policy, edited by Tom Regan and Donald VanDeVeer (Totowa, NJ: Rowan and Littlefield, 1982), pp. 116–118. Reprinted by permission of the publisher.

Most of us would roundly condemn such an action. What might the consigner of the parcel say to try to justify it? He might say that it is *not certain* that the gas will escape, or that the world needs his product and it is his duty to supply it, or that in any case he is not responsible for the train or the people on it. These sorts of excuses, however, would normally be seen as ludicrous when set in this context. Unfortunately, similar excuses are often not so seen when the consigner, again a (responsible) businessman, put his workers' health or other peoples' welfare at risk.

Suppose he says that it is his own and others' pressing needs which justify his action. The company he controls, which produces the material as a by-product, is in bad financial straits, and could not afford to produce a better container even if it knew how to make one. If the company fails, he and his family will suffer, his employees will lose their jobs and have to look for others, and the whole company town, through loss of spending, will be worse off. The poor and unemployed of the town, whom he would otherwise have been able to help, will suffer especially. Few people would accept such grounds as justification. Even where there are serious risks and costs to oneself or some group for whom one is concerned one is usually considered not to be entitled to simply transfer the heavy burden of those risks and costs onto other uninvolved parties, especially where they arise from one's own, or one's group's chosen life-style.

The matter of nuclear waste has many moral features which resemble the train case. How fitting the analogy is will become apparent as the argument progresses. There is no known proven safe way to package the highly toxic wastes generated by the nuclear plants that will be spread around the world as large-scale nuclear development goes ahead. The waste problem will be much more serious than that generated by the 50 or so reactors in use at present, with each one of the 2000 or so reactors envisaged by the end of the century producing, on average, annual wastes containing 1000 times the radioactivity of the Hiroshima bomb. Much of this waste is extremely toxic. For example, a millionth of a gramme of plutonium is enough to induce a lung cancer. A leak of even a part of the waste material could involve much loss of life, widespread disease and genetic damage, and contamination of immense areas of land. Wastes will include the reactors themselves, which will have to be abandoned after their expected life times of per-

haps 40 years, and which, some have estimated, may require 1½ million years to reach safe levels of radioactivity.

Nuclear wastes must be kept suitably isolated from the environment for their entire active lifetime. For fission products the required storage period averages a thousand years or so, and for transuranic elements, which include plutonium, there is a half million to a million year storage problem. Serious problems have arisen with both short-term and proposed long-term methods of storage, even with the comparatively small quantities of waste produced over the last twenty years. Short-term methods of storage require continued human intervention, while proposed longer term methods are suject to both human interference and risk of leakage through non-human factors.

No one with even a slight knowledge of the geological and climatic history of the earth over the last million years, a period whose fluctuations in climate we are only just beginning to gauge and which has seen four Ice Ages, could be confident that a rigorous guarantee of safe storage could be provided for the vast period of time involved. Nor does the history of human affairs over the last 3000 years give ground for confidence in safe storage by by methods of requiring human intervention over perhaps a million years. Proposed long-term storage methods such as storage in granite formations or in salt minds, are largely speculative and relatively untested, and have already proved to involve difficulties with attempts made to put them into practice. Even as regards expensive recent proposals for first embedding concentrated wastes in glass and encapsulating the result in multilayered metal containers before rock deposit, simulation models reveal that radioactive material may not remain suitably isolated from human environments. In short, the best present storage proposals carry very real possibilities of irradiating future people and damaging their environment. . . .[2]

The risks imposed on the future by proceeding with nuclear development are, then, *significant*. Perhaps 40,000 generations of future people could be forced to bear significant risks resulting from the provision of the (extravagant) energy use of only a small proportion of the people of 10 generations. . . .

Notes

1. This paper is a condensation of an early version of our "Nuclear power—ethical, social, and political

dimensions" (ESP for short, available from the authors). . . . For help with the condensation we are very considerably indebted to the editors.

In the condensation, we simplify the structure of the argument and suppress underlying political and ideological dimensions (for example, the large measure of responsibility of the USA for spreading nuclear reactors around the world, and thereby enhancing the chances of nuclear disasters, including nuclear war). We also considerably reduce a heavy load of footnotes and references designed and needed to help make good many of our claims. Further, in order to contain references to a modest length, reference to primary sources has often been replaced by references through secondary sources. Little difficulty should be encountered however in

tracing fuller references through secondary sources or in filling out much important background material from work cited herein. For example, virtually all the data cited in sections I and VII are referenced in Routley. At worst ESP can always be consulted. . . .

2. Naturally the effect on humans is not the only factor that has to be taken into account in arriving at moral assessments. Nuclear radiation, unlike most ethical theories, does not confine its scope to human life and welfare. But since the harm nuclear development may afflict on nonhuman life, for example, can hardly *improve* its case, it suffices if the case against it can be made out solely in terms of its effects on human life in the conventional way.

61. Sustainability: An Economist's Perspective

Robert M. Solow

This talk is different from anything else anyone has heard at Woods Hole; certainly for the last two days. Three people have asked me, "Do you plan to use any transparencies or slides?" Three times I said, "No," and three times I was met with this blank stare of disbelief. I actually have some beautiful aerial photographs of Prince William Sound that I could have brought along to show you, and I also have a spectacular picture of Michael Jordan in full flight that you would have liked to have seen. But in fact I don't need or want any slides or transparencies. I want to talk to you about an idea. The notion of sustainability or sustainable growth (although, as you will see, it has nothing necessarily to do with growth) has infiltrated discussions of long-run economic policy in the last few years. It is very hard to be against sustainability. In fact, the less you know about it, the better it sounds. That is true of lots of ideas. The questions that come to be connected with sustainable development or sustainable growth or just sustainability are genuine and deeply felt and very complex. The combination of deep feeling and complexity breeds buzzwords, and sustainability has certainly become a buzzword. What I thought I might do, when I was

invited to talk to a group like this, was to try to talk out loud about how one might think straight about the concept of sustainability, what it might mean and what its implications (not for daily life but for your annual vote or your concern for economic policy) might be.

Definitions are usually boring. That is probably true here too. But here it matters a lot. Some people say they don't know what sustainability means, but it sounds good. I've seen things on restaurant menus that strike me the same way. I took these two parts of a definition from a UNESCO document: ". . . every generation should leave water, air and soil resources as pure and unpolluted as when it came on earth." Alternatively, it was suggested that "each generation should leave undiminished all the species of animals it found existing on earth." I suppose that sounds good, as it is meant to. But I believe that kind of thought is fundamentally the wrong way to go in thinking about this issue. I must also say that there are some much more carefully thought out definitions and discussions, say by the U.N. Environment Programme and the World Conservation Union. They all turn out to be vague; in a way, the message I want to leave with you today is that sustainability

This paper was presented as the Eighteenth J. Stewart Johnson Lecture to the Marine Policy Center, Woods Hole Oceanographic Institution, at Woods Hole, Massachusetts, on June 14, 1991. *Economics Of The Environment: Selected Readings*, edited by Robert Dorfman and Nancy S. Dorfman, 3rd edition (NY: W. W. Norton & Company, Inc., 1993), pp. 179–187. Reprinted by permission.

is an essentially vague concept, and it would be wrong to think of it as being precise, or even capable of being made precise. It is therefore probably not in any clear way an exact guide to policy. Nevertheless, it is not at all useless.

Pretty clearly the notion of sustainability is about our obligation to the future. It says something about a moral obligation that we are supposed to have for future generations. I think it is very important to keep in mind—I'm talking like a philosopher for the next few sentences and I don't really know how to do that—that you can't be morally obligated to do something that is not feasible. Could I be morally obligated to be like Peter Pan and flap my wings and fly around the room? The answer is clearly not. I can't have a moral obligation like that because I am not capable of flapping my arms and flying around the room. If I fail to carry out a moral obligation, you must be entitled to blame me. You could properly say unkind things about me. But you couldn't possibly say unkind things about me for not flying around the room like Peter Pan because you know, as well as I do, that I can't do it.

If you define sustainability as an obligation to leave the world as we found it in detail, I think that's glib but essentially unfeasible. It is, when you think about it, not even desirable. To carry out literally the injunction of UNESCO would mean to make no use of mineral resources; it would mean to do no permanent construction or semi-permanent construction; build no roads; build no dams; build no piers. A mooring would be all right but not a pier. Apart from being essentially an injunction to do something that is not feasible, it asks us to do something that is not, on reflection, desirable. I doubt that I would feel myself better off if I had found the world exactly as the Iroquois left it. It is not clear that one would really want to do that.

To make something reasonable and useful out of the idea of sustainability, I think you have to try a different kind of definition. The best thing I could think of is to say that it is an obligation to conduct ourselves so that we leave to the future the option or the capacity to be as well off as we are. It is not clear to me that one can be more precise than that. Sustainability is an injunction not to satisfy ourselves by impoverishing our successors. That sounds good too, but I want you to realize how problematic it is—how hard it is to make anything precise or checkable out of that thought. If we try to look far ahead, as presumably we ought to if we are trying to obey the injunction to sustainability, we realize that the tastes, the preferences, of future generations are something that we don't know about. Nor do we know anything very much about the technology that will be available to people 100 years from now. Put yourself in the position of someone in 1880 trying to imagine what life would be like in 1980 and you will see how wrong you would be. I think all we can do in this respect is to imagine people in the future being much like ourselves and attributing to them, imputing to them, whatever technology we can "reasonably" extrapolate—whatever that means. I am trying to emphasize the vagueness but not the meaninglessness of that concept. It is not meaningless, it is just inevitably vague.

We are entitled to please ourselves, according to this definition, so long as it is not at the expense (in the sense that I stated) of future well-being. You have to take into account, in thinking about sustainability, the resources that we use up and the resources that we leave behind, but also the sort of environment we leave behind including the built environment, including productive capacity (plant and equipment) and including technological knowledge. *To talk about sustainability in that way is not at all empty.* It attracts your attention, first, to what history tells us is an important fact, namely, that goods and services can be substituted for one another. If you don't eat one species of fish, you can eat another species of fish. Resources are, to use a favorite word of economists, fungible in a certain sense. They can take the place of each other. That is extremely important because it suggests that we do not owe to the future any particular thing. There is no specific object that the goal of sustainability, the obligation of sustainability, requires us to leave untouched.

What about nature? What about wilderness or unspoiled nature? I think that we ought, in our policy choices, to embody our desire for unspoiled nature as a component of well-being. But we have to recognize that different amenities really are, to some extent, substitutable for one another, and we should be as inclusive as possible in our calculations. It is perfectly okay, it is perfectly logical and rational, to argue for the preservation of a particular species or the preservation of a particular landscape. But that has to be done on its own, for its own sake, because this landscape is intrinsically what we want or this species is intrinsically important to preserve, not under the heading of sustainability. Sustainability doesn't require that any *particular* species of owl or any *particular* species of fish or any *particular* tract of forest be preserved. Substitutability is also important on the production side. We know that one kind of input can be substituted for another in production. There is no reason for our society to feel guilty about using up aluminum as long as we leave behind a capacity to perform the same or analogous functions using other kinds of materials—plastics or other natural or artificial materials. In making policy decisions we can take advantage of the principle of substitutability, remembering that what we are obligated to leave behind is a generalized capacity to create well-being, not any particular thing or any particular natural resource.

If you approach the problem that way in trying to make plans and make policies, it is certain that there will be mistakes. We will impute to the future tastes that they don't have or we will impute to them technological capacities that they won't have or we will fail to impute to them tastes and technological capacities that they do have. The set of possible mistakes is usually pretty symmetric.

That suggests to me the importance of choosing robust policies whenever we can. We should choose policies that will be appropriate over as wide a range of possible circumstances as we can imagine. But it would be wrong for policy to be paralyzed by the notion that one can make mistakes. Liability to error is the law of life. And, as most people around Woods Hole know, you choose policies to avoid potentially catastrophic errors, if you can. You insure wherever you can, but that's it.

The way I have put this, and I meant to do so, emphasizes that sustainability is about distributional equity. It is about who gets what. It is about the sharing of well-being between present people and future people. I have also emphasized the need to keep in mind, in making plans, that we don't know what they will do, what they will like, what they will want. And, to be honest, it is none of our business.

It is often asked whether, at this level, the goal or obligation of sustainability can be left entirely to the market. It seems to me that there is no reason to believe in a doctrinaire way that it can. The future is not adequately represented in the market, at least not the far future. If you remember that our societies live with real interest rates of the order of 5 or 6 percent, you will realize that that means that the dollar a generation from now, thirty years from now, is worth 25 cents today. That kind of discount seems to me to be much sharper than we would seriously propose in our public capacity, as citizens thinking about our obligation to the future. It seems to me to be a stronger discount than most of us would like to make. It is fair to say that those people a few generations hence are not adequately represented in today's market. They don't participate in it, and therefore there is no doctrinaire reason for saying, "Oh well, ordinary supply and demand, ordinary market behavior, will take care of whatever obligation we have to the future."

Now, in principle, government could serve as a trustee, as a representative for future interests. Policy actions, taxes, subsidies, regulations could, in principle, correct for the excessive present-mindedness of ordinary people like ourselves in our daily business. Of course, we are not sure that government will do a good job. It often seems that the rate at which governments discount the future is rather sharper than that at which the bond market does. So we can't be sure that public policy will do a good job. That is why we talk about it in a democracy. We are trying to think about collective decisions for the future, and discussions like this, not with just me talking, are the way in which policies of that kind ought to be thrashed out.

Just to give you some idea of how uncertain both private and public behavior can be in an issue like this, let me ask you to think about the past, not about the future. You could make a good case that our ancestors, who were considerably poorer than we are, whose standard of living was considerably less than our own, were probably excessively generous in providing for us. They cut down a lot of trees, but they saved a lot and they built a lot of railroad rights-of-way. Both privately and publicly they probably did better by us than a sort of fair-minded judge in thinking about the equity (whether they got their share and we got our share or whether we profited at their expense) would have required. It would have been okay for them to save a little less, to enjoy a little more and given us a little less of a start than our generation has had. I don't think there is any simple generalization that will serve to guide policy about these issues. There is every reason to discuss economic policy and social policy from this point of view, and anything else is likely to be ideology rather than analysis.

Once you take the point of view that I have been urging on you in thinking about sustainability as a matter of distributional equity between the present and the future, you can see that it becomes a problem about saving and investment. It becomes a problem about the choice between current consumption and providing for the future.

There is a sort of dual connection—a connection that need not be intrinsic but is there—between environmental issues and sustainability issues. The environment needs protection by public policy because each of us knows that by burdening the environment, by damaging it, we can profit and have some of the cost, perhaps most of the cost, borne by others. Sustainability is a problem precisely because each of us knows or realizes that we can profit at the expense of the future rather than at the expense of our contemporaries and the environment. We free-ride on each other and we free-ride on the future. Environmental policy is important for both reasons. One of the ways we free-ride on the future is by burdening the environment. And so current environmental protection—this is what I meant by a dual connection—will almost certainly contribute quite a lot to sustainability. Although, I want to warn you, not automatically. Current environmental protection contributes to sustainability if it comes at the expense of current consumption. Not if it comes at the expense of investment, of additions to future capacity. So, there are no absolutes. There is nothing precise about this notion but there are perhaps approximate guides to public policy that come out of this way of reasoning about the idea of sustainability. A correct principle, a correct general guide is that when we use up something—and by we I mean our society, our country, our civilization, however broadly you want to think—when we use up something that is irreplaceable, whether it is minerals or a fish species, or an environmental amenity, then we should be thinking about providing a substitute of equal value, and the vagueness comes in the notion of value. The something that we provide in exchange could be knowledge, could be technology. It needn't even be a physical object.

Let me give you an excellent example from the recent past of a case of good thought along these lines and also a case of bad thought along these lines. Commercially usable volumes of oil were discovered in the North Sea some years ago. The two main beneficiaries of North Sea oil were the United Kingdom and Norway. It is only right to say that the United Kingdom dissipated North Sea oil, wasted it, used it up in consumption and on employment. If I meet Mrs. Thatcher in heaven, since that is where I intend to go, the biggest thing I will tax her with is that she blew North Sea oil. Here was an asset that by happenstance the U.K. acquired. If the sort of general approach to sustainability that I have been suggesting to you had been taken by the Thatcher government, someone would have said, "It's okay we are going to use up the oil, that's what it is for, but we will make sure that we provide something else in exchange, that we guide those resources, at least in large part, into investment in capacity in the future." That did not happen. As I said, if you ask where (and by the way the curve of production from the North Sea fields is already on the way down; that asset is on its way to exhaustion) it went, it went into maintaining consumption in the United Kingdom and, at the same time, into unemployment.

Norway, on the other hand, went about it in the typical sober way you expect of good Scandinavians. The Norwegians said, here is a wasting asset. Here is an asset that we are going to use up. Scandinavians are also slightly masochistic, as you know. They said the one thing we must avoid is blowing this; the one thing we must avoid is a binge. They tried very hard to convert a large fraction of the revenues, of the rentals, of the royalties from North Sea oil into investment. I confess I don't know how well they succeeded but I am willing to bet that they did a better job of it than the United Kingdom.

This brings me to the one piece of technical economics that I want to mention. There is a neat analytical result in economics (mainly done by John Hartwick of Queen's University in Canada) which studies an economy that takes what we call the rentals, the pure return to a non-renewable resource, and invests those rentals.[1] That is, it uses up a natural asset like the North Sea oil field, but makes a point of investing whatever revenues intrinsically inhere to the oil itself. That policy can be shown to have neat sustainability properties. In a simple sort of economy, it will guarantee a perpetually constant capacity to consume. By the way, it is a very simple rule, and it is really true only for very simple economies; but it has the advantage, first of all, of sounding right, of sounding like justice, and secondly, of being practical. It is a calculation that could be made. It is a calculation that we don't make and I am going to suggest in a minute that we should be making it. You might want to do better. You might feel so good about your great-grandchildren that you would like to do better than invest the rents on the non-renewable resources that you use up. But in any case, it is, at a minimum, a policy that one could pursue for the sake of sustainability. I want to remind you again that most environmental protection can be regarded as an act of investment. If we were to think that our obligation to the future is in principle discharged by seeing that the return to non-renewable resources is funnelled into capital formation, any kind of capital formation—plant and equipment, research and development, physical oceanography, economics or environmental investment—we could have some feeling that we were about on the right track.

Now I want to mention what strikes me as sort of a paradox—as a difficulty with a concept of sustainability. I said, I kind of insisted, that you should think about it as a matter of equity, as a matter of distributional equity, as a matter of choice of how productive capacity should be shared between us and them, them being the future. Once you think about it that way you are almost forced logically to think about equity not between periods of time but equity right now. There is something inconsistent about people who profess to be terribly concerned about the welfare of future generations but do not seem to be terribly concerned about the welfare of poor people today. You will see in a way why this comes to be a paradox. The only reason for thinking that sustainability is a problem is that you think that some people are likely to be shortchanged, namely, in the future. Then I think you really are obligated to ask, "Well, is anybody being short-changed right now?"

The paradox arises because if you are concerned about people who are currently poor, it will turn out that your concern for them will translate into an increase in current consumption, not into an increase in investment. The logic of sustainability says, "You ought to be thinking about poor people today, and thinking about poor people today will be disadvantageous from the point of view of sustainability." Intellectually, there is no difficulty in resolving that paradox, but practically there is every difficulty in the world in resolving that paradox. And I don't have the vaguest notion of how it can be done in practice.

The most dramatic way in which I can remind you of the nature of that paradox is to think about what it will mean for, say, CO_2 discharge when the Chinese start to burn their coal in a very large way; and, then, while you are interested in moral obligation, I think I should invent for yourself how you are going to explain to the Chinese that they shouldn't burn the coal, even living at their standard of living they shouldn't burn the coal, because the CO_2 might conceivably damage somebody in 50 or 100 years.

Actually the record of the U.S. is not very good on either the intergenerational equity or the intragenerational equity front. We tolerate, for a rich society, quite a lot of poverty, and at the same time we don't save or invest a lot. I've just spent some time in West Germany, and there is considerably less apparent poverty in the former Federal Republic than there is here; and at the same time they are investing a larger fraction of their GNP than we are by a large margin.

It would not be very hard for us to do better. One thing we might do, for starters, is to make a comprehensive accounting of rents on non-renewable resources. It is something that we do not do. There is nothing in the national accounts of the U.S. which will tell you what fraction of the national income is the return to the using up of non-renewable resources. If we were to make that accounting, then we would have a better idea than we have now as to whether we are at least meeting that minimal obligation to channel those rents into saving and investment. And I also suggested that careful attention to current environmental protection is another way that is very likely to slip in some advantage in the way of sustainability, provided it is at the expense of current consumption and not at the expense of other forms of investment.

I have left out of this talk, as some of you may have noticed until now, any mention of population growth; and I did that on purpose, although it might be the natural first order concern if you are thinking about sustainability issues. Control of population growth would probably be the best available policy on behalf of sustainability. You know that, I know that, and I have no particular competence to discuss it any further; so I won't, except to remind you that rapid population growth is fundamentally a Third World phenomenon, not a developed country phenomenon. So once again, you are up against the paradox that people in poor countries have children as insurance policies for their own old age. It is very hard to preach to them not to do that. On the other hand, if they continue to do that, then you have probably the largest, single danger to sustainability of the world economy.

All that remains for me is to summarize. What I have been trying to say goes roughly as follows. Sustainability as a moral obligation is a general obligation, not a specific one. It is not an obligation to preserve this or preserve that. It is an obligation, if you want to make sense out of it, to preserve the capacity to be well off, to be as well off as we. That does not preclude preserving specific resources, if they have an independent value and no good substitutes. But we shouldn't kid ourselves, that is part of the value of specific resources. It is not a consequence of any interest in sustainability. Secondly, an interest in sustainability speaks for investment generally. I mentioned that directing the rents on nonrenewable resources into investment is a good rule of thumb, a reasonable and dependable starting point. But what sustainability speaks for is investment, investment of any kind. In particular, environmental investment seems to me to correlate well with concerns about sustainability and so, of course, does reliance on renewable resources as a substitute for non-renewable ones. Third, there is something faintly phony about deep concern for the future combined with callousness about the state of the world today. The catch is that today's poor want consumption not investment. So the conflict is pretty deep and there is unlikely to be any easy way to resolve it. Fourth, research is a

good thing. Knowledge on the whole is an environmentally neutral asset that we can contribute to the future. I said that in thinking about sustainability you want to be as inclusive as you can. Investment in the broader sense and investment in knowledge, especially technological and scientific knowledge, is as environmentally clean an asset as we know. And the last thing I want to say is, don't forget that sustainability is a vague concept. It is intrinsically inexact. It is not something that can be measured out in coffee spoons. It is not something that you could be numerically accurate about. It is, at best, a general guide to policies that have to do with investment, conservation and resource use. And we shouldn't pretend that it is anything other than that.

Thank you very much.

Note

1. John M. Hartwick, "Substitution among exhaustible resources and intergenerational equity," *Review of Economic Studies* 45(2): 347–543 (June 1978).

References

World Commission on Environment and Development, *Our Common Future* (The Brundtland Report). Oxford: Oxford University Press, 1987.

World Conservation Union, *Caring for the Earth*. Gland, Switzerland, 1991; see especially p.10.

World Resources Institute, *World Resources 1992–93: Toward Sustainable Development*. New York: Oxford University Press, 1992. See especially Ch. 1.

62. Sustainability

Robert E. Goodin

The green case is also couched increasingly commonly in terms of the sustainability of ecologically sound strategies and, conversely, the unsustainability of unsound ones.[1] It is in our collective self-interest to manifest "biocentric wisdom" and show "respect for self-regulating natural systems," if we do not wish to "destroy the stability of the ecosystem" on which we ourselves depend. And that, on these accounts, is what green politics is all about.

The overriding, unifying principle, some would say, "is that all human activities must be indefinitely sustainable."

One familiar gloss on those themes, redolent of the mid-1960s and early 1970s, evokes the image of the earth as a "spaceship." The imagery, however quaint, is nonetheless apt. Spaceships are paradigmatically closed systems. Being closed systems, we can neither import additional resources into them

From *Green Political Theory*, by Robert E. Goodin (Cambridge: Polity Press, 1992), pp. 62–73. Reprinted by permission. [Footnotes have been reduced and renumbered.—Eds.]

nor expel unwanted wastes from them; and that, in turn, makes notions of "materials balance" and "stationary state" obviously crucial in governing such systems. Denizens of "spaceship earth" must, on the rhetoric that this imagery inspired, realize that there is "only one earth," and they must adopt the sorts of steady-state policies that are sustainable over the long term accordingly. From the first Earth Day to this day, "sustainability" and "steady-state economics" have continuously been the catchwords of green economic policy statements.

This style of argument has recently been resurrected by the World Commission on Environment and Development, chaired by the sometime Norwegian Prime Minister, Grø Harlem Brundtland. That Commission coined the catchphrase "sustainable development," with the aim of suggesting that environmentally responsible practices are actually in the interests of developing nations themselves—or at least of any of them that want to keep on developing. Largely through the influence of that Commission, the phrase has spread among centre-left commentators and centre-right governments alike.

Whether or not sustainability is an independent value is an open question, though. There is something to be said for stability in people's lives, in general, to be sure. It facilitates planning, both on their own part and on the part of those that rely on them. It allows them to see some order and coherence within their own lives, which is satisfying to themselves and useful to others. It enables them to make promises and commitments that others can count on being kept. In all of those ways, the sheer fact of stability in their lives is important to people.

But none of that argues for stability over the very long time horizons that ecologists seem to have in view. The sorts of earnings stabilization schemes that operate in our social welfare policies seem to suggest that the crucial thing is to protect against very rapid changes in people's lives. After a year or at most two, we seem to expect people to adapt to their new circumstances, radically different though they may be. If they want more—if they want sustainability over decades rather than days, over millennia rather than months—then environmentalists cannot simply appeal to the commonplace desires people have for stability in their own lives.

Neither do those familiar sorts of concerns for macro-stability in the overall course of a person's life lead to the environmentalist's concerns for the micro-stability of very particular patterns and processes. Those simply demanding stability in the overall course of their lives are usually willing to accept substitutes. They might be indifferent between getting to work by car or train or telephone. Environmentalists fixated on sustainability are less inclined to tolerate such trade-offs. They have no doubt that, through the interrelated connections that characterize the system as a whole, if any one factor is altered compensating variations in various other factors are bound to occur. But they are rather inclined to dread rather than welcome that fact.[2] While accepting that such processes can never be suppressed completely, the whole point of their trying to achieve sustainability, system balance and a homeostatic equilibrium is to suppress such alterations as much as they can. Again, if environmentalists want micro-stability, then environmentalists must offer some further justifications beyond appeals to the commonplace that people desire stability in their lives.

Sometimes environmentalists try to appeal to brute facts to settle that matter. The ecological balance, they say, is enormously delicate. Even slight deviations—or, anyway, deviations of the not-so-slight sort that humanity is currently imposing—risk provoking intolerably large reactions that are unprecedented in human history and incompatible with continued life as we know it. The *Limits to Growth* literature of the 1970s took as its theme that we are standing on just such a precipice. Those themes are echoed today in models of climate change or ozone depletion and, in a less modest fashion, in various forms of the Gaia hypothesis.

Brute facts, if factually true, can sometimes settle arguments over principles. But, by their nature, these facts are such that we cannot afford to wait to see whether or not they turn out to be true. And in any case, if it can be shown that we should do the same things for reasons of principle and, perhaps, of brute fact as well then that constitutes a pretty clear case for supposing that we should do it *tout court*.

The principles to which environmentalists need to appeal to carry their case for sustainability, though strong, seem not to be independent principles. In so far as their argument for sustainability of particular processes is an argument for accepting no substitutes, their case for sustainability hinges on arguments concerning irreplaceability just discussed. In so far as their argument for sustainability is an argument for adopting longer time horizons, their case for sustainability hinges on the argument from futurity to be discussed below. And both of those other arguments, in turn, are best understood as mere corollaries of the green theory of value developed in earlier sections. Seen in that light, the value of sustainability—far from constituting an independent moral basis for environmental ethics—would seem to constitute little more than a second-order derivative from the true basis.

Another crucial component of the environmentalist ethic is concern for the further future. "How can we induce people and institutions to think in terms of the long-range future, and not just in terms of their short-range selfish interest?" asks the umbrella group for American greens, who reckon that a "future focus" ought to figure conspicuously among "key green values." The 1983 Manifesto of the German Greens echoes these themes:

> The pillage of nature brings about long-term damage, part of which can never be restored. This is accepted in the interest of short-term profit. The very basis of people's lives is endangered by nuclear installations, by air, water and soil pollution, by storage of dangerous waste products and by the squandering of raw materials. . . . We stand for an economic system geared to the vital needs of human beings and future generations, to the preservation of nature and a careful management of natural resources.[3]

This is no mere matter of worrying about one's own future or that of one's own immediate family. There are good grounds for that, too, environmentalists would argue. Pollution is imprudent. It amounts to fouling our own nests, and we or those whom we care about will (or may well) ultimately suffer in consequence.

Such concerns stretch only a little way into the future, however. They are consistent with activities that create environmental time bombs of colossal proportions, so long as they have moderately long fuses. Full-blooded environmentalists would worry about those, too, however long their fuses. Greens are concerned with entire future generations, not just with their own progeny, and with distant generations, not just their own children and their children's children. Their concern, as they standardly say, is with the long-term future of life on earth.[4]

In this as in so many other matters, the environmentalist's principal opponent in policy debates is the economist. On the question of the proper treatment of the further future, the environmental ethic is counterposed most directly to the standard economic practice of discounting the future.[5] Economists standardly advise us to weigh future pay-offs (costs or benefits) less heavily—indeed, disproportionately less heavily—the further in the future they come. Technically expressed, they discount future income streams according to a discount function that is exponential (that is, geometrical) in form.[6]

The consequence of that practice is obvious. Costs and benefits that are relatively near to hand weigh relatively heavily. The £1 million that will accrue next year has a present value of £952,400, assuming a (relatively modest) 5 per cent discount rate. But the further in the future a cost or benefit is, the disproportionately less heavily will it weigh with us now. Thus, for example, the present value of the same £1 million twenty years away is reckoned to be merely £376,000 and the same sum a century away appears in current accounts with a paltry present value of only £761.

(The cynical may say that sounds about right. Inured as we all are to the fact of inflation, we rightly regard large sums in the distant future as "funny money." But all these calculations—and all that follow later in this section—are expressed in terms of "constant prices." The effects of inflation have already been factored out. The suggestion is that, even after inflation has been taken into account, we should regard £1 million next century as equivalent to no more than £761 today.)

Discounting in that way is commended, virtually as a hallmark of rationality itself, in just about every economics text and development manual in print.[7] But is it so obviously rational to ignore almost completely what the consequences of our present actions will have beyond a few generations? That is not a long time, even in terms of human history much less in terms of geological time. On economistic calculations of present values, though, consequences that come in a century or two—however large or however certain they may be—are treated as being simply of no proper concern to us.

There are many ways to resist such conclusions, of course. Perhaps the most obvious strategy—and certainly the one most often employed by writers on ethics in general, and on environmental ethics in particular—is to shift the terms of discourse. Essentially, the aim is to concede the low ground of pragmatics to economists, while claiming for oneself the high moral ground.

Perhaps, this line goes, it is peculiarly efficient—peculiarly rational, even, in some narrowly economistic sense of that term—to discount the future as economists would recommend. Here as elsewhere, though, a trade-off must be made between equity and efficiency, between the maximization of total social utility and its just distribution. Hence, philosophers deploying this device would say, it may be economically efficient for us to shortchange the future; but it is nonetheless wrong for us to do so. It would amount to unjust treatment of future generations.

Of course, those taking this tack must then provide some theory of intergenerational justice strong enough to sustain such a claim. Many avenues have been explored but most, it is probably fair to say, are variations on one basic theme. Justice, it is standardly said, ought to be blind to facts about people that are truly arbitrary from a moral point of view. Among those arbitrary facts is the precise timing of one's birth. Indeed, the century of one's birth is as irrelevant from a moral point of view as the precise microsecond. Justice therefore requires that we weigh equally in our present decisions the interests of all generations, whenever they come in human history.[8]

If that sort of argument goes through, the upshot is that high morality requires that we not discount—or, as economists would put it, that we apply a "zero discount rate"—whereas the low morality of economic rationality requires some positive rate of time discounting. How well the argument goes through, in the first place, depends on the relative weight of arguments for both moralities (high and low) on these questions.

Even if the philosophers' arguments go through, though, the form of their rejoinder has conceded some important ground to the economists. There is a trade-off to be made, they will have implicitly agreed. And that is in itself a costly concession. Maybe the moralistic arguments against discounting will prevail in nine cases out of ten, or ninety out of a hundred. But in casting their rejoinder as the other side of an important value trade-off, philosophers are conceding that there is always going to be something to be said for the

economists' case. That being so, it will inevitably sometimes prevail—if only occasionally, and if only at the margins.[9]

Environmentalists would therefore be well advised to look for some better way of resisting the economists' devil-may-care conclusions about the further future. Ideally, they should try to meet the economists on their own ground, and to undermine their case for discounting from within. On inspection, it turns out that there is indeed some considerable scope for exposing obvious flaws in the justifications that economists themselves offer for discounting.

Those justifications are, of course, many and varied. Some hardly count as justifications at all. Perhaps the most standard among them appeals to nothing more than people's blind prejudice in favour of the present over the future, in a way that many economists themselves cannot quite countenance.[10]

Other economistic arguments for discounting the further future turn on just plain sloppy thinking. They confuse the argument in favour of discounting for time *per se*—which is what they are seeking—with arguments in favour of discounting future pay-offs on account of things that merely correlate (and then only imperfectly) with the passage of time. Thus, it may well be true that the further we are looking into the future, the more uncertain we will be what the pay-offs actually will be and whether we will ourselves be around to experience them; or the later the pay-offs come the more resources we are likely to have to cushion us against, or at least to compensate us for, their evil effects. But all those things—increased uncertainty, technology, wealth—are only contingently connected with the passage of time. They therefore provide no reason for supposing that it will necessarily be proper to discount later pay-offs.

Furthermore, and in a way more importantly, none of these considerations—not even the first-mentioned brute psychological fact—provides any reason at all for the rapidly progressive form that the economist's geometric discount function ordinarily takes. There is no reason to suppose that uncertainty or technological progress or wealth or even people's psychological attachment to the future alters at some fixed rate of r per cent per year, compounding continually on into the further future. Yet, of course, if the rate varies then the case for compounding collapses and (depending on the details of the formula we use instead) the further future may well loom larger in our present calculations than the standard economic formula suggests.

Environmentalists can get a long way towards undermining disregard for the further future merely by attacking the bad arguments that economists themselves give for discounting. Economists do, however, have one good argument to justify discounting in that powerfully exponential form. And it is this argument that environmentalists, and friends of the further in general, must be principally concerned to address.

This one good argument for exponential discounting of future costs and benefits treats discounting as a form of a compound interest in reverse. A smaller sum now ought, on this argument, be seen as equivalent to—ought be deemed the "present value" of—a larger sum later, simply because if you put that smaller sum into the bank earning compound interest now it will actually have grown into that larger sum by the later date. Thus, £761 now ought be seen as equivalent to—the present value of—£1 million next century, simply because £761 invested now at 5 per cent per year, compounded, will amount to £1 million in a hundred years' time. So money, or anything that can be bought and sold for money, ought be discounted at a rate that is equal to the long-term interest rate.[11]

That way of summarizing the conclusion, however, only serves to highlight what is most wrong with this argument. First, it requires us to guess what the interest rate really will be over the (possibly very) long term. Real interest rates have, in fact, been highly variable, so there is no good way of knowing what discount rate to use.[12] Second and more important is the fact that that argument for discounting applies, first and foremost, to money and things that can be bought and sold in exchange for money.

The argument for discounting the future value of things that can be bought and sold goes like this. We should be indifferent between being given £37,600 today or the guarantee of a £100,000 house in twenty years' time, because we can put that smaller sum on compound interest and (assuming a constant 5 per cent interest rate over the entire period[13]) have in hand at the end of twenty years £100,000 with which to buy that exact house. By the same token, we should be indifferent between being given a £37,600 house today or the guarantee of a £100,000 house in twenty years' time, because

(ignoring transaction costs and making the same heroic assumptions about interest rates) we could sell the cheaper house today, put the money on compound interest in the bank, and buy the more expensive house later.

But obviously that argument only works for things, like houses, that really can be bought and sold. Consider, by way of contrast, the case of something that cannot: human lives. That is not to deny that lives have "monetary equivalent." Of course they do, in all sorts of ways. We might look at the sum for which people insure their lives, or at the compensation payments that courts order when someone has been killed. Suppose such measures suggest that the going rate for the life of someone like Mr. Smith is £100,000.

Even if we can, in such ways, come up with a monetary equivalent of non-tradable commodities, it would be fallacious to use those sums in any scheme of discounting justified in the way sketched above.[14] Adapting the house example, devout discounters might reason as follows. Mr. Smith should be indifferent between getting—£37,600 now or medical treatment to remove a latent tumour that will cause his certain death in twenty years' time; that would be equivalent to conferring on him a benefit worth £100,000 (what his life is worth) in twenty years, and £37,600 invested at 5 per cent compound interest will grow to £100,000 by the end of twenty years.

But what is not true in the case of the life, in a way that it is in the case of the house, is that invested proceeds of the smaller sum could later be used to buy the greater good. Mr. Smith may have an extra £100,000 in the bank on the day he dies, thanks to the workings of compound interest. But he cannot use it to buy off the Grim Reaper, in a way that the person in the earlier example could use it to buy exactly the same house.

What makes discounting rationally mandatory, in the case of things like houses that genuinely can be bought and sold, is that money put on compound interest can buy exactly the same things later. Then it really would be irrational—it would be to distinguish between things that are indistinguishable—categorically to refuse the offer of a smaller sum now which will yield exactly the same goods later.

In the case of things that cannot be bought and sold, though, that is not what will happen. Money invested on compound interest will not buy us exactly the same thing later. It will buy us something that is "equivalent" or "as good," perhaps. But what it will buy us will undeniably be something that is different.

It follows from that fact alone that it is not necessarily irrational to reject discounting for nontradable commodities. It is not irrational, at least, in the sense that it does not amount to drawing distinctions between things that are literally indistinguishable. Clearly, in the case of things that cannot be bought and sold, we will be getting things that are different—albeit "equivalent"—if we discount than if we do not.

That is to say that discounting is not necessarily rational, in such cases. That is not to say, though, that discounting is necessarily not rational. Everything depends, in these cases, on just how close is the "equivalence" between what we would be getting and what we would be losing if we discounted the present value of future losses of nontradable commodities.[15]

At this point, then, the case against economistic discounting of the further future links up with previous discussions of irreplaceability. The losses that, on the argument just sketched, we may rightly refuse to discount are losses of things for which there are no good substitutes or equivalents. If something is replaceable, or if there are good substitutes for it, then there is no reason in principle not to discount the prospect of its future loss. It is only the irreplaceable whose future is potentially immune to the solvent of compound interest calculations.[16]

A theory of irreplaceability is therefore what is needed to resist the economists' strongest argument for discounting the future. And a theory of irreplaceability is precisely what the green theory of value, sketched above, has provided. It is a partial theory, in the sense that there may be other things (like human lives, or anyway the lives of particular human individuals) that are also irreplaceable.[17] But the green theory of value gives us grounds for supposing that at least some things produced by natural forces are irreplaceable, precisely because they have a history of having been produced by those natural forces. The things might be replicated artificially. But history cannot be so replicated.

Depending on exactly what it is about natural creation we value, some limited discounting might still be justifiable on compound-interest-in-reverse style arguments. Suppose that our reason for valuing natural creation is, as I have suggested, that we want to see our lives as being set in some larger context. Suppose that what we value about nature is therefore its general order. That is to say, suppose our concern is with natural types rather than with mere tokens. We do not much care about the deaths of individual animals. We do care powerfully about the loss of whole species.

Then we might be prepared to tolerate a certain limited discounting of future streams of resources. In this discounting, we would be limited to trading like for like—whales for whales, baboons for baboons. So long as what we care about is types rather than tokens—natural order, rather than the particular animals—we should regard them as good substitutes for one another. And so long as those populations have the characteristics of an interest-bearing resource, growing with time if not destroyed now (as biological populations obviously do), then the compound-interest-in-reverse case for discounting applies. We should care less about saving a single baboon in the future than in the present simply because, if the one in the present lives and mates, then it will produce many more in the future.

This sort of argument, notice, applies only to particular sorts of environmental assets. It applies only to those akin to interest-bearing resources. It discounts each resource according to a different rate, depending on the growth rate of that resource itself. And since no resource (no biological population, even) continues growing at exponential rates indefinitely into the future, neither can our discounting of such resources. The structure—the formula—as well as the rate at which we discount these sorts of resources must match the pattern of growth in those resources themselves. Hence, discounting justified in these resource-specific ways cannot display the marked unconcern for the further future that geometric discounting implies.

If our concern is for the general shape of the natural order, a second consequence for resource futures follows. Suppose our basic aim is, in so far as possible, to "leave no footprints." Suppose that we are therefore trying to preserve distinct natural types into the indefinite future, not worrying too much about the fate of particular tokens of those types (individual animals, as distinct from whole species). Then we may cream off only as much of the resource flow as is consistent with leaving enough to reproduce at least as much in the future.[18] In biological terms, we should take only as much as is consistent with leaving a breeding population. In economic terms, we should be striving to "maximize sustainable yield."

Notes

1. Many might be tempted to place at the core of green values the need for modes of existence (economic, social and political) that are sustainable in the face of natural limits to growth in material consumption. . . . However, those who would make sustainability a fundamental axiom rather than a mere corollary must explain . . . why sustainability ought be valued (except, obviously, in the human-instrumental terms that greens so clearly want to eschew).

2. That is rather the implication of the Gaia hypothesis, for example: nature will survive all right; the only question is whether humanity will be able to tolerate the changes it makes in response to our interventions. . . .

3. Die Grünen 1983, p. 9.

4. Thus, for example, Ophuls (1977, p. v) dedicates his *Ecology and the Politics of Scarcity* to "the posterity that has never done anything for me.". . .

5. There have always been some economists opposing those practices, of course (see e.g., p. 1977). With the "second environmental crisis" and growing concerns about global warming or destruction of the ozone layer, more and more are coming around to such longer-term perspectives. . . .

6. Technically, the standard formula is $PV = X/(1 + r)^t$, where PV is present value, X is the sum that will accrue in t years and r is the discount rate.

7. For just two of the most influential examples, see the OECD manual on *Project Appraisal and Planning for Developing Countries* (Little and Mirrlees 1974, secs 1.7 and 4.1) and the textbook for the required course on policy analysis at Harvard's Kennedy School of Government. . . .

8. Such arguments are of course inspired by, though typically go well beyond [see John Rawls, *A Theory of Justice*, sec. 44] . . . .

9. If they have further consented to the economistic way of putting their point against discounting—as an argument for a "zero discount rate"—then there will be yet more room for compromise between the contending principles, each of which has something to be said for it. If moral principle requires a zero discount rate and economic efficiency a 10 per cent discount rate, and economic efficiency is say one-tenth as important as moral principle in the case at hand, then the obvious compromise is to apply a discount rate one-tenth of the way between what moralists and economists recommend—that is, a 1 per cent discount rate.

10. This is what economists call "pure time discounting." Some economists would themselves reject discounting grounded in no more than this: Pigou . . . lambasts pure time discounting as a mere failure of the "telescopic faculty," and Ramsey . . . says plainly that it "is ethically indefensible and arises merely from the weakness of the imagination." Others bemoan that as "an authoritarian rejection of individual preferences," arguing that if individuals discount the future for no good reason in this way then so too should democratic governments committed to reflecting faithfully their preferences. . . . What that argument overlooks is that the people themselves, who would now have us discount future pay-offs, would wish come the time the pay-off occurs that we had not done so; it is not a case of substituting planners' judgement for citizens' own, but rather a case of planners choosing which of citizens' conflicting judgements to track in their plans. . . . As Sen [Amartya] astutely puts it, "If the difference is only due to the distance in time, then the position is symmetrical. A future object looks less important now, and similarly, a present object will look less important in the future. . . . [T]here is no necessary reason why today's discount of tomorrow should be used, and not tomorrow's discount of today."

11. Environmental costs and benefits are standardly treated in this way. Similarly, the standard resource-economic advice is to exhaust exhaustible resources up to the point at which their increase in scarcity value equals the market interest rate. . . .

12. In a way, it might not matter much. The nature of exponential decay functions of this sort is such that, just about whatever rate you use, costs and benefits in the distant future will virtually disappear from present calculations. But that is true only so long as you can be reasonably certain that on average interest rates will at least be positive over the relevant period. (Were they negative, then the present value of £1 tomorrow would be more—not less—than the value of £1 received today.) If the darker fears of the eco-doomsayers prove well founded, even that may well not be true. There are some circumstances under which we should contemplate a negative interest rate. . . .

13. Or—what is more realistic in some ways, but less so in others—a constellation of varying interest rates over the period with the same practical consequences.

14. It is no mere "straw man" that is here being attacked. Notice, for example, health economists

writing, "The reason for discounting future life years is precisely that they are being valued relative to dollars, and since a dollar in the future is discounted relative to a present dollar, so must a life year in the future be discounted relative to a present dollar." . . .

15. In the case of £100,000 for Mr. Smith's life, it is essentially a question of whether he would be willing to commit suicide for that sum.

16. That point is sometimes phrased, somewhat misleadingly, in terms of "sustainability"—i.e. the sustainability of the particular resource flows which we regard as irreplaceable and non-substitutable. . . .

17. And for analogous reasons: the reason that still-fertile parents, distraught at the loss of a child, suppose that they cannot just have another to take that child's place is that the new child will have a different personality shaped by a different history than the first.

18. "May," notice—not "should." This argument permits discounting, of this distinctly limited sort. It does not require it—or, indeed, provide any positive justification at all for it.

ENVIRONMENTAL PROBLEMS AND POLICIES

VI.A PRESERVING BIODIVERSITY

63. PREVIEW

As extinction spreads, some of the lost forms prove to be keystone species, whose disappearance brings down other species and triggers a ripple effect through the demographies of the survivors. The loss of a keystone species is like a drill accidentally striking a power line. It causes the lights to go out all over.[1]

E. O. Wilson

Death is one thing; an end to birth something else?[2]

Michael Soulé and David Wilcox

Imagine that we are about to enter a conference room in a large hotel, Hotel Gaia if one likes, the only one in the cosmos, and all living creatures live somewhere in this huge hotel. As we enter to discuss the destiny of many of these fellow beings (not to mention our own species), we note that parts of the hotel are on fire. Some of the fires were started by members of "our" group, our species. We know that we cannot put out all these fires, and stop starting new ones, without persuading others that many lives must be saved and that we must stop starting these fires. And we know that as we reflect on these matters and explore these problems, the fires will spread and many will die, and in some cases, the last of a certain kind will die and that group will be no more, as extinction is forever. That is what is meant by the "death of birth." In that context we go

into the conference room to discuss the issues; "further studies" have their costs. We must figure out how bad the fire is and what is threatened and what we can do about it. Well, at least some must do that; others go to put out a few fires.

We do not seem to mourn the extinction of certain groups of biological organisms. Some we tend to view as insignificant. Recall that talk of species includes various types of fauna (mammals, marsupials, insects, and so on) as well as flora (such as trees, grass). The skeptic may ask whether it matters if the earth contains one less type of horned toad or one less type of mosquito. Given its role as a carrier of disease, should we regret, or should we celebrate, the extinction of the Norwegian rat? In short, what's so bad about the disappearance of certain species (other than *Homo sapiens!*)? Alternatively, are there compelling reasons to draw the moral conclusion that we ought to make strenuous efforts to preserve species and foster a biodiverse world? One might ask as well, "What's so great about people?" "Why preserve *Homo sapiens?*" If we could imagine things from the viewpoint of a grizzly bear or a coyote, perhaps we would not mourn the extinction of those superpredators classified as *Homo sapiens*. We need to survey and reassess the reasons for and against preservation. The selections in this section will facilitate the development of a considered view on these matters. We organize our thoughts in these segments:

451

1. The concept of species

2. Empirical data about the rate of extinction and the effects of extinction

3. Arguments for and against preservation

4. A sketch of the essays in the section

THE CONCEPT OF SPECIES

Not everyone will recall a common biological taxonomy: kingdom, phylum, class, order, family, genus, and species. We might ask whether the classification "species" is the relevant one with which to be concerned, but we shall set aside that question in favor of others. There are some slippery differences between considering our relations to species and to *current members* of a species. There is a distinction between focus on an open class (such as a species) and a closed one (such as the 1984 U.S. Supreme Court). A closed class ceases to be the class that it is if its membership changes. Ignoring this difference is likely to generate confusion. It is of interest that a given species can continue to exist at time t^{n+1} even though all the members of that species at t^n have ceased to exist at t^{n+1} (suppose that new members are on the scene at t^{n+1}).

The concept of a species, then, is unlike that of concepts designating certain groups, such as the 1984 U.S. Olympic women's volleyball team (a closed class). In contrast, the species designated as "the humpback whale" is not to be understood as the set of currently existing whales. Killing all such existing whales would be sufficient to extinguish the species (barring later reconstitution from residual genetic materials, such as frozen cells), but such an event is not necessary for the species to cease to exist. Even if there is a negative duty not to kill any whale and even if that duty were not (henceforth) violated, the whale might cease to exist. Another type of act, sterilization of all the members of a species, could cause the species to cease to exist (even though such an act would not vio-

late any duty not to kill members of that species). There is, then, a certain asymmetry between considering the relations we may have toward members of a species and relations to the species as such. Further, a negative duty not to extinguish a species is not identical with a possible duty not to kill members of that species. In further contrast, a positive duty to preserve a given species, the humpback whale for example, might be carried out (in principle) by preserving only a small number of humpbacks. Some who advocate a duty to "preserve species" no doubt have in mind something stronger—a duty to help many members of a species thrive and reproduce.

Another conceptual matter, closely related to a focus on species, concerns whether a species can have moral rights, and not merely legal rights. Even if it is clear that individuals of certain sorts (you, but not your thumb) can have rights, it is less clear that a complex entity such as a species can. Those who claim that we have duties to preserve certain species may claim (at this juncture) that moral rights intelligibly and reasonably can be attributed to entities other than individuals (for example, corporations, governments, or families). But what sorts of complex entities can have rights? One may maintain that not all duties are correlative to rights possessed by the entity to whom the duty is owed. For example, some assert that we have certain duties to human infants, comatose humans, and even dead humans (such as not to deal recklessly with the corpse), even though they are not bearers of rights. The questions of whether a species conceptually can possess rights (as opposed to individual members of the species possessing them) and whether any species does are questions requiring further exploration. These distinctions are relevant to the larger moral issue of whether we are failing in any duties we might have to preserve any or all species. What is it, however, about the current situation that is thought to be deserving of great concern?

PROSPECTIVE EXTINCTION

Most in the public spotlight is the threatened extinction of certain "charismatic megafauna," such as the tiger, blue whale, whooping crane, giant panda, orangutan, cheetah, and northern spotted owl.[3] Less dramatic, but of equal or greater significance, is the probable current loss of a dozen species per day. What is often not recognized—in discussions of the prospective fate of different species—is the very dramatic historical turnabout that has developed in recent years and that is continuing. The data on why the current era is undergoing an extinction spasm are found in the striking Essay 64 excerpted from E. O. Wilson's book *The Diversity of Life* (see also Essay 77, "Tropical Forests and Their Species: Going, Going . . ." by Norman Myers). Briefly, due to human activity and intervention in natural processes, there is a radical increase in the number of members of one species, *Homo sapiens,* and a radical increase in the rate of extinction of other species. Whether these changes are good or bad, a reason to celebrate or mourn, is a matter of evaluation; we regard it as a largely unrecognized megatragedy of modern times. It seems fair to say that our species, numbering over 6 billion and weighing over 200 million tons, temporarily dominates the planet (if we ignore the little creatures discussed earlier by E. O. Wilson, in Essay 19). Current population projections suggest that we could number 8 to 10 billion people by the year 2025. In spite of the evident problems (say, the need for adequate food, shelter, and health care) attending large and dense populations of people, the propensity of humans to "be fruitful and multiply" has led to both the direct and indirect destruction (intentional or not; foreseen or not) of many species of plants and animals by the cramping, erosion, or elimination of their habitats or food supplies.

What is new under the sun is a significant increase in the rate of extinction caused by human activity. Between 1600 and 1900, a species became extinct about once every four years. From 1900 to 1960, the rate was about one per year. Since then, estimates have ranged from 100 per year up to 40,000 per year in the last quarter of this century. This last figure is based in part on the projected destruction of prairie land, wetlands, and tropical moist forests (some assume the latter to contain 2 to 5 million species each). Even if these estimates are seriously in error, radical changes are under way.

SKETCHING THE ARGUMENTS

As we noted, one view of the demise of thousands, or even millions, of species, of habitats, and of ecosystems is "So what?" Should we be concerned? Should we act differently? Why? If so, how? Or why not? The arguments in favor of our making efforts to preserve species, or certain species, tend to fall into two broad categories—as one might surmise. First are the purely anthropocentric considerations; other species should be preserved because they are valuable to us human beings. Some argue that we should, for purely prudential reasons, protect or promote our human interests now. Some urge that we have duties to other, indeed now nonexistent, humans (is it not wrong to turn the earth into a garbage dump for future generations of humans?); recall the essays in Section V.E. Second, as we noted in Part III, powerful arguments can be marshaled on behalf of the view that members of at least some other species have moral standing (or are intrinsically valuable). If so, we have duties not to harm them—duties not derivative from, or dependent on, contingent facts about whether the preservation of animals in the long or short run promotes human interests.

As noted in the Preview to "The Other Animals" (Part III), the criteria for possession of moral standing such as sentience, possession of consciousness, or self-consciousness will not "confer" moral standing on all animals. Furthermore, on the widely held assumption that plants lack these traits, such grounds provide no basis for concluding that we owe direct duties to plants or many animals (for example, thousands of insect species). Thus, according to such views, there is no direct duty to preserve thousands of plants and animal species. Some defenders of the "land ethic" and some biocentric, egalitarians (of both an individualist and holist bent; see Section IV.A) take a contrary view. This type of dispute is often alluded to in terms of a conflict between animal liberationists and defenders of "the land ethic" (or, in somewhat misleading terminology, "defenders of" an "environmental ethic"). A closer examination of this matter is in Part IV. If it is true that individual animals (or some) have rights, or intrinsic value, or moral standing (as the case may be), is it also the case that any species (or ecosystem) has rights, intrinsic value, or moral standing? In Essay 66, Lilly-Marlene Russow defends a negative answer to this question.

Even if (but we are not assuming this) there are no direct duties to individual animals, to individual plants, to species, or to ecosystems, there are evident advantages to our preservation of many species, other things being equal. The advantages accruing to humans from having certain animals and plants around to exploit are enormous. Much of this exploitation (recall the essays in Part III) may be morally justifiable, but it is reasonable to believe that much human "use" of plants and animals is permissible, for example, shearing sheep for wool, keeping dogs and cats for pets, making valuable drugs from plants, and harvesting trees from farms (not to be confused with the National Forests). There is, then, a consequentialist line of argument for preserving certain species.[4] Sometimes doing so may maximize utility (whether the

utilities accruing to sentient animals are weighed in here—as in classic Utilitarianism—is, of course, an important matter). In some cases the benefit of preserving a species cannot be "cashed" readily in terms of the value of experimenting on, eating, or making products from its members. Sometimes the value of preservation seems to be mainly, or solely, of an aesthetic sort. The question arises as to whether this is a rational basis for urging the preservation of the giant panda, the blue whale, the Florida cougar, or old forests. Even if the appeal to the preservation of aesthetic values succeeds in the just mentioned cases, it is less likely to provide a plausible ground for preserving ugly, or very small, nocturnal creatures (or species). Indeed, it is hard, and perhaps impossible, to defend the preservation or conservation of certain species on the ground that they themselves are valuable as economic resources. At least some species seem to be useless as aesthetic, economic, or ecological resources. On the latter point, compare Russow's query about the ecological role of a species all of whose members are in zoos—or all of which were bred to live briefly only in a laboratory (such as lab rats). Still, some species or other entities are part of an ecosystem or habitat that is itself valuable. If we are to preserve a certain species, then we cannot blithely, or ruthlessly, continue to destroy their habitats. Analogously, it would be absurd to maintain that we cared about whooping cranes and then allowed their nesting places to be turned into yet another shopping mall or condominium complex. We have already discussed the conflict between so acting and maintaining the "license to kill" conception of property rights that is popular in the United States.

An obvious difficulty is inherent in trying to measure the aesthetic value of experiences. A standard "measuring rod," of course, is the "cash value" of a thing. How many dollars, for example, is it worth to preserve a blue whale (or heighten the probability of its preservation) so that our grandchildren might see it—and not just a film or a photograph? Economists have suggestions, of course, about how to assign a monetary value to things whose value we find hard to measure, or even regard as incommensurable—not measurable in terms of alien stuff (for example, human life in terms of dollars). What one would be willing to pay to lower the probability of premature death (for example, accepting a lower income to have a safer job) is often suggested as a useful measure of the cash value of "life" (or enhanced likelihood of a longer life). These matters were explored somewhat in Section V.A, "Letting the Market Decide" and in V.B, "Cost–Benefit Analysis."

As noted earlier, some maintain that certain species have intrinsic value. There are, however, various obscurities surrounding the concept of intrinsic value. Generally it seems that when it is claimed that "X has intrinsic value" what is meant is that "X is valuable in itself and apart from whatever valuation of X is made by others" (such as people). But sometimes an alternative interpretation is employed. To say that "X is intrinsically valuable" means that "X is valued *by others* for X's own sake" (in contrast with what philosophers often mean when they claim that pleasure is intrinsically good or valuable). This latter interpretation, unlike the former, requires valuers to be around. Would the Grand Canyon or the giant panda lack intrinsic value if people (valuers) did not exist? Or if possession of the capacity to live a meaningful life (one in which how things went was not a matter of indifference to the possessor) is necessary for something to possess intrinsic value, it would seem that only sentient, or perhaps only conscious, entities could have intrinsic value. This would include most people (but not the brain-dead or anencephalic infants) and many animals, but little else would have intrinsic value based on this criterion. If we allow that all tigers have intrinsic value and that that consideration is the only

basis for concluding that we owe them certain direct duties, say, not to cause them premature death or foster their living under certain circumstances, then there is no obvious nonanthropocentric basis for saying that we have special duties to preserve those kinds of tigers that may be on an endangered species list as opposed to those which are not. This consideration is surely one motivation for examining whether some sort of intrinsic value can sensibly be ascribed to species as such.

In short, there is no easy path to finding common ground for the conclusion that most or all species ought to be preserved—indeed for identifying a rational justification for the somewhat powerful preservationist instincts many of us share. One final item for reflection: If it is argued that X (a dog, say) has intrinsic value and Y (a very valuable diamond ring, for example) does not, should we automatically preserve X instead of Y if for some reason we have to choose one or the other (imagine that a house is on fire and that we can save only the dog or the ring)? Consider another example. Suppose that instead of a diamond ring, what might be saved is the only accessible antidote for a poison that a child has just ingested. Many practical environmental problems involve a similar kind of conflict; that is, we must sacrifice one thing of value (of some sort) to preserve something else of value (of some sort). Just how to resolve the tradeoffs in a nonarbitrary manner is a most difficult matter; recall once more the discussions in Part III, "The Other Animals."

A SKETCH OF THE ESSAYS

We have noted the focus of Lilly-Marlene Russow's "Why Do Species Matter?" (Essay 66) as well as some of the appalling data on the severe decline in biodiversity noted by E. O. Wilson (Essay 64). A major attempt to try to halt the loss of species in the United States was the passage of the Endangered Species Act (ESA) of 1973. The act sought to protect, evidently, those species thought to be endangered. It has been criticized by some for focusing only on species, instead of on all animals or all sentient animals (criticisms, in different ways, of some defenders of animal rights and some biocentrists). The ESA requires that federal agencies ensure that their actions are not likely to jeopardize the continued existence of threatened or endangered species or adversely modify or destroy their habitats. Many who support the intent of the act suggest that what is needed is an "endangered habitat act" because it is foolish to continue to destroy the places where animals live and then go to sometimes very expensive and desperate lengths to rescue some species whose prognosis for recovery may be a guarded one. In part, the suggestion is that we must engage in more *preventive* action (including the stopping of our regular, deliberate destruction of habitats), and not just in rescue efforts. Restraint imposes costs—the costs of forgone opportunities—but it is by no means obvious that the costs outweigh the benefits to humans, even on a purely anthropocentric basis. They may, however, depending on modes of accounting and limited time frames. It is clear that many defenders of logging the old growth forests in the northwest United States assign no intrinsic value to the preservation of the northern spotted owl or other species of fauna in that habitat and that they see great 100- to 300-year-old trees as only so many board feet, as a mere commodity whose value is utterly wasted when the trees finally fall to the ground and rot (the rotting trees, themselves, however, provide habitat for many creatures).

Between 1979 and 1991, there were 120,000 "consultations" between federal agencies and appropriate reviewers (often the U.S. Fish and Wildlife Service) over whether species would be jeopardized by proposed activities. The findings in 99 percent of those cases were one of no jeopardy, and only 34 projects were canceled in that period.[5] All this

suggests that industrial complaints over constraints imposed by the ESA are misplaced. One might also infer, given all that we know about federal deregulation and the probusiness attitude that prevailed during that period, that the ESA was not strongly enforced by a largely antienvironmental federal administration. Still, of the 600 or so species in the U.S. (1,100 worldwide) listed as threatened or endangered, 238 are said to be stable or improving.[6] It is worth noting that the ESA's restraints have little effect on uses of "private property" that result in habitat destruction or similar situations in areas over which no nation has full sovereignty, such as the oceans.

It is natural to wonder what sort of entity a species is, and are we not arbitrarily picking out some collection of creatures when we employ the notion of species. Alternatively, do species correspond to eternal essences in the mind of God as some insist? Should concern about preservation not focus on subspecies or genera or some other grouping? Essay 65, from Stephen Jay Gould, "What Is a Species?" addresses the question of the reality of species, and he defends the view that what we call *species* are almost always objective entities in nature. Holmes Rolston III, in an excerpt we have entitled "Why Species Matter" (Essay 67), suggests reasons for valuing the continued existence of species beyond those for preserving the existence of individual plants and animals.[7] Indeed, he claims that it is difficult to separate the value of individuals from the ecosystem pyramid that is the matrix for the existence of individuals. Some people defend the view that species or ecosystems are living entities with morally significant interests in their own right. There is an important question of how such entities can be said to possess interests even though they do not seem to be goal oriented, or to "have goals," in the way that individual animals or plants might.[8] Further, what seems conducive to the survival of the genotype (one kind of construal of species identity) may be destructive to the individual animal whose genotype is in question.

For reasons discussed throughout this book (see also Essay 64, excerpt from *The Diversity of Life,* by E. O. Wilson), it seems reasonable to believe that the preservation of any, or virtually all, species is a good in itself (however weighty). We note here that some mainstream economists, among others, propose another approach, the adoption of a *safe-minimal standard* (SMS). It is: We should maintain a safe minimal standard (the minimal level of preservation that ensures survival) unless the opportunity costs (those goods humans would have to forgo if resources went to maintaining preservation) are intolerably high. This proposal sounds tautologous, but it is nevertheless of some interest. If not tautologous, it seems straightforwardly moral in nature, and one wonders whether it is to be thought of as derivative from some other principle or basic (nonderivative) in nature. We leave the question for the reader. One advocate of this view, Richard C. Bishop, defends the principle, in part, on the basis of considerations from game theory, and in particular the consideration that in situations such as this in which one cannot ascertain the expected cost or expected benefit of preservation or nonpreservation (due to uncertainties and the inability to estimate certain probabilities of harm or benefit), one ought to minimize maximum losses (choose the alternative: preservation) whose worst outcome is better than the worst outcome of any other available alternative (irreversible loss of that which is of great value).[9] What is lost now may be a loss only to this generation; what is lost via extinction is a loss for all future generations. Should we, or should we not, mourn the permanent loss of the last remaining smallpox virus?[10]

Critics of the mainstream economic approach emphasize the danger (indeed the impossibility) of trying to put a "dollar value" on biodiversity and the perhaps concurrent

assumption that "doing so the right way" will lead to the appropriate preservation of biodiversity. Market incentives may lead some corporations to act so as to preserve species on some occasions but not others. There is little reason to believe that the so-called Invisible Hand will invariably connect in an optimal manner profit maximization to preservation of biodiversity. Economists tend to agree that the Invisible Hand (markets) will not lead to the right level of diversity; in their view, the key question is whether one will arrive there after externalities are corrected.[11] Critics insist that, even so, it is both dangerous and wrong to deny the inherent value of biodiversity and to try to gauge its value solely in terms of economic benefit.

The task of learning the relevant facts, gaining perspective, and weighing matters in an all-things-considered manner is not quickly accomplished. Our selection by E. O. Wilson helps us to understand the extent to which the loss of species diversity is "irreversible." Our time frame is important here. Suppose that someone took your car or bike and told you, "Don't worry, I'll have it back shortly . . . a few days before you are 100 years old." For your purposes, the loss would be complete and irreversible. How long will it take for comparable biodiversity to return after the massive extinctions currently underway and increasing? Wilson considers the record after the explosion at Krakatau in 1883, a volcanic eruption equivalent to 100–150 tons of TNT, which left an island without life on it. Other evidence is derived from the five major extinctions that have occurred in the history of our planet. The five mass extinctions, according to E. O. Wilson, are, in terms of geological period and time before the present: Ordovician, 440 million years; Devonian, 365 million years; Permian, 245 million years; Triassic, 210 million years; and Cretaceous, 66 million years. Of what relevance is it that life in some forms and some degree of diversity has returned or continued? Wilson reviews some of the data on the rate at which many species are disappearing, especially due to the destruction of those habitats that are the richest of all in species diversity, the tropical forests.[12] As difficult as it may be to formulate the most reasonable view as to what should be done to halt or slow "the silent hemorrhage," we are forced to pause and reflect deeply when Wilson observes: "The creation of that diversity came slow and hard: 3 billion years of evolution to start the profusion of animals that occupy the seas, another 350 million years to assemble the rain forests in which half or more of the species on earth now live. . . . Young or old, all living species are direct descendants of the organisms that lived 3.8 billion years ago."

On the face of it, collective human behavior sustained over decades poses greater risks of harm to the diversity of life than does what many of us were raised to think of as the greatest danger of all, nuclear war. Yet a certain ignorant and mindless cynicism is often expressed by those who ridicule thinking beyond one's own life and beyond the present generation. Perhaps we should rethink just who deserves one often-used label, namely, "prolife," and what it would really mean to favor the life process.

NOTES

1. Edward O. Wilson, *The Diversity of Life* (Cambridge, MA: Harvard University Press, 1992).

2. Attributed to Michael Soulé and David Wilcox by Norman Myers in "Tropical Forests and Their Species," in *Biodiversity*, edited by E. O. Wilson and Frances M. Peter (Washington, DC: National Academy Press, 1988), p. 32.

3. The expression "charismatic megafauna" is attributed to Dennis Murphy of the Center of Conservation Biology at Stanford in the essay "The Butterfly Problem," by Charles Mann and Mark Plummer in the *Atlantic Monthly*, January 1992, p. 49.

4. On the notion of consequentialism, see "An Introduction to Ethical Theory," Section 2.4, and also the Glossary.

5. The figures are from the "Endangered Species Act: Bulwark Against the Tide of Extinction," distributed by the National Wildlife Federation.

6. Ibid.

7. The Rolston selection here is the latter portion of his essay "Environmental Ethics: Values in and Duties to the Natural World," in *Ecology, Economics, Ethics: The Broken Circle*, edited by F. Herbert Bormann and Stephen R. Kellert (New Haven: Yale University Press, 1991), pp. 82–96.

8. On this matter, see Lawrence E. Johnson, "Toward the Moral Considerability of Species and Ecosystems," *Environmental Ethics* 14(2) (Summer 1992), 145–57.

9. The rule of rational choice under situations of uncertainty, noted in the text, is also called the "maximin rule." It is also relevant to choices we confront in policy decisions about global warming; on this see the discussion in Section VI.E. See also Richard C. Bishop, "Endangered Species and Uncertainty: The Economics of a Safe Minimal Standard," *American Journal of Agricultural Economics* 60(l) (February 1978), 10–18.

10. This interesting question was posed by one of our reviewers.

11. This point would have been overlooked but for a reminder by Talbot Page.

12. On this topic see the essay by Norman Myers in the following section, Essay 77.

64. The Diversity of Life _____

E. O. Wilson

. . . [D]iversity, the property that makes resilience possible, is vulnerable to blows that are greater than natural perturbations. It can be eroded away fragment by fragment, and irreversibly so if the abnormal stress is unrelieved. This vulnerability stems from life's composition as swarms of species of limited geographical distribution. Every habitat, from Brazilian rain forest to Antarctic bay to thermal vent, harbors a unique combination of plants and animals. Each kind of plant and animal living there is linked in the food web to only a small part of the other species. Eliminate one species, and another increases in number to take its place. Eliminate a great many species, and the local ecosystem starts to decay visibly. Productivity drops as the channels of the nutrient cycles are clogged. More of the biomass is sequestered in the form of dead vegetation and slowly metabolizing, oxygen-starved mud, or is simply washed away. Less competent pollinators take over as the best-adapted bees, moths, birds, bats, and other specialists drop out. Fewer seeds fall, fewer seedlings sprout. Herbivores decline, and their predators die away in close concert.

In an eroding ecosystem life goes on, and it may look superficially the same. There are always species able to recolonize the impoverished area and exploit the stagnant resources, however clumsily accomplished. Given enough time, a new combination of species—a reconstituted fauna and flora—will reinvest the habitat in a way that transports energy and materials somewhat more efficiently. The atmosphere they generate and the composition of the soil they enrich will resemble those found in comparable habitats in other parts of the world, since the species are adapted to penetrate and reinvigorate just such degenerate systems. They do so because they gain more energy and materials and leave more offspring. But the restorative power of the fauna and flora of the world as a whole depends on the existence of enough species to play that special role. They too can slide into the red zone of endangered species.

Biological diversity—"biodiversity" in the new parlance—is the key to the maintenance of the world as we know it. Life in a local site struck down by a passing storm springs back quickly because enough diversity still exists. Opportunistic species evolved for just such an occasion rush in to fill the spaces. They entrain the succession that circles back to something resembling the original state of the environment.

This is the assembly of life that took a billion years to evolve. It has eaten the storms—folded them into its genes—and created the world that created us. It holds the world steady. When I rose at dawn the next morning, Fazenda Dimona had not changed in any obvious way from the day before.* The same high trees stood like a fortress along the forest's edge; the same profusion of birds and insects foraged through the canopy and understory in precise individual timetables. All this seemed timeless, immutable, and its very strength posed the question: how much force does it take to break the crucible of evolution?

*

Krakatau, earlier misnamed Krakatoa, an island the size of Manhattan located midway in the Sunda Strait between Sumatra and Java, came to an end on Monday morning, August 27, 1883. It was dismembered by a series of powerful volcanic eruptions. The most violent occurred at 10:02 A.M., blowing upward like the shaped explosion of a large nuclear bomb, with an estimated force equivalent to 100–150 megatons of TNT. The airwave it created traveled at the speed of sound around the world, reaching the opposite end of the earth near Bogotá, Colombia, nineteen hours later, whereupon it bounced back to Krakatau and then back and forth for seven recorded passages over the earth's surface. The audible sounds, resembling the distant cannonade of a ship in distress, carried southward

*Fazenda Dimona is a place on the edge of a rain forest in Brazil, one of the locations of E. O. Wilson's research.

The Diversity of Life, by Edward O. Wilson (Cambridge, MA: Harvard University Press, 1992), pp. 14–17, 19, 24, 25, 29, 31, 344–48, 351. Reprinted by permission of the publishers. ©1992 by Edward O. Wilson.

across Australia to Perth, northward to Singapore, and westward 4,600 kilometers to Rodriguez Island in the Indian Ocean, the longest distance traveled by any airborne sound in recorded history.

As the island collapsed into the subterranean chamber emptied by the eruption, the sea rushed in to fill the newly formed caldera. A column of magma, rock, and ash rose 5 kilometers into the air, then fell earthward, thrusting the sea outward in a tsunami 40 meters in height. The great tidal waves, resembling black hills when first sighted on the horizon, fell upon the shores of Java and Sumatra, washing away entire towns and killing 40,000 people. The segments traversing the channels and reaching the open sea continued on as spreading waves around the world. The waves were still a meter high when they came ashore in Ceylon, now Sri Lanka, where they drowned one person, their last casualty. Thirty-two hours after the explosion, they rolled in to Le Havre, France, reduced at last to centimeter-high swells.

The eruptions lifted more than 18 cubic kilometers of rock and other material into the air. Most of this tephra, as it is called by geologists, quickly rained back down onto the surface, but a residue of sulfuric-acid aerosol and dust boiled upward as high as 50 kilometers and diffused through the stratosphere around the world, where for several years it created brilliant red sunsets and "Bishop's rings," opalescent coronas surrounding the sun.

Back on Krakatau the scene was apocalyptic. Throughout the daylight hours the whole world seemed about to end for those close enough to witness the explosions. At the climactic moment of 10:02 the American barque *W. H. Besse* was proceeding toward the straits 84 kilometers east northeast of Krakatau. The first officer jotted in his logbook that "terrific reports" were heard, followed by

> a heavy black cloud rising up from the direction of Krakatoa Island, the barometer fell an inch at one jump, suddenly rising and falling an inch at a time, called all hands, furled all sails securely, which was scarcely done before the squall struck the ship with terrific force; let go port anchor and all the chain in the locker, wind increasing to a hurricane; let go starboard anchor, it had gradually been growing dark since 9 A.M., and by the time the squall struck us, it was darker than any night I ever saw; this was midnight at noon, a heavy shower of ashes came with the squall, the air

being so thick it was difficult to breathe, also noticed a strong smell of sulfur, all hands expecting to be suffocated; the terrible noises from the volcano, the sky filled with forked lightning, running in all directions and making the darkness more intense than ever; the howling of the wind through the rigging formed one of the wildest and most awful scenes imaginable, one that will never be forgotten by any one on board, all expecting the last days of the earth had come; the water was running by us in the direction of the volcano at the rate of 12 miles per hour, at 4 P.M. wind moderating, the explosions had nearly ceased, the shower of ashes was not so heavy; so was enabled to see our way around the decks; the ship was covered with tons of fine ashes resembling pumice stone, it stuck to the sails, rigging and masts like glue.

In the following weeks, the Sunda Strait returned to outward normality, but with an altered geography. The center of Krakatau had been replaced by an undersea crater 7 kilometers long and 270 meters deep. Only a remnant at the southern end still rose from the sea. It was covered by a layer of obsidian-laced pumice 40 meters or more thick and heated to somewhere between 300° and 850°C, enough at the upper range to melt lead. All traces of life had, of course, been extinguished.

Rakata, the ash-covered mountain of old Krakatau, survived as a sterile island. But life quickly enveloped it again. In a sense, the spinning reel of biological history halted, then reversed, like a motion picture run backward, as living organisms began to return to Rakata. Biologists quickly grasped the unique opportunity that Rakata afforded: to watch the assembly of a tropical ecosystem from the very beginning. Would the organisms be different from those that had existed before? Would a rain forest eventually cover the island again?

The first search for life on Rakata was conducted by a French expedition in May 1884, nine months after the explosions. The main cliff was eroding rapidly, and rocks still rolled down the sides incessantly, stirring clouds of dust and emitting a continuous noise "like the rattling of distant musketry." Some of the stones whirled through the air, ricocheting down the sides of the ravines and splashing into the sea. What appeared to be mist in the distance turned close up into clouds of dust stirred by the falling debris. The crew and expedition members eventually found a safe landing site and fanned out to learn what they could. After searching for organisms in particular, the ship's naturalist wrote that "notwithstanding all my researches, I was not able to observe any symptom of animal life. I only discovered one microscopic spider—only one; this strange pioneer of the renovation was busy spinning its web." . . .

*

What was the greatest blow ever suffered by life through all time? Not the 1883 explosions at Krakatau, which were not even the worst in recorded history. An 1815 eruption at Tambora, 1,400 kilometers to the east of Krakatau on the Indonesian island of Sumbawa, lifted five times as much rock and ash as Krakatau. It inflicted more environmental destruction and killed tens of thousands of people. About 75,000 years ago a still greater eruption occurred in the center of northern Sumatra. It blew out a phenomenal 1,000 cubic kilometers of solid material, creating an oval depression 65 kilometers long that filled with fresh water and persists to this day as Lake Toba. Paleolithic people lived on the island then. We can only imagine what they felt in the presence of an eruption one hundred times the magnitude of Krakatau, and what stories of gods and apocalypse proliferated in the culture afterward.

Great eruptions are likely to have occurred repeatedly across long stretches of geological time. A simple form of statistical reasoning leads to this conclusion. The frequency curve of the intensity of volcanic eruptions around the world, like so many chance phenomena, peaks near the low end and tapers off for a long distance toward the high end. This means that most eruptions are relatively minor perturbations, consisting of a plume of vapor from a fumarole here, a minor lava flow there. Lava fountains and big flows, the next step up, are less common but still occur on a yearly basis somewhere in the world. An event the size of the Krakatau explosion happens once or twice a century. An eruption as big as the one at Toba is far rarer but, over millions of years, probably inevitable.

The same statistical reasoning applies to the fall of meteorites. A large number ranging in size from dust particles to pebbles reach the earth's surface each year, streaking in at 15 to 75 kilometers a second. A much smaller number range in size from baseballs to soccer balls. They account for the majority of the thirty or so meteorites worldwide that can be seen traveling all the way down and are then located by searchers on foot. A very few are much more massive. The largest ever observed in the United States was a 5,000-kilogram meteorite that fell in Norton County, Kansas, on February 18, 1948. Over millions of years only a few truly gigantic meteorites reach the earth's surface. One with a diameter of 1,250 meters gouged out Canyon Diablo in Arizona. Another monster, 3,200 meters in diameter, created the Chubb Depression at Ungava, Quebec.

By extrapolation upward along the scale of violence, it is conceivable and even likely that a volcanic eruption or a meteorite strike occurs once every 10 million or 100 million years so great as to literally shake the earth, drastically change its atmosphere, and as a result extinguish a substantial portion of the species then living. Something of that kind might have happened at the end of the Mesozoic era 66 million years ago, when dinosaurs and a few other prevailing groups of animals were set back or extinguished altogether. . . .

[T]he Cretaceous extinction was only one of five such catastrophes that occurred over the last half-billion years, and it was not the most severe. Furthermore, the earlier spasms appear not to have been associated with meteorite strikes or unusually heavy volcanism. The five mass extinctions occurred in this order, according to geological period and time before the present: Ordovician, 440 million years; Devonian, 365 million years; Permian, 245 million years; Triassic, 210 million years; and Cretaceous, 66 million years. There have been a great many second- and third-order dips and rises, but these five are at the far end of the curve of violence, and they stand out. They are to other episodes as a catastrophe is to a misfortune, a hurricane to a summer squall. . . .

To summarize: life was impoverished in five major events, and to lesser degree here and there around the world in countless other episodes. After each downturn it recovered to at least the original level of diversity. How long did it take for evolution to restore the losses after the first-order spasms? The number of families of animals living in the sea is as reliable a measure as we have been able to obtain from the existing fossil evidence. In general, five million years were enough only for a strong start. A complete recovery from each of the five major extinctions required tens of millions of years. In particular the Ordovician dip needed 25 million years, the Devonian 30 million years, the Permian and Triassic (combined because they were so close together in time) 100 million years, and the Cretaceous 20 million years. These figures should give pause to anyone who believes that what *Homo sapiens* destroys, Nature will redeem. Maybe so, but not within any length of time that has meaning for contemporary humanity. . . .

For the green prehuman earth is the mystery we were chosen to solve, a guide to the birthplace of our spirit, but it is slipping away. The way back seems harder every year. If there is danger in the human trajectory, it is not so much in the survival of our own species as in the fulfillment of the ultimate irony of organic evolution: that in the instant of achieving self-understanding through the mind of man, life has doomed its most beautiful creations. And thus humanity closes the door to its past.

The creation of that diversity came slow and hard: 3 billion years of evolution to start the profusion of animals that occupy the seas, another 350 million years to assemble the rain forests in which half or more of the species on earth now live. There was a succession of dynasties. Some species split into two or several daughter species, and their daughters split yet again to create swarms of descendants that deployed as plant feeders, carnivores, free swimmers, gliders, sprinters, and burrowers, in countless motley combinations. These ensembles then gave way by partial or total extinction to newer dynasties, and so on to form a gentle upward swell that carried biodiversity to a peak—just before the arrival of humans. Life had stalled on plateaus along the way, and on five occasions it suffered extinction spasms that took 10 million years to repair. But the thrust was upward. Today the diversity of life is greater than it was 100 million years ago—and far greater than 500 million years before that.

Most dynasties contained a few species that expanded disproportionately to create satrapies of lesser rank. Each species and its descendants, a sliver of the whole, lived an average of hundreds of thousands to millions of years. Longevity varied according to taxonomic group. Echinoderm lineages, for example, persisted longer than those of flowering plants, and both endured longer than those of mammals.

Ninety-nine percent of all the species that ever lived are now extinct. The modern fauna and flora are composed of survivors that somehow managed to dodge and weave through all the radiations and extinctions of geological history. Many contemporary world-dominant groups, such as rats, ranid frogs, nymphalid butterflies, and plants of the aster family Compositae, attained their status not long before the Age of Man. Young or old, all living species are direct descendants of the organisms that lived 3.8 billion years ago. They are living genetic libraries, composed of nucleotide sequences, the equivalent of words and sentences, which record evolutionary events all across that immense span of time. Organisms more complex than bacteria—protists, fungi, plants, animals—contain between 1 and 10 billion nucleotide letters, more than enough in pure information to compose an equivalent of the *Encyclopaedia Britannica.* Each species is the product of mutations and recombinations too complex to be grasped by unaided intuition. It was sculpted and burnished by an astronomical number of events in natural selection, which killed off or otherwise blocked from reproduction the vast majority of its member organisms before they completed their life spans. Viewed from the perspective of evolutionary time, all other species are our distant kin because we share a remote ancestry. We still use a common vocabulary, the nucleic-acid code, even though it has been sorted into radically different hereditary languages. . . .

Organisms are all the more remarkable in combination. Pull out the flower from its crannied retreat, shake the soil from the roots into the cupped hand, magnify it for close examination. The black earth is alive with a riot of algae, fungi, nematodes, mites, springtails, enchytraeid worms, thousands of species of bacteria. The handful may be only a tiny fragment of one ecosystem, but because of the genetic codes of its residents it holds more order than can be found on the surfaces of all the planets combined. It is a sample of the living force that runs the earth—and will continue to do so with or without us.

We may think that the world has been completely explored. Almost all the mountains and rivers, it is true, have been named, the coast and geodetic surveys completed, the ocean floor mapped to the deepest trenches, the atmosphere transected and chemically analyzed. The planet is now continuously monitored from space by satellites; and, not least, Antarctica, the last virgin continent, has become a research station and expensive tourist stop. The biosphere, however, remains obscure. Even though some 1.4 million species of organisms have been discovered (in the minimal sense of having specimens collected and formal scientific names attached), the total number alive on earth is somewhere between 10 and 100 million. No one can say with confidence which of these figures is the closer. Of the species given scientific names, fewer than 10 percent have been studied at a level deeper than gross anatomy. The revolution in molecular biology and medicine was achieved with a still smaller fraction, including colon bacteria, corn, fruit flies, Norway rats, rhesus monkeys, and human beings, altogether comprising no more than a hundred species.

Enchanted by the continuous emergence of new technologies and supported by generous funding for medical research, biologists have probed deeply along a narrow sector of the front. Now it is time to expand laterally, to get on with the great Linnean enterprise and finish mapping the biosphere. The most compelling reason for the broadening of goals is that, unlike the rest of science, the study of biodiversity has a time limit. Species are disappearing at an accelerating rate through human action, primarily habitat destruction but also pollution and the introduction of exotic species into residual natural environments. I have said that a fifth or more of the species of plants and animals could vanish or be doomed to early extinction by the year 2020 unless better efforts are made to save them. This estimate comes from the known quantitative relation between the area of habitats and the diversity that habitats can sustain. These area–biodiversity curves are supported by the general but not universal principle that when certain groups of organisms are studied closely, such as snails and fishes and flowering plants, extinction is determined to be widespread. And the corollary: among plant and animal remains in archaeological deposits, we usually find extinct species and races. As the last forests are felled in forest strongholds like the Philippines and Ecuador, the decline of species will accelerate even more. In the world as a whole, extinction rates are already hundreds or thousands of times higher than before the coming of man. They cannot be balanced by new evolution in any period of time that has meaning for the human race.

Why should we care? What difference does it make if some species are extinguished, if even half of all the species on earth disappear? Let me count the ways. New sources of scientific information will be lost. Vast potential biological wealth will be destroyed. Still undeveloped medicines, crops, pharmaceuticals, timber, fibers, pulp, soil-restoring vegetation, petroleum substitutes, and other products and amenities will never come to light. It is fashionable in some quarters to wave aside the small and obscure, the bugs and weeds, forgetting that an obscure moth from Latin America saved Australia's pastureland from overgrowth by cactus, that the rosy periwinkle provided the cure for Hodgkin's disease and childhood lymphocytic leukemia, that the bark of the Pacific yew offers hope for victims of ovarian and breast cancer, that a chemical from the saliva of leeches dissolves blood clots during surgery, and so on down a roster already grown long and illustrious despite the limited research addressed to it.

In amnesiac revery it is also easy to overlook the services that ecosystems provide humanity. They enrich the soil and create the very air we breathe. Without these amenities, the remaining tenure of the human race would be nasty and brief. The life-sustaining matrix is built of green plants with legions of microorganisms and mostly small, obscure animals—in other words, weeds and bugs. Such organisms support the world with efficiency because they are so diverse, allowing them to divide labor and swarm over every square meter of the earth's surface. They run the world precisely as we would wish it to be run, because humanity evolved within living communities and our bodily functions are finely adjusted to the idiosyncratic environment already created. Mother Earth, lately called Gaia, is no more than the commonality of organisms and the physical environment they maintain with each passing moment, an environment that will destabilize and turn lethal if the organisms are disturbed too much. A near infinity of other mother planets can be envisioned, each with its own fauna and flora, all producing physical environments uncongenial to human life. To disregard the diversity of life is to risk catapulting ourselves into an alien environment. We will have become like the pilot whales that inexplicably beach themselves on New England shores.

Humanity coevolved with the rest of life on this particular planet; other worlds are not in our genes. Because scientists have yet to put names on most kinds of organisms, and because they entertain only a vague idea of how ecosystems work, it is reckless to suppose that biodiversity can be diminished indefinitely without threatening humanity itself. Field studies show that as biodiversity is reduced, so is the quality of the services provided by ecosystems. Records of stressed ecosystems also demonstrate that the descent can be unpredictably abrupt. As extinction spreads, some of the lost forms prove to be keystone species, whose disappearance brings down other species and triggers a ripple effect through the demographies of the survivors. The loss of a keystone species is like a drill accidentally striking a powerline. It causes lights to go out all over.

These services are important to human welfare. But they cannot form the whole foundation of an enduring environmental ethic. If a price can be put on something, that something can be devalued, sold, and discarded. It is also possible for some to dream that people will go on living comfortably in a biologically impoverished world. They suppose that a prosthetic environment is within the power of technology, that human life can still flourish in a completely humanized world, where medicines would all be synthesized from chemicals off the shelf, food grown from a few dozen domestic crop species, the atmosphere and climate regulated by computer-driven fusion energy, and the earth made over until it becomes a literal spaceship rather than a metaphorical one, with people reading displays and touching buttons on the bridge. Such is the terminus of the philosophy of exemptionalism: do not weep for the past, humanity is a new order of life, let species die if they block progress, scientific and technological genius will find another way. Look up and see the stars awaiting us.

But consider: human advance is determined not by reason alone but by emotions peculiar to our species, aided and tempered by reason. What makes us people and not computers is emotion. We have little grasp of our true nature, of what it is to be human and therefore where our descendants might someday wish we had directed Spaceship Earth. Our troubles, as Vercors said in *You Shall Know Them*, arise from the fact that we do not know what we are and cannot agree on what we want to be. The primary cause of this intellectual failure is ignorance of our origins. We did not arrive on this planet as aliens. Humanity is part of nature, a species that evolved among other species. The

more closely we identify ourselves with the rest of life, the more quickly we will be able to discover the sources of human sensibility and acquire the knowledge on which an enduring ethic, a sense of preferred direction, can be built.

The human heritage does not go back only for the conventionally recognized 8,000 years or so of recorded history, but for at least 2 million years, to the appearance of the first "true" human beings, the earliest species composing the genus *Homo*. Across thousands of generations, the emergence of culture must have been profoundly influenced by simultaneous events in genetic evolution, especially those occurring in the anatomy and physiology of the brain. Conversely, genetic evolution must have been guided forcefully by the kinds of selection rising within culture.

Only in the last moment of human history has the delusion arisen that people can flourish apart from the rest of the living world. Preliterate societies were in intimate contact with a bewildering array of life forms. Their minds could only partly adapt to that challenge. But they struggled to understand the most relevant parts, aware that the right responses gave life and fulfillment, the wrong ones sickness, hunger, and death. The imprint of that effort cannot have been erased in a few generations of urban existence. I suggest that it is to be found among the particularities of human nature, among which are these:

- People acquire phobias, abrupt and intractable aversions, to the objects and circumstances that threaten humanity in natural environments: heights, closed spaces, open spaces, running water, wolves, spiders, snakes. They rarely form phobias to the recently invented contrivances that are far more dangerous, such as guns, knives, automobiles, and electric sockets.

- People are both repelled and fascinated by snakes, even when they have never seen one in nature. In most cultures the serpent is the dominant wild animal of mythical and religious symbolism. Manhattanites dream of them with the same frequency as Zulus. This response appears to be Darwinian in origin. Poisonous snakes have been an important cause of mortality almost everywhere, from Finland to Tasmania, Canada to Patagonia; an untutored alertness in their presence saves lives. We note a kindred response in many primates, including Old World monkeys and chimpanzees: the animals pull back, alert others, watch closely, and follow each potentially dangerous snake until it moves away. . . .

Wilderness is a metaphor of unlimited opportunity, rising from the tribal memory of a time when humanity spread across the world, valley to valley, island to island, godstruck, firm in the belief that virgin land went on forever past the horizon.

I cite these common preferences of mind not as proof of an innate human nature but rather to suggest that we think more carefully and turn philosophy to the central questions of human origins in the wild environment. We do not understand ourselves yet and descend farther from heaven's air if we forget how much the natural world means to us. Signals abound that the loss of life's diversity endangers not just the body but the spirit. If that much is true, the changes occurring now will visit harm on all generations to come.

The ethical imperative should therefore be, first of all, prudence. We should judge every scrap of biodiversity as priceless while we learn to use it and come to understand what it means to humanity. We should not knowingly allow any species or race to go extinct. And let us go beyond mere salvage to begin the restoration of natural environments, in order to enlarge wild populations and stanch the hemorrhaging of biological wealth. There can be no purpose more enspiriting than to begin the age of restoration, reweaving the wondrous diversity of life that still surrounds us.

The evidence of swift environmental change calls for an ethic uncoupled from other systems of belief. Those committed by religion to believe that life was put on earth in one divine stroke will recognize that we are destroying the Creation, and those who perceive biodiversity to be the product of blind evolution will agree. Across the other great philosophical divide, it does not matter whether species have independent rights or, conversely, that moral reasoning is uniquely a human concern. Defenders of both premises seem destined to gravitate toward the same position on conservation.

The stewardship of environment is a domain on the near side of metaphysics where all reflective persons can surely find common ground. For what, in the final analysis, is morality but the command of conscience seasoned by a rational examination of consequences? And what is a fundamental precept but one that serves all generations? An enduring environmental ethic will aim to preserve not only the health and freedom of our species, but access to the world in which the human spirit was born.

65. What Is a Species? _____

Stephen Jay Gould

I had visited every state but Idaho. A few months ago, I finally got my opportunity to complete the roster of 50 by driving east from Spokane, Washington, into western Idaho. As I crossed the state line, I made the same feeble attempt at humor that so many of us try in similar situations: "Gee, it doesn't look a bit different from easternmost Washington." We make such comments because we feel the discomfort of discord between our mental needs and the world's reality. Much of nature (including terrestrial real estate) is continuous, but both our mental and political structures require divisions and categories. We need to break large and continuous items into manageable units.

Many people feel the same way about species as I do about Idaho—but this feeling is wrong. Many people suppose that species must be arbitrary divisions of an evolutionary continuum in the same way that state boundaries are conventional divisions of unbroken land. Moreover, this is not merely an abstract issue of scientific theory but a pressing concern of political reality. The Endangered Species Act, for example, sets policy (with substantial teeth) for the preservation of species. But if species are only arbitrary divisions in nature's continuity, then what are we trying to preserve and how shall we define it? I write this article to argue that such a reading of evolutionary theory is wrong and that species are almost always objective entities in nature.

Let us start with something uncontroversial: the bugs in your backyard. If you go out to make a complete collection of all the kinds of insects living in this small discrete space, you will collect easily definable "packages," not intergrading continua. You might find a kind of bee, three kinds of ants, a butterfly or two, several beetles, and a cicada. You have simply validated the commonsense notion known to all: in any small space during any given moment, the animals we see belong to separate and definable groups—and we call these groups species.

In the eighteenth century this commonsense observation was translated, improperly as we now know, into the creationist taxonomy of Linnaeus. The great Swedish naturalist regarded species as God's created entities, and he gathered them together into genera, genera into orders, and orders into classes, to form the taxonomic hierarchy that we all learned in high school (several more categories, families and phyla, for example, have been added since Linnaeus's time). The creationist version reached its apogee in the writings of America's greatest nineteenth-century naturalist (and last truly scientific creationist), Louis Agassiz. Agassiz argued that species are incarnations of separate ideas in God's mind, and that higher categories (genera, orders, and so forth) are therefore maps of the interrelationships among divine thoughts. Therefore, taxonomy is the most important of all sciences because it gives us direct insight into the structure of God's mind.

Darwin changed this reverie forever by proving that species are related by the physical connection of genealogical descent. But this immensely satisfying resolution for the great puzzle of nature's order engendered a subsidiary problem that Darwin never fully resolved: If all life is interconnected as a genealogical continuum, then what reality can species have? Are they not just arbitrary divisions of evolving lineages? And if so, how can the bugs in my backyard be ordered in separate units? In fact, the two greatest evolutionists of the nineteenth century, Lamarck and Darwin, both questioned the reality of species on the basis of their evolutionary convictions. Lamarck wrote, "In

vain do naturalists consume their time in describing new species"; while Darwin lamented: "we shall have to treat species as . . . merely artificial combinations made for convenience. This may not be a cheering prospect; but we shall at least be freed from the vain search for the undiscovered and undiscoverable essence of the term *species*" (from the *Origin of Species*).

But when we examine the technical writings of both Lamarck and Darwin, our sense of paradox is heightened. Darwin produced four long volumes on the taxonomy of barnacles, using conventional species for his divisions. Lamarck spent seven years (1815–1822) publishing his generation's standard, multivolume compendium on the diversity of animal life—*Histoire naturelle des animaux sans vertebrès*, or *Natural History of Invertebrate Animals*—all divided into species, many of which he named for the first time himself. How can these two great evolutionists have denied a concept in theory and then used it so centrally and extensively in practice? To ask the question more generally: If the species is still a useful and necessary concept, how can we define and justify it as evolutionists?

The solution to this question requires a preamble and two steps. For the preamble, let us acknowledge that the conceptual problem arises when we extend the "bugs in my backyard" example into time and space. A momentary slice of any continuum looks tolerably discrete; a slice of salami or a cross section of a tree trunk freezes a complexly changing structure into an apparently stable entity. Modern horses are discrete and separate from all other existing species, but how can we call the horse (*Equus caballus*) a real and definable entity if we can trace an unbroken genealogical series back through time to a dog-size creature with several toes on each foot? Where did this "dawn horse," or "eohippus," stop and the next stage begin; at what moment did the penultimate stage become *Equus caballus*? I now come to the two steps of an answer. First, if each evolutionary line were like a long salami, then species would not be real and definable in time and space. But in almost all cases large-scale evolution is a story of branching, not of transformation in a single line—bushes, not ladders, in my usual formulation. A branch on a bush is an objective division. One species rarely turns into another by total transformation over its entire geographic range. Rather, a small population becomes geographically isolated from the rest of the species—and this fragment changes to become a new species while the bulk of the parental population does not alter. "Dawn horse" is a misnomer because rhinoceroses evolved from the same parental lineage. The lineage split at an objective branching point into two lines that became (after further events of splitting) the great modern groups of horses (eight species, including asses and zebras) and rhinos (a sadly depleted group of formerly successful species).

Failure to recognize that evolution is a bush and not a ladder leads to one of the most common vernacular misconceptions about human biology. People often challenge me: "If humans evolved from apes, why are apes still around?" To anyone who understands the principle of bushes, there simply is no problem: the human lineage emerged as a branch, while the rest of the trunk continued as apes (and branched several more times to yield modern chimps, gorillas, and so on). But if you think that evolution is a ladder or a salami, then an emergence of humans from apes should mean the elimination of apes by transformation.

Second, you might grasp the principle of bushes and branching but still say: Yes, the ultimate products of a branch become objectively separate, but early on, while the branch is forming, no clear division can be made, and the precursors of the two species that will emerge must blend indefinably. And if evolution is gradual and continuous, and if most of a species' duration is spent in this state of incipient formation, then species will not be objectively definable during most of their geologic lifetimes.

Fair enough as an argument, but the premise is wrong. New species do (and must) have this period of initial ambiguity. But species emerge relatively quickly, compared with their period of later stability, and then live for long periods—often millions of years—with minimal change. Now, suppose that on average (and this is probably a fair estimate), species spend one percent of their geologic lifetimes in this initial state of imperfect separation. Then, on average, about one species in a hundred will encounter problems in definition, while the other 99 will be discrete and objectively separate—cross sections of branches showing no confluence with others. Thus, the principle of bushes, and the speed of branching, resolve the supposed paradox: continuous evolution can and does yield a world in which the vast majority of species are separate from all others and clearly definable at any moment in time. Species are nature's objective packages.

I have given a historical definition of species—as unique and separate branches on nature's bush. We also need a functional definition, if only because historical evidence (in the form of a complete fossil record) is usually unavailable. The standard criterion, in use at least since the days of the great French naturalist Georges de Buffon (a contemporary of Linnaeus), invokes the capacity for interbreeding. Members of a species can breed with others in the same species but not with individuals belonging to different species.

This functional criterion is a consequence of the historical definition: distinct separateness of a branch emerges only with the attainment of sufficient evolutionary distance to preclude interbreeding, for otherwise the branch is not an irrevocably separate entity and can amalgamate with the parental population. (Exceptions exist, but the reproductive criterion generally works well and gives rise to the standard one-liner for a textbook definition of a species: "a population of actually or potentially reproducing organisms sharing a common gene pool.")

Much of the ordinary activity of evolutionary biologists is devoted to learning whether or not the groups they study are separate species by this criterion of "reproductive isolation." Such separateness can be based on a variety of factors, collectively termed "isolating mechanisms": for example, genetic programs so different that an embryo cannot form even if egg and sperm unite; behaviors that lead members of one species to shun individuals from other populations; even something so mundane as breeding at different times of the year, or in different parts of the habitat—for example, on apple trees rather than on plum trees—so that contact can never take place. (We exclude simple geographic separation—living on different continents, for example—because an isolating mechanism must work when actively challenged by a potential for interbreeding through spatial contact. I do not belong to a separate species from my brethren in Brazil just because I have never been there. Similarly, reproductive isolation must be assessed by ordinary behavior in a state of nature. Some truly separate species can be induced to interbreed in zoos and laboratories. The fact that zoos can make tiglons—tiger-lion hybrids—does not challenge the separate status of the two populations as species in nature.)

Modern humans (species *Homo sapiens*) fit these criteria admirably. We are now spread all over the world in great numbers, but we began as a little twig in Africa (the historical criterion). We may look quite different from one another in a few superficially striking aspects of size, skin color, and hair form, but there is astonishingly little overall genetic difference among our so-called races. Above all (the functional criterion), we can all interbreed with one another (and do so with avidity, always, and all over the world), but not with any member of another species (movies about flies notwithstanding). We are often reminded, quite correctly, that we are very similar in overall genetic program to our nearest cousin, the chimpanzee—but no one would mistake a single individual of either species, and we do not hybridize (again, various science fictions notwithstanding).

I do not say that these criteria are free from exceptions; nature is nothing if not a domain of exceptions, where an example against any clean generality can always be found. Some distinct populations of plants, for example, can and frequently do interbreed with others that ought to be separate species by all other standards. (This is why the classification of certain groups—the rhododendrons for example—is such a mess.) But the criteria work in the vast majority of cases, including humans. Species are not arbitrary units, constructed for human convenience, in dividing continua. Species are the real and objective items of nature's morphology. They are "out there" in the world as historically distinct and functionally separate populations "with their own historical role and tendency" (as the other textbook one-liner proclaims).

Species are unique in the Linnaean hierarchy as the only category with such objectivity. All higher units—genera, families, phyla, et cetera—are human conventions in the following important respect. The evolutionary tree itself is objective; the branches (species) emerge, grow, and form clusters by subsequent branching. The clusters are clearly discernible. But the status we award to these so-called higher taxa (clusters of branches with a single root of common evolutionary ancestry) is partly a matter of human decision. Clusters A and B in the figure are groups of species with a common parent. Each branch in each cluster is an objective species. But what are the clusters themselves? Are they two genera or two families? Our decision on this question is partly a matter of human preference constrained by the rules of logic and the facts of nature.

(For example, we cannot take one species from cluster A and one from cluster B and put them together as a single genus—for this would violate the rule that all members of a higher taxon must share a common ancestor without excluding other species that are more closely related to the common ancestor. We cannot put domestic cats and dogs in one family while classifying lions and wolves in another.)

The taxonomic hierarchy recognizes only one unit below species—the subspecies. Like higher taxa, subspecies are also partly objective but partly based on human decision. Subspecies are defined as distinctive subpopulations that live in a definite geographic subsection of the entire range of the species. I cannot, for example, pluck out all tall members of a species, or all red individuals, wherever they occur over the full geographic range, and establish them as subspecies. A subspecies must be a distinct geographic subpopulation—not yet evolved far enough to become a separate species in its own right but different enough from other subpopulations (in terms of anatomy, genetic structure, physiology, or behavior) that a taxonomist chooses to memorialize the distinction with a name. Yet subspecies cannot be irrevocably unique natural populations (like full species) for two reasons: First, the decision to name them rests with human taxonomists, and isn't solely dictated by nature. Second, they are, by definition, still capable of interbreeding with other subpopulations of the species and are, therefore, impermanent and subject to reamalgamation.

This difference between species and subspecies becomes important in practice because our Endangered Species Act currently mandates the protection of subspecies as well. I do not dispute the act's intention or its teeth, for many subspecies do manifest distinctly evolved properties of great value and wonder (even if these properties do not render them reproductively isolated from other populations of the species). We would not, after all, condone the genocide of all Caucasian human beings because members of other races would still exist; human races, if formally recognized at all, are subspecies based on our original geographic separations. But since subspecies do not have the same objective status as species (and since not all distinct local populations bear separate names), argument over what does and does not merit protection is inevitable. Most of the major ecological wrangles of recent years—rows over the Mount Graham red squirrel or the northern spotted owl—involve subspecies, not species.

The taxonomic issues were once abstract, however important. They are now immediate and vital—and all educated people must understand them in the midst of our current crisis in biodiversity and extinction. I therefore close with two observations.

By grasping the objective status of species as real units in nature (and by understanding why they are not arbitrary divisions for human convenience), we may better comprehend the moral rationale for their preservation. You can expunge an arbitrary idea by rearranging your conceptual world. But when a species dies, an item of natural uniqueness is gone forever. Each species is a remarkably complex product of evolution—a branch on a tree that is billions of years old. All the king's horses and men faced an easy problem compared with what we would encounter if we tried to reconstitute a lost species. Reassembling Humpty-Dumpty is just an exceedingly complex jigsaw puzzle, for the pieces lie at the base of the wall. There are no pieces left when the last dodo dies.

But all species eventually die in the fullness of geologic time, so why should we worry? In the words of Tennyson (who died exactly 100 years ago, so the fact is no secret):

> From scarped cliff and quarried stone
> She cries, "A thousand types are gone:
> I care for nothing. All shall go."

(From *In Memoriam*)

The argument is true, but the time scale is wrong for our ethical concerns. We live our lives within geologic instants, and we should make our moral decisions at this proper scale—not at the micromoment of thoughtless exploitation for personal profit and public harm; but not at Earth's time scale of billions of years either (a grand irrelevancy for our species' potential tenure of thousands or, at most, a few million years).

We do not let children succumb to easily curable infections just because we know that all people must die eventually. Neither should we condone our current massive wipeout of species because all eventually become extinct. The mass extinctions of our geologic past may have cleared space and created new evolutionary opportunity—but it takes up to 10 million years to reestablish an interesting new world, and what can such an interval mean to us? Mass extinctions may have geologically distant benefits, but life in the midst of such an event is maximally unpleasant—and that, friends, is where we now reside, I fear.

Species are living, breathing items of nature. We lose a bit of our collective soul when we drive species (and their entire lineages with them), prematurely and in large numbers, to oblivion. Tennyson, paraphrasing Goethe, hoped that we could transcend such errors when he wrote, in the same poem:

> I held it truth, with him who sings
> To one clear harp in divers tones
> That men may rise on stepping-stones
> Of their dead selves to higher things.

66. Why Do Species Matter?

Lilly-Marlene Russow

I. Introduction

Consider the following extension of the standard sort of objection to treating animals differently just because they are not humans: the fact that a being is or is not a member of species S is not a morally relevant fact, and does not justify treating that being differently from members of other species. If so, we cannot treat a bird differently *just* because it is a California condor rather than a turkey vulture. The problem, then, becomes one of determining what special obligations, if any, a person might have toward California condors, and what might account for those obligations in a way

Environmental Ethics, Vol. 3, No. 2 (Summer 1981) 101–12. Reprinted by permission of the publisher and author.

that is generally consistent with the condemnation of speciesism. Since it will turn out that the solution I offer does not admit of a direct and tidy proof, what follows comprises three sections which approach this issue from different directions. The resulting triangulation should serve as justification and motivation for the conclusion sketched in the final section.

II. Species and Individuals

Much of the discussion in the general area of ethics and animals has dealt with the rights of animals, or obligations and duties toward individual animals. The first thing to note is that some, but not all, of the actions normally thought of as obligatory with respect to the protection of vanishing species can be recast as possible duties to individual members of that species. Thus, if it could be shown that we have a *prima facie* duty not to kill a sentient being, it would follow that it would be wrong, other things being equal, to kill a blue whale or a California condor. But it would be wrong for the same reason, and to the same degree, that it would be wrong to kill a turkey vulture or a pilot whale. Similarly, if it is wrong (something which I do not think can be shown) to deprive an individual animal of its natural habitat, it would be wrong, for the same reasons and to the same degree, to do that to a member of an endangered species. And so on. Thus, an appeal to our duties toward individual animals may provide some protection, but they do not justify the claim that we should treat members of a vanishing species with *more* care than members of other species.

More importantly, duties toward individual beings (or the rights of those individuals) will not always account for all the actions that people feel obligated to do for endangered species—e.g., bring into the world as many individuals of that species as possible, protect them from natural predation, or establish separate breeding colonies. In fact, the protection of a species might involve actions that are demonstrably contrary to the interests of some or all of the individual animals: this seems true in cases where we remove all the animals we can from their natural environment and raise them in zoos, or where we severely restrict the range of a species by hunting all those outside a certain area, as is done in Minnesota to protect the timber wolf. If such efforts are morally correct, our duties to pre-serve a species cannot be grounded in obligations that we have toward individual animals.

Nor will it be fruitful to treat our obligations to a species as duties toward, or as arising out of the rights of, a species thought of as some special superentity. It is simply not clear that we can make sense of talk about the interests of a species in the absence of beliefs, desires, purposeful actions, etc.[1] Since having interests is generally accepted as at least a necessary condition for having rights,[2] and since many of the duties we have toward animals arise directly out of the animals' interests, arguments which show that animals have rights, or that we have duties towards them, will not apply to species. Since arguments which proceed from interests to rights or from interests to obligations make up a majority of the literature on ethics and animals, it is unlikely that these arguments will serve as a key to possible obligations toward species.

Having eliminated the possibility that our obligations toward species are somehow parallel to, or similar to, our obligations not to cause unwarranted pain to an animal, there seem to be only a few possibilities left. We may find that our duties toward species arise not out of the interests of the species, but are rooted in the general obligation to preserve things of value. Alternatively, our obligations to species may in fact be obligations to individuals (either members of the species or other individuals), but obligations that differ from the ones just discussed in that they are not determined simply by the interests of the individual.

III. Some Test Cases

If we are to find some intuitively acceptable foundation for claims about our obligations to protect species, we must start afresh. In order to get clear about what, precisely, we are looking for in this context, what obligations we might think we have toward species, what moral claims we are seeking a foundation for, I turn now to a description of some test cases. An examination of these cases illustrates why the object of our search is not something as straightforward as "Do whatever is possible or necessary to preserve the existence of the species"; a consideration of some of the differences between cases will guide our search for the nature of our obligations and the underlying reasons for those obligations.

Case 1. The snail darter is known to exist only in one part of one river. This stretch of river would be destroyed by the building of the Tellico dam. Defenders of the dam have successfully argued that the dam is nonetheless necessary for the economic development and well-being of the area's population. To my knowledge, no serious or large-scale attempt has been made to breed large numbers of snail darters in captivity (for any reason other than research).

Case 2. The Pére David deer was first discovered by a Western naturalist in 1865, when Pére Armand David found herds of the deer in the Imperial Gardens in Peking: even at that time, they were only known to exist in captivity. Pére David brought several animals back to Europe, where they bred readily enough so that now there are healthy populations in several major zoos.[3] There is no reasonable hope of reintroducing the Pére David deer to its natural habitat; indeed, it is not even definitely known what its natural habitat was.

Case 3. The red wolf (*Canis rufus*) formerly ranged over the southeastern and southcentral United States. As with most wolves, they were threatened, and their range curtailed, by trapping, hunting, and the destruction of habitat. However, a more immediate threat to the continued existence of the red wolf is that these changes extended the range of the more adaptable coyote, with whom the red wolf interbreeds very readily; as a result, there are very few "pure" red wolves left. An attempt has been made to capture some pure breeding stock and raise wolves on preserves.[4]

Case 4. The Baltimore oriole and the Bullock's oriole were long recognized and classified as two separate species of birds. As a result of extensive interbreeding between the two species in areas where their ranges overlapped, the American Ornithologists' Union recently declared that there were no longer two separate species; both ex-species are now called "northern orioles."

Case 5. The Appaloosa is a breed of horse with a distinctively spotted coat; the Lewis and Clark expedition discovered that the breed was associated with the Nez Peroé Indians. When the Nez Peroé tribe was defeated by the U.S. Cavalry in 1877 and forced to move, their horses were scattered and interbred with other horses. The distinctive coat pattern was almost lost; not until the middle of the twentieth century was a concerted effort made to gather together the few remaining specimens and reestablish the breed.

Case 6. Many strains of laboratory rats are bred specifically for a certain type of research. Once the need for a particular variety ceases—once the type of research is completed—the rats are usually killed, with the result that the variety becomes extinct.

Case 7. It is commonly known that several diseases such as sleeping sickness, malaria, and human encephalitis are carried by one variety of mosquito but not by others. Much of the disease control in these cases is aimed at exterminating the disease-carrying insect; most people do not find it morally wrong to wipe out the whole species.

Case 8. Suppose that zebras were threatened solely because they were hunted for their distinctive striped coats. Suppose, too, that we could remove this threat by selectively breeding zebras that are not striped, that look exactly like mules, although they are still pure zebras. Have we preserved all that we ought to have preserved?

What does an examination of these test cases reveal? First, that our concept of what a species *is* is not at all unambiguous; at least in part, what counts as a species is a matter of current fashions in taxonomy. Furthermore, it seems that it is not the sheer diversity or number of species that matters: if that were what is valued, moral preference would be given to taxonomic schemes that separated individuals into a larger number of species, a suggestion which seems absurd. The case of the orioles suggests that the decision as to whether to call these things one species or two is not a moral issue at all.[5] Since we are not evidently concerned with the existence or diversity of species in *this* sense, there must be something more at issue than the simple question of whether we have today the same number of species represented as we had yesterday. Confusion sets in, however, when we try to specify another sense in which it is possible to speak of the "existence" of a species. This only serves to emphasize the basic murkiness of our intuitions about what the object of our concern really is.

This murkiness is further revealed by the fact that it is not at all obvious what we are trying to preserve in some of the test cases. Sometimes, as in the case of the Appaloosa or attempts to save a subspecies like the Arctic wolf or the Mexican wolf, it is not a whole species that is in question. But not all genetic subgroups are of interest—witness the case of the laboratory rat—and sometimes the preservation of the species at the cost of one of its externally obvious features (the stripes on a zebra) is not our only concern. This is not a minor puzzle which can be resolved by changing our question from "why do species matter?" to "why do species and/or subspecies matter?" It is rather a serious issue of what makes a group of animals "special" enough or "unique" enough to warrant concern. And, of course, the test cases reveal that our intuitions are not always consistent: although the cases of the red wolf and the northern oriole are parallel in important respects, we are more uneasy about simply reclassifying the red wolf and allowing things to continue along their present path.

The final point to be established is that whatever moral weight is finally attached to the preservation of a species (or subspecies), it can be overridden. We apparently have no compunction about wiping out a species of mosquito if the benefits gained by such action are sufficiently important, although many people were unconvinced by similar arguments in favor of the Tellico dam.

The lesson to be drawn from this section can be stated in a somewhat simplistic form: it is not simply the case that we can solve our problems by arguing that there is some value attached to the mere existence of a species. Our final analysis must take account of various features or properties of certain kinds or groups of animals, and it has to recognize that our concern is with the continued existence of individuals that may or may not have some distinctive characteristics.

IV. Some Traditional Answers

There are, of course, some standard replies to the question "Why do species matter?" or, more particularly, to the question "Why do we have at least a *prima facie* duty not to cause a species to become extinct, and in some cases, a duty to try actively to preserve species?" With some tolerance for borderline cases, these replies generally fall into three groups: (1) those that appeal to our role as "stewards" or "caretakers," (2) those that claim that species have some extrinsic value (I include in this group those that argue that the species is valuable as part of the ecosystem or as a link in the evolutionary scheme of things), and (3) those that appeal to some intrinsic or inherent value that is supposed to make a species worth preserving. In this section, with the help of the test cases just discussed, I indicate some serious flaws with each of these responses.

The first type of view has been put forward in the philosophical literature by Joel Feinberg, who states that our duty to preserve whole species may be more important than any rights had by individual animals.[6] He argues, first, that this duty does not arise from a right or claim that can properly be attributed to the species as a whole (his reasons are much the same as the ones I cited in Section II of this paper), and second, while we have some duty to unborn generations that directs us to preserve species, that duty is much weaker than the actual duty we have to preserve species. The fact that our actual duty extends beyond our duties to future generations is explained by the claim that we have duties of "stewardship" with respect to the world as a whole. Thus, Feinberg notes that his "inclination is to seek an explanation in terms of the requirements of our unique station as rational custodians of the planet we temporarily occupy."[7]

The main objection to this appeal to our role as stewards or caretakers is that it begs the question. The job of a custodian is to protect that which is deserving of protection, that which has some value or worth.[8] But the issue before us now is precisely *whether* species have value, and why. If we justify our obligations of stewardship by reference to the value of that which is cared for, we cannot also explain the value by pointing to the duties of stewardship.

The second type of argument is the one which establishes the value of a species by locating it in the "larger scheme of things." That is, one might try to argue that species matter because they contribute to, or form an essential part of, some other good. This line of defense has several variations.

The first version is completely anthropocentric: it is claimed that vanishing species are of concern to us because their difficulties serve as a warning that we have polluted or altered the environment in a way that is potentially dangerous or undesirable for us. Thus, the California condor, whose eggshells are weakened due to the absorption of DDT, indicates that something is wrong: presumably we are being affected in subtle ways by the absorption of DDT, and that is bad for us. Alternatively, diminishing numbers of game animals may signal overhunting which, if left unchecked, would leave the sportsman with fewer things to hunt. And, as we become more aware of the benefits that might be obtained from rare varieties of plants and animals (drugs, substitutes for other natural resources, tools for research), we may become reluctant to risk the disappearance of a species that might be of practical use to us in the future.

This line of argument does not carry us very far. In the case of a subspecies, most benefits could be derived from other varieties of the same species. More important, when faced with the loss of a unique variety or species, we may simply decide that, even taking into account the possibility of error, there is not enough reason to think that the species will ever be of use; we may take a calculated risk and decide that it is not worth it. Finally, the use of a species as a danger signal may apply to species whose decline is due to some subtle and unforeseen change in the environment, but will not justify concern for a species threatened by a known and foreseen event like the building of a dam.

Other attempts to ascribe extrinsic value to a species do not limit themselves to potential human and practical goods. Thus, it is often argued that each species occupies a unique niche in a rich and complex, but delicately balanced, ecosystem. By destroying a single species, we upset the balance of the whole system. On the assumption that the system as a whole should be preserved, the value of a species is determined, at least in part, by its contribution to the whole.[9]

In assessing this argument, it is important to realize that such a justification (a) may lead to odd conclusions about some of the test cases, and (b) allows for changes which do not affect the system, or which result in the substitution of a richer, more complex system for one that is more primitive or less evolved. With regard to the first of these points, species that exist only in zoos would seem to have no special value. In terms of our test cases, the David deer does not exist as part of a system, but only in isolation. Similarly, the Appaloosa horse, a domesticated variety which is neither better suited nor worse than any other sort of horse, would not have any special value. In contrast, the whole cycle of mosquitoes, disease organisms adapted to these hosts, and other beings susceptible to those diseases is quite a complex and marvelous bit of systematic adaption. Thus, it would seem to be wrong to wipe out the encephalitis-bearing mosquito.

With regard to the second point, we might consider changes effected by white settlers in previously isolated areas such as New Zealand and Australia. The introduction of new species has resulted in a whole new ecosystem, with many of the former indigenous species being replaced by introduced varieties. As long as the new system works, there seems to be no grounds for objections.

The third version of an appeal to extrinsic value is sometimes presented in Darwinian terms: species are important as links in the evolutionary chain. This will get us nowhere, however, because the extinction of one species, the replacement of one by another, is as much a part of evolution as is the development of a new species.

One should also consider a more general concern about all versions of the argument which focus on the species' role in the natural order of things: all of these arguments presuppose that "the natural order of things" is, in itself, good. As William Blackstone pointed out, this is by no means obvious: "Unless one adheres dogmatically to a position of a 'reverence for all life,' the extinction of some species or forms of life may be seen as quite desirable. (This is parallel to the point often made by philosophers that not all 'customary' or 'natural' behavior is necessarily good.)"[10] Unless we have some other way of ascribing value to a system, and to the animals which actually fulfill a certain function in that system (as opposed to possible replacements), the argument will not get off the ground.

Finally, then, the process of elimination leads us to the set of arguments which point to some *intrinsic value* that a species is supposed to have. The notion that species have an intrinsic value, if established, would allow us to defend much stronger claims about human obligations toward threatened species. Thus, if a species is intrinsically valuable, we should try to preserve it even when it no longer has a place in the natural ecosystem, or when it could be replaced by another species that would occupy the same niche. Most important, we should not ignore a species just because it serves no useful purpose.

Unsurprisingly, the stumbling block is what this intrinsic value might be grounded in. Without an explanation of that, we have no nonarbitrary way of deciding whether subspecies as well as species have intrinsic value or how much intrinsic value a species might have. The last question is meant to bring out issues that will arise in cases of conflict of interests: is the intrinsic value of a species of mosquito sufficient to outweigh the benefits to be gained by eradicating the means of spreading a disease like encephalitis? Is the intrinsic value of the snail darter sufficient to outweigh the economic hardship that might be alleviated by the construction of a dam? In short, to say that something has intrinsic value does not tell us *how much* value it has, nor does it allow us to make the sorts of judgments that are often called for in considering the fate of an endangered species.

The attempt to sidestep the difficulties raised by subspecies by broadening the ascription of value to include subspecies opens a whole Pandora's box. It would follow that any genetic variation within a species that results in distinctive characteristics would need separate protection. In the case of forms developed through selective breeding, it is not clear whether we have a situation analogous to natural subspecies, or whether no special value is attached to different breeds.

In order to speak to either of these issues, and in order to lend plausibility to the whole enterprise, it would seem necessary to consider first the justification for ascribing value to whichever groups have such value. If intrinsic value does not spring from anything, if it becomes merely another way of saying that we should protect species, we are going around in circles, without explaining anything.[11] Some further explanation is needed.

Some appeals to intrinsic value are grounded in the intuition that diversity itself is a virtue. If so, it would seem incumbent upon us to create new species wherever possible, even bizarre ones that would have no purpose other than to be different. Something other than diversity must therefore be valued.

The comparison that is often made between species and natural wonders, spectacular landscapes, or even works of art, suggest that species might have some aesthetic value. This seems to accord well with our naive intuitions, provided that *aesthetic value* is interpreted rather loosely; most of us believe that the world would be a poorer place for the loss of bald eagles in the same way that it would be poorer for the loss of the Grand Canyon or a great work of art. In all cases, the experience of seeing these things is an inherently worthwhile experience. And since diversity in some cases is a component in aesthetic appreciation, part of the previous intuition would be preserved. There is also room for degrees of selectivity and concern with superficial changes: the variety of rat that is allowed to become extinct may have no special aesthetic value, and a bird is neither more nor less aesthetically pleasing when we change its name.

There are some drawbacks to this line of argument: there are some species which, by no stretch of the imagination, are aesthetically significant. But aesthetic value can cover a surprising range of things: a tiger may be simply beautiful; a blue whale is awe-inspiring; a bird might be decorative; an Appaloosa is of interest because of its historical significance; and even a drab little plant may inspire admiration for the marvelous way it has been adapted to a special environment. Even so, there may be species such as the snail darter that simply have no aesthetic value. In these cases, lacking any alternative, we may be forced to the conclusion that such species are not worth preserving.

Seen from other angles, once again the appeal to the aesthetic value of species is illuminating. Things that have an aesthetic value are compared and ranked in some cases, and commitment of resources may be made accordingly. We believe that diminishing the aesthetic value of a thing for mere economic benefit is immoral, but that aesthetic value is not absolute—that the fact that something has aesthetic value may be overridden by the fact that harming that thing, or destroying it, may result in some greater good. That is, someone who agrees to destroy a piece of Greek statuary for personal gain would be condemned as having done something immoral, but someone who is faced with a choice between saving his children and saving a "priceless" painting would be said to have skewed values if he chose to save the painting. Applying these observations to species, we can see that an appeal to aesthetic value would justify putting more effort into the preservation of one species than the preservation of another; indeed, just as we think that the doodling of a would-be artist may have no merit at all, we may think that the accidental and unfortunate mutation of a species is not worth preserving. Following the analogy, allowing a species to become extinct for *mere* economic gain might be seen as immoral, while the possibility remains open that other (human?) good might outweigh the goods achieved by the preservation of a species.

Although the appeal to aesthetic values has much to recommend it—even when we have taken account of the fact that it does not guarantee that all species matter—there seems to be a fundamental confusion that still affects the cogency of the whole argument and its application to the question of special obligations to endangered species, for if the value of a species is based on its aesthetic value, it is impossible to explain why an endangered species should be more valuable, or more worthy of preservation, than an unendangered species. The appeal to "rarity" will not help, if what we are talking about is species: each species is unique, no more or less rare than any other species: there is in each case one and only one species that we are talking about.[12]

This problem of application seems to arise because the object of aesthetic appreciation, and, hence, of aesthetic value, has been misidentified, for it is not the case that we perceive, admire, and appreciate a *species*—species construed either as a group or set of similar animals or as a name that we attach to certain kinds of animals in virtue of some classification scheme. What we value is the existence of individuals with certain characteristics. If this is correct, then the whole attempt to explain why species matter by arguing that *they* have aesthetic value needs to be redirected. This is what I try to do in the final section of this paper.

V. Valuing the Individual

What I propose is that the intuition behind the argument from aesthetic value is correct, but misdirected. The reasons that were given for the value of a species are, in fact, reasons for saying that an individual has value. We do not admire the grace and beauty of the species *Panthera tigris;* rather, we admire the grace and beauty of the individual Bengal tigers that we may encounter. What we value then is the existence of that individual and the existence (present or future) of individuals like that. The ways in which other individuals should be "like that" will depend on why we value that particular sort of individual: the stripes on a zebra do not matter if we value zebras primarily for the way they are adapted to a certain environment, their unique fitness for a certain sort of life. If, on the other hand, we value zebras because their stripes are aesthetically pleasing, the stripes do matter. Since our attitudes toward zebras probably include both of these features, it is not surprising to find that my hypothetical test case produces conflicting intuitions.

The shift of emphasis from species to individuals allows us to make sense of the stronger feelings we have about endangered species in two ways. First, the fact that there are very few members of a species—the fact that we rarely encounter one—itself increases the value of those encounters. I can see turkey vultures almost every day, and I can eat apples almost every day, but seeing a bald eagle or eating wild strawberries are experiences that are much less common, more delightful just for their rarity and unexpectedness. Even snail darters, which, if we encountered them every day would be drab and uninteresting, become more interesting just because we don't—or may not—see them every day. Second, part of our interest in an individual carries over to a desire that there be future opportunities to see these things again (just as when, upon finding a new and beautiful work of art, I will wish to go back and see it again). In the case of animals, unlike works of art, I know that this animal will not live forever, but that other animals like this one will have similar aesthetic value. Thus, because I value possible future encounters, I will also want to do what is needed to ensure the possibility of such encounters—i.e., make sure that enough presently existing individuals of this type will be able to reproduce and survive. This is rather like the duty that we have to support and contribute to museums, or to other efforts to preserve works of art.

To sum up, then: individual animals can have, to a greater or lesser degree, aesthetic value: they are valued for their simple beauty, for their awesomeness, for their intriguing adaptations, for their rarity, and for many other reasons. We have moral obligations to protect things of aesthetic value, and to ensure (in an odd sense) their continued existence; thus, we have a duty to protect individual animals (the duty may be weaker or stronger depending on the value of the individual), and to ensure that there will continue to be animals of this sort (this duty will also be weaker or stronger, depending on value).

I began this paper by suggesting that our obligations to vanishing species might appear inconsistent with a general condemnation of speciesism. My proposal is not inconsistent: we value and protect animals because of their aesthetic value, not because they are members of a given species.

Notes

1. Cf. Joel Feinberg, "The Rights of Animals and Future Generations," in *Philosophy and Environmental Crisis*, ed. William Blackstone (Athens: University of Georgia Press, 1974), pp. 55–57.

2. There are some exceptions to this: for example, Tom Regan argues that some rights are grounded in the intrinsic value of a thing in "Do Animals Have a Right to Life?" in *Animal Rights and Human Obligations*, eds. Tom Regan and Peter Singer (Englewood Cliffs, NJ: Prentice-Hall, 1975), pp. 198–203. These and similar cases will be dealt with by examining the proposed foundations of rights; thus, the claim that species have intrinsic value will be considered in Section III.

3. The deer in China were all killed during the Boxer rebellion; recently, several pairs were sent to Chinese zoos.

4. *Predator 7*, no. 2 (1980). Further complications occur in this case because a few scientists have tried to argue that all red wolves are the result of inter-breeding between grey wolves (*Canis lupus*) and coyotes (*C. latans*). For more information, see L. David Mech, *The Wolf* (Garden City, NY: Natural History Press, 1970), pp. 22–25.

5. Sometimes there are moral questions about the practical consequences of such a move. The recent decision to combine two endangered species—the seaside sparrow and the dusky seaside sparrow—aggravates the difficulties faced by attempts to protect these birds.

6. Joel Feinberg, "Human Duties and Animal Rights," in *On the Fifth Day: Animal Rights and Human Ethics*, Richard Knowles Morris and Michael W. Fox, eds. (Washington: Acropolis Books, 1978), p. 67.

7. Ibid, p. 68.

8. Cf. Feinberg's discussion of custodial duties in "The Rights of Animals and Future Generations," *Philosophy and Environmental Crisis*, pp. 49–50.

9. A similar view has been defended by Tom Auxter, "The Right Not to Be Eaten," *Inquiry* 22 (1979): 222–23.

10. William Blackstone, "Ethics and Ecology," *Philosophy and Environmental Crisis*, p. 25.

11. This objection parallels Regan's attack on ungrounded appeals to the intrinsic value of human life as a way of trying to establish a human right to life. Cf. Thomas Regan, "Do Animals Have a Right to Life?" *Animal Rights and Human Obligations*, p. 199.

12. There is one further attempt that might be made to avoid this difficulty: one might argue that species do not increase in value due to scarcity, but that our duties to protect a valuable species involve more when the species is more in need of protection. This goes part of the way toward solving the problem, but does not yet capture our intuition that rarity does affect the value in some way.

67. Why Species Matter

Holmes Rolston III

Sensitivity to the wonder of life . . . can sometimes make an environmental ethicist seem callous. On San Clemente Island, the U.S. Fish and Wildlife Service and the Natural Resource Office of the U.S. Navy planned to shoot two thousand feral goats to save three endangered plant species (*Malacothamnus clementinus, Castilleja* *grisea*, and *Delphinium kinkiense*), of which the surviving individuals numbered only a few dozen. After a protest, some goats were trapped and relocated. But trapping all of them was impossible, and many thousands were killed. In this instance, the survival of plant species was counted more than the lives of individual mam-

This selection is the latter portion of "Environmental Ethics: Values in and Duties to the Natural World," by Holmes Rolston III, in *Ecology, Economics, Ethics: The Broken Circle*, edited by F. Herbert Bormann and Stephen R. Kellert (New Haven: Yale University Press, 1991), pp. 82–96. Reprinted by permission.

mals; a few plants counted more than many thousands of goats.

Those who wish to restore rare species of big cats to the wild have asked about killing genetically inbred, inferior cats presently held in zoos, in order to make space available for the cats needed to reconstruct and maintain a population that is genetically more likely to survive upon release. All the Siberian tigers in zoos in North America are descendants of seven animals; if these tigers were replaced by others nearer to the wild type and with more genetic variability, the species might be saved in the wild. When we move to the level of species, sometimes we decide to kill individuals for the good of their kind.

Or we might now refuse to let nature take its course. The Yellowstone ethicists let the bison drown, in spite of its suffering; they let the blinded bighorns die. But in the spring of 1984 a sow grizzly and her three cubs walked across the ice of Yellowstone Lake to Frank Island, two miles from shore. They stayed several days to feast on two elk carcasses, and the ice bridge melted. Soon afterward, they were starving on an island too small to support them. This time the Yellowstone ethicists promptly rescued the grizzlies and released them on the mainland, in order to protect an endangered species. They were not rescuing individual bears so much as saving the species.

Coloradans have declined to build the Two Forks Dam to supply urban Denver with water. Building the dam would require destroying a canyon and altering the Platte River flow, with many negative environmental consequences, including further endangering the whooping crane and endangering a butterfly, the Pawnee montane skipper. Elsewhere in the state, water development threatens several fish species, including the humpback chub, which requires the turbulent spring runoff stopped by dams. Environmental ethics doubts whether the good of humans who wish more water for development, both for industry and for bluegrass lawns, warrants endangering species of cranes, butterflies, and fish.

A species exists; a species ought to exist. An environmental ethic must make these assertions and move from biology to ethics with care. Species exist only instantiated in individuals, yet they are as real as individual plants or animals. The assertion that there are specific forms of life historically maintained in their environments over time seems as certain as anything else we believe about the empirical world. At times biologists revise the theories and taxa with which they map these forms, but species are not so much like lines of latitude and longitude as like mountains and rivers, phenomena objectively there to be mapped. The edges of these natural kinds will sometimes be fuzzy, to some extent discretionary. One species will slide into another over evolutionary time. But it does not follow from the fact that speciation is sometimes in progress that species are merely made up and not found as evolutionary lines with identity in time as well as space.

A consideration of species is revealing and challenging because it offers a biologically based counterexample to the focus on individuals—typically sentient and usually persons—so characteristic in classical ethics. In an evolutionary ecosystem, it is not mere individuality that counts; the species is also significant because it is a dynamic life-form maintained over time. The individual represents (re-presents) a species in each new generation. It is a token of a type, and the type is more important than the token.

A species lacks moral agency, reflective self-awareness, sentience, or organic individuality. The older, conservative ethic will be tempted to say that specific-level processes cannot count morally. Duties must attach to singular lives, most evidently those with a self, or some analogue to self. In an individual organism, the organs report to a center; the good of a whole is defended. The members of a species report to no center. A species has no self. It is not a bounded singular. There is no analogue to the nervous hookups or circulatory flows that characterize the organism.

But singularity, centeredness, selfhood, and individuality are not the only processes to which duty attaches. A more radically conservative ethic knows that having a biological identity reasserted genetically over time is as true of the species as of the individual. Identity need not attach solely to the centered organism; it can persist as a discrete pattern over time. From this way of thinking, it follows that the life the individual has is something passing through the individual as much as something it intrinsically possesses. The individual is subordinate to the species, not the other way around. The genetic set, in which is coded the telos, is as evidently the property of the species as of the individual through which it passes. A consideration of species strains any ethic fixed on individual organisms, much less on sentience or persons. But the result can be biologically sounder, though it revises what was formerly thought logically permissible or ethically binding. When ethics is informed by this kind of biology, it is appropriate to attach duty dynamically to the specific form of life.

The species line is the vital living system, the whole, of which individual organisms are the essential parts. The species too has its integrity, its individuality, its right to life (if we must use the rhetoric of rights); and it is more important to protect this vitality than to protect individual integrity. The right to life, biologically speaking, is an adaptive fit that is right for life, that survives over millennia. This idea generates at least a presumption that species in a niche are good right where they are, and therefore that it is right for humans to let them be, to let them evolve.

Processes of value that we earlier found in an organic individual appear at the specific level: defending a particular form of life, pursuing a pathway through the world, resisting death (extinction), regenerating, maintaining a normative identity over time, expressing creative resilience by discovering survival skills. It is as logical to say that the individual is the species' way of propagating itself as to say that the embryo or egg is the individual's way of propagating itself. The dignity resides in the dynamic form; the individual inherits this form, exemplifies it, and passes it on. If, at the specific level, these processes are just as evident, or even more so, what prevents duties from arising at that level? The appropriate survival unit is the appropriate level of moral concern.

A shutdown of the life stream is the most destructive event possible. The wrong that humans are doing, or allowing to happen through carelessness, is stopping the historical vitality of life, the flow of natural kinds. Every extinction is an incremental decay in this stopping of life, no small thing. Every extinction is a kind of superkilling. It kills forms (species) beyond individuals. It kills essences beyond existences, the soul as well as the body. It kills collectively, not just distributively. It kills birth as well as death. Afterward nothing of that kind either lives or dies.

Ought species x to exist? is a distributive increment in the collective question, ought life on Earth to exist? Life on Earth cannot exist without its indi-

viduals, but a lost individual is always reproducible; a lost species is never reproducible. The answer to the species question is not always the same as the answer to the collective question, but because life on Earth is an aggregate of many species, the two are sufficiently related that the burden of proof lies with those who wish deliberately to extinguish a species and simultaneously to care for life on Earth.

One form of life has never endangered so many others. Never before has this level of question—superkilling by a superkiller—been deliberately faced. Humans have more understanding than ever of the natural world they inhabit and of the speciating processes, more predictive power to foresee the intended and unintended results of their actions, and more power to reverse the undesirable consequences. The duties that such power and vision generate no longer attach simply to individuals or persons but are emerging duties to specific forms of life. What is ethically callous is the maelstrom of killing and insensitivity to forms of life and the sources producing them. What is required is principled responsibility to the biospheric Earth.

Human activities seem misfit in the system. Although humans are maximizing their own species interests, and in this respect behaving as does each of the other species, they do not have any adaptive fitness. They are not really fitting into the evolutionary processes of ongoing biological conservation and elaboration. Their cultures are not really dynamically stable in their ecosystems. Such behavior is therefore not right. Yet humanistic ethical systems limp when they try to prescribe right conduct here. They seem misfits in the roles most recently demanded of them.

If, in this world of uncertain moral convictions, it makes any sense to assert that one ought not to kill individuals without justification, it makes more sense to assert that one ought not to superkill the species without superjustification. Several billion years' worth of creative toil, several million species of teeming life, have been handed over to the care of this late-coming species in which mind has flowered and morals have emerged. Ought not this sole moral species do something less self-interested than count all the produce of an evolutionary ecosystem as nothing but human resources? Such an attitude hardly seems biologically informed, much less ethically adequate. It is too provincial for intelligent humanity. Life on Earth is a many-splendored thing; extinction dims its luster. An ethics of respect for life is urgent at the level of species.

Ecosystems

A species is what it is where it is. No environmental ethics has found its way on Earth until it finds an ethic for the biotic communities in which all destinies are entwined. "A thing is right," urged Aldo Leopold (1968 [1949]), "when it tends to preserve the integrity, stability, and beauty of the biotic community. It is wrong when it tends otherwise." Again, we have two parts to the ethic: first, that ecosystems exist, both in the wild and in support of culture; second, that ecosystems ought to exist, both for what they are in themselves and as modified by culture. Again, we must move with care from the biological assertions to the ethical assertions.

Giant forest fires raged over Yellowstone National Park in the summer of 1988, consuming nearly a million acres despite the efforts of a thousand fire fighters. By far the largest ever known in the park, the fires seemed a disaster. But the Yellowstone land ethic enjoined: "Let nature take its course; let it burn." So the fires were not fought at first, but in midsummer, national authorities overrode that policy and ordered the fires put out. Even then, weeks later, fires continued to burn, partly because they were too big to control but partly too because Yellowstone personnel did not really want the fires put out. Despite the evident destruction of trees, shrubs, and wildlife, they believe that fires are a good thing—even when the elk and bison leave the park in search of food and are shot by hunters. Fires reset succession, release nutrients, recycle materials, and renew the biotic community. (Nearby, in the Teton wilderness, a storm blew down fifteen thousand acres of trees, and some people proposed that the area be disclassified from wilderness to allow commercial salvage of the timber. But a similar environmental ethic said, "No, let it rot.")

Aspen are important in the Yellowstone ecosystem. Although some aspen stands are climax and self-renewing, many are seral and give way to conifers. Aspen groves support many birds and much wildlife, especially beavers, whose activities maintain the riparian zones. Aspen are rejuvenated after fires, and the Yellowstone land ethic wants the aspen for their critical role in the biotic community.

Elk browse the young aspen stems. To a degree this is a good thing, because it provides the elk with critical nitrogen, but in excess it is a bad thing. The elk have no predators, because the wolves are gone, and as a result the elk overpopulate. Excess elk also destroy the willows, and that destruction in turn destroys the beavers. So, in addition to letting fires burn, rejuvenating the aspen might require park managers to cull hundreds of elk—all for the sake of a healthy ecosystem.

The Yellowstone ethic wishes to restore wolves to the greater Yellowstone ecosystem. At the level of species, this change is desired because of what the wolf is in itself, but it is also desired because the greater Yellowstone ecosystem does not have its full integrity, stability, and beauty without this majestic animal at the top of the trophic pyramid. Restoring the wolf as a top predator would mean suffering and death for many elk, but that would be a good thing for the aspen and willows, the beavers, and the riparian habitat, and would have mixed benefits for the bighorns and mule deer (the overpopulating elk consume their food, but the sheep and deer would also be consumed by the wolves). Restoration of wolves would be done over the protests of ranchers who worry about wolves eating their cattle; many of them also believe that the wolf is a bloodthirsty killer, a bad kind. Nevertheless, the Yellowstone ethic demands wolves, as it does fires, in appropriate respect for life in its ecosystem.

Letting nature take its ecosystemic course is why the Yellowstone ethic forbade rescuing the drowning bison but required rescuing the sow grizzly and her cubs, the latter case to insure that the big predators remain. After the bison drowned, coyotes, foxes, magpies, and ravens fed on the carcass. Later, even a grizzly bear fed on it. All this is a good thing because the system cycles on. On that account, rescuing the whales trapped in the winter ice seems less of a good thing, when we note that rescuers had to drive away polar bears that attempted to eat the dying whales.

Classical, humanistic ethics finds ecosystems to be unfamiliar territory. It is difficult to get the biology right and, superimposed on the biology, to get the ethics right. Fortunately, it is often evident that human welfare depends on ecosystemic support, and in this sense all our legislation about clean air, clean water, soil conservation, national and state forest policies, pollution controls, renewable resources, and so forth is concerned about ecosystem-level processes. Furthermore, humans find much of value preserving wild ecosystems, and our wilderness and park system is impressive.

Still, a comprehensive environmental ethics needs the best, naturalistic reasons, as well as the good, humanistic ones, for respecting ecosystems. Ecosystems generate and support life, keep selection pressures high, enrich situated fitness, and allow congruent kinds to evolve in their places with sufficient containment. The ecologist finds that ecosystems are objectively satisfactory communities in the sense that organismic needs are sufficiently met for species to survive and flourish, and the critical ethicist finds (in a subjective judgment matching the objective process) that such ecosystems are satisfactory communities to which to attach duty. Our concern must be for the fundamental unit of survival.

An ecosystem, the conservative ethicist will say, is too low a level of organization to be respected intrinsically. Ecosystems can seem little more than random, statistical processes. A forest can seem a loose collection of externally related parts, the collection of fauna and flora a jumble, hardly a community. The plants and animals within an ecosystem have needs, but their interplay can seem simply a matter of distribution and abundance, birth rates and death rates, population densities, parasitism and predation, dispersion, checks and balances, and stochastic process. Much is not organic at all (rain, groundwater, rocks, soil particles, air), and some organic material is dead and decaying debris (fallen trees, scat, humus). These things have no organized needs. There is only catch-as-catch-can scrimmage for nutrients and energy, not really enough of an integrated process to call the whole a community.

Unlike higher animals, ecosystems have no experiences; they do not and cannot care. Unlike plants, an ecosystem has no organized center, no genome. It does not defend itself against injury or death. Unlike a species, there is no ongoing telos, no biological identity reinstantiated over time. The organismic parts are more complex than the community whole. More troublesome still, an ecosystem can seem a jungle where the fittest survive, a place of contest and conflict, beside which the organism is a model of cooperation. In animals the heart, liver, muscles, and brain are tightly integrated, as are the leaves, cambium, and roots in

plants. But the so-called ecosystem community is pushing and shoving between rivals, each aggrandizing itself, or else seems to be all indifference and haphazard juxtaposition—nothing to call forth our admiration.

Environmental ethics must break through the boundary posted by disoriented ontological conservatives, who hold that only organisms are real, actually existing as entities, whereas ecosystems are nominal—just interacting individuals. Oak trees are real, but forests are nothing but collections of trees. But any level is real if it shapes behavior on the level below it. Thus, the cell is real because that pattern shapes the behavior of amino acids; the organism, because that pattern coordinates the behavior of hearts and lungs. The biotic community is real because the niche shapes the morphology of the oak trees within it. Being real at the level of community requires only an organization that shapes the behavior of its members.

The challenge is to find a clear model of community and to discover an ethics for it: better biology for better ethics. Even before the rise of ecology, biologists began to conclude that the combative survival of the fittest distorts the truth. The more perceptive model is coaction in adapted fit. Predator and prey, parasite and host, grazer and grazed, are contending forces in a dynamic process in which the well-being of each is bound up with the other—coordinated as much as heart and liver are coordinated organically. The ecosystem supplies the coordinates through which each organism moves, outside which the species cannot really be located.

The community connections are looser than the organism's internal interconnections but are not less significant. Admiring organic unity in organisms and stumbling over environmental looseness is like valuing mountains and despising valleys. The matrix that the organism requires to survive is the open, pluralistic ecological system. Internal complexity—heart, liver, muscles, brain—arises as a way of dealing with a complex, tricky environment. The skin-out processes are not just the support; they are the subtle source of the skin-in processes. In the complete picture, the outside is as vital as the inside. Had there been either simplicity or lockstep concentrated unity in the environment, no organismic unity could have evolved. Nor would it remain. There would be less elegance in life.

To look at one level for what is appropriate at another makes a mistake in categories. One should not look for a single center or program in ecosystems, much less for subjective experiences. Instead, one should look for a matrix, for interconnections between centers (individual plants and animals, dynamic lines of speciation), for creative stimulus and open-ended potential. Everything will be connected to many other things, sometimes by obligate associations but more often by partial and pliable dependencies, and, among other things, there will be no significant interactions. There will be functions in a communal sense: shunts and crisscrossing pathways, cybernetic subsystems and feedback loops. An order arises spontaneously and systematically when many self-concerned units jostle and seek to fulfill their own programs, each doing its own thing and forced into informed interaction.

An ecosystem is a productive, projective system. Organisms defend only their selves, with individuals defending their continuing survival and with species increasing the numbers of kinds. But the evolutionary ecosystem spins a bigger story, limiting each kind, locking it into the welfare of others, promoting new arrivals, increasing kinds and the integration of kinds. Species increase their kind, but ecosystems increase kinds, superposing the latter increase onto the former. Ecosystems are selective systems, as surely as organisms are selective systems. The natural selection comes out of the system and is imposed on the individual. The individual is programmed to make more of its kind, but more is going on systemically than that; the system is making more kinds.

Communal processes—the competition between organisms, statistically probable interactions, plant and animal successions, speciation over historical time—generate an ever-richer community. Hence the evolutionary toil, elaborating and diversifying the biota, that once began with no species and results today in five million species, increasing over time the quality of lives in the upper rungs of the trophic pyramids. One-celled organisms evolved into many-celled, highly integrated organisms. Photosynthesis evolved and came to support locomotion—swimming, walking, running, flight. Stimulus-response mechanisms became complex instinctive acts. Warm-blooded animals followed cold-blooded ones. Complex nervous systems, conditioned behavior, and learning emerged. Sentience appeared—sight, hearing, smell, taste, pleasure, pain. Brains coupled with hands. Consciousness and self-consciousness arose. Culture was superposed on nature.

These developments do not take place in all ecosystems or at every level. Microbes, plants, and lower animals remain, good of their kinds and, serving continuing roles, good for other kinds. The understories remain occupied. As a result, the quantity of life and its diverse qualities continue—from protozoans to primates to people. There is a push-up, lock-up ratchet effect that conserves the upstrokes and the outreaches. The later we go in time, the more accelerated are the forms at the top of the trophic pyramids, the more elaborated are the multiple trophic pyramids of Earth. There are upward arrows over evolutionary time.

The system is a game with loaded dice, but the loading is a pro-life tendency, not mere stochastic process. Though there is no Nature in the singular, the system has a nature, a loading that pluralizes, putting natures into diverse kinds: $nature_1$, $nature_2$, $nature_3$ . . . $nature_n$. It does so using random elements (in both organisms and communities), but this is a secret of its fertility, producing steadily intensified interdependencies and options. An ecosystem has no head, but it heads toward species diversification, support, and richness. Though not a superorganism, it is a kind of vital field.

Instrumental value uses something as a means to an end; intrinsic value is worthwhile in itself. No warbler eats insects to become food for a falcon; the warbler defends its own life as an end in itself and makes more warblers as it can. A life is defended intrinsically, without further contributory reference. But neither of these traditional terms is satisfactory at the level of the ecosystem. Though it has value *in* itself, the system does not have any value *for* itself. Though it is a value producer, it is not a value owner. We are no longer confronting instrumental value, as though the system were of value instrumentally as a fountain of life. Nor is the question one of intrinsic value, as though the system defended some unified form of life for itself. We have reached something for which we need a third term: systemic value. Duties arise in encounters with the system that projects and protects these member components in biotic community.

Ethical conservatives, in the humanistic sense, will say that ecosystems are of value only because they contribute to human experiences. But that mistakes the last chapter for the whole story, one fruit for the whole plant. Humans count enough to have the right to flourish in ecosystems, but not so much that they have the right to degrade or shut down ecosystems, not at least without a burden of proof that there is an overriding cultural gain. Those who have traveled partway into environmental ethics will say that ecosystems are of value because they contribute to animal experiences or to organismic life. But the really conservative, radical view sees that the stability, integrity, and beauty of biotic communities are what are most fundamentally to be conserved. In a comprehensive ethics of respect for life, we ought to set ethics at the level of ecosystems alongside classical, humanistic ethics.

Value Theory

In practice the ultimate challenge of environmental ethics is the conservation of life on Earth. In principle the ultimate challenge is a value theory profound enough to support that ethics. In nature there is negentropic construction in dialectic with entropic teardown, a process for which we hardly yet have an adequate scientific theory, much less a valuational theory. Yet this is nature's most striking feature, one that ultimately must be valued and of value. In one sense, nature is indifferent to mountains, rivers, fauna, flora, forests, and grasslands. But in another sense, nature has bent toward making and remaking these projects, millions of kinds, for several billion years.

These performances are worth noticing, are remarkable and memorable—and not just because of their tendencies to produce something else; certainly not merely because of their tendency to produce this noticing in certain recent subjects, our human selves. These events are loci of value as products of systemic nature in its formative processes. The splendors of Earth do not simply lie in their roles as human resources, supports of culture, or stimulators of experience. The most plausible account will find some programmatic evolution toward value, and not because it ignores Darwin but because it heeds his principle of natural selection and deploys it into a selection exploring new niches and elaborating kinds, even a selection upslope toward higher values, at least along some trends within some ecosystems. How do we humans come to be charged up with values, if there was and is nothing in nature charging us up so? A systematic environmental ethics does not wish to

believe in the special creation of values or in their dumbfounding epigenesis. Let them evolve. Let nature carry value.

The notion that nature is a value carrier is ambiguous. Much depends on a thing's being more or less structurally congenial for the carriage. We value a thing and discover that we are under the sway of its valence, inducing our behavior. It has among its strengths (Latin: *valeo*, "be strong") this capacity to carry value. This potential cannot always be of the empty sort that a glass has for carrying water. It is often pregnant fullness. Some of the values that nature carries are up to us, our assignment. But fundamentally there are powers in nature that move to us and through us.

No value exists without an evaluator. So runs a well-entrenched dogma. Humans clearly evaluate their world; sentient animals may also. But plants cannot evaluate their environment; they have no options and make no choices. A fortiori, species and ecosystems, Earth and Nature, cannot be bona fide evaluators. One can always hang on to the assertion that value, like a tickle or remorse, must be felt to be there. Its *esse* is *percipi*. To be, it must be perceived. Nonsensed value is nonsense. There are no thoughts without a thinker, no percepts without a perceiver, no deeds without a doer, no targets without an aimer.

Such resolute subjectivists cannot be defeated by argument, although they can be driven toward analyticity. That theirs is a retreat to definition is difficult to expose, because they seem to cling so closely to inner experience. They are reporting, on this hand, how values always excite us. They are giving, on that hand, a stipulative definition. That is how they choose to use the word *value*.

If value arrives only with consciousness, experiences in which humans find value have to be dealt with as appearances of various sorts. The value has to be relocated in the valuing subject's creativity as a person meets a valueless world, or even a valuable one—one able to be valued but one that before the human bringing of valuableness contains only possibility and not any actual value. Value can only be extrinsic to nature, never intrinsic to it.

But the valuing subject in any otherwise valueless world is an insufficient premise for the experienced conclusions of those who respect all life. Conversion to a biological view seems truer to world experience and more logically compelling. Something from a world beyond the human mind, beyond human experience, is received into our mind, our experience, and the value of that something does not always arise with our evaluation of it. Here the order of knowing reverses, and also enhances, the order of being. This too is a perspective but is ecologically better-informed. Science has been steadily showing how the consequents (life, mind) are built on their precedents (energy, matter), however much they overleap them. Life and mind appear where they did not before exist, and with them levels of value emerge that did not before exist. But that gives no reason to say that all value is an irreducible emergent at the human (or upper-animal) level. A comprehensive environmental ethics reallocates value across the whole continuum. Value increases in the emergent climax but is continuously present in the composing precedents. The system is value-able, able to produce value. Human evaluators are among its products.

Some value depends on subjectivity, yet all value is generated within the geosystemic and ecosystemic pyramid. Systemically, value fades from subjective to objective value but also fans out from the individual to its role and matrix. Things do not have their separate natures merely in and for themselves, but they face outward and co-fit into broader natures. Value-in-itself is smeared out to become value-in-togetherness. Value seeps out into the system, and we lose our capacity to identify the individual as the sole locus of value.

Intrinsic value, the value of an individual for what it is in itself, becomes problematic in a holistic web. True, the system produces such values more and more with its evolution of individuality and freedom. Yet to decouple this value from the biotic, communal system is to make value too internal and elementary; this decoupling forgets relatedness and externality. Every intrinsic value has leading and trailing *and*'s. Such value is coupled with value from which it comes and toward which it moves. Adapted fitness makes individualistic value too system-independent. Intrinsic value is a part in a whole and is not to be fragmented by valuing it in isolation.

Everything is good in a role, in a whole, although we can speak of objective intrinsic goodness wherever a point–event—a trillium, for example—defends a good (its life) in itself. We can speak of subjective intrinsic goodness when such an event registers as a point-experience, at which point humans pronounce both their experience and what

it is to be good without need to enlarge their focus. Neither the trilliums nor the human judges of it require for their respective valuings any further contributory reference.

When eaten by foragers or in death resorbed into humus, the trillium has its value destroyed, transformed into instrumentality. The system is a value transformer where form and being, process and reality, fact and value, are inseparably joined. Intrinsic and instrumental values shuttle back and forth, parts-in-wholes and wholes-in-parts, local details of value embedded in global structures, gems in their settings, and their setting-situation a corporation where value cannot stand alone. Every good is in community.

In environmental ethics one's beliefs about nature, which are based upon but exceed science, have everything to do with beliefs about duty. The way the world is informs the way it ought to be. We always shape our values in significant measure in accord with our notion of the kind of universe that we live in, and this process drives our sense of duty. Our model of reality implies a model of conduct. Differing models sometimes imply similar conduct, but often they do not. A model in which nature has no value apart from human preferences will imply different conduct from one in which nature projects fundamental values, some objective and others that further require human subjectivity superimposed on objective nature.

This evaluation is not scientific description; hence it is not ecology per se but metaecology. No amount of research can verify that, environmentally, the right is the optimum biotic community. Yet ecological description generates this valuing of nature, endorsing the systemic rightness. The transition from *is* to *good* and thence to *ought* occurs here; we leave science to enter the domain of evaluation, from which an ethics follows.

What is ethically puzzling and exciting is that an *ought* is not so much derived from an *is* as discovered simultaneously with it. As we progress from descriptions of fauna and flora, of cycles and pyramids, of autotrophs coordinated with heterotrophs, of stability and dynamism, on to intricacy, planetary opulence and interdependence, unity and harmony with oppositions in counterpoint and synthesis, organisms evolved within and satisfactorily fitting their communities, and we arrive at length at beauty and goodness, we find that it is difficult to say where the natural facts leave off and where the natural values appear. For some people at least, the sharp *is–ought* dichotomy is gone; the values seem to be there as soon as the facts are fully in, and both values and facts seem to be alike properties of the system.

There is something overspecialized about an ethic, held by the dominant class of *Homo sapiens*, that regards the welfare of only one of several million species as an object and beneficiary of duty. If the remedy requires a paradigm change about the sorts of things to which duty can attach, so much the worse for those humanistic ethics no longer functioning in, or suited to, their changing environment. The anthropocentrism associated with them was fiction anyway. There is something

Newtonian, not yet Einsteinian, besides something morally naive, about living in a reference frame in which one species takes itself as absolute and values everything else relative to its utility. If true to its specific epithet, which means wise, ought not *Homo sapiens* value this host of life as something that lays on us a claim to care for life in its own right?

Only the human species contains moral agents, but perhaps conscience on such an Earth ought not to be used to exempt every other form of life from consideration, with the resulting paradox that the sole moral species acts only in its collective self-interest toward all the rest. Is not the ultimate philosophical task the discovery of a whole great ethic that knows the human place under the sun?

VI.B Food and Agriculture _____

68.   PREVIEW

Here you are creating millions of novel organisms, organisms that the Earth has never seen, and then releasing them into the environment. They are exactly analogous to exotic organisms like kudzu vine or those responsible for chestnut blight or Dutch elm disease. Any time you introduce an exotic organism into a new environment you are throwing the ecological dice. . . . Many of us have spent much of our working lives addressing the terrible ecological problems created by chemical pollution. [But] chemical pollution, however horrible, does dilute over time, and it can often be contained. However, once you release an organism into the environment it cannot be recalled or contained. It will not dilute but rather will reproduce, disseminate, and mutate. It is unstoppable.

Andrew Kimbrell

What kind of society isn't structured in greed? The problem of social organization is how to set up an arrangement under which greed will do the least harm; capitalism is that kind of a system.

Milton Friedman

What six billion people on the planet eat and *how* their sources of food grow—(typi-

cally grown by deliberate human effort as opposed to the simple harvesting of wild plants and animals) has enormous impact on our environment. Disease, the dust bowl, loss of biodiversity, extinction, malnutrition, starvation, obesity, mortality rates all are affected by agriculture and further processes of food production and distribution. In turn, these are much affected by commercial enterprises that range from selling burgers to seed, as well as correlative efforts by governments to foster or constrain the activities of private enterprise— both within countries and between countries. Prior discussions of animal rights issues and factory farming techniques, habitat destruction, the appeal to "efficiency" or "progress" and so on, evidently affect one's judgment about the acceptability of certain widespread agricultural practices. In this section, the focus is on questions about how food is produced as an end product but also on the way plants and seeds are created and marketed.

In recent decades scientists have learned to introduce the genes from one species into host organisms of other species. The technique, a type of *genetic engineering*, results in a *transgenic* organism. Many people have been surprised to learn of the reality of *cloning* techniques and the reasons for a moral dispute over *stem cell* research. Perhaps more startling is the fact that genes can be taken from flounders and introduced into an entirely different species—tomatoes—to enhance the latter's ability to withstand cold. To develop a desirable yellow color in certain tomatoes, scientists can look for colors in butterflies or other organisms for gene transfer to the tomato—and look not just among other tomatoes. Many corporations have jumped on the high tech bandwagon in altering agricultural techniques. A prime example is Monsanto, a company that produced seeds that can be used for only one season but were alleged to have offsetting advantages such as enhanced herbicide resistance; due to criticism of these "terminator" seeds, Monsanto has backed away from its project as of 2001. One dispute concerns the increasing power that large corporations have over farmers all over the world. Some of the protests against globalization and the World Trade Organization are motivated by the concerns that are discussed in this section.

Many economists and many conservatives celebrate the "sovereign" consumer and tend to assume that "more choice is better." Presumably they have in mind *informed* choices—as opposed to those offered by con artists. Thus we are tempted to think that we should allow consumers to choose to purchase *genetically modified foods*—the latter perhaps labeled with the slippery terms *natural* or *organic*. Curiously, the U.S. government has refused to require such labels—ones that would foster "eyes-wide-open risk-taking" and avoid certain more paternalistic types of intervention (in which restrictions are defended on the ground that they are *for the chooser's own good*). One might note an extraordinary contrast here between such foods and the requirements of drug labeling. Thus there is a moral dispute over labeling.

More fundamental disputes concern the "ecological risks of engineered crops," as one recent book is entitled. There are a number of important "pros and con," as addressed here in three discussions by Stephen R. Palumbi, professor of biology at the Museum of Comparative Zoology at Harvard University; Wes Jackson, head of the Land Institute in Kansas; and Richard Lewontin, evolutionary biologist at the Museum of Comparative Zoology at Harvard University. One basic question concerns the magnitude of the alleged extensive benefits of such crops either across the board or in particular cases. Are they part of the much heralded Green Revolution, which promises to alleviate the significant and tragic starvation of humans? (In contrast, recall biologist Garret Hardin's contrary reasons for letting masses die, discussed in Essay 47, "The Tragedy of the Commons.") Are those worrying about the ecological risks of such crops simply fussy, affluent Westerners who are indifferent to the plight of the world's poor and hungry? One question here concerns whether or not existing or future transgenic crops will actually help with problems of starvation; some, the "flavr saver" tomato designed for a longer shelf life, seem aimed at quite different results. Further, transgenic crops can produce large amounts of pollen, which can then alter the genetic structure of wild relatives; this can result in a loss of biodiversity or "weedy," resistant, out-of-control crops. Southerners are especially familiar with the history of the introduction of nonindigenous (nonnative) Kudzu, a Japanese plant introduced for the fine purposes of garden ornamentation and controlling erosion. As to its vigor, poet James Dickey in his poem "Kudzu" said "In Georgia . . . you must close your windows at night to keep it out of the house." Adoption of genetically modified seeds also can increase the tendency toward the creation of monocultures and their attendant risks (having one type of crop increases risk; the potato blight in 19th-century Ireland caused, in part, the widespread famine). But ask an Irishman about British policies at that time.

"Whether [genetic engineering] is a good thing or a bad thing for the plants (or for us), it is unquestionably a new thing,[1] according to Michael Pollan, an award-winning environmental journalist and contributing writer to *The New York Times Magazine*. In Essay 69, "A Plant's-Eye View of the World" makes concrete his exploration of the many issues surrounding genetic engineering by discussing what the Monsanto Corporation has done to the potato. As he reports, Monsanto's NewLeaf potatoes have within them a gene that resists a certain potato bug. The fact that Monsanto owns the gene in the potato raises ethical questions about the patenting of forms of life. Monsanto's ownership of the gene has also allowed them to investigate crops and prosecute farmers whom Monsanto accuses of stealing their property.[2] As Pollan explains, "the contracts farmers must sign to buy Monsanto seeds grant the company the right to perform . . . tests at will to prove they're the company's intellectual property." In one dramatic case, Vandana Shiva comments that a farmer's "fields were invaded by Monsanto's Roundup Ready canola. . . . But instead of paying [the farmer] for biological pollution, Monsanto is suing him for 'theft' of its property."[3] Perhaps most surprising of all is the fact that the NewLeaf is itself registered as a pesticide. This phenomenon bears out Patricia Hyne's 1992 prediction that biotechnology will not free us from chemical solutions. (See the commentary on *Silent Spring* in the Preview to Section VI.E.)

As he eats his potato salad, Pollan reports that he wonders, ". . . which ingredient was more likely to be hazardous to my health, the NewLeafs or the . . . Russets I *knew* to be full of poison. . . ."[4] It seems that there are three ways to grow potatoes: (1) dousing them with chemicals, (2) using genetically engineered seeds that allow for fewer chemical sprayings, or (3) using organic methods. In his discussion of alternative ways to farm, Pollan introduces us to farmer Danny Forsyth. Forsyth grows acres of potatoes for commercial use by conventional methods (1 and 2 above) because he feels he has no choice. But he uses organic methods for his personal food. He says, "I like to eat organic food, and in fact I grow a lot of it at the house. The vegetables we buy at the market we just wash and wash and wash. I'm not sure I should be saying this, but I always plant a small area of potatoes without any chemicals. By the end of the season, my field potatoes are fine to eat, but any potatoes I pulled today are probably still full of systemics. I don't eat them."[5] One might consider Forsyth's choice and the options he faces.

We mentioned Monsanto's patent, but it is an astonishing fact of modern life that forms of life may be legally patented. Often when no one owns something it is neglected and not taken care of; compare the usual state of public versus private bathrooms (see Essay 47) — as economists often remind us. Thus, a fuller distribution of property rights over things we want protected seems like a good thing. But are there no limits here? Life itself? English philosopher John Locke (1632–1704) claimed that we acquire a moral right to something previously unowned if we *mix our labor* with it for example, a plot of land. But does one *own* a feral dog if one feeds it? Does one own her kidney? Does one own his children? If one finds an abandoned child and feeds it for two months, does one come to have property rights in it? A parody of the news (at theonion.com) reported that Bill Gates had patented ones and zeroes. Are not some things the common heritage of all humankind? Today, Monsanto owns nearly half of the seed supply, and much of the rest is owned by Dupont.[6] Should seeds be part of our common heritage or the intellectual property of corporations? Does the view that it is all right to patent things never before patented presuppose a we-are-lords-of-all-creation attitude? Should we allow the patenting of any or all forms of life? As transgenic organisms are created, and as research on stem cells proceeds, these are serious moral and legal questions.

Readers are directed to Essay 70 by Claudia Mills, "Patenting Life," for help in beginning to explore these issues.

Stephen Palumbi, author of the book, *The Evolution Explosion*, and Essay 71, "Brute-Force Genetic Engineering," discusses further the closely related case in point: the development and use of genetically modified crops. *Artificial selection* produces genetic change—as the breeding of pedigreed dogs shows. So does *genetic modification*. The U.S. Department of Agriculture treats the latter as if it is not relevantly different from the former. The matter is not uncontroversial. Palumbi notes that "Brute-force genetic manipulation seeks to alter a solitary gene in a small number of plants and immediately produce a population-wide desirable trait—but selection almost never works so single-mindedly. Typically *many interacting genes,* not to mention environmental conditions, affect the production of an overt macrotrait; in this respect see his striking example of the extraordinary adaptation of Tibetan Yaks to function at altitudes above 10,000 feet. Artificial selection typically produces changes slowly—over many generations; genetic engineering can cause instant change. Plug a gene in and see what happens. A key concern is what the result will be—over the long and short term—and the uncertainty and difficulty of predicting. An effort to overcome this problem involves initially testing new plants *in the field.* But genes can escape their host plants, for example by the spread of pollen, and enter weed species. What might occur? Can this result possibly be avoided by available techniques? Are the private corporations that do this playing Russian roulette? Is this not a new, indeed radical intrusion into natural processes? We accept many intrusions of course, but have we correctly estimated the potential costs in this type of case? Can the policy of the U.S. Department of Agriculture—to treat genetically modified crops as subject to the same standards as other crops—be

defended? Protests over "globalization" are in part protests over the great power that corporations have over our lives and the lives of people in all nations. Global trade agreements make it difficult or impossible for people in many nations to reject the importation of foods created by methods that many think immoral and over which there is dubious democratic control. In the fall of 2001, the administration of President George W. Bush complained to European nations belonging to the European Union that their regulations on importing genetically modified foods "discriminate against U.S. products in violation of World Trade Organization requirements."[7] One wonders if U.S. efforts to prevent the importing of British cattle into the United States, because of fears of hoof and mouth disease, analogously "discriminate" against British policies. Thus, there is here an intertwined set of issues concerning genetic risks, fair trade, and controls over corporate and national power.

Evolutionary biologist Richard Lewontin critically reviews some recent discussions of the risks of using genetic engineering in agriculture. He notes that traditional, domestic modification of plants and animals has made many of them "unnatural." For example, maize with tightly adhering seeds would not survive in the wild. *Transgenic engineering* in plants, which inserts DNA from quite unrelated organisms into the plant to be modified, has mainly been aimed at producing pesticide resistance and pest resistance. He notes that ". . . any gene in any species can be transferred to any other species." How far has it all come? Lewontin observes that over 100 million acres are already planted in a variety of transgenic crops. Are the benefits worth the costs? Lewontin sides with those who believe "it has never been possible to come to a general agreement on the dollar cost of sickness and death." (Discussions in Section V.B focus on these matters.) Further, the parties that benefit are not identical with those on whom the burdens fall. Hence, a question of distributive justice or fairness arises.

Lewontin reviews reports on genetic engineering policy issued by the National Research Council, the research arm of the National Academy of Science (in the United States). He maintains that a "chief deficiency" with governmental regulatory policy is that *the relevant data on safety is not produced by the federal agencies themselves but by those seeking approval*—those concerned with private interests. One may speculate on the chances of a lack of bias here. He asserts further that no one has paid sufficient attention to the fact that *where a gene is inserted* in a recipient's genome is an important matter; the result could be that a protein normally produced in small quantity is now produced in large quantity, the possible consequence being a toxin in part of a plant normally eaten instead of a part not normally eaten (with tomatoes the stems and leaves are toxic, for example). Lewontin mentions a close call in this respect with genetic alterations of the Brazil nut. Finally, he calls attention to the larger economic context in which industrial capital with its new techniques has transformed agriculture, and the independent farmer is being converted into "an industrial employee." His final words are not filled with optimism for pursuing any other path. Lewontin aside, we note a theme that runs throughout many of these matters, the *loss of control*, loss by ordinary people over what they eat, over even *knowing* what they are eating, of nations in determining what they import, of farmers of a way of life, and of regulatory agencies knowing that the data they use are unbiased. Who is gaining control? In spite of all their benefits from time to time, one has to say: certain large corporations.

Is there a way to practice agriculture that avoids such risks and that can be sustained over generations? The research projects of Wes Jackson (biologist, environmental historian, and President of the Land Institute in Kansas)

are designed to answer this very question. Jackson's approach to good farming is to learn from the earth, to work with nature instead of against it. More specifically, Jackson maintains that "the best agriculture for any region is one that best mimics the region's natural ecosystems." In studying the differences between prairies and agricultural fields, Jackson proceeds on the assumption that good farming adapts to the environment instead of making the environment adapt to what we as consumers, corporate executives, or genetic engineers want.

Pollan makes a similar point in his critique of industrial agriculture's reliance on monocultures. Huge fields of identical plants are more vulnerable to disease and insects, and yet huge fields of Russets are what McDonald's requires to make the long, spot-free French fries that are desired by consumers and corporations alike. As individual consumers we demand long, "perfect" fries that can only be grown in a monoculture even though a monoculture is "poorly fitted to the way nature seems to work." It is vulnerable to the potato bug so the fields have been treated with chemical sprays, which in turn create problems that are being solved by engineering pesticide-resistant plants. "Fast food" practices are so influential in what many people eat and how that food is produced that a discussion of contemporary agriculture must examine them.

"Fast food" fulfills our need for calories, tasty food, and saving time. Concerns about such food sometimes focus on the long-term effects on human health, sometimes on the way in which large companies transform agriculture. As Eric Schlosser comments in his best seller, *Fast Food Nation*, McDonalds rose from a small business to become the largest private landholder in the United States. When McDonalds demands a potato that yields perfect French fries, one can bet that thousands of farmers dance to their tune. Ronald McDonald is said to be second in name recognition only to Santa Claus among young children in the United States. Even as many people who were reared as Catholics are questionably free to become Muslims or Jews or atheists as adults, one wonders to what extent widespread adult preferences for burgers by those weaned on "happy meals" since elementary school can be said to be "free choice" by the "sovereign" consumer.

In his wide-ranging book, Schlosser discusses not only social and marketing issues but also seems to be "channeling the spirits of Upton Sinclair and Rachel Carson," as the *San Francisco Chronicle* puts it. The selection included here by Schlosser—"What's in the Meat?"(Essay 74) —is frighteningly similar to Upton Sinclair's 1906 classic *The Jungle* that describes the unhealthy practices and horrible working conditions of the early 20th-century meat-packing industry: "the routine slaughter of diseased animals, the use of chemicals such as borax and glycerin to disguise the smell of spoiled beef, the deliberate mislabeling of canned meat, the tendency of workers to urinate and defecate on the kill floor."[8] Not so very different are Schlosser's observations on today's treatment of cattle, meat processing, and the working conditions in many fast-food restaurants where that meat is ultimately sold.

> The cattle now packed into feedlots get little exercise and live amid pools of manure. . . . Feedlots have become an extremely efficient mechanism for "recirculating the manure," which is unfortunate, since *E coli* 0157:H7 can replicate in cattle troughs and survive in manure for up to ninety days. Far from their natural habitat, the cattle in feedlots become more prone to all sorts of illnesses. And what they are being fed often contributes to the spread of disease.[9]

As one government health official put it, ". . . the sanitary conditions in a modern feedlot [compare] to those in a crowded European city during the Middle Ages when people dumped their chamber pots out the window, raw sewage ran in the streets, and epidemics raged."[10]

Schlosser attributes the problems of food safety and bad working conditions to the industrialization and centralization of agriculture. Many independent producers have been replaced by a few agribusiness firms. Centralization of production into just a few powerful companies allows those companies to oppose regulation, unions, and antitrust legislation. With few legal restraints on their operations, food production corporations can keep jobs such as those in meat-packing plants and fast-food restaurants as ones with little or no safety oversight, very low wages and few required skills. As Schlosser points out, even the work itself reflects centralization: fast food is "'assembled,' not prepared."[11] His critique extends to the quality of fast food:

> In May of 2000, three teenage employees at a Burger King in Scottsville, New York, were arrested for putting spit, urine, and cleaning products such as Easy-Off Oven Cleaner and Comet with Bleach into the food. . . . A Taco Bell employee said that food dropped on the floor was often picked up and served. An Arby's employee told me that one kitchen worker never washed his hands after doing engine repairs on his car. And several employees at [a] McDonald's restaurant in Colorado Springs independently provided details about a cockroach infestation in the milk-shake machine and about armies of mice that urinated and defecated on hamburger rolls left out to thaw in the kitchen every night.[12]

In addition to centralized production, meat-packing safety lapses, and fast-food factory jobs, turning farming into an industry has altered the raw material itself by genetic engineering. Another such alteration is the bio-engineered development of a bovine growth hormone (BGH) known scientifically as bovine somatotropin (BST). In their book on agricultural biotechnology, Sheldon Krimsky and Roger P. Wrubel note, "Recombinant BST was largely motivated by a few multinationals that invested heavily in the idea of a veterinary growth hormone for raising milk productivity. . . . [T]he large mechanized farms were receptive to innovations that could easily be integrated into their technological milking processes and would offer a profit without compromising the quality of the milk. The market for BST was the milk producers and not the consumers, who see no added value."[13]

"No added value" is hardly the pressing issue. What about the disvalue if BST does compromise the quality of the milk? The worry here is not only about the hormone residue in the milk but also the residue of antibiotics used to treat some illnesses of cows, such as mastitis that may be caused by BST. "Increas[ing] the rate at which cows contract mastitis, an infection of the udders that can be treated by antibiotics," is, according to Krimsky and Wrubel "among the most forceful and frequently cited arguments against the use of rBST."[14] Interestingly, "[i]n the [farmer] package insert of Monsanto's rBST product (Posilac®), mastitis, increased body temperature, and localized swelling are listed as possible side effects."[15]

In a 1993 review of the safety data on rBST, Professor of Agriculture and Veterinary Medicine David Kronfield concluded that ". . . pathologic changes in cows cannot be accounted for by increased milk production but are from rBST treatment."[16] His colleague, a toxicological pathologist, ". . . identified five pathologic lesions affecting the mammary, lung, kidney and joint tissue that increased linearly with dose."[17] Moreover, mad cow disease may be indirectly related to BST:

> . . . Cows receiving rBST require more energy-dense food than ordinary cows. One of the major sources of energy-dense food are the proteins from rendered

animals. If, as expected, BST will increase the amount of rendered protein fed to dairy cows, there is a likelihood that more cows will be contaminated with bovine spongiform encephalopathy (a pathogen found in rendered animals), and therefore rBST use will indirectly increase the spread of this organism.[18]

Industry and government reports, the authors maintain, tend to "gloss over" or give less attention to adverse effects on cows and "the indirect health consequences of new technologies."[19]

Krimsky and Wrubel note further that "[r]eputable scientific opinion, albeit a minority, remains skeptical over the official government conclusion on such key issues as safety of rBST to cows, the appearance of rBST in milk, the nutritional quality of milk, and the relationship between the synthetic growth hormone and residues of antibiotics and other secondary products in the milk."[20] These remarks remind us, as do Lewontin's, that scientists do not always agree.[21]

In a way reminiscent of Peter Singer's urged boycott of factory farm products (see Essay 15), Eric Schlosser maintains that consumers, despite the centralization of agriculture, do not have to accept bad food. "Nobody in the United States is forced to buy fast food. The first step toward meaningful change is by far the easiest: stop buying it. . . . [Businessmen] will sell free-range, organic, grass-fed hamburgers if you demand it. They will sell whatever sells at a profit."[22] Interestingly, consumers themselves could strike a blow against animal cruelty were they in sufficient numbers willing and able to alter their choices of food.

NOTES

1. Michael Pollan, *The Botany of Desire: A Plant's-Eye View of the World* (New York: Random House, 2001), p. 197.

2. For an extended discussion of this issue, see Vandana Shiva, *Stolen Harvest: The Hijacking of the*

Global Food Supply (Cambridge, MA: South End Press, 2000), pp. 90–93.

3. Ibid., pp. 92, 93.

4. Pollan, p. 221.

5. Ibid., p. 220.

6. Shiva, p. 81–82.

7. Alan Sipress and Marc Kaufman, "U.S. Challenges EU's Biotech Food Standards" (*Washington Post,* August 26, 2001).

8. Eric Schlosser, *Fast Food Nation: The Dark Side of the All-American Meal* (New York: Houghton Mifflin Company, 2001), p. 204.

9. Ibid., p. 202.

10. Ibid., p. 201.

11. Ibid., p. 269.

12. Ibid., p. 222.

13. Sheldon Krimsky and Roger P. Wrubel, *Agricultural Biotechnology and the Environment* (Urbana: University of Illinois Press, 1996), p. 190.

14. Ibid., p. 176.

15. Ibid., p. 178.

16. Ibid.

17. Ibid.

18. Ibid., p. 179.

19. Ibid.

20. Ibid., p. 188.

21. It is a good thing that scientists do not always agree; in 2001 the leader of the Max Planck Society apologized for the grisly medical experiments carried out in the name of science during Hitler's Third Reich [See *The News & Observer,* June 17, 2001]. These included forced sterilizations, and the killing of the retarded and the handicapped allegedly to improve the human gene pool. It should give one pause that outstanding scientists could do this, that today some science is "mandated" by corporations, which may not have defensible moral outlooks. No commitment to a method seems to preclude rationalization and callous disregard for rights. There is an admittedly limited but noteworthy parallel between current genetic experimentation done to improve the genes of plants and earlier eugenic movements.

22. Schlosser, p. 269.

69.   A Plant's-Eye View of the World

Michael Pollan

The garden is still a site for experiment, a good place to try out new plants and techniques without having to bet the farm. . . .

. . . Recently I planted something new—something very new, as a matter of fact—and embarked on my most ambitious experiment to date. I planted a potato called "NewLeaf" that has been genetically engineered (by the Monsanto corporation) to produce its own insecticide. This it does in every cell of every leaf, stem, flower, root, and—this is the unsettling part—every spud. . . .

The industry simultaneously depicts these plants as the linchpins of a biological revolution—part of a "paradigm shift" that will make agriculture more sustainable and feed the world—and, oddly enough, as the same old spuds, corn, and soybeans, at least so far as those of us at the eating end of the food chain should be concerned. The new plants are novel enough to be patented, yet not so novel as to warrant a label telling us what it is we're eating. It would seem they are chimeras: "revolutionary" in the patent office and on the farm, "nothing new" in the supermarket and the environment. . . .

Here at the planter's end of the food chain, where I began my experiment after Monsanto agreed to let me test-drive its NewLeafs, things certainly look new and different. After digging two shallow trenches in my vegetable garden and lining them with compost, I untied the purple mesh bag of seed potatoes Monsanto had sent and opened the grower's guide tied around its neck. Potatoes, you will recall from kindergarten experiments, are grown not from actual seeds but from the eyes of other potatoes, and the dusty, stone-colored chunks of tuber I carefully laid at the bottom of the trench looked much like any other. Yet the grower's guide that comes with them put me in mind not so much

From *The Botany of Desire: A Plant's-Eye View of the World* (New York: Random House, 2001). ©2001 by Michael Pollan. Reprinted by permission of Random House, Inc.

of planting vegetables as booting up a new software release.

By "opening and using this product," the card informed me, I was now "licensed" to grow these potatoes, but only for a single generation; the crop I would water and tend and harvest was mine, yet also not mine. That is, the potatoes I would dig come September would be mine to eat or sell, but their genes would remain the intellectual property of Monsanto, protected under several U.S. patents, including 5,196,525; 5,164,316; 5,322,938; and 5,352,605. Were I to save even one of these spuds to plant next year—something I've routinely done with my potatoes in the past—I would be breaking federal law. (I had to wonder, what would be the legal status of any "volunteers"—those plants that, with no prompting from the gardener, sprout each spring from tubers overlooked during the previous harvest?) The small print on the label also brought the disconcerting news that my potato plants were *themselves* registered as a pesticide with the Environmental Protection Administration (U.S. EPA Reg. No. 524–474). . . .

What is to rescue the American food chain is a new kind of plant. Genetic engineering promises to replace expensive and toxic chemicals with expensive but apparently benign genetic information: crops that, like my NewLeafs, can protect themselves from insects and diseases without the help of pesticides. In the case of the NewLeaf, a gene borrowed from one strain of a common bacterium found in the soil—Bacillus thuringietisis, or "Bt" for short—gives the potato plant's cells the information they need to manufacture a toxin lethal to the Colorado potato beetle. This gene is now Monsanto's intellectual property. With genetic engineering, agriculture has entered the information age, and Monsanto's aim, it would appear, is to become its Microsoft, supplying the proprietary "operating systems"—the metaphor is theirs—to run this new generation of plants. . . .

. . . Monsanto likes to depict genetic engineering as just one more chapter in the ancient history of human modifications of nature, a story going back to the discovery of fermentation. . . .

Yet this new biotechnology has overthrown the old rules governing the relationship of nature and culture in a plant. Domestication has never been a simple one-way process in which our species has controlled others; other species participate only so far as their interests are served, and many plants

(such as the oak) simply sit the whole game out. That game is the one Darwin called "artificial selection," and its rules have never been any different from the rules that govern natural selection. The plant in its wildness proposes new qualities, and then man (or, in the case of natural selection, nature) selects which of those qualities will survive and prosper. But about one rule Darwin was emphatic; as he wrote in *The Origin of Species*, "Man does not actually produce variability."

Now he does. For the first time, breeders can bring qualities at will from anywhere in nature into the genome of a plant: from fireflies (the quality of luminescence), from flounders (frost tolerance), from viruses (disease resistance), and, in the case of my potatoes, from the soil bacterium known as *Bacillus thuringiensis*. Never in a million years of natural or artificial selection would these species have proposed those qualities. "Modification by descent" has been replaced by . . . something else.

Now, it is true that genes occasionally move between species; the genome of many species appears to be somewhat more fluid than scientists used to think. Yet for reasons we don't completely understand, distinct species do exist in nature, and they exhibit a certain genetic integrity—sex between them, when it does occur, doesn't produce fertile offspring. Nature presumably has some reason for erecting these walls, even if they are permeable on occasion. Perhaps, as some biologists believe, the purpose of keeping species separate is to put barriers in the path of pathogens, to contain their damage so that a single germ can't wipe out life on Earth at a stroke.

The deliberate introduction into a plant of genes transported not only across species but across whole phyla means that the wall of that plant's essential identity—its irreducible wildness, you might say—has been breached, not by a virus, as sometimes happens in nature, but by humans wielding powerful new tools.

For the first time the genome itself is being domesticated—brought under the roof of human culture. . . .

Uncertainty is the theme that unifies most of the questions now being raised about agricultural biotechnology by environmentalists and scientists. By planting millions of acres of genetically altered plants, we're introducing something novel into the environment and the food chain, the consequences of which are not completely understood. Several of these uncertainties have to do with the fate of the grains of pollen these bumblebees are carting off from my potatoes.

For one thing, that pollen, like every other part of the plant, contains Bt toxin. The toxin, which is produced by a bacterium that occurs naturally in the soil, is generally thought to be safe for humans, yet the Bt in genetically modified crops is behaving a little differently from the ordinary Bt that farmers have been spraying on their crops for years. Instead of quickly breaking down in nature, as it usually does, genetically modified Bt toxin seems to be building up in the soil. This may be insignificant; we don't know. (We don't really know what Bt is doing in soil in the first place.) We also don't know what effect all this new Bt in the environment may have on the insects we *don't* want to kill, though there are reasons to be concerned. In laboratory experiments scientists have found that the pollen from Bt corn is lethal to monarch butterflies. Monarchs don't eat corn pollen, but they do eat, exclusively, the leaves of milk-weed (*Asclepias syriaca*), a weed that is common in American cornfields. When monarch caterpillars eat milkweed leaves dusted with Bt corn pollen, they sicken and die. Will this happen in the field? And how serious will the problem be if it does? We don't know. . . .

Yet what will happen if Peruvian farmers plant Bt potatoes? Or if I plant a biotech crop that does have local relatives? Scientists have already proved that the Roundup Ready gene can migrate in a single generation from a field of rapeseed oil plants to a related weed in the mustard family, which then exhibits tolerance to the herbicide; the same has happened with genetically modified beets. This came as no great surprise; what did is the discovery, in one experiment, that transgenes migrate more readily than ordinary ones; no one knows why, but these well-traveled genes may prove to be especially jumpy.

Jumping genes and superweeds point to a new kind of environmental problem: "biological pollution," which some environmentalists believe will be the unhappy legacy of agriculture's shift from a chemical to a biological paradigm. (We're already familiar with one form of biological pollution: invasive exotic species such as kudzu, zebra mussels, and Dutch elm disease.) Harmful as chemical pollution can be, it eventually disperses and fades, but biological pollution is self-replicating. Think of it as the difference between an oil spill and a disease.

Once a transgene introduces a new weed or a resistant pest into the environment, it can't very well be cleaned up: it will already have become part of nature.

In the case of the NewLeaf potato, the most likely form of biological pollution is the evolution of insects resistant to Bt, a development that would ruin one of the safest insecticides we have and do great harm to the organic farmers who depend on it.* . . .

I was surprised to learn that the specter of Bt resistance has forced Monsanto to temporarily lay aside its mechanistic habits of thought and approach the problem more like, well, a Darwinian. Working with government regulators, the company has developed a "'Resistance Management Plan" to postpone Bt resistance. Farmers who plant Bt crops must leave a certain portion of their land planted in non-Bt crops in order to create "refuges" for the targeted bugs. The goal is to prevent the first Bt-resistant Colorado potato beetle from mating with a second resistant bug and thereby launching a new race of superbugs. The theory is that when that first Bt-resistant insect does show up, it can be induced to mate with a susceptible bug living on the refuge side of the tracks, thereby diluting the new gene for resistance. The plan implicitly acknowledges that if this new control of nature is to last, a certain amount of no-control, or wildness, will have to be deliberately cultivated. The thinking may be sound, but an awful lot has to go right for Mr. Wrong to meet Miss Right. No one can be sure how big the refuges have to be, where they should be located, and whether farmers will cooperate (creating safe havens for your most destructive pests is counterintuitive, after all)—not to mention the bugs.

Monsanto executives voice confidence that the plan will work, though their definition of success will come as small comfort to organic farmers: the company's scientists say that, if all goes well, resistance can be postponed for thirty years. . . .

. . . Monsanto is acknowledging that, in the case of Bt, it plans on simply using up not just another patented synthetic chemical but a natural resource,

---

*What the emergence of Bt resistance might mean for the environment is harder to say. We have lots of experience with pests developing resistance to man-made pesticides, but what will happen if one of nature's own "pest controls" loses its effectiveness?

one that, if it belongs to anyone, belongs to everyone. The true cost of this technology is being charged to the future—no new paradigm there. Today's gain in control over nature will be paid for by tomorrow's new disorder, which in turn will become simply a fresh problem for science to solve. *We can cross that bridge when we come to it.* Of course, it was precisely this attitude toward the future that encouraged us to build nuclear power plants before anybody had figured out what to do with the waste—a bridge we now badly need to cross but find we still don't have any idea how to. . . .

Beginning this month, [farmer Danny] Forsyth will hire a crop duster to spray for aphids at fourteen-day intervals. The aphids are harmless in themselves, but they transmit the leaf roll virus, which causes "net necrosis" in Russet Burbanks, a brown spotting of the potato's flesh that will cause a processor to reject a whole crop. Despite all his efforts to control it, this happened to Forsyth just last year. Net necrosis is a purely cosmetic defect, yet because McDonald's believes—with good reason—that we don't like to see brown spots in our french fries, farmers like Danny Forsyth must spray their fields with some of the most toxic chemicals now in use, including an organophosphate called Monitor.

"Monitor is a deadly chemical," Forsyth told me; it is known to damage the human nervous system. "I won't go into a field for four or five days after it's been sprayed—not even to fix a broken pivot." That is, Forsyth would sooner lose a whole circle to drought than expose himself or an employee to this poison. . . .

After I talked to farmers like Danny Forsyth . . . while walking fields made sterile by a drenching, season-long rain of chemicals, Monsanto's New-Leafs began to look like a blessing. Set against current practices, genetically modified potatoes represent a more sustainable way of growing food. The problem is, that isn't saying much. . . .

Organic farmers like Mike Heath have turned their backs on what is unquestionably the greatest strength—and still greater weakness—of industrial agriculture: monoculture and the economies of scale it makes possible. Monoculture is the single most powerful simplification of modern agriculture, the key move in reconfiguring nature as a machine, yet nothing else in agriculture is so poorly fitted to the way nature seems to work. Very simply, a vast field of identical plants will always be exquisitely vulnerable to insects, weeds, and disease—to all

the vicissitudes of nature. Monoculture is at the root of virtually every problem that bedevils the modern farmer, and from which virtually every agricultural product is designed to deliver him.

To put the matter baldly, a farmer like Mike Heath is working hard to adjust his fields to the logic of nature, while Danny Forsyth is working even harder to adjust his fields to the logic of monoculture and, standing behind that, the logic of an industrial food chain. One small case in point: when I asked Mike Heath what he did about net necrosis, the bane of Danny Forsyth's potato crop, I was disarmed by the simplicity of his answer. "That's only really a problem with Russet Burbanks," he explained. "So I plant other kinds." Forsyth can't do that. He's part of a food chain—at the far end of which stands a perfect McDonald's french fry—that demands he grow Russet Burbanks and nothing else.

This, of course, is where biotechnology comes in, to the rescue of Forsyth's Russet Burbanks and, Monsanto is betting, to the whole industrial food chain of which they form a part. Monoculture is in crisis. The pesticides that make it possible are rapidly being lost, either to resistance or to worries about their dangers. As the fertility of the soil has declined under the onslaught of chemicals, so too in many places have crop yields. "We need a new silver bullet," an entomologist with the Oregon Extension Service told me, "and biotech is it." Yet a new silver bullet is not the same thing as a new paradigm. Rather, it's something that will allow the old paradigm to survive. That paradigm will always construe the problem in Danny Forsyth's field as a Colorado beetle problem, rather than what it is: a problem of potato monoculture. . . .

It's only in the last few decades, with the introduction of modern hybrids, that farmers began to buy their seeds from big companies. Even today a great many farmers save some seed every fall to replant in the spring. "Brown bagging," as this practice is sometimes called, allows farmers to select strains particularly well adapted to local conditions.* Since these seeds are typically traded among farmers, the practice steadily advances the state of the genetic art. Indeed, over the centuries it has given us most of our major crop plants.

Infinitely reproducible, seeds by their very nature don't lend themselves to commodification,

---

*Worldwide, it's estimated that some 1.4 billion people depend on saved seed.

which is why the genetics of most of our major crop plants have traditionally been regarded as a common heritage rather than as "intellectual property." In the case of the potato, the genetics of the important varieties—the Russet Burbanks and Atlantic Superiors, the Kennebecs and Red Norlings—have always been in the public domain. Before Monsanto got involved, there had never been a national corporation in the potato seed business. There simply wasn't enough money in it.

Genetic engineering changes this. By adding a new gene or two to a Russet or Superior, Monsanto can now patent the improved variety. Legally, it's been possible to patent a plant for several years now, but biologically, these patents have been almost impossible to enforce. Genetic engineering has gone a long way toward solving this problem, since it allows Monsanto to test the potato plants growing on a farm to prove they're the company's intellectual property. The contracts farmers must sign to buy Monsanto seeds grant the company the right to perform such tests at will, even in future years. To catch farmers violating its patent rights, Monsanto has reportedly paid informants and hired Pinkertons to track down gene thieves; it has already sued hundreds of farmers for patent infringement. With a technology such as the Terminator, the company will no longer have to go to all that trouble.*

With the Terminator, seed companies can enforce their patents biologically and indefinitely. Once these genes are widely introduced, control over the genetics of our crop plants and the trajectory of their evolution will complete its move from the farmer's field to the seed company—to which the world's farmers will have no choice but to return year after year. The Terminator allows companies like Monsanto to enclose one of the last great commons in nature: the genetics of the crop plants that civilization has developed over the past ten thousand years. . . .

*I say "such as the Terminator" because, after an international barrage of criticism, Monsanto has forsworn the technology. However, it has not forsworn a group of related technologies that achieve the same end: Genetic Use Restriction Technologies (GURT), which make it possible to turn genetic traits on and off by applying certain proprietary chemicals to genetically modified plants in the field. So even if the plant in question still produces viable seed, those seeds will produce worthless plants—plants with their disease or herbicide resistance turned off unless the farmer buys the chemical activator.

. . . The Food and Drug Administration told me that, because it operates on the assumption that genetically modified plants are "substantially equivalent" to ordinary plants, the regulation of these foods has been voluntary since 1992. Only if Monsanto feels there is a safety concern is it required to consult with the agency about its NewLeafs. I'd always assumed the FDA had tested the new potato, maybe fed a bunch of them to rats, but it turned out this was not the case. In fact, the Food and Drug Administration doesn't even officially regard the NewLeaf as a food. *What?* It seems that since the potato contains Bt, it is, at least in the eyes of the federal government, not a food at all but a pesticide, putting it under the jurisdiction of the Environmental Protection Agency. Feeling a bit like Alice in a bureaucratic wonderland, I phoned the EPA to ask about my potatoes. As the EPA sees it, Bt has always been a safe pesticide, the potato has always been a safe food, so put the two together and you've got something that should be safe both to eat and to kill bugs with. Evidently the machine metaphor has won the day in Washington too: the NewLeaf is simply the sum of its parts—a safe gene added to a safe potato.

I also phoned Margaret Mellon at the Union of Concerned Scientists in Washington, D.C., to ask her advice about my spuds. Mellon is a molecular biologist and lawyer and a leading critic of biotech agriculture. She couldn't offer any hard scientific proof that my NewLeafs were unsafe to eat, but she pointed out that there was also no scientific proof for the notion of "substantial equivalence."*

"That research simply hasn't been done."

Mellon talked about genetic instability, a phenomenon which strongly suggests that a biotech plant is *not* simply the sum of its old and new genes, and she talked about the fact that we know nothing about the effect of Bt in the human diet, a place it has never been before. I pressed: Was there any reason why I shouldn't eat these spuds?

"Let me ask *you* a question: why would you want to?"

*In fact, internal documents that have come to light as part of a consumer suit against the FDA reveal that several of the agency's own scientists also reject the notion of "substantial equivalence."

70.　Patenting Life

Claudia Mills

The inventiveness of the human spirit knows few limitations, but the patentability of its inventions is carefully regulated by certain key provisions of patent law. Any "process, machine, manufacture, or composition of matter" awarded a patent must be useful for some purpose and must be a genuine, non-obvious innovation. It must be truly human-made and not a "law of nature" or a "product of nature." In addition, the invention must lend itself to a precise, written description. Within these confines, patents have been awarded to millions of innovations, ranging from the neutrino reactor to purified vitamin B-12. But in the last few years controversy has arisen over whether patent protections should extend to tinkerers who create, not a new gadget, but a new form of life.

The question of whether existing statutes do allow at least some life forms to be patented was settled in 1980, when the Supreme Court upheld a patent awarded to geneticist Ananda Chakrabarty for a new strain of bacteria particularly suited for cleaning up oil spills. The Court ruled that Chakrabarty's discovery "is not nature's handiwork, but his own. . . . the relevant distinction [is] not between living and inanimate things, but between products of nature, whether living or not, and human-made inventions." In a similar case, *In re Bergy,* a lower court was even blunter: "the fact that microorganisms . . . are alive is a distinction without legal significance." The Chakrabarty decision, however, was a narrow ruling based on arguments about Congress's intent in drafting the relevant legal provisions. The question remains open: should current law be amended to bar the patenting of life?

Opposition to patenting life forms can arise from two distinct objections to it (among others). One is that even the lowliest of life forms has a dignity that should render it unpatentable. The second is that patenting lower life forms will lead to far more serious tampering with the workings of nature, which we would do well to resist while we can.

The Sacredness of Life

Activist Ted Howard, coauthor with Jeremy Rifkin of *Who Should Play God?*, inveighs against the Bergy decision for its denial that life has any sacred status. He charges that the court, in calling a living microorganism "a useful industrial tool," in essence pronounced that "life does not have to be treated as life at all." The claim seems to be that life itself, even at its lowliest, is invested with a sanctity that the patent process defiles.

What does this claim amount to? Certainly whatever sacredness is ascribed to life has to be squared with the fact that human beings are permitted to own all manner of individual (nonhuman) living things—and even to kill most of them, as wantonly as we please. With every step we take legions of microorganisms perish, and we are not judged the worse for it.

At issue here, however, are not individual creatures, but whole species. Does this make matters better or worse for the defender of life's sanctity? Philosopher Bryan Norton cautions that it is very difficult to argue that species as such have any intrinsic moral worth, since most moral systems are based, at bottom, on respect for the rights and interests of *individuals:* "to apply the concepts of rights and interests to species as collectives radically alters their very logic." Yet we do reserve special moral condemnation for genocide, the deliberate extermination of a *group,* as a worse evil than the random killing of the same number of isolated individuals. And we do have policies aimed at preserving species. So there may be some special worth attaching to a life form that is not possessed by its individual members.

But wherein does the sacredness of life reside? Just how sacred is some all but invisible strain of slime? What is there about the sheer fact of being alive that matters so much? It is hard enough, some argue, to draw a line between living and nonliving, let alone to claim that the line, once drawn, is of any momentous moral concern. Thus an amicus brief

Reprinted with permission from the Report from the Center for *Philosophy & Public Policy,* University of Maryland, vol. 5, no. 1, Winter 1985.

filed by the University of California at Berkeley in *Bergy* asserts: "Recognition of the difficulty that skilled scientists are experiencing in drawing a bright line between life and its absence effectively destroys the argument that life itself is not only *the essential characteristic* of *any* living being . . . but *the one* which . . . precludes patentability." On this view, it would have to be some other, further characteristic that makes the real difference, such as being able to feel, or suffer, or care, or reason. But these characteristics are absent from lower life forms.

Others, however, see respect for lower life forms as respect for our own distant ancestors in a great, unbroken chain of life—theirs is the vital spark passed on to us through eons of evolution. Leon Kass, writing in *Commentary,* suggests that "reacquiring a respect for our relatives, the ever-changing living forms, could regain for us a much needed recognition and appreciation of the natural and unchanging source of all change."

At this point one might ask: is disrespect for life shown by taking out patents on new life forms, or does the real disrespect lie in performing the research that leads to their creation in the first place? The research itself is where we "play God"; the ensuing patent may seem so much frosting on the cake. But Douglas MacLean, director of the Center for Philosophy and Public Policy, points out that respect for sacred values is exhibited in a variety of socially acknowledged ways. We show respect for the sanctity of human life, for example, by "forming conventions and ritualizing certain behavior and activities to transcend . . . the necessity of using and exploiting one another." These may take the form of taboos: collective societal decisions that there are some things we will not do. Refusing to patent life forms as so many more "industrial tools" may, then, be one way of expressing our respect for the value inherent in all of life. But it remains to be shown that prohibiting patents does in fact have this kind of social meaning.

After Microorganisms, the Deluge

A second group of objections is motivated by fear of what the patenting of lower life forms will bring in its wake. The possible adverse consequences cited are of two kinds: the nightmarish shift in our values and attitudes that might result one day in granting patents to the creators of genetically altered human beings; and the massive evolutionary disruption that might be wreaked once human beings dabble too far in God-playing.

In the dispute over patenting life, the question is repeatedly raised: if lower life forms are patentable, where will we draw the line? What meaningful distinction can be made to avoid extending the same patentability to higher forms of life? However, meaningful distinctions do not seem hard to come by, even if present law offers no grounds for making them. (As a matter of fact, the difference in complexity alone between microorganisms and higher animals makes it very unlikely that the latter will ever be capable of the "full, clear, concise, and exact" description currently required in a patent application.) If we believe that there is nothing in itself troubling about patenting microorganisms, but there is something in itself troubling about patenting species of higher animals, or ultimately human beings, we can point to whatever differences lead us to give a different answer in the two cases: differences such as sentience, consciousness, social relationships, reason. It may be difficult to pinpoint any precise break in the life continuum where we feel confident that all and only species to one side of that line deserve special protection. But that it is difficult to draw a precise line does not mean that it is impossible to make some rough, but workable, distinctions.

It is harder to answer the question: where can we draw the line to make sure that our genetic meddling doesn't have far-reaching and disastrous consequences? Jonathan Glover, Fellow in philosophy at New College, Oxford, thinks that this is the real worry behind the otherwise obscure charge that geneticists who create new life forms are "playing God." For if the prohibition on playing God "tells us not to interfere with natural selection at all, this rules out medicine, and most other environmental and social changes. [But] what makes [genetic engineering,] and not the others, objectionably God-like?" One answer may be, Glover suggests, that genetic changes may be both more drastic and less reversible than environmental ones, and we object to "a particular group of people, necessarily fallible and limited, taking decisions so important to our future."

Granted that fears of irreversible tinkering in the evolutionary process are valid ones, in what way are they addressed by a decision to place new limits on the patentable? The Supreme Court in *Chakrabarty* acknowledged the possible dangers of genetic research, but decided that "the grant or denial of patents on microorganisms is not likely to put an end to genetic research. . . . Legislative or judicial fiat as to patentability will not deter the scientific mind from probing into the unknown any more than Canute could command the tides." Kass agrees: "denial of individual patent applications seems a poor way for society to decide questions about allegedly dangerous research and technology. . . . As they are instruments for encouraging innovation, they are poorly designed for regulating or controlling it."

How, then, should the pace and direction of technological change be regulated and controlled? Threats to health and safety posed by new technologies can be dealt with by the sorts of regulations promulgated by agencies like the Food and Drug Administration and the Nuclear Regulatory Commission. But Kass argues that this focus on health and safety unduly constricts the full mea-

sure of our concern: "We have few means of assessing and regulating with regard to the massive consequences of new technologies to our mores, institutions, and ways of life." MacLean adds: "Our regulatory agencies are designed to protect the public from the harmful consequences of technological failure. With genetic engineering, our deepest fears seem to be directed toward the consequences of technological success. We are concerned about the ultimate ramifications of increased knowledge, and its applications. Neither our current regulatory laws nor the agencies that enforce them seem well equipped to address these social issues."

Patent law in any form is certainly inadequate to acknowledge these deeper concerns. Our challenge is to design institutional mechanisms that will allow us to express our respect for whatever it is we take to be sacred about all life and to control the growth and direction of new technology in a way that will allow human life to flourish to its fullest.

71. Brute-Force Genetic Engineering

Stephen R. Palumbi

Genetically modified crops stand at the center of an intense debate between consumers and industrial developers, and between governments touting the benefits of high-tech agribusiness and citizens unsure about the safety of genetic manipulation. The biggest question centers on whether gene-altered crops are any different from artificially selected ones. The U. S. Department of Agriculture, for example, considers genetic engineering just another form of selective breeding, likening the insertion of a bacterial gene into a sugar beet to artificially selecting beets for the same characteristics. Consumer advocates and scientific watchdogs such as the Union of Concerned Scientists are not yet convinced. They call for more comprehensive testing of potential genetically modified crops, and more careful consideration of potential risks before widespread environmental release.

Some caution seems warranted. Already, genes for herbicide resistance have escaped from their host plants to enter weed species through hybridization with pollen from crop plants. Such genes have also been up your nose if you've walked past a pollen-filled field of modified crops. Each bee carries those genes back to the hive in pollen sacks: They will be in honey. Each seed that escapes the thresher carries the gene into exile in next year's hedgerows or roadside verge.

Worry about such escapes rings throughout the agricultural world. But do these evolutionary manipulations differ from Mayan selection of corn thousands of years ago? Or French vintners crossing different vines to produce cabernet sauvignon grapes? Both artificial selection and genetic manipulation are a kind of evolutionary change. The first is an accidental mimicry of the forces of natural

Reprinted from *The Evolution Explosion: How Humans Cause Rapid Evolutionary Change* (London: W. W. Norton and Company, 2001).

selection, the second a purposeful mimicry of the imagined power of special creation. These similarities have prompted the U.S. Food and Drug Administration to regulate genetically modified crop plants in the same "generally recognized as safe" category it uses for strains developed by artificial selection. Whether genetic engineering and artificial selection are actually the same has turned into a battle for a very valuable high ground.

The major difference between artificial selection and brute-force genetic manipulation lies in the complexity of interlocking, multiple evolutionary changes that underlies most of the important differences we see between species. Brute-force manipulation seeks to alter a solitary gene in a small number of plants and immediately produce a populationwide desirable trait—but selection almost never works so simple-mindedly.

Usually, several genes contribute to any given trait, including many that control trait expression in an organism. For example, sexual maturity may be expressed early or late in the life of an individual—say, in a male salmon—which matures after six months at sea instead of a year and a half. Or expression of a trait may occur only in certain tissues, like the red color in Christmas poinsettias—but only in leaves surrounding the nondescript flowers. Virtually all genes are orchestrated by other genes, and without such controls, gene expression would be like the whole orchestra playing every note of a symphony at once rather than letting the music flow out one harmony at a time. Because of this, a quick fix to a genetic problem frequently is like a hasty patch of a tire blowout during a road trip—the fix will take you some distance, but probably not the whole way.

The Tibetan yak has a meaty magnificence coated in rough fur and wrapped in stoic power. The term "beast of burden" perfectly suits these biological machines of Himalayan survival, hooves and hair and lungs that thrive in the thin, high air, ferrying immense loads through mountain passes higher than many airplanes dare go.

Tibetan culture has marched on these animals' backs for millennia. Yak oil and butter are household staples—yak leather becomes clothing—yak horns are ground to make mortar. Yak strength powers the plow, spent to pull iron through stony soil and till fields closer to the sun than any other on earth.

Over the generations, Tibetan yaks have become so adapted to high altitudes that they suffer poor health below 10,000 feet. Their coarse hair, hanging in ragged, insulating cascades, combines with other integrated features of yak physiology to protect these animal from the rigors of the Himalayas. As described in Christopher Wills's book, *Children of Prometheus,* they have immense lungs—three times larger than those of similar sized cows—to pull oxygen from the miserly air. They have less hemoglobin in their red blood cells and fewer red cells in their blood than their lowland relatives. Thin blood allows higher capacity for temporary dehydration in the dry air and prevents blood cells from being forced out of ruptured capillaries by the high blood pressure required in high-altitude environments. Even the microstructure of their lungs differs. Yaks have thin-walled arterioles in their lungs, allowing better transport of oxygen into their bloodstreams.

Yaks have been altered in many ways by artificial selection over the centuries of Tibetan dependence. All these changes combine to allow yaks freedom on the high Tibetan plateau—no single change would suffice. The search for a "high-altitude gene" that would make regular mammals well suited to Tibetan rigors would fail—because no such single gene exists.

This example is not unusual. Evolutionary changes brought about by natural or artificial selection usually craft an entire suite of complementary attributes working together to produce an effective change in lifestyle. Seldom does a single genetic change suffice to create a major ecological difference in an organism. Should unicorns exist, they would differ from horses in more than a single "horn" gene. And in the heart of the yak, artificial selection must have acted on many genes at once to produce a domesticated beast where none other can live.

Artificial selection simultaneously selects for the genes providing a trait plus all the genes that control it. This inclusion of regulatory genes in the evolutionary process happens automatically because selection acts on the whole organism, not just a single gene. Desirable features and any potentially undesirable complications are balanced by the process of selection, an evolutionary personification of the human adage "You have to take the bad with the good." As a result, artificial selection must work on the end-product of all of an organism's genes as they act together to produce stems, roots, and flowers. The sum total is the most important—the way the pieces fit together determining success.

Artificial selection for fundamentally new traits crawls along because it must work on the balance of so many genes at once. While we can see rapid evolution in a generation or two for many traits, selecting for wildly different characteristics—like single-stalked corn from a candelabra-shaped teosinte plant—might take many generations and involve populations in the hundreds or thousands.

By contrast, genetic manipulation can be fast—inserting a trait never-before possessed by a plant almost instantly—and might involve the generation of only a few genetically modified individuals to act as Adam and Eve of a new crop variety. In the first case, artificial selection sorts among many genetically different individuals, each with a slightly different version of the desired features. In the second case, genetic manipulation generates a very small number of take-it-or-leave-it test plants.

These three differences between selection and engineering—inclusion of the necessary regulatory genes, selection for whole-organism success over several generations, and large population sizes with multiple variants—result in very different evolutionary processes and potentially very different outcomes.

Suppose your town wanted a practice area for the Girl Scout rifle team. One option would be to develop a rifle range, complete with professional operators, ear protectors, training classes, and unimpeded targets. Different sites could be compared, evaluated, and tested. Regulations could be developed to fit your community's priorities and altered as needed to fit emerging needs. That's one way of proceeding. Another way involves dropping the guns on Main Street and hoping that everything sorts itself out.

The brute force of genetic engineering is like dropping guns on Main Street. Engineers drop the trait into the organism, loaded with potential impact, and everyone hopes for the best. Usually, no regulatory genes are added except the few that activate the new genes. The complex and species-specific set of genes that control the timing of gene expression—or the tissues in which expression occurs—are in general unknown.

As a result, engineering a new gene into a plant does not guarantee that the plant will embody features planned by the molecular engineers—or envisioned by the stockholders. Engineering focuses on understanding the single genetic mechanism that controls a desired change, not the total regulatory machinery necessary to control it. Such engineering solutions might produce the wanted change—they might turn a plant into the desired evolutionary product. But most of the engineering effort has gone into the gene for the trait itself, not the regulatory genes. Because of this tendency, many engineering approaches focus on the rifles, not the rifle range.

Brute-force engineering has produced surprising results in one case. Joy Bergelson of the University of Chicago discovered in 1998 that a genetically modified mustard plant began to fertilize seeds of other plants 20 times more commonly than normal. Normally these plants produce pollen that fertilizes their own seeds, but in one mustard variety that had a herbicide resistance gene, use of pollen from other plants increased enormously. For reasons still not well understood, the gene-insertion procedure had multiple effects on the plant's fertilization system—effects not predictable by bioengineers.

Thus, when we use brute-force evolution, we must build in a stage for culling and sorting. In the final analysis, inserting genes merely engineers variation that can fuel the evolutionary engine. True evolution still must select among these variants. But the biggest difference between natural evolution and brute-force evolution lives here. Natural evolution is profligate with its variants, and cavalier about failures of individual, experiments, For every successful mutation—for every new trait that fits harmoniously into the whole organism like a new soprano in the choir—many, many fail. Evolution in natural populations is a great tinkerer. Selection sorts through hundreds, even thousands of combinations of different genes to find ones that work best—that work longest, in different climates, at different ages. The winning regulatory genes and trait genes function together in the plant to produce more seeds than other plants with other gene combinations. The winners declare themselves through higher levels of reproduction and survival.

Working within large populations, selection from generation to generation patiently culls the failures, waiting for a truly successful new combination of genes to arise. All mutant genes have to prove themselves in combination with all the other genes. Many combinations are discarded as failures before any are good enough to survive. Trial and error works in this selection process because there are so many gene combinations to choose from, and because the failures can die in droves. Evolution's dustbin overflows with partial successes.

Brute-force evolution produces fewer variants for selection to sort among. You wanted the gene to metabolize glyphosate in your soybeans? Here it is—inserted into a single plant, or maybe a small family. How many different ways of inserting genes are tried? How many different genes are employed? How many different ways to accomplish this crop goal are engineered? The costs of molecular development being so high, I'd be surprised if hundreds of different engineered products are generated for the same new trait. I'd be surprised if there were 10 different origins for the glyphosate gene in soybeans or the Bt gene in corn.

When these variants are so rare they also become more valuable—more difficult to discard. Here lies the biggest difference between selection of natural variants and a bioengineered crop—the willingness to discard products if they are not the desired result. Natural or artificial selection weeds brutally among the partially successful variants, but human engineers do not. Instead, human engineering has a long and successful history of tinkering failures into successes.

If failures are not discarded—if new gene combinations that have surprising or dangerous effects are not detected and eliminated—then modern genetic technology differs enormously from evolution by selection. Ironically, extensive field testing stands nowadays at the fulcrum of the environmental debate. Gene-technology producers, eager to expedite field trials, usually short-circuit normal evolutionary trial and error of their products by producing genetically homogeneous stocks that cannot evolve. Environmental groups, especially in Europe, object to the whole field-trial business, and have taken to farm sabotage against experimental crops. Ironically, both the bioengineers and the natural-varieties advocates hold evolution prisoner on the sidelines, given no opportunity to sort through genetic combinations that work best for the whole organism.

Humans use poisons to control the rest of the biological world, and they've worked, increasing food production enormously, and preparing us to feed the 10 billion people we expect for dinner within 50 years. Toxin-delivery ability has grown along with our batteries of genetic and chemical weapons, and now centers on the delivery of exquisitely designed poisons through a handful of manipulatable genes. Evolution has already played a prominent role in our development as chemical farmers, changing the potency of most herbicides and insecticides by producing resistant populations. Evolution certainly will play a more complex role in future development of genetically modified crops.

The question is not whether to use this technology to help double the world's food supply—burgeoning humanity leaves us little choice. But how do we best use genetic technologies? How will evolution of the crops by brute force, and evolution of weeds and insects by normal selection or escaping genes, change the face of agriculture? Biological engineers must admit their profession differs fundamentally from civil engineering, because bridges don't evolve but plants do—often in unexpected ways. The success of the unexpected is evolution's favorite trick, and engineering solutions must learn to accommodate astonishment.

72. Genes in the Food!

Richard Lewontin

1.

The introduction of methods of genetic engineering into agriculture has caused a public reaction in Europe and North America that is unequaled in the history of technology. Not even the disasters at Three Mile Island and Chernobyl were sufficient to produce such heavy and effective political pressure to prohibit or further regulate a technology, despite the evident fact that uncontained radioactivity has caused the sickness and death of very large numbers of people, while the dangers of genetically engineered food remain hypothetical. . . .

The uproar about so-called genetically modified organisms (GMOs) has been the direct consequence of the development of a radically new way to manipulate heredity. Human beings have been genetically modifying organisms since the first domestication of plants and animals. The results of those ancient modifications have been organisms that are not only very different from their wild ancestors, but are in many characteristics the very opposite of the organisms from which they were derived. The compact ear of maize with large kernels adhering tightly to the cob is very useful in a grain that needs to be gathered and to be stored for long periods, but a plant with such a seed head would soon disappear in nature because it could not disperse its seed. The history of domestication is precisely the history of the genetic modification of organisms to make them most "unnatural."

Until recently the method for producing new varieties of plants or animals has been to search for desirable variants and to propagate them selectively. The naturally occurring variation within species can also be augmented by matings with closely related species that do not ordinarily interbreed in nature, but will do so under conditions of domestication. So classical methods of plant and animal breeding have included "unnatural" transgression of species boundaries. But the use of the genetic variation available only from closely related organisms limits what can be accomplished precisely because they are closely related and therefore quite similar. Moreover, introducing genetic variation by crossing between organisms is imprecise. A cross between two varieties is indiscriminate in the hereditary characteristics that are transmitted. Thus if one attempts to introduce disease resistance into an especially high-yielding variety of wheat by crossing that variety with one that has the disease resistance but not the high yield, the result will be a variety with improved resistance but lower yield. The ideal of the plant or animal engineer is to be able to remake the heredity of an organism to order, so as to produce just those variants that the occasion seems to require.

Apparently the secret of genetic engineering was known to the ancients. Genesis 30 tells us that in order to retain the services of his son-in-law Jacob, who was apparently quite good at animal husbandry, Laban agreed to let him keep all the speckled and streaked goats and sheep that were born in the flocks that he tended. Jacob, the ur-biotechnologist, then peeled some twigs to make them speckled and streaked and held them up before the eyes of the plain-colored ewes just as they were about to conceive. This produced the desired result and Jacob became very rich indeed.

Being of little faith, we seem to have lost the twig trick, but have invented a new one. Modern genetic engineering consists in extracting the DNA corresponding to a particular gene from a donor organism and then inserting it into the cells of a recipient in such a way that it becomes incorporated into the recipient's genome. This insertion can be carried out by coating tiny metal particles with the DNA and shooting them into the recipient cells or by first putting the DNA into microorganisms and then infecting the recipient with them. If the source of the DNA is a distant species that cannot be intercrossed with the recipient, the engineered result is said to be a transgenic organism. The donor and recipient need not be anything like each other for the trick to work.

Thus the human gene for insulin has been successfully inserted into the genome of bacteria, and these bacteria, grown in industrial vats, are now churning out human insulin for the market. Despite the fears about the human ingestion of the products of genetic engineering, no one appears to be worried about the large number of diabetics who are injecting bacterially produced insulin twice a day. As far as anyone knows, no one has been harmed by this product of genetic engineering; but then, as far as anyone knows, no one has yet been harmed by any product of genetic engineering.

The chief use of transgenic DNA transfers in agriculture up to the present has been to provide crop plants with resistance to insect pests or to make the plants resistant to herbicides used to control weeds. The resistance to insects has been created by inserting into plants the genes coding for powerful toxins, the Bt proteins, from a bacterium, *Bacillus thuringensis*. When insects begin to nibble the plants, they ingest the Bt toxin and die. Resistance to herbicides has also been transferred into a variety of crop plants from bacteria, as well as from a variety of unrelated plants that happen to be resistant to particular chemicals. One of the ironies of the current struggle over GMOs is that advocates of organic farming practices who strongly oppose the introduction of transgenic crops containing the Bt genes have for many years promoted the dusting of the bacteria themselves on plants as an organic substitute for chemical insecticides.

While an irony, it is hardly the contradiction that proponents of GMOs suggest. The dusting of a toxin on the outside of plants, from which it could be washed away, is not the same thing as having the plants manufacture it internally. Although pest and herbicide resistance have been the main focus of transgenic engineering until now, anything seems possible. What makes the technique so attractive and so productive of anxiety is that any gene in any species can be transferred to any other species. Of course, some of these transfers will be harmful or even lethal to the recipient organism so that no practical use can be made of them; but there are no general rules to tell us what will work.

The critical point is that there is no limit to what could be done if it were worth someone's while to do it. Hundreds of plant varieties created by genetic engineering have been tested under guidelines approved by federal agencies, and several dozen transgenic varieties are commercially available, including corn, cotton, squash, potatoes,

canola, soybeans, and sugar beets. It has only been six years since the first transgenic crops were planted commercially, yet now more than 20 percent of maize acreage in the United States is planted in transgenic corn and worldwide there are about 100 million acres sown in a variety of transgenic crops, including cotton and soybeans.

The usual reaction of the federal government to widespread public agitation about public health and environmental issues is to tinker with already existing regulatory procedures. When scientific questions are involved, federal agencies or Congress will often request that the National Academy of Sciences, through its research arm, the National Research Council, produce an expert report to guide regulatory policy. Sometimes, however, the Academy will act even without such a request. The National Academy of Sciences is a self-perpetuating body of the American scientific elite that provides technical advice to the government. Its leadership, conscious of its legitimacy as a font of supposedly disinterested and expert opinion on scientific questions, will sometimes arrange for National Research Council reports unbidden, on the assumption that their weight of authority will have an effect on public policy.

The NRC has issued, without a formal request, several reports on genetic engineering since 1974, when it became clear that recombinant DNA techniques would be important as tools of genetic research and technology. Three of those reports have been directly concerned with the application of the techniques in agriculture, one in 1987 on the release of GMOs into the environment, one in 1989 on the safe field testing of transgenic varieties, and, in 2000, *Generally Modified Pest-Protected Plants*, which includes a discussion of both the environmental issues and threats to human health.

The creation of a scientific report on a contentious issue presents a special difficulty. On the one hand the drafting committee must include representatives of various constituencies with opposing views. So the committee that wrote the new report included academics involved in genetics, economics, and agriculture, a representative of a public interest environmental action group, a lawyer who helps clients to obtain regulatory approvals, and a state government environmental regulator. On the other hand, there cannot be a majority and a minority report, since after all we are dealing with Objective Science, and scientists either know the truth or they don't. NRC reports always speak with one voice. Such reports, then, can produce only a slight rocking of the extremely well gyrostabilized ship of state, no matter how high the winds and waves. Any member of the crew who mutinies is put off at the first port of call.

While usually artfully concealed, the machinery of forced consensus is apparent in the pest-protected plant report. The economist on the committee, Erik Lichtenberg, clearly felt that the sorts of regulation recommended by the report were not worthwhile and, indeed, would have costs not justified by any claimed benefits. He and his cost–benefit analysis are quarantined in an appendix and referred to only in a footnote: "This appendix was authored by an individual committee member and is not part of the committee's consensus report. The committee as a whole may not necessarily agree with all of the contents of appendix A." Of course, appendix A is merely economics, while the "committee as a whole" must necessarily agree with the contents" of the rest of the report or it wouldn't be a scientific report. In fact, the committee could have discounted the appendix on substantive grounds. Like so much of cost–benefit analysis, it fails to take account of the fact that the costs, possible ill-health, fall on different parties than the benefits, profits to corporate entities who produce the inputs into agriculture. More fundamentally, it avoids the deep problem that to provide a quantitative balancing of the books, the costs and benefits would have to be assessed in the same currency, while it has never been possible to come to a general agreement on the dollar cost of sickness and death.

2.

There are five general issues that are in contention in the struggle over GMOs. Three of these, threats to human health, possible disruption of natural environments, and threats to agricultural production from a more rapid evolution of resistant pests, comprise the agenda of the NRC report. The other two, disruption of third-world agricultural economies and principled objections to "unnatural" interventions, are deliberately excluded. Page 2 of the report states in italics: *The study does not address philosophical and social issues surrounding the use of genetic engineering in agriculture, food labeling, or international trade in genetically modified plants.*" In

analyzing the risks of GMOs the committee follows a general principle established in previous Academy reports, a principle that it regards as fundamental, namely that it is the product and not the process that matters. For the NRC it is irrelevant whether a variety has been produced by conventional genetic manipulations or by transgenic transfer of DNA. What counts is whether the new property of the resultant organism is harmful to health or the environment.

The NRC authors point out, quite properly, that the conventional methods of breeding, including sexual crosses between species that do not ordinarily cross in nature, might produce varieties with some heightened toxicity to humans or other species, or with unusual invasive abilities, or with greater resistance to pests that would hasten the evolution of more effective pest species. Jane Rissler and Margaret Mellon, in their extremely informative *The Ecological Risks of Engineered Crops*, give many examples of new troublesome weeds that have arisen from the hybridization of crop plants with their wild relatives and several where rare wild species have been driven to extinction by hybridization with crop plants.

Indeed, the only examples we have so far of the adverse effects of agricultural varieties on any animal or plant species in nature, including on human health, have been from conventionally bred organisms or from the introduction of invasive species from distant geographical areas, or from foods like peanuts or milk to which some people are naturally allergic. So if the usual products of agricultural practice already provide numerous examples of adverse effects, why is there the massive popular and political anxiety centered on genetically engineered crops in particular? None of the authors of the reports and books seems to have noticed that if it were really only the product and not the process that matters, then nothing has changed. The NRC report itself provides a protocol for protecting consumers against new food toxins and allergens (i.e., substances causing allergies) that applies irrespective of the genetic method used in variety development and which makes use of the already existing federal apparatus for the approval of new plant varieties.

First, one asks whether a new substance is found in parts of a plant that consumers eat or with which workers come in contact. If not, the substance is "exempt from health concerns." If it is found in such parts, then does it have chemical properties common to many allergens? If it does, then safety assessment is needed. If not, then is it similar to other substances that people eat? If not, then again we need safety assessment. The real problem revealed in the NRC report, although it did not seem to bother the panel, is that the data on which "safety assessment" is currently based are not produced by the federal agencies themselves but are provided by the very parties who are asking for approval to distribute the new variety in the first place. Moreover, no one seems to have noticed that there is, in fact, an aspect of the process of genetic engineering that does make that process unusually likely to produce unpredictable results.

All the attention has been paid to the physiological effect of the gene that has been put into the recipient, but none to the effect of where it is inserted in the recipient's genome. Genes consist of two functionally different adjacent stretches of DNA. One, the so-called structural gene, has information on the chemical composition of the protein that the cell will manufacture when it reads the gene. The other, the so-called regulatory element, is part of a complex signaling system that concerns where and when and how much protein will be produced. When DNA is inserted into the genome of a recipient by engineering methods it may pop into the recipient's DNA anywhere, including in the middle of some other gene's regulatory element. The result will be a gene whose reading is no longer under normal control.

One consequence might be that the gene is never read at all, in which case it will probably be bad for the recipient and will never be part of a useful agricultural variety. But another possibility is that the cell will now produce vast amounts of a protein that ordinarily is produced in very low amount, and this high concentration could be toxic or be involved in the biochemical production of a toxin. Yet another possibility is that a toxic substance that used to be produced only in one part of a plant, not ordinarily eaten, could now be manufactured in another part. Tomatoes are delicious, but you would be ill-advised to eat the leaves and stems because they contain toxins. It is not impossible that a genetically engineered tomato might, by bad luck, start to produce these toxins in the fruit. Thus the process of genetic engineering itself has a unique ability to produce deleterious effects and, contrary to the recommendations of the NRC

report, this justifies the view that, all varieties produced by recombinant DNA technology need to be specially scrutinized and tested for such effects. Exactly how one would go about doing that, in view of the unknown nature of the danger, is uncertain. Even extensive testing on a variety of animals provides no guarantee of safety since there are plant substances that are toxic to some species and not to others.

As yet no one that we know of has been poisoned by a transgenic plant. There have been a couple of close calls, however. The most widely cited case is the Brazil nut protein produced by a transgenic soybean. In some subsistence agricultural communities, for example in West Africa, diets are severely deficient in an essential amino acid, methionine. Brazil nuts produce a protein that is rich in methionine and so it was thought that inserting the appropriate gene from Brazil nuts into soybeans would provide an easy fix for West African malnutrition. Unfortunately the Brazil nut protein is known to be allergenic and the transgenic soybean proved to be so as well, so the variety was never released.

Proponents of recombinant DNA technology like Alan McHughen point to this case as a proof that self-policing by a variety developer can be counted on to avoid disaster. One's confidence in self-policing is somewhat diminished, however, by the realization that the allergenic properties of the protein were well known before the Pioneer Hi-bred seed company ever started to develop the variety in the first place. At some point they must have realized that the Food and Drug Administration would have refused approval of the variety even under our present system of regulation. How one wishes for a transcript of the discussions in the company board room.

A major part of the NRC report and the entirety of Rissler and Mellon's book are concerned with ecological issues in the broad sense. One anxiety is that "superweeds" will be produced, dominant plants that will spread en masse either through cultivated fields or through natural habitats. Sometimes what is meant by "weeds" is unwanted species that are growing in cultivated fields. At other times these are confused with introduced invasive species like the European purple loosestrife that has taken over so many American wetlands. There are no known examples of hybrids between cultivated plants and wild relatives becoming superweeds that have destroyed natural habitats, largely because too many of the characteristics selected during domestication make cultivars—cultivated varieties of plant species—dependent on the tender loving care given to them by farmers. Nor will the addition of a gene conferring herbicide resistance or pest resistance change that dependence. Plants growing in natural habitats are not subject to herbicides, nor are they attacked regularly by the hordes of predatory insects attracted to the concentrated free lunch offered in cultivated fields.

On the other hand, more difficult weeds of cultivated fields certainly will evolve if herbicide resistance becomes incorporated by natural crossing into species that are already weeds. The fear of superweeds is promoted by the metaphor of "escape"' used to describe the passage of an engineered gene into a wild species. The image is of the mad scientist (or not-so-mad germ warfare biologist) who has created a virulent disease organism, ready at any moment to create a major epidemic unless it is rigorously confined to the laboratory or, better yet, destroyed. But transgenes are not spread like microbes, entering the body from outside. They are transmitted by reproduction of the entire genome of an organism, and if a cross occurs between an engineered plant and a wild relative, the result is an offspring that is hybrid in every respect, including all those characteristics that make cultivated varieties so ill-adapted to survival in nature, such as their demands for unnaturally high levels of nitrogen fertilizer.

The opponents of GMOs are not alone in the misuse of the image of "escape." McHughen, in his manifesto against the regulation of biotechnology, claims that spatial isolation of fields in which transgenic crops are growing is utterly useless because the transgenes have already escaped onto roadsides and other fields through seed that is inevitably spilled from sacks, trucks, and machinery in the very process of transportation and planting. But this small amount of spilled seed is irrelevant. What is properly of concern is not the escape of a virulent infection, but that a constant rain of millions of pollen grains produced by hundreds of acres of a transgenic crop will over and over produce hybrids with weedy species at the margins of cultivated fields and eventually result in a new weedy form that will be unusually invasive or competitive.

3.

Most of what is written about GMOs is quite parochial, concentrating on their effects in North America and Europe. While we expect nothing more from the National Research Council or from an indignant Canadian plant engineer, the general lack of interest in the effects of biotechnology on the third world seems in contradiction to the rather moralistic tone of the public discourse. Predictably, the most famous example of a piece of biotechnology that is supposed to be good for subsistence agricultures is cited by McHughen, but, unfortunately, it does not do the work intended. A serious problem of nutrition in some rice-producing regions, causing blindness, is a lack of vitamin A. A transgenic variety, Golden Rice, has been created with the promise that if it is ever cultivated, it will provide the missing vitamin. But Golden Rice—not to be confused with Green Revolution rice—does not, in fact, provide vitamin A. It is enriched in beta carotene, a precursor of the vitamin (hence the golden color), which can only be converted to vitamin A in the body of an already well-nourished person. The developers of Golden Rice have not dealt with this problem in their publicity releases. Rissler and Mellon have a brief final chapter entitled "International Implications," but these are largely the extension of the ecological risk arguments already made for the United States and do not deal with promised nutritional benefits. . . .

The real present danger to third-world agriculture from transgenics, is elsewhere. Much of the agricultural economy of these countries depends on growing specialty commodities like lauric acid oils used in soaps and detergents, once found only in tropical species. Now, with recombinant DNA, these are produced by canola. Why buy palm oils from the politically unstable Philippines, where 30 percent of the population depends on it economically, when we can grow it in Saskatchewan? Caffeine genes have been put into soybeans. Why not Nescafé from Minnesota?

*

No unequivocal conclusions can be drawn about the overall effect of genetic engineering technologies. It is clear that any manipulation of organisms, whether by conventional means or by genetic engineering, poses some danger to human health, to present systems of agricultural production, and to natural environments. All of these potential effects have led to a fairly effective apparatus of government regulation whose chief deficiency is its dependence on data supplied to it by parties whose prime concern is not the public good but private interest. Nothing is significantly changed in this situation by the introduction of genetic engineering. The technology provides a method for transferring a specific gene into a crop, rather than the uncontrolled mixture of entire genomes that takes place when two varieties or species are crossed. On the other hand the random disruptions of regulatory genes of the recipient that may take place are totally uncontrolled. On balance, it is impossible to say whether we have achieved greater or lesser control over the unintended consequences of mucking around with nature.

We find ourselves in a puzzling situation. None of the books on the subject of GMOs gives us any reason to think that the known dangers to human health and natural ecosystems posed by agriculture have become radically greater because of the introduction of genetic engineering as a technique.

Nor do we even have a single case of a catastrophe that might have engendered widespread public anxieties. . . .

. . . The independent family farmer, tilling the soil, in touch with nature, making decisions about what and when to plant and harvest from his craft knowledge, sitting down at dinner to a groaning board of home-grown victuals prepared by his aproned wife, is our last connection with an authentic life. We want to preserve it. Unfortunately, we are a hundred years too late and GMOs are the wrong target. To understand the situation we need more mental fight and fewer arrows of desire.

The history of American and European agriculture over the last hundred years has been a history of the increasing dominance of industrial capital over farming. In 1900 the inputs into farming were predominantly self-produced. The farmer saved seed from the previous year's crop to plant, the plow and tillage machinery was pulled by mules fed on forage grown on the farm, 40 percent of planted acreage was in feed crops, and livestock produced manure to go back on the fields. Now the seed is purchased from Pioneer Hi-bred, the mules from John Deere, the feed from Exxon, and the manure from Terra. The rise in purchased industrially produced inputs has had two effects. A major

increase in yields per acre has driven down the price paid to farmers for their product. Simultaneously the farmers' costs of production have risen. There has been no escape from this dilemma for an individual farmer. Because the price paid for a farm product is determined by the aggregate production from all farms, no individual farmer can push prices up by holding down production. Thus he must increase production when other farmers do, but the result of all these individually economically rational acts is mass suicide. Smaller and smaller margins between farm income and expenses have led to increasing farm debt and bankruptcies.

The consequence of the growing dominance of industrial capital in agriculture for the classical "family farm" has been the progressive conversion of the independent farmer into an industrial employee. More and more farm operators and their spouses are only part-time farmers, trying to support their farming from outside income. That is why the confusion between farm family income and income from farming in the appendix to the NRC report is so misleading. In 1997, 60 percent of farm operators were also employed off the farm and 40 percent worked at alternative employment for more than two hundred days a year. They work as truck drivers, salespeople, secretaries, and factory workers. Car companies now put their assembly plants in the rural counties of the farm belt to take advantage of this labor force. It is not Jerusalem that has been built in the green and pleasant land, it is the dark Satanic Mills.

The creation and adoption of genetically modified organisms are the latest steps in this long historical development. of capital-intensive industrial agriculture. Roundup Ready herbicide-resistant soybeans have been created by Monsanto so that farmers will be able to use its powerful herbicide, Roundup, while at the same time buying Monsanto seed. The farmers accept the cost of the new variety and its chemical partner because the use of such a powerful general weed killer will reduce the number of herbicide treatments or mechanical tillage passages through the fields, freeing them for the hours in the automobile assembly plant that they need to keep their farms. For the farmer there is no escape from engineering, whether it be mechanical, chemical, electrical, or genetic.

73. Nature as the Measure
for a Sustainable Agriculture

Wes Jackson

At the Land Institute in Salina, Kansas, we use the prairie as our standard or measure in attempting to wed ecology and agriculture. When Wendell Berry dedicated our new greenhouse in March 1988, he traced the literary and scientific history of our work at the institute. To set the stage for understanding the institute's place in the grand scheme of things, I shall review the history he provided (Berry, 1990).

Berry first cited Job:

> . . . ask now the beasts, and they shall teach
> thee; and the fowls of the air, and they shall
> tell thee:
>   Or speak to the earth, and it shall teach thee;
> and the fishes of the sea shall declare unto thee.

Later Berry mentioned other writings. At the beginning of *The Georgics* (36–29 B.C.), Virgil advised that

> . . . before we plow an unfamiliar patch
> It is well to be informed about the winds,
> About the variations in the sky,
> The native traits and habits of the place,
> What each locale permits, and what denies.

Toward the end of the 1500s, Edmund Spenser called nature "the equall mother" of all creatures, who "knittest each to each, as brother unto brother." Spenser also saw nature as the instructor of creatures and the ultimate earthly judge of their behavior. Shakespeare, in *As You Like It*, put the forest in the role of teacher and judge; Touchstone remarks, "You have said; but whether wisely or no, let the forest judge."

Milton had the lady in *Comus* describe nature in this way:

> She, good cateress,
> Means her provision only to the good
> That live according to her sober laws
> And holy dictate of spare Temperance.

And Alexander Pope in his *Epistle to Burlington*, counseled gardeners to "let Nature never be forgot" and to "consult the Genius of the Place in all."

"After Pope," Berry (1990) has stated, "so far as I know, this theme departs from English poetry. The later poets were inclined to see nature and humankind as radically divided, and were no longer much interested in the issues of a *practical* harmony between the land and its human inhabitants. The romantic poets, who subscribed to the modern doctrine of the preeminence of the human mind, tended to look upon nature, not as anything they might ever have practical dealings with, but as a reservoir of symbols."

In my own region of the prairies, I think of Virgil's admonition: "Before we plow an unfamiliar patch/It is well to be informed about the winds." What if the settlers and children of settlers who gave us the dust bowl on the Great Plains in the 1930s had heeded that two-thousand-year-old advice? What if they had heeded Milton's insight that nature "means her provision only to the good / That live according to her sober laws / And holy dictate of spare Temperance"? Virgil was writing about agricultural practices, whereas Milton was writing of the spare use of nature's fruits. It is interesting that the poets have spoken of both practice in nature and harvest of nature.

Berry pointed out that this theme surfaced again among the agricultural writers, first in 1905 in a book by Liberty Hyde Bailey entitled *The Outlook to Nature*. The grand old dean at Cornell wrote, "If nature is the norm then the necessity for correcting and amending abuses of civilization become baldly apparent by very contrast. The return to nature affords the very means of acquiring the incentive and energy for ambitious and constructive work of a high order." In *The Holy Earth* (1915) Bailey advanced the notion that "most of our difficulty with the earth lies in the effort to do what perhaps ought not to be done." He continued, "A good part of agriculture is to learn how to adapt one's work to nature. . . . To live in right relation with his natural conditions is one of the first lessons that a wise farmer or any other wise man learns."

J. Russell Smith's *Tree Crops*, published in 1929, contributed to the tradition. Smith was disturbed with the destruction of the hills because

From *Ecology, Economics, Ethics: The Broken Circle*, ed. F. Herbert Bormann and Stephen R. Kellert (New Haven, CT: Yale University Press, 1991). Reprinted with permission of Yale University Press.

"man has carried to the hills the agriculture of the flat plain." Smith too believed that "farming should fit the land."

In 1940 Sir Albert Howard's *An Agriculture Testament* was published. For Howard, nature was "the supreme farmer": "The main characteristic of Nature's farming can therefore be summed up in a few words. Mother earth never attempts to farm without live stock; she always raises mixed crops; great pains are taken to preserve the soil and to prevent erosion; the mixed vegetable and animal wastes are converted into humus; there is no waste; the processes of growth and the processes of decay balance one another; ample provision is made to maintain large reserves of fertility; the greatest care is taken to store the rainfall; both plants and animals are left to protect themselves against disease."

It may appear that our work at the Land Institute is part of a succession in a literary and scientific tradition, for we operate with the assumption that the best agriculture for any region is one that best mimics the region's natural ecosystems. That is why we are trying to build domestic prairies that will produce grain. We were ignorant of this literary and scientific tradition, however, when we began our work. I did have a background in botany and genetics and could see the difference between a prairie and a wheat field out my windows at the Land Institute, but as Berry said about the poets and scientists he quoted, understanding probably comes out of the familial and communal handing down of agrarian common culture rather than from any succession of teachers and students in the literary culture or in the schools. As far as the literary and scientific tradition is concerned, Berry pointed out that it is a series, not a succession. The succession is only in the agrarian common culture. I came off the farm out of a family of farmers, and apparently my "memory" of nature as measure is embedded in that agrarian common culture. George Bernard Shaw said that, "perfect memory is perfectful forgetfulness." To know something well is not to know where it came from. That is probably the nature of succession in the nonformal culture.

"Unwitting Accessibility to the World"

It is always easier to think of a better way to produce either food or a consumer item than it is to propose how to avoid using food or a gadget wastefully. Of all the poets mentioned here, Milton is the only one who wrote about human consumption. Yet if nature is to be our measure, we must be attentive to the "holy dictate of spare Temperance." This is where I see humankind's split with nature widening, and therefore an examination of what is at work is in order.

I believe that we live in a fallen world. By that, I mean that to meet our food and fiber needs, we have changed the face of the earth. We employed human cleverness to make the earth yield up an unbounded technological array that has produced even more countless things. In agriculture we have hot-wired the landscape, bypassing nature's numerous control devices. What drives us to do this in the face of the evidence all around that we are destroying our habitat? Carlos Castaneda's Don Juan called it our "unwitting accessibility to the world." I should explain my interpretation of that phrase.

A few years ago on the last page of *Life*, I saw a memorable photograph of a near-naked and well-muscled tribesman of Indonesian New Guinea, staring at a parked airplane in a jungle clearing. The caption noted the Indonesian government's attempt to bring such "savages" into the money economy. A stand had been set up at the edge of the jungle and was reportedly doing a brisk business in beer, soda pop, and tennis shoes.

We can imagine what must have followed for the members of the tribe, what the wages of their "sin," their "fall," must have been—decaying teeth, anxiety in a money system, destruction of their social structure. If they were like most so-called primitive peoples, then in spite of having a hierarchical structure, their society was much more egalitarian than industrialized societies today.

Unlike Adam and Eve, who partook of the tree of knowledge, the New Guinea tribesmen did not receive an explicit commandment to avoid the goodies of civilization. They were simply given unwittingly accessibility to the worldly items of beer, soda pop, and tennis shoes. In the Genesis version, the sin involves disobedience, an exercise of free will. In the latter version, the "original sin" is our unwitting accessibility to the material things of the world. I perceive that to be the largest threat to our planet and to our ability to regard nature as the standard.

In *Beyond the Hundredth Meridian* (1953), Wallace Stegner described the breakdown of American Indian culture:

> For however sympathetically or even sentimentally a white American viewed the Indian, the industrial culture was certain to eat away at

the tribal cultures like lye. One's attitude might vary, but the fact went on regardless. What destroyed the Indian was not primarily political greed, land hunger, or military power, not the white man's germs or the white man's rum. What destroyed him was the manufactured products of a culture, iron and steel, guns, needles, woolen cloth, *things that once possessed could not be done without* (italics added).

It was not the continuity of the Indian race that failed; what failed was the continuity of the diverse tribal cultures. These exist now only in scattered, degenerated reservation fragments among such notably resistant peoples as the Pueblo and Navajo of the final, persistent Indian Country. And here what has protected them is aridity, the difficulties in the way of dense white settlement, the accident of relative isolation, as much as the stability of their own institutions. Even here a Hopi dancer with tortoise shells on his calves and turquoise on his neck and wrists and a kirtle of fine traditional weave around his loins may wear down his back as an amulet a nickel-plated Ingersoll watch, or a Purple Heart medal won in a white man's war. Even here, in Monument Valley where not one Navajo in ten speaks any English, squaws may herd their sheep through the shadscale and rabbitbrush in brown and white saddle shoes and Hollywood sunglasses, or gather under a juniper for gossip and bubblegum. The lye still corrodes even the resistant cultures.

This reality—things that once possessed cannot be done without—is so powerful that it occupies our unconscious, and yet we know that nature "means her provision only to the good / That live according to her sober laws / And holy dictate of spare Temperance."

Voluntary Poverty as a Path toward Insight

Lynn White (1967) has proposed Saint Francis of Assisi as the patron saint of ecologists. Francis held the radical position that all of creation was holy. Yet nothing in the record shows that he arrived at that position because he was initially endowed with the wilderness psyche of a Henry David Thoreau or a John Muir or an Aldo Leopold. In fact, his entry point was from a nearly opposite end of the spectrum—this son of a well-to-do man chose poverty. Apparently, Francis took

seriously the words of Jesus of Nazareth, "If you have done it unto the least of these my brethren, you have done it unto Me." Francis's intimate identification with the least, his joining the least, must have prepared him psychologically to be sensitively tuned to all of creation—both the living and the nonliving world. He was a Christian pantheist who believed that birds, flowers, trees, and rocks had spiritual standing.

Francis, the founder of the most heretical brand of Christianity ever, began his journey with a marriage to poverty. This poverty, voluntarily chosen, apparently was the prerequisite for making what White (1967) called "the greatest spiritual revolutionary in Western history." His marriage to poverty and his sparing use of the earth's resources led to deep ecological insight. You may remember the legend of the famous wolf of Gubbio, which had been eating livestock and people. Francis approached the wolf and asked him, in the name of Jesus Christ, to behave himself. The wolf gave signs that he understood. Francis then launched into a description of all that the wolf had done, including all the livestock and people he had killed, and told him, "You, Friar Wolf, are a thief and a murderer" and therefore "fit for the gallows." The wolf made more signs of understanding, and Francis continued, stating in effect, "I see you have a contrite heart about this matter, and if you promise to behave, I'll see to it that you are fed." The wolf showed signs that he promised, and the legend has it that the wolf came to town, went in and out of people's houses as a kind of pet, and lived that way two years before he died. The townspeople all fed him, scratched his ears, and so on. It was life at the dog food bowls of Gubbio.

In light of that story, I once thought that Saint Francis might more properly be regarded as the patron saint of domesticators. Anyone able to encourage a wolf to quit acting like a wolf should act, given everything from its enzyme system to its fangs, is not likely to be regarded as an ecologist, let alone a patron saint for such.

A few weeks ago, at about three in the morning, the barking of our two dogs woke me up. Soon there was hissing and growling and more barking right on the back porch. I went outside and saw a raccoon cowering under a step stool by the dog food bowl. I chased it away with a stick, sicced our border collie Molly on him, and went back to bed. I confidently went to sleep. A few minutes later I heard more barking, more hissing, more growling. Once again I went outside, and the dogs and I ran the coon off. Back to bed, and sure enough the same story. This time, however, I left the porch light on for this nocturnal animal. I lay in bed and listened, and there was no more ruckus. I felt pleased with myself for having solved the problem with a light switch by means of my biological knowledge about nocturnal animals, and I went to sleep. The next morning, I headed out the back door to begin the day's work, and there in a box of tinder on a table was the coon, sleeping away. Both dogs were asleep under the table. Each time I returned to the house during the day, I expected to see that the coon had gone. But he didn't leave. And as he slept that day, the dogs would walk by, look up, and sniff, well on their way toward accepting their new fellow resident.

What was going on here? We are taught to consider recent changes when something unusual breaks a pattern. And so I might have an answer. Late in the afternoons this winter I have been going to my woods with a chain saw, some gasoline, and matches to burn brush. I am clearing out most of the box elder trees that have grown up there over the last forty years. They are early-stage succession trees that have mostly covered the area where the former tenant logged out all the walnuts and burr oaks. The box elders are the first trees to green up in the spring, and they accommodate woodpeckers. But they are no good for lumber, and though we burn them, they are very low in fuel value. I want to accelerate succession by planting some walnuts and oaks for my grandchildren. Nearly every box elder I took down was hollow. The woods are less than a quarter of a mile from my house along the Smoky Hill River, and I suspect that I destroyed the home of Friar Coon and that Friar Coon, looking for a new home, simply moved into mine.

Now back to Gubbio. Why was the thieving, murdering wolf forgiven and then given a life at the dog food bowls? I suspect that the ecological context necessary to accommodate proper wolfhood around Gubbio had been destroyed, that the usual predator-prey relationship had been somehow disrupted, and that Francis realized it. If so, Francis's deeper ecological insight was a derivative of his respect and love for nature. He could, after all, have organized a posse to eliminate the killer wolf, but instead his love and respect for nature—in turn at least partly derived from his identification with poverty—made him forgiving and compassionate.

But there is still an item on our agenda for discussion. Was Saint Francis engaged in an act of domestication? It appears so, but if harmony with nature is what we seek, should we not be willing to be in harmony any way we can? The wolf's tame behavior demonstrates that nature is not rigid. Humanity (Francis) reached out to nature (the wolf), and the wolf responded. If we insist that wild nature be so rigid, we are denying one of the most important properties of nature—resilience. The unanswered question here is, Once the wolf comes to town, can he ever return to the wild? Life at a dog bowl in Gubbio may be easier than life that relies on the fang and the occasional berry. If the wolf is unable to return, then that particular wolf is a fallen creature. Would it matter that he was made that way initially by the fallen ecological context of humanity's making? Wolves and coons, unable to return to their original context because they have gained unwittingly accessibility to the world, may be little different from the New Guinea tribesmen or the native Americans. Stegner's phrase, "things that once possessed could not be done without," can be applied beyond people. Grizzlies in the garbage at Yellowstone and elephants in African dump heaps come to mind as modern expressions of the same problem. A wolf, or any other creature, unable to return is a fallen animal dependent on fallen humanity. And so another ethical question comes on the agenda: What right do we have to create a fallen world for other species when we know that life at the dog food bowl is second best? Following that line of thinking, our crops and livestock represent fallen species that accommodate fallen humanity.

Interpenetration of the Domestic and the Wild

The stories about the wolf in Gubbio and the coon on the porch illustrate the problem of trying to use nature as measure, for in those examples the interpenetration of the domestic and the wild is total. During the last five hundred years or so, the ratio of the domestic to the wild has increased so much, especially in the Western Hemisphere, that wilderness is becoming an artifact of civilization.

Civilization is all that can save wilderness now. The wild that produced us, that we were dependent upon, is now dependent on us. We pay homage to wildness in the United States by regarding pristine wilderness as a kind of a saint. But that presents some problems, too.

In Christianity the tradition of sainthood calls upon the faithful to stand or kneel before an image of a saint, light a candle, meditate, think, and perhaps whisper some words before departure. Often these faithful go in peace, perhaps thinking, "Well, that's covered," and they carry on more or less as before. This isolation of virtue can also be found in countless wilderness advocates who clamor to have wilderness set aside as pristine. They will stand in forest wilderness, soak up its silence, walk out, and send money to defend it. They may say little in protest, however, about the spread of lethal farm chemicals over more than half a million square miles of the best agricultural land in the world, and soil erosion may be no concern of theirs. I do not object to either saints or wilderness, but to keep the holy isolated from the rest, to treat our wilderness as a saint and to treat Kansas or East Saint Louis otherwise, is a form of schizophrenia. Either all the earth is holy, or it is not. Either every square foot deserves our respect, or none of it does.

Would Earth First! activists or Deep Ecologists be as interested in cleaning up East Saint Louis, for example, as they are in defending wilderness? Would Earth First! activists be as fervent about defending a farmer's soil conservation effort or chemical-free crop rotation as they are about spiking a tree or putting sugar in the fuel tank of a bulldozer?

It is possible to love a small acreage in Kansas as much as John Muir loved the entire Sierra Nevada. That is fortunate, for the wilderness of the Sierra will disappear unless little pieces of nonwilderness become intensely loved by lots of people. In other words, Harlem and East Saint Louis and Iowa and Kansas and the rest of the world where wilderness has been destroyed will have to be loved by enough of us, or wilderness is doomed. Suddenly we see we are dealing with a range of issues. For that reason Saint Francis's entire life becomes an important example. People who struggle for social justice by working with the poor in cities and people out to prevent soil erosion and save the family farm are suddenly on the same side as the wilderness advocate. All have joined the same fight.

Nature as Measure in Agricultural Research

Rather than deal with problems *in* agriculture here and now, we at the Land Institute address the problem *of* agriculture, which began when agriculture began some eight to ten thousand years ago. We have seen that nature is an elusive standard. Nevertheless, it seems to us at the Land Institute less elusive than any other standard when sustainability is our primary objective. The nature we look to at the Land Institute is the never-plowed native prairie.

We have around one hundred acres of such land at the institute, and when we compare prairie with the ordinary field of corn or wheat, important differences become apparent. From our typical agricultural fields, valuable nutrients run toward the sea, where for all practical purposes most of them are gone for good. The prairie, on the other hand, by drawing nutrients from parent rock material or subsoil, all the while returning chemicals produced by life, actually builds soil. The prairie, like nearly all of nature, runs mostly on contemporary sunlight, whereas our modern agricultural fields benefit from the stored sunlight of extinct ancient floras. Diversity does not necessarily yield stability overall; nevertheless, the chemical diversity inherent in the diverse plant species of the prairie confronts insects and pathogens, making epidemics, so common to agricultural monocultures, rare on the prairie. Because no creature has an all-consuming enzyme system, diversity yields some protection. The prairie therefore does not require the introduction of chemicals with which species have had no evolutionary experience.

So what are the basic differences between a prairie and an agricultural field? A casual examination of the ordinary differences will help us to see that the prairie features perennials in a polyculture, whereas modern agriculture features annuals in a monoculture. Our work at the Land Institute is devoted primarily to exploring the feasibility of an agriculture that features herbaceous perennials grown in a mixture for seed production—that is, domestic prairies—as substitutes for annual monocultures grown in rows on ground that can erode.

We address four basic questions in our experiments at the institute. First, can herbaceous perenniality and high seed yield go together? Because perennial plants must divert some photosynthate to belowground storage for overwintering, it may be difficult to breed perennials to produce as much seed as annual crops that die after reproducing. Perennial species differ greatly in both relative and absolute amounts of energy devoted to seed production, however, so theoretically there seems to be no reason why a fast-growing, well-adapted species could not yield adequate seed while retaining the ability to overwinter.

Before we begin to breed for stable high seed yields in an herbaceous perennial, we determine its genetic potential. Whether we start with a wild introduced species or a wild native, the development of perennial seed-producing polycultures will require that we select for varieties that perform well in polyculture. The potential improvement, therefore, depends on the range of existing genetic variability in the wild. To assess this variation requires an adequate sample drawn from the geographic range of the species and then an evaluation of the collection within a common garden.

Now our second question: Can a polyculture of perennial seed producers outyield the same species grown in monoculture? Overyielding occurs when interspecific competition in a plant community is less intense than intraspecific competition. Thus, we believe that through differences in resource use and timing of demand, multispecies fields typically yield more per unit area than do monospecific stands.

Our third question is, Can a perennial polyculture provide much of its own fertility? Specifically, can such internal factors as nitrogen fixation and weathering of primary minerals compensate for nutrients removed in harvested seed? To answer this question, we must document nutrient cycling in the soil, nutrient content of seed, and capacity of crop plants to enrich the soil.

As our fourth and final question we ask, Can a perennial mixture successfully contend with phytophagous insects, pathogens, and weeds? If we are to protect a crop, a combination of breeding for resistant lines and studies on the effects of species diversity must converge. Insect pests can be managed through a combination of attracting predators and preventing insects from locating host plants. A mixture of species, and of genotypes within species, may reduce the incidence and spread of disease. Weeds may be controlled either allelopathically or via continuous shading of the soil surface by the perennials.

Though we keep all four of these questions in mind, the most pressing biological question at the Land Institute is whether perennials and high seed yield can go together. To answer this question, we started a plant inventory that had the following steps: (1) we reviewed the literature of seed yield in winter-hardy herbaceous perennials; (2) we collected seed and plants in nature and developed an herbary of approximately three hundred species, each grown in five-meter-long rows; and (3) we planted more than forty-three hundred accessions of more than one hundred species representing seven grass genera. Our inventory continues even though we are currently focusing on five species plus a hybrid of our making.

The relationship between perennials and high yield also involves the issue of sustained production. Prairies, after all, feature perennials, but they do not feature high seed yield. Ultimately, we have to explore the optimum balance between sustainability and yield.

In addition to the inventory of potentially high-yielding species, other sorts of inventories, such as an inventory of the vegetative structure, are necessary for long-term considerations. Because perennial roots are a major feature of our work, an inventory of the soil relationships in the prairie and in our plots is also essential. The ecological inventory includes more than analysis of the phytomass ratios; it also includes an ongoing inventory of the insects and pathogens in our herbary and in our experimental plots. We always compare the results with those from our prairie, the system that represents the least departure from what was here before white settlement.

The inventory phase will probably never end. The ecological inventory is particularly long-lasting because of the countless number of interactions over time. Even research on the question of perennials and high yield will require several years, for it amounts to an investigation of long-term demographic patterns in perennial seed production, a field that is largely unexplored. Studies thus far at the Land Institute have shown increases, decreases, and oscillations in seed yield over time. But we always come back to these questions: What was here? What will nature permit us to do here? And what will nature help us to do here? Wendell Berry once wrote in a letter, "When we cut the forest and plowed our prairies we never knew what we were doing because we never knew what we were undoing." It is now a matter of practical necessity to learn what we were undoing.

In a 1986 preliminary investigation, Jon Piper, the institute's ecologist, asked, How much above-ground plant life is supported each year by the prairie, and what are the proportions of grasses, legumes, and composites? Those plant families comprise most of our temperate agricultural species. Net production of the plants at Piper's grassland sites (five hundred to seven hundred grams per square meter) was similar to that of many midwestern crops. At their peaks, grasses composed 67 to 94 percent of plant matter, and legumes and composites represented 16 and 11 percent of vegetation, respectively. Piper concluded from these encouraging results that "a sustainable agricultural system for central Kansas is feasible if perennial grasses were featured followed by nearly equal proportions of legumes and composites."

In 1985 we began to examine insects and plant pathogens qualitatively in nine experimental plots at the Land Institute. Every week from May through August, and every other week from September through October, insects were collected with a sweep net or from individual plants. All diseased plants were sent to the Disease Diagnosis Laboratory at Kansas State University for pathogen identification. All sampled plots showed a diversity of both beneficial and harmful insects. Several foliar diseases were present, but few were serious. We continued that inventory in 1986 but with important modifications. The prairie was sampled using sweep nets every third week. Over the years, we have sampled the prairie, the herbary, and the experimental plots for insects and pathogens and have made numerous comparisons.

A final example of this soft approach to sustainable-agriculture research is the design of the large polyculture experiment we intend to establish in 1991. For that experiment, we think about the species components we intend to introduce, the planting density of each species, the ratios of species to one another, and so forth.

Three Final Questions

We have three final questions to consider. First, is perennial polyculture or ecosystem agriculture inherently more complicated and therefore less likely to succeed than monoculture agriculture, be it of the annual or the perennial variety?

My answer is, not necessarily. The disciplines of science are divided to explore the various levels in the hierarchy of structure from atoms to molecules, cells, tissues, organs, organ systems, and organisms. At each level of aggregation, it is the emergent qualities more than the contents that define the discipline. A physicist may have learned about the structure and workings of an atom in great detail. Though some understanding of atoms is necessary for a chemist, the chemist does not need to know the atom with the same intricacy of detail as the physicist. A chemist mostly studies reactions. On up the hierarchy, we see that chemistry is important to a cell biologist but does not define cell biology, and a good cell biologist does not need to have a chemist's detailed knowledge. Cell biology as a field is not more complicated than chemistry or physics, though cells are more complex than molecules or atoms. Likewise, ecosystem agriculture will be more complex than monoculture agriculture, but the management of agro-ecosystems may not be more complicated. Ecosystem agriculturalists will take advantage of the natural integrities of ecosystems worked out over the millennia.

When we deal with nature's designs, a great deal of ignorance on our part is tolerable. Much error is forgiven. Ignorance is tolerable until we begin to impose our own designs on nature's landscape. Even then certain kinds of ignorance and large amounts of forgetfulness will be tolerated. (Not knowing is a kind of ignorance preferred over knowing things that just are not so. At least one does not have to unlearn what is not known.) When we impose our own designs on nature's landscape, we do so with the presumption that we know what we are doing, and we have to assume responsibility for our mistakes. By imitating nature's patterns, we should be able to reduce error by taking advantage of nature's complexity, thus minimizing complications for ourselves. Farmers and scientists alike may not know why certain associations of plants and animals grant sustainability, just that they do. And though there is little wrong with finding out why certain associations work, from the point of view of a farmer interested in running a sustainable farm, knowing why is not always necessary.

Our second question is, How crucial is species diversity, and if it is necessary, how much and what kind are optimum? As mentioned earlier, diversity does not necessarily lead to stability. Numerous diverse ecosystems are less stable than simpler ones. We can raise a question about the inherent value of diversity by considering two extremes. At one extreme, we could assemble a diverse hodge-podge of species, plants that have never grown together in an ecosystem. At the other extreme, we could assemble plant species that have histories of growing together—on the prairie, let us say. In the latter case natural integrities have evolved to the point that large numbers of genetic ensembles interact in a species mix. This area warrants much research.

Another important consideration is associated with the diversity question. As species are selected for future experimentation, we may need to determine to what extent the genetic profile is tuned to interspecific versus intraspecific complementarity. In all of our important domestic grains, the genetic assembly of an individual plant resonates against members of its own kind (intraspecific complementarity). On a prairie, that is not the case. Prairie plants are more tuned to interact with different species (interspecific complementarity).

The third question we ask is this: Is it true that, for any biotic system, internal control uses material and energy resources more efficiently than external control? In a hierarchy of structure—beginning with an individual plant, then the field (an ecosystem), then the farm (a larger ecosystem), and then the farm community (an even larger ecosystem) — it will be necessary to think about the efficient use of material and energy resources.

This philosophical consideration is of great practical importance. Consider a plant's resistance to an insect. If a plant uses its genetic code to make a chemical that is distasteful to an insect, thereby granting itself protection, we would call that internal control. If we, perhaps unknowingly, remove that ability through breeding, the plant is susceptible and we apply an insecticide on the plant's surface to grant it protection. That is external control. Yield increases, but the resource cost for protection is paid from the outside, and seemingly the total cost would be greater.

Another example is nitrogen fertility. If the feedstock for commercial nitrogen fertilizer is natu-

ral gas, the total energy cost would be higher than if the plant fixed its own nitrogen. In the first case, we are using what we might call vertical energy, or time-compressed energy; in the second case, we are using horizontal, or contemporary, energy from the sun. As our supplies of vertical energy run out and we are forced to use horizontal energy, then the answer to our major question becomes crucial, for at that point the energy source becomes a land-use problem.

A third example is weed control. If the roots of a plant produce an herbicide to keep back most weeds, then weed protection comes from within the plant (allelopathy). The plant's production of such an herbicide will come at a cost in yield. But let us say that a plant lacks the ability to produce the herbicide and that mechanical weeding is necessary. If we pay the cost on the farm the way we used to—that is, harvest biomass from a pasture or field to feed horses supplying the power for mechanical weed removal—then it seems obvious that the overall cost will be higher.

We are faced with extremely difficult choices and, I believe, extremely difficult times. Our goal must be a harmony between the human economy and nature's economy that will preserve both. In the greenhouse dedication speech mentioned earlier, Wendell Berry pointed out that such a goal is traditional: "The world is now divided between those who adhere to this ancient purpose and those who by intention do not, and this division is of far more portent for the future of the world than any of the presently recognized national or political or economic divisions."

Recalling his outline of the literary and scientific traditions, Berry concluded, "The remarkable thing about this division is its relative newness. The idea that we should obey nature's laws and live harmoniously with her as good husbanders and stewards of her gifts is old. . . . And I believe that until fairly recently our destructions of nature were more or less unwitting—the by-products, so to speak, of our ignorance or weakness or depravity. It is our present principled and elaborately rationalized rape and plunder of the natural world that is a new thing under the sun."

74. What's in the Meat

Eric Schlosser

On July 11, 1997, Lee Harding ordered soft chicken tacos at a Mexican restaurant in Pueblo, Colorado. Harding was twenty-two years old, a manager at Safeway. His wife Stacey was a manager at Wendy's. They were out to dinner on a Friday night. When the chicken tacos arrived, Harding thought there was something wrong with them. The meat seemed to have gone bad. The tacos tasted slimy and gross. An hour or so after leaving the restaurant, Harding began to experience severe abdominal cramps. It felt like something was eating away at his stomach. He was fit and healthy, stood six-foot-one, weighed two hundred pounds. He'd never felt pain this intense. The cramps got worse, and Harding lay in bed through the night, tightly curled into a ball. He developed bad diarrhea, then bloody diarrhea. He felt like he was dying, but was afraid to go to the hospital. If I'm going to die, he thought, I want to die at home.

The severe pain and diarrhea lasted through the weekend. On Monday evening Harding decided to seek medical attention; the cramps were getting better, but he was still passing a good deal of blood. He waited three hours in the emergency room at St. Mary-Corwin Hospital in Pueblo, gave a stool sample, and then finally saw a doctor. It's probably just a "summer flu," the doctor said. Harding was sent home with a prescription for an antibiotic. Tuesday afternoon, he heard a knock at his front door. When Harding opened it, nobody was there. But he found a note on the door from the Pueblo City–County Health Department. It said that his stool sample had tested positive for *Escherichia coli* 0157:H7, a virulent and potentially lethal foodborne pathogen.

The next morning Harding called Sandra Gallegos, a nurse with the Pueblo Health Department. She asked him to try and remember what foods he'd eaten during the previous five days. Harding mentioned the dinner at the Mexican restaurant and the foul taste of the chicken tacos. He was sure that was where he had gotten food poisoning. Gallegos disagreed. *E. coli* 0157:H7 was

rarely found in chicken. She asked if Harding had consumed any ground beef lately. Harding recalled having eaten a hamburger a couple of days before visiting the Mexican restaurant. But he doubted that the hamburger could have made him ill. Both his wife and his wife's sister had eaten the same burgers, during a backyard barbecue, and neither had become sick. He and his wife had also eaten burgers from the same box the week before the barbecue without getting sick. They were frozen hamburgers he bought at Safeway. He remembered because it was the first time he'd ever bought frozen hamburgers. Gallegos asked if there were any left. Harding said there just might be, checked the freezer, and found the package. It was a red, white, and blue box that said "Hudson Beef Patties."

A Pueblo health official went to Harding's house, took the remaining hamburgers, and sent one to a USDA laboratory for analysis. State health officials had noticed a spike in the number of people suffering from *E. coli* 0157:H7 infections. At the time Colorado was one of only six states with the capability to perform DNA tests on samples of *E. coli* 0157:H7. The DNA tests showed that at least ten people had been sickened by the same strain of the bug. Investigators were searching for a common link between scattered cases reported in Pueblo, Brighton, Loveland, Grand Junction, and Colorado Springs. On July 28, the USDA lab notified Gallegos that Lee Harding's hamburger was contaminated with the same strain of *E. coli* 0157:H7. Here was the common link.

The lot number on Harding's package said that the frozen patties had been manufactured on June 5 at the Hudson Foods plant in Columbus, Nebraska. The plant seemed an unlikely source for an outbreak of food poisoning. Only two years old, it had been built primarily to supply hamburgers for the Burger King chain. It used state-of-the-art equipment and appeared to be spotlessly clean. But something had gone wrong. A modern factory designed for the mass production of food had instead become a vector for the spread of a deadly

Reprinted with permission from Eric Schlosser's *Fast Food Nation: The Dark Side of the All-American Meal* (New York: Houghton Mifflin Co., 2001).

disease. The package of hamburger patties in Lee Harding's freezer and astute investigative work by Colorado health officials soon led to the largest recall of food in the nation's history. Roughly 35 million pounds of ground beef produced at the Columbus plant—enough meat to provide every single American with a tainted fast food hamburger—was voluntarily recalled by Hudson Foods in August of 1997. Although public health officials did a fine job of tracing the outbreak to its source, the recall proved less successful. By the time it was announced, about 25 million pounds of the ground beef had already been eaten.

An Ideal System for New Pathogens

Every day in the United States, roughly 200,000 people are sickened by a foodborne disease, 900 are hospitalized, and fourteen die. According to the Centers for Disease Control and Prevention (CDC), more than a quarter of the American population suffers a bout of food poisoning each year. Most of these cases are never reported to authorities or properly diagnosed. The widespread outbreaks that are detected and identified represent a small fraction of the number that actually occurs. And there is strong evidence not only that the incidence of food-related illness has risen in the past few decades, but also that the lasting health consequences of such illnesses are far more serious than was previously believed. The acute phase of a food poisoning—the initial few days of diarrhea and gastrointestinal upset—in many cases may simply be the most obvious manifestation of an infectious disease. Recent studies have found that many foodborne pathogens can precipitate long-term ailments, such as heart disease, inflammatory bowel disease, neurological problems, autoimmune disorders, and kidney damage.

Although the rise in foodborne illnesses has been caused by many complex factors, much of the increase can be attributed to recent changes in how American food is produced. Robert V. Tauxe, head of the Foodborne and Diarrheal Diseases Branch at the CDC, believes that entirely new kinds of outbreaks are now occurring. A generation ago, the typical outbreak of food poisoning involved a church supper, a family picnic, a wedding reception. Improper food handling or storage would cause a small group of people in one local area to get sick. Such traditional outbreaks still take place. But the nation's industrialized and centralized system of food processing has created a whole new sort of outbreak, one that can potentially sicken millions of people. Today a cluster of illnesses in one small town may stem from bad potato salad at a school barbecue—or it may be the first sign of an outbreak that extends statewide, nationwide, or even overseas.

Much like human immunodeficiency virus (HIV) responsible for causing AIDS, the E. coli 0157:H7 bacterium is a newly emerged pathogen whose spread has been facilitated by recent social and technological changes. E. coli 0157:H7 was first isolated in 1982; HIV was discovered the following year. People who are infected with HIV can appear healthy for years, while cattle infected with E coli 0157:H7 show few signs of illness. Although cases of AIDS date back at least to the late 1950s, the disease did not reach epidemic proportions in United States until increased air travel and sexual promiscuity helped transmit the virus far and wide. E. coli. 0157:H7 was most likely responsible for some human illnesses thirty or forty years ago. But the rise of huge feedlots, slaughterhouses, and hamburger grinders seems to have provided the means for this pathogen to become widely dispersed in the nation's food supply. American meat production has never before been so centralized: thirteen large packinghouses now slaughter most of the beef consumed in the United States. The meat-packing system that arose to supply the nation's fast food chains—an industry molded to serve their needs, to provide massive amounts of uniform ground beef so that all of McDonald's hamburgers would taste the same—has proved to be an extremely efficient system for spreading disease.

Although E. coli 0157:H7 has received a good deal of public attention, over the past two decades scientists have discovered more than a dozen other new foodborne pathogens, including *Campylobacter jejuni, Cryptosporidium parvum, Cyclospora cayetanensis, Listeria monocytogenes*, and Norwalk-like viruses. The CDC estimates that more than three-quarters of the food-related illnesses and deaths in the United States are caused by infectious agents that have not yet been identified. While medical researchers have gained important insights into the links between modern food processing and the spread of dangerous diseases, the nation's leading agribusiness firms have resolutely opposed any further regulation of their food safety practices. For years the large meatpacking companies have managed to avoid the sort of liability routinely imposed on the manufacturers of most consumer products. Today the U.S. government can demand the nationwide recall of defective softball bats, sneakers, stuffed animals, and foam-rubber toy cows. But it cannot order a meatpacking company to remove contaminated, potentially lethal ground beef from fast food kitchens and supermarket shelves. The unusual power of the large meatpacking firms has been sustained by their close ties and sizable donations to Republican members of Congress. It has also been made possible by a widespread lack of awareness about how many Americans suffer from food poisoning every year and how these illnesses actually spread.

The newly recognized foodborne pathogens tend to be carried and shed by apparently healthy animals. Food tainted by these organisms has most likely come in contact with an infected animal's stomach contents or manure, during slaughter or subsequent processing. A nationwide study published by the USDA in 1996 found that 7.5 percent of the ground beef samples taken at processing plants were contaminated with *Salmonella*, 11.7 percent were contaminated with *Listeria monocytogenes*, 30 percent were contaminated with *Staphylo-coccus aureus*, and 53.3 percent were contaminated with *Clostridium perfringens*. All of these pathogens can make people sick; food poisoning caused by *Listeria* generally requires hospitalization and proves fatal in about one out of every five cases. In the USDA study 78.6 percent of the ground beef contained microbes that are spread primarily by fecal material. The medical literature on the causes of food poisoning is full of euphemisms and dry scientific terms: coliform levels, aerobic plate counts, sorbitol, MacConkey agar, and so on. Behind them lies a simple explanation for why eating a hamburger can now make you seriously ill: There is shit in the meat. . . .

Instead of focusing on the primary causes of meat contamination—the feed being given to cattle, the overcrowding at feedlots, the poor sanitation at slaughterhouses, excessive line speeds, poorly trained workers, the lack of stringent government oversight—the meatpacking industry and the USDA are now advocating an exotic technological solution to the problem of foodborne pathogens. They want to irradiate the nation's meat. Irradiation is a form of bacterial birth control, pioneered in the 1960s by the U.S. Army and by NASA. When microorganisms are zapped with low levels of gamma rays or x-rays, they are not killed, but their DNA is disrupted, and they cannot reproduce. Irradiation has been used for years on some imported spices and domestic poultry. Most irradiating facilities have concrete walls that are six feet thick, employing cobalt 60 or cesium 137 (a waste product from nuclear weapons plants and nuclear power plants) to create highly charged, radioactive beams. A new technique, developed by the Titan Corporation, uses conventional electricity and an electronic accelerator instead of radioactive isotopes. Titan devised its SureBeam irradiation technology during the 1980s, while conducting research for the Star Wars antimissile program.

The American Medical Association and the World Health Organization have declared that irradiated foods are safe to eat. Widespread introduction of the process has thus far been impeded, however, by a reluctance among consumers to eat things that have been exposed to radiation. According to current USDA regulations, irradiated meat must be identified with a special label and with a radura (the internationally recognized symbol of radiation). The Beef Industry Food Safety Council—whose members include the meatpacking and fast food giants—has asked the USDA to change its rules and make the labeling of irradiated meat completely voluntary. The meatpacking industry is also working hard to get rid of the word "irradiation," much preferring the phrase "cold pasteurization.". . .

Steven Bjerklie, the former editor of *Meat & Poultry*, opposes irradiation. . . . He thinks it will reduce pressure on the meatpacking industry to make fundamental and necessary changes in their production methods, allowing unsanitary practices to continue. "I don't want to be served irradiated feces along with my meat," Bjerklie says.

VI.C WILDERNESS AND FORESTS _____

75. PREVIEW

I'm the Lorax who speaks for the trees
which you seem to be chopping as fast as
you please.

Dr. Seuss, The Lorax[1]

Even on the eve of the end of the world,
plant a tree.

The Qur'an

The term *wilderness* is not easy to define,
but a useful working definition is "an area of
the earth substantially untrammeled or
unmodified by human beings." Virtually no
one suggests that an area must be entirely
untouched by humans to qualify as wilderness. For example, in defining the context of
wilderness, the Wilderness Act of 1964 recognized human beings as visitors who do not
remain.[2] Val Plumwood, in her comment on
John Passmore's remark that the presence of
recreationists converts wilderness into "man-
made landscape," maintains: "The occasional
human presence and evidence of human activity around trails do not convert an area to
"man-made landscape,"—anymore than the
presence of a wombat trail creates a wombat-
made landscape."[3]

What is it that is so especially valuable
about wilderness? Does its existence fill a need
in the human psyche? Is there some value in
just knowing that it is there to go into if we
should want to do that? Must its existence be
good for us at all? Is there a moral obligation
to preserve wilderness and wildness?

Many of the arguments that are given in
defense of preserving the wild are labeled utilitarian. Here *utilitarian* carries one of its traditional meanings, that of identifying as good
those things that are useful or "of utility" to
human beings (consider "utility companies").
For example, the scientific, recreational, aesthetic, and spiritual arguments are all utilitarian in this sense. Perhaps, according to a

utilitarian view, there is an optimal amount of
wilderness.

One argument related to scientific concerns maintains that wilderness should be preserved because it contains a reservoir of
genetic diversity. Norman Myers in Essay 77,
"Tropical Forests and Their Species: Going,
Going . . . ?," explains in rich detail a mass
extinction episode that we are witnessing due
to worldwide deforestation.

Recreational, aesthetic, and spiritual arguments for wilderness preservation center on
the importance of wilderness experience.
Wilderness often evokes responses of awe,
wonder, even terror. For much of human history, wilderness denoted a harsh environment
"cursed by God, and commonly occupied by
foul creatures."[4] The same scenes that once
elicited fear, contempt, and alienation are at
other times touted as the source of inspiration,
spiritual catharsis, and therapy from the stress
and strain of civilized life. For example, the
Derbyshire peak region in England was once
considered unfit for viewing. "Travelers . . .
were advised to keep their coach blinds drawn
while traversing the region so as not to be
shocked by its ugliness and wildness. Within a
few decades, however, the very same region
came to be regarded as so attractive that it
inspired lines of extravagant praise by nineteenth-century poets."[5]

Aesthetic considerations can be powerful,
but they have their limitations. For example,
John Rodman points out that aesthetic arguments are particularly plausible in arguing for
the preservation of the Sierra and the Grand
Canyons, but not with respect to saving the
marshes and brushlands.[6] He further asserts
that some, but not all, sacred spaces are
informed by an aesthetic of the sublime and
the beautiful. Thus, if we rely on aesthetic considerations, what we save depends in part on
our conception of what is beautiful or ugly,

awe inspiring or threatening, clarifying or puzzling.

Wilderness, it is claimed, has a positive influence on human character: "Wilderness can teach us moral lessons; we can learn humility and gratitude, but we also can gain self-reliance, independence, and courage in facing the challenge of the wild. Wilderness has molded us as a nation; Daniel Boone, the Oregon Trail, and the Western frontier are all part of our national heritage."[7] The loss of wilderness may mean the loss of freedom in a sense quite different from freedom as a cultural symbol. Freedom will be lost in that our choices among environments will be limited to those we create ourselves.[8]

As the title of his book—*Toward Unity Among Environmentalists*—indicates, Bryan G. Norton sees general agreement and accord among contemporary environmentalists in their policy proposals for preserving forests or wilderness. In his short section on Forest Service policy (Essay 79), he says that both the Forest Service and organizations such as The Wilderness Society and the Sierra Club now recognize that managing national forests is "a balancing act."[9] He means by this that both have accepted that national forests will have a "productive" use (the Pinchot influence), and both accept the importance of aesthetic and amenity values (the Muir influence). Preservation organizations, he says, argue "for wilderness whenever possible as a counterforce against a perceived bias of foresters toward timber production over other aesthetic and moral goals."[10]

Perri Knize, in her "The Mismanagement of the National Forests" (Essay 78), does not sanction a balancing act. She thinks the Forest Service should get out of the timber industry altogether. Grinding up our ancient trees into pulp "to make disposable diapers and cellophane for cigarette packs"[11] is inexcusable when, among other considerations, "we don't need the lumber, . . . the timber program loses money, . . . the program is used to prop up fal-

tering local economies artificially, and . . . we have a biological stake in an end to logging our national forests."[12] Knize would replace the funds the Forest Service now receives from timber sales with recreation fees. She says, "Without fees, all taxpayers are paying for the destruction of the national forests. With fees, those who used the national forests would be paying to preserve their integrity."[13] Knize's article in *The Atlantic Monthly* was one of several essays in high-profile magazines in the early 1990s that, according to Ed de Steiguer, brought the U.S. Forest Service to its knees.[14] Forestry, he says, used to be about wood products. The magazine disclosures created pressures for amenity values and environmental values. Now, he says, the profession is trying to redefine itself

It is easy to assume after amassing all these reasons for wilderness preservation, that the case we have made applies globally. The work of Ramachandra Guha (Essay 76), however, makes clear that in exporting our valuing of wilderness preservation to third-world countries as in our supporting tiger preserves, Americans fail to recognize how culture-bound their values are. America, as a large and rich country, can afford to preserve wilderness. As Guha sees it, doing so is just one more consumer luxury and one that third-world countries cannot afford. They must give higher priority to the "integration of ecological concerns with livelihood and work."[15] Here and in his concern for equity and social justice, Guha agrees with Vandana Shiva. Guha would in all likelihood agree with Ian Barbour's statement that "wilderness has molded [the United States] as a nation." Perhaps Guha would even agree that wilderness has taught Americans some virtues, but social justice and moderation in consumption have not been among them.

NOTES

1. Dr. Seuss, *The Lorax* (New York: Random House, 1971).

2. Public Law 88-577 in U.S., *Statutes at Large,* 78, pp. 890–96.

3. Val Routley [now Val Plumwood], "Critical Notice of John Passmore's *Man's Responsibility for Nature,*" *Australasian Journal of Philosophy* 53 (1975), 182.

4. René Dubos, *The Wooing of the Earth* (New York: Scribner's 1980), p. 10.

5. Ibid., p. 14. See Essay 10, by Nina Rosenstand, in Part II for further elaboration.

6. John Rodman, "Four Forms of Ecological Consciousness Reconsidered," *Ethics and the Environment,* edited by Donald Scherer and Thomas Attig (Englewood Cliffs, NJ: Prentice Hall, 1983), p. 86.

7. Ian Barbour, *Technology, Environment, and Human Values* (New York: Praeger, 1980), p. 83.

8. See Edward B. Swain for a defense of freedom in this sense, "Wilderness and the Maintenance of Freedom," *The Humanist* 43(2) (March–April 1983), 26–30.

9. Bryan G. Norton, *Toward Unity Among Environmentalists* (New York: Oxford University Press, 1991), p. 106.

10. Ibid.

11. Perri Knize, "The Mismanagement of the National Forests," *The Atlantic Monthly* (October 1991), p. 100.

12. Ibid., p. 108.

13. Ibid., p. 112.

14. These comments are from a conversation with Professor J. E. de Steiguer, Department of Forestry, North Carolina State University.

15. Ramachandra Guha, "Radical American Environmentalism and Wilderness Preservation: A Third World Critique," *Environmental Ethics* 11(1) (Spring 1989), 81.

76. Radical American Environmentalism and Wilderness Preservation: A Third World Critique

Ramachandra Guha

I. Introduction

The respected radical journalist Kirkpatrick Sale recently celebrated "the passion of a new and growing movement that has become disenchanted with the environmental establishment and has in recent years mounted a serious and sweeping attack on it—style, substance, systems, sensibilities and all."[1] The vision of those whom Sale calls the "New Ecologists"—and what I refer to in this article as deep ecology—is a compelling one. Decrying the narrowly economic goals of mainstream environmentalism, this new movement aims at nothing less than a philosophical and cultural revolution in human attitudes toward nature. In contrast to the conventional lobbying efforts of environmental professionals based in Washington, it proposes a militant defence of "Mother Earth," an unflinching opposition to human attacks on undisturbed wilderness. With their goals ranging from the spiritual to the political, the adherents of deep ecology span a wide spectrum of the American environmental movement. As Sale correctly notes, this emerging strand has in a matter of a few years made its presence felt in a number of fields: from academic philosophy (as in the journal *Environmental Ethics*) to popular environmentalism (for example, the group Earth First!).

In this article I develop a critique of deep ecology from the perspective of a sympathetic outsider. I critique deep ecology not as a general (or even a foot soldier) in the continuing struggle between the ghosts of Gifford Pinchot and John Muir over control of the U.S. environmental movement, but as an outsider to these battles. I speak admittedly as a

Centre for Ecological Sciences, Indian Institute of Science, Bangalore 560 012, India. This essay was written while the author was a visiting lecturer at the Yale School of Forestry and Environmental Studies. He is grateful to Mike Bell, Tom Birch, Bill Burch, Bill Cronon, Diane Mayerfeld, David Rothenberg, Kirkpatrick Sale, Joel Seton, Tim Weiskel, and Don Worster for helpful comments. *Environmental Ethics*, Vol. 11, No. 1 (Spring 1989), 71–83. Reprinted by permission.

partisan, but of the environmental movement in India, a country with an ecological diversity comparable to the U.S., but with a radically dissimilar cultural and social history.

My treatment of deep ecology is primarily historical and sociological, rather than philosophical, in nature. Specifically, I examine the cultural rootedness of a philosophy that likes to present itself in universalistic terms. I make two main arguments: first, that deep ecology is uniquely American, and despite superficial similarities in rhetorical style, the social and political goals of radical environmentalism in other cultural contexts (e.g., West Germany and India) are quite different; second, that the social consequences of putting deep ecology into practice on a worldwide basis (what its practitioners are aiming for) are very grave indeed.

II. The Tenets of Deep Ecology

While I am aware that the term *deep ecology* was coined by the Norwegian philosopher Arne Naess, this article refers specifically to the American variant.[2] Adherents of the deep ecological perspective in this country, while arguing intensely among themselves over its political and philosophical implications, share some fundamental premises about human–nature interactions. As I see it, the defining characteristics of deep ecology are fourfold.

First, deep ecology argues that the environmental movement must shift from an "anthropocentric" to a "biocentric" perspective. In many respects, an acceptance of the primacy of this distinction constitutes the litmus test of deep ecology. A considerable effort is expended by deep ecologists in showing that the dominant motif in Western philosophy has been anthropocentric—i.e., the belief that man and his works are the center of the universe—and conversely, in identifying those lonely thinkers (Leopold, Thoreau, Muir, Aldous Huxley, Santayana, etc.) who, in assigning man a more humble place in the natural order, anticipated deep ecological thinking. In the political realm, meanwhile, establishment environmentalism (shallow ecology) is chided for casting its arguments in human-centered terms. Preserving nature, the deep ecologists say, has an intrinsic worth quite apart from any benefits preservation may convey to future human generations. The anthropocentric–biocentric distinction is accepted as axiomatic by

deep ecologists, it structures their discourse, and much of the present discussions remains mired within it.

The second characteristic of deep ecology is its focus on the preservation of unspoilt wilderness—and the restoration of degraded areas to a more pristine condition—to the relative (and sometimes absolute) neglect of other issues on the environmental agenda. I later identify the cultural roots and portentous consequences of this obsession with wilderness. For the moment, let me indicate three distinct sources from which it springs. Historically, it represents a playing out of the preservationist (read *radical*) and utilitarian (read *reformist*) dichotomy that has plagued American environmentalism since the turn of the century. Morally, it is an imperative that follows from the biocentric perspective; other species of plants and animals, and nature itself, have an intrinsic right to exist. And finally, the preservation of wilderness also turns on a scientific argument—viz., the value of biological diversity in stabilizing ecological regimes and in retaining a gene pool for future generations. Truly radical policy proposals have been put forward by deep ecologists on the basis of these arguments. The influential poet Gary Snyder, for example, would like to see a 90 percent reduction in human populations to allow a restoration of pristine environments, while others have argued forcefully that a large portion of the globe must be immediately cordoned off from human beings.[3]

Third, there is a widespread invocation of Eastern spiritual traditions as forerunners of deep ecology. Deep ecology, it is suggested, was practiced both by major religious traditions and at a more popular level by "primal" peoples in non-Western settings. This complements the search for an authentic lineage in Western thought. At one level, the task is to recover those dissenting voices within the Judeo-Christian tradition; at another, to suggest that religious traditions in other cultures are, in contrast, dominantly if not exclusively "biocentric" in their orientation. This coupling of (ancient) Eastern and (modern) ecological wisdom seemingly helps consolidate the claim that deep ecology is a philosophy of universal significance.

Fourth, deep ecologists, whatever their internal differences, share the belief that they are the "leading edge" of the environmental movement. As the polarity of the shallow/deep and anthropocentric/biocentric distinctions makes clear, they see themselves as the spiritual, philosophical, and political vanguard of American and world environmentalism.

III. Toward a Critique

Although I analyze each of these tenets independently, it is important to recognize, as deep ecologists are fond of remarking in reference to nature, the interconnectedness and unity of these individual themes.

(1) Insofar as it has begun to act as a check on man's arrogance and ecological hubris, the transition from an anthropocentric (human-centered) to a biocentric (humans as only one element in the ecosystem) view in both religious and scientific traditions is only to be welcomed.[4] What is unacceptable are the radical conclusions drawn by deep ecology, in particular, that intervention in nature should be guided primarily by the need to preserve biotic integrity rather than by the needs of humans. The latter for deep ecologists is anthropocentric, the former biocentric. This dichotomy is, however, of very little use in understanding the dynamics of environmental degradation. The two fundamental ecological problems facing the globe are (i) overconsumption by the industrialized world and by urban elites in the Third World and (ii) growing militarization, both in a short-term sense (i.e., ongoing regional wars) and in a long-term sense (i.e., the arms race and the prospect of nuclear annihilation). Neither of these problems has any tangible connection to the anthropocentric–biocentric distinction. Indeed, the agents of these processes would barely comprehend this philosophical dichotomy. The proximate causes of the ecologically wasteful characteristics of industrial society and of militarization are far more mundane: at an aggregate level, the dialectic of economic and political structures, and at a micro-level, the life-style choices of individuals. These causes cannot be reduced, whatever the level of analysis, to a deeper anthropocentric attitude toward nature; on the contrary, by constituting a grave threat to human survival, the ecological degradation they cause does not even serve the best interests of human beings! If my identification of the major dangers to the integrity of the natural world is correct, invoking the bogy of anthropocentrism is at best irrelevant and at worst a dangerous obfuscation.

(2) If the above dichotomy is irrelevant, the emphasis on wilderness is positively harmful when applied to the Third World. If in the U.S. the preservationist/utilitarian division is seen as mirroring the conflict between "people" and "interests," in countries such as India the situation is very nearly the reverse. Because India is a long settled and densely populated country in which agrarian populations have a finely balanced relationship with nature, the setting aside of wilderness areas has resulted in a direct transfer of resources from the poor to the rich. Thus, Project Tiger, a network of parks hailed by the international conservation community as an outstanding success, sharply posits the interests of the tiger against those of poor peasants living in and around the reserve. The designation of tiger reserves was made possible only by the physical displacement of existing villages and their inhabitants; their management requires the continuing exclusion of peasants and livestock. The initial impetus for setting up parks for the tiger and other large mammals such as the rhinoceros and elephant came from two social groups, first, a class of ex-hunters turned conservationists belonging mostly to the declining Indian feudal elite and second, representatives of international agencies, such as the World Wildlife Fund (WWF) and the International Union for the Conservation of Nature and Natural Resources (IUCN), seeking to transplant the American system of national parks onto Indian soil. In no case have the needs of the local population been taken into account, and as in many parts of Africa, the designated wildlands are managed primarily for the benefit of rich tourists. Until very recently, wildlands preservation has been identified with environmentalism by the state and the conservation elite; in consequence, environmental problems that impinge far more directly on the lives of the poor—e.g., fuel, fodder, water shortages, soil erosion, and air and water pollution—have not been adequately addressed.[5]

Deep ecology provides, perhaps unwittingly, a justification for the continuation of such narrow and inequitable conservation practices under a newly acquired radical guise. Increasingly, the international conservation elite is using the philosophical, moral, and scientific arguments used by deep ecologists in advancing their wilderness crusade. A striking but by no means atypical example is the recent plea by a prominent American biologist for the takeover of large portions of the globe by the author and his scientific colleagues. Writing in a prestigious scientific forum, the *Annual Review of Ecology and Systematics,* Daniel Janzen argues that only biologists have the competence to decide how the tropical landscape should be used. As "the representatives of the natural world," biologists are "in charge of the future of tropical ecology," and only they have the expertise and mandate to "determine whether the tropical agroscape is to be populated only by humans, their mutualists, commensals, and parasites, or whether it will also contain some islands of the greater nature—the nature that spawned humans, yet has been vanquished by them." Janzen exhorts his colleagues to advance their territorial claims on the tropical world more forcefully, warning that the very existence of these areas is at stake: "if biologists want a tropics in which to biologize, they are going to have to buy it with care, energy, effort, strategy, tactics, time, and cash."[6]

This frankly imperialist manifesto highlights the multiple dangers of the preoccupation with wilderness preservation that is characteristic of deep ecology. As I have suggested, it seriously compounds the neglect by the American movement of far more pressing environmental problems within the Third World. But perhaps more importantly, and in a more insidious fashion, it also provides an impetus to the imperialist yearning of Western biologists and their financial sponsors, organizations such as the WWF and IUCN. The wholesale transfer of a movement culturally rooted in American conservation history can only result in the social uprooting of human populations in other parts of the globe.

(3) I come now to the persistent invocation of Eastern philosophies as antecedent in point of time but convergent in their structure with deep ecology. Complex and internally differentiated religious traditions—Hinduism, Buddhism, and Taoism—are lumped together as holding a view of nature believed to be quintessentially biocentric. Individual philosophers such as the Taoist Lao Tzu are identified as being forerunners of deep ecology. Even an intensely political, pragmatic, and Christian-influenced thinker such as Gandhi has been accorded a wholly undeserved place in the deep ecological pantheon. Thus the Zen teacher Robert Aitken Roshi makes the strange claim that Gandhi's thought was not human-centered and

that he practiced an embryonic form of deep ecology which is "traditionally Eastern and is found with differing emphasis in Hinduism, Taoism and in Theravada and Mahayana Buddhism."[7] Moving away from the realm of high philosophy and scriptural religion, deep ecologists make the further claim that at the level of material and spiritual practice "primal" peoples subordinated themselves to the integrity of the biotic universe they inhabited.

I have indicated that this appropriation of Eastern traditions is in part dictated by the need to construct an authentic lineage and in part a desire to present deep ecology as a universalistic philosophy. Indeed, in his substantial and quixotic biography of John Muir, Michael Cohen goes so far as to suggest that Muir was the "Taoist of the [American] West."[8] This reading of Eastern traditions is selective and does not bother to differentiate between alternate (and changing) religious and cultural traditions; as it stands, it does considerable violence to the historical record. Throughout most recorded history the characteristic form of human activity in the "East" has been a finely tuned but nonetheless conscious and dynamic manipulation of nature. Although mystics such as Lao Tzu did reflect on the spiritual essence of human relations with nature, it must be recognized that such ascetics and their reflections were supported by a society of cultivators whose relationship with nature was a far more *active* one. Many agricultural communities do have a sophisticated knowledge of the natural environment that may equal (and sometimes surpass) codified "scientific" knowledge; yet, the elaboration of such traditional ecological knowledge (in both material and spiritual contexts) can hardly be said to rest on a mystical affinity with nature of a deep ecological kind. Nor is such knowledge infallible; as the archaeological record powerfully suggests, modern Western man has no monopoly on ecological disasters.

In a brilliant article, the Chicago historian Ronald Inden points out that this romantic and essentially positive view of the East is a mirror image of the scientific and essentially pejorative view normally upheld by Western scholars of the Orient. In either case, the East constitutes the Other, a body wholly separate and alien from the West; it is defined by a uniquely spiritual and nonrational "essence," even if this essence is valorized quite differently by the two schools. Eastern man exhibits a spiritual dependence with respect to nature—on the one hand, this is symptomatic of his prescientific and backward self, on the other, of his ecological wisdom and deep ecological consciousness. Both views are monolithic, simplistic, and have the characteristic effect—intended in one case, perhaps unintended in the other—of denying agency and reason to the East and making it the privileged orbit of Western thinkers.

The two apparently opposed perspectives have then a common underlying structure of discourse in which the East merely serves as a vehicle for Western projections. Varying images of the East are raw material for political and cultural battles being played out in the West; they tell us far more about the Western commentator and his desires than about the "East." Inden's remarks apply not merely to Western scholarship on India, but to Orientalist constructions of China and Japan as well:

> Although these two views appear to be strongly opposed, they often combine together. Both have a similar interest in sustaining the Otherness of India. The holders of the dominant view, best exemplified in the past in imperial administrative discourse (and today probably by that of 'development economics'), would place a traditional, superstition-ridden India in a position of perpetual tutelage to a modern, rational West. The adherents of the romantic view, best exemplified academically in the discourses of Christian liberalism and analytic psychology, concede the realm of the public and impersonal to the positivist. Taking their succour not from governments and big business, but from a plethora of religious foundations and self-help institutes, and from allies in the 'consciousness industry,' not to mention the important industry of tourism, the romantics insist that India embodies a private realm of the imagination and the religious which modern, western man lacks but needs. They, therefore, like the positivists, but for just the opposite reason, have a vested interest in seeing that the Orientalist view of India as 'spiritual,' 'mysterious,' and 'exotic' is perpetuated.[9]

(4) How radical, finally, are the deep ecologists? Notwithstanding their self-image and strident rhetoric (in which the label "shallow ecology" has an opprobrium similar to that reserved for "social democratic" by Marxist-Leninists), even within the American context their radicalism is limited and it manifests itself quite differently elsewhere.

To my mind, deep ecology is best viewed as a radical trend within the wilderness preservation movement. Although advancing philosophical rather than aesthetic arguments and encouraging political militancy rather than negotiation, its practical emphasis—viz., preservation of unspoilt nature—is virtually identical. For the mainstream movement, the function of wilderness is to provide a temporary antidote to modern civilization. As a special institution within an industrialized society, the national park "provides an opportunity for respite, contrast, contemplation, and affirmation of values for those who live most of their lives in the workaday world."[10] Indeed, the rapid increase in visitations to the national parks in postwar America is a direct consequence of economic expansion. The emergence of a popular interest in wilderness sites, the historian Samuel Hays points out, was "not a throwback to the primitive, but an integral part of the modern standard of living as people sought to add new 'amenity' and 'aesthetic' goals and desires to their earlier preoccupation with necessities and conveniences."[11]

Here, the enjoyment of nature is an integral part of the consumer society. The private automobile (and the life style it has spawned) is in many respects the ultimate ecological villain, and an untouched wilderness the prototype of ecological harmony; yet, for most Americans it is perfectly consistent to drive a thousand miles to spend a holiday in a national park. They possess a vast, beautiful, and sparsely populated continent and are also able to draw upon the natural resources of large portions of the globe by virtue of their economic and political dominance. In consequence, America can simultaneously enjoy the material benefits of an expanding economy and the aesthetic benefits of unspoilt nature. The two poles of "wilderness" and "civilization" mutually coexist in an internally coherent whole, and philosophers of both poles are assigned a prominent place in this culture. Paradoxically as it may seem, it is no accident that Star Wars technology and deep ecology both find their fullest expression in that leading sector of Western civilization, California.

Deep ecology runs parallel to the consumer society without seriously questioning its ecological and socio-political basis. In its celebration of American wilderness, it also displays an uncomfortable convergence with the prevailing climate of nationalism in the American wilderness movement. For spokesmen such as the historian Roderick Nash, the national park system is America's distinctive cultural contribution to the world, reflective not merely of its economic but of its philosophical and ecological maturity as well. In what Walter Lippman called the American century, the "American invention of national parks" must be exported worldwide. Betraying an economic determinism that would make even a Marxist shudder, Nash believes that environmental preservation is a "full stomach" phenomenon that is confined to the rich, urban, and sophisticated. Nonetheless, he hopes that "the less developed nations may eventually evolve economically and intellectually to the point where nature preservation is more than a business."[12]

The error which Nash makes (and which deep ecology in some respects encourages) is to equate environmental protection with the protection of wilderness. This is a distinctively American notion, borne out of a unique social and environmental history. The archetypal concerns of radical environmentalists in other cultural contexts are in fact quite different. The German Greens, for example, have elaborated a devastating critique of industrial society which turns on the acceptance of environmental limits to growth. Pointing to the intimate links between industrialization, militarization, and conquest, the Greens argue that economic growth in the West has historically rested on the economic and ecological exploitation of the Third World. Rudolf Bahro is characteristically blunt:

> The working class here [in the West] is the richest lower class in the world. And if I look at the problem from the point of view of the whole of humanity, not just from that of Europe, then I must say that the metropolitan working class is the worst exploiting class in history. . . . What made poverty bearable in eighteenth- or nineteenth-century Europe was the prospect of escaping it through exploitation of the periphery. But this is no longer a possibility, and continued industrialism in the Third World will mean poverty for whole generations and hunger for millions.[13]

Here the roots of global ecological problems lie in the disproportionate share of resources consumed by the industrialized countries as a whole *and* the urban elite within the Third World. Since it is impossible to reproduce an industrial monoculture worldwide, the ecological movement in the West must begin by cleaning up its own act. The Greens advocate the creation of a "no growth" economy, to be achieved by scaling down current (and clearly unsustainable) consumption levels.[14] This radical shift in consumption and production patterns requires the creation of alternate economic and political structures—smaller in scale and more amenable to social participation—but it rests equally on a shift in cultural values. The expansionist character of modern Western man will have to give way to an ethic of renunciation and self-limitation, in which spiritual and communal values play an increasing role in sustaining social life. This revolution in cultural values, however, has as its point of departure an understanding of environmental processes quite different from deep ecology.

Many elements of the Green program find a strong resonance in countries such as India, where a history of Western colonialism and industrial development has benefited only a tiny elite while exacting tremendous social and environmental costs. The ecological battles presently being fought in India have as their epicenter the conflict over nature between the subsistence and largely rural sector and the vastly more powerful commercial-industrial sector. Perhaps the most celebrated of these battles concerns the Chipko (Hug the Tree) movement, a peasant movement against deforestation in the Himalayan foothills. Chipko is only one of several movements that have sharply questioned the nonsustainable demand being placed on the land and vegetative base by urban centers and industry. These include opposition to large dams by displaced peasants, the conflict between small artisan fishing and large-scale trawler fishing for export, the countrywide movements against commercial forest operations, and opposition to industrial pollution among downstream agricultural and fishing communities.[15]

Two features distinguish these environmental movements from their Western counterparts. First, for the sections of society most critically affected by environmental degradation—poor and landless peasants, women, and tribals—it is a question of sheer survival, not of enhancing the quality of life. Second, and as a consequence, the environmental solutions they articulate deeply involve questions of equity as well as economic and political redistribution. Highlighting these differences, a leading

Indian environmentalist stresses that "environmental protection per se is of least concern to most of these groups. Their main concern is about the use of the environment and who should benefit from it."[16] They seek to wrest control of nature away from the state and the industrial sector and place it in the hands of rural communities who live within that environment but are increasingly denied access to it. These communities have far more basic needs, their demands on the environment are far less intense, and they can draw upon a reservoir of cooperative social institutions and local ecological knowledge in managing the "commons"—forests, grasslands, and the waters—on a sustainable basis. If colonial and capitalist expansion has both accentuated social inequalities and signaled a precipitous fall in ecological wisdom, an alternate ecology must rest on an alternate society and polity as well.

This brief overview of German and Indian environmentalism has some major implications for deep ecology. Both German and Indian environmental traditions allow for a greater integration of ecological concerns with livelihood and work. They also place a greater emphasis on equity and social justice (both within individual countries and on a global scale) on the grounds that in the absence of social regeneration environmental regeneration has very little chance of succeeding. Finally, and perhaps most significantly, they have escaped the preoccupation with wilderness preservation so characteristic of American cultural and environmental history.[17]

IV. A Homily

In 1958, the economist J. K. Galbraith referred to overconsumption as the unasked question of the American conservation movement. There is a marked selectivity, he wrote, "in the conservationist's approach to materials consumption. If we are concerned about our great appetite for materials, it is plausible to seek to increase the supply, to decrease waste, to make better use of the stocks available, and to develop substitutes. But what of the appetite itself? Surely this is the ultimate source of the problem. If it continues its geometric course, will it not one day have to be restrained? Yet in the literature of the resource problem this is the forbidden question. Over it hangs a nearly total silence."[18]

The consumer economy and society have expanded tremendously in the three decades since

Galbraith penned these words; yet his criticisms are nearly as valid today. I have said "nearly," for there are some hopeful signs. Within the environmental movement several dispersed groups are working to develop ecologically benign technologies and to encourage less wasteful life styles. Moreover, outside the self-defined boundaries of American environmentalism, opposition to the permanent war economy is being carried on by a peace movement that has a distinguished history and impeccable moral and political credentials.

It is precisely these (to my mind, most hopeful) components of the American social scene that are missing from deep ecology. In their widely noticed book, Bill Devall and George Sessions make no mention of militarization or the movements for peace, while activists whose practical focus is on developing ecologically responsible life styles (e.g., Wendell Berry) are derided as "falling short of deep ecological awareness."[19] A truly radical ecology in the American context ought to work toward a synthesis of the appropriate technology, alternate life style, and peace movements.[20] By making the (largely spurious) anthropocentric–biocentric distinction central to the debate, deep ecologists may have appropriated the moral high ground, but they are at the same time doing a serious disservice to American and global environmentalism.[21]

Notes

1. Kirkpatrick Sale, "The Forest for the Trees: Can Today's Environmentalists Tell the Difference," *Mother Jones* 11, no. 8 (November 1986): 26.

2. One of the major criticisms I make in this essay concerns deep ecology's lack of concern with inequalities *within* human society. In the article in which he coined the term *deep ecology*, Naess himself expresses concerns about inequalities between and within nations. However, his concern with social cleavages and their impact on resource utilization patterns and ecological destruction is not very visible in the later writings of deep ecologists. See Arne Naess, "The Shallow and the Deep, Long-Range Ecology Movement: A Summary," *Inquiry* 16 (1973): 96 (I am grateful to Tom Birch for this reference).

3. Gary Snyder, quoted in Sale, "The Forest for the Trees," p. 32. See also Dave Foreman, "A Modest Proposal for a Wilderness System," *Whole Earth Review*, no. 53 (Winter 1986–87):42–45.

4. See, for example, Donald Worster, *Nature's Economy: The Roots of Ecology* (San Francisco: Sierra Club Books, 1977).

5. See Centre for Science and Environment, *India: The State of the Environment 1982: A Citizens Report* (New Delhi: Centre for Science and Environment, 1982); R. Sukumar, "Elephant-Man Conflict in Karnataka," in Cecil Saldanha, ed., *The State of Karnataka's Environment* (Bangalore: Centre for Taxonomic Studies, 1985). For Africa, see the brilliant analysis by Helge Kjekshus, *Ecology Control and Economic Development in East African History* (Berkeley: University of California Press, 1977).

6. Daniel Janzen, "The Future of Tropical Ecology," *Annual Review of Ecology and Systematics* 17 (1986): 305–06; emphasis added.

7. Robert Aitken Roshi, "Gandhi, Dogen, and Deep Ecology," reprinted as appendix C in Bill Devall and George Sessions, *Deep Ecology: Living as if Nature Mattered* (Salt Lake City: Peregrine Smith Books, 1985). For Gandhi's own views on social reconstruction, see the excellent three-volume collection edited by Raghavan Iyer, *The Moral and Political Writings of Mahatma Gandhi* (Oxford: Clarendon Press, 1986–87).

8. Michael Cohen, *The Pathless Way* (Madison: University of Wisconsin Press, 1984), p. 120.

9. Ronald Inden, "Orientalist Constructions of India," *Modern Asian Studies* 20 (1986): 442. Inden draws inspiration from Edward Said's forceful polemic, *Orientalism* (New York: Basic Books, 1980). It must be noted, however, that there is a salient difference between Western perceptions of Middle Eastern and Far Eastern cultures, respectively. Due perhaps to the long history of Christian conflict with Islam, Middle Eastern cultures (as Said documents) are consistently presented in pejorative terms. The juxtaposition of hostile and worshiping attitudes that Inden talks of applies only to Western attitudes toward Buddhist and Hindu societies.

10. Joseph Sax, *Mountains Without Handrails: Reflections on the National Parks* (Ann Arbor: University of Michigan Press, 1980), p. 42. Cf. also Peter Schmitt, *Back to Nature: The Arcadian Myth in Urban America* (New York: Oxford University Press, 1969), and Alfred Runte, *National Parks: The American Experience* (Lincoln: University of Nebraska Press, 1979).

11. Samuel Hays, "From Conservation to Environment: Environmental Politics in the United States since World War Two," *Environmental Review* 6 (1982): 21. See also the same authors book entitled *Beauty, Health and Permanence: Environmental Politics in the United States, 1955–85* (New York: Cambridge University Press, 1987).

12. Roderick Nash, *Wilderness and the American Mind,* 3rd ed. (New Haven: Yale University Press, 1982).

13. Rudolf Bahro, *From Red to Green* (London: Verso Books, 1984).

14. From time to time, American scholars have themselves criticized these imbalances in consumption patterns. In the 1950s, William Vogt made the charge that the United States, with one-sixteenth of the world's population, was utilizing one-third of the globe's resources. (Vogt, cited in E. F. Murphy, *Nature, Bureaucracy and the Rule of Property* [Amsterdam: North Holland, 1977 p. 29]). More recently, Zero Population Growth has estimated that each American consumes thirty-nine times as many resources as an Indian. See *Christian Science Monitor,* 2 March 1987.

15. For an excellent review, see Anil Agarwal and Sunita Narain, eds., *India: The State of the Environment 1984–85: A Citizens Report* (New Delhi: Centre for Science and Environment, 1985). Cf. also Ramachandra Guha, *The Unquiet Woods: Ecological Change and Peasant Resistance in the Indian Himalaya* (Berkeley: University of California Press, forthcoming).

16. Anil Agarwal, "Human–Nature Interactions in a Third World Country," *The Environmentalist* 6, no. 3 (1986): 167.

17. One strand in radical American environmentalism, the bioregional movement, by emphasizing a greater involvement with the bioregion people inhabit, does indirectly challenge consumerism. However, as yet bioregionalism has hardly raised the questions of equity and social justice (international, intranational, and intergenerational) which I argue must be a central plank of radical environmentalism. Moreover, its stress on (individual) *experience* as the key to involvement with nature is also somewhat at odds with the integration of nature with livelihood and work that I talk of in this paper. Cf. Kirkpatrick Sale, *Dwellers in the Land: The Bioregional Vision* (San Francisco: Sierra Club Books, 1985).

18. John Kenneth Galbraith, "How Much Should a Country Consume?" in Henry Jarrett, ed., *Perspectives on Conservation* (Baltimore: Johns Hopkins Press, 1958), pp. 91–92.

19. Devall and Sessions, *Deep Ecology,* p. 122. For Wendell Berry's own assessment of deep ecology, see his "Amplications: Preserving Wildness," *Wilderness* 50 (Spring 1987): 39–40, 50–54.

20. See the interesting recent contribution by one of the most influential spokesmen of appropriate technology—Barry Commoner, "A Reporter at Large: The Environment," *New Yorker,* 15 June 1987. While Commoner makes a forceful plea for the convergence of the environmental movement (viewed by

him primarily as the opposition to air and water pollution and to the institutions that generate such pollution) and the peace movement, he significantly does not mention consumption patterns, implying that "limits to growth" do not exist.

21. In this sense, my critique of deep ecology, although that of an outsider, may facilitate the reassertion of those elements in the American environmental tradition for which there is a profound sympathy in other parts of the globe. A global perspective may also lead to a critical reassessment of figures such as Aldo Leopold and John Muir, the two patron saints of deep ecology. As Donald Worster has pointed out, the message of Muir (and, I would argue, of Leopold as well) makes sense only in an American context; he has very little to say to other cultures. See Worster's review of Stephen Fox's *John Muir and His Legacy*, in *Environmental Ethics* 5 (1983): 277–81.

77. Tropical Forests and Their Species: Going, Going . . .?

Norman Myers

There is strong evidence that we are into the opening stages of an extinction spasm. That is, we are witnessing a mass extinction episode, in the sense of a sudden and pronounced decline worldwide in the abundance and diversity of ecologically disparate groups of organisms.

Of course extinction has been a fact of life since the emergence of species almost 4 billion years ago. Of all species that have ever existed, possibly half a billion or more, there now remain only a few million. But the natural background rate of extinction during the past 600 million years, the period of major life, has been on the order of only one species every year or so (Raup and Sepkoski, 1984). Today the rate is surely hundreds of times higher, possibly thousands of times higher (Ehrlich and Ehrlich, 1981; Myers, 1986; Raven, 1987; Soulé, 1986; Western and Pearl, in press; Wilson, 1987). Moreover, whereas past extinctions have occurred by virtue of natural processes, today the virtually exclusive cause is *Homo sapiens*, who eliminates entire habitats and complete communities of species in super-short order. It is all happening in the twinkling of an evolutionary eye.

To help us get a handle on the situation, let us take a lengthy look at tropical forests. These forests cover only 7% of Earth's land surface, yet they are estimated to contain at least 50% of all species (conceivably a much higher proportion). Equally important, they are being depleted faster than any other ecological zone.

Tropical Forests

There is general agreement that remaining primary forests cover rather less than 9 million square kilometers, out of the 15 million or so that may once have existed according to bioclimatic data. There is also general agreement that between 76,000 and 92,000 square kilometers are eliminated outright each year, and that at least a further 100,000 square kilometers are grossly disrupted each year (FAO and UNEP,1982; Hadley and Lanley,1983; Melillo et al., 1985; Molofsky et al., 1986; Myers,1980,1984). These figures for deforestation rates derive from a data base of the late 1970s; the rates have increased somewhat since then. This means, roughly speaking, that 1% of the biome is being deforested each year and that more than another 1% is being significantly degraded.

The main source of information lies with remote-sensing surveys, which constitute a thoroughly objective and systematic mode of inquiry. By 1980 there were remote-sensing data for approximately 65% of the biome, a figure that has risen today to 82%. In all countries where remote-sensing information has been available in only the past few years—notably Indonesia, Burma, India, Nigeria, Cameroon, Guatemala, Honduras, and Peru—we find there is greater deforestation than had been supposed by government agencies in question.

Tropical deforestation is by no means an even process. Some areas are being affected harder than others; some will survive longer than others. By the end of the century or shortly thereafter, there could be little left of the biome in primary status with a full complement of species, except for two large remnant blocs, one in the Zaire basin and the other in the western half of Brazilian Amazonia, plus two much smaller blocs, in Papua New Guinea and in the Guyana Shield of northern South America. These relict sectors of the biome may well endure for several decades further, but they are little likely to last beyond the middle of next century, if only because of sheer expansion in the numbers of small-scale cultivators.

Rapid population growth among communities of small-scale cultivators occurs mainly through immigration rather than natural increase, i.e., through the phenomenon of the shifted cultivator. As a measure of what ultrarapid growth rates can already impose on tropical forests, consider the situation in Rondonia, a state in the southern sector of Brazilian Amazonia. Between 1975 and 1986, the population grew from 111,000 to well over 1 million, i.e., a 10-times increase in little more than 10 years. In 1975, almost 1,250 square kilometers of forest were cleared. By 1982, this amount had grown to more than 10,000 square kilometers, and by late 1985, to around 17,000 square kilometers (Fearnside, 1986).

It is this broad-scale clearing and degradation of forest habitats that is far and away the main cause of species extinctions. Regrettably, we have no way to know the actual current rate of extinction, nor can we even come close with accurate estimates. But we can make substantive assessments by looking at species numbers before deforestation and then applying the analytic techniques of island biogeography. To help us gain an insight into the scope and scale of present extinctions, let us briefly consider three particular areas: the forested tracts of western Ecuador, Atlantic-coast Brazil, and Madagascar. Each of these areas features, or rather featured, exceptional concentrations of species with high levels of endemism. Western Ecuador is reputed to have once contained between 8,000 and 10,000 plant species with an endemism rate somewhere between 40 and 60% (Gentry, 1986). If we suppose, as we reasonably can by drawing on detailed inventories in sample plots, that there are at least 10 to 30 animal species for every one plant species, the species complement in western Ecuador must have amounted to 200,000 or more in all. Since 1960, at least 95% of the forest cover has been destroyed to make way for

banana plantations, oil exploiters, and human settlements of various sorts. According to the theory of island biogeography, which is supported by abundant and diversified evidence, we can realistically expect that when a habitat has lost 90% of its extent, it will eventually lose half its species. Precisely how many species have actually been eliminated, or are on the point of extinction, in western Ecuador is impossible to say. But ultimate accuracy is surely irrelevant, insofar as the number must total tens of thousands at least, conceivably 50,000—all eliminated or at least doomed in the space of just 25 years.

Very similar baseline figures for species totals and endemism levels, and a similar story of forest depletion (albeit for different reasons and over a longer time period), apply to the Atlantic-coastal forest of Brazil, where the original 1 million square kilometers of forest cover have been reduced to less than 50,000 square kilometers (Mori et al., 1981). Parallel data apply also to Madagascar, where only 5% of the island's primary vegetation remains undisturbed—and where the endemism levels are rather high (Rauh, 1979).

So in these three tropical forest areas alone, with their roughly 600,000 species, the recent past must have witnessed a sizeable fallout of species. Some may not have disappeared as yet, due to the time lag in equilibration, i.e., delayed fallout effects stemming from habitat depletion. But whereas the ultimate total of extinctions in these areas in the wake of deforestation to date will presumably amount to some 150,000 species, we may realistically assume that already half, some 75,000 species, have been eliminated or doomed.

Deforestation in Brazil's Atlantic-coastal forest and Madagascar has been going on for several centuries, but the main damage has occurred during this century, especially since 1950, i.e., since the spread of broad-scale industrialization and plantation agriculture in Brazil and since the onset of rapid population growth in Madagascar. This all means that as many as 50,000 species have been eliminated or doomed in these areas alone during the last 35 years. This works out to a crude average of almost 1,500 species per year—a figure consistent with the independent assessment of Wilson (1987), who postulates an extinction rate in all tropical forests of perhaps 10,000 species per year. Of course many reservations attend these calculations. More species than postulated may remain until a new equilibrium is established and causes their disappearance. Conversely, more species will presumably have disappeared during the later stages of the 35-year period than during the opening stage. Whatever the details of the outcome, we can judiciously use the figures and conclusions to form a working appraisal of the extent that an extinction spasm is already under way.

Extinction Rates: Future

The outlook for the future seems all the more adverse, though its detailed dimensions are even less clear than those of the present. Let us look again at tropical forests. We have seen what is happening to three critical areas. We can identify a good number of other sectors of the biome that feature exceptional concentrations of species with exceptional levels of endemism and that face exceptional threat of depletion, whether quantitative or qualitative. They include the Choco forest of Colombia; the Napo center of diversity in Peruvian Amazonia, plus seven other centers (out of 20-plus centers of diversity in Amazonia) that lie around the fringes of the basin and hence are unusually threatened by settlement programs and various other forms of development; the Tai Forest of Ivory Coast; the montane forests of East Africa; the relict wet forest of Sri Lanka; the monsoon forests of the Himalayan foothills; northwestern Borneo; certain lowland areas of the Philippines; and several islands of the South Pacific (New Caledonia, for instance, is 16,100 square kilometers, almost the size of New Jersey, and contains 3,000 plant species, 80% of them endemic).

These various sectors of the tropical forest biome amount to roughly 1 million square kilometers (2.5 times the size of California), or slightly more than one-tenth of the remaining undisturbed forests. As far as we can best judge from their documented numbers of plant species, and by making substantiated assumptions about the numbers of associated animal species, we can estimate that these areas surely harbor 1 million species (could be many more) —and in many of the areas, there is marked endemism. If present land-use patterns and exploitation trends persist (and they show every sign of accelerating), there will be little left of these forest tracts, except in the form of degraded remnants, by the end of this century or shortly thereafter. Thus forest depletion in these areas alone could well eliminate large numbers of species, surely hundreds of thousands, within the next 25 years at most.

Looking at the situation another way, we can estimate, on the basis of what we know about plant numbers and distribution together with what we can surmise about their associated animal communities, that almost 20% of all species occur in forests of Latin America outside of Amazonia and that another 20% are present in forests of Asia and Africa outside the Zaire basin (Raven, 1987). That is, these forests contain some 1 million species altogether, even if we estimate that the planetary total is only 5 million. All the primary forests in which these species occur may well disappear by the end of this century or early in the next. If only half the species in these forests disappear, this will amount to several hundred thousand species.

What is the prognosis for the longer-term future? Could we eventually lose at least one-quarter, possibly one-third, or conceivably an even larger share of all extant species? Let us take a quick look at Amazonia (Simberloff, 1986). If deforestation continues at present rates until the year 2000, but then comes to a complete halt, we could anticipate an ultimate loss of about 15% of the plant species and a similar percentage of animal species. If Amazonia's forest cover were to be ultimately reduced to those areas now set aside as parks and reserves, we could anticipate that 66% of the plant species will eventually disappear together with almost 69% of bird species and similar proportions of all other major categories of species.

Of course we may learn how to manipulate habitats to enhance survival prospects. We may learn how to propagate threatened species in captivity. We may be able to apply other emergent conservation techniques, all of which could help to relieve the adverse repercussions of broad-scale deforestation. But in the main, the damage will have been done. For reasons of island biogeography and equilibration, some extinctions in Amazonia will not occur until well into the twenty-second century, or even further into the future. So a major extinction spasm in Amazonia is entirely possible, indeed plausible if not probable.

Tropical Forest and Climatic Change

Protected areas are not likely to provide a sufficient answer for reasons that reflect climatic factors. In Amazonia, for instance, it is becoming apparent that if as much as half the forest were to be safeguarded in some way or another (e.g., through multiple-use conservation units as well as protected areas), but the other half of the forest were to be developed out of existence, there could soon be at work a hydrologic feedback mechanism that would allow a good part of Amazonia's moisture to be lost to the ecosystem (Salati and Vose, 1984). The remaining forest would likely be subjected to a steady desiccatory process, until the moist forest became more like a dry forest, even a woodland—with all that would mean for the species communities that are adapted to moist forest habitats. Even with a set of forest safeguards of exemplary type and scope, Amazonia's biotas would be more threatened than ever.

Still more widespread climatic changes with yet more marked impact are likely to occur within the foreseeable future. By the first quarter of the next century, we may well be experiencing the climatic dislocations of a planetary warming, stemming from a buildup of carbon dioxide and other so-called greenhouse gases in the global atmosphere (Bolin and Doos, 1986; DOE, 1985). The consequences for protected areas will be pervasive and profound. The present network of protected areas, grossly inadequate as it is, has been established in accord with present-day needs. Yet its ultimate viability will be severely threatened in the wake of a greenhouse effect as vegetation zones start to migrate away from the equator with all manner of disruptive repercussions for natural environments (Peters and Darling, 1985).

These, then, are some dimensions of the extinction spasm that we can reasonably assume will overtake the planet's biotas within the next few decades (unless of course we do a massively better job of conservation). In effect we are conducting an irreversible experiment on a global scale with Earth's stock of species.

Repercussions for the Future of Evolution

The foreseeable fallout of species, together with their subunits, is far from the entire story. A longer-term and ultimately more serious repercussion could lie in a disruption of the course of evolution, insofar as speciation processes will have to work with a greatly reduced pool of species and their genetic materials. We are probably being optimistic when we call it a disruption; a more likely outcome is that certain evolutionary processes will be suspended or even terminated. In the graphic phrasing of Soule and Wilcox (1980), "Death is one thing; an end to birth is something else."

From what little we can discern from the geologic record, a normal recovery time may require millions of years. After the dinosaur crash, for instance, between 50,000 and 100,000 years elapsed before there started to emerge a set of diversified and specialized biotas, and another 5 to 10 million years went by before there were bats in the skies and whales in the seas (Jablonski, 1986). Following the crash during the late Permian Period, when marine invertebrates lost about half their families, as many as 20 million years elapsed before the survivors could establish even half as many families as they had lost (Raup, 1986).

The evolutionary outcome this time around could prove even more drastic. The critical factor lies with the likely loss of key environments. Not only do we appear ready to lose most if not virtually all tropical forests, but there is also progressive depletion of coral reefs, wetlands, estuaries, and other biotopes with exceptional biodiversity. These environments have served in the past as preeminent power-houses of evolution, in that they have supported the emergence of more species than have other environments. Virtually every major group of vertebrates and many other large categories of animals have originated in spacious zones with warm, equable climates, notably tropical forests. In addition, the rate of evolutionary diversification—whether through proliferation of species or through the emergence of major new adaptations—has been greatest in the tropics, again most notably in tropical forests.

Of course tropical forests have been severely depleted in the past. During drier phases of the recent Ice Ages (Pleistocene Epoch), they have been repeatedly reduced to only a small fraction, occasionally as little as one-tenth, of their former expanse. Moreover, tropical biotas seem to have been unduly prone to extinction. But the remnant forest refugia usually contained sufficient stocks of surviving species to recolonize suitable territories when moister conditions returned (Prance, 1982). Within the foreseeable future, by contrast, it seems all too possible that most tropical forests will be reduced to much less than one-tenth of their former expanse, and their pockets of holdout species will be much less stocked with potential colonizers.

Furthermore, the species depletion will surely apply across most if not all major categories of species. This is almost axiomatic, if extensive environments are eliminated wholesale. The result will contrast sharply with the end of the Cretaceous Period, when not only placental mammals survived (leading to the adaptive radiation of mammals, eventually including humans), but also birds, amphibians, and crocodiles, among other nondinosaurian reptiles. In addition, the present extinction spasm looks likely to eliminate a sizeable share of terrestrial plant species, at least one-fifth within the next half century and a good many more within the following half century. By contrast, during most mass-extinction episodes of the prehistoric past, terrestrial plants have survived with relatively few losses (Knoll, 1984). They have thus supplied a resource base on which evolutionary processes could start to generate replacement animal species forthwith. If this biotic substrate is markedly depleted within the foreseeable future, the restorative capacities of evolution will be all the more reduced.

In sum, the evolutionary impoverishment of the impending extinction spasm, plus the numbers of species involved and the telescoped time scale of the phenomenon, may result in the greatest single setback to life's abundance and diversity since the first flickerings of life almost 4 billion years ago.

References

Bohn, B., and B. R. Doos, eds. 1986. *The Greenhouse Effect: Climatic Change and Ecosystems*. Wiley, New York. 541 pp.

DOE (U.S. Department of Energy). 1985. *Direct Effects of Increasing Carbon Dioxide on Vegetation*. U.S. Department of Energy, Washington, DC.

Ehrlich, P. R., and A. H. Ehrlich. 1981. *Extinction: The Causes and Consequences of the Disappearance of Species*. Random House, New York. 305 pp.

FAO and UNEP (Food and Agriculture Organization and United Nations Environment Programme). 1982. *Tropical Forest Resources*. Food and Agriculture Organization of the United Nations, Rome, Italy, and United Nations Environment Programme, Nairobi, Kenya. 106 pp.

Fearnside, P. M. 1986. *Human Carrying Capacity of the Brazilian Rain Forest*. Columbia University Press, New York. 293 pp.

Gentry, A. H. 1986. Endemism in tropical versus temperate plant communities. Pp. 153–181 in M. E. Soulé, ed. *Conservation Biology: The Science of Scarcity and Diversity*. Sinauer Associates, Sunderland, MA. 584 pp.

Hadley, M., and J. P. Lanley. 1983. Tropical forest ecosystems: Identifying differences, seeing similarities. *Nat. Resour.* 19:2–19.

Jablonski, D. 1986. Causes and consequences of mass extinction: A comparative approach. Pp. 183–230 in D. K. Elliot, ed. *Dynamics of Extinction*. Wiley Interscience, New York.

Knoll, A. H. 1984. Patterns of extinction in the fossil record of vascular plants. Pp. 21–68 in M. H. Nitecki, ed. *Extinctions*. University of Chicago Press, Chicago.

Melillo, J. M., C. A. Palm, R. A. Houghton, G. M. Woodwell, and N. Myers. 1985. A comparison of recent estimates of disturbance in tropical forests. *Environ. Conserv.* 12(1):37–40.

Molofsky, J., C. A. S. Hall, and N. Myers. 1986. *A Comparison of Tropical Forest Surveys*. U.S. Department of Energy, Washington, DC.

Mori, S. A., B. M. Boom, and G. T. Prance. 1981. Distribution patterns and conservation of eastern Brazilian coastal forest tree species. *Brittonia* 33(2):233–245.

Myers, N. 1980. *Conservation of Tropical Moist Forests*. A report prepared for the Committee on Research Priorities in Tropical Biology of the National Research Council. National Academy of Sciences, Washington, DC. 205 pp.

Myers, N. 1984. *The Primary Source: Tropical Forests and Our Future*. W. W. Norton, New York. 399 pp.

Myers, N. 1986. *Tackling Mass Extinction of Species: A Great Creative Challenge*. Albright Lecture, University of California, Berkeley. 40 pp.

Peters, R. L., and J. D. S. Darling. 1985. The greenhouse effect and nature reserves. *BioScience* 35(11):707–717.

Prance, G. T., ed. 1982. *Biological Diversification in the Tropics*. Proceedings of the Fifth International Symposium of the Association for Tropical Biology, held at Macuto Beach, Caracas, Venezuela, February 8–13, 1979. Columbia University Press, New York. 714 pp.

Rauh, W. 1979. Problems of biological conservation in Madagascar. Pp. 405–421 in D. Bramwell, ed. *Plants and Islands*. Academic Press, London, U.K.

Raup, D. M. 1986. Biological extinction in earth history. *Science* 231:1528–1533.

Raup, D. M., and J. J. Sepkoski. 1984. Periodicity of extinction in the geologic past. *Proc. Natl. Acad. Sci. USA* 81:801–805.

Raven, P. H. 1987. *We're Killing Our World*. Keynote paper presented to Annual Conference of the

American Association for the Advancement of Science, Chicago, February 1987. Missouri Botanical Garden, St. Louis.

Salati, E., and P. B. Vose.1984. Amazon basin: A system in equilibrium. *Science* 25:129–138.

Simberloff, D. 1986. Are we on the verge of a mass extinction in tropical rain forests? Pp. 165–180 in D. K. Elliot, ed. *Dynamics of Extinction.* Wiley, New York.

Soulé, M. E. 1986. *Conservation Biology, The Science of Scarcity and Diversity.* Sinauer Associates, Sunderland, MA.

Soulé, M. E., and B. A. Wilcox, eds. 1980. *Conservation Biology: An Evolutionary-Ecological Perspective.* Sinauer Associates, Sunderland, MA, 395 pp.

Western, D., and M. Pearl, eds. In press. *Conservation 2100.* Proceedings of International Conference on Threatened Wildlife and Species, Manhattan, October 1986, organized by the New York Zoological Society. Oxford University Press, New York.

Wilson, E. O. 1987. Biological diversity as a scientific and ethical issue. Pp. 29–48 in Papers Read at a Joint Meeting of the Royal Society and the American Philosophical Society. Volume 1. Meeting held April 24, 1986, in Philadelphia. American Philosophical Society, Philadelphia.

78. The Mismanagement of the National Forests

Perri Knize

There once was a time when if a tree was felled in the forest, nobody saw, and business went on as usual. But now a tree can't be felled anywhere in the national forests without causing violent tremors all the way to Washington, D.C. There the bureaucrats at the once-proud and formerly revered U.S. Forest Service, the administrators of the national forests, are losing credibility as forty years of forest devastation come to light.

While our government supports schemes to trade Third World debt for intact Third World rain forests and dispatches American foresters to Ecuador and Honduras to aid those countries in proper forest management, the Forest Service is deforesting our national timberlands at a rate that rivals Brazil's. What remains of America's original virgin forests is being clipped away daily in our public lands, lands that contain the most biomass per acre of any forests on the planet. We are losing intact ecosystems, watersheds, fish habitat, wildlife habitat, recreation lands, and native-species diversity to a degree that may be irreparable.

Once, the land could accommodate this "management" without attracting much notice. The national forests, unlike national parks, have traditionally provided wood, grass, and minerals to the private sector. But population growth, shifting demographics, and reduced resources mean that foresters are increasingly hard-pressed to find forest areas where nobody will see the clear-cuts.

When I joined the U.S. Forest Service as a volunteer wilderness guard, in the summer of 1983, I, like most Americans, thought the Forest Service was a conservation organization dedicated to preserving the nations wild lands. I was vaguely aware that the Forest Service sold trees, but was unprepared for the extensive logging roads and cutting I saw on the Beaverhead and Bitterroot national forests, in southwest Montana. Entire mountainsides were shorn of cover, and rough roads crisscrossed their faces, creating terraces that bled topsoil into the rivers when the snows melted in spring. Since that summer I've traveled to national forests all over the United States, from the Carolinas to Alaska, and seen the same and worse: Entire mountain ranges have their faces shaved in swaths of forty to a hundred acres which from the air resemble mange. From the ground these forests, charred and smoking from slash burning, look like battlefields.

I was shocked: the Forest Service seemed more concerned about selling trees than about the vitality of the public's forests. Yet I met many dedicated Forest Service employees at all levels of the agency who were terribly unhappy about the emphasis on timber, and I felt compelled to learn as much as I

The Atlantic Monthly, Vol. 268, No. 4 (October 1991), 98–100, 103–104, 107–108, and 111–112. Reprinted by permission of International Creative Management, Inc. Copyright 1991 by Perri Knize.

could about why the Forest Service was pursuing such an apparently destructive policy.

After all, the national forests supply only about 15 percent of the nation's wood, and Forest Service research shows that if that timber were removed from the market, half of the loss would be replaced by wood from private industrial tree farms and half by wood substitutes that are already on the market. Seventy-two percent of all the timberland in the United States is privately owned. This land is far better suited to tree farming than federal land—it is fertile, low-elevation, accessible, and for the most part does not have the intact ecosystems found on public land. Our national forests, although they are richer in biological diversity, have comparatively little value as tree farms. They are for the most part thin-soiled, steep, high-elevation, less accessible lands that produce low-quality timber. They are the lands nobody would take, even for nothing, when the government was divvying up the West.

Despite the abundance of merchantable private timber and the relatively low value of public timber, no one has seriously considered ending national-forest logging. With the exception of a tiny minority of passionate nature lovers who are considered extremist, virtually everyone I've interviewed over the past eight years says that ending national-forest logging is impractical if not impossible.

A thoughtful look at the condition of our forests, the needs of our communities, and the national demand for wood products reveals that ending national-forest logging is not only possible but also highly pragmatic. In fact, we can end logging on the national forests and at the same time improve the future economic stability of small communities now dependent on timber dollars, stabilize our wood supply, save and spend more wisely the billions now pouring out of the federal Treasury, and preserve the health of our virgin forests—if we decide to. We can do it because, contrary to conventional wisdom, we don't need national-forest timber—not for jobs, certainly not for the income, and not for the nation's wood supply. Most commercial-timber owners would actually benefit if the government were no longer competing with them: as prices rose, long-term forest planning would become more feasible and profitable. The Forest Service itself would benefit, as it escaped the endless and expensive forest-management planning with an emphasis on timber which

inevitably lands it in court. Forest Service employees could begin to inventory and study the national forests, as they were mandated to do in the National Forest Management Act of 1976, though without adequate funding for the job. They could begin repairing the damage of the past forty years, instead of trying to produce board feet that can no longer be cut in an environmentally responsible fashion.

Timber Mythology

In view of these benefits, why isn't the Forest Service eager to end national-forest logging? Why is it adamant that that cannot or should not be done? The Forest Service rebuffs all such suggestions with three arguments that I call collectively the Great Federal Timber Mythology.

> Myth No. 1: Federal timber is needed to meet an ever-escalating demand for wood fiber.
>
> Myth No. 2: Timber sales overall make a profit for the federal Treasury.
>
> Myth No. 3: Federal timber, even if sold at a loss, aids timber-dependent communities.

Last year the Forest Service once again predicted, as it has since its founding, in 1905, that demand for national-forest timber would continue to rise and that timber would remain in short supply. In fact the demand for timber has declined since the invention of the internal-combustion engine and since we began using electricity and fuel oil instead of wood for our energy needs. Many privately held forests logged in the nineteenth century are now regrown. Horse pasture and farmland have returned to forest. We actually have more standing trees today than we did ninety years ago. So whereas the old-growth trees that provide the softwood lumber used for products like fine furniture and musical instruments are indeed in short supply, particularly in the Pacific Northwest, we have plenty of wood fiber that can be made into less-refined products. Most of our ancient trees are not made into pianos and armoires anyway, but are ground into pulp to make disposable diapers and cellophane for cigarette packs. Obviously, small-diameter trees from tree farms would serve that purpose just as well. As for building materials, we can also create them from small-diameter trees. Oriented-strand board, chipboard, finger-joint board, and particle board—made from chips or small pieces of wood—are already available; they are stronger than regular wood and can be made from very young trees grown in rows like a corn crop.

"Crop forests are where our timber supply really comes from," says a former logging manager at Weyerhauser Corporation, who asked not to be named. He explains that the industry wants the old timber on the national forests only because with minimal processing these logs bring a premium price overseas. "As to old growth, everyone has gored that fatted calf long enough. Weyerhauser made a fortune from old growth, but you can't cut the last one and say, 'Gee, that was nice. What do we do now?'"

One sign that we have a glut of wood fiber in the United States is that although we exported 4.2 billion board feet of raw logs last year, we can still find plentiful, cheap toilet paper in the supermarket. Timber has such a low market value in this country that owners of private timberland often find that growing trees doesn't pay—the rate of return isn't high enough. Many are selling off their forests and using the profits to reduce their debt. If timber were scarce—and valuable—this would be a poor business practice.

The Forest Service exacerbates the situation by flooding the market with cheap national-forest timber, driving prices down. One could argue reasonably that the national-forest timber program, by competing with the private sector, is destroying the environmental quality of our private timberlands as well.

It also empties the federal purse. "If we simply gave the loggers fourteen thousand dollars a year not to cut the trees, we'd be a lot better off," says K. J. Metcalf, a retired Forest Service planner in Alaska, about his review of the Tongass forest plan in 1978. He echoed the sentiments of many of the agency's critics. The Forest Service has long claimed that the government makes money on timber sales, but an analysis performed at the request of the House Government Operations Subcommittee on the Environment, Energy, and Natural Resources shows that the Forest Service timber program has lost $5.6 billion over the past decade. Robert Wolf, a retired staffer at the Congressional Research Service, a forester, and a road engineer, analyzed the Forest Service's timber-income accounting system at the request of Representative Mike Synar, the chairman of the subcommittee. At the time this was written, Wolf expected to submit his testimony in September. He says his original intention was to show that sales of national-forest timber were profitable and beneficial. Instead, he found that most of the 122 national forests have never earned a dime on timber, and only fifteen showed a profit last year. The Forest Service claims that it made $630 million on its timber program last year; that claim, Wolf says, stems from inflated revenues and discounted costs.

The "net" revenue figure doesn't make allowances for the 25 percent of gross receipts ($327 million last year) that must be paid to counties from which timber has been removed, as compensation for property taxes lost because those lands aren't privately owned. Nor does it take into consideration road-maintenance expenses—another $80 million. Land-line location (surveying to confirm national-forest boundaries) cost another $24 million. The Forest Service also overlooked some $60 million spent on protection against insects and disease, maintenance of staff buildings, map-making, and fire protection.

Another $575 million—funds earmarked for reforestation, brush disposal, timber salvage sales, roads built to accommodate timber buyers, and other programs—was depreciated over more years than appropriate for accounting purposes. The Forest Service has used a number of creative accounting gimmicks, including amortizing roads over 240 years. (One year roads on the Chugach National Forest, in Alaska, were amortized over 1,800 years.) The typical life of a logging road, however, is twenty-five years; that's why 60 percent of each year's road-building budget is earmarked for reconstruction. Last year the Forest Service received appropriations of $700 million for the timber program from the federal Treasury, yet spent more than $1 billion. According to Wolf's calculations, after a realistic amortization of costs, the timber program actually generated a net *loss* to the federal Treasury of $186 million last year.

One reason timber sales don't make money is that most national-forest timber is virtually worthless. Short growing seasons and poor, unstable soils mean that a national-forest tree may need 120 years to reach maturity. "No one in his right mind would pay what it costs to grow it," says Wolf, who now calls the Forest Service timber program "a fraud." Since the Forest Service was founded on the promise that the timber program would make money, to admit losses after so many years of false claims would threaten not only the agency's timber program, and therefore about a third of its 45,000 jobs, but quite probably the existence of the Forest Service itself.

Even in the face of evidence that the timber market is glutted, and that its operations run at a net loss, the Forest Service will justify selling trees as a way to provide small communities with jobs. But national-forest timber isn't keeping people employed; although timber production and logging on federal lands have increased, industry employment has declined. Automation, exports of raw lumber, and competition for foreign labor are the causes. As for small community sawmills wholly dependent on old-growth national-forest timber, their timber supply is limited. The small family mill is destined to go the way of the small family farm, and leveling the national forests won't save it.

The loggers and mill workers who depend on national-forest timber are, like the forests, victims of federal policy. Since the end of the Second World War the Forest Service has fostered in their communities an expectation that federal timber would be available indefinitely, and a way of life has evolved around that expectation. If the Forest Service and the loggers' elected representatives had been honest with their constituents even ten years ago, and warned them that the supply of trees could not support their industry forever, mill owners and loggers might not have invested further in lumber operations that are doomed, national-forest timber or no. These communities were misled, and they deserve aid in adjusting to what is for them a catastrophe.

But aiding those affected by an end to national-forest logging is less problematic than it seems. The jobs that would be lost are not irreplaceable, nor are they as numerous as claimed by the timber industry, which wants to maintain the flow of cheap national-forest old-growth lumber. A study funded by the timber industry predicted that 100,000 jobs would be lost in the Pacific Northwest as a consequence of restrictions to protect the spotted owl. But according to a Forest Service assessment written for other purposes, the true number is closer to 6,000. The industry study counted jobs projected for the year 2000 if logging continued to increase as was once planned, and it included a loss of secondary jobs, such as pumping gas and waiting tables, though the relatively healthy economy of the Pacific Northwest is creating new jobs in many other sectors.

The Forest Service says that only 106,000 jobs nationwide—including approximately 15,000 in the agency itself—are related to national-forest timber. An agency report speculated that these jobs would be replaced in part by new logging jobs when wood production shifted to private industrial lands. And in communities without nearby industrial timberland new jobs could be created, including jobs rehabilitating the national forests, with federal funds saved when national-forest timber was no longer being sold at a loss.

Inevitably, the small communities dependent on national-forest logging must diversify their economies or die. But if we do not end logging before their timber supply is exhausted, the clearcuts that surround these communities will bankrupt their future. Once the forests are gone, they will have neither the timber industry nor property values nor the recreation potential that could help them build a stable economic future. Logging the national forests results in the loss, rather than the strengthening, of community stability.

So if jobs are being lost despite increased logging, and the U.S. government loses millions a year on that logging, and we don't even need the lumber, why does the Forest Service persist in logging the national forests? When environmentalists, economists, forest planners, and policy-makers say it is not practical to end national-forest logging, they mean it is not practical *politically*.

Political Realities

The National Forest Management Act of 1976 stipulates that those who are most intimate with the national forests—the public and the local Forest Service team—should work together to decide how they are to be managed. But in practice the forests are ruled by competing and complementary agendas in Washington, D.C. Forest Service administrators are concerned with maximizing their budgets, holding on to their jobs, and preserving the status quo. Congressmen want jobs in their districts and continued timber-industry support for their reelection campaigns. And the White House wants to take care of its friends. All use national-forest timber as a means to achieve their aims.

More than a quarter of the money the Forest Service spends comes from selling timber—

whether the sales make money or not—through a little-known law called the Knutson-Vandenberg Act of 1930. The K-V Act allows the Forest Service to retain virtually all its gross timber receipts in order to fund projects like tree-planting, wildlife-habitat improvement, and trail-building, and to buy equipment like computers, refrigerators, and so on. It is a back-door way of funding the agency without going through the appropriations process. Last year K-V money and similar timber funds added $475 million to the Forest Service budget, above and beyond congressional appropriations. Because Congress has limited its funding to timber-sales development, fire fighting, and road-building on the national forests, and has resisted the agency's requests for support of other programs, K-V money is often the only resource on which the Forest Service can rely to finance many of its non-timber activities. Erosion control, campground improvements, and plant and animal inventory, for example, are all funded by timber sales.

For this reason the K-V Act has led to absolutely perverse management. According to Randal O'Toole, a natural-resource economist and the author of a tendentious book titled *Reforming the Forest Service*, mismanagement in the pursuit of K-V money is rampant. O'Toole has analyzed the management of more than half the national forests. He found, for example, that when Gallatin National Forest, in Montana, needed funds to close roads to protect grizzly-bear habitat, its managers held timber sales and built roads in other prime grizzly habitat. When the Medicine Bow National Forest, in Wyoming, needed funds to inventory ancient Indian archaeological sites, it sold timber on those very sites, destroying them in the process. And in the Sequoia National Forest, in California, when foresters needed funds for a prescribed burn to protect giant-sequoia groves from wildfire, à la Yellowstone National Park, they sold timber in the groves to get the money they needed to pay for the prescribed burn. But the clear-cuts left only a few giant trees, surrounded by devastation. Instead of burning, the foresters had to replant the area, at a cost of $1,000 an acre. The point of these seemingly pointless exercises was to get and spend money. Like most bureaucracies, the Forest Service is deeply concerned with keeping overhead accounts full and maximizing its budget.

Since a third of all K-V money is spent on administrative overhead for every level of the Forest Service, from the Washington office down to the local districts, the promise of K-V funds encourages everyone in the Forest Service, including wildlife biologists and recreation specialists, to support timber sales, even if those sales damage the resources they are charged with protecting.

Because the Forest Service is so heavily dependent on timber sales, ensuring the future of the timber program is critical to the agency. That future depends on a vast network of access roads. In addition to the annual budget appropriation and the K-V money, the Forest Service has a capital-investment fund—known as hard money—set aside by Congress just for building and reconstructing roads. Last year this fund was $270 million. In addition to the 360,000 miles of roads already on the national forests—nearly one mile of road for every square mile of forest, or a system about eight times the length of the U.S. interstate highway system—the Forest Service has ambitious plans to build another 43,000 miles of roads over the next fifty years. Depending on the type of road and terrain, building these roads can cost as little as $5,000 or as much as $500,000 a mile. The agency is anxious to get roads into even marginally productive areas, critics say, because a roadless area can become a designated wilderness, off limits to logging forever.

Another way the Forest Service hopes to protect the timber program is by rewarding forest managers with promotions for meeting their timber quotas. Congress sets these quotas as a means of accounting for the money it has given the Forest Service. If the agency has said it will sell 11 billion board feet of timber in return for its $700 million congressional appropriation, at the close of the fiscal year Congress will want to know that in fact the agency has sold the trees. To make sure they are sold, the Forest Service assigns sales targets to the nine national-forest regions, according to their capacity. Each regional forester's performance rating depends in part on coming within five percent of his target.

Congress's concern about jobs is of a different nature. To get votes, a public servant needs to get jobs and money for his or her district, and in small communities in the West timber sales mean jobs, and money in the county coffers for roads and schools. Counties are entitled to 25 percent of gross receipts from the national forests within their boundaries, so county commissioners are deeply interested in national-forest programs that generate receipts, and many cannot meet their budgets without them. These officials exert tremendous pressure on members of Congress and agency officials to keep the volume of timber cut in the national forests as high as possible. Congressmen from states with lots of national forest are usually zealous about complying if they want to stay in office.

They are also ready to express gratitude to the timber industry for its campaign contributions. The industry contributes to the campaigns of several key congressmen on the appropriations committees who go to bat for timber interests every year when the timber and roads budget comes up for review. Last fall, for example, the soon-to-be retired Senator James McClure, of Idaho, added to the 1991 appropriations bill a promise of a five percent funding bonus for wildlife and recreation to any Forest Service region that meets or exceeds its timber targets—this at a time when regional foresters throughout the West were insisting that they could no longer meet federally mandated targets without damaging the land and violating environmental laws.

The 9.5 billion board feet of timber scheduled for sale on the national forests this year, and the more than 2,000 miles of timber roads scheduled to be built, will continue to make following environmental standards and guidelines difficult. Former Forest Service officials have admitted to overcutting in the past, and timber targets remain high, causing some in the agency to protest that not enough trees are left to meet them. On a day I spent on the Willamette National Forest last year, no one was in the Blue River Ranger District office. The district had three days left to meet its timber target, and the rangers were out on the ground, scrambling to find trees that met specifications for cutting.

"Anybody—on the back of an envelope—could have figured out that the rate of [timber] harvest cannot be sustained," said Max Peterson, a former Forest Service chief, when he met with agency employees at the Wenatchee National Forest in 1989. He said the cut should go down at least 25 percent; some forest planners, knowing the Forest Service to be extremely conservative on such matters, understood that to mean the cut should go down at least 75 percent.

Heavy cutting in much of the Pacific Northwest over the past decade was caused in part by congressional orders to the Forest Service which resulted in a cut far larger than the agency itself recommended. Last year Oregon's congressional delegation attached a rider to the federal appropriations bill allowing the Forest Service to sell more timber than existing laws allowed, and greatly reducing the possibilities of judicial review. A federal appeals court recently declared the rider unconstitutional.

But the impact of Congress on national-forest management is mild compared with the negative influence of the White House. My season with the Forest Service coincided with the era of John Crowell, Jr., a former timber-industry attorney and lobbyist appointed by President Reagan, as assistant secretary of commerce for natural resources and the environment—the official who oversees the Forest Service. Crowell, who had worked for Louisiana-Pacific Corporation, one of the largest buyers of federal timber, dedicated his term in office to doubling the amount of timber cut on the national forests, and he ordered the Forest Service to ignore federal court orders and national environmental laws to meet that goal.

Logging and road-building in forbidden areas was a familiar occurrence in the national-forest system during the Crowell era, and it continues to this day. Logging in a designated wilderness has been discovered several times on the Willamette National Forest. Crowell's successor, George Dunlop, another Reagan appointee, refused to approve any national-forest plan in the Pacific Northwest that didn't increase logging. As a result, Forest Service Region Six is now under such pressure to meet its targets that some districts have wandered into areas off limits to timber sales.

The President's influence on timber management can be far more direct. In June of last year the Forest Service was about to endorse the Jack Ward Thomas report, a study prepared by a team of scientists from the Forest Service and other natural-resource agencies. The Thomas report spelled out which lands should be spared from logging in the Pacific Northwest in order to save the northern spotted owl from extinction. The week before Dale Robertson, the chief of the Forest Service, was to announce the agency's endorsement of the report, timber-industry representatives paid a visit to the White House. Shortly thereafter the Bush Administration announced that it was ordering its own special task force, chaired by Clayton Yuetter, the Secretary of Agriculture, to study the spotted-owl situation further and to come up with more options. Months later Bush's task force announced its conclusions: the Thomas report's recommendations should be accepted in principle, and the cut should be reduced, but less old-growth forest should be protected than the Thomas report implied. The delay meant that timber sales in spotted-owl habitat continued unrestricted by either report all summer; by the time Bush's task force made its announcement, the logging season was just about over.

The stalling continues. The Forest Service says it may need another two or three years to come up with a management plan for the spotted owl. And last May a court ordered the agency to withdraw sales planned for 66,000 acres of prime spotted-owl habitat. Those acres would have been in addition to the 400,000 acres of owl habitat already logged since 1984, when the agency began preparing guidelines for the spotted owl. William L. Dwyer, the U.S. district judge presiding over the case in Seattle (also, ironically, a Reagan appointee), wrote a stunning denunciation of the White House in his decision:

> More is involved here than a simple failure by an agency to comply with its governing stature. The most recent violation of the National Forest Management Act exemplifies a deliberate and systematic refusal by the Forest Service and the Fish and Wildlife Service to comply with the laws protecting wildlife. This is not the doing of the scientists, foresters, rangers, and others at the working levels of these agencies. It reflects decisions made by higher authorities in the executive branch of government.

Biological Costs

Judge Dwyer's decision underscores the fundamental reason why we should not be harvesting the national forests. Aside from the facts that we don't need the lumber, that the timber program loses money, that the program is used to prop up faltering local economies artificially, and that the real reasons for timber cutting continue to be unacknowledged, we have a biological stake in an end to logging on our national forests.

The greatest threat represented by our current national-forest policy is that it will destroy biological diversity on public lands. Forest scientists say that the national forest are most valuable to us as founts of life. Our native and old-growth forests are intricate, fragile webs encompassing everything from bacteria, fungi, and insects to grizzly bears, wolves, and ancient sequoias. They constitute a complex, interdependent plant and animal community that is the foundation upon which we human beings eat and breathe. Scientists say they understand little about forest biological systems, but they do know that the fresh air and clean water our forests produce are essential to our survival, because they are basic components of the food chains that keep all species alive. As species die off, the ecosystem is simplified, and the more simplified it becomes, the less life it is capable of supporting.

We are learning more about the value of the national forests every day. For example, scientists have recently concluded that forests play a major role in the absorption and storage of carbon dioxide. When very old trees, those more than 200 years old, are cut down, vast stores of carbon are released, owing to soil disturbance, decay, and the burning that accompanies tree harvesting. The resulting climatic changes are called global warming.

With global warming, habitats that will nurture biological diversity become an even more pressing need. When climates change, species must migrate if they are to survive, and land-based species must have connecting corridors of undisturbed forest through which to move unmolested. The burden of protecting habitat that can nurture diversity must fall on the public natural-resource agencies, because virtually all the original, intact ecosystems remaining in the United States are on our public lands.

Our national forests also embody other important values. A national forest is a place where you might awaken to find a bull elk staring you down, startled from his drink at a glacier-fed lake. Snow-tipped crags and rocky cirques reflect in pools and creeks and waterfalls of penetrating clarity; the water is so clear that to look at it is to be mesmerized and merged with it. Sometimes the only sound is the wind, roaring through the giant firs like a locomotive. At other times the silence is so deep and inviolate that you can hear, seemingly, to infinity. To visit a national forest is to let a bit of the harmony lacking in our contemporary lives seep in. A lifelong New Yorker visiting a Montana national forest last summer said that camping there was like staying in a five-star hotel—a city-dweller's ultimate compliment, and a measure of how claustrophobic and diminished our everyday surroundings have become. The wildness, solitude, and silence of the national forests are now among our country's greatest luxuries.

The Forest Service's predominant logging method, clear-cutting, destroys the visual beauty of the national forests. But the threat to biological diversity is more subtle. By law, clear-cuts must be reforested, and they are usually replanted with one favored tree species. These plantings then grow into even-aged monocultures—they are tree farms, not forests. Diversity is reduced, and wildlife is stressed as nesting sites, dens, and cover from predators are lost. Although the young grasses growing in clearcuts do provide food for deer and elk, the loss of cover drives away bear, turkey, squirrels, and other species. Clear-cutting is also dangerous where rains are heavy and terrain is steep, as in southeast Alaska, on the western slope of the Cascade Mountains, and in the northwest corner of the Rockies. Flooding, soil erosion, water contamination, and loss of fisheries as sediment flushes into spawning streams are often the result. In some areas washouts and mud slides occur, and soil is removed down to bedrock. Clear-cutting changes the flow of streams, causing flooding during rains and drought during dry periods. It also interferes with recreation: no one wants to go hiking or camping in a clear-cut, and clear-cutting often obliterates recreation trails.

We know that clear-cutting destroys the complexity of forest ecology because we have the example of Europe, which was essentially deforested more than 300 years ago. Foresters there are still trying to figure out how to bring the forests back. Modern forestry techniques have evolved from the attempts, beginning in eighteenth-century Germany, to regenerate old-growth forests like the ones that we are logging here. The forests that European foresters so painstakingly tend are sterile: birds don't sing in them; sticks, not logs, are harvested from them; and now Europeans are worried about the long-term fertility of their soil. "Look to Europe for what the future holds," says Paul Alaback, a research biologist for the Forest Service in Juneau, Alaska. "Is it really necessary to cut all the forests down before we learn from others' mistakes?"

The Forest Service is now experimenting with an alternative to clear-cutting called new forestry.

New forestry is an attempt to protect diversity by simulating natural events like windstorms and fires. As I've seen it practiced at the Andrews Experimental Forest, in Oregon, new forestry looks like a messy version of clear-cutting. Instead of clearing the land of all timber and burning the remaining debris, the foresters leave dead and living trees standing in clusters, slash unburned, and dead trees and debris on the ground and in streams. This new method can be just as ugly as a clear-cut and more expensive, because it requires being more careful and yields fewer board feet per acre. And no one knows for sure if it helps preserve long-term biological diversity, the purpose for which it was created by Jerry Franklin, a Forest Service scientist. It may not be biologically destructive, but new forestry is almost always aesthetically destructive, and if it is adopted in place of clear-cutting, more timber will be sold below cost and net returns will be reduced on those forests that do earn money. We'll lose more money on the national forests than ever.

All of this points toward the conclusion that the Forest Service shouldn't be in the timber business. Managing the land to sustain its ecology is inherently incompatible with managing it to turn a profit. The time frame allowed under today's short-sighted economic system is far too limited to take biological diversity into account, and alternatives to clear-cutting will only increase deficit timber sales. Without regulation or financial incentives, most private industry will never manage its land to enhance biological diversity—long rotations (the number of years trees grow before harvest) don't help short-term profit margins—so this role must fall to the Forest Service. But as long as the Forest Service is in the timber business, its time horizon, too, will be far too short.

A Proposal

We need to reconsider the purpose of the national forests. Most people agree that public lands should exist to benefit the public, with private use permitted only when it does not reduce that public benefit. Yet the Forest Service's timber program is beneficial chiefly to politicians in Washington, to a small segment of the timber industry, and to the Forest Service's administrators. Taxpayers, small communities, recreationists, the owners of private timberland—and the land itself—all lose. The national forests without logging would not be the same as the national parks: hunting, grazing, mining, irrigation, and other private uses that don't interfere with the public's right to enjoy its land would continue. But without the logging program the Forest Service could, like the National Park Service, emphasize a stronger conservation ethic.

Such a shift in management cannot be achieved without confronting the political realities. That is why any legislation to reform national-forest management must change the incentives that motivate the Forest Service and private users of the forests. If the Forest Service gets funds for its programs by selling timber, and timber management is destroying the national forests for other uses, then we must find a means other than timber to fund the national forests. The most logical approach would be to charge recreation fees.

In its 1990 planning paper the Forest Service estimated that if it were allowed to charge fees for recreation, the income to the agency could be more than $5 billion a year, or three times what it earns in gross timber receipts. The estimate is based on fees that national-forest users have said they would be willing to pay, ranging from a few dollars for picnicking to nearly thirty dollars a day for big-game hunting. As Randal O'Toole has pointed out, this income, combined with the money saved by ending logging on the national forests, would fund the agency entirely from its own receipts; tax dollars would no longer be needed to support the Forest Service. Instead, only those who used the national forests would pay, and their fees would ensure that the forests were managed in the best interests of recreationists.

When the agency's funding no longer came from Congress, pork-barrel politics would no longer dictate how the forests were managed. County commissioners would stop putting pressure on their congressmen to appropriate funds for timber sales, because counties that depend on timber receipts for their roads and schools would get even more money from recreation than they did from timber. Private industry and landowners would benefit, because the value of their land and their timber would increase, and they, too, could charge recreation fees. With part of the billions of taxpayer dollars we were no longer investing in the Forest Service, we could easily create programs to help communities dependent on national-forest timber make the transition to a more diverse local economy, one that would serve them for the long term.

Without fees, all taxpayers are paying for the destruction of the national forests. With fees, those who used the national forests would be paying to preserve their integrity. Hikers, hunters, fishermen, backpackers, and skiers would begin to get the resources and management they need to enjoy the national forests, instead of getting leftovers after the interests of the timber industry have been served. With this new emphasis we could fund an inventory of, research on, and monitoring of national-forest species and ecosystems to help us repair the damage done by forty years of overcutting.

To accomplish this revolution in national-forest management, Congress must be persuaded that recreation fees and an end to national-forest logging are a sensible and practical way to ensure a healthy future for our national forests. Environmental groups should endorse these recommendations as a means to preservation. County governments should support this plan because it would more than double their revenues from national-forest use. Large industrial timber farmers like Weyerhauser and International Paper should favor it because it would increase the value of their lands and their timber. Fiscal conservatives and those worried about the national debt should support this plan because it would save taxpayers the yearly cost of managing the national forests. An unprecedented coalition of these interests would stop national-forest logging in its tracks. Congress and the White House would have to comply.

79. Forest Service Policy

Bryan G. Norton

[Gifford] Pinchot[1] conflated his own career goal, to institute and lead an active, effective, and productive forestry profession, with the public goals of resource conservation. Following Pinchot's lead, the wise-use wing of the environmental movement initially excluded aesthetic and other "non-economic" goals from its category of uses. Concern for fair and farsighted resource use, as it was institutionalized under Pinchot's influence in the governmental bureaucracies, centered on narrow commodity-oriented values. The bureaucracies therefore failed to develop a conception of "resources" broad enough to comprehend [John] Muir's aesthetic/spiritual concerns.

Muir had equal difficulty explaining how wise use of forests for productivity fit into his more preservationist approach—he discussed these matters less and less as his opposition to Pinchot's narrow utilitarianism grew. Muir's followers and Pinchot's followers increasingly talked past each other, unable to comprehend the other's viewpoint within their own worldview. In the early environmental movement, no positive program of environmental policy emerged beyond shared opposition to unrestrained exploitation; no common moral and aesthetic vocabulary evolved, much less a shared vision of what it would be like for humans to live *in* true harmony with the world of nature, even while living *on* nature's resources. [Aldo] Leopold made bold steps toward a unification of these approaches but, even today, the environmentalists' dilemma, reflected as a lack of common vocabulary and common positive vision, affects discourse on resource policy.

In the intervening years, however, the lines of separation between the policies of the two traditions have blurred. For example, during the 1920s the Park Service—created as a counterforce against the orientation toward productivity in the Forest Service—succumbed to boosterism and emphasized development and road-building. Meanwhile the Forest Service, under the influence of Leopold and Arthur Cathart (who was hired as a consulting "recreational engineer"), set aside wilderness and roadless areas in the National Forests. Preservationists, therefore, allied themselves for a time with the Forest Service in opposition to the Park Service. By the end of World War II, however, Pinchot's emphasis on productivity had reasserted itself in the Forest Service, and the process of designating Forest Service lands as wilderness virtually ended. The Forest Service once again pursued a policy of unrestrained road-building and cheap timber sales through the 1940s and 1950s, until the revolution in consumer tastes, especially a rapidly growing demand for outdoor recreation, once again altered the Forest Service approach.[2]

John McGuire, whose career in the Forest Service began before World War II and who served as Chief of the Forest Service from 1972 until his retirement in 1979, says: "A major change in the goals of forestry during my time in the Forest Service has been a growing acceptance of valuing nonmarket resources. These still cannot be readily analyzed in the benefit-cost sense, but these values are much more likely to be recognized by people in general today."

Furthermore, he believes, these changes affect policy:

> Now, if the American people want more of something such as timber or forage from the National Forests, the Forests Service goes to budget-makers and Congressmen and says: "Here are some of the costs that will be incurred." We then insist on funds to support recreation, to mitigate effects on wildlife, and to protect other values that may be threatened. If we get the added funds, we can probably off-set the costs to these other values.

McGuire sees these changes as intimately tied with the important changes in public attitudes that occurred during the 1960s and 1970s: "The growth in the public perception of nonmarket values has in a way both led to, and supported, the growth of the second environmental movement that occurred during the 60s and 70s. And these changes have had a profound effect on Forestry."[3]

As Samuel Hays argues, concern had shifted from production to consumption, and consumer interest in amenities pushed conservationists in the government resource agencies toward a broader conception of the public good. For example, in 1960, Congress approved the Multiple Use–Sustained Yield Act, which mandated the Forest Service to consider recreational uses as well as timber production in the National Forests; four years later Congress extended the idea of multiple use to Bureau of Land Management lands as well. In that same year it also passed the Wilderness Bill, committing the government to "managing" wilderness areas without concern for productivity.[4]

Today, resource managers are forced to make every decision with an eye on the effects it will have on broader social values. Foresters who think of their profession simply as timber production are badly out of step—forestry has instead become a balancing act, a balancing of timber production against recreation, of forest management against wilderness values, of productivity of single-stand forestry against the goals of ecological diversity.[5] Foresters have therefore abandoned the assumption that they can manage forests for a particular purpose such as timber production while paying no heed to other social values.

Especially important is acceptance of responsibility among forest managers to protect biological diversity. Throughout the Forest Service there are popping up small cadres of researchers and managers who specialize in protecting biological diversity. By accepting this responsibility, the Forest Service opens itself to criticism of its methods from outside the forestry profession. While foresters can claim to be experts on timber production, they cannot claim overriding expertise in protecting biological diversity. Whereas Pinchot's Forest Service could ignore outside criticism, insisting that their expertise gave them the right to manage forests without outside interference, today's forester is liable to be shown wrong by an academic biologist or a restoration ecologist if a management plan causes serious disruption in the composition of species in the forest.

This new responsibility for protecting biological diversity also forces forest managers to transcend single-species management. The early forays of foresters into wildlife management mostly involved attempts, such as Leopold's, to maximize one or a few game species, each with its own man-agement plan. Over the decades, foresters have recognized the futility of atomistic, single-species management and have gradually accepted whole-habitat management as essential in most cases. Management for protecting biological diversity completes this trend—a forest manager, in the final analysis, is responsible for managing every species in the forest. This implies that the manager must be a forest ecologist as well as a timber manager.

Nor do I mean to suggest that all of the movement toward a consensus has been from the conservationist side. Preservationists, who once thought they could preserve natural systems by isolating them, have been forced to admit that even the largest parks do not constitute whole ecosystems, so wildlife management must range over park boundaries. But this quickly implies that the mix of uses around the park will determine the qualities of the park. This in turn implies that the parks must be seen as one element of the larger pattern of land use and that they can be protected only if that larger pattern is devised with an eye toward their protection from spillover of the activities surrounding the park.[6] Preservationists have therefore been drawn into debates about the proper complex of land uses around park boundaries and into society-wide debates about clean air and clean water. The preservationists, like the timber managers, have been driven toward management of whole ecosystems rather than isolated portions of those systems.

It is important not to paper over real differences. Attacks on the Forest Service by modern preservationists for below-value timber sales, for superfluous road-building, and for short-selling recreational values have never been more intense. Further, wildlife- and wilderness-oriented organizations fault the service for doing a miserable job of protecting diversity on the lands they manage. But the differences, however rancorous, are no longer all-or-nothing disputes. The Forest Service has clearly and explicitly accepted the legislative mandate that makes its management a balancing act. Likewise, preservation organizations such as the Wilderness Society and the Sierra Club have accepted the same formulation of the problem, accepting that the national forests will have some productive use, but arguing for wilderness wherever possible as a counterforce against a perceived bias of foresters toward timber production over other, aesthetic and moral goals.

The arguments now represent disagreements of degree and, as in the early days of conservation, these policy disagreements play themselves out as disputes regarding the appropriateness of particular uses for particular lands: What is the proper mix of economic management and contribution to non-commercial values for a public agency? While these issues are not easy, they are now discussed in a context of both sides accepting that management will involve finding a balance, and that the Forest Service will be held accountable for the effects of its activities on the whole range of social values. Essential to this consensus is the agreement that contextual management must supersede atomistic management—that management must take into account the important role of health and stability of the larger landscape in which productive and recreational units are embedded.

While this shift in values can be considered a victory of Muir over Pinchot, the victory is by no means complete. First of all, once a narrow worldview is entrenched in a bureaucracy, new legislation and broader leadership from the top will at best alter it slowly. On a deeper level, however, the methodological innovations of hypothetical market techniques for measuring amenity values represent a response to only one aspect of Muir's and Leopold's disagreement with the early resource managers. The Axiom of Usefulness performed two key functions in the early conservationists' worldview: It focused their efforts on commodity production, but reliance on the unquestioned value of maximizing sustainable production also encouraged resource managers to believe that their enterprise of "scientific resource management" was a value-free discipline. Since scientific resource managers merely maximized measurable outputs of desirable products, their professional tasks seemed to them to involve no value judgments.

The acceptance of aesthetic and amenity values has broadened the mission of resource managers, but many of them never questioned the underlying assumption that social preferences can be measured scientifically and can be used to determine what values public agencies should pursue. The broadening of values that took place in the post-Pinchot resource agencies therefore involved no attack on the assumption that economics, perhaps supplemented by questionnaires to determine nonmarket preferences, could scientifically determine the goals of the profession.

One might say that the Axiom of Usefulness was replaced with the Axiom of Consumer Value in their minds and in their management approach. The Axiom of Consumer Value, unlike its predecessor, countenances a broad conception of human value—a product or experience is valuable to the public if some members of the public desire it. But the Axiom of Consumer Value shares with its predecessor the implication that the task of resource managers is to maximize public satisfactions, and it views those satisfactions as "givens." Wide acceptance of the Axiom of Consumer Value among resource managers, therefore, represents a broadening of management goals to include aesthetic, recreational, and amenity values, but does not represent an acceptance of science as ecstatic and normative. Nor does it represent an acceptance of Leopold's conception of conservation biology and environmental management as a value-laden search for a culturally adequate conception of man's ethical relation to land. . . .

Notes

1. For a discussion of Pinchot and his beliefs, see the Preview to IV.A: "Historical Movements."

2. See T. H. Watkins, "Untrammeled by Man," *Audubon*, November 1989, pp. 78ff., for a history of this episode in Forest Service history.

3. Interview with author, Washington, DC, May 21, 1986; also see Hays, *Beauty, Health.*

4. William K. Wyant, *Westward in Eden: The Public Lands and the Conservation Movement* (Berkeley: University of California Press, 1982), pp. 279–81.

5. See Hays, *Beauty, Health,* chap. 4, especially pp. 123–28, for a more detailed account of how the Forest Service, although showing bureaucratic resistance, has gradually accepted that its task is one of "a broker among conflicting demands" (p. 128).

6. See Alston Chase, *Playing God in Yellowstone* (Boston: Atlantic Monthly Press, 1986), for a detailed account of the problems caused when the Park Service designed management plans on the (false) assumption that Yellowstone National Park could be managed as a self-sufficient ecosystem.

VI.D CORPORATE RESPONSIBILITY

80. PREVIEW

I have given presentations to industry groups . . . and I always begin by asking them to accept the truth of the statement "Air pollution is bad." . . . And you see everybody swallowing their olives, and their martinis start coming out of their ears, because a certain segment of corporate society is paid to say exactly the opposite.

Charles E. Little[1]

In the Spring of 1988, Northern Telecom . . . adopt[ed] the slogan "Free in Three," meaning free of CFCs [chlorofluorocarbons] in three years. . . . By reaching its goal ahead of time, Northern Telecom saved the atmosphere from 9000 tonnes of CFCs while eliminating over $50 million in costs.

David Suzuki[2]

There is no doubt about it: While corporations are driven by the vast engine of consumer satisfaction, many are also responsible significant environmental destruction. Most Americans can recall the oil spill in Prince William Sound by the *Exxon Valdez*, an icon of the potential disasters inherent in the fossil fuel business. They may not, however, be as aware of the corporate role in America's "hamburger habit." To keep up a continuous flow of beef from South America to the United States, millions of acres of ancient rain forests have been razed and burned to create pasture land for grazing cattle. Corporations and businesses also generate pollution, contributing to what has been called "the trash crisis" in North America.[3] Part of the trash problem is due to overconsumption in so-called northern countries. Carl Pope, executive director of the Sierra Club, says, "Since [corporations] exist to maximize profits . . . they are compelled by their nature to grow and grow, consuming more natural resources and encouraging more

consumption."[4] It might also be noted that corporations work within the existing economic structure, and economists propose (for the most part) that a successful economy must always be expanding. On this issue, see Section V.E. In the selection "Consumption as a Theme in the North-South Dialogue" (Essay 83), Luis Camacho details how the problems posed by consumption are not universal but are in fact different for different parts of the globe.

Corporations have been accused not only of generating trash, but of environmental racism, a charge that turns our attention to where that trash is going and has gone. There has been, says Benjamin F. Chavis, Jr., "a deliberate targeting of people of color communities for toxic waste facilities" and an "official sanctioning of the life-threatening presence of poisons and pollutants in our communities."[5] "[M]inorities bear a greater burden from lead poisoning, airborne toxins and contaminated drinking water," says Deeohn Ferris, an attorney for the National Wildlife Federation. "The condition is called 'environmental racism.'"[6] Explaining further, environmental researcher Hope Taylor says, "Small dirty industries have a tendency to locate in minority communities for two reasons: One, cheap labor. And two, their relative lack of knowledge about environmental concerns."[7]

Karl Grossman, in Essay 81, "Environmental Racism," analyzes the pattern of placing hazardous facilities in black and Native American communities in the United States; he also makes the connection between this phenomenon and the dumping of hazardous wastes in third-world countries.[8] One striking example is found in an internal memo written by Lawrence Summers, former chief economist of the World Bank. Leaked to the press, the December 12, 1991, memo begins, "Just between you and me, shouldn't the World

Bank be encouraging more migration of the dirty industries to the LDCs [less developed countries]?"[9]

Often a discussion of ethics in business or corporate responsibility is reduced to a stark conflict between making profits for shareholders versus assuming social responsibilities to an entire community. In a well-known article from 1970, Nobel Prize-winning economist Milton Friedman addressed the question of whether business has social responsibilities.[10] Some business people have expressed the view that they ought not merely be concerned with maximizing profits but also concerned about "discrimination" and "avoiding pollution." Friedman's response to what he referred to as such "catchwords" is that they were "preaching pure and unadulterated socialism" and were "unwitting puppets" of forces undermining the basis of a free society. Friedman allowed that that artificial person, the corporation, can have "artificial responsibilities" (legal ones?) but not "business as a whole."[11] In practice, his question focuses on whether corporate executives have responsibilities; Friedman argues that they are employees of the stockholders and that their duty is to make as much money as possible compatible with "the basic rules of society"—those embodied in law and those "embodied in ethical custom."[12] The executive is thus an *agent* of those who own the corporation, and his "primary responsibility" is to them. He (or she) must not, so Friedman claims, make corporate decisions in any manner that does not promote "the best interests of his employers"; if he does, he is spending someone else's money to promote a "social objective."[13] In Friedman's view, this amounts to taxation, a function reserved in our political system to the government. If an executive so acts, he is taxing people without their being represented; Friedman thinks this is typical of socialism. He further claims that executives may lack expertise to make such decisions, for example, about how to fight inflation—or to ascertain

how much of the stockholders' money to spend on such matters. In those cases in which some stockholders advocate pursuit of social objectives, he claims that they are trying to spend money belonging to other stockholders in pursuit of the favored causes of the "activists." Such is the gist of Friedman's position and his arguments.

In Essay 85, legal theorist Christopher Stone responds in detail to Friedman's view and to others like it. All these views, he says, assume that "the managers of the corporation are to be steered almost wholly by profit, rather than what they think proper for society on the whole."[14] In the end, Stone takes the position that it may be better to leave the running of corporations to the market and the law rather than "to have corporate managers implementing their own vague and various notions of what is best for the rest of us."[15] However, this view applies *only* if the law and the market can keep corporations within "desirable bounds." Stone asks, "[A]re [the 'antiresponsibility' forces] blind to the fact that there are circumstances in which the law—and the forces of the market—are simply not competent to keep the corporation under control?"[16]

One example of these circumstances is the displacing of third-world farmers by huge agribusiness companies in order to grow crops for export to Japan, Europe, and the United States. By pressure, by force, and with the complicity of corrupt government officials, many small locally owned subsistence farms become one giant corporate farm. The farmers have next to nothing to eat, no place to live decently. Thousands move to the cities to live in shacks, scrounging food from garbage dumps. The corporations, although many bear well-known American names, are beyond the reach of U.S. law. They are free from local law as well to the extent that third-world governments are aligned with the corporations against the interests of their poorest citizens. The market appears to favor these practices of agribusiness, although at least one corporation has included space for local farms within corporate farms so that people living in the area can feed themselves. Perhaps when conditions get to the point of food riots—as they have in some countries—corporations can find different ways to make profits or even live with less profits. For reading on this issue, see Essay 36, by Vandana Shiva, in the section on ecofeminism. Also, we recommend the video *Hungry for Profit,* a 1990 production that details certain practices of agribusiness worldwide.

The idea of a *stakeholder* is also a response to Friedman-type views. *Stakeholder* is a relatively new term invented to contrast with *shareholder* and to suggest that many individuals and groups beside shareholders have an interest in how business is done (employees, retirees, host communities, and customers, to name a few). In a sense, what is being asked here is the same question Peter Singer posed in a different context, namely, "Whose interests count?" Even as Singer wanted us to see that all sentient beings, not just human beings, have an interest in not having unwanted pain and suffering heaped on them, so Lisa Newton (and others) maintain that many interests *other than those of shareholders* are at stake in the context of business activities.

In Essay 84, Newton develops the story of the hostile corporate takeover of the well-managed Pacific Lumber Company, a change that in turn brought about massive environmental destruction and social dislocation. Interestingly, corporate takeovers as a business practice have been justified on grounds that *efficient* management of the acquired company results. Defenders of takeovers claim that well-managed companies are not raided; takeovers only clean up mistakes of the past. Some have even used the religious language of "cleansing" when discussing the merits of takeovers.[17] The "efficiency defense" crumbles, however, in the case of Pacific Lumber Company, a corporation that had clearly exhibited personal, social, and environmental responsibility. It was raided for the sake of profit for a few.

Corporate takeovers, mergers, acquisitions, and leveraged buyouts are business phenomena of the 1980s that persist into the twenty-first century. Most often, their justification or lack thereof is discussed in terms of utilities. The main argument in favor of corporate takeovers is the one just given: to oust inefficient management. Reasons offered against include the disruption to the lives of individuals and communities, the elimination of jobs, and the claim that no new wealth is created; takeovers merely shift ownership and replace equity with debt.

Social critic Barbara Ehrenreich, in her book *Fear of Falling: The Inner Life of the Middle Class,* offers a unique discussion on corporate takeovers as a matter of character rather than as a question of evaluating the consequences of the practice. She says the following of the character displayed by the corporate raiders in their games of hostile takeovers:

> None of these speculative activities generates new wealth, new jobs (except for legions of corporate lawyers), new products, or new technology. They are games of chance, carried on at an unprecedented scale, whose only tangible result is a reshuffling of existing wealth and power among a tiny group of players. . . . In the speculative frenzy that has taken the place of industrial capitalism, it is the corporate-financial elite that most clearly exhibits the supposed defects of the poor: present-time orientation and the incapacity to defer gratification. . . . Our corporate elite has been entrusted with an unseemly share of the nation's wealth . . . and they are gambling it away.[18]

On the other hand, middle-class people, she argues, regularly defer gratification—for example, enduring temporary poverty to get a college education in the hopes of a secure future. That control is motivated by a real fear of falling out of the middle class into permanent poverty, hence her book's title. The irony built into the system is that despite their willpower, whether or not those in the middle class will in fact remain there depends in part on how money changes hands when the very rich—the corporate elite—gamble and speculate with the wealth entrusted to them.

Like Ehrenreich, Mark Sagoff, in "I Am No Greenpeacer, But . . . or Environmentalism, Risk Communication, and the Lower Middle Class" (Essay 86), addresses issues of environmentalism and class. Sagoff challenges the long-standing view that only upper-middle class suburban professionals support laws protecting the environment, and that the lower middle class oppose such laws. His lively examples from *Car and Driver, Farm Journal,* and other sources show that "environmentalism plays as well in Peoria as on Martha's Vineyard."[19] Arguing that the environment has become a populist issue, Sagoff goes on to show how the populist movement has influenced environmental regulation of industry. Moreover, he is optimistic about the prospects of environmentalists and corporate executives working together to restructure environmental law.

Sagoff and Newton respectively refer to Greenpeace and Earth First! A history and comparison of these activist groups is provided in the Preview to Part VII, "Varieties of Activism."

NOTES

1. Charles E. Little, "On Top of Mount Mitchell," in *The Dying of the Trees: The Pandemic in America's Forests* (New York: Viking Press, 1995), p. 50.

2. David Suzuki, *Time to Change* (Toronto: Stoddart, 1994), pp. 139–140.

3. See Paul H. Connett, "The Disposable Society," *Ecology, Economics, Ethics: The Broken Circle,* edited by F. Herbert Bormann and Stephen R. Kellert (New Haven: Yale University Press, 1991).

4. Carl Pope, *Sierra,* November–December 1996, p. 14.

5. Benjamin Chavis, Jr., quoted in "Black and Green," by William Rees, *The New Republic* March 2, 1991, p. 15.

6. "Some See Racism in Waste Decisions," *The News and Observer* (Raleigh, NC), November 12, 1992, p. 1A.

7. Ibid., p. 12A.

8. Karl Grossman, "Environmental Racism," *The Crisis* 98(4) (April 1991), p. 17.

9. "Let Them Eat Pollution," *The Economist,* February 8, 1992, p. 66.

10. Milton Friedman, "The Social Responsibility of Business Is to Increase Its Profits," *The New York Times Magazine,* September 13, 1970, pp. 33, 122, 124, 126.

11. Ibid., p. 33.

12. Ibid.

13. Ibid.

14. Christopher D. Stone, *Where the Law Ends: The Social Control of Corporate Behavior* (New York: HarperCollins, 1975), p. 80.

15. Ibid., pp. 86–87.

16. Ibid., p. 87.

17. See the video *Anatomy of a Corporate Takeover,* Ethics in America Series, 1988. Annenberg-cpb collection, produced by Columbia University, distributed by Intelimation, P.O. Box 1922, Santa Barbara, CA 93116–1922.

18. Barbara Ehrenreich, *Fear of Falling: The Inner Life of the Middle Class* (New York: Pantheon Books, 1989), pp. 254–55.

19. Mark Sagoff, "'I Am No Greenpeacer, But . . .'or Environmentalism, Risk Communication, and the Lower Middle Class," in *Business Ethics and the Environment: The Public Policy Debate,* edited by W. Michael Hoffman, Robert Frederick, and Edward S. Petry, Jr. (New York: Quorum Books, 1990), p. 109.

81. Environmental Racism

Karl Grossman

"We're sitting in a center of a donut surrounded by a hazardous waste incinerator that gives off PCB's, seven landfills that are constantly growing—they look like mountains," Hazel Johnson was saying. "There are chemical plants, a paint factory, two steel mills which give off odors, and lagoons filled with all kinds of contaminants that emit 30,000 tons of poison into the air each year. And there's a water reclamation district where they dry sludge out in the open. The smell is horrible, like bodies decomposing."

Mrs. Johnson was describing Atgeld Gardens, a housing project in which 10,000 people, nearly all African-Americans, reside on the Southeast Side of Chicago, surrounded on every side by sources of pollution.

The result: environmental diseases and death.

"We have lots of cancer, respiratory problems, birth deformities," Mrs. Johnson went on. "Just the other day, there were three cancer deaths. Then more. We've been having babies born with brain tumors. One baby was born with her brain protruding from her head. She's two now, blind and she can't walk. My daughter was five months pregnant. She took ultra-sound and the doctors found the baby had no behind, no head," said Mrs. Johnson, the mother of seven. "The baby had to be aborted."

Mrs. Johnson has no doubt that "the terrible health problems we have in our community are related to the pollution," the product of trying to live amid one of the most concentrated areas of environmental contamination in the U.S.

And she is clear about why her area gets dumped on because it is largely inhabited by African-Americans and Hispanics. "In Chicago, everything is mostly dumped out in this area where we are. They figure that we're not going to come out and protest and disagree." But Mrs. Johnson has, for 10 years now, as the head of People for Community Recovery, been fighting back.

"Atgeld Gardens symbolizes environmental racism," the Rev. Benjamin Chavis, Jr., the noted civil rights leader and executive director of the United Church of Christ's Commission for Racial Justice, declared. "The community is surrounded on all four sides by pollution and has one of the highest cancer rates in the nation. The public officials in Chicago are well aware of the circumstances that these people are forced to live in, yet, because of their race, the city has no priority in stopping this type of environmental injustice."

Rev. Chavis was the first to use the term "environmental racism" in 1987 with the release of what has become a landmark study by the commission, "Toxic Wastes and Race in the United States." It has taken several years for the import of the report, notes Rev. Chavis, to take hold.

But now that has well begun. There have been a series of important events, including a week long tour by the Rev. Jesse Jackson, shortly before Earth Day 1990, of low-income minority communities struck by pollution. He stressed the "relationship between environment and empowerment" and declared it "a new day and a new way. No longer will corporations be allowed to use job blackmail to poison poor people be they black, brown, yellow, red, or white. We are demanding that all corporate poisoners sign agreements to stop the poisoning of our communities."

Rev. Jackson was accompanied by Dennis Hayes, a principal organizer of both the original Earth Day, in 1970, and last year's event, and John O'Connor, executive director of the National Toxics Campaign, who emphasized that "for the environmental movement to be successful in saving the planet, it must include all races, ethnic groups, rich and poor, black and white, and young and old. When our movement to clean up the nation is truly a reflection of all people in the country, it is at that point that we will succeed in stopping the poisoning of America."

Issuing a report in 1990, at a National Minority Health Conference in Washington on environmental contamination, describing how "a marriage of the movement for social justice with environmentalism" was taking place was the Panos Institute. "Organizing for environmental justice among people of color has grown from a small group of

The Crisis, Vol. 98, No. 4 (April 1991), 14–17, 31–32. Reprinted by permission of the publisher.

activists in the 1970s to a movement involving thousands of people in neighborhoods throughout the U.S.," said Dana A. Alston, director of the Environment, Community Development and Race Project of Panos, an international group that works for "sustainable development." She added in the report, "We Speak for Ourselves: Social Justice, Race and Environment," that "communities of color have often taken a more holistic approach than the mainstream environmental movement, integrating 'environmental' concerns into a broader agenda that emphasizes social, racial, and economic justice."

In Atlanta in 1990, at a conference on environmental problems in minority areas sponsored by the federal Agency for Toxic Substances and Disease Registry and others, attended by 300 community leaders, doctors and governmental officials, Dr. Aubrey F. Manley, deputy assistant secretary of the Department of Health and Human Services, stated, "Poor and minority organizations charged eight major national environmental groups with racism in their hiring practices and demanded that they substantially increase the number of people of color on their staffs. The environmental groups acknowledged the problem—"The truth is that environmental groups have done a miserable job of reaching out to minorities," said Frederick D. Krupp, executive director of the Environmental Defense Fund—and set up an Environmental Consortium for Minority Outreach.

And last year, too, the Commission for Racial Justice organized a workshop on racism and the environment for the Congressional Black Caucus, whose members, unbeknownst to many, are rated as having among the best pro environmental voting records in Congress by the League of Conservation Voters, which scores Congressional representatives on their environmental records.

A key event to be held this year will be the first National Minority Environmental Leadership Summit in Washington, D.C., in October. "We want to bring together leaders of community groups, environmental groups, civil rights organizations and academic, scientific, governmental and corporate organizations to participate in this three-day corporate meeting," says Charles Lee, research director of the Commission for Racial Justice, which is organizing the gathering. "The purpose of this summit is to develop a comprehensive and tangible national agenda of action that will help reshape and redirect environmental policy-making in the United States to fully embrace the concerns of minority Americans."

People of color have been the worst victim of environmental pollution for a long time. Lee tells of the building of the Gauley Bridge in West Virginia in the 1930s: "Hundreds of African-American workers from the Deep South were brought in by the New Kanawha Power Company, a subsidiary of the Union Carbide Corporation, to dig the Hawks Nest tunnel. Over a two year period, approximately 500 workers died and 1,500 were disabled from silicosis, a lung disease similar to Black Lung. Men literally dropped on their feet breathing air so thick with microscopic silica that they could not see more than a yard in front of them. Those who came out for air were beaten back into the tunnel with ax handles. At subsequent Congressional hearings, New Kanawha's contractor revealed, "I knew I was going to kill these niggers, but I didn't know it was going to be this soon."

Lee relates how "an undertaker was hired to bury dead workers in unmarked graves" and of his agreeing "to perform the service for an extremely low rate because the company assured him there would be a large number of deaths."

But it was not until recent years that this and other horror stories of environmental racism started to be examined in their systematic context.

It was in 1982 that residents of predominantly African-American Warren County, North Carolina asked the Commission for Racial Justice for help in their protests against the siting of a dump for PCB's—the acronym for polychlorinated biphenyls, a carcinogen. In a campaign of civil disobedience that ensued, there were more than 500 arrests, including the commission's Rev. Chavis, Dr. Joseph Lowery of the Southern Christian Leadership Conference, and Congressman Walter Fauntroy of Washington.

It was during that effort that Rev. Chavis began considering the connection between the dumping in Warren County and the federal government's Savannah River nuclear facility, long a source of radioactive leaks and located in a heavily African-American area of South Carolina, and the "largest landfill in the nation" in the mainly black community of Emelle, Alabama. "We began to see evidence of a systematic pattern which led us to a national study," recounted Rev. Chavis.

That study—"Toxic Wastes and Race in the United States"—clearly shows what Rev. Chavis suspected: communities of color are where most of America's places of poison are located. In detail, the analysis looked at a cross-section of the thousands of U.S. "commercial hazardous water facilities" (defined by the U.S. Environmental Protection Agency as places licensed for "treating, storing or disposing of hazardous wastes") and "uncontrolled toxic waste sites" (defined by EPA as closed and abandoned sites), and correlated them with the ethnicity of the communities in which they are located.

Some of the study's major findings:

- "Race proved to be the most influential among variables tested in association with the location of commercial hazardous waste facilities. This represented a consistent national pattern."

- "Communities with the greatest number of commercial hazardous wastes facilities had the highest composition of ethnic residents."

- "Although socio-economic status appeared to play an important role in the location of commercial hazardous waste facilities, race still proved to be more significant."

- "Three out of every five black and Hispanic Americans lived in communities with uncontrolled toxic waste sites."

- "Blacks were heavily overrepresented in the populations of metropolitan areas with the largest number of uncontrolled toxic waste sites"—Memphis, St. Louis, Houston, Cleveland, Chicago, and Atlanta.

- "Approximately half of all Asian/Pacific Islanders and American Indians lived in communities with uncontrolled toxic waste sites."

The analysis called for change. "This report firmly concludes that hazardous wastes in black, Hispanic and other racial and ethnic communities should be made a priority issue at all levels of government. This issue is not currently at the forefront of the nation's attention. Therefore, concerned citizens and policy-makers, who are cognizant of this growing national problem, must make this a priority concern."

It called for the U.S. president "to issue an executive order mandating federal agencies to consider the impact of current policies and regulations on racial and ethnic communities"; state governments "to evaluate and make appropriate revisions in their criteria for the siting of new hazardous waste facilities to adequately take into account the racial and socio-economic characteristics of potential host communities"; the U.S. Conference of Mayors, the National Conference of Black Mayors and the National League of Cities "to convene a national conference to address these issues from a municipal perspective"; and "civil rights and political organizations to gear up voter registration campaigns as a means to further empower racial and ethnic communities to effectively respond to hazardous wastes in racial and ethnic communities at the top of state and national legislative agendas."

Environmentalist Barry Commoner commented that the report showed the "functional relationship between poverty, racism and powerlessness and the chemical industry's assault on the environment."

It was in 1978 that sociologist Robert Bullard first began exploring environmental racism. He was asked by Linda McKeever Bullard, his wife, to conduct a study on the siting of municipal landfills and incinerators in Houston for a class-action lawsuit challenging a plan to site a new landfill in the "solid middle class" mostly African-American Houston neighborhood of Northwood Manor, notes Bullard. Just out of graduate school, a new professor at Texas Southern University, he found that from the 1920s to that time, all five of Houston's landfills and six out of eight of its incinerators were sited in black neighborhoods. That led to wider studies by Dr. Bullard on how "black communities, because of their economic and political vulnerability, have been environmental hazards."

He wrote several papers and, last year, his book, *Dumping in Dixie: Race, Class, and Environmental Quality*, came out. Black communities are consistently the ones getting dumped on "because of racism, plain and simple," says Dr. Bullard, now a professor at the University of California at Riverside.

Often it is a promise of "jobs, jobs, and jobs that are held out as a savior" for these communities although, in fact, "these are not labor-intensive industries." The companies involved, meanwhile, figure they can "minimize their investment" by avoiding the sort of lawsuit more likely to be brought by a white community faced with having a toxic dump, an incinerator, a paper mill, a slaughterhouse, a lead smelter, a pesticide plant, "you name it," said Dr. Bullard. Also, with planning and zoning boards commonly having "excluded people of color," the skids are further greased. And to top it off, "because of housing patterns and limited mobility, middle-income and lower-income blacks," unlike whites, often cannot "vote with their feet" and move out when a polluting facility arrives. "Targeting certain communities for poison is another form of discrimination," charged Dr. Bullard.

He tells in *Dumping in Dixie* of how African-Americans in Houston and Dallas; in Alsen, Louisiana; Institute, West Virginia; and Emelle, Alabama, "have taken on corporate giants who would turn their areas into toxic wastelands." He is enthused by the existence of how "literally hundreds of environmental justice groups are made up of people of color."

One of the many organizations is the Gulf Coast Tenants Association. "We have not only the dumping here, but we get the up-front stuff; this is where much of the petrochemical industry is centered, and where they produce a lot of the stuff," says Darryl Malek-Wiley, the New Orleans-based group's director of research. "Cancer Alley is the nickname for this area," speaking of the 75-mile swath along the Mississippi from Baton Rouge to New Orleans. The group offers courses in environmental education and assists people to fight environmental hazards in their communities and block the siting of new ones. The placement of hazardous facilities in black communities in the South follows a pattern of subjugation going back "hundreds of years," notes Malek, with "the industrial age" giving this a new translation. And, he says, it should be viewed in connection with the dumping of hazardous waste in Third World countries.

Up North, in the middle of America's biggest city, New York—Peggy Shepard has been challenging environmental racism as a leader of West Harlem Environmental Action (WHE ACT). Obnoxious, "exploitive" facilities placed in our area in recent years, she notes, have included a huge sewage treatment plant, a "marine transfer station" for garbage, and yet another bus storage depot. "We organized around a series of issues in our community that turned out to be all environmental [in] nature." WHE ACT has been "networking with organizations around" New York City and found that what had happened to West Harlem is typical of what has occurred to other African-American and Hispanic neighborhoods. "We get so used to the stereotype that what environmentalism means is wildlife and the preservation of open space. There had not been sufficient movement on urban environmental problems: incinerators, sewage treatment plants, factories polluting the air, devastating occupational exposure."

Sulalman Mahdi is southeast regional director of the Center for Environment, Commerce and Energy in Atlanta. "Our work involves educating the African-American community around the whole question of the environment. I am particularly interested in bridging the civil rights movement and the environmental justice movement," says Mahdi.

He became involved in the "green" movement while working in the campaign for reparations in land for African-Americans for the injustices committed against them. Living in southern Georgia, near Brunswick, "a papermill town and smelling the sulfur all the time" from the papermill lands, he concluded as he choked on the putrid air, that "we need to fight for environmental protection or the land we seek might not be of any real value once it's returned."

He takes the African-American perspective on nature right back to Africa, and indeed is writing a book on African ecology. The African approach to nature "is very similar to that of the Native Americans," says Mahdi. He speaks of the "founder of agriculture, the founder of botany" both ancient Egyptians. He sees a solid "relationship between our freedom struggle" and battling the environmental abuse subjected on African-Americans, what he terms "environmental genocide."

Genocide is also the word used by Lance Hughes of Native Americans for a Clean Environment. "As states and various municipalities have been closing down a lot of dumps because of public opposition, the companies have been descending on the reservations across the country," says Hughes. Indian reservations are seen as good dump sites by their firms because they are considered sovereign entities not subject to local or state environmental restrictions.

The group of which he is director was formed six years ago because of radioactive contamination caused by a twin set of nuclear production facilities run by Kerr-McGee in northeast Oklahoma amid a large concentration of Native Americans. One produces nuclear fuel for weaponry, the other for nuclear power plants. Further, some of the nuclear waste generated at them is put in fertilizer throughout the state, and also by Kerr-McGee on 10,000 acres surrounding the nuclear facilities.

"The hay and cattle from that land is sold on the open market," says Hughes. The Native Americans who live in the area have many "unusual cancers" and a high rate of birth defects from "genetic mutation. It gets pretty sad," says Hughes, "with babies born without eyes, babies born with brain cancers."

Wildlife is also born deformed. "We found a nine-legged frog and a two-headed fish. And there was a four-legged chicken." Hughes emphasizes that the subjugation of Native Americans "is still going on. The name of the game has been changed, but I would call it the same—genocide, because that is exactly what the result is."

The Southwest Organizing Project (SWOP) is a multi-ethnic, multi-issue organization which began a decade ago in a predominantly Chicano area of Albuquerque, New Mexico. "We have a municipal landfill, the largest pig farm in the city of Albuquerque, a dogfood plant, Texaco, Chevron, General Electric, a sewage plant," says Richard Moore, SWOP co-director. This, he said, is typical of Hispanic and African-American communities in the Southwest.

"Wherever you find working class, ethnic communities you find environmental injustice," says Moore, whose group has grown to fight environmental racism throughout New Mexico. "We have been organizing door-to-door, building strong organizations, going up against pretty major organizations." Non-partisan voter registration has been a key tool. The group was also the founding organization of the Southwest Network of Environmental and Economic Justice, which Moore co-chairs, that brings together people in seven Southwest states also on a multi-ethnic, multi-issue basis.

Moore was one of the signatories of the letter sent to eight major environmental organizations protesting their lack of minority representation (example: of the 315 staff members of the Audubon Society, only three were black).

Importantly, not scored in that letter were three prominent national environmental groups: Greenpeace, the National Toxics Campaign, and Earth Island Institute. In a breakthrough, in contra-diction to the pattern elsewhere, the president of Earth Island Institute is an African-American.

Carl Anthony is not only president of Earth Island Institute, headquartered in San Francisco, but director of its Urban Habitat program. "We're very interested in issues at two ends of the spectrum: global warming, the ozone layer, depletion of global resources—and the negative environmental impacts on communities of poor people and people of color. In order to bring these two concerns together," says Anthony, "we have to develop a new kind of thrust and a new kind of leadership in communities of color to address the needs of our communities and also the larger urban community in making a transaction to more sustainable urban patterns." Urban Habitat is "basically a clearing-house for a lot of people all over the country who want to work on these issues. And it helps alert people from our community to the issues that concern them: toxics, energy issues, air quality, water quality."

Anthony, an architect who says he has "always been aware of environmental issues," is a designer of buildings and a professor of architecture at the University of California at Berkeley, where he is now teaching a new course for the school, Race, Poverty, and the Environment. He speaks with great pleasure of his involvement with Earth Island Institute, but is dubious about whether some of the other national environmental groups will become fully multiethnic. They have long taken an "elitist perspective. I doubt that Audubon, for instance, will ever make a big push in this direction."

Chicago's Hazel Johnson has worked closely with Greenpeace, the national environmental group most committed to direct action. "I have a very good working relationship with Greenpeace. It is more than an action group. I have gone with Greenpeace to many places and they have come out to assist us." She spoke of one recent demonstration carried on by her People for Community Recovery against yet one more incinerator planned for her community in which, with Greenpeace, "we chained ourselves to trucks."

"Unequivocally," says Lee, of the Commission for Racial Justice, "minority communities are the communities most at risk to environmental pollution." He paints in words the panorama of pollution. There is the heavy exposure to pesticides of Hispanic farmworkers, including those in Delano, California, where "there is an estimated

300,000 pesticide-related cancers among farm-workers each year."

There are the effects of radioactive contamination on Native Americans, especially the Navajos, the nation's primary work force in the mining of uranium—who have extreme cancer rates as a result. "There is lead poisoning of children in urban areas—with an estimated 55 percent of the victims being African-Americans," says Lee. There is the mess in Puerto Rico, "one of the most heavily polluted areas in the world," with U.S. petrochemical and pharmaceutical companies long having discharged toxics on a massive scale. All the people in the island's town of La Ciudad Cristiana were forced to be relocated due to mercury poisoning. The terrible stories go on and on. Says Lee: "We still have a long way to go in truly addressing this issue."

"To understand the causes of these injustices, it is important to view them in a historical context," he notes. "Two threads of history help to explain the disproportionate impact of toxic pollution on racial and ethnic communities. The first is the long history of oppression and exploitation of African-Americans, Hispanic Americans, Asian-Americans, Pacific Islanders, and Native Americans. This has taken the form of genocide, chattel slavery, indentured servitude, and racial discrimination in employment, housing and practically all aspects of life in the United States. We suffer today from the remnant of this sordid history, as well as from new and institutionalized forms of racism. The other thread of history is the massive expansion of the petrochemical industry since World War II."

"Environmental racism is racial discrimination in environmental policy-making," says Rev. Chavis. "Wherever you find non-white people, that's where they want to dump stuff. And it's spreading all over the world. A lot of toxic chemicals have been going for dumping in the Pacific Islands, and Africa; it recently was revealed that Kenya has been allowing us to dump nuclear wastes." (The Organization of African Unity has denounced the dumping by the U.S. and European countries of hazardous waste in Africa as "toxic terrorism" and "a crime against Africa and the African people.")

"I think when we define the freedom movement, it now includes the environmental issues," says Rev. Chavis. "We now understand the insidious nature of racism. Fighting it does not just involve getting civil rights laws on the books. It goes beyond that. Racism has so permeated all facets of American society. We see the struggle against environmental racism as being an ongoing part of the civil rights and freedom movement in this country, something we are going to make part of our agenda, not a side issue but a primary issue. We must be just as vigilant in attacking environmental racism as racism in health care, housing, and schools."

82. Consumption and the Environment

Herman E. Daly

[C]oncern about unlimited resource use is hardly new. Yet there is also a history of wishful thinking on these matters. Consider, in this light, the theory of the "demographic transition," which holds that population growth will stop if only per capita consumption reaches a certain level. Some believers in the demographic transition urge us to count on economic growth alone to reduce population pressures and forestall resource scarcities. But it is not very reassuring to hear that one term of a product will stop growing if only the other term grows faster, when it is the product of the two terms that must be limited. Will the average Indian's consumption have to rise to that of the average Swede before Indian fertility falls to the Swedish level? Can the eroded and crowded country of India support that many cars, power plants, buildings, and so on?

One way out of this dilemma is the technological fix frequently referred to as "dematerialization." The Wuppertal Institute in Germany, one of the places where interesting work is being done on the subject, used this somewhat extravagant term

The Ethics of Consumption, Report from the Institute for Philosophy & Public Affairs, Vol. 15, No. 4 (Fall 1995), p. 5. Published by the University of Maryland. Reprinted by permission.

to mean "improved resource use." The Institute explicitly calls for technology to improve resource productivity by a factor of ten—a reasonable goal and a way to buy valuable time to deal with more fundamental problems. But some technological optimists get carried away with dematerialization; they seem to imagine that soon we will have no use for material resources at all. To hear them talk, one would think that McDonald's was about to introduce the "info-burger," consisting of a thick patty of information between two slices of silicon, thin as communion wafers so as to emphasize the symbolic and spiritual nature of consumption. But in truth, though we can certainly eat lower on the fool chain, we cannot eat recipes. The Information Reformation, like the demographic transition before it, expands a germ of truth into a whale of a fantasy.

While all countries must worry about both population and per capita consumption, it is evident that the South needs to focus more on population, and the North more on per capita consumption. This fact will continue to play a major role in North/South treaties and discussions. Why should the South control its population if the resources saved thereby are merely gobbled up by Northern overconsumption? Why should the North control its overconsumption if the saved resources will merely allow a larger number of poor people to subsist at the same level of misery? Without for a moment minimizing the necessity of population control, it is nevertheless incumbent on the North to get serious about consumption control, and not simply wish that dematerialization and the demographic transition will come to the rescue.

83. Consumption as a Theme in the North–South Dialogue

Luis N. Camacho

In connection with consumption, three issues seem especially relevant for the North–South dialogue: (a) What is the relation between mass consumption in the North and mass destitution in the South? (b) Is there an ongoing discussion in the South on the influence of patterns of Northern consumption and, if there is one, what can we learn from it? (c) Is there something like a perspective on consumption typical of the South?

Two remarks may be useful before any answer to these questions is attempted:

(1) "North" and "South," like "West" and "East" before them, are to be taken as very imprecise designations. In addition to the truism that there is no correspondence between geography and economics (New Zealand is in the geographic South but in the economic North; Russia is in the geographic North but in the economic South), there is another, more important fact: intra-regional differences are almost as great as regional ones. Any characterization of "the South," then, must be understood as an approximation. The only justifica-

tion for the use of such terms is usual practice and lack of a better terminology.

(2) Twenty years ago in Latin America, many theorists tried to explain the underdevelopment of the South by pointing to its extreme dependency on developed countries. One answer to this dependency, they argued, was the creation of a non-consumerist society. Such a society would affirm local traditions against the encroachments of modernization, and insist that development in imitation of the North was not necessarily the best course for the non-industrial world.

This "dependence theory" was undoubtedly one-sided. In stressing Southern dependency, it failed to consider the ways in which relations between developed and underdeveloped regions are reciprocal; and in placing so strong an emphasis on external dependency, it tended to miss the internal contradictions that are characteristic of the developing world. Nonetheless, the theory performed a useful function by asking what an alternative society might look like. It is not difficult to

The Ethics of Consumption, Report from the Institute for Philosophy & Public Policy, Vol. 15, No. 4 (Fall 1995), pp. 32–34. Published by the University of Maryland. Reprinted by permission.

locate examples of wasteful consumption, on the one hand, and severe deprivation, on the other. But is there not a third option, one that would be open to the majority?

Real Options and Unfulfilled Desires

Unfortunately, in the South today, a privileged minority engage in ostentatious consumption while large sectors of the population remain in dire poverty. Patterns of wasteful consumption by elites in the South have come to mimic and exaggerate usual consumption in the North.

The promotion of high consumption in the South is, of course, advantageous to Northern industrial and service companies. It has been argued that consumption patterns in the North are likewise beneficial to Southern countries, since exports sold in the North provide developing countries with badly needed hard currencies. Indeed, one rationale for signing North–South trade agreements like NAFTA is that an increase in international commerce is good business for all concerned.

However, the fact that international trade may lead to more consumption in the South does not necessarily mean that poverty will be reduced. For millions of destitute persons in the world, consumption is primarily something that a few inhabitants of their countries can engage in as a privilege; with respect to the majority, it is denied or severely restricted—either because of rampant unemployment or because of great disparities between wages and prices. From a Southern perspective, then, what is of primary interest is not so much the distinction between good and bad consumption, but the distinction between consumption as a real option for some and as an unfulfilled desire for most.

This approach to the issue gives us a start toward an answer to the third of the initial questions. As seen from the North, consumption is largely associated with the pleasures of shopping, and perhaps with the depression resulting from not finding happiness in what can be bought. As seen from the South, consumption is connected to the ostentation of the rich, daydreams of the poor, and food riots by hungry crowds.

In the South, the external signs of the latest onslaught in the battle for a consumer society are very visible. Huge closed malls take the place of open shopping centers, which in turn had taken the place of small grocery stores; flashy cars substitute for inexpensive public transportation; designer clothes are worn by a small minority. Malls are especially interesting because they represent such a massive disruption of local conditions—both climatological and social. Only a profound distortion of the economy and of social values (together with a modification of political conditions) can explain the existence of these huge air-conditioned buildings in countries where the temperature is comfortable all year round. Within the shopping malls, English is the written language, even in countries where people do not speak it; giant parking lots accommodate dozens of cars, while outside most of the roads are filled with potholes.

The visual impact of these monstrous buildings is likewise remarkable; both their size and style—or lack thereof—amount to a violent imposition on the landscape. To attract customers, they are often built in populated neighborhoods, which instantly become noisy, exhaust-filled places and lose any human intimacy they may have had in the past. Everything inside the malls is geared toward selling and buying; all human transactions are reduced to a single function, and the scale of the whole enterprise seems to foster no behavior other than buying as much as possible. However, the prices tend to be astronomical for a substantial majority of the population, who are reduced thereby to gawking without buying.

The few remaining traditional grocery stores, and even the more modern supermarkets which began to sprout in the 1950's, were and continue to be visited by people with specific needs and wants, as well as the money to pay for what they buy. The malls, on the contrary, give rise to a new phenomenon: the reduction of most people to passive onlookers, who dream of the day when they will be able to buy many gadgets whose purpose they do not fully understand. If *Homo sapiens* becomes *homo economicus* inside the malls, there by necessity appears what Ivan Illich calls *homo miserabilis*—persons who are reduced to a marginal condition, not because they cannot perform as an economic agent in another type of society, but because the social conditions are such that they are forced to remain on the periphery of the new economy. It is hard to imagine hordes of visitors getting into supermarkets and grocery stores just to look and to long for the time when they will be able to buy. Yet this has become the everyday occurrence in Third

World malls. Physically similar to those in the North, socially they are very different.

The combination of closed spaces, a great variety of imported goods, and English labels is probably intended to give visitors the impression that they are somewhere in the North and not in a country where shantytowns and beggars are all too common. For many years now, movies, magazines, and television shows have depicted a blissful part of the world where most people live in happiness amid plenty of goods and services; now the malls are just those places. The North has moved South.

The South in the North

But now let us take a look at the other side of the coin. If the presence of Northern consumption patterns in the South is so blatant and disruptive, is there something like a Southern presence in the North? Here I can only offer a highly speculative suggestion. It is likely that for many people in the North, the picture of the destitution in the South operates as a deterrent to change, as a powerful image of what they might become if they do not keep doing what they do every day—working endless hours in jobs they find meaningless or oppressive, jobs whose only justification seems to be the income they provide. So, in the same way that consumption in the North has become a utopian dream for the South, perhaps the Southern destitution has become a dreaded possibility for the North. This symmetry is worth exploring. In both cases, an image of life as it is lived elsewhere in the world provides the motive for misguided sentiment or action: a pursuit of the worst features of industrial society for some, a reluctance to change toward more meaningful lives for some others. There is a more tangible symmetry as well: just as showy shops full of consumer goods are the visible part of the North in the South, homeless people and inner-city slums may be taken as the South in the North.

Mechanisms of Survival

The questions I have addressed about the relation between North and South have largely been bypassed, unfortunately, in recent discussions and debates. What we often find in their stead is the complaint that the South has too many people and the North too much consumption. This slogan has become a powerful political weapon because of its simplicity and its facile use of imagery. It has been voiced in important international gatherings and in policy documents. As usually happens with over-simplified visions, it hides a complex web of related problems, while at the same time it becomes either an excuse for avoiding action or a device for the justification of hasty polices. The North is said to consume more than it needs and the South to need more than it consumes. But since there is a North in the South, external problems of unequal relations become internal contradictions.

Expensive consumption has been looked upon with suspicion by many Latin American thinkers as one of the causes of recurrent economic crisis. It is seen as a grave danger for the well-being of society, which is thought to be more secure in a simple life of frugality. One finds such a concern in the 1973 book *The Poverty of Nations*, by the Costa Rican politician José ("Pepe") Figueres (1906–1990), twice President of his country. Figueres saw the consumption of expensive imported goods as an obstacle to the all-important task of creating decent jobs for the population, especially for landless peasants. The cover of his book—a reproduction of a 1936 drawing by a local artist—summarizes this idea. In the drawing, a barefooted peasant, bearing a heavy sack of coffee beans on his back, tries to cross a city street while a luxury car passes by. Coffee exports make it possible to buy the imported car, but this luxury item contributes nothing either to the productive capacity of the country or to the improvement of the conditions of the peasant.

There is one final aspect of the Southern perspective which merits some attention. In spite of all the adverse conditions in which they live, millions of poor people survive with very low levels of consumption. How do they manage to survive? How is it possible to find laughter and joy in poverty? If their mechanisms of survival were well understood in the North, perhaps the fear associated with personal and social change, sometimes perceived as threatening, would abate. Consumption, then, provides a point of entry to a complex set of realities—especially in a world where survival may well be a shared problem.

84. The Chainsaws of Greed: The Case of Pacific Lumber

Lisa H. Newton

The bare facts of the Pacific Lumber Company chronicle are shortly told and widely known: once, there was a very traditional company, Pacific Lumber, based in its company town of Scotia in Humboldt County, California, home of the legendary 2000 year old Sequoia trees. And it took care of its workers, conserved its giant redwood trees, turned a modest but steady profit, planned for the long term, and, in brief, made none of the mistakes that all the short-sighted lumber companies made. A California Newsreel documentary, "Mad River: Hard Times in Humboldt County," made in 1982, excoriated the entire industry for its miscalculations of its market, its failures toward its workers and its destruction of its trees—but took time out to mention Pacific Lumber, as proof of the fact that good business and good citizenship could, with wise management, go hand in hand. Then came the villains, jetting in from Wall Street: the takeover artists, the sharks, Charles Hurwitz' Maxxam Inc, recently spun out of Federated, soon to be joined with MCO, who gobbled up the company's stock, bought off the management, threatened the workers' jobs and benefits, and immediately doubled the timber harvest to pay down the junk-bond-financed debt. Overtime pay fattened the workers' wallets but threatened long term security; environmentalists were horrified; state and national legislatures contemplated action but took none; the courts, to whom all resorted almost immediately, tentatively fumbled through new territory, not supporting any side consistently.

Despite, or because of, the fairytale quality of its story, Pacific Lumber crystallizes several of the most important ethical issues confronting American Business, in particularly poignant and understandable form: the company is small, the trees are large and well loved, the loggers are folk heroes, the financiers are folk villains, and covering it all, the press and the senators are highly articulate commentators and critics of the whole affair, a Greek Chorus with power of subpoena. From the materials available to us chronicling this case, we recognize

five familiar issues, and the organization of this presentation will follow them in logical order:

1. At the outset: Is the traditional (paternalistic) American company worth preserving, as the traditional American Family Farm is held to be? Or is profit, return on investment to the shareholders, the only measure of good business practice?

2. Should "hostile takeovers" financed by "junk bonds" be outlawed, in light of the crime they invite and the injury they produce? Or are they just good business, working for the interests of the shareholders and the efficiency of the American economy?

3. What shall we do to save our national natural resources? Can we rely on business to protect them? Or is state regulation absolutely essential for anything of value? If the interests of a single state are not served by conservation, does the country as a whole have a right to dictate such policies?

4. In the present structure of the judicial branch and the corporate sector, it is entirely possible that resources might be irretrievably lost in the process of seeking legal means to protect them. Under the circumstances, are extreme and illegal tactics like those of Earth First! justified? How should a business deal with such tactics?

5. Who speaks for the worker? What courses are open to the employee in this confusion? To form a union? Join with management to drive out the environmentalists? Join with the environmentalists to drive out management? Or try to buy the company themselves?

1. Old Fezziwig vs. Ebenezer Scrooge: How to Run a Business

No one denies that Pacific Lumber Company was an exemplar of all the virtues traditionally professed by American Business. Founded a century

Reprinted by permission of the author. [Notes have been reduced and renumbered.—Eds.]

ago, run from the turn of the century by one family, the firm undertook to protect equally the shareholders, the workers and the natural environment, and was doing well at all of those tasks.

a. From the point of view of the shareholders, the firm had shown profits steadily since its founding, and stood to show profits steadily into the future. Financial statements for the years through 1984 show small cyclical adjustments to demand, but steady earnings on its outstanding shares.[1] Prudent management of its assets, 189,000 acres of the redwood forests of Humboldt County, California, including the largest virgin redwood stands still in private hands, ensured that no more was cut each year than grew, and avoided the boom-and-bust cycle endured by the rest of the lumber industry.

b. From the point of view of the workers, that policy worked out to steady employment; but PL was famous for employment policies that went far beyond the certainty of a job. The town of Scotia, in the center of the lumbering area, was one of the last of the company towns, wholly built and owned by PL; the houses were rented to the workers at rents that were low even for that area, and in hard times the company forgot to collect the rent. No one ever got laid off, or faced retirement or medical emergency without funds to cover them. A worker's children were assured jobs with the company, if that's what they wanted, or a full scholarship to college. Company loyalty came easy, and no union ever got a foothold in PL. "They always treated everyone so well, why rock the boat?" explained a former employee. "You knew you'd retire from there, and if your kids wanted to work there, they would. . . . People cared for the company and wanted to see it prosper."[2] We hear the echoes of Old Fezziwig, Ebenezer Scrooge's first employer in Charles Dickens' *A Christmas Carol,* who ran a business as a service for customers, employees, and the community at large; people came before profits in this operation. . . .

c. From the point of view of the environment, PL's record was excellent: not only was the selective cutting good for business in the long run, but it spared the hillsides the devastation wrought by clearcutting. Since the 1930's, it has been known that cutting all the trees on a hillside leads to the immediate dispersal or destruction of the wildlife, the erosion of the soil to the point where new trees will grow poorly or not at all, the consequent silt-ing of the streams and the destruction of the fish, and, from the increasingly rapid runoff of the rain into the silted streams, the undermining of the downstream forests. The environmental deterioration proceeds quite without limit; and in the very steep and rainy forests of the Pacific Northwest, it proceeds very quickly. Most lumber companies in this area, in the rush to capitalize on the sudden demand for lumber for housing after the second World War, had moved to clearcutting as a more efficient way to get lumber out of the forest quickly, and had severely degraded their lands. PL had not done this; it stood as a living demonstration that prudent business practices equal sound labor relations equal sound environmental practices. Beyond sound conservationist cutting policy, PL had contributed substantially to the State Park system. Pursuant to an agreement with the Save-the-Redwoods League in 1928, PL set aside many of its most scenic groves for purchase by the State of California, for inclusion in the Humboldt Redwoods State Park. When the money was slow collecting, PL "held on to the land it had agreed to preserve, patiently paying taxes on it, letting people use it as if it were already a part of the park," until the money finally came through and the acquisition was complete—in the case of the last parcel, 40 years after the original agreement.[3]

So from the point of view of the usual list of "stakeholders" in the operations of any corporation, then, PL exemplified that "excellence," of which we made so much in the early 1980's, when the new breed of management consultants started writing their bestsellers.[4] But should management be working for "excellence"? The New Greed has driven anything approaching that description off the Bottom Line in fashionable circles. Scrooge's single-minded approach to business was not new in Dickens' time. Since Adam Smith, those who stand to profit from massive financial transactions have argued that capital is "most efficiently put to use" in that employment where it yields its highest monetary return in the shortest possible time, and that therefore the general welfare is best served by leaving financiers free to seek such a return.[5] Even the notion of the "stakeholder" is disagreeable to Scrooge's children, the defenders of the new business orientation: John Boland, writing in the *Wall Street Journal* in February, 1988, complains that shareholders have a right to protest the "diminished status" of "stakeholders" assigned to them by the community-oriented managers of the companies whose shares they hold; "the only direct, clear legal obligation of corporate fiduciaries (beyond obeying civil law and contractual constraints in general) is to corporate owners who pay them."[6] If return to shareholders can be significantly increased by management practices which are not to the advantage of the workers, or the community, or the natural environment, are the corporate fiduciaries—the officers of the corporation—obliged to adopt them?

Such a question is ordinarily academic: a company which has undertaken to consider the welfare of workers, community, forests and future, in all its decisions for a century and more, will not suddenly change to suit the new imperatives from the business Right. But in the Reagan-era climate of hands-off regulatory policies, there arose another way to direct cash into the shareholders' pockets: the hostile takeover. In the "takeover," for those who have been in the Amazonian jungle for the last ten years, a "raider" (elsewhere "shark") with truly astonishing amounts of cash, most of it borrowed at very high interest from investment banks that specialize in this sort of transaction, offers to buy up the stock of a corporation (the "target") at a level well above the market price. The shareholders of the moment get a much better price for their stock, should they tender it for sale, than they might have expected. Where the stock is held by institutional funds, and most outstanding stock is these days, the fund manager is under a fiduciary obligation to the fund's owners to get that price, and to tender the stock; loyalty to the company whose shares are in question is nowhere on the manager's possible list of obligations. Having (therefore) obtained a majority of the stock with rather little effort, the raider takes control of the company, then pays down the debt with the assets of the target. Of course, once in control, he can do anything else he likes with the assets. And the attractiveness of that control, especially where the assets are large and surely profitable, may tempt the raider to marginally legitimate means in pursuit of his ends. Such, at least, were the allegations in PL's case.

2. Shady Deals in the Canyons: Michael Milken and the Sharks

In 1985, Pacific Lumber was debt-free, cash-rich (including a workers' pension fund overfunded by $50–$60 million), resource-rich beyond the knowledge of the Board of Directors (it had been 30 years since the last timber cruise, or inventory of its timber resources), and complacent in the knowledge that its practices were sound and well accepted by the community. Meanwhile, merger mania was in full swing, and Michael Milken was riding high at Drexel Burnham Lambert. On October 2, 1985, backed by Milken's "junk bonds"—the high-risk, high-yield notes that were Milken's specialty—the New York based Maxxam Group, led by Charles Hurwitz, an investor from Houston, Texas, made a tender offer of $38.50 per share for the company, almost $10 more than the then current market price of $29. PL's board of directors, led by CEO Gene Elam, obviously stunned by the attack, rejected the offer as not only "inadequate" but "unconscionable." Two weeks later, they accepted a Maxxam offer just 4% higher than the first, or $40 per share. Many analysts were surprised by the acceptance; they had reckoned the company as worth far more than that, and indeed, the entire increase from the first offer was funded, with change left over, from the pension plan. What had happened? Speculation turns on the following questions:

a. How was the board of directors taken by surprise? Were the infamous arbitragers Ivan Boesky and Boyd Jeffries involved with a scheme to "park" stock in friendly parking lots while the motives of all concerned were concealed from those who were charged with protecting the company? (How come, just as the deal got under way, Jeffries sold about 439,000 shares of PL stock to Maxxam at $29.10 per share, when the market was closing at about $33 per share?)

b. What kind of advice did they get? They hired Salomon Brothers to advise them, on a curious arrangement whereby Salomon would receive 2.25 million to keep PL independent but almost twice that if PL was sold at any bid higher than the $38.50 per share then offered. Maxxam was clearly willing to go higher; what incentive did Salomon Brothers have to oppose them?[7]

c. The major new provision in Maxxam's final offer of $40 per share included agreement to indemnify the Board of Directors against shareholder lawsuits, and to fund severance packages of up to two years' pay for 34 middle managers and "key people." When President Elam quietly left the company in June, 1986, he took with him $400,000 in such severance. Were all those people really thinking about the interests of the company when they hastily agreed to a friendly merger?[8]

How does a financier run a lumber company? Everyone knew, by the time the last suit was settled, that Hurwitz would abandon the old careful schedule of cutting in order to raise cash. Of the $840 million he had spent for the company, $770 million was debt, of which $575 million was financed through Milken's junk bonds; that debt had to be paid with predictable results for the workers and for the environment; see below. It is doubtful that even the Board of Directors foresaw the financial transformations that were to follow. For a start, Hurwitz terminated the employees' pension plan. Of the total $90 million in assets in the plan at the time of the takeover, Maxxam took $50 million for the debt and spent the remainder to buy annuities for the 2,861 plan participants. In a move that alarmed some of the executives covered by the plan, Hurwitz chose to buy those policies from the Executive Life Insurance Company of Los Angeles, which has, according to *New York Times* writer Robert Lindsey, "provided annuities to employees at several companies taken over with Drexel Burnham financing. According to investigators, that insurance company was chosen for the annuities contract despite missing a bidding deadline." The executives were alarmed because "a large proportion of its assets are in high-risk securities, among them a significant share of the bonds issued for Maxxam's takeover of Pacific Lumber."[9] . . .

Hurwitz explained to his public that the cash generated from the accelerated harvest was to be used to pay down PL's debt. But tremendous amounts of cash can be generated from an established company with uncounted timber resources, and the New Finance avoids such tedious uses as payment of debt when new opportunities present themselves. . . .

3. Who Speaks for the Trees? The Logger and the State

The Law has already figured largely in this case, as the vehicle for private parties to express, and attempt to validate, their conviction that their rights have been violated. There is another place for the law, of course: not as instrument of the remedial rights of offended private parties, but as creator of primary rights for the society as a whole, to protect what we value as our common inheritance and to provide for the common good in the future. Presumably our elected representatives are the authorized determiners of that public interest, and ultimate protectors of the resources of the nation. Presumably, to come to the point, when we are dealing with unique and irreplaceable resources like stands of 2000-year old redwoods, we might expect that the public authorities will determine what policy for those redwoods best serves the public, and private profit-oriented enterprises will operate within the guidelines set down in accordance with that policy.

That expectation is not generally fulfilled in a country dedicated to free enterprise. On the contrary, the presumption has been that anything that can be privately owned, like land, will be privately owned; and that whatever owners have traditionally been permitted to do with their land, like cut down trees and sell the lumber, the owners shall be permitted to do. The burden is on the public to prove that private control of the uses of land is so contrary to the public safety that the situation cries out for regulation and public control. On the question, who speaks for the trees?, the lumber industry has answered with a single voice: we do, and we need no public regulation and environmentalist criticism to teach us how to protect our resources.

This voice can be heard in the lumber industry's publications from the origins of the industry, and especially since 1970, when the nascent environmental movement descended upon logging operations with renewed energy. When Maxxam took over PL, with obvious plans to go after the older stands of timber protected by the old owners, the debate over the need for state protection of the lumber took on new urgency. An ecologist with the Northcoast Environmental Center, Andy Alm, summarized the areas of danger from the new practices: depletion of the timber supply, erosion of the watershed areas, increased sediment loads on area streams (endangering the fish, all species that depend on the fish, all species that depend on the streams), and the possible extinction of many endangered wildlife species such as the spotted owl.[10] A cautious scientist, Alm conceded that at that point, the projected impact on the environment "is speculative." More assertive was Earth First!'s Greg King, who advocates the complete cessation of harvest of old growth timber. The spokespersons for PL, predictably, immediately presented views in opposition to the environmentalists: statements from a consulting firm hired by Maxxam reassure that PL "could easily continue to harvest its timber at the current doubled rate for the next 20 years," and that "PL is just helping to fill in the gap left by the other companies whose capacity in production was reached shortly after World War II." The county should be happy, the consultant concluded ominously, that there was a company like PL who was "there to fill the gaps when other companies are not only dropping off production but laying off workers."[11] David Galitz, the company's manager of public affairs, was similarly reassuring, concluding on the familiar note:

> We're here to protect the land. Our resource is that land and we know it. The trees are a crop, and they keep coming back. If you want to meet a group of environmentalists, come within the Pacific Lumber Company . . . I think we practice more environmental protection methods and have more concern for the environment than the Greg Kings of this world.[12]

The dispute inspires reflection, to be conducted, very briefly, in three questions: First, where, if anywhere, does private enterprise get the right to speak for the trees? aren't they naturally suspect in such a case? Second, if the trees are to be guarded for the sake of the people, where do the people stand on the issue? and if the people are divided, do those on the spot have more right to vote than the others? Third, given that the California Department of Forestry is supposed to be appointed especially to speak for the trees, where is its position on the issue and why don't we just listen to it?

a. Private enterprise's claim derives from the ancient truth of Galitz's statement: "our resource is that land and we know it. The trees are a crop, and they keep coming back." We come from a long line of farmers and herdsmen—about 800 generations, probably. Only since the last century, three or four generations, has it become possible for any but a tiny percentage of us to live any other way. The imperatives of the farmer and herdsman are abundantly plain: conserve the land, the flock, the ability of the farm to produce more in future, or die. Owners and caretakers of property in land or livestock, whether or not they were the same persons, had interests in common, closely tied, on a daily

basis, to obedience to those imperatives. Cultures which disobeyed the imperatives died out; cultures which obeyed them well flourished, and produced us, who carry the same commands by now in all our understanding of our cultural inheritance. For the best of economic reasons, then, in that inheritance, the property owner has properly been trusted with the care and preservation of his property, and barring a few municipal regulations to preserve residential peace and quiet, the legal system has incorporated few restrictions on how he may use that property.

But ancient truth does not mean present workability. The business community took note of the "separation of ownership and control" of the modern corporation earlier in this century, largely to call attention to the troubling fact that those who run the corporation (management) may, on occasion, reprehensibly deviate from the desires of the proper owners (shareholders). Of more interest to the environment, specifically to the owned land and livestock, is the fact that, once separated from control and daily management, the owners may have no interest at all in the care of the property, which will be consigned to hired stewards. Such stewardship has itself a long tradition, and becomes problematic only when the steward is given responsibility, not for land or stock or factory or corporation, but for a sum of money. This is the position of the institutional funds, mentioned above, whose stewards must, on pain of breach of fiduciary responsibility, tender shares to raiders on evidence that they are likely to see no higher price. When the raider himself, as is usually the case, has no interest in the property except to drain it of cash for his next ventures, his own future welfare disappears from the imperatives above, and the property is no longer safe in its owner's hands. Ought we to take it away from him? Do we have the legal structure to do so? We know that under the doctrine of "eminent domain" we can seize the redwoods for a new park; but can we seize all that land just to continue a more conservative commercial logging operation? Or is that choice necessarily Owners' Option, a case of "different management philosophies and needs which need to be addressed," as David Galitz put it?[13]

b. What do the people want? Most of the people in the area are employees of Pacific Lumber.

Almost by definition, they want their jobs, and they want wages as high as possible. The rest of the people are the shopkeepers, craftsmen and service personnel who take care of the employees and the towns in which the employees live. Their interests are as intimately tied to the company as those of the loggers. The very limited options of the loggers will be taken up in section 5 below; for the present, we may ask how the people affected by these policies see the issue, without taking specifics of employment into account.

One indication of the will of the people turned up in May 1987, in the California State Legislature in Sacramento. State Senator Barry Keene had submitted a bill, SB1641, which would "limit sudden increases of timber harvesting and clear-cutting brought on by potential change of ownership of logging companies."[14] No one who favored, or opposed, the bill had any doubts about whose ownership was being discussed. PL's executive vice president was one of those who spoke against it, predicting a "whole new round of timber industry layoffs" should the bill be adopted. It was not; it had some support, especially from environmentalist groups like the Sierra Club, but was voted down in Committee.

Legislatures can be influenced, of course, by persistent popular effort. As is typical in such political exchanges, the corporations organized first: the sawmills, logging and trucking companies got their representatives to the May 1987 meetings and defeated the Keene bill. The environmental groups, all volunteer, organize much more slowly. As summer turned to fall, these groups got an unexpected publicity boost from the congressional investigations into Maxxam's tangled financial history. By Spring of 1988, the country had begun to notice what was happening in Humboldt County. An article by Richard Lovett in the *Sacramento Bee* in February told the PL story to a statewide audience. "While the future of old-growth forests is very much in doubt, one thing is certain," Lovett concluded, "The Pacific Lumber takeover is a frightening cautionary tale—an example of how progressive business management can be replaced virtually overnight, with decades of conservationist practices likely to be erased in only a few years."[15] Alarm went nationwide with an article by Robert Lindsey, dramatically entitled "They Cut Redwoods Faster to Cut the Debt Faster," in *The New York Times* in March,

citing not only the extensive environmental damage caused by the new logging policies, but also the dubious financial maneuvers behind the takeover.[16] And in April, Earth First! staged some very public demonstrations on PL land, getting themselves headlines in California newspapers.

By May, 1988, Byron Sher, Chairman of the Assembly Natural Resources Committee for the California State Assembly, was able to launch a campaign to get PL to stop clearcutting (at least) the remaining stands of virgin redwood (at least). The demand seems minimal; yet even this would have been impossible without the negative publicity of the last six months. Under those circumstances, he was able to muster enough clout (he thought) to enforce a reasonable agreement. Such an agreement was made, on May 26, 1988, and proudly announced by Sher, Assemblyman Dan Hauser of Humboldt County, and Pacific Lumber: "Pacific Lumber has agreed to stop clearcutting its remaining stands of virgin redwood. . . . This is the practice it followed for decades and earned it a reputation as a model timber company in the eyes of many Californians. . . ."[17] Sher's office simultaneously released a hopeful statement on the agreement, as did PL's public relations office (". . . the agreement reflects the Company's sensitivity to concerns expressed by Assemblymen Sher and Hauser, as well as others, over the aesthetic effect of clear-cutting in virgin old growth redwood stands"). *The New York Times* found the agreement sufficiently newsworthy to record—and recorded also the scepticism of local environmentalists and Woody Murphy: "If the wolf tells you that he no longer wants to eat chickens, who are you going to believe?" Indeed, with time, the volunteers go home and the paid agents return to the saw. By January, 1989, Sher was sponsoring a new bill calling for the whole industry to stop clearcutting older trees or face $50,000 fines for each incident. "Pacific Lumber has reneged on last year's agreement," said Sher. "They are moving as quickly as they can to destroy the old-growth characteristic of their virgin redwood holdings." In hindsight, he regretted the May 1988 agreement that had ended his pursuit of similar legislation.[18]

Letters to local newspapers during the period in which it was pending overwhelmingly opposed the bill. One letter, chilling in its naivete, shows how much the new owners relied on the old for their early support:

Inasmuch as the cutting of trees is the timber companies' main source of revenue, surely Senator Keene does not think that they would purposely shorten their own existence by clear cutting their timber without a definite reforestation plan in mind. As far as the Pacific Lumber Company is concerned, they would not have been so attractive an acquisition were it not for the fact that, through careful timber management, they have built a solid reputation spanning a hundred years or more for good business practices which include long range goals benefiting both themselves and their community. In conclusion, I feel that we need to have enough faith in the experts of the timber industry to allow them to continue to make the necessary, intelligent decision regarding the future of the logging in this area.

This was four months before Hurwitz's move to merge Maxxam and MCO, stripping the cash from PL to feed more takeover attempts, was made public. Another, from the owner of a local sawmill that purchased logs from PL, pointed out that his sawmill would be out of business if PL stopped cutting, and that "there will be less jobs!" if the sales should stop. "Instead of kicking a good neighbor and generous community supporter, let's get behind Pacific Lumber and give them all the support we can." A third, to finish this quick sampling of local sentiment, had

> a few thoughts on the Barry Keene "Maxxamshutdown" bill. . . . As we all know by looking at a map of California, a majority of the land is owned by some form of government, i.e. national parks or state parks. Now that Maxxam owns The Pacific Lumber Company "private land," Maxxam should be able to use it in the way the present guidelines are set up. They were good enough for everyone else, why not Maxxam? We don't need government harassment in Humboldt County! The county has been hurting enough these past few years. Is the Barry Keene bill another "land grab" by the government? By forcing Maxxam into bankruptcy, are they going to buy the land for yet another rotting park? I am really tired of government and their "screw up of everything they touch" record. My only consolation is that when Pacific Lumber closes down, my family and I can mooch off the government instead of paying taxes, and I'll have a lot of time to get involved in demonstrations to shut down other private industries.

From a sociological perspective, that letter is a delight. All the notes of blue-collar conservatism are there: anti-parks, anti-welfare, anti-government in general, pro-private industry, above all pro-jobs. The next section of this paper discusses the environmental movement; this letter shows as clearly as may be shown the agenda that the environmentalists faced in their public education activities.

Simultaneously, the Fortuna Town Council convened a special meeting, ostensibly to debate the Keene bill, but actually (in the absence of any supporters) to denounce it and pass a resolution to that effect. The participants in the denouncing were not, significantly, employees of PL, but residents of the town and officers of local trucking companies and sawmills; the entire area's dependence on the logging industry, and on the freedom of that industry to bring in cash, could not have been more emphatically underlined.[19]

Yes, but what of all the *other* people, like me, here on the East Coast, or in the South, or anywhere at all except in Scotia, or Fortuna, Eureka, Arcata, or Humboldt County generally? Don't we have an interest in the redwoods? If the people of the area only want to speak for Maxxam, can't *we* speak for the trees? Whose are they, anyway? Can't our ownership, as Americans, be taken into account somehow? How should it be balanced against the need in Humboldt County for jobs, security, a steady economic and political setting in which to raise children and carry on communities with a hundred years and more of settled existence? Their interests are more immediate, but there are a lot more of us. Do we have a way to allot votes in such situations? Do we even have a candidate for a way?

c. Recognizing some years ago that redwoods were sort of special, California had passed legislation requiring the lumber companies to file Timber Harvest Plans (THPs) with the state, and charged its Department of Forestry (the CDF) with the task of reviewing these THPs for environmental soundness and compatibility with the long-term benefit of the industry and the state of California. This the department had done, without much controversy, for years, until the takeover of PL.

The CDF makes an early appearance in the PL affair, as participant in the debate, quoted above, between Greg King and David Galitz on the wisdom of trusting private enterprise with the care of the trees. The CDF's position might surprise those accustomed to chilly relations between industries and the state agencies appointed to regulate them: "To date, the department has found no significant impacts to the various biological or environmental resources as a result of The Pacific Lumber Company timber harvesting. Whether it be clearcutting or selection, this harvesting has been ongoing since the turn of the century. Hopefully, it will continue on indefinitely into the future. The actions of The Pacific Lumber Company are not expected to deter this prospect." So said Tom Osipowich, the forest practice officer with the CDF. One wonders why Maxxam felt it had to hire private consultants to present its case.[20] When the new PL started submitting THPs, the issue revived. Shortly after the Keene bill failed in Committee, the Environmental Protection Information Center, one of numerous environmental organizations active in this case, brought suit against PL and the CDF to oppose state approval of some of those THPs. In company with other environmental organizations, EPIC was worried not only about the amount of timber that would be taken, but about the old-growth dependent wildlife that would be displaced. "You have specific species of wildlife that are dependent upon old-growth stands," explained John Hummel, a wildlife biologist attached to the California Department of Fish and Game to a public meeting on the THPs. "If their habitat is taken away from them you're going to lose a significant number of the population of certain species."[21] Specifically, EPIC wanted to send its own experts into the forests to see if matters were as the company said they were, and to see if damage to the environment would be as slight as the CDF said it would be. On that issue, Judge Frank Peterson of the Superior Court ruled in favor of the company: no independent experts traipsing through private property second-guessing the authorized foresters. But on the larger issue, of the methods used by the CDF to reach its determinations, the judge was unsparing:

> . . . one can conclude that no cumulative impact study or findings were adequately made and no alternative to clear-cutting was considered. It appears that the CDF rubber-stamped the timber harvest plans as presented to them by Pacific Lumber Company and their foresters. It is to be noted, in their eagerness to approve two of these harvest plans (230 and 241), they approved them before they were completed. . . . As to the effect on wildlife, there was no evidence presented except the conclusion of the Foresters that there were no *concerned* or endangered species affected. Both the Water Quality personnel and Fish and Game relied on the information provided by the professional foresters hired by Pacific Lumber and the Department of Forestry. Fish and Game's position was, if the forester saw something that needed their attention, he or she would inform them. That is not compliance with the law. That is not only naive, it was a total failure to exercise any discretion by those agencies who by law are to make findings and recommendations upon which the director is to base and exercise reasonable discretion. . . . What is most distressing to the Court is the position of the Water Quality and Fish and Game personnel, that any suggestions by them would not be considered by Forestry, and in fact Forestry would consider it to be ill advised. . . . In this case it is apparent that California Department of Forestry, the State Board of Forestry, its resource manager and director, as the *lead agency* does not want Fish and Game or Water Quality to cause any problems or raise any issues which would deter their approval of any timber harvest plan. Again it must be emphasized, this is not following the law; it is not only an abuse of discretion, but an absolute failure to exercise discretion, which the law demands. . . .[22]

The CDF was not a little miffed by the public scolding, but promised reporters that the whole matter would be straightened out soon: "We'll just change the documentation of what we do so the judge will have less difficulty in understanding it," said staff forester Harold Slack.[23]

The story of the CDF is familiar, almost a paradigm for American politics. Underfunded and understaffed, the CDF cannot monitor the forests it is supposed to monitor even if it wanted to, which it does not. Given the leg-hold restraints on its operation, it cannot keep the bright young idealists that periodically pass through its doors, but settles for career government men who know that satisfaction in life depends on not rocking the boat. The boat, of course, is the huge and rich industry that they minister to, source of colleagues, support in the legislature, and jobs when they retire from government work. As long as the industry is kept happy, the only threat to their existence is turf infringement by other government agencies in the same line of work. So we find the CDF, like any typical "regulatory" agency, dividing its time between pacifying its legislature (to avoid scandal), adjusting its delicate relationship with its industry (attempting to balance its eager cooperation with a show of control in the public interest), and fighting turf wars with other agencies, like Fish and Game and Water Quality.

Why did we ever expect anything better? When we set up task forces within a company to get a job done, we know enough to structure the incentives so that it will at least be to the interests of the task force members to do the job. But in the CDF, we have an agency, and again, not an unusual agency, whose employees are rewarded both in daily dealings and in long-term career prospects for *not* doing their job: for ignoring what they are supposed to know, for concealing what they are supposed to reveal, for handing over for destruction what they are supposed to protect, and in general, for serving as advocate, not for the people, but for the industry the people hired them to control. . . .

The unfairness of it all brings tears to the eyes. The state appointed and taxpayer bankrolled agencies openly admit that only public exposure and humiliation brought about by pressure from private groups will make them do their jobs; for the rest, they serve the industry. Let them actually be frightened into conscientious action for a change, and their action can be overruled by a taxpayer-financed but politically sensitive Board, well aware of where the votes are next election day. And so, having paid for the Board, and paid for the agency, to protect the trees, if we really want, after all, to save the trees, we must sue as private citizens the very same public servants, and pay the tab for the private litigation as well. There has to be a better method—a more direct and effective method.

4. Do Earth's Ends Justify Extra-Legal Means? Enter Earth First!

Who, then, speaks for the trees? Once, the lumber companies, but no more. Legitimately, the people, but with no single voice. Authoritatively, the California Department of Forestry, but not well. Yet the trees need protection now, immediately, not in some rosy future when we will have responsible business practices and an enlightened people and dedicated public agencies. Each day that goes by means that responsibility, enlightenment and dedication will arrive too late for yet more groves of redwoods. And a grove of redwoods is not like other things your bulldozer might accidentally run over. It's more like you.

Ordinarily we will stop the bulldozer if you are in front of it. The reason we will stop it is complex: it is not just a matter of law, not just a matter of prudent use of resources, and certainly not just a matter of tender feelings for you—it is more a perception of the dignity of the unique in life, and some permanent injunction against destruction of that uniqueness, an injunction to be breached only prayerfully and in strict necessity. . . .

It seems to have something to do with respect for that which we cannot create, a totally unique center of life and spirit which, once gone, is gone forever. I can grow other human beings to replace you, of course, but they just won't be the same; there is no combination of individuals that will ever add up to, or duplicate you, do what you did or be what you were. This uncreatable uniqueness properly inspires in us reverence and respect, and leads us to agonize over every deliberate taking of human life, no matter how justified by law and conduct (witness, for instance, the extreme reluctance of the states to bring back capital punishment, and their even greater queasiness at applying it in an instant case).

Now, by this criterion, an old grove of redwoods has all the bulldozer-, or chainsaw-, stopping rights of a human being. (We will adopt as correct the environmentalists' assumption, that from the point of view of the environment, it is the ecosystem as a whole, not the individual tree, that is the viable unit, including all its soil mass, wildlife, water, air, even its insects, as well as flowers, moss, trees. By "grove," then, we will understand a stand of trees of sufficient size to support itself indefinitely, barring interference from outside.) It is unique and uncreatable, certainly uncreatable by us. We can plant redwoods, but we cannot plant 1000-year-old redwoods. We can plant trees, but we cannot restore the soil that has been washed away after the last clearcutting, and therefore we cannot replace the floral ground cover, nor bring back the animals that lived on that assortment of plants dependent upon the shade and moisture of that grove. It is very difficult to create any ecosystem, let alone to recreate a particular ecosystem, and I think it could be argued that it is by definition impossible to recreate one that has been slowly coming to be over a millennium. When we are dealing with groves of this complexity and antiquity, we do not need to ask for the solution to a cost–benefit analysis, although some interesting analyses of the cost of extinction of species have been presented. We need only note that the grove in front of the saw can in no way be created or recreated by us, that it deserves our respect, and that we have no right to destroy it.

All of the above is by way of philosophical background to spikes in the trees. Earth First! (the punctuation is part of the name) is not one of your polite conservation-minded groups. Its specialty is "monkey-wrenching," tossing monkey wrenches into or otherwise fouling up any and all activities that destroy the environment. In addition to the usual suits and injunctions, the group's program includes burning billboards, pulling up developers' landmark stakes, and crippling bulldozers with nasty substances like maple syrup.[24] It should be noted that Earth First!'s actions on PL property were restricted to sitting in trees, talking to loggers, and occasionally serenading the company with guitar-accompanied renditions of "Where Are We Gonna Work When the Trees Are Gone," led by folk singer Darryl Cherney. (Cherney was at that time a candidate for the state legislature.) Occasionally arrested and sued at least once by the company, Earth First! quietly settled the suit and volunteered for community service instead of jail.[25] But they are not always so nonviolent. In their efforts to prevent other logging operations, their activities have been known to include spiking roads to cripple the logging trucks, and tree-spiking, driving a twenty-penny nail into a tree. The nail is easily concealed, and the operation doesn't hurt a living tree. But it does render the tree useless for lumber, because the nail chews up the blades of the saws. If the authorities are informed that a grove is spiked, and tells the logging company about it, a prudent company would not log that grove, until the spikes could be removed. If the spiking is sufficiently persistent, it may be impossible to log the grove.

Is this good environmentalist activity? "They are outlaws," says Jay Hair, President of the National Wildlife Federation, of Earth First!, "they are terrorists; and they have no right being considered environmentalists." "A terrorist organization," echoes Michael Kerrick, supervisor for the

Willamette National Forest in Oregon; Cecil Andrus, former Secretary of the Interior, calls them "a bunch of kooks."[26] It is hard to find supporters for these tactics in the ranks of the traditional conservationist organizations, and even harder in the ranks of the government agencies charged with enforcing environmental regulation. But has anything else worked, for individual groves or ecosystems? Sometimes we can get tradeoffs—we agree not to press the matter on 15 or 20 acres of old-growth redwoods, and they will preserve some particularly desirable stretches in Alaska. But if it is a grove of trees more than a millennium old that is slated for destruction today, and the lumber company is in the hands of a Wall Street financier who wants only cash now, and local councils and legislatures are dominated by sawmill owners and the like, and the CDF approved the THP even before it was drafted, what other than terrorist tactics will work to preserve it?

Perhaps the notion of a "tradeoff" is not entirely appropriate to the situation of the irreplaceable grove. If we trade off a grove for another today, what shall we trade tomorrow? For it is impossible to grow something of equal value to satisfy the appetite of the company. Only complete preservation will preserve the status quo ante, the balance that trades try to maintain. We do not, after all, always insist on tradeoffs in all matters, even in the political system. We never tried to get the Ku Klux Klan to lynch *fewer* Blacks, or only rural Blacks or Blacks in the Deep South states. Sometimes we had to endure lynchings, but the notion of a legal and accepted compromise on the numbers of lynchings never came up. It may just be that when we are dealing with fragile ecosystems, as when we are dealing with human beings, the rule of compromise, applicable elsewhere in environmental matters and in political matters generally, will have to be scrapped in favor of a rule of strict preservation, and no lobbying or legislative efforts should be spent in attempts to reach "compromise solutions." If this is the move of the future for the environmentalist community, we will owe, perhaps, more of a debt than we are willing to acknowledge to Earth First!.

Meanwhile, how should a legitimate business react to terrorist tactics? If PL by now does not seem to be legitimate, the question can be raised about any other company or industry. How should we react to Pro-Life threats to smash all windows in the pharmacies that sell abortifacients? to Vegetarian threats to poison the cattle herds? to Muslim threats to firebomb the bookstores? The usual counsel, and indeed, *my* counsel, under all other circumstances, is to take the strongest possible measures to arrest and disable the terrorists, while conducting business as usual to show that terrorism is unavailing. Should that be our advice to Maxxam in its dealings with Earth First!?

5. Tell Me, Which Side Are You On? The Tragic Options of the Loggers

While the well-oiled machines of finance whir on Wall Street, and the salvoes fly between environmentalists and the industry, what is the worker to do? The communications identifiably from loggers and their families in the local newspapers reveal above all a sense of loss for the destruction of the company they knew, and which they expected to take care of them until retirement and beyond. Above all, they want to preserve the lifestyle and security they had. But that, of course, is the one thing they cannot do. Beyond that loss, all other options lead to more loss.

a. *Onward and Upward with Private Enterprise.* They can side with the company, and applaud the wasteful acceleration of the logging. After all, it leads to plenty of work now, including overtime, and that feeds the wallet enough to block out that empty feeling in the soul when the clearcut hillside is finished and abandoned. . . .

b. *Save the Trees.* The loggers can side with the environmentalists and try to get the trees, especially the old growth, preserved forever under some state umbrella. This course is not so immediately unlikely as it sounds; most loggers genuinely love the woods and streams among which they live, and enjoy outdoor recreation by choice. But it was never a real option for the PL loggers. First, there was the visceral hatred of the environmentalists: long-haired, dirty, foul-mouthed, middle class and instinctively contemptuous of workers, to all appearances Communist and drug-abusers, these hippies repelled the loggers from the day they bumped into town in their Volkswagens. . . . Second, and more enduringly important, saving the trees meant instant unemployment and the necessity of leaving the area for a very uncertain

future elsewhere. The loggers were never for one minute unaware of this; as the sampling above indicates, PL spokespeople never opened their mouths without reminding the workers that if the environmentalists had their way, there wouldn't be any jobs. To a young head of a family, without any educational qualifications, such forced relocation is equivalent to suicide; environmentalism had very few friends among the ranks of the loggers.

c. *Solidarity Forever.* There had never been a union at Pacific Lumber. Was it worth a try after the takeover? One article, filed two weeks after the takeover was announced, reported that Local 3-98 of the International Woodworkers of America, AFL-CIO, was considering an organizing effort in response to a few requests from frightened workers. About all the union could do, its business agent conceded, was make sure that layoffs took place in an orderly manner, respecting seniority. . . .

d. *The Dream of Ownership.* By September of 1988, the extent of the destruction of the timber lands was evident to everyone, and the workers had begun to talk about alternatives to unwavering support of present management. Could they take over the company? The ESOP, or Employee Stock Ownership Plan, was a new idea for the workers, but organizer Patrick Shannon assured them it was feasible. . . . Shannon is urging a hostile takeover by workers, requiring that they raise hundreds of millions of dollars to buy up shares on the open market until they have a majority. Is this even remotely possible? . . . "Employees who want to pursue the dream of an ESOP takeover have every right to do so," editorialized the *Times-Standard* in October, 1988, "Circumstances, however, suggest it's an impossible dream—one fraught with the potential for great disappointment and financial loss."[27]

Conclusion

Whatever facet of this case we have under consideration—the traditional company, with its rich inheritance of social responsibility and compassion for its workers and its land, the loggers, once secure in a relatively carefree existence, the community, once assured of a prosperous future, the financial institutions, once reliable custodians of conservative fiscal practices, or the giant redwoods themselves, that we always assumed would last forever—"great disappointment and financial loss" seem to be among the outcomes. At this point it is not clear whether criminal acts were involved in the takeover that opens our story, whether shameful betrayal is the correct characterization of the acts of the Board of Directors, whether the government agencies charged with regulating the timber industry are up to the job, whether the radical environmentalists are right in their employment of extreme measures, and whether, eventually, the workers will be able to get off the rollercoaster and take control of their situation. In these and other unclarities, the case raises questions about the conduct of a business in every one of its areas of constituent relations, and serves as a prism through which a multitude of issues may be seen in exemplar.

Notes

1. In the third quarter of 1984, for instance, less than a year before the takeover, PL reported that its net earnings rose 50 percent over the previous year ($11,337,000, or 47 cents per share, compared to $7,547,000, or 31 cents per share, for the third quarter a year ago). Sources include annual reports from the years 1981 through 1984.

2. Ilana DeBare, "Old Redwoods, Traditions Felled in Race for Profits," *Los Angeles Times*, April 20, 1987.

3. The source for this statement is a brochure published by Pacific Lumber, no date visible.

4. See Thomas J. Peters and Robert H. Waterman, Jr., *In Search of Excellence*, New York: Harper & Row, 1982, Daddy of them all; then progeny, Terrence E. Deal and Allan A. Kennedy, *Corporate Cultures*, Reading: Addison-Wesley, 1982; John Naisbitt and Patricia Aburdene, *Re-inventing the Corporation*, New York: Warner Books, 1985; Tom Peters and Nancy Austin, *A Passion for Excellence*, New York: Random House, 1985; Buck Rodgers, *The IBM Way*, New York: Harper & Row, 1986; Robert H. Waterman, Jr., *The Renewal Factor*, New York: Bantam Books, 1987.

5. The orthodox capitalist approach is possibly best captured by Milton Friedman, in his oft-reprinted "The Social Responsibility of Business is to Increase its Profits," *The New York Times Magazine*, September 13, 1970.

6. *Wall Street Journal*, February 10, 1988.

7. Testimony of William G. Bertain, Attorney at Law, attorney of record for the Murphy great-grandchildren in the suit to retain control of the company, before Congress, on October 5, 1987; investigation of Drexel Burnham Lambert's major customers.

8. "Pacific Accepts Maxxam Bid," *The New York Times*, October 24, 1985; "PL agrees to buyout deal: New York firm's offer of $40-a-share accepted," *Times-Standard*, Eureka, CA, October 23, 1985; "Money Talks," *Wall Street Journal*, November 13, 1985; "PL chief quits; gets $400,000," *Times-Standard*, June 10, 1986.

9. Robert Lindsey, "They Cut Redwoods Faster to Cut the Debt Faster," *The New York Times*, March 2, 1988. Attempts to secure PL comment on the allegations were unsuccessful; Mr. Hurwitz was "not available" for comment. The company lawyer, however, Howard Bressler, "said the company had complied 'meticulously' with all applicable laws in the merger," and that there was "nothing improper" about the handling of the pension plan.

10. Enoch Ibarra, "Pacific Lumber Timber Harvest Causes Concern," *The Humboldt Beacon*, Fortuna, California, January 27, 1987.

11. Ibid.

12. Ibid.

13. Ibid.

14. *Times-Standard* of Eureka, California, May 5, 1987.

15. Richard A. Lovett, "The Real Costs—to All of Us— of a Corporate Buyout," *The Sacramento Bee*, February 21, 1988.

16. Robert Lindsey, "They Cut Redwoods Faster to Cut the Debt Faster," *The New York Times*, March 2, 1988.

17. Statement on Pacific Lumber Old-Growth Agreement, Governor's Press Conference Room State Capitol, May 26, 1988.

18. See also, "Company Eases Its Policy on Logging of Redwoods," *The New York Times*, Friday, May 27, 1988; PALCO news release, The Pacific Lumber Company, PO Box 37, Scotia, CA 95565, May 26, 1988; "Bill to Stop Clearcutting in the Works," *San Francisco Chronicle*, January 28, 1989; "Bill would restrict PL clearcutting of virgin redwoods," *Times-Standard*, Eureka, CA, January 31, 1989.

19. Letters to *Times-Standard*, May 5, May 13, and June 4, 1987. "Timber bill opposed," *Times-Standard*, May 2, 1987.

20. Enoch Ibarra, "Pacific Lumber Timber Harvest Causes Concern," *Humboldt Beacon*, January 27, 1987.

21. Greg King, "Fish and Game Says Pacific Lumber/CDF Eliminating Wildlife," *Humboldt News Service*, May 11, 1987.

22. Superior Court of the State of California for the County of Humboldt, case #79879, Ruling on Petition for Writ of Mandamus, Nov. 5, 1987.

23. See also "Judge sides with PL and CDF, " *Times-Standard* (Eureka, CA), July 10, 1987; "Suit Against Pacific Lumber to Be Fought on PL Terms," *North*

Coast News, July 16, 1987; "CDF won't appeal ruling," November 13, 1987, "CDF upset by court's decision," *Times-Standard,* November 15, 1987.

24. David Foreman, *Ecodefense: A Field Guide to Monkeywrenching,* 1985; cited in Jamie Malanowski, "Monkey-Wrenching Around," *The Nation,* May 2, 1987.

25. *Times-Standard,* Eureka, CA, April 8, 1988; May 1, 1988; April 14, 1988 ("20 Arrested in Kneeland Anti-Logging Protest"); Publications from Darryl Cherney for Congress, PO Box 9, Percy, CA 95467.

26. Malanowski, *op. cit.* p. 569.

27. *Times-Standard,* Eureka, CA, October 11, 1988.

85. Why Shouldn't Corporations Be Socially Responsible?

Christopher Stone

. . . [T]he opposition to corporate social responsibility comprises at least four related though separable positions. . . . Each assumes in its own degree that the managers of the corporation are to be steered almost wholly by profit, rather than by what they think proper for society on the whole. Why should this be so? So far as ordinary morals are concerned, we often expect human beings to act in a fashion that is calculated to benefit others, rather than themselves, and commend them for it. Why should the matter be different with corporations?

The Promissory Argument

The most widespread but least persuasive arguments advanced by the "antiresponsibility" forces take the form of a moral claim based upon the corporation's supposed obligations to its shareholders. In its baldest and least tenable form, it is presented as though management's obligation rested upon the keeping of a promise—that the management of the corporation "promised" the shareholders that it would maximize the shareholders' profits. But this simply isn't so.

Consider for contrast the case where a widow left a large fortune goes to a broker, asking him to invest and manage her money so as to maximize her return. The broker, let us suppose, accepts the money and the conditions. In such a case, there would be no disagreement that the broker had made a promise to the widow, and if he invested her money in some venture that struck his fancy for any reason other than it would increase her fortune, we would be inclined to advance a moral (as well, perhaps, as a legal) claim against him. Generally, at least, we believe in the keeping of promises; the broker, we should say, had violated a promissory obligation to the widow.

But that simple model is hardly the one that obtains between the management of major corporations and their shareholders. Few if any American shareholders ever put their money into a corporation upon the express promise of management that the company would be operated so as to maximize their returns. Indeed, few American shareholders ever put their money directly *into* a corporation at all. Most of the shares outstanding today were issued years ago and found their way to their current shareholders only circuitously. In almost all cases, the current shareholder gave his money to some prior shareholders, who, in turn, had gotten it from B, who, in turn, had gotten it from A, and so on back to the purchaser of the original issue, who, many years before, had bought the shares through an underwriting syndicate. In the course of these transactions, one of the basic elements that exists in the broker case is missing: The manager of the corporation, unlike the broker, was never even offered a chance to refuse the shareholder's "terms" (if they were that) to maximize the shareholder's profits.

There are two other observations to be made about the moral argument based on a supposed promise running from the management to the shareholders. First, even if we do infer from all the circumstances a "promise" running from the management to the shareholders, but not one, or not one of comparable weight running elsewhere (to the company's employees, customers, neighbors, etc.), we ought to keep in mind that as a moral matter (which is what we are discussing here) sometimes it is deemed morally justified to break promises (even to break the law) in the furtherance of other social interests of higher concern. Promises can advance moral arguments, by way of creating presumptions, but few of us believe that promises, per se, can end them. My promise to appear in class on time would not ordinarily justify me from refusing to give aid to a drowning man. In other words, even if management *had* made an express promise to its shareholders to "maximize your profits," (a) I am not persuaded that the ordinary person would interpret it to mean "maximize *in every way you can possibly get away with*, even if that means polluting the environment, ignoring or breaking the law"; and (b) I am not persuaded that, even if it were interpreted as so blanket a promise, most people would not suppose it ought—morally—to be broken in some cases.

Finally, even if, in the face of all these considerations, one still believes that there is an overriding, unbreakable, promise of some sort running from management to the shareholders, I do not think that it can be construed to be any stronger than one running to *existent* shareholders, arising from *their* expectations as measured by the price *they* paid. That is to say, there is nothing in the argument from promises that would wed us to a regime in which management was bound to maximize the income of shareholders. The argument might go so far as to support compensation for existent shareholders if the society chose to announce that henceforth management would have other specified obligations, thereby driving the price of shares to a lower adjustment level. All future shareholders would take with "warning" of, and a price that discounted for, the new "risks" of shareholding (i.e., the "risks" that management might put corporate resources to *pro bonum* ends).

The Agency Argument

Related to the promissory argument but requiring less stretching of the facts is an argument from agency principles. Rather than trying to infer a promise by management to the shareholders, this argument is based on the idea that the shareholders

designated the management their agents. This is the position advanced by Milton Friedman in his *New York Times* article. "The key point," he says, "is that . . . the manager is the agent of the individuals who own the corporation. . . ."[1]

Friedman, unfortunately, is wrong both as to the state of the law (the directors are *not* mere agents of the shareholders)[2] and on his assumption as to the facts of corporate life (surely it is closer to the truth that in major corporations the shareholders are *not*, in any meaningful sense, selecting the directors; management is more often using its control over the proxy machinery to designate who the directors shall be, rather than the other way around).

What Friedman's argument comes down to is that for some reason the directors ought morally to consider themselves more the agents for the shareholders than for the customers, creditors, the state, or the corporation's immediate neighbors. But why? And to what extent? Throwing in terms like "principal" and "agent" begs the fundamental questions.

What is more, the "agency" argument is not only morally inconclusive, it is embarrassingly at odds with the way in which supposed "agents" actually behave. If the managers truly considered themselves the agents of the shareholders, as agents they would be expected to show an interest in determining how their principals wanted them to act—and to act accordingly. In the controversy over Dow's production of napalm, for example, one would expect, on this model, that Dow's management would have been glad to have the napalm question put to the shareholders at a shareholders' meeting. In fact, like most major companies faced with shareholder requests to include "social action" measures on proxy statements, it fought the proposal tooth and claw.[3] It is a peculiar agency where the "agents" will go to such lengths (even spending tens of thousands of dollars of their "principals'" money in legal fees) to resist the determination of what their "principals" want.

The Role Argument

An argument so closely related to the argument from promises and agency that it does not demand extensive additional remarks is a contention based upon supposed considerations of *role*. Sometimes in moral discourse, as well as in law, we assign obligations to people on the basis of their having assumed some role or status, independent of any specific verbal promise they made. Such obligations are assumed to run from a captain to a seaman (and vice versa), from a doctor to a patient, or from a parent to a child. The antiresponsibility forces are on somewhat stronger grounds resting their position on this basis, because the model more nearly accords with the facts—that is, management never actually promised the shareholders that they would maximize the shareholders' investment, nor did the shareholders designate the directors their agents for this express purpose. The directors and top management are, as lawyers would say, fiduciaries. But what does this leave us? So far as the directors are fiduciaries of the shareholders in a legal sense, of course they are subject to the legal limits on fiduciaries—that is to say, they cannot engage in self-dealing, "waste" of corporate assets, and the like. But I do not understand any proresponsibility advocate to be demanding such corporate largesse as would expose the officers to legal liability; what we are talking about are expenditures on, for example, pollution control, above the amount the company is required to pay by law, but less than an amount so extravagant as to constitute a violation of these legal fiduciary duties. (Surely no court in America today would enjoin a corporation from spending more to reduce pollution than the law requires.) What is there about assuming the role of corporate officer that makes it immoral for a manager to involve a corporation in these expenditures? A father, one would think, would have stronger obligations to his children by virtue of his status than a corporate manager to the corporation's shareholders. Yet few would regard it as a compelling moral argument if a father were to distort facts about his child on a scholarship application form on the grounds that he had obligations to advance his child's career; nor would we consider it a strong moral argument if a father were to leave unsightly refuse piled on his lawn, spilling over into the street, on the plea that he had obligations to give every moment of his attention to his children, and was thus too busy to cart his refuse away.

Like the other supposed moral arguments, the one from role suffers from the problem that the strongest moral obligations one can discover have at most only prima facie force, and it is not apparent why those obligations should predominate over some contrary social obligations that could be advanced.

Then, too, when one begins comparing and weighing the various moral obligations, those running back to the shareholder seem fairly weak by comparison to the claims of others. For one thing, there is the consideration of alternatives. If the shareholder is dissatisfied with the direction the corporation is taking, he can sell out, and if he does so quickly enough, his losses may be slight. On the other hand, as Ted Jacobs observes, "those most vitally affected by corporate decisions—people who work in the plants, buy the products, and consume the effluents—cannot remove themselves from the structure with a phone call."[4]

The "Polestar" Argument

It seems to me that the strongest moral argument corporate executives can advance for looking solely to profit is not one that is based on a supposed express, or even implied promise to the shareholder. Rather, it is one that says, if the managers act in such fashion as to maximize profits—if they act *as though* they had promised the shareholders they would do so—then it will be best for all of us. This argument might be called the polestar argument, for its appeal to the interests of the shareholders is not justified on supposed obligations to the shareholders per se, but as a means of charting a straight course toward what is best for the society as a whole.

Underlying the polestar argument are a number of assumptions—some express and some implied. There is, I suspect, an implicit positivism among its supporters—a feeling (whether its proponents own up to it or not) that moral judgments are peculiar, arbitrary, or vague—perhaps even "meaningless" in the philosophic sense of not being amenable to rational discussion. To those who take this position, profits (or sales, or price–earnings ratios) at least provide some solid, tangible standard by which participants in the organization can measure their successes and failures, with some efficiency, in the narrow sense, resulting for the entire group. Sometimes the polestar position is based upon a related view—not that the moral issues that underlie social choices are meaningless, but that resolving them calls for special expertise. "I don't know any investment adviser whom I would care to act in my behalf in any matter except turning a profit. . . . The value of these specialists . . . lies in their limitations; they ought not allow themselves to see so much of the world that they become distracted."[5] A slightly modified point emphasizes not that the executives lack moral or social expertise per se, but that they lack the social authority to make policy choices. Thus, Friedman objects that if a corporate director took "social purposes" into account, he would become "in effect a public employee, a civil servant. . . . On grounds of political principle, it is intolerable that such civil servants . . . should be selected as they are now."[6]

I do not want to get too deeply involved in each of these arguments. That the moral judgments underlying policy choices are vague, I do not doubt—although I am tempted to observe that when you get right down to it, a wide range of actions taken by businessmen every day, supposedly based on solid calculations of "profit," are probably as rooted in hunches and intuition as judgments of ethics. I do not disagree either that, ideally, we prefer those who have control over our lives to be politically accountable; although here, too, if we were to pursue the matter in detail we would want to inspect both the premise of this argument, that corporate managers are not *presently* custodians of discretionary power over us anyway, and also its logical implications. Friedman s point that "if they are to be civil servants, then they must be selected through a political process"[7] is not, as Friedman regards it, a *reductio ad absurdum*—not, at any rate, to Ralph Nader and others who want publicly elected directors.

The reason for not pursuing these counterarguments at length is that, whatever reservations one might have, we can agree that there is a germ of validity to what the "antis" are saying. But their essential failure is in not pursuing the alternatives.

Certainly, *to the extent* that the forces of the market and the law can keep the corporation within desirable bounds, it may be better to trust them than to have corporate managers implementing their own vague and various notions of what is best for the rest of us. But are the "antis" blind to the fact that there are circumstances in which the law—and the forces of the market—are simply not competent to keep the corporation under control? The shortcomings of these traditional restraints on corporate conduct are critical to understand, not merely for the defects they point up in the "antis" position. More important, identifying where the traditional forces are inadequate is the first step in the design of new and alternative measures of corporate control.

Notes

1. *New York Times,* September 12, 1962, sect. 6, p. 33, col. 2.
2. See, for example, *Automatic Self-Cleansing Filter Syndicate Co. Ltd. v. Cunninghame* (1906) 2 Ch. 34.
3. "Dow Shalt Not Kill," in S. Prakash Sethi, *Up Against the Corporate Wall* (Englewood Cliffs, N.J.: Prentice-Hall, 1971), pp. 236–266, and the opinion of Judge Tamm in *Medical Committee for Human Rights v. S.E.C.,* 432 F.2d 659 (D.C. Cir. 1970), and the dissent of Mr. Justice Douglas in the same case in the U.S. Supreme Court, 404 U.S. 403, 407–411 (1972).
4. Theodore J. Jacobs, "Pollution, Consumerism, Accountability," *Center Magazine* 5, 1 (January–February 1971): 47.
5. Walter Goodman, "Stocks Without Sin," *Harper's,* August 1971, p. 66.
6. *New York Times,* September 12, 1962, sect. 6, p. 122, col. 3.
7. Ibid., p. 122, cols. 3–4.

86. "I Am No Greenpeacer, But . . ." or Environmentalism, Risk Communication, and the Lower Middle Class

Mark Sagoff

Car and Driver, a magazine popular among macho motorists, has come out for "the global environment."[1] For two decades, the magazine railed against "safety twits,"[2] Ralph Nader,[3] the Clean Air Act,[4] eco-fascists,[5] endangered species programs,[6] seat belts and air bags,[7] speed limits,[8] welfare cheats,[9] and all regulations devised by "the bloated civil service, the feeders at the public trough" who "still thrive in all their pompous, isolated, self-serving, over-stuffed glory."[10] In the November 1988 issue, however, Brock Yates, who for years assailed the bureaucracy, wrote:

> Like it or not, our beloved car is an irksome source of pollution, urban congestion, and excessive fossil-fuel consumption. Calls for an end to the CAFE [corporate average fuel economy] standards—recently heard from no less an eminence than General Motors president Robert Stempel—seem selfish and simple-minded. I am no Greenpeacer, but I believe we face larger problems on this globe than the search for more horsepower-per-cubic-inch or the financial welfare of the auto industry.[11]

In the August 1989 *Car and Driver,* William Jeannes, a columnist who historically echoed Yates's diatribes against environmental regulations, joined the bandwagon: "If you are concerned about planet Earth and the cars you drive on it," he wrote, "you understand that an efficient automobile is one that . . . contributes as little carbon dioxide as possible to fuel the greenhouse effect."[12]

Tough-minded, hard-working American men, the kind who know how to strap a twelve-gauge shotgun on the back of a pickup, could always count on a few magazines—*Sport Truck, Car and Driver,* and *Motor Trend,* for example—to stand up against doomsaying environmental and bureaucratic wimps. These magazines, which have long defended the oil and automotive industry against the likes of Ralph Nader and the Sierra Club, have now gone over to the enemy. The November 1989 issue of *Sport Truck* calls on Detroit to provide technology that is friendly to the environment. "Even if performance has to be compromised by clean air legislation," an editorial concedes, "we're just going to have to bite the bullet. Because when our enthusiasm butts heads with our health, something has to give."[13]

Four Rules for Risk Communication

In supporting CAFE standards, *Car and Driver* did not lose all the old-time religion.[14] It still fulminates volcanically against governmental efforts to improve safety of any kind, especially highway safety. Brock Yates recently praised "Peach State libertarian marksmen" who potshotted unattended radar units "Smokey" had set up to slow down Georgia drivers.[15] In rhetoric his readers have come to expect, Yates celebrated "the latent anarchism of the American people,"[16] who will pick up a rifle before letting anyone tell them how fast to drive their cars."[17]

Car and Driver, which out-Herods the *American Rifleman* in trying to keep the government off our backs, nevertheless has adopted an environmentalist image.[18] Why? Why are environmental restrictions acceptable when all other regulations, especially safety regulations, remain anathema to this popular journal? How can such a macho magazine extol risk taking and at the same time speak for the trees?

Readers of *Car and Driver* were quick to pose these questions. "An endorsement of tighter CAFE standards from the magazine obsessed with

Reprinted with permission of the publisher from *Business, Ethics, and the Environment: The Public Policy Debate,* ed. by W. Michael Hoffman et al. (Quorum Books, an imprint of Greenwood Publishing Group, Inc., Westport, CT, 1990), pp. 101–123. ©1990 by the Center for Business Ethics at Bently College. [Notes have been reduced and renumbered.—Eds.]

performance and freedom from government regulation. What gives?" wrote a man from Conyers, Georgia, in a letter in the October 1989 issue. "When it comes to breaking the speed limit and opposing radar detector bans, you're right there. Now you become de facto Naderites by endorsing a regulation that threatens the lives of Mustangs, ZR-1s, etc."[19]

Readers may rest assured that *Car and Driver* continues to oppose paternalistic regulations, such as air bag and seat belt requirements, that try to make driving less dangerous. CAFE standards, however, do not attempt to limit one's personal freedom to drive as one likes. Rather, these standards seek to protect nature from pollution and, perhaps, to make America less dependent on the Organization for Petroleum Exporting Countries (OPEC). Accordingly, in calling for tougher CAFE standards, *Car and Driver* does not necessarily endorse safety regulations but supports nature, nationalism, patriotism, and so on. These values are right up there with breaking speed limits and ignoring radar detector bans.

Readers of *Car and Driver* are not, in general, risk averse. They oppose speed limits and air bags. That they may court danger personally implies nothing, however, about their attitude toward nature and the environment. You do not have to be risk averse to favor policies that promote energy independence or protect the integrity and beauty of the natural environment. You do not have to be a "safety twit" to want fuel economy; people who drive fast can brake for animals.

A person who owns a fast car and drives it that way—a person who likes to take risks—may be as concerned about nature as someone who drinks Perrier and watches birds for fun. This concern is likely to lie in a moral, cultural, or even religious respect for nature rather than in a quest for personal safety. This environmental ethic has little to do with risk assessment, risk management, and risk perception. Rather, it lies in a collective sense of moral responsibility many of us feel toward each other and toward the natural world.

First, I examine political attitudes among lower-middle-class Americans, particularly white men, who, according to public opinion surveys, are swelling the ranks of the environmental movement. I want to use what some people may describe as "the greening of the rednecks" as an occasion to propose four theses as cardinal rules of risk communication:

1. Risk communicators need to address concerns, values, and problems that may have little to do with risk.
2. Risk communicators have to communicate about risk primarily in ethical, not economic, terms.
3. Nature is more important than the environment.
4. Law can be a powerful legitimating instrument.

The first thesis—that risk communication may have less to do with risk than is commonly thought—will not sound paradoxical to those who know the literature. The literature of risk analysis distinguishes between risk as an objective physical property of events (one may call this the magnitude of a risk) and risk as a social construct (the meaning of a risk).[20] Thus, the risks involved, say, in jumping and being pushed from the same window may carry exactly the same objective magnitudes but have entirely different meanings. Indeed, the meaning of a risk, which arises from its social and moral circumstances, can depend as little on its objective magnitude as its objective magnitude depends on its social meaning.

Efforts at risk communication (I believe many experts will agree) cannot succeed if they address only the objective magnitude of various technological risks. Rather, the decisive concerns may lie in the relationships of power, culture, and mutual respect or disrespect among various participants within a political process. These participants may argue over the objective assessment of risk, but the deeper conflict often lies in political disagreements—that is, in differing conceptions of our national goals and the way we should achieve them. One may express doubts, for example, about the safety of genetic engineering but be concerned more fundamentally about the moral character of "artificial" animals or "man-made" life.[21]

The second rule follows as a corollary from the first. Many experts, even those who urge the relevance of economic risk–benefit calculations, concede that ethical and cultural factors are often more decisive than economic ones in making people accept or resent various hazards. Arguments over the objective magnitude of a particular hazard, indeed, may skirt the main question, which is whether the risk, whatever its magnitude, is politically and ethically acceptable. Risk communicators have to be able to discuss hazards in ethical and cultural rather than just in economic and scientific terms. The objective magnitude of a risk, within wide limits, may not really matter.

In 1969 Chauncey Starr pointed out that a lot of moral factors influence the acceptability of a risk, "the most obvious being the difference by several orders of magnitude in society's willingness to accept 'voluntary' and 'involuntary' risk."[22] The concepts of voluntary and involuntary are themselves open to a great deal of interpretation, moreover, and may implicate many other values. Accordingly, scholars have described scores of ethical concerns besides voluntariness that endow hazards with different meanings—reasons that explain why some hazards remain culturally acceptable while others are not, even if their costs and benefits are the same.[23] These values include the familiarity of a risk, its connection (however slight) to something dreadful, like cancer, the remoteness of its source, and the uncertainty surrounding it. Pollution, which is primarily an aesthetic or cultural rather than a scientific concept, particularly engages ethical and political sentiments, whether it is dangerous or not.[24] We may resist or resent pollution more because of aesthetic and cultural revulsion than any kind of fear, even if we continue to talk about pollution in the technical context of risk.

To see this possibility, imagine that you spit continually into a large glass, which you keep in the refrigerator, until it is full. Now imagine that someone asks you to drink it down, explaining that must be perfectly safe since you swallow your spit all the time. You may not relish drinking it even though it is safe, and you might even resent being told you are irrational for not swigging it down. Perhaps we are irrational, in a sense, to decide what we are willing to eat, drink, or breathe on grounds other than those of objective safety and health. Yet it also seems foolish to dismiss as irrational the cultural, aesthetic, and moral distinctions on which social life may ultimately depend.

Nature, Law, and the Environment

We now come to the third rule, which emphasizes the importance of nature as distinct from environment. The concept of nature suggests our common birthright or the legacy of the past—perhaps a gift from God. The concept of the environment, on the other hand, refers to surroundings that we may manipulate according to our interest and profit. Thus, we may perceive nature as an object of love and respect, while we regard the environment as a collection of resources to be managed prudently and efficiently over the long run. In that event, moral concerns we may have about the preservation of nature may be well expressed in the context of managing, say, the environmental commons.

Consider, for example, the way Exxon handled its public relations after the recent unpleasantness in Prince William Sound. The corporation pointed out, correctly I assume, that the environment would bounce back after a few years. Natural resources (fishing, for example) would sustain no long-term damage, and Exxon promised to compensate those who suffered short-term economic loss. Exxon could not understand what upset people so much, since stocks of fish would return to normal levels in a few years and everyone would be paid off for interim losses.

This response ignored what many Americans, on seeing the dead otters on television, may have perceived as the most serious crime: the crime against nature. Many Americans felt Exxon should have recognized and apologized for the sin of defiling the beauty, integrity, and innocence of nature on such a large scale. That recognition and that apology never came. Moral concepts like sin and forgiveness may be central to our culture and history as a people. These concepts may not always be available, however, to corporate executives. They may speak the positive language of economics; they may be less comfortable with the concepts of good and evil than the concepts of benefits and costs. The American people, however, are not afraid of—and may even expect—normative or ethical discourse. Americans are not embarrassed by talk about good and evil; they are not hesitant to discuss moral judgments in moral terms.

At one time, perhaps, the concepts of economics—risk–benefit analysis, efficient allocation of resources, and so on—might have carried a normative significance. In the years prior to the New Deal, for example, environmentalism coincided generally with conservationism, a movement, represented, for example, by Gifford Pinchot, which sought to make efficient use of resources in order to maximize the long-run benefits nature offers people. Pinchot and others argued that society would be happier or somehow better off if it maximized in this way the production of goods and services that consumers wanted to buy. A literature of environmental economics developed during the 1960s that extended this normative argument to pollution control and other problems of environmental policy.[25]

During the New Deal and after, however, the environmental movement returned to its roots in Puritanism and romanticism, as represented, for example, by Henry David Thoreau, Ralph Waldo Emerson, and John Muir, to emphasize the religious idea that humanity is rich in relationship to the number of things it can afford to leave alone. During the 1970s and 1980s, environmentalists argued that consumption is not itself a value and that societies that maximize consumption or consumer satisfaction do not become better off in any morally meaningful sense. Money, after basic needs are met, does not buy happiness. Environmentalists argued that we will be happier, healthier, and wiser if we try to live in respectful harmony with nature rather than exploit it, however efficiently that is done.

Readers of magazines like *Sport Truck* and *Car and Driver* may also tend to make judgments in moral terms—in terms of some ethical or cultural rule or principle—rather than according to academic theories. *Car and Driver* does not print risk–benefit calculations about seat belts and speed limits because it knows its readers regard these as matters not of prudence but of principle. Arguments framed in terms of resource economics—analyses of costs, benefits, efficiency, social discounting—are likely to appall rather than to appeal to environmentalists who view obligations to nature in ethical rather than in economic terms. The protection of nature seems to them to be a question of principle, not just a question of prudence.

Finally, industry would be much better served, I shall argue, if it looked on pollution control law as an opportunity to protect nature in cost-effective ways. Industry now pays high costs associated with pollution control policies that are proved failures. Industry now has the opportunity to join the political mainstream in developing a regulatory system that will work incrementally and efficiently to decrease wastes and emissions. The conservatism of industry, however, may lead it to oppose

rather than to propose legislation that could make more environmental progress at lower costs. Industry might rather bear those ills it has, in other words, than to rush to others that it knows not of.

In the past, corporations have enjoyed a strong bargaining position with the government under statutes—the Clean Air Act is a good example—that are so cumbersome that they are nearly impossible to enforce.[26] Statutory amendments now under consideration (the permitting requirements of President Bush's proposed Clean Air Act, for example) may be easier to enforce and therefore are more likely to lead to the environmental improvements the public expects. Industry might do well to support rather than to oppose more cost-effective and more enforceable statutes, including permit systems, that will work to reduce waste and pollution. By helping to frame and to enact these statutes—statutes that not only promise but also can deliver a cleaner environment—industry could join the political mainstream and reap the legitimacy and credibility that comes with supporting environmentally sound regulation.

The alternative will involve deeper dousing in strict and joint-and-several liability schemes and the prospect of even tougher criminal sanctions. Thus, business leaders have every reason to join with environmentalists and other Americans generally in getting behind statutes that will give us progress and not just promises in protecting nature and improving the environment.

Do Real Americans Care About the Environment?

At the time *Car and Driver* announced for "the global environment," the *London Economist* cited a speech by Margaret Thatcher "that marked her conversion from Iron Lady to Green Goddess":

> Hard on her heels trod Mikhail Gorbachev, who made the environment a theme of an address to the United Nations; George Bush, who built part of his election campaign on a promise to clean up America; and the EEC Commission, trying to outdo its member governments in greenery. Never have so many politicians seized so quickly on one idea.[27]

Politicians, according to the *Economist*, "are responding to an extraordinary shift in public opinion, apparent all over the world."[28] Public opinion polls amply document this trend, at least in the

United States. A *New York Times*–CBS poll in June 1989 found 80 percent of those polled agreed while 14 percent disagreed with the statement, "Protecting the environment is so important that requirements and standards cannot be too high, and continuing environmental improvements must be made at all costs."[29] These results show an increase since 1981, when yeas and nays were nearly equal.[30]

What may strike us as surprising about the rush of politicians to the environment is that they need not (and they do not) change their other political colors when they paint themselves green. President Bush, for example, planted trees in Spokane, yet he spoke against gun control and for a constitutional amendment against desecrating the flag.

A pro-environment position, then, seems not to imply anything about any other salient political issue. In defending the environment, therefore, the president did not have to become more liberal with respect, say, to the death penalty, abortion rights, or the drug problem. The environmental bandwagon—unlike gun control or abortion rights—apparently has room for everybody. Environmentalism plays as well in Peoria as on Martha's Vineyard.

Where, then, does environmentalism fit in the political spectrum? Some have argued that environmentalism fits best within upper-middle-class suburban liberalism, particularly in its opposition to laissez-faire capitalism and its support for paternalism and the welfare state.[31] Social scientists, however, have described environmental concern as a belief system strongly held by the American public but only weakly constrained by or integrated in broader political ideologies. As two researchers put this thought, environmentalism is "an issue in search of a home."[32]

A lot may depend on how one characterizes or measures the concept of environmental concern.[33] Scholars have long observed a tension, even an antagonism, between a prudential conservation ethic or gospel of efficiency, which endorses long-run, cost–benefit accounting, and a moral environmental ethic, which rebels against utilitarian thinking and might be associated historically with Aldo Leopold and John Muir. This distinction can be drawn politically today between prudential and ethical environmentalism or, roughly, those who seek to protect nature for the sake of exploiting resources efficiently and those who wish to protect nature for its own sake.

The distinction between prudential and ethical environmentalism may help to explain an anomaly that has long puzzled social scientists. Environmentalism has become an overwhelming political force even though "traditional American values and beliefs pose barriers to the development of a strong pro-environment orientation."[34] According to this analysis, as Americans squared off against the apparently limitless natural frontier, they formed a "dominant social paradigm" (to use Dennis Pirages's term) around values like materialism, unfettered progress, and personal liberty.[35] Researchers have established that in many aspects, this dominant social paradigm (e.g., support for laissez-faire government, insistence on property rights, faith in science and technology, commitment to individual liberty, and faith in economic growth and material abundance) relates strongly, but negatively, to environmental concerns.[36] Environmentalists themselves have called for a paradigm shift away from "the basic values which have built our society" and lie "at the root of the ecological crisis."[37]

Social scientists and analysts even today reason that since lower-middle-class Americans—the "silent" or "populist" majority—strongly share the dominant social paradigm and since this paradigm conflicts so deeply and thoroughly with a protective approach to nature, the lower middle class has to oppose laws protecting the environment. Only upper-middle-class suburban professionals, who prefer the welfare state over the dominant paradigm, could favor environmental protection. "This reaffirms the importance of liberalism as a component of the broader ideological systems from which environmental attitudes are drawn."[38]

As candidate Reagan campaigned for the White House, his advisers, following this plausible analysis, construed environmental concern as a crochet of upper-middle-class professionals, mostly suburbanites who sought to protect the amenities they enjoyed. These advisers aimed the campaign, then, at farmers, workers, businessmen, and lower-middle-class whites who, they thought, sought to be free from environmental constraints. Swept into office by this constituency, President Reagan entered the White House intent on rolling back environmental regulations.

During the early Reagan years a group of writers made explicit what his campaign implied: environmentalism represented the "conservativism of the liberals" and expressed itself as a suburban agrarianism in opposition to industry, farming, business, and other forms of production that might swell the numbers of the privileged class.[39] In short, environmentalists constituted a new aristocracy, opposed to traditional American values, who sought to maintain their privileged status against economic and social growth.[40] "Having made it to the top, they become far more concerned with preventing others from climbing the ladder behind them, than in making it up a few more rungs themselves."[41]

Several social scientists in the 1970s, aware of this political analysis, tested whether environmental concern was indeed rooted in the upper-middle-class intelligentsia. These writers quickly dismissed conclusions drawn from evidence that "environmental groups . . . have an upper-middle-class membership."[42] Rather, these scientists have reached a virtual consensus that "the link between the upper-middle class and environmental activism is a link between socioeconomic status and factors of political activism, rather than a link between the upper-middle class and environmental concern."[43] Indeed, as one writer notes, the most vocal, coordinated opposition to environmentalism comes from the top levels or corporate management; therefore, "the *opponents* of environmentalism come closer to being an elite than do core environmentalists."[44]

Recent studies and public opinion polls point unambiguously to the conclusion that "support for environmentalism is diffuse in the population as a whole."[45] These studies, according to one review article, "are showing that environmental concern is broad-based in American society, cutting across nearly all socioeconomic categories."[46]

The question arises, then, why environmentalism plays as well in Peoria as on Martha's Vineyard. Are the issues the same? Are lower-middle-class workers, farmers, and small businessmen in Birmingham and Baton Rouge defending the same environment as well-to-do liberals in Brookline and Bethesda? Are political constituencies that disagree on nearly everything else truly united behind one environmental banner? Are environmentalists motivated primarily by prudential concerns about safety, health, and the coming ecological crisis? Have longstanding religious and ethical beliefs,

which may be consistent with the dominant social paradigm, in contrast, brought the lower middle class into the environmental consensus?

It is reasonable to conjecture that if Americans in the dominant paradigm are optimistic, freedom-loving, risk-taking, wealth-seeking individualists, then they would tend to scoff at warnings about the so-called ecological crises. The scientific evidence, for example, about the greenhouse effect remains uncertain and even contradictory; why, then, listen to a lot of nattering nabobs of negativity? If Americans were secure in their local communities—if the air they breathe and the streams in which they fish remained the same—they might not worry about purveyors of doom who prognosticated global change.

Faced with persistent ecological and environmental degradation in their own immediate communities, however, Americans may not so quickly dismiss concerns about the global environment. Love of community belongs to the dominant social paradigm. People within that paradigm may regard the continuity of nature as necessary for the maintenance and identity of communities to which they belong. When communities are threatened by large technological, economic, and political changes, therefore, people may find predictions of environmental disaster more credible. Security of a moral and visceral sort requires that nature—in a romantic and religious sense, not merely as a collection of resources—remain intact. It should be no surprise, therefore, that the environment has become a populist issue throughout the world.

Environmentalism and the Lower Middle Class

To examine more closely the place of environmentalism in the political spectrum, let us turn to the *Farm Journal*, in which, during the 1970s, farmers voiced resentment against "government controls" that "engulf our every move."[47] An Indiana farmer writing in the *Journal* in January 1976 described an attitude then prevalent toward environmental regulations among farmers:

> EPA is another non-elected, self-perpetuating group with awesome power. No one dares question them. Congressmen. How can Russell Train be permitted to use dirty tricks, scare tactics and unproven theories to influence people to support him?[48]

The following month, the *Farm Journal*, in an editorial titled "'Organic Foods': Today's Big Rip-Off," notes that "only ignorance of nature leads one to label as 'artificial' fertilizers which are mined from the earth or made from 'natural' gas."[49] In the following issue, an article titled "Will You Go to Jail over Erosion?" inveighs against agricultural zoning regimes that prevent farmers from selling their land to developers. According to the article, environmentalists "want to preserve open land because they like to look at it, but they're trying to preserve the farms without preserving the farmers."[50]

How does the *Farm Journal* view environmentalism today? At about the same time *Car and Driver* started speaking for the trees, the *Farm Journal* also greened. In the June–July 1989 issue, the editors proudly introduced a regular column, titled "Environment Today," to let farmers know, for example, that the overapplication of fertilizers by corn growers accounts for the bulk of groundwater nitrate problems. In 1976 the *Journal* castigated organic foods; in 1989 it praised organic and low-input farming as the ways farmers may make themselves less dependent on the chemical industry. In 1976 a typical *Journal* article carried the title "Coming: A New Wave of Hard-Hitting Insecticides." Twelve years later, a representative title reads, "Are Pesticides Losing Their Punch?"

For one explanation of this change, look in the January 1989 issue, where an editorial breaks ranks with the past.[51] "Before I say anything else," the author, Gene Logson, begins, "understand that I eat red meat; red, white and medium rare. I know which side my bread is buttered on, because I spread it a quarter-inch thick." Logson establishes his credentials as a two-fisted cattleman with no patience for "diet dillies, organic nuts, and Bambi lovers" and others overconcerned about risk. "Having said that," he continues, "allow me to say a good word for animal rightists." The good word is that animal rights advocates threaten not the independent family livestock farmer but animal megafactories. Logson believes that if factory farm practices continue, competition may drive the world's egg production into four counties in Arkansas. All beef will be fed in five counties in Colorado and Texas. All hogs will be born in Missouri and fattened in Iowa:

> If large-scale animal factories continue to have their way, you will slowly be pushed out of the hog and beef business just as happened to 95% of the chicken farmers.

On the other hand, if animal rightists have their way, the livestock industry will return to smaller, family-sized farms.[52]

This argument takes up a familiar populist theme: the resentment small and middle-sized farmers direct against larger, better-capitalized operations that use economies of scale to undersell them. It also relates a love-of-nature issue, animal rights, to concerns about protecting the economic viability of small farmers and farming communities.

Similarly, articles in which the *Farm Journal* reversed its view of organic farming do not argue that low-input methods will produce a safer or a more nutritious product. Rather, the *Journal* advocates low-input farming just insofar as it liberates farmers from their dependence on chemicals and thus allows them to keep the money that would otherwise pass through to the chemical industry. The argument for low-input farming, if it concerns health at all, concerns the economic health of farming communities. To protect the land, to maintain traditional technologies, and to engage in labor-intensive husbandry makes sense economically for small farmers who want to stay in business. Without the environmental brake, the technological treadmill in agriculture would lead quickly to the industrialization of production and therefore to the demise of the small operator. Farmers have good reasons to side with environmentalists against this process.

A century ago, southern populists excoriated corporations and trusts that, "in their insatiate greed," plundered the wealth of America and drove farmers into poverty.[53] The ethical and political sentiments that united farmers in the West and South against the trusts a century ago may be alive and well today. When large agrichemical businesses show big profits, farmers may treat them with suspicion, especially when those farmers, who grow the crops, have nothing to show for their pains but debt. Environmentalism is a populist issue; the protection of nature could become a rallying call today as free silver was a hundred years ago.

Exactly a century ago, when the populist movement in the United States grew to its height, the People's party formed in the South. By 1896 the party established a coalition with the Democrats, representing farmers, workers, and members of the lower middle class who "looked around them and saw what seemed to them an unhealthy growth of big business, monopolistic industries brought into existence by the demands of Civil War technology, saw changing mores and class alignments, [and] saw a breakneck pace of national life that seemed to be leaving the farmer and his ways behind."[54]

The populist fusion party lost the presidential election in 1896 but not by a large margin. In later political campaigns, this alliance did help to elect presidents, including two Roosevelts, who combined the reform of capitalism and the protection of nature in one program. Teddy Roosevelt was elected as both a conservationist and a trust-buster; Franklin Roosevelt stood strongly for environmental protection and the regulation of industry. Thus, it may be a cyclical event—it surely seems to be an American tradition—that political movements arise that combine distrust of big business and desire to protect nature and the environment. Analogies may be drawn between populism historically and the environmental movement today.

The central ideological commitment of populism in the past, as one commentator has said, follows from the "deification of nature."[55] He continues:

> The natural/artificial dichotomy, one suspects, also underlies much of the emotional reaction of populism to such things as banks, gold, Eastern manners, lace cuffs, tie wigs, and foppery of all kinds. . . . The impression is conveyed that everything good, decent, homely, simple, honest, in a word *natural*, is about to be felled, murdered, raped, crucified by something phony, mannered, effete, superfluous, in a word artificial.[56]

Sentiments of this sort mix easily with the resentments of the small against the great—resentments small farmers, small businessmen, and those who live in small towns direct against the rich and powerful who live in distant cities. These beliefs reflect, in a way, problems with the way power (not just risk) is distributed in society. If technologies, whether represented by railroads, banks, or factories, confer too much power on too few people, if the many have no sense of participating in the decisions the few make about how these technologies are used, then the many are likely to regard these technologies as nefarious.

The populist crusade in America stands as well on a second principle: egalitarianism and the ethic of hard work. This idea, again a Jeffersonian theme, sees virtue as residing in the simple people, who make up the overwhelming majority of Americans,

and in their collective traditions. The simple people are continually victimized, according to this populist mythology, by greedy and evil persons who control finance, industry, and technology. These captains of industry are not to be trusted. As Woody Guthrie put the thought, they rob you not with a gun but with a fountain pen.

Small-town and lower-middle-class Americans of the kind who joined the populist cause, moreover, have little tolerance for theories and analyses. They trust the tangible and the immediate; they think more in anecdotes than in abstractions. President Reagan caught this aspect of his constituency perfectly. These Americans, moreover, tend to read moral meanings into events. The idea that good or bad things could happen by chance—that there might be disasters for which no one is morally responsible—might seem absurd to them. There must be a hero or villain; there is someone to repay or someone to blame.

It is no accident that the dumping of hazardous waste (as at Love Canal) became the primary battleground on which lower-middle-class Americans first sided with environmentalists. Waste (whether hazardous or not) imposes the excrescence of technology and industry on nature; once this kind of waste is produced, it can never be gotten rid of.[57] Only nature can degrade waste—return it to nature—but the rubbish produced by technology today, such as radioactive wastes, may not be degraded in the foreseeable future. Waste of this sort constitutes a stain on nature that will not wash out.

Risk assessment cannot address this conceptual or moral problem. If chemical wastes, as at Love Canal, constitute a stain, they are morally perverse, and, therefore, as the residents of Love Canal concluded, they must be hurting adults and children in the community, whatever any report may say. When natural and human communities are presumed to have an integrity that has been violated, the resulting political issues cannot be discussed persuasively in risk–benefit or even scientific terms.

Americans who made up the bulk of the Reagan majority sought to preserve the moral sentiments and ideals they cherished against an attack from the government and from the liberal intelligentsia they thought owned the government. It may be fair to say that the locus of this grievance has now shifted from the government to large-scale technologies, which seem to be intruding, through their economic and environmental effects, on the integrity of nature and the viability of local communities. If so, environmental regulations, particularly in their insistence that interventions in nature be *safe*, give otherwise powerless Americans a weapon with which to protect their communities and their ways of life. And any technology thought to threaten those ways of life, along with the conception of the natural on which they are based, cannot possibly be safe enough.

What Sort of Statutes Should Industry Support?

Environmental law began to reflect the force of environmentalism as a populist issue starting in about 1980 after Love Canal, the dumping of kepone in the James River, and several other unfortunate episodes led many Americans to believe (correctly) that statutes enacted in the 1970s were not working. Public resentment and a growing conviction that something had to be done forced Congress to restructure environmental legislation from prospective command-and-control strategies to regulations based in retroactive liability and criminal penalties. Industries were put on notice not to contaminate or pollute except in permissible ways—or face severe legal penalties after the fact. In previous legislation, industry was permitted to do anything it was not prohibited from doing. More recent laws reverse the approach, making industry strictly liable for any environmental problem it was not permitted to create.

During the 1970s, most federal environmental laws were prospective; that is, they told industry what sorts of pollution control technology to install. Economists and others criticized such command-and-control approaches as inefficient since industry itself, rather than the government, is in the best position to manage pollution. Congress acted on this criticism with a vengeance, probably not in the way the critics intended, by enacting a series of laws that assigned liability retroactively to any corporation that might be involved in causing a pollution problem.[58] Under strict liability statutes, as one commentator points out, "responsible parties are liable for environmental contamination regardless of individual degrees of fault," and, one may add, regardless of the extent of the risk or hazard the contamination creates. According to this environmental lawyer:

The effect of these laws is to shift much of the responsibility for planning for a dangerous and uncertain environmental future to that segment of society most capable of finding innovative and efficient solutions—the private sector. Regardless of its perceived fairness, if carried through, this approach will result in a quantum leap in the effectiveness of environmental laws.[59]

Which kind of statutes should industry support?[60] The old command and control had the advantage, for industry, that they did not work; they were far too cumbersome to implement or enforce. Their unenforceability, however, led to an even greater disadvantage: the public demanded something tougher. And so we have liability-based laws that are tougher—they may hurt industry a lot more—but may not help us make progress toward a cleaner, more healthful, more natural environment.

It seems plausible to suppose that industrial associations such as the Chemical Manufacturers Association and the American Petroleum Institute should use their considerable power and expertise to support laws that work to clean up the environment in cost-effective ways. Laws of this kind may require industry to pollute only with a permit; they may also have to empower citizens' groups to enforce compliance with those statutes through the courts. At the same time, these laws would allow industry, for example, through the use of permit trading schemes and other market incentives, to ratchet down pollution to lower levels by the most efficient and least costly methods. Industry, bureaucracy, environmentalists, and the public are ready to support laws that get results rather than laws that simply appeal to particular ideologies. Industry should now support workable and enforceable legislation that will ratchet down the amount of waste and pollution in the most cost-effective ways.[61]

Representatives from industrial and from environmentalist associations now have many interests in common. The primary common goal must be to find a regulatory framework that will work to control and eventually decrease emissions. Industry must support laws that make this kind of progress in cost-effective ways or face further toughening of liability-based and criminal sanctions, which, in the continued absence of progress, will become vindictive. Environmentalists, who may now be weary of making the best the enemy of the good, no longer insist on statutes that promise the moon but are so unrealistic that they defeat all prospects of progress. Environmentalists must desire a regulatory framework that gives us efficient improvement, even if it does not, for example, solve the ozone problem in Los Angeles in five years.

If environmentalists and corporate executives have these strong interests in common, why don't they work together? Part of the reason is cultural: these groups have a long history of suspicion and antagonism. Another problem arises from the growth of industries that live off this antagonism. Public relations firms, for example, must describe environmentalists as fire-breathing dragons in order to get large retainers from industry to slay or tame them. If environmentalists and executives worked together for common legislative purposes, they would overcome the distrust that makes business for public relations firms. There would be no dragon to slay.[62]

If environmentalists and corporate executives cut a political deal, for example, to pursue workable statutes, they would eliminate much of the work not only of public relations experts but also of experts in risk assessment, risk analysis, risk management, risk communication, and so on. The idea behind workable laws is to make the environment safer, cleaner, and more natural in enforceable but cost-effective ways. We can do this without supporting an establishment of theorists to answer questions—like "how safe is safe enough?" —that no one will ever answer because they always require more research.[63]

It is time for business leaders and environmental leaders to deal directly with one another, without the benefit of academic and public relations experts who have made a niche for themselves by forcing these two sides further apart. We have the necessary experience with environmental law—we have learned enough by trial and error, which is the only way—to write statutes that work. This kind of experience, if we rely on it, can turn opposition to cooperation between industry leaders and environmental groups in restructuring environmental law.

Notes

The research reported in this chapter received support from a grant from the Ethics and Values Studies Program of the National Science Foundation, Grant BBS 8619104. The views expressed are those of the author only and not necessarily of any institute or agency.

1. Brock Yates, *Car and Driver* 35(2) (August 1989): 16.

2. William Jeannes, "Eye on the Road," *Car and Driver* 34(1) (July 1988): 11.

3. See, for example, "The Rise and Fall of Ralph Nader," *Car and Driver* 28(3) (September 1982): 64–71. "To the Naderites, the automobile and the corporations that foist it off on the innocent public are nothing less than public enemy number one" (p. 64).

4. "Driver's Seat," *Car and Driver* 26(2) (August 1980): 5–6.

5. Ibid.

6. Ibid.

7. *Car and Driver* has inveighed relentlessly against passive restraints and other safety devices as decidedly nonmacho; see, for example, Patrick Bedard, "Stalking the Wild Bureaucrat," *Car and Driver* 24(10) (April 1979): 17.

8. Virtually any issue, but for a recent example, see Brock Yates, "Miscellaneous Fulminations," *Car and Driver* 34(10) (April 1989): 20.

9. Patrick Bedard, "Take an Endangered Species to Lunch," *Car and Driver* 25(10) (April 1980): 16.

10. Brock Yates, "Say 'Cheese,'" *Car and Driver* 33(9) (March 1988).

11. Brock Yates, "Would You Draw to This Pair," *Car and Driver* 34(5) (November 1988): 23.

12. William Jeannes, "Eye on the Road," *Car and Driver* 35(2) (August 1989): 7.

13. *Sport Truck* (November 1989): 18.

14. Brock Yates, "I Take Pen in Hand," *Car and Driver* 35(2) (August 1989): 16 (an open letter to American carmakers defending CAFE standards as necessary "to reduce automobile carbon-dioxide emissions, a significant contributor to the greenhouse effect and global warming"). See also William Jeannes, "Eye on the Road," *Car and Driver* 35(1) (July 1989): 5 (conceding that "the buying public *must* somehow be talked out of buying too-large cars").

15. Brock Yates, "Say 'Cheese,'" *Car and Driver* 33(9) (March 1988): 25.

16. Ibid.

17. Brock Yates, *Car and Driver* 34(8) (February 1989): 19.

18. Patrick Bedard, "The Gipper Boots Big Brother off Our Dashboards," *Car and Driver* 28(4) (October 1982): 14 (conceding, however, that "President Reagan has yet to achieve his campaign promise of getting big government off our backs").

19. Letters to *Car and Driver* 35(4) (October 1989):10. The editors responded by printing another letter from a California man who wrote: "The only way to cut down on the global production of CO_2 is to

drastically reduce the amount of fuel being burned." This reader continues: "I'm an enthusiast, and I like to drive as fast as you guys, but let's face it: we keep this up and nobody's going to be left alive to drive anything."

20. For the distinction between the study of risk as a physical fact and as a social construct, see H. J. Otway and K. Thomas, "Reflections on Risk Perception and Policy," *Risk Analysis* 2(1982): 69–82.

21. For discussion, see Usher Flesing, "Risk and Culture in Biotechnology," *Trends in Biotechnology* 7(March 1987): 56.

22. Chauncey Starr, "Social Benefit versus Technological Risk," *Science,* September 19, 1969, p. 1235.

23. See, for example, W. C. Clark, "Witches, Floods, and Wonder Drugs: Historical Perspectives on Risk Management," in *Societal Risk Assessment: How Safe Is Safe Enough?* ed. R. C. Schwing and W. A. Albers (New York: Plenum, 1980), pp. 287–313; J. Conrad, "Society and Risk Assessment: An Attempt at Interpretation," in J. Conrad, ed., *Society, Technology, and Risk Assessment* (New York: Academic Press, 1980), pp. 241–76; and S. Raynor, "Disagreeing about Risk: The Institutional Cultures of Risk Management," in *Risk Analysis, Institutions, and Public Policy,* ed. S. G. Hadden (Fort Washington: Associated Faculty Press, 1984), pp. 150–68.

24. See, for example, Mary Douglas and Aaron Wildavsky, *Risk and Culture* (Berkeley: University of California Press, 1982).

25. For a useful bibliography of this literature, see Anthony Fisher and Frederick Peterson, "The Environment in Economics: A Survey," *Journal of Economic Literature* 14(1976): 1–33.

26. For a discussion of how and why the Clean Air Act proved too cumbersome to implement and enforce, see, for example, R. Shep Melnick, *Regulation and the Courts: The Case of the Clean Air Act* (Washington, D.C.: Brookings, 1983); David Schoenbrod, "Goals Statutes and Rules Statutes: The Case of the Clean Air Act," *UCLA Law Review* 30 (1983): 720–828; and William Pedersen, "Why the Clean Air Act Works Badly," *University of Pennsylvania Law Review* 129(1981):1059–1105.

27. "The Politics of Posterity," *Economist,* September 2, 1989, p. 3.

28. Ibid.

29. *New York Times,* July 2, 1989, p. 1.

30. Similarly, a September 1988 Gallup Poll found that 84 percent of Americans are very concerned about water pollution—a 36 percentage point increase since 1970. In April 1989, the *Washington Post* and ABC News completed a survey that found that nine Americans in ten ranked "taking stronger action to clean up the nation's air and water" as a top priority for government and business leaders. According to recent Roper and Cambridge Research studies, a majority of Americans favor tougher environmental laws and regulations—up from a less than 30 percent minority in the late 1970s. A National Opinion Research Center survey found that almost two-thirds of all Americans believe that the country spends too little to protect the environment; a Harris Poll in February 1989 determined that a greater than two-thirds majority favors increased government spending to control acid rain and toxic waste dumping even if it means higher taxes. Several other surveys confirm the same trend: that Americans are willing to pay as much as a thousand dollars each in higher taxes, for example, to clean up toxic wastes. For documentation of these surveys, see Louis Harris et al., *The Rising Tide: Public Opinion, Policy and Politics,* Section 5 (Washington, D.C.: Sierra Club Press, 1989).

31. For a review of the sources of this popular belief, see D. L. Sills, "The Environmental Movement and Its Critics," *Human Ecology* 39 (1975): 1–41.

32. J. F. Springer and E. Costantini, "An Issue in Search of a Home," in S. Nagel, ed., *Environmental Politics* (New York: Praeger, 1974), pp. 195–224.

33. For analysis, see Kent D. Van Liere and Riley Dunlap, "Environmental Concern: Does It Make a Difference How It's Measured?" *Environment and Behavior* 13(6) (1981): 651–76.

34. Riley E. Dunlap and Kent D. Van Liere, "Commitment to the Dominant Social Paradigm and Concern for Environmental Quality," *Social Science Quarterly* 65(4) (1984): 1023. These authors add (p. 1025): "Our results suggest that the traditional values and beliefs constituting our society's dominant social paradigm are important sources of opposition for environmental protection."

35. Dennis C. Pirages, "Introduction: A Social Design for Sustainable Growth," in D. C. Pirages, ed., *The Sustainable Society* (New York: Praeger, 1977), pp. 1–13.

36. For a recent review of these studies, see Diane M. Samdahl and Robert Robertson, "Social Determinants of Environmental Concern," *Environment and Behavior* 21(1) (1989): 57–81.

37. James A. Swan, "Environmental Education: One Approach to Resolving the Environmental Crisis," *Environment and Behavior* 3(1971): 225. For similar views, see William Ophuls, *Ecology and the Politics of Scarcity* (San Francisco: Freeman, 1977), and Dennis Pirages, *The Evolution of Societies* (Englewood Cliffs, N.J.: Prentice-Hall, 1977).

38. Samdahl and Robertson, "Environmental Concern," p. 61.

39. William Tucker, *Progress and Privilege: America in the Age of Environmentalism* (Garden City, N.Y.: Doubleday, 1982).

40. For excellent analysis and debunking of this view, see Denton E. Morrison and Riley Dunlap, "Environmentalism and Elitism: A Conceptual and Empirical Analysis," *Environmental Management* 10(5) (1986): 581–89.

41. Tucker, *Progress and Privilege,* p. 15. According to this interpretation, the liberal middle class directed a series of policies against the interests of lower-middle-class people during the 1970s. These policies included forced integration (well-off liberals live in or can move to white suburbs not implicated in busing); affirmative action (the members of the privileged classes are unlikely to be the marginal applicants who lose their jobs to blacks); and urban renewal or "removal" (gentrifying ethnic communities). According to this account, environmentalist policies to limit economic growth, such as through pollution control and energy conservation, also served the interests of the upper against those of the lower middle class. These policies created jobs in high-paying professions for the college educated at the expense of farmers, blue-collar workers, small business people, and others who strove to improve themselves by producing wealth rather than by entering privileged professional castes.

      Several political scientists . . . interpreted ecological doomsaying, even more prevalent in the 1970s than today, as a scare tactic through which liberal elites tried to control social progress and cut off or abort the economic growth that would make others equally well off. See, for example, S. Epstein, *The Politics of Cancer,* rev. ed. (Garden City, N.J.: Anchor Press, 1979); James Ridgeway and Alexander Cockburn, *The Politics of Ecology* (New York: Dutton, 1971); and John Whitaker, *Striking a Balance* (Washington, D.C.: AEI-Hoover Institute, 1976).

42. For an example of this kind of argument, see B. J. Frieden, *The Environmental Protection Hustle* (Cambridge, Mass.: MIT Press, 1979).

43. Paul Mohai, "Public Concern and Elite Involvement in Environmental-Conservation Issues," *Social Science Quarterly* 66(14) (1985): 820–38. This article reviews a large number of studies that test relevant hypotheses.

44. Morrison and Dunlap, "Environmentalism and Elitism," p. 583.

45. Ibid.

46. Mohai, "Public Concern and Elite Involvement," p. 836.

47. Bill Copeland, "We Don't Elect Those Who Control Us," *Farm Journal* (January 1976): 17.

48. Ibid.

49. Editorial, "'Organic Foods': Today's Big Rip-Off," *Farm Journal* (February 1976): 66.

50. Laura Lane, "Will You Go to Jail over Erosion?" *Farm Journal* (Mid-February 1976): 23.

51. Gene Logson, "Maybe the Animal Rights Movement Is Good for Us." *Farm Journal* (January 1989): 26-D.

52. *Farm Journal* (December 1988): 4 prints this letter from Iowa farmers Mark and Brenda Dagel: "Lately we've been annoyed about all the corporate hog farms being built: National in Nebraska now wanting to expand to Colorado, Smithfield planning to build 100 units with 1,000 sows to produce two million hogs per year. (That will replace 666 family operations of 150 sows each.)

      "We have felt that the animal welfare people were fighting us, threatening to take our farrowing crates and gestation stalls. Maybe we should join them. It might be the only way to stop corporate hog farms. Wouldn't it be fun to watch the big corporations farrow pigs in open pens that would have to be bedded and cleaned out?"

53. Bruce Palmer, *"Man over Money": The Southern Populist Critique of American Capitalism* (Chapel Hill: University of North Carolina Press, 1980), p. 9.

54. George McKenna, *American Populism* (New York: Putnam, 1974), p. 85.

55. Ibid., p. 3.

56. Ibid., p. 4.

57. This is an aesthetic and conceptual thesis; it has nothing to do with technology. To make waste conceptually something different, one must perceive it differently. This is what happens when junk becomes identified as antiques or when hideous slums are converted, by an act of perception and a little gentrification, into glorious heritage. For an excellent study of the conceptual boundaries among useful object, waste, and art, see Michael Thompson, *Rubbish Theory* (New York: Oxford University Press, 1979).

58. Before 1980 the government found its capacity to implement pollution control statutes severely limited by the difficulties it faced in identifying environmental problems and in creating workable and enforceable regulations to deal with them. Laws enacted after 1980, for example, the Hazardous and Solid Waste Amendments of 1984 and the Superfund Amendments and Reauthorization Act of 1986, shift the burden of identifying and solving problems to the private sector. These statutes provide the necessary incentives by establishing joint and several liability, as well as criminal penalties for any problems that industry might create and might be identified later on.

59. Adam Babich, "Restructuring Environmental Law," *Environmental Law Reporter* 19 (February 1989): 10057.

60. It would be irresponsible for industry not to lobby for or against any policy or program, that is, to abandon the field to environmentalists and other lobbies. One reason, of course, is that environmentalists have again and again made the best the enemy of the good and in the statutory quest for environmental perfection have squandered opportunities for environmental progress. Environmentalists have shown their enthusiasm for ideology (e.g., a minimal risk or no-risk society) and, with it, their inability to deal with reality (the economic, political, and technological realities that quickly turn laws consistent with this ideology into fictions honored in the breach rather than in the observance). If we are going to have laws that work to clean up the environment—rather than laws that announce noble aspirations but are utterly unenforceable—we need to have input from industry, as well as from agency bureaucrats and environmentalists. Laws that industry did not help to write, I fear, it will find ways to ignore. For further argument along these lines, see Mark Sagoff, *The Economy of the Earth: Philosophy, Law and the Environment* (New York: Cambridge University Press, 1988), esp. chap. 9.

61. I believe that the permitting program (Title IV) of the Clean Air Act President Bush has proposed has these virtues. The Chemical Manufacturers Association has supported (or at least does not oppose) this strategy. The American Petroleum Institute (API) has come out against it. The only reason I can imagine the API opposes a permitting program is that such a program is far more enforceable than state implementation plans as they are now set up. The API apparently does not want an enforceable law even if that law, being based on a marketable permit scheme, allows industry to control pollution in the most cost-effective ways.

62. I recently visited a large public relations firm as part of a seminar on risk assessment in biotechnology. The panel of public relations experts represented the environmentalist lobby, led primarily by the National Wildlife Federation, as ideological and religious fanatics with great powers of controlling Congress. This is nonsense. The National Wildlife Federation and environmental groups generally have taken very moderate and responsible positions. (These groups are not to be confused with Jeremy Rifkin, American author and activist, who has his own agenda.) It seemed to me that these experts have a built-in conflict of interest with the corporations they serve. To get corporate business, they must represent environmentalists as much more unreasonable and antagonistic than they really are.

63. For an interesting critique of the literature of risk analysis, see Judith A. Bradbury, "The Policy Implications of Different Conception of Risk," *Science, Technology, and Human Values* 14(4) (1989): 380–99.

VI.E SLIDING TO GLOBAL CATASTROPHE

87. PREVIEW

[I] thought she was a spinster. What's she so worried about genetics for?

Member of the Federal Pest Control Review Board
(about Rachel Carson)[1]

[W]hat the computer models are suggesting is that children born today may see a climate change approximately the size of an Ice Age.[2]

Jonathan Weiner, *The Next 100 Years*

Warwick Fox dates "[t]he birth of the environmental movement . . . to the virtual explosion of interest that attended the 1962 publication of Rachel Carson's *Silent Spring*."[3] A best-seller and much celebrated in the cartoons of the day, *Silent Spring* is about the contamination of the environment with chemical poisons, especially the widespread practice of aerial spraying with toxic pesticides such as DDT. Poisons used to kill certain insects, Carson argued, become embedded in the food chain. Notably birds eat the contaminated insects and die. Eventually no birds sing; hence, the title, *Silent Spring*.

The book begins with a fable warning us of what could happen if we fill our world with poisonous chemicals. Interestingly, H. Patricia Hynes, in her book, *The Recurring Silent Spring*, says, "Since . . . 1985 there have been at least three publicized 'Silent Springs,' in Bhopal, Chernobyl, and the Rhine River, two of which involved pesticides. Many of the major ecological disasters of the past two decades have occurred in the manufacture, storage, use, and disposal of pesticides or chemical compounds with deadly biocidal components."[4] Carson ends her book by admonishing scientists not to take the disastrous road of the chemical control of insects, but instead to take the road of "biological solutions, based on understanding of the living organisms they seek to control, and of the whole fabric of life to which these organisms belong."[5]

In his foreword to the twenty-fifth-anniversary edition of *Silent Spring,* Paul Brooks points out that the reception of Carson's book was "as bitter and unscrupulous as anything of the sort since the publication of Charles Darwin's *Origin of Species* a century before." A review from *Time* magazine from September 28, 1962, for example, calls the book "unfair, one-sided, and hysterically overemphatic" and argues that Carson's "emotional and inaccurate outburst . . . may do harm by alarming the nontechnical public."[7]

It is in this heated response to the book that its most significant message to the reader lies, for surely the virulent reactions of Carson's critics speak of more than a difference of opinion on chemicals. Her claim that neither scientists nor government officials nor the public understood the dangers of pesticides and agricultural chemicals obviously touched some raw nerves. Again quoting Paul Brooks, "It was not simply that she was opposing indiscriminate use of poisons but—more fundamentally—that she had made clear the basic irresponsibility of an industrialized technological society toward the natural world."[8] Carson concluded, says H. Patricia Hynes, "that the arrogant control of nature by science and technology was at the root of pollution and the silencing of spring."[9]

Paul Brooks concludes his foreword with the following: "*Silent Spring* will continue to remind us that in our overorganized and overmechanized age, individual initiative and courage still count: change can be brought about . . . by altering the direction of our thinking about the world we live in."[10] After completing her manuscript, Carson herself said in a letter to Dorothy Freeman:[11]

> I took Jeffie [her cat] into the study and played the Beethoven violin concerto—one of my favorites, you know. And suddenly the tension of four years was broken and I let the tears come. I think I let you see last summer what my deeper feelings are about this when I said I could never again listen happily to a thrush song if I had not done all I could. And last night the thoughts of all the birds and other creatures and all the loveliness that is in nature came to me with such a surge of happiness, that now I had done what I could—I had been able to complete it—now it had its own life.[12]

Looking at Carson's work through the commentators' eyes, one can see the parallel between Carson and Lynn White, Jr., deep ecologists, Native American (American Indian) writers, and others who call for a fundamental change in attitude toward the environment, an openness to the voices of birds and the land that would make possible some reciprocal relationship between human beings and the earth that is precluded, indeed, silenced by an attitude of arrogance and domination.[13]

President John F. Kennedy's Science Advisory Committee was critical of pesticide use in industry and government, acknowledging its debt to *Silent Spring.*[14] As a consequence, DDT was taken off the U.S. market. However, as Hynes and others point out, the continued manufacture of DDT in the United States for export to foreign countries still comes home to roost. "Nearly 50 million pounds of DDT have been manufactured in the U.S. each year and exported to foreign countries since the chemical was suspended here. It is then imported back on fruits and vegetables in what has been labeled a 'circle of poison.'"[15] We could benefit, Hynes says, from a fresh reading of *Silent Spring* in light of the work of a relatively new U.S. industry—biotechnology. An ecology centered agriculture, as advanced in *Silent Spring*, is arguably not part of a biotech future. In 1992, Hynes noted that, "Developing herbicide-tolerant plant lines—that is, plants genetically modified to survive being sprayed with a herbicide—constitutes about 40 percent of the U.S. biotechnology research in agriculture."[16] Hence, chemical solutions were and are still viewed with approval. In passing, we note that fear of harming the biotechnology industry was the main reason former president George Bush gave for the United States not signing the "biodiversity agreement" at the Earth Summit. Pesticides are problems that quite literally will not go away, but other forms of pollution are more visible and perhaps more compelling.

Characterizing pollution as a problem of justice and fairness, says Bryan G. Norton, is "in the tradition of Rachel Carson's moralism."[17] In support of his claim, Norton quotes Carson on pollution and the Bill of Rights:

> We have subjected enormous numbers of people to contact with these poisons, without their consent and often without their knowledge. If the Bill of Rights contains no guarantee that a citizen shall be secure against lethal poisons distributed either by private individuals or by public officials, it is surely only because our forefathers, despite their considerable wisdom and foresight, could conceive of no such problem.[18]

According to Norton, Richard Ayers, senior staff attorney at the National Resources Defense Council and chair of the National Clean Air Coalition, is speaking in this tradition when he says, "Pollution is somebody's garbage, somebody's unwanted material and polluters have no right to impose, involuntarily on me, an exposure to those materials for their profit."[19] To pass on unconsented to, nontrivial costs to others is to violate what many philosophers refer to as the Harm Principle. A crude version of the Harm Principle is that it is wrong to harm others (on balance) without their voluntary, informed consent.[20] So if by "pollution" we understand such passing on of costs, then doing so is morally problematic, to say the least, and there is a parallel between so polluting and cases of burglary, embezzlement, assault, or rape.[21] As was discussed in "An Introduction to Ethical Theory," paradigmatic harms such as theft typically happen in a short span of time, have a single, readily identifiable causal agent and a single, readily identifiable recipient or victim. In contrast, much pollution imposes harms over a long period of time on many recipients, and sometimes the occurrence of a bad outcome is not certain—it occurs only after a long period of deterioration and sometimes only in conjunction with other similar forms of pollution. Recall the slow effects of exposure to nuclear radiation, toxic chemicals, or asbestos particles.

It is important to note that the main types of pollution we have been discussing—poisons and toxic waste—do not represent everything that could be classified as pollution. Arguably, all factories, most food production, and all cars pollute. Broadening the conception of what counts as pollution increases the plausibility that some pollution is acceptable and that what we need is an *optimal* amount of pollution. For example, there is a cost in not polluting. One moral question concerns under what conditions it is permissible to generate wastes, what kinds, and at what rate.

If Socrates or Aristotle were alive today, we are confident that neither would be surprised by talk of "ethics and climate." The expression will become more familiar as it becomes clear that our actions are powerfully affecting the world's climate, and we can no longer think of the earth as some fixed, unalterable stage on which lives come and go and on which human activities have only a negligible effect. Arguably, one of the greatest threats to humankind and much of the biota is the threat of global warming. "What threat?" one might ask, for many deny that there is any such threat and claim that the warnings of environmentalists amount only to the same old doomsday talk, a mere device to place new restrictions on "free" enterprise.

The situation is this. Due to the emission of certain gases, "greenhouse gases," such as methane, carbon dioxide, and nitrous oxide, many of the warming rays of the sun that would otherwise bounce off the earth and be radiated back into the stratosphere are "trapped" in the earth's atmosphere by the layer of these gases accumulating there.[22] That is the "greenhouse effect." There is no significant controversy about whether it occurs. The phenomenon is millions of years old; without the greenhouse effect, the oceans would be solid ice.[23] The phenomenon makes most, if not all, life on earth possible. It is also widely agreed that the data show the earth warmed about 1 degree Fahrenheit or 1/2 degree Celsius (centigrade) between 1860 and the 1980s. The year 1981 was the warmest in 100 years (remember, we speak of average global surface temperature and not local extremes). And 1983 was even warmer.[24] The hottest year prior to 1993 was 1988. It is this latter increase in average global surface temperature which people today are commonly referring to when they speak of "global warming." Some degree of global warming is, then, noncontroversial. It does not follow that these warm years were caused by an intensification of the greenhouse effect; they could just be random occurrences.

What is clear is that a warming trend has occurred over the last 130 years. That is not controversial. What is a matter of some dispute is *why* this phenomenon has occurred. Is an intensification of the greenhouse effect the correct explanation of that increase?[25] Is there a more plausible explanation, or only some reluctance to embrace the greenhouse explanation? Corporations, major emitters of the most important greenhouse gases, have powerful vested interests in denying that they are imposing a cosmic-sized risk on humankind, and they would rather not engage in costly procedural changes. Also having vested inter-

ests are those politicians who profit from the support of those interests; it is predictable, then, that whatever the facts are, such voices will tend to deny that there is a problem, will insist that only "further study" is called for, that the costs of change are too great, that those who predict otherwise are fearmongers, or that they rely on bad science.

To speak of a trend is sometimes to suggest not just that there has been a trend in the past but that forces at work will bring about a certain stream of events in the future. So there is not only a dispute about the explanation for past occurrences but also what is going to happen in, say, the next 100 years. This source of disagreement is evidently connected with the view that the evident warming trend of 130+ years is due to recent human industrial activities and growing population that have intensified the greenhouse effect. If that is the explanation, then we can only expect that trend to continue until and unless natural events alter that trend (we observe that there is evidence that an even *longer-term trend* [over tens of thousands, if not millions, of years] may be one in the direction of a much *colder* planet) or humans collectively alter their behavior so significantly as to cease contributing to those factors that increase global warming.

The average global surface temperature of the planet has waxed and waned radically over the eons. At one time sea creatures swam in the waters that once existed in what are now hot and dry African deserts. In Mecca, Indiana, fossil remains of 13-foot-long sharks have been found.[26] In Greenland there are fossils of alligators that once roamed there.[27] On the top of Mt. Everest, now 5 miles above sea level, and usually covered in snow, is a layer of limestone that resulted from the fossils of plantlike animals that lived in shallow seas some 300 million years ago.[28] The Finger Lakes of New York State were formed by giant glaciers as they receded during the end of the last Ice Age.[29] At the peak of that period, about 20,000 years ago, the earth was, of course, comparatively colder. At the end of that period, about 16,000 years ago, the ice on

Manhattan Island (New York City) was half a mile deep.[30] The marks of retreating glaciers can be observed today on the rocks in that city's Central Park. The ice covered 11 million square miles of land on the globe that is today free of ice; concomitantly, sea levels fell 350 feet. The striking fact is that at the depth of that Ice Age, the average global temperature was 5 degrees Celsius colder than today.[31] A 1.5-degree Celsius increase in the global average would make the earth warmer than it has been in 100,000 years.[32] As noted, the increase in the last 130 years has been about ½ degree Celsius. If the 5 billion tons of carbon (to take one example) we humans collectively emit into the atmosphere each year significantly contributes to the increase in warming, then we are playing a kind of global Russian roulette; that is, we are engaged collectively in behavior that seriously increases the risks to life on earth.[33] Luxembourg has a ratio of about two persons per car. Imagine what might happen if the 1 billion Chinese, for example, came to own one automobile for every two persons. Yet people who live in affluent societies cannot readily say, "Do as we preach, but not as we do." Once again we need to ask whether our lifestyle is ecologically sustainable.

A series of important questions must be dealt with, the leading ones of which are the following:

1. Will the increase in global warming continue?

2. If so, for how long and at what rate?

3. Is the recent trend caused mainly by an increase in the emission of greenhouse gases?

4. If so, what are the benefits of taking steps to avoid contributing to, or halting, this trend?

5. What will be the costs of so acting? The costs of not acting?

6. What is a reasonable and morally acceptable choice to make under the circumstances?

So we confront questions concerning the magnitude of the benefits and harms that increased warming might bring. In addition, there are evidently questions concerning the probability that warming will intensify and, if so, at what rate. Omitting details, the magnitude of harm associated with a rise of 3 degrees Celsius (centigrade) by late in the next century would probably be catastrophic for large parts of the planet.

In exploring the question of what we ought to do, one might consider analogous cases. What one should do personally, for example, about the possibility of one's house burning down; getting tetanus, the flu, smallpox, AIDS—or biological warfare; or sustaining serious injury in an automobile accident. There may be low-cost ways of avoiding serious harm; in a few of the cases just mentioned, one might simply get a vaccination. Analogously, there are some low-cost ways of reducing carbon emissions, and alternatively, there are high-cost ways of avoiding serious harms; for example, one might undergo a series of rather painful shots to ensure that one will not suffer the worst effects of being bitten by a possibly rabid dog. Analogously, the extremely high cost of having a powerful military is a price the United States has chosen to pay as a means of warding off attack, and so on.

In many if not all cases in which one faces the possibility of being subjected to a serious harm of unclear probability, it is prudent to hedge one's bets, and to do so in some cases by undertaking activities that are, in fact, quite costly—all depending on the magnitude of the threat. Recall once again the national defense example or the case of purchasing expensive health insurance to avoid financial disaster. Contemporary decision theory distinguishes two kinds of decision-making scenarios. In one, *"decision-making under risk,"* the probabilities of certain outcomes are known; here the rule of rationality to be followed is said to be, maximize expected utility. What is crucial if this rule is to be followed is to estimate accurately the benefits and costs of the different paths we can pursue (to emphasize a point, including the costs of not acting to slow or halt human-generated increases in global warming). The other decision-making scenario (often called *"decision-making under uncertainty"*) is that in which it is not possible to estimate the probabilities of the different outcomes associated with a choice of one path or another. Here many people think (the point is controversial) that the rational choice is to choose the alternative whose worst outcome is better than the worst outcome of any other available alternative—that is, *"maximin,"* or maximize the minimum. Here again an enormous nest of empirical "economic" (broadly understood) questions arise, for one must compare, roughly, the costs and benefits of choosing the path of (1) doing little to halt increases in warming, the benefits of such inaction, and the costs of future increased warming if it occurs, and (2) doing a lot to prevent future increases in warming, the costs of such action, and the benefits of halting or diminishing the warming if one succeeds in doing so. Again, all this is oversimplified, but we hope to have identified the extremes between which one can choose.

In his excellent book *The Next 100 Years,* Jonathan Weiner shrewdly observes, "We do not respond to emergencies that unfold in slow motion. We do not respond adequately to the invisible."[34] Again, it may be worth comparing the horror of the Holocaust, the fury it evoked, the massive effort to fight the Nazis, and the slower, more passive reaction to the threat of HIV, which almost certainly has killed more people than died in the Holocaust. There is good reason to believe that we humans collectively are engaged in a massive transformation of the planet and are flirting with a human and ecological disaster of horrendous proportions. Yet we cannot point to it. We do not hear it. We cannot film it. We do not see the blood in the streets. We do not see the torn bodies of little children as in a war. It is not on television. It is not like September 11, 2001. We have powerful incentives to deny the very existence of a problem.

As noted, wealthy corporate and political interests will use their enormous influence to control what people will think and what they will do.

There are subtleties and disputes about the empirical bases for concluding that an enhanced greenhouse effect is occurring. Patrick Michaels, an environmental scientist at the University of Virginia, makes the case in Essay 90 in this section that the general circulation models (GCMs) used in the 1980s to simulate climatic change, although predicting dire consequences, are in fact defective due to the way they employed certain "fudge factors." He argues that there are further dubious assumptions made by those who make such predictions. There has been little additional warming during the period in which there has been the most noticeable increase in greenhouse gases, roughly in the last half-century, so he avows. Moreover, he asserts that the use of GCMs were at the basis of the 1990 "Report of the Intergovernmental Panel on Climate Change" of the United Nations Environment Programme, which served as the basis of the Rio Treaty. Michaels is critical of the Rio Declaration, as well as proposals by former U.S. President Clinton, to limit greenhouse gases. He in effect poses a dilemma; either the GCM predictions are correct and proposed solutions are ineffectual, or they are incorrect—in which case the proposed changes are unnecessary and too costly. In addition, Michaels makes a case that some of the science supporting harsh predictions has been politicized and is therefore unreliable.

Christopher Flavin, vice president of the Worldwatch Institute, responds to Michaels's views (Essay 91). Flavin notes that political conservatives, of which Michaels is one, are normally known for being (1) risk averse, and (2) advocates of conserving what is of established value. One would think then, given this view, that conservatives might be reluctant to dismiss serious evidence that profound disruptions to the earth's atmosphere may be occurring. Flavin compares the dismissal of the results of GCM use—because they are admittedly imperfect—to the dismissal of results of medical exams on the ground that they are imperfect. He notes much counterevidence; to mention only one example, the ten warmest years in the past century have occurred since 1980. Flavin challenges the position that because there is a good deal of uncertainty about a potential disaster, we therefore should do little or nothing to avoid it.

One key issue concerns the magnitude of a disaster, if one occurs. Clearly some are inclined to minimize the harshness of a worst case scenario—that is, to evaluate it as a noncatastrophic matter. Others are not inclined to regard the consequences (such as the submerging of all the world's coastal cities), were they to occur, as noncatastrophic, and view the more important issue as the one concerning the probability of certain predicted consequences. Given, however, that virtually everyone admits the possibility of a catastrophic outcome, Flavin defends reliance on the "precautionary principle"—taking prudent steps to minimize substantial risks—as, he notes, a prudent nation would do in going to war, or Bill Gates did in entering the software business.[35] As Flavin notes, it is worth considering the parallel with principles employed by insurance companies, aspiring rational agents that also face the possibility of dealing with hard-to-predict catastrophic events. Two other comparisons (admittedly viewed from hindsight) are mentioned; one concerns the question of the justification of huge U.S. defense expenditures during the Cold War period when again there was the uncertain possibility of catastrophic events occurring. Another analogy concerns how to navigate a large ship, perhaps like the Titanic, through waters possibly containing huge, hidden icebergs. Highly relevant to such questions also is the cost of acting in a cautious manner—as well as the cost of *not* doing so. Here one might reflect on the questionable claim that if one's house does not catch fire, the money spent on fire insurance was wasted.

The excerpt "Climate Change Science" that follows (Essay 92) draws from a full report by the same title published in the summer of 2001 by the National Research Council of the National Academy of Sciences in the United States. It notes that global temperatures are rising, in recent decades is "likely mostly due to human activities," and is "particularly strong within the past twenty years." The mid-range estimate is a rise of 3 degrees Centigrade (5.4 Fahrenheit) by the end of the twenty-first century. Always noting the uncertainties and the frequent scarcity of data, the National Academy does not object to the view of the earlier Intergovernmental Panel on Climate Change that warming in the Northern hemisphere during the twentieth century "is likely to have been the largest of any century in the past thousand years." The exact causes are elusive and the National Academy does not purport to say what *ought* to be done about global warming.

In July 2001 in Bonn, Germany, 178 nations agreed to a weakened version of the Kyoto Protocol. The agreement requires 38 industrialized nations to reduce greenhouse gas emissions 5.2 percent below 1990 levels by 2012 or face tougher goals and some penalties for failure. Credits for having large forests (which function as a sink for CO_2) allowed Japan, Russia, and Canada to achieve lower levels of reduction of emissions. Somewhat surprisingly, companies with nuclear power plants supported reductions because nuclear power, other risks aside, does not emit greenhouse gases at the stage of energy production. President George W. Bush of the United States (which generates about 25 percent of the world's greenhouse gas emissions) viewed the treaty as "fatally flawed" and the United States refused to sign the treaty. *Time* magazine queried whether the United States was being a "rogue nation." One European official noted that the treaty had many flaws but said, "I prefer an imperfect agreement that is living than a perfect agreement that doesn't exist." Another commentator said, "If the United States will not lead, Europe can and will."[36] Skeptics remarked that President Bush apparently preferred at that time the imperfections and "uncertain science" of a missile defense system to the imperfections and "uncertain science" of a treaty to slow global warming. More positively, one journalist observed "Whatever the treaty's imperfections, there was a collective sense of achievement among the overwhelming majority of the world's industrialized and developing nations at the fact that they'd fashioned an epic international consensus on global warming despite the objections of the one nation that still aspires to global leadership."[37]

In brief, we confront a number of basic, distinct questions: (1) What view about the probability of enhanced global warming is best supported by the best science? (2) Can we agree that the events suggested by comparatively worst-case scenarios would be catastrophic (if they were to occur), even if not uniform in their worldwide effects? and (3) How ought we to proceed if we cannot reach agreement about the probabilities?

NOTES

1. H. Patricia Hynes, *The Recurring Silent Spring* (New York: Pergamon Press, 1989), pp. 18–19.

2. Jonathan Weiner, *The Next 100 Years* (New York: Bantam Books, 1991), p. 103.

3. Warwick Fox, *Toward a Transpersonal Ecology* (Boston: Shambhala, 1990), p. 4.

4. H. Patricia Hynes, *The Recurring Silent Spring*, p. 13.

5. Rachel Carson, *Silent Spring* (Boston: Houghton Mifflin, 1962), p. 278.

6. Paul Brooks, Foreward to *Silent Spring* (Boston: Houghton Mifflin, 1962), p. xii.

7. *Time*, 80(13) (September 28, 1962), 45, 48.

8. Paul Brooks, Foreword to *Silent Spring*, p. xii.

9. H. Patricia Hynes, *The Recurring Silent Spring*, p. 24.

10. Paul Brooks, Foreword to *Silent Spring*, pp. xiii–xiv.

11. Rachel Carson and Dorothy Freeman spent ten consecutive summers together in Maine where "they met for beach picnics, found wild haunts, lay on the rocks and in sunny, grassy enclaves where they watched migrating birds, read to each other, and discuss[ed] Carson's [work]" (Hynes, p. 30). Carson's letters to Freeman are held by Freeman and are unavailable to the public (Hynes, p. 2).

12. Paul Brooks, *The House of Life: Rachel Carson at Work* (Boston: Houghton Mifflin, 1972), pp. 271–12.

13. Thanks to Anthony Weston for our conversations about attitudes toward the environment. Note Warwick Fox's remarks on the similarities between Rachel Carson and Lynn White, Jr., vis-à-vis the Western attitude of arrogance toward the environment in *Toward a Transpersonal Ecology*, pp. 4–5.

14. Paul Brooks, *The House of Life: Rachel Carson at Work*, p. 305.

15. H. Patricia Hynes, "'Spring' Lessons Timeless and Ignored," *The News and Observer* (Raleigh, NC, September 14, 1992.

16. Ibid.

17. Bryan G. Norton, *Toward Unity Among Environmentalists* (New York: Oxford University Press, 1992), p.123.

18. Rachel Carson, *Silent Spring*, pp. 12–13.

19. Bryan G. Norton, *Toward Unity Among Environmentalists*, p. 123.

20. Another "rights variant" on the Harm Principle would be that it is wrong to infringe the rights of others without their voluntary, informed consent. The latter version requires the elaboration of a theory of rights specifying what rights the "others" have. The perceptive reader will note that who or what counts as a relevant other raises the absolutely fundamental question of what sorts of things have moral standing. Traditional ethical theorizing, with the notable exception of J. S. Mill and Jeremy Bentham, often has assumed that the relevant other was a human, often an adult, perhaps a property owner, and head of household. Any essential reference to the relevance of consent requires a good deal of elaboration as well, that is, an addressing of some questions about who is capable of giving or withholding voluntarily informed consent, what counts as voluntary consent, what counts as informed, and so on. We note that both plants and some humans are incapable of consent, such as babies or comatose humans. In part we are suggesting that the widespread supposition, shared by most economists and most people, that at least many forms of the passing on of the costs of pollution are wrong rests on a number of moral suppositions that may constitute a kind of hidden moral theory on which much economic reasoning tacitly relies. The complexities of the Harm Principle are discussed in Joel Feinberg's outstanding book *Harm to Others* and in the series of which it is a part (New York: Oxford University Press, 1984).

21. In contrast, one might "foul one's own nest," that is, pollute it and, hence, not pass on costs to others.

22. The amount of methane has doubled in the last 150 years, due in large part to cattle production and

humans' consumption of beef There are over a billion cows on the planet according to one estimate. Their contribution to the emission of methane is not trivial. See Weiner, *Planet Earth* (Toronto: Bantam Books, 1986), p. 139.

23. Ibid.

24. Ibid., p. 74.

25. As the editors use the terms *hypothesis* and *theory*, we do not mean to imply that that which receives such a label is not true or is not known to be true; we take, for example, Darwin's theory and the theory of continental drift to be true in their basic outlines.

26. See Louise B. Young's wonderfully written book, *The Blue Planet* (Boston: Little, Brown, 1983), p. 169.

27. Jonathan Weiner, *Planet Earth*, p. 128.

28. Young, pp. 13–14.

29. That was the most recent of five identified major glacial epochs. Ibid., p. 141.

30. In the 1960s, French archaeologists found glacier-scarred rocks in southern Algeria that are dated 400 million years ago. See Young, p. 138.

31. Weiner, *The Next 100 Years*, pp. 102–103. Weiner relies in part on John Imbrie and Katharine Imbrie, *Ice Ages: Solving the Mystery* (Short Hills, NJ: Enslow, 1979).

32. Ibid., p. 103.

33. Global warming even in worst-case scenarios may pose no threat at all to the continuation of life on earth, in that life of some sort would survive it. But if biodiversity is radically altered (and opportunist creatures reign, such as lice, fleas, and ticks) and tens of millions of humans suffer and prematurely die, then it would be of little solace that life would go on. Thus the central threat is not to life as such.

34. Weiner, *The Next 100 Years*, p. 241.

35. Compare the view of certain Christians who believe (1) the world will soon end in an apocalypse, and (2) they themselves will be saved from harm, and thus such events are indeed desirable ones. Some who may agree with the empirical claim (1), may not make the same evaluation, (2). Those who preach "Repent, the end is near" but allow the difficulty of predicting the end more precisely (thus, the use of the vague "near") may presuppose something like the Precautionary Principle.

36. Some remarks on the climate accord in July 2001 are drawn from "178 Nations Reach Climate Accord; U.S. Only Looks On" in the *New York Times* July 24, 2001.

37. Tony Karon, "When It Comes to Kyoto, the U.S. is the 'Rogue Nation'" in *Time*.com July 24, 2001.

88. Silent Spring

Rachel Carson

A Fable for Tomorrow

There was once a town in the heart of America where all life seemed to live in harmony with its surroundings. The town lay in the midst of a checkerboard of prosperous farms, with fields of grain and hillsides of orchards where, in spring, white clouds of bloom drifted above the green fields. In autumn, oak and maple and birch set up a blaze of color that flamed and flickered across a backdrop of pines. Then foxes barked in the hills and deer silently crossed the fields, half hidden in the mists of the fall mornings.

Along the roads, laurel, viburnum and alder, great ferns and wildflowers delighted the traveler's eye through much of the year. Even in winter the roadsides were places of beauty, where countless birds came to feed on the berries and on the seed heads of the dried weeds rising above the snow. The countryside was, in fact, famous for the abundance and variety of its bird life, and when the flood of migrants was pouring through in spring and fall people traveled from great distances to observe them. Others came to fish the streams, which flowed clear and cold out of the hills and contained shady pools where trout lay. So it had been from the days many years ago when the first settlers raised their houses, sank their wells, and built their barns.

Then a strange blight crept over the area and everything began to change. Some evil spell had settled on the community: mysterious maladies swept the flocks of chickens; the cattle and sheep sickened and died. Everywhere was a shadow of death. The farmers spoke of much illness among their families. In the town the doctors had become more and more puzzled by new kinds of sickness appearing among their patients. There had been several sudden and unexplained deaths, not only among adults but even among children, who would be stricken suddenly while at play and die within a few hours.

There was a strange stillness. The birds, for example—where had they gone? Many people spoke of them, puzzled and disturbed. The feeding stations in the backyards were deserted. The few birds seen anywhere were moribund; they trembled violently and could not fly. It was a spring without voices. On the mornings that had once throbbed with the dawn chorus of robins, catbirds, doves, jays, wrens, and scores of other bird voices there was now no sound; only silence lay over the fields and woods and marsh.

On the farms the hens brooded, but no chicks hatched. The farmers complained that they were unable to raise any pigs—the litters were small and the young survived only a few days. The apple trees were coming into bloom but no bees droned among the blossoms, so there was no pollination and there would be no fruit.

The roadsides, once so attractive, were now lined with browned and withered vegetation as though swept by fire. These, too, were silent, deserted by all living things. Even the streams were now lifeless. Anglers no longer visited them, for all the fish had died.

In the gutters under the eaves and between the shingles of the roofs, a white granular powder still showed a few patches; some weeks before it had fallen like snow upon the roofs and the lawns, the fields and streams.

No witchcraft, no enemy action had silenced the rebirth of new life in this stricken world. The people had done it themselves.

This town does not actually exist, but it might easily have a thousand counterparts in America or elsewhere in the world. I know of no community that has experienced all the misfortunes I describe. Yet every one of these disasters has actually happened somewhere, and many real communities have already suffered a substantial number of them. A grim specter has crept upon us almost unnoticed, and this imagined tragedy may easily become a stark reality we all shall know. . . .

The Obligation to Endure

The history of life on earth has been a history of interaction between living things and their surroundings. To a large extent, the physical form and the habits of the earth's vegetation and its animal life have been molded by the environment. Considering the whole span of earthly time, the opposite effect, in which life actually modifies its surroundings, has been relatively slight. Only within the moment of time represented by the present century has one species—man—acquired significant power to alter the nature of his world.

During the past quarter century this power has not only increased to one of disturbing magnitude but it has changed in character. The most alarming of all man's assaults upon the environment is the contamination of air, earth, rivers, and sea with dangerous and even lethal materials. This pollution is for the most part irrecoverable; the chain of evil it initiates not only in the world that must support life but in living tissues is for the most part irreversible. In this now universal contamination of the environment, chemicals are the sinister and little-recognized partners of radiation in changing the very nature of the world—the very nature of its life. Strontium 90, released through nuclear explosions into the air, comes to earth in rain or drifts down as fallout, lodges in soil, enters into the grass or corn or wheat grown there, and in time takes up its abode in the bones of a human being, there to remain until his death. Similarly, chemicals sprayed on croplands or forests or gardens lie long in soil, entering into living organisms, passing from one to another in a chain of poisoning and death. Or they pass mysteriously by underground streams until they emerge and, through the alchemy of air and sunlight, combine into new forms that kill vegetation, sicken cattle, and work unknown harm on those who drink from once pure wells. As Albert Schweitzer has said, "Man can hardly even recognize the devils of his own creation."

It took hundreds of millions of years to produce the life that now inhabits the earth—eons of time in which that developing and evolving and diversifying life reached a state of adjustment and balance with its surroundings. The environment, rigorously shaping and directing the life it supported, contained elements that were hostile as well as supporting. Certain rocks gave out dangerous radiation; even within the light of the sun, from which all life draws its energy, there were short-wave radiations with power to injure. Given time—time not in years but in millennia—life adjusts, and a balance has been reached. For time is the essential ingredient; but in the modern world there is no time.

The rapidity of change and the speed with which new situations are created follow the impetuous and heedless pace of man rather than the deliberate pace of nature. Radiation is no longer merely the background radiation of rocks, the bombardment of cosmic rays, the ultraviolet of the sun that have existed before there was any life on earth; radiation is now the unnatural creation of man's tampering with the atom. The chemicals to which life is asked to make its adjustment are no longer merely the calcium and silica and copper and all the rest of the minerals washed out of the rocks and carried in rivers to the sea; they are the synthetic creations of man's inventive mind, brewed in his laboratories, and having no counterparts in nature.

To adjust to these chemicals would require time on the scale that is nature's; it would require not merely the years of a man's life but the life of generations. And even this, were it by some miracle possible, would be futile, for the new chemicals come from our laboratories in an endless stream; almost five hundred annually find their way into actual use in the United States alone. The figure is staggering and its implications are not easily grasped—500 new chemicals to which the bodies of men and animals are required somehow to adapt each year, chemicals totally outside the limits of biologic experience.

Among them are many that are used in man's war against nature. Since the mid-1940's over 200 basic chemicals have been created for use in killing insects, weeds, rodents, and other organisms described in the modern vernacular as "pests"; and they are sold under several thousand different brand names.

These sprays, dusts, and aerosols are now applied almost universally to farms, gardens, forests, and homes—nonselective chemicals that have the power to kill every insect, the "good" and the "bad," to still the song of birds and the leaping of fish in the streams, to coat the leaves with a deadly film, and to linger on in soil—all this though the intended target may be only a few weeds or insects. Can anyone believe it is possible to lay down such a barrage of poisons on the surface of the earth without making it unfit for all life? They should not be called "insecticides," but "biocides."

The whole process of spraying seems caught up in an endless spiral. Since DDT was released for civilian use, a process of escalation has been going on in which ever more toxic materials must be found. This has happened because insects, in a triumphant vindication of Darwin's principle of the survival of the fittest, have evolved super races immune to the particular insecticide used, hence a deadlier one has always to be developed—and then a deadlier one than that. It has happened also because destructive insects often undergo a "flareback," or resurgence, after spraying, in numbers greater than before. Thus the chemical war is never won, and all life is caught in its violent crossfire.

Along with the possibility of the extinction of mankind by nuclear war, the central problem of our age has therefore become the contamination of man's total environment with such substances of incredible potential for harm—substances that accumulate in the tissues of plants and animals and even penetrate the germ cells to shatter or alter the very material of heredity upon which the shape of the future depends.

Some would-be architects of our future look toward a time when it will be possible to alter the human germ plasm by design. But we may easily be doing so now by inadvertence, for many chemicals, like radiation, bring about gene mutations. It is ironic to think that man might determine his own future by something so seemingly trivial as the choice of an insect spray.

All this has been risked—for what? Future historians may well be amazed by our distorted sense of proportion. How could intelligent beings seek to control a few unwanted species by a method that contaminated the entire environment and brought the threat of disease and death even to their own kind? Yet this is precisely what we have done. . . .

The Other Road

We stand now where two roads diverge. But unlike the roads in Robert Frost's familiar poem, they are not equally fair. The road we have long been traveling is deceptively easy, a smooth superhighway on which we progress with great speed, but at its end lies disaster. The other fork of the road—the one "less traveled by"—offers our last, our only chance to reach a destination that assures the preservation of our earth.

The choice, after all, is ours to make. If, having endured much, we have at last asserted our "right to know," and if, knowing, we have concluded that we are being asked to take senseless and frightening risks, then we should no longer accept the counsel of those who tell us that we must fill our world with poisonous chemicals; we should look about and see what other course is open to us.

A truly extraordinary variety of alternatives to the chemical control of insects is available. Some are already in use and have achieved brilliant success. Others are in the stage of laboratory testing. Still others are little more than ideas in the minds of imaginative scientists, waiting for the opportunity to put them to the test. All have this in common: they are *biological* solutions, based on understanding of the living organisms they seek to control, and of the whole fabric of life to which these organisms belong. Specialists representing various areas of the vast field of biology are contributing—entomologists, pathologists, geneticists, physiologists, biochemists, ecologists—all pouring their knowledge and their creative inspirations into the formation of a new science of biotic controls. . . .

Through all these new, imaginative, and creative approaches to the problem of sharing our earth with other creatures there runs a constant theme, the awareness that we are dealing with life—with living populations and all their pressures and counterpressures, their surges and recessions. Only by taking account of such life forces and by cautiously seeking to guide them into channels favorable to ourselves can we hope to achieve a reasonable accommodation between the insect hordes and ourselves.

The current vogue for poisons has failed utterly to take into account these most fundamental considerations. As crude a weapon as the cave man's club, the chemical barrage has been hurled against the fabric of life—a fabric on the one hand delicate and destructible, on the other miraculously tough and resilient, and capable of striking back in unexpected ways. These extraordinary capacities of life have been ignored by the practitioners of chemical control who have brought to their task no "high-minded orientation," no humility before the vast forces with which they tamper.

The "control of nature" is a phrase conceived in arrogance, born of the Neanderthal age of biology and philosophy, when it was supposed that nature exists for the convenience of man. The concepts and practices of applied entomology for the most part date from that Stone Age of science. It is our alarming misfortune that so primitive a science has armed itself with the most modern and terrible weapons, and that in turning them against the insects it has also turned them against the earth.

Principal Sources

"Report on Environmental Health Problems," *Hearings*, 86th Congress, Subcom. of Com. on Appropriations, March 1960, p. 170.

Swanson, Carl P., *Cytology and Cytogenetics*. Englewood Cliffs, NJ: Prentice-Hall, 1957.

89. The Case That the World Has Reached Limits

Robert Goodland

Mahatma Gandhi [when asked if, after independence, India would attain British standards of living]: "It took Britain half the resources of the planet to achieve its prosperity; how many planets will a country like India require . . . ?"

The aim of this chapter is to present the case that limits to growth have already been reached, that further input growth will take the planet further away from sustainability, and that we are rapidly foreclosing options for the future, possibly by overshooting limits (Catton 1982). This chapter seeks to convince the reader of the urgent need to convert to a sustainable economy, rather than the related and equally or more important need of poverty alleviation. The political will to transit to sustainability will be mustered only when the need for the transition is per-

Granted with permission from *Population, Technology, and Lifestyle: The Transition to Sustainability,* edited by Robert Goodland, Herman E. Daly, Salah El Serafy, Copyright © Island Press, 1992. Published by Island Press, Washington, DC, & Covelo, California.

ceived. The crucial next step—how to muster that political will—is deferred to a subsequent book.

To begin, plaudits for Brundtland's heroic achievement: elevating sustainability as a planetary goal now espoused by practically all nations, the United Nations family, and the World Bank. In July 1989, leaders of the Group of Seven major industrialized nations called for "the early adoption, worldwide, of policies based on sustainable development." The world owes Brundtland an enormous debt for this tremendous feat, and we admire her political wisdom. This chapter builds on Brundtland's lead and explores the implications of sustainability. We assume as given that the world is being run unsustainably now—being fueled by inherited fossil fuels is the best single example. Nonrenewable oil and gas provide 60 percent of global energy with barely fifty years of proven reserves.

Brundtland stated that meeting essential needs requires "a new era of economic growth" for nations in which the majority are poor. The report (WCED 1987) anticipates "a five- to tenfold increase in world industrial output." Two years later, this "sustainable growth" conclusion was reemphasized by the secretary general of the Brundtland Commission: "A fivefold to tenfold increase in economic activity would be required over the next 50 years" to achieve sustainability (MacNeill 1989).

The Global Ecosystem and the Economic Subsystem

A single measure—population times per capita resource consumption—encapsulates what is needed to achieve sustainability. This is the scale of the human economic subsystem with respect to that of the global ecosystem on which it depends and of which it is a part. The global ecosystem is the source of all material inputs feeding the economic subsystem and is the sink for all its wastes. Population times per capita resource consumption is the total flow—throughput—of resources from the ecosystem to the economic subsystem, then back to the ecosystem as waste. . . . Population times per capita resource use is refined by Tinbergen and Hueting (1992) and by Ehrlich and Ehrlich (1990).

The global ecosystem's source and sink functions have limited capacity to support the economic subsystem. The imperative, therefore, is to maintain the size of the global economy to within the capacity of the ecosystem to sustain it. Speth (1989) calculates that it took all of human history to grow to the $600 billion global economy of 1900. Today, the world economy grows by this amount every two years. Unchecked, today's $16 trillion global economy may be five times bigger only one generation or so hence.

It seems unlikely that the world can sustain a doubling of the economy, let alone Brundtland's "five- to tenfold increase." We believe that throughput growth is not the way to reach sustainability; we cannot "grow" our way into sustainability. The global ecosystem, which is the source of all the resources needed for the economic subsystem, is finite and has limited regenerative and assimilative capacities. It looks inevitable that the next century will be occupied by double the number of people in the human economy consuming sources and burdening sinks with their wastes.

The global ecosystem is the sink for all the wastes created by the economic subsystem, and this sink has limited assimilative capacity. When the economic subsystem was small relative to the global ecosystem, then the sources and sinks were large and limits were irrelevant. Leading thinkers, such as Ehrlich and Ehrlich (1990), Hardin (1991), Boulding (1991), Daly (1990a, 1990b, 1991a, 1991b), as well as the Club of Rome (Meadows et al. 1974), have shown for years that the world is no longer "empty," the economic subsystem is large relative to the biosphere, and the capacities of the biosphere's sources and sinks are being stressed.

Localized Limits to Global Limits

This chapter presents the case that the economic subsystem has reached or exceeded important source and sink limits. We take as agreed that we have already fouled our nest: practically nowhere on this earth are signs of the human economy absent. From the center of Antarctica to the top of Mount Everest, human wastes are obvious and increasing. It is impossible to find a sample of ocean water with no sign of the 20 billion tons of human wastes added annually. PCBs and other persistent toxic chemicals, such as DDT and heavy metal compounds, have already accumulated throughout the marine ecosystem. One-fifth of the world's population breathes air more poisonous than WHO standards recommend, and an entire generation of Mexico City children may be intellectually stunted by lead poisoning (Brown et al. 1991).

Since the Club of Rome's 1972 report "Limits to Growth," the constraints have shifted from source limits to sink limits. Source limits are more open to substitution and are more localized. Since then, the case has substantially strengthened for limits to throughput growth. There is a wide variety of limits. Some are tractable and are being tackled, such as the CFC phase-out under the Montreal Convention. Other limits are less tractable, such as the massive human appropriation of biomass (see below). The key limit is the sink constraint of fossil energy use. Therefore, the rate of transition to renewables, including solar energy, parallels the rate of transition to sustainability. Here the optimists add the possibility of cheap fusion energy by the year 2050. We are agnostic on technology and want to encourage it by energy taxes. . . . Hitherto, technology has only started to focus on input reduction and even less on sink management, which suggests there is scope for improvements.

Land-fill sites are becoming harder to find; garbage is shipped thousands of miles from industrial to developing countries in search of unfilled sinks. It has so far proved impossible for the U.S. Nuclear Regulatory Commission to find anywhere to rent a nuclear waste site for U.S. $100 million per year. Germany's Kraft-Werk Union signed an agreement with China in July 1987 to bury nuclear waste in Mongolia's Gobi Desert. These facts prove that land-fill sites and toxic dumps—aspects of sinks—are increasingly hard to find, that limits are near.

First Evidence of Limits: Human Biomass Appropriation

The best evidence that there are other imminent limits is the calculation by Vitousek et al. (1986) that the human economy uses—directly or indirectly—about 40 percent of the net primary product of terrestrial photosynthesis today. (This figure drops to 25 percent if the oceans and other aquatic ecosystems are included.) And desertification, urban encroachment onto agricultural land, blacktopping, soil erosion, and pollution are increasing—as is the population's search for food. This means that in only a single doubling of the world's population (say, thirty-five years) we will use 80 percent, and 100 percent shortly thereafter.

As Daly (1991a, 1991b) points out, 100 percent appropriation is ecologically impossible and socially highly undesirable. The world will go from half-empty to full in one doubling period, irrespective of the sink being filled or the source being consumed. Readers refusing to recognize such overfullness that has appropriated 40 percent for humans already should decide when between now and 100 percent they would be willing to say "enough." What evidence will they require to be convinced? Although the Vitousek et al. evidence has not been refuted during the last five years, this single study is so stark that we urge prompt corroboration and analysis of the implications.

Second Evidence of Limits: Global Warming

Evidence of atmospheric carbon dioxide accumulation is pervasive, as geographically extensive as possible, and unimaginably expensive to cure if allowed to worsen. In addition, the evidence is unambiguously negative and strongly so. There may be a few exceptions, such as plants growing faster in CO_2-enriched laboratories where water and nutrients are not limiting. However, in the real world, it seems more likely that crop belts will not shift with changing climate, nor will they grow faster, because some other factor (for example, suitable soils or water) will become limiting. The prodigious North American breadbasket's climate may indeed shift north; but this does not mean that the breadbasket will follow, because the rich prairie soils will stay put, and Canadian boreal soils and muskeg are very infertile.

The second evidence that limits have been exceeded is global warming. The year 1990 was the warmest year in more than a century of record-keeping. Seven of the hottest years on record all occurred in the last 11 years. The 1980s were 1 degree Fahrenheit warmer than the 1880s, while 1990 was 1.25 degrees Fahrenheit warmer. This contrasts alarmingly with the pre-industrial constancy in which the earth's temperature did not vary more than 2 to 4 degrees Fahrenheit in the last 10,000 years. Humanity's entire social and cultural infrastructure over the last 7000 years has evolved entirely within a global climate that never deviated as much as 2 degrees Fahrenheit from today's climate (Arrhenius and Waltz 1990).

It is too soon to be absolutely certain that global "greenhouse" warming has begun: normal climatic variability is too great for absolute certainty. There is even greater uncertainty about the possible effects. But all the evidence suggests that global warming may well have started, that CO_2 accumulation started years ago, as postulated by Svante Arrhenius in 1896, and that it is worsening fast. Scientists now practically universally agree that such warming will occur, although differences remain on the rates. The U.S. National Academy of Science warned President Bush that global warming may well be the most pressing international issue of the next century. A dwindling minority of scientists remain agnostic. The dispute concerns policy responses much more than the predictions.

The scale of today's fossil-fuel-based human economy seems to be the dominant cause of greenhouse gas accumulation. The biggest contribution to greenhouse warming—carbon dioxide released from burning coal, oil, and natural gas—is accumulating fast in the atmosphere. Today's 5.3 billion people annually burn the equivalent of more than one ton of coal each.

Next in importance in contributing to greenhouse warming are all other pollutants released by the economy that exceed the biosphere's absorptive capacity: methane, CFCs, and nitrous oxide. Relative to carbon dioxide these three pollutants are orders of magnitude more damaging, although their amount is much less. Today's price to polluters for using atmospheric sink capacity for carbon dioxide disposal is zero, although the real opportunity cost may turn out to be astronomical.

The costs of rejecting the greenhouse hypothesis, if true, are vastly greater than the costs of accepting the hypothesis, if it proves to be false. By the time the evidence is irrefutable, it is sure to be too late to avert unacceptable costs, such as the influx of millions of refugees from low-lying coastal areas (55 percent of the world's population lives on coasts or estuaries), damage to ports and coastal cities, an increase in storm intensity, and, worst of all, damage to agriculture. Furthermore, abating global warming may save money, not cost it, according to Lovins (1990), when the benefit from lower fuel bills is factored in. The greenhouse threat is more than sufficient to justify action now, even if only in an insurance sense. The question to be resolved is how much insurance to buy?

Admittedly, great uncertainty prevails. But uncertainty cuts both ways. "Business as usual" or "wait and see" approaches are thus imprudent, if not foolhardy. Underestimation of greenhouse or ozone shield risks is just as likely as overestimation. Recent studies suggest that we are underestimating risks, rather than the converse. In May 1991, the U.S. EPA upped by *twentyfold* their estimate of UV-radiation cancer deaths, and the earth's ability to absorb methane was estimated *downward by 25 percent* in June 1991. In the face of uncertainty about global environmental health, prudence should be paramount.

The relevant component here is the tight relationship between carbon released and the scale of the economy. Global carbon emissions have increased annually since the Industrial Revolution, currently at nearly 4 percent per year. To the extent that energy use parallels economic activity, carbon emissions are an index of the scale of the economy. Fossil fuels account for 78 percent of U.S. energy. Of course, there is tremendous scope for reducing the energy intensity of industry and of the economy in general; that is why reductions in carbon emissions are possible without reducing standards of living. A significant degree of decoupling economic growth from energy throughput appears substantially achievable. Witness the 81 percent increase in Japan's output since 1973 using the same amount of energy. Similarly, the United States achieved nearly a 39 percent increase in GNP since 1973 with only a modest increase in energy use. This means energy efficiency increased almost 26 percent. Sweden—cold, gloomy, industrialized, and very energy-efficient—is the best example of how profitable it is to reduce CO_2. The Swedish State Power Board found that doubled electric efficiency, a 34 percent decrease in CO_2, and the phase-out of the nuclear power that supplies 50 percent of the country's electricity actually *lowers* consumers' electricity bills by U.S. $1 billion per year (Lovins 1990). Other, less efficient nations should be able to do even better.

Reducing energy intensity is possible in all industrial economies and in the larger developing economies, such as China, Brazil, and India. The scope of increasing energy use without increasing CO_2 means primarily the overdue transition to renewables: biomass, solar, and hydro. The other major source of carbon emissions—deforestation—also parallels the scale of the economy. More people needing more land push back the frontier. But there are vanishingly few geopolitical frontiers left today.

Greenhouse warming is a compelling argument that limits have been exceeded because it is globally pervasive, rather than disrupting the atmosphere in the region where the CO_2 was produced. In comparison, regional evidence of limits includes acid rain damaging parts of the United States and Canada, and those parts of Scandinavia downwind from the United Kingdom, and the "Waldsterben," or U.S. $30 billion loss of much of Europe's forest.

The nearly 7 billion tons of carbon released into the atmosphere each year by human activity (from fossil fuels and deforestation) accumulate in the atmosphere, which suggests that the ecosystem's sinks capable of absorbing carbon have been exceeded, and carbon accumulation appears for all practical purposes irreversible on any relevant time frame; hence it is of major concern for sustainability for future generations. Removal of carbon dioxide by liquefying it or chemically scrubbing it from stacks might double the cost of electricity. Optimistically, technology may reduce this cost, but still at a major penalty.

Third Evidence of Limits: Ozone Shield Rupture

The third evidence that global limits have been reached is the rupture of the ozone shield. It is difficult to imagine more compelling evidence that human activity has already damaged our life-support systems than the cosmic holes in the ozone shield. That CFCs would damage the ozone layer was predicted as far back as 1974 by Sherwood Rowland and Mario Molina. But when the damage was first detected—in 1985 in Antarctica—disbelief was so great that the data were rejected as coming from faulty sensors. Retesting and a search of hitherto undigested computer printouts confirmed that not only did the hole exist in 1985, but that it had appeared each spring since 1979. The world had failed to detect a vast hole that threatened human life and food production and that was more extensive than the United States and taller than Mount Everest (Shea 1989).

The single Antarctic ozone hole has now gone global. All subsequent tests have proved global ozone layer thinning far faster than models predicted. A second hole was subsequently discovered over the Arctic, and recently ozone shield thinning has been detected over both north and south temperate latitudes, including over northern Europe and North America. Furthermore, the temperate holes are edging from the less dangerous winter into the spring, thus posing more of a threat to sprouting crops and to humans. The incidence of blindness in Chilean sheep and Patagonian rabbits in the Andes soared in 1991.

The relationship between the increased ultraviolet "B" radiation leaking through the impaired ozone shield and skin cancers and cataracts is relatively well known—every 1 percent decrease in the ozone layer results in 5 percent more of certain skin cancers—and alarming in neighboring regions (for example, Queensland, Australia). The world seems destined for 1 billion additional skin cancers, many of them fatal, among people alive today. The possibly more serious human health effect is depression of our immune systems, increasing our vulnerability to an array of tumors, parasites, and infectious diseases. In addition, as the shield weakens, crop yields and marine fisheries will decline. But the gravest effect may be the uncertainty, such as upsetting normal balances in natural vegetation. Keystone species—those on which many others depend for survival—may decrease, leading to widespread disruption in environmental services and accelerating extinctions.

The 1 million or so tons of CFCs annually dumped into the biosphere take about 10 years to waft up to the ozone layer, where they destroy it with a half-life of 100 to 150 years. The tonnage of CFCs and other ozone-depleting gases released into the atmosphere is increasing damage to the ozone shield. Today's damage, although serious, only reflects the relatively low levels of CFCs released in the early 1980s. If CFC emissions cease today, the world still will be gripped in an unavoidable commitment to 10 years of increased damage. This would then gradually return to predamage levels over the next 100 to 150 years.

This seems to be evidence that the global ecosystem's sink capacity to absorb CFC pollution has been vastly exceeded. The limits have been reached and exceeded; mankind is in for damage to environmental services, human health, and food production. This is a good example because 85 percent of CFCs are released in the industrial North, but the main hole appeared over Antarctica in the ozone layer twenty kilometers up in the sky, showing the damage to be widespread and truly global in nature.

Fourth Evidence of Limits: Land Degradation

Land degradation—decreased productivity such as caused by accelerated soil erosion, salination, and desertification—is only one of the many topics that could be included here. It is not new; land degraded thousands of years ago (for example, the Tigris-Euphrates Valley) remains unproductive today. But the scale has mushroomed and is important because practically all (97 percent) food comes from land rather than from aquatic or ocean systems. As 35 percent of the earth's land already is degraded, and since this figure is increasing and is largely irreversible in any time scale of concern to society, such degradation is a sign that we have exceeded the regenerative capacity of the earth's soil source.

Pimentel et al. (1987) found that soil erosion is serious in most of the world's agricultural areas and that this problem is worsening as more marginal land is brought into production. Soil loss rates, generally ranging from 10 to 100 tons per hectare per year, exceed soil formation rates by at least tenfold. Agriculture is leading to erosion, salination, or waterlogging of possibly 6 million hectares per year: "a crisis seriously affecting the world food economy."

Exceeding the limits of this particular environmental source function raises food prices and exacerbates income inequality at a time when 1 billion people are already malnourished. As one-third of developing-country populations now face fuel wood deficits, crop residues and dung are diverted from agriculture to fuel. Fuel wood overharvesting and this diversion intensify land degradation, hunger, and poverty.

Fifth Evidence of Limits: Decrease in Biodiversity

The scale of the human economy has grown so large that there is no longer room for all species in the ark. The rates of takeover of wildlife habitat and of species extinctions are the fastest they have ever been in recorded history and are accelerating. The world's richest species habitat, tropical forest, has already been 55 percent destroyed; the current rate exceeds 168,000 square kilometers per year. As the total number of species extant is not yet known to the nearest order of magnitude (5 million or 30 million or more), it is impossible to determine precise extinction rates. However, conservative estimates put the rate at more than 5000 species of our inherited genetic library irreversibly extinguished each year. This is about 10,000 times as fast as prehuman extinction rates. Less conservative estimates put the rate at 150,000 species per year (Goodland 1991). Many find such anthropocentrism to be arrogant and immoral. It also increases risks of overshoot. Built-in redundancy is a part of many biological systems, but we do not know how near thresholds are. Most extinctions from tropical deforestation (for example, colonization) today increase poverty—tropical moist forest soils are fragile—so we do not even have much of a beneficial tradeoff with development here.

Population

Brundtland is sensible on population: adequate food is too expensive for one-fourth of the earth's population today. Birthweight is declining in places. Poverty stimulates population growth. Direct poverty alleviation is essential; "business as usual" on poverty alleviation is immoral. MacNeill (1989) states it plainly: "reducing rates of population growth" is an essential condition to achieve sustainability. This is as important, if not more so, in industrial countries as it is in developing countries. Industrial countries overconsume per capita, hence overpollute, and thus are responsible for by far the largest share of limits being reached. The richest 20 percent of the world consumes more than 70 percent of the world's commercial energy. Thirteen nations already have achieved zero population growth, so it is not utopian to expect others to follow.

Developing countries contribute to exceeding limits because they are so populous today (77 percent of the world's total) and are increasing far faster than their economies can provide for them (90 percent of world population growth). Real incomes are declining in some areas. If left unchecked, it may be halfway through the twenty-first century before the number of births will fall back even to current high levels. Developing-countries' population growth alone would account for a 75 percent increase in their commercial energy consumption by 2025, even if per capita consumption remained at current inadequate levels (OTA 1991). These countries need so much growth due to the population increase that this can be freed up only by the transition to sustainability in industrial countries.

The poor must be given the chance, must be assisted, and will justifiably demand to reach at least minimally acceptable living standards by access to the remaining natural resource base. When industrial nations switch from input growth to qualitative development, more resources and environmental functions will be available for the South's needed growth. This is a major role of the World Bank. It is in the interests of developing countries and the world commons not to follow the fossil fuel model. It is in the interests of industrial countries to subsidize alternatives, and this is an increasing role for the World Bank. This view is repeated by Dr. Qu Wenhu, of Academica Sinica, who says: "If 'needs' includes one automobile for each of a billion Chinese, then sustainable development is impossible." Developing-countries' populations account for only 17 percent of total commercial energy now, but unchecked this will almost double by 2020 (OTA 1991).

Merely meeting the unmet demand for family planning would help enormously. Educating girls and providing them with credit for productive purposes and employment opportunities are probably the next most effective measures. A full 25 percent of U.S. births, and a much larger number of developing-country births, are to unmarried mothers, hence providing less child care. Most of these births are unwanted, which also tends to result in less care. Certainly, international development agencies should assist high-population-growth countries in reducing to world averages as an urgent first step, instead of trying only to increase infrastructure without population measures.

Growth Versus Development

To the extent that the economic subsystem has indeed become large relative to the global ecosystem on which it depends, and the regenerative and assimilative capacities of its sources and sinks are being exceeded, then the growth called for by Brundtland will dangerously exacerbate surpassing the limits outlined above. Opinions differ. MacNeill (1989) claims "a minimum of 3% annual per capita income growth is needed to reach sustainability during the first part of the next century," and this would need higher growth in national income, given population trends. Hueting (1990)

disagrees, concluding that for sustainability "what we need **least** is an increase in national income." Sustainability will be achieved only to the extent that quantitative throughput growth stabilizes and is replaced by qualitative development, holding outputs constant. Reverting to the scale of the economy—population times per capita resource use— per capita resource use must decline, as well as population.

Brundtland is excellent on three of the four necessary conditions for sustainability. First, the production of more with less (for example, conservation, efficiency, technological improvements, and recycling). Japan excels in this regard, producing 81 percent more real output than it did in 1973 using the same amount of energy. Second, the reduction of the population explosion. Third, the redistribution from overconsumers to the poor. Brundtland was probably being politically astute in leaving fuzzy the fourth necessary condition to make all four sufficient to reach sustainability. This is the transition from input growth and growth in the scale of the economy to qualitative development, holding the scale of the economy consistent with the regenerative and assimilative capacities of global life-support systems. In several places the Brundtland Report hints at this. In qualitative, sustainable development, production replaces depreciated assets, and births replace deaths, so that stocks of wealth and people are continually renewed and even improved (Daly 1990b). A developing economy is getting better: the well-being of the (stable) population improves. An economy growing in throughput is getting bigger, exceeding limits, and damaging the self-repairing capacity of the planet.

To the extent our leaders recognize the fact that the earth has reached limits and decide to reduce further expansion in the scale of the economy, we must prevent hardship in this tremendous transition for poor countries. Brundtland commendably advocates growth for poor countries. But only raising the bottom without lowering the top will not permit sustainability (Haavelmo 1990).

The poor need an irreducible minimum of basics: food, clothing, and shelter. These basics require throughput growth for poor countries, with compensating reductions in such growth in rich countries. Apart from colonial resource drawdowns, industrial country growth historically has increased markets for developing countries' raw materials, hence presumably benefiting poor countries, but it is industrial country growth that has to contract to free up ecological room for the minimum growth needed in poor country economies. Tinbergen and Hueting (1992) put it plainest: "no further production growth in rich countries." All approaches to sustainability must internalize this constraint if the crucial goals of poverty alleviation and halting damage to global life-support systems are to be approached.

Conclusion

When economies change from agrarian through industrial to more service-oriented, then smokestack throughput growth may improve to growth less damaging of sources and sinks: from coal and steel to fiber optics and electronics, for example. We must speed to production that is less throughput-intensive. We must accelerate technical improvements in resource productivity— Brundtland's "producing more with less. " Presumably this is what the Brundtland Commission and subsequent follow-up authors (for example, MacNeill 1989) label "growth, but of a different kind." Vigorous promotion of this trend will indeed help the transition to sustainability and is probably essential. It is also largely true that conservation and efficiency improvements and recycling are profitable and will become much more so the instant environmental externalities (for example, carbon dioxide emissions) are internalized.

But this approach will be insufficient for four reasons. First, all growth consumes resources and produces wastes, even Brundtland's unspecified new type of growth. To the extent that we have reached limits to the ecosystem's regenerative and assimilative capacities, throughput growth exceeding such limits will not herald sustainability. Second, the size of the service sector relative to the production of goods has limits. Third, even many services are fairly throughput-intensive, including tourism, universities, and hospitals. Fourth, and highly significant, less throughput-intensive growth is "hi-tech"; hence the places where there has to be more growth—tiny, impoverished, developing-country economies—are less likely to be able to afford Brundtland's "new" growth.

Part of the answer will be massive technology transfer from industrial countries to developing countries to offer them whatever throughput-neutral or throughput-minimal technologies are available. This transfer is presaged by the U.S. $1.5 billion Global Environment Facility of the United Nations Environment Program (UNEP), the United Nations Development Program (UNDP), and the World Bank that will start in 1991 to finance improvements not yet fully "economic," but which benefit the global commons.

This chapter is not primarily about how to approach sustainability: that is well documented elsewhere (Adams 1990, Agarwal and Narain 1990, Chambers et al. 1990, Conroy and Litvinoff 1988, Goldsmith, Hildyard, and Bunyard 1990). Nor is it about the economic and political difficulties of reaching sustainability, such as the pricing of the infinite (the ozone shield, for example), the endlessly debatable (biodiversity, for example), or pricing for posterity what we cannot price today. That is admirably argued by Daly and Cobb (1989), Daly (1990a, 1991a, 1991b), El Serafy (1991), and Costanza (1991). It is about the need to recognize the imminence of limits to throughput growth, while alleviating poverty in the world. Many local thresholds have been broached because of population pressures and poverty; global thresholds are being broached by industrial countries' overconsumption.

To conclude on an optimistic note: the Organization for Economic Cooperation and Development (OECD) found in 1984 that environmental expenditures are good for the economy and good for employment. The 1988 Worldwatch study (Brown 1988) speculated that most sustainability could be achieved by the year 2000 with additional annual expenditures increasing gradually to U.S. $150 billion in 2000. Money is available: World Bank President Barber Conable calculated early in 1991 that industrial country trade barriers cost developing countries about U.S. $100 billion in foregone income—twice the interest paid annually by developing countries on their international debt. Most measures needed to approach sustainability are beneficial also for other reasons (fuel efficiency, for example). The world's nations have annually funded UNEP with about U.S. $30 million, although they propose now "to consider" increasing this sum to U.S. $100 million. It is not financial capital shortage that limits the economy anymore. It is shortages of both natural capital as well as of political will in the industrialized world. Yet we fail to follow economic logic and invest in the limiting factor.

Many nations spend less on environment, health, education, and welfare than they do on arms, which now annually total U.S. $1 trillion worldwide. Global security is increasingly prejudiced by source and sink constraints as recent natural resource wars have shown, such as the 1974 "cod" war between the United Kingdom and Iceland, the 1969 "football" war between overpopulated El Salvador and underpopulated Honduras, and the 1991 Persian Gulf war. As soon as damage to global life-support systems is perceived as far riskier than military threats, more prudent reallocation will promptly follow.

References

Adams, W. M. *Green Development: Environment and Sustainability in the Third World.* London: Routledge,1990.

Agarwal, A., and S. Narain. *Towards Green Villages.* Delhi: Center for Science and Environment, 1990.

Arrhenius, E., and T. W. Waltz. *The Greenhouse Effect: Implications for Economic Development.* Discussion Paper 78. Washington, D.C.: World Bank, 1990.

Boulding, K. "Ecological Paramountcy." In *Ecological Economics,* edited by R. Costanza. New York: Columbia University Press, 1991.

Brown, L. R., et al. *State of the World.* Washington, D.C.: Worldwatch Institute, 1988. (See also *State of the World* for 1989, 1990, and 1991.)

Catton, W. R. *Overshoot: The Ecological Basis of Revolutionary Change.* Chicago: University of Illinois Press, 1982.

Chambers, R., N. C. Saxena, and T. Shah. *To the Hands of the Poor.* London: Intermediate Technology, 1990.

Conroy, C., and M. Litvinoff. *The Greening of Aid: Sustainable Livelihoods in Practice.* London: Earthscan, 1988.

Costanza, R., ed. *Ecological Economics: The Science and Management of Sustainability.* New York: Columbia University Press, 1991.

Court, T. de la. *Beyond Brundtland: Green Development in the 1990s.* London: Zed Books, 1990.

Daily, G. C., and P. R. Ehrlich. "An Exploratory Model of the Impact of Rapid Climate Change on the World Food Situation." *Proceedings Royal Society* (1990): 232–44.

Daly, H. E. "Toward Some Operational Principles of Sustainable Development." *Ecological Economics* 2(1990): 1–6.

Daly, H. E. "Boundless Bull." *Gannett Center Journal* 4(3) (1990): 113–18.

Daly, H. E. "Ecological Economics and Sustainable Development." In *Ecological Physical Chemistry,* edited by C. Rossi and E. Tiezzi. Amsterdam: Elsevier, 1991.

Daly, H. E. "Towards an Environmental Macroeconomics." In *Ecological Economics,* edited by R. Costanza. New York: Columbia University Press, 1991.

Daly, H. E. "Sustainable Development: From Conceptual Theory Towards Operational Principles." *Population and Development Review.* Forthcoming.

Daly, H. E., and J. B. Cobb. *For the Common Good: Redirecting the Economy Toward Community, the Environment, and a Sustainable Future.* Boston: Beacon Press, 1989.

Ehrlich, P. "The Limits to Substitution: Meta-Resource Depletion and a New Economic-Ecologic Paradigm." *Ecological Economics* 1(1) (1989): 9–16.

Ehrlich, P., and A. Ehrlich. *The Population Explosion.* New York: Simon & Schuster, 1990.

El Serafy, S. "The Environment as Capital." In *Ecological Economics,* edited by R. Costanza. New York: Columbia University Press, 1991.

Foy, G. "Economic Sustainability and the Preservation of Environmental Assets." *Environmental Management* 14(6) (1990): 771–78.

Goldsmith, E., N. Hildyard, and P. Bunyard. *5000 Days to Save the Planet.* London: Hamlyn, 1990.

Goodland, R. *Tropical Deforestation: Solutions, Ethics and Religion.* Environment Department Working Paper 43. Washington, D.C.: World Bank, 1991.

Goodland, R., E. Asibey, J. Post, and M. Dyson. "Tropical Moist Forest Management: The Urgency of Transition to Sustainability." *Environmental Conservation* 17(4) (1991): 303–18.

Goodland, R., and G. Ledec. "Neoclassical Economics and Sustainable Development." *Ecological Modelling* 38(1987): 19–46.

Goodland, R., and H. E. Daly. "The Missing Tools (for Sustainability)." In *Planet Under Stress: The Challenge of Global Change,* edited by C. Mungall and D. J. McLaren. Toronto: Oxford University Press, 1990.

Haavelmo, T. "The Big Dilemma, International Trade and the North–South Cooperation." In *Economics Policies for Sustainable Development.* Manila: Asian Development Bank, 1990.

Hardin, G. "Paramount Positions in Ecological Economics." In *Ecological Economics,* edited by R. Costanza. New York: Columbia University Press, 1991.

Hueting, R. "The Brundtland Report: A Matter of Conflicting Goals." *Ecological Economics* 2(2) (1990): 109–18. Lovins, A. B. "Does Abating Global Warming Cost or Save Money?" *Rocky Mountain Institute* 6(3) (1990): 1–3.

MacNeill, J. "Strategies for Sustainable Development." *Scientific American* 261(3) (1989): 154–65.

Meadows, D. H., et al. *The Limits to Growth: A Report for the Club of Rome's Project on the Predicament of Mankind.* 2d ed. New York: Universe Books, 1974.

Office of Technology Assessment. *Energy in Developing Countries.* Washington, D.C.: OTA, 1991.

Pimentel, D., et al. "World Agriculture and Soil Erosion." *BioScience* 37(4) (1987): 277–83.

Shea, C. P. "Protecting Life on Earth: Steps to Save the Ozone Layer." Worldwatch Paper No. 87. Washington, D.C.: Worldwatch Institute, 1989.

Speth, J. G. "A Luddite Recants: Technological Innovation and the Environment." *The Amicus Journal* (Spring 1989): 3–5.

Tinbergen, J., and R. Hueting. "GNP and Market Prices: Wrong Signals for Sustainable Economic Success That Mask Environmental Destruction."

Vitousek, Peter M., et al. "Human Appropriation of the Products of Photosynthesis." *BioScience* 34(6) (1986): 368–73.

World Commission on Environment and Development. "Our Common Future" (The Brundtland Report). Oxford: Oxford University Press, 1987.

90. The Climate-Change Debacle: The Perils of Politicizing Science

Patrick J. Michaels

During the past decade much has been said about the "greenhouse effect," whereby a portion of the heat energy radiated from the earth is recycled near the earth's surface; carbon dioxide, methane, water vapor, and other gases in the atmosphere prevent some of this energy from directly passing out to space. The combustion of fossil fuels (petroleum, coal, natural gas) is the primary cause of the increases in these gases. The enhanced greenhouse effect, also known as "global warming," potentially represents the greatest environmental disturbance ever associated with our species.

Concern that climate may be changing and that human beings are the cause is not new. Thomas Jefferson hypothesized that the deforestation of the Mid-Atlantic region resulted in changed wind patterns as far west as the Blue Ridge Mountains. (He was wrong.) A hundred years later, the British physicist John Tyndall performed pioneering laboratory experiments on the absorption of infrared energy by certain constituents of the atmosphere, including carbon dioxide and water vapor. In 1896, the Swedish chemist Svante Arrhenius generalized Tyndall's findings to the globe and concluded that if the atmospheric carbon dioxide were to double, the mean temperature of the planet would rise some five degrees Celsius.

Half a century later, the invention of the digital computer allowed Arrhenius's findings to be generalized to specific regions and seasons. The result was "General Circulation Models" (GCMs), which can simulate the atmosphere disturbed by an enhanced greenhouse effect. For estimating future climatic change, these simulations form the only quantitative scientific formulation of sufficient resolution that does not rely upon past temperature records or geological results of limited accuracy. They are the basis for the United Nations Framework Convention on Climate Change, the "Rio Treaty," described below. The GCMs, and the rather dire pictures they paint, are the most important component of the call for action on global warming.

Rarely acknowledged in any debate are several important points concerning the substantial limitations and unreliability of the simulations. This omission probably occurs, not out of an attempt to mislead the public, but because many in the environmental community lack the training required to appreciate some important subtleties.

The primitive mid-1980s versions of these models were the ones most featured in congressional hearings about global warming that began around 1985. These models predicted, on the

Creation at Risk? Religion, Science, and Environmentalism, edited by Michael Cromartie, ©1995 The Michigan Ethics and Public Policy Center. Used by permission of Wm. B. Eerdmans Publishing Co., Grand Rapids, Michigan.

average, that the mean surface temperature of the earth will warm up 4.2°C (7.6°F) if the concentration of atmospheric carbon dioxide is doubled. In the high latitudes of the Northern Hemisphere, the projected winter changes average around 8°C (14.4°F), and in some areas are nearly 20°C (36°F). The most recent generation of these models predicts a somewhat reduced average warming of 3.4°C (6.1°F) for a doubling of CO_2.

The Fudge Factors

In 1994 three MIT scientists investigated what *Science* magazine now refers to as the "fudge factors" in these climate models. Left to their own devices and working solely with known scientific principles, the models simulate a climate that simply does not exist. To correct for this, modelers introduced artificial changes in the amount of warming radiation moving poleward. Removing the "fudge factor" after getting the "right" answer then resulted in unreliable forecasts of the future (which should come as no surprise).

Consider one of the most advanced American GCMs, the coupled atmosphere-ocean model published in the August 1991 *Journal of Climate*.[1] In order to achieve a realistic nineteenth-century climate, this GCM assumes that the energy coming from the sun is some 20 watts per square meter less than it really is. Normally, around half of the sun's radiation actually goes to warm the atmosphere as it passes through, so the effect of unrealistically decreasing the sun's output by 20 watts actually translates to about 10 watts per square meter at the surface of the planet. But enhancing the greenhouse effect by doubling the carbon dioxide in the atmosphere is equivalent to increasing radiation at the earth's surface by about 4.0 watts per square meter. Consequently, the "adjustment" factor used to get the right temperature before an increase in CO_2 is factored in is in fact over twice as large as the change expected to be caused by a change in CO_2.

Thus we cannot simulate the current climate from known scientific principles. Therefore the question "how much do we expect the climate to change?" becomes impossible to answer with confidence. In recognition of this problem, a facile switch was made in all GCMs that few people outside the climate-modeling community are aware of: model output is presented, not as the expected change from, say, the current climate, or even the

global climate around 1900, but as the difference between two model runs, one using "$1 \times CO_2$" and the other using "$2 \times CO_2$." The "forecast" is actually one model, complete with the systematic errors described above (and many more), subtracted from an equally flawed "background" model.

Imagine that today's weather forecast for the Corn Belt was, say, ten degrees too hot, but that the forecaster knew it and arbitrarily subtracted away from the error. This is what occurs in climate models. In the weather-forecast situation, all subsequent computer products that were made public, ranging from the probability of severe thunderstorms to the agricultural forecast for crop spraying, would appear reasonable; yet they would be driven by a model that was producing known and large errors of agricultural consequence. Knowing that an error of this magnitude was lurking in the weather forecast, would society make expensive plans as a result?

Similar and unfortunately very real problems (unlike the fabricated one in our weather-forecasting example) are present in the GCMs, and, on the basis of these faulty models, we have signed a treaty that has the potential to force the most dramatic managing of the American economy in the nation's history.

It is not surprising that the amount of global warming predicted by the average of current GCMs—3.4°C for a doubling of CO_2—is in the range of Arrhenius's original calculation. But he also calculated that the temperature rise at the point halfway to a doubling of pre-industrial CO_2, which is where we stand today, would be 3.0°C. Even scientists who are not fluent with the temperature history of the planet know that it has not warmed nearly this amount since the enhancement began.

Examining the Assertions

A forecast is nothing but a scientific hypothesis, and hypotheses stand or fall on objective fact rather than on other computer simulations. Let us look at the assertions that accompany the GCM forecasts:

1. The history of climatic warming should be consonant with the enhancement of the greenhouse effect.

2. Water warms more slowly than land. Therefore the Southern Hemisphere, which is mostly

water at its surface, should warm much more slowly than the Northern Hemisphere, which contains almost all of the planetary landmass.

3. Warming should be greatest in the high latitudes of both hemispheres.

The combination of several greenhouse-enhancing gases (carbon dioxide, methane, chlorofluorocarbons, nitrous oxide, in descending order) has raised the CO_2 level in the atmosphere from the natural 270 parts per million to approximately 410 (expressed as CO_2 equivalents to allow for the different characteristics of the various greenhouse gases). Almost half of this increase has been since World War II.

Approximately 13 per cent of the current "warming potential" arises from chlorofluorocarbons (CFCs). These compounds, once used widely as aerosol propellants and refrigerants, are being phased out of production in accordance with the Montreal Protocol on substances that deplete stratospheric ozone. They are very effective greenhouse gases; had they been left unchecked, their increase would have made them responsible for 20 per cent of the warming potential by the middle of the next century. Although the elimination of CFCs clearly will reduce the rise in the greenhouse effect, the United Nations does not take account of this in its reckoning.

Projections vs. Observations

The surface-temperature histories for the Southern and Northern Hemispheres published by the U.S. Department of Energy support a rise of 0.45°C plus or minus .10° in the last 100 years, on a global scale.[2] But the mid-1980s GCM projections produce an expected warming—given the observed trace-gas change—of around 2.0°C.

In addition, the "water" (Southern) hemisphere should warm up more slowly. While most of its measuring stations are on land, the fact that so much of the hemisphere is water means there is more oceanic influence on the record there than occurs in the Northern Hemisphere. However, the Southern Hemisphere shows the *greater* "greenhouse-like" effect.

Trend analysis of the global surface-temperature records demonstrates, in a statistical sense, that much of the observed warming was realized prior to 1945.[3] In 1945 the concentration of greenhouse gases was approximately 310ppm,

compared to today's 410; only a quarter of the enhancement of the greenhouse gases (from the natural 270ppm) that we observe today had occurred. This means, then, that there has been relatively little additional warming during the period in which three-quarters of the greenhouse-effect change has taken place.

Even the United Nations concurs. In the famous 1990 report of the Intergovernmental Panel on Climate Change, page 246 makes it quite apparent that during the last fifty years the global temperature has *never* been on the warming track projected by the mid-1980s GCMs.[4] The report states that if the rise in twentieth-century temperatures were caused only by changing the greenhouse effect, then the net rise for doubled CO_2 would be only 1.3°C.

Furthermore, it is not known how much of the warming measured in surface-based records is attributable to the "urban warming effect," a common problem that results because cities tend to grow around weather-observing stations. Satellite data, which began in 1979, show no statistically significant warming of either hemisphere between 1979 and 1995, though the ground-based records for the same period in the Southern Hemisphere do show some warming. . . .

The surface-based records also show very little difference in the overall ground-based temperature changes in the two hemispheres, even though the predominance of land in the Northern Hemisphere should result in a more rapid warming.

Polar temperature histories are also inconsistent with the prime assertions about climatic change. In the coupled ocean-atmosphere GCM of Manabe et al. in which the greenhouse effect changes more realistically than in previous models, the high latitudes of the Northern Hemisphere are predicted to have warmed by 2.0°C since 1950.[5] But the Department of Energy compendium of temperature records indicates a rapid rise in Arctic temperatures *prior* to most of the greenhouse-gas emissions. In most polar records, the rise in temperature is followed by a decline, from the 1940s to the mid-70s, similar in proportion to the rise.

All GCMs suggest that the polar warming will be magnified in winter. Nonetheless, there has been a substantial decline in winter temperatures over the Atlantic Arctic since 1920,[6] and there has been no change in polar night temperatures averaged over Antarctica.[7] Kahl et al. found no net warming of the Arctic, and there was even some evidence for a cooling of winter temperatures.[8] Conversely, Kalkstein et al. have documented that, while there has been no net warming of the North American Arctic, the coldest air masses, whose mean surface temperatures are approximately –40°, have warmed some two degrees .[9]

Is the Warming "Hidden"?

Most scientists who are conversant with both the GCMs and the temperature histories now acknowledge the discrepancies between greenhouse assertions about climatic warming and the observed temperatures. As a result, some have argued that the predicted effect has been obscured by the "anti-greenhouse" products of combustion, such as sulfate aerosol.[10] If this is true, then the GCMs should perform significantly better in sulfate-free environments, such as the Southern Hemisphere or both polar regions, and poorer in the sulfate regions of eastern North America, Europe, and East Asia.

Sulfate aerosols hypothetically counter greenhouse warming by increasing the reflectivity of the lower atmosphere (via direct aerosol backscattering) so that more heat is radiated away from the earth's surface, or by serving as condensation nuclei that increase the amount of low-level (stratiform) clouds. In either case the prime effect is reflective, so the sulfate effect should be more pronounced in the summer, when the clouds have the longest length of day to reflect radiation.

In a recent paper, we examined the detailed behavior of the *Journal of Climate* GCM cited earlier. We divided our study into the polar regions, the earth's hemispheres, and the sulfate region of the Northern Hemisphere.[11] Studies were separated into winter and summer. If sulfates were mitigating the warming predicted by the model, the following should be observed:

1. The model should perform worst where sulfates are highly concentrated.

2. The model should perform better in the Southern Hemisphere, as almost all sulfate emissions are in the Northern Hemisphere.

3. The model should perform best in the polar regions, which are virtually sulfate-free.

In general, we found that we could no longer entertain the primary hypothesis that underlies policy proposals on global warming: that the *observed* patterns of climatic change resemble those that were *predicted*.

Further, we found no support for the hypothesis that the counter-effect of sulfate aerosol is a sufficient cause of this failure. None of the three hypotheses concerning GCM behavior difference over the sulfate region, between hemispheres, and between the poles and the hemispheres is supported by the data. In fact, in the sulfate region the only patterns in which what was forecast resembled what was observed occurred in the summer—when the model should be most compromised by sulfates. In this case, the model correctly captures the statistically most important pattern of observed climatic change, thus *countering* the sulfate hypothesis.

The addition to a GCM of any type of parameter that reduces the predicted warming, particularly in the mid-latitudes of the Northern Hemisphere (where the sulfate density is greatest), will increase the correspondence between the model and reality. Thus we can expect a number of simulations to appear in which reflectivity or low cloud cover is increased in these regions, and consequent reduced warming will be initially forecast, followed by a more rapid warming as the compensating parameter is removed. But our results suggest that calculating this compensation in a sulfate-region GCM, as was done by Hansen et al.,[12] will make the GCM "right" for the wrong reason, for its failure was in fact greater in the sulfate-free polar region. This alteration of GCMs will make them even more unreliable as estimators of future climate than they had been in their more pristine state.

The Rio Treaty

Most nations in the world have ratified the 1992 United Nations Framework Convention on Climate Change, first signed in Rio de Janeiro at the Earth Summit. The stated purpose of the treaty is to "achieve . . . stabilization of greenhouse gas concentrations in the atmosphere at a level that would prevent dangerous anthropogenic interference with the climate system."

So we have agreed to stabilize greenhouse gases at a level that would prevent man's "dangerous interference" with the climate. But GCMs indicate that we have already interfered with the climate in a "dangerous" fashion, while the observed data are in large part counter to GCM forecasts. If we are at the "danger" level, the required reduction in greenhouse-gas emissions from today's level would be 60 to 80 per cent. In the United States, for example, this would require emission rates somewhere around the 1930 level. In developing nations, there would be virtually no fossil-fuel combustion.

No one knows how to do this. In October 1993, President Clinton announced a "voluntary" program, known as the "Climate Change Action Plan," to meet one goal of the Rio Treaty: the reduction of emissions to 1990 levels by the year 2000. Even if successful, this plan will not advance the overall treaty objective, because it will not contribute to "stabilization of greenhouse-gas concentrations." All it says is that we will reduce our emissions to 1990 levels. In 1990, greenhouse-gas concentrations were increasing by approximately 25 parts per million in equivalent CO_2 every ten years; reducing emissions to that level merely maintains that level of increase, rather than "stabilizing" the concentrations.

Even though the GCM forecasts appear to have overestimated warming, we can use them to estimate how much warming this policy will prevent. If their forecasts are assumed to be correct it is a very small amount: if all the nations succeeded in implementing Clinton's program, the amount of warming that would be prevented through the year 2025 would be approximately 0.2°C.

The "voluntary" program, not surprisingly, is failing. Writing in Spring 1994 in the newsletter *Energy, Economics and Climate Change,* analyst Nick Sundt calculated that, by the end of 1993, U.S. emissions had reached levels that would have occurred in 1996 without any attempt to limit them. According to Howard Geller of the American Council for an Energy Efficient Economy, this resulted because of the "rapid economic growth, low energy prices, and unfavorable weather" (meaning the cold winter of 1993–94, not global warming).

The objective of the Rio Treaty, as stated above, is to stabilize greenhouse-gas concentrations in the atmosphere "at a level that would prevent dangerous anthropogenic interference with the climate system." More important are some provisions in its various articles. A number of these are quoted and (in most cases) commented on below.

From Article 3: Principles

ARTICLE 3.1 and ARTICLE 3.2: "The Parties should protect the climate system . . . on the basis of equity. . . . Accordingly, the developed country Parties should take the lead in combating climate change and the adverse effects thereof" (3.1). "The specific needs and special circumstances of developing country Parties . . . should be given full consideration" (3.2).

Comment: Twenty-five nations with a high Gross Domestic Product (Russia and the other former Soviet states are notably excepted) will have the goal of reducing emissions to 1990 levels by the year 2000. (This will hereafter be referred to as the 1990/2000 goal.) All others, whose emissions are growing at a much faster rate than those of the high-GDP states, are not constrained by any goal, even though their emissions will be the largest of any group of nations by early in the twenty-first century.

ARTICLE 3.3: "Where there are threats of serious or irreversible damage, lack of full scientific certainty should not be used as a reason for postponing . . . measures [to anticipate, prevent, or minimize the causes of climate change and mitigate its adverse effects]."

Comment: As long as an argument can be made that there is some "threat" of serious damage, action may not be postponed despite the existence of scientific data that may not be consistent with that threat. Signatories can therefore be forced to reduce emissions in spite of any evidence that it might not be necessary.

ARTICLE 3.4: "Policies and measures to protect the climate system . . . should be integrated with national development programmes."

Comment: The U.N. assumes that all nations centrally plan their development.

From Article 4: Commitments

ARTICLE 4.1a: "[The signatories will] develop. . . national inventories of anthropogenic emissions by sources and removals by sinks of all greenhouse gases not controlled by the Montreal Protocol."

Comment: This important clause was designed to keep the nations (notably the United States) that have produced considerable amounts of chlorofluorocarbons (CFCs), which are being eliminated by the Montreal Protocol for stratospheric ozone protection, from counting those eliminations as reductions in global-warming potential. Yet they *are* reductions in warming potential, and the United States could easily meet the 1990/2000 goal with the phase-out of CFCs that has already been mandated by Congress.

ARTICLE 4.1c: "Promote and cooperate in the development, application and diffusion, *including transfer,* of technologies . . . that . . . reduce or prevent anthropogenic emissions of greenhouse gases [emphasis added]."

Comment: This treaty can mandate the *transfer* (which does not mean the sale) of energy technologies to nations that are relatively inefficient. The result of this clause has been to enlist the support of many lobbying organizations associated with energy technology, because, if the technology is "transferred" without cost to a foreign country, it will still have to be purchased here—by taxpayer dollars—before it is transferred.

ARTICLE 4.1i: "Promote and cooperate in education . . . and . . . awareness related to climate change and encourage the widest participation in the process, including that of non-governmental organizations."

Comment: Virtually all the "non-governmental organizations" represented at the Rio Earth Summit (where the treaty was signed) were either environmental groups, such as Greenpeace, or group-rights advocates. The signatories are therefore bound to "encourage . . . participation" in the environmental educational process by these groups.

ARTICLE 4.2a: "[Each of the signatory developed countries shall] adopt national policies and take corresponding measures on the mitigation of climate change, by limiting its anthropogenic emissions of greenhouse gases and protecting and enhancing its greenhouse sinks and reservoirs."

Comment: Here the signatories commit themselves to reducing greenhouse-gas emissions and "protecting and enhancing" sinks, which by and large means forested land. In other words, the developed nations may violate this treaty if they do not limit emissions or if they do not increase their forested land. This article is an open invitation for environmental organizations to bring suit against the signatories, as has already occurred in Australia.

ARTICLE 4.2b: "[Each of the signatory developed countries] in order to promote progress towards this end [Article 4.2a] shall communicate, within six months of the entry into force of the convention . . . detailed information on its policies on greenhouse gases not controlled by the Montreal Protocol [see 4.1a, above] . . . with the aim of returning to [the 1990/2000 goal]."

Comment: This meeting took place in Berlin in March 1995. Signatories agreed to set specific emission reductions (beyond the 1990/2000 goal) at Tokyo in 1997. This commits the United States to some type of increased reduction, but specific targets and scheduling were not announced.

ARTICLE 4.3: "The developed country Parties . . . shall provide *new and additional* financial resources to meet the agreed full costs incurred by the developing countries under Article 12, Paragraph 1 [emphasis added]. They shall also provide such financial resources, including for the transfer of technology, needed by the developing country parties to meet the agreed full incremental costs of implementing measures that are covered by Paragraph 1 of this article. The implementation of these commitments shall take into account the need for adequacy . . . in the flow of funds and the importance of appropriate burden sharing among the developed country parties."

Comment: Article 12, Paragraph 1, states, among other things, that each signatory will communicate a description of steps taken to implement the convention. Article 4.3 can therefore be used to compel the developed nations to pay for whatever the developing nations say they must do to comply with the convention.

ARTICLE 4.4: "The developed country Parties . . . shall also assist the developing country Parties that are particularly vulnerable to the adverse effects of climate change in meeting costs of adaptation to those adverse effects [emphasis added]."

Comment: Because no climate model can confirm or deny that a particular phenomenon—say, increased drought frequency in Sahelian Africa—is related to greenhouse emissions, developed nations may simply assert such a claim and demand compensation based on this treaty.

ARTICLE 4.5: "The developed country Parties. . . shall take all practicable steps to promote, facilitate and *finance* . . . the transfer of, or access to, environmentally sound technologies and know-how to other Parties, particularly developing country Parties . . . [emphasis added]."

Comment: This important clause states that the developed nations will subsidize the purchase of technologies and "know-how" (which may mean patented processes) to other nations. This means, in the United States, that companies that produce more efficient energy technology will have that technology exported at taxpayer expense. It is therefore not surprising that an industrial consortium has arisen that strongly supports the treaty, despite its ultimate goal. This clause can require that public monies be used to purchase privately held technology that is ultimately given or lent to Third World nations.

ARTICLE 4.6: "In the implementation of their commitments . . . a certain degree of flexibility shall be allowed by the Conference of the Parties to the Parties included in Annex I undergoing the transition to a market economy. . . ."

Comment: The parties listed in Annex I, those to be allowed "flexibility," are Belarus, Bulgaria, Czechoslovakia, Estonia, Hungary, Latvia, Lithuania, Poland, Romania, Russia, and Ukraine. And so these articles really apply only to the industrialized democracies; the formerly Communist countries are relieved of their responsibilities.

ARTICLE 6(a)(i): "The parties shall promote . . . the development and implementation of educational and public awareness programmes on climate change and its effects and (iii) public participation in addressing climate change and its effects and developing adequate responses."

From Article 21: Interim Arrangements

ARTICLE 21.2: "The head of the interim secretariat . . . will cooperate closely with the Intergovernmental Panel on Climate Change (IPCC) to ensure that the Panel can respond to the need for objective scientific and technical advice. Other relevant scientific bodies could also be consulted."

Comment: The IPCC, a United Nations entity that is used to define scientific "consensus," can serve as the sole scientific advisory panel for this treaty.

From Article 25: Withdrawal

ARTICLE 25.1: "At any time after three years from the date on which the Convention has entered into force . . . a . . . party may withdraw . . . by giving written notification. . . ."

Comment: Any of the signatories, including the United States, can legally withdraw from the Framework Convention on Climate Change by sending a letter after March 21, 1997.

Future Policy

The Clinton administration has stated that the commitments made in the Rio Treaty are not adequate because they do not address what will happen beyond the year 2000. Indeed, as noted above, if the "danger" argument is cited, the commitments are clearly insufficient and will have little effect on the predicted global warning. In early 1995 Germany proposed a 20 per cent reduction in emissions (from 1990 levels) by the year 2005 as the new goal for the treaty. The DRI-McGraw-Hill econometric firm has estimated that by the year 2020 this would cost $2,500 per capita per year (in 1989 dollars) in the United States. Ironically, this reduction in emissions would have only a modest effect on global warming.

We have entered into a treaty designed to prevent a "dangerous" climate change that is predicted by models that aren't working, and we have produced a policy that cannot succeed. How did this happen?

It seems obvious that there is a considerable disconnection between early forecasts and recent observations of climate change. Yet GCM forecasts were at the core of the 1990 "Report of the Intergovernmental Panel on Climate Change" of the United Nations Environment Programme, which served as the scientific basis for the Rio Treaty.

As we saw in looking at Article 3.3, "where there are threats of serious or irreversible damage," the signatories may not postpone action on the basis of a "lack of full scientific certainty." Many have taken this to mean that the normal process of verification of hypotheses (that is, of forecasts) by observation is not required before the nations of the world undertake expensive steps to reduce greenhouse emissions.

Why didn't scientists object to this clear perversion of their professional ethic? In my opinion, the answer lies in the nature of science funding. Virtually every active academic researcher in the environmental sciences is supported by the federal government. Large amounts of research support have been directed towards the issue of global climate change.

Since this support would stop if the research community were to say that much of the concern about this issue was misplaced, the policy community received little if any signal indicating that the models were not being verified by observed data.

Diversification: A Solution?

The current situation resulted in large part because scientists are forced to work in a "single provider" research funding system. All of the imbalances that attend a monopoly can be expected to occur: politicization, disequilibrium between true and perceived need, and disproportionate funding of those who express agreement with the monopoly's goals. Because this monopoly is publicly funded and is administered by agencies that require congressional oversight, there is certain to be some political bias with respect to the programs that receive the most funding.

Particularly with applied research, it was not always the case that funding came from a single provider, the federal government. In fact, the federalization of science was relatively inconsequential until the advent of the Manhattan Project, which built the atomic bomb during World War II. Before that, most science was funded by industry, either in-house or at universities. The change from private to public funding was seen by many as a good thing because it gave scientists some freedom from the presumed biases of industry. As long as there was a reasonable mix of the two sources, some type of competition between biases—industry and federal—could create a fertile mix for scientific progress.

That mix, or dynamic equilibrium, does not exist today in the environmental sciences, particularly with respect to climate change. There is virtually no private funding, and the federal biases are obvious. While serving in the Senate, for example, Albert Gore was chairman of the Subcommittee on Science, Space and Technology, which oversees the budgets of both the National Science Foundation and NASA. It is difficult to envision these agency heads testifying at budget hearings in front of the senator-environmentalist that global climate change is not so important an issue that it merits a substantial increase in their budgets!

The States' Interests

The policies that result from this type of bias are often at odds with the interests of certain states. One would be hard put to imagine, for example,

that Virginia, West Virginia, Pennsylvania, and Wyoming—major coal-producing states—would enthusiastically support some type of tax on the carbon content of fuels, which is what *must* ultimately be mandated to reduce emissions enough to stabilize CO_2 concentration at or slightly above the current level.

One solution to the problem of federal-monopoly bias is to encourage the reappearance of the competing-industry bias. However, it would seem inappropriate to foster such an effort at the federal level, because the federal bias would ultimately reappear. Rather, states should undertake such a program.

The 1994 session of the Pennsylvania State Legislature saw the passage of a bill designed to create a bias that would compete with the federal bias on funding for climate research. The Bill, called the "Interstate Climate Change Research Act," was passed by the legislature but vetoed by the governor, who said he was committed to funding no new programs during that legislative cycle. (A similar bill was introduced in the 1995 Illinois legislature.)

The Pennsylvania bill had some interesting provisions. It pointed out that climate change could be either deleterious or beneficial, that a great deal of uncertainty surrounds the issue, that the cost of regulation to inhibit prospective changes may be severe, that the impact of regulation would fall disproportionately, and that "certain states may have a differential interest in this issue between them and the federal government." The proposed research would address both negative and positive aspects of climate change in an evenhanded fashion. Funding would originate from for-profit corporations that could reduce their state tax burden by an equivalent amount.

The intent of the Pennsylvania bill was clearly to encourage private industry to fund a basic research pool on climate change. If industry perceived that its contributions were not being well spent (i.e., were not funding research that was appropriate for their bias), then it is likely that their financial support would cease.

It will be interesting to see whether analogous legislation will be submitted in other states that are particularly affected by climate-change regulation.

A Modest Proposal

We have sown the wind—making politics the prime determinant of scientific research targets, using planned science as a vehicle for national planning—and we are now reaping the whirlwind. The political recognition has begun that perhaps federal management is not the only solution to our scientific problems—that, in fact, a single-provider federal science system necessarily produces skewed results and consequent bad policy.

The climate-change debacle—where politicized science created impossible policy—should serve as a model of what is wrong with government monopolies in the information business. Besides leading the United States to sign a treaty it cannot uphold without disrupting its own energy economy, it is also likely to result in a great deal of public distrust of science in general.

A modest proposal: As a public signal that this will no longer be tolerated, perhaps we should legally withdraw from the Rio Treaty, then disburse treaty costs to the states for enhanced research, and start over with a more diverse science base. That might be one benefit that accrues from the great climate-change debacle.

Notes

1. S. Manabe et al., "Transient Responses of a Coupled Ocean-Atmosphere Model to Gradual Changes of Atmospheric CO_2: Part One: Annual Mean Response," *Journal of Climate* 4 (1991): 785–818.

2. R. C. Bailing and S. B. Idso, "100 Years of Global Warming?," *Environmental Conservation* 17 (1990): 165.

3. Ibid.

4. Intergovernmental Panel on Climate Change, "Scientific Assessment of Climate Change" (U.N. Environment Programme, 1990).

5. Manabe, "Transient Responses."

6. J. C. Rogers, Proceedings, 13th Annual Climate Diagnostics Workshop (U.S. Department of Commerce, 1989).

7. J. Samson, "Antarctic Surface Temperature Time Series," *Journal of Climate* 2 (1989): 1164–72.

8. J. D. Kahl et al., "Absence of Evidence for Greenhouse Warming Over the Arctic Ocean in the Past Forty Years," *Nature* 361 (1993): 335–37.

9. L. S. Kalkstein, T. C. Dunne, and R. S. Vose, "Detection of Climate Change in the Western North American Arctic Using a Synoptic Climatological Approach," *Journal of Climate* 3 (1990): 1154–67.

10. T. M. L. Wigley, "Could Reducing Fossil-Fuel Emissions End Global Warming?," *Nature* 349 (1991): 503–5; R. J. Charlson et al., "Climate Forcing by Anthropogenic Aerosols," *Science* 225 (1992): 423–30.

11. Patrick J. Michaels, D. C. Knappenberger, and D. A. Gay, "General Circulation Models: Testing the Forecast," *Technology: Journal of the Franklin Institute* 331A (1994): 123–33.

12. J. E. Hansen, M. Sato, and R. Ruedy, "Long-Term Changes of the Diurnal Temperature Cycle: Implications About Mechanisms of Global Climate Change," U.S. Department of Energy Conf. 9309350, 1993, 313–25.

91. A Response

Christopher Flavin

One of the things I wonder about when listening to Pat Michaels and his "conservative" supporters is why it is considered conservative to view with complacency the idea of profoundly disrupting the world's atmosphere, while assuming (or hoping) that the consequences will be benign. Most conservatives are risk averse and want to protect what we have. Why then would a conservative go out of his way to dismiss all the scientific evidence pointing to climate change, and search obsessively for bits of data that indicate even the slimmest chance that humanity might survive the unprecedented experiment we are conducting with the earth's atmosphere? Conservatives also consider themselves the custodians of values and ethics. But is it ethical to disrupt the natural world without regard to the impact on our descendants or on Creation itself?

Creation at Risk? Religion, Science, and Environmentalism, edited by Michael Cromartie, ©1995 The Ethics and Public Policy Center. Used by permission of Wm. B. Eerdmans Publishing Co., Grand Rapids, Michigan.

Michaels's debating style is to pick a few holes in the vast body of scientific evidence on climate change and assume that listeners will not notice that most of the evidence remains unchallenged. The enormous complexity and inevitable uncertainty entailed in atmospheric science make this approach an easy one to pursue, but it results in a profoundly incomplete and dangerous view of the climate issue.

Michaels's presentation relies heavily on his opinion that the Global Circulation Models used by scientific teams to understand climate change are inconsistent with the record of actual temperature changes in the last century or so. Indeed, all scientists agree that the climate models in use today are imperfect. They do not fully represent the earth's extraordinarily complex atmospheric system, and are not capable of predicting exactly what the climate will be in Washington, D.C., a hundred years from now.

Yet to ignore the climate models because they are not perfect is akin to refusing to have a medical checkup because you can't be sure the doctor will predict precisely what your health will be in the future. Imperfect though they are, the climate models provide invaluable insights into the fundamentals of climate change. It is also notable that there have been substantial improvements in climate modeling in the past few years, so that the latest models are able to emulate the historic climate record much more closely than ever before. These models were also vindicated when the cooling effect of the Mount Pinatubo eruption in the early 1990s closely paralleled the magnitude predicted by climate modelers shortly after the eruption. In 1994, the IPCC released a draft of its second major climate-change assessment, confirming the likelihood of a rapid warming in the coming decade.[1]

Scientists have recently managed to integrate oceanic and atmospheric models, and are now able to incorporate the cooling effect of sulfate aerosols. The model developed by the Hadley Center for Climate Prediction and Research at the Meteorological Office in Bracknell, England, which includes the effects of sulfates, shows that the historic temperature record over the past century correlates very closely with their model's predictions, demonstrating a 0.6°C rise in global temperatures since the onset of the Industrial Revolution.[2] The Max Planck Institute in Germany has used similar data to conclude that there is now a 95 per cent

probability that the rise in temperature over the past century is caused by rising concentrations of greenhouse gases.[3] Indeed, even the layman has a hard time accepting the notion that it is a mere coincidence that the ten warmest years in the past century have all occurred since 1980.

Signs of Climate Change

Regional climate changes that have been detected recently are also consistent with the projections of Global Circulation Models. For example, the rapid warming of Antarctica projected by many models has been clearly detected in recent years and is causing deglaciation in some areas. North America, on the other hand, should not be experiencing much warming at this point—as a result of heavy sulfur emissions—which is in fact the case. The rapid warming of Europe in recent decades is also consistent with the climate models.

Other evidence also indicates change. Pine trees in northern Finland have begun a dramatic advance north into tundra areas in apparent response to warmer temperatures—at a rate of about forty meters per year, according to a scientist at the University of Helsinki. In Switzerland and Austria, researchers have documented a rapid retreat of many glaciers, uncovering areas that have been under deep ice for thousands of years. Oceanographers at the Hopkins Institute in Monterey, California, which has been tracking undersea life for sixty years, say that marine snails and other mollusks normally found in warm waters are now expanding their ranges north along the Pacific Coast, while coldwater species retreat.

Climate change is also indicated by a new space-based measuring device—an orbiting radar gun—that during the past three years has been able to detect a small but significant rate of increase in sea level, a trend that is consistent with the thermal expansion that occurs as a result of warming. Scientists have detected other "fingerprints" of climate change that suggest that greenhouse warming is under way. For example, in many parts of the world, tropical corals, which are highly sensitive to water temperature, are dying. Large-scale die-offs of oceanic plankton have also been detected. Health impacts are also being observed, according to some scientists. Researchers at Harvard University believe that recent outbreaks of cholera in South America, Hanta virus in the U.S.

Southwest, and pneumonic plague in India may all be connected to rising temperatures.

The timing of the earth's seasons, which is crucial to agriculture, may also be affected. A recent study by David J. Thomson, a scientist at AT&T's Bell Labs, demonstrates a profound shift in the timing of seasons that began in 1940, reversing a pattern of relative stability that had lasted for three hundred years.[4] Dr. Thomson believes there is an extremely high probability that this shift is related to the rapid rise in greenhouse-gas concentrations in recent decades. Another recent study demonstrates that since 1980, the climate of the United States has become substantially more extreme.[5]

Such evidence has convinced Thomas Karl, senior scientist at the National Oceanic and Atmospheric Administration, who was once the darling of Patrick Michaels and other skeptics, that "the data are consistent with the general trends expected from a greenhouse-enhanced atmosphere."[6] He puts the odds that the observed changes are merely a statistical blip at less than 10 per cent. Benjamin Santer, an atmospheric physicist at the Lawrence Berkeley National Laboratory, says, "The circumstantial evidence is getting stronger that the global warming signal is here."[7]

The Danger in Uncertainty

Of course, even as the scientific evidence has strengthened, many aspects of future climate change remain uncertain. But anyone who has studied the way complex science develops—and this is one of the *most* complex fields today—knows that this situation is quite routine. Such complexity almost always entails large degrees of uncertainty. Michaels argues that this uncertainty should make us complacent. According to his theorem, whenever we face a potentially disastrous but uncertain outcome, we should assume the best. "Don't worry, be happy," he tells us.

What the contrarians fail to acknowledge is that the very uncertainty associated with climate change is the biggest danger we face. If we knew for sure whether we will face a 2° or 6° change in global average temperature in the next century, and knew exactly what the effects of that change would be, then we would have a challenging but manageable problem. We could invest in dikes, build new water systems, and perhaps even develop new agricultural technologies.

It is, of course, possible, even likely, that the mean rate of climate change projected by the Intergovernmental Panel on Climate Change (IPCC), the official body of scientists that assesses these issues for the United Nations, will not be realized. Michaels argues that there may be a negative feedback effect, whether it be increased cloud cover or a carbon "sink" that might develop. This cannot be ruled out, but there is also a strong possibility that the rate of climate change and the degree of disruption to human societies might be greater than what the IPCC projects. For example, many scientists are concerned that warming could cause an extensive loss of northern boreal forests, releasing large additional quantities of carbon dioxide.[8] Moreover, warming of the tundra could release large quantities of methane. Either effect could accelerate the rate of climate change beyond what the IPCC is projecting. It is also possible that unanticipated, severe regional effects may occur if, for instance, a major oceanic current were to shift as a result of climate change. Some scientists, for example, hypothesize that a rapid temperature rise could melt both the west and east ice sheets of Antarctica, raising sea levels by up to 150 feet and submerging all the world's coastal cities.[9] In other words, there is a real chance that climate change will be more severe than most scientists currently predict.

We have seen this happen before. In the early 1970s, when the issue of depletion of the ozone layer first emerged as a scientific concern, scientists developed models to anticipate what might happen to the ozone layer as a result of chlorofluorocarbon emissions. Looking back, those models seem incredibly primitive—and ended up being dead wrong. The ozone-depletion problem turned out to be far *more* severe than had been projected. The biggest scientific surprise was the emergence of the "hole" in the ozone layer over Antarctica. This hole was so far from anything scientists had contemplated that when the first satellite observations began to come in showing a severe depletion of the Antarctic ozone layer, scientists assumed it was an artifact of damaged instruments. Only later did they learn that they had discovered a serious new threat.

One of the questions we now face is whether global warming will result in climatic changes that are as dramatic and unwelcome as the hole in the ozone layer. Growing evidence suggests that in the real world, climate change is likely to be spasmodic, unexpected, and so complex that you really have to get into the fields of chaos and complexity theory to begin to understand it. That is, environmental systems can cross thresholds in which a set of gradual trends may be completely disrupted and move in unexpected directions. Extreme climatic events might become more common in a substantially warmer world. These include catastrophic storms of various kinds, particularly those that are fed by warm tropical waters. Droughts could become more severe and last for many years, disrupting agriculture. Heat waves could also kill off crops and forests. The catastrophic wildfires seen in many parts of the world in recent years could also become routine.

As a result of such climatic changes, the coastal development that has expanded so dramatically over the past few decades might suddenly become more vulnerable than before, a problem that is exacerbated by the unprecedented concentrations of human populations in many parts of the world today. Low-lying areas that are dangerous to inhabitants even at current sea levels might become substantially more so with sea levels already rising by 0.3 cm per year. At a time when global food supplies are likely to be relatively tight over the next few decades, climate change could further reduce food security—damaging fisheries as well as crops. And as mentioned earlier, climate change could encourage the spread of deadly infectious diseases.

The Precautionary Principle

Given that even Patrick Michaels cannot deny the possibility of such events, it seems to me that we should invoke what is called "the precautionary principle." That is, we should take prudent steps to ensure that we minimize what could be substantial risks. It is interesting to ask how many of us in our personal or business dealings insist on the kind of certainty Michaels does when considering disastrous outcomes. For example, does a country go to war with absolute certainty of the outcome? Did Bill Gates decide to go into the software business because he knew for sure that he would be more successful than his competitors? Just asking these questions makes the point. Virtually everything we do in this world today involves a substantial degree of uncertainty.

There is one industry that understands this kind of uncertainty well, and that views the issue of climate change with growing alarm. It is one of the world's largest—roughly the same size as the fossil-fuel industry. I am referring of course to the insurance industry, which insures many of the properties most vulnerable to climate change, and has suffered record damages in recent years. The general manager of Swiss Re, one of Europe's largest insurance companies, says, "There is a significant body of scientific evidence indicating that last year's record insured loss from natural catastrophes was not a random occurrence. . . . Failure to act would leave the insurance industry and its policyholders vulnerable to truly disastrous consequences."[10]

Note that Swiss Re and other insurers are not saying that climate change is certain. Rather, they are saying that as an uncertain trend with potentially disastrous consequences, climate change has many similarities with the other risks with which the insurance industry deals on a daily basis. When an insurance company decides to insure your house, it does not know whether or not the house is going to burn down. The kinds of principles used to evaluate risk and decide what premium to charge suggest a good analogy to the way society should be looking at global climate change.

Michaels is a lot less conservative than the average insurance executive. His argument is that we should throw out the precautionary principle, ignore the risk of climate change, and hope for the best. The bottom line is that Michaels has his own forecast, which happens to be at odds with most of the hundreds of climate scientists that are working on these issues. I simply ask you: Does it make sense to bet the planet on the optimistic assumptions of one contrarian? Indeed, a real conservative would argue that we should act now to slow the dangerous rise in greenhouse-gas emissions rather than risk having to reduce emissions drastically in the future, which really could disrupt the economy.

The Policy Options

In the same way that he has mischaracterized the science of climate change, so has Michaels distorted the policy options. The way he has framed the debate, I guess I would have to describe myself as being part of a "conspiracy" involving the vice-president of the United States, several hundred scientists around the world, and probably the Trilateral Commission as well. According to the Michaels theorem, we are all desperate to foster a government takeover of the economy—presumably in order to reduce everybody's wealth, revive Karl Marx, and so on.

Within the policy community there is actually a broad spectrum of views on how we ought to address the problem of climate change. Even within the environmental community, there are groups that favor carbon taxes, and others that favor regulation, or tradable permits. In other words, there is a range of opinions that do not necessarily correlate with how much alarm those holding the views feel about the problem itself. The majority opinion is that some sort of market mechanism is the most efficient way to reduce carbon dioxide emissions—for example, higher energy taxes that would be offset by a decline in labor and income taxes.

A grand governmental solution is not the way we are going to achieve the kind of energy system that is needed. I simply do not think that that is the pattern for successful innovation in any sector. Certainly there are government policies that can help spur efficient change, however. For example, the huge existing subsidies to coal and oil are clearly an impediment to the development of new renewable energy technologies. To spur private businesses and allow them to accelerate the move away from carbon-intensive energy systems, the key is to free up the energy markets, and get away from the public and private monopolies that control oil, gas, and electricity. We are beginning to see this happen in a number of countries, where innovative technologies have been fostered by such beneficial government policies. India and Germany, for example, are building numerous wind farms today.

In my opinion, reducing carbon emissions—even by the 60–80 per cent that will ultimately be required to stabilize carbon dioxide concentrations—will end up being a lot easier and less expensive than most economists and industry groups currently expect. In support of that argument, it is worth noting that there is a century-long trend of gradually lowering the carbon intensity of energy systems. When you learn that the Russian economy has five times the carbon intensity of the Japanese economy, you realize that the level of national carbon emissions is *inversely* related to economic success. Rising energy efficiency tends to

reduce emissions, as does the broader trend from carbon-laden coal to progressively less carbon-intensive fuels such as oil, then to natural gas, and finally to renewable energy sources that emit no carbon. The many advanced electronic and materials technologies that have appeared in recent years provide opportunities to accelerate that trend. In fact, in 1994 we at the Worldwatch Institute published a book entitled *Power Surge: A Guide to the Coming Energy Revolution,* which makes the case for a gradual transition away from the kind of energy system we have today.[11]

Far from slowing global economic progress, the Framework Convention on Climate Change has the potential to accelerate it, by spurring countries to speed up investment in more energy-efficient infrastructure, to eliminate counterproductive energy subsidies, and to accelerate the development of new technologies. Already, in the two and a half years since the so-called Rio Treaty was signed, we have seen a dramatic acceleration in the development of renewable energy sources and natural gas in many parts of the world, while dependence on coal is being reduced in some nations. In many industrial and developing countries, the treaty has helped reform outdated domestic energy policies.

If it is implemented constructively—and aggressively—the Rio Treaty could turn out to be one of the best things that ever happened to the global economy. If the United States wants to be successful in the expanding energy markets of the next century, it will need to take a leading role in developing a sustainable energy system and stabilizing the earth's atmosphere. In that endeavor, ignoring the misguided words of Patrick Michaels would be a productive first step.

Notes

1. Intergovernmental Panel on Climate Change, "IPCC Second Scientific Assessment," draft, Zurich, 1994.

2. The Hadley Centre, *Modelling Climate Change* (Bracknell, U.K., 1995).

3. Charles Petit, "New Hints of Global Warming," *San Francisco Chronicle,* April 17, 1995.

4. David J. Thomson, "The Seasons, Global Temperature, and Precision," *Science,* April 7, 1995.

5. William K. Stevens, "More Extremes Found in Weather, Pointing to Greenhouse Gas Effect," *New York Times,* May 23, 1995.

6. Charles Petit, "New Hints of Global Warming," *San Francisco Chronicle*, April 17, 1995.

7. Ibid.

8. George M. Woodwell and Fred T. Mackenzie, *Biotic Feedbacks in the Global Climatic System: Will the Warming Feed the Warming?* (New York: Oxford University Press, 1995).

9. Walter Sullivan, "New Theory on Ice Sheet Catastrophe Is the Direst One Yet," *New York Times*, May 2, 1995.

10. Swiss Reinsurance Company, *Global Warming: Element of Risk* (Zurich, 1994).

11. Christopher Flavin and Nicholas Lenssen, *Power Surge: A Guide to the Coming Energy Revolution* (New York: W. W. Norton 1994).

92. Climate Change Science

The National Academy of Sciences

Greenhouse gases are accumulating in Earth's atmosphere as a result of human activities, causing surface air temperatures and subsurface ocean temperatures to rise. Temperatures are, in fact, rising. The changes observed over the last several decades are likely mostly due to human activities, but we cannot rule out that some significant part of these changes are also a reflection of natural variability. Human-induced warming and associated sea level rises are expected to continue through the 21st century. . . .

The mid-range model estimate of human induced global warming by the Intergovernmental Panel on Climate Change (IPCC) is based on the premise that the growth rate of climate forcing[1] agents such as carbon dioxide will accelerate. The predicted warming of 3°C (5.4°F) by the end of the 21st century is consistent with the assumptions about how clouds and atmospheric relative humidity will react to global warning. . . .

Because there is considerable uncertainty in current understanding of how the climate system varies naturally and reacts to emissions of greenhouse gases and aerosols, current estimates of the magnitude of future warming should be regarded as tentative and subject to future adjustments (either upward or downward). . . .

It is more difficult to estimate the natural variability of global mean temperature because of the sparse spatial coverage of existing data and difficulties in inferring temperatures from various proxy data. Nonetheless, evidence suggests that global warming rates as large as 2°C (3.6°F) per millennium may have occurred during retreat of the glaciers following the most recent ice age. . . .

Of the greenhouse gases that are directly influenced by human activity, the most important are carbon dioxide, methane, ozone, nitrous oxide, and chlorofluorocarbons (CFCs). Aerosols released by human activities are also capable of influencing climate. . . .

Concentrations of carbon dioxide (CO_2) extracted from ice cores drilled in Greenland and Antarctica have typically ranged from near 190 parts per million by volume (ppmv) during the ice ages to near 280 ppmv during the warmer "interglacial" periods like the present one that began around 10,000 years ago. Concentrations did not rise much above 280 ppmv until the Industrial Revolution. By 1958, when systematic atmospheric measurements began, they had reached 315 ppmv, and they are currently ~370 ppmv and rising at a rate of 1.5 ppmv per year (slightly higher than the rate during the early years of the 43-year record). Human activities are responsible for the increase. The primary source, fossil fuel burning, has released roughly twice as much carbon dioxide as would be required to account for the observed increase. Tropical deforestation also has contributed to carbon dioxide releases during the past few decades. The excess carbon dioxide has been taken up by the oceans and land biosphere.

From *Climate Change Science: An Analysis of Some Key Questions*, Committee on the Science of Climate Change of the U.S. National Academy of Sciences (Washington, DC: National Academy Press, 2001).

Like carbon dioxide, methane (CH_4) is more abundant in Earth's atmosphere now than at any time during the 400,000 year long ice core record, which dates back over a number of glacial/interglacial cycles. . . .

About two-thirds of the current emissions of methane are released by human activities such as rice growing, the raising of cattle, coal mining, use of land-fills, and natural gas handling, all of which have increased over the past 50 years. . . .

Virtually all the 20th century warming in global surface air temperature occurred between the early 1900s and the 1940s and during the past few decades. The troposphere warmed much more during the 1970s than during the two subsequent decades, whereas Earth's surface warmed more during the past two decades than during the 1970s. The causes of these irregularities and the disparities in the timing are not completely understood. . . .

The IPCC's conclusion that most of the observed warming of the last 50 years is likely to have been due to the increase in greenhouse gas concentrations accurately reflects the current thinking of the scientific community on this issue. The stated degree of confidence in the IPCC assessment is higher today than it was ten, or even five years ago, but uncertainty remains because of (1) the level of natural variability inherent in the climate system on time scales of decades to centuries, (2) the questionable ability of models to accurately simulate natural variability on those long time scales, and (3) the degree of confidence that can be placed on reconstructions of global mean temperature over the past millennium based on proxy evidence. Despite the uncertainties, there is general agreement that the observed warming is real and particularly strong within the past twenty years. . . .

In the near term, agriculture and forestry are likely to benefit from carbon dioxide fertilization and an increased water efficiency of some plants at higher atmospheric CO_2 concentrations.

With higher sea level, coastal regions could be subject to increased wind and flood damage even if tropical storms do not change in intensity. A significant warming also could have far reaching implications for ecosystems. . . .

Global warming could well have serious adverse societal and ecological impacts by the end of this century, especially if globally-averaged temperature increases approach the upper end of the IPCC projections. . . .

A diverse array of evidence points to a warming of global surface air temperatures. Instrumental records from land stations and ships indicate that global mean surface air temperature warmed by about 0.4–0.8°C (0.7–1.5°F) during the 20th century. The warming trend is spatially widespread and is consistent with the global retreat of mountain glaciers, reduction in snow-cover extent, the earlier spring melting of ice on rivers and lakes, the accelerated rate of rise of sea level during the 20th century relative to the past few thousand years, and the increase in upper-air water vapor and rainfall rates over most regions. A lengthening of the growing season also has been documented in many areas, along with an earlier plant flowering season and earlier arrival and breeding of migratory birds. Some species of plants, insects, birds, and fish have shifted towards higher latitudes and higher elevations. The ocean, which represents the largest reservoir of heat in the climate system, has warmed by about 0.05°C (0.09°F) averaged over the layer extending from the surface down to 10,000 feet, since the 1950s.

Pronounced changes have occurred over high latitudes of the Northern Hemisphere. Analysis of recently declassified data from U.S. and Russian submarines indicates that sea ice in the central Arctic has thinned since the 1970s. . . .

Some of these high latitude changes are believed to be as much or more a reflection of changes in wintertime wind patterns as a direct consequence of global warming per se. The rate of warming has not been uniform over the 20th century. Most of it occurred prior to 1940 and during the past few decades. The Northern Hemisphere as a whole experienced a slight cooling from 1946–75, and the cooling during that period was quite marked over the eastern United States. The cause of this hiatus in the warming is still under debate. . . .

This result is based on several elevations. The western part of the nation is highly dependent on the amount of snow pack and the timing of the runoff. The noted increased rainfall rates have implications for pollution run-off, flood control, and changes to plant and animal habitat. Any significant climate change is likely to result in increased costs because the nation's investment in water supply infrastructure is largely tuned to the current climate.

Health outcomes in response to climate change are the subject of intense debate. . . .

[C]hanges in the agents that transport infectious diseases (e.g. mosquitoes, ticks, rodents) are likely to occur with any significant change in precipitation and temperature. Increases in mean temperatures are expected to result in new record high temperatures and warm nights and an increase in the number of warm days compared to the present. . . .

. . . Significant climate change will cause disruptions to many U.S. ecosystems, including wetlands, forests, grasslands, rivers, and lakes. Ecosystems have inherent value, and also supply the country with a wide variety of ecosystem services. . . .

Notes

1. A climate forcing is defined as an imposed perturbation of the Earth's energy balance. Climate forcing is typically measured in watts per square meter (W/m^2)

93. SIDELIGHT: Let's Transform the Military

David Suzuki

Accountants tell me that responsible companies plan ahead for the coming year by projecting curves based on the current state of business and on the best- and worst-case possibilities. To ensure long-term success, a company must anticipate the worst possible disasters and marshal the resources and versatility to survive such scenarios.

Military leaders do the same thing. We, as a society, make expensive defence commitments based on predictions of threats to our security posed by erratic human behaviour and social, economic, and political events around the world. It is accepted as sound economic and national defence strategy to take seriously in our planning the crudest of worst-case projections. Surely then, at the very least, we ought to be applying that caution and commitment to much more palpable threats to all life that were so urgently raised at Rio.

Even though the United States is a wealthy nation, the expenditure of a third of its federal budget for defence has meant restrictions to much-needed environmental and social programs. Many analysts point out that forced demilitarization of a defeated Japan was a critical factor in the country's remarkable economic recovery. So military preparedness exacts costs that are more than just dollars and cents.

Seven years ago, only the most prescient political analyst or wild-eyed optimist could have anticipated the explosive changes within the late Soviet Union and its allies with an astonishingly small number of lives lost. For decades, the two superpowers held the world hostage to the terror of nuclear weapons and delivery systems that were on such a scale of speed, power, and number as to be literally beyond human control.

Military budgets often dwarf most other government expenditures. In spite of government concern over a growing deficit, Canada's defence budget increased by $680 million in 1990 alone, reaching a total of $12.8 billion in 1991. As global perceptions of military threats shift, defence budgets represent a potential windfall to be tapped for more pressing issues. We have a historic opportunity to reassess the role of the military and the global threats we face. I believe we still need a strong Department of National Defence, but today, the "'mother of all battles" is environmental, not military. A simple change in title to the Department of *Environmental* Defence would signal a radical shift in our perceptions and priorities. "War" is more than a metaphor; we are in a very real struggle to protect the life-support systems of the planet from a degradation that is every bit as threatening as a bomb or bullet.

After Pearl Harbor, people had no choice but to make profound changes in the way they lived in order to protect their way of life. Today, the daily

Time to Change by David Suzuki (Toronto: Stoddart Publishing Company, LTD., 1994), pp. 12–16.
Reprinted by permission of Stoddart Publishing Co., Ltd.

assaults on the environment around the world add up to the threat of a far greater holocaust than the world wars. The challenge is to make that threat as real and obviously dangerous to the public as an actual pitched military battle. In the eco war, the front lines are fires in tire dumps or PCB tanks, marine oil and chemical spills, vast tracts of deforested land, eroding farmland, wild game poaching, illegal dumping of toxic material, and the "biological war" for protein being fought at the boundaries of our ocean territory. That's where we need to marshal our troops.

As we approach a new millennium with a different perspective on the place of humans in nature and a heightened concern for our planetary home, we must reexamine our traditional military assumptions. Iraq is a good place to start.

The Gulf War was like no other in history: television enabled millions of viewers to see the events at the battlefront; the array of technological armaments was awesome, and the loss of life was spectacularly one-sided. But like all wars, it was a human and ecological disaster. The intimate close-ups of shorebirds being sucked under a wave of thick oil and the footage of the inferno of deliberately set well fires galvanized an outcry of horror.

For a few weeks in early 1991, most of us were glued to radios and television sets. In the United States, President George Bush and the media invoked the name of Hitler in reference to Iraq's president, Saddam Hussein. The name of the Nazi leader immediately conjured up images of a brutal butcher bent on genocide with weapons of terror. A more appropriate name to invoke would have been Frankenstein. Remember that Frankenstein was the doctor who applied all of the powers of science to concoct an improved kind of being, only to create a monster. Like modern-day Frankensteins, politicians, businessmen, and military leaders generated the frightening figure that Hussein had become. They armed him to the teeth with the most advanced inventions of military science and technology. The United States, Britain, France, West Germany, and the Soviet Union attempted to impose their political sphere on Iraq while amassing enormous profits from the sale of machines of death. And like Dr. Frankenstein, they created a horrifying man who was no longer predictable or controllable. It was even more appalling to realize that tinpot monsters like Hussein have been created all over the world by the same merchants of war.

Television reveals that like little boys, our political and military leaders are enthralled with their deadly toys—cruise missiles, nerve gas, Patriot rockets, laser guided "smart" bombs, Stealth bombers. The horror of the destructive power and dexterity of modern weaponry becomes amplified by the realization that those who will decide how to use this arsenal—Saddam Hussein, George Bush, Brian Mulroney—are just human beings. In spite of our great scientific advances and technological prowess, the people attempting to control this power possess the same minds and emotions of our Stone Age ancestors.

As we reflect on the incredible array of military personnel and armaments focused in the Persian Gulf, consider the staggering cost of war. In times of peace, $1,750,000 is spent on the military around the world every *minute*. The Worldwatch Institute in Washington, D.C., estimates that a mere 15 percent ($150 billion) of the annual global military budget would save the planet from environmental collapse. Yet governments continue to plead poverty as the excuse for ignoring environmental destruction. The United States, with disastrously skewed priorities, spends $300 on the military for every $1 on the environment. Even Canada invests $14 on national defence for every $1 on the environment. If only a fraction of the global defence budget was used for environmental protection, there would be money to reduce national debt, forgive foreign loans, purchase wilderness, and create new kinds of employment.

A handful of politicians is now seriously proposing the transformation of our defence department. One of them is former federal environment minister Charles Caccia, who has written a paper outlining the economics and politics of such a shift. The Liberal MP's rationale is simple and convincing:

> What good is it to enjoy the protection of military alliances . . . when at the same time holes in the ozone layer, atmospheric pollution, destruction of the rainforests, desertification, soil erosion, water contamination, badly stored toxic waste, to name a few . . . threaten our very survival? What good is it for Europe to have four million Soviet and two million NATO troops on its soil for military security, while at the same time the Rhine, the Loire, the Baltic Sea, the Po River, and Adriatic Sea, you name it, are going belly up? The fact of the matter is that we are now on a dual path of

mutually assured destruction, driven by environmental as well as nuclear threats.

Caccia says Canada should augment its role in global security by pressing for "'elimination of famine, poverty, desertification; stopping soil erosion, water contamination, forest, grassland, and fisheries depletion; putting the economies of developing countries on a healthy footing . . . using resources in a careful way." He points out that "a stronger stand on international environmental issues must be based on an improvement of environmental performance at home. We would have to rethink our energy policies . . . policies in agriculture, forestry, fisheries, transport, and taxation." To that end, he recommends that the men and women in the armed forces be used to enforce environmental security.

Caccia has presented an important set of challenges and specific recommendations that have to be debated in the political arena. My generation grew up with the Cold War and nuclear weapons, but today's youngsters know the real battle is to save the planet's environment.

It is the misdirection of intellectual effort that is our greatest tragedy. The scale and scope of the weaponry used in the Vietnam War to assault that tiny country showed our species at its most imaginative—in the invention of ways to kill and destroy. And the long-term environmental and human costs were monumental. Vietnam's countryside is still pocked and scarred with the craters of millions of bombs, while its soil remains poisoned by massive spraying of defoliants. One of Southeast Asia's richest tropical rainforests has been transformed into a barren desert, while malformed babies and diseased adults continue to pay for a war two decades later. What a perverted way to use the resourceful genius of human intellect.

Faced with an ecological crisis on the scale of a nuclear war, we still choose to expend our money, technology, and lives to kill. And so like Mary Shelley's tragic character, Dr. Frankenstein, our leaders, with all the best intentions, end up fighting the brute they made.

The metaphor of war serves the global ecocrisis well. It emphasizes the battle going on and underlines the fact that, as in times of war, we have no choice but to act on a massive scale. And if we do, money is the least of our problems.

VII

VARIETIES OF ACTIVISM

94. PREVIEW

Monkeywrenching is a proud American
tradition . . . going all the way back to the
Boston Tea Party in 1773.[1]

Dave Foreman

Henry David Thoreau [was] sent to jail
for refusing to pay his poll tax to protest
the U.S. war against Mexico. When Ralph
Waldo Emerson came to bail him out,
Emerson called through an open window
and said, "Henry, what are you doing in
there?" Thoreau quietly replied, "Ralph,
what are you doing out there?"[2]

Dave Foreman

Radical forms of environmental activism
can be found in groups such as Earth First!
and the Sea Shepherds. Earth First! is often
associated with its founder, Dave Foreman,[3]
as well as with tactics called "monkeywrenching." Monkeywrenching or ecological
sabotage (alternatively called *ecotage* or *night-
work*) is a name, as Foreman explains, "for the
destruction of machines or property that are
used to destroy the natural world."[4] It
includes wrecking heavy equipment, spiking
trees (driving nails into trees to damage saw
blades), and sinking holes in whaling ships, as
the Sea Shepherds do.

Although Earth First!ers engage in many
nondestructive protests, such as chaining
themselves to a bulldozer or sitting in a tree
scheduled to be cut down, the events publicized in the name of Earth First! center on
property destruction. Foreman is perhaps best
known for his 1987 book *Ecodefense: A Field
Guide to Monkeywrenching*. A how-to book, it
contains, as Rik Scarce nicely summarizes,

"detailed instructions for destroying just
about anything used to ruin wild places,
including heavy equipment, power and seis-
mographic lines, and snowmobiles. Jamming
locks, making smoke bombs, engaging in sabotage in an urban environment, and protecting oneself against discovery are among the
other topics exhaustively discussed."[5]

Both Earth First! and the Sea Shepherds
claim to be committed to nonviolence,
although they condone limited property
destruction. Neither group considers destruction of property to be violence. In contrast, a
more mainstream environmental organization
such as Greenpeace, originally known as the
"Don't Make a Wave Committee,"[6] is committed to the principle of no property destruction.
Scarce, in his book on the radical environmental movement, illustrates the difference:
"Greenpeace led an ultimately successful boycott against Icelandic fish products to protest
that nation's whaling policy, and some of its
activists even stalled the off-loading of
Icelandic fish from a freighter to publicize the
issue; the Sea Shepherds' approach was to
sink half of the Icelandic whaling fleet."[7]

Like Earth First! and the Sea Shepherds
before them, a group known as the Earth
Liberation Front (ELF) has claimed responsibility for millions of dollars of property
destruction in the last few years. "Sport utility
vehicles have been destroyed, fast-food
restaurants and Starbucks outlets vandalized.
Fields of genetically engineered wheat have
been cut down. Chicken farms and mink
ranches have been raided and the animals
released."[8] Luxury homes built in environmentally sensitive areas have been torched.[9]

Mentioning environmental concerns and protection of the lynx habitat, ELF took credit in 1998 for burning buildings and ski lifts in Vail, Colorado worth $12 million.[10] The FBI has had little success locating members of ELF who have no organizational structure and "seem to exist only in cyberspace."[11]

In contrast, Greenpeace is a large, well-organized, hierarchical structure with chapters capable of generating direct mailings on a national and international scale. Although Greenpeace has been in the forefront of guerrilla theater—going to the site of a seal clubbing or a whaling ship to get media attention—the organization expelled board of directors member Paul Watson for throwing a wooden club and pelts into the water during a protest of the killing of baby harp seals.[12] Watson, who went on to found the Sea Shepherds, calls Greenpeace "the Avon ladies of the environmental movement." In a more temperate statement about the relationship between radical and more mainstream groups, Dave Foreman recently said, "I think we have allowed the Sierra Club and other groups to actually take stronger positions than they would have before and yet appear to be more moderate than ever."[13]

People disagree about the appropriate description of the activities of radical environmentalists. For example, *Newsweek*, in a 1982 piece on Earth First!, described the actions of the group as "pranks."[14] Michael Martin, in his essay, "Ecosabotage and Civil Disobedience,"[15] sees ecological sabotage as at least close to (fitting an expanded version of) civil disobedience. Ecotage, he says, is markedly different from the standard case of civil disobedience in that the illegal actions performed are not public. As Edward Abbey, author of *The Monkey Wrench Gang*, said, "I'm not advocating illegal activity . . . . [except] at night."[16] However, as Martin points out, the underground railroad is thought by some to be an example of civil disobedience, and this effort to free slaves was not, indeed, could not be,

conducted in public. Nor would anyone likely call the activities of the underground railroad "pranks" for they were not amusing, playful, or malicious in intent. Eugene C. Hargrove, editor of *Environmental Ethics*, condemned monkeywrenching as "paramilitary operations . . . closer to terrorism than civil disobedience."[17] The charge of terrorism is heard fairly often. Eco-warriors reject the label of terrorist, as Rik Scarce says, because of "the precautions they take to avoid injuring others."[18]

There are many accounts of terrorism, but looking at just one contemporary example—Bat-Ami Bar On's "Why Terrorism Is Morally Problematic"—is helpful in determining whether it makes sense or is stretching a point to call monkeywrenchers ecoterrorists. Bar On says that "terrorism produces people who are afraid . . . [it] places its victims in a life threatening situation in which one feels both a need to do something to save oneself and helplessness."[19] Having in mind the context of state terrorism and such actions as bombing a city, shooting indiscriminately in an airport, and abducting and killing people, Bar On compares terrorism to seasoning (the process used by pimps to form prostitutes) and torture as practices that "involve the intentional erosion of selves and the intentional breaking of wills."[20] She speaks of the "daily fears for . . . survival and physical well-being."[21] We must ask ourselves whether these consequences seem an apt description of the results of ecosabotage. In his book, *Green Rage*, Christopher Manes reports that "President of Louisiana-Pacific Harry Merlo remarks, 'Terrorism is the name of the game for radical environmental goals.'" [Mike] Roselle . . . [replies], "Real terrorists would not be spiking trees . . . but spiking Merlo."[22]

When the Greenpeace ship *Rainbow Warrior* was bombed and sunk by the French government and a member of the crew drowned, nobody described the incident as terrorism.[23] When a member of the British Parliament said to then Prime Minister Margaret Thatcher,

"It's a British ship with a British flag and a British captain and a British crew in a British Commonwealth harbor sunk by the French government," she said, "It's none of our concern."[24] Unsurprisingly, Paul Watson, who told this story, finds Margaret Thatcher's remark hypocritical.[25] Certainly, the choice to describe people as terrorists may depend in part on the ends they are trying to accomplish. Conor Cruise O'Brien sums up this point nicely: "We reserve the use [of the words 'terrorism' and 'terrorist'] in practice for politically motivated violence of which we disapprove. The words imply a judgment about the political context in which those who we decide to call terrorists operate, and above all about the nature of the regime under which and against which they operate. We imply that the regime itself is legitimate. If we call them 'freedom fighters' we imply that the regime is illegitimate."[26]

Often little if any controversy surrounds the recommendations of legal ways to help the environment. Nonetheless, the ways suggested in Essays 98 and 97, by Guy Claxton and Kristin Shrader-Fréchette, respectively, have potential in this regard. In her defense of environmental and ethical advocacy by scholars, Shrader-Fréchette warns that "those who 'rock the boat' are often subject to the disapproval of the academy and the violence of vested interests."[27]

Ethical advocacy, Shrader-Fréchette explains, is "taking a stand, in a partisan sense, in one's professional writing or speaking; taking a stand on a specific, practical issue and defending that stance as rational and ethical rather than merely pointing out the assets and liabilities of alternative positions, rather than merely maintaining a stance of informed neutrality."[28] Shrader-Fréchette begins her argument for ethical advocacy by suggesting that the playing field is tilted. For example, enormous amounts of corporate money given to universities make them beholden to special interests: "Universities appear to be selling their integrity in much the same way as medieval churches sold pardons and indulgences."[29] Shrader-Fréchette develops her argument with subtlety and care, examining concepts such as objectivity and neutrality. She considers both deontological and consequentialist arguments for scholars assuming positions of ethical advocacy. She invites us to think about how to deal with "an academic and industrial playing field heavily tilted against environmental interests, against fair play, and against open exchange."[30]

In the final selection (Essay 98), Guy Claxton suggests methodologies of self-transformation that may allow us to voluntarily seek a life of (more) simplicity. Claxton explores the considerable psychological obstacles to altering those of our personal habits that satisfy our immediate desires but that have unfortunate environmental consequences—collectively and in the long run. His article raises many interesting questions for discussion. Should simplicity be our goal? (See also Luis N. Camacho in VI.D, Shrader-Fréchette on consumption here in VII.) Is "consumerism" similar to drug addiction? Is there a legitimate desire for a comfortable life that is not equivalent to "I shop, therefore I am"? Can one love material things—say, a well-built and beautiful piece of furniture that lasts over the course of a lifetime, or lifetimes—and still not overconsume? Lastly, and here Claxton is most helpful, if simplicity ought to be a goal for countries of the North, how can we achieve it and why do we so often fail?

NOTES

1. Dave Foreman, *Confessions of an Eco-Warrior* (New York: Harmony Books, 1991), pp. 118–19.

2. Dave Foreman, *Defending the Earth: A Dialogue Between Murray Bookchin and Dave Foreman*, edited by Steve Chase (Boston: South End Press, 1991), pp. 70–71.

3. No longer associated with Earth First!, Foreman subsequently joined environmentalists who support the North American Wilderness Recovery Project, alternatively known as the Wildlands Project.

4. Dave Foreman, *Confessions of an Eco-Warrior*, p. 118.

5. Rik Scarce, *Eco-Warriors: Understanding the Radical Environmental Movement* (Chicago: Noble Press, 1990).

6. Ibid., p. 47.

7. Ibid., pp. 103–104.

8. Scott Sunde and Paul Shukovsky, "Elusive Radicals Escalate Attacks in Nature's Name," *Seattle Post Intelligencer*, 18 June 2001, http://seattlep-i.nwsource.com.

9. Ibid.

10. Ibid.

11. Ibid.

12. Doing so was a crime under Canadian law, and Greenpeace lost its tax-exempt status as a result. See Scarce, p. 101.

13. Dave Foreman, *Defending the Earth*, p. 39.

14. See *Newsweek*, July 19, 1982, pp. 26, 27.

15. Michael Martin, "Ecosabotage and Civil Disobedience," *Environmental Ethics 12*(4) (Winter 1990), 291–310.

16. *Denver Post*, July 5, 1982, quoted in *Green Rage: Radical Environmentalism and the Unmaking of Civilization* (Boston: Little, Brown, 1990), p. 81.

17. Eugene C. Hargrove, "Ecological Sabotage: Pranks or Terrorism?" *Environmental Ethics 4* (1982), 292.

18. Scarce, *Eco-Warriors*, p. 77.

19. Bat-Ami Bar On, "Why Terrorism Is Morally Problematic," *Feminist Ethics*, edited by Claudia

Card (Lawrence: University of Kansas Press, 1991), pp. 111, 112.

20. Ibid., p. 116.

21. Ibid., p. 122.

22. Christopher Manes, *Green Rage*, p. 177. The Louisiana-Pacific Corporation is the largest purchase of timber from the national forests. Mike Roselle is cofounder of Earth First!.

23. See Scarce, p. 112. See also Roderick Frazier Nash, *The Rights of Nature: A History of Environmental Ethics* (Madison: University of Wisconsin Press, 1989), p. 180.

24. Scarce reported this statement from an interview with Paul Watson, p. 113.

25. Ibid.

26. Bar On, p. 109, quoting Conor Cruise O'Brien, "Terrorism Under Democratic Conditions: The Case of the IRA," in *Terrorism, Legitimacy, and Power: The Consequences of Political Violence*, edited by Martha Creshnaw (Middleton, CT: Wesleyan University Press, 1983), p. 91.

27. Kristin Shrader-Fréchette, "An Apologia for Activism: Global Responsibility, Ethical Advocacy, and Environmental Problems," *Ethics and Environmental Policy: Theory Meets Practice*, edited by Frederick Ferré and Peter Hartel (Athens: University of Georgia Press, 1994), p. 179.

28. Ibid., pp. 179, 180.

29. Ibid., p. 180.

30. Ibid., p. 179.

95. Strategic Monkeywrenching

Dave Foreman

. . . Only one hundred and fifty years ago, the Great Plains were a vast, waving sea of grass stretching from the Chihuahuan Desert of Mexico to the boreal forest of Canada, from the oak-hickory forests of the Ozarks to the Rocky Mountains. Bison blanketed the plains—it has been estimated that 60 million of the huge, shaggy beasts moved across the grass. Great herds of pronghorn and elk also filled this Pleistocene landscape. Packs of wolves and numerous grizzly bears followed the immense herds.

One hundred and fifty years ago, John James Audubon estimated that there were several *billion* birds in a flock of passenger pigeons that flew past him for several days on the Ohio River. It has been said that a squirrel could travel from the Atlantic seaboard to the Mississippi River without touching the ground, so dense was the deciduous forest of the East.

At the time of the Lewis and Clark Expedition, an estimated 100,000 grizzlies roamed the western half of what is now the United States. The howl of the wolf was ubiquitous. The condor dominated the sky from the Pacific Coast to the Great Plains. Salmon and sturgeon filled the rivers. Ocelots,

Ecodefense: A Field Guide to Monkeywrenching, by Dave Foreman (Tucson, AZ: Ned Ludd, 1987), pp. 10–17. Reprinted by permission of the author.

jaguars, margay cats and jaguarundis roamed the Texas brush and Southwestern deserts and mesas. Bighorn sheep in great numbers ranged the mountains of the Rockies, Great Basin, Southwest and Pacific Coast. Ivory-billed woodpeckers and Carolina parakeets filled the steamy forests of the Deep South. The land was alive.

East of the Mississippi, giant tulip poplars, chestnuts, oaks, hickories and other trees formed the most diverse temperate deciduous forest in the world. On the Pacific Coast, redwood, hemlock, Douglas fir, spruce, cedar, fir and pine formed the grandest forest on Earth.

In the space of a few generations we have laid waste to paradise. The tall grass prairie has been transformed into a corn factory where wildlife means the exotic pheasant. The short grass prairie is a grid of carefully fenced cow pastures and wheat fields. The passenger pigeon is no more. The last died in the Cincinnati Zoo in 1914. The endless forests of the East are tame woodlots. The only virgin deciduous forest there is in tiny museum pieces of hundreds of acres. Six hundred grizzlies remain and they are going fast. There are only three condors left in the wild and they are scheduled for capture and imprisonment in the Los Angeles Zoo. Except in northern Minnesota and Isle Royale, wolves are known merely as scattered individuals drifting across the Canadian and Mexican borders (a pack has recently formed in Glacier National Park). Four percent of the peerless Redwood Forest remains and the monumental old growth forest cathedrals of Oregon are all but gone. The tropical cats have been shot and poisoned from our southwestern borderlands. The subtropical Eden of Florida has been transformed into hotels and citrus orchards. Domestic cattle have grazed bare and radically altered the composition of the grassland communities of the West, displacing elk, moose, bighorn sheep and pronghorn and leading to the virtual extermination of grizzly, wolf, cougar, bobcat and other "varmints." Dams choke the rivers and streams of the land.

Nonetheless, wildness and natural diversity remain. There are a few scattered grasslands ungrazed, stretches of free-flowing river undammed and undiverted, thousand-year-old forests, Eastern woodlands growing back to forest and reclaiming past roads, grizzlies and wolves and lions and wolverines and bighorn and moose roaming the backcountry; hundreds of square miles that have never known the imprint of a tire, the bite of a drill, the rip of a 'dozer, the cut of a saw, the smell of gasoline.

These are the places that hold North America together, that contain the genetic information of life, that represent sanity in a whirlwind of madness.

In January of 1979, the Forest Service announced the results of RARE II [its Roadless Area Review and Evaluation]: of the 80 million acres of undeveloped lands on the National Forests, only 15 million acres were recommended for protection against logging, road building and other "developments." In the big tree state of Oregon, for example, only 370,000 acres were proposed for Wilderness protection out of 4.5 million acres of roadless, uncut forest lands. Of the areas nationally slated for protection, most were too high, too dry, too cold, too steep to offer much in the way of "resources" to the loggers, miners and graziers. Those roadless areas with critical old growth forest values were allocated for the sawmill. Important grizzly habitat in the Northern Rockies was tossed to the oil industry and the loggers. Off-road-vehicle fanatics and the landed gentry of the livestock industry won out in the Southwest and Great Basin. . . .

The BLM [Bureau of Land Management] wilderness review has been a similar process of attrition. It is unlikely that more than 9 million acres will be recommended for Wilderness out of the 60 million with which the review began. Again, it is the more spectacular but biologically less rich areas that will be proposed for protection.

During 1984, Congress passed legislation designating minimal National Forest Wilderness acreages for most states (generally only slightly larger than the pitiful RARE II recommendations and concentrating on "rocks and ice" instead of crucial forested lands). In the next few years, similar picayune legislation for National Forest Wilderness in the remaining states and for BLM Wilderness will probably be enacted. The other roadless areas will be eliminated from consideration. National Forest Management Plans emphasizing industrial logging, grazing, mineral and energy development, road building, and motorized recreation will be implemented. Conventional means of protecting these millions of acres of wild country will largely dissipate. Judicial and administrative appeals for their protection will be closed off. Congress will turn a deaf ear to requests for additional Wildernesses so soon after disposing of the thorny issue. The effectiveness of conventional political lobbying by conservation groups to protect endangered wild lands will evaporate. And in half a decade, the saw, 'dozer and drill will devastate most of what is unprotected. The battle for wilderness will be over. Perhaps 3% of the United States will be more or less protected and it will be open season on the rest. Unless . . .

Many of the projects that will destroy roadless areas are economically marginal. It is costly for the Forest Service, BLM, timber companies, oil companies, mining companies and others to scratch out the "resources" in these last wild areas. It is expensive to maintain the necessary infrastructure of roads for the exploitation of wild lands. The cost of repairs, the hassle, the delay, the down-time may just be too much for the bureaucrats and exploiters to accept if there is a widely-dispersed, unorganized, *strategic* movement of resistance across the land.

It is time for women and men, individually and in small groups, to act heroically and admittedly illegally in defense of the wild, to put a monkeywrench into the gears of the machine destroying natural diversity. This strategic monkeywrenching can be safe, it can be easy, it can be fun, and—most importantly—it can be effective in stopping timber cutting, road building, overgrazing, oil and gas exploration, mining, dam building, powerline construction, off-road-vehicle use, trapping, ski area development and other forms of destruction of the wilderness, as well as cancerous suburban sprawl.

But it must be strategic, it must be thoughtful, it must be deliberate in order to succeed. Such a campaign of resistance would follow these principles:

Monkeywrenching Is Non-Violent

Monkeywrenching is non-violent resistance to the destruction of natural diversity and wilderness. It is not directed toward harming human beings or other forms of life. It is aimed at inanimate machines and tools. Care is always taken to minimize any possible threat to other people (and to the monkeywrenchers themselves).

Monkeywrenching Is Not Organized

There can be no central direction or organization to monkeywrenching. Any type of network

would invite infiltration, *agents provocateurs* and repression. It is truly individual action. Because of this, communication among monkeywrenchers is difficult and dangerous. Anonymous discussion through this book and its future editions, and through the Dear Ned Ludd section of the *Earth First! Journal*, seems to be the safest avenue of communication to refine techniques, security procedures and strategy.

Monkeywrenching Is Individual

Monkeywrenching is done by individuals or very small groups of people who have known each other for years. There is trust and a good working relationship in such groups. The more people involved, the greater are the dangers of infiltration or a loose mouth. Earth defenders avoid working with people they haven't known for a long time, those who can't keep their mouths closed, and those with grandiose or violent ideas (they may be police agents or dangerous crackpots).

Monkeywrenching Is Targeted

Ecodefenders pick their targets. Mindless, erratic vandalism is counterproductive. Monkeywrenchers know that they do not stop a specific logging sale by destroying any piece of logging equipment which they come across. They make sure it belongs to the proper culprit. They ask themselves what is the most vulnerable point of a wilderness-destroying project and strike there. Senseless vandalism leads to loss of popular sympathy.

Monkeywrenching Is Timely

There is a proper time and place for monkeywrenching. There are also times when monkeywrenching may be counterproductive. Monkeywrenchers generally should not act when there is a non-violent civil disobedience action (a blockade, etc.) taking place against the opposed project. Monkeywrenching may cloud the issue of direct action and the blockaders could be blamed for the ecotage and be put in danger from the work crew or police. Blockades and monkeywrenching usually do not mix. Monkeywrenching may also not be appropriate when delicate political negotiations are taking place for the protection of a certain area. There are, of course, exceptions to this rule. The Earth warrior always thinks: Will monkeywrenching help or hinder the protection of this place?

Monkeywrenching Is Dispersed

Monkeywrenching is a wide-spread movement across the United States. Government agencies and wilderness despoilers from Maine to Hawaii know that their destruction of natural diversity may be met with resistance. Nation-wide monkeywrenching is what will hasten overall industrial retreat from wild areas.

Monkeywrenching Is Diverse

All kinds of people in all kinds of situations can be monkeywrenchers. Some pick a large area of wild country, declare it wilderness in their own minds, and resist any intrusion against it. Others specialize against logging or ORV's [off-road vehicles] in a variety of areas. Certain monkeywrenchers may target a specific project, such as a giant powerline, construction of a road, or an oil operation. Some operate in their backyards, others lie low at home and plan their ecotage a thousand miles away. Some are loners, others operate in small groups.

Monkeywrenching Is Fun

Although it is serious and potentially dangerous activity, monkeywrenching is also fun. There is a rush of excitement, a sense of accomplishment, and unparalleled camaraderie from creeping about in the night resisting those "alien forces from Houston, Tokyo, Washington, DC, and the Pentagon." As Ed Abbey says, "Enjoy, shipmates, enjoy."

Monkeywrenching Is Not Revolutionary

It does *not* aim to overthrow any social, political or economic system. It is merely non-violent self-defense of the wild. It is aimed at keeping industrial "civilization" out of natural areas and causing its retreat from areas that should be wild. It is not major industrial sabotage. Explosives, firearms and other dangerous tools are usually avoided. They invite greater scrutiny from law enforcement agencies, repression and loss of public support. (The Direct Action group in Canada is a good example of what monkeywrenching is *not*.) Even Republicans monkeywrench.

Monkeywrenching Is Simple

The simplest possible tool is used. The safest tactic is employed. Except when necessary, elaborate commando operations are avoided. The most effective means for stopping the destruction of the wild are generally the simplest: spiking trees and spiking roads. There are obviously times when more detailed and complicated operations are called for. But the monkeywrencher thinks: What is the simplest way to do this?

Monkeywrenching Is Deliberate and Ethical

Monkeywrenching is not something to do cavalierly. Monkeywrenchers are very conscious of the gravity of what they do. They are deliberate about taking such a serious step. They are thoughtful. Monkeywrenchers—although non-violent—are warriors. They are exposing themselves to possible arrest or injury. It is not a casual or flippant affair. They keep a pure heart and mind about it. They remember that they are engaged in the most moral of all actions: protecting life, defending the Earth.

A movement based on these principles could protect millions of acres of wilderness more stringently than any Congressional act, could insure the propagation of the grizzly and other threatened life forms better than an army of game wardens, and could lead to the retreat of industrial civilization from large areas of forest, mountain, desert, plain, seashore, swamp, tundra and woodland that are better suited to the maintenance of natural diversity than to the production of raw materials for overconsumptive technological human society.

If loggers know that a timber sale is spiked, they won't bid on the timber. If a Forest Supervisor knows that a road will be continually destroyed, he won't try to build it. If seismographers know that they will be constantly harassed in an area, they'll go elsewhere. If ORVers know that they'll get flat tires miles from nowhere, they won't drive in such areas.

John Muir said that if it ever came to a war between the races, he would side with the bears. That day has arrived.

96. The Sea Shepherds: Bringing Justice to the High Seas

Rik Scarce

Paul Watson says he doesn't remember when he first heard of the *Sierra,* an infamous pirate whaling ship that prowled the waters of the Atlantic for nearly twenty years. It was like an archetypal specter that was always *out there,* menacing the waves in the collective consciousness of anti-whaling activists. In the summer of 1979, with little more than a "gut feeling" to go on, Watson set out to change all that by tracking down and destroying the 678-ton killer/factory ship that haunted him. His bond with whales was strong, having been cemented by a vision in an Oglala Sioux sweat lodge when he was initiated into the tribe following the Indian uprising at Wounded Knee in 1973. A bison appeared to Watson, who was made a member of the tribe after he snuck into the besieged encampment during the seventy-one day rebellion and worked as a medic. The buffalo told him that he should "concentrate on the mammals of the sea, especially whales."[1]

It was a profound visitation, Watson says, especially because of the messenger. "The Plains Indians were the first people to ever fight a war to save something other than themselves—the buffalo."[2]

In this parable of the high seas, the *Sierra* was a seagoing version of the rapacious foreigners who wiped out Indians and bison in their relentless drive to "conquer the west." Like Buffalo Bill, the *Sierra* was a terrorist practicing genocide, bound by no written or moral law. In one three-year period the *Sierra* slaughtered 1,676 whales, selling the meat to Japan for 138,000 yen per metric ton. At a time of increasing international pressure to halt all whaling, the *Sierra* operated with impunity toward the unenforceable strictures and quotas established by the International Whaling Commission (IWC).[3] Watson felt that such lawlessness could be stopped only by taking the fight to the high seas. Only months before, he had convinced Cleveland Amory, a philanthropist and president of the Fund for Animals, to put up the money for

a ship that Watson re-christened the *Sea Shepherd.* Amory had an abiding love for all animals and a strong urge to protect them through whatever non-violent means were available. As he wrote in the introduction to Watson's book, *Sea Shepherd,* "I wanted a tough team able to take on—head-on, if need be—the major cruelties to which so many animals are regularly and ruthlessly subjected."[4] In Watson, Amory saw an ideal warrior for the animals of the sea. During a June 1979 meeting, Amory asked his captain to take the ship to the Aleutians and block a fur seal kill there. But the barrel-chested, baby-faced, blunt-spoken Watson felt the *Sierra* gnawing at his bones. His ship was ready to go. "Give me a month," Watson pleaded with his benefactor. He wanted to search out the *Sierra* and send it to the depths to avenge the gentle leviathans who had met their end at the point of the pirate's harpoon. Amory relented, and the desperate chase soon was on.[5]

The *Sea Shepherd* began life in 1960 as a 779-ton, 206-foot-long deep-water trawler, a cod fishing ship that Watson purchased with Amory's money in December 1978 for $120,000. Its time on the ocean ended barely a year later at the bottom of the harbor at Leixoes, Portugal, scuttled by order of its own Captain Watson to avoid having it turned over to the pirate whalers. But that is the denouement to the hunt for the *Sierra.* The story begins on July 15, 1978, when Watson discovered the whaling vessel off the Portuguese coast. The twenty-eight-year-old commander found his adversary after a cross-ocean hunt lasting twelve days, guided only by some vague information that the *Sierra* would be somewhere off the Iberian peninsula. The excitement over the imminent end of the chase must have been tremendous, but the ships were too far from shore for Watson to act. His strict code of non-violence prevented him from smashing into his antagonist then and there, on a cold and frothy sea far from port, risking the lives of the *Sierra's* crew and his

Eco-Warriors: Understanding the Radical Environmental Movement, by Rik Scarce (Chicago: The Noble Press, 1990), pp. 97–100. Reprinted by permission of the author.

own. Watson figured he would soon enough have his opportunity.

The next day that chance came, but was nearly lost. After following the outlaw ship all night as it slowly made for shore, Watson was tricked into port by the Portuguese authorities around noon. They had him believe that the *Sierra* was heading in as well, when in reality it was soon to leave. Watson, more determined than ever to get the pirates, dashed the *Sea Shepherd* out of the harbor without permission. He had been docked for one hour, which was long enough to discharge nearly all of his twenty-person crew—only two chose to stand with him and risk the uncertain punishment that would befall them. Then it was onward after the *Sierra*.

Watson sailed out of the mouth of the port to find the pirate whaler sitting languidly at anchor a quarter-mile from shore, biding its time until the appointed hour to steam out and meet a Japanese cargo ship into which it would disgorge its whale flesh. Watson wasted no time in heading straight for the *Sierra*, whose crew was sunbathing on deck. On the first attack he used the *Sea Shepherd's* concrete-reinforced bow to smash into the *Sierra's* leading edge in the hope of severing the pendent harpoon platform; the collision left major damage to the whaler but failed to take off the executioner's stand. Watson banked his ship hard and took aim amidships of the *Sierra*. Its crew ran about frantically. They must have been trying to start the engines, but no wake could be seen. Sitting there idle, the *Sierra* was an easy target. "When you ram another ship and you can control it in calm waters," Watson explains, "it's not like two cars hitting each other. You've got 750 tons of metal hitting 680 tons of metal. That's a lot of steel to absorb the shock of the impact."[6] Gentle though it might have felt, the second charge was devastating, the combination of speed and mass as powerful as a bomb. The collision ripped open a hole in the hull six feet wide by eight feet long. Whale meat could be seen hanging inside. As Watson turned to administer the *coup de grâce*, his adversary finally got underway and limped the short distance to the harbor.

Suddenly, it was Watson's turn to play the outlaw. He and his tiny crew ran the *Sea Shepherd* at full speed up the coast in hopes of reaching Spanish territorial waters, thereby avoiding any penalties which the Portuguese might levy. Their desperate dash ended eight miles short of the mark, when a

Portuguese naval destroyer demanded that Watson turn his ship around or be fired upon. The *Sea Shepherd* was escorted back to Leixoes and docked at the far end of the harbor from the critically damaged, listing *Sierra*.

The *Sea Shepherd* sat there for four and a half months while the Portuguese debated what to do. Maritime law dictated that the ship, not the captain or the crew, was to blame for certain high seas crimes, so Watson was released. He spent much of his time on television and radio shows telling of his exploit. Then in December, Watson was finally given the terms, or term, under which the *Sea Shepherd* would be returned to him: pay $750,000 in damages and fines. Refusal to pay would mean the *Sea Shepherd* would be forfeited to the *Sierra's* owners. Watson flew to Portugal to inspect his ship and found that many vital components had been stripped by thieves, including the port police, who had stolen the ship's radio.

Even if he had been able to raise three-quarters of a million dollars to get his $120,000 ship back, the repair expenses would be enormous. Giving up the ship to the whalers was out of the question. Watson's way was clear. As close to heartbroken as the tough merchant marine could ever be, Watson realized that his only choice was to scuttle his pride and joy, sending it to the bottom of the harbor and then running like hell.

Amidst the pandemonium of New Year's Eve, *Sea Shepherd* Chief Engineer Peter Woof crept aboard the vessel at night, stealing into the engine room. There he opened a valve that, when closed, kept sea water from entering the engine. Brine gushed into the ship. Woof escaped from the vessel before it sank. He immediately left the country; Watson, however, wanted one last look at his vessel. The day after the scuttling, he drove by the port. Police were everywhere; it was obvious the job was well-done. Watson avoided extraordinary security measures by the incensed Portuguese authorities and escaped to London.[7]

On February 6, 1980, a bomb tore open the hull of the fully-refitted *Sierra* as it sat in Lisbon's harbor, ready to sail and kill once more. It sank in 10 minutes. An anonymous caller to United Press International said, "The *Sierra* will kill no more whales! We did it for the *Sea Shepherd*." Within weeks, two of Spain's five whalers were sunk by the same three saboteurs who did-in the *Sierra*. Watson was an ocean away at the time of all three bombings. No one was injured, and the perpetrators were never caught.[8] . . .

Notes

1. Paul Watson, *Sea Shepherd* (New York: W. W. Norton, 1982), p. 70.
2. Interview with Paul Watson, Poulsbo, Washington, November 26, 1989.
3. Watson, *Sea Shepherd,* pp. 214–215.
4. Ibid., p. 11.
5. Ibid., p. 212.
6. Watson interview.
7. Watson, *Sea Shepherd,* pp. 225–251.
8. Ibid., p. 250.

97. An Apologia for Activism: Global Responsibility, Ethical Advocacy, and Environmental Problems

Kristin Shrader-Fréchette

One of the most difficult *theoretical* problems in normative ethics is understanding and resolving conflicts over collective responsibility for global environmental crises. It is difficult both because the precise contribution of each member of a collectivity (a group, nation, or planet) in causing and alleviating planetary problems is hard to determine and because environmental goods are both public and indivisible. One of the most difficult *practical* problems in normative ethics is how to achieve authentic collective responsibility. It is problematic both because international laws and sanctions are difficult to formulate and enforce and because the tragedy of the commons and the appeal of being a "free rider" are typically more powerful motivators than ethical suasion. I shall address the second, more practical, problem.

Apart from devising legal, governmental, and institutional strategies for creating and enforcing solutions to problems of the global environmental commons, the other main strategy for environmental action (a noninstitutional strategy) is education and advocacy, especially through nongovernmental organizations. Advocacy of any kind, however, is viewed as inimical both to objectivity in general and to the academy in particular. In this essay I argue that environmental advocacy by scientists, philosophers, and other intellectuals is not only permissible but perhaps ethically mandatory. My conclusion is based on at least four premises for which I shall argue: (1) because decision making in industry, government, and the academy is highly partisan and often contrary to environmental interests and fair play, alleged neutrality (rather than advocacy) actually serves the status quo; (2) scholarly objectivity regarding environmental issues is not achieved by neutrality; (3) provided certain conditions are met, there are sound deontological arguments for scholars assuming positions of environmental advocacy; and (4) provided certain conditions are met, there are sound consequentialist arguments for scholars assuming positions of environmental advocacy.

In sum: the world has grown too small and too troubled to be served by an ivory tower, if, indeed, it ever served us. The ivory tower model of objectivity is clearly wrong, in part because there is no tower, but instead there is an academic and industrial playing field heavily tilted against environmental interests, against fair play, and against open exchange. This is illustrated easily by a recent experience of Peter Singer's.

The Playing Field Is Tilted

In May 1991, Peter Singer was standing in an auditorium at the University of Zurich, about to give a lecture on animal rights. Before he could begin, a massive group of leftists and anarchists—including a large number of disabled persons in wheelchairs—disrupted this lecture. They accused Singer, because of one chapter in his *Practical Ethics,*

Ethics and Environmental Policy: Theory Meets Practice, edited by Frederick Ferré and Peter Hartel. Athens: The University of Georgia Press, 1994, pp. 178–194. Reprinted by permission.

of advocating active euthanasia for severely disabled newborn infants. Singer said that one-third to one-fourth of the auditorium began to chant "Singer *'raus! Singer 'raus!"* in a deafening roar. As he rose and tried to speak, one of the euthanasia protesters came up from behind him, tore Singer's glasses off his face, threw them to the floor, and broke them.[1]

Part of the Singer case is similar to that of other advocates, including my own—in having my phone bugged and in being threatened, intimidated, and harassed by industry and government groups who have tried to stop some of my writing and speaking on nuclear power and hazardous waste. Although I won't discuss these experiences here, they, like Singer's, illustrate that environmental or ethical advocates, especially those who "rock the boat," are often subject both to the disapproval of the academy and to the violence of vested interests. Yet, the very violence and power of these vested interests is precisely one of the reasons why advocacy, especially environmental advocacy, is so needed in the academy if we are to solve our global environmental problems.

What is environmental advocacy? It is taking a stand, in a partisan sense, in one's professional writing or speaking; taking a stand on a specific, practical issue and defending that stance as rational and ethical rather than merely pointing out the assets and liabilities of alternative positions, rather than merely maintaining a stance of informed neutrality. Environmental advocacy might be exemplified by taking a stand in favor of a solar economy or unilateral disarmament or against commercial nuclear fission or deep geological disposal of hazardous wastes.

Because the justifiability of normative and partisan stances in one's research is proportional to the degree to which the research game is already played in an ideological and highly partisan way, it is important to know something about who controls academic research. Academia is no longer an ivory tower, if indeed it ever was. Adam Smith has co-opted it. In 1981, for example, the West German pharmaceutical company Hoechst gave $70 million to Harvard's Department of Molecular Biology in exchange for rights to market all discoveries made in the department and to exclude all funding and research that interfered with Hoechst's proprietary position. In the same year, Jack Whitehead gave MIT $125 million in exchange for MIT's relinquishing control over patent rights, finances, hiring, and choice of research at its biotechnology research center. Likewise, at Carnegie Mellon, 60 percent of the research funds are from the U.S. Department of Defense.[2] Hence, any environmentalist who takes a particular stand against certain uses of biotechnology or military technology is already speaking within a highly partisan framework created by special interest groups.

Part of the reason for the power of special interest groups, particularly those that are antienvironment, is that of all corporate monies given to United States universities, one-third is provided by only ten corporations, and one-fifth of all industry funds—millions of dollars—is provided by only two corporations.[3] Faculty in molecular biology at Harvard are indentured servants to Hoechst. MIT biotechnologists are hired hands of entrepreneur Jack Whitehead; at Carnegie Mellon, they comprise a branch of the army and the air force.

Universities appear to be selling their integrity in much the same way as medieval churches sold pardons and indulgences. Typically, they give the most power and internal support to departments that have the most corporate monies behind them. As noted Harvard biologist Richard Lewontin put it when he heard about Harvard's deal with Hoechst: "What about the rest of us who are so foolish as to study unprofitable things like poetry, Sanskrit philology, evolutionary biology and the history of the chansons? Will the dean have time to hear our pleas for space and funds between meetings with the university's business partners?"[4] Indeed, will academic administrators even give such researchers a "fair shake" if their scholarship leads them to question the research methods, assumptions, and politics of the government and industry groups, typically antienvironment groups, that funnel their money into the university?

In universities dominated by narrow technical, governmental, and industrial concerns and driven by extramural funding from corporate sources, environmental awareness is almost nonexistent, and liberal education has become progressively more narrow. As Nobelist Isidore Rabi warned, this narrowness is paving the way for a repetition of what happened in Germany during the 1930s when the rise of militaristic nationalism, fueled by the dominance of narrow technical and professional training, eroded ethical values and liberal university education, thus laying the foundation for

Hitler's rise. Given such a restrictive conception of the university and scholarship, it was no accident that in 1937 the Prussian Academy of Sciences condemned Albert Einstein because he criticized the violations of civil liberties in the Nazi regime. (The academy said that he should have remained silent, neutral, and objective.) Once an Einstein, or any disinterested academic, is condemned for speaking out in the public interest, then the narrowing of the ivory tower begins to strangle democracy as well. No country can survive the theft of its universities' capacity to criticize. Democratic institutions are fed by the free flow of information and criticism, and government and science, as well as the public, require universities to provide this independent perspective. Otherwise government must blindly choose the answers offered by individuals and corporations, who are by nature self-interested. Because they are self-interested, they cannot be trusted to judge what is in the common interest. Democracy needs the Socratic gadfly, the detached observer, and the social critic. Neither society nor the university can afford to become the whore for special interest groups.[5] The way to avoid their domination by antienvironmental industrial or militaristic special interest groups is for scholars themselves to take partisan stands and advocate positions that are ethically defensible, especially when the positions run counter to those of the interest groups.

Objectivity Is Not Achieved by Neutrality

One reason why scholars so often fail to engage in environmental advocacy through their speaking and writing is probably that they have accepted the antiquated positivistic model of objectivity as neutrality. A corollary of the outmoded positivist tradition of research is that whatever scholarship is not neutral is also subjective in a reprehensible way. If it makes sense for philosophers and other scholars to be advocates and partisans, however, and not merely neutral observers of society, then obviously the acceptability of advocacy presupposes that neutrality is not objectivity. Thanks to Thomas Kuhn, Michael Polanyi, Stephen Toulmin, Paul Feyerabend, and others, we now know that complete objectivity is impossible and that there is no value-free inquiry, at least not free from cognitive or methodological values.[6]

Philosophical analysis, moreover, can show that not all methodological and ethical values deserve equal respect, and therefore not all values are subjective in a reprehensible way. Not all values deserve equal respect—or disrespect, as the positivists would have it—because formulation of any scientific theory is incompatible with the avoidance of methodological values, because there is no fact–value dichotomy, and because values alone never determine all the facts or all aspects of the facts. Just as there are rational reasons, short of empirical confirmation, for accepting one theory over another—reasons such as simplicity and heuristic power—so also are there rational reasons—such as consistency or equal treatment—for accepting one value over another.[7]

If not all ethical and methodological values are subjective in a reprehensible way, then advocating some values and being a partisan on their side is philosophically defensible on both epistemological and ethical grounds.[8] In other words, objectivity does not equal neutrality, for at least six reasons:

1. Failure to criticize indefensible or questionable values gives implicit assent to them in practising ethics or public policy. Hence, once one admits that methodological and ethical values are unavoidable in all research, including scientific research, then not to assess those values is to become hostage to them or at least implicitly to sanction them. Hence, to avoid uncritical acceptance of status quo values one must criticize values rather than remain ethically neutral in all cases.

2. Not all ethical and methodological positions are equally defensible. If they are not, then real objectivity requires one to represent indefensible positions as indefensible and less defensible positions as less defensible.

3. To represent objectivity as neutrality in the face of a great hazard or threat is simply to serve the interests of those responsible for the threat.

4. To represent objectivity as neutrality is also to encourage persons to mask evaluational and ethical assumptions in their research and policy and hence to avoid public disclosure of, and control over, those assumptions.

5. To represent objectivity as neutrality is also to presuppose that objectivity is somehow delivered from on high rather than negotiated and

discovered socially through the give-and-take of alternative points of view, point and counter point.

6. Most disturbing of all, to represent objectivity as neutrality is to sanction ethical relativism and therefore injustice. This is exactly what happened during World War II when some anthropologists from Columbia University were asked about their position on the actions of the Nazis. They said that because conflicts between the Nazis and others represented a controversy over value systems, they had "to take a professional stand of cultural relativity"; they said that they had to be "skeptics" with respect to all judgments of value.[9]

At least three groups in contemporary society would agree that the Columbia University anthropologists should have been skeptics with respect to judgments of value. They would support a resounding no to the question of whether philosophers should be advocates: (1) the fashionable "deconstructive" postmodernists who have tried to destroy the foundations of ethical, social, and epistemological criticism; (2) the unfashionable positivists who nevertheless lurk in the closets of most natural scientists; and (3) the relativist social scientists who have confused silence with objectivity and neutrality. Someone else can have the task of telling how and why these three positions go wrong. For now, I'd like to provide several consequentialist arguments, followed by a number of contractarian or deontological arguments, for advocacy and partisanship in selected cases of environmental scholarship.

Consequentialist Arguments for Advocacy

One of the most powerful consequentialist arguments in favor of environmental advocacy is that without it greater harm would occur, more persons would be hurt, and more important values would be sacrificed. Although it would be difficult to prove, for example, it is arguable that the Nazis' experimentation on prisoners and brutality against Jews, gypsies, and leftists could have been stopped or at least hampered had the Columbia University anthropologists and other scholars taken a different ethical stance and condemned the atrocities. Likewise, it is reasonable to believe that environmental abuses such as global warming, destruction of the ozone layer, and pollution of air and water could be stopped or at least hampered if scholars would take a partisan stance against them.

Of course, the obvious objection to taking a partisan stance on environmental or other issues is that such stances are often wrong and that careful, conservative scholars ought never move beyond the facts. If knowing that one were correct were a necessary condition for taking a position of advocacy, however, then many evils would be so advanced that it would be impossible to stop them. Moreover, in a situation of uncertainty, advocacy encourages counterarguments and public discussion and hence is often itself an important way to resolve uncertainties.

In other words, an important consequentialist argument in favor of environmental advocacy on specific issues is that such advocacy would help to educate the public. Even if particular scholars were wrong in advocating certain courses of action, the advocacy itself would draw out public debate, analysis of the issues, and a will to know the truth. Environmental advocacy would also help to reverse a status quo dominated by the vested interests of industry, greed, big government, and the military. Without such advocacy, our silence or neutrality likely would serve the status quo, especially what is ethically and environmentally indefensible in the status quo. As Abraham Lincoln put it: Silence makes men cowards. Silence or neutrality makes us cowards in telling the truth about the evils that surround us, and therefore our silence sanctions those evils. Scholars' failure to adopt positions of environmental advocacy also might encourage the consequence that less educated persons, some serving their own vested interests, would dictate public policy debate. If scholars and those most lacking in self-interest do not become advocates, then the advocacy will become the prerogative of the worst elements of society, just as a volunteer army has often become the prerogative of ne'er-do-wells and politics has often become the prerogative of the corrupt.

Environmental advocacy is also defensible on largely prudential grounds. If environmental hazards are threatening our lives and well-being, then a purely prudential argument in favor of scholars adopting positions of environmental advocacy is that such advocacy would lead to better protection of human and environmental welfare. It is arguable, following this line of reasoning, that environmental advocacy is justifiable on the grounds of self-defense. We have the obligation to do whatever is necessary to defend our lives and welfare. Therefore, as a consequence, we have the obligation as scholars to engage in environmental advocacy. In other words, one consequence of our acting as environmental advocates is that we would be better able to protect human rights to bodily security and equal protection, both of which are threatened by environmental degradation.[10]

Deontological Arguments for Advocacy

There are also good deontological reasons for believing that those who oppose the advocacy of scholars are wrong. For example, by virtue of their position, the anthropologists who failed to oppose Hitler were being neither objective nor neutral. It is not objective to say that committing atrocities is neither right nor wrong. It is not objective to say that one should be neutral regarding experimentation on prisoners without their consent. It is not objective to be neutral in the face of systematic discrimination against persons on the basis of their religion or race. Genuine objectivity requires calling a spade a spade. An important deontological argument for ethical advocacy of scholars is that objectivity does not require treating a questionable ethical position and a more reasonable one the same. Indeed, as Aristotle recognized, equal treatment does not mean the same treatment; equal treatment means treating equals the same. By virtue of trivializing and treating morally different positions equally, proponents of alleged neutrality actually discriminate and practice bias.

Failure to practice advocacy often amounts to bias. "Telling it the way it is" frequently requires us to take a stand precisely because certain governmental, political, and economic interests are taking either a reprehensible stand or no stand at all against great evils. Vested interests often exercise a highly questionable sort of advocacy, and our raising questions about their stances typically amounts to advocacy for the other side. No one can evaluate the social science methodology of risk perception studies done near the proposed Yucca Mountain radioactive waste site, for example, without examining and condemning the massive, one-sided advertising campaign mounted against the citizens

of Nevada by every nuclear utility in the country. When the nuclear industry spends $5.5 million per year (in rate-payer funds) in one state in an attempt to control the results of social science surveys, the students of social science methodology cannot ignore that fact.[11] Scholars need to condemn such bias. In doing so they act as advocates for alternative action.

One reason that researchers need to act as advocates for alternative action is that, often, researchers are the only people with the requisite information to make an informed decision about the rights and wrongs of a particular situation. In other words, an important deontological reason for scholars acting as environmental advocates is that they often have the ability to make a difference; they have a "responsibility through ability." Following the reasoning of moral philosophers such as Peter Singer, if we have the ability to make a difference, and if it would cause us no serious hardship to do so, then we have the duty to attempt to make a difference.[12]

We also have a responsibility through complicity. We have a responsibility to act as environmental advocates because often we have benefitted from environmental harm. Frequently, for example, we are responsible for correcting environmental harms because we have paid less for goods produced by manufacturers who fail to curb their pollution. Hence, our monetary benefits have been purchased at the price of harms to the environmental commons. Scholars in developed, Western nations bear a special responsibility through complicity because our standard of living and luxuries frequently are made possible only through environmental degradation and through our using a disproportionate share of environmental resources. Hence, we have a responsibility through complicity to help reverse the environmental damage from which we have profited.[13]

Even if scholars had no responsibility through complicity to act as environmental advocates, we would clearly have a responsibility by virtue of third-party professional obligations. Professional ethics dictates that by virtue of the benefits professionals receive from society, we have an obligation to the public to protect its interests and serve its welfare. Indeed, professionals' obligations to third parties often supersede obligations to first and second parties. In the case of employees of state universities, this third-party obligation is particularly strong and is, indeed, even a first-party obligation, because the people—the taxpayers of the state—are literally our employers. Hence, we have an obligation to protect their interests, a main part of which includes environmental well-being.[14] And if we have an obligation to protect the interests of the public in environmental well-being, then we may have an obligation to engage in environmental advocacy.

Restrictions on Advocacy

Admittedly, of course, if one takes a position of advocacy, then one is bound to provide equal consideration of all relevant interests and to answer all relevant objections of "the other side." This is perhaps the greatest failing of applied philosophers and environmental scholars who take positions of advocacy. They sometimes are more interested in preaching to the converted than in examining both sides, in order to show which is ethically or methodologically preferable. A corollary to presenting alternative sides and to answering relevant objections is to put one's own methodological and ethical judgments up front to determine whether they can bear scrutiny. This again seems to me to be a common failing of applied philosophers working in environmental ethics. They sometimes are more interested in speculative, and often undefended, metaphysics and ethics than in the epistemological justifications for their positions.

Another necessary condition for environmental advocacy is that we meet William Frankena's criterion for discrimination: it must lead to greater overall equality and good, over the long term, for everyone. Otherwise, any discriminatory or partisan arguments, even for environmental goods, are not justifiable and may merely use other persons and their positions as means to our own partisan ends.[15] But herein lies the problem. Those who want to build Yucca Mountain radioactive waste repository and jeopardize our descendants in perpetuity, or those who want to continue destroying thousands of species per day, typically *agree* with principles of equal consideration of interests and with achieving greater equality and good, over the long term. Usually, however, they disagree with us over the facts. They disagree over whether Yucca Mountain will leak over tens of thousands of years, whether species extinction is a natural process, or whether humans can accommodate themselves to increasing numbers of carcinogens. Therefore, one

of the most important tasks of the environmental advocate is to understand and defend the factual assumptions that he or she makes.[16]

Indeed, Paul Gomberg argues quite persuasively that moralists can be advocates and even partisans whose killing of others can be ethically justified provided that certain factual and ethical considerations are satisfied.[17] The factual conditions for justifiable advocacy (according to Gomberg) have to do with the gravity of the physical threat and the guilt of those responsible for it.[18] The gravity of the physical threat is an especially important condition in justifying advocacy regarding a particular environmental situation because the graver the threat, all things being equal, the more justified is a partisan position against it. This is why, for example, in his *Just and Unjust Wars*, Michael Walzer claims that "the survival and freedom of political communities . . . are the highest values of international society," and therefore we can countenance even the killing of civilians when the existence of a nation is up for grabs.[19]

But what about Earth First!'s actions? Is one justified in being an advocate and a partisan if one's goal is to protect a greater environmental good—survival of the planet and its resources? If civil disobedience is justifiable, and I think that there are occasions when it is, then analogous arguments might reveal when philosophical disobedience to the alleged norms of disinterested scholarship is likewise justifiable. Also, if Walzer is correct, then one could argue analogously that if the survival of the earth and its inhabitants is the highest of all values, then even the most extreme forms of advocacy and partisanship, such as killing civilians, can be countenanced when survival is at stake. Obviously, advocating killing is an extreme position. Equally obviously, it is justified only in the gravest of situations. Hence, much of the key to the justification of scholarly advocacy is the factual context in which it takes place.

Although he did not write about philosophical partisanship, John Locke appears to justify the partisan conception of human relationships when he says: "One may destroy a man who makes war upon him, or has discovered an enmity to his being, for the same reason that he may kill a wolf or a lion, because they are not under the ties of the common law of reason, have no other rule but that of force and violence, and so may be treated as a beast of prey."[20]

Few, if any, of us are likely to find ourselves in situations in which, because others are making war on us, we therefore have the right to destroy them or to advocate their destruction. Nevertheless, those who justify Earth First!'s actions appear to believe that they are in such a situation. Partisan scholarship and advocating particular ethical and policy positions, both amounting to a form of coercion, are obviously more justifiable to the degree that they are necessary to prevent some greater evil. The greater the evil needing to be prevented, the greater the justification for the coercive or partisan scholarship. Although I have doubts about whether he succeeded, that is how Garrett Hardin, for example, attempted to justify the highly coercive measures he defends in "The Tragedy of the Commons" and "Living on a Lifeboat."[21]

One could probably say, however, that the views of persons like Garrett Hardin and Edward Abbey—who said that he would sooner shoot a man than a snake because snakes are important members of ecological communities—and Earth First! members are highly ideological. Because they are highly ideological, one would probably argue that they are incapable of being justified by means of the numerous causal inferences necessary to show that some personal or environmental catastrophe is at stake.

Indeed, epistemological conservatism keeps most of us from assenting to, much less joining in, the actions of Earth First! We also believe that the environmental world is not quite so simple as Earth First! members believe, just as the political world is not so simple as Marxist revolutionaries claim; neither worldview obviously and easily justifies highly partisan actions. It does not seem to be the case, for example, as R. P. Dutt claims,[22] that fascist deeds and acts of war are inevitable under capitalism, because there is never any pure capitalism. Fascism sometimes exists with some degree of democracy because many acts of war are at least partially justifiable. Likewise, I believe that there are few totally unjustifiable acts of environmental degradation. Rather, many environmental actions often involve uncertainty regarding their causal effects, or, if the effects are certain but harmful, their proponents sometimes justify them by appealing to the greater good. In other words, in many cases of environmental controversy there are no "smoking guns."

Although I believe strongly in environmental advocacy, it is not always obvious or provable that environmental catastrophe is inevitable unless we engage in partisan scholarship and activism to promote particular causes, for example, stopping use of all potential carcinogens. We simply do not have that great a fix on the causal chain that results in various environmental damages. Because we don't, our advocacy is never wholly or easily justifiable. For example, recent news reports tell us that there is a cluster of primary brain cancers among residents near the Los Alamos National Laboratory in New Mexico, where nuclear weapons research is conducted. We know radiation causes cancer, and we have a dose–response curve to measure the effects of radiation exposure. We also know that there is a statistically significant increase in the disease rate in the Los Alamos area. The epidemiological studies are inconclusive, however, because we cannot link the effect, cancer, to the alleged cause, radiation exposure, in all cases. For one thing, cancer typically has a latency period and takes several years to show up, because the exposed population often is not studied for a long period of time. Moreover, researchers frequently cannot rule out intervening factors and alternative causes of the cancer, even though increases in the cancer are statistically significant.[23] In other words, many environmental situations are characterized by massive scientific uncertainty. This means that in order to justify environmental advocacy in such a case, one must justify choosing the environmental actions least likely to cause the most serious harm. One must defend a personal rule of scholarship that is based on maximin decisions rather than on utilitarianism or on average expected utility. I shall not take the time to defend such a maximin ethics, both because I have done so elsewhere and because John Rawls has given persuasive arguments that seem to me to be convincing. For both of us, however, perhaps the main key to the acceptability of advocacy directed at maximin choices is the severity of the environmental catastrophe we face. In other words, the key is the factual situation:[24] the greater the catastrophe we face, the greater is the acceptability of advocacy to prevent catastrophe.

If we do engage in partisan scholarship—work that defends and examines only one side of an issue—independent of the correct factual situation, then we should recognize that such coercive tactics may not lead to environmental education. Instead, they may lead to bias, to an inability to engage in rational analysis, and, ultimately, to diminished autonomy and decreased civil liberties for those who seek to be heard on all sides of an issue. Often, the first casualty of those who seek to preserve us from a great social or political evil is civil liberties. Likewise, the first casualty of those who seek to preserve us from a great environmental evil may be loss of autonomy and the ability to rationally analyze a situation.

From a consequentialist point of view, it is possible to defend both partisanship and avoidance of partisanship. Partisan scholarship could lead to the consequences (1) that we as a society lose the ability to engage in rational analysis of a situation, and (2) that because we lose part of our rational abilities, we lose some of our autonomy and some of our capacity for free, informed consent both to environmental hazards and to government actions. Partisan scholarship could also lead to the consequence (3) that from a pragmatic and prudential point of view, experts whose warnings about environmental disaster are proved wrong thereby lose their credibility. Such a loss of credibility would hurt not only society but the profession as a whole.

Avoidance of advocacy and partisan scholarship, on the other hand, could also lead to dangerous consequences. For example, the U.S. Office of Technology Assessment claims that up to 90 percent of all cancers are environmentally induced and theoretically preventable,[25] and we know that one in three persons will die of cancer. Had more people spoken out to advocate reduction of suspected environmental carcinogens, these rates might not be what they are today. Had more moral philosophers argued about the ethical constraints of behavior in a situation of scientific uncertainty, then the carcinogens might not have been so easily accepted. Other consequences of avoiding advocacy might be that those in a position to correct environmentally catastrophic situations would not do so.

For example, when the Chernobyl accident took place, officials in the former USSR said (and continue to say) that only 31 casualties occurred as a result of the accident. They ignored all nonimmediate fatalities, and they forbade medical doctors from inscribing the cause of death on the death certificates of those killed by radiation-related causes. Even the U.S. Department of Energy has admitted that Chernobyl fatalities are likely to go as high as

28,000, and academics at the University of California, Berkeley, have argued that once the statistical casualties are counted, the fatalities could go as high as 475,000.[26] Failure to address the silence of the nuclear industry in such a situation, and failure to be an advocate for the four million persons living near Chernobyl, whose premature deaths could be prevented, were they moved out of contaminated areas, is reprehensible. Environmental advocacy seems required of every scholar who knows the situation.

Sometimes we also might be able to justify our advocacy or our partisanship on the grounds that totally objective dialogue or argument is impossible. The argument here is that those who need to hear nonpartisan analysis would not listen to it, and some of those at fault in situations of environmental degradation have not listened for a long time. This is the same justification suggested by John Locke, who believed that it cannot be taken for granted that two human beings are bound by the same morality of common law of reason. Not all human beings are capable of listening to each other. Rather, a common bond of morality depends on the actual relationships among people, including their intentions toward each other.[27]

In other words, in order to treat "persons on the other side" as being responsible for their actions and able to change, we must believe in their susceptibility to ethical dialogue.[28] If I engage in ethical dialogue with another, I treat the other as ethically responsible. Dialogue both helps to establish and is presupposed by a moral community of agents seeking agreement. Hence, if we understand ascriptions of moral responsibility as entailing the belief that some persons can be affected by dialogue and criticism, then we need to know whether these persons can be so affected. This is a factual question. If they cannot be so affected, and if rational persuasion is impossible, then, presumably, one is not required to present totally neutral, nonpartisan rational arguments in order to persuade them. As Paul Gomberg puts it, if fascist brutality and fascist mindsets are inevitable, then morality is useless.[29]

According to the partisan conception of morality, there may be others with whom one does not share a morality and to whom one's moral duties are limited. This may be why, for example, the quadriplegics and paraplegics who helped to attack Peter Singer in Switzerland did not believe that they shared a common morality with him, whereas they were convinced that he was their enemy, a person whose ideas about euthanasia could result in their destruction. Conversely, persons who were convinced that others did share a common morality with them would not be likely to behave like those who disrupted Singer's talk because they would see no causal connection between a philosopher's beliefs about euthanasia and exterminating the disabled. If one is committed to a universalist morality, one would have trouble believing that another person is "out to get one" or has a design on one's life. In Reuben Ainsztein's words, "Because [Jews] . . . believed in progress and the perfectibility of man, they were the last to realize how bestial the Germans were."[30]

The obvious questions are whether actions are bestial or not and whether people can be written off or not. The obvious problem with environmental advocacy is the epistemological question of whether the factual situation is catastrophic enough to justify advocacy. On the one hand, because most of us do not understand fully the factual conditions around us, we often cannot determine whether or not advocacy is justified. On the other hand, factual uncertainty requires ethically conservative actions, actions not likely to harm either persons or the environment. Hence, factual uncertainty can be grounds for advocating ethically conservative actions.

Because we believe in progress and the perfectibility of humans, we likewise are often too slow to recognize the need for advocacy or the extremity of the environmental catastrophe that we face. This is somewhat like what Kris Kristofferson (the same Kristofferson who wrote "Me and Bobbie McGee" and "Help Me Make It Through the Night") said of his own transformation. He went from being an army brat and volunteering for Vietnam to being a Rhodes scholar, a longtime antiwar activist, a supporter of the United Farm Workers, and an opponent of United States policy in Central America. His own idealism about both humans and the government, however, kept him from recognizing the severity of the military and environmental dangers around him and therefore from taking a position of advocacy. He says: "Growing up, I was never aware of the fact that only white males who owned property were covered in the Constitution and could vote, and the whole country was built on genocide, the murder of natives. I've often thought that the more I read, the more I realized that our Government may never have stood for the things I believe in. But they made a mistake. Somewhere along the line they taught me that's what we stood for, and now I demand it."[31] We must demand it as well.

Notes

1. Peter Singer, "On Being Silenced in Germany," *New York Review of Books* 38, August 15, 1991, 36–42.

2. Kristin Shrader-Fréchette, "Helping Science Serve Society," in *Hoe Toonaangevend is de Universiteit?* ed. H. de Ward (Groningen, Netherlands: University of Groningen Press, 1989), 75, 78.

3. Shrader-Fréchette, "Helping Science Serve Society," 79.

4. Shrader-Fréchette, "Helping Science Serve Society," 77–78.

5. Shrader-Fréchette, "Helping Science Serve Society," 78.

6. See Helen Longino, *Science as Social Knowledge* (Princeton: Princeton University Press, 1990); also Shrader-Fréchette, *Science Policy, Ethics, and Economic Methodology* (Boston: Reidel, 1984), 73. Finally, see Shrader-Fréchette, *Risk and Rationality* (Berkeley: University of California Press, 1991), 40ff.

7. Shrader-Fréchette, *Science Policy,* 73–74.

8. Shrader-Fréchette, *Science Policy,* 183.

9. Shrader-Fréchette, *Science Policy,* 88.

10. A. Gewirth, *Human Rights: Essays on Justification and Applications* (Chicago: University of Chicago Press, 1982), 181ff.

11. Yucca Mountain PR expenditures were revealed through the investigative reporting of D. Olinger, in "Nuclear Industry Targets Nevada," *St. Petersburg Times,* December 1, 1991, D1, D5.

12. Shrader-Fréchette, *Risk,* 160–62.

13. Shrader-Fréchette, *Risk,* 162–63.

14. See Michael Bayles, *Professional Ethics* (Belmont, Calif.: Wadsworth, 1981), 92–109.

15. William Frankena, "The Concept of Social Justice," in *Social Justice,* ed. R. Brandt (Englewood Cliffs, N.J.: Prentice-Hall, 1962), 15; see also Shrader-Fréchette, *Risk,* chap. 8, for discussion of this argument.

16. Paul Gomberg, "Can a Partisan Be a Moralist?" *American Philosophical Quarterly* 27 (January 1990): 71.

17. Gomberg, "Partisan," 71–79. Following Gomberg, I take *partisan* to mean "a division of human beings into those on my side, whose interests or judgments count positively, and my enemies" (75).

18. Gomberg, "Partisan," 72–73. What principle of pro-portionality is relevant to justify partisanship and advocacy? Clearly what is not appropriate is partisanship and advocacy that somehow exceed the gravity of the harm arising from the situation one advocates. What is not appropriate is what Hersh Smoliar, a leader of partisans from the Minsk Ghetto, describes: "Each one of them had his own account to square. . . . Two eyes for one, the whole mouth for one tooth" (quoted in Gomberg, "Partisan," 73). This attitude bespeaks revenge rather than impartial justice; presumably such revenge is appropriate only in the most extreme cases in which one's enemy is outside one's moral community and is bent on annihilation.

19. Michael Walzer, *Just and Unjust Wars* (New York: Basic Books, 1977), 254.

20. Quoted in Gomberg, "Partisan," 75.

21. See Garrett Hardin, "The Tragedy of the Commons," *Science* 162 (1968): 1243–48; and Hardin, "Living on a Lifeboat," *BioScience* 24 (1974): 561–68.

22. R. P. Dutt, *Fascism and Social Revolution* (Chicago: Proletarian Publishers, 1978), 16ff., 44ff., 91, 296ff.

23. J. M. Cousteau, "Nuclear Weapons Testing Casts a Deadly Shadow on the Environment," *Calypso Log* 18 (October 1991): 3.

24. See Shrader-Fréchette, *Risk*, chap. 8.

25. See Shrader-Fréchette, *Risk*.

26. Cousteau, "Nuclear Weapons Testing," 5.

27. Cited in Gomberg, "Partisan," 75.

28. See Lawrence Stern, "Freedom, Blame, and Moral Community," *Journal of Philosophy* 71 (1974): 72–84.

29. Gomberg, "Partisan," 75.

30. Quoted in Gomberg, "Partisan," 76.

31. Rosa Jordan, "Kris Kristofferson," *Progressive* 55 (September 1991): 36–38.

98. Involuntary Simplicity: Changing Dysfunctional Habits of Consumption

Guy Claxton

> When our ruling passion is no longer survival it becomes comfort. To someone whose passion *is* survival our preoccupation with comfort is ignoble and trivial; there is no way it can be justified. It can't even be understood.
>
> Nicholas Freeling, *A City Solitary*

In non-abundant societies, where the prerogative of survival leaves little room for choice, people's patterns of consumption are predominantly dictated by the nature of their circumstances. When there is little to eat, how one acts is largely determined by agricultural or ecological forces beyond individual control. But in the affluent countries of the North, what people consume, what they waste, what long and short-term considerations are or are not taken into account in making consumption decisions—these betray the powerful influence of the cultural and individual assumptions and beliefs that are resident in people's minds. And if dysfunctional habits of consumption are driven by psychological factors, then a satisfactory solution is not going to be found in either technological innovation or in ecopolitical reorganisation, but in the liberation of individuals, in their millions, from the sway of an unconsciously self-destructive worldview.

This obvious starting-point for any discussion about ways of averting further ecological catastrophes is summed up by Laszlo (1989):

> There are hardly any world problems that cannot be traced to human agency and which could not be overcome by appropriate changes in human behaviour. The root cause even of physical and ecological problems are the inner constraints on our vision and values. . . . Living on the threshold of a new age, we squabble among ourselves to acquire or retain the privileges of bygone times. We cast about for innovative ways to satisfy obsolete values. We manage individual crises while heading towards collective catastrophes. We contemplate changing almost anything on this earth

Environmental Values 3 (Cambridge, UK: The White Horse Press, 1994), pp. 71–78. Reprinted by permission.

except ourselves. . . . A new insight must dawn on people: you do not solve world problems by applying technological fixes within the framework of narrowly self-centered values and short-sighted national institutions. Coping with mankind's current predicament calls for inner changes, for a human and humanistic revolution mobilizing new values and aspirations, backed by new levels of personal commitment and political will. (pp. 46–7)

Voluntary Simplicity

Those who have seen that this individual process of *reprioritisation* is the nub of the problem have tended to take two routes. One involves making explicit the tacit dysfunctional beliefs that have driven heedless overconsumption and waste (as Laszlo does), in the hope that "making the unconscious conscious" (in Freud's famous phrase) will do the trick. The other relies more on extolling the virtues of "voluntary simplicity." Elgin (1981), who coined the phrase, has argued irrefutably *why* changes in personal lifestyle are vital for planetary well-being, and has persuasively shown how such changes can be construed not as sacrifice but as a joyous reorientation of life away from "having" and towards "being" (c.f. Fromm, 1978). "To live more frugally on the material side of life is to be enabled to live more abundantly on the psychological and spiritual side of life" (Elgin, ibid). And he offers in his book plenty of good, practical advice, not just about what we should be doing, but about how to get started and put it into effect. He has recently (Elgin, 1992) returned to the theme, and the mixture is as before: scary facts and prognostications acting as the "stick"; glowing exhortations about the joys of frugality to provide the "carrot"; and tips as to how to do it.

Yet while the spirit, as a result of reflecting on these considerations, may, for many people, be willing, the flesh remains often and indubitably weak. In this area of personal lifestyle, as in many others such as dieting or giving up smoking, to *know* what to do, to *agree* that it is a good idea, even to *want* to change, seem over and over again to be insufficient. A new course of action is enthusiastically embraced, but somehow, as T. S. Eliot (1962) said in "The Hollow Men," "between the idea and the reality, between intention and the act, falls the Shadow." That which is adopted *voluntarily* has, it seems, little power to resist being shouldered aside

by a deeper impulse that remains involuntary. The vital tactical question, then, in considering any attempt to save humankind from itself, focuses not on information or exhortation, but on the resilience of habits and beliefs that are "embodied," in the face of contrary principles that are "espoused." One *wants*, and one *wants not to want*; the problem is how to translate the *wanting not to want* into *not wanting*.

To see how to enable oneself to change it is necessary to understand the psychology of addiction, for people's involuntary rejection of their "better natures" can be seen as reflecting an addiction to luxury, or comfort, that relies on the psychological (though not of course the same physiological) dynamics as that of heroin addicts, whose need may require them, in the heat of the moment, continually to over-ride their aversion to lying to, and stealing from, those they love. In the long run it may be no less destructive—to the sustainability of the planet, if not to individual well-being—to be unable to give up flushing the toilet after every visit, or to drop the attachment to being able to pop into town on a whim, which creates the addiction to the second car. For neither the drug addict nor the comfort addict is the combination of *voluntary* effort—"will-power"—self-talk and guilt adequate to the task.

Traps

This problem arises when the dysfunctional habit is locked in place by an underlying system of belief which determines, to a significant extent, a person's worldview. Such a belief system is called by Stolzenberg (1984) a "trap," which he defines as:

> a closed system of attitudes, beliefs and habits of thought for which one can give an objective demonstration that certain of the beliefs are incorrect, and in which certain of the attitudes and habits of thought prevent this from being recognised.

Such a system constitutes, in effect, one's vantage point; while the system is operating "upstream" of perception, its assumptions are built in to the "reality" that is experienced, and its constituents are not visible, and not open to question. One might say that the word-processing program that is currently installed on my computer is a "trap" in the same sense. Its instructions and subroutines are nowhere to be seen; yet they determine absolutely the "reality" that appears on the screen in front of me. Unless I become aware (as in fact I am) that the "belief system" embodied by WordPerfect 5.1 is simply one amongst many, and that there are many alternative "realities" that my laptop is potentially capable of revealing to me, then I am "trapped" into confusing the view according to WordPerfect with the way things "really" (i.e. inevitably, unquestionably) are. It is possible (as I am about to do) to type, in WordPerfect, a "heretical" statement like "I wish I could be working in Microsoft Word; it's so much better." But whatever I type *within* WordPerfect can have absolutely no effect on the program itself.

Just so, when the mind habitually runs a particular belief system, and when that belief system is instrumental in creating (editing, selecting, interpreting) *experience,* then everything that happens can only be understood in terms of the presuppositions of the system—or it cannot be understood at all. As the programmers say, "it does not compute." To quote Stolzenberg (ibid.) again:

> A belief system has this one distinguishing feature: all acts of observation, judgment etc., are performed solely from the particular standpoint of the system itself. Therefore, once any belief or operating principle has been accepted, that is, is seen as "being so," any argument for not accepting it will be rejected unless it can be shown that there is something "wrong" with it from the standpoint of the system itself. . . . And any such demonstration would collapse as soon as it had been given because its force would depend upon the correctness of the very methodology that has just been found to be incorrect.
>
> When an outside observer is in a position to see that such a system contains an incorrect belief and also that no proof of its incorrectness can be given in terms of the system itself, then he is in a position to say that this system has become a trap. In such a situation, the outside observer will see those within as being dogmatic, while those on the inside will see the observer as someone who refuses to accept what is "obviously so." And, in fact, both will be right. (pp. 269, 272)

The Trap of Competitive Needs

We might argue that comfort-addicts are in exactly this situation. Their view of the world embodies a nest of assumptions that link together identity, preference and material comfort in such a way that denial of preference is experienced as a mortal blow to personal efficacy, and discomfort is experienced as a threat to physical survival. Xenos (1989), for example, shows how Europeans' "normal" experience of themselves—and their experience of themselves as "normal"—was shifted, in the eighteenth century, by the rise of manufacturing industry and the invention of fashion, towards a constant state of relativised need or scarcity. One's sense of self, and self-worth, came to depend on possession and consumption. As fashions changed, so those one aspired to be like threatened to pull further away, while the hot breath of those one was striving *not* to be like could perpetually be felt on the back of one's neck.

> Needs that are conceived to be naturally based, such as needs for food, shelter, sex, etc., can be approached discretely. . . . But when these needs become intertwined with a fluid, ever-changing social world of emulation and conspicuous consumption, they become transformed into an indiscrete desire constantly shifting its focus from one unpossessed object to another.
>
> Among the social needs constitutive of modern commercial societies are those of recognition and prestige, and even if some of them run up against absolute limits to their satisfaction, others, particularly those tied to fashion, are capable of apparently infinite expansion. Thus the boundlessness of desire is realised in the proliferation of social needs. For us, the denizens of this world of desire, it is no longer a question of episodic insufficiency; out of our affluence we have created a social world of scarcity. (Xenos, ibid., pp. 5, 10)

Put simply, "individual consumerism" has become a cornerstone of modern Northern/Western identity, so that living in a spiral of escalating affluence is no longer experienced as a fortunate option, but as a matter of absolute necessity. This belief installs consumption at the heart of human identity, as a core trait that is now not the servant, but the master, of survival. The idea of *not* being able to continue to consume in the style, and at the rate, that has been prescribed, therefore, can *only* be experienced as loss, sacrifice and threat, because the perceptual apparatus has been programmed to see that way.

This is true even when the conscious, voluntary mind is espousing alternative values and dispositions. One can *try* to cut down consumption, but if underneath the intention to live frugally there is the buried belief that "I shop; therefore I am," the commitment to the conscious intention will be fragile and half-hearted, and can only manifest as a "gesture" that may placate the espoused belief while, on a deeper level, validating the embodied belief. I *know* I should be buying recycled toilet paper, but somehow, when I get home from the supermarket, I find, almost to my surprise, that yet again it is the softer, whiter product that I have actually bought.

Whilst the underlying trap is in place, the attempt to live frugally is bound to be experienced, however faintly, as *painful*, as a deprivation of what is "needed," and as soon as this occurs, the system as a whole seeks to rectify the situation. The lack of comfort or of choice becomes an itch that demands scratching; and because the "motive" is still in place, there are no good-enough grounds for resisting the urge to "scratch." The Buddhist monk Nanavira Thera (1987) uses again the analogy of the drug addict:

> If (the addict) decides that he must give up his addiction to the drug (it is too expensive; it is ruining his reputation or his career; it is undermining his health; and so on) he will make the decision only when he is in a fit state to consider the matter, that is to say *when he is drugged*; and it is from this (for him, *normal*) point of view that he will envisage the future. But as soon as the addict puts his decision into effect and stops taking the drug he ceases to be "normal," and decisions taken when he was normal now appear in quite a different light—and this will include his decision to stop taking the drug. *Either*, then, he abandons his decision as invalid ("How could I possibly have decided to do such a thing? I must have been off my head.") and returns to his drug-taking, *or* (though he approves the decision) he feels it urgently necessary to return to the state in which he originally took the decision (which was when he was drugged) *in order to make the decision seem valid again*. In both cases the result is the same—a return to the drug. And so long as the addict takes his "normal" drugged state for granted at its face value—i.e. *as* normal—the same thing will happen whenever he tries to give up his addiction. (pp. 205–6)

The foregoing discussion has tried to make clear that any espousal of "voluntary simplicity" is doomed if it is overlaid on an embodied belief system to which it is antithetical. It follows that encouraging people to see voluntary simplicity as a "good idea," and offering them advice as to how to put it in to practice, is a waste of time if, for the vast majority of the audience, the underlying addiction is not treated. But how is this to be done? How can one truly experience the value of simplicity, when one's experience itself is the product of a belief in the necessity of luxury?

Getting Out of Jail

There are a number of possible methods for escaping from the trap. One is to *require* people to behave in a way that respects ecological values. If they are prevented from retreating into the familiar, sensible, normal, comfortable way, when the going gets tough, and are forced to put up with the withdrawal symptoms (to "go cold turkey"), without any apparent hope of returning to "the good (bad) old days," then a shift in underlying assumptions and priorities can take place which makes it possible for the value of simplicity to be experienced and appreciated. The problems and risks with this eco-dictatorial solution are, however, too numerous and too obvious to make it either a viable or a sensible option.

Another strategy is to engage a different motivation, so that the discomfort of acting *as if* one were un-trapped is made worth bearing. Like the first method, the idea is to arrange things so that people will for a sustained period act in line with the espoused belief rather than the embodied one. As the benefit of the new way of acting cannot be experienced to begin with, and therefore cannot act as the *reward* for putting up with the disruption and discomfort, some *other* form of reward can be used to keep the new behaviour going while it "takes root."

These rewards may be either positive or negative, and there are risks associated with each. Lepper and Greene (1975), in their studies of the so-called "undermining effect," have shown that when people are positively reinforced for doing something that they themselves would have voluntarily undertaken anyway, the habit can be "appropriated" by the extrinsic reinforcement, and when the reward stops, the original motivation is now no longer strong enough to keep the behaviour going. So giving people money back on returnable bottles, to encourage them to recycle, is a self-limiting expedient if it turns out that as soon as you stop the cash everybody stops recycling. This of course is why Elgin and others have emphasised that the simplification of lifestyles should be "voluntary." The use of negative reinforcement—punishment— on the other hand, tend towards the eco-fascist option, which we have already discarded.

A third option is to create a special context within which the value of a simplified lifestyle can be experienced; a context within which people's purpose or activity is framed in such a way that the materialistic trap is weakened or unactivated. On a camping holiday, or a meditation retreat, for example, one's expectations and habits of consumption may be radically different from those that are compulsive within the normal routines of life. The problem with this is that there is often little or no carry-over from one context to the other. We seem to be constructed psychologically in such a way that we can happily manifest different priorities in different contexts without feeling obliged to achieve any reconciliation (e.g. Lave, 1988). As Sheldrake (1990) has pointed out, many people sense no contradiction between working all week for a multinational oil company or a merchant bank, and on Friday evening dashing down the M4 in the Range Rover to a country home where the pin-stripe is immediately exchanged for working jeans, and Nature is celebrated, respected (and occasionally, without any felt contradictions, shot) for a couple of days.

This analysis of the causes of resistance to lifestyle changes makes the role of "self-help" and "support" groups very clear. Normal relationships, and the normal routines or life, readily reinforce both each other *and* the beliefs that underpin normal habits of consumption. But the power of *example* and *support,* in the suspension of this package of self-fulfilling, mutually-reinforcing life structures, is formidable, and certainly much greater than rational assent or individual resolve. Religious communities have long known the value of congregation and of *sangha* (Rahula, 1967), but in the lay world this kind of support has often been seen as a comforting *addition* to other strategies for life change, rather than as one of the few strategies that actually addresses the heart of the psychological difficulty.

The final approach to making voluntary simplicity a reality which I shall discuss here is the cultivation of *mindfulness,* a term which Elgin (1981)

has borrowed from Buddhist scripture. I have argued elsewhere (Claxton, 1994) that sharpening awareness of the immediate present is a prerequisite for the uncovering of tacit presuppositions. It is only an acquired (and therefore reversible) habit of perceptual imprecision that allows these unrecognised assumptions to be continually dissolved in the process whereby experience is fabricated. We can "leap to conclusions," and mistake those conclusions for "reality," only if we do not see that "leaping to conclusions" is what we are doing. By attending precisely to the minute detail of experience, the nest of assumptions that link identity, security and consumption can be brought to light— not just in an intellectual fashion, but within the realm of spontaneous perceptions and dispositions.

Conclusions

The main conclusion of this analysis, then, is that those who wish to promote what they see as healthier lifestyles, and more sustainable patterns of consumption, must acknowledge that giving information, advice and encouragement have to be seen as just one component of a much wider strategy. To write your book, and then stand back in puzzled confusion while the mass of enthusiastic readers continue much as before, is only possible given an ignorance of the depth of the psychological challenge which a change of lifestyle poses. To become either angry, despondent or exhausted are the reactions of one who has grievously underestimated the magnitude and subtlety of the problem.

The second conclusion is that the practical wisdom that is often associated with spiritual traditions such as Buddhism is "wise" not because it relies on a particular theology, but because it understands the psychological dynamics of inertia, denial and self-deception, and is designed to engage with the issue at the requisite depth (see Fox, 1990). The Three Jewels of Buddhism— Buddha, Dharma and Sangha—represent the power of inspiration and living example, the power of mindfulness, and the power of supportive friendship, respectively. Advocacy of "voluntary simplicity," or any other significant lifestyle change, which does not understand that what is required is not *just* a change of habits, but that these habits are the visible tip of a massive and intricate belief system, is bound to increase frustration, guilt, hostility, and thereby to generate heat and friction—in the manner of one who releases the clutch, only to depress simultaneously the accelerator and the brake—but not much motion.

References

Claxton, G. L. 1994 *Noises from the Darkroom: The Science and Mystery of the Mind*. London, HarperCollins/Aquarian Press.

Elgin, D. 1981 *Voluntary Simplicity: Toward a Way of Life That Is Outwardly Simple, Inwardly Rich*. New York, Morrow.

Elgin, D. 1992 "Ecological Living and the New American Challenge." *Elmwood Quarterly* 8(1):11–12.

Eliot, T. S. 1962 *Selected Poems*. London, Faber & Faber.

Fox, W. 1990 *Toward a Transpersonal Ecology*. London and Boston, Shambhala.

Fromm, E. 1978 *To Have or to Be*. London, Cape.

Laszlo, E. 1989 *The Inner Limits of Mankind*. London, Oneworld Publications.

Lave, J. 1988 *Cognition in Practice*. Cambridge, Cambridge University Press.

Lepper, M., and Green, D. 1975 "Turning Play into Work," *Journal of Personality and Social Psychology* 31: 479–86.

Nanavira Thera. 1987 *Clearing the Path*. Colombo, Sri Lanka, Path Press.

Rahula, W. 1967 *What the Buddha Taught*. London, Gordon Fraser.

Sheldrake, R. 1990 *The Rebirth of Nature*. London, Century.

Stolzenberg, G. 1984 "Can an Inquiry into the Foundations of Mathematics Tell Us Anything Interesting about Mind?" in *The Invented Reality*, edited by P. Watzlawick. New York, W. W. Norton.

99. SIDELIGHT: A Resistance Movement of One's Own

There are moments in life when all or most may seem lost, when one seems overwhelmed by the obstacles at hand or the forces by which one appears to be surrounded. Moments when one seems faced with overwhelming odds. What if one cares about the planet, about the extinction spasm we are in, about the loss of cleaner air, of purer lakes, of great old growth forests? Given the widespread indifference about environmental degradation, the passivity of fellow citizens, the times when corporations and governmental agencies are a menace, and the periods when the prolific market system seems designed to generate excesses, it is tempting to sadly and pessimistically feel, that *there is nothing one can do* and that individual citizens are powerless against such forces. Sometimes private efforts such as an occasional letter to a member of congress, conscientious recycling, or a contribution to The Nature Conservancy seem no more significant, as they say, than spitting in the ocean. The ocean does not seem to notice. Why not surrender in despair? Maybe apathy or fatalism would be the more durable stance.

But let us reflect. We really do have this choice: We can either be part of the problem or part of the solution. We can either "roll over" or fight back. If you have worked through many of the issues in this book, you may have some strong opinions about which is the better or the worse course.

Questions arise. *Where is the guarantee that our individual efforts will bear fruit?* The answer would seem to be, There is none. If one needs guarantees, perhaps a job at the post office is in order. But marriage does not come with guarantees, nor do the efforts of the farmer, the entrepreneur, or the physician or nurse who labors twenty straight hours to save a patient's life.

What difference can one person make? It is hard to tell ahead of time, is it not? One thinks of the efforts of Ralph Nader—hardly a charismatic personality—in changing the direction of the auto industry. One thinks of Rosa Parks, the courageous black woman from Alabama who refused to sit on the back of the bus, the students who sat in protest at a segregated lunch counter in Greensboro, North Carolina, in 1960. Great transformations ensued—but not overnight. And the work is not over.

Still, one might think, *how can I ever hope to know enough to contribute to the solution of environmental issues?* After all, some seem quite perplexing, and scientists often dispute the facts. One kind of contribution is *directly* to the solution of a scientific puzzle; to do that one has to make a serious commitment—namely, to professional training in the sciences. Not a path for everyone, but a path for some. However, figuring out which side to be on does not always require direct scientific expertise but rather an intelligent decision about which authorities to trust. And this is not a new problem or one especially associated with environmental issues. After all, most of us are not trained in medicine or dentistry, but we need to figure out who is a reliable authority in such fields; there are clearly smart and foolish ways to go about these tasks. In some cases the key policy question does not seem to turn on what the facts are. The facts about how veal calves are raised, or how fetuses develop, are not at issue in disputes about the treatment of such animals or in the dispute about abortion. Working through these issues, and the arguments, is not a domain restricted to scientists, and the scientifically trained have not always distinguished themselves at that task. Consider, for example, the number of Nazi physicians in Germany in World War II, or the number of anthropologists who pleaded scientific neutrality rather than condemn the Nazi movement.

Aside from professional paths one might take, we all have the role of citizen and some obligation to be informed about the issues at hand. Otherwise, we simply "roll the dice" and let others decide our collective fate. But we come back to our difficulty once more. As individual citizens, we feel intellectually overwhelmed. How can the ordinary, nonacademic citizen find the time and the will and the opportunity to investigate the spread of AIDS; the Ebola virus; global warming; ozone problems; population and famine issues; war in Rwanda, the Near East, Afghanistan, East Timor; terrorism here and around the world; the after-effects of Chernobyl; the nuclear wastes at Rocky Flats, Colorado; the proposed nuclear waste depository in Yucca Mountain, Nevada; the decline of fish and crabs in the Chesapeake Bay; the red tide off the coast of North Carolina; the loss of species in the Everglades in Florida; the slaughter of elephants and rhinoceros in Africa; the burning of the rain forests in Brazil; environmental racism; and so on—for starters? The answer, simply, is, One cannot. But one can pick his battles and one can pick an area of

desired competence. We cannot all be advocates for, or highly informed students of, Alzheimer's patients, cancer research, AIDS, underweight babies, those born blind, abused animals, rape victims, and so on. Aside from the impossibility of addressing all these concerns in any serious and direct manner, there is, beside the option of despair, choosing to do what one can about a small number of issues, of deciding to learn about them over time and to make one's presence felt. This requires saying no to lots of worthy causes—for example, giving money to environmental causes instead of giving to fight muscular dystrophy. There are hard choices here; the trick *would seem to be not to do nothing just because one cannot do everything*. There may be some truth in "Think globally, act locally." There is strength in numbers, and one task is to organize those who care. Much remains undone here.

As most people know, salmon travel hundreds or thousands of miles to reach their goal, much of it upstream. If they knew the odds and could think about it, they would be tempted to give in to a self-defeating prediction, that is, "since I'll never succeed, I'll quit right now"—a choice ensuring that the prediction is true and thus self-fulfilling. When enough people choose to swim upstream, and to fight in an organized manner, great changes occur. Regardless of one's views about the morality of U.S. involvement in Vietnam, there is little doubt that the efforts of thousands of individual students and others in the United States had a profound effect on U.S. foreign policy—and over time turned it around. Thoreau once said that "the United States must cease to hold slaves and to make war on Mexico—though it costs them their existence as a people." That kind of noncalculating commitment can make a difference. In any case, one can only choose one's own course, his or her own code. One can give in to despair—and ensure one's own political impotence, or one can be part of the resistance.

LEARNING AND RESEARCH TOOLS

100. GLOSSARY

Some terms are often used in both a technical *and* non-technical sense (such as *valid* or *sound* in and out of philosophy, and *irritable* in and out of biology) and readers need to be on the alert for this; often the only way, if at all, to tell how a term is being used is from the context. Furthermore, even technical, or stipulative, terms may not be used in precisely the same manner by all writers and one needs to be wary here as well. Of course, undergraduates will recognize the usual conspiracy here to make life hard for them. What follows is a more or less standard definition of possibly unfamiliar terms.

anthropoid apes Chimpanzees, orangutans, gorillas, and gibbons.

argument As used technically by philosophers, mathematicians, and logicians: two or more, usually explicit statements in which one is intended as the main claim (the *conclusion*) and the others (the *premises*) are thought to provide a reason for accepting it. Its appraisal is a further matter. Thus, the neighbors' fight is not an argument in this sense.

anthropocentrism *Anthropocentrism* is used technically in moral philosophy to refer to the view that all and only members of *Homo sapiens* have moral standing. Sometimes the term refers to a less bold view to the effect that humans should have pride of place, so to speak, in a world in which other beings have some, albeit lesser, standing or significance. Some writers use the term simply to mean "human centered" or "from the viewpoint of humans," but then all of physics, mathematics, chemistry, and so on, are no less "anthropocentric" (in this sense) than any ethical theory or "values" that we might invoke.

anthropomorphic Views are anthropomorphic if they involve projecting particularly human traits onto living nonhumans. If a trait such as sexuality or sentience is shared by the animal or plant in question, the projection may hit a target of course.

atmosphere The layers of air surrounding the earth.

biocentrism The view that any living thing has moral standing. The view may allow that different living things have different magnitudes of intrinsic value (*biocentric inegalitarism*) or it may hold that all living things have the same magnitude (*biocentric egalitarism*).

biological integrity Roughly the "wholeness of a biological system," including appropriate (naturally evolved assemblages of) elements, and processes occurring at appropriate rates. This explication seems problematic, given the ostensibly evaluative term *appropriate*.

biosphere Those layers of the earth and the earth's atmosphere in which living things are located.

biodiversity Roughly, the diversity of different sorts of living creatures, possibly defined in terms of ecosystems, species, subspecies, some other taxonomic level, or genetic variability among individuals.

biome A region characterized by a distinct kind of vegetation, such as grasslands, forests.

capital Usually refers to machinery, factories, and so on, that is, human artifacts useful in production; the term *human capital* has come to be used, usually referring to the stock of human skills and capacities useful in production of a good or service. The term *labor* is also used for the latter; another recognized category in economics is *land*: The latter term usually refers to anything that is not *labor* or *capital*.

care-based ethic An ethical outlook according to which there are important deficiencies in a rights-based ethic or one focusing on justice, because the latter fails to be complete and thus omits a significant aspect of morality.

carrying capacity The theoretical limit as to how much a given population can be supported by a certain habitat.

chlorofluorocarbons (CFCs) Compounds made up of carbon, chlorine, and fluorine; in gaseous form they react with ozone molecules to deplete the ozone layer in the stratosphere.

conclusion The main claim, or central contention, in an argument.

consequentialist Ethical theories are labeled consequentialist if they suppose that *only* the consequences of an act matter (in some fashion) to determining the morality of the act. Prime examples: Utilitarianism and Ethical Egoism.

contractualism An ethical theory is contractualist if it supposes that the morality of an act depends on whether certain parties have agreed to the principles that support it—or perhaps would agree to the principles under certain conditions, e.g., if fully informed, free, and so on. John Rawls's well-known theory of justice gives central place to what rational negotiators would agree to while not knowing their own class, nationality, or into which generation they were born (they are under a "veil of ignorance").

cost–benefit analysis The attempt to measure the balance of benefits (or advantages—often cashed in terms of *human satisfaction* and measured in some unit of currency) and costs (or disadvantages).

criterion of moral standing The feature or trait (or set of such) in virtue of which something possesses moral standing. There is debate here over various proposed criteria, such as being alive, being sentient, being rational, and so on.

Deep Ecology The view, associated with Norwegian philosopher Arne Naess, that we should care about the earth not just as a means to our human ends but for its own sake and that the boundaries between humans and other living things, and perhaps nonliving things, are arbitrary; hence, a larger sense of one's self is fitting. Thus to care about one's larger self is to care about the earth. The expression "Deep Ecology" is contrasted with "shallow ecology." Thus the use of these labels tends to suggest that one view is superior to the other; without arguments, this move tends to try to win the day by "theft rather than honest toil," as Bertrand Russell often said. To be fair, defenders of Deep Ecology do give arguments.

demographics The study of the structure and size of various populations, usually human.

deontological Deriving from the Greek *deontos*, "duty," this term is used technically to refer to ethical theories that assume that one's duties are not to be determined solely by weighing up the consequences of different courses of action (that is, in "consequentialist" fashion).

development See growth.

discounting The practice of assigning some current economic value to future benefits (costs) in a manner (at some rate) that typically makes those values much less than their future value (or disvalue). The calculation is done at "constant rates," that is, independently of the effects of inflation. Economists often claim that "rationality" itself requires one to do so.

diversity–stability hypothesis The view that the more diverse an ecosystem is in terms of some measure of biodiversity, then the more stable it is; this view is now widely thought outdated.

ecofeminism The view that there are important connections between the domination of nature and the domination of women. Thus, an understanding of these connections is thought to be important to both environmental ethics and feminism.

ecology The study of the interaction of living things with one another and with their nonliving environment.

economic good Sometimes defined as any service or material that gives people satisfaction. Note that, thus, assassination, torture, vandalism, and genocide will count as "economic goods," and one may wonder about the desirability of "increasing the sum of economic goods" or "growing the economy" in just any fashion.

ecosphere The collection of living things on the planet.

ecosystem Community of living things of diverse species interacting with one another and their inorganic environment.

efficient Nontechnically, the term often means that a process or object yields more benefit per unit of cost than another, which is then said to be less efficient. In economics a situation A is said to be more efficient than (a Pareto improvement over) another situation B if one can go from B to A and at least one person is better off in A than in B *and* no one is worse off in A than in B. It is often claimed that whenever free and informed persons make an exchange then the result is more efficient than the situation prior to it; this step may be thought of as increasing total net utility. It is well worth scrutinizing the widespread assumption that we *should* do what is maximally efficient. There are further assumptions that people always act in their own interests, and that people know whether a given purchase, for example, will promote their own interests on balance. Further, *efficiency* so understood just concerns the welfare of members of *Homo sapiens*.

entropy Disorder or diffusion; the scattering of energy in the form of heat is an increase in entropy.

environmental holism The view that not merely individual living things but certain sorts of "collective" entities also have moral standing, such as species or ecosystems, and that we owe duties to them as well. There is a related "environmental contextualism," which asserts that duties are not just to promote individual welfare but something like a harmony between individuals and certain environmental processes across generations and different scales of concern.

environmental individualism   The view that only individual living things of one kind or another have moral standing, and that it is thus only to them that we directly owe duties.

environmental pragmatists   Typically this term refers to those who for one reason or another think we should focus our efforts on solving particular environmental policy problems and not try to resolve, or respectively focus on resolving, theoretical issues. Thus, one can have "convergence" at a policy level without "consensus" about the theoretical foundations for that convergence.

epistemological   Having to do with knowledge. The central questions of epistemology, or theory of knowledge, are What can we know as opposed to merely believe? and What is the criterion for what counts as knowing something?

estuary   Area where freshwater at mouth of a river mixes with salty seawater.

eukaryotic   A cell with a nucleus; contrast "prokaryotic"—cells without a distinct nucleus.

evolution   In biology, the generation over time of organisms genetically unlike their predecessors such that new species come into existence.

externalities   Social benefits or harms not reflected in the market price of that good; for example, a polluter may not have to pay for the cost of his or her pollution, which gets passed on to others. One might note the resemblance here to what is often classified as a crime.

first law of thermodynamics   In (nonnuclear) physical or chemical changes, no energy is lost but only changed in form.

future generations   Usually the reference is to those people who will be born at a later date, not yet conceived, and not merely possible persons. Compare future generations of plants and animals.

Gaia theory   The view that the earth is alive and maintains a certain stability by means of positive or negative feedback between its living and nonliving elements. The principal advocate is James Lovelock, a British chemist. Sometimes this view is taken as a reason not to worry about human induced pollution, but the envisioned maintenance of balance need not be at all favorable to the well-being of the human species.

gene pool   The hereditary information encoded in a particular species over time.

genus   The taxonomic level between that of species and family.

great apes   Chimpanzees, orangutans and gorillas.

greenhouse effect   The trapping of heat in the atmosphere by the presence of certain gases (carbon dioxide, chlorofluorocarbons, ozone, and so on) and radiated back toward the surface of the earth.

Gross National Product (GNP)   The sum of market values of all goods and services produced in a country for final use in a given year. Contrast *net economic welfare* (NEW), which would subtract the market value of those that decrease the quality of life for humans.

growth   An important but slippery notion; in one sense the increase in the size of something (like the GNP or cancer), but often used to imply a positive evaluation. Some people talk as if "growth is good" is a tautology; "metastasizing GNP" sounds odd. Sometimes the term *development* may be used in contrast to refer to qualitative improvements without increase in size; for example, one might develop one's novel without increasing its length. The terms may be used so as to slide from technical to nontechnical usage; this fact is one source of confusion in debates over "sustainable development."

homeostasis   The tendency of an organism to maintain certain traits at a constant level (such as temperature) under variable external conditions.

hominid   A member of the family Hominidae, erect bipedal primates consisting of humans and related extinct forms, now represented by one living species, *Homo sapiens.*

hominoid   A member of the Hominoidae , a superfamily of primates including great apes and humans.

impartialist theories   Some views advocate promoting the well-being of all people (or even some broader category) regardless of race, sex, nationality, class, sexual preferences, family membership, or other narrowing traits. Utilitarianism and certain rights theories seem to be impartialist; contrary views promote in an exclusivist and often condemnatory manner, such as being white, being black, being American, or French, being straight, being Christian, being Islamic, and so on.

island biogeography   Study of the way in which the breaking up of animal and plant habitats into smaller and smaller parcels (perhaps by roads or buildings) affects these populations—for example, leads to species loss.

justice, theory of   A theory about the appropriate or morally obligatory pattern of *distribution* of benefits or burdens across some population (compare to fair distribution). A most influential theory was posed by John Rawls in *A Theory of a Justice* in 1971. Such considerations are often thought to conflict with maximizing policies, which only seek to maximize the sum or *magnitude* of something, such as GNP, utility, growth, or wealth.

K-strategists   Species that invest much energy in rearing few offspring until they reach reproductive age; contrast *R-strategists*, which produce many offspring often with short lives.

keystone species   Species on which the functioning of many other organisms depend.

kingdoms   The most basic of the taxa or categories of living things.

lithosphere   Outer layers of the earth made up of the crust and the outer portion of the mantle (the layer between the core and the crust).

Lamarckism   The claim of Jean Baptiste de Lamarck that organisms can acquire traits during their lifetimes and transmit them directly to their offspring.

LDC   Less developed country (with respect to technology, GNP, and so on).

mammal   A taxonomic category of vertebrates that includes those animals that suckle their young with milk secreted through mammary glands.

mature community   Comparatively stable, self-sustaining community of organisms.

maximax principle   See maximin principle.

maximin principle   In cases in which one cannot reasonably estimate the probability of the consequences of one's action ("decision making under uncertainty"), many people recommend one or the other of two principles as capturing what it is to choose *rationally*. One such principle is the *maximin principle*, which says choose the alternative whose worst outcome is better than the worst outcome of any other available alternative; thus one "maximizes the minimum." The other principle, by way of contrast, is the *maximax principle*, which says, choose the alternative whose consequences are better than those of any other available alternative. These principles have a bearing on what to do about global warming, or building nuclear plants—as any insurance company might tell you. See the Preview to Section VI.E.

metaphysical   Originally this term was used to refer to Aristotle's book after (*meta*) the one he wrote on physics (*nature* in the Greek). The term now alludes to the kinds of questions he took up there, namely abstract questions such as what kinds of things are there (mental and physical or ?), do we have freedom of choice, and so on. "Can computers think? Do animals or humans have souls? Could I be identical with the fetus from which I derived?" are often classified as metaphysical questions.

moral monism   The view that there is a single moral value or moral principle we should follow.

moral pluralism   The view that there is not, or may not be, a single moral principle or value but rather a small number of irreducible values or principles to which we should give weight in decision making.

moral standing   (often defined) An entity has moral standing if and only if its interests are intrinsically valuable or valuable for their own sake.

natural   This term and *nature* are indeed slippery ones. Sometimes what is meant by *natural* is what is not the result of human intervention; alternatively, sometimes what is meant is what is typical of a large number of members of a certain group (compare: "going to outer space is unnatural," or "being over six feet eight inches tall is unnatural for a human," or "being resurrected").

natural law   Sometimes the reference is just to a scientific law (for example, the second law of thermodynamics), but in ethics the reference is to a normative principle concerning how one should live, one that is thought to derive from the way nature works or be "readable" from an examination of natural processes. However, see Essay 33, "Do What's Natural, You Say?"

natural right   A right to do (or be) X is often thought to be possession of a moral permission to do X and correlatively an impermission for others to disrupt one's doing so (compare: "right to live" or "right to form one's opinion"); if claimed to be natural, it is thought to be something one possesses at birth because of the kind of being one is (compare: "human right" or "right of all sentient creatures") and not something one has to earn or purchase.

natural selection   The process whereby the offspring of a certain species exhibit some degree of genetic diversity, thus some offspring have an advantage in reaching the age of reproduction and hence some genotypes or genetic programs get passed on at a higher rate than others. There is no "selector" on this view; so perhaps it is not the most fortunate term to have been adopted.

net primary production (NPP)   The amount of solar energy captured in photosynthesis by primary producers, less the amount they use up in their own growth; so NPP is the basic food resource of all living things not capable of photosynthesis. It has been estimated that one species, *Homo sapiens*, now uses 25 percent of global NPP, or 40 percent if only terrestrial NPP is considered. Consider what will happen with two or more doublings of the human population.

old-growth forests   Forests that are hundreds of years old or older; some can be found in the northwestern United States in northern California, Oregon, and Washington. Contrast "tree farm."

ontogeny   The development of any individual organism from egg to senescence.

optimality   A term that nontechnically may mean "the best" but in economic theory a situation is described as optimal (or "Pareto optimal") if it is one in which it is impossible to make someone better off without making someone worse off (in his or her own estimation). Orthodox economists tend to view as desirable policies those that lead to optimal outcomes, and may advocate such policies even if they are not sustainable. But watch out for a slide from technical to nontechnical usage or vice versa. See **efficient.**

ozone layer   The thin layer of ozone (O_5) in the stratosphere that protects living things from certain harmful rays of the sun. Evidence of human destruction of this layer, especially in the Antarctic, by generations of chlorofluorocarbons (CFCs), has led to international agreements to halt this process, which, nevertheless, is expected to continue for decades or more.

phylogeny   The evolutionary history of any taxon (that is, any taxononomic group such as a species).

plate tectonics   The theory first widely accepted only in the 1960s explaining geophysical processes (such as earthquakes) by reference to the movements of plates of the earth's lithosphere.

pollution   A process or material that causes destructive effects on some population, usually humans.

pragmatism   The outlook that what works successfully (according to some criteria) in practice is most important; therefore, one should be wary of overemphasis on abstract theorizing. Agreement about policy is the crucial thing even if divergent reasons may support it.

premises   The claim or claims in an argument other than the conclusion.

prima facie duty   A genuine duty but one justifiably overridable on the basis of weightier, morally relevant considerations; thus a duty not to use someone's car without her consent might be overridable to rush someone to the hospital to save her life. Sometimes contrasted with "absolute duty" (but "absolute" tends to be used in wildly diverse ways).

primate   A member of the order Primates, which includes apes, lemurs, monkeys, marmosets, and humans.

punctuated equilibrium   The view that evolution does not always proceed very slowly and incrementally but rather occasionally by comparatively large leaps.

R-strategists   See **K-strategists.**

resource   Again, a term typically defined from the standpoint of the interests of one species: whatever humans find instrumentally useful. If certain processes or objects in nature are valuable on their own, it is misleading to think of them simply as resources for humans. Analogously, an Ethical Egoist might think of all *other* humans merely as "natural resources"; slaveowners at various times may think of slaves as their "natural resources." Thus the typical use of *natural resource* by many economists, among others, presupposes a certain theory of value—one often not recognized as such.

rights theory   Generally a theory about some set of beings possessing the prerogative to act, choose, or be in a certain state (to live, to speak, to choose, to vote, and so on) and asserting the duty of moral agents to accord, or not interfere with, the prerogatives (respect the rights). On these views there are moral constraints on what any agent permissibly may do to seek certain goals—even otherwise attractive ones such as increasing happiness, promoting efficiency, and so on. Associated historically with Thomas Hobbes, John Locke, Immanuel Kant, Jean Jacques Rousseau, and Mary Wollstonecraft.

risk   The probability that something harmful will occur.

second law of thermodynamics   The tendency of energy in concentrated forms (dense ones) to disperse into less useful forms, such as low-temperature forms dispersed in the environment.

sentient   Capable of experiencing satisfaction or dissatisfaction; a trait that may vary in degree.

shallow ecology   See **Deep Ecology.**

social ecology   A somewhat liberal-to-leftish, democratic, egalitarian view that advocates enlightenment ideals (autonomy, reason, and so forth) along with a recognition of the importance of the environment; it opposes ostensive mystical, intuitionist, and misanthropic elements it discerns in Deep Ecology and ecofeminism and elsewhere.

social traps   Situations in which the short-run local reinforcements guiding our behavior lead to the subversion of the long-run best interests of the individual or society (as in smoking, addiction to fried foods, gas-guzzling cars, unprotected sex, very large families, and so on).

sound argument   An argument is (technically) sound if and only if it (1) is valid and (2) has *all* true premises. Both *valid* and *sound* have a common, *nontechnical meaning,* that is, good, correct, or according to a rule (as in "a valid move in chess").

speciation   The formation over time of two species from one species as a result of genetic variation and natural selection.

species   One standard definition: A population of organisms that interbreed naturally in the wild; but see the essay by Stephen Jay Gould in the section on biodiversity in this book.

speciesism   The view that the members of one species or their interests are more valuable than the interests of other species—or more extremely, that the interests of only one species has any intrinsic value; the prime example is anthropocentrism. Views said to be speciesist are often claimed to be arbitrary in the manner of racism or sexism.

stratosphere   Area about 11 to 30 miles above the earth that contains the ozone layer, which filters out harmful, cancer-causing, UV solar radiation.

sustainability   A slippery and important term. One general characterization: A sustainable economy is one whose essential practices can be carried on indefinitely while maintaining its population of humans and other species at a certain level of well-being. It is not clear that there is a plausible characterization of *sustainability* that is not, in part, evaluative. Because "continual growth" in one sense may be incompatible with such sustainability, many think "sustainable growth" is, on one interpretation ("indefinitely sustainable growth"), an incoherent notion.

tautology   A label for statements thought to be true simply in virtue of their structure such as "It's square or it is not" or in virtue of the meaning of the key terms such as "All red things are colored." Such claims convey no non-linguistic information about the world.

taxonomy   A hierarchical classification in biology; normally that of the 18th Century Swedish naturalist Carolus Linnaeus; he classified living things into kingdoms, phyla, classes, orders, families, genera, and species. Further refinements or newer clarifications are often used.

teleological   In one sense: purposive or goal-directed—with no necessary implication of the existence of conscious purposes. Thus, a thermostat or heat-seeking missile may be said to be teleological. Teleological explanations of events are often thought to differ from "causal explanations." In sharp contrast, in moral philosophy the term is sometimes used interchangeably with *consequentialist* to refer to ethical theories that assume that the moral value of an act depends (in some manner) solely on its consequences.

thermodynamics   The study of mechanical or heat changes. The first law of thermodynamics is the *law of conservation of energy:* In any exchange of energy the total amount of energy remains the same. The second law is the *law of entropy* (disorder): In energy changes, there is an increase in the diffusion of energy from more to less concentrated forms.

tragedy of the commons   The view that when a resource is not privately held (by established property rights) but is "commonly owned" or readily accessible to the public, it will be overused—resulting in its serious degradation or complete loss.

trophic level   The distance from the original source of energy; all organisms that are the same number of energy transfers away from the original source of energy are at the same level; thus, "producers" are in the first level, and herbivores at the second level, and so on.

Utilitarianism   The classical theory of Jeremy Bentham and John Stuart Mill according to which the right act is whichever one will bring about the greatest balance of utility (or happiness) over disutility (unhappiness) for all those affected by the action (which for Bentham and Mill included all sentient creatures—thus, some nonhumans as well).

valid argument   An argument is valid if and only if it is one in which the conclusion must be true if the premises are. Understanding this definition and distinguishing valid from invalid (not valid) arguments takes practice; a logic course is recommended.

value-laden term   A term that is explicitly evaluative such as *good; bad; right*—or less obviously so, such as *natural; unnatural; overpopulation; efficient; primitive; pollutant; pest; weed; invaders;* and *resource;* and perhaps *poverty; growth; sustainable;* and *development* as well.

virtue-based ethics   Those ethical outlooks or theories that focus on questions of what it is to be a good person, or to exhibit virtuous character (honesty, courage, integrity, and so on) as opposed to focusing on policy questions or questions about which action is right. Dating back to Aristotle, these views have had a certain revival in the last decade or so.

101. TIME CHART _____

THE BEGINNING OF THE UNIVERSE UNTIL 200,000 YEARS AGO (YA)[1]

15 billion ya	The universe is formed.[2]
4.6 billion ya	The earth comes into existence.
3.5 billion ya	Life on earth (bacterial life) begins.
1.3 billion ya	Complex nucleated life exists.
700 million ya	Multicelled animal life appears in fossil record. Note: for almost 90 percent of the earth's existence, there was no animal life.
535 million ya	Lifeforms vastly expand ("the Cambrian[3] explosion").
500 million ya	First vertebrates appear.
390 million ya	Bony fishes appear.
210-225 million ya	Earliest dinosaurs and mammals appear.
65 million ya	Massive die off of dinosaurs occurs near this time.
60 million ya	First living primate species appears.
30 million ya	Monkeys date back to this period.
23 million ya	Ape specimens date back this far.
6 to 7 million ya	Molecular estimate places the split of African apes and first hominids about 5 mya [million years ago]. *Australopithecus ramidus* is the earliest named hominid species.
4 to 5 million ya	Genus Homo appears. Species *Homo sapiens* appears.

200,000 YEARS AGO UNTIL THE PRESENT

150,000 ya	Anatomically modern humans arise in Africa.
10 to 12,000 ya	Humans become less dependent on local ecosystems with the development of agriculture.
1200 to 1000 B.C.E.	Book of Genesis is probably written.
5th–4th century B.C.E.	Socrates, Plato, Aristotle.
4 B.C.E.	Jesus is born; about *250 million* humans exist.
1500 C.E.	60 to 125 million bison roam North America (500 ya); Columbus arrives. Descartes is born in 1496.
1689 C.E.	Isaac Newton's *Mathematical Principles of Natural Philosophy* is published.
1775 or so C.E.	Industrial revolution (275 ya). Adam Smith's *Wealth of Nations* is published in 1776. Jeremy Bentham's *Principles of Morals and Legislation* is published in 1789, the year of the French Revolution.
1798 C.E.	Thomas Malthus's essay *On Population* is published. In 1817 David Ricardo's publishes *Principles of Political Economy and Taxation*.

---

[1]*Abbreviations:* ya stands for years ago; C.E. stands for Common Era, also often known by A.D.; B.C.E. stands for Before the Common Era.

[2]For dates, etc. we have relied on Niles Eldredge, Dominion (New York: Holt, 1995; G. Tyler Miller, *Living in the Environment* (Belmont, CA: Wadsworth, 1994), Robert Foley, *Humans Before Humanity* (Oxford: Blackwell, 1995), David Suzuki, *A Time to Change* (Toronto: Stoddart, 1994), and the Museum of Paleontology web site of the University of California at Berkeley. For more detail you can access this useful site at: *http://wvv.ucmp.berkeley.edu/index.html.* Another useful site is *http://geologyone.com/esa/geotime/time/geotime2.html.* The dates are periodically revised as new evidence comes to light.

[3]The vast expanse of time is usually divided by paleontologists into eons, eras, periods, epochs, and ages; thus these terms are used technically and not as they are commonly and nontechnically used (loosely and vaguely). Remembering this fact helps avoid confusion. We ignore such subdivisions here.

1838 C.E.	Darwin formulates the notion of evolution by natural selection. In 1848 Karl Marx's *Communist Manifesto* and John Stuart Mill's *Principles of Political Economy* are published.
1850 C.E.	*1 billion* humans exist (150 ya). Time for our species to reach this number is *3 to 5 million years*. Darwin's *Origin of Species* is published in 1859. In the early 1860s the Civil War begins in the United States.
1895 C.E.	About 85 bison left in North America (100 ya). Sigmund Freud's first writings appear.
1900 C.E.	Einstein formulates the theory of relativity.
1930 C.E.	*2 billion* humans exist. Time for the human population to double since 1 billion is *80 years*.
1940s C.E.	Nuclear weapons are created.
1950s C.E.	DNA structure is discovered.
1958 C.E.	*3 billion* humans exist.
1960s C.E.	The theory of plate tectonics is accepted. "Environmental economics" emerges. Rachel Carson's *The Silent Spring* is published in 1962.
1970 C.E.	The first "Earth Day" is celebrated in the United States.
1975 C.E.	*4 billion* humans exist. Time to double since 2 billion is *45 years*.
1980s C.E.	A recognizable domain of academic inquiry, "environmental ethics," develops. In 1987, the "Brundtland Report," *Our Common Future,* is published, urging environmentally sustainable practices.
1988 C.E.	*5 billion* humans exist.
2000 C.E.	*6 billion* humans exist.

PROJECTED FUTURE:

2017 C.E.	Speculative figure: *8 billion* humans exist. Time to double since 4 billion is *42 years*; projections depend on whether the recent growth rate is sustained.
2030–2040 C.E.	Grandchildren born for many of those graduating from a university around 2001 to 2005.
2060 C.E.	*10 to 12 billion* humans exist? No decrease in doubling time assumed for this estimate since the last period.

102. INTERNET AND OTHER ENVIRONMENTAL RESOURCES _____

I. SEARCH ENGINES/ DIRECTORIES

In this third edition there is much less need for guidance as to how to search for relevant material on the Internet. Procedures here are widely known and used. It is essential to know how use the main search engines and how to refine search techniques. A staggering increase exists in available information. The following is a list of some of the major search engines. Their approaches vary somewhat; hence, one might try several.

alltheweb.com

askjeeves.com

directhit.com

dogpile.com

google.com

mamma.com

metacrawler.com

teoma.com

wisenut.com

We strongly encourage the reader to look up, with any search engine, whatever terms strike one as relevant, for example, *environmental ethics, rain forest, animal rights, gaia, great apes, justice, environmental racism, Greenpeace, Earth First!, natural law, ecological sustainability, ecosystem health, E. O. Wilson, BBC, Economist, National Geographic, Scientific American, Pareto Principle, biotech, ozone layer, when life began,* etc.

II. WEB SITES ADDRESSING ENVIRONMENTAL ISSUES

The directories at Refdesk [outstanding], Yahoo, About.com, and elsewhere are also worth checking. The *New York Times, Washington Post,* the *Atlantic Monthly,* and other magazines or papers (see *thepaperboy.com* also) are worth exploring.

Most of the links cited in the second edition of this volume can be found as hot links at *http://www.cortland.edu/www/philosophy/elinks.htm*. This site thus may save some actual typing of URLS.

On environmental ethics as such, check the many links on Ethics Updates at *http://ethics.acusd.edu/environmental_ethics.html*. A directory of web sites with over 600 links may be found at *http://www.ulb.ac.be/ceese/meta/cds.html*. Another fine location is the *Center for Environmental Philosophy* at *http://www.cep.unt.edu/*. Or search the archives at the *International Society for Environmental Ethics* at *http://www.phil.unt.edu/bib/*.

We also note here the valuable newsletter concerning news, books, events, meetings, etc. The British journal, *Environmental Values*, may be found at *http://www.erica.demon.co.uk/EV.html*.

Excellent links can be found at the site for the Center for Applied Ethics at the University of British Columbia: *http://www.ethics.ubc.ca/resources/environmental/*.

On religion: *http:/www.acton.org*

Scientific wealth can be found at the site for the American Museum of Natural History: *http://www.amnh.org*

The National Audobon Society: *http://www.audobon.org*

On transgenic crops: *http://www.colostate.edu/programs/lifesciences/TransgenicCrops*

Society for Conservation Biology: *http://conbio.net/scb/*

Duke University Primate Center: *http://www.duke.edu/web/primate/*

Earth First! Journal is at *http://www.earthfirstjournal.org/*

Good links are at *http://www.ecoethics.net/hsev/200002res.htm*

Useful, extensive, often conservative, archives can be found at *The Economist: http://www.economist.com*

Environmental News Network at *http://www.enn.com*

The International Association for Environmental Philosophy is at *www.environmentalphilosophy.org*.

On factory farming and to see dramatic slides (also further links): *http://www.factoryfarming.com/gallery.htm*

Friends of the Earth: *http://www.foe.co.uk/*

Greenpeace: *http://www.greenpeace.org*

Professor Ernest Partridge's site on environmental ethics, with essays, news, and further links, is at *http://www.igc.org/gadfly/*

EcoNet is at *http://www.igc.org/igc/gateway/enindex.html*

On religious skepticism, see *http://www.infidels.org/library/historical/robert_ingersoll/why_i_am_agnostic.html*

The Intergovernmental Panel on Climate Change can be found at *http://www.ipcc.ch/*

On agriculture: see the Land Institute: *http//www.landinstitute.org*

The well-known journal of science, *Nature*, can be found at *http://www.nature.com/nature/*

See the sections Nature & Wildlife, as well as Science and Technology, on the Public Broadcast System at *http://www.pbs.org*

The Nature Conservancy: *http://www.nature.org*

Pesticide Action Network: *http://www.panna.org/*

People for the Ethical Treatment of Animals: *http://www.peta.org/*

Rainforest Action Network: *http://www.ran.org*

On mad cow disease, see *http://www.theatlantic.com/cgi-bin/o/issues/98sep/madcow.htm*

The Ecologist: http://www.theecologist.org

Thoreau Center for Sustainability: *http://www.Thoreau.org/home.html*

The Union of Concerned Scientists: *http://www.ucsusa.org/index.html*

Project Vote Smart has dozens if not hundreds of links at *http://www.vote-smart.org/issues/ENVIRONMENT/*

Worldwatch Institute is at *http://www.worldwatch.org/*

Zero Population Growth: *http://www.zpg.org*

III. PHILOSOPHY WEB SITES

The *Electronic Journal of Analytic Philosophy: http://ejap.louisiana.edu/EJAP/1995.spring/contents.html* Finally, there are live members of our species—reference librarians—who can be of great assistance.

IV. SITES ESPECIALLY RELEVANT TO CITIZEN ACTIVISM

The Aristotle Project: *http://www.Aristotle.org*

Free Expression Clearing House: *http://FreeExpression.org*

InterActivism: *http://www.InterActivism.com*

The Liberty Net: *http://www.libertynet.org/community/phila/natl.html*

Vox Populi: *http://www.voxpop.org*

V. A NOTE ON "ENVIRONMENTAL ORGANIZATIONS"

The expression *environmental organization* suggests an organization that aims at preserving or protecting some aspect of the environment. Thus one might be tempted to think that organizations with names like B. C. Forest Alliance, Environmental Conservation Organization, The Evergreen Foundation, The Global Climate Coalition, Mothers Watch, Science and Environmental Policy Project, The Sea Lion Defense Fund, and so on are all aimed at protecting the environment from threats—including human generated ones. However, all of these organizations are listed in a volume published by Greenpeace called *The Greenpeace Guide to Anti-Environmental Organizations*. According to Greenpeace, the Evergreen Foundation, for example, is an organization of the timber industry, located in the heart of Oregon's forest country, that publishes *Evergreen*, a magazine that mixes fly-fishing stories, attractive wildlife photographs and insinuates the message that environmental protection laws are harmful. Whether a particular organization actually represents groups with narrow economic interests but is in reality a cover for the promotion of these interests in particular, must be decided on an individual basis. According to Greenpeace, the Sea Lion Defense Fund is a legal arm of the Alaska fishing industry.

Reckless organizations often try to portray themselves as ecologically sensitive ones. Thus one needs to be skeptical, look into membership on editorial boards when possible, and check out whether the scientists or experts quoted are misquoted or whether they are of the familiar "for hire" variety. Despite the pedigree of the organization, green or otherwise, presented arguments (if any) deserve careful assessment. The use of smear tactics, personal attacks, insinuation, the failure to even consider objections, and the lack of scholarly documentation is a good clue that an organization or writer lacks reasonable arguments and is thus inclined and willing to resort to fraud, cardstacking, misdirection, or something like it to influence readers.

VI. MEDIA RESOURCES

Bullfrog Films (environmental videos): *www.bullfrogfilms.com*

The Video Project (environmental videos and CD-ROMS): *www.videoproject.net*

103. BIBLIOGRAPHY

We call attention to the journal *Environmental Ethics*, a pioneering periodical from the early days of an emerging field of study. The founding editor, Eugene Hargrove, is in the Department of Philosophy and Religious Studies at the University of North Texas in Denton, Texas. We also call attention to these more recent periodicals with similar focus: the British journal *Environmental Values*, and the American journal *Ethics and the Environment*.

We further mention the *Journal of the Society for Conservation Biology, Ecological Economics, Between the Species,* and the *Trumpeter*. Other philosophical journals that occasionally focus on environmental issues are *Inquiry*, the *Monist*, the *American Philosophical Quarterly, Ethics*, the *Journal of Value Inquiry,* and *Philosophy and Public Affairs*. Bibliographies are springboards from which to jump; the materials cited here, notoriously "incomplete" in many respects, will lead the reader to other important works. There are extensive references available on the Internet; see the prior section—especially the online Bibliography available from the journal *Environmental Ethics* web site.

Also, there are two annotated bibliographies drawn up by Eric Katz: (1) "Environmental Ethics: A Select Annotated Bibliography, 1983–1987," in *Research in Philosophy & Technology 9*, 251–285; and (2) "Environmental Ethics: A Select Annotated Bibliography: II: 1987–1990," in *Research in Philosophy & Technology 12*, 287–324.

For current bibliographic references, reviews, videotape information, and current announcements about conferences on, or related to, environmental ethics, see the lively and downright essential *International Society for Environmental Ethics Newsletter*. The editor is Professor Jack Weir; his e-mail address is: j.weir@morehead-st.edu. On a broad variety of topics in ethics, the excellent two-volume *Encyclopedia of Ethics*, 2nd ed., edited by Lawrence Becker and Charlotte Becker (New York: Routledge, 2001), will prove extremely useful.

I. An Introduction to Ethical Theory

Feldman, Fred. *Introductory Ethics* (Englewood Cliffs, NJ: Prentice Hall, 1978).

Gilroy, John Marin. Justice & Nature; Kantian Philosophy; *Environmental Philosophy and the Law* (Baltimore, MD: Georgetown University Press, 2001).

Hargrove, Eugene. *Foundations of Environmental Ethics* (Englewood Cliffs, NJ: Prentice Hall, 1989).

Miller, Harlan B., and William H. Williams, eds. *The Limits of Utilitarianism* (Minneapolis: University of Minnesota Press, 1982).

Mutz, Kathryn, Gary C. Bryner, and Douglass S. Kenney, eds. *Justice and Natural Resources: Concepts, Strategies, and Applications* (Washington, DC: Island Press, 2001).

Nash, Roderick, F. *The Rights of Nature: A History of Environmental Ethics* (Madison: University of Wisconsin Press, 1989).

Palmer, Clare. *Environmental Ethics and Process Thinking* (New York: Oxford University Press, 1998).

Rachels, James, ed. *The Elements of Moral Philosophy* (New York: McGraw-Hill, 1993).

———. *The Right Thing to Do* (New York: Random House, 1989).

Regan, Tom, and Donald VanDeVeer, eds. *And Justice For All* (Totowa, NJ: Rowman & Littlefield, 1982).

Ruggiero, Vincent. *Thinking Critically About Ethical Issues* (Mountain View, CA: Mayfield, 1992).

Sen, Amartya, and Bernard Williams, eds. *Utilitarianism and Beyond* (Cambridge, MA: Cambridge University Press, 1982).

Sher, George, ed. *Moral Philosophy* (San Diego: Harcourt Brace Jovanovich, 1987).

Singer, Peter. *Applied Ethics* (Oxford: Oxford University Press, 1988).

———. *Practical Ethics* (Cambridge, MA: Cambridge University Press, 1979).

Sterba, James. *Morality in Practice* (Belmont, CA: Wadsworth, 1988).

Taylor, Paul. *Problems of Moral Philosophy* (Belmont, CA: Dickenson, 1967).

II. Religious and Cultural Perspectives

Allen, Paula Gunn. *The Sacred Hoop: Recovering the Feminine in American Indian Traditions* (Boston: Beacon Press, 1986).

Ames, Roger T., and J. Baird Callicott, eds. *Nature in Asian Traditions of Thought: Essays in Environmental Philosophy* (Albany: State University of New York Press, 1989).

Aquinas, Thomas. *Summa Contra Gentiles,* trans. Anton Pegis et al. (5 vols.) (Garden City, NY: Image Books, 1955–57).

———. *Summa Theologica (60 vols.)* (London: Eyre and Spottiswoode; and New York: McGraw-Hill, 1964).

Attfield, Robin. *The Ethics of Environmental Concern*, 2nd ed. (Athens: The University of Georgia Press, 199 1).

———. *God and the Secular: A Philosophical Assessment of Secular Reasoning from Bacon to Kant* (Cardiff, UK: University College Cardiff Press, 1978).

Berry, Thomas. *The Dream of the Earth* (San Francisco: Sierra Club Books, 1988).

Birch, Charles, William Eakin, and Jay McDaniel, eds. *Liberating Life: Contemporary Approaches to Ecological Theology* (Maryknoll, NY: Orbis Books, 1990).

Black, John. *The Dominion of Man: The Search for Ecological Responsibility* (Edinburgh: University of Edinburgh Press, 1970).

Callicott, J. Baird. *Earth's Insights: A Survey of Ecological Ethics from the Mediterranean Basin to the Australian Outback* (Berkeley: University of California Press, 1994).

Callicott, J. Baird, and Roger Ames, eds. *Nature in Asian Traditions of Thought* (Albany: State University of New York Press, 1989).

Clark, Stephen R. L. *How to Think about the Earth: Philosophical and Theological Models for Ecology* (New York: Mowbray, 1993).

Dombrowski, Daniel. *Hartshorne and the Metaphysics of Animal Rights* (Albany: State University of New York Press, 1981).

Ehrenfeld, D. *The Arrogance of Humanism* (New York: Oxford University Press, 1981).

Gottfried, Robert R. *Economics, Ecology, and the Roots of Western Faith* (Lanham, MD: Rowman & Littlefield, 1995).

Gottlieb, Roger S., ed. *This Sacred Earth: Religion, Nature, Environment* (New York: Routledge, 1996).

Hume, C.W. *The Status of Animals in the Christian Religion* (London: Universities Federation for Animal Welfare, 1957).

Hessel, Dieter T. and Rosemary Radford Ruether. *Christianity and Ecology: Seeking the Well-Being of Earth and Humans* (Cambridge, MA: Harvard University Press, 2000)

Kahn, Jr., Peter H. *The Human Relationship with Nature: Development and Culture* (Cambridge, MA: The MIT Press, 1999).

Karrer, Otto, ed. *St. Francis of Assisi, The Legends and the Lauds,* trans. N. Wydenbruck (London: Sheed & Ward, 1977).

Linzey, Andrew. *Animal Rights: A Christian Assessment of Man's Treatment of Animals* (London: SCM Press, 1976).

———. *Animal Theology* (Urbana: University of Illinois Press, 1995).

———. *Christianity and the Rights of Animals* (New York: Crossroads, 1987).

Linzey, Andrew and Tom Regan, eds. *Animals and Christianity: A Book of Readings* (London; Crossroad, NY: SPCK, 1989).

Martin, Calvin. *Keepers of the Game: Indian Animal Relationships and the Fur Trade* (Berkeley: University of California Press, 1978).

McDaniel, Jay B. *Of God and Pelicans: A Theology of Reverence for Life* (Louisville: Westminster/John Knox Press, 1989).

McFague, Sallie. *The Body of God: An Ecological Theology* (Minneapolis: Augsburg Fortress Press, 1993).

Midgley, Mary. *Evolution as Religion: Strange Hopes and Stranger Fears* (London: Methuen, 1985).

Milton, Kay. *Environmentalism and Cultural Theory* (London: Routledge, 1996).

Moltmann, Jürgen. *Creating a Just Future: The Politics of Peace and the Ethics of Creation in a Threatened World* (London, SCM Press; Philadelphia, PA: Trinity International Press, 1989).

Neihardt, John G. *Black Elk Speaks: Being the Life Story of a Holy Man of the Oglala Sioux* (Lincoln: University of Nebraska Press, 1961).

Passmore, John. *Man's Responsibility for Nature* [MRN] (London: Duckworth, 1974; 2nd edition, 1980).

Peacocke, Arthur R. *Creation and the World of Science: The Bampton Lectures, 1978* (Oxford: Clarendon Press, 1979).

———. *God and the New Biology* (San Francisco: Harper & Row Publishers, 1986).

Rachels, James. *Created from Animals: The Moral Implications of Darwinism* (New York: Oxford University Press, 1990).

Regan, Tom, ed. *Animal Sacrifices: Religious Perspectives on the Use of Animals in Science* (Philadelphia, PA: Temple University Press, 1986).

Rockefeller, Steven C., and John C. Elder, eds. *Spirit and Nature: Why the Environment Is a Religious Issue* (Boston: Beacon Press, 1992).

Rolston, Holmes, III. ed. *Science and Religion: A Critical Survey* (New York: Random House, 1987).

Santmire, H. Paul. *Nature Reborn: The Ecological and Cosmic Promise of Christian Theology* (Minneapolis: Fortress Press, 2000).

———. *The Travail of Nature: The Ambiguous Ecological Promise of Christian Theology* (Philadelphia, PA: Fortress Press, 1985).

Schweitzer, Albert. R. H. Fuller, ed. *Reverence for Life* (London: Society for Promoting Christian Knowledge, 1970).

Spring, David, and Eileen Spring, eds. *Ecology and Religion in History* (New York: Harper & Row, 1974).

Tucker, Mary Evelyn and John A. Grim, eds., *Worldviews and Ecology: Religion, Philosophy, and the Environment* (Mayknoll, NY: Orbis Books, 1994).

Westra, Laura and Tom Robinson, eds. *The Greeks and the Environment* (Lanham, MD: Rowman & Littlefield, 1997).

White, Lynn, Jr. *Medieval Technology and Social Change* (Oxford: Clarendon Press, 1962).

III. The Other Animals (also Darwin, humans, and human origins)

Adams, Carol J. *Neither Man Nor Beast: Feminism and the Defence of Animals* (New York: Continuum, 1994).

———. *The Sexual Politics of Meat: A Feminist-Vegetarian Critical Theory* (New York: Continuum, 1990).

The Animals' Agenda: The International Magazine of Animal Rights and Ecology. P.O. Box 6809, Syracuse, NY 13217.

Beston, Henry. *The Outermost House: A Year of Life on the Great Beach of Cape Cod* (New York: Viking Press, 1962).

———. *Between the Species.* P.O. Box 254, Berkeley, CA 94701.

Clark, Stephen. *The Moral Status of Animals* (Oxford: Clarendon Press, 1977).

Coetzee, J. M. Introduction by Amy Gutmann, ed. *The Lives of Animals* (Princeton, NJ: Princeton University Press, 1999).

Cohen, Carl and Tom Regan. *The Animal Rights Debate* (Lanham, MD: Rowman & Littlefield Publishers, Inc., 2001).

Crosby, Alfred W. *Ecological Imperialism* (New York: Cambridge University Press, 1986).

Dawkins, Marian. *Animal Suffering: The Science of Animal Welfare* (New York: Routledge, Chapman, and Hall, 1980).

de Grazia, David. *Taking Animals Seriously: Mental Life and Moral Status* (New York: Cambridge University Press, 1996).

de Waal, Frans. *Good Natured: The Origins of Right and Wrong in Humans and Other Animals* (Cambridge, MA: Harvard University Press, 1996).

Dombrowski, Daniel A. *Babies and Beasts: The Argument from Marginal Cases* (Champaign: University of Illinois Press, 1997).

Ehrenfeld, D. *The Arrogance of Humanism* (New York: Oxford University Press, 1981).

Eldredge, Niles. *Dominion* (New York: Holt, 1995).

————. *Reinventing Darwin: The Great Debate at the High Table of Evolutionary Theory* (New York: Wiley, 1995).

Farber, Paul Lawrence. *The Temptations of Evolutionary Ethics* (Berkeley: University of California Press, 1994).

Farrington, Benjamin. *What Darwin Really Said* (New York: Schocken Books, 1982).

Foley, Robert. *Humans Before Humanity* (Oxford: Blackwell, 1995).

Fox, Michael. *Returning to Eden: Animal Rights and Human Responsibility* (New York: Viking Press, 1980).

Fox, Michael, and Nancy Wiswall. *The Hidden Costs of Beef* (Washington, DC: Humane Society of the United States, 1989).

Francione, Gary L. *Rain Without Thunder: The Ideology of the Animal Rights Movement* (Philadelphia, Temple University Press, 1996).

Frey, R. G. *Interests and Rights: The Case Against Animals* (Oxford: Clarendon Press, 1980).

————. *Rights, Animals and Suffering* (Oxford: Blackwell, 1983).

Godlovitch, Stanley, Roslind Godlovitch, and John Harris, eds. *Animals, Men, and Morals* (New York: Taplinger, 1972).

Hargrove, Eugene. *The Animal Rights/Environmental Ethics Debate: The Environmental Perspective* (Albany: State University of New York Press, 1992).

Harrison, Ruth. *Animal Machines: The New Factory Farming Industry* (London: Stuart, 1964).

Hughes, J. Donald. *American Indian Ecology* (El Paso: Texas Western Press, 1983).

Inquiry, 22, (1–2) (Summer 1979). Includes a useful bibliography; the entire issue is about animals

Johnson, Edward. *Species and Morality*, unpublished doctoral dissertation in philosophy at Princeton University (1976); see University Microfilms International, 1977, Ann Arbor, Michigan.

Kroc, Ray. *Grinding it Out: The Making of McDonald's* (Chicago: Henry Regnery, 1977).

Landsbury, Coral. *The Old Brown Dog: Women Workers and Vivisections in Edwardian England* (Madison: University of Wisconsin Press, 1985).

Lappe, Frances Moore. *Diet for a Small Planet* (New York: Ballantine Books, 1982).

Lappe, Frances Moore, and Joseph Collins. *Food First: Beyond the Myth of Scarcity* (New York: Ballantine Books, 1978).

Linzey, Andrew. *Animal Theology* (Urbana: University of Illinois Press, 1995).

Linzey, Andrew and Tom Regan, eds. *Animals and Christianity: A Book of Readings* (London and Crossroad, New York: Society for Promoting Christian Knowledge, 1989).

Lovejoy, Arthur O. *The Great Chain of Being: A Study of the History of an Idea* (Cambridge, MA: Harvard University Press, 1936).

Magell, Charles. *A Bibliography on Animal Rights and Related Matters* (Washington, DC: University Press of America, 1981).

Mason, Jim, and Peter Singer. *Animal Factories* (New York: Crown, 1980).

Midgley, Mary. *Animals and Why They Matter* (Harmondsworth, England: Penguin Books, 1983).

————. *Beast and Man* (Ithaca, NY: Cornell University Press, 1979).

————. *The Ethical Primate: Humans, Freedom and Morality* (New York: Routledge, 1994).

Pluhar, Evelyn. *Beyond Prejudice: The Moral Significance of Human and Nonhuman Animals* (Durham, NC: Duke University Press, 1997).

Rachels, James. *Created from Animals: The Moral Implications of Darwinism* (New York: Oxford University Press, 1990).

Regan, Tom. *All That Dwell Therein: Animal Rights and Environmental Ethics* (Berkeley: University of California Press, 1982).

————. *The Case for Animal Rights* (Berkeley: University of California Press, 1983).

————. *The Thee Generation: Reflections on the Coming Revolution* (Philadelphia, PA: Temple University Press, 1991).

Regan, Tom, and Peter Singer, eds. *Animal Rights and Human Obligations* (Englewood Cliffs, NJ: Prentice Hall, 1976).

Rifkin, Jeremy. *Beyond Beef: The Rise and Fall of the Cattle Culture* (New York: Dutton, 1992).

Rollin, Bernard. *Animal Rights and Human Morality*, Rev. ed. (Buffalo, NY: Prometheus Press, 1992).

Rollin, Bernard E. *The Frankenstein Syndrome: Ethical and Social Issues in the Genetic Engineering of Animals* (New York: Cambridge University Press, 1995).

————. *The Unheeded Cry: Animal Consciousness, Animal Pain and Science.* (Oxford: Oxford University Press, 1989).

Rosenfield, Lenora. *From Beast-Machine to Man-Machine* (New York: Columbia University Press, 1968).

Ryder, Richard. *Speciesism: The Ethics of Vivisections* (Edinburgh: Scottish Society for the Prevention of Vivisection, 1974).

———. *Victims of Science: The Use of Animals in Research* (London: Davis-Poynter, 1975).

Sapontzis, Steve. *Morals, Reason, and Animals* (Philadelphia, PA: Temple University Press, 1987).

Scarce, Rik. *Fishy Business: Salmon, Biology, and the Social Construction of Nature* (Philadelphia, PA: Temple University Press, 1999).

Serpell, James. *In the Company of Animals: A Study of Human-Animal Relationships* (Oxford: Basil Blackwell, 1986).

Shepard, Paul. *The Others: How Animals Made Us Human* (Washington, DC: Island Press, 1996).

Singer, Peter. *Animal Liberation* (New York: A New York Review Book, distributed by Random House, 1975).

———. *The Expanding Circle* (New York: Farrar, Straus, & Giroux, 1981).

———, ed. *In Defense of Animals* (New York: Blackwell, 1987).

———. *Practical Ethics* (Cambridge, MA: Cambridge University Press, 1979).

Sorrell, Roger D. *St. Francis of Assisi and Nature: Tradition and Innovation in Western Christian Attitudes toward the Environment* (New York: Oxford University Press, 1988).

Spiegel, Marjorie. Preface by Alice Walker. *The Dreaded Comparison: Human and Animal Slavery* (New York: Mirror Books, 1988).

Warren, Mary Anne. *Moral Status: Obligations to Persons and Other Living Things* (New York: Oxford University Press, 1998).

White, Michael, and John Gribbin. *Darwin: A Life in Science* (New York: Penguin Books, 1995).

Yaffe, Martin E., ed. *Judaism and Environmental Ethics* (Blue Ridge Summit, PA: Lexington Books, 2001).

IV.A The Broader, Biotic Community

Callicott, J. Baird, *Beyond the Land Ethic: More Essays in Environmental Philosophy.* (Albany: State University of New York Press, 1999).

———, ed. *Companion to a Sand County Almanac: Interpretive and Critical Essays* (Madison: University of Wisconsin Press, 1987).

Engberg, Robert, and Donald Wesling, eds. *John Muir: To Yosemite and Beyond: Writings from the Years 1863 to 1875* (Madison: University of Wisconsin Press, 1980).

Flader, Susan L. *Thinking Like a Mountain: Aldo Leopold and the Evolution of an Ecological Attitude Toward Deer, Wolves, and Forests* (Columbia: University of Missouri Press, 1974).

Goodin, Robert. *Green Political Theory* (Oxford: Blackwell Polity Press, 1992).

Hays, Samuel P. *Conservation and the Gospel of Efficiency: The Progressive Conservation Movement, 1890–1920* (Cambridge, MA: Harvard University Press, 1959).

Jacoby, Karl. *Crimes Against Nature: Squatters, Poachers, Thieves, and the Hidden History of American Conservation* (Berkeley: University of California Press, 2001).

Lovelock, James. *Gaia: A New Look at Life on Earth* (New York: Oxford University Press, 1981).

Marsh, George Perkins. *Man and Nature* (Cambridge, MA: Harvard University Press, 1965).

The Monist 75(2) (April 1992); special issue on the intrinsic value of nature.

Pinchot, Gifford. *The Fight for Conservation* (Seattle: University of Washington Press, 1910).

Schultz, Robert C., and J. Donald Hughes, eds. *Ecological Consciousness: Essays from the Earthday X Colloquium, University of Denver, April 21–24, 1980* (Washington, DC: University Press of America, 1981).

Westra, Laura. *Living in Integrity: A Global Ethic to Restore a Fragmented Earth* (Lanham, MD: Rowman & Littlefield Publishers, Inc., 1998).

Wright, Larry. *Teleological Explanation* (Berkeley: University of California Press, 1976).

IV.B. Deep Ecology and Social Ecology

Bookchin, Murray. *The Ecology of Freedom: The Emergence and Dissolution of Hierarchy* (Palo Alto, CA: Cheshire Books, 1982).

———. *The Philosophy of Social Ecology: Essays on Dialectical Naturalism* (Toronto: Black Rose Books, 1990).

———. *Post-Scarcity Anarchism* (San Francisco: Ramparts Press, 1971).

———. *Remaking Society: Pathways to a Green Future* (Boston: South End Press, 1990).

———. *Toward an Ecological Society* (Montreal: Black Rose Books, 1980).

———. *Which Way for the Ecology Movement?* (San Francisco: AK Press, 1994).

Bradford, George. *How Deep Is Deep Ecology? A Challenge to Radical Environmentalists* (Ojai, CA: Times Change Press, 1989)

Clark, John, ed. *The Anarchist Moment: Reflections on Culture, Nature, and Power* (Toronto: Black Rose Books, 1984).

———. *Renewing the Earth: The Promise of Social Ecology* (London: Green Print, 1990).

Devall, Bill. *Simple in Means, Rich in Ends, Practicing Deep Ecology* (Salt Lake City: Peregrine Smith Books, 1988).

Devall, Bill, and George Sessions. *Deep Ecology Living as if Nature Mattered* (Salt Lake City: Peregrine Smith Books, 1985).

Drengson, Alan R. *Beyond Environmental Crisis: From Technocratic to Planetary Person* (New York: Peter Lang, 1989).

Ehrenfeld, David. *Beginning Again: People and Nature in the New Millennium* (New York: Oxford University Press, 1993).

Evemden, Neil. *The Natural Alien* (Toronto: University of Toronto Press, 1985).

Fox, Warwick. *Toward a Transpersonal Ecology: Developing New Foundations for Environmentalism* (Boston: Shambhala, 1990).

Glasser, Harold, ed. *The Selected Works of Arne Naess* (Kluwer Academic Publishers, 2001).

Gore, Al, Jr. *Earth in Balance: Ecology and the Human Spirit* (Boston: Houghton Mifflin, 1992)

Gray, Gary G. *Wildlife and People: The Human Dimensions of Wildlife Ecology* (Champaign: University of Illinois Press, 1995).

Katz, Eric, Andrew Light, and David Rothenberg. *Beneath the Surface: Critical Essays in the Philosophy of Deep Ecology* (Cambridge, MA: The MIT Press, 2000).

Harbinger: *The Journal of Social Ecology*. P.O. Box 89, Plainfield, VT 05667.

Naess, Arne. *Ecology, Community and Lifestyle: Outline of an Ecosophy*. Trans. David Rothenberg (New York: Cambridge University Press, 1989).

Nash, Roderick Frazier. *American Environmentalism: Readings in Conservation History*, 3rd. ed. (New York: McGraw-Hill, 1990).

Sale, Kirkpatrick. *Dwellers in the Land: The Bioregional Vision* (San Francisco: Sierra Club Books, 1985).

Seed, John, Joanna Macy, Pat Fleming, and Arne Naess. *Thinking Like a Mountain: Towards a Council of All Beings* (Philadelphia, PA: New Society Publishers, 1988).

Snyder, Gary. *The Old Ways* (San Francisco: City Lights Books, 1977).

———. *The Practice of the Wild* (San Francisco: North Point Press, 1990).

———. *Turtle Island* (New York: New Directions Books, 1977).

Spretnak, Charlene, and Fritjof Capra. *Green Politics*. rev. ed. (Santa Fe: Bear and Company, 1986).

Tobias, Michael, ed. *Deep Ecology* (San Diego: Avant Books, 1977).

The Trumpeter. LightStar, P.O. Box 5853, Victoria, BC, Canada V8R-6S8.

IV.C Ecofeminism

Adams, Carol J., ed. *Ecofeminism and the Sacred* (Maryknoll, NY: Orbis Books, 1992).

Allen, Paula Gunn. *The Sacred Hoop: Recovering the Feminine in American Indian Tradition* (Boston: Beacon Press, 1986).

Biehl, Janet. *Rethinking Ecofeminist Politics* (Boston: South End Press, 1991).

Brown, Wilmette. *Roots: Black Ghetto Ecology* (London: Housewives in Dialogue, 1986).

Caldecott, Leonie, and Stephanie Leland, eds. *Reclaim the Earth: Women Speak Out for Life on Earth* (London: The Women's Press, 1983).

Cuomo, Chris. *Feminism and Ecological Communities* (London, Routledge, 1998).

Diamond, Irene, and Gloria Feman Orenstein, eds. *Reweaving the World: The Emergence of Ecofeminism* (San Francisco: Sierra Club Books, 1990).

Easlea, Brian. *Science and Sexual Oppression: Patriarchy's Confrontation with Women and Nature* (London: Weidenfeld and Nicholson, 1981).

Environmental Review. Special issue on Women and Environmental History, guest editor, Carolyn Merchant, 8(1),1984.

Gaard, Greta, ed. *Ecofeminism: Women, Animals, Nature* (Philadelphia, PA: Temple University Press, 1993).

Gray, Elizabeth Dodson. *Green Paradise Lost* (Wellesley, MA: Roundtable Press, 1979).

Griffin, Susan. *Women and Nature: The Roaring Inside Her* (New York: Harper & Row, 1978).

Held, Virginia, ed. *Justice and Care: Essential Readings in Feminist Ethics* (Boulder, CO: Westview Press, 1995).

Heresies 13(4) *Feminism and Ecology* 4(1981).

Hypatia. Special issue on Ecological Feminism 6 (Spring 1991).

Kolodny, Annette. *The Lay of the Land: Metaphor as Experience and History in American Life and Letters* (Chapel Hill: University of North Carolina Press, 1975).

List, Peter C., ed. *Radical Environmentalism: Philosophy and Tactics* (Belmont, CA: Wadsworth, 1993).

Merchant, Carolyn. *The Death of Nature: Women, Ecology, and the Scientific Revolution* (New York: Harper & Row, 1983).

———. *Ecological Revolution: Nature, Gender, and Science in New England* (Chapel Hill: University of North Carolina Press, 1990).

———. *Radical Ecology: The Search for a Livable World* (New York: Routledge, 1992).

The New Catalyst 1987–88 (Winter). Special issue on Women/Earth Speaking: Feminism and Ecology.

Plant, Judith, ed. *Healing the Wounds: The Promise of Ecofeminism* (Santa Cruz, CA: New Society Publishers, 1989).

Reuther, Rosemary Radford. *Gaia and God: An Ecofeminist Theology of Earth Healing* (London: SCM Press, 1993).

———. *New Women, New Earth: Sexist Ideologies and Human Liberation* (New York: Seabury Press, 1975).

Studies in the Humanities 15(2) (1988). Special issue on Feminism, Ecology, and the Future of the Humanities. Edited by Patrick Murphy.

Warren, Karen J. *Ecofeminist Philosophy: A Western Perspective on What it is and Why it Matters* (Lanham, MD: Rowman & Littlefield Publishers, Inc., 2000)

———. *Ecofeminism: Women, Culture, Nature* (Bloomington: Indiana University Press, 1997).

———. *Ecological Feminism* (New York: Routledge, 1994).

———. *Ecological Feminist Philosophies* (Bloomington: Indiana University Press, 1996)

V. Economics, Ethics, and Ecology (Sections V.A and V.B combined)

Ackerman, Frank, David Kiron, Neva R. Goodwin, Jonathan M. Harris, and Kevin P. Gallagher, eds. *Human Well-Being and Economic Goals* (Washington, DC: Island Press, 1997).

Arthur, John, and William H. Shaw, eds. *Justice and Economic Distribution* (Englewood Cliffs, NJ: Prentice Hall, 1978).

Berry, Wendell. *Home Economics* (San Francisco: North Point Press, 1987).

Bormann, F. H., and Stephen R. Kellert, eds. *Ecology, Economics, and Ethics: The Broken Circle* (New Haven: Yale University Press, 1991).

Broome, John. *Weighing Goods* (Cambridge, MA: Blackwell, 1991).

Brundtland, G. *Our Common Future* (New York: Oxford University Press, 1987).

Costanza, Robert. *Ecological Economics* (New York: Columbia University Press, 1991).

Daily, Gretchen C., ed. *Nature's Services: Societal Dependence on Natural Ecosystems* (Washington, DC: Island Press, 1997).

Daly, Herman E. *Steady-State Economics: The Economics of Biophysical Equilibrium and Moral Growth* (San Francisco: Freeman, 1977).

Daly, Herman, and John Cobb. *For the Common Good: Redirecting the Economy Toward Community, the Environment, and a Sustainable Future* (Boston: Beacon Press, 1989).

de la Court, Thijs. *Beyond Brundtland: Green Development in the 1990s* (New York: New Horizons Press, 1990).

De Steiguer, J. E. *Age of Environmentalism* (New York: McGraw-Hill, 1997).

Douglas, Mary, and Baron Isherwood. *The World of Goods* (New York: Basic Books, 1979).

Dryzek, John S. *Rational Ecology: Environment and Political Economy* (New York: Blackwell, 1987).

Elkington, John, and Jonathan Shopley. *The Shrinking Planet: U.S. Information Technology and Sustainable Development* (Holmes, PA: World Resources Institute, 1988).

Elkins, Paul. *Green Economics* (New York: Doubleday, 1992).

Elster, J., and E. Hylland, eds. *Foundations of Social Choice Theory* (Cambridge, MA: Cambridge University Press, 1983).

Freeman, A. Myrick, III, Robert Haveman, and Allen Kneese. *The Economics of Environmental Policy* (New York: Wiley, 1973).

Fusfield, Daniel. *The Age of the Economist* (Glenview, IL: Scott Foresman, 1986).

Goodland, Robert, ed. *Race to Save the Tropics: Ecology and Economics for a Sustainable Future* (Covelo, CA: Island Press, 1990).

Gupta, Avijit. *Ecology and Development in the Third World* (New York: Routledge, 1988).

Heal, Geoffrey. *Nature and the Marketplace: Capturing the Value of Ecosystem Services* (Washington, DC: Island Press, 2000).

Kneese, A., S. Ben-David, and W. D. Shulze, eds. *The Ethical Foundations of Benefit–Cost Analysis* (Washington, DC: Resources for the Future, 1983).

Krishnan, Rajaram, Jonathan M. Harris, and Neva R. Goodwin, eds. *A Survey of Ecological Economics* (Washington, DC: Island Press, 1995).

Krutilla, John, and Anthony Fisher. *The Economics of Natural Environments* (Washington, DC: Resources for the Future, 1985).

Leonard, H. Jeffrey, et al. *Environment and the Poor: Development Strategies for a Common Agenda* (New Brunswick, NJ: Transaction Publishers, 1989).

MacLean, Douglas, ed. *Values at Risk* (Totowa, NJ: Rowman & Littlefield, 1986).

MacNeil, Jim, Pieter Winsenuus, and Taizo Yakushiju. *Beyond Interdependence* (New York: Oxford University Press, 1991).

Milbrath, Lester. *Envisioning a Sustainable Society* (Albany: State University of New York Press, 1989).

Mishan, Edward J. *The Cost of Economic Growth* (Harmondsworth, UK: Penguin Books, 1969).

Okun, Arthur M. *Equality and Efficiency: The Big Tradeoff* (Washington, DC: Brookings Institution, 1975).

Orr, David W. *Ecological Literacy: Education and the Transition to an Environmental Postmodern World* (Albany: State University of New York Press, 1992).

Panayotou, Theodore. *Green Markets* (San Francisco: ICS Press, 1993).

Pearce, David, Edward Barbier, and Anil Markandya. *Blueprint for a Green Economy* (London: Earthscan Publications, 1989).

———. *Sustainable Development: Economics and Environment in the Third World* (Brookfield, VT: Gower, 1990).

Pepper, David. *Eco-Socialism* (London: Routledge,1993).

Perrings, Charles. *Economy and Environment* (Cambridge, MA: Cambridge University Press, 1987).

Posner, Richard. *The Economics of Justice* (Cambridge, MA: Harvard University Press, 1981).

Rawls, J. *A Theory of Justice* (Cambridge, MA: Harvard University Press, 1971).

Sagoff, Mark. *The Economy of the Earth* (Cambridge, MA: Cambridge University Press, 1988).

Schelling, Thomas. *Micromotives and Macrobehavior* (New York: Norton, 1978).

Schumacher, E. F. *Small Is Beautiful* (New York: Harper & Row, 1973).

Sen, A. K. *Collective Choice and Social Welfare* (San Francisco: Holden-Day, 1970).

———. *On Ethics and Economics* (New York: Blackwell, 1987).

Seneca, Joseph, and Michael Taussig. *The Environmental Economics* (Englewood Cliffs, NJ: Prentice Hall, 1979).

Shrader-Fréchette, K. S. *Burying Uncertainty: Risk and the Case Against Geological Disposal of Nuclear Waste* (Berkeley: University of California Press, 1993).

———. *Risk and Rationality* (Berkeley: University of California Press, 1991).

Stokey, Edith, and Richard Zeckhauser. *A Primer for Policy Analysis* (New York: Norton, 1978).

Tribe, Laurence H., Corinne S. Schelling, and John Voss, eds. *When Values Conflict: Essays on Environmental Analysis, Discourse, and Decision* (Cambridge, MA: Ballinger, 1976).

Waring, Marilyn. *If Women Counted: A New Feminist Economics* (San Francisco: HarperCollins, 1988).

Willis K. G., and J. T. Corkindale, eds. *Environmental Valuation: New Perspectives* (United Kingdom: CAB International, 1995).

V.C From the Commons to Property

Ackerman, Bruce A., ed. *Economic Foundations of Property Law* (Boston: Little & Brown, 1975).

———. *Private Property and the Constitution* (New Haven, CT: Yale University Press, 1977).

Barnes, Peter. *Who Owns the Sky?: Our Common Assets and the Future of Capitalism* (Washington, DC: Island Press, 2001).

Becker, Lawrence C. *Property Rights: Philosophical Foundations* (London, Routledge & Kegan Paul, 1977).

Blumenfeld, Samuel L. *Property in a Humane Economy* (La Salle, IL: Open Court, 1974).

Burger, Joanna, Elinor Ostrom, Richard B. Norgaard, David Policansky, and Bernard D. Goldstein, eds. *Protecting the Commons: A Framework for Resource Management in the Americas* (Washington, DC: Island Press, 2000).

Geisler, Charles and Gail Daneker, eds. *Property and Values: Alternatives to Public and Private Ownership* (Washington, DC: Island Press, 2000).

Gewirth, Alan. *Human Rights: Essays in Justification and Application* (Chicago: University of Chicago Press, 1982).

Hardin, Garrett, and John Baden, eds. *Managing the Commons* (San Francisco: Freeman, 1977).

MacPherson, C. B. *The Political Theory of Possessive Individualism: Hobbes to Locke* (Oxford: Oxford University Press, 1962).

Nozick, Robert. *Anarchy, State, and Utopia* (New York: Basic Books, 1974).

Ostrom, Elinor. *Governing the Commons: The Evolution of Institutions for Collective Action* (New York: Cambridge University Press, 1990).

Pennock, J. R., and J. W. Chapman, eds. *Property* (New York: New York University Press, 1980).

Waldron, Jeremy. *The Right to Private Property* (Oxford: Clarendon Press, 1988).

Weber, Michael L. *From Abundance to Scarcity: A History of U.S. Marine Fisheries Policy* (Washington, DC: Island Press, 2001).

V.D Human Population and Pressure on "Resources"

Aiken, William, and Hugh LaFollette, eds. *World Hunger and Morality,* 2nd ed. (Englewood Cliffs, NJ: Prentice Hall, 1996).

Bayles, Michael D., ed. *Ethics and Population* (Cambridge, MA: Schenkman, 1976).

Cole, H. et al. *Thinking About the Future: A Critique of the Limits to Growth* (London: Chatto & Windus and Sussex University Press, 1973).

Donaldson, Peter J. *Nature Against Us: The United States and the World Population Crisis* (Chapel Hill: University of North Carolina Press, 1990).

Ehrlich, Paul R. *The Population Bomb* (London: Pan Books/Ballantine, 1971).

Ehrlich, Paul R., and Anne H. Ehrlich. *The Population Explosion* (New York: Simon & Schuster, 1990).

———. *Population, Resources, Environment: Issues in Human Ecology,* 2nd ed. (San Francisco: Freeman, 1972).

George, Susan. *How the Other Half Dies: The Real Reasons for World Hunger* (Montclair, NJ: Allanheld, Osmun, 1977).

Hardin, Garrett. *Exploring New Ethics for Survival: The Voyage of the Spaceship Beagle* (New York: Viking Press, 1972).

Hartman, Betsy. *Reproductive Rights and Wrongs: The Global Politics of Population Control and Contraceptive Choice* (New York: Harper & Row, 1987).

Harrison, Paul and Gred Pearce. *AAAS Atlas of Population and Environment* (Berkeley: University of California Press, 2001).

Lappe, Frances Moore, and Joseph Collins. *World Hunger: Twelve Myths* (New York: Grove Press, 1986).

Malthus, Thomas Robert. *Population: The First Essay* (Ann Arbor: Ann Arbor Paperbacks, University of Michigan Press, 1959).

McKibben, Bill. *Maybe One: A Case for Smaller Families* (New York: Penguin Putnam Inc., a Plume Book, 1998).

Orr, David, and Marvin S. Soroos. *The Global Predicament* (Chapel Hill: University of North Carolina Press, 1979).

Partridge, Ernest, ed. *Responsibilities to Future Generations* (New York: Prometheus Books, 1981).

Sen, Arnartya. *Poverty and Famines* (New York: Oxford University Press, 1981).

Simon, Julian L. *The Ultimate Resource* (Princeton, NJ: Princeton University Press, 1981).

Simon, Julian, and Herman Kahn, eds. *The Resourceful Earth* (Oxford: Blackwell, 1984).

Telfer, Elizabeth. *Food for Thought: Philosophy and Food* (New York: Routledge, 1996).

V.E Future Generations and Sustainability Questions

Beckerman, Wilfred. *Small Is Stupid* (London: Duckworth, 1995).

———. *Through Green-Colored Glasses* (Washington, DC: CATO Institute, 1996).

Cooper, David, and Joy Palmer. *Just Environments: Intergenerational, International and Interspecies Issues* (New York: Routledge, 1995).

Costanza, Robert, ed. *Ecological Economics: The Science and Management of Sustainability* (New York: Columbia University Press, 1991).

Cromartie, Michael, ed. *Creation at Risk? Religion, Science, and Environmentalism* (Washington, DC: Ethics and Public Policy Center, 1995).

Davion, Victoria, ed. *Ethics and the Environment.* (Greenwich, CT: JAI Press) 1(1) (Spring 1996).

de-Shalit, Avner. *Why Posterity Matters: Environmental Policies and Future Generations* (New York: Routledge, 1995).

Fishkin, James S., and Peter Laslett, eds. *Justice Between Age Groups and Generations* (New Haven: Yale University Press, 1992).

Goodland, Robert, Herman Daly, and Sarah El Serafy, eds. *Population, Technology and Lifestyle* (Washington, DC: Island Press, 1992).

Holmberg, John. *Making Development Sustainable: Redefining Institutions, Policy, and Economics* (Washington, DC: Island Press, 1992).

Kennedy, Paul. *Preparing for the Twenty-First Century* (New York: Random House, 1993).

Krishnan, Raj-am, Jonathan Harris, and Neva Goodwin, eds. *A Survey of Ecological Economics* (Washington, DC: Island Press, 1995).

Partridge, Ernest, ed. *Responsibilities to Future Generations* (New York: Prometheus Books, 1981).

Pearce, David W., and Jeremy J. Warford. *World Without End: Economics, Environment, and Sustainable Development* (New York: Oxford University Press, 1993).

Pearl, Mary C., and David Wesbem, eds. *Conservation for the Twenty-first Century* (New York: Oxford University Press, 1989).

Peet, John. *Energy and the Ecological Economics of Sustainability* (Washington, DC: Island Press, 1992).

Van den Bergh, Jeroen C. J. M., and Jan Van der Straaten. *Toward Sustainable Development: Concepts, Methods and Policy* (Washington, DC: Island Press, 1994).

VI. Environmental Problems and Policies

VI.A Preserving Biodiversity

Barbier, Edward, Joanne Burgess, Timothy Swanson, and David Pearce. *Elephants Ivory and Economics* (London: Earthscan Publications, 1990).

Cohnvaux, Paul. *Why Big Fierce Animals Are Rare* (Princeton, NJ: Princeton University Press, 1978).

Ehrenfeld, David W. *The Arrogance of Humanism* (New York: Oxford University Press, 1978).

———. *Conserving Life on Earth* (New York: Oxford University Press, 1972).

Ehrlich, Paul, and Anne Ehrlich. *Extinction* (New York: Random House, 1981).

Leslie, John. *The End of the World: The Science and Ethics of Human Extinction* (New York: Routledge, 1996).

McNeely, J. A. *Economics and Biological Diversity* (Gland, Switzerland: International Union for the Conservation of Nature and Natural Resources, 1988).

McNeely, Jeffrey A., Kenton R. Miller, Walter V. Reid, Russell Mittermeier, and Timothy B. Werner. *Conserving the World's Biological Diversity* (Washington, DC: WRI, 1990).

Myers, Norman. *A Wealth of Wild Species: Storehouse for Human Welfare* (Boulder, CO: Westview Press, 1983).

Norton, Bryan, ed. *The Preservation of the Species* (Princeton, NJ: Princeton University Press, 1985).

———. *Why Preserve Natural Variety?* (Princeton, NJ: Princeton University Press, 1987).

Regenstein, Lewis. *The Politics of Extinction* (New York: Macmillan, 1975).

Sharpe, Virginia A., Bryan Nortan, and Strachan Donnelley, eds. *Wolves and Human Communities: Biology, Politics, and Ethics* (Washington, DC: Island Press, 2001).

Wilson, E. O., ed. *Biodiversity* (Washington, DC: National Academy Press, 1986).

———. *Biophilia* (Cambridge, MA: Harvard University Press, 1984).

———. *The Diversity of Life* (Cambridge, MA: Harvard University Press, 1992).

VI.B Food and Agriculture

Behand, Richard W. *Plundered Promise: Capitalism, Politics, and the Fate of the Federal Lands* (Washington, DC: Island Press, 2001).

Biotechnology and Sustainable Agriculture: A Bibliography (SRB-94-13) (Beltsville, MD: USDA National Agricultural Library, 1994).

Dallmeyer, Dorinda G. *Values at Sea: Ethics for the Marine Environment* (Athens, GA: University of Georgia Press, 2003).

Dawkins, K. *Gene Wars: The Politics of Biotechnology* (New York: Seven Stories Press, 1998).

Ehrlich, Paul R. *Human Natures: Genes, Cultures, and the Human Prospect* (Washington, DC: Island Press, 2000).

Fox, Michael W. *Beyond Evolution: The Genetically Altered Future of Plants, Animals, the Earth and Humans* (New York: The Lyons Press, 1999)

———. *Eating With Conscience: The Bioethics of Food* (Troutdale, OR: New Sage Press, 1997).

———. *Superpigs and Wondercorn* (New York: St. Martin's Press, 1992).

Hallberg, M., ed. *Bovine Somatotropin and Emerging Issues: An Assessment* (Boulder, CO: Westview Press, 1992).

Hill, Julia Butterfly. *The Legacy of Luna: The Story of a Tree, a Woman, and the Struggle to Save the Redwoods* (San Francisco: Harper Collins Publishers, 2000).

Ho, Mae-Wan. *Genetic Engineering: Dream or Nightmare?* (Bath, UK: Gateway Books, 1998)

Jackson, Wes, Wendell Berry, and Bruce Colman, eds. *Meeting the Expectations of the Land: Essays in Sustainable Agriculture and Stewardship* (San Francisco: North Point Press, 1984).

Kemmis, Daniel. *This Sovereign Land: A New Vision for Governing the West* (Washington, DC: Island Press, 2001).

Krimsky, Sheldon and Roger Wrubel. *Agricultural Biotechnology and the Environment: Science, Policy, and Social Issues* (Champaign: University of Illinois Press, 1996).

Leopold, Aldo. Edited by J. Baird Callicott and Eric T. Freyfogle. *For the Health of the Land: Previously Unpublished Essays and Other Writings* (Washington, DC: Island Press, 1999).

Lewis, Charles A. *Green Nature/Human Nature: The Meaning of Plants in our Lives* (Champaign: University of Illinois Press, 1996).

McHughen, Alan. *Pandora's Picnic Basket: The Potential and Hazards of Genetically Modified Foods* (New York: Oxford University Press, 2000).

Mellon, Margaret and Jane Rissler, eds. *Now or Never: Serious New Plans to Save a Natural Pest Control* (Cambridge, MA: Union of Concerned Scientists, 1998)

Mepham, Ben, ed. *Food Ethics* (London: Routledge, 1996).

Palumbi, Stephen R. *The Evolution Explosion: How Humans Cause Rapid Evolutionary Change* (New York: W. W. Norton & Co, 2001).

Pollan, Michael. *The Botany of Desire: A Plant's-Eye View of the World* (New York: Random House, 2001).

Porritt, Jonathon. *Playing Safe: Science and the Environment* (New York: Thames and Hudson, Inc., 2000).

Rissler, Jane and Margaret Mellon. *The Ecological Risks of Engineered Crops* (Cambridge, MA: MIT Press, 1996).

———. *Perils Amidst the Promise: Ecological Risks of Transgenic Crops in a Global Market* (Cambridge, MA: Union of Concerned Scientists, 1991).

Schlosser, Eric. *Fast Food Nation: The Dark Side of the All-American Meal* (New York: Houghton Mifflin Company, 2001).

Shiva, Vandana. *Monocultures of the Mind: Perspectives on Biodiversity and Biotechnology* (London: Zed Books, 1993).

———. *Stolen Harvest: The Hijacking of the Global Food Supply* (Cambridge, MA: South End Press, 2000)

Thompson, Paul. B. *Agricultural Ethics: Research, Teaching, and Public Policy* (Ames: Iowa State University Press, 1998).

———. *Food Biotechnology in Ethical Perspective* (London: Chapman Hall, 1997).

Ticciati, Laura and Robin Ticciati. *Genetically Engineered Foods: Are They Safe? You Decide* (New Canaan, CT: Keats Publishing, 1998).

Wilson, Duff. *Laying Waste* (New York: Harper Collins, 2001).

Wilson, Edward O. *Consilience: The Unity of Knowledge* (New York: Alfred A. Knopf, Inc., 1998).

World Bank. *Agricultural Biotechnology: The Next Green Revolution?* (Washington, DC: World Bank, 1990).

VI.C Wilderness and Forests

Agarwal, Bina. *Cold Hearths and Barren Slopes: The World Fuel Crisis in the Third World* (New Delhi: Allied Publishers, 1986).

Barney, Daniel R. *The Last Stand, Ralph Nader's Study Group on the National Forests* (New York: Grossman, 1974).

Beeman, Randal S. and James A. Pritchard. *A Green and Permanent Land: Ecology and Agriculture in the Twentieth Century* (Lawrence: University Press of Kansas, 2000).

Best, Constance and Laurie A. Wayburn. *America's Private Forests: Status and Stewardship* (Washington, DC: Island Press, 2001).

Dietrich, William. *The Final Forest: The Battle for the Last Great Trees of the Pacific Northwest* (New York: Simon & Schuster, 1992).

Frome, Michael. *Battle for the Wilderness* (New York: Praeger, 1974).

Gradwohl, Judith, and Russell Greenberg. *Saving the Tropical Forests* (Washington, DC: Island Press, 1988).

Gregersen, Hans, Sydney Draper, and Dieter Elz, eds. *People and Trees: The Role of Social Forestry in Sustainable Development* (Washington, DC: World Bank Publications, 1989).

Guha, Ramachandra. *The Unquiet Woods: Ecological Change and Peasant Resistance in the Himalaya* (Berkeley: University of California Press, 1990).

Hanson, Victor Davis. *Fields Without Dreams: Defending the Agrarian Idea* (New York: Free Press, 1996).

Hurst, Philip. *Rainforest Politics: Ecological Destruction in South-East Asia* (London: Zed Books, 1990).

Mahar, Dennis J. *Government Policies and Deforestation in Brazil's Amazon Region* (Washington, DC: World Bank, 1989).

Myers, Norman. *The Primary Source: Tropical Forests and Our Future* (New York: Norton, 1984).

Nash, Roderick, ed. *American Environmentalism: Readings in Conservation History*, 3rd ed. (New York: McGraw-Hill, 1990).

———. *Wilderness and the American Mind* (New Haven: Yale University Press, 1973).

Nations, James D. *Tropical Rainforests, Endangered Environment* (New York: Franklin Watts, 1988).

Norse, Elliot A. *Ancient Forests of the Pacific Northwest* (Washington, DC: Island Press, 1990).

Repetto, R., and M. Gillis, eds. *Public Policies and the Misuse of Forest Resources* (New York: Cambridge University Press, 1988).

Routley, Richard, and Val Routley. *The Fight for the Forests* (Canberra: Australian National University Press, 1974).

Schwartz, William, ed. *Voices for the Wilderness* (New York: Ballantine Books, 1969).

Seuss, Dr. *The Lorax* (New York: Random House, 1971).

Shiva, Vandana. *Forestry Crisis and Forestry Myths: A Critical Review of Tropical Forests: A Call for Action.* (Tropical Forests: A Call for Action is a joint report of The World Bank, UNDP, and World Resources Institute.) (Malaysia: World Rainforest Movement, 1987).

Snyder, Gary. *A Place in Space: Ethics, Aesthetics, and Watersheds* (Washington, DC: Counterpoint, 1995).

———. *The Practice of the Wild* (San Francisco: North Point Press, 1990).

Thompson, Paul B. *The Spirit of the Soil: Agriculture and Environmental Ethics* (New York: Routledge, 1995).

True, Alianor, ed. *Wildfire: A Reader* (Washington, DC: Island Press, 2001).

Valenti, Peter. *Reading the Landscape: Writing a World* (New York: Harcourt Brace College Publishers, 1996).

World Commission on Forests. *Our Forests, Our Future* (Cambridge, MA: Cambridge University Press, 1999).

VI.D Corporate Responsibility (see items in V.A and V.E as well)

Bullard, Robert D., ed. *Unequal Protection: Environmental Justice and Communities of Color* (San Francisco: Sierra Club Books, 1994).

French, Peter A. *Corporate Ethics* (New York: Harcourt Brace College Publishers, 1995).

Hoffman, W. Michael, Robert Frederick, and Edward S. Petry, Jr., eds. *Business, Ethics, and the Environment: The Public Policy Debate* (New York: Quorum Books, 1990).

———. *Business Ethics, Readings and Cases in Corporate Morality* 3rd ed. (New York: McGraw-Hill, 1995).

———. *The Corporation, Ethics and the Environment* (New York: Quorum Books, 1990).

Houck, John W. and Oliver Williams, eds. *Is the Good Corporation Dead?* (Lanham, MD: Rowman & Littlefield, 1996).

Pfeiffer, Raymond S. *Why Blame the Organization?* (Lanham, MD: Rowman & Littlefield, 1995).

Stone, Christopher D. *Where the Law Ends: The Social Control of Corporate Behaviour* (New York: Harper & Row, 1975).

Westra, Laura and Patricia H. Werhane, eds. *The Business of Consumption: Environmental Ethics and the Global Economy* (Lanham, MD: Rowman & Littlefield Publishers, Inc., 1998).

Westra, Laura and Peter S. Wenz, eds. *Faces of Environmental Racism: Confronting Issues of Global Justice* 2nd edition (Lanham, MD: Rowman & Littlefield Publishers, Inc., 2001).

VI.E Sliding to Global Catastrophe

Abrahamson, D. *The Challenge of Global Warming* (Washington, DC: Island Press, 1989).

Benedick, Richard E., et al. *Greenhouse Warming: Negotiating a Global Regime* (Washington, DC: World Resources Institute, 1991).

———. *Ozone Diplomacy: New Directions in Safeguarding the Planet* (Cambridge, MA: Harvard University Press, 1991).

Brown, Michael H. *Toxic Cloud: The Poisoning of America's Air* (New York: HarperCollins, 1988).

Brown, Wilmette. *Roots: Black Ghetto Ecology* (London: Housewives in Dialogue, 1986).

Cobb, John B., Jr., and Herman E. Daly. *For the Common Good: Redirecting the Economy Toward Community, the Environment, and a Sustainable Future*, 2nd ed., rev. (Boston: Beacon Press, 1994).

Dotto, Lydia. *The Ozone War* (Garden City, NY: Doubleday, 1978).

Durham, William, Robert M. Hollingworth, and Gino J. Marco, eds. *Silent Spring Revisited* (Washington, DC: American Chemical Society, 1987).

Fisher, David E. *Fire and Ice: The Greenhouse Effect, Ozone Depletion, and Nuclear Winter* (New York: Harper & Row, 1990).

Gibson, Mary, ed. *To Breathe Freely: Risk, Consent and Air* (Totowa, NJ: Rowman & Allanheld, 1985).

Hynes, H. Patricia. *The Recurring Silent Spring* (New York: Pergamon Press, 1989).

Larabee, Ann. *Decade of Distaster* (Champaign: University of Illinois Press, 2000).

Leggett, Jeremy. *Global Warming: The Greenpeace Report* (New York: Oxford University Press, 1990).

MacLean, Doug, ed. *Energy and the Future* (Totowa, NJ: Rowman & Littlefield, 1983).

Oppenheimer, M., and R. Boyle. *Dead Heat* (New York: Basic Books, 1990).

Reid, Walter V. *Drowning the National Heritage: Climate Change and the U.S. Coastal Biodiversity* (Washington, DC: World Resources Institute, 1991).

———. *Keeping Options Alive: The Scientific Basis for Conserving Biodiversity* (Washington, DC: World Resources Institute, 1989).

Schneider, Stephen H. and Terry L. Root, eds. *Wildlife Responses to Climate Change: North American Case Studies* (Washington, DC: Island Press, 2001).

Schneider, Stephen H, Armin Rosencranz, and John O. Niles, eds. *Climate Change Policy: A Survey* (Washington, DC: Island Press, 2002).

Schneider, Stephen H. *Global Warming: Are We Entering the Greenhouse Century?* (San Francisco: Sierra Club Books, 1989).

Shrader-Fréchette, K. S. *Nuclear Power and Public Policy* (Dordrecht, Netherlands: Reidel, 1989).

VII. Varieties of Activism (lifestyle, political strategy, and theory)

Abbey, Edward. *Abbey's Road* (New York: Dutton, 1979).

———. *Hayduke Lives!* (Boston: Little, Brown, 1990).

———. *The Monkey Wrench Gang* (New York: Avon Books, 1976).

Arnold, Ron. *Ecology Wars: Environmentalism as if People Mattered* (Bellevue, WA: Free Enterprise Press, 1987).

Birnie, Patricia W., and Alan E. Boyle. *International Law and the Environment* (New York: Clarendon Press, 1994).

Brown, Michael, and John May. *The Greenpeace Story* (New York: Dorling Kindersley, 1991).

Chase, Steve, ed. *Defending the Earth: A Dialogue Between Murray Bookchin and Dave Foreman* (Boston: South End Press, 1991).

Crocker, David A. and Toby Linden, eds. *Ethics of Consumption: The Good Life, Justice, and Global Stewardship* (Lanham, MD: Rowman & Littlefield Publishers, Inc., 1997).

Davis, John, and Dave Foreman, eds. *The Earth First! Reader: Ten Years of Radical Environmentalism* (Salt Lake City: Peregrine Smith, 1991).

Day, David. *The Environmental Wars* (New York: St. Martin's Press, 1989).

———. *The Whale War* (San Francisco: Sierra Club Books, 1987).

Dobson, Andrew, and Paul Lucardie, eds. *The Politics of Nature* (London: Routledge, 1993).

Eckersley, Robyn. *Environmentalism and Political Theory* (Albany: State University of New York Press, 1992).

Editors of Ramparts. *Eco-Catastrophe* (San Francisco: Canfield Press, 1970).

Ehrlich, Paul and Anne H. Ehrlich. *Betrayal of Science and Reason* (Washington, DC: Island Press, 1996).

Foreman, Dave. *Confessions of an Eco-Warrior* (New York: Harmony Books, 1991).

Goodin, Robert. *Green Political Theory* (Oxford: Blackwell Polity Press, 1992).

Goodland, Robert, Herman Daly, and Sarah El Serafy, eds. *Population, Technology, and Lifestyle* (Washington, DC: Island Press, 1992)

Hays, Samuel P. *Beauty, Health, and Performance: Environmental Politics in the United States* (Cambridge, MA: Cambridge University Press, 1987).

Hepworth, James, and Gregory McNamee, eds. *Resist Much, Obey Little: Some Notes on Edward Abbey* (Salt Lake City: Dream Garden Press, 1985).

Hunter, Robert. *Warriors of the Rainbow: A Chronicle of the Greenpeace Movement* (New York: Holt, Rinehart and Winston, 1979).

Hunter, Robert, and Paul Watson. *Cry Wolf* (Vancouver, BC: Shepherds of the Earth, 1985).

Irvine, Sandy and Alec Ponton. *A Green Manifesto* (London: Macdonald, 1989).

Kerrick, Michael. *Ecotage from Our Perspective: An Explanation of the Willamette National Forest's Policy on Environmental Sabotage Known as Ecotage.* A Report for Civil Leaders (Eugene, OR: Willamette National Forest, 1985).

Light, Andrew, and Eric Katz, eds. *Environmental Pragmatism* (New York: Routledge, 1996).

List, Peter. *Radical Environmentalism: Philosophy and Tactics* (Belmont, CA: Wadsworth, 1993).

Lewis, Martin W. *Green Delusions: An Environmentalist Critique of Radical Environmentalism* (Durham, NC: Duke University Press, 1992).

Love, Sam, ed. *Earth Tool Kit: A Field Manual for Citizen Activists* (New York: Pocket Books, 1971).

Love, Sam, and David Obst, eds. *Ecotage!* (New York: Pocket Books, 1972).

Manes, Christopher. *Green Rage* (Boston: Little, Brown, 1990).

Marietta, Don, Jr., and Lester Embree, eds. *Environmental Philosophy and Environmental Acivism* (Lanham, MD: Bowman & Littlefield, 1995).

McKibben, Bill. *Hope, Human and Wild: True Stories of Living Lightly on the Earth* (New York: Little, Brown, 1995).

Mitchell, John G., with Constance L. Stallings. *Ecotactics: The Sierra Club Handbook for Environment Activists* (New York: Pocket Books, 1970).

Norton, Bryan G. *Toward Unity Among Environmentalists* (New York: Oxford University Press, 1991).

Paehlke, Robert. *Environmentalism and the Future of Progressive Politics* (New Haven, CT: Yale University Press, 1989).

Porritt, Jonathon. *Seeing Green* (Oxford: Blackwell, 1985).

Ritter, Don. *Ecolinking: Everyone's Guide to Online Environmental Information* (Berkeley, CA: Peachpit Press, 1992).

Scarce, Rik. *Eco-Warriors: Understanding the Radical Environmental Movement* (Chicago: The Noble Press, 1990).

Sea Shepherd Log. Newsletter of the Sea Shepherd Conservation Society, 1314 2nd St., Santa Monica, CA 90401.

Student Action Coalition. *The Student Environmental Action Guide: 25 Simple Things We Can Do* (Berkeley: Earth Works Press, 1991).

Tokar, Brian. *The Green Alternative: Creating an Ecological Future* (San Pedro, CA: R. & E. Miles, 1987).

Watson, Paul, and Warren Rogers. *Sea Shepherd: My Fight for Whales and Seals* (New York: Norton, 1982).

Weston, Joe, ed. *Red and Green* (London: Pluto Press, 1986)

About the Planet (science; Darwin here and in Part III)

Baarschers, William H. *Eco facts and Eco-fiction* (London: Routledge, 1996).

Brown, Lester. *The World-Watch Reader on Global Environmental Issues* (New York: Norton & Company, 1991).

Ehrlich, Paul R., and Anne H. Ehrlich. *Healing the Planet* (Reading, MA: Addison-Wesley, 1991).

Ehrlich, Paul R., Anne H. Ehrlich, and J. P. Holdren. *Ecoscience: Population, Resources, Environment* (San Francisco: Freeman, 1977).

Ehrlich, P. R., and J. Roughgarden. *The Science of Ecology* (New York: Macmillan, 1987).

Gould, Stephen Jay. *Dinosaur in a Haystack: Reflections in Natural History* (New York: Harmony Books, 1995).

Hull, David. *Darwin and His Critics* (Cambridge, MA: Harvard University Press, 1973).

Imbrie, John, and Katherine Imbrie. *Ice Ages: Solving the Mystery* (Short Hulls, NJ: Enslow, 1979).

Jamieson, Dale, and Marc Bekoff, eds. *Readings in Animal Cognition* (Cambridge, MA: The MIT Press, 1996).

Kohn, David. *The Darwinian Heritage* (Princeton, NJ: Princeton University Press, 1985).

Lappe, Francis Moore. *Diet for a Small Planet*, 10th ed. (New York: Ballantine Books, 1985).

Lovelock, J. E. *Gaia: A New Look at Life on Earth* (New York: Oxford University Press, 1987).

Meadows, Dennis. *Beyond the Limits* (Post Mills, VT: Chelsea Green, 1992).

Miller, J. T. *Living in the Environment* (Belmont, CA: Wadsworth, 1988).

Odum, E. P. *Fundamentals of Ecology* (Philadelphia, PA: Saunders, 1969).

Reaka-Kudia, Marjorie, Don E. Wilson, and Edward O. Wilson, eds. *Biodiversity II* (Washington, DC: Joseph Henry Press, 1997).

Rolston, Holmes, III. *Biology, Ethics, and the Origins of Life* (Boston: Jones & Bartlett, 1994).

Sagan, Carl. *The Demon-Haunted World* (New York: Random House, 1995).

Schmidt, Victor A. *Planet Earth and the New Geoscience* (Dubuque, IA: Kendall-Hunt, 1985).

Shepard, Paul. *Subversive Science* (Boston: Houghton Mifflin, 1969).

Shrader-Fréchette, K. S., and E. D. McCoy. *Method in Ecology: Strategies for Conservation* (New York: Cambridge University Press, 1993).

Simon, Noel. *Nature in Danger: Threatened Habitats and Species* (New York: Oxford University Press, 1995).

Weiner, Jonathan. *The Next 100 Years* (New York: Bantam Books, 1990).

———. *Planet Earth* (New York: Bantam Books, 1986).

Wilson, E. O. *In Search of Nature* (Washington, DC: Island Press, 1996).

Woodwall, George. *The Earth in Transition* (Cambridge, MA: Cambridge University Press, 1990).

Young, Louise. *The Blue Planet* (Boston: Little, Brown, 1983).

General Works by Single Authors and Collections

Armstrong, Susan J., and Richard G. Botzler, eds. *Environmental Ethics: Divergence and Convergence* (New York: McGraw-Hill, 1992).

Attfield, Robin. *The Ethics of Environmental Concern*, 2nd ed. (Athens: University of Georgia Press, 1991).

———. *The Ethics of the Global Environment* (West Lafayette, IN: Purdue University Press, 1999).

Attfield, Robin and Katharine Dell, eds. *Values, Conflict, and the Environment* 2nd ed. (Brookfield, VT: Ashgate Publishing Co., 1996).

Barbour, Ian. *Technology, Environment, and Human Values* (New York: Praeger, 1980).

Biehlm, Janet and Peter Staudenmaier. *Ecofascism: Lessons from the German Experience* (San Francisco: AK Press, 1995)

Blackstone, William T., ed. *Philosophy and Environmental Crisis* (Athens: University of Georgia Press, 1974).

Brennan, Andrew. *Thinking About Nature: An Investigation of Nature, Value and Ecology* (London: Routledge; and Athens: University of Georgia Press, 1988).

Caldicott, Helen. *If You Love This Planet: A Plan to Heal the Earth* (New York: Norton, 1992).

Callicott, J. Baird. *In Defense of the Land Ethic: Essays in Environmental Philosophy* (Albany: State University of New York Press, 1989).

Cooper, David E., and Joy A. Palmer, eds. *The Environment in Question* (London: Routledge, 1992).

Desjardins, Joseph R. *Environmental Ethics: An Introduction to Environmental Philosophy* (Belmont, CA: Wadsworth, 1993).

Dillingham, Catherine K. and Lisa H. Newton. *Watersheds: Classic Cases in Environmental Ethics* (Belmont, CA: Wadsworth, 1994).

Dobson, Andrew. *Green Political Thought,* 2nd ed. (London: Routledge, 1992).

Drengsom, Alan R. *Beyond Environmental Crisis: From Technocrat to Planetary Person* (New York: Peter Lang, 1989).

Eckersley, Robyn. *Environmentalism and Political Theory: Toward an Ecocentric Approach* (Albany: State University of New York Press, 1992).

Elliot, Robert ed. *Environmental Ethics* (New York: Oxford University Press, 1995).

Elliot, Robert, and Arran Gare, eds. *Environmental Philosophy: A Collection of Readings* (University Park: Pennsylvania State University Press, 1983).

Ferre, Frederick, and Peter Hartel, eds. *Ethics and Environmental Policy: Theory Meets Practice* (Athens: University of Georgia Press, 1994).

Goodpaster, K. E., and K. M. Sayre, eds. *Ethics and Problems of the 21st Century* (Notre Dame, IN: University of Notre Dame Press, 1979).

Gunn, Alastair S., and Aarne Vesilind, eds. *Environmental Ethics for Engineers* (Chelsea, MI: Lewis, 1986).

Gruen, Lori, and Dale Jamieson, eds. *Reflecting on Nature: Readings in Environmental Philosophy* (New York: Oxford University Press, 1994).

Hansom, Philip P., ed. *Environmental Ethics: Philosophical and Policy Perspective* Vol. I (Burnaby, BC: Simon Fraser University, 1986).

Hart, Richard E., ed. *Ethics and the Environment* (Lanham, MD: University Press of America, 1992).

Jamieson, Dale, ed. *A Companion to Environmental Philosophy* (Malden, MA: Blackwell Publishers, 2001).

Johnson, Lawrence E. *A Morally Deep World: An Essay on Moral Significance and Environmental Ethics* (Cambridge, MA: Cambridge University Press, 1991).

Katz, Eric. *Nature and Subject: Human Obligations and Natural Community* (Lanham, MD: Rowman & Littlefield Publishers, Inc., 1997).

Light, Andrew, and Eric Katz, eds. *Environmental Pragmatism* (New York: Routledge, 1996).

McCloskey, H. J. *Ecological Ethics and Politics* (Totowa, NJ: Rowman & Littlefield, 1983).

Miller, Alan S. *Gaia Connections: An Introduction to Ecology, Ecoethics, and Economics* (Totowa, NJ: Rowman & Littlefield, 1991).

Mills, Claudia. *Values & Public Policy* (New York: Harcourt Brace Jovanovich, 1992).

Norton, Bryan G. *Toward Unity Among Environmentalists* (New York: Oxford University Press, 1991).

O'Neill, John. *Ecology, Policy and Politics: Human Well-Being and the Natural World* (New York: Routledge, 1993).

Passmore, John. *Man's Responsibility for Nature: Ecological Problems and Western Traditions* (New York: Scribner's, 1974).

Pojman, Louis. *Environmental Ethics: Readings in Theory and Application* (Boston: Jones & Bartlett, 1996).

Potter, Van Rensselaer. *Global Bioethics: Building on the Leopold Legacy* (Lansing: Michigan State University Press, 1989).

Regan, Tom, ed. *Earthbound: New Introductory Essays in Environmental Ethics* (New York: Random House, 1984).

Rolston, Holmes, III. *Environmental Ethics* (Philadelphia, PA: Temple University Press, 1988).

———. *Philosophy Gone Wild: Essays in Environmental Ethics* (Buffalo, NY: Prometheus Books, 1986).

Sapontzis, Stephen F. *Morals, Reason and Animals* (Philadelphia, PA: Temple University Press, 1987).

Satris, Stephen, ed. *Taking Sides: Clashing Views on Controversial Moral Issues* (Guilford, CT: Dushkin/Brown & Benchmark, 1996).

Scherer, Donald. *Upstream/Downstream: Issues in Environmental Ethics* (Philadelphia, PA: Temple University Press, 1990).

Scherer, Donald, and Thomas Attig, eds. *Ethics and the Environment* (Englewood Cliffs, NJ: Prentice Hall, 1983).

Serres, Michel. *The Natural Contract.* Trans. Elizabeth MacArthur and William Paulson (Ann Arbor: University of Michigan Press, 1995).

Shrader-Fréchette, K. S., ed. *Environmental Ethics* (Pacific Grove, CA: Boxwood Press, 1981).

Sterba, James P. *Earth Ethics: Environmental Ethics, Animal Rights, and Practical Applications* (Englewood Cliffs, NJ: Prentice Hall, 1995).

———. *Three Challenges to Ethics: Environmentalism, Feminism, and Multiculturalism* (New York: Oxford University Press, 2000).

Stone, Christopher F. *Earth and Other Ethics: The Case for Moral Pluralism* (New York: Harper & Row, 1987).

VanDeVeer, Donald, and Christine Pierce. *People, Penguins and Plastic Trees: Basic Issues in Environmental Ethics* (Belmont, CA: Wadsworth, 1986; 2nd ed., 1995).

Varner, Gary E. *In Nature's Interests? Interests, Animal Rights and Environmental Ethics* (New York: Oxford University Press, 1998).

Wellington, Alex, Allen Greenbaum, and Wesley Cragg, eds. *Canadian Issues in Environmental Ethics* (Peteborough, Ontario: Broadview Press, 1997).

Wenz, Peter S. *Environmental Ethics Today* (New York: Oxford University Press, 2000).

———. *Environmental Justice* (Albany: State University of New York Press, 1988).

Weston, Anthony. *Toward Better Problems: New Perspectives on Abortion, Animal Rights, the Environment, and Justice* (Philadelphia: Temple University Press, 1992).

Westra, Laura. *An Environmental Proposal for Ethics: The Principle of Integrity* (Lanham, MD: Rowman & Littlefield, 1994).

Zimmerman, Michael, J. Baird Callicott, George Sessions, Karen J. Warren, and John P. Clark, eds. *Environmental Philosophy: From Animal Rights to Radical Ecology* (Englewood Cliffs, NJ: Prentice Hall, 1993).